encyclopedia of millennialism and Millennial Movements

ROUTLEDGE ENCYCLOPEDIAS OF RELIGION AND SOCIETY

David Levinson, *Series Editor*

The Encyclopedia of Millennialism and Millennial Movements

Richard A. Landes, *Editor*

The Encyclopedia of African and African American Religions

Stephen D. Glazier

The Encyclopedia of Fundamentalism

Brenda E. Brasher, *Editor*

encyclopedia of millennialism and Millennial Movements

Richard A. Landes, Editor

Religion and Society
A Berkshire Reference Work

ROUTLEDGE
NEW YORK LONDON

Published in 2000 by

Routledge
29 West 35th Street
New York, NY 10001
A Berkshire Reference Work

Printed in the United States of America on acid-free paper.

10 9 8 7 6 5 4 3 2 1

Library of Congress Cataloging-in-Publication Data

Encyclopedia of millennialism and millennial movements / Richard A. Landes, editor.
p. cm. – (Religion and society)
"A Berkshire Reference work."
Includes bibliographical references and index.
ISBN 0-415-92246-1 (acid-free paper)
1. Millennialism–Encyclopedia. I. Landes, Richard Allen. II. Berkshire Reference Works (Firm) III. Religion and society (New York, N.Y.)
BT891.E53 2000
306'1–dc21 99-052373

Contents

Editorial Advisory Board

List of Entries

Introduction

The *Encyclopedia of Millennialism and Millennial Movements* is a guide to the religious or spiritual social movements throughout history and around the world that have promised to create a better world or usher in a new one. These movements are given many names: crisis cults, nativistic movements, messianic cults, cargo cults, chiliastic movements, revitalization movements, utopian movements, apocalyptic movements, and millennial movements. All share a number of common features. They are collective movements, drawing people together in a common belief and often a common cause. They depend on what are known as millennial or millenarian beliefs—the idea that the world can, and will, be transformed or improved or saved. They look to the supernatural or spiritual world—whether to a god or to aliens from another galaxy—for assistance and guidance.

Throughout history and across cultures millennial movements have been a common form of social protest and a mechanism for seeking societal change. In fact, all of the major world religions, with the exception of Hinduism, began as millennial movements. And even when they are small—like the Ghost Dance or the Branch Davidians—millennial movements often draw considerable attention from society in general. Such movements often draw much attention because they are perceived by those in power to be a threat to the existing social and political order. In part motivated by such perceptions, the United States government sent more than half of its cavalry forces in pursuit of a few thousand Plains Indian Ghost Dancers in 1890; similarly, heavily armed federal agents attacked the Branch Davidian compound in Waco, Texas in 1993.

Many millennial movements have, naturally enough, been triggered by calendar dates considered of spiritual or magical significance. The concept of the millennium has long fascinated people in the Christian world. But a millennial time or moment can be determined by non-European calendars, by signs in the stars or in nature, by numerology, or by particular events that a group considers to be millennial. The explosion at the Chernobyl nuclear power plant in the Soviet Union in 1986, for example, is considered by some a millennial event.

The desire for magical transformation—of individual lives, of communities and groups, of entire societies, or of the whole world—is not new. Nor is it fading in this age of technological and scientific advance. Even as technology influences every aspect of our lives, and science explains and alters human genes and human behavior, technology and science inspire new anxieties and fears. Social change—such as women and minority groups achieving greater rights and more significant roles in private and public life—can lead to millennialism in others threatened by these changes. Readers who seek a general introduction to millennialism and millennial movements should consult the article "Millennialism in the Western World," which provides a broad overview of the rise, spread, and various manifestations of millennialism.

The encyclopedia is historical, cross-cultural, and interdisciplinary, covering movements in the Western World and also in Africa, Asia, and Oceania, and among native North and South Americans. It draws upon the work of anthropologists, historians, sociologists, political scientists, religious scholars, and others who study millennial movements. Millennial studies is still a young field. First launched by the anthropologists who studied cargo cults in the post-World War II period, developed by medievalists like Norman Cohn and Marjorie Reeves, and theoretically refined by sociologists like Leon Festinger, it has, in the past generation, become an international field of research. Because of the unusual dynamics of millennial manifestations—the brief intensity, the seemingly irrational passions, the range of responses to apocalyptic disappointment—the study of them often demands counterintuitive thinking and calls for a multidisciplinary approach that engages a wide range of fields and specialties. At the approach of the third millennium, however, the field is popular not only among scholars, but also among policymakers.

The *Encyclopedia of Millennialism and Millennial Movements* covers dozens of movements, including many associated with Christianity and the Western World as well with other world religions including Islam, Judaism, Buddhism, Daoism, Confucianism, Baha'i, Mormonism, and Zoroastrianism. It also gives much attention to non-Western movements including those among indigenous peoples in the Americas, the cargo cults of Melanesia, and indigenous churches in sub-Saharan Africa. Although much attention is given to the history of millennialism, equal attention is given to movements in the modern world, including Seventh-Day Adventism, Christian Identity, Heaven's Gate, Peoples Temple, Davidians, numerous UFO cults, and millennial thinking connected with the technological threat known as Year 2000, the Millennial Bug, or Y2K.

In addition to descriptions of specific movements, there are also articles covering the concepts and theories that guide the scholarly study of millenarianism, such as utopia, cult, and end signs; articles on general topics such as charismatic leadership, the role of women, and markers of millennial moments; and articles on relevant theological topics such as dispensationalism, premillennialism, and defilement. By including articles on this broad range of topics we have tried to provide a full summary of the state of our knowledge of millennialism at the year 2000 and to enhance the reader's understanding of the interaction of religion and society. While most of the articles were written prior to the beginning of the year 2000, articles have been updated and the article "Year 2000 Celebrations" was added after the beginning of the year 2000 to make the volume as up to date as possible.

There are many people to acknowledge and thank for their contributions to this encyclopedia. The volume as well as the Religion and Society series were developed by David Levinson and Karen Christensen of Berkshire Reference Works and then refined through consultation with Routledge. The key event in the development of this work was the Conference on "Knowing *of* a Time, Knowing *the* Time," convened by the Center for Millennial Studies (CMS) at Boston University in December 1998. At that conference the plans for the encyclopedia were publicly announced for the first time, and scholars were first asked to participate. And participate they did. Several dozen people at the conference met with us to revise the preliminary headword list, suggest scholars to write the articles, and many volunteered or agreed to write and review articles. And after the conference, as word of the project spread, other scholars came on board with more suggestions and a willingness to participate themselves. While these people are listed here as authors of articles, we also want to acknowledge their other contributions in helping the project develop and move along to completion. In this regard, deserving of special thanks are Michael Barkun, Chip Berlet, Gene Gallagher, Tom Long, Cathy Wessinger, and Robert Whalen.

Also deserving of special acknowledgment and thanks are those at the Center for Millennial Studies and Berkshire Reference Works who brought this volume to fruition. At BRW the project was ably managed by Ben Manning, and at CMS David Kessler and Beth Forrest were especially helpful with promoting the project in its early stages and in getting various ends wrapped up at the conclusion of the project. We also want to thank Kevin Ohe at Routledge for his support and help in developing the project and in bringing it to fruition.

Richard A. Landes and David Levinson

666

"This calls for wisdom: let him who has understanding reckon the number of the beast, for it is a human number, its number is six hundred and sixty-six."

No passage of biblical prophecy has been subjected to more futile debate than Revelation 13:18, the verse quoted above. Those Christians who take every word of the Bible as divinely inspired believe that Satan will be reincarnated as a human Antichrist prior to the Battle of Armageddon and the Lord's Second Coming. During the Antichrist's temporary domination of the Earth, he will be assisted by another malevolent entity called the beast. According to Revelation 13:16–17, the Antichrist will stamp 666 on the right hand or forehead of every living person.

Almost all biblical scholars suspect that the author of Revelation was referring to a method for extracting 666 from the name of a wicked person who at the time was thought to be either the beast or the Antichrist. Such numerology, known as *gematria*, originated among Hebrew cabalists, and persisted in later centuries among Jews, Christians, and Muslims. Numbers were assigned to the letters of a word or phrase, then the values summed. The most likely interpretation of 666, historians believe, is that the number applied to Nero, the Roman emperor of the first century. Numbers assigned to NRN KSR, Nero's name in Hebrew (which has no vowels), add to 666.

Ever since Revelation was written, Christians have found 666 in the names of dozens of evil political leaders as well as the names of founders and leaders of rival religious faiths. During the Reformation, Protestants extracted 666 from the names of hated popes. Catholics retaliated by finding 666 in the names of Luther, Calvin, and other famous Protestants. In later centuries Napoleon, Hitler, Mussolini, Stalin, and other dictators have had their names translated to 666. The technique applied to Hitler is amazingly simple. Using the cipher A = 100, B = 101, C = 102, and so on, HITLER adds to 666.

Early Seventh-day Adventists found 666 in the Latin phrase for the pope, *Vicarious filii dei* ("In place of the Son of God"). This was done by adding the letters that are also Roman numerals. (Because the Romans used V for U, both U and V are taken as 5.) Adventists dropped this from their literature after someone discovered that Roman numerals in

The Beast of the Apocalypse: 666

A gigantic auto-programming computer

One will need the number of the Beast to buy and sell

It is already set up at Brussels, Belgium, the Beast of the Apocalypse. It is a gigantic computer that makes its own programs. "By using three entries of six digits each, each citizen of the whole world will see himself attributed a distinct credit card number". Three entries of six digits each: 666.

Saint John's Apocalypse speaks of two Beasts, the Beast of the sea and the Beast of the earth, that will make up the "Antichrist" couple, at the end of times. The commentators say that the Beast coming from the sea, it is the political power, Satan's redoubtable ally. And the Beast coming from the earth, it is the power of money. The Beast of the earth, the financial power, will bring about that

"it will cause all, the small and the great, and the rich and the poor, and the free and the bond, to have a mark on their right hand or on their foreheads, and it will bring it about that no one may be able to buy or to sell except him who has the mark, either the name of the beast or the number of its name. Here is wisdom. He who has understanding, let him calculate the number of the beast, for it is the number of a man; and its number is six hundred and sixty-six.
(The Apocalypse)

Well! The number 666 is not a mystery anymore. We know that it designates the gigantic computer that will be the great controller of all the men of the earth for their purchases and sales.

Following is a text from the Moody Magazine, that reveals to us where the international financiers have led so far, the peoples, and in what slavery they propose to chain them.

MICHAEL JOURNAL, 1101 PRINCIPALE ST., ROUGEMONT, QUE., CANADA J0L 1M0. REPRODUCED BY PERMISSION.

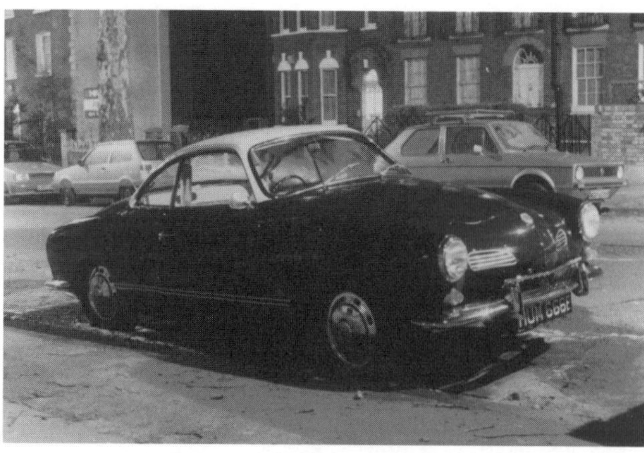

This Karmann Ghia retains its 1967 license plate number HUM666E. The British DVLC no longer issues license plates with the number 666 because many people do not want a number linked in common parlance with the devil.

the name of Ellen Gould White, one of their founders, also add to 666, taking W to be "double U" or two Vs.

Today's Fundamentalists avoid attaching 666 to any individual or institution. Billy Graham, for example, has preached many sermons on the Antichrist and the immanence of the Second Coming. He points out that because 7 is a biblical symbol of perfection, the triple 6 may indicate a falling from perfection, but he admits there is a mystery about 666 not yet revealed.

Other Fundamentalists are less cautious. In recent years they have discovered 666 all over the lot, especially in bar codes, and even in the pattern of stars in the logo of Proctor and Gamble Company. Their boycott of Proctor and Gamble products was so bothersome that the company spent a sizeable sum in the 1980s defending their logo and filing lawsuits against those who spread rumors about the company's alleged link to Satan.

The symbolism of 666 has now spilled over into daily life. Car owners in North America and Europe regularly return license plates with 666, and England has stopped issuing such plates. In 1996 the Social Security Administration announced that anyone with 666 in their number could ask for a new number. On 6 June 1996, thousands of citizens in Bogota, Columbia, rushed to churches to have themselves or their children baptized because of a rumor that on 6/6/96 the Antichrist would be born. President Reagan, after leaving office, changed his address on St. Cloud Drive, Bel Air, CA, from 666 to 668. "No one knows," Reagan said during a debate, "whether . . . Armageddon is a thousand years away or the day after tomorrow."

Martin Gardner

See also Antichrist

Bibliography

Caird, George Bradford. (1966) *A Commentary on the Revelation of St. John the Divine.* New York: Harper and Row.

Gardner, Martin. (1988) *The New Age: Notes of a Fringe Watcher.* Buffalo, NY: Prometheus Books.

Aetherius Society

Founded in England in 1954 by George King, the Aetherius Society combines an eclectic blend of the world's religions, yoga, and a belief in UFOs, making it one of the oldest and best organized ongoing millennial UFO religions. Born in Shropshire, England, on 23 January 1919, King alleges that one morning in 1954 a loud voice rang out telling him that he was to become the voice of the "Interplanetary Parliament." King became a channel for extraterrestrial beings from other planets, including Jesus, whom the Aetherians believe to be an ascended space master from the planet Venus. At the direction of these beings, King founded the metaphysical order called The Aetherius Society.

The beliefs and goals of the Aetherius Society center on the cooperation of humankind and the extraterrestrial intelligences, in order to devise techniques to manipulate and enhance spiritual energy for the benefit of life on Earth. Like other millennial ufologists, the Aetherians believe that humanity bears most of the blame for the current atmosphere of global social and environmental decay and that the human race has again reached a crossroad. A document on the Web site for the Aetherius Society, entitled "Why and How are the Space Masters Helping Us Now," reads: "One road leads to disaster, self-inflicted by his [humankind's] own science and materialism. . . . In these days there is again a danger of his technology, in the hands of the few, causing mass destruction to the many."

Through extraterrestrial communication the Aetherians have come to believe that the aliens will save us from the ultimate destruction of the planet and extinction of humankind. Like other millennial ufology religions, the Aetherians argue that the alien visitors are benevolent saviors, sent to help us overcome the restrictions of our "humanness" and assist us in the transition from the old world to a new one. Members of the Aetherius Society believe that these extraterrestrials have been helping us for many centuries and consider us to be their younger, less evolved brothers. The notion of an intergalactic Christ, foretold by King in 1958, has all the markings of a biblical prophecy.

July 8th is considered the holiest day of the year for Aetherians, because it is believed that on this day in 1964,

A COSMIC PROPHECY

"There will shortly come Another among you.

He will stand tall among men with a shining countenance. This One will be attired in a single garment of the type now known to you. His shoes will be soft-topped, yet not made of the skin of animals.

He will approach the Earth leaders. They will ask of Him, His credentials. He will produce these.

His magic will be greater than any upon Earth—greater than the combined materialistic might of all the armies.

And they who heed not His words, shall be removed from the Earth.

This Rock is now Holy—and will remain so for as long as the World exists.

Go ye forth and spread My Word throughout the World, so that all men of pure heart may prepare for His coming."

Delivered to Dr. George King on the Holy mountain Brown Willy in Cornwall, England on 23 November 1958 by a spiritually evolved extraterrestrial known as a Lord of Karma.

Source: http://www.aetherius.org/avatar.htm.

Mother Earth was given an "Initiation" in which she received more energy than she had ever received before in order for the Earth to advance into higher and more spiritual realms in the new millennium. While the Aetherius Society is more than thirty years old, has followers throughout the world, numerous publications, and sponsored activities, its membership is relatively small.

Philip Lamy

Bibliography

Aetherius Society. (1999) "Sir George King: A Western Master of Yoga for the Aquarian Age." http://www.aetherius.org/bio.htm.

———. (1999) "Why and How are the Space Masters Helping Us Now?" http://www.aetherius.org/intro.htm.

Ellwood, Robert, and Harry Partin. (1988) *Religious and Spiritual Groups in Contemporary America*. Englewood Cliffs, NJ: Prentice Hall.

Africa, Sub-Saharan

The indigenous religions of Sub-Saharan Africa have been much influenced by Christianity and Islam. Thus, it is now intellectually false to consider these two religions as foreign to African life, although both religions have been reinterpreted through the idioms and cultural precepts of Africa.

Christianity

The millennial impulse in Sub-Saharan Africa is an integral part of the African initiatives in Christianity. The mid-twentieth century witnessed the rapid proliferation of indigenous religious movements in Africa. Within Christianity, the most radical reinterpretation of the faith and indigenization of forms occurred in the independent movements initiated by African prophets. These prophets invoke a profound sense of *homo ex machina:* they were extremely charismatic individuals who were able to relate to the hopes and aspirations of the people. They were able to attract many followers. The independent religious movements that were formed by these prophets have been interpreted by many scholars as an authentic African understanding of the Christian faith. They were able to create religious movements that were symptomatic of the yearnings of Africa to feel at home within Christianity. They were also veritable responses to the religious, political, economic, and psychological domination engendered by colonialism.

Lumpa Church

One of the early prophetic movements that had a millennial note was the Lumpa Church, established by Alice Lenshina Mulenga (c. 1919–78) in Zambia. She was from the Chinsali District in northern Zambia. Alice Lenshina, the wife of Petro Chintankawa, came back from the dead in September 1954 with a religious calling. She studied in the same primary school at the Presbyterian Mission of Lubwa as

Kenneth Kaunda, whose father had been its first African minister. She started her mission after her incredible religious experience. She was seen as a visionary prophetess and healer who spoke about the imminent return of Jesus Christ. Like Simon Kimbangu (1889–1951) in Zaire (Congo), she was able to draw many former teachers and catechists to her movement. She called her mission Lumpa, meaning, in the Bemba language, the highest, the supreme, or to excel or to go far. For a while, she stayed within the Presbyterian Church. Within two years, however, her strong antiwitchcraft views and millennial impulse brought about a separation with Presbyterianism.

She promised spiritual wholeness and a new life to those who abandoned traditional magic and witchcraft to follow her. She condemned polygamy, sorcery, and divination. Like Isaiah Shembe (c. 1870–1935) in South Africa, she was an inspired composer of hymns in Bemba. Lenshina established a holy village at Kasomo called the New Zion. Many people believed that God had given her a sacred book specifically for Africans, since white missionaries had hidden the book that should have been given to them. Her followers were opposed to government taxation and political authority. They believed that the end of all things was near and, increasingly, pulled away from a sinful world. The Lumpa Church was proscribed in 1964 after staging an armed insurrection against the government, now led by Kenneth Kaunda, shortly before Zambia gained independence from Britain in October 1964. Alice Lenshina died in detention in 1978. Shortly before her death, she complained that her political proclivities obscured her original message of conversion and intense spirituality.

Apostolic Church of John Masowe

Another religious movement with messianic and millennial tendencies was formed by Shoniwa or John Masowe (1915–73) in October 1932, in the Hartley district of southern Rhodesia (Zimbabwe). He called himself John the Baptist and claimed to have been resurrected from death and consequently gifted with healing and prophetic powers. He emerged from this experience with a new identity, wearing long white garments and carrying a staff and a Bible.

He moved from village to village baptizing people who accepted his message of healing and a golden age. The golden age involved political and spiritual liberation for the peoples of Africa. He commanded his followers to refrain from wage labor for the colonial authorities and to confront colonial religious and political structures. He promised a new glorious period of freedom, justice, and self-sufficiency. He rejected all Christian sacraments except baptism. As the leader of the religious movement, he had the prerogative of baptizing all new converts. His followers worship Jehovah, observe Old Testament dietary rules, and keep the Sabbath. Polygamous marriages are encouraged, and John Masowe is called the "Word," "Spirit," or "Star of God." His followers, also known as *vahosanna* (the "hosannas") or as Basketmakers, live in their own separate communities. They make baskets, install their own electric generators, and make furniture and metalware of different kinds. Women wear white gowns and turbans, while men go around with long beards and shaven heads. Under political threat in southern Rhodesia, the Apostolic Church of John Masowe, immigrated to the Korsten suburb of Port Elizabeth, South Africa, in 1943. Masowe is often referred to as the "secret messiah" because his followers did not know his precise whereabouts much of the time.

After the late 1940s, he only made sporadic appearances to baptize new converts. Many stories developed around him, the most enduring one was that he had died and then returned to life. In 1960, his church was abolished in South Africa. Most of his members moved to Lusaka and Nairobi. Masowe died in Ndola, Zambia, in 1973 leaving behind a compelling millennial promise of freedom and a golden age. The general consensus among scholars of African religions is that the figure of Masowe is one of the strangest in history. He moved from one country to another creating much lore around himself and for much of his life his whereabouts were unknown. Even after his death, his messianic and millennial ideas were perpetuated as a means of strengthening the faith of his followers. His widespread acceptance was rooted in the messages of hope, healing, and abundant life he offered to his followers.

Watchtower

The most persistent millenarian movement in sub-Saharan Africa is the organization called the Watchtower, or *Kitawala*. This movement is closely connected to the American Jehovah's Witnesses who started their missionary foray in Africa in the twentieth century. Since 1910, several Watchtower movements sprang up across eastern, central, and southern Africa. The Watchtower movement in Africa is unique because it does not consider itself a church, or even a sect, but an organization. It teaches that it is the religious responsibility of every member to try to convert nonbelievers, especially the lost followers of other religions. It neither seeks any accommodation with the world nor expects affirmation by the state. The best known was the Watchtower group established by Elliot Kamwana of Nyasaland (in present-day Malawi) in 1908. This group hoped for the coming of a spiritually glorious age. The group was also a formidable response to colonial ideological hegemony.

The basic doctrinal foundation of the Watchtower movement is the imminent expectation of the end of all things when the Kingdom of God will be established on earth, to be ruled over by Christ and the witnesses of His truth. Earthly principalities and powers represent the power of the Devil who is the invisible ruler of the earth. These powers will eventually be defeated by Jesus Christ and all His Hosts in the battle of Armageddon (this is an ever-present reality represented by political chaos in the world). This is the absolute truth. Members are encouraged to await the Kingdom. The gory news of the First World War was a ringing suggestion that Armageddon was, indeed, at hand. Members believed that Jesus Christ will soon return (the precise date has been changed several times). In this new spiritual dispensation, sickness, death, and war will disappear. This promise of an imminent golden age was very appealing in many countries during the colonial period in Africa. The Watchtower movement was against colonial authoritarianism. It was particularly critical of the blatant racism of colonial authorities in southern and central Africa.

The millennial agenda set forth by the Watchtower movement in many parts of Africa is a sort of expectation that social and economic problems would be obliterated by a supernatural intervention. Members of this movement define the state as basically evil. They are to avoid all commitments to it other than the common civic duty of paying tax and keeping the peace.

The Watchtower movement is still prominent in Zambia, Zaire, Tanzania, and Angola. They are organized in village groups under the control of a charismatic prophet. They are closely connected to the people at the grass roots. They have given a credible expression to the hopes and aspirations of common people. This movement has a long history in Africa. The relationships between African political elites and the Watchtower movement has to be seen against the background of a protracted and continuing involvement of this movement in Africa. The movement, as it known today, consists not only in recruits to a well-organized sect managed from the United States, but in age-long members who have brought up their families as Witnesses. Many African nations do not see the movement as foreign and exotic but as a local means of addressing the yearnings of the people.

Islam: The Maitatsine Sect

The Maitatsine religious movement in northern Nigeria best represents the millennial impulse in Islam in Sub-Saharan Africa. Maitatsine was the name given by the people of Kano in northern Nigeria to Muhammadu Marwa, the leader of an Islamic sect that started a riot in that city in December 1980. The name is derived from a Hausa phrase he usually used against his critics, *Alla ya tsine maka albarka*, meaning, "May God deprive you of his blessing." Because the group was wary of outsiders, and because the riots in Kano gave rise to bizarre innuendoes, little reliable information exists about the movement or its leader.

Muhammadu Marwa was reportedly from the region of Marwa, a city in northern Cameroon. He is said to have come to the city of Kano in 1945, but nothing is known of his activities in the city until the early 1960s. By this time, he had gained considerable reputation for Qur'anic interpretation and commentary, and was given the honorific title of "*Mallam Mai Tafsiri*" meaning someone well versed and well respected in the interpretation of the Qur'an. The religious and political situation in Kano in the years after Nigeria's independence in 1960 was chaotic and Muhammadu Marwa took full advantage of this precarious situation. He told people to resist the message of orthodox Islam. In 1962, the ruler of Kano, Emir Muhammadu Sanusi had Marwa brought before a Muslim judge on allegations of illegal preaching and an offense known in Arabic jurisprudence as *shatimati*, or abusive language. Marwa was sentenced to three months in prison and was later deported to Cameroon. In the late 1960s, Marwa returned to Kano. He lived in an area of Kano called Yan Awaki. Many of his followers lived with him. Many young people were attracted to Marwa's radical message. Many of his followers were also Qur'anic students, known as *almajirai* or *gardawa*.

This sect clearly falls within the mahdist-millenarian tradition. The idea of a Madhi, one rightly guided by God, is well established in Sunni and Shi'ah Islam. The idea rests on the affirmation that at a certain point in time a Deliverer or Savior would come to reestablish order, peace, justice, and true religion to a morally corrupt world torn asunder by dissension. This Deliverer or Savior is the Madhi. In restoring justice and peace, the Madhi will also reshape Islam into its pristine form. The belief that a Madhi would come to destroy the infidel, get rid of injustice, ensure prosperity and well-being, and bring about the ascendancy of Islam has been well entrenched in the minds of many Muslims in West Africa since the latter half of the eighteenth century. Maitatsine was able to tap into this deep-seated religious belief. He saw himself as the forerunner of the Madhi.

Apart from indicting both religious and political authorities, Maitatsine condemned all those who enjoyed modern Western consumer goods such as television sets, radios, watches, and automobiles. He rejected the Hadith and preached against facing Mecca during the *salat*, the daily prayer requirement in Islam. He also condemned any Muslim who includes "Allah Akbar," meaning "God is Great," in his or her prayer. There were reports that after his death, copies of the Qur'an found in his house had the name of the Prophet replaced by his own. Maitatsine's followers believed that he was their true prophet. They called upon Muslims in northern Nigeria to stop mentioning the name of Prophet Muhammad whom they referred to as an Arab. Marwa accepted the Qur'an as an authentic source of religious teaching and instruction, but as a prophet he also claimed the prerogative to promulgate new religious commandments, or new interpretations of the Qur'an.

Many people saw Marwa's message as a menace. There were persistent rumors that Marwa planned to take over the city's two mosques. On 26 November 1980, the governor of Kano State issued an ultimatum stipulating the breakup of the community Marwa had built in the Yan Awaki section in Kano. The governor did not however take any immediate action on the expiration of this ultimatum. In December 1980, there was a violent encounter between the followers of Maitatsine and the Nigerian police. Almost four thousand people were killed in this mayhem. The Nigerian army was finally called upon to douse this raging fire of bedlam and confusion. Marwa was shot in the leg, and died as a result of his injury. His followers buried his body but it was later exhumed and cremated by the government in the vain hope of permanently eliminating this movement. In October 1982, another violent occurrence connected to Maitatsine took place in the city of Maidiguri in northeastern Nigeria. Other disturbances occurred at Yola in March 1984 and in Gombe in April 1985. There are stories that Maitatsine followers continue to operate surreptitiously in northern Nigeria.

There is no gainsaying the fact that millennial movements have had an exciting history in many parts of Africa. They have been very attractive to many followers who longed for the coming of a golden age; a time when the rule of God will reign supreme.

Akintunde E. Akinade

See also Islam

Bibliography

Barrett, David B. (1968) *Schism and Renewal in Africa: An Analysis of Six Thousand Contemporary Religious Movements.* London and Nairobi: Oxford University Press.

Clarke, Peter B. (1972) *West Africa and Islam.* London: Edward Arnold Publishers.

Coker, S. A. (1917) *The Rights of Africans to Organize and Establish Indigenous Churches Unattached to and Uncontrolled by Foreign Church Organizations.* Lagos: Tika-Tore Printing Works.

Hastings, Adrian. (1994) *The Church in Africa 1450–1950.* Oxford: Clarendon Press.

Isichei, Elizabeth. (1995) *A History of Christianity in Africa.* Michigan: Wm. B. Eerdmans Publishing Co.

Lubeck, Paul. (1987) *Islam and Urban Labor in Northern Nigeria: The Making of a Muslim Working Class.* Cambridge: Cambridge University Press.

Martin, Marie-Louise. (1954) *The Biblical Concept of Messianism, and Messianism in Southern Africa.* Morija, Basutoland (Lesotho): Morija Sesuto Book Depot.

Welbourn, F. (1962) *East African Rebels.* London: SCM Press.

Wishlade, R. L. (1964) *Sectarianism in Southern Nyasaland.* London: Oxford University Press.

Age of Mary

The Age of Mary refers to a conglomeration of apocalyptic and millennial beliefs associated with the popular Catholic piety springing from alleged apparitions and miracles of the Virgin Mary in the nineteenth and twentieth centuries. Devotees, a politically conservative, loosely knit group within the larger church, describe the Age as a special, circumscribed time in history when the Mother of God comes to her children to grant them special favors and to herald the Second Coming of Jesus Christ. They explain the present and the near future in millennial and apocalyptic terms, although the exact contents of their eschatological convictions change with historical, sociological, and even personal circumstances. Throughout the Age, believers associate Mary with sentimental piety, ultramontane Catholicism, and Victorian moral values, while they connect her enemies to atheistic rationalism, cultural secularization, and moral decline. Many of the believers point to the Enlightenment and the French Revolution as the intellectual sources of what they see as cultural degeneration in the nineteenth and twentieth centuries. Ultimately, the devotional life and apocalyptic imaginings of the Age constitute an ongoing romantic response to societal changes brought on by the Industrial Revolution.

Development of the Idea of the Age of Mary

The idea of the epoch first became popularized in mid-nineteenth-century France. Pious writers connected an apparent surge in Marian devotion with the idea that Mary and the values of the church had conquered Marianne, a feminine figure representing democratization in France and the ideals of the French Revolution. Believers saw eschatological implications in the Marian renewal, which signaled for many of them the nearness of the Second Coming of Christ. Following the guidance of eighteenth-century prophets, some devotees took Rome's 1854 declaration of the Dogma of the Immaculate Conception (which announced as an article of

Catholic faith that Mary was conceived in her mother's womb without the stain of original sin) to mean that a millennial triumph of the church through Mary was actually underway. Although believers clearly saw and disliked anticlericalism, anti-Victorian values, and extreme positivism, all of which they understood as intellectual vestiges of the Enlightenment and the Revolution, they nonetheless felt confident that the new sentimental piety in the country signaled victory for the faith and the church, a victory they described in millennial terms. In many ways, the confidence and optimism they expressed in Marian piety could be likened to the same many others of the period felt for science and invention.

Although the nineteenth century first popularized the idea of an Age of Mary, the notion has its roots in the European missions of Tridentine Catholicism. The Council of Trent (1545–63) mandated that every Catholic learn at least the rudiments of the faith. Missionaries traveled to remote villages across Europe until the early nineteenth century to teach the peasant population the catechism, encourage the devout life, and replace practices they considered to be pagan or superstitious with ones deemed to be less so. The missionaries fostered, among other practices, a highly spiritualized Marian piety as both a means to a holy life and as an alternative to local religious practices that Tridentine reform could no longer tolerate. Reformers replaced devotion to saints of doubtful historical origin with devotion to Mary. Although the Virgin had long been associated with salvation, in particular with saving undeserving sinners from the fires of hell at the last possible moment, she became connected in the Tridentine era to a lifestyle of righteousness that brought one closer to Christ inwardly and revealed one's salvation outwardly. Connecting her to the church's mission to universalize the faith and to convert the entire world, some Tridentine writers began to associate her not only with individual salvation but also with the ultimate redemption of the social body.

The most directly influential of these authors on nineteenth- and twentieth-century ideas of an Age of Mary is the French missionary, Louis-Marie Grignion de Montfort (1673–1716). De Montfort's *Treatise on the True Devotion to the Blessed Virgin,* unpublished until its discovery in 1842, became a French devotional bestseller, going through no less than fourteen editions by 1895. De Montfort wrote that an "Age of Mary" would precede the Second Coming of Christ; and he characterized the epoch as a period of revelation of the glories of Mary and warfare between her and Satan. God, he argued, wished Mary to be known in the latter days as both the pinnacle of creation and chief guide to Jesus Christ. She would battle demons and be joined by the elite "Apostles of the Latter Times," her faithful children, who would destroy heresy, convert many people, and be the greatest saints in the history of Christianity. In many ways, de Montfort's prophesies are heir to the most influential apocalypticist of the Middle Ages, Joachim of Fiore (c.1135–1202), who taught that an Age of the Holy Spirit would preface the Second Coming. De Montfort's ideas about an End Times spiritual battle between Mary and Satan, a special elite who would provide devotional leadership for the Last Days, and Mary as a herald of the End Times struck a chord with the nineteenth-century Marian faithful who understood widespread devotion to the Madonna and Rome's declaration of the dogma of the Immaculate Conception as evidence that the Age of Mary had dawned.

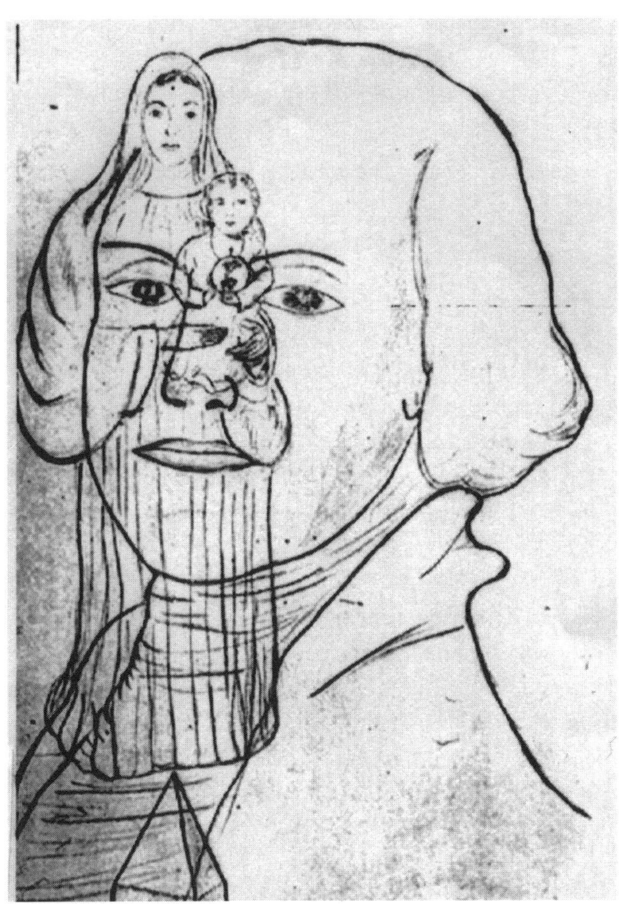

Age of Mary piety has participated in nationalistic fervor ever since the French understood nineteenth-century apparitions within their borders to be special gifts from the Blessed Virgin. Seer Mary Ann Van Hoff of Necedah, Wisconsin, who began seeing the Madonna in the 1950s, drew this portrait of the "Mother of God" superimposed over "The Father of Our Country." Van Hoof claimed that the Virgin Mary appeared to Washington himself during his lifetime and predicted that his country would eventually endure a horrific and bloody "Fifth Siege." VAN HOOF, MARY ANN. (1977) *MY WORK WITH NECEDAH*. 4 VOL. NECEDAH, WI: FOR MY GOD AND MY COUNTRY.

AGE OF MARY VS. ERA OF AIRLINE TRANSPORTATION

A staple of Age of Mary apocalyptic scenarios of the past two and a half decades has been a "great miracle" to occur at Garabandal, Spain. Visionary Conchita Gonzalez will announce the date eight days in advance. Such short notice puts non-European devotees in a bind, as the writer of this letter to the editor, published in *Garabandal* in the early 1990s, explains:

> **. . . [T]he time in which one will be able to make travel arrangements and set his personal affairs in order so that he can attend the Miracle will be very short. It would seem to be of great advantage, and perhaps even necessary, to have all travel arrangements made ahead of time. However, it is almost impossible to make firm travel commitments with a commercial carrier ahead of time when departure time is contingent on a future happening of a now uncertain date.**
>
> **I am wondering whether you might have established some arrangements for providing such travel services. . . .**

Although the *Garabandal* staff regretfully could not help at the time, at least one Marian organization, the 101 Foundation, now plans to charter planes to Spain once the date of the miracle is announced. The price is $1000 before the warning (a future worldwide experience of seeing one's sins as God sees them) and $1500 afterwards.

Christy A. Cousineau

By the last two decades of the nineteenth century, the Age was associated with a series of highly publicized French apparitions, beginning with one to a novice of the Daughters of Charity in Paris in 1830. Despite the widely divergent circumstances and messages accompanying each of these sets of visions, devotees connected them together into an interrelated narrative in which Mary was granting special favors to the historical period. Producing new shrines, devotions, and sacramentals, her appearances were understood as a sign of the millennial Triumph of both church and country during an age of anti-Christian rationalism. The humble faith of the visionaries offered a romantic alternative to the scientific expertise that was setting the foundation of the Second Industrial Revolution. Devotees connected the visionary events to nationalistic pride and understood the celebrated French apparitions to signal the glories of Gaul and her role as the "Eldest Daughter of the Church." The annual national pilgrimage to Lourdes, France (the most famous worldwide apparition site of the nineteenth and twentieth centuries), attracted groups of people representing countries from around the world and revealed the extent to which Marian millennialism was tied to nationalistic fervor. At the same time, brewing underneath the chiliastic anticipation was persistent apocalyptic anxiety: the Madonna gave stern warnings in some of her appearances about punishments to befall society if there was no repentance.

Age of Mary in the Twentieth Century

French devotional literature and members of religious orders carried their version of Marian piety to other countries, including the United States. During the first half of the twentieth century, the phrase "Age of Mary" went into decline, although devotees in France and other countries to which the devotion had spread still understood the apparitions of the period to form an interrelated narrative. Writers added new church-sanctioned visionary experiences to the on-going apparition saga: one to three shepherd children in Fatima, Portugal (1917), one to five children in Beauraing, Belgium (1932), and one to a young girl at her home in Banneaux, Belgium (1933). Devotional materials continued to follow many of the trends present in the nineteenth century, although without explicit millennial allusions. Relentless references to miraculous cures, especially at such healing shrines as the apparition site in Lourdes, France, continued to offer ample evidence to the devout reader that rationalism and science had crippling limitations in the face of the Virgin Mary. The endless cures critiqued secular culture as well, since many devotees understood atheistic rationalism to be at its roots. Pious writers also continued to set visionary meaning within the realm of contemporary happenings. The apparitions at Banneaux, for example, where the Madonna called herself the "Virgin of the Poor," was understood as a compassionate gift from a heavenly Mother sympathizing with her children as they suffered during the Great Depression.

After World War II, the idea of the Age gained a newfound popularity during the cold war, and in America the phrase "Age of Mary" enjoyed its greatest prominence between 1945 and the Second Vatican Council (1962 to 1965). Believers invested the notion so heavily in ideas of a future apocalypse that some embarrassed Catholic writers sought to redefine the concept as simply a time of special devotion to the Virgin. During this period, the "Age of Mary" implied not only the general sense that the Madonna is a special benefactor of the people of the industrial era, but also that she has come specifically to save the planet from the immediate threats of communism and nuclear catastrophe. Many Western Catholics imagined the Madonna as an angelic warrior Virgin protecting them against the horrors of satanic Bolshevism. They turned to the narrative of the 1917 apparitions to three shepherd children in Fatima, Portugal, for ritual practices to save the world from communism and a possible nuclear apocalypse. They imagined that an unrevealed "secret" of the Virgin to one of the seers contained prophesies of impending apocalyptic doom. Believers also awaited another Fatima prediction, the millennial "Triumph of Mary's Immaculate Heart," a postcommunist period of earthly peace and religious devotion to the Madonna. The narrative of the apparitions at Fatima was so important to cold-war Marian devotion that some commentators claimed that the Age of Mary had its origins in the 1917 visions in Portugal. At the same time that believers worried about the communist threat from without, they also grew increasingly more anxious about the secular threat from within. They criticized fashions, the media, consumerism, leftist political movements, and other aspects of Western culture that appeared to jeopardize traditional morals. Secularization seemed to be leading society increasingly on a downward slide, one that would end in communist takeover or supernatural punishment.

The interpretation of Vatican II and the political turmoil of the sixties promoted spiritual values that clashed with those that had supported Marian devotion in the 1950s in the West. The more intellectual, antiauthoritarian, individualistic American Catholicism that arose during the period had little room for imagining God sending fiery punishments. The idea of a Marian Age declined, but did not disappear. Disaffected Catholics, alarmed at the spread of what they saw as a degenerative spirituality, took comfort in devotion to the Madonna and accompanying apparition narratives. They considered many of the changes in the church to be further signs of the nearness of the apocalypse. Organizations such as the Blue Army (which had risen after World War II to promote the messages of Fatima) continued to publish anticommunist tracts hinting at the potential for nuclear attack and an unspecific future apocalypse based on the unrevealed secret. Other associations, such as The Workers of Our Lady of Mount Carmel and Our Lady of the Roses, sprung up to promote new apparition narratives and their popularization of new End Times scenarios.

By the late 1980s, the notion of an "Age of Mary" took root again in American devotional life. The meaning of the Age changed from a Virgin saving the planet from heinous communism to a Madonna pleading with her children to give up the prideful sins that abject rationalism had brought into the world. Inspired in part by a deeply Marian pope who both negotiated with communist leaders and criticized the consumer-driven West, believers turned to new apparition narratives as they grappled spiritually with a complex and changing political landscape. The popularization of the story of the Virgin's appearances to six young people in the town of Medjugorje in the former Yugoslavia marked this important turning point. The apparitions, beginning in 1981 and still ongoing as of late 1999, formed a narrative which embodied Pope John Paul II's critique of East and West by both portraying Marxist repression and criticizing American-style materialism. The initially hostile communist Yugoslav government imprisoned the parish pastor and a publicist of the messages, but eventually permitted pilgrims to visit the town, who returned home to describe an idyllic pastoral village offering spiritual nourishment to a world obsessed with material consumption.

Although the transformation of Russian communism through glasnost and the eventual collapse of the Soviet Union has not completely allayed anxieties about a communistic takeover among believers, it has led most to spend more time focusing on the supposed ills of Western society as signs of the upcoming apocalypse heralded by Mary and her Age. The renewed emphasis on societal conversion, the employment of emerging computing technologies, and the willingness of devotees to accept roles as leaders in the post-Vatican II church all helped popularize new apparition sites and apocalyptic scenarios. The abrogation of canon laws in 1966 requiring that all publication and dissemination of information about private revelation be approved by church authorities made it easier for the newly energized faithful to write newsletters, organize conferences, and establish prayer groups based on preternatural experience without fear of ecclesiastical sanction. As the list of visionaries and available material proliferated, many devotees understood the growth as renewed pleas from heaven for conversion and as yet another sign of an impending denouement to the Marian epoch. Marian compilers, such as Michael H. Brown in *The Final Hour* (1992), Ted and Maureen Flynn in *The Thunder of Justice* (1993), and Thomas W. Petrisko in *Call of the Ages* (1995), integrated the new apocalyptic stories and apparition accounts with the long-standing Age of Mary narrative. They describe Mary's many mystical appearances to diverse visionaries at the end of the twentieth century as wake-up calls for the need for conversion and as portents announcing the proximity of Armageddon.

The Age of Mary and Millennial Expectations

In part because of the large assortment of prophesies and in part because the institutional church rarely sanctions or condemns Marian predictions, conviction in a particular series of upcoming events can vary widely from believer to believer. Those who have apocalyptic leanings, much like their Protestant evangelical cousins, generally expect that the widespread life of material comfort industrialization and secularization brought to Western culture will erode through a series of tumultuous events, such as war, financial collapse, catastrophic climatic change, or the establishment of an oppressive one-world government. Next, divine forces will intervene to purify society of the supposed ill effects of secularization. Heaven will send final, supernatural calls to repentance and conversion; a purifying punishment; and, finally, a millennial utopia.

The most popular version of this future narrative in the last decade of the twentieth century is perhaps best summarized by the Flynns in the subtitle of their devotional manual as "the Warning, the Miracle, the Chastisement, [and] the Era of Peace." The first of the set, the warning, will be a terrifying interior experience sent from heaven to members of the entire human race, who will see their sins and understand them as they would before the eyes of God. Shortly thereafter, great miracles will occur at the apparition sites of Medjugorje and Garabandal, Spain. If neither the warning nor the miracles lead to general repentance, then a chastisement will visit the earth, most likely in the form of the Three Days of Darkness, when, for seventy-two hours, there will be no light, whether natural or artificial. Electric and fire-based technologies will fail, and many people will die in the planetary chaos. The chastisement deprives the world of control over fire, a fundamental technology which fueled the Industrial Revolution and ensuing cultural changes. After this destructive punishment, a chiliastic era of peace will reign. Although notions of what the millennium will look like are various and often vague, the reiterating theme of agricultural utopia suggests a world in which believers are finally rescued from the perils of industrial life. Thus we can read the Age of Mary of the last decade of the twentieth century much as we would read its nineteenth century manifestations as longing for a nostalgic and romantic return to a time before the onslaught of rationalism introduced the era of the machine.

Christy A. Cousineau

See also Bayside (Our Lady of the Roses), Fatima Cult, Marianism, Prophecy, Roman Catholicism, Secular Millennialism

Bibliography

Brown, Michael H. (1992) *The Final Hour.* Milford, OH: Faith Publishing.

Cuneo, Michael W. (1997) *The Smoke of Satan: Conservative and Traditionalist Dissent in Contemporary American Catholicism.* New York: Oxford University Press.

Flynn, Ted, and Maureen Flynn. (1993) *The Thunder of Justice: The Warning, the Miracle, the Chastisement, the Era of Peace: God's Ultimate Acts of Mercy.* Sterling, VA: MaxKol Communications.

Grignion de Montfort, Louis Marie. ([1987] 1997) "True Devotion to Mary." In *God Alone: The Collected Writings of St. Louis Marie de Montfort,* edited and translated by the staff of Montfort Publications. Bay Shore, NY: Montfort Publications, 289–397.

Kselman, Thomas A. (1983) *Miracles and Prophesies in Nineteenth-Century France.* New Brunswick, NJ: Rutgers University Press.

Perry, Nicholas, and Loreto Echeverria. (1988) *Under the Heel of Mary.* London: Routledge.

Petrisko, Thomas W. (1995) *Call of the Ages.* Santa Barbara, CA: Queenship.

Savart, Claude. (1972) "Cent ans après: Les apparitions mariales en France au XIXe siècle, un ensemble?" *Revue d'histoire de la spiritualité* 48: 205–20.

Zimdars-Swartz, Sandra. (1991) *Encountering Mary: From La Salette to Medjugorje.* Princeton, NJ: Princeton University Press.

Akkadian and Babylonian Apocalypses

The area of Akkad is now that of central Iraq, while Assyria is in north-central Iraq and Babylon is in southern Iraq. These three kingdoms were all of Semitic ancestry and supplanted the previous Sumerian kingdoms of southern Iraq in 2350 BCE, when Sargon of Akkad conquered them. His dynasty lasted approximately until 2000 BCE, and was eventually supplanted by the Old Babylonian Dynasty (2000–1763 BCE). Over a period of hundreds of years, the Assyrian dynasties came to dominate Iraq, and eventually most of the Near East between 746–607. Their domination was followed by that of the New Babylonian Dynasty (626–539 BCE), known best for its part in taking the people of the Kingdom of Judah (the Jews) into captivity. The New Babylonian Dynasty was eventually overthrown by the Persians.

Babylonian apocalyptic texts in the Akkadian language are the oldest known to date. They consist of purported predictions in an affected historical style. Whether they are actually *post eventum* (after the fact) is the subject of a good deal of debate, since the events described are frequently so vague that interpretation on the basis of historical events is impossible. Some have been identified with the reign of Nebuchadnezzar I (1124–1103 BCE) of the Old Babylonian Dynasty, who defeated the Elamites (a people located in the mountains to the east of Babylonia, who were among the principal foes of the Babylonians), and recovered the statue of the god Marduk, which the Elamites had taken previously. While the following generalizations will not cover all of the prophecies, the texts usually describe a situation of chaos brought about by the misrule of an evil king, which leads to natural disasters and celestial omens on the part of the gods warning the people to repent. Invaders come (either Elamites, Amorites, or Hittites), sacking and destroying the land, frequently plundering the temples of the gods, and taking the contents of these temples back to their own lands. There is then a renewal in the country, and a new king or dynasty comes to the fore. The gods bless the new rulers and allow them to retake the plundered treasures and return them to their rightful places either in Nippur or Uruk or one of the other holy cities. These last are the liberation apocalyptic prophecies which date from the time of Nebuchadnezzar I, prophesying the end of kingdoms and the restoration of the primary position of the god Marduk and the city of Babylon. Occasionally there are simply long predictions of the qualities of certain kings, some good and some bad, accompanied by astrological omens.

The place of this literature is uncertain in the context of Akkadian life; there is no evidence that these texts were designed for popular consumption. Usually the parallels are to the Akkadian and Babylonian omen texts, which saw history cyclically, and thus found value in lore of this nature, as it was bound to happen again in the future. Some have also seen these texts as part of the beginnings of apocalyptic literature, which was to blossom over a thousand years later. It is possible that the texts represented some form of conflict between the religious and royal elite, but there is no evidence concerning this. There is no evidence of literary dependency at this point between Akkadian/Babylonian apocalyptic and either Jewish apocalyptic or Zoroastrian apocalyptic. Later Assyrian rulers also used apocalyptic texts of the imperial type, usually glorifying the ruler and giving him divine legitimacy. Prophecies are recorded concerning the later Assyrian rulers Esarhaddon and Assurbanipal (681–650 BCE), which are sometimes oracles of encouragement or dominion: "Mullissu [a prophetess] has said: you [Esarhaddon] shall rule over the kings of the lands; you shall show them their frontiers and set the courses they take" (Parpola 1997, 38). This type of apocalyptic literature is important because it formulated the type of what imperial (progovernment) apocalyptic patterns would be like for all time: the sin-punishment-repentance-renewal-victory process so central to Biblical and Muslim apocalyptic cycles.

David Cook

See also Apocalypse

Bibliography

Biggs, Robert D. (1967) "More Akkadian Prophecies." *Iraq* 29: 117–32.

Grayson, A. K., and W. G. Lambert. (1964) "Akkadian Prophecies." *Journal of Cuneiform Studies* 18: 7–23.

Hallo, William W. (1966) "Akkadian Apocalypses." *Israel Exploration Journal* 16: 131–42.

Hunger, Hermann, and Stephen Kaufman. (1975) "A New Akkadian Prophecy Text." *Journal of the American Oriental Society* 95: 371–75.

Lambert, Wilferd G. (1978) *The Background of Jewish Apocalyptic*. London: The Athlone Press.

Parpola, Sima. (1997) *Assyrian Prophecies*. Helsinki: Helsinki University Press.

Anabaptists

The name "Anabaptists" was given by its opponents to a loosely connected grouping of evangelical Christians in the sixteenth century. It is a translation of the German "*Wiedertäufer*," and means rebaptizers. The name was first applied to a group that formed in Switzerland around Conrad Grebel and, after Grebel's death, Michael Sattler, in the 1520s. It is now applied, especially in English-speaking scholarship, to much of the so-called Radical Reformation of the sixteenth century.

The Radical Reformation, sometimes called the "left wing" of the Reformation, is considered one of four major types of church grouping to grow out of the breakaway from Rome alongside of Lutheranism, the Reformed churches (Zwinglian and Calvinist), and Anglicanism. The term "radical" is appropriate to the degree that, at least in externalities, the Anabaptists and others made a cleaner break with Roman Catholicism than the other branches of the Reformation. On the other hand, parallels between their stress on discipleship and medieval asceticism suggest that their understanding of Christianity remained structurally close to that of the Middle Ages.

Anabaptism is primarily associated with apocalypticism because of an experiment in theocratic rule at Münster, Germany, 1534–35, that ended in its bloody suppression. This incident has been called the "most sensational expression of popular apocalypticism in the sixteenth century" (Barnes 1996: 64), and the movement as a whole "the gravest danger to an orderly and comprehensive reformation of Christendom" (Williams 1992: xxviii). Millennialism—chiliasm in the strict sense of an explicit belief in a thousand-year reign of Christ on earth before the last judgment—was rare but did surface in a few figures.

Location in Time and Space

The Reformation began when Martin Luther (1483–1546), an Augustinian monk and theology professor, began to question many of the teachings and practices of the Church of Rome. Yet Luther believed—as did almost all Western Europeans of his time—that this church was the church that Jesus Christ had founded. Nevertheless, he began to call his fellow Christians out of what he called the Babylonian captivity of that church.

Soon, however, the Reformation took on aspects that Luther, a basically conservative man, could not control. He began a bitter controversy with Swiss reformer Ulrich Zwingli (1484–1531) over the meaning of the bread and wine in the Lord's Supper. But in one point they were agreed: other leaders and groups that tried to move the Reformation closer to their vision of the true church were even more dangerous than the "papists." Prominent among these were the Anabaptists.

The key difference between mainstream reformers such as Luther and Zwingli on the one hand and the radicals on the other was a different understanding of the church. Despite their criticism of Rome, Luther and Zwingli still held to medieval picture of the church as basically synonymous with the population of a Christian state. The "radicals" sought a church that was made up of committed believers.

Luther and Zwingli's resistance to radical groups such as the Anabaptists was based not only on theological, but also on strategic considerations. They were aware that Rome could mobilize the military might of the Holy Roman Empire to crush religious nonconformity. It had only been a century since Bohemian reformer John Hus (c. 1372–1415) had been burned at the stake. Luther and Zwingli knew that without the support of princes and city councils that they could suffer the same fate. To allow the Reformation camp to further splinter could jeopardize the support of the nobility and burghers that they needed—especially if those splinter groups believed, as some of them did, that the day of God's vengeance upon the mighty of the world had come and that they were its instruments.

The first identifiably Anabaptist movement arose in Zürich among zealous erstwhile supporters of Zwingli. They became disillusioned with him when it became clear that he would defer to the civil authorities of the city in the matter of concrete reforms such as the abolition of images and the mass. Disappointed over Zwingli's hesitation, they presented him with a program calling for a church of believers, in which real sanctification would be promoted. In the course of 1524, infant baptism became an issue, possibly because of the influence in Switzerland of writings by Andreas Bodenstein von Karlstadt, a former colleague of Luther's, and Thomas Müntzer, who would soon gain notoriety for his role in the Peasants' War.

The founding act of Anabaptism was Conrad Grebel's baptism of Georg Blaurock, a former priest, in Zürich on 21 January 1525. This adult baptism occurred immediately following the Zürich government's decision that this group's objections to infant baptism were unfounded, and were considered acts of defiance by Zwingli and the city council.

Although the beginning of the movement can be precisely located in time and space, it was not a unitary movement. Current scholarship identifies six major, and twenty lesser, movements, which can be broadly grouped into three families: the Swiss Brethren (those stemming from Conrad Grebel and Michael Sattler); the groups inspired by Hans Denck and Hans Hut, beginning at Augsburg in 1526; and the Melchiorites, inspired by the apocalyptic preaching of Melchior Hoffman. Within these broad groupings there are many groups, "most of them making exclusivist claims and condemning the others" (Stayer 1996: 32). Anabaptist congregations were radically decentralized, a trait common to many of their descendants today.

Key Beliefs and Actions

The Anabaptists combined a literal understanding of the Bible with a belief in the direct inspiration of ordinary people by the holy spirit. This view of scripture included a mistrust of university-trained theologians. Anabaptist leader Pilgram Marpeck chided Caspar Schwenckfeld in a letter written in 1544 for the lack of the simplicity that Christ said was necessary to receive God's revelation:

> Just as God has always begun so will God conclude: with the faithful and simple people. Thus, He will save man by means of true language and teaching. All the more so, because the world in these last days is becoming increasingly more crafty and more cunning, more scribal and more evil. Therefore, God also conceals His true, unadulterated, pure understanding of salvation behind so much deeper, truer simplicity, and brings about the realization of faith in Christ in the simple hearts. . . . Therefore, to learn the language of the simple, faithful, truly believing hearts is now, in these last dangerous times, when the fullness of the Gentiles has come in, a thousand times more necessary and useful than to learn Latin, Greek, Hebrew, or other languages. (Marpeck 1978: 371)

One result of this emphasis was a willingness to reopen all theological questions, especially those whose resolution in earlier centuries had depended more on philosophical argumentation than appeal to clear scriptural teaching. For this reason, some combined their Anabaptism with anti-Trinitarianism, and a few adopted the practice of the seventh-day Sabbath.

The belief that there would be an outpouring of the spirit in the last days was not only grounded in scriptures such as Acts 2:17–18, but also on the prophecies of Joachim of Fiore, a twelfth-century Cistercian monk who divided history according to a Trinitarian scheme. He understood his own day as the waning of the second age, the age of the Son. This would be succeeded by a third age, the age of the Spirit.

Based on Acts 3:21, Anabaptists expected that the age immediately preceding the return of Jesus Christ would be one of the restitution of all things. To them, this meant above all a restoration of the faith and practice of the New Testament church. Ever since the conversion of Roman emperor Constantine in the fourth century, the church had no longer been a sect of committed believers, a church of martyrs, but a state church. In such a church, the distinction between clergy and laity would disappear; in its place, the direct inspiration of the Holy Spirit would guide men and women in matters of faith and practice.

Anabaptists understood Christianity as obedience to Christ. They placed more emphasis on ethical practice, as outlined in the Sermon on the Mount and the idealized view of the early church in the book of Acts, than on dogma. This concentration on ethical practice led to social radicalism as well as a withdrawal from civic duties.

The understanding of the nature of the church as a gathering of committed believers, in combination with the emphasis on strict ethical practice, resulted in the practice of shunning. Anabaptists and their successors have retained an understanding that moral failure not only affects the individual in his or her relation to God, but is also in some way a sin against the fellowship he or she has pledged to uphold.

All Anabaptists lived with the certainty that they were living in the last time. The prophecy in 2 Timothy 3:1–5 that in the last days perilous times would come was so ingrained in Anabaptist thinking that the phrase "these dangerous last days" was a common expression among them to refer to the times they lived in. They shared this expectation, however, with many of their contemporaries, including Luther, so that while it is a characteristic trait, it was not unique to them. In addition, a distinction between activist and contemplative forms of apocalypticism can be made. On the one hand, there were those such as Bernhard Rothmann, theoretician of the Münster Anabaptists, who believed that just as Elijah slew the prophets of Baal (1 Kings 18:40), so now the time of God's vengeance had come, and his true followers on earth were to be the instruments of it. On the other hand, many Anabaptists, such as Menno Simons, believed in passively waiting for God to establish his kingdom.

The first Anabaptist known to have set a date for the end was Hans Hut, who believed that Jesus Christ would return on Pentecost 1528 and that the elect would then exterminate the godless. The most widespread scenario was that of Melchior Hoffman, who expected the end of the age in 1533.

Growth and Spread during the Reformation

The Zurich authorities suppressed and scattered the first Anabaptist group, but not before an Anabaptist conference led by Michael Sattler drafted a statement of beliefs in February 1527, known at the Schleitheim Confession. In the meantime, similar movements sprang up in other German-speaking areas and in the Netherlands. The movement was condemned at the Diet of Speyer (April 1529), attended by leaders of both Protestant and Catholic areas. Emperor Charles V instructed imperial officials to deal severely with them, but the severity of repression varied widely from area to area. Protestant civil leaders generally had less zeal to execute dissenters than did Catholic.

Strasbourg, a relatively tolerant city, became an early center of Anabaptism. Melchior Hoffman, in his interpretation of the book of Revelation, proclaimed the city the location of the spiritual temple that would be attacked by the beast (the pope), the dragon (the emperor), and the false prophet (the monks), but successfully defended, leading to the return of Jesus Christ to establish his eternal kingdom.

By the time Hoffman's predicted date of 1533 arrived, Anabaptist expectations centered on another city. Münster, in northwest Germany, despite being a bishop's seat, had been receptive to reform. When Anabaptist refugees arrived there in September 1532, they were received readily, and leading clergy, led by Bernhard Rothmann, accepted their views, although baptisms were not carried out because Hoffman had suspended the practice pending the onset of the end. Melchiorite apostles sent from Holland by Jan Matthijs, who had resumed baptizing, arrived there in January 1534. Within a few days of their arrival, they baptized most of the clergy there and roughly one-quarter of the populace. Matthijs sent Jan of Leiden with revelations and instructions, then traveled personally to the city in February. On 23 February, the Anabaptists gained control of the city through civic elections. Matthijs moved immediately to suppress dissent by declaring that all who refused baptism should be killed. City leaders, supported by Jan of Leiden, argued that they should be merely expelled without their possessions. Many accepted baptism at this point, but others left.

Anabaptists from other parts, especially the Netherlands, responded to an appeal to gather there to escape God's wrath, but many of them were turned back on the way by authorities. When the expected end did not come on Easter (5 April), Matthijs went out of the city with a few followers to attack the combined Catholic-Lutheran army that by then had assembled to besiege the city and restore its prince-bishop, Franz von Waldeck. If God routed the numerous enemy through these few, Matthijs would be vindicated, despite his failed prediction. Instead, he and his men were killed. Nevertheless, some expected that he would rise and visibly ascend to heaven. This did not happen, and Jan van Leiden was proclaimed king in early September 1534. He reinforced the community of goods that Matthijs had instituted; in addition, he instituted polygamy. The Anabaptists were betrayed from within the city and the bishop was restored in June 1535.

Meanwhile, Anabaptists in Holland, inspired by the example of Münster, twice attempted to take over Amsterdam. In reaction, the city, once tolerant of religious dissent, began repressive measures, through which Anabaptists of all kinds, peaceful as well as violent, suffered.

Survival to the Present Day

Münster can be regarded as a turning point in the Anabaptist movement. In its wake, many recanted. Others fled to Moravia, where the ruling lords desired colonists, or to Poland and, later, the Ukraine. The pacifist Anabaptists in the Netherlands and northern Germany rallied under the leadership of Menno Simons, a former priest, and his helper Dirk Philips. Although these men and others continued to believe they were living in the endtimes, they refused all attempts at date setting and categorically rejected all thought that humans should actively seek to bring God's kingdom.

Anabaptists continued to be harried on the Continent. The Peace of Augsburg (1555) allowed for Lutheranism and Catholicism in the empire—but not Anabaptism (nor the Reformed followers of Zwingli or Calvin, for that matter, although they were later included among the tolerated religions). The Anabaptists found political freedom first in Holland under William of Orange (1574), then in England. The effect of Dutch tolerance was, first, a dramatic increase in numbers. By 1700 there were 160,000 baptized members in the Netherlands. The second effect, though, was assimilation. Now called Mennonites, they were strongly influenced by the Enlightenment, and by 1837 membership had declined to about 15,300.

Persecution in Switzerland continued into the eighteenth century. Anabaptists there left for southern Germany, Alsace, the Netherlands, and North America (beginning in 1663). In contrast to their brethren in Holland and northern Germany, who became urbanized and included many successful businessmen, the Anabaptists in southern Germany and Alsace lived in semiclosed rural communities with an agrarian economy.

By World War I, Mennonite communities in Russia numbered over 120,000 members and were largely autonomous. In the Soviet Union the communities were either destroyed during World War II or dissolved by the government soon after. Because of the German ancestry of many, they were eligible to be repatriated to the Federal Republic of Germany. Many had earlier emigrated to North and South America.

Mennonites, Hutterites (as the Moravian Anabaptists came to be called), and the Amish (a breakaway from the Mennonites in the late seventeenth century), survived through a strategy of withdrawal from society, combined with a rigorous internal discipline. Although they can be found in many parts of the world, their largest concentration is in North America.

Major Anabaptist Leaders

Conrad Grebel (c. 1498–1526)

Grebel was a Zürich patrician with a humanist education at Basel, Vienna, and Paris who was at first an enthusiastic supporter of Zwingli. The radicals crystallized into a group under his leadership during 1524. His main interest was the practical reforms he believed were the consequence of Zwingli's preaching, such as the abolition of tithes, images, and mass. His conviction that the church should be an assembly of committed believers grew out of his disappointment when Zwingli bowed to the wishes of the city council to delay action on these issues. Opposition to infant baptism became a further issue when a Reformed pastor near Zürich began preaching against it and some families refused to have their newborn infants baptized. After the city council condemned this, Grebel performed the first adult baptism in January 1525. He was imprisoned, then escaped, but died of the plague while a fugitive.

Melchior Hoffman (c. 1500–1543?)

Hoffman was a furrier from Swabia (southwestern Germany). He became a Lutheran lay preacher in the Baltic lands, especially the present-day Tartu, Estonia, but his radical apocalyptic version of Lutheranism led to his banishment in the summer of 1526. Before leaving, he completed his first major written work, a commentary on Daniel 12. We do not know who baptized him, although he had contact with Hut-Denck Anabaptists in Strasbourg in 1529 and may have been baptized there. He identified himself with the angel (the Greek word also means messenger) of Revelation 14:6–7, who proclaimed the everlasting gospel, as well as with the angel of Revelation 10:1–7. He brought Anabaptism to northern Germany and Holland in 1530 and gained many followers. He taught that the world would end in 1533 and that the new age would begin in Strasbourg. When he returned there to await the end he was imprisoned and probably died there in 1543, although there is some evidence that he recanted and returned to his home city of Schwäbisch Hall.

Jan Matthijs (c. 1480–1534)

A baker from Haarlem, Matthijs rose to prominence among the Melchiorites in Amsterdam, to which he had secretly fled with his young mistress (he had abandoned his legal wife, who had not shared his religious views). In the uncertainty of 1533, when Hoffmann's prediction of the end of the age had not been fulfilled, Matthijs claimed that God had revealed to him that he was Enoch and that he and "Elijah" (Melchior Hoffmann) were to be the two witnesses of Revelation 11. He moved to Leiden, where he met Jan Bockelszoon, and from where he sent out pairs of apostles to rally the Melchiorites. Two Matthijs apostles arrived in Münster on 5 January 1534 and achieved immediate success. Matthijs went there personally in February and became the dominant figure in the city. He initiated the destruction of images and the burning of books to purify the city before the day of God's wrath on the world, which would come that Easter. When this did not occur, he went out of the city to confront the enemy with a handful of supporters and was killed.

Thomas Müntzer (c. 1490–1525)

Müntzer's relation to Anabaptism is controversial. He was never formally a part of the movement, although Luther saw him as one. While Mennonite historians long kept their distance, in more recent times they have reassessed his role. An early supporter of Luther, his first notoriety was as a reformation preacher in Zwickau, an economically depressed mining and weaving town in Saxony, where he stressed the direct access of all to God. Lack of education was no hindrance, since the Spirit of God spoke in each person. After he was expelled from Zwickau, he moved to Prague, where, in 1521, he published his Prague Manifesto, in which he called on the people of that city to initiate a true, spirit-led reformation. As opposition grew, he left that city, eventually settling in Allstedt, in Thuringia, where, as pastor, he had an opportunity to work as a reformer. He published his first two booklets, which were read by Grebel and his circle in Zürich. In one of them, he attacked infant baptism. He was asked to preach before Duke John, and used the occasion to expound Daniel 2 and to try to enlist the Saxon court for his views. At that time, the Peasants' War began, and Müntzer saw in it the beginning of God's judgment on the world. He joined the peasants, was captured at the decisive battle of Frankenhausen, and beheaded.

Bernhard Rothmann (d. 1535?)

The leading reformer, preacher, and theologian in Münster, Rothmann was won over to a Melchiorite Anabaptism when refugees arrived in the city in September 1532. His defense of believer's baptism, *Confession of the Two Sacraments*, may have been influential in causing Jan Matthijs to end Hoffman's suspension of the practice. Rothmann and others were then baptized by the Melchiorite apostles when they arrived in January 1534. Rothmann was the leading theological apologist for the Anabaptist experiment in theocracy during the next eighteen months. He elaborated and modified the Melchiorite endtime scheme. Although his death was not confirmed, it is likely that he died when Münster was overtaken.

Michael Sattler (c. 1490–1527)

Together with Conrad Grebel, Sattler is identified as founder of one of three main groupings of Anabaptists, the Swiss Brethren. A former Benedictine prior, he joined the Zürich group in 1525. The Schleitheim Confession (February 1527), a document in which the main tenets of the Swiss movement are set out in seven articles, was prepared under his leadership. Schleitheim is a village on the Swiss border near Schaffhausen. Interestingly, it lies directly across the Wutach River from Stühlingen in Germany, where the Peasants' War had broken out in 1525. He was executed in Rottenburg on the Neckar in May 1527.

Menno Simons (1496–1561)

A Dutch priest, Simons long sympathized with the Anabaptists and finally joined the movement in 1536. He rallied the Anabaptists in the Netherlands and northern Germany after the Münster debacle. Born into a peasant family in Friesland, he entered the priesthood in 1524; and seven years later, became the parish priest of his hometown, Witmarsum, although by this time he was known as an evangelical preacher. During his first year in the priesthood he began to doubt the real presence of Christ in the Eucharist. His subsequent study of the Bible and the writings of Martin Luther led to other convictions, such as the need for believer baptism and a church committed to living a holy life. The turning point in his life came in 1535 when members of his parish, including Peter Simons, who may have been his brother, were killed when a cloister they had occupied was stormed. When Münster fell a few months later he spoke out on behalf of those whom he felt were misguided spirits. He went into hiding and spent a year deciding what the future course of his life should be. After being asked to lead a group of pacifist Anabaptists he traveled widely and wrote prolifically. He died in Oldesloe, northeast of Hamburg, where he had established a base of operations late in life. The Mennonites take their name from him.

Anabaptist Membership

Anabaptists in Switzerland and southern Germany were originally urban rather than rural. In the early days of the movement, there was a fairly high proportion of leaders with intellectual or pastoral backgrounds. This changed significantly after 1550, as the effects of persecution took their toll. At no time, however, were the Anabaptists numerically significant.

In Austria, Anabaptism appears to have drawn its support from the peasantry. Some estimate that as many as two-thirds of the population of the Upper Inn in Tirol, especially among the miners, held Anabaptist beliefs in the 1520s. One prominent convert was Pilgram Marpeck, an imperial mine inspector. Many either recanted or fled in the face of Habsburg severity, and the movement quickly lost its potential to gain a mass following.

As for Holland, most early Anabaptists there were artisans, a segment of society especially hard hit by the social, economic, political, and religious problems of the third and fourth decades of the sixteenth century. "The large numbers of artisans who joined the Anabaptist movement, their enthusiastic adoption of apocalypticism, their almost complete lack of an educated leadership, and the desperate nature of their hope and migrations, all attest to the fact that most of those who joined the Anabaptist movement in the Netherlands did so out of a profound sense of crisis" (Waite 1990: 29).

Descendants of the Anabaptists have nourished a martyrology of their forebears in the sixteenth century. Modern research, however, has reduced the number of those executed for Anabaptist belief. Claus-Peter Clasen has been able to document 845 certain and probable executions of Anabaptists in Switzerland, southern and central Germany, and Austria between 1525 and the Thirty Years' War; he concedes the possibility of two or three hundred additional executions. Estimates for the Netherlands vary from fifteen hundred to at least twenty-five hundred.

Cultural, Social, and Political Aspects

The belief that the end of human history was approaching was widespread in the early sixteenth century. Luther, for one, believed it, and accepted the conviction of some of his followers that he was the spiritual Elijah who was to come before the return of Jesus Christ. While there were some religious leaders who did not have a great interest in it (Erasmus and Zwingli are two examples), they were in the minority. The Anabaptists shared the conviction of their time.

The return to scripture as norm for faith and practice was common to the whole Reformation, as well. In the Anabaptists it found its most thoroughgoing adherents, combined with an insistence that scripture—newly available in the languages of the common people—could be understood, and therefore interpreted, by all.

The Anabaptists are often considered the first proponents of the separation of church and state, and therefore the progenitors of religious freedom. While the influence of the Anabaptist movement, both directly and indirectly via England, should not be underestimated, its adherents hardly envisioned the religious landscape as it developed in the United States. When their original vision of a society thoroughly renewed by the gospel was denied, they recognized in themselves the restitution of the one true church of the New Testament, not as one of a plurality of religions.

Summary

Endtime movements in Christianity are often characterized by a triad of beliefs: a literal understanding of the scriptures; the conviction of living in the last generation (or that the end is "near"); and that the essence of Christianity lies in convicted discipleship, leading in many cases to a striving for perfectionism. These three elements were present in all expressions of Anabaptism. Various strands differed as to whether one should passively await God's intervention, or whether the faithful should take action to help initiate these events.

The name Anabaptist is a misnomer for two reasons. First, in the eyes of those who practiced believer baptism, it was the only true baptism. Only for their opponents, who maintained the efficacy of infant baptism, was it a repeat baptism. For this reason, recent German-language scholarship prefers to refer to them as *Täufer* (Baptists). English-language scholarship has not followed in this practice, to avoid confusion with the more widely known Baptist churches that had their origin slightly later in England. Second, and more importantly, it is reductionist. It focuses on one tenet and does not describe the whole program (although that tenet is emblematic for the overall program). The Anabaptists were an endtime-oriented movement, yet to consider them only in those terms would be equally reductionist.

Henry Sturcke

See also Protestantism

Bibliography

Primary sources

Much has been done in the twentieth century to edit and publish documentation of the movement. The stricture in 1 Peter 3:15 to be in a continual state of readiness to "give an answer to every man that asks you a reason of the hope that is in you" was taken seriously by Anabaptists, and they were very open in court interrogations, which for them were opportunities to witness. These records form the bulk of the series of source documents that have been published.

Marpeck, Pilgram. (1978) *Writings (WPM)*, translated and edited by William Klassen and Walter Klaassen. Scottdale, PA, and Kitchener, Ontario: Herald Press.

Mellink, A. F., ed. (1975–1985) *Documenta Anabaptistica Neerlandica*. Vol. 1: *Friesland en Groningen, 1530–1550*. Vol. 2: *Amsterdam, 1536–1578*. Vol. 5: *Amsterdam, 1531–1536*. Leiden: E.J. Brill.

Müntzer, Thomas. (1988) *The Collected Works of Thomas Müntzer*, edited and translated by Peter Matheson. Edinburgh, U.K.: T. & T. Clark.

Sattler, Michael. (1973) *The Legacy of Michael Sattler*, edited by John H. Yoder. Scottdale, PA: Herald Press.

Secondary sources

Barnes, Robin B. (1996) S.v. Apocalypticism. In *The Oxford Encyclopedia of the Reformation*. New York and Oxford: Oxford University Press.

Bender, Harold S. (1950) *Conrad Grebel, c. 1498–1526: The Founder of the Swiss Brethren, Sometimes Called Anabaptists*, Goshen, IN: Mennonite Historical Society.

Clasen, Claus-Peter. (1972) *Anabaptism: A Social History, 1525–1618; Switzerland, Austria, Moravia, and South and Central Germany*. Ithaca, NY: Cornell University Press.

Davis, Kenneth R. (1974) *Anabaptism and Asceticism*. Scottdale, PA: Herald Press.

Deppermann, Klaus, Werner O. Packull, and James M. Stayer. (1975) "From Monogenesis to Polygenesis: The Historical Discussion of Anabaptist Origins." *Mennonite Quarterly Review* 49: 83–122.

Goertz, Hans-Jürgen. (1989) *Thomas Müntzer: Mystiker, Apokalyptiker, Revolutionär*. Munich: Beck.

Goertz, Hans-Jürgen, ed. (1982) *Profiles of Radical Reformers*. Kitchener, Ontario: Herald Press.

Klaassen, Walter. (1992) *Living at the End of the Ages: Apocalyptic Expectation in the Radical Reformation*. Lanham, MD: University Press of America.

Packull, Werner O. (1977) *Mysticism and the Early South German-Austrian Anabaptist Movement, 1525–1531*. Studies in Anabaptist and Mennonite History, 19. Scottdale, PA, and Kitchener, Ontario: Herald Press.

Stayer, James M. (1996) S.v. Anabaptists. In *The Oxford Encyclopedia of the Reformation*. New York and Oxford, U.K.: Oxford University Press.

Stayer, James M., and Werner O. Packull, eds. (1980) *The Anabaptists and Thomas Müntzer*. Dubuque, IA: Kendall/Hunt.

Waite, Gary K. (1990) *David Joris and Dutch Anabaptism 1524–1543*. Waterloo, Ontario: Wilfrid Laurier University Press.

Williams, George H. (1992) *The Radical Reformation*. Sixteenth Century Essays and Studies, 15. Kirksville, MO: Thomas Jefferson University Press.

Ancient World

Millenarianism or millennialism is the belief in the end of this world or age and the arrival of a New Age or New World of perfected harmony, free of tragedy, suffering, evil, and even death itself. This view of the future is to be distinguished from notions of an escape or release from this world, and an entrance into a perfected existence in a heavenly realm beyond, though these views are often intertwined and related. The earliest fully developed expressions of millenarianism in the ancient Western world are found in the Prophets of the Hebrew Bible (OT), beginning in the eighth century BCE. The early Christians expanded and developed these views, relating them to the Second Coming of Jesus Christ and his one thousand year (Latin *mille*, "thousand") reign before the creation of a New Heavens and New Earth (Revelation 20–22). However, we can find elements of millenarian thinking, or perhaps what might be called protomillenarianism, in ancient Egyptian, Babylonian, Persian, Greek, and Roman texts as well. In the ancient Eastern world, we also find within Hindu, Buddhist, and Taoist traditions, ideas about unfolding cycles and epochs of history, but since they never involve the permanent transformation of *this* world, but either an escape therefrom, or a merging into the cosmos itself, they are not properly classified as millenarian—at least not in the Western sense. This article will concentrate, accordingly, on the ancient Western world.

Near Eastern Millennial Visions

The Ancient Near Eastern (Egyptian, Babylonian, Hebrew) view of history generally places emphasis on an ordered world, shaped out of primordial chaos, that is essentially unchanging. The gods have created things so that humans have their place on earth, death is an inevitable part of their lot, and the future, though subject to the periodic fluctuations of floods, drought, war, and disease, is essentially immutable. History is an endless repetition of the cycles of the past. The Sumerian poem of the Pickax (third millennium BCE) puts it well:

> The lord, he who truly created the normal order,
> The lord, whose decisions are inalterable,
> Enlil, who bring up the seed of the land from the earth,
> Took care to move away heaven and earth . . .
> So that the seed from which grew the nations could sprout up from the field . . .
> So that humankind could grow from the earth . . .
> He introduced labor and decreed fate,
> The pickman's way of life . . . its fate decreed by father Enlil. (Kramer 1944: 51–53)

This order, established from the beginning, provides humankind its proper place. Within that allotted place are decreed a whole set of fates or ways of life, here illustrated by the lowly pickman. The duty of humankind is to affirm and fulfill that place, both in society and in the larger cosmos, as servants of the gods. The ancient Mesopotamian hero Gilgamesh (second millennium BCE), who vainly searches for the secret of eternal life, is admonished at one point in his quest by the barmaid Siduri:

> Gilgamesh, why do you wander?
> The life you pursue you will not find.
> When the gods created humankind,
> Death for humankind they decreed,
> Life in their own hand retaining.
> You Gilgamesh, let your belly be full,
> Make merry by day and by night,
> Of each day make a feast of rejoicing,
> Day and night dance and play. (*Gilgamesh Epic* 10.3)

In ancient Egyptian texts the ordered cycle of the seasons, with the regular flooding of the Nile, mirrored the balance within the cosmos, created and guaranteed by the gods. The birth of Rameses II (1300 BCE) was celebrated by his divine father Amum-Ra: "I have put justice *(ma'at)* into its place, so that the earth is made firm, heaven is satisfied, and the gods are content" (Breasted 1907: 4, 26). This general view of things is echoed in the older parts of the Hebrew Bible—as Psalm 115:16–17 puts it: "The heavens are Yahweh's heavens, but the earth he has given to human beings. The death do not praise Yahweh, nor do any that go down into silence." After the Flood, humans are given the guarantee: "As long as earth endures, seedtime and harvest, cold and heat, summer and winter, day and night shall not cease" (Genesis 8:22).

It is against this decidedly nonmillenarian view of history that one can find minor deviations. The Middle Kingdom (second millennium BCE) delivered Egypt from the severe social disruptions of civil war and anarchy so that the pharaohs who reestablished order were celebrated with a sense of messianic salvation. In the most important text of this type, *The Prophecy of Neferti*, foretells the downfall of the Old Kingdom and the reestablishment of order by Amenemhet I, the first king of the new dynasty. Both society and nature are disorder in this text:

> Lo, the great no longer rule the land . . .
> All happiness has vanished,
> The land is bowed down in distress . . .
> I show you the land in turmoil:
> The weak is strong-armed,
> One salutes him who saluted . . .
> The beggar will gain riches,
> The great will [will rob] to live . . .
> Dry is the river of Egypt,
> One crosses the water on foot . . .
> Re will withdraw from humankind:
> Though he will rise at his hour,
> One will not know when noon has come;
> No one will discern his shadow. (Pritchard: 1969 444–45)

The text closes with a triumphant celebration of Amenemhet I: "It is then that a King will come from the south, Ameni, the triumphant, his name. Rejoice you people of his time. . . . Asiatics will fall to his sword, and the Libyans will fall to his flame, and the treacherous of heart will be in awe of him, . . . and justice will come into its place while wrongdoing is driven out" (Pritchard 1969: 446). Although one might call this text protoapocalyptic, because of its declaration of hope and sudden deliverance in the midst of despair, it lacks a fully developed millenarian view of the future. The "salvation" or transformation brought by the new pharaoh is still wholly of this world. It is essentially the reestablishment of the order that has always prevailed since creation.

One also finds, in Middle Kingdom texts from Egypt, the possibility of a blissful afterlife in a world beyond, but any actual transformation of this world, with its ordered cycles of birth, death, and duty, is never envisioned. This holds true throughout the Ancient Near Eastern world—whether one is dealing with Egyptian, Babylonian, or Hebrew views of the cosmos.

Greco-Roman Millennial Visions

One finds a remarkably similar view of the cosmos and the human place therein in our oldest Greek materials. Hesiod's *Theogony* (eighth century BCE) celebrates the removal of chaos in the founding of earth, "the ever-sure foundation of all." Zeus banishes the Titans, guaranteeing to humankind that the present order will last forever (lines 713–35). The Homeric Hymns (eighth century BCE) likewise celebrate the earth as the abiding and proper place for humankind, with the established cycle of the seasons of nature maintained forever for the benefit of all creatures (1936: 456–57).

Plato's "Great Year," which became a commonplace in Classical Greek materials, does represent a type of "end of the world" thinking in this otherwise orderly scheme of things. When all the cycles of the planets and constellations complete an entire revolution (usually put at about 36,000 years), there was to be a "return" to the beginning (*Timaeus* 39D, Cicero, *The Nature of the Gods* 2.51). Given Hesiod's scheme of a Golden Age, followed by the declining epochs of silver, bronze, and iron, this notion of a kind of "revolution of the ages" offered a remote hope for future renewal (Plato, *Republic* 546). The Book of Daniel gives a decidedly apocalyptic interpretation to such a scheme, with its succession of four kingdoms (Babylon, Persia, Greek, and Rome), followed by the eternal Kingdom of God (Daniel 2). Josephus, the first-century CE Jewish historian, adapted these Greek ideas to his own apocalyptic notions of resurrection of the dead: "to those who observe the laws, and if they must needs die for them, willingly meet death, God has granted a renewed existence and in the *revolution of the ages*, the gift of a better life" (*Against Apion* 2. 218; *Jewish War* 3.374).

We do find a fully apocalyptic adaptation of Greek cosmology in the Latin *Asclepius*, a second-century BCE work of Egyptian provenance and related to the Greek *Corpus Hermetica*. There the disciple Asclepius is told:

> Such will be the old age of the world: irreverence, disorder, disregard for everything good. When all this comes to pass . . . the God whose power is primary . . . will take his stand against the vices and perversion in everything, righting wrong, washing away malice in a flood or consuming it in fire or ending it by spreading pestilential disease everywhere. Then he will restore the word to its beauty of old so that the world itself will again seem deserving of worship and wonder. (Copenhaver 1992: 82–83)

Book III of the *Sibylline Oracles* (second century BCE), weaves together Greek and Hebrew traditions, predicting a time of moral decline, unprecedented disasters, wars, and cosmic disruptions, followed by the Kingdom of God:

> And then, indeed, he will raise up a kingdom for all
> ages among men,
> He who once gave the holy Law to the pious,
> To all of whom he promised to open the earth and the
> world
> And the gates of the blessed and all joys
> And immortal intellect and eternal cheer. (3:767–71,
> Charlesworth 1983: 1, 379)

Virgil (first century BCE) takes these general Greek ideas of the transformation of the world and adapts it to Roman political propaganda, celebrating the age of the Emperor Augustus. His Fourth *Eclogue* celebrates the arrival of a messianic world ruler:

> The great order is born anew from the line of the ages.
> The Virgin has now returned; Saturn's reign has
> returned;
> Now a new offspring is sent from Heaven on High.
> You alone grant favor at the birth of the boy,
> By whom the iron age shall cease,
> And a golden race shall rise up on the world . . .

The Iranian prophet Zarathustra (sixth century BCE), or Zoroaster as the Greeks called him, is apparently the first Western figure to develop a fully eschatological view of the future that included a cosmic battle between the forces of good and evil, the cleansing of the world through fire, resurrection of the dead, and final judgment, and a new transformed immortal world of perfect harmony for the righteous of all ages.

Judeo-Christian Millennial Visions

Isaiah's "Little Apocalypse," (chapters 24–27) contains all of these elements, and most scholars see it as a later interpolation, heavily influenced by Persian ideas, inserted into the main body of Isaiah's eighth-century BCE work. Within the Hebrew tradition Isaiah 2:1–4 and 11:1–9 appear to be our earliest texts that reflect a rather fully developed messianic millenarianism. The Prophet sees a time when Jerusalem becomes the spiritual capital of the world and as a result the nations "beat their swords into plowshares, and their spears into pruning hooks, nation shall not lift up sword against nations, neither shall they learn war any more" (2:4). This universal reign of peace and justice is ushered in by a Messiah of the lineage of King David, and the world is transformed into a utopian harmony that effects both humans and animals: "The wolf will dwell with the lamb, the leopard shall lie down with the kid, the calf and the lion and the fatling together, and a little child shall lead them . . . for the earth will be full of the knowledge of Yahweh, as the waters cover the sea (11:6–9).

Such hopes and dreams of apocalyptic transformation of the world and the arrival of the Kingdom of God, are found in a host of Jewish texts from the third century BCE into the early Christian era. The book of Daniel (second century BCE) predicts the coming of the Kingdom of God that will stand forever, including a resurrection of "those who sleep in the dust, some to everlasting life, and others to everlasting shame and contempt" (Daniel 2:44; 12:2–3). 1 Enoch (third–second century BCE) traces human history from Noah's Flood to the Messianic kingdom, which the author expects to arrive shortly after the Maccabean revolt (1 Enoch 83–90). 2 (Slavonic) Enoch (first century BCE) is one of our earlier texts that appears to predict that the present world is to last seven days of a thousand years each, modeled upon the six days of creation with the seventh day of Sabbath rest.

It is the New Testament book of Revelation, written in the last decades of the first century CE, that offers us our first clear and explicit scheme of a *one thousand year* messianic reign, or millennium, followed by a final judgment and the creation of a New Heavens and New Earth (Revelation 20–22). The author John writes:

> I saw an angel coming down from heaven . . . he seized the dragon, that ancient serpent, who is the Devil and Satan, and bound him for a thousand years . . . so that he would deceive the nations no more, until the thousand years were ended . . . They [righteous martyred dead] came to life and reigned with Christ a thousand years. The rest of the dead did not come to life until the thousand years were ended. This is the first resurrection. . . . (20:1–6)

This scheme of six thousand years of human history, to be culminated in a one thousand year "Sabbath" seems to be in the mind of the unknown author of the New Testament book of Hebrews (4:4–11) and is possibly implied in 2 Peter 3:8–9 where the author recommends patience in waiting for the End: "a day with the Lord is a thousand years, and a thousand years is a day." The letter of Barnabas (second century CE) declares:

> the Lord will make an end of everything in six thousand years, for a day with him means a thousand years . . . so then children, in six days, that is in six thousand years, everything will be completed . . . when his Son comes he will destroy the time of the wicked one, and will judge the godless, and will change the sun and the moon and the stars, and then he will truly rest on the seventh day. (15. 3–5)

This general scheme of things becomes the pillar of all millenarian-oriented Christian traditions, even into the modern age.

James D. Tabor

See also Judaism, Zoroastrianism

Bibliography

Breasted, James H. (1906–7) *Ancient Records of Egypt.* 5 vols. Chicago: University of Chicago Press.

Charlesworth, James, ed. (1983) *The Old Testament Pseudipgrapha.* 2 vols. Garden City, NY: Doubleday & Co.

Cohn, Norman. (1993) *Cosmos, Chaos, and the World to Come: The Ancient Roots of Apocalyptic Faith.* New Haven, CT: Yale University Press.

Copenhaver, Brian. (1992) *Hermetica.* Cambridge, U.K.: Cambridge University Press.

Hesiod. (1936) *The Homeric Hymns and Homerica,* translated by Hugh G. Evelyn-White. Loeb Classical Library. Cambridge, MA: Harvard University Press.

Kramer, S. N. (1944) *Sumerian Mythology.* Philadelphia: The American Philosophical Society.

Pritchard, James B., ed. (1969). *Ancient Near Eastern Texts Relating to the Old Testament.* Princeton, NJ: Princeton University Press.

Antichrist

Many cultures believe that evil is present in the world. There are many myths that describe figures who personify evil, and how their existence impacts the course of events. The Western world is no different, and a fascination with evil can be found throughout the history of Christianity, from its beginnings up to the present day.

In Christianity, beliefs about evil are shaped by a rich lore of legends about Satan and Antichrist. They are two different entities. As God sent Christ to earth to do his work, so Satan sends Antichrist to do his. Like Christ, Antichrist is often conceived of as a human being who is able to do things ordinary humans cannot. Traditional Christian eschatology holds that a period of wickedness will precede salvation and the final judgment. In the endtime period of wickedness, Antichrist will reign on earth. If a Christian believes that the end is near, it is quite likely that he or she has identified a contemporary political figure as Antichrist. Nero, Muhammad, Napoleon, and Hitler, among others, have all been called Antichrist. But to better appreciate Antichrist we need to survey its biblical origins.

The Prehistory of Antichrist

In the Hebrew Bible, evil, like everything else, comes from God: "I am the Lord, and there is none other. I make the light, I create the darkness; author alike of well-being and woe" (Isaiah 45:6–7) (the Hebrew word for "woe," *ra'*, can also be translated as "evil"). Evil is not attributed to a demonic figure. One does however find "Satan" in the Hebrew Bible. There it is not a proper noun, but *satan*, a Hebrew word that means "adversary." The adversary is a member of God's heavenly court (see Job 1; Zechariah 3). The *satan* questions God or his faithful, but he is not evil.

More important than the *satan* for the development of the Antichrist myth is the legend of the final tyrant. Ezekiel 38–39, written in the sixth century BCE, tells the story of Gog, king of Magog, which was far to the north of Israel. It prophecies that one day Gog will lead his country and other nations in an ultimate battle against Israel. Then God will vanquish Gog and his armies. It was later understood that this final war between Gog and Israel would take place in the endtime (see Revelation 20:8). Daniel 7, written in the second century BCE, became a central text for Antichrist speculation. In this chapter Daniel has a vision of four beasts. The fourth is the most powerful and has ten horns. Then a "little horn" will sprout from the beast, displacing three of the original ten horns. The fourth beast is understood as symbolizing a tyrannical "kingdom on earth" and the little horn will persecute the faithful and insult God (7:23–4; 11:36). Then the horn will be dethroned and judged, and the faithful will rule the entire world. People who in their own times identify a tyrant, such as Hitler, as the little horn or the fourth beast of Daniel, often believe they are living in the endtime period of wickedness preceding the final judgment and salvation.

In the second century BCE, Jews increasingly began to believe that there was an evil entity, separate from God, who was responsible for the wickedness of the world. This entity was known by various names: Mastema, Beliar, or Belial; Belial being the most common. Belial is mentioned quite frequently in the Dead Sea Scrolls, most of which date to the first and second centuries BCE. The authors of these texts, members of a Jewish sect known as the Essenes, feared Belial. In the *Community Rule*, which explains the rules the group lived by, it is explained that these rules are to be followed "in order not to stray from following him [God] for any fear, dread, grief, or agony (that might occur) during the dominion of Belial" (1:18). The War Scroll describes the final eschatological battle between the Gentiles and the Dead Sea community, led by angels. It emphasizes that the Gentiles represent wickedness manifest in the world and are the "army of Belial" (1:13; cf. 2 Corinthians 6:15).

Antichrist, the New Testament, and Early Christian Literature

The word "Antichrist" occurs only five times in the New Testament. These occurrences are found in the First and Second Epistles of John, which were probably written at the end of the first century CE. Their author believed that there are many antichrists: "You were told that an antichrist was to come. Well, many antichrists have already appeared, proof to us that this is indeed the last hour" (1 John 2:18). This is related to the widespread belief that the final days will be characterized by false prophets and deceit (cf. Matthew 24:23). 1 and 2 John use the word "antichrist" to describe heretics—those who deny "both the Father and the Son"

The Great Red Dragon and the Beast from the Sea. William Blake, c. 1805.

NATIONAL GALLERY OF ART, WASHINGTON, D.C.

ONE WORLD ECONOMY

The Antichrist's economy will be a cashless society in which every financial transaction can be electronically monitored. John, author of the book of Revelation, describes the situation: "He causes all, both small and great, rich and poor, free and slave, to receive a mark on their right hand or on their foreheads, and that no one may buy or sell except one who has the mark or the name of the beast, or the number of his name" (Rev. 13:16-17).

The cashless society may ostensibly be presented to the world as a way to control drug lords, tax evaders, and the like, and so it will be. It may be presented as a foolproof way to end theft or as the ultimate in convenience for the shopper who can go to the supermarket without even a wallet. He will simply have his hand or forehead scanned by an electronic device that reflects the amount of cash he has in the bank, makes the deduction for his purchase, and gives him a current balance.

This scenario doesn't sound nearly as far-fetched as it used to, does it? My bank today offers a debit card; even today I don't need money to go to the grocery store. Everything is scanned these days, from library cards to thumbprints, and it doesn't require a great leap of imagination to see how this cashless, computerized system of buying and selling will be placed into operation. A day is coming when you will not even be able to buy Rolaids without the proper approval, without having a mark upon your hand or forehead scanned.

Source: Hagee, John. (1996) *Beginning of the End: The Assassination of Yitzhak Rabin and the Coming Antichrist.* Nashville: Thomas Nelson Publishers.

(1 John 2:22; 4:3; 2 John 7). The term "antichrist" here does not refer to a mythological figure who personifies evil.

The Antichrist legend is based on texts that include a mythological figure of evil. Second Thessalonians, probably written at the end of the first century CE, describes Christians being led astray. It attributes this rise of waywardness to "the man of lawlessness, the son of perdition, the adversary" (2:3–4). He is also called "the wicked one." He will perform "counterfeit miracles" for those who would not accept "the love of truth" or salvation, leading them astray (2:10). Many also have interpreted the "abomination of desolation" *(bdelugma tes eremoseos)* of Mark 13:14 as the Antichrist (see also Matthew 24:15; also Daniel 9:27 and 11:31). Mark 13, Matthew 24, and Luke 21 are parallel accounts of the final tribulations and the return of Jesus. The abomination of desolation in these stories (except Luke) is a sign that the unparalleled distress of the endtimes is beginning.

The main source for the Antichrist legend is the Book of Revelation, although it does not use the word "Antichrist." It was probably written at the end of the first century CE on the island of Patmos (1:9). The book depicts the tribulations before the Day of Judgment. When seven angels blow their trumpets in succession, the fifth trumpet signals the unlocking of the Abyss; this unleashes an army of locusts led by their emperor, Abaddon (Hebrew for "destruction"; 9:1–12). Revelation 11 predicts that the beast *(therion)* that comes out of the Abyss will kill two prophets sent by God. The people, under the sway of the beast, will celebrate the death of these prophets. Revelation 12 depicts a dragon that represents Satan (12:9; 20:2) that is hurled by the archangel Michael into the Abyss. While the dragon continues to wage war against the faithful (12:17), much of this work is continued by a beast who emerges from the sea (13:1). Borrowing imagery from Daniel 7, this beast will have seven heads and ten horns. The dragon hands over its authority to this beast (13:2). It will make boasts and blasphemies for forty-two months (a symbolic length of time taken from Daniel 7:25 that represents a period of persecution) and acquire power over "every race, people, language and nation" (13:7). All whose names are not written in the Book of Life will worship this beast. Then a second beast shall appear. He is understood as a false prophet who will trick Christians into worshipping the first beast (13:14; 16:13; 19:20; 20:10). He encourages people to make a statue of the first beast and makes it illegal for anyone to buy or sell anything who is not branded with the mark of the first beast (13:17). This mark is the number 666.

While many believe that this is the mark that will identify the beast, in Revelation the mark is a sign of the beast that is upon all the people who are under his power. This number in Hebrew (where each letter also has a numeric value) spells out "Nero Caesar." Nero (b. 37 CE), emperor of the Roman Empire, was reviled by Jews and Christians because he persecuted them. *The Martyrdom of Isaiah*, a Jewish text written originally in the second century BCE with sections added in subsequent centuries, identified Nero with Beliar (see 4:1–7). The *Sibylline Oracles*, which contain Jewish and Christian prophecies expressed in pagan style, predict that one day Nero will return to commit acts of unparalleled destruction (4:119–129; 4:138–9; 5:137–160, and others). It is dated to the second century BCE with later additions. It also associates Nero with Beliar (3:63). None of these early legends about Nero use the word "Antichrist" but utilize traditions about Beliar and the final tyrant that are antecedents to the Antichrist myth. The historical connection between Nero and Antichrist is clear in Armenian, for example, where the word for Antichrist is *nerhn*, which is based on the word "Nero."

The beast is identified with Rome in general in Revelation 17. This chapter contains a vision of the Whore of Babylon riding the beast with seven heads and ten horns mentioned in chapter 13. She represents the Roman Empire and is "drunk from the blood of the saints," a reference to Rome's persecution of Christianity (17:6). Here the beast is interpreted allegorically. An angel tells John that the seven heads signify seven emperors (of Rome) and the ten horns signify ten kings of nations who will be allied with Rome. The beast is taken prisoner in the final eschatological battle between good and evil. He and the false prophet are thrown alive into the lake of burning sulfur (19:20). Then the dragon is thrown into the Abyss, after which begins the 1,000 year reign of Christ on earth (the origin of the term "millennialism"). The beast's rise to power signals the coming of Christ, and the beast's downfall.

Other early Christian literature shows the development of the Antichrist legend. The *Didache*, a collection of Christian teachings from the end of the first century CE, ends with the assertion that in the final days "the deceiver of the world" will claim to be the messiah, perform miracles, and will acquire power. The second century CE *Apocalypse of Peter* also predicts that false Christs will appear in the endtime and that there is one "deceiver who must come into the world and do signs and wonders in order to deceive" (chapter 2). *The Apocalypse of Elijah*, which may come from the second or third centuries CE, predicts that the "son of lawlessness" (a term from 2 Thessalonians) will come and perform every miracle that Christ performed except raising the dead (3:5–13). The "son of lawlessness" will be killed by Enoch and Elijah, which will advent the millennial reign of Christ on earth (5:30–39).

The first systematic treatments of Antichrist were written by Saint Irenaeus (c. 130–c. 200) and Hippolytus (c. 170–c. 236). Irenaeus's discussion of Antichrist is found in his five volume *Against Heresies* (c. 175–80), a work of orthodox theology that is polemical against gnosticism (see esp. 5:30:1–4). Hippolytus's views can be found in his *Commentary on Daniel* and *On the Antichrist*, both written around 200 CE. *On the Antichrist* is the oldest known treatise on this topic. In it, Hippolytus writes that "the Deceiver seeks to liken himself in all things to the Son of God. Christ is a lion, so Antichrist is a lion; Christ is a king, so Antichrist is also a king. The Savior was manifested as a lamb, so he too, in like manner, will appear as a lamb, though within he is a wolf" (chapter 6). Antichrist is a warped imitation of Christ. The biblical stories about an evil ruler and deceiver coming to power at the end of days never call these figures Antichrist. A long-standing tradition holds that these stories describe with different names the same figure—Antichrist. This is a tradition to a great extent established by Irenaeus and Hippolytus.

Antichrist in History

There have been many other important contributions to the Antichrist tradition, of which only a few can be mentioned. The Latin *Tiburtine Sibyl*, which circulated widely as early as the fourth century CE, helped popularize the belief that Antichrist will appear before Jesus' return. Adso, a French monk, wrote in 950 a *vita* (life) of Antichrist, in the manner that *vitas* were written of saints. In the fifteenth century *Book of Lismore*, written in Ireland, Antichrist is a monster, 600 fathoms high, with fire coming from his nose, a mouth that goes down to his chest, and wheels on his feet.

While accounts of Antichrist generally agree that he will wield power at the end of days, there are significant differences of opinion on more specific details. One tradition holds that Antichrist will be a Jew, from the tribe of Dan (one of the twelve tribes of Israel). Exegetically, this is based on Jeremiah 8:16 and Revelation 7:5–8, which names the tribes of Israel who will be spared from the coming destruction. Dan is not mentioned. This identification of Antichrist is also based on the anti-Semitic view that Jews are anti-Christian. There is also a tradition that Antichrist is a Catholic. Critics of the papacy have named the pope Antichrist as early as the thirteenth century. The papal Antichrist is a centerpiece of Luther's theology, and a standard feature of the Protestant polemic against Catholicism. There is also a tradition that Antichrist is a Muslim. Christian foes of Islam have often identified Muhammad as Antichrist. Some Fundamentalists at the end of the twentieth century asserted that Saddam Hussein was Antichrist.

Judaism and Islam have figures that parallel the Antichrist. The Jewish "Antichrist" is Armillus. The name is probably related to Romulus, the mythological founder of Rome, and perhaps the tradition of the (Roman) final emperor. Armillus will fight Israel and be slain by Messiah ben David. Islam has many traditions about a figure named Dajjal. He will wage war against Islam, perform miracles, and spread apostasy. According to some traditions he is king of the Jews. Most traditions hold that Dajjal will be slain by Jesus, who is revered in Islam as an eschatological prophet. The arrival of both Armillus and Dajjal, like the Christian Antichrist, is a feature of the tribulations that characterize the endtime.

Antichrist at the End of the Twentieth Century

The twentieth century was rich in Antichrist speculation, which showed no sign of abating at century's end. One of the basic convictions of Fundamentalism and premillennialism is that the current generation is the terminal generation, or not far from it. Premillennialism holds that the Tribulations are at hand and that Christ will return before his millennial reign begins. For premillennialists, events foretold in biblical prophecy about the endtime unfold in our own time. Televangelists such as Jerry Falwell and Pat Robertson endorsed such views at the end of the twentieth century to thousands of supporters.

Premillennialists often view the rise of secularism and modernity as the apostasy and lawlessness that is a feature of the endtime. Father Vincent Miceli, in his *Antichrist* (1981), complains how modern thought has led people astray from the church. He writes that the modern world "has a deathwish to be dominated by the Antichrist." In this view, women's liberation, counterculture morals, New Age religion, or the political left are proof of Antichrist's influence. Peter Lalonde, in his *One World Under Antichrist* (1991) sees the stamp of the beast everywhere in modern culture, regarding MTV and the Teenage Mutant Ninja Turtles as the work of Antichrist.

During the cold war, Fundamentalists routinely wrote the Soviet Union into their views on Antichrist and the endtimes. The final war of Gog and Magog in Ezekiel prefigured for them the nuclear war between the United States and Russia (Reagan's evil empire). In the final days of the Soviet Union, Gorbachev was occasionally taken to be Antichrist.

Premillennialists also often view the modern political and economic institutions of our time as the reign of Antichrist. The formation of the United Nations in 1948 is interpreted in light of Revelation 13's beast who will acquire power of the entire world. The European Economic Community (EEC) is viewed similarly. Hal Lindsey in his *The 1980s: Countdown to Armageddon* (1981), viewed Greece's induction to the EEC as its tenth member as the fulfillment of the ten horns of the fourth beast of Daniel 7. He asserted that Antichrist will lead the EEC and is currently a member of the EEC Parliament. A similar distrust in the world economy is seen in Mary Stewart Relfe's *When Your Money Fails* (1981). She calls the modern economy the "666 System" and identifies the ubiquitous bar code as the mark of the beast (Revelation 13:17). Similarly, premillennial preachers such as John Hagee today tell their congregations that the "one-world government" of the Antichrist is "New World Order."

Conclusion

Such assessments of current events assume that Antichrist is either among us now or will arrive soon. Pat Robertson in 1981 wrote that "[T]here is a man alive today, approximately 27 years old, who is now being groomed to be the Satanic messiah" (Fuller 1995: 166). The Reverend Jerry Falwell in January 1999 proclaimed that the Antichrist is alive today and a male Jew. Astrologer and psychic Jeanne Dixon asserted that Antichrist was born on 5 February 1962. Movies such as *Omen* (1976) and rock musicians like Marilyn Manson and his Church of Antichrist Superstar show that the American fascination with Antichrist extends beyond premillennialists.

Naming the Antichrist is a venerable Christian practice. The Antichrist legend gives the Christian a paradigm of evil that legitimates the hatred of an enemy. The Christian can mythologize his or her foe by placing him in an eschatological scenario where evil threatens the faithful but is ultimately vanquished. According to this view the Bible provides a "road map" to the endtime tribulations that will precede salvation and final judgment. Antichrist is an important feature of this map. If a person believes that we are living in the final days, the question is not if Antichrist will appear, but how soon.

Matthew Goff

See also 666, Messianism, New World Order, Premillennialism

Bibliography

Bousset, Wilhelm. ([1896] 1999) *The Antichrist Legend: A Chapter in Christian and Jewish Folklore.* London: Hutchinson and Company; reprint, Atlanta: Scholars Press.

Fuller, Robert C. (1995) *Naming the Antichrist: The History of an American Obsession.* New York and London: Oxford University Press.

Jenks, Gregory C. (1991) *The Origins and Early Development of the Antichrist Myth.* Berlin and New York: Walter de Gruyter.

Lietaert Peerbolte, Lambertus J. (1996) *The Antecedents of Antichrist: A Traditio-Historical Study of the Earliest Christian Views on Eschatological Opponents.* Leiden: E.J. Brill.

Malone, Peter. (1990) *Movie Christs and Antichrists.* New York: Crossroads Publishing Company.

McGinn, Bernard. (1994) *Antichrist: Two Thousand Years of the Human Fascination with Evil.* San Francisco: Harper San Francisco.

——. (1998) *Visions of the End: Apocalyptic Traditions in the Middle Ages,* 2d ed. New York: Columbia University Press.

Wright, Rosemary Muir. (1995) *Art and Antichrist in Medieval Europe.* Manchester, U.K., and New York: Manchester University Press.

Apocalypse

The word "apocalypse" comes from the Greek, *apokalypsis,* which means unveiling hidden information or revealing secret knowledge concerning unfolding human events. The word "revelation" is another way to translate the idea of *apokalypsis.* Thus, the words "apocalypse," "revelation," and "prophecy" are closely related. Prophets, by definition, are apocalyptic.

In its more common and generic usage, the word "apocalypse" has come to mean the belief in an approaching confrontation, cataclysmic event, or transformation of epochal proportion, about which a select few have forewarning so they can make appropriate preparations. Those who believe in a coming apocalypse might be optimistic about the outcome of the apocalyptic moment, anticipating a chance for positive transformational change; or they might be pessimistic, anticipating a doomsday; or they might anticipate a period of violence or chaos with an uncertain outcome.

Apocalypticism relates to millennialism in complex ways. The period immediately prior to a millennial date can be marked by people turning inward in preparation for apocalyptic events, removing themselves from society, and in extreme cases, committing suicide. Conversely, some who believe the end of time means there will be literally no time for punishment, may act out on their anger by demonizing or killing their enemies. Other people swept up in apocalyptic millennial expectation target scapegoated groups for discrimination or violence to ritually cleanse the society, or push it toward the final showdown. During the period after an anticipated millennial transformation, people can turn outward, and express anger over failed expectations by blaming scapegoated groups for having prevented the transformation. Others might express their disappointment by turning inward and reformulating some continuing basis for apocalyptic beliefs. Some become disillusioned altogether.

The Varieties of Apocalypse

In Christianity, the Apocalypse usually refers to a gigantic global battle with Satanic forces that are defeated by the faithful, followed by a millennium of godly rule. The apocalyptic tradition also exists in Judaism, Islam, and other religions that predated Christianity. Christian premillennialists often generate apocalypticism through their expectation that the endtimes bring the return of Christ who reigns for one thousand years. Christian postmillennialists can be apocalyptic in their quest to take over secular society and hold it for the thousand years they believe is required to bring the return of Christ.

All millennial movements are apocalyptic in some sense, even when positive and hopeful; but not all apocalyptic movements are millennial. Apocalyptic themes can be found today in the Christian Right, the Patriot and armed militia movements, and the far right. Apocalypticism can also be found among New Age devotees, environmental activists, and UFO groups.

Apocalyptic themes are certainly evident in popular culture where films such as *Armageddon* and *Apocalypse Now* and the TV series *Millennium* name the tradition while mainstreaming the ideas. Films including *Rambo, Mad Max, Red Dawn, Die Hard, Terminator,* and their sequels reinterpret apocalyptic visions while obscuring their origins. The *X-Files* film and its related TV series are quintessential apocalyptic narratives. *Buffy the Vampire Slayer* stomps incarnate evil in a weekly TV series. Prophetic scripture provides the paradigm for sensational scripts. What is entertainment for some, however, is spiritual and political reality for others.

This is not a new phenomenon in U.S. history. Apocalyptic ideas of demonic possession fueled the witch-hunts that swept New England starting in the 1600s. Now Salem, Massachusetts—which put suspected witches to death—is a center for modern witchcraft and other New Age beliefs. Many antislavery abolitionists around the time of the Civil War were mobilized by Christian apocalyptic beliefs, and that theme was reflected in the rhetoric of "The Battle Hymn of the Republic."

Given its widespread influence in both historical and contemporary culture and events, it is surprising that apocalypticism has not been studied further. According to Landes, apocalyptic activities rarely "receive more than a passing mention in 'mainstream' analyses, and even fuller discussions tend to 'fence off' the phenomenon from the analysis of the truly consequential deeds of the age. Given that, in favorable circumstances, apocalyptic beliefs can launch mass movements capable of overthrowing (and forming) imperial dynasties and creating new religions, such an approach seems rather inadequate" (Landes 1996: 49). For instance,

SELECTIONS FROM THE NEW TESTAMENT (RSV) ABOUT THE APOCALYPSE

Isaiah 2.4

4. He shall judge between the nations, and shall decide for many peoples; and they shall beat their swords into plowshares, and their spears into pruning hooks; nation shall not lift up sword against nation, neither shall they learn war any more.

Isaiah 11.1–9

1. There shall come forth a shoot from the stump of Jesse, and a branch shall grow out of his roots.
2. And the Spirit of the LORD shall rest upon him, the spirit of wisdom and understanding, the spirit of counsel and might, the spirit of knowledge and the fear of the LORD.
3. And his delight shall be in the fear of the LORD. He shall not judge by what his eyes see, or decide by what his ears hear;
4. but with righteousness he shall judge the poor, and decide with equity for the meek of the earth; and he shall smite the earth with the rod of his mouth, and with the breath of his lips he shall slay the wicked.
5. Righteousness shall be the girdle of his waist, and faithfulness the girdle of his loins.
6. The wolf shall dwell with the lamb, and the leopard shall lie down with the kid, and the calf and the lion and the fatling together, and a little child shall lead them.
7. The cow and the bear shall feed; their young shall lie down together; and the lion shall eat straw like the ox.
8. The sucking child shall play over the hole of the asp, and the weaned child shall put his hand on the adder's den.
9. They shall not hurt or destroy in all my holy mountain; for the earth shall be full of the knowledge of the LORD as the waters cover the sea.

Revelation 21.1–5

1. Then I saw a new heaven and a new earth; for the first heaven and the first earth had passed away, and the sea was no more.
2. And I saw the holy city, new Jerusalem, coming down out of heaven from God, prepared as a bride adorned for her husband;
3. and I heard a loud voice from the throne saying, "Behold, the dwelling of God is with men. He will dwell with them, and they shall be his people, and God himself will be with them;
4. he will wipe away every tear from their eyes, and death shall be no more, neither shall there be mourning nor crying nor pain any more, for the former things have passed away."
5. And he who sat upon the throne said, "Behold, I make all things new." Also he said, "Write this, for these words are trustworthy and true."

Kovel observes that many historians have overlooked the apocalyptic dimensions of anticommunism, especially its dualism and conspiracism (Kovel 1994). Damian Thompson, argues that "Richard Hofstadter was right to emphasise the startling affinities between the paranoid style and apocalyptic belief—the demonisation of opponents, the sense of time running out, and so on. But he stopped short of making a more direct connection between the two. He did not consider the possibility that the paranoia he identified actually derived from apocalyptic belief" (1996: 307).

There have been numerous theories put forward for explaining apocalyptic beliefs, including psychological factors, social or economic crisis, natural disasters or other hardships, relative deprivation, and loss of status. Strozier (1994) takes the psychological approach, claiming apocalyptic thinking reflects a broken self-identity within a person, leading to an inability to deal with the present on a personal, societal, and metaphysical level. Lamy (1996) and Thompson (1996) argue that while apocalyptic millennialism has many sources, it generally can be tied to some type of societal conflict or resistance to change. Fuller says apocalyptic fervor is complex, and part of a "literary and theological tradition," that is "transmitted through a variety of cultural institutions that are relatively immune" to certain "social or economic forces" (1995: 9–10, 191–200). Fenn sees apocalyptic rituals both as a way to mediate social change and transfer power between generations; and to challenge, at least metaphorically, death itself.

According to Fenn, fascism is a virulent form of apocalyptic belief rooted in resistance to the transformation of economic and social relations: "Fascist tendencies are most likely to flourish wherever vestiges of a traditional community, bound together by ties of race and kinship, persist in a society largely dominated by large-scale organizations, by an industrial class system, and by a complex division of labor. Under these conditions the traditional community itself becomes threatened; its members all the more readily dread and demonize the larger society" (1997: 224). Wistrich (1985) also traces the apocalyptic paradigm of Nazism and writes of the millennial roots of their plans for a thousand-year Reich.

O'Leary has constructed a theory of how millennial rhetoric is used to manage concepts of time, authority, and evil. Thus the "mythic narrative of Apocalypse can be used to justify the existence of evil on a cosmic scale by pointing to the promised restoration of an earthly Kingdom of God, while individual experience of evil is itself [a sign and a] proof . . . that the cosmic drama of evil is nearing its resolution" (1994: 20). Apocalyptic beliefs that demonize, says O'Leary, flow from a specific literal viewpoint regarding how good and evil function in society, and how and when God exercises ultimate judgment. "The problem is not the mythological character of Revelation; rather, it is that any interpretation of the [apocalyptic] myth (whether by skeptics or by dogmatists) that reduces it to literal and factual content inevitably distorts the deliberately metaphorical language of prophecy" (1994: 42). O'Leary calls this the tragic interpretation of apocalyptic myth and says only a sense of comedic can compete by accepting the irony that God's judgment of good and evil has already occurred, is occurring even now, and is always about to occur, thus making calendar dates and specific timetables beyond the ability of humans to predict.

Revelation Interpreted as Apocalyptic Narrative

Christian apocalypticism is based on many sources in the Bible, including the Old Testament Books of Daniel and Ezekiel, and the New Testament Gospel of Matthew. The primary biblical source, however, is the Book of Revelation, the last book of the Christian New Testament. Revelation, the chronicle of an apocalyptic vision, was written about 95 CE, but parts derive from prophetic elements of the book of Daniel and other Old Testament books. The identity of John of Patmos, the author of Revelation, is disputed, but most experts suggest it was not the same John, the disciple of Jesus, who authored the fourth Gospel.

Revelation describes in graphic terms what will happen when an angry God finally intervenes in human affairs at the end of time. The narrative describes the end times as a period of widespread sinfulness, moral depravity, and crass materialism. The Four Horsemen of the Apocalypse ride in bringing God's wrath in the form of wars, disease, civil strife, and natural disasters. Satan's chief henchman appears in human form as the Antichrist, a popular world leader who secretly harbors sympathy for the Devil. He promises peace and unity of all nations under one world government, but it's a trick. His agents are tracking down and punishing Christians who refuse to abandon their faith. Satan's allies receive a mark—the Mark of the Beast—represented by the number 666. This period of hard times are called "the Tribulations" and culminate in a final cataclysmic doomsday confrontation of massed armies in the Middle East, at a place named Armageddon. Good triumphs over evil at the battle of Armageddon, ushering in a millennium of Christian rule.

The narrative of Revelation provides important clues for understanding the rhetoric and actions of devout Christians who are influenced by apocalypticism and millennialism. Among Christians, belief in an actual coming apocalypse is particularly strong among those Fundamentalists who not only read the Bible literally, but also consider prophetic Biblical text to be a coded timetable or script revealing the future.

Those that believe the Apocalypse is at hand can act out those theological beliefs in social, cultural, and political arenas. An example might be when believers view current world events as "signs of the endtimes" or see those with whom they disagree as agents of the Antichrist. Apocalyptic movements in the United States often have reflected a Manichaean framework of absolute good versus absolute evil that leads to demonization of opponents. Kaplan notes: "A manichaean framework requires the adherent to see the world as the devil's domain, in which the tiny, helpless 'righteous remnant' perseveres through the protection of God in the hope that, soon, God will see fit to intervene once and for all in the life of this world" (1997: 171).

This perspective can promote a passive, fatalist response, or can lead some to be proactive and interventionist, seeking to prepare the way for the anticipated confrontation. Believers can be optimistic or pessimistic about the outcome. Today, apocalyptic themes influence many diverse Christian groups, including those who do not think the endtimes are close at hand. Paul Boyer (1992: 148–49) argues that Christian apocalypticism must be factored into both cold war and post–cold war political equations.

The mainstreaming of apocalypticism received a major boost when, in 1983, Ronald Reagan cited scriptural authority to demonize the Soviet Union as an "evil empire." Halsell (1986) noted that some evangelists, including Jerry Falwell, Hal Lindsey, and Pat Robertson, hinted that use of atomic weapons might be part of the inevitable final battle of Armageddon. There are hundreds of books with apocalyptic themes aimed at Christian evangelicals and fundamentalists, see, for example, Lindsey and Carlson (1970), Lindsey (1997), Graham (1983), and Jeffrey (1994). By the time the 1974 prophecy book, *Armageddon, Oil, and the Middle East Crisis* was revised and republished during the Gulf War, it had sold over one million copies.

Two Apocalyptic Traditions in Christianity

Quinby argues that "Apocalypticism in each of its modes fuels discord, breeds anxiety or apathy, and sometimes causes panic," and that "this process can occur at the individual, community, national, or international level." "What makes apocalypse so compelling," argues Quinby, "is its promise of future perfection, eternal happiness, and godlike understanding of life, but it is that very will to absolute power and knowledge that produces its compulsions of violence, hatred, and oppression" (1994: 162).

Yet not all contemporary Christian interpretations of Revelation promote apocalyptic demonization. Within Christianity, there are two competing views of how to interpret the apocalyptic themes in the Bible. One view identifies evil with specific persons and groups, seeking to identify those in league with the Devil. This view easily lends itself to demonization. A more positive form of interpreting apocalyptic prophecy is not based on demonization; it is promoted by those Christians who see evil in the will to dominate and oppress. Apocalyptic thinking, in this case, envisions a liberation for the oppressed. The two interpretations represent a deep division within Christianity.

Even some relatively conservative and orthodox Christians look to the prophetic tradition of siding with the poor and oppressed, and these themes can be found in both the New and Old Testaments. This is the tradition of the social gospel in Protestantism and liberation theology in Catholicism. It can be found in today's Sojourners group and the tradition of "prophetic anger" coupled with "evangelical populism." Social justice activist Daniel Berrigan uses apocalyptic discourse in the Bible as a tool in challenging oppression, corruption, and tyranny. Philosopher René Girard argues that the New Testament can be used to help unravel scapegoating. Author and activist Cornel West identifies himself with a prophetic tradition rooted in African-American Christianity and the struggle for black civil rights. The Rev. Martin Luther King, Jr. preached from this tradition when he spoke truth to power.

Within mainstream denominations, independent evangelical churches, progressive Christian communities, and followers of liberation theology are many Christians who are painfully aware of those historic periods when some Christian leaders sided with oppression and used demonization as a tool to protect and extend power and privilege. It is not accurate to stereotype all Christians as continuing that heritage. Some of the most vocal critics of apocalyptic demonization and conspiracist scapegoating come from within Christianity. One such critique by Gregory S. Camp is impressive both as a historical and theological work. Camp warns of the "very real danger that Christians could pick up some extra spiritual baggage" by credulously embracing conspiracy theories (1997: 190).

Conclusion

O'Leary points out "the study of apocalyptic argument leads to the conclusion that its stratagems are endless, and not susceptible to negation through rational criticism" (O'Leary: 221–22). He suggests patience, a sense of tragedy in history, and a sense of humor in interaction as the best strategies for mending communities that experience the trauma of apocalyptic confrontation.

Christian apocalypticism refers to a broad range of ideas. The dangerous dynamic arises primarily among the sector of Christians who combine biblical literalism, apocalyptic timetables, demonization, and oppressive prejudices. Scapegoating that is generated or enhanced by apocalyptic fears has distinctive features and targets. Scapegoating always needs to be taken seriously when it bullies its way into political and social discourse. Any group can be framed as doing evil or being evil, given enough creative energy on the part of the scapegoater. Apocalyptic views that demonize by naming specific groups of people as evil pose a threat to civil society.

The history of apocalyptic fervor is written by those secure in their knowledge that all previous predictions of terminal cataclysm have turned out to be false. After all, if the end of time ever arrives, it will leave behind no historians or sociologists, thus making skepticism an appealing and safe alternative. While believers prepare for the spiritual tsunami that will wash away both sins and sinners, skeptics make the assumption that it is just another wave that will eventually collapse, seeping away through the infinite sands of time. Yet no matter what we believe, we are all destined to experience the effects of the apocalypse, because it invents itself in the maelstrom of the human mind, and no logical arguments can stop the storm.

Chip Berlet

Bibliography

Berrigan, Daniel. (1997) *Ezekiel: Vision in the Dust.* Maryknoll, NY: Orbis Books.

Boyer, Paul. (1992) *When Time Shall Be No More: Prophecy Belief in Modern American Culture.* Cambridge, MA: Belknap/Harvard University Press.

Camp, Gregory S. (1997) *Selling Fear: Conspiracy Theories and End-Times Paranoia.* Grand Rapids, MI: Baker Books.

Cohn, Norman. (1993) *Cosmos, Chaos and the World to Come: The Ancient Roots of Apocalyptic Faith.* New Haven, CT: Yale University Press.

Fenn, Richard K. (1997) *The End of Time: Religion, Ritual, and the Forging of the Soul.* Cleveland, OH: Pilgrim Press.

Fuller, Robert. (1995) *Naming the Antichrist: The History of an American Obsession.* New York: Oxford University Press.

Graham, Billy. (1983) *Approaching Hoofbeats: The Four Horsemen of the Apocalypse.* Minneapolis, MN: Grason.

Halsell, Grace. (1986) *Prophecy and Politics: Militant Evangelists on the Road to Nuclear War.* Westport, CT: Lawrence Hill.

Jeffrey, Grant R. (1994) *Apocalypse: The Coming Judgement of Nations.* New York: Bantam.

Johnson, George. (1995) *Fire in the Mind: Science, Faith, and the Search for Order.* New York: Knopf.

Kaplan, Jeffrey. (1997) *Radical Religion in America: Millenarian Movements from the Far Right to the Children of Noah.* Syracuse, NY: Syracuse University Press.

Kovel, Joel. (1994) *Red Hunting in the Promised Land: Anticommunism and the Making of America* New York: Basic Books.

LaHaye, Tim. (1975) *Revelation: Illustrated and Made Plain.* Grand Rapids, MI: Zondervan.

Lamy, Philip. (1996) *Millennium Rage: Survivalists, White Supremacists, and the Doomsday Prophecy.* New York: Plenum.

Landes, Richard. (1996) "On Owls, Roosters, and Apocalyptic Time: A Historical Method for Reading a Refractory Documentation." *Union Seminary Quarterly Review* 49:1–2, 49–69.

Lindsey, Hal, with C. C. Carlson. (1970) *The Late Great Planet Earth.* Grand Rapids, MI: Zondervan.

Lindsey, Hal. (1997) *Apocalypse Code.* Palos Verdes, CA: Western Front.

O'Leary, Stephen. (1994) *Arguing the Apocalypse: A Theory of Millennial Rhetoric.* New York: Oxford University Press.

Quinby, Lee. (1994) *Anti-Apocalypse: Exercise in Genealogical Criticism.* Minneapolis: University of Minnesota Press.

Robbins, Thomas, and Susan J. Palmer, eds. (1997) *Millennium, Messiahs, and Mayhem: Contemporary Apocalyptic Movements.* New York: Routledge.

Smith, Christian, ed. (1997) *Disruptive Religion: The Force of Faith in Social Movement Activism.* New York: Routledge.

Strozier, Charles B. (1994) *Apocalypse: On the Psychology of Fundamentalism in America.* Boston: Beacon Press.

Thompson, Damian. (1996) *The End of Time: Faith and Fear in the Shadow of the Millennium.* Great Britain: Sinclair-Stevenson.

Walvoord, John F. (1990) *Armageddon, Oil, and the Middle East Crisis.* Revised. Grand Rapids, MI: Zondervan.

Wistrich, Robert. (1985) *Hitler's Apocalypse: Jews and the Nazi Legacy.* New York: St. Martin's.

The Apostles of Infinite Love

The Apostles of Infinite Love is a schismatic conservative Catholic monastic order and an apocalyptic Marian movement organized under the authority of a mystical pope, Gregory XVII, whom disciples refer to as "Brother John." The motherhouse of this new order was established in 1958 on a 500-acre estate located 100 kilometers northeast of Montreal in St.-Jovite, Quebec, where around five hundred monks and nuns reside. A few small communities also are located in Quebec's rural areas and in Latin America.

The original mystical pope was the late Michael Collins, known as Clement XV, who also founded the Order of the Magnificat of the Mother of God in France (to which the Apostles in Quebec are closely related). Gregory XVII is Clement XV's successor.

The community at St.-Jovite sees itself as the Apostles living in the last days, and they follow the thirty-three rules of Our Lady of Salette, as dictated in 1846 to Melamie Calvat, the visionary of La Salette, France, whose prophecies were ratified by Pope Leo XIII in 1879.

The Origins in France

Michael Collins (1905–75) was born in Bechy, France. He was a priest in the order of the Congregation du Sacre Couer who, in 1935, received a vision of Jesus Christ celebrating the mass. Jesus then proceeded to consecrate Collins as a mystical bishop. After founding the Apostles of Infinite Love in 1933, Collins received a vision of the Trinity in 1950, and was blessed with the "consécration pontificale." Eventually, Collins adopted the title Clement XV, the 108th consecrated pope, he whom St. Malachie had prophesied in the sixteenth century under the title, *flos florum*. Clement XV appears to have demonstrated considerable charisma, for his followers claimed they saw hosts of angels and saints swirl around him and heard celestial voices. Statues came to life in his presence, and he performed miracles of healing. Collins attracted a substantial following, distributed mainly throughout French-speaking Europe and Guadalupe. The motherhouse, the Petit Vatican de Marie Corédemptrice in Clemery Nomeny, has become a pilgrimage center.

Clement XV enlisted the sympathy of several Catholic bishops and cardinals, and his charismatic claims were confirmed in 1966 by the Archbishop of Meaux, successor to Saint Peter at Antioch and of Jacque Benigne Bossuet. After Paul VI ascended to the papal throne, Clement XV launched a campaign criticizing the corruption of the Vatican. With the assistance of his friend, Maurice Guignard, a Normandy food importer, he sent out letters to European leaders and politicians denouncing Paul VI as a quadruple agent who was working for the Nazis, Zionists, Fascists, and the Chinese simultaneously. His letters impugned the "Antipope's" private morals, claiming that he was a homosexual and morphine addict who kept, in the heart of the Vatican, a brothel of little boys. He also launched a vigorous campaign against the Hachette chain of bookstores and called the Minister of Education a "pornographer."

The Mystical Pope's Successor

According to an esoteric Catholic tradition, the secret of Fatima was meant to be divulged in 1960. For Jean-Gaston Tremblay, a young priest, born in Rimouski, Quebec, in 1938, one of Fatima's secrets was that the successor of John XXIII would be a mystical pope chosen by God not man, to direct His true church. Known as Pere Jean at the time, Tremblay founded the Congregation des Freres de Jesus et de Marie in 1953 in Quebec, based on the writings of an eighteenth-century mystic, Louis Mary de Monfort, namely his *True Devotion to Mary*, which was rediscovered in 1842. Tremblay was also influenced by the prophecies that issued from an 1846 apparition of the Virgin in La Salette in France. The Virgin's chief confidant was Melanie Calvat (1831–1904) an "ignorant shepherd girl," who wrote letters describing the prophecies she received, and later codified them in a document presented to Pope Leo XIII at his request.

In 1949 Tremblay beheld a vision of a pope chosen by God. By 1960 he had gathered together a community in Quebec of priests, monks, and nuns who disagreed with Vatican II. Tremblay first met Collins in 1961 and recognized him as the mystical pope he had seen in his vision, and they spoke of merging their two orders into one. In 1968 the Virgin Mary appeared to an "unknown mystical individual" in Canada to reveal that the successor of St. Peter was Father Jean of the Trinity, and he would someday hold the name Gregory XVII. Clement XV confirmed these revelations and proclaimed Tremblay as his legitimate successor. On 9 May 1969 they signed a document validating the succession.

Membership

In 1978 the community in St.-Jovite numbered between 450–500 with 150 children, and claimed fifty-five missions in Latin America. Since members have taken vows of silence and, more specifically, are not permitted to talk about their former lives, it is impossible to conduct membership surveys or interviews. It appears that most are elderly and were already in monastic orders (Grey Sisters, Dominicans) before joining. The membership is divided into Apostles, Disciples, and Cenacle Homes, representing three degrees of commitment. The Apostles are celibate brothers and sisters who vow poverty, chastity, and obedience. They combine a contemplative life with a more active life of selling calendars door-to-door, teaching children, and performing charitable acts. Their children (from before their celibacy), the "Juvenists" (youth between the ages of seven and sixteen) and the "Cherubim" (younger children) board on the premises and attend the monastery school. The Disciples are men and women still living in nuclear families, who reside in trailers or small houses near the monastery. They wear a distinctive habit and share all their goods in common. All attend the daily masses and work side by side. Disciples follow the same thirty-three rules as the Apostles, but these are adapted to their secular and married state. The Cenacle Homes comprise families who live in the secular world, retain their own property, but receive the mass in their own homes. Gregory XVII has ordained married men and women as "sacramental priests" who are authorized to administer the sacraments in their own homes, but not to preach or offer spiritual guidance. Many couples also have been admitted to the diaconate.

The monastery is almost self-sufficient, since the Apostles build their own buildings out of granite blocks, fieldstone, and logs, repair their own cars, weave their own fabric and sew their medieval-style garments, grow their own food (making their own wine, bread, pickles, and cheese) operate a printing press, and have their own radio and television. They have their own hydroelectric plant and, until the mid-eighties they ran their own school.

The Apostles are traditionalists in some respects. They celebrate the Roman mass of St. Pius V, observe the rosary, and adore the sacred Host, but in other respects they are modernists. Gregory XVII ordains women as priests and allows priests to marry. The Apostles have a charter from the Quebec government and are recognized as a religious corporation.

Beliefs

The aims of the Apostles are threefold: to warn humanity about the coming chastisement for those who live in sin; to gather monastics and laity into a new order detached from the wicked spirit of the age to follow the example of St. John the Evangelist in all his purity and simplicity; to rally after destruction and "purification" of the world in the rebuilding of a united Christendom.

Gregory XVII's millenarian expectations are based on the revelations of the Virgin Mary at Salette. In his 270-page encyclical *Peter Speaks to the World* (first published in 1975), the mystical pope cites the Virgin's warning that "Rome will lose its faith and become the seat of the Antichrist." Due to the secularization and liberalism of the Catholic faith since Vatican II, he argues, the Church of Rome has fallen into apostasy and has become the "tarp of the Antichrist" (Gregory XVII 1993). This leaves him, the mystical pope as the supreme ruler of the universal church in the Last Days. The small size of the Apostles as well as the persecution they have suffered, is regarded as proof that they are the righteous remnant destined to escape the impending Divine wrath, while the rest of humanity will be destroyed. Gregory XVII compares his following to Noah's family, and his "True Church of Jesus Christ" to the Ark, and quotes Our Lady of Salette: "Fight, children of light, you little number who see; for behold the time of times, the end of ends" (Gregory XVII 1993).

In the Apostles' apocalyptic drama there will be three stages: the "First Chastisement" when the "Antipope" will be installed in Rome, and the true Christians will be reduced to a tiny, persecuted remnant. Cataclysms and tribulations will mark this stage resulting in the death of a significant portion of humanity, and the communists, or some other alien power, will rule the world. Next, the mystical pope or his successor will lead a crusade against the forces of the Antichrist, depose the atheistic world order, and establish a New Catholic Christendom on earth. The "Period of Peace" will follow, in which millions convert to the renewed Catholic faith and a peaceful and prosperous theocracy will rule the earth. The "Second Chastisement" soon follows this utopian phase when, due to humanity's lapse into sin and apostasy, wars and natural disasters will break out signifying God's renewed Wrath, and the Day of Judgment will conclude history.

The Virgin Mary plays a central role in this final apocalyptic drama for, by true devotion to her, the Apostles will bring about her reign on earth. Like the first apostles in the primitive church, Mary will be their leader, during which she will produce the greatest saints of the latter times. In an interesting version of bridal theology, the prophecy claims that the Holy Spirit is her "faithful and inseparable Spouse," and will only enter into a human soul permeated with love for her, and will then "perform starting wonders in our souls."

The Apostles' literature awards the Virgin Mary a firm place in the Trinity, thus creating a kind of Quaternity that "feminizes" the godhead. Clement XV claimed he beheld the Virgin merging simultaneously into the Father, Son, and Holy Spirit, and suggested: "She is all of three Persons . . . she now permeates the interior of all Three" (Gregory XVII 1993).

Conflicts and Controversies

Gregory XVII is guided by a "voice from the sky" that warns him, among other things, that he will be humiliated "like Me climbing to Calvary and . . . your mitre will be a crown of thorns" (1993). For the Apostles, this prophecy has been confirmed in a series of legal battles, negative news reports, and criminal charges leveled against them and their pope.

First, their internal schools and childcare methods and facilities have been a source of concern since 1967, and the Quebec government and the Laurentian School Commission have launched investigations. In 1968 the Social Services investigated the children's quarters and reported finding them unduly Spartan. In 1974 the Minister of Education decided the school did not fulfill the provincial requirements and refused to reissue a *permis d'enseignement.*

A dramatic series of custody battles have generated conflict and the roots of this conflict lie in the patterns of commitment and communalism peculiar to this group. Married couples are permitted to join and cohabit together as disciples but, as their commitment deepens, they take vows of celibacy and become Apostles, and their children are raised in same-sex children's quarters, taught and presided over by monks or nuns. When one parent decides to leave the monastery, he or she will then sue for custody of the children, one side accusing the other of brainwashing and child abuse, and the other reluctant to surrender their children to a wicked world about to receive the wrath of God. In 1967–68 Gregory XVII was charged with "sequestration des enfants" or abducting the seventy children that a judge had placed under the protection of the court. Some of these children were eventually found, as they had been placed in different houses belonging to the Order.

In 1977 there was a police raid on the St.-Jovite Monastery, in response to a private complaint by one father, a Mr. Currier, who had been granted legal custody of his three children but was denied permission to visit and had no knowledge of their whereabouts. After twenty warrants to appear in court had been served and ignored, Gaston Tremblay was charged with "sequestration des enfants" and warrants were issued against him, the mother, and other members. The police flew over the walls of the monastery in helicopters and arrested "accomplices" who were then imprisoned. Pope Gregory was not to be found, but a year later in April 1978 he was picked up accidentally by traffic police and was sentenced to six months in prison on 10 August 1978 for the illegal detention of children and contempt of court. One of the children was returned to his father, and the other two remain within the Order.

On 14 April 1999, sixty police cars drew up at the monastery in St.-Jovite with warrants for the arrest of four Apostles, two nuns who were charged with the physical abuse of girls, one monk wanted for sexual abuse of minors charges, and one pope wanted for gross indecency charges; all allegations by ex-members who were once children raised in the monastery, involving events that allegedly occurred between 1964 and 1975. Finding the suspects absent, the police seized documents and searched the premises. Fourteen children were taken into custody, and Gregory XVII turned himself in a week later and, as of September 1999, was awaiting trial.

Susan J. Palmer

Bibliography

Barette, Jean-Marie. (1988) *The Prophecy of the Apostles of the Latter Times.* St.-Jovite, Quebec: Éditions Magnificat.

Cuneo, Michael. (1997) "The Vengeful Virgin." In *Millennium, Messiahs and Mayhem,* edited by Thomas Robbins and Susan J. Palmer. New York: Routledge, 175–94.

Gregory XVII. ([1975] 1993) *Peter Speaks to the World,* 2d ed. St.-Jovite: Monastery of the magnificat, 211–12.

The Order of the Magnificat of the Mother of God. (1999) http://magnificat.qc.ca/english/index.html.

Armageddon Time Ark Base

To the members of the Armageddon Time Ark Base Operations (ATA), a ufology religion located in Weslaco, Texas, it is not the aliens who are to blame for the sorry state of planet Earth, but earthlings. The group believes that humans were placed on Earth by extraterrestrial "cosmic engineers" under the direction of a prime creator and given free moral will over six thousand years ago. Since then the inhabitants of planet Earth have been found by the "outer dimensional" beings to be abusing themselves and the Earth, a consequence of deficient evolution. Enslaved by costly and time-wasting experimental research and industrial development, humans have created a new world of waste, pollution, disease, war, and death.

Freely borrowing from the Book of Revelations, the ATA commonly employs apocalyptic language in reference to corrupted humanity as "Babylon" and the final collapse of human civilization as "Armageddon." The ATA predicts the inevitability of planetary collapse, a time in which they will escape the destruction of the planet in their "Time Arks" (spaceships), presumably at some time prior to Armageddon.

There is a conspiracy element to the beliefs of ATA, as well. For example, the group sees in the emergence of national and international political and economic organizations the specter of "Big Brother." An article entitled "State of Time Station Earth," from the Internet website of the Armageddon Time Ark Base, reveals details of this cosmic conspiracy:

> The jailers who force the humatons to sweat and exist in this stone age "juzgado"... are the false prophets of the many of the End Time, who are preventing you from knowing by restricting you to belief and faith, and the Big Brother Police State to insure that you remain in the Dark Stone Age of The Wheel, with its friction, pollution, disease and death as a reward for being a good bondslave. (ATA 1997)

While most ufology religions share the concern over the fate of the Earth and its inhabitants and predict that the aliens will prevent global destruction or initiate some form of evolutionary or cosmic transformation, ATA is less sanguine about the salvation of Earth or humankind. Likewise, Heaven's Gate theology referred to the ultimate destruction of the planet Earth as a "spading under," while Armageddon Time Ark Base sees it as a "chiropractic adjustment" of the Earth's "spine." The only way to survive this destruction is to evacuate, as the Heaven's Gate group believed they were doing in their mass suicide. For Armageddon Time Ark Base, the evacuation of the Earth will occur when group members don their space suits and blast off from Earth in their own spaceships, allegedly being built by the group in preparation for "S-day."

Philip Lamy

Bibliography

Kooks Museum (http://www.teleport.com/~dkossy/nodrog.html)

Art

The related themes of the Apocalypse, the Last Judgment, and the millennium have inspired twenty centuries of Western art. Other religious traditions, among them Buddhism and Hinduism, skillfully use art to portray the tortures of the damned and the bliss of the saved. Representation of demonic forces is, likewise, a staple of primitive and folk art, some of it remarkably poignant. Christianity, however, is nearly unique in its extensive artistic treatment of apocalypticism. This does not surprise, since eschatology is far more important to its theological and historical heritage than for other world religions. The other Abrahamic faiths, Judaism and Islam, share at least some of Christianity's preoccupation with the Last Judgment. However, their religious scruple on visual representation of divine images inhibits creation of sacred art. Most importantly, they possessed nothing comparable to the Christian doctrine of the Second Advent for thematic inspiration.

Eschatological Christian art especially thrives because of that religion's extraordinarily vivid sacred texts which treat with the Apocalypse. The most notable among these is, of course, the late-first-century CE Revelation to John, a book crammed with lurid imagery, which all but cries out for artistic representation. The evangelist's mention of "a woman clothed with the sun, with the moon under her feet, and on her head a crown of twelve stars" (Revelation 12:1) is merely one of dozens of motifs that for centuries have inspired artists. Eschatological passages in the Gospels, as well, offer inspiration. So potent, though, is Revelation in summoning the imagination, and so liable is its imagery to fanciful representation, that Byzantine Christianity quietly withdrew the book from circulation. In the West, however, it proved a creative fount for artistic expression.

Antiquity

Artistic representation of apocalyptic and millennial themes appeared in mosaic form on Roman churches as early as the fourth century CE, as well as on sarcophagi, small ivories, and other minor art works. The motifs were usually taken from Revelation and several entered Christian iconography. The Alpha and Omega symbol, S, which one historian calls "probably the oldest apocalyptic symbol in art," and which expresses Christ's stature as the beginning and end of all things ("I am the Alpha and the Omega," Revelation 1:8) became especially common. The S, which closes the Greek alphabet, symbolized Christ's agency in bringing Creation to its close at the Parousia. It was, however, only one of several eschatologically significant signs used by artists and craftsman of the ancient world.

The Middle Ages

Apocalyptic art abounded throughout the long medieval era, which followed the end of the ancient world in Western history. Motifs drawn from Revelation are common in surviving illuminated manuscripts, small work such as caskets and ivories, stained glass, and, most especially, the carving and stonework of the great cathedrals. From the early Middle Ages until the fourteenth century, Romanesque and then Gothic cathedrals were commonly decorated with statutes and bas-relief, which illustrated such apocalyptic themes as the dragon (Revelation 12:3) or the rider of death (Revelation 6:8). During the later Middle Ages, apocalyptic imagery drew heavily from the Gospel of St. Matthew.

The great Christian themes of judgment and apocalypse were leavened in medieval art by the even more prominent teachings of mercy and compassion. An example is the tympanum of the central bay in the south portal at Chartres. Here, Christ sits in judgment. But, he prominently displays as well his wounds suffered willingly on behalf of humanity. At his either side, St. John and the Virgin still beseech mercy, even though the world is about to end, to show that, as Emile Mâle observed, "Grace is stronger than law." The damned are, indeed, led dolefully away to their fate; but, the eye is also drawn to the saved, raised from death and overwhelmed with light and joy. Christ's return in judgment, in other words, is not solely the Day when "there will be great tribulation, such as has not been from the beginning of the world until now" (Matthew 24:21). For those who persevere in the faith, it will be a time of unutterable happiness and fulfillment. For Christians, in other words, the apocalypse is not dreaded but welcomed.

Apocalyptic themes were so common in late medieval art that even such an inherently grim subject was translated by skilled artists into a thing of beauty. The artists chosen by Jean, Duc de Berry, in the fifteenth century CE to illustrate his *Très Riches Heures* lavished their talents on a gorgeous rendering of the fourth rider of the Apocalypse. They portrayed Death as a handsome nobleman, seated upon a white charger, who drives from their tombs a skeletal troupe of the dead. The arisen cross a verdant lawn, to the astonishment of a group of soldiers, whose armor is gorgeously rendered with shimmering gold leaf. Behind the scene are dainty turreted and crenellated battlements, and beyond these loom forested hills and a clear sky, both done in rich blue. Here, the apocalypse entertains as much as terrifies.

The Renaissance and Reformation

Renaissance art continued the traditional reliance on religious themes. Now, however, artists worked with ever-increasing skill and sophistication to render the Apocalypse for appreciative patrons. Fra Angelico (1387–1455) created a magnificent Last Judgment, dominated by a Christ in Glory who at the end of all things summons his saints, while the damned trudge disconsolately into Hell. Hubert Van Eyck (?–1426) elaborated the same thing in an extraordinary painting in which Death, portrayed as a bat-winged skeleton, dominates the center plane. Here, terror is restored to the Apocalypse.

Apocalyptic art was common as well during the Reformation and often used as religious propaganda. Woodcuts combined with the newly invented printing press to produce countless illustrations, some sophisticated, more quite crude, which depicted the pope or Luther as the Antichrist or some notorious beast from Revelation. The German engraver Albrecht Dürer (1471–1528) used his grotesque but hugely impressive manner to create well-known renderings of St. John's Apocalypse. His technically superb work so strikingly, if somewhat slavishly, portrayed the Last Judgment that it smothered other representations for generations, except for a few hardy or immensely talented artists. It took an El Greco, especially his stylized *Opening of the Fifth Seal* with its typically fluid and elongated human torsos, or a Corregio, working on an immense scale inside the cupola of the church of St. Giovanni in Parma, to successfully separate from Dürer's endlessly reproduced engravings.

Eighteenth and Nineteenth Centuries

Religious themes faded somewhat in Western art during the Enlightenment, among them the Apocalypse. Prophecy briefly returned to fashion as a fit subject for artistic treatment toward the nineteenth century, though more for its spookiness than religiosity, as part of the Romantic movement. William Blake's metal relief etchings for his own *Europe: A Prophecy* (1794) offered striking millenarian imagery, which, while it drew on Christian eschatology, essentially purloined its elements to illustrate the artist's own idiosyncratic philosophy.

During the nineteenth century, millennial prophecy inspired works of craft, often by humble folk, which dispensed with the stereotyped themes of Christian iconography to honor Scripture with mundane but beautiful forms. The American Shakers, technically the Millennial Church of the United Society of Believers, rested on the literal interpretation of the Bible, most especially passages of prophecy and revelation, favored by the founder, "Mother" Ann Lee Stanley. She taught that the millennium was at hand and insisted her followers lead a life of utmost simplicity, in imitation, as she believed, of the earliest Christians. Her eschatological faith was manifested by believers in their creation of exquisitely simple things for everyday use. Items as mundane as a common chair, or even a broom, were crafted into objects of haunting grace and honesty.

The American artist Edward Hicks (1780–1849) produced dozens of representations of the millennial era, drawn from the prophecy of Isaiah: "The wolf shall dwell with the lamb, and the leopard shall lie down with the kid . . . and a little child shall lead them" (Isaiah 11:6). Hicks painted variations on this theme, nearly all of which gently portray an infant surrounded by slightly comical, naturally fierce beasts, now rendered benign in God's "Peaceable Kingdom." His is perhaps the most widely known visual representation of the millennium.

The Twentieth Century

The twentieth century saw an enormous outpouring of millenarian folk art, more so than ever before in history, in the American evangelical and Fundamentalist communities. Themes drawn from Revelation were illustrated and reproduced countless millions of times to illuminate confusing prophetic imagery for believers. A typical portrayal showed a bizarre multiheaded "beast from the sea" (Revelation 13:1–4), replete with requisite horns and diadems, ferociously breaking through the waves. The simple draftsmanship and literal representation of such productions disqualifies them as serious art. They do, however, belong in the long and vital tradition of Western folk illustration. Like their distant medieval counterparts, these works are essentially didactic and in their naïve fashion serve as efficient teaching tools for believers. As such, the twenty-century Western tradition of apocalyptic and millennial art has never been more alive than at the dawn of the twenty-first century.

Robert K. Whalen

Bibliography

Bjelajac, David. (1988) *Millennial Desire and the Apocalyptic Vision of Washington Allston.* Washington, D.C.: Smithsonian Institution Press.

Mâle, Emile. (1958) *The Gothic Image: Religious Art in France of the Thirteenth Century.* New York: Icon Editions.

Price Mather, Eleanore. (1983) *Edward Hicks: His "Peaceable Kingdom" and Other Paintings.* Newark, DE: American Art Journal/Kennedy Galleries Books.

Van der Meer, Frederick. (1978) *Apocalypse: Visions from the Book of Revelation in Western Art.* New York: Alpine Fine Arts Collection, Ltd.

Asia

Millenarian expectation of an age of redemption, in which the evils and travails of a wicked world will be miraculously supplanted by a utopian order of supreme justice and moral perfection, is as deeply rooted in the societies of Asia as it is in those of the Western world. As in the West, it is often believed that this new age will be ushered in by a messianic deliverer, whose sacred mission is conceived to manifest the will of a transcendent, providential spiritual reality. In Asia, this form of millenarianism normally draws its shape and inspiration from Hinduism, Buddhism, Confucianism, or one of the lesser religious or philosophical traditions of the Asian world. Historically, millennialism in Asia was embodied most commonly in radical religious movements that were directed principally toward fundamental social reform or political rebellion—movements which frequently culminated in peasant uprisings against intolerable economic inequities or dynastic corruption and incompetence.

China

Ancient China presents us with one of the earliest and most influential prototypes of Asian millenarianism in the form of the "mandate of Heaven." This cosmic principle of dynastic succession was enshrined in a set of compilations associated with the venerated philosopher Confucius (551–479 BCE), who looked backward to a golden age of antiquity for ideal models of public and private morality. The legendary past envisioned in the Confucian Classics dated back to the twenty-third century BCE and was marked by the rule of the sage-kings Yao and Shun and the virtuous founder of the Xia dynasty, YŸ. The worldly authority of these early cultural heroes was sanctified and sustained through their ritualized linkage with the providential power of Heaven *(Tian)*, and their pervasive wisdom and benevolence was seen to epitomize the highest ideals of human culture.

According to the Confucian *History Classic (Shujing)*, the Xia dynasty established by YŸ was eventually deposed when its last ruler, the cruel and tyrannical King Jie, had so abused his powers that Heaven transferred the mandate to rule to Tang, the virtuous founder of the Shang dynasty. King Tang brought Heaven's retribution to his evil predecessor and reconstituted the traditional moral framework of Chinese society. Likewise, the degenerate final ruler of the Shang dynasty lost the mandate of Heaven and was overthrown by King Wen, the upright founder of the Zhou dynasty, whose lineage still reigned in China at the time of Confucius.

Winning and retaining the mandate of Heaven thus became the basis of political legitimacy in traditional China, and the public perception that the ruler had forsaken the virtuous benevolence of the "son of Heaven" provided political contenders with a cosmological justification for political rebellion. Throughout the succeeding centuries, this millenarian scheme would be repeated time and time again and remain one of the major cultural forces sustaining the cyclical pattern of China's dynastic history.

By the end of the Han dynasty (206 BCE–220 BCE), popular Daoism (Taoism) had emerged as the basis of another form of Chinese millennialism. The origins of Daoism are traced by most historians to the teachings of the philosopher Lao-Tsu, a contemporary of Confucius. Lao-Tsu's teachings, which in many respects were the very antithesis of Confucianism, were recorded in the *Classic of the Way and Its Power (Dao De Jing)*. Whereas Confucius stressed the importance of maintaining a rigid social hierarchy sustained by an elaborate observance of traditional rites and proprieties, Daoism longed for a primitive egalitarianism that was free of the oppressive strictures, superfluous conventions, and pretentious ritualism of the Confucian order. In the centuries following Lao-Tsu's original formulation of his philosophy, a form of folk Daoism emerged that combined his teachings with a pantheon of folk deities and an emphasis on the power of magical spells and practices.

Daoism thus evolved into the ideal vehicle for peasant protest against the growing political oppression and economic inequity of late Han society; particularly when the cosmological significance of the times was confirmed by calamitous portents such as comets, floods, earthquakes, and poor harvests. The Yellow Turban uprising of 184 BCE, a name derived from the head-dress adopted by its members, was one of the earliest examples of this sort of popular Daoist millenarianism. The messianic patriarch of the movement, Zhang Jue, deliberately invoked the communal egalitarianism of the Daoist golden age by naming his sect the Great Peace *(Taiping)*. This sect focused its worship upon the Lord Huang Lao, a deified synthesis of Lao-Tsu and the legendary sovereign Huang Di (the Yellow Emperor). The group also practiced the confession of sins and spirit possession and believed in the protective virtues of magic potions and amulets. At the height of their power, the Yellow Turbans claimed 360,000 armed supporters and were suppressed by the Han only after great cost and struggle.

As Mahayana Buddhism spread from the land of its birth in India to penetrate the farthest reaches of East Asia, it too provided a fertile vision and ideology for millenarian movements. Among the most noteworthy of these were the diverse religious sects, which historians group together as White Lotus societies. This form of millenarian Buddhism assumed great importance as a distinctive religious tradition during the middle of the fourteenth century, at which time the

THE CHINESE "MANDATE OF HEAVEN" CONCEPT

Heaven and Earth is the parent of all creatures; and of all creatures man is the most highly endowed. The sincere, intelligent, and perspicacious [among men] becomes the great sovereign; and the great sovereign is the parent of the people. [But] now, Zhou, the king of Shang [dynasty], does not reverence Heaven above, and inflicts calamities on the people below. He has been abandoned to drunkenness, and reckless in lust. He has desired to exercise cruel oppression. Along with criminals he has punished all their relatives. He has put men into office on the hereditary principle. He has made it his pursuit to have palaces, towers, pavilions, embankments, ponds, and all other extravagances, to the most painful injury of you the myriad people. He has burned and roasted the loyal and good. He has ripped up pregnant women.

. . . The iniquity of Shang is full. Heaven gives command to destroy it. If I did not comply with Heaven, my iniquity would be as great.

I, who am a little child, early and late am filled with apprehensions. I have received charge from my deceased father Wan [King Wen]; I have offered special sacrifice to God [*Shangdi*]; I have performed the due services to the great Earth;–and I lead the multitude of you to execute the punishment appointed by Heaven. Heaven compassionates the people. What the people desire, Heaven will be found to give effect to. Do you aid me, the one man, to cleanse forever [all within] the four seas. Now is the time!–it may not be lost.

Source: *History Classic,* "The Books of Zhou," "The Great Declaration [of King Wu, co-founder of the Zhou dynasty]." Legge, James, trans. (1991) *The Chinese Classics.* Vol. III. Taipei, Taiwan: SMC Publishing, 283–88.

Mongol Yuan dynasty was violently overthrown by the founders of the Ming dynasty. These early White Lotus sects of heterodox Buddhists anticipated the return of the messianic Buddha Maitreya, who at the end of an era of unprecedented calamity and tribulation would bring salvation to the faithful and establish a new order of supreme justice and felicity.

The rebellious Red Turbans of the lower Yellow River region, whose leader Han Shantong was regarded as an incarnation of the Maitreya, were among the most notable of these millenarian sects. Beginning in 1351, following a period of repeated flooding in the region, the Red Turbans led a series of massive peasant insurrections that spread widely throughout the central provinces and contributed greatly to the eventual overthrow of the Yuan. Even the vigorous Ming dynasty founder himself, Zhu Yuanzhang, was a former monk who had been deeply influenced by messianic Buddhism and had once allied his forces with the Red Turbans.

By the middle of the sixteenth century, White Lotus sectarians began to focus their worship on an Eternal Venerable Mother *(Wusheng Laomu)*, a figure drawn from Chinese folk religion that was described as the progenitor of all humanity. According to sectarian literature, this Eternal Venerable Mother arranged for her descendents to live in the "Eastern world," where, in time, they became "indulged in vanity and lost their original nature." Wishing for her children to return to their "original home in the world of true emptiness," she vowed to send the Buddha Maitreya *(Mile fo)* to guide them back to the "Pure Land." This was to occur after the duration of a lengthy historical era of thousands of years known as a "kalpa," at the end of which the world would succumb increasingly to wickedness and disorder until, finally, a cosmic catastrophe would destroy all evil and clear the way for the followers of the Eternal Venerable Mother to rise to power.

This latter form of White Lotus sectarianism provided the ideological impetus for the massive peasant rebellions of the late eighteenth and early nineteenth centuries. During this period, Chinese society was beginning to degenerate under the pressures of an expanding population and the declining leadership of the Qing dynasty, causing many among the lower classes to turn to White Lotus religious sects for mutual support and joint resistance. In 1774, a martial arts and healing expert named Wang Lun invoked the support of the Eternal Venerable Mother during his leadership of a major rebellion that managed to capture several towns before Qing forces were able to muster the power to suppress them. A rash of similarly inspired uprisings occurred between 1796 and 1803, until they too were brutally suppressed by the imperial government. In the autumn of 1813, yet another White Lotus sect calling themselves the Eight Trigrams likewise arose to overthrow the Qing and establish a new era of "endless blessings."

Southeast Asia

Millennialism in Southeast Asia followed some of the same patterns as those in China, particularly in Vietnam where the sinicized social and political orders were deeply influenced by such notions as the mandate of Heaven and other aspects of the Confucian or Daoist traditions. Millenarian movements in Southeast Asia also absorbed a range of influences from Hinduism and Islam, both of which contributed greatly to the rich cultural landscape of the region. The idea of the Hindu *avatara* (Divine incarnation), drawn from the classical works of India such as the *Ramayana* and the *Bhagavad Gita,* maintained that gods or cultural heroes of India's past will incarnate themselves as great messianic leaders during times of social crisis or decline. It is not surprising, therefore, to find even in Vietnam a pagoda keeper of the early sixteenth century declaring himself to be a reincarnation of Indra and winning a large enough following to nearly overthrow the decadent Le dynasty rulers.

Islamic traditions recorded in the Hadith also held out the promise of a messianic figure, or Mahdi, who would appear during a time of great social turmoil and spiritual degeneracy to reunite the faithful and revitalize the fortunes of the Muslim community. In nineteenth-century Java, Prince Dipanagara, a regional *kyai* (venerated teacher of Islam) from a *priyayi* (Javanese aristocratic) background, amalgamated native and Islamic millenarian ideas by claiming the messianic title of the pre-Islamic *ratu adil,* or just king, who in Javanese folklore would arrive during a period of severe decline to institute a new age of justice and prosperity. In 1825, Prince Dipanagara won devout and determined support among his countrymen for a revolt against the Dutch, whose colonial encroachments had severely disrupted the traditional order of Javanese society. This Java War, as it is known, was won by the Dutch only after five years of bitter fighting, after which the Dutch colonial authorities took measures to channel such popular religiosity by establishing a strictly regulated religious bureaucracy for native Islamic clerics.

In Burma and Siam (Thailand), religious millennialism was most likely to be shaped by ideas drawn from the classical Buddhist tradition, particularly those notions associated with the archetypal *cakkavatti,* or Universal Ruler. Modeled upon orthodox accounts of the reign of the Indian emperor Ashoka, who ruled during the glory days of the Mauryan dynasty in the third century BCE, the *cakkavatti* was venerated as the ideal patron of the Buddhist *sangha* (monkhood) and the supreme propagator of the *dharma* (religious law). Southeast Asian Buddhists, like their counterparts in China, also believed in the Buddha Maitreya, who would arrive at the end of the kalpa to inaugurate an era of peace and justice. These two key traditions were frequently combined to form the ideological basis of premodern millenarianism in the Buddhist kingdoms of mainland Southeast Asia.

The founder of the Kongbaung dynasty in eighteenth-century Burma imbued his military campaigns with millenarian significance by taking the title of *Alaung Mintayagi,* or embryo Buddha, and justified a major war against the Thai kingdom of Ayutthaya on the basis that the Thai rulers had not fulfilled their traditional obligation to support Buddhism. His son and successor, Bodawpaya (c. 1781–1819), claimed the title of both Maitreya and *cakkavatti,* declaring himself to be the long-awaited messianic harbinger of a new religious epoch destined to succeed the allotted five thousand year span of the current religion. Even as late as 1931, a former monk, fortune teller, and practitioner of folk

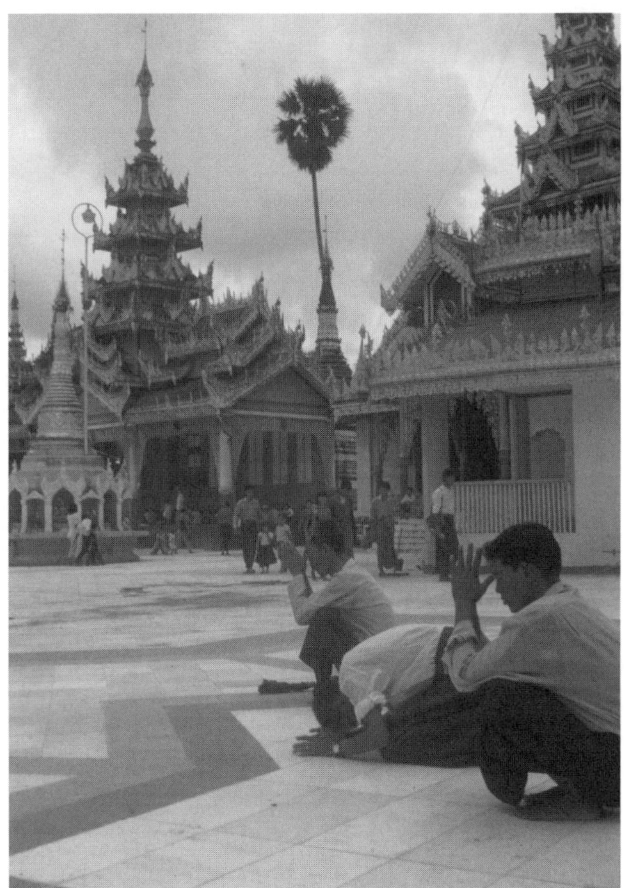

Buddhists praying at Shwedegun Pagoda in Yangon, Myanmar (Burma). Buddhism has been a source of numerous millennial movements across Asia. STEPHEN G. DONALDSON.

EXCERPT FROM THE *BHAGAVAD GITA* 4:5–8

5. **I have been born many times, Arjuna, and many times hast thou been born. But I remember my past lives, and thou hast forgotten thine.**
6. **Although I am unborn, everlasting, and I am the Lord of all, I come to my realm of nature and through my wondrous power I am born.**
7. **When righteousness is weak and faints and unrighteousness exults in pride, then my Spirit arises on earth.**
8. **For the salvation of those who are good, for the destruction of evil in men, for the fulfillment of the kingdom of righteousness, I come to this world in the ages that pass.**

medicine named Saya San led a massive peasant-based rebellion against British colonialism in Burma during which he declared himself a *Min-laung,* (embryo king) and *Setkya-min* (Burmanization of *cakkavatti*). Saya San further inspired the religious frenzy of his followers by adopting all the paraphernalia of divine kingship, even building a humble palace that incorporated all the symbolic imagery of a traditional Buddhist capital.

Christian-Inspired Millennial Movements

During the era of Western colonialism, Asian millennialism even found expression through the religious symbols and ideas of Christianity. In the Philippines, a country that had been largely converted to Catholicism in the early years of Spanish colonialism, the popularization of Catholic teachings through the public dramatization of Christ's passion, death, and resurrection *(Pasyon)*, generated a popular faith in the essential interconnectedness of the human and divine and opened the possibility of appropriating the messianic imagery of Christ as the basis of anticolonial rebellion. The *Pasyon* also introduced an eschatological scheme to the Filipino peasantry by suggesting a biblical progression of three eras *(panahon)* presided over by the Father, Son, and Holy Spirit—the latter ending with the cataclysmic arrival of the apocalypse and the return of Christ.

The most sensational radical movement associated with these beliefs was that which began as the Cofradia de San José (Confraternity of St. Joseph). Under the leadership of Apolinario de la Cruz, a charismatic lay brother who was deeply inspired by Catholic mysticism, the movement grew independent of church control and rapidly attracted a mass following as Apolinario became increasingly recognized as a messianic holy man, or a Tagalog Christ, with traditional powers of healing and invulnerability. Retreating to the sacred slopes of Mount Banahao, Apolinario organized his followers into a vast commune to prepare for the impending apocalyptic upheaval and lay the foundations for the new order that would succeed it. Proscribed by Spanish church authorities in 1840, the Cofradia was finally suppressed with great violence once its heretical independence had begun to openly challenge the cultural and political hegemony of the Spanish colonial authorities. Its teachings were nevertheless kept alive as survivors of the movement were scattered to the remote villages and enclaves of islands to the south.

The Taiping Rebellion of nineteenth-century China was undoubtedly the most spectacular example of Christian-inspired millennialism in Asia. The leader of the Taiping's, Hong Xiuquan, fashioned a messianic image for himself on the basis of some Protestant missionary tracts presented to him while attending the imperial examinations in Canton in 1833. Correlating the evangelical message contained in these tracts with an independently experienced vision of his own, Hong Xiuquan claimed to be the younger brother of Christ, commissioned by the Lord of Heaven to slay the devil-demons (Manchus) whose rule had brought ruin to China and, finally, to establish a Christian-based Heavenly Kingdom of Great Peace *(Taiping Tianguo)*. This task would involve purifying China of the influence of those false religions (Confucianism and Buddhism), which throughout Chinese history have led the people astray from the worship of the one true (Judeo-Christian) God.

The rapidly disintegrating condition of Chinese society around the mid-nineteenth century opened the possibility for the rise of revolutionary alternatives to Manchu (Qing) rule. It is not that surprising, therefore, that Hong Xiuquan's puritanical, communistic ideology was able to win a large enough following to mount a serious challenge to the Qing dynasty rulers. Establishing his "Heavenly Capital" at Nanjing in 1853, the Taiping rebels came very close to overthrowing the Qing state and revolutionizing the traditional ethical and religious foundations of Chinese society. But, ironically, Hong Xiuquan was unable to win the support of Western missionaries and merchants in China, who became increasingly suspicious of his heretical claims and imperious behavior. In the end, this allowed the Qing to rebound and with Western aid crush the Taipings after a decade of unceasing war and devastation that caused as many as twenty million deaths.

Conclusion

Throughout the centuries, millennialism in Asia has assumed many forms, and while it has normally been fashioned on the basis of beliefs and traditions indigenous to the region, it has often seized syncretically on millenarian conceptions embodied in the religions and philosophies of the West. Some historians have even interpreted the 1949 Communist Revolution in China as a combined expression of traditional Chinese and Marxist millenarianism. On the other hand, millenarian movements have arisen also as an effort to reaffirm those cherished religious traditions that in the colonial era and afterward were subjected to the onslaught of alien cosmologies from the West. The millenarian dimensions of some of the Hindu and Islamic fundamentalist movements currently gaining ascendancy in South Asia have been interpreted as examples of this. Whatever the case may be, the beliefs and aspirations associated with Asian millennialism appear destined to continue to exert a profound influence on the fortunes of Asian society, just as they continue to do in the Western world.

Michael C. Lazich

See also Aum Shinrikyo, Chen Tao, China, Islam, Japan, Zoroastrianism

Bibliography

Ileto, Reynaldo Clemena. (1979) *Pasyon and Revolution.* Quezon City, Philippines: Ateneo de Manila University Press.

Naquin, Susan. (1976) *Millenarian Rebellion in China.* New Haven, CT: Yale University Press.

Rinehart, James F. (1997) *Revolution and the Millennium.* Westport, CT: Praeger Publishers.

Spence, Jonathan D. (1996) *God's Chinese Son.* New York: W. W. Norton & Company.

Tarling, Nicholas, ed. (1992) *The Cambridge History of Southeast Asia.* Cambridge, U.K.: Cambridge University Press.

Assaulted Millennial Groups

An assaulted millennial group is assaulted by persons in mainstream society, because the members' religious views and actions are misunderstood, feared, and despised. The group is assaulted because it is viewed as being dangerous to society. The group's members are not seen as practicing a valid religion worthy of respect. The group might be assaulted by law enforcement agents or civilians. Today, such a group is likely to be labeled with the pejorative term "cult." While some assaulted groups bear part of the responsibility for the violence that engulfs them, the primary responsibility for the violence rests upon those in mainstream society who assault them. Mormons in nineteenth-century America, the Lakota Sioux at Wounded Knee, the Israelites at Bulhoek, South Africa, and the Branch Davidians of Waco, Texas, are examples of assaulted millennial groups and movements.

Assaulted millennial groups often contribute to the violence that engulfs them by possessing arms. Also, the catastrophic millennial group's radical dualistic worldview in which stark good is seen as pitted against stark evil leads to an "us vs. them" perspective that contributes to conflict situations. A millennial group's allegiance to God over civil authority increases the likelihood that the group will come into conflict with law enforcement agents.

The unnecessary assault of millennial groups can be avoided if law enforcement agents learn to recognize the power of religious commitment and how millennial beliefs can contribute to violent episodes. Law enforcement agents can learn to handle millennial groups more skillfully by consulting credentialed experts on religions.

Catherine Wessinger

See also Catastrophic Millennialism, Progressive Millennialism.

Bibliography

Tabor, James D., and Eugene V. Gallagher. (1995) *Why Waco? Cults and the Battle for Religious Freedom in America.* Berkeley, CA: University of California Press.

Wessinger, Catherine. (2000) *How the Millennium Comes Violently.* Chappaqua, NY: Seven Bridges Press.

——, ed. (2000) *Millennialism, Persecution, and Violence: Historical Cases.* Syracuse, NY: Syracuse University Press.

Aum Shinrikyo

Aum Shinrikyo, or Aum Supreme Truth as it refers to itself in English, is a Japanese millennial movement founded in the

1980s by the blind charismatic prophet Asahara Shoko (b.1955). It had about ten thousand members in Japan, of whom just over one thousand had renounced the world to live in Aum's communes. It gained international notoriety in 1995 because of the attack it carried out using sarin nerve gas on the Tokyo underground. It transpired that Aum had committed a number of other attacks on opponents and had manufactured chemical weapons on a large scale, apparently in order to defend itself against what it believed was a vast conspiracy against it and in order to fight in the sacred war between good and evil that it believed would engulf the world and herald the end of contemporary materialist civilization. Aum is highly significant in millennial terms because of its espousal of weapons of mass destruction (the first case, it is believed, by a private organization) and because it is a movement that began with an optimistic form of millennialism that became progressively more catastrophic and destructive in nature until it finally came to seek destruction and death on a grand scale.

Aum in the Japanese Context: Millennialism and Mission

Aum was one of the new religions that grew in Japan in the late twentieth century. It combined elements of Buddhism, Hinduism, folk religion, and mysticism, and its followers sought spiritual transcendence through yoga and meditation techniques. Asahara himself claimed to have achieved supreme enlightenment when visiting India in 1986. He identified himself with the Hindu deity Shiva and was considered in Aum to be a supremely enlightened being capable of transferring his spiritual power to others through initiation rituals. The movement had a strong world-negating view, believing that the material world was corrupt and evil and that the normal consequence of living in it would be to absorb bad karma which would pull the spirit into lower spiritual realms after death. The only way to avoid this was to withdraw from the world and engage in ascetic practices to eradicate one's bad karma. Aum developed a monastic system to this end, in which members severed all ties with their families, took on a new religious name, pledged absolute devotion to Asahara, and lived in Aum's communes, where they sought to purify their bodies and minds and to take on the spiritual power and characteristics of their guru.

The movement was infused by a belief that the current age was coming to an end and that the world was threatened by cataclysms that would herald a new age. Its millennialism was also influenced by Christian images and by the prophecies of Nostradamus, which had been translated into Japanese and had an effect on the popular Japanese religious consciousness of the era. Originally Aum's millennialism was optimistic, and it believed that it had a mission to accomplish a peaceful transition to a new and more spiritual age. Asahara's early visions foresaw a cosmic struggle in which the forces of evil would be defeated by those of good, and in this cosmic struggle he and his followers (who called themselves "true victors") would save the world from imminent disasters and play a leading role in the transformation into a new spiritual age. In the late 1980s Aum began to build "Lotus villages" (communes in rural Japan) that would be the basis for the development of a utopian new world (Shambhala, named after the Buddhist paradise).

The Development of Violent and Confrontational Millennial Views

Aum was unable, however, to attract the followers it believed necessary to accomplish this mission, and became increasingly pessimistic in its worldview. Moreover it ran into trouble due to conflicts with the parents of commune members who had cut ties with their families. It fell afoul of the authorities for breaking various laws when it acquired the land for its communes and faced several lawsuits as a result. This apparent rejection of its message coupled with external opposition led Asahara to conclude that the world at large was neither worthy nor capable of being saved, and that only the Aum faithful were capable of salvation. He developed a persecution complex in which he believed that hostile forces were conspiring against Aum; and while such interpretations helped "explain" why his messages were not getting across to the wider public, they increased the pressure on the movement and made it feel increasingly beleaguered.

Aum also developed a dark secret: a follower died accidentally during ascetic practice. This death was covered up to prevent the news harming Aum's reputation, but when another follower who had been present decided to go public with the news, he was killed by Aum devotees in order to silence him. The killing was legitimated doctrinally on the grounds that it was necessary to kill him in order to save him from accruing the bad karma that would have come through jeopardizing Aum's mission, and to save him from falling into the hells as a result. This was a catalyst to further cycles of violence inside the movement that only came to light years later. Aum's essentially polarized view of the world became increasingly rigid as its fears of exposure grew, while Asahara's visions of the final struggle between good and evil became more dramatic and violent in scope as he became convinced that a final war, Armageddon, would erupt in the 1990s. While it was Aum's sacred mission to fight against evil in this war, Asahara was convinced that it faced enormous odds because the whole world was turning against it and because a vast conspiracy was planning to destroy it using futuristic weapons. In this spiral of paranoid visions, Aum further developed its doctrinal position that its "true victors" could kill in order to defend their mission and also to "save" the unworthy who, by living in this corrupt world, were accumulating bad karma which would cause their inevitable fall into the hells after death. Aum thus became enveloped in a philosophy of violence, backed with deeds such as manufacturing chemical weapons that it planned to use in defense of its mission.

Aum's initial optimistic millennialism thus gave way to a bleak, catastrophic view, in which the primary images that drove the movement's leaders were those of destruction. Its behavior became more and more confrontational, and by the spring of 1995 it was widely suspected of having committed a number of attacks and murders of opponents and an attack using nerve gas in Matsumoto, a town in central Japan. Police raids were widely expected, but before they could occur Asahara ordered a preventative strike on the Tokyo subway using nerve gases made by the movement's devotees. The station targeted was right at the heart of Japan's government office district and the use of nerve gas at the nerve center of Japanese life thus appeared to be highly symbolic. Twelve people were killed and thousands injured. Immediately afterward Aum's centers were raided by the police and 180 leading members, including Asahara, were arrested. Several of the most senior figures, including Asahara, have been charged with crimes including murder, and several face the death penalty as a result.

The Future of Aum

The arrest of Asahara and other senior figures in the movement in 1995, and the public revelation of their activities, were severe blows to Aum. The majority of followers, who had been unaware of their leaders' activities, left the movement. Within a year the number of faithful had dropped to around nine hundred, a figure that appears to have remained fairly constant. Aum's status as a registered religious organization was revoked in 1995, although members are still allowed to meet and pursue collective worship. Asahara officially stepped down as leader in 1996 and, while incarcerated, has no contact with current members. Reflecting the common belief of Japanese new religions that charisma is an inherited trait, however, his two young sons are officially now the leaders of the movement. But Asahara remains a major focus of worship for members, many of whom believe that whatever activities Aum was involved in were parts of an inspired or divine plan whose truth will become known eventually. While many feel unhappy at being deprived of contact with their guru, they remain unperturbed about his possible fate: many

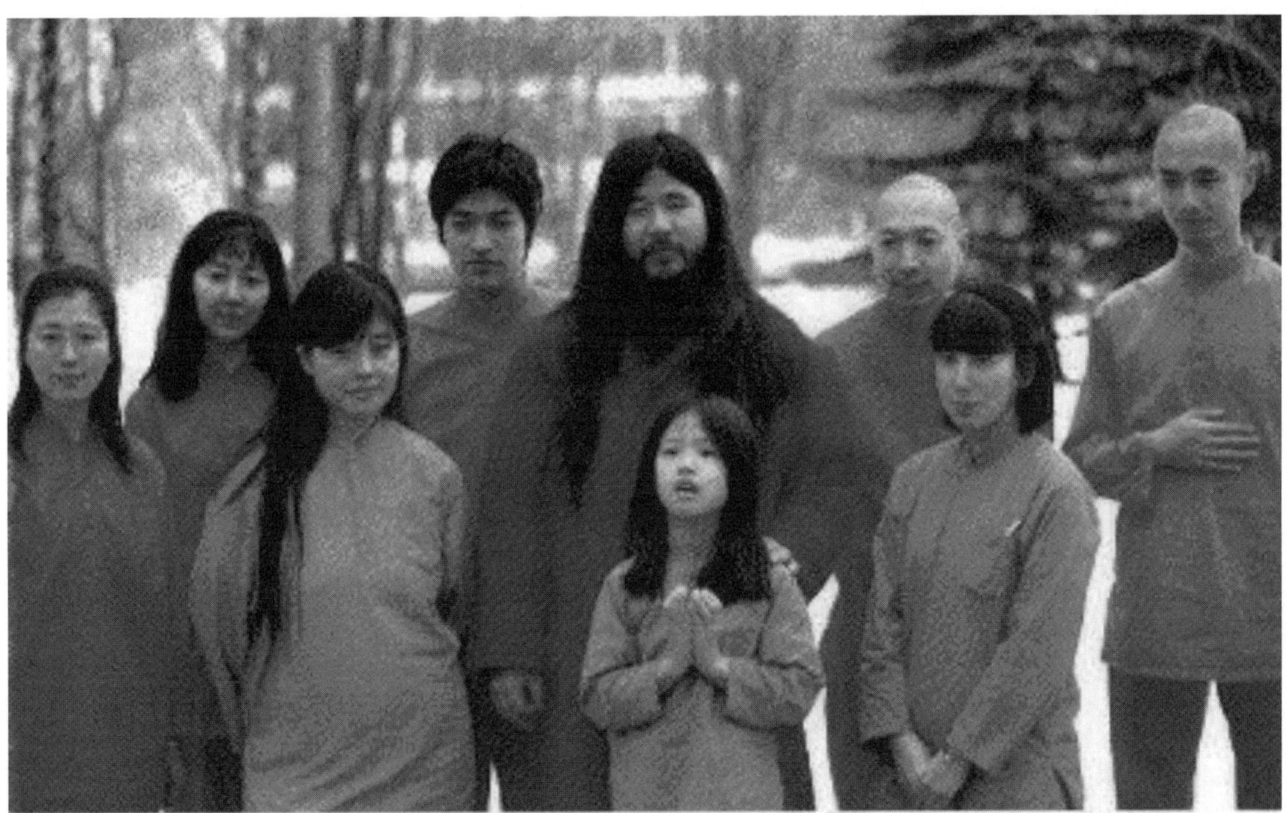

Shoko Asahara and close disciples in Russia in 1992. "SINRI" JAPANESE MAGAZINE, 1992.

assume he will be executed but consider that this fits in with their (and Asahara's) understandings of the corrupt nature of the world. They continue to espouse an ascetic path of world rejection, to focus on their ascetic practice, and to believe in the eventual occurrence of an apocalypse. The future of the movement is uncertain, given the lack of Asahara's charismatic presence and the hostility of the general public, which makes proselytizing difficult. However, Aum's current members also believe that the events that brought their movement such infamy also have accorded it a profound significance, bringing worldwide attention to its messages and enabling it "to be in the history books." As such, they feel that even if the movement disappears due to lack of members in the future, it has attained a form of immortality and will not be forgotten.

Besides further research into Aum's history, a number of areas relating to Aum after the subway attack require further research. The continuing faith of members in a guru who has been publicly discredited, and the capacity of movements to survive catastrophes as profound as that which engulfed Aum, are topics worthy of consideration, as is the extent to which members who had been unaware of their movement's criminal activities have, after the fact, been able to accept the movement's justifications for violence. In addition the impact of the Aum affair on Japanese millennialism is worthy of further study: the evidence on hand suggests that other millennial groups have, in the wake of the affair, altered their perspectives away from the radical forms of catastrophic millennialism prevalent in the early 1990s, to more benign forms.

Ian Reader

See also Catastrophic Millennialism, Japan

Bibliography

Kisala, Robert. (1998) "The AUM Spiritual Truth Church in Japan." In *Wolves Within the Fold: Religious Leadership and Abuses of Power,* edited by Anson Shupe. New Brunswick, NJ: Rutgers University Press, 33–48.

Metraux, Daniel. (1995) "Religious Terrorism in Japan: The Fatal Appeal of Aum Shinrikyô." *Asian Survey* 35, 12: 1140–54.

Mullins, Mark R. (1997) "The Political and Legal Response to Aum-related Violence in Japan." *Japan Christian Review* 63: 37–46.

Reader, Ian. (1996) *A Poisonous Cocktail? Aum Shinrikyô's Path to Violence.* Copenhagen: NIAS Books.

———. (2000) *Religious Violence in Contemporary Japan: The Case of Aum Shinrikyô.* London: Curzon and the University of Hawaii Press.

Shimazono Susumu. (1995) "In the Wake of Aum: The Formation and Transformation of a Universe of Belief." *Japanese Journal of Religious Studies* 22, 3–4: 343–80.

Baha'i Faith

The Baha'i religion and its precursor, the Babi religion, emerged from Shi'a Islam during the nineteenth century in Iran. It has its own divine founders, scriptures, institutions, practices, laws, principles, and calendar. Its followers number some six million worldwide.

Its first stage—the Babi religion—began in Shiraz in 1844. The Bab (Arabic, "Gate"—title of Sayyid 'Ali-Muhammad, 1819–50) claimed to fulfill the eschatological hopes of Shi'ism, founded an independent religion, and said that he was the forerunner of the supreme messiah for all faiths. Its second stage—as the Baha'i religion—was initiated in Baghdad in 1863 and publicly proclaimed in Edirne in 1867 when the Persian Babi exile Baha'u'llah (Arabic, "Glory of God"—title of Mirza Husayn-'Ali Nuri, 1817–92) said that he was the messenger promised by the Bab, and the expected messiah of all religions.

Babi Phase

The Ithna-'Ashari (Twelver) branch of Shi'a Islam believed that the Prophet Muhammad designated the lineage of 'Ali and Fatimah as Imams to provide infallible guidance. Persecutions of the Imams by non-Shi'a dynasties invested the imamate with messianic import. Upon the death of the eleventh Imam in AH 260 (874 CE), his son Muhammad al-Mahdi was believed to have gone into hiding. A series of four intermediaries, known as *babs* ("gates") or *vakils* ("trustees") to name two designations, acted as his voice to the faithful. Millennialist expectation for the return of the Hidden Imam was running high one thousand years later in AH 1260 (1843–44). The Shaykhi school, led by Shaykh Ahmad al-Ahsa'i (1763–1826) and Sayyid Kazim-i-Rashti (d. 1843), anticipated this appearance relying heavily on arcane Shi'a philosophy and mysticism to express this expectation. The mood of expectation went far beyond the confines of Shaykhi thought and was expressed in a series of religious and cultural developments from popular preaching to the Shah's preoccupation with the Imam's return.

From the Shaykhi movement came the initial followers of the Bab, among them Mulla Husayn-i-Bushru'i (1813–49) who in 1844 first accepted Sayyid 'Ali-Muhammad of Shiraz as the Bab and the promised one. The Bab's title signified a new gate to the Hidden Imam, the gate to another messenger, the gate of God himself, or all three simultaneously. He was later understood to be the possessor of a divine mission like that of Muhammad, Jesus, and Moses. The Bab's messianic role was attractive to a significant minority of Persians, especially the merchant classes.

The Bab proclaimed the abrogation and replacement of Islamic law by the laws of his own revelation, set down in such works as the Bayan. Thus there can be no question of any claim to be a merely sectarian Shi'a development. It had assumed an independent religious existence. The Mahdi, according to Islamic expectation, was to have authority over rulers and clerics. The Babi claims were inherently revolutionary in the eyes of the Persian court and Islamic divines. State and religious authorities forced the Babis into a defensive series of conflicts, and the Bab himself was executed in 1850 for his claims. The Bab's main intentions, according to Baha'is, were to break the strictures of Islamic orthodoxy, to convince the world that he was a source of divine revelation, and to prepare the way for another messenger whose appearance was imminent.

Baha'i Phase

Despite ferocious persecution of the Babis, the staying power of millennialism made possible the survival of Babism and its transformation into a world religion through the leadership of Baha'u'llah. He had become an early follower of the Bab and an articulate exponent of his teaching. After the execution of the Bab, Baha'u'llah was influential in the Babi community, despite being imprisoned in Tehran and then exiled to Ottoman Iraq in 1853. Baha'u'llah announced in 1863 that he was "He Whom God shall manifest," the messianic figure promised by the Bab. Most Babis became Baha'is. He was successively exiled to Istanbul, Edirne in Turkey, and the citadel of Acre in Syria (now Israel).

Baha'u'llah claimed to be the latter-day messiah for all religions. He proclaimed that the millennial kingdom came into being spiritually at the assumption of his mission and would be established by his followers in the visible world over a period of a thousand years. The Baha'i faith focuses on the establishment of institutions, social structures, and community life as a basis for global civilization.

The Baha'i World Centre in Haifa, Israel. BAHAI WORLD CENTRE, ARC PROJECT OFFICE.

A PASSAGE FROM BAHÁ'Í SCRIPTURE ANNOUNCING THE COMPLETION OF ISLAMIC PROPHECIES

Among them are those who have said: 'Have the verses been sent down?' Say: 'Yea, by Him Who is the Lord of the heavens!' 'Hath the Hour come?' 'Nay, more; it hath passed, by Him Who is the Revealer of clear tokens! Verily, the Inevitable is come, and He, the True One, hath appeared with proof and testimony. The Plain is disclosed, and mankind is sore vexed and fearful. Earthquakes have broken loose, and the tribes have lamented, for fear of God, the Lord of Strength, the All-Compelling.' Say: 'The stunning trumpet blast hath been loudly raised, and the Day is God's, the One, the Unconstrained.' 'Hath the Catastrophe come to pass?' Say: 'Yea, by the Lord of Lords!' 'Is the Resurrection come?' 'Nay, more; He Who is the Self-Subsisting hath appeared with the Kingdom of His signs'... They that have gone astray have said: 'When were the heavens cleft asunder?' Say: 'While ye lay in the graves of waywardness and error'... And among them is he who saith: 'Have I been assembled with others, blind?' Say: 'Yea, by Him that rideth upon the clouds!'

Source: Bahá'u'lláh. (1941, 1953, 1988) *Epistle to the Son of the Wolf.* Wilmette, IL: Bahá'í Publishing Trust, 131–34.

Baha'u'llah enunciated progressive theological and social principles in dozens of scriptural volumes, including the Kitab-i-Aqdas (Most Holy Book) and Kitab-i-Iqan (Book of Certitude): (1) God, the Creator, is unknowable to humanity except as his attributes are revealed through a series of messengers or "Manifestations" (e.g., Moses, Zoroaster, Buddha, Jesus Christ, Muhammad, the Bab, and Baha'u'llah). (2) The fundamental aims and purposes of the world's religions are one; their differences are due to the exigencies of the times and places in which they appear. (3) The human soul is immortal. The individual's goal is to develop spiritual attributes that will permit the soul to progress. (4) The social goal of humanity in this age is world unification and a permanent lasting peace. (5) The social principles on which this unification depend include elimination of prejudice, gender equality, moral rectitude, compulsory education, elimination of extremes of wealth and poverty, harmony of religion and science, development of an international language and script, sustainable development, and individual initiative.

Baha'u'llah provided for succession of leadership and an administrative structure regarded as divine in origin. He appointed his son, 'Abdu'l-Baha (1844–1921), as head of the religion, authorized interpreter of its sacred texts, and exemplar of Baha'i life. 'Abdu'l-Baha in turn appointed his grandson Shoghi Effendi (1897–1957) as Guardian of the religion and its authoritative scriptural interpreter. These leaders outlined the means for creating an international elected administrative structure of local, national, and international "Houses of Justice." The council at the head of the faith, the nine-member Universal House of Justice, has been elected every five years since 1963. It legislates on questions not already revealed in Baha'i scripture or authoritative interpretation. Obedience and loyalty to the successive heads of the religion is embodied in "the Covenant," which binds the believer to the community's leadership. Baha'is consider the faith's governance a pattern for a future world commonwealth to be established during a thousand-year period.

The Baha'i faith was established in most of the Middle East and South Asia by the 1880s, reached Europe and North America in the 1890s, was flourishing in Latin America, Africa, Asia, and the Pacific by the 1970s, and was well established in countries of the former communist bloc in the 1990s. In 1999, there were elected national Baha'i councils in 179 countries. Its world spiritual and administrative center is in the cities of Haifa and Acre, Israel.

Millennialist Motif: Catastrophism and Progressivism

The Baha'i religion offers a test-case for sociological theory about millennialism in a non-Christian context. Millennialism may be defined as imminent collective salvation accomplished according to a divine plan, or the expectation of a future time free from cares, imperfections, and suffering. Millennialism is a primary motif of the religion. The Bab's writings presupposed the eventual setting up of Babi state and community institutions following the destruction of a corrupt contemporary order. Baha'u'llah and 'Abdu'l-Baha advocated long-term creation of a divine world order with sacred institutions. Shoghi Effendi reiterated this view, while raising in some of his work the apocalyptic possibilities of World War II and the cold war's threat of nuclear cataclysm. Baha'i scriptures make metaphorical use of many apocalyptic images from the Bible and the Qur'an.

Millennialism in the Christian context has been defined as either premillennial (Christ returns to establish the millennial kingdom suddenly) or postmillennial (Christ returns after the believers have established the millennial kingdom). The Bab and Baha'u'llah claimed to fulfill prophecies of the return of Christ; their appearance was to be followed by the spiritual and earthly salvation of humanity. Baha'is nevertheless plan to construct the millennial kingdom over a long period, rather than through immediate catastrophic apocalypse.

In more generic terms, millennialism may be considered either catastrophic or progressive. The Babi religion, which Shoghi Effendi termed a religious and social revolution, represented to many followers the catastrophic expectation of an immediate overthrow of the established order and its replacement by a divine one. Although the Babis' trust in a sudden break with the old order was dampened by the execution of the Bab and the massacre of their fellow believers, their fervor served to ensure the community's survival through persecution into its global community-building phase. The Baha'i religion into which the Babi movement evolved represents the progressive expectation demonstrated by a community that internalizes spiritual principles and constructs the "kingdom of God on earth" under a divine plan. The Baha'i Faith is thus premillennialist by definition, operationally postmillennialist, and over time modulates from catastrophic to progressive millennialism.

Although Baha'i millennialism is progressive and optimistic about the future, it retains elements of catastrophism for the short term. Shoghi Effendi characterized modern society as undergoing two processes: integration (represented by the Baha'i faith and other progressive movements) and disintegration (represented by collapsing outmoded social structures). Integration is progressive, disintegration is catastrophic. Shoghi Effendi, drawing on apocalyptic statements by Baha'u'llah, wrote that global unrest must culminate in a world upheaval that will create a consciousness of world citizenship upon which a lasting peace must depend. The Baha'i millennium is built out of the chaos of a dying order inadequate to the needs of the time, through the kingdom-building efforts of Baha'is to spread their faith, and the hidden hand of God working behind the scenes.

Millennial Dating

Historicist premillennialism was the predominant method of interpreting biblical time prophecy in the early nineteenth century in the English-speaking world. Through the day-for-a-year principle and the synchronization of all biblical texts that could be used in any way for predicting dates, it was possible to extrapolate dates for future events based on known historical occurrences. William Miller (1782–1849) used this method to predict the return of Jesus Christ in 1843–44 CE. The coincidence of Miller's prediction with the Shaykhi expectation of the Mahdi in AH 1260 is significant for Baha'is by its apparent confirmation of two disparate millennialist traditions and their methods of scriptural prediction. The appearance of the Bab in 1844/1260 is thought to substantiate the Baha'i claim that the new messenger fulfilled Christianity and Islam. It also confirmed a Baha'i version of historicist premillennial time-prophecy interpretation of the Bible still widely used as a tool to convert Christians to Baha'i beliefs.

The Bab devised the calendar used by Baha'is today. The year 2000 CE does not equate to a millennial year in the Baha'i calendar, bridging as it does the Baha'i years 156 and 157. The end of the second millennium CE is a nonevent in the Baha'i calendar. However, some statements in the Baha'i writings indicate that a form of political peace called the Lesser Peace (see below) is to have been established by the end of the twentieth century. This has caused speculation that such a political change requires calamitous events first—a view that has not gained overwhelming influence due to discouragement by the Universal House of Justice.

Millennial Kingdom

The word "millennium" rarely appears in authoritative Baha'i texts. Baha'u'llah is termed the inaugurator of the long-awaited millennium when "the kingdoms of this world shall have become the Kingdom of God Himself, the Kingdom of Baha'u'llah" (Shoghi Effendi 1991: 157). Baha'i authoritative texts anticipate a two-stage process toward the millennium, with several milestones within each stage. The first is the Lesser Peace, a political cessation of hostility entered into by nations independently of the Baha'is. The second stage is the Most Great Peace, a millennial age in which a world commonwealth, suffused with Baha'i ideals, unites all nations, races, and religions. The millennial condition is thus envisioned as a stable, peaceful, and prosperous human civilization operating under divine principles.

Baha'is also anticipate the appearance of future "Manifestations of God" (divine messengers, prophets) at least one thousand solar years after Baha'u'llah was made conscious of his divine mission in October 1852. The millennial kingdom is not a static attainment of perfection, but a new integrative step in human social development. In the particular instance of the appearance of the Bab and Baha'u'llah, Baha'is believe that spiritual civilization will flourish and will not decline as has happened in religious cycles of the past. Each new stage in human development nevertheless brings problems that must be solved beyond the established system. Therefore Baha'is expect new divine messengers approximately every thousand years. This appearance is viewed as a perennial spiritual phenomenon—future religious development as cyclical progressive millennialism. The coming of the next messenger does not currently engender specific millennialist expectations for Baha'is.

Conclusion

The Babi-Baha'i religious development is based on a continuing and creative millennialist motif. The religion has grown steadily in widely disparate cultures and among people of every religious and social origin. Baha'i progressivism is attractive in industrialized countries where growth nevertheless remains slow. Its spiritual life, inclusiveness, empowering institutions, and growing social presence results in the majority of its membership living in developing countries. India has the largest national community of around two million; countries with large percentages of Baha'i population include Guyana, Bolivia, Tuvalu, and Kiribati. The Baha'i community is completing a major expansion of its world center, and has a growing number of houses of worship, schools, and local centers. If the religion's growth rate continues, it may surpass several other world religions of small population during the early twenty-first century and become more universally recognized.

William P. Collins

See also Islam

Bibliography

'Abdu'l-Baha. (1984) *Some Answered Questions.* Wilmette, IL: Baha'i Publishing Trust.

Amanat, Abbas. (1989) *Resurrection and Renewal: The Making of the Babi Movement in Iran, 1844–1850.* Ithaca, NY: Cornell University Press.

Baha'u'llah. (1983) *Kitab-i-Iqan: The Book of Certitude,* 2d ed. Wilmette, IL: Baha'i Publishing Trust.

Balyuzi, H. M. (1980) *Baha'u'llah: The King of Glory.* Oxford: George Ronald.

Matthews, Gary L. (1996) *He Cometh with Clouds: A Baha'i View of Christ's Return.* Oxford, U.K.: George Ronald.

Nabil Zarandi. (1932) *The Dawn-Breakers: Nabil's Narrative of the Early Days of the Baha'i Revelation,* translated from the original Persian and edited by Shoghi Effendi. Wilmette, IL: Baha'i Publishing Trust.

Piff, David, and Margit Warburg. (1997) "Millennial Catastrophism in Popular Baha'i Lore." Paper delivered at the Eleventh Annual Conference of the Center for the Study of New Religions (CESNUR), Amsterdam, Netherlands.

Sears, William. (1961) *Thief in the Night, or The Strange Case of the Missing Millennium.* Oxford, U.K.: George Ronald.

Shoghi Effendi. (1991) *The World Order of Baha'u'llah: Selected Letters.* Wilmette, IL: Baha'i Publishing Trust.

Shoghi Effendi. (1996) *The Promised Day Is Come.* Wilmette, IL: Baha'i Publishing Trust.

Smith, Peter. (1987) *The Babi and Baha'i Religions: From Messianic Shi'ism to a World Religion.* Cambridge, U.K.: Cambridge University Press.

Smith, Peter. (1982) "Millenarianism in the Babi and Baha'i Religions." In *Millennialism and Charisma,* edited by Roy Wallis. Belfast: The Queen's University, 231–83.

Sours, Michael. (1991) *The Prophecies of Jesus.* Oxford, U.K.: Oneworld.

Stockman, Robert H. (1996) "The Vision of the Baha'i Faith." In *Ultimate Visions: Reflections on the Religions We Choose,* edited by Martin Forward. Oxford, U.K.: Oneworld, 266–74.

Universal House of Justice. (1996) *Messages from the Universal House of Justice, 1963–1986: The Third Epoch of the Formative Age,* compiled by Geoffry W. Marks. Wilmette, IL: Baha'i Publishing Trust.

Bayside (Our Lady of the Roses)

Since the mid-1970s, thousands of Catholic pilgrims have visited Flushing Meadows-Corona Park in the borough of Queens, New York City, to attend the apocalyptic Marian apparitions of Mrs. Veronica Lueken. For more than twenty years, until her death in 1995, Lueken communicated end-time prophecies from the Virgin Mary, Jesus, and numerous saints, to humanity. The group of devotees that follow these visions call themselves Baysiders, and the shrine as well the visitations from the Virgin Mary are referred to as "Our Lady of the Roses."

The Bayside phenomenon began on 5 June 1968, the day that Robert F. Kennedy was assassinated. Lueken, a housewife and mother of five children from Queens, New York, experienced a perfume of roses in her car as she prayed for the dying New York senator. Shortly thereafter, she had a vision of St. Thérèse of Lisieux, who later gave her sacred writings and poems by dictation. On 7 April 1970, the Virgin Mary appeared to Lueken in her home, instructing her to establish a shrine on the grounds of the St. Robert Bellarmine Church in Bayside, New York, and promising to make a personal appearance if rosary vigils were held there on 18 June 1970. The Virgin Mary requested that this shrine be named "Our Lady of the Roses, Mary Help of Mothers." The Virgin Mary also promised to appear and speak through Lueken (who would act as a "voice box," repeating words from heaven) in the evenings of all the great feast days of the Catholic Church, if vigils were faithfully kept on those days. In addition, the Virgin Mary told Lueken to spread the messages from heaven throughout the world.

Beginning in 1970, vigils were held regularly at the Bayside shrine. Several hundred missives were transmitted by Lueken until her death on 3 August 1995. She claimed that she repeated the Virgin Mary's messages word-for-word, although she often would add her own descriptions of what she saw in her visions. In 1975 the apparition site was moved from Bayside to Flushing Meadows-Corona Park, because of the objections of church officials and Bayside residents to the Saturday night vigils. Despite the new location, the visions are still referred to as the "Bayside apparitions," and Lueken's followers continue to call themselves "Baysiders." The number of Baysiders is difficult to estimate. Throughout the 1980s and the 1990s, the shrine's mailing list consisted of roughly fifty-five thousand names worldwide; the shrine's publications claim that there are more than forty thousand Baysiders throughout the world.

The Bayside apparitions address a litany of subjects, but the most prominent topics are the evils of contemporary society, corruption within the Catholic Church and the Vatican itself, the urgent need for worldwide atonement, and especially, the approach of an apocalyptic scenario. The apparitions assert that "a worldwide Warning, Miracle, and fiery Chastisement in the form of a 'Ball of Redemption'—a comet which will strike the earth, and along with World War III and other disasters, will remove three-quarters of mankind—are very near at hand" (*Our Lady of the Roses Booklet* n.d.: i). The signs of the end are everywhere, according to the apparitions: nuclear weapons, natural disasters, abortion, AIDS, famine, pornography, terrorism, communism, rampant murder and drug abuse, and corruption in the government and especially in the Catholic Church. The coming worldwide cataclysm, or what Baysiders refer to as the "Great Chastisement," may be averted through personal penance, prayer, and a return to traditional Catholic teachings.

Although the imminence of worldly annihilation is a predominant theme in the Bayside messages, other disasters are emphasized as well, such as earthquakes, floods, drought, famine, starvation, and epidemics, all of which are regarded as punishments from God and further proof that the endtimes are at hand. Lueken's apparitions also provide divine commentary on a wide range of various satanic influences in American society, including discussions of things like rock music, drugs, immodest dress, sex education, television, the Illuminati, UFOs, and test tube babies. Some of the shrine's literature addresses contemporary issues, but much of the distributed material attempts to establish the shrine's legitimacy in terms of previous Marian apparitions and often highlights the supernatural phenomena associated with the apparition site.

Lueken's visions have antecedents in a tradition of apocalyptic Marian prophecies, particularly the apparitions at Fatima (in 1917), and the ecclesiastically unsanctioned apparitions at Garabandal, Spain (1961–65); San Damiano, Italy (1964–81); and Necedah, Wisconsin (during the 1950s). According to Sandra Zimdars-Swartz, this transcultural, apocalyptic tradition involves the belief that Mary's recent appearances are part of a pattern of endtime warnings that reveal an "all-encompassing divine plan" occurring at the end of history before the return of Christ (1991: 246). In these apparitions, the Virgin Mary warns of imminent divine chastisements to be unleashed because people are so sinful and have rejected God. The Bayside apparitions, possibly the most apocalyptic of Marian visitations, represent an intensification of the eschatological, anticommunist, and conspiratorial themes of this modern Marian worldview, with Mary appearing in the roles of intercessor and nurturing mother, intervening on behalf of her children to rescue them from the apocalyptic punishments of an angry God.

The Catholic Church traditionally has taken a very restrained position toward the acceptance of Marian sightings, especially apocalyptic ones, sanctioning only a few of the thousands of visions that have been reported. The Bayside apparitions are among those that have not been approved. After an investigation in 1973 and again in 1986, the Diocese of Brooklyn declared that it had no basis for belief that Veronica Lueken had seen the Virgin Mary, and it issued a statement directing the faithful to "refrain from participating in the 'vigils' and from disseminating any propaganda related to the 'Bayside apparitions'" (Mugavero 1989: 209–11).

Around the same time as this church declaration, Lueken's detractors, some of whom had once been Baysiders, accused her of being a charlatan, an occultist, a paranoid psychotic, and a tool of satanic forces (Cuneo 1997: 163–68). Other critics asserted that she had consciously plagiarized or unconsciously imitated previous Marian messages, such as those of Mary Ann Van Hoof, the seer in Necedah, Wisconsin during the 1950s. However, these accusations and the lack of ecclesiastical approval of the apparitions did not appear to discourage belief in the prophecies among Baysiders, and in fact may have motivated many of them to increase their efforts to disseminate the Bayside messages and gain acceptance for Lueken's visions.

The Bayside apparitions are promoted at a grassroots level through mass-produced religious tracts, books, videos, audiocassettes, radio broadcasts, cable television, and the Internet. Advertisements for the apparitions have appeared on highway billboards, subway posters, national newspapers, and tabloid magazines such as the *Weekly World News*. The shrine's latest prophecy tracts, videos, and other devotional materials also may be ordered twenty-four hours a day from various organizations affiliated with the apparitions. Groups dedicated to promoting the Bayside messages have formed in numerous cities in the United States and throughout the world; a radio program about the Bayside prophecies, entitled "These Last Days," airs in various cities in over thirty states; and the Bayside prophecies have been translated into more than twenty languages.

Doomsday Admonitions and Conditional Apocalypticism

The most prominent theme in the Bayside prophecies is the imminence of divine punishment and worldly catastrophe. The apocalyptic scenario presented in the apparitions describes a global "Warning," followed by a "Great Miracle," and then a "Chastisement" that will destroy three-fourths of humanity. Like other aspects of the apparitions, Lueken's predictions of these events have precedents in previous Marian prophecies. Popular beliefs about a comet chastisement have been a part of Catholic folk apocalypticism for years, and Lueken's visions of the Warning are similar to descriptions of the sun hurling toward the earth at Fatima, which was interpreted by some who experienced it as a terrifying chastisement from heaven and a prelude to the end of the world. Beliefs about the Great Miracle, said to occur in the sky after the Warning, are also associated with other apparitions. According to Lueken, if humanity does not change its sinful behavior after this supernatural spectacle, the Chastisement will follow and consist of two parts. The first will be World War III; the second, a "Fireball of Redemption" in the form of a comet unleashed by the fury of God. According to the Bayside apparitions, as humanity becomes increasingly sinful and violent, God will repay human violence with the violence of apocalypse.

Although the Bayside prophecies express the view that human history is unfolding according to a divine endtime plan, the messages assert that human beings may avert the day of doom if they act in accordance with God's will and if God permits that the world not be destroyed. Such beliefs are an expression of "conditional apocalypticism," characterized by the idea that apocalypse is imminent but may be forestalled if human beings behave in ways prescribed by God or a superhuman power. In this scenario, human will is effectual in averting worldly destruction when it corresponds to God's decrees.

Popular Roman Catholic prophecy beliefs, because of the emphasis on the personal relationship between the saints in heaven and the faithful on earth, appears to be less overtly fatalistic than other forms of apocalypticism (such as Protestant premillennial dispensationalism), which assert that history is predetermined and that apocalypse is inevitable and unalterable by human effort. Dispensationalists, for example, interpret the signs of the endtime as noncausal markers on a foreordained timetable of irreversible doom; the messages of Lueken, and other Catholic visionaries, maintain that apocalypse is imminent but that the divine timetable may be postponed if people repent and return to God's ways. The apocalypse predicted by Lueken will occur at a specific historical moment not because it is preordained to occur at that time but because of God's anger at humanity's increasing sinfulness. In this view, the Virgin Mary can petition God and intercede on behalf of the faithful, and Baysiders, like many other Roman Catholics, believe that through Mary the destiny of the world may be altered. But the Bayside prophecies reiterate that if worldly sin reaches a specific anti-Christian critical mass, Mary's merciful pleas will be powerless to hold back the punishing hand of God.

In contrast to the apocalyptic anger of God in these apparitions, the tone of the Virgin Mary is that of concern and love for humanity gone astray. Lueken's prophecies fluctuate between visions of devastation, with Mary depicted as a warrior deity who will lead the battle against Satan and ultimately crush him beneath her heel, and Mary as compassionate mother, pleading with her children to prevent the prophesied catastrophes through repentance, prayer, and conversion. Despite the apocalyptic ethos and violence of the visions at Bayside, Baysiders tend to emphasize the role of the Virgin Mary as the forgiving and loving Mother, the Mother who nurtures all, who suffers and weeps over her children, and protects them from the wrath of God the Father. Devotion to the Virgin Mary, at Flushing Meadows Park and elsewhere, is appealing not only because it may represent the worship of the feminine side of God, but perhaps because it expresses the yearning for divine maternal protection otherwise denied in the Christian tradition dominated by male deities and principles.

Emergent Folk Traditions and the Bayside Movement

Although the Bayside apparitions have antecedents in previous Marian apparitions, they also have new elements that modify the existing corpus of beliefs and narratives and that further contribute to the tradition of Marian sightings. One

THE MESSAGE FROM HEAVEN

Our Lady has been chosen by the Eternal Father to alert mankind now of the scriptural predictions of a cleansing of the earth with fire unless mankind makes a complete reversal of his sinful ways. A world-wide Warning according to Our Lady shall precede this Chastisement in an effort to recall God's children to a life of grace. She has also promised that God will perform a great Miracle after this Warning, and if men still refuse to change, then God will be forced to send the Chastisement.

The following pages contain excerpts of what Our Lord and Our Lady have said on these and other important matters.

THE WARNING

On April 21, 1973, Veronica experienced the coming Warning while in ecstasy: It's as though everything has exploded in the sky. There is a great flash! Then it's very hot—very warm—and it feels like you're burning. There is a huge explosion, and the sky becomes very white. . .and then there are colors—blues, purples. . . .Finally, there is a voice within you: Your warning before the Chastisement. Flash, fire, and the voice within you.

"Man will feel that the very powers of the elements have shaken the very foundations of his being. So great will be the impact of this Warning from the Father but none will doubt that it had come from the Father. . . .It will be a major awakening to many. The rumbling and the shaking of the elements will set fright into many hearts. . . .Hearts will shudder with fear and men will drop from fright. . . .Many signs of an angry God will appear before you. . . ."

On June 12, 1976, the Blessed Virgin Mary told Mrs. Lueken that the Warning was at hand: "My child, you must pray more; do much penance, for the Warning is coming upon mankind. There will be a tremendous explosion and the sky shall roll back like a scroll. This force shall go within the very core of the human. He will understand his offenses to his God. However, this Warning will be of short duration, and many shall continue upon their road to perdition, so hard are the hearts hardened now, My child . . . .

BEWARE OF THE SUNRISE!

"As the day follows night, so shall this Warning follow soon. Beware of the sunrise! Do not look up to the sky, the flash!!! Beware of the sunrise! Do not look up to the sky, the flash!!! Close your windows! Draw your shades! Remain inside; do not venture outside your door, or you will not return! Pray! Prostrate yourselves upon your floor! Pray with arms outstretched and beg for mercy of your God, the Father. Do not seek or receive your animals into your homes, for the animals of those who have remained of well spirit will be taken care of.

WHAT YOU SHOULD STORE

"O My children, how many will try to go back and restore their homes when it is too late? Keep blessed candles, water, blankets, food within your homes. The candles of those who have remained in the state of grace shall not be extinguished, but the candles in the homes of those who have given themselves to Satan shall not burn! Amen, I say to you, as night follows day a great darkness shall descend upon mankind."

TIMING OF THE WARNING

Jesus - " . . . I give you one indication that the time is ripe: When you see, when you hear, when you feel the revolution in Rome; when you see the Holy Father fleeing, seeking a refuge in another land, know that the time is ripe."

-Sept. 14, 1976

"As you know, as I have told you (which must remain secret until it is profitable to be told — and I will tell you, My child), there is little time left before the Warning."

July 25, 1978

"OUR LADY OF THE ROSES: MARY HELP OF MOTHERS," INTRODUCTORY BOOKLET. LOWELL, MI: THESE LAST DAYS.

such element, for instance, is the belief in the concept of the Rapture, normally associated with premillennial dispensationalism. Like dispensationalist beliefs, Lueken's prophecies imply that a select group of the chosen few will not have to endure the horrors of apocalypse because they will have been raptured prior to this event.

Lueken's extensive and detailed accounts of what she sees in her visions is another distinctive aspect of the Bayside apparitions. In the past, most visionaries have briefly described the Virgin Mary and conveyed Mary's concise messages; Lueken not only communicates lengthy messages from a profusion of saints and holy figures in the Roman Catholic pantheon, but she describes the color of the sky, the clothing, the gestures, and the expressions of these divine beings as well.

The widespread use of photography by Baysiders to document the miraculous phenomena associated with the shrine is perhaps the most notable technological innovation on previous Marian traditions concerning miraculous images. Since the 1970s, taking photographs of the miraculous phenomena at the apparition site has been central to the religious experiences of many of the shrine's followers. Referred to as "miracle photos" or "Polaroids from Heaven" by Baysiders, these images are said to contain allegorical and apocalyptic symbols and are interpreted as divine communications offering insights of prophetic and personal relevance. Like Marian devotees at other apparition sites, Baysiders have adapted the image-making and apparitional qualities of photography to document revelatory experiences, produce "proofs" of the endtime, and reproduce tangible manifestations of the sacred.

Like many of the Baysiders' beliefs and practices, the use of cameras to document miraculous phenomena may be usefully thought of as an expression of folk belief, a vernacular religious phenomenon promoted apart from institutional doctrines and outside the official sanction of clerical authorities. Similar to other Catholic apocalypticists, the Baysiders derive the ultimate authority for their beliefs not so much from current doctrinal theology but from prophetic messages and charismatic experiences that exist outside ecclesiastical sanction.

The Bayside Movement, Roman Catholic Traditionalism, and Nativism

The Bayside phenomenon is an expression of the broader Roman Catholic traditionalist movement that arose after the reforms initiated during the Second Vatican Council (1962 and 1965). Catholic traditionalism developed as a response to the liberalizing changes in Church doctrine and policy, such as the Mass being said entirely in the vernacular, the priest facing the congregation during the consecration of the Holy Eucharist, increased participation in services by members of the congregation, and less emphasis on religious ceremony and more on the word of God. Although the majority of Roman Catholics welcomed these changes, the Council's *aggiornamento* ("updating") was regarded by some as a betrayal of the Catholic faith and the abandonment of a rich heritage of sacred traditions.

Like many traditionalist Catholics, most Baysiders regard Vatican II as heretical or the result of a conspiracy and reject its modernist theology, its liturgical changes, and its sacramental rites. Although traditionalists may condemn Pope Paul VI, who approved the reforms of Vatican II, the Bayside literature states that the authentic pope, Paul VI, was poisoned and replaced by an imposter pope who, with his satanic allies, then implemented the modernist changes in the church. Consequently, Baysiders believe that they do not oppose the authority of the actual pope, Paul VI, because, they maintain, he had nothing to do with the progressive reforms of the church brought about by the "Antipope."

Conspiracy theories about the changes instituted by the Second Vatican Council are a persistent feature of traditionalist Catholic worldview. Traditionalist literature consistently proclaims that the church is infiltrated by the evil forces and that the reforms of Vatican II are a part of a plot by the enemies of Christ to destroy the church, with communists and Freemasons as ubiquitous conspirators. Like other traditionalists, Baysiders regard the struggle for the restoration of traditional Catholic doctrines and rites as a conflict between good and evil, an eschatological battle between the sinister minions of Satan and righteous army of Christ.

The Bayside phenomenon is not unique among apocalyptic movements in its emphasis on a return to previous traditions. Numerous apocalyptic groups in the past have advocated a restoration of traditional values when accepted systems of meaning were being destroyed by change or when the world was perceived to be in a state of severe spiritual, moral, or cultural crisis. In such situations, established beliefs and practices are reasserted, while individuals await the imminent and supernaturally ordained destruction of the present world, which is regarded as irredeemably corrupt. Ralph Linton identifies such worldviews as expressions of "nativistic movements," defined as any "conscious, organized attempt on the part of a society's members to revive or perpetuate selected aspects of its culture" (1943: 230). Although this concept is usually applied to non-Western societies to describe responses to cultural contact, conflict, and oppression, it seems to be an appropriate characterization of the themes expressed in the Bayside apparitions as well as the behavior of Baysiders. Like previous nativistic movements (such the Ghost Dance movement of various Native American tribes in the 1890s), the emphasis on the restoration of traditions that characterizes the Bayside phenomenon is a response to a sense of religious and cultural crisis, and especially a sense of loss—the loss of one's religious heritage and one's religious identity.

The nativistic aspects of the Bayside apparitions are illustrated by the repeated assertions that contemporary society is in a state of social crisis and decay. Lueken's visions enumerate the ways that traditional Catholic attitudes about God, morality, community, family, sexuality, and the roles of women and men, among other things, have been challenged or destroyed. The restoration of traditional beliefs, practices, and spirituality is regarded as the only means of averting worldly annihilation. Like other Marian apparitions, the Bayside visions condemn modernist and secularist ideas as the source of contemporary ills, and give expression to traditionalist and supernaturalist beliefs attacked by scientific and rational criticism.

Lueken's Death and Schism in the Bayside Movement

After the death of Veronica Lueken in 1995, the Bayside movement not only lost its charismatic visionary, but some of its direction and sense of purpose as well. Lueken's followers have split into two groups and have fought over control of the Bayside shrine facilities, permission to use the apparition site, and the shrine statue of the Virgin Mary, among other things. One group, Our Lady of the Roses Corporation, is headed by Lueken's husband, Arthur, while the other group, Saint Michael's World Apostolate, is led by Michael Mangan, the former shrine director and workshop coordinator. Mangan was told by the shrine's attorney to resign his position in October 1997, after accusations that he had been altering the actual content of Lueken's messages, adding his own personal interpretations, and stealing and misinterpreting some of Lueken's miraculous photos. Mangan also predicted that Lueken's prophecy of the worldwide Warning would be fulfilled in 1997 and that a revolution in Rome would occur. When nothing happened, Mangan announced that the prayers of the faithful had postponed this global admonition. Arthur Lueken's group accused Mangan of being delusional and stated that the "Warning '97" message was not an officially approved Bayside prophecy. Mangan also was accused of taking the shrine's vans and computers, illegally withdrawing and spending $130,000 of shrine money, and usurping Mr. Lueken's authority by proclaiming himself president of the shrine organization in a general mailing to followers.

New York park authorities initially granted Mangan control of the Bayside shrine for prayer vigils and holy hours; Lueken won a court battle to keep the Lueken name, as well as the shrine statue and other shrine materials. In 1998 the New York City Parks Department ruled that the two groups must share the apparition grounds and alternate control of each prayer vigil and holy hour. Throughout the rift, "miracle photos" have played a central role, with new photographs produced by each group that are then used to condemn the opposing faction. Both groups seem to agree, however, that the schism is a part of a satanic plot to discredit the Bayside prophecies and demoralize Baysiders. Since the conflict, attendance at the vigils and holy hours has decreased, and some followers interpret the schism as the final sign that the end is at hand.

Daniel Wojcik

See also Age of Mary, Dispensationalism, Fatima Cult, Marianism, Nativist Millennial Movements

Bibliography

Carroll, Michael P. (1986) *The Cult of the Virgin Mary: Psychological Origins.* Princeton, NJ: Princeton University Press.

Cuneo, Michael W. (1997) *The Smoke of Satan: Conservative and Traditionalist Dissent in Contemporary American Catholicism.* New York: Oxford University Press.

Dinges, William D. (1991) "Roman Catholic Traditionalism." In *Fundamentalisms Observed,* edited by Martin E. Marty and R. Scott Appleby. Chicago: University of Chicago Press, 66–101.

Greeley, Andrew. (1977) *The Mary Myth: On the Femininity of God.* New York: Seabury Press.

Jung, Carl G. (1970) *Four Archetypes: Mother, Rebirth, Spirit, Trickster.* Princeton, NJ: Princeton University Press.

Kselman, Thomas A., and Steven Avella. (1986) "Marian Piety and the Cold War in the United States." *The Catholic Historical Review* 72 (July): 403–24.

Linton, Ralph. (1943) "Nativistic Movements." *American Anthropologist* 45: 230–40.

Mugavero, Bishop Francis. (1989) "Declaration Concerning the 'Bayside Movement.'" In *Cults, Sects, and the New Age,* edited by Rev. James J. LeBar. Huntington, IN: Our Sunday Visitor Publishing Division, 209–11.

Our Lady of the Roses, Mary, Help of Mothers: An Introductory Booklet on the Apparitions of Bayside. (No date) Bayside, NY: Our Lady of the Roses, Mary, Help of Mothers Shrine.

Our Lady of the Roses, Mary, Help of Mothers: A Book about the Heavenly Apparitions to Veronica Lueken at Bayside, New York. ([1981] 1986) Lansing, MI: Apostles of Our Lady, Inc.

Primiano, Leonard Norman. (1995) "Vernacular Religion and the Search for a Method in Religious Folklife." *Western Folklore* 54, 1: 37–56.

Turner, Victor W., and Edith Turner. (1978) *Image and Pilgrimage in Christian Culture: Anthropological Perspectives.* New York: Columbia University Press.

Wojcik, Daniel. (1996) "Polaroids from Heaven: Photography, Folk Religion, and the Miraculous Image Tradition at a Marian Apparition Site." *Journal of American Folklore* 109, 432: 129–48.

——. (1997) *The End of the World As We Know It: Faith, Fatalism, and Apocalypse in America.* New York and London: New York University Press.

Yoder, Don. (1974) "Toward a Definition of Folk Religion." *Western Folklore* 33: 2–15.

Zimdars-Swartz, Sandra L. (1991) *Encountering Mary: From La Salette to Medjugorje.* Princeton, NJ: Princeton University Press.

Burned-over District

Upstate New York, the area west of the Catskill and Adirondack mountains, was said to have been repeatedly "burned over" by the fires of religious revivalism and millennial enthusiasm in the first half of the nineteenth century. Excitement peaked during several decades of rapid settlement and population growth that followed completion in 1825 of the 363 mile long Erie Canal linking the Hudson River near Albany to Lake Erie near Buffalo. The region's foremost interpreter, Whitney Cross, characterized it as a "storm center," a "psychic highway" upon which congregated a diverse group of settlers, largely from the hill country of western New England, a people "peculiarly devoted to crusades aimed at the perfection of mankind and the attainment of millennial happiness" (1950: ix, 1). Virtually every religious and secular cause of the antebellum years either originated or found strong support in this hotbed of revivalist and reform movements that may be seen as a nineteenth-century analogue to what California would become in the twentieth century.

Revivalism in the Burned-over District

The millenarian ethos of upstate New York, as well as of other similarly "burned-over" regions extending from western New England to the upper Ohio Valley and beyond, owed much to the distinctive post-Revolutionary War era revivalism known as the Second Great Awakening. That movement increasingly rejected Calvinist predestinarianism in favor of Arminian beliefs that individuals could and must actively seek their own salvation, while looking toward the imminence of the kingdom of heaven on earth. Revivalists such as Charles Grandison Finney conducted more than 1,300 revivals in New York state alone during the decade after 1825. Among the "new measures" that Finney and others developed or utilized so effectively were direct, blunt speech, "protracted meetings" where excitement built up night after night, testimony by women in public meetings, and "anxious benches" in the front of churches where individuals seeking to be converted could receive special attention. These revivals proved most effective in areas largely settled by Yankees from western New England, who combined a complex blend of moral intensity with deep but idiosyncratic religious concern and credulity.

The period during which such revivals flourished was characterized by John Higham (1969) as "an age of boundlessness" in which virtually every aspect of American economic, political, social, intellectual, and religious life was in flux. As upstate New York moved even more rapidly than the rest of the country toward economic and social maturity following completion of the Erie Canal, individuals sought to come to terms with rapid social change and find a new basis for order. Women, whose lives were undergoing dramatic transformations as the developing market economy freed them to pursue concerns beyond simple survival, were a key factor in the religious enthusiasm, contributing a substantial majority of those involved in revival activity.

Influential Groups of the Burned-over District

A precursor and contributor to the later excitements in the Burned-over District was a group popularly known as the Shakers, which established its first settlements at Watervliet (near Albany) and New Lebanon, New York, in the aftermath of the American Revolution. Best known for their revivalistic shaking, their commitment to celibacy, their successful communal settlements, their granting of full equality to women in religious leadership, and their veneration of their founder Ann Lee, whom they viewed as the second embodiment of Christ's spirit in human form, the Shakers would exercise a profound influence on later perfectionist and communitarian groups in the region.

Another precursor to the main millenarian activity in the region was the religious movement started by Joseph Smith, a young farm boy from the Palmyra, New York, area. He saw visions during the early 1820s, dictated his new scripture called the Book of Mormon in the late 1820s, and founded his Church of Jesus Christ of Latter-day Saints, popularly known as Mormons, in 1830. After leaving New York in 1831, the Mormons settled in Ohio, Missouri, and Illinois. Eventually, led by Brigham Young, this "afterclap of Puritanism," as Ralph Waldo Emerson characterized the Mormons, would migrate to the valley of the Great Salt Lake and settle much of the intermountain West after 1847 as their controversial American Zion. The Mormons created a church-dominated society and practiced their version of Old Testament patriarchal polygamy until 1890, after which they began to give up both polygamy and direct church control over politics, gradually reintegrating themselves into mainstream American society.

Leading up to and subsequently influenced by the devastating economic depression precipitated by the banking Panic of 1837 were extreme millenarian and social reform tendencies that Whitney Cross called "ultraism." Drawing on revivalistic techniques that stressed all-or-nothing commitment, numerous Finney-influenced revivalists and social reformers such as Theodore Dwight Weld argued not only for religious but also for social "perfection." They became involved throughout New York in the large and highly successful temperance movement, which demanded immediate and complete abstinence from alcoholic beverages, and in the militant abolitionist movement, which called for the immediate, uncompensated abolition of slavery. Also influenced by such concerns was the social activism that expressed itself in the first women's rights convention in America at Seneca Falls, New York, in 1848. These and many other movements for radical social reform would eventually have an impact far beyond the Burned-over District itself.

One controversial form of religious ultraism in upstate New York was that of the Baptist minister William Miller. Aided by the skillful publicist Joshua Himes and others, Miller eventually convinced at least fifty thousand direct followers and as many as a million "skeptically expectant" others throughout the nation of his Bible-based prediction that the world would literally end between 21 March 1843 and 21 March 1844. After the world failed to end then or on a later, recalculated, 22 October 1844 date, the "Great Disappointment" led to a falling away of supporters. Eventually, however, under the leadership of Ellen G. White, a successful Seventh-Day Adventist movement would arise out of the ashes of the apparently "failed" Millerite prophecy.

Another manifestation of religious and social ultraism was the Oneida Community, founded by John Humphrey Noyes and his perfectionist followers in central New York in 1848. Arguing that the second coming of Christ had already occurred in 70 CE and that the heavenly perfection could therefore be realized immediately on earth, Noyes set up an enlarged communal family numbering more than two hundred in which all individuals in the community considered themselves married to the group rather than to a monogamous partner. For more than thirty years, all members lived together in one large communal Mansion House, ate together, worked together, and exchanged adult heterosexual partners frequently, while breaking up any exclusive monogamous attachments.

Also influenced by the depression of the early 1840s were several dozen Fourierist communities, six of them in New York state, inspired by the secular millenarianism of the eccentric French social theorist Charles Fourier, as interpreted by his American disciple Albert Brisbane. Fourier had been convinced that the cure for the evils of competitive capitalism was the creation of elaborately planned cooperative communities or "phalanxes." Although most American Fourierist communities were far simpler than Fourier envisioned and typically lasted only a few years, the movement contributed to a variety of other economic and social reforms in New York state and the nation.

The Spiritualist movement, inspired by the mysterious rappings in the home of the Fox sisters near Hydesville, New York, in 1848, created a popular sensation. Spiritualism, which purported to provide direct communication with the dead through seances, eventually became an organized religious movement that supported women's active participation in religion, the dissemination of unorthodox religious ideas, and various types of social and sexual radicalism with many parallels to the twentieth-century New Age movement.

Explaining the Burned-over District

Scholars have debated whether and in what ways the Burned-over District of western and central New York was more prone to millenarian enthusiasms than adjacent regions of the young United States. Despite Cross's claim for New York state's primacy in the number and diversity of its revivalistic movements, more recent scholarship by David Rowe (1978, 1985) and Linda Pritchard (1984) suggests that other "burned-over districts" developed at different times throughout the entire area influenced by the westward expansion of New England settlement between the American Revolution and the Civil War and that such areas may have been associated with similar processes of economic, social, and religious maturation. The religious and social excitements of upstate New York and related "burned-over districts," however, do not conform easily to any single-cause explanations of millenarian movements based on theories such as social deprivation, psychological stress, or the impact of nascent industrialism. Whatever the explanations for the millenarian excitements of the Burned-over District of upstate New York, the area was undoubtedly one of the most diverse, dynamic, and influential in the young American Republic during its heyday before the Civil War.

Lawrence Foster

See also Millerites, Utopia

Bibliography

Andrews, Edward Deming. (1963) *The People Called Shakers*, new enl. ed. New York: Dover.

Barkun, Michael. (1986) *Crucible of the Millennium: The Burned-over District of New York in the 1840s*. Syracuse, NY: Syracuse University Press.

Braude, Ann. (1989) *Radical Spirits: Spiritualism and Women's Rights in Nineteenth-Century America*. Boston: Beacon Press.

Brewer, Priscilla J. (1986) *Shaker Communities, Shaker Lives*. Hanover, NH: University Press of New England.

Brodie, Fawn M. (1972) *No Man Knows My History: The Life of Joseph Smith, the Mormon Prophet*, 2d ed. New York: Knopf.

Bushman, Richard L. (1984) *Joseph Smith and the Beginnings of Mormonism*. Urbana, IL: University of Illinois Press.

Butler, Jon. (1990) *Awash in a Sea of Faith: Christianizing the American People*. Cambridge, MA: Harvard University Press.

Carden, Maren Lockwood. (1969) *Oneida: Utopian Community to Modern Corporation*. Baltimore, MD: Johns Hopkins University Press.

Carroll, Bret E. (1997) *Spiritualism in Antebellum America*. Bloomington, IN: Indiana University Press.

Cott, Nancy F. (1977) *The Bonds of Womanhood: "Women's Sphere" in New England, 1780–1835*. New Haven, CT: Yale University Press.

Cross, Whitney. (1950) *The Burned-over District: The Social and Intellectual History of Enthusiastic Religion in Western New York, 1800–1850*. Ithaca, NY: Cornell University Press.

Foster, Lawrence. (1984) *Religion and Sexuality: The Shakers, the Mormons, and the Oneida Community*. Urbana, IL: University of Illinois Press.

Gaustad, Edwin D., ed. (1974) *The Rise of Adventism: Religion and Society in Mid-Nineteenth Century America*. New York: Harper.

Guarneri, Carl. (1991) *The Utopian Alternative: Fourierism in Nineteenth Century America*. Ithaca, NY: Cornell University Press.

Hammond, John L. (1979) *The Politics of Benevolence: Revival Religion and Voting Behavior*. Norwood, NJ: Ablex.

Hardman, Keith J.(1987) *Charles Grandison Finney: Revivalist and Reformer*. Syracuse, NY: Syracuse University Press.

Hatch, Nathan O. (1989) *The Democratization of American Christianity*. New Haven, CT: Yale University Press.

Higham, John. (1969) *From Boundlessness to Consolidation: The Transformation of American Culture, 1848–1860*. Ann Arbor, MI: William I. Clements Library.

Johnson, Charles A. (1955) *The Frontier Camp Meeting: Religion's Harvest Time*. Dallas, TX: Southern Methodist University Press.

Johnson, Curtis D. (1989) *Islands of Holiness: Rural Religion in Upstate New York, 1790–1860*. Ithaca, NY: Cornell University Press.

Johnson, Paul E. (1978) *A Shopkeeper's Millennium: Society and Revivals in Rochester, New York, 1815–1837*. New York: Hill and Wang.

Ludlum, David M. (1939) *Social Ferment in Vermont, 1791–1850*. New York: Columbia University Press.

Marini, Stephen A. (1982) *Radical Sects of Revolutionary New England*. Cambridge, MA: Harvard University Press.

Matthews, Lois Kimball. (1909) *The Expansion of New England: The Spread of New England Settlement and Institutions to the Mississippi River, 1620–1865*. Boston: Houghton Mifflin.

McLoughlin, William G. (1978) *Revivals, Awakenings, and Reforms: An Essay on Religion and Social Change in America*. Chicago: University of Chicago Press.

Numbers, Ronald L., and Jonathan M. Butler, eds. (1986) *The Disappointed: Millerism and Millenarianism in the Nineteenth Century*. Bloomington: Indiana University Press.

Parker, Robert Allerton. (1935) *A Yankee Saint: John Humphrey Noyes and the Oneida Community*. New York: Putnam's.

Pitzer, Donald L., ed. (1997) *America's Communal Utopias*. Chapel Hill, NC: University of North Carolina Press.

Pritchard, Linda. (1984) "The Burned-over District Reconsidered." *Social Science History* 8 (summer 1984): 243–65.

Rossi, Alice S. (1973) "Social Roots of the Women's Movement in America." In *The Feminist Papers*, edited by Alice S. Rossi. New York: Columbia University Press, 243–81.

Roth, Randolph A. (1987) *The Democratic Dilemma: Religion, Reform, and the Social Order in the Connecticut River Valley of Vermont, 1791–1850*. Cambridge, U.K.: Cambridge University Press.

Rowe, David L. (1978) "A New Perspective on the Burned-over District: The Millerites in Upstate New York." *Church History* 47 (December 1978): 408–20.

———. (1985) *Thunder and Trumpets: Millerites and Dissenting Religion in Upstate New York, 1800–1850*. Chico, CA: Scholars Press.

Ryan, Mary P. (1981) *Cradle of the Middle Class: The Family in Oneida County, New York, 1790-1865*. Cambridge, U.K.: Cambridge University Press.

Stein, Stephen J. (1992) *The Shaker Experience in America: A History of the United Society of Believers*. New Haven, CT: Yale University Press.

Stewart, James Brewer. (1976) *Holy Warriors: The Abolitionists and American Society*. New York: Hill and Wang.

Tyler, Alice Felt. (1944) *Freedom's Ferment: Phases of American Social History to 1860*. Minneapolis, MN: University of Minnesota Press.

Wallace, Anthony F. C. (1970) *The Death and Rebirth of the Seneca*. New York: Alfred A. Knopf.

Walters, Ronald G. (1978). *American Reformers, 1815–1860*. New York: Hill and Wang.

Camp Meetings

Camp meetings were among the most popular and well-attended religious phenomena of nineteenth-century American cultural life. These "festivals of democracy" (as Michael Chevalier has called them) were great outdoor gatherings lasting four to ten days, usually in the late summer. Tens of thousands would attend them each year, staying in canvas tents that were arranged in close proximity to create an intimate sense of community. Each day during camp meeting participants would gather for continuous services of worship held in open-air clearings or "bush arbors." Rough preacher's stands were often constructed with trees providing a natural canopy, while wooden planks set across stumps served as benches. The major portion of the religious services consisted of preaching, exhortation, testimonies, and popular singing. Overt physical displays of emotions, such as shouting, braying, and sometimes even dancing, were encouraged by speakers and participants alike, giving the camp meetings some of their most distinguishing characteristics.

Elsewhere in American Protestantism, millennial expectations ran high in the first half of the nineteenth century. In the camp meetings, however, as in the wider Holiness movement of which they were a part, millennial themes were relatively muted. It wasn't until the latter decades of the nineteenth century that millennial doctrines became a topic on many camp meeting programs, or began to impact the overall theology of the movement. Yet the camp meeting movement was not far removed from the wider currents of millennial expectation in American Protestant theology. The purpose of the camp meetings was to call sinners to conversion and personal holiness. They were one of the major methods employed by the leading names of what is often called the Second Great Awakening in American history (c. 1800–50). A number of the techniques that came to characterize revivalism in America in general were first developed in the context of camp meetings, including the extensive use of testimonies, popular singing, and the "mourners bench" (or later the altar rail) for practicing repentance.

Camp meetings were designed to lead those who participated in them into an experience of personal repentance that resulted in sanctification, often described as a baptismal experience of spiritual proportions. They were therefore concerned with achieving at a personal spiritual level what millennial Christian doctrines taught was to be achieved at a social and political level by the Christianizing effect of America upon the world. To this end the camp meeting sought to bring the kingdom of God to bear upon individuals at a personal level, but they did so in service to the realization of the kingdom of God that was expected soon to come at a larger social, political, and even cultural level.

A second major consideration regarding camp meetings and millennialism is that, while camp meetings were often interdenominational in character, the Methodists played a dominant institutional role overall within them. Bishop Francis Asbury, the guiding force in the American Methodist movement during the first decades of the nineteenth century, was the major ecclesial proponent of camp meetings. Asbury promoted them as a primary method for church growth, and indeed through them a large number of individuals were introduced into the Methodist connection. Asbury had little interest in millennial doctrines, and most Methodists in the first decades of the nineteenth century appear to have followed him in this regard. The marriage of millennialism and camp meeting came only after the movement gained a wider institutional basis among Protestant churches. In this regard, the claim to have held the first explicitly millennial camp meeting fell to the Millerites who held a Second Advent Camp Meeting in 1842.

During the second half of the nineteenth century, camp meetings became more closely identified with millennial teachings on a number of fronts. The most important was the growing collaboration between camp meetings and the new Bible prophecy conference movement in North America. Eventually a number of Bible prophecy conference speakers came on the programs at camp meetings. The Niagara Bible Conference met on the campgrounds of Old Orchard, Maine, and in 1888 Leander W. Munhall brought the first "Inter-Denominational Bible Conference" to the camp meeting at Ocean Grove, New Jersey. After that an increasing number of camp meeting programs took up the task of studying Scripture to discern the prophecies concerning the imminent end of the age, the second coming of Christ, and the advent of his millennial kingdom on earth.

History of American Camp Meetings

The history of the camp meeting in America reaches back into the earliest days of the nation. Precedents for American camp meetings can be found in Scottish history, in the Holy Fairs conducted outdoors by dissident Presbyterian Church leaders during the time of Episcopal restoration. These Scottish open-air services also lasted several days and were primarily sacramental events. In the English Awakenings of the eighteenth century, led by George Whitefield and John Wesley, outdoor preaching was a common practice (although Wesley did not engage in sacramental practices in such settings). In America, Methodists and others held services of worship outdoors in the eighteenth century. In both the Carolinas and Georgia, toward the end of eighteenth century, several Methodist clergy appear to have begun holding services outdoors in the summer to attract converts. The Grassy Branch Camp Meeting at Rehobeth, North Carolina, for instance, claims to be a site of summer camp meetings from 1794.

The most important early camp meeting in America was held at Cane Ridge, Kentucky, in 1801. Led by John McGee, James McGready, and Barton Stone, the Cane Ridge Camp Meeting drew an estimated 25,000 persons that summer, and attracted attention throughout the Protestant churches of America. Many of the reports from Cane Ridge focused on the overt displays of emotion that characterized the meetings, leading to controversy over both their methods and outcomes. Nevertheless, their popularity increased rapidly. By the summer of 1810, Bishop Francis Asbury reported that according to his count, from three to four million persons had attended that summer. If even the lower number of this estimate was correct, that would make one out of three Americans a participant in them.

Many of the Americans who attended camp meetings were of African descent. Slaves came with their masters to these summer gatherings, participating in worship and experiencing what amounted to a period of rest from labor during the busiest period of the agricultural season. Organizers of camp meeting usually tried to separate Africans from Europeans at the events by segregating tents and even erecting fences, but more often than not the segregation failed to keep blacks and whites entirely apart. The relatively free form of worship and opportunities for extensive lay involvement through testimony and singing favored black participation in camp meetings. African cultural forms of spirited worship were often communicated spontaneously to European participants, leading to a greater mixing of both practices and ideas. Indeed, camp meetings were perhaps the single most important events of interracial worship and cross-cultural religious influences in nineteenth-century American life.

Later in the century, African-American churches developed their own separate camp meetings, such as that at Tuckers Grove in North Carolina, which was first opened by the African Methodist Episcopal Zion church in 1876. Still, even during the period of reconstruction and Jim Crow legislation at the end of the century, African Americans continued to participate and lead in predominantly European American camp meetings. The African Methodist Episcopal church evangelist, Amanda Berry Smith, was a regular leader in such camp meetings during the last quarter of the nineteenth century, and was even given a cottage to stay for a month by the board of the predominantly white Ocean Grove Camp Meeting Association in New Jersey.

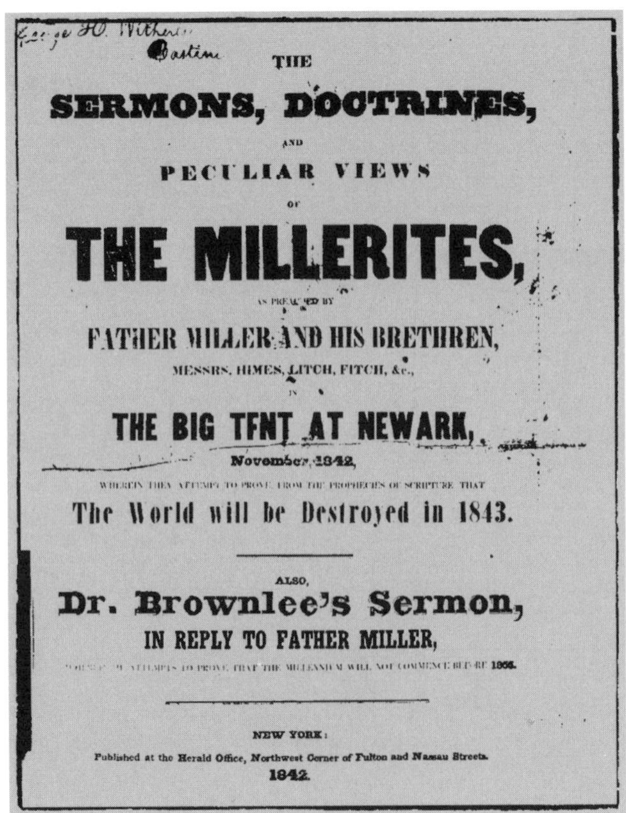

A poster announcing a tent meeting at which Dr. William C. Brownlee, pastor of the Collegiate Protestant Reformed Church in New York City, preached against Millerite prophecy of the end of the world. NUMBERS, RONALD L., AND JONATHAN M. BUTLER, EDS. (1987) *THE DISAPPOINTED: MILLERISM AND MILLENARIANISM IN THE NINETEENTH CENTURY.* BLOOMINGTON: UNIVERSITY OF INDIANA, 124.

In the post-Civil War era, many of the established camp meeting grounds in America began to change their emphasis, adopting more of an atmosphere of recreational centers. The family camping movement and scouting were both direct outgrowths of the religious camp meetings of the earlier part of the century. Many permanent grounds began to appear more as summer resorts than religious centers for revival. It was partially in response to this changing emphasis that a group of Methodist clergy from the New York, Philadelphia, and Scranton areas met in Vineland, New Jersey, in 1867 to establish the National Camp Meeting Association for the Promotion of Holiness (later simply called the National Holiness Association). They began holding a series of national camp meetings on various camp grounds across the nation the following summer, seeking to revive the holiness emphasis.

Two years after the founding of the national association a group of their leadership founded the Ocean Grove Camp Meeting in a half-mile-long section of shorefront property south of Long Branch, New Jersey. In the words of Elwood Stokes, Ocean Grove's first president, its founders were looking for a place where ministers and other religious persons who were not necessarily of means could find recreational and spiritual retreat at a place that was not a "fashionable watering hole." Camp meetings were the center of Ocean Grove's summer program, but a full array of religious and leisure activities were planned from May through September. Like other Holiness camp meetings, this camp was governed by strict rules that forbid worldly activities deemed sinful. Commercial and recreational activities were strictly forbidden on Sunday and were otherwise governed by regulations of modesty or holiness. In its own way, Ocean Grove and other Holiness camp grounds at the end of the nineteenth century sought to realize in a limited measure the godly vision of the millennial kingdom they expected would one day be established over all the earth.

Dale T. Irvin

See also Holiness Movement, Millerites, Pentecostalism

Bibliography

Brown, Kenneth O. (1992) *Holy Ground: A Study of the American Camp Meeting.* New York: Garland Press.

Dieter, Melvin Easterday. (1996) *The Holiness Revival of the Nineteenth Century.* Studies in Evangelicalism, No. 1, 2d ed. Metuchen, NJ: Scarecrow Press.

Hughes, George. ([1973] 1975) *Days of Power in the Forest Temple: A Review of the Wonderful Work of God at Fourteen National Camp-Meetings from 1867 to 1872.* Boston: J. Bent; reprint, Salem, Ohio: Allegheny Wesleyan Methodist Connection.

Johnson, Charles A. (1955) *The Frontier Camp Meeting: Religion's Harvest Time.* Dallas: Southern Methodist University Press.

Messenger, Troy. (1999) *Holy Leisure: Recreation and Religion in God's Square Mile.* Minneapolis: University of Minnesota Press.

Cargo Cults

In the final scenes of the film *Mondo Cane*, Gualtiero Jacopetti's original "shockumentary," we see eager Papua New Guinea islanders clustered around a huge, roughly made model of an airplane. They are high up in the mountains, sitting on a new airstrip they carved out of the forest. Their eyes search the skies, so the film tells us, for airplanes full of wonderful "cargo" that they expect will soon arrive. But they are destined to be disappointed. No planes will land. These islanders are the misguided followers of a cargo cult.

Anthropologists, journalists, and others have used the term "cargo cult" since 1945 to describe various South Pacific social movements. Cargo cults blossomed in the postwar 1940s and 1950s throughout the Melanesian archipelagoes of the southwest Pacific. People turned to religious ritual (which was sometimes traditional and sometimes innovative) in order to obtain "cargo." The term cargo (or *kago* in Melanesian Pidgin English) is rich in meaning. Sometimes cargo meant money or various sorts of manufactured goods (vehicles, packaged foods, refrigerators, guns, tools, and the like). And sometimes, metaphorically, cargo represented the search for a new moral order that often involved an assertion of local sovereignty and the withdrawal of colonial rulers. In either case, people expected and worked for a sudden, miraculous transformation in their lives. Cargo cult prophets commonly drew on Christian millenarianism, sometimes conflating the arrival of cargo with Christ's second coming and Judgment Day (locally often called "Last Day"). Among the most notable cargo cults are the John Frum and Nagriamel movements of Vanuatu, the Christian Fellowship Church of the Solomon Islands, and the Paliau and Yali movements, Hahalis Welfare Society, Pomio Kivung, and Peli Association of Papua New Guinea.

The Cargo Cult Label

The term "cargo cult" first appeared in a 1945 issue of the colonial news magazine *Pacific Islands Monthly.* That year, a disgruntled Australian resident of Papua New Guinea wrote to warn against outbreaks of cargo cult should the government dare to liberalize its native affairs policies. Anthropologists and others quickly adopted the term to label almost any sort of organized village-based social movement with religious and political aspirations. Before the war, observers had occasionally used the term "Vailala Madness," borrowed from anthropologist F. E. William's early analysis of a 1920s movement that had excited people around Vailala, Papua New Guinea (Williams 1923).

Although an improvement over Vailala Madness, "cargo cult" also is problematic in several ways. People involved in such movements always aspired to many things beyond simple material goods. And the organizations of these movements were ill-described by the word "cult." Moreover, people within the Pacific and beyond also quickly adopted the term

HANOVER AWAITS CHRIST

Hundreds of people are pouring onto the island of New Hanover off New Ireland for "the return of Jesus Christ" on Friday.

Supporters of the Tutukuval Isukal Association are expecting to receive K200 million on that day, according to people in Kavieng, the main town of New Ireland.

The people of New Hanover are best remembered for their support of the bizarre activities of the Johnson cult in the 1960s.

Thousands of people on the island dropped all normal activities to await the arrival on a mountain top of the then US president, Lyndon Johnson.

They expected President Johnson to rule over them and bestow all of the wealth of the United States on their island.

Later investigations found the mass indoctrination of villagers stemmed from distortions of conversations with US Army surveyors who spent a short time on the mountain top preparing for the establishment of communications equipment.

In later years, activities of the cult followers were steered into business ventures within the operations of the TIA [Tutukuval Isukal Association].

Their leader Mr. Walla Gukguk served a term in Parliament as the Member for Kavieng.

Mr. Gukguk was removed from his seat late last year for failure to attend meetings of Parliament.

The MV Danlo has been sailing between Kavieng and Taskul since Monday taking people for Friday's "celebrations."

The boat has been travelling fully loaded, and many disappointed followers have been left at Kavieng.

Details of the proposed celebrations could not be confirmed yesterday, but officials in Kavieng expect Taskul to host the occasion.

The cult's quasi-religious aspects have often been linked to the strong influence on the island of the Catholic Church, but members of the church maintain that any involvement by priests has only been to assist the TIA member[s] to start business ventures. ***(PC 1983c, 3)***

Source: *Post-Courier* (August 1983) Papua New Guinea, c, 3.

as a form of political abuse: politicians today may belittle the plans and aspirations of their rivals by labeling these as "cargo cultist."

Despite the popularization of cargo cult as a label for South Pacific movements, from the beginning anthropologists sought out alternative terms. These included nativistic movements, revitalization movements, messianic movements, millenarian movements, crisis cults, Holy Spirit movements, protonationalist movements, culture-contact movements, and the like. These broader labels appreciated cargo cult's affinities with social movements elsewhere that also appeared to be sparked by the global spread of the colonialist and capitalist systems. Cargo cults, thus, were in significant ways similar to the North American Ghost Dance, or China's Boxer Rebellion, or the Mau Mau of East Africa. "Cargo Cult," nonetheless, remains as the now standard label for the South Pacific version of global millenarian movements.

Cargo Belief

The defining aspect of cargo cult beliefs, or ideology, was of course cargo itself. Cultists, supposedly, strove for the arrival of planes and ships full of cargo: manufactured goods and tinned foods, vehicles, weapons, and money. However, lists of desired cargo, as reported, reflected both Pacific aspirations and European presumptions of what islanders should want. Refrigerators, for example, occupied a suspiciously prominent place in many such reported cargo lists.

Details of cargo ideology varied from movement to movement. Common themes, however, included the belief that the ancestors were somehow involved in the production of manufactured goods. In some places, people believed that a technologically wise ancestor long ago had sailed away to America, or Europe, or Australia to teach the secrets of cargo to people there. In others, cargo myth presumed that Europeans had stolen industrial knowledge from Pacific ancestors, or were stealing cargo itself that ancestors were shipping back to the islands. In either case, people invented new rituals to induce the dead to provide cargo and, sometimes, to come back to life and return home with cargo-filled ships and planes.

After the Pacific War, the American military occasionally came to take on the role of cargo provider. Many Melanesians, particularly those recruited to work at Allied bases on Efate and Espiritu Santo in the New Hebrides (Vanuatu), Guadalcanal in the Solomon Islands, and Manus, Hollandia, and elsewhere in New Guinea, received better pay and obtained a variety of new wartime goods and services. After the militaries withdrew from most of the southwest Pacific in 1946, money and goods became scarcer. John Frum supporters on Tanna (Vanuatu), began predicting the return of the American military and the cargo that they had enjoyed as labor corps recruits. John Frum leaders also incorporated their experience of military routines and symbols into cult ritual and liturgy, including drill team marching, bamboo rifles, red crosses (from army ambulances), khaki uniforms, and U.S. flags.

Many movements, in addition to material goods, also pursued various sorts of world transformation. This, too, partly reflected political conditions at the end of the Pacific War. The Japanese advance had dislodged the Dutch and the Australians from much of New Guinea along with the British from the Solomon Islands. Large American occupation forces similarly weakened colonial authority in the New Hebrides and, to a degree, in New Caledonia and Fiji. At war's end, in all these countries, the colonial powers moved to reestablish their authority in island hinterlands. Not surprising, people who had largely governed themselves during the war resisted this reassertion of European control. Cargo cult prophets predicted that ancestors, or returning Americans, would drive the colonial powers from the region. Cults were, as Jean Guiart argued, "forerunners of Melanesian nationalism" (1951).

In addition to articulating people's desires for freedom, dignity, and independence from European domination, some cult prophets predicted more millenarian sorts of change. Mountains would flatten and valleys would rise up. Land would become sea, and the seas would become land. People expected the coming of a new world, with remade people, and many cult rituals included elements of rebirth, or baptism, to mark the creation of a new order. Two very common prophesies were that the dead would come back to life and that the skins of the faithful would turn white. The first of these prophecies reflected the importance of ancestors in traditional religion and their connections with fertility and production. The second responded to the stark racial

Ritual gate on the cargo road in Tanna. LAMONT LINDSTROM.

inequalities of colonialist regimes where Europeans controlled access to money, goods, and education.

Cargo Organization

An oral rather than literate tradition continues to characterize much of Melanesia. People communicate by talking. All sorts of rumor and speculation flow from village to village—some of this about mysterious sightings, dreams of the future, or statements of prophesy. Only some of these stories attract much public attention, however. Anthropologists have attempted to figure why cargo movements occurred in one village while bypassing another. Two important factors were the degree of people's sense of "relative deprivation"—how unhappy they are with their lives—and the absence of a strong, local power structure. Where village leaders were in firm control of a village or clan (whether these leaders were chiefs or what, in Melanesian Pidgin, are called "big-men"), they usually could deflect cargo cult enthusiasm and stifle the local spread of a movement.

Cargo "prophets" foretold the return of ancestors and typically explained what people must do in order to obtain cargo, instigating, for example, dance and other ritual. Some cargo movements revived traditional ceremonies that European missionaries and officials had devalued. Others focused on a ritual miming of European practices and styles, including dinner tables, dress, and literacy. Cargo prophets instructed people to drill and march. They and the faithful cleared new airfields and built makeshift cargo warehouses. Prophets advised followers that the ancestors required new offerings of food, or flowers, or money to be left in graveyards before cargo will arrive. They demanded that people dig up their crops, kill their animals, and discard all European money in order to open the gate to the cargo road. Sometimes they commanded the abolition of marriage and incest prohibition, and people engaged in unrestrained sexuality. Elsewhere, they forbade sex entirely as ritually necessary to ensure cargo's arrival.

Prophetic messages of all sorts, in fact, are not unusual in Melanesia. Most people, even though today largely Christian, continue to sense the presence of ancestral ghosts. It is common for men and women to receive knowledge and information from ancestors—and also from God and the Holy Spirit—in their dreams. Those whose messages were accepted became leaders of the movements that formed around them. It was also common that other men, who organized and distributed prophetic messages, might assume control of a movement. Women have also been cargo prophets, although men typically appropriated and broadcast the messages that women received in dreams or otherwise.

In much of Melanesia, knowledge remains a politically valued resource. Men achieve a personal reputation and also political status by having good knowledge of family genealogy, history, personal and place names, ritual procedures, curing, and divination. Knowledge of cargo has similar political weight. Prophets—or those who controlled their messages—organized large, regional movements of thousands of people who desired to learn the secrets of cargo. Cargo prophesies have united people—at least temporarily—into large organizations that conjoin villages and kin groups from across a region. These movements were much larger than traditional Melanesian social groups. Cult ideology, typically, focused on social cooperation and standardization. Prophets and leaders worked to get everyone involved in cult ritual, e.g., mass dances and marches to invite ancestral arrival, or ritual procedures to wash and bless money to promote its reproduction. They also often preached against socially divisive practices of sorcery and other threats to group unity. The lack of movement solidarity served sometimes to excuse the failure of prophecy. Cargo does not arrive because followers have not fully observed the ancestors' commands.

The history of most cargo cults was short. Followers would often abandon a prophet and his movement when cargo failed to arrive, or the world did not transform. Some leaders, however, have successfully institutionalized their movements. John Frum on Tanna, for example, which began in the late 1930s, sixty years later is managed by third-generation leaders and has elected members to Vanuatu's national parliament. Other cargo cults have similarly been institutionalized as political parties, or new religions, or both. The Peli Association and Pomio Kivung in Papua New Guinea are successful political organizations at the local level. The Christian Fellowship Church continues today on New Georgia, Solomon Islands, as a syncretic church.

Cargo Cults and Melanesian Culture

Cargo belief and cult organization reflect enduring, fundamental patterns in Melanesian cultures. Everywhere, the exchange of goods and wealth objects is an important aspect of creating and maintaining social relationships. People give one another garden produce, pigs, mats and baskets, traditional shell and contemporary money, and other valuables to celebrate births and marriages and to mourn deaths. Moreover, men and women earn social reputation and political influence through generous giving. Cultic focus on wealth, thus, elaborated traditional concern with the political management of economic production and exchange. And, because people believe that ancestral powers ensure the fertility of people, gardens, and pigs, it made sense to turn to ancestors also to acquire money or shotguns or tinned peaches. Cargo cult rituals were similar to traditional ceremonies that ensure ancestral benevolence.

Islanders also continue to believe that ancestors speak to them in dreams, providing important knowledge, hints of the future, and instruction for proper living. Ancestral messages about the arrival of cargo ships and planes were similar to other sorts of spiritual communication. Furthermore, Lawrence (1964) and others have suggested that Melanesian structures of time and social transformation are "episodic" rather than developmental. People presume that sudden transformations are normal; that one cosmic order at any moment may replace another. Prophecies of cargo's arrival, the return of the dead, and the emergence of a new world are more compelling where people do not believe that the future must develop incrementally over time from the present. Finally, cultic organization—a society of believers who follow cult prophets and leaders—resembled ordinary social organization in much of Melanesia where big-men attract followers by managing the exchange of goods and information. Cargo prophets, along these lines, were just another sort of traditional island leader.

If cargo cults are a Pacific version of millenarian movements that erupt everywhere in times of uncertainty and change, then these aspects of Melanesian culture help explain the particular organizational form of cults and the details of cargo belief. More than this, some have suggested that cargo culting is an indigenous Melanesian form of politicking that predates colonial interference in the region. If this is the case, cargo cults may not quiet down and ultimately disappear as the era of colonialism passes into that of postcolonialism.

Cargo Cult Futures

Cargo cults may continue to erupt, or they may prove to have been a twentieth-century reaction to colonial inequalities and the disruptions of world war. The most successful movements, however, will certainly survive into the twenty-first century, now institutionalized as political parties and churches in Vanuatu, Solomon Islands, and Papua New Guinea. Beginning in the 1980s, fundamentalist Christian missions based in Australia, New Zealand, and the United States strengthened their presence in the Pacific. Influenced by this Christian millenarianism, many islanders have become involved in Holy Spirit movements. In these, cargo expectations are muted. Instead, people seek to be possessed by the Holy Spirit to bring about the transformation of self, society, and world. Typically, these movements also undertake campaigns against sorcery, cleansing villages of hidden sorcery paraphernalia believed to be causing illness, death, and disorder. Holy Spirit prophets predict the Last Day—the return not so much of cargo but of Christ—and the impending establishment of a new cosmos.

Whatever happens to cargo cults themselves in the Pacific, the label "cargo cult" is now widely applied—and not just in Melanesia. Any fervid desire today for wealth or goods that people pursue with apparently irrational means can be condemned as cargo cultic. As people everywhere are absorbed into a global, capitalist order where economic inequalities persist, and even deepen, it may be that cargo culting will indeed spread beyond Melanesia. As we learn to desire goods that are impossible to obtain, we may turn in despair to our gods and prophets. Insofar as that global order limits our freedom and dignity, we may join with others in organized protest. We, too, may be searching the skies for our cargo.

Lamont Lindstrom

See also John Frum Movement

Bibliography

Burridge, Kenelm. (1960) *Mambu: A Study of Melanesian Cargo Movements and Their Social and Ideological Background.* London: Methuen.

———. (1960) *New Heaven, New Earth: A Study of Millenarian Activities.* New York: Schocken Books.

Cochrane, Glynn. (1970) *Big Men and Cargo Cults.* Oxford: Clarendon Press.

Guiart, Jean. (1951) "Forerunners of Melanesian Nationalism." *Oceania* 22:81–90.

Lattas, Andrew. (1998) *Cultures of Secrecy: Reinventing Race in Bush Kaliai Cargo Cults.* Madison, WI: University of Wisconsin Press.

Lawrence, Peter. (1964) *Road Belong Cargo: A Study of the Cargo Movement in the Southern Madang District, New Guinea.* Manchester, U.K.: Manchester University Press.

Lindstrom, Lamont. (1993) *Cargo Cult: Strange Stories of Desire from Melanesia and Beyond.* Honolulu: University of Hawaii Press.

———. (1996) "Cargo Inventories, Shopping Lists, and Desire." In *Talking about People: Readings in Contemporary Cultural Anthropology*, 2d ed., edited by William Haviland and Robert Gordon. Mountain View, CA: Mayfield Publishing, 35–39.

Maher, Robert. (1961) *New Men of Papua: A Study of Culture Change.* Madison, WI: University of Wisconsin Press.

McDowell, Nancy. (1988) "A Note on Cargo Cults and Cultural Constructions of Change." *Pacific Studies* 11:121–34.

Mead, Margaret. (1966) *New Lives for Old: Cultural Transformation—Manus, 1928–1953.* New York: Morrow.

Rimoldi, Max. (1992) *Hahalis and the Labour of Love: A Social Movement on Buka Island.* Oxford, U.K.: Berg.

Steinbauer, Friedrich. (1979) *Melanesian Cargo Cults: New Salvation Movements in the South Pacific.* St. Lucia, Australia: University of Queensland Press.

Trompf, Garry W. (1990) *Cargo Cults and Millenarian Movements: Transoceanic Comparisons of New Religious Movements.* Berlin: Mouton de Gruyter.

Whitehouse, Harvey. (1995) *Inside the Cult: Religious Innovation and Transmission in Papua New Guinea.* New York: Oxford University Press.

Williams, Frances E. (1923) *The Vailala Madness and the Destruction of Native Ceremonies in the Gulf Division.* Anthropology Report No. 4. Port Moresby: Territory of Papua.

Worsley, Peter. (1957) *The Trumpet Shall Sound: A Study of "Cargo" Cults in Melanesia.* London: Macgibbon & Kee.

Catastrophic Millennialism

"Millennialism" has become an academic term used to refer to belief in an imminent transition to a collective salvation in which the elect will experience well-being and the limitations of the human condition will be transcended. The collective salvation is often expected to be earthly, but it can also be heavenly. If physical events thoroughly disconfirm the establishment of the millennial kingdom on earth, the millennialists may shift to focusing on a heavenly collective salvation. The terms "millennialism" or "millenarianism" derive from Christianity, because the New Testament book of Revelation states that the kingdom of God will exist on earth for one thousand years (a millennium). Increasingly, "millennialism" is a term applied to particular religious patterns found in a variety of religious traditions. Catastrophic millennialism has existed for several thousand years, and will continue as a religious pattern past the 2000 date that is exciting religious imaginations, because it appeals to the perennial human desire to achieve permanent well-being that is at the heart of the religious quest.

Catastrophic millennialism is the most common millennial religious pattern. In the catastrophic millennial pattern, there is belief in an imminent and catastrophic transition to the millennial kingdom. Catastrophic millennialism involves a pessimistic view of human nature and society. Humans are so evil and corrupt that the old order has to be destroyed violently to make way for the perfected millennial kingdom. Catastrophic millennialism involves a radical dualistic worldview; reality is seen in terms of the opposition of good and evil, and this easily translates into a perspective of "us vs. them."

Catastrophic millennial beliefs often develop in response to the experience of repeated disasters, including natural disasters, political disasters, technological disasters, and the disasters a religious group experiences such as defections and persecutions. But even when obvious disasters are not contributing factors, people find the catastrophic millennial worldview appealing, because it explains the disasters of finite existence—illness, old age, disappointment, strife, loss, and death. The millennial kingdom is a promise of the transcendence of life's suffering and the attainment of total well-being. Salvation is a condition of permanent well-being, and catastrophic millennialism offers that salvation to collectivities of people as opposed to individuals. Catastrophic millennialism is a worldview that offers the hope that the experience of evil is not meaningless and that the righteous will be vindicated and included in salvation.

Catastrophic millennial beliefs have the power to motivate people to take actions. If the world is going to end soon and there will be a judgment to determine who will be admitted to the millennial kingdom, then it is urgent to get one's life in order and to be of the right faith. Often catastrophic millennial beliefs have been strong at the time of the founding of a new religion. This was the case with Christianity, Islam, Baha'i, Mormonism, and a multitude of smaller religions. The sense of the imminence of the catastrophic destruction likely will diminish as the new religion institutionalizes and becomes accommodated to society and perhaps even becomes the dominant religion. But the catastrophic millennial beliefs will be preserved in the religion's scriptures, and thus they will remain accessible as resources to be utilized by future new religious movements and their leaders within that tradition.

Catastrophic millennialism, as with other forms of millennialism, is religious, because it involves an "ultimate concern," which can be defined as "a concern which is more important than anything else in the universe for the person [or the group] involved" (Baird 1971: 18). The ultimate concern is the religious goal, and for catastrophic millennialists, the religious goal is to be included in the collective salvation, however that is defined. People may change their ultimate concerns over time, or abandon an ultimate concern if it is disconfirmed or if they are pressured, but some people cling to their ultimate concern so tightly that they become willing to kill or die for it.

Because so many catastrophic millennialists believe that the imminent millennial kingdom will be earthly, they often find themselves in conflict with civil authorities. Millennialists may attempt to create their millennial kingdom, live out its principles in their daily lives, or, in some cases, attempt to overthrow the current political order to establish the divinely mandated rule. Catastrophic millennialists regard civil authority as secondary to their ultimate authority.

Catastrophic millennialism and progressive millennialism are not mutually exclusive religious patterns. Often a movement's theology will contain some elements of each. Millennial beliefs change in reaction to circumstances. A group's experience of repeated disasters including opposition, hostility, and persecution from society will increase catastrophic millennial expectations. Progressive millennialism, the belief that the imminent transition to the collective salvation will be noncatastrophic, is likely to become more prominent when a group becomes comfortable in society and experiences some success in building the millennial kingdom.

In the catastrophic millennial pattern, the catastrophic transition to the collective salvation often is believed to be accomplished by a superhuman agent, who might be God, a messiah, the collective will and efforts of the people, and increasingly, extraterrestrials. A "messiah" is an individual who is believed to possess the power to create the millennial kingdom. A messiah also will be a "prophet," someone who receives divine revelation, but prophets are not necessarily messiahs. Both prophets and messiahs have "charisma," i.e., access to an unseen divine or superhuman source of authority. An individual will not possess charismatic authority unless people believe her or his claim to that revelation. Increasingly in millennial religions, extraterrestrials are cast in the roles formerly played by God, Satan, angels, and devils. This is a contemporary expression of the ages-old religious belief that there are normally unseen beings who affect humans for good or ill.

In Christianity, "apocalypse" refers to biblical literature that reveals the catastrophic events at the end of the world as we know it. In popular language, apocalypse has become synonymous with the expected catastrophe, therefore "apocalyptic" is synonymous with "catastrophic millennialism."

Catastrophic millennialists have different views about the roles humans will play in the apocalyptic transition to the millennial kingdom. Many catastrophic millennialists wait in faith for divine intervention to violently destroy the world.

Some catastrophic millennialists wait for divine intervention to establish the millennial kingdom, but they are armed for self-defense during the anticipated tribulation period; if they are attacked, they will fight. Some catastrophic millennialists are revolutionaries, who believe they are called to fight in the plan of the divine or superhuman agent to destroy the current government and thereby establish the millennial kingdom.

Catastrophic millennialism is not necessarily related to violence, but catastrophic millennial groups involved in violence will either be assaulted millennial groups, fragile millennial groups, or revolutionary millennial movements.

Catherine Wessinger

See also Assaulted Millennial Groups, Fragile Millennial Groups, Progressive Millennialism, Revolutionary Millennial Movements.

Bibliography

Baird, Robert D. (1971) *Category Formation and the History of Religions.* The Hague: Mouton.

Barkun, Michael. (1974) *Disaster and the Millennium.* New Haven, CT: Yale University Press.

Wessinger, Catherine. (1997) "Millennialism With and Without the Mayhem: Catastrophic and Progressive Expectations." In *Millennium, Messiahs, and Mayhem: Contemporary Apocalyptic Movements,* edited by Thomas Robbins and Susan J. Palmer. New York: Routledge, 47–59.

——. (2000) *How the Millennium Comes Violently.* Chappaqua, NY: Seven Bridges Press.

——, ed. (2000) *Millennialism, Persecution, and Violence: Historical Cases.* Syracuse, NY: Syracuse University Press.

Wojcik, Daniel. (1997) *The End of the World As We Know It: Faith, Fatalism, and Apocalypse in America.* New York: New York University Press.

Century, Centennial, Centenarium

"Century" signifies a period of 100 years. For the most part it is calculated from a received chronological epoch, especially from the assumed date of the birth of Christ. The series of historical centuries counted forward and backward from the birth of Christ has become a common means of orientation in history and chronology. Over time the century has advanced to a frame of reference for memories, experiences, and expectations. The idea of the century gained its biggest impact on the public mind in the wake of the French Enlightenment, where the eighteenth century or *siècle* was associated with the familiar state of the world *(notre siècle)* or at least as a certain stage of historical development *(siècle des lumières, siècle philosophique* or *philosophe).* The idea of the "close of the century" gained influence at the end of the nineteenth century, when the slogan "fin de siècle" intensified existing doubts about the progress of civilization. In this case the tradition of the century took an apocalyptic point of view, as far as it drew the attention to an expected end, which at the same time opened the idea of a threshold, leading into a new era.

The period of 100 years forms not only the chronological framework of history, but also determines our modern culture of public remembrance and historical celebration. The centennial is, as the hundredth anniversary of a certain person or institution, often accompanied by retrospective jubilee celebrations. The modern use of the century derives from older sources. One is the late medieval use of the notion of *centenarium.* It stood originally for "containing a hundred" and achieved the meaning "hundred years" at least in the discipline of calendar reckoning. The notion developed in accordance with *millenarium* (containing a thousand), a term that was sometimes used in late medieval times. Whereas the *millenarium* or millennium acquired a high apocalyptic significance due to its reference in Revelation 20 the *centenarium* (century) remained, with one or two exceptions, insignificant. Thus the boundaries of the centuries were never particularly favored in millenarian predictions. It is necessary to take the history of terms like *centenarium* and the vivid tradition of centennial celebrations into account to understand the whole range of meaning included in the modern idea of the century. Furthermore the year 2000 should be seen as the point of intersection between the two different traditions of the millennium and the century.

Ancient 100-year Traditions

The century as a historical unit is a distinctly modern focus of awareness. Nevertheless we find early beginnings in Roman antiquity. A very long human life can extend, according to Varro, up to 100 years. This idea stood in accordance to the Etruscan idea of the *saeculum* as the maximum time of a certain generation. The Etruscan model of the *saeculum* led into the tradition of *ludi saeculares* (secular games), which where celebrated by the Romans at the assumed end of a *saeculum.* The intervening period between the Roman secular games varied between exactly 100 years, 110 years, or shorter periods. Thus the Roman *saeculum* failed to establish a series of historical centuries.

The Apocalyptic Meaning of the Century

An apocalyptic meaning of the century appeared in some rather remote contexts. A first trace is to be found in an anonymous tract of a German monk, *De semine scripturarum*, which divided time into twenty-three centuries, according to the twenty-three letters of the Roman alphabet. These alphabetical centuries did not coincide with our modern historical centuries, since the monk started his counting with the founding of the city of Rome (752 BCE). Each letter or *centenarium* was supposed to lead mankind into a new spiritual state, which was why many early readers ascribed *De semine scriptuarum* to Joachim of Fiore. So did Arnold of Villanova, a Catalan physician, who commented on the tract in the last years of the thirteenth century. Arnold replaced the letters with numbers and started counting with the incarnation of Christ. As a result, he was one of the first to perceive and indicate the turn of the century as a turn of the century. It should be pointed out, that neither Arnold nor his contemporaries showed any fear of this special year, since they related apocalyptic dates to traditional categories, such as the *annus mundi* (year of the world) and the Millennium. In spite of the tract *De semine scripturarum*, which recommended the century as a key to apocalyptic reckoning, the century never became an important eschatological category at least in the Christian culture. Thus there has been no tradition of a centenarianism comparable to millenarianism.

The Century as Historical Time Unit

In medieval times the word *saeculum* only meant "world" or "age." We cannot find it again in its ancient meaning of "century" until about 1235, when John of Sacrobosco defined the *saeculum* again as a *spatium centum annorum* (space of hundred years). Nevertheless it remained uncommon to translate *saeculum* as a period of 100 years until the seventeenth century. The older, more technical *centenarium*, often explained by the collocation *annorum* (of years), fell into disuse. It was used most frequently in calendar reckoning *(computus)*, from where it might have been lent to the eschatological tract *De semine scripturarum*. Up to the sixteenth century, *centuria* was a collective noun referring to a hundred similar things. It could be a military unit, like the subdivision of a Roman legion. But the primary use of the notion *centuria* has been as a classification of textual materials into centuries or *centuriae* of poems, prayers, stories, etc. At least until the so-called Magdeburg Centuriators, a group of German Protestant writers gathered in Magdeburg, assigned one volume to each one hundred years of church history and called each volume a *centuria*. Their church history, issued between 1559 and 1574, was the first printed work to separate history into centuries. The series became known as the *Magdeburg Centuries* and established the meaning of "100-year period" to the term *centuria* which was absorbed in the English term "century." Once in use, the century soon captured a key position, and the habit of referring to the sequence of centuries became a common element of historical narration.

The Turn of the Century

The earliest public awareness of the century is to be found in the year 1300 when Boniface VIII opened the first Holy Year, an indulgence to all pilgrims to Rome, to be granted every hundredth year. Boniface's move was new, both in fixing the importance of the century as a unit and in associating this unit with the expectation of momentous new spiritual opportunities. But later popes shortened the intervening period to fifty, then thirty-three and finally twenty-five years, so that the Holy Year failed to establish a series of turn-of-the-century celebrations. With little exceptions, the turns of the centuries were not celebrated or even perceived until 1600, when the idea of historical centuries found use in historiography. Although this practice was somewhat new when the sixteenth century ended, the Protestants had a good reason to care about the year 1600: flocks of Roman Catholic pilgrims went to Rome in order to acquire the indulgence of the Holy Year. Some Protestant preachers used the beginning of the year 1600 as an opportunity to take up the challenge of the Holy Year. They emphasized in special new-year sermons the - historical dignity of their own church and made the first historical reviews of a century at its end.

The importance of the turn of the century grew with the importance of the idea of history itself in the eighteenth century. Whereas only a few contemporaries alluded to the year 1700 and especially to the question of, whether the *saeculum* ends with the year 1699 or 1700, the year 1800 was awaited as a meaningful step in progress itself. Even small villages celebrated the turn of the century with at the least special sermons by their parsons. The United States had comparatively few celebrations, which might be attributed to the death of George Washington on 14 December 1799.

The years before the next turn of the century shaped the phenomenon of the fin de siècle. Despite its pessimism in literature and art, this was not evident at the moment of the changing century, when again thousands of cities celebrated the arrival of a new century.

Millenarian and Centenarian Traditions

Apart from the series of turning centuries, the idea of the 100-year period supported the tradition of centennials. The habit of celebrating jubilees and round anniversaries became more and more common from early modern times. Centennial consciousness is rooted in the sociological functions of the jubilee, which underlines the identity of one's own group linked to a calculated optimism for the future. The turn of the century has been celebrated at least since 1800 as a "jubilee of mankind." Taking this into account, the year 2000 stands at the point of intersection between a millenarian and a centenarian tradition. Whereas the millennium tended to encourage a tradition of fear, the concept of century, which emerged later and in different contexts, strengthens the idea of celebration.

Arndt Brendecke

See also Fin de Siècle

Bibliography

Brendecke, Arndt. (1999) *Die Jahrhundertwenden: Eine Geschichte ihrer Wahrnehmung und Wirkung*. Frankfurt am Main and New York: Campus.

Krauss, Werner. (1963) *Studien zur deutschen und französischen Aufklärung*. Berlin: Rütten & Loenig.

Milo, Daniel Shabetaï. (1991) *Trahir le temps* (histoire). Paris: Les Belles Lettres.

Reeves, Marjorie. ([1969] 1993) *The Influence of Prophecy in the Late Middle Ages: A Study in Joachimism*. Oxford, U.K.: Clarendon Press; new edition, Notre Dame, IN: University of Notre Dame Press.

Rusconi, Roberto. (1984/85) "Millenarismo e centenarismo: tra due fuochi." In *Annali della Facoltá di Lettere e Filosofia della Universitá degli Studi di Perugia*, vol. 22, N. S. 8, 2 (Studi storico-antropologici, Perugia): 49–64.

Schwartz, Hillel. (1996) *Century's End: A Cultural History of the Fin de Siècle from the 990s through the 1990s*. New York: Doubleday.

———. (1996) *Century's End: An Orientation Manual Toward the Year 2000*. New York: Doubleday.

Charisma

The approach of the millennium provided the circumstances which characteristically give rise to charismatic groups and movements. The concept of charisma has evolved over the years, progressively shifting from the predominantly leader-centered focus of Max Weber.

When Weber first introduced the concept of charismatic authority in 1922, he addressed the psychology of the followers, but only in cursory fashion. He made it clear that he considered that the predominant determinant of the relationship between the charismatic leader and his followers was the compelling forcefulness of the leader's personality, in the face of which the followers were essentially choiceless, and felt compelled to follow. Schiffer (1973) has observed that later commentators on the phenomenon of charismatic authority have also focused disproportionately on the magnetism of the leader, failing to make the fundamental observations that all leaders—*especially* charismatic leaders—are at heart the creation of their followers. A notable exception to this criticism is the corpus of work of Abse and Ulman (1977). They give important attention to the psychological qualities of the followers which render them susceptible to the force of the charismatic leader and lead to collective regression. In so doing, Abse and Ulman draw attention to the relationship between the psychological qualities of narcissistically wounded individuals and charismatic leader-follower relationships.

Wilner (1984) has observed that the concept of charisma has been much abused and watered down since Weber (1922) first introduced it. The media indeed often use charisma as synonymous with popular appeal, whereas Weber defined charismatic authority as a personal authority deriving from "devotion to the specific sanctity, heroism or exemplary character of an individual person and of the normative patterns or order revealed or ordained by him." To operationalize the concept, Wilner surveyed the vast (and often contradictory) literature bearing on charismatic leadership. She emerges with this definition:

> Charismatic leadership is a relationship between a leader and a group of followers that has the following properties:
> 1. The leader is perceived by the followers as somehow superhuman.
> 2. The followers blindly believe the leader's statements.
> 3. The followers unconditionally comply with the leader's directives for action.
> 4. The followers give the leader unqualified emotional support.

It should be observed that each of these properties relates to a perception, belief, or response of the followers. Wilner dismisses as interesting but unproven hypotheses that "in times of crisis, individuals regress to a state of delegated omnipotence and demand a leader [who will rescue them, take care of them]" and that "individuals susceptible to [the hypnotic attraction of] charismatic leadership have themselves fragmented or weak ego structures."

There is indeed, however, powerful support for these hypotheses. Clinical work with individuals with narcissistic personality disorders, the detailed studies of individuals who join charismatic religious groups, and psychodynamic observations of group phenomena all provide persuasive support for these hypotheses concerning the psychological makeup and responses of individuals susceptible to charismatic leadership—the "lock" of the follower for the "key" of the leader. Indeed, rather than speak of charismatic leaders it is more appropriate to speak of charismatic leader-follower relationships.

Psychological Characteristics of Charismatic Leaders and their Followers

At the core of the charismatic leader-follower relationship is the charismatic leader, a "mirror-hungry" individual. Arrogant and dogmatic on the surface, he or she hungers for confirming and admiring responses to counteract an inner sense of worthlessness and lack of self-esteem. The "mirror-hungry" leader requires a continuing flow of admiration from an audience in order to nourish a famished self. Central to his or her ability to elicit that admiration is an ability to convey a sense of grandeur, omnipotence, and strength. Charismatic leaders display an apparently unshakeable self-confidence and voice their opinions with absolute certainty. These individuals who have had feelings of grandiose omnipotence awakened within them are particularly attractive to individuals seeking idealized sources of strength. They convey a sense of conviction and certainty to those who are consumed by doubt and uncertainty. This mask of certainty is no mere pose. In truth, so profound is the inner doubt that a wall of dogmatic certainty is necessary to ward it off. For them, preserving grandiose feelings of strength and omniscience does not allow of weakness and doubt. No matter how positive the response, they cannot be satisfied and will continue seeking new audiences from whom to elicit the attention and recognition they crave.

A complement to the "mirror-hungry" personality is the "ideal-hungry" personality of individuals who feel incomplete unto themselves and only feel complete when attached to an idealized other: in Crayton's formulation, "If I am not perfect, I will at least be in a relationship with something perfect" (1983). These individuals can experience themselves as worthwhile only so long as they can relate to individuals whom they can admire for their prestige, power, beauty, intelligence, or moral stature. They forever search for such idealized figures. The mirror-hungry leader comes to the psychological rescue of the ideal-hungry followers. Taking on heroic proportions and representing what the followers wish to be, the leader protects them from confronting themselves and their fundamental inadequacy and alienation. The leader's success becomes the follower's success, a succor to the latter's self-esteem. But the inner void cannot be filled. Inevitably, the ideal-hungry find that this God is merely human, that this hero has feet of clay. Disappointed by the discovery of defects in a previously idealized object, the followers cast it aside and search for a new hero, to whom they attach themselves in the hope that they will not be disappointed again.

Gallanter's studies of charismatic religious groups provide confirmation for the hypothesis that narcissistically wounded individuals are specially attracted to charismatic leader-follower relationships. He found that the more lonely and isolated individuals were before joining, the more apt they were to affiliate strongly with the Unification Church and stay through the entire recruitment process. There was a tendency to suspend individual judgment and follow unquestioningly the dictates of the leader. Moreover, the more psychological relief that was experienced on joining, the less likely individuals were to question the leader's requirement for actions and behavior which ran counter to their normal social values and practices.

The phenomenon of the charismatic leader-follower relationship is surely too complex to lend itself to a single overarching psychodynamic personality model. In addition to features of the leader, the followers, and their relationships, one must take into account complex sociocultural, political, and historical factors. But at the core of charismatic movements are wounded followers following the banner of a dramatic leader who provides a sense of meaning and direction.

The Charismatic Leader as Group Hypnotist

There is a quality of mutual intoxication in the leader's reassuring his followers who in turn reassure him. One is reminded of the relationship between hypnotist and subject. Manifesting total confidence, the hypnotist instructs his subject to yield control to him and to suspend volition and judgment. Observers of the powerful mesmerizing effect of Hitler on his followers at the mass rallies have likened him to a hypnotist who placed his entire audience into a trance. But the power of the hypnotist ultimately depends upon the eagerness of his subjects to yield to his authority, to cede control of their autonomy, to surrender their will to the hypnotist's authority.

Charisma and Paranoia

Phyllis Greenacre (1971) observed that in order to be effectively charismatic, it is a great asset to possess paranoid conviction. While there is no necessary relation between charisma and paranoia, when the two are linked some of the most fearful excesses of human violence in history have occurred. For the charismatic leader with paranoid characteristics who is projecting his inner aggression, the rhetoric becomes the basis for justifying attacking the outside enemy: *we* are not weak. The problem is out there, with *them*. By destroying *them*, by expelling *them* from our midst, *we* will be the strong people we want to be. And each time the admiring crowd shouts its approval in response to his externalizing rhetoric, the leader's facade of certainty is strengthened and his inner doubts assuaged.

The Rhetoric of Charismatics is Polarizing and Absolutist

There is the "me" and the "not me." Analysis of the speeches of charismatic leaders repeatedly reveals such all-or-nothing polar absolutism—good versus evil, strength versus weakness, us versus them. Either/or categorization, with the leaders on the side of the angels, is a regular characteristic of charismatic evocative rhetoric. Bychowski has observed the predominance of the theme of strength and weakness in Hitler's speeches: the emphasis upon the strength of the German people, the reviling of weakness, the need to purify the race of any contamination or sign of weakness. But what could be the barrier to the German people achieving its full measure of greatness? "If we Germans are the chosen of God, then they (the Jews) are the people of Satan" (1948). Here the polarity is between good and evil, between children of God and the people of Satan. Hitler invokes the cult of strength and reviles weakness. "One must defend the strong who are menaced by their inferiors. . . . A state which, in a period of racial pollution, devotes itself to caring for its best racial elements must someday become the lord of the earth." The fear of appearing weak is projected upon the nation with whom he identifies.

Being on the side of God and identifying the enemy with Satan is a rhetorical device found regularly in the speeches of charismatic leaders. Ayatollah Khomeini continued to identify the United States as "the great Satan." Wilner sees this as an identifying feature of the speeches of the charismatic leader which heightens his identity as a leader with supernatural force. She observed the frequency of biblical references in the speeches of Franklin Delano Roosevelt. In the second inaugural address, for example: "We of the Republic pledged ourselves to drive from the temple of our ancient faith those who had profaned it. . . . Our Convenant with ourselves did not stop there." And, in the stirring conclusion, "I shall do my utmost to speak their purpose and do their will, seeking Divine guidance to help us and everyone to give light to them that sit in darkness and to guide our feet into the way of peace." As Wilner points out, not only is the authority of the Bible invoked, but also there are suggestions of God speaking through the mouth of the prophet Franklin. He identified himself with Moses as well in asking, "Shall we pause now and turn our back upon the road that lies ahead? Shall we call this the promised land?"

The invocation of divine guidance and use of biblical references are surely the currency of political rhetoric, and no politician worth his salt would ignore them. What is the difference between the leader whose use of such rhetoric rings false, as hollow posturing, and the politician whose religious words inspire? Is this related to Wildenmann's (1984) distinction between Charisma and Pseudocharisma? The narcissistic individual who does indeed consciously believe that he has special leadership gifts and accordingly has a special role to play may utilize religious rhetoric much more convincingly. Most convincing of all is its use by leaders like Ayatollah Khomeini who are indeed genuinely convinced they have a religious mission to perform.

While the ability to convey belief is an important asset, genuine belief is most convincing. This is also true of the polarization of good and evil, *us* versus *them*. Again, while it is a common political tactic to attempt to unify the populace against the outside enemy, the rhetoric of polarization is most effective when, as in the case of Hitler, *they* are absolutely believed to be the source of the problem, *they* are evil, and to eliminate *them* is to eliminate *our* problems.

Societal Crisis and the Social Psychology of the Followers

The ideal-hungry followers without whose uncritical response the charismatic leader would be but an empty shell, have, of course, sociopsychological patterns worth considering. It is important to make a distinction between those "ideal-hungry" narcissistically injured personalities who are permanently prone to enter such relationships and those who are, by virtue of external circumstances, rendered temporarily susceptible to enter into a charismatic leader-follower relationship.

At moments of societal crisis, otherwise mature and psychologically healthy individuals may temporarily come to feel overwhelmed and in need of a strong and self-assured leader. But when the historical moment passes, so too does the need. Few would omit Winston Churchill from the pantheon of charismatic leaders. The sense of conviction and assuredness he conveyed provided a rallying point to Great Britain and the Western Alliance during their darkest hours. During the crisis, Churchill's virtues were exalted and idealized. But when the moment passed and the need for a strong leader abated, how quickly the British people demystified the previously revered Churchill, focused on his leadership faults, and cast him out of office.

Indeed the process of idealization carries within it the seeds of disillusion. And the intensity of disengagement from the charismatic leader can be every bit as powerful as the attraction, a reflection of the cyclic course of history and the changing needs of the populace. Charismatic leader-follower relationships are particularly apt to occur at such historical moments, when the ranks of dependent followers will be swollen by normally self-sufficient individuals who have temporarily been rendered psychologically vulnerable by external events.

There is a special attraction to the banner of charismatic leaders in times of societal stress. When one is feeling overwhelmed, besieged by fear and doubt, it is extremely attractive to be able to suspend individual judgment and repose one's faith in the leadership of someone who conveys his conviction and certainty that he has the answers, that he knows the way—be it Reverend Moon, Jim Jones or David Koresh, Adolph Hitler or Ayatollah Khomeini. Through skillful use of rhetoric, they persuade their needy audiences: Follow me and I will take care of you. Together we can make a new beginning and create a new society. The fault is not within us but out there, and the only barrier to the happiness, peace, and prosperity we deserve is the outside enemy out to destroy us.

There is an additional bonus for the potential follower lured by the siren song of the leader's strength and conviction. Promised leadership and identification with a group, the follower draws additional strength from sharing allegiance with others. The identity of follower becomes a badge of honor, a statement of membership in a collective self. And in having merged with the collective others, the success of fellow followers becomes the success of the individual followers, as well. For isolated individuals with damaged self-esteem and weak ego boundaries, the sense of *we* creates and imparts a coherent sense of identity. For such individuals, the self and "the we" are fused so that the self is experienced as the relationship. This leads to a tendency of individuals to merge themselves with the group. In a figurative manner, a group mind or group ego is developed. The group becomes idealized and the standards of the group, as articulated by the leader and his disciples, take over and become the norm. This helps explain the startling degree to which individuals can suspend their own standards and judgment and participate in the most violent of actions when under the sway of the psychology of the group, if persuaded that the cause of the group is served by their actions. Even that most basic of human needs—the drive for self-preservation—can be suspended in the service of the group, as was horrifyingly evidenced by the phenomena of Jonestown and Ranch Apocalypse of the Branch Davidians.

Destructive and Reparative Charismatics

The phenomena of Jonestown, Ranch Apocalypse, and Germany under Hitler, convey the false impression that charismatic leader-follower relationships are only a force for human destructiveness. They certainly are so if the narcissistically wounded leader rages at the world for depriving him of "mirroring" and enlists his followers in attacking it. This is the destructive charismatic, as exemplified by Hitler.

By contrast, charismatic leader-follower relationships can also catalyze a reshaping of society in a highly positive and creative fashion, what Volkan (1984) has termed reparative leadership. He has persuasively demonstrated in his study of Ataturk of Turkey that the narcissistically wounded "mirror-hungry" leader, in projecting a personal psychic split upon society, may be a force for healing. While attempting to heal personal narcissistic wounds through the vehicle of leadership, the leader may indeed be resolving splits in a wounded society.

Just as the temporarily needy person may adopt an idealized object at trying moments of personal psychological development, so too a temporarily needy nation may need the leadership of an idealized object at trying moments of historical development. And just as the object of individual veneration is inevitably dethroned as worshippers achieve psychological maturity, so too the idealized leader will be discarded when the moment of historical need passes, as evidenced by the rise and fall of Winston Churchill.

But whatever fluctuations in the external circumstances of whole populations, within them there will always be individuals whose internal needs lead them to seek out idealized leaders. And when these "ideal-hungry" followers find a "mirror-hungry" leader, the elements of a charismatic leader-follower relationship exist. During times of relative societal repose, these relationships frequently regarded as peculiar aberrations, as cults. Microscopic in scale at first, in times of social crisis these powerful relationships can become the nuclei for powerful transforming social movements, as was the case with the revolutionary leadership of Ataturk and Khomeini.

With the end of the cold war and the superpower rivalry, the international system has entered an unstable transitional period, with major social and economic dislocations producing widespread challenges to the bases of social identity. As the millennium approaches, some messianic personalities will find this a fertile medium to attract followers to their cause, be it passively waiting for the arrival of the messiah, or actively attempting to precipitate the final struggle, as did Shoko Asahara with his religious cult Aum Shinrikyo. It is a ripe climate for the development of charismatic leader-follower relationships; the growth of fundamentalist cults and the development of new religions and social movements is likely.

Jerrold M. Post

See also Aum Shinrikyo, Davidians, Peoples Temple

Bibliography

Abse, D. W., and R. B. Ulman (1977) "Charismatic Political Leadership and Collective Regression." In *Psychopathology and Political Leadership,* edited by R. S. Robins. Tulane Studies in Political Science, Vol. 16. New Orleans: Tulane University Press.

Bychowski, O. (1948) *Dictators and Disciples.* New York: International Universities Press.

Crayton, J. (1983) "Terrorism and Self-Psychology." In *Terrorism and Violence,* edited by Y. Alexander and D. Friedman.

Galanter, M. (1978) "The 'Relief Effect': A Sociobiological Model for Neurotic Distress and Large Group Therapy." *American Journal of Psychiatry* 135: 5.

——. (1979) "The Moonies: A Psychological Study of Conversion and Membership in a Contemporary Religious Sect." *American Journal of Psychiatry* 136: 2.

——. (1980) "Psychological Induction into the Large Group: Findings from a Modern Religious Sect." *American Journal of Psychiatry* 137: 12.

——. (1986) "Engaged Members of the Unification Church: Impact of a Charismatic Large Group on Adaptation and Behavior." *Arch. Gen. Psychiat.*

Greenacre, P. (1971) Personal Communication.

Post, J. (1984) "Dreams of Glory and the Life Cycle: REFLECTIONS on the Life Course of Narcissistic Leaders." J. *Polit. Mil. Sociol.* 12, 1: 49–60.

——. (1986) "Narcissism and the Charismatic Leader-Follower Relationship." *Political Psychology* 7, 4.

Robins, R., and J. Post. (1997) *Political Paranoia: The Psychopolitics of Hatred.* New Haven, CT: Yale University Press.

Schiffer, I. (1973) *Charisma.* Toronto: University of Toronto Press.

Ulman, R. B., and D. W. Abse. (1983) "The Group Psychology of Mass Madness: Jonestown." *Political Psychology* 4, 4: 637–61.

Volkan, V. (1980) "Narcissistic Personality Organization and Reparative Leadership." *International Journal of Group Psychotherapy* 30: 131–52.

Volkan, V., and N. Itzkowitz. (1984) *The Immortal Ataturk.* Chicago: University of Chicago Press.

Weber, Max. ([1922] 1963) *The Sociology of Religion.* Boston, MA: Beacon Press.

Wildenmann, W. (1984) Personal Communication.

Wilner, A. R. (1984) *The Spellbinders.* New Haven, CT: Yale University Press.

Chen Tao (God's Salvation Church)

Chen Tao ("True" or "Right Way," pronounced "jun dao") is a small new religious movement from Taiwan whose adherents as of this writing were in the United States awaiting salvation from the end of this world. The group provides a prime example of the way new religious movements (NRMs) in many societies are fusing elements of science, science fiction, and technology with established religious traditions to create technologically credible spiritualities. Chen Tao combines Jai-ling ("Perfect Heart") Buddhism, apocalyptic Christianity, flying saucer ideology, and technological metaphors for the spirit. The methods of the group are also a contemporary example of how NRMs become involved with the media and how these groups attempt to publicize prophecy through the media.

Chen Tao began as a quasi-academic "client cult" (an organization geared toward service or therapy for—and demanding only partial commitment from—a clientele) known as the Research Group for the Study of Soul Light, in southern Taiwan in the 1950s. Its mission was the quantification and cultivation of "soul-light," or spiritual energy. The current leader Hon-ming Chen, then on the social science faculty of Chianan (some news reports say Chiayi) Pharmaceutical College, joined the Research Group in 1993. Chen developed a reportedly lifelong psychic ability into full-blown prophetic leadership, predicting in February 1996 the end of the present age, to be preceded by the descent of "the Kingdom of God" on Taiwan and, later, the United States. His prophetic and healing skills convinced up to 160 members to move to the United States late in 1996. The group was first based in San Dimas, California from December 1996 to July 1997, and then in Garland, Texas from August 1997 to April 1998. In May 1998, they moved to Lockport, New York. Though nearly half its members returned to Taiwan in April 1998, and more left after the move to Lockport, a core of believers continued to await the arrival of "God's space aircrafts."

As a religious organization, Chen Tao attracted people both unsatisfied with traditional religions and wealthy enough to shop around Taiwan's religious marketplace; academics, students, physicians, and engineers who found a technologically credible religion appealing. Teacher Chen offered both an explanation for the apparent moral decay of the world and a means to escape it while attempting to remedy it. Members cultivate their souls through meditation, modified traditional exercises, and working to save all living beings. They believe that through multiple incarnations, these practices will allow them to escape from the cycle of death and rebirth and merge with the Heavenly Father. Their more immediate concern was warning others about the "Great Tribulation" late in 1999, a cataclysm brought on by the negative collective karma (actions) of humanity.

Having taken "the role and responsibility of God" to assist in salvation (Chen 1995), Teacher Chen and his followers have fostered a relationship with the mass media through

NEWS RELEASE
March 28, 1998

THE KINGDOM OF GOD
3117 Ridgedale Dr.
Garland, TX, 75041

Tel: (972)864-0667
Fax: (972)864-0667

ANNOUNCEMENT FROM GOD, THE HEAVENLY FATHER:

The Significance of the Salvation of God's Changing into Human Form and the Descending of God'sKingdom

Dear lovely people:

From today (March 31st) on, God is going to start His salvation by means of changing into the human form as well as the descending of God's Kingdom on American continents. But how is His salvation to be operated?

1. It shall start from the spiritual world, followed by people's realization of the truth that "the spiritual body is at the same time the physical body, and the physical body is the spiritual body, too." God shall commence His operation by inspiring the conscience in people's soul. Anyone in American continents may see, in sleep, the other One dressed in white clothing with exactly the same appearance with "this one"--me, wearing a "cowboy hat," or "Chinese straw hat," shaking hands with you, smiling in regard to you, or conversing with you. People will begin receiving, in a gradual way, the teaching from God about how to cultivate ourselves by means of the conscience in our soul so as to become God ourselves, and about the fact that the great tribulation of nuclear wars is going to happen in 1999. After the coming July, people will quite often witness God delivering His regard and salvation to people all over the American Continents.

2. All material things on earth will become alive with their own spiritual life. People may find such objects as TV sets, refrigerators, beds, blankets, shoes, toys, dolls, computers, houses, etc. becoming alive with their own spiritual life or even walking at the house, looking at you, playing with you, chatting with you, and the like.

The first page from a Chen Tao document setting forth the group's ideology and mission. THE KINGDOM OF GOD.

which the group publicized prophetic information and created good karma for themselves. In this arrangement, Chen elicited media interest to spread his millennial message, but that interest resulted in the press garbling his message with unfounded references to "suicide cults" like Heaven's Gate. This garbling is what other groups have sought to avoid by getting direct access to electronic media (creating websites, for example).

Ryan J. Cook

Bibliography

Hon-ming Chen. (1995) *Practical Evidence and Study of the World of God and Buddha: God's Salvation and Education.* Privately published.

——. (1997) *God's Descending in Clouds (Flying Saucers) on Earth to Save People.* Garland, TX: privately published.

——. (1998) *The Arrival of God and the Descending of the Kingdom of God.* Lockport, NY: privately published.

Cook, Ryan J., Dereck M. Daschke, Carrie B. Dohe, and Matthew J. Goff. (1998) "God and Grad Students Descend on Texas: A Field Report on Chen Tao." *Millennial Prophecy Report* 7, 2.

Covert, James. (1997) "Sect Leader Denies Suicide Plan." *Garland News* (25–27 December): 1A, 7A.

——. (1998) "Prepared for Flight with God: Group Talks about Beliefs that Christ Is Coming to Visit." *Garland News* (13 March): 1A–2A.

——. (1998) "Officials Ponder Religious Group's Next Move." *Garland News* (29 March): 5A.

——. (1998) "Religious Leader Draws Media Crowd." *Garland News* (2 April): 1A, 12A.

Festinger, Leon et al. (1956) *When Prophecy Fails.* Minneapolis: University of Minnesota Press.

Stark, Rodney, and William Sims Bainbridge. (1987) *The Future of Religion: Secularization, Revival, and Cult Formation.* Berkeley: University of California Press.

Chernobyl

On the banks of the Pripyat River in Ukraine, near the border of Belarus, a nuclear power plant was hastily constructed in 1983, utilizing outdated 1960s technology. On 26 April 1986, an explosion occurred blowing the lid off the reactor and releasing seven tons of radioactive particles into the atmosphere. A mile-high nuclear cloud rained down isotopes on an unsuspecting population of five million. Because of the direction of the winds after the explosion, Belarus received 70 percent of the fallout (Ukraine received 20 percent and Russia 10 percent). The rest fell on Western Europe.

The Chernobyl disaster is internationally regarded as the world's worst nuclear accident. The actual explosion was only the size of a small atomic bomb. However, in terms of fallout, Chernobyl produced 200 times the radioactive contamination of the atomic bombs dropped on Hiroshima and Nagasaki combined, and one million times the emissions of Three Mile Island in Pennsylvania. While the atmospheric radiation has returned to normal, hot particles of plutonium and cesium remain in the soil, in the water supply, and in plant and animal life. Much of the land will be contaminated for hundreds of thousands of years.

At the end of the twentieth century, two of the four reactors of the Chernobyl Nuclear Power Station remained operational. There were at least fifteen other Chernobyl-type reactors in Eastern Europe and the former Soviet Union, posing a threat for future generations. At least three fires have erupted at the Chernobyl plant since the initial incident. The sarcophagus encasing reactor No. 4 is cracked and still emitting radiation. The International Atomic Energy Agency (IAEA) had warned the world that the reactor site remained unstable, and the United States, Japan, and other nations had pledged funds to help Ukraine permanently shut it down, but the closure of the plant never happened.

In the years following the 1986 Chernobyl disaster, a popular antinuclear and environmental movement began in Ukraine and Belarus, and soon took on apocalyptic characteristics. For pessimists, Chernobyl became associated with biblical prophecy of the end of the world. For optimists, Chernobyl was a watershed event that marked the end of the nuclear era (and the cold war between East and West), as well as the advent of new millennial thinking about a coming global age of peace and security. At the end of the twentieth century, the verdict was still out whether the Chernobyl prophecy was a warning bell which the world heeded, or the unheeded birth pangs of nuclear disasters yet to come.

The Chernobyl Prophecy

> Then the third angel sounded: And a great star fell from heaven, burning like a torch, and it fell on a third of the rivers and on the springs of water. The name of the star is Wormwood. A third of the waters became wormwood, and many people died from the water, because it was made bitter. (Revelation 8:10–11)

"Wormwood" is the English name for a variety of the plant absinthe, with a red-brown or deep-purple bitter stem that makes fresh water undrinkable. Absinthe, the main ingredient of which is vermouth (*vermes* = worm) was used for medicinal purposes to cure intestinal worms. The word "amnesia" (forgetfulness) is derived from the Greek *absinthe.* The botanical associations of the bitter medicinal plant serve as a biblical metaphor for the bitterness and forgetfulness of sin resulting in divine judgment. (Other biblical references to the bitter wormwood plant include Proverbs 5:4; Jeremiah 9:15; 23:15; Lamentations 3:15–19; and Amos 5:7; 6:12.) The Greek word *apsinthos* in Revelation 8:11, translated "wormwood" in English, is often translated *Chornobyl* in Ukrainian Bibles.

The Ukrainian name for the wormwood plant is *Chornobyl* (Ukrainian spelling). In Russian, the name of the plant is *Polyn,* also known as *Chernobyl. Chernyi* means dark or black, while *byl* literally means story (the past tense of existence) and connotes the bitterness of being, the blackness of existence, the darkness of reality. In Slavic languages, the meaning of a word is found in its associations, allusions, and connotations. "To the Russian ear," according to Russian journalist Andrey Illesh, "the word Chernobyl is rich in meanings and tones." Beyond its historical and philological meanings, it also has botanical associations: "*Bylka,* or *bylinka,* is a blade of grass. And the *chernaya bylka,* or *Chernobyl* is another name for wormwood—which invites its popular association with the 1986 disaster near the historic town of Chernobyl" (Illesh 1987: 69).

Chernobyl is first mentioned in twelfth-century manuscripts as a settlement near the River Pripyat in Lithuania (later Poland and Ukraine) and was settled by an apocalyptic sect of Old Believers in 1775, under the headship of one Illarian Petrov. The "Chernobylites" preached the arrival of the Antichrist and the imminent end of the world. Whether they migrated to Chernobyl because they believed the end centered around that town, we do not know. Illarian Petrov, according to Illesh, "bore the rather strange nickname 'Cows Legs' and was known for his extreme fanaticism." The Chernobylites were persecuted because they "refused to pray for the tsar, acknowledge passports, forbade military service and oaths, and behaved in a contrary manner." At the end of the nineteenth century, invited by the Emperor Josef II (who freed Old Believers from taxation), the sect emigrated to Austria (72–73).

The symbolic (or prophetic) connection between nineteenth-century Chernobylites and twentieth-century Chernobyl apocalypticism is a natural one for those who are familiar with the town of Chernobyl in Ukraine. The so-called Chernobyl prophecy is known by practically everyone who lives in the Chernobyl-contaminated region of Ukraine and Belarus. Predictions of the 1986 Chernobyl disasters are thought to be found in the Bible (Revelation 8:10,11 quoted above). The Chernobyl prophecy is also located in the writings of Nostradamus—the famous sixteenth-century French astrologer who some sources believe foresaw and recorded in coded quatrains future world events with remarkable accuracy, including the rise of Hitler, the fall of the Soviet Union, and the end of an age in July 1999.

How Chernobyl Was Interpreted

On a widespread and popular level in Ukraine and Belarus, according to documentary evidence, the 1986 Chernobyl nuclear disaster is considered "an act of God" and assigned religious significance. Chernobyl is interpreted as prophetic (fatalistic or predictive) and apocalyptic (cataclysmic or revelatory) in harmony with a long, popular tradition of Russian apocalyptic eschatology.

In the history of popular apocalyptic interpretation, Revelation 8:10–11 has been identified with a volcanic eruption, a meteorite or comet striking the earth, and global nuclear war. In the refectory of Dionysiou Monastery on Mount Athos (which influenced Russian Orthodox monasticism), there is a fresco illustrating the falling Wormwood star. During the 1950s, the monks interpreted the Wormwood prophecy in terms of atomic bombs. The Wormwood or Chernobyl Star figures prominently in Orthodox Christian apocalyptic eschatology, and the Chernobyl nuclear plume which rained down radioactive isotopes over much of Belarus and Ukraine has been depicted in Russian art and literature as a fatal, falling, prophetic, poisonous star.

In a 1994 national poll, 1,550 Belarusian citizens (including a quota sample of 244 institutional leaders) were asked a variety of questions, including how strongly they disagreed or agreed with the following statement: "The Chernobyl disaster was prophesied in the Revelation of John and was therefore inevitable." On a scale from 1 to 5, the mean response was 2.56 (1=Strongly Disagree, 5= Strongly Agree). The surprisingly high number of "Agree" and "Strongly Agree" responses among certain segments of the population was considered significant (Clark 1994:34). According to a survey of 485 Belarusian citizens commissioned in April 1996 (during the tenth anniversary of Chernobyl), nearly one-third (31.2 percent) considered the Chernobyl nuclear disaster a prophecy specifically predicted in the Bible. In the same survey, 31.5 percent of the respondents answered "yes" to the question: "The 1986 Chernobyl disaster is specifically mentioned (predicted) as a prophecy in the writings of Nostradamus." Only 6.8 percent answered "no" and 61.4 percent "I don't know" (Christensen 1997).

A Spectrum of Interpretations

The sound of the third trumpet in Revelation, announcing the fall of the bitter Wormwood Star from heaven, generally was understood on a popular level in Belarus and Ukraine as an ancient prophecy revealing the end of *something*. What was the end that it signified or warned was coming?

Ethnographic field research in the contaminated region (1991–96) suggests that the Chernobyl explosion and its aftermath was interpreted by significant segments of the Belarusian population (especially retired persons and youth in the contaminated region) as an apocalyptic symbol of divine judgment, national doom, and prophetic warning of the coming final Apocalypse. A variety of religious views were expressed to researchers about what the Chernobyl prophecy meant and about what exactly was coming to an end. Some claimed that the third trumpet of Revelation 8:10–11—announcing the fall of the Wormwood star—referred specifically to the end of time and history. Others hoped it signaled the end of the present time of pain and suffering. Some understood Chernobyl as a divine punishment for Soviet policies of abuse; for others, the symbol pointed to the inevitable consequences of technological and environmental neglect for which humanity is responsible. For some, the trumpet sounded out divine judgment on sin; for others, another Chernobyl may happen unless there are radical changes in the Republic and in the world. While some offered purely secular and rational interpretations of Chernobyl's meaning, others favored distinctly religious apocalyptic interpretations of the nuclear disaster—the only escape from which is public repentance and divine intervention.

To what extent can the spectrum of popular interpretations of Chernobyl be categorized in reference to assumed biblical prophecy (or the prophecies of Nostradamus) about the end of the world? Comparative analysis of published texts and oral history revealed a pattern of interpretation and categories of response that suggested a continuum: nonapocalyptic, prophetic, or apocalyptic (see eschatological matrix).

Religious philosopher, Nikolai Berdyaev, delineates two basic orientations in popular Russian eschatology (nihilistic and apocalyptic thinking) with two polarities (passive and active) (1992: 257). Berdyaev identifies himself as an active and creative apocalyptic thinker (located as "B" on the eschatological matrix). In a 1996 ethnographic study, representative responses to the question—"Do you have a religious opinion about Chernobyl?"—were coded and organized into an eschatological matrix modeled after Berdyaev's basic insight. The matrix was constructed to locate the full spectrum of apocalyptic—prophetic—nonapocalyptic interpretations of Chernobyl, with rational, mythological, and active-passive polarities (Christensen 1997: 160).

Interpretations that fit the *apocalyptic orientation* tended to be passive, pessimistic, or fatalistic. Representative responses include: "Chernobyl is a plague sent by God to punish evil-doers . . ."; "God has forgotten our country"; "We are being punished for the sins of our leaders . . ." (Christensen 1997: 164).

Interpretations that fit the *prophetic orientation* tended to be more optimistic in outlook, hopeful in attitude, responsible in action, provisional in reason, and encouraging in emotion. Prophetic interpreters felt that a catastrophe was imminent. Yet a crisis for them disclosed new opportunities for survival and transformation. In this interpretation, God may signal warning and dispense judgment, but there is divine provision for remedial action on humanity's part to avert a final apocalypse. There is a certain religious activity and willingness to accept responsibility for the future of the world in this view. The words or concepts associated with the prophetically oriented respondents were these: optimism in the midst of crisis; human destiny not absolutely determined; Chernobyl as a "changeable prophecy" or a "prophetic warning" (e.g., God may be trying to warn humanity of potential danger in order to avert a future global disaster).

A third category of nonapocalyptic interpretations was also identified, represented by comments such as these: Chernobyl is the work of human hands; People, not God, are

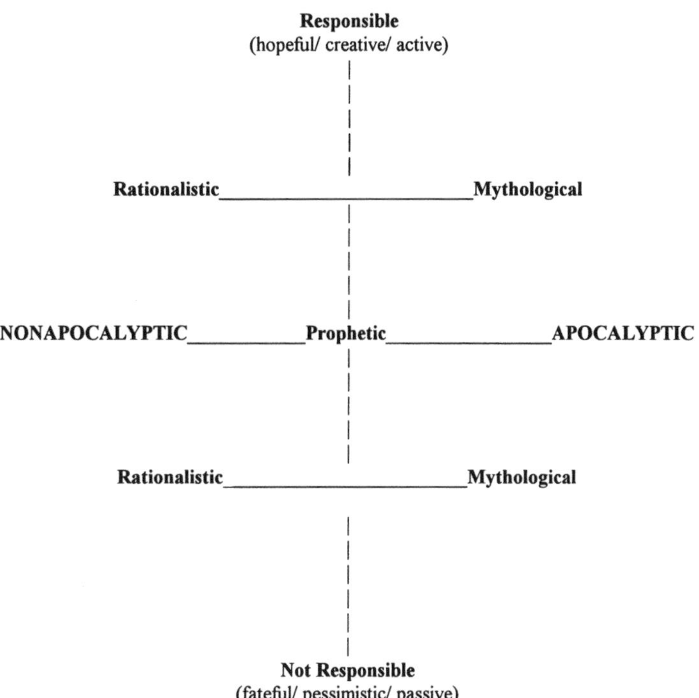

Religious philosopher Nikolai Berdyaev delineates two basic orientations in popular Russian eschatology (nihilistic and apocalyptic thinking) with two polarities (fatalistic and hopeful). Representative responses to the question "Do you have a religious opinion about Chernobyl?" were coded and organized into a full spectrum of interpretations. © CHRISTENSEN 1997.

responsible; Chernobyl was an accident, that is all; The fact that it happened has nothing to do with prophecy. If it's in the Bible, it's a coincidence or misunderstanding. The Russian journalist, Andrey Illesh, in his chapter on "Chernobyl, the Mysticism, 1986," documents popular apocalyptic interpretations of the nuclear disaster but calls such notions "ancient" and "superstitious" (1987: 70).

Conclusion: For Whom the Bell Tolls

At the end of the twentieth century, Chernobyl was understood widely as a preordained and prophetically fulfilled moment in Soviet history, this regardless of the original intent of the biblical writer or the later historical-critical interpretations of Revelation 8:10–11. In the context of post-Soviet Ukraine and Belarus, the so-called Chernobyl prophecy was considered apocalyptic, especially among retired persons and youth (at least in the sense that the Soviet State came to an end in 1991, and the independent statehood of Belarus may also end). There were many who imagined the Chernobyl apocalypse as the end of the present generation of the children whose compromised immune systems and genetic abnormalities may render them unlikely to live out their otherwise natural lives.

In the aftermath of Chernobyl, popular calendars in Minsk and Kiev distinguished the years before and after Chernobyl. Digital clocks in Belarus continued to flash the current time, temperature, and radiation level. Citizens remembered their former life and anticipated future sufferings. The passing of time had not changed apocalyptic consciousness as much as it changed the *meaning* of the End for different segments of the population. In striking apocalyptic language, Russian journalist Alla Yaroshinskaya writes how Chernobyl has changed the course of personal histories, national history, and perhaps even sacred history:

> . . . this ancient wonderland, this forest, these fields and meadows, our whole lives . . . from now on life on earth would not only be divided into epochs and eras, civilizations, religions and political systems, but also into "before" and "after" Chernobyl. The earth would never be the same as it had been before 26 April 1986 at twenty-four minutes past one . . . . (1965:16)

In a case study of Russian apocalyptic eschatology, both statistical and ethnographic research in the Chernobyl region in the 1990s revealed a full continuum of Nonapocalyptic/Prophetic/Apocalyptic tendencies among the general

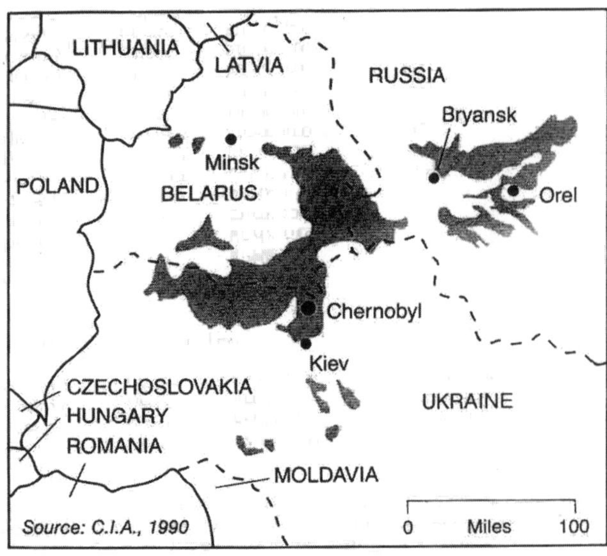

Areas contaminated by radiation from Chernobyl. HTTP://WWW.CYBER-ACADEMY.COM.

population of Belarus. In addition to the Responsible/Not Responsible dialectic of Berdyaev, Rationalistic/Mythological polarities were found. Survey results and ethnographic narratives support the conclusion that the Chernobyl disaster was a historical marker, a turning point in Ukrainian, Belarusian, and Soviet history.

The United Soviet Socialist Republic came to an abrupt end five years after the Chernobyl catastrophe. The official Russian Communist Party ended after the 19 August 1991 coup, and the Soviet Union officially ended when Gorbachev resigned and transferred political (and nuclear) power to Yeltsin in December 1991. But, in terms of millennial markers, the Soviet utopian dream died on 26 April 1986.

Elsewhere in this volume (Marking Millennial Moments), Christensen and Savage argue that the Chernobyl catastrophe of 26 April 1986 was a decisive apocalyptic event in the history of Rus, marking the end of an age. The disaster certainly served as a revelatory moment in Russia and around the world, a ringing of the bell that called for global attention, as Mikhail Gorbachev recorded in his 1996 *Memoirs:*

> *Chernobyl was a bell* calling mankind to understand what kind of age we live in. It made people recognize the danger of careless or even criminally negligent attitudes towards the environment. . . . Chernobyl shed light on many of the sicknesses of our system as a whole. Everything that had built up over the years converged in this drama . . . . (1996: 193, emphasis mine)

Michael J. Christensen

See also Marking Millennial Moments

Bibliography

Berdyaev, Nikolai. ([1947] 1992) *The Russian Idea.* New York: Lindisfarne Press.

Boym, Svetlana. (1994) *Common Places: Mythologies of Everyday Life in Russia.* Cambridge, MA: Harvard University Press.

Calian, Carnegie S. (1965) *The Significance of Eschatology in the Thoughts of Nicolas Berdyaev.* Leiden: E.J. Brill.

Christensen, Michael J. (1997) "The Chernobyl Apocalypse: A Theological Case Study." Ph.D. diss., Drew University, Madison, NJ.

Clark, Peter. (1994) "Belarus—Let's Understand Ourselves and Our Future: Summary of the Descriptive Statistics from a Survey of National Public Opinion." Gomel, Belarus: The Center for Sociological Research—ORACUL, World Vision International, (Cornell University).

Gale, Robert. (1988) *Final Warning: The Legacy of Chernobyl.* New York: Warner Books.

Gofman, John. (1993) *Radiation and Chernobyl.* San Francisco: Committee for Nuclear Responsibility, Inc.

Gorbachev, Mikhail. (1996) *Memoirs.* New York: Double Day.

Gould, Peter. (1990) *Fire in the Rain: The Democratic Consequences of Chernobyl.* Cambridge, U.K.: Polity Press in association with Basil Blackwell, Oxford.

Illesh, Andrey V. (1987) *Chernobyl: A Russian Journalist's Eye Witness Account.* New York: Richardson and Steirman.

Kull, Steven. (1992) *Burying Lenin: The Revolution in Soviet Ideology and Foreign Policy.* Boulder, CO: Westview Press.

Lifton, Robert Jay. (1987) *The Future of Immortality and Other Essays for a Nuclear Age.* New York: Basic Books.

Mackay, Louis, ed. (1988) *Something in the Wind: Politics After Chernobyl.* London: Pluto Press.

Marples, David. (1986) *Chernobyl and Nuclear Power in the USSR.* New York: St. Martin's Press.

———. (1988) *The Social Impact of the Chernobyl Disaster.* New York: St. Martin's Press.

———. (1996) *Belarus: From Soviet Rule to Nuclear Catastrophe.* New York: St. Martin's Press.

Medvedev, Grigori. (1991) *The Truth about Chernobyl.* New York: Basic Books.

Medvedev, Zhores A. (1990) *The Legacy of Chernobyl.* New York: Norton.

Read, Piers P. (1993) *Ablaze: The Story of Chernobyl.* New York: Random House.

Richard, Graham. (1989) *The Chernobyl Catastrophe.* Great Disasters Series. New York: Bookwright Press.

Robert, Henry C., ed. (1982) *The Complete Prophecies of Nostradamus,* new rev. ed. New York: Nostradamus & Co.

Sich, Alexander R. (1994) "The Chernobyl Accident Revisited: Source Term Analysis and Reconstruction of Events During the Active Phase." Ph.D. diss., Massachusetts Institute of Technology.

Ulam, Adam. (1992) *The Communists: The Story of Power and Lost Illusions 1948–1991*. New York: Scribner's.

Valentin, Jacques. (1960) *The Monks of Mount Athos*, translated by Diana Athill. London: Andre Deutsch.

Yaroshinskaya, Alla. (1995) *Chernobyl: The Forbidden Truth*, translated by Michelle Kahn and Julia Sallabank. Lincoln, NE: University of Nebraska Press.

Zaprudnik, Jan. (1993) *Belarus at a Crossroads in History*. Boulder, CO: Westview Press.

China

Messianic and millenarian movements have been a powerful force in Chinese history since at least the second century CE. Indeed, several times such movements have been instrumental in hastening the demise of a ruling dynasty.

Most Chinese messianic movements reflect a longing for a Perfect Ruler *(Zhen Wang)*, a "sage king," who will rid the world of evil and injustice and establish a reign of peace, harmony, and benevolent government. The ideal of the Perfect Ruler, traceable to the classical thinkers of China's antiquity, merged with Buddhist messianism in the first century CE and profoundly affected all subsequent millenarian movements. Such movements appeared especially, though not always, in times of intense, disruptive social change or dynastic decline, and were usually led by charismatic figures who mobilized mass movements around the notion that salvation for the faithful was imminent.

The earliest Chinese examples of utopian thinking are the philosophical schools of the Eastern Zhou era (770–256 BCE), the classical age of Chinese thought. Classical philosophers looked to the past for the ideal society or envisioned it in a remote inaccessible land. Confucius (551–479 BCE), for example, thought the solution to the social problems of his age was to recreate the golden age of the Sage Kings Yao and Shun, the benevolent mythical rulers of remote antiquity who oversaw a realm of peace and justice. On the other hand, Laozi (Lao-tzu), legendary father of philosophical Daoism (Taoism), maintained that utopia was a world in which people returned to their original state of primitive innocence, and led simple lives in small, isolated communities without interference from government. A third school, the Moists, promoted a philosophy of universal love, and most important for our purposes believed in creating the "Great Unity" *(Datong)*, a world of peace, harmony, wise rule, and equality. The idea was later incorporated into Confucian thought and used to recast Confucius as a visionary reformer, most recently in the 1890s by the philosopher Kang Youwei.

In addition to the more philosophically oriented utopian ideas, the ancient Chinese believed that utopias existed in remote regions to the west and east of China proper. The first deity actually linked to millenarian themes, Queen Mother of the West (Xi Wang Mu), controlled both immortality and the stars, and lived in a perfect world on Mount Kunlun in the far northwest. Originally a deity of the privileged elite, by the Han dynasty (202 BCE–220 CE) she had been transformed into a popular savior goddess venerated by ordinary Chinese. Her following was such that in 3 BCE, as the Han dynasty entered a period of decline and social disorder, processions of thousands of believers converged on the capital, Chang'an (modern Xi'an), thinking that the end of the world was at hand and that only those who possessed a magic talisman to demonstrate their faith would be spared and granted immortality when she arrived.

The Chinese also believed that a number of fairy islands lay off the east coast of China. The islands of Penglai (Proliferating Weeds), Fangzhang (Square Fathom), and Yingzhou (Ocean Continent) all were said to be inhabited by immortals, but, again, these idyllic lands were the province of the elite, not the average Chinese peasant. In fact, the First Emperor of Qin (259–210 BCE), unifier of China, famously spent the last years of his life in a fruitless quest for the islands hoping to achieve his own immortality. In the end, his immortality came instead through the monumental tomb in which he tried to recreate his entire empire to take into the afterlife.

Early Chinese Millenarian Movements

At the end of the Latter Han dynasty, in the second century CE, the first genuine millenarian movements emerged in which the faithful believed that a divinely inspired individual would deliver them from social chaos and create a paradise on earth. Two important movements led by Daoist masters arose in response to the calamitous disorder of the period.

The Yellow Turban uprising of 184, the first religiously motivated rebellion in Chinese history, which emerged mainly in central and eastern China, envisioned the imminent arrival of the Yellow Lord, who would establish the era of Great Peace (Taiping). Their leader, Zhang Jue, a faith healer, based his movement on the *Classic of Great Peace (Taiping Jing)*, a Daoist text that described the ideal society that would be established through the intervention of the Yellow Lord, but only afterward would pass through a series of cataclysmic events. The leaders of the revolt were captured and executed in 184, but adherents to the movement continued sporadic uprisings for the next several decades and were instrumental in hastening the fall of the declining dynasty.

The year of the revolt, 184, has special significance for millenarian movements, because it was a *jiazi* year, the first year in the sixty-year cycle of the Chinese calendar. *Jiazi* years, therefore, carried with them a sense of transition and renewal similar to the millennial mark in the Christian tradition, and were for this reason often the date calculated for uprisings to assist the arrival of the apocalypse and the new era.

The second major movement, the Five Pecks of Rice (Wu Dou Mi), later known as the Way of the Celestial Masters (Tian Shi Dao), derived its name from the contribution the faithful were expected to make to the communal coffers. The movement was founded by Zhang Daoling (34?–156? CE), who is revered as the first Daoist patriarch. Zhang's source of inspiration was a vision in which Laozi brought him a new scripture, the *Orthodox One (Zhengyi)* or the Authority of the Sworn Oath, and ordered him to rid the world of decadence and return it to its original perfect state for believers, the chosen. The movement spread throughout Sichuan and Shaanxi under the leadership of Zhang's son and later his grandson, Zhang Lu (fl. 190–220), and resulted in the creation of an independent theocratic state that existed from 186 to 216 CE. Followers were organized in communal organizations in which they were registered and ranked according to a strict hierarchy of the elect based on religious merit. Recitation of sacred texts, such as the *Classic of the Way and Its Power (Dao De Jing)*, the practice of special breathing exercises, and performance of communal religious ceremonies, among other things, gained adherents religious merit and absolution of their sins. In addition, the state promoted work for the public good, such as providing free food for the needy. While not always able to achieve their ends, the programs were intended to assist in creating a utopia on earth. Unlike their rebellious counterparts, the Way of the Celestial Masters survived by a political accommodation with the warlord Cao Cao whereby Zhang Lu relinquished political authority in exchange for recognition of the religious authority of the movement. For this reason, the movement continued to thrive and eventually became recognized as the orthodox Daoist tradition in China.

Between the fall of the Han dynasty in 220 CE and reunification in 589, China was divided into many small, mutually hostile states. This was a period of intense religious fervor. Confucianism, a form of which had become official orthodoxy during the Han, lost credibility as a value system. People sought refuge—from unrelenting internecine warfare as well as periodic invasions from steppe people to the north—in religious Daoism and Buddhism, the latter having been introduced from India in the first century CE.

During the fourth and fifth centuries periodic Daoist-inspired popular rebellions were carried out in the name of Li Hong, the Perfect Lord, who was said to be the reincarnation of Laozi. The transformation of Laozi into a savior, a "sage on the throne," appears to have been part of an effort by a family once associated with the Celestial Masters movement to legitimize its own dynastic pretensions. Eventually, however, the sage was transformed into the popular messianic figure, who would appear to save believers from the cataclysm of floods, epidemics, wars, and famine that would accompany the apocalyptic struggle to rid the world of evil and reign over an empire of great peace and abundance.

Li Hong-inspired rebellions occurred as late as the Song dynasty (960–1279), but by the late second century, many Buddhist beliefs had become part of the Chinese worldview in what Erik Zürcher has called the "Buddho-Daoist hybridization" (1981: 34). Buddhist conceptions of cycles of time ending in *kalpic* transitions—transitions characterized by plagues, terrifying storms that darken the world, and demon warriors to cleanse the world of evil—became part of popular religious belief. This was accompanied by prophesies that the Buddha's doctrine *(dharma)* would become corrupted over a three-stage period and the world would descend into decadence and corruption, only to be revived with the appearance of the future Buddha, known as Maitreya.

Chinese believers, imbued with Daoist notions of periodic cosmic crises, transformed these ideas in a number of important ways that formed a new and potentially volatile strain of popular belief. Most significantly, in the popular imagination, Maitreya became the world redeemer thought to be waiting for final days of the *dharma*, when he would descend to earth to save all believers, rid the world of evil, and usher in the new golden age on earth. Maitreya differed from other Buddhas in that salvation entailed radically transforming this world. Believers need not await being transported to an other-worldly paradise, such as the Pure Land of the Buddha Amitabha. For most believers this mattered little, since Maitreya was not prophesied to arrive for tens of thousands of years. However, others saw in the political corruption, social chaos, and natural disasters of this world signs of the imminent turn of the *kalpa* and arrival of Maitreya. The cult of Maitreya and its later permutations were particularly subversive in the eyes of the state, since they became the symbol of many antidynastic movements intent on helping to speed up the arrival of the new world. This sort of apocalyptic vision, and particularly the idea of messianic saviors or "Enlightened Ones," was also extended to some bodhisattvas, beings who have experienced enlightenment but chosen to stay in the sentient world to assist others to achieve it as well. A messianic figure known as "Prince Moonlight" (Yueguang tongzi), who was contemporaneous with the appearance of

EXCERPT FROM THE *TAI-PING CHIU-SHIN-KO* (TAIPING SONGS ON WORLD SALVATION)

[I]n ancient times men's minds were still clear and their true origin had not yet been lost; they all knew how to honor and worship our Heavenly Father, the Supreme Lord and Great God. At that time every family was instructed and every household properly taught, so that no one was ignorant of his duty to praise His merit and virtue and give thanks for the favor of Heaven. But coming to later generations, the farther removed in point of time, the more their origin was lost, until they gradually became deluded by the demons and suddenly strayed into the demons' path, molding images in clay and dressing wooden idols in gold; their various evil practices are beyond enumeration. Therefore, our Heavenly Father, the Supreme Lord and Great God, angered at man's perversity and deploring the loss of the true doctrine, especially sent his first-born son, the Heavenly Elder Brother, Jesus, down into the world to save mankind and to suffer extreme misery and grief in order to redeem mankind's sins.

. . . Our Heavenly Father loved the world most fervently and was fearful lest men of the world should not be speedily converted, all to revert to the true Way and unitedly to enjoy true happiness; therefore, He sent our Sovereign, the T'ien Wang [Hong Xiuquan], into the world, as the true mandated Sovereign to exterminate the demons [Manchu/Qing rulers of China], awaken the world, and soothe the myriad states that they might equally enjoy true felicity. His wisdom and intelligence are endowed by Heaven; his knowledge far exceeds that of the common man; generously benevolent and compassionate, his liberality is vast and boundless. In eradicating the demons and in tranquilizing the good, his rule and his teachings are all in conformity with Heaven's law; in decapitating the evil and in preserving the correct, the right to preserve and to kill is exercised with extreme justice. Hence, since the commencement of the righteous uprising at Chin-t'ien, the people have exultingly rejoiced; he has exterminated the host of demons, burned and destroyed demon temples, swept away all that is corrupt and abominable, and caused men to revert to the pure and the true. These, his magnificent exploits and virtues, have not been equaled over the previous several thousand years.

Source: Michael, Franz, and Zhang Lizhong, eds. (1971) *The Taiping Rebellion: History and Documents.* Vol. 2. Seattle: University of Washington Press, 239–40.

the Li Hong cults, is a prime example of this tendency and also shows how extensively Chinese religions borrowed from each other and overlapped at the popular level. In this case, the Chinese took what had been a minor figure in Indian accounts of the life of the Buddha and endowed him with all the messianic features of his Daoist counterpart, the True King. Prince Moonlight was eventually superseded in the popular imagination by Maitreya, though some scholars argue that even as late as the nineteenth century he figures in the mythology of secret societies.

Manichaeism, introduced from Persia into western China during the Tang dynasty (618–907), was a second possible important foreign religion affecting millenarian thought in China. However, it should be noted that recent scholarship has downplayed its influence, arguing that the idea of a struggle between the forces of good and evil characteristic of Manichaeism can be found in indigenous apocalyptic thinking that predates the Tang dynasty. Its founder, Mani (c. 216–74), also believed that history progressed through a three-stage struggle between the forces of Light (God; Good) and Darkness (Satan; Evil). Light would emerge victorious in the third stage, but only if believers led a pure and puritanical life, achieved through strict vegetarianism, fasting, and prayer.

The White Lotus Teachings

Over the next several centuries the above traditions interacted and evolved producing the religious tradition collectively known as the White Lotus teachings. The origins of the White Lotus teachings are still debated, but many scholars trace them back to Mao Ziyuan (1086–1166), a practitioner of Pure Land Buddhism, who founded a pious vegetarian group by that name. Over the next three centuries, the movement took a more popular turn, giving rise to a wide variety of religious groups that incorporated elements of religious Daoism, Maitreyism, and folk religion into their belief system. At the end of the Yuan dynasty (1280–1368), some of these groups had metamorphosed into a vast, multifaceted millenarian movement known as the Red Turbans, intent on driving the Mongols from China. The leader of one wing of the movement, Han Shantong (d. 1355), declared the imminent arrival of Maitreya and the birth of the "Young Prince of Light." Eventually Han was captured and executed, but others carried on, and out of the movement emerged the founder of the succeeding dynasty, Zhu Yuanzhang, who promptly proscribed the teachings once he ascended the throne. Some scholars argue that the very name of the dynasty Ming (1368–1644), which means "Illumination," is indicative of Manichaean influence on the founder, while others point to the Han precedent of "Prince Moonlight," as the most important influence.

Although proscribed, the White Lotus tradition underwent extensive development during the Ming dynasty. The main elements of the teachings are as follows. The principal deity, the Eternal Venerable Mother *(Wusheng Laomu)*, is the progenitor of the human race. Over the eons humans have forgotten their origin and fallen from grace. Distressed, the Venerable Mother vows to spare the repentant from the coming apocalypse and return them to the "native land of true emptiness" *(zhenkong jiaxiang)*, where they will enjoy peace and affluence forever. Before the elect are reunited with the Venerable Mother they must attend the Dragon Flower Assembly, which is convened to verify who are the chosen. White Lotus eschatology also incorporated the three-stage progression of Buddhas, but diminished the role of Maitreya to that of Venerable Mother's messenger during the *kalpic* transition. By the seventeenth century, a substantial body of religious tracts, known as "Precious Scrolls" *(baojuan)*, had been written by numerous authors containing various formulations of this basic myth. Since possession of these scriptures was punishable by death, they were secretly copied by hand and distributed around northern China.

Religious sects were a constant source of concern for imperial governments, especially after the mid-eighteenth century when they began to appear in ever greater numbers. The sects were by force of circumstance secret and had no centralized organization, which made it very difficult for the government to control them. Even so, they were still capable of forming extensive regional networks based on shared beliefs and master-disciple relationships. While most sects were usually small and localized, in some cases families became hereditary religious practitioners with geographically broad networks of followers developed over many generations. For example the descendants of Wang Sen (d. 1619) of Stone Buddha Wharf in modern Hebei province, carried on for several centuries despite periodic government persecutions.

White Lotus sects were persecuted by imperial governments, because their belief Venerable Mother was subversive of the universal authority of the imperial order. In addition, orthodox Confucians considered sectarian relationships heretical, because they were based on one's seniority in the sect, rather than age or kinship, as well as their relatively egalitarian attitude toward gender relations. Many sects never acted upon the millenarian aspects of the teachings. Nevertheless, governments were always suspicious of them because periodically ambitious and charismatic individuals would use the teachings to incite rebellion. Significant rebellions associated with variations of the White Lotus teachings occurred in 1644, 1774, 1796, and 1814. Most were of brief duration, though the rebellion of 1796 took nearly eight years to bring under control, covered parts of five provinces, nearly bankrupted the imperial treasury, and is considered by many to be the first significant indication of the decline of the Qing dynasty.

Millenarian themes were also a part of the ritual and ideology of China's famous secret societies, which, though initially founded in the eighteenth century as mutual-aid societies, came to be associated with organized crime. The most famous of these, the Heaven and Earth society *(Tiandihui)* also known as the "Triads," had as at least part of its ideology similar notions of a coming apocalypse. However, as with many of the strictly religious sects, the millenarian themes while important in their ritual and foundation myths were for the most part downplayed and never acted upon.

The Taiping Rebellion

The most spectacular millenarian movement in late imperial China was the Taiping Rebellion (1850–64), which brought together indigenous and Christian messianic beliefs. It was led by Hong Xiuquan (1813–64) a frustrated scholar of the Hakka minority, who had repeatedly failed the imperial examinations. After one such failure he received a Christian tract from a Chinese convert, which he read only after a subsequent failure brought on a hallucinatory dream. The tract convinced him that he was Jesus Christ's younger brother. Subsequently he created a religious movement known as the God-worshipers Society that was a mixture of traditional Chinese eschatology and Christian salvationism. In 1850, they rebelled, in part reacting to anti-Hakka ethnic tensions. Instilled with Hong's sense of mission the rebel army captured much of Central China. In 1853, Hong made Nanjing his Heavenly Capital, the "New Jerusalem" promised in the Christian book of Revelation. However, factional struggles combined with the renewed vigor of Qing armies finally resulted in their defeat in 1864.

The name Hong chose for his movement clearly shows the multiple sources of Taiping ideology. The Heavenly Kingdom of Great Peace (*Taiping Tianguo*) combines "Taiping," the ideal that inspired the Yellow Turbans in 184, and "Tianguo," the Judeo-Christian vision of God's kingdom on earth. In short, Hong believed that he was the instrument through which God's Kingdom, in the form of the Great Peace, could be realized on earth. Other important characteristics of the Taiping ideology were the equality of men and the liberation of women, though this was not always the case in practice. The same should be said of Taiping reform of the land tenure system that was supposed to provide equitable land distribution, with no distinction between the sexes in terms of allotments. Nevertheless, Hong's brand of messianic salvationism, which was both anti-Confucian and anti-Manchu, was without question the most radical imperial China ever witnessed.

Twentieth-Century Chinese Revolutionaries

In a certain sense, twentieth-century Chinese revolutionaries, particularly the communists, have operated much in the same mode as the earlier millenarian sectarians in their attempt to change the world. The religious fervor of the Red Guard movement unleashed against the Chinese Communist party in 1966 by Mao Zedong (1893–1976), had many of the trappings of a millenarian movement. Youthful Red Guards, after having experiences approaching religious ecstasy at gigantic rallies in Beijing, fanned out across China to spread Mao's message of salvation and crush anyone who opposed him. Mao in the eyes of his followers was the savior of China, the "Great Helmsman," who would steer China toward realization of a selfless communist paradise on earth.

Since the death of Mao and the relative easing of the party's control over China in the final decades of the twentieth century messianic sects of the more traditional sort have begun to reappear in China, sometimes led by charismatic figures offering salvation. This has been a particular response to the social disruption caused by the ongoing effort to shift to a market economy. People are once again seeking solace in messianic cults, especially in the rural areas of the country. Only time will tell whether social conditions will push one of these movements to the forefront to develop a mass following that will once again threaten the established order.

Conclusion

Chinese millenarian movements have a history that can be traced at least to the second century. Generally such movements appeal to marginalized elements, who are alienated from the prevailing orthodoxy. Sectarian movements, as they do in other cultures, provide such people with a sense of group solidarity. In some instances, the leadership of such movements can lead to power and influence by irregular means. Usually they interpret times of economic distress, social turmoil, and natural disasters as signals of the advent of the new age, an age in which they would be free of exploitation and injustice. Frequently, these beliefs would lead to open rebellion. Therefore, since they are subversive of the established order, such movements were for most of Chinese history branded as heterodox and persecuted by governments.

Blaine Gaustad

See also Asia, Messianism

Bibliography

Bauer, Wolfgang. (1976) *China and the Search for Happiness: Recurring Themes in Four Thousand Years of Chinese Cultural History*, translation of *China und die Hoffung auf Glück* (Munich: Carl Hanser Verlag, 1971) by Michael Shaw. New York: Seabury.

de Groot, Jan Jacob Maria. ([1940] 1976) *Sectarianism and Religious Persecution in China.* 2 vols. Amsterdam: Johannes Muller; reprint, Taipei: Ch'eng Wen Publishing Co.

Gaustad, Blaine. (1994) "Religious Sectarianism and the State in Mid-Qing China: Background to the White Lotus Uprising of 1796–1804," Ph.D. diss., University of California at Berkeley.

Ma Xisha, and Han Bingfang. (1992) *Zhongguo Minjian Zongjiao Shi* (History of Chinese popular religion). Shanghai: Shanghai People's Press.

Naquin, Susan. (1976) *Millenarian Rebellion in China: The Eight Trigrams Uprising of 1813.* New Haven, CT: Yale University Press.

——. (1981) *Shantung Rebellion: The Wang Lun Uprising of 1774.* New Haven, CT: Yale University Press.

——. (1982) "Connections Between Rebellions: Sect Family Networks in Qing China." *Modern China* 8: 3.

——. (1985) "The Transmission of White Lotus Sectarianism in Late Imperial China." In *Popular Culture in Late Imperial China*, edited by D. Johnson, A. Nathan, and E. Rawski. Berkeley: University of California Press.

Overmyer, Daniel. (1976) *Folk Buddhist Religion: Dissenting Sects in Late Traditional China.* Cambridge, MA: Harvard University Press.

——. (1999) *Precious Volumes: An Introduction to Chinese Sectarian Scriptures of the Sixteenth and Seventeenth Centuries.* Cambridge, MA: Harvard University Press.

Ownby, David. (1999) "Chinese Millenarian Traditions: The Formative Age," *American Historical Review* (December) 104: 5.

Robinet, Isabelle. (1997) *Taoism: Growth of a Religion*, translated by Phyllis Brooks. Stanford, CA: Stanford University Press.

Seidel, Anna. (1969–70) "The Image of the Perfect Ruler in Early Taoist Messianism: Lao-tzu and Li Hung." *History of Religions* 9: 216–47.

Shek, Richard. (1980) "Religion and Society in Late Ming: Sectarianism and Popular Thought in Sixteenth and Seventeenth Century China." Ph.D. diss., University of California at Berkeley.

Suzuki Chusei. (1982) "Shincho Chuki ni okeru Minkan Shukyo Kessha to sono Sennen okoku Undo e no Keisha" (Popular religious societies in the mid-Qing and their tendencies towards millenarianism). In *Sennen Okoku Teki Minshu Undo no Kenkyu* (Studies on millenarian popular movements), edited by Suzuki Chûsei. Tokyo: Tokyo Daigaku Shuppankai.

ter Haar, Barend J. (1992) *The White Lotus Teaching in Chinese Religious History*. Leiden: E.J. Brill.

——. (1998) *The Ritual and Mythology of the Chinese Triads: Creating an Identity*. Leiden: E.J. Brill.

Zürcher, Erik. (1981) "Eschatology and Messianism in Early Chinese Buddhism." In *Leyden Studies in Sinology* edited by Wilt L. Idema. Leiden: E. J. Brill.

——. (1982) "'Prince Moonlight': Messianism and Eschatology in Early Medieval Chinese Buddhism." *T'oung Pao* 68, 1–3: 1–75.

Christian Identity

Christian Identity is the most influential religious position among White supremacists. It is, however, difficult to precisely describe because of its lack of any central organization. It is not organized as a denomination and has no central institutions. Hence there is no authority structure capable of definitively distinguishing orthodox beliefs from heretical ones. This makes Identity a community with unclear boundaries, knit together only by beliefs that have a common family resemblance to one another.

The beliefs most commonly associated with Christian Identity are the following: (1) persons of northwestern European ancestry are considered the direct, biological descendants of the biblical tribes of Israel; (2) Jews are regarded as the offspring, through Cain, of a sexual liaison between Eve and Satan; and (3) the present is believed to be at or near the endtimes, which will feature a final battle between "Israelites" (i.e., white "Aryans"), on the one hand, and Jews and non-Whites, on the other.

History

The immediate origins of Christian Identity lie in the British-Israel (or Anglo-Israel) movement, which developed in Great Britain during the second half of the nineteenth century and subsequently spread to other parts of the English-speaking world, including the United States. British-Israelism asserted that the inhabitants of the British Isles as well as descendants of northwestern Europeans in general were direct offspring of the "ten lost tribes of Israel." The tribes, they believed, had wandered north and west to eventually populate Great Britain and adjacent areas. British-Israelism was initially well disposed toward the Jewish people, whom they saw as literal relatives.

Nonetheless, twentieth-century British-Israelism became increasingly anti-Semitic, particularly in the United States and western Canada. The major American British-Israel organization, the Anglo-Saxon Federation of America, founded by Howard Rand about 1930, spread an overtly anti-Semitic version of British-Israelism throughout the country during the Depression years. Rand was greatly aided in this effort by William J. Cameron, a Ford Motor Company executive who had earlier edited Henry Ford's notoriously anti-Semitic newspaper, the *Dearborn Independent*. Rand and Cameron established the organizational infrastructure from which Christian Identity arose.

Christian Identity began to emerge as a distinct religious tendency in America after World War II. Its separation from British-Israelism, however, was never complete. Some American groups continued to advance the highly anti-Semitic Anglo-Israelism developed by Rand and Cameron (e.g., the America's Promise Ministry, under Sheldon Emry and David Barley). Christian Identity's initial nucleus consisted of three preachers in Southern California: Bertrand Comparet, William Potter Gale, and Wesley Swift. All were closely associated with the anti-Semitic political organizer Gerald L. K. Smith.

Identity gradually spread from its West Coast beginnings, but, like British-Israelism, it never developed a denominational structure. Consequently, it appeared in many variants, including not only churches but also different styles of right-wing extremism. These have included neo-Nazi groups, such as Richard Girnt Butler's Aryan Nations; Ku Klux Klan organizations, such as Thom Robb's; and local paramilitary groups, such as elements of the Posse Comitatus. Hence Identity now overlaps upon many other styles of extremist organization.

While Identity may be found throughout the United States, it has been weakest in the Northeast and strongest in

INDEX

CHRISTIAN IDENTITY AND MANUAL OF ARMS

CHRISTIAN BASICS

1 Baptism: Into the name of the Father,of the Son,by the Holy Spirit!
2 Begotten (not born)!
3 Christian, what is?
4 Church, (Out-Called) Civil Government.
5 The Commandments
6 The Law,i.e., Civil,Ceremonial,Commandments, and Dietary.
7 Covenant, [Old] & [New].
8 Faith,
9 Fasting
10 Gospel
11 Grace, the unmerited Gift!
12 Healing
13 Hell
14 Holy Spirit
15 Holy Days
16 Kingdom of God
17 Laying on of hands!
18 Marriage, Divorce, Child rearing and domesticity.
19 Millennium
20 Overcoming, and Obedience by the Holy Spirit!
21 Prayer
22 Prophecy
23 Repentence
24 Resurrection
25 Reconciliation
26 Sabbath, [the test commandment]
27 Salvation
28 Satan, Demons, Angels.
29 Sin, which is NOT transgression!
30 Transgression
31 Soul
32 Tithing
33 Trials
34 Worldiness
35 Prosperity
36 OUR FATHER IN HEAVEN!

Jesus Christ certified and approved the entire Bible when He returned from the Father with His curriculum...which He gave to His disciples...Luke 24:44.

God is calling out certain ones to take His Truth to the world. Those who study His Word and apply its meaning...will be called for duty. To each of us there comes'in our lifetime a special moment when we are figuratively tapped on the shoulder and offered that opportunity to do a very special thing which is unique...yet fitted for our talent. What a tragedy if that moment finds' us unprepared and unqualified for our FATHER'S WORK!

Index of the "Christian Identity and Manual of Arms," a basic outline of the beliefs of the movement. THE DIDACHE FOUNDATION OF TRUTH.

parts of the Ozarks, southern Appalachians, Southwest, and Pacific Northwest. Because of its fragmented character, all estimates of total size have been guesses based upon such factors as the known size of some groups, number of groups, and periodicals and websites. These estimates generally cover a substantial range—from about 10,000 to 100,000—but even at the upper limits of the range, suggest a movement that remains extremely small. Its influence, however, has been far greater than its size suggests.

Data is comparably fragmentary concerning social background. Evidence to date (much of it anecdotal) suggests that members of Identity groups are not significantly different from surrounding populations in terms of such variables as age, income, education, and marital status. Some Identity groups have made concerted efforts to recruit from populations thought to be particularly alienated or marginalized. These have included economically troubled farmers, skinheads, and White prison inmates. While such efforts have enjoyed some success, the numbers drawn in do not appear to have been large enough to change Identity's overall composition.

Political Activities

The political orientations of Identity adherents have ranged from complete withdrawal to violent engagement. Withdrawal has taken the form of "survivalism," i.e., the cultivation of a lifestyle marked by both physical withdrawal and self-sufficiency. Those who adopt such a lifestyle have sometimes done so as individual families and sometimes as small communities.

Communal separation has had varied political consequences. In some cases, such as that of Pastor Dan Gayman's Church of Israel in Schell, Missouri, it has been accomplished with minimum friction with the authorities. In other cases, however, the separation has been accompanied by the failure to observe legal requirements. A case in point was the predominantly Identity Freemen compound near Jordan, Montana, which was the scene of a standoff with the FBI in 1996.

While most Identity believers appear to live in ways that do not bring them into conflict with the authorities, there have been conspicuous exceptions. These have tended to be among those who believe in the inevitability of a war between "Aryan Israelites" on one side and Jews and non-Whites on the other. While some survivalists also believe such a war will eventually take place, others in Identity have felt compelled to try to set the struggle off through deliberate violent acts. The most dramatic case was that of "The Order" (also called "The Silent Brotherhood" or "Bruders Schweigen") which, in the mid-1980s, engaged in a brief insurgency against the federal government. While only about half the organization's members were Identity, those that were saw such an undertaking as consistent with their religious commitments.

Since the late 1980s, more vigorous government intelligence gathering and prosecutions have reduced the propensity of Identity followers to engage in violence. However, an unknown number of Identity believers are also members of militia groups. Consequently, it is extremely difficult to determine the degree of Identity influence in these paramilitary organizations.

The 1990s have presented particularly acute challenges to Christian Identity. By this decade, the leadership generation that had assumed its roles in the 1950s and 1960s had died or was on the verge of retirement. The 1995 bombing of the Oklahoma City Federal Building greatly increased public concern about right-wing terrorism. Although it was never clear whether Timothy McVeigh had any Christian Identity associations, the bombing made the antigovernment subculture a major public concern for the first time. Partly in response to these stresses, the label "Christian Identity" itself has fallen out of favor within the movement (indeed, there were always Identity figures who used other terms, such as "Kingdom Message"). "Identity" was seen as a term so stigmatizing and so closely associated with violent political dissent that even figures whose belief system was clearly Identity, such as Pastor Dan Gayman, do not use it.

Beliefs

Because of their conviction that they are the biological descendants of the biblical Israelites, Identity believers think of themselves as God's elect, the instruments for the fulfillment of his will on earth. British-Israelism held a similar view, but tended to identify nations, especially Great Britain and the United States, as the divine agents. Identity has been much more overtly racial, imputing to White "Aryans" a special status in the divine scheme and implicitly or explicitly devaluing non-Whites.

A theology of anti-Semitism lies at the heart of Christian Identity, for whom Jews are essentially non-White. More significantly, they see Jews as impostors, masquerading as Israelite descendants. The most fully developed version of this theology—found in such Identity writers as Wesley Swift, William Potter Gale, and Dan Gayman—is its so-called two-seed theology. According to the two-seed theory, Adam and Eve were the parents of Abel and Seth, but not of Cain. Cain's parents were supposedly Eve and Satan, Satan having sexually seduced Eve in the Garden of Eden. Identity regards the Jews as the literal, biological descendants of Satan, through Cain. Hence they posit a continuing state of war between the White seedline of Adam and the diabolical seedline of Cain. Blacks and other non-Whites are assumed to have resulted from separate creations in which neither Adam nor Eve was involved.

Identity Millennialism

The war between the seedlines is believed to be reaching its climax. This leads to an endtime scenario conceived in terms of race war (again, based upon Identity's view of Jews as racially non-White). As the earlier discussion suggested, this view of history has been used to support both radical withdrawal and violent engagement. It can be used to justify survivalism, in which Identity believers seek separation in order to avoid the dangers of conflict in the last days; and it can be used to justify violent attacks on Jews, non-Whites, and governmental authority, on the grounds that Satanic forces are poised to destroy God's people.

These differing orientations toward the endtimes can be better understood in terms of Identity's relationship to broader millenarian currents in American society. While Identity is sometimes considered part of fundamentalism, it in fact is quite different. The relationship between Christian Identity and Protestant fundamentalism has generally been one of mutual hostility. That is because they differ radically about two important theological issues: the role of the Jewish people, and the doctrine of the Rapture.

The great majority of Protestant fundamentalists accept the millenarian system devised in the late nineteenth century by John Nelson Darby called "dispensational premillennialism." It was Darby's contention that Christ's Second Coming would precede the millennium, but that the Second Coming could not take place until biblical prophecies concerning the Jewish people were fulfilled. There was no sign of this in Darby's time, and he and other dispensationalists believed the "prophetic clock" had stopped for an indefinite period. However, the creation of the State of Israel in 1948 and the reunification of Jerusalem in 1967 persuaded many fundamentalists that the "prophetic clock" was now ticking and that consequently the world was moving rapidly toward the final events of history.

Darby believed that these events would include a seven-year period of conflict and persecution, known as the "Tribulation," the final half of which would be dominated by the figure of the Antichrist. However, dispensationalists have held that the saved would not have to endure the rigors of the Tribulation, because they would be "raptured." That is, they would be taken up into heaven at the beginning of the Tribulation, be with Christ for the seven years, and then return with him at the time of the battle of Armageddon.

Christian Identity totally rejects this scenario. Since it believes Jews to be satanic impostors, it does not believe that biblical prophecies concerning "Israel" refer to them. Indeed, it believes such prophecies refer to White "Aryans." Thus, Identity adherents believe that the support shown by Christian fundamentalists for the State of Israel signifies that the Christian community has been duped or co-opted by Jews. Identity also rejects the doctrine of the Rapture as a major theological error. It does not believe the faithful will be lifted off the earth. Instead, the saved (again, themselves) will have to live through the harrowing events of the Tribulation. This belief has significantly reinforced separatist tendencies, since a survivalist lifestyle is deemed to be not merely a way of escaping a society regarded as sinful, but also as a way of protecting themselves against what they see as the dangers to come. It also fuels paramilitary tendencies, for they believe that during the Tribulation, public order will break down and/or the government will become the enemy of believers. Consequently, they see guns as an essential means of defense against encircling enemies.

The result is a millennialism resembling that of other Protestants only in its belief that the end of history is imminent. In virtually all other respects, it deviates from prevalent millenarian beliefs. These differences have created difficulties not only for Identity recruiting but also for coalition building with other segments of the right-wing/antigovernment subculture, since Identity has coupled its theological disagreements with the charge that the Christian clergy has "sold out." This has led in some instances to a muting of doctrinal issues by Identity leaders in the hope that less emphasis on the distinctiveness of its religious teachings would allow Identity to assume a greater leadership role in the larger right-wing community. The Colorado-based Identity pastor, Pete Peters, has been particularly adept at presenting himself to non-Identity audiences, notably after the 1992 Ruby Ridge, Idaho, shootout involving Randy Weaver and his family.

Summary

Throughout the roughly fifty years of its history, Christian Identity has shown itself to be capable of rapid and unpredictable changes. Because its constituent groups operate independently of one another, individual pastors and political organizers have been free to develop their own interpretations and programs. By closely interweaving anti-Semitism and racism with millennial expectation, Christian Identity has provided a theological rationalization for racial and religious conflict and inequality. Its assertion that these positions have a divine mandate has given to Identity an influence in extremist circles far beyond the relatively small number of adherents.

Michael Barkun

Bibliography

Aho, James. (1990) *The Politics of Righteousness: Idaho Christian Patriotism.* Seattle, WA: University of Washington Press.

Barkun, Michael. (1997) *Religion and the Racist Right: The Origins of the Christian Identity Movement,* rev. ed. Chapel Hill, NC: University of North Carolina Press.

——. (1997) "Millenarians and Violence: The Case of the Christian Identity Movement." In *Millennium, Messiahs, and Mayhem: Contemporary Apocalyptic Movements,* edited by Thomas Robbins and Susan J. Palmer. New York: Routledge, 247–60.

Jeansonne, Glen. (1988) *Gerald L. K. Smith: Minister of Hate.* New Haven, CT: Yale University Press.

Kaplan, Jeffrey. (1997) *Radical Religion in America: Millenarian Movements from the Far Right to the Children of Noah.* Syracuse, NY: Syracuse University Press.

Robins, Robert A., and Jerrold M. Post. (1997) *Political Paranoia: The Psychopolitics of Hatred.* New Haven, CT: Yale University Press.

Christian Reconstructionists and Dominionists

Christian Reconstructionism is a politically potent theology that in its forty-year history, has served as an ideological catalyst for the Christian right political movement in the United States. While professing Reconstructionists are few in number, the significance of this movement rests not in its numbers but in the power and resonance of its ideas. Laying claim to God's covenant, the theological tradition of Calvin, and the intellectual rigor of Reformed Presbyterianism, Christian Reconstructionism has gained a pivotal, if controversial place in American evangelicalism, as it offers an explicitly theocratic view of governance and politics. As the strongest body of literature in the field, it has become a standard to which others evaluate their stance.

Reconstructionism generally proposes that contemporary application of the laws of Old Testament Israel, or "Biblical Law," is the only basis for reconstructing society toward the Kingdom of God on Earth. As such, they see Bible as the "blueprint" for reconstructing all areas of life, from the arts and education, to economic and government along the lines they have fashioned. They generally refer to this as holding a "Biblical worldview" and applying "Biblical principles" to examine contemporary matters.

Reconstructionism has grown out of the works of a small group of scholars working in the 1960s and 1970s to inform a wide swath of conservative Christian thought and action. One scholar reports that Reconstructionism has "had substantial influence among . . . fundamentalists and evangelical Christians, especially among independent Baptist congregations and within smaller Reformed denominations," as well as the charismatic movement, "homeschoolers, libertarians, and the Religious Right" (Smith 1989: 18).

Reconstructionism's modern antecedents trace to a 1936 schism in Presbyterianism in the United States between Fundamentalists and modernists. J. Gresham Machen led the breakaway faction out of the mainline Presbyterian Church, and formed the Orthodox Presbyterian Church and Westminster Theological Seminary.

Seminal Thinkers and Writers

The original and defining text of Reconstructionism is *Institutes of Biblical Law,* published in 1973 by Rousas John Rushdoony. *Institutes* is an 800-page explanation of the Ten Commandments, the biblical "case law" that derives from them, and their application today. "The only true order," writes Rushdoony, "is founded on Biblical Law. All law is religious in nature, and every non-Biblical law-order represents an anti-Christian religion." Moreover, "Every law-order is a state of war against the enemies of that order, and all law is a form of warfare" (Rushdoony 1973: 113, 93). Reconstructionist writers take such aggressive ideas literally in the context of history, and often express the notion that such warfare has both spiritual and physical (Whitehead 1977: 165), even military dimensions (North 1989: 93–94; Clarkson 1997: 117–19, 148–50).

The main body of Reconstructionism defines itself with five main points: presuppositionalism, the idea that all of reality must be informed by a "biblical worldview"; covenantalism, that the primary social relationships of family church and civil government are directed by this contractual relationship with God and adherence to his laws; postmillennialism, the belief that the return of Jesus will crown 1,000 years of Christian rule, when the world has become perfectly Christian; and biblical law, that the statutes found in the Old Testament can be codified, serve as a blueprint for modern society in all areas of life. Finally, personal regeneration, conversion through the Holy spirit, or as Gary DeMar wrote, "God's spirit must be in us before we can walk in his statutes" (DeMar 1988: 63).

Rushdoony, perhaps the leading theocratic Christian thinker of the twentieth century, is the son of Armenian immigrants. He was born in New York City in 1916, served for a time as a minister and missionary in the Orthodox Presbyterian Church, and since 1964, he has headed a think tank in Vallecito, California, called The Chalcedon Foundation. His several dozen books, and those he has published through his Ross House Books, are the seminal source of Reconstruction's literature. Other significant publishing enterprises associated with leading Reconstructionist thinkers are Gary North's Dominion Press in Tyler, Texas, and Gary DeMar's American Vision, in Atlanta, Georgia.

Rushdoony and younger American theologian, Greg Bahnsen, were both students of Cornelius Van Til who taught at Princeton and Westminster Theological Seminary. Although Van Til never himself became a Reconstructionist, Reconstructionists nevertheless claim him as the father of their movement because of his advocacy of the doctrine of presuppositionalism. Gary North, describes Van Til's argument "There is no philosophical strategy that has ever worked, except this one: to challenge the lost in terms of the revelation of God in his Bible . . . by what standard can man know anything truly? By the Bible, and only by the Bible" (Bahnsen 1985, Prologue, XV). Van Til stopped short of proposing what a biblical society might look like or how to get there. That is where Reconstructionism begins, charting a course for world conquest or "dominion," claiming a biblically prophesied inevitable victory. Reconstructionist theologian David Chilton asserts: "The Christian goal for the world is the universal development of Biblical theocratic republics, in which every area of life is redeemed and placed under the Lordship of Jesus Christ and the rule of God's law" (House and Ice 1988: 65).

As a movement primarily of ideas, Reconstructionism has no one denominational or institutional home. Nor is it defined by a single charismatic leader, or even a single text. Rather it is defined by a small group of scholars who are identified primarily with Reformed or Orthodox Presbyterianism. The movement networks primarily through magazines, conferences, publishing houses, think tanks, and bookstores. As a matter of strategy, it is decentralized and avoids publicity, but nevertheless now informs a wide swath of conservative Christian thought and action. Reconstructionists have created a comprehensive program, with biblical justifications for far-right political action and public policy initiatives. However, Reconstructionism calls on conservatives to be Christians first, and to build a church-based political movement from there. In this it has been notably successful, influencing such major figures of the Christian Right as Rev. Jerry Falwell, founder of the Moral Majority, and Pat Robertson founder of the Christian Coalition, and Reformed Presbyterian author, Francis Schaeffer. Robert Billings, a founder of the Moral Majority said, "If it weren't for [Rushdoony's] books, none of us would be here" (Cantor 1994: 120).

For much of Reconstructionism's short history, it has been an ideology in search of a constituency. But its influence has grown rapidly. Gary North observes, "We once were shepherds without sheep. No longer" (House and Ice 1988: 352). One pastor wrote that that the leadership of the movement is passing to hundreds of small local churches that are "starting to grow both numerically and theologically. Their people are being trained in the Reconstructionist army. And at least in Presbyterian circles . . . we're Baptizing and catechizing a whole generation of Gary Norths, R. J. Rushdoonys and David Chiltons" (House and Ice 1988: 20).

God's New Chosen, Covenant People

Reconstructionists also believe that "the Christians" are the "new chosen people of God," and "are commanded to do that which Adam in Eden, and Israel in Canaan failed to do . . . create the society that God requires" (Rushdoony 1973: 4). Further, the Jews, once the "chosen people" according to Reconstructionists, failed to live up to God's covenant, and therefore are no longer God's chosen. Christians, of the correct sort, now are, as declared in Charles Provan's *The Church is Israel Now* (1987).

Reconstructionism shares in common the notion of the shift in the covenant with the White supremacist Christian Identity movement, which specifies that only White Christians are the chosen people, but otherwise embraces the notion of biblical law. Lacking a systematic theology of their own, the more amorphous Identity movement has been influenced by Rushdoony.

Rushdoony's *Institutes of Biblical Law* echoes a major work of the Protestant Reformation, John Calvin's *Institutes of the Christian Religion.* In fact, the theocracy Calvin created in Geneva, Switzerland, in the 1500s is one of the political models Reconstructionists look to, along with Old Testament Israel, and the Puritanism of the Massachusetts Bay Colony. These inform Reconstructionist thought on the program for an American Christian theocracy.

Generally, Reconstructionists break down the structure of governance under biblical law into three parts: family government, civil government, and church government. Under God's covenant, the nuclear family is the basic unit. The husband is the head of the family, and the wife and children are "in submission" to him. In turn, the husband "submits" to Jesus and God's laws as detailed in the Old Testament. The church has its own ecclesiastical structure and governance. Civil government exists to implement God's laws. All three institutions are under biblical law, the implementation of which is called "theonomy."

War of the Worldviews

Epitomizing the Reconstructionist idea of biblical "warfare" is the centrality of capital punishment under biblical law. Doctrinal leaders, notably Rushdoony, North, and Bahnsen insist on a long list of capital crimes, advocating death as punishment not only for such contemporary capital crimes as rape, kidnapping, and murder but such acts as striking a parent, and incorrigible juvenile delinquency and a series of religious crimes—apostasy (abandonment of the faith), propagating false doctrines, idolatry, heresy, blasphemy, witchcraft, and astrology; and sex crimes, including adultery, homosexuality, incest, and in the case of women, "unchastity before marriage" (Rushdoony 1973: 235, 402). North argues that women who have abortions should be publicly executed, "along with those who advised them to abort their children" (North 1989: 627). Rushdoony concludes: "God's government prevails, and His alternatives are clear-cut: either men and nations obey His laws, or God invokes the death penalty against them" (Rushdoony 1973: 237). While some Reconstructionists demur slightly on the death penalty, insisting that it would be "the maximum not necessarily the mandatory penalty," they nevertheless insist that biblical theocratic Republics would be "happy" places to which people would flock because "capital punishment is one of the best evangelistic tools of a society" (Sutton 1987: 188).

The biblically approved methods of execution include burning (at the stake, for example), stoning, hanging, and "the sword" (Rushdoony 1973: 237). Punishments for noncapital crimes generally involved whipping, restitution in the form of indentured servitude, or slavery. Prisons would likely be only temporary holding tanks, prior to the imposition of the actual sentence. Many who are influenced by Reconstructionism flee the label because of the controversial scope of the list of capital crimes and the methods of execution. Others are ambivalent on the particulars, such as the execution of sinners and nonbelievers.

Rushdoony's notion that nations are punished or perish for failing to adhere to biblical law, is an animating aspect of the political activities of Reconstructionists and their political allies on such matters as abortion, homosexuality, and even the 1997–99 drive to impeach President Bill Clinton.

Reconstructionism also adheres to a revisionist view of history which holds that history is predestined from creation until the inevitable arrival of the Kingdom of God. "Christian history" is written by means of retroactively discerning "God's providence," in light of history's predestined conclusion. Rushdoony calls this "Christian revisionism" (Rushdoony 1965: iv). Reconstructionists are not uniform in their discerning of God's providence. Rushdoony and DeMar, for example, believe that the notion of the United States as a "Christian nation," is enshrined in the U.S. Constitution. Gary North, who holds doctorate in history, argues that Article VI of the Constitution, which bars "religious tests" for public office, signaled a "judicial break from Christian America," and presented a "legal barrier to Christian theocracy" which led "directly to the rise of religious pluralism" (North 1985: 681–85). Indeed, prior to the ratification of the Constitution, most of the colonies had been theocracies of various sorts, and required Christian "oaths" for public officials. All Reconstructionists agree however, that such ideas as religious pluralism and separation of church and state are Satanic doctrines designed to thwart Christian rule.

Reconstructionism appeals to some elements of conservative Christianity because it provides a unifying framework for conspiracy theories. "There is one conspiracy," writes Gary North, "Satan's. And it must fail. Satan's supernatural conspiracy is the conspiracy; all other visible conspiracies are merely outworkings of this supernatural conspiracy" (North 1986: 15). "The view of history as conspiracy," according to Rushdoony, ". . . is a basic aspect of the perspective of orthodox Christianity" (1965: 156–57). Blaming the failure of Christians with millennial ambitions to achieve or sustain political power on Satanically inspired conspiracies has a long tradition in the United States. The blame for this is most often assigned to the Masons, particularly an eighteenth-century Masonic group called the Illuminati, and ultimately Satan.

Reconstructionism's role in transforming the theological landscape of American evangelicalism is epitomized by the 1982 formation of the Coalition on Revival. The Coalition, which over the years has brokered a series of theological compromises, aimed at forging a transdenominational theology for American evangelicalism and a modern Reformation. While the Coalition has produced numerous documents, its main focus and perhaps its major accomplishment, has been to substantially reconcile the two main eschatological (end-times) camps, the premillennialists and the postmillennialists. The premillennialists generally hold that it is impossible to change the world for the better until Jesus returns (the Second Coming) which will be followed by a thousand-year reign of Jesus with the Christians. This other-worldly orientation has tended to keep most evangelicals on the sidelines of politics. While the postmillennialists, including the Reconstructionists and the wider Reformed Presbyterian community, are actively working to build the Kingdom of God on Earth. The Coalition on Revival's theological dialog was able to get the eschatological factions to agree to disagree on the timing of the Second Coming. They were then able to agree on the need to work for the Kingdom of God "in so far as it is possible" until Jesus returns. This language allowed people to agree to work on common interests in public policy without having to agree on exactly how much could be accomplished and how soon. The diminishment of this theological barrier to political action has been crucial to the surge of political activity in the charismatic and Pentecostal communities, which form the base of Pat Robertson's Christian Coalition. The political engagement of large sectors of the premillennialist evangelicals remains one of the greatest religious and political shifts of the latter half of the twentieth century.

Many individual Reconstructionists are prominent in public life. Howard Ahmanson, heir to a large savings and loan fortune, has long been the largest donor and board member of both Rushdoony's Chalcedon Foundation, and the California Republican Party, and has spent millions of dollars on candidates and conservative ballot initiatives. Ahmanson once declared, "My purpose is total integration of Biblical law into our lives" (Clarkson 1997: 111). Howard Phillips is the founder and two-time presidential candidate of the nationally organized U.S. Taxpayers Party. Randall Terry, the founder of the antiabortion group, Operation Rescue, continues to lead mediagenic and militant theocratic activism nationwide. Rev. Paul Lindstrom, of Arlington Heights, Illinois, is a pioneer and leader in the Christian homeschooling movement. John Whitehead, a disciple of Rushdoony, became one of the most famous lawyers in America, when he represented Paula Jones in her sexual harassment case against President Bill Clinton. Paul Hill, who studied with Greg Bahnsen at Reformed Theological Seminary in Jackson Mississippi, is scheduled to die in Florida's electric chair for his 1994 assassination of an abortion provider in Pensacola, Florida. Though most Reconstructionists rejected Hill's seeming vigilante action, Hill nonetheless presented himself as a role model for others to begin to foment theocratic revolution against what all Reconstructionists view as the Godless state. Finally, Gary North developed a public persona in the media as an "expert" on the Y2K computer bug, and predicted that it would crash the economic system.

Christian Reconstructionism is notable in the context of millennial movements because it is generally antiapocalyptic and views the turn of the century with about as much interest as the turn of the odometer on a car or truck: one more digit marking time on God's calendar, the only one that counts. At the same time, Reconstructionism adds political heft to those animated by premillennialist visions of the endtimes. It has been increasingly acceptable to be a theonomist, without being a postmillennialist. There is no sign at century's end that the young Reconstructionist movement, led by the octogenarian Rushdoony, has peaked in influence, or the spread of its ideas.

Frederick Clarkson

See also Christian Identity, Fundamentalism

Bibliography

Bahnsen, Greg. (1985) *By This Standard: The Authority of God's Law Today*, prologue by Gary North. Tyler, TX: Institute for Christian Economics.

Barron, Bruce. (1992) *Heaven on Earth?* Grand Rapids, MI: Zondervan.

Boston, Robert. (1988) "Paula's Pals." *Church & State* (March).

Cantor, David. (1994) *The Religious Right and the Assault on Tolerance & Religious Pluralism.* New York: Anti-Defamation League.

Clapp, Rodney. (1987) "Democracy as Heresy." *Christianity Today* (20 February).

Clarkson, Frederick. (1997) *Eternal Hostility: The Struggle Between Theocracy and Democracy.* Monroe, ME: Common Courage Press.

——. (1999) "John Whitehead." *I.F. Magazine.*

DeMar, Gary. (1988) *The Debate over Christian Reconstruction.* Atlanta, GA: American Vision Press.

DeMar, Gary. (1993) *America's Christian History, The Untold Story.* Atlanta, GA: American Vision.

Diamond, Sara. (1995) *Roads to Dominion: Right-Wing Movements and Political Power in the United States.* New York: The Guilford Press.

Grant, George. (1987) *The Changing of the Guard: Biblical Principles for Political Action.* Ft. Worth, TX: Dominion Press.

House, H. Wayne, and Thomas Ice. (1988) *Dominion Theology: Blessing or Curse? An Analysis of Christian Reconstructionism.* Multnomah Press.

McCullagh, Declan. (1999) "There's Something About Gary." *Wired News* (7 January). http://www.wired.com/news/news/culture/story/17193.html.

North, Gary. (1985) *Political Polytheism: The Myth of Pluralism.* Institute for Christian Economics. (North's works, and others he has published, are available for downloading at www.freebooks.com).

——. (1986) *Conspiracy: A Biblical View.* Ft. Worth, TX: Dominion Press Texas.

——. (1986) *The Sinai Strategy: Economics and the Ten Commandments.* Tyler, TX: Institute for Christian Economics.

——. (1989) *When Justice Is Aborted: Biblical Standards for Non-Violent Resistance.* Tyler, TX: Dominion Press.

Provan, Charles D. (1987) *The Church Is Israel Now: The Transfer of Conditional Privilege.* Vallecito, CA: Ross House Books.

Rushdoony, Rousas John. (1965) *The Nature of the American System.* Fairfax, VA: Thoburn Press.

——. (1973) *Institutes of Biblical Law.* Presbyterian and Reformed Publishing Company.

——. (1982) *Law and Society: Volume II of the Institutes of Biblical Law.* Vallecito, CA: Ross House Books.

Rushdoony, Rousas John, ed. (1998) "Christian Home Schooling: Raising a Victorious Army for Jesus Christ." *The Chalcedon Report* (March).

Shupe, Anson. (1989) "Prophets of a Biblical America." *The Wall Street Journal* (12 April).

Smith, Gary Scott, ed. (1989) *God and Politics: Four Views on the Reformation of Civil Government.* Phillipsburg, NJ: Presbyterian and Reformed Publishing.

Sutton, Rev. Ray. (1987) *That You May Prosper: Dominion By Covenant.* Tyler, TX: Institute for Christian Economics.

Thoburn, Robert L. (1986) "The Children Trap." *Biblical Blueprint Series.* Tyler, TX: Dominion Press, Thomas Nelson Publishers.

Whitehead, John W. (1977) *The Separation Illusion: A Lawyer Examines the First Amendment,* foreword by R. J. Rushdoony. Milford, MI: Mott Media.

Chronology and Dating

There are three types of calendars: solar, lunisolar (a lunar calendar with adjustments made to make up for the missing days between it and the solar year), and lunar, and three types of chronologies: absolute (dating from the assumed beginning of the world), fixed (tied to an important event usually of political or religious significance), and variable (usually either regnally based or cyclical). The solar year lasts 365.25636 days (although there have been minute variants during the past five millennia), while the lunar year is approximately 354 days. Lunisolar calendars usually add on a set number of days or a month at given intervals in order to stabilize the months in their given seasons (known as intercalation).

Any type of calendar can lend itself to apocalyptic interpretations, but chronologies of either the absolute or fixed type are most suited for this purpose. However, it is not unknown for variable chronologies to also be interpreted in an apocalyptic manner—usually to give legitimacy to a dynasty or ruler or sometimes to show the cyclical nature of predicting the future. In order for this interpretation to have credibility, the chronology must be tied in some fashion to a form of revelation, or to the assumed beginning of the messianic age itself. In general, monotheistic systems lend themselves most easily to apocalyptic interpretation, Judaism using an absolute chronology, while both Christianity and Islam use fixed ones. Many chronologies have had apocalyptic significance because there was assumed to be some correlation between the number of ages (usually assumed to be six, with the seventh being the millennium) and the days of creation (Genesis 2:2). This pattern of seven ages for humanity is oftentimes called the "world year." All apocalyptic chronologies are attempts to understand, order, and explain the meaning of past events and to sense a pattern in the course of human history that leads inexorably to an end.

Historians and religious figures who work with history usually have to confront the problem of the meaning of history and often have chosen to order and interpret the events in an apocalyptic fashion. Some sought to use the historical events as a timetable for increasing apocalyptic expectation, while others sought to dim the ardor of the believers by denying this option. Apocalyptic chronology is slightly different from regular chronology, since it assumes the knowledge of the future. Many historians in the past saw their work in terms of both past events and future events, and sought to encompass the entirety of human history within their compositions. Apocalyptic writers who sought to promote a consciousness of the proximity of the end either used these schemes or sometimes produced new ones of their own. Certain important apocalyptic dates will be noted in the discussion.

Ancient Systems

Ancient systems are usually chronologically variable and can be based on either a solar, lunisolar, or a lunar calendar. It is not unusual for there to be a great deal of scholarly debate about certain variable chronologies, since there are few firmly datable events which can be used as guideposts. In many cases astronomical events are the solution to this problem, or the use of outside sources, if there happen to be any, to fix a certain date. When some of these systems had little apocalyptic relevance when they were current, it is not unusual for them to be resurrected during our own time for use by apocalyptic groups (the principal example being the Mayan chronology).

Mesopotamian (Akkadian, Babylonian, and Assyrian) Systems

Mesopotamian systems are usually lunar (though not always) and variable. The day began at sunset, and the month began with the sighting of the new moon. This leads to variation (between 28 and 31 days) in the length of the month, and sometimes to additional variation because of bad weather, making the lunar crescent sighting impossible. Chronological systems are well developed and begin with the impressive Sumerian king-lists from before the Flood (tentatively dated to previous to 3000 BCE) showing kings reigning for periods up to 64,800 years before (all numbers are given in multiples of 3,600 years). Later chronologies have gaps during interdynastic periods or periods of chaos, but good coverage is available for most of the two major Babylonian dynasties (2000–1600 and 747–539 BCE). Assyrian chronology can be traced back to approximately 1100 BCE. Although these lists are not directly related to apocalyptic, it is clear that the kings did see these chronologies as a form of legitimizing imperial apocalyptic.

Bibliography

De Meis, Salvo, and Hermann Hunger. (1998) *Astronomical Dating of Assyrian and Babylonian Reports.* Rome: Instituto Italiano per l'Africa e l'Oriente.

Huber, Peter. (1982) *Astronomical Dating of Babylon I and Ur III.* Occasional Papers on the Near East, 1, 4. Malibu, CA: Undena Publications.

Meer, P. E. van der (1955) *The Chronology of Ancient Western Asia and Egypt,* 2d rev. ed. Leiden: Brill.

Egyptian

Egyptian calendars are lunisolar and the chronologies are variable, with the first day of the year tied to the appearance of the star Sirius (in Egyptian: Sothis) on the eastern horizon just before the rising of the sun. It is very likely that the year (of 365 days) was adopted in the distant past because of the conjunction of the Nile inundation and the rising of the star. Months are twelve in number and last for thirty days each, with five days extra—with the result that the months moved forward at the rate of about one day per four years. This chronology, known as the Sothic cycle, apparently begins in 4242 BCE and does a complete revolution around the calendar every 1460 years, approximately. However, insofar as is known, this chronology had no relation to apocalyptic beliefs or texts.

Bibliography

Hornung, Erik. (1964) *Untersuchungen zur Chronologie und Geschichte des neuen Reiches.* Wiesbaden: Harrasowitz.

Redford, Donald. (1986) *Pharonic King-Lists, Annals and Day-Books.* Mississauga, Canada: Benden.

Spalinger, Anthony, ed. (1994) *Revolutions in Time: Studies in Ancient Egyptian Calendrics.* San Antonio, TX: Van Seelen Books.

Greek and Roman

At their base, both Greek (using the Athenian calendar as representative of the multiplicity of calendars available in classical times) and Roman calendars are lunar. While the Greek one was never accepted beyond the confines of Greece, the Roman one was eventually adapted by the Alexandrine calendar (see below) to form the basis for the Christian calendar of medieval times. For chronology, Herodotus, the "father of history," used the generational scheme, assuming that three generations was a century. In general, however, chronological organization of history was chaotic for the period previous to Alexander the Great (d. 333 BCE). A wide range of Jewish and Christian chronological schemes are based on the Seleucid chronology which begins on 1 October 312–11 BCE, but this was most widely developed in apocalyptic usage by the eastern Christians (see below).

Bibliography

Meimaris, Yiannis. (1992) *Chronological Systems in Roman-Byzantine Palestine and Arabia.* Athens: Kentron Hellenikes.

Paulys realencyclopädie der classischen Alterumswissenschaft. (1997) Munich: Alfred Drucken Müller Verlag, s.v. "Kalendar."

Indian and Iranian

Indian calendars are either solar or lunisolar and variable as to their chronologies. Hindu rulers used dynastic schemes to calculate chronology, while Buddhist chronologies begin with 544 BCE (the presumed death of the Buddha), and Jain chronology begins in 528 BCE. Currently the chronology used throughout India is that of the Saka or Salivahana era, beginning in 78 CE. During classical times, astronomers calculated a much longer set of periods (lasting a total of 4,320,000 years), divided into four stages (*yugas*), of which the fourth, the Kali, has been computed to have begun in 3102 BCE. It will last 432,000 years. There is no evidence that this chronology has been used for apocalyptic purposes, but there is no reason why it could not be. Certain Buddhists have used their calendar for apocalyptic calculations, probably under the influence of Zoroastrianism.

The ancient Iranian calendar was a lunisolar calendar of 360 days, which employed an as yet unidentified method of intercalation. During the post-Alexander period this was modified to one very closely tied to that of the Egyptians, employing a solar calendar of 365 days (12 months of 30, with 5 days extra). There is some disagreement as to what exactly the date is fixed at. Zoroastrian apocalyptic chronologies are well developed and include the *Denkard* (vol. 6), and most especially the *Bundahisn,* which describes history in a "world-year" fashion leading up to the end of time, and the revelation of the messiah. In astrology as well, there was some attempt to calculate the years into meaningful cycles. By this method it was decided that there were 3,679 years between the Flood and the coming of Islam (by the time these calculations were made most Iranians were Muslim), and from that point Muslim calculations were used. However, most Zoroastrians assumed that Zoroaster only received his revelation at the beginning of the last 1,000 years, and so the dating from the Flood was meaningless to them.

Bibliography

Chakravarty, Apurba (1975) *Origin and Development of Indian Calendrical Science.* Calcutta: Indian Studies, Past and Present.

Kennedy, Edward S., and B. L. van der Waerden. (1963) "The World-Year of the Persians." *Journal of the American Oriental Society* 83: 315–27.

Sewell, Robert. (1924) *The Siddhantas and the Indian Calendar.* Calcutta: Government of India.

Sewell, Robert, and S. B. Dikshita. (1926) *The Indian Calendar.* London: S. Sonnenschein.

Chinese, Japanese, and Turkic

The Chinese and Japanese calendars are lunisolar and are a mixture of fixed and variable chronologies. The calendars run in cycles of twelve years, each of which has the name of an animal (Rat, Ox, Tiger, Rabbit, Dragon, Serpent, Horse, Sheep, Monkey, Fowl, Dog, and Pig), whereupon the cycle starts anew. Chronology is also fixed regnally (from the regnal year of the emperor), and is fixed to the twelve-year animal cycle (for example, one could say "in the fourteenth year of the reigning emperor, during the year of the Monkey"). For more lengthy periods of time, there is a cyclical system which begins in 2637 BCE, although scholars feel that it was probably not adopted until the twelfth century BCE. Therefore, years are named by their animal names and keyed to the regnal years of either the Chinese or the Japanese emperors on the basis of this long system. Japanese mythological chronology goes back to the emperor Jimmu Tenno in approximately 660 BCE; however this date has been disputed, and might be several centuries too early.

Turkish-Mongolian calendars also used the Chinese twelve-year animal cycle, though chronology was not developed until the time of Genghis Khan (d. 1227). This chronology is used to give a messianic aura to the Mongol rulers in *The Secret History of the Mongols.* All of these calendars have been used for the purposes of legitimization of rulers, but there is no evidence that they were apocalyptically significant.

Bibliography

Bazin, Louis. (1991) *Les systemes chronologiques dans le monde turc ancien.* Paris: Éditions du CNRS.

Bramsen, William. (1880) *Japanese Chronological Tables.* Tokyo: Printed at the "Seishi Bunsha" office.

Hoang, Pierre. (1968) *Concordance des chronologies néoméniques: Chinoise et Europeenne.* Taiwan: Kuangchi Press.

Yachita Tsuchihashi. (1952) *Japanese Chronological Tables 601–1872.* Tokyo: Tokyo University.

Meso-American and South American

Mayan calendars worked from a solar calendar of 365 days divided into 18 months of 20 days each, with five extra "nameless" days (similar to those of the Egyptians and the Iranians) to fill out the year. The chronology starts with a fixed point at 10 August 3113 BCE, and divides the periods up into groups of multiples of twenty (*tun*, a year, *katun*, 20 years, *baktun*, 400 years, and so forth). The earliest calendar inscription dates from 292 CE. However, side by side with this solar calendar, there was another calendar of 260 days divided up into 13-day periods (weeks). This calendar corresponds to the preceding solar calendar once every 52 years; hence the importance of the numbers 13 and 52. In the longer scheme, the number 13 is keyed to the starting point of 3113 above, and goes through 13 cycles of 394–95 years each, and each of these cycles is comprised of 10 parts of 19–20 years each (for example, the year 1934 is in the twelfth cycle and the sixteenth part). This is known as the Long Count, and serves for long-term chronologies. It goes back millions of years according to the Mayan codexes which have been deciphered. Certain aspects of the Mayan calendar cycles resemble those of the Chinese animal twelve-year cycle; however, the relationship between the two remains uncertain. Although there is no evidence that the Mayan calendar was used apocalyptically, today adherents of New Age movements frequently use it for this purpose.

Bibliography

Douglas, Paul Campbell. (1992) *Astronomy and the Mayan Calendar Correlation.* Laguna Hills, CA: Aegean Press.

Thompson, John Eric Sidney, Sir. (1937) *Maya Chronology: The Correlation Question.* Washington, D.C.: Carnegie Institution of Washington.

Whittaker, Gordon. (1990) "Calendar and Script in protohistorical China and Mesoamerica." Ph.D. diss., University of Bonn.

Monotheistic

Monotheistic systems are those which believe in a single God, and have their basis in His revelations to humanity of His will concerning them through prophets.

Jewish

Judaism uses a lunisolar calendar and has an absolute chronological system, which was probably adopted in the ninth century CE, but has its roots as far back as the first century BCE. The lunar calendar is corrected with the addition of an intercalary month after the seventh month out of a lunar cycle of nineteen years (now fixed at years 3, 6, 8, 11, 14, 17, and 19). Days begin at sundown, and the year begins in the fall, usually in late September. The most widely used chronological system has its basis in the book of Genesis, and all later monotheistic chronological systems base themselves on it, even when they occasionally differ as to details. This absolute chronology, according to the dating system used currently, would assume the creation of the world in 3761 BCE (on 7 October). Other calendars have been briefly in use as a result of messianic movements: those of the First (66–70 CE) and Second (132–35) Jewish Revolts are the best known.

Apocalyptic chronology in Judaism has a long history. Since the calendar uses a numerical system based on letters (in which each letter is assumed to have a numerical value), it is not infrequent that years are actually words with meaning. When this meaning is ominous (or sometimes blessed), then apocalyptic considerations are strong. For Judaism, therefore, the lure of even dates (such as the year 1000 or other dates based on the decimal system), which has such strength in Christianity and Islam, is weakened and focused on those dates with meaning in terms of words. Gematrical (or Talmudic) calculations on the basis of dates are not unusual in apocalyptic speculation. For example, the absolute date of 5426 for the Shabbetai Zvi messianic movement (1665–66) does not seem attractive at first glance, but the meaning of the word makes the apocalyptic pull greater.

Apocalyptic chronologies, which are well known, are the *Seder Olam Rabba,* probably composed in the second century CE; and a *Seder Olam Zuta,* which continues until 804 CE. In Spain, the *Sefer ha-Kabbalah,* composed by the Spanish Abraham b. Da'ud (c. 1180 CE) provides much the same function. These chronologies were designed to show God's plan for Jewish history and usually present it in terms of cycles of similar length (twenty-one years for example, in *Sefer ha-Kabbalah*). Samaritans also composed chronologies of this sort; an example is the *Sefer ha-asatir* (Book of Secrets) which traces Samaritan history from the beginning of the world to the early Muslim period.

Bibliography

Encyclopedia Judaica. (n.d.) Jerusalem: Ariel, s.v. "Chronology" (Benjamin Isaacson).

Ben-Hayim, Zeev, ed. (1943 and 1944) "Kitab al-asatir." *Tarbitz* 14: 174–90, and 15: 71–87 (in Hebrew).

Benish, Hayyim. (1995) *ha-Zmanim bi-halacha.* Bnei Brak (no publisher listed).

Cohen, Gershon, ed. (1967) *Sefer ha-Kabbalah.* Philadelphia: Jewish Publication Society.

Frank, Edgar. (1956) *Talmudic and Rabbinical Chronology.* New York: P. Feldheim.

Kahana, Sh. Z. (1993) *ha-Geula bi-Sod hodshei ha-shana.* Tel Aviv: Histadrut ha-Poel ha-Mizrahi be-Erets-Yisrael.

Christian

Christianity uses a solar calendar with a fixed (and occasionally an absolute) chronological system, and is currently the most widespread calendar and chronological system in use, and the one most apocalyptic calculations are keyed to. However, there have been important variants as to the fixation point of the chronological system.

Eastern Christian Systems Eastern Christians used the Seleucid chronology with 1 CE equal to 312–13, and gradually modified it by tying it to the "world-era" in which at first creation was dated to 5493 BCE, known as the Alexandrine world-era. This was modified at a later period, and creation was redated to 5507. This chronology was known as the Byzantine world-era, and was generally accepted throughout the eastern churches. However, the Ethiopian church dated 1 CE equal to 8 BCE (which we now know to be more accurate).

Apocalyptic chronologies in eastern Christianity are well developed and began as a response to the Muslim conquests which traumatized the entire community. One of the earliest known is that of Pseudo-Methodius (c. 690 CE), which sought to explain all of history in terms of the apocalyptic events about to occur during the author's lifetime. The apocalypse was quickly translated into Greek and was probably brought to Western Europe by Luitprand of Cremona (visiting Constantinople in 968 CE), where it has been very influential for apocalyptic chronologies.

Other examples of apocalyptic chronologies are those of Matthew of Edessa (d. c. 1144), who documented the Crusades from an Armenian point of view and who sought to prove that the end of the world was near through chronology. When in 1022 a large meteor fell in Armenia, terrifying the entire country, he had this to say, citing John Kozern, a monk (note that the Armenians at this time used a form of the Iranian chronology instead of the Byzantine one):

> "Oh children, listen to me. Misfortune and disaster has come to all mankind, for today is the thousandth year of the imprisonment of Satan, which our Lord Jesus Christ had brought about by his crucifixion and especially by his holy baptism in the Jordan river. Now Satan has been released from his imprisonment according to the testimony of the vision of the evangelist John, who was told by the angel of God that Satan would be imprisoned for one thousand years and then would be released from his imprisonment. Lo, today Satan has been released from his thousand year imprisonment. This is the year 473 of the Armenian era [14 March 1029–13 March 1030]; add to it the first 552 years which comes out to 1030 years; then subtract 30 years for the period before the baptism of Christ and you have 1000 years at the present.
> (in Doustourian 1972: 60–61)

It is easy to see that here the speculation is tied to the year 1000, and shortly afterwards, he notes the thousandth anniversary of the Crucifixion, when a comet appears. Many other apocalyptic chronologies are known from Eastern churches.

Bibliography

Bagnall, Roger S., and K. A. Worp. (1978) *The Chronological Systems of Byzantine Egypt.* Zutphen, Netherlands: Terra.

Doustourian, Ara. (1972) "The Chronicle of Matthew of Edessa." Ph.D. diss., Rutgers University.

Reinink, G. "Ps. Methodius: A Concept of History in Response to the Rise of Islam." In *The Byzantine and Early Islamic Near East,* edited by Averill Cameron and Lawrence I. Conrad. Princeton, NJ: Darwin Press, 149–87.

Wustenfeld, Heinrich. (1961) *Vergleichungs-tabellen zur muslimischen und iranischen Zeitrechung mit tafeln zur Umrechung orient-christlicher Ären.* Wiesbaden: Franz Steiner.

Western Christian Systems Western Christians have used a number of chronologies, among them the Seleucid one used by the Eastern Christians (in those areas dominated culturally by the Byzantine), and the Spanish one which dated from 38 BCE, the conquest of Spain by Caesar Augustus. After 526, as a result of the influence of Dionysius Exiguus, the dating from the birth of Christ (1 CE, rather than the 4 BCE to which it is usually dated today) was adopted. This is known as the Julian calendar and was comprised of a year of 365 and one-fourth days. There was no consensus as to when the beginning of the year occurs and at different times and places either 25 December, 1 January, 25 March, or the day of Easter (which is itself dependent upon the Jewish calendar) has been recognized as the first day of the year. In 1582, Pope Gregory XIII ordered a reform of the calendar to correct the inaccuracies in the Julian one, and thus ten days (between 4 and 15 October 1582) were eliminated, and gradually over the next three centuries this calendar was accepted throughout Europe and then most of the rest of the world.

Apocalyptic interest in the calendar was focused upon the end of centuries and most especially upon the turn of the millennium (1000 CE). After the year 1300, each turn of a century has had excitement attached to it, and many times this has spilled over to divisions of the century (at breaks such as 25, 50, 75, etc.). As in the East, apocalyptic chronologies were very early on accepted by Western Christians. No attempt will be made here to be thorough, but a few examples from different time periods will be adduced. Among the first to demonstrate an awareness of apocalyptic chronology was Augustine of Hippo (d. 430 CE), who sought to show that the last millennium was about to arrive. There was a pattern of a tension concerning dating of the apocalypse during the middle ages; as one grew closer to the date proposed by earlier generations, nervous scholars sought to move it further into the distant future.

During the twelfth century Joachim of Fiore promoted an apocalyptic chronology, dividing the history of the world into three ages, and sought to identify the end on this basis. Much later, the English bishop James Ussher made an attempt to establish an absolute date for creation, dated it to 4004 BCE, as part of his world chronology. Isaac Newton sought to find these patterns in the history of ancient peoples, and to date the apocalypse on the basis of Daniel 7. Many others have followed in his footsteps, usually using Daniel or other Gematrical biblical calculations.

Bibliography

Archer, Peter. (1941) *The Christian Calendar and the Gregorian Reform.* New York: Fordham University.

Bloomfield, Morton. (1975) "Joachim of Fiore: A Critical Survey of his Canon, Teachings, Sources, Biography and Influence." In *Joachim of Fiore in Christian Thought,* edited by Delno West. New York: Burt Franklin, 29–92.

Grumel, V. (1958) *La Chronologie.* Paris: Presses Universitaires de France.

Hampson, Robert T. (1841) *Medii aevi Kalendarium.* London: H. K. Causton.

Kelly, Aidan, Peter Dresser, and Linda Ross. (1993) *Religious Holidays and Calendars.* Detroit: Omnigraphics.

Landes, Richard. (1988) "Lest the Millennium be Fulfilled. . . ." In *Use and Abuse of Eschatology in the Middle Ages,* edited by W. Verbeke, Daniel Verhelst, and A. Welkenhuysen. Louvain: Louvain University, 141–211.

Newton, Isaac. (1728) *The Chronology of Ancient Nations.* London: J. Osborn and T. Longman.

Ussher, James (1847) *The Whole Works,* edited by Charles Elrington. London: Whittaker.

Muslim

Islam uses a lunar calendar and a fixed chronological system starting with the Hijra (the emigration of the Prophet Muhammad to Medina), and intercalation is forbidden by Qur'an 9: 36. The assumed date is 16 July 622 CE, which is about two months previous to the accepted date of the emigration. The lunar month loses between ten to thirteen days each year and thus travels around the seasonal calendar, and each month does not start until the lunar crescent has been sighted. Dates from pre-Islamic times are calculated on the basis of a named-year system. For example, Muhammad is said to have been born in the "Year of the Elephant" (assumed to be 570 CE), so named because of the use of an elephant to attack the city of Mecca. There is no consensus about dates in the Prophet Muhammad's life previous to the Hijra. The earliest recorded date independent of the Muslim tradition is an Egyptian papyrus of 22 AH/643 CE, making it virtually certain that Hijra dates were widely accepted within the first two decades of Islam. No other calendar has ever received such general acceptance in Islam, although there have been several attempts, primarily by Turkish or Mongol rulers, to initiate new systems (cf. the Chinese twelve-year animal cycle in Persia, and the solar calendar promoted by the Indian Mughal Akbar in 1556, which lasted until the end of the dynasty).

No apocalyptic events are known to have been calculated from these calendars; however, Akbar's calendar was in itself an apocalyptic event, heralding as it did the second millennium of Islam (occurring in 1591). Although currently all Muslims use the Hijri calendar, for several centuries Muslim governments have been using a lunisolar version of it, and during the past century, the Christian calendar. Today even Muslim fundamentalists calculating the apocalypse frequently use the Christian calendar or mix the two.

Apocalyptic traditions began using the Hijri chronological system to calculate the end no later than 35 AH/655–56 CE, and continue to our own time. Most apocalyptic dates are easily guessed at: 70 AH/689–90 CE and multiples thereof, 100/718–9 and multiples thereof, 500/1106–7, 1000/1591, 1500/2076, but numerous other dates are available. A typical example of apocalyptic chronological prediction is the following keyed to the century of 200–300 AH/815–912 CE:

> In the 210s there will be bombardment, swallowing up by the earth and metamorphosis, in the 220s there will be death among the religious leadership of the world–until none are left . . . in the 230s the sky will rain hail like eggs and the cattle will perish, in the 240s the Nile and the Euphrates will cease to flow, so that they will sow in their river-courses, in the 250s there will be brigandage, wild animals will dominate humans and everybody will stay in their own towns, in the 260s the sun will cease (shining) for half an hour and half of humanity and *jinn* will perish, in the 270s no-one will be born, and no female will be pregnant, in the 280s women will be like donkeys—so that 40 men will have intercourse with one woman and no one will think anything of it, in the 290s the year will be like a month, the month like a week, the week like a day, the day like an hour, an hour like the burning of an ulcer such that a man would leave his house and not arrive at the city gate until sunset and in 300 the rising of the sun from the west. (Nu'aym, *Fitan:* 427)

Most Muslim histories are chronologies which try and cover the history of the world from creation, but dates previous to the Hijra are lacking. The chronological sequence used is that of the Judeo-Christian tradition, and the system of the "world day" mentioned above is prevalent in apocalyptic calculations (cf. Qur'an 22:47: "but a day with the Lord is as a thousand years of your counting"). Since the year 1000 AH, apocalyptic speculation has largely been deferred to the year 1500. Chronological apocalyptic speculation can be most obviously seen with the fourteenth-century Syrian historian Ibn Kathir, whose book *The Beginning and the End (al-Bidaya wa-l-nihaya)* sought to bridge the entirety of human history. In the Black Muslim version of Islam current in the United States a considerably different chronology obtains, which places the beginning point many trillions of years in the past, and dates world history back 6,000 years. This is deemed to be the period (until the year 2000) of the white man's rule upon the earth, when the apocalypse will occur.

Bibliography

Encyclopedia of Islam (1960–) Leyden: Brill, s.v. "ta'rikh" (F. de Blois).

'Abduh, Muhamamd. (n.d.) *Tafsir al-Manar.* Cairo: al-Manar.

Ansari, Z. I. (1981) "Aspects of Black Muslim Theology." *Studia Islamica* 53: 137–76.

Bashear, Suleiman. (1993) "Muslim Apocalypses." *Israel Oriental Studies* 13: 75–99.

Conrad, L. I. (1987) "Muhammad and Abraha." *Bulletin of the School of Oriental and African Studies* 50: 215–40.

Kennedy, E. S. (1983) "The World-Year Concept in Islamic Astrology." In *Studies in the Exact Sciences.* Beirut: American University of Beirut, 351–71.

Melville, Charles. (1994) "The Chinese-Uighur Animal Calendar in Persian Historiography of the Mongol Period." *Iran* 32: 83–98.

Nu'aym bin Hammad. (1993) *Kitab al-fitan.* Beirut: Dar al-Fikr.

Sinh, Raghubir. (1984) *The Julusi Sanehs of the Mughal Emperors of India 1556-1857.* Malwa, India: Shri Natnagar Shodh-Samsthan.

Wustenfeld, *Vergleichungs-tabellen,* op. cit.

Other Systems

Certain systems are unusual in that they do not predict a messianic age, they inaugurate it. Such a one was the Calendar of the French Revolution lasting between 22 September 1792 and 31 December 1805. The months used were not those of the Christian year, but entirely new configurations, with French seasonally based names. Certain New Age beliefs take the Mayan calendar mentioned above and continue calculations on the basis of it. Humanity has been divided into epochs, and has entered the "Age of Aquarius" in May 1948, which is characterized by harmony rather than the previous Piscean Epoch, which was said to have been bitter and divisive. Adherents of this view feel free to use many ancient methods of calculation, and based their "Harmonic convergence" of August 1987 on the Mayan calendar (although according to Thompson's calculations it should have occurred in 1986). The next event should be the end of the present cycle of 394 years, which will occur in 2012. Many of their calculations are based on "ancient systems" which are deemed to be more authoritative than the monotheistic systems currently in use.

Bibliography

Barton, Tamsyn. (1994) *Ancient Astrology*. London: Routledge.

Braden, William. (1970) *The Age of Aquarius*. Chicago: Quadrangle.

Ferguson, Marilyn. (1981) *The Aquarian Conspiracy*. Los Angeles: St. Martin's Press.

Gordon, Melton. (1990) *New Age Encyclopedia*. Detroit: Gale Research.

Kessen, A. (1937) *Le Calendier de la République française*. Paris: (no publisher listed).

Dating and chronologies are an important (but not an absolutely essential) part of an apocalypse. By using dates and chronologies, the apocalyptist builds a sense of proportion, and a scale which adds immensely to the other proofs and signs he can adduce. If the calendar or chronology is perceived to be the result of divine intervention, then the authority of the apocalyptist is strengthened immeasurably. It is almost on the level of a revelation for his purposes.

David Cook

Church Universal and Triumphant

The Church Universal and Triumphant emerged as a lineal descendant of earlier esoteric groups in the Ascended Master tradition. Founded as The Summit Lighthouse in 1958, the small, Washington, D.C.-based group assumed the character of a religio-political movement from its inception. Organized by Wisconsin native Mark L. Prophet (1919–73), a onetime Army Air Corps veteran and railway laborer who had been associated with other metaphysical religious movements, The Summit Lighthouse constructed a theology which blended together strident anticommunism and patriotism with a vision of human transcendence to the Godhead. As the organization matured, its esoteric outlook became dominated by images of enemies who were believed to oppose its millennial dream for America's rebirth as a chosen nation.

Mark Prophet's marriage in 1963 to Elizabeth Clare Ytreberg, a twenty-one-year-old student attending Boston University, marked the beginning of a growth period for The Summit Lighthouse during which its membership increased and its publication of theological literature expanded. Functioning as the charismatic spiritual leaders of the movement, Mark and Elizabeth Clare Prophet infused their following with the belief that conspiratorial forces were succeeding in their efforts at destroying the country and that a world catastrophe would soon take place as a sign of God's Judgment against those responsible for America's decline. In response to these perceived threats, the organization adopted a separatist existence, divorced both geographically and psychologically from a society that it perceived as corrupted and on the verge of a cataclysmic event. Its strategy of group separation compelled the group to undertake a series of relocations, first to Colorado, then, shortly following the death of Mark Prophet in 1973, to southern California.

In 1986 the membership of the renamed Church Universal and Triumphant established a spiritual headquarters on an expansive ranch property in Paradise Valley, Montana—a location thought to offer believers safety from the imminent earthly catastrophe predicted by Elizabeth Clare Prophet. Despite its flight to Montana, the membership residing at the communal headquarters site (The Royal Teton Ranch) further descended into the conspiratorial and apocalyptic worldview which had defined the group's past. These attitudes culminated in Elizabeth Clare Prophet's prediction of a Soviet nuclear attack on the U.S. on March 15, 1990. In order to withstand the event, group members embarked upon a survival plan which included constructing underground shelters and purchasing emergency supplies. Although the group possessed weapons, it theology steered it away from a violent encounter with outsiders during the chaotic episode of millennial excitement leading to the expected disaster. The church's mobilization for catastrophe draws attention to the disaster-prone beliefs adhered to by some countercultural groups. Its brush with the apocalypse in Montana offers insights into the crisis psychology that pervades catastrophic millennial movements.

The Lineage of the Church Universal and Triumphant

The Church Universal and Triumphant inherited from Theosophy its theological understanding of universal truth. Theosophical doctrine combined elements of Eastern and Western mysticism, "secrets" obtained from arcane texts, and occultic belief into a syncretic philosophy detached from what its adherents viewed as the rigid orthodoxy of established churches. Its followers comprised a small but well-educated body of upper-middle-class esoteric seekers who desired a new path to spiritual development. Crediting history's secret societies as being the bearers of ancient wisdom possessing mysterious lost truths, the early Theosophists maintained that the hidden knowledge of the universe could be understood by those who studied the esoteric. Taking the name the Theosophical Society, a group founded in New York in 1875 by Helena Petrovna Blavatsky (1813–91) and Henry Steel Olcott (1832–1907), the circle of initiates became the period's most significant expression of ancient wisdom belief. Looking to The Knights Templar and the Masonic Lodge, among others, as groups of the Elect possessing an eternal divine wisdom, Theosophical thought fostered a sense of intrigue and spiritualized elitism among its followers. At the core of the Theosophical belief system was a conviction in the existence of a Brotherhood of Eastern Masters who were thought to steer the evolution of the universe. Dwelling on a higher spiritual plane than that of material man, the Masters were believed to provide Elect disciples with the knowledge necessary to lead humanity to a more sublime state of spiritual evolution.

Theosophy established the metaphysical roots from which the Church Universal and Triumphant would develop, but the church's patriotism and anticommunist ideology came from another source. These features of the church's theology were inherited directly from the I AM movement, founded by Guy Ballard (1880–1939) in the early 1930s. Ballard's I AM organization, whose doctrine borrowed heavily from Theosophy, may have claimed as many as one hundred thousand members at its peak of popularity during the Depression. Asserting the existence of a Great White Brotherhood of spiritual entities (known as Ascend Masters) responsible for directing the spiritual development of the world, Ballard's I AM movement followed in the same occultic tradition advanced by Blavatsky. Like Blavatsky, who claimed to receive messages from the spiritual entities governing the universe, Ballard was recognized in his movement as the "Messenger" of the Ascended Masters, a position he maintained was conferred upon him by the key figure in the group's pantheon of deities, the legendary Saint Germain.

Aside from the act of absorbing several rather well-established esoteric concepts (such as reincarnation and communication with the Masters) into a unified belief system, Ballard's group broke ground with the Theosophical movement by espousing an avowedly political philosophy. The I AM movement envisioned a special destiny for America reflecting its chosen status conferred by the Ascended Masters. Its stridently anticommunist and nationalistic political attitudes were enmeshed within a framework of Theosophically inspired religion, a synthesis which led the I AM following to harbor a vision for America in which its political leaders were guided by the authority of the Ascended Masters. Within the movement, it was believed that obstacles impeding America's path to glory were attributable to the forces of worldly dissension. Notably, leftist political groups and the "antipatriotic" Franklin Delano Roosevelt government were perceived as threats imperiling the grand designs the Ascended Masters had for the country and for the new society the spiritual deities were believed to be orchestrating. Like all millenarian movements, the central beliefs of the I AM sect contained both transcendent and this-worldly aspects. Blending elements of a strong political agenda with its concept of the divine, the message of the I AM religious activity attracted a considerable following at least partially due to its timely appearance on the American historical scene. Appearing during the Depression years, the movement succeeded in tapping into the larger culture's frustration and sense of angst with America's condition.

The Development of the Church Universal and Triumphant

The millennial tendencies of the I AM movement found expression in the voices of others who claimed to receive messages from the Ascended Masters following Guy Ballard's death in 1939. Among these new Messengers was Mark Prophet, who had been associated with some I AM splinter groups which formed several years following Ballard's death. The Washington, D.C.-based Summit Lighthouse, which Prophet founded in 1958 and dedicated to teaching and publishing the word of the Ascended Masters, shared most of the doctrinal beliefs of the I AM movement. Among the similarities between the organizations were their patriotic civil religion, anticommunism, and the view that their members constituted a new spiritual elect. Following his marriage to Elizabeth Clare Ytreberg, Mark Prophet moved his sect to a communal site in Colorado Springs in 1966. The westward relocation represented an important turning point in the psychological worldview of the organization. As opponents of what they saw as the decadent and depraved interests of the Eastern power elite class, the Prophet's brand of populist, Ascended Master religion was not well suited to Washington, D.C. Wary of the existence of an "International Capitalist/Communist Conspiracy" thought to be responsible for America's decline, the group's migration to Colorado symbolized the Prophets' desires to separate the group from a surrounding culture thought to be contaminated by the country's decaying political culture.

The Summit Lighthouse headquarters remained in Colorado Springs until 1975. During this period, some major changes took place within the group which would later prove to have major ramifications for its future development. Mark Prophet's untimely death in 1973 as a result of a massive stroke left the organization under the stewardship of his thirty-three-year-old widow. Declaring that her deceased husband had graduated to the status of Ascended Master, Elizabeth Clare Prophet began to receive and deliver his messages. Mark Prophet's departure became the occasion for the introduction of an apocalyptic tenor to the group's teachings. Claiming that the deceased Messenger had revealed to her images of impending disaster, Elizabeth Clare Prophet began to emphasize preparation for an expected earthly calamity. This scenario involved not only the appearance of naturally occurring phenomena (such as floods and earthquakes), but the likely future persecution of the group by the armed forces of the government.

In the time immediately following her husband's death, Elizabeth Clare Prophet emerged as the sole charismatic leader of the movement. Renaming the sect the Church Universal and Triumphant, she directed its relocation to southern California in 1975. The church counted a worldwide membership of some 25,000 members by this point—the majority of whom, however, were only affiliated with the organization to the degree that they subscribed to church publications. The California phase of the church's history included an initial move to Los Angeles, and then to Pasadena and Malibu, respectively. Because of it financial success, which was bolstered by membership tithes and income derived from the sale of its literature, the church possessed assets sufficient to purchase in 1978 the 218-acre property of the defunct St. Thomas Aquinas College. The move to the Malibu site was accompanied by a wave of negative media coverage, most of which was directed to the alleged misdeeds of the organization. These reports, which charged the group with extorting money from members and engaging in "brainwashing" practices, were usually attributed to defectors who left the church during this period.

The Exodus to Montana and Apocalyptic Mobilization

As the media's criticism became more pronounced, the church's apocalyptic impulses were ratcheted to higher levels. Citing astrological signs pointing to the arrival of a dangerous "karmic acceleration," Elizabeth Clare Prophet informed her following that the 1980s would likely be marked by sweeping catastrophic events. In order to remain safe from the anticipated disasters, the group purchased a 12,000-acre ranch (formerly owned by Malcolm Forbes) in southwestern Montana. Using the proceeds from the sale of the Malibu property to buy the $7 million tract, the church established its 600-member communal settlement in the Paradise Valley region at a location near Yellowstone National Park. The decision to migrate to Montana was not arbitrary. The Teton Mountains, located near the ranch, have always held a special importance for spiritual movements following in the I AM tradition. Believing the Tetons to be the hollow dwelling-place of Saint Germain, I AM followers routinely visited the site during the 1930s and 1940s in the hope that the opening of the mountains would allow the faithful to ascend to the ethereal plane on which the Great White Brotherhood resided.

Although the relocation to the isolated property provided group members with geographical separation from the threat-filled world they envisioned, Prophet continued to warn the movement's most devoted following on the ranch about the likelihood of future world emergencies. Shortly after the move to Montana, Prophet delivered to the membership a dire statement from Saint Germain which conveyed the Ascended Master's suspicion that the Soviet Union was readying to launch a surprise nuclear strike on the United States. Pointing initially to March and April 1990 as a "danger period" for the attack, but later designating 15 March as the date for the event, the Messenger propelled the church on a desperate survivalist initiative. By November 1988, church members had secretly begun work on a massive underground shelter designed to offer security for the ranch residents both during the nuclear war and for several years afterward. The structure, which cost in excess of $10 million to build, was situated on a particularly remote and highly elevated part of the ranch. A similar construction effort began at the same time at Glastonbury, a tract of church-owned property located approximately 20 miles from the Royal Teton Ranch. At this site, which was occupied by 400 group members who sought to live near the organization's headquarters, Prophet's following pooled their resources to build smaller fallout shelters. In an effort to save fellow church members from the disaster, many of the Glastonbury shelters had spaces reserved for those residing outside Montana.

As the shelter construction project continued, between one and two thousand group members flocked to the region to prepare for a nuclear war. From points as distant as Australia, Europe, and South America, members of the church fled their homes in response to the organization's warnings about the expected catastrophe. Arriving ready to participate in an extended prayer vigil designed to psychically ward off the oncoming disaster, believers braced for the attack while, at the same time, desperately seeking to prevent it.

Although the building of the shelter on the Royal Teton Ranch escaped public attention for some time, the July 1989 arrest of group member Vernon Hamilton in Spokane, Washington, alerted the local population to the church's survivalist preparations. News of Hamilton's arrest for conspiring to buy $150,000 worth of assault weapons under a false name immediately focused unwanted attention on the group and its furtive construction effort. While Prophet claimed no knowledge of Hamilton's plan and reported that the illegal affair was not authorized by the church, both local media in Montana and law enforcement officials remained skeptical. The failed attempt to augment the stockpile of firearms, legally owned by individual church members, drew more attention when Edward Francis, the husband of Elizabeth Clare Prophet and an officeholder in the organization, admitted his complicity in the plot. Official church documents obtained through a Freedom of Information Act request by a local newspaper indicated that the group had long believed it would have to defend itself against outsiders in a survivalist struggle following an apocalyptic event. However, no evidence surfaced in the documents that the church ever countenanced striking out against the nonbelieving surrounding society.

Despite the flurry of negative media treatment the church received in the wake of the embarrassing weapons-buying fiasco, the panic-stricken members living on and nearby the ranch continued to prepare themselves to weather the Soviet strike. So powerful was the imagery of the destruction of the existing world that the group practiced emergency drills in anticipation of a nuclear Armageddon. When the predicted time for the event had arrived, the church ordered its members to report to the shelters, where they remained until the morning of 16 March. In the aftermath of the non-event, it is reported that people emerged from the shelters in a state of emotional exhaustion and that many openly rejoiced in amazement that the disaster had not occurred. When the episode passed without incident, many of the group's members experienced a feeling of bewilderment about the dramatic activity in which they had participated. In some cases, the discomforting evidence of life as usual following Elizabeth Clare Prophet's dire warning proved too much to bear. According to recent reports from a high-ranking official in the organization, the church lost 30 percent of its total membership in the days after the nonappearance of the catastrophe.

The Post-Disaster Experience and the Future of the Church Universal and Triumphant

In 1992, after completing a three-year audit of the organization, the IRS revoked the church's tax-exempt status. This was only a temporary setback for the group, however, since the tax-exemption issue was settled in June 1994 when the government agency agreed to restore the church's officially designated standing as a religious organization. The IRS decision to restore the tax exemption came with a number of stipulations. In addition to requiring the church to pay income taxes on some unreported business enterprises, the agency mandated that all communally owned weapons were to be sold and that two years of tax revocation (from 1988–90) be observed as a penalty.

The resolution of the tax issue proved to be a rare piece of news in what otherwise was a decade-long period of problems for the church. By 1995 reports surfaced that many of the ranch residents had grown weary with Prophet's rigid management practices and began to reject the rigorous, monastic lifestyle historically practiced by the church's core adherents. In order to stem a growing tide of defections by disgruntled members, the organization announced publicly that it would begin a sweeping overhaul of its management structure. As part of the plan, Prophet resigned as president of the church, but retained her position as its spiritual leader. Her former post was assumed by Gilbert Cleirbaut, a longtime member and Canadian management consultant once employed by Union Carbide. Cleirbaut soon charted a new public relations strategy which focused on creating a less authoritarian organization with a reduced emphasis on survivalism.

The sudden decline in membership was compounded by the group's inability to market itself to a wider audience. Since its founding, the Prophets had pointed to world communism (and the Soviet Union) as manifestations of pure evil challenging the Forces of Light. The political dissolution of the Soviet Union in 1991, along with American political culture's adoption of a post–Cold-War mindset, adversely impacted the church's recruiting efforts. By far, however, the most serious problem faced by the group since the 1990 apocalyptic mobilization pertains to its ability to survive without the guiding presence of Elizabeth Clare Prophet. In 1998 the church revealed that Prophet was diagnosed with Alzheimer's Disease and that she would soon retire from her role as Messenger. Her imminent absence leaves open the question of how the church will function in the future.

Brad Whitsel

Bibliography

Braden, Charles. (1949) *These Also Believe: A Study of American Cults and Minority Religious Movements.* New York: Macmillan.

Bryan, Gerald. (1940) *Psychic Dictatorship in America.* Burbank, CA: New Era Press.

"Church Regains Tax Status." (1994) *Bozeman Daily Chronicle* (3 June): 1.

"CUT Documents Show Church's Long History of Arms Purchases." (1990) *Livingston Enterprise,* Livingston, MT, (5 March): 1.

"CUT's Theology Hasn't Changed." (1998) *Bozeman Daily Chronicle* (18 March): 1.

Ellwood, Robert. (1979) *Alternative Altars: Unconventional and Eastern Spirituality in America.* Chicago: University of Chicago Press.

"Guru Ma: Leader of A Multi-Million Dollar Church." (1980) *Los Angeles Times* (11 February): 7.

"Leaders Deny CUT Bought Guns." (1995) *Billings Gazette* (16 February): 1.

Melton, Gordon. (1990) *New Age Encyclopedia,* 1st ed. Detroit: Gale Research.

——. (1994) "The Church Universal and Triumphant: Its Heritage and Thoughtworld." In *Church Universal and Triumphant in Scholarly Perspective,* edited by James Lewis and Gordon Melton. Stanford, CA: Center for Academic Publication.

Pearls of Wisdom. (1973) Summit Lighthouse, 16, 21 (May 27): 1.

Prophet, Elizabeth Clare. (1980) *Prophecy for the 1980s: The Handwriting on the Wall.* Malibu, CA: Summit University Press.

——. (1991) *The Astrology of the Four Horsemen.* Livingston, MT: Summit University Press.

Shepherd, Gary, and Lawrence Lilliston. (1994) "Children of the Church Universal and Triumphant: Some Preliminary Impressions." In *Church Universal and Triumphant in Scholarly Perspective,* edited by James Lewis and Gordon Melton. Stanford, CA: Center for Academic Publication.

Washington, Peter. (1993) *Madame Blavatsky's Baboon: A History of the Mystics, Mediums, and Misfits Who Brought Spiritualism to America.* New York: Schocken Books.

Columbus/Colon

Christopher Columbus has served for five centuries as the icon of the modern, adventurous spirit of discovery. It is quite recent that those peoples who had already inhabited the so-called New World have enabled a "rediscovery" of the Americas: the hero can now be read also as a villain, the discovery as a theft. In the attempt to come to terms with the meaning of European colonialism and American identity, we attend here to another facet of the colon/ial mythology embodied in the figure of Columbus (whose name in Spanish, extraordinarily, is Colon). Contrary to the image of the purely rational navigator, with his new scientific cartography, it turns out that he was motivated by beliefs most Americans today would consider wildly irrational: Columbus was inspired by an apocalyptic millennialist vision.

Colon's Millennial Vision

Of course his journals show him driven by multiple motives: huge doses of courage, opportunism, and greed mingle with his apocalypticism. But his extraordinary effect upon history cannot be understood without reference to a particular medieval tradition of millennialism. It is not that he was a member or leader of a millenarian sect. Rather, he was inspired by certain apocalyptic texts and helped in his interpretation by Spanish Franciscans. Given his unparalleled impact upon world history, his simultaneous obsession—whether one deems it grand or grotesque—with apocalyptic and geopolitical calculations reveals something of the spirit of the modern West.

"Of the New Heaven and Earth which our Lord made, as St. John writes in the Apocalypse, after He had spoken in by the mouth of Isaiah, He made me the messenger thereof and showed me where to go" (Morison 1963: 291). This is a startling scriptural interpretation: the future time of apocalypse is collapsed into the space of Colon's own discovery. Colon wrote these words in 1500, during the third expedition. He had managed funding despite what his rulers recognized as scandalous mismanagement of the colony on Hispaniola (the site of his 1498 colonization, where his leadership had seen not only mass murders and suicides of the indigenous Tainos, but also executions of Spaniards). Sailing southward, he has encountered evidence of a continent *(tierra firma)* at the mouth of the Orinoco River. While charting out accurate maps of the coastline, he decides that the earth is not round after all, but shaped "like a woman's breast," or a pear: the perennial fantasy of the world as a woman to be conquered, seems to merge in his imagination with the intensive rape and plunder that had characterized his prior two journeys.

But suddenly he falls into, in his own words, a "state of disarray," pivoting in the waters, sailing suddenly back to Hispaniola, even though he had been forbidden to return there. He gives practical reasons publicly, but in his journal writes: "I am completely persuaded in my own mind that the Terrestrial Paradise is the place I have said." He believes he has in fact found the Lost Eden. The four tributaries of the Orinoco are a perfect match, he believes, for the four rivers flowing from the biblical Eden. There was a medieval tradition of the lost paradise as still extant, waiting to be rediscovered, inhabited by a blessed people living at the fringes of Eden. These Columbus identifies with the people he spots from the ship, whom he describes as "whiter than any others I have seen in the Indies (still his term for the Americas)," and "more intelligent" (Sale 1990: 175). The religious mythology, tinged with the color-coded racism of modernity, serves his voracious opportunism: he is confident they will have (despite his prior disappointments) "plenty of gold." Yet nonetheless he panics: it is the prospect of entering paradise without a directive from God that causes him to flee.

Colon's small library, moreover, contained a still extant volume of Pierre d'Ailly's *Imago Mundi*, which intertwines legends of Eden and of the adjacent land of blessed peoples with the eleventh-century chiliast prophecies of Joachim of Fiore. Colon had pored over this book, consistently marking the Joachite prophecies of a new age. Yet contrary to Joachim, Colon assumed that the "new heaven and earth" were already created, waiting to be discovered—by none other than himself.

Colon's sense of apocalyptic vocation did not just emerge amidst the psychological dysfunctions and dishonor following the first two expeditions. Already in 1493, he had adopted a clever identity sign, reminiscent of adolescent experiments with signature: using the Greek abbreviation for "Christ," to emphasize the Christ in Christopher, he signed his name "XRO-ferens," "Christ-carrier." Choosing a single name in the style of saints and royalty, he makes of himself a messianic sign/nature. As Christopher, patron saint of sailors, had borne Christ across the river, he now would bear Christendom across an ocean. Colon was not developing his theology single-handedly. He boarded often at a Franciscan monastery, to which he had also entrusted his son's care.

The strongest evidence for Colon's millennialism has only recently come to light, with the publication for the first time of a book he authored, *The Prophecies*, in which he unfolds a full millennialist narrative, with himself as its messianic hero. Significantly, he simultaneously wrote a companion volume, *The Privileges*, frantic to claim for himself and his ancestors the glory and money he believed Spain owed him for his colossal achievements. This is the prophetic plot: the Lord chose Colon as the divine instrument for the fulfillment of the biblical prophecies. He would be the one to rescue Christianity before the end of the world, which Colon calculated as due in 155 years, i.e., 1650. He would accomplish this mission by spreading Christianity to the unsaved pagan populations around the world. As he converted he would also conquer, therefore providing the gold for financing the crusade to recapture the Holy Sepulcher from the infidels. To this end, God bestowed upon his herald not only the requisite marine talents, but also the special illumination characteristic of apocalyptic prophets: a "light, which comforted me with its rays of marvelous clarity . . . and urged me onward with great haste continuously and without a moment's pause." "You may rejoice," he wrote to Ferdinand and Isabella, "when I tell you by the same authorities [the prophetic precedents] that you are assured of certain victory in the enterprise of Jerusalem if you have faith" (Sale 1990: 58f). They apparently did not, however, and the future of his millennialism would be left to others "messengers."

Thus in Colon's reading the new creation is the site not of hope, as for many Joachites, but of an impending deadline, leaving little time for the conversion of the earth. But however bizarre his biblical interpretation, he may have fulfilled his own prophecy: he may be described as the prime agent in the Christianization of the globe. And by the same token, he may be counted as the prime agent of Armageddon for Native America. Ironically, the population of 250,000 Tainos was down to 50,000 by 1515 and by his date for doom, none. The tragic ironies continue: Joachim and the Franciscan Radicals he first influenced anticipated a "third status," a new age of economic egalitarianism and monastery style, with no private property; and from here they would build upon the radical critique of imperialist economics of the "Whore of Babylon" allegory in the Book of Revelation. But Colon is the "messenger" of a new age of unprecedented economic growth funded largely by gold, silver, and labor commandeered from the Americas. The identification of the "third age" with the lost paradise seems to have merged with the crude refrain that runs through Colon's journals: "There may be many things that I don't know, for I do not wish to delay but to discover and go to many islands to find gold" (Sale 1990: 197). He failed to turn up the quantities he tirelessly sought, but those who followed in his wake would so flood Europe with the gold and silver of America that a new economic system, that of modern capitalism, would arise. The global growth economy is directly indebted to the native peoples, with the silver, gold, and resources yielded by their slave labor. The "New Heaven and Earth" of which Colon was the messenger would liberate Europeans not from private property but for its limitless pursuit.

Conclusion

As Noam Chomsky notes, the "fundamental themes of the conquest retain their vitality and resilience, and will continue to do so until the reality and causes of the 'savage injustice' [Adam Smith] are honestly addressed" (1993: 5). Considering the millennialism that energizes the "conquest of paradise" (Sale) belongs to such honesty. For that vitality springs at least in part from the fusion of Edenic return-to-the-breast with apocalyptic future-drive.

Catherine Keller

See also Joachism

Bibliography

Chomsky, Noam. (1993) *Year 501: The Conquest Continues.* Boston: South End Press.

Columbus, Christopher. (1991) *The "libro de las profecias" of Christopher Columbus / translation and commentary by Delno C. West and August Kling.* Gainesville, FL: University of Florida Press.

Keller, Catherine. (1996) *Apocalypse Now and Then: A Feminist Guide to the End of the World.* Boston: Beacon.

Morison, Samuel Eliot, ed. and trans. (1963) *Journals and Other Documents on the Life and Voyages of Christopher Columbus.* New York: Heritage Press.

Sale, Kirkpatrick. ([1990] 1991) *The Conquest of Paradise: Christopher Columbus and the Columbian Legacy.* New York: Plume.

Communism

Communist movements can only be considered millenarian in the broadest sense, and more often they are classified as secular revolutionary movements. Socialist and communist revolutions have had serious global impact since the nineteenth century. Karl Marx (1818–83) and his adherents envisioned the historic struggle for a worker paradise to be carried out without any supernatural intervention. Marxists place a strictly materialist faith in the ability of the proletariat to bring about a new age of human emancipation and universal equality. However, certain precursor movements qualify as millenarian because they advocated chiliastic prophecy and communistic land reform. Nevertheless, specific aspects of communist movements, such as charismatic leadership and zeal of followers resemble millenarian expression.

Early Millenarian Tendencies

Millenarian tendencies have been noted in the forerunners of communist movements. Social historian Norman Cohn traced the original meaning of millenarianism to the earliest traditions of religious dissent, specifically to the visions of Jewish and Christian apocalyptic prophecies that called for a messianic and egalitarian kingdom on earth. In a future golden age, people would live in an idyllic state without war or want. Cohn recognized many of these movements, the Anabaptists, the Taborites, and particularly the followers of Thomas Münzer, as forerunners to modern communism. In the early 1500s, the Anabaptists wished to set up separate societies of egalitarian Christian communalism. The Taborites were the most radical part of the Hussite movement of the fifteenth century. While Taborites demanded clerical reform, they also fought against the feudalist exploitation. These groups all believed in the Second Coming of Christ and the inevitability of the new millennium.

The radical Protestant Thomas Münzer (c. 1490–1525) published revolutionary tracts and manifestos. While his rebellion was primarily religious in nature, he supported the peasants against the upper classes and joined a peasant revolt in 1524. He founded a revolutionary organization called the League of the Elect which was organized to lead peasant revolts by force of arms. The League of the Elect charged its disciplined believers with the mission of inaugurating the millennium of true equality. Cohn notes that Friedrich Engels "inflated Münzer into a giant symbol, a prodigious hero in the history of the class war" (1970, 251). In *The Peasant War in Germany*, Karl Marx's friend and collaborator, Engels (1820–95) pointed out that Thomas Münzer's sixteenth-century political program anticipated later interpretations of communism.

Communist Theory

Communism theory analyzes a society with respect to the structure its class system, and it identifies which social class takes advantage of the other by exploiting its labor. Since labor creates all wealth, any profits or surpluses rightfully belong to the workers. Historically, the exploitative class (ruling class) robbed common people of the fruits of the labor, but they consistently had been opposed. Communism views this phenomenon of class struggle as the motivating force of all history. During the class struggle of the modern age, the economic and human contradictions of capitalism would give way to the pinnacle of true socialism, communism. This ideal classless society would be brought about by the efforts of the working class, the proletariat. Communist ideology stressed that the proletariat would bring about a new age where the workers lived in peace and prosperity, but this would not come about without conflict.

As Marx and Engels expounded in many of their works from *The German Ideology* to *The Communist Manifesto*, class struggle over the ownership of the means of production (tools and raw materials needed to earn a living) had shaped history in stages from its simple communal beginning to the perverse inequity of individualistic economics. Throughout the ages, society had moved from a universal stage of tribal communalism to a phase of slavery, then into feudalism, and finally into capitalism. Under capitalism, labor was exploited by the bourgeoisie, but under socialism laborers would finally reap the benefits of their work. Many Marxists believed the transition from capitalism to communism was inevitable. The communistic ideal contains some prophecies of the coming of a perfect society.

In the *Economic and Philosophic Manuscripts of 1844*, Karl Marx defined the new communist society as the reconciliation of humanity with nature and with its fellows. Marx

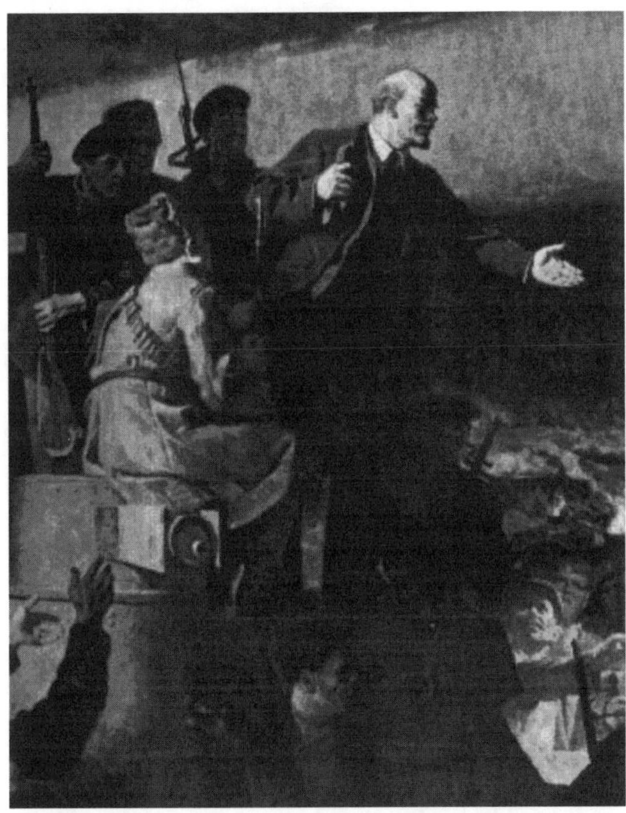

Lenin addressing workers. Although communism is classified as a form of secular millennialism, this and other works are sometimes interpreted as examples of communist religious art. HTTP://WWW.ANU.EDU.AU/POLSCI/MARX/GRAPHICS/VIEWGRAPHICS.HTML.

anticipated that the important feature of this new society would be dignified labor that would emerge when exploited labor was abolished. Marx states, "Communism is the riddle of history solved, and it knows itself to be this solution" (1844, 135). A communist society would be classless without the need for a repressive state or a disadvantageous division of labor. In a communist society, people would live without alienation, or estrangement from self, others, creativity, and work. Alienated labor would vanish. One could fish in the morning and be a social critic in the afternoon. Such a society would eliminate scarcity, as well as allow for the optimal development of human potential. After a period when the "dictatorship of the proletariat" would forcefully insure the construction of communism, the state itself would "wither away."

Karl Marx's historical prophecy said that before communism could be established, capitalism would necessarily destroy itself. The anarchy of production under capitalism would lead to crisis and slumps, and to the turmoil of economic depression. In the process, the system would naturally produce its own gravediggers, the proletariat. The organized representative of the proletariat would be the communist party that would provide leadership, instruction, and discipline for the revolutionary masses.

Communist Movements

Some of communist history centers on the International, which functioned through its social networks, national organizations, and coalitions of local movements to sustain political debate and recommend action. The First International met in London in September, 1864. Marx made the inaugural address and wrote its declaration of principles. The Second International met in 1889 and floundered over discussions of reform and adaptation to the bourgeois state. Debates and schisms among the communist factions continued until 1943 when the Third International voted to dissolve itself. The Fourth International was dominated by Trotsky's followers and the demand for world revolution.

No single entity represents the whole of communist movements, however, the Soviet Union played a significant role. With the success of the Bolshevik Revolution in 1917, communism was attempted on a mass scale. Vladimir Ilich Lenin (1870–1924) came to power and predicted that all countries would imitate the Soviet model. Following the revolution, Marxism became established as the official state ideology. Along with Leon Trotsky (1879–1940), Lenin believed that revolutionary social change would transform their economically backward nation. Trotsky argued for "permanent revolution" throughout the world as the only hope for the survival of communism. After Lenin's demise in 1924, Joseph Stalin instituted a reign of terror in the Soviet state until his death in 1953. Stalin banished Trotsky, forcing him into exile where he was assassinated in 1940 by Stalin's agents.

Although Soviet communism never lived up to the Marxist ideal, it did manage to export and support communist movements throughout the world. During the cold war, the Soviet Union and the Eastern Bloc held the world in an economic and technological stalemate with the United States and its NATO allies. Communist movements took hold most notably in China, Cuba, Vietnam, Central America, South America, and in Africa. There communist rebels fought to rid their respective countries of colonial domination and oppressive class structures.

Similarities to Millenarian Movements

Social thinkers, like Albert Camus and Eric Hoffer, have often drawn parallels between the beliefs and practices of communists and those of true believers and millennial followers. Moreover, communist movements have produced numerous charismatic leaders who invoked the type of zeal once only associated with religious fervor. The devotional nature of some genres of communist art, in which such leaders as Lenin or Mao Zeodong are depicted as divinely idealized, reminds viewers of religious representations. Notwithstanding, most social scientists would be cautious about such comparisons because communist movements are so typically political and secular in nature.

Charismatic leaders abound in communist movements. One such leader was American journalist John Reed (1887–1920), who wrote a first-hand account of the Bolshevik Revolution, *Ten Days That Shook the World.* In Germany, the courageous Rosa Luxemburg (1871–1919) influenced most of the important political debates of her day until she was murdered by the state. In China, Mao Zeodong (1893–1976) led the Communist Revolution in 1947 and the Cultural Revolution in 1966, but his influence did not end there. His little red book, *The Quotations of Chairman Mao,* was widely read in the United States during the sixties, initially because it was sold by the Black Panther Party. During his lifetime, Mao enjoyed a venerated status among the common people. A symbol of revolution in many parts of the world, Ernesto Che Guevara (1928–1967) exported guerrilla warfare to the Third World where communist movements have had their greatest effect by helping to overthrow colonialism.

Diana Tumminia

See also Russian Millennialism, Secular Millennialism

Bibliography

Anderson, Jon Lee. (1997) *Che Guevara: A Revolutionary Life.* New York: Grove Press.

Borkenau, Franz. (1962) *World Communism: A History of the Communist International.* Ann Arbor: University of Michigan Press.

Camus, Albert. (1956) *The Rebel.* New York: Vintage Books.

Cohn, Norman. (1970) *The Pursuit of the Millennium.* London: Oxford University Press.

Deutscher, Isaac. (1954) *The Prophet Armed: Trotsky 1879–1921.* London: Oxford University Press.

Engels, Friedrich. ([1850] 1967) *The Peasant War in Germany.* New York: International Publishers.

Guevara, Ernesto Che. (1985) *Guerrilla Warfare.* Lincoln and London: University of Nebraska Press.

Hoffer, Eric. (1951) *The True Believer: Thoughts on the Nature of Mass Movements.* New York: Harper and Row.

Laidler, Harry W. (1968) *History of Socialism.* New York: Thomas Y. Crowell Company.

Marx, Karl. ([1844] 1971) *Economic and Philosophic Manuscripts of 1844.* New York: International Publishers.

Reed, John. (1935) *Ten Days That Shook the World.* New York: Modern Library.

Trostsky, Leon. (1965) *The Permanent Revolution, and Results and Prospects.* New York: Pioneer Publishers.

Tse-tung, Mao. (1972) *Quotations from Chairman Mao Tse-tung.* Peking: Foreign Language Press.

Urban, George. (1971) *The Miracles of Chairman Mao: A Compendium of Devotional Literature 1966–1970.* Los Angeles: Nash Publishing.

Conspiracism

Conspiracism in a public setting is a narrative form of scapegoating. It justifies the blaming of societal problems on a stigmatized "Them" who are demonized as wholly evil for plotting against the good "Us." Meanwhile, the scapegoater is acclaimed as a hero for revealing the plot against the common good.

There are real conspiracies throughout history, but there are also people who believe in conspiracies that do not actually exist, or are grossly exaggerated in form or outcome. The word "conspiracy" is from the Latin term for "breathing together," and, as it suggests, a real conspiracy requires two or more individuals. Conspiracism, however, requires only one person with a fertile imagination.

"Conspiracism serves the needs of diverse political and social groups in America and elsewhere," writes Mintz, "it identifies elites, blames them for economic and social catastrophes, and assumes that things will be better once popular action can remove them from positions of power" (1995: 199). Conspiracism can flourish in a mass movement, be used as a tool in a power struggle between competing elites, or as a justification for state agencies to engage in repressive actions against alleged subversives.

Most of the conspiracist allegations in Western culture are variations on the themes propounded in the late 1700s by Robison and Barruel, who saw a vast secret plot to spread the subversive Enlightenment ideas of liberty, democracy, and freedom.

Both authors were religious philosophers who claimed that a Bavarian-based secret society called the Illuminati worked through the Freemasons to undermine church and state as part of a global conspiracy to create a one-world government.

In the early 1900s many of the same charges concerning the Freemasons were incorporated into allegations of secret plots by international Jewish bankers, an idea spread by the hoax text, *The Protocols of the Secret Elders of Zion.*

The Protocols was a propaganda plot by the Russian secret police to scapegoat Jews as subversives as the cause of political unrest. The text purports to be secret minutes of meetings held by a supreme international Jewish council conspiring to control the world. No such meetings took place, the council does not exist, the charge of conspiracy is false, and the entire document is a fraud. Yet, as Cohn, Mintz, and Johnson observe, *The Protocols* has a life of its own and continues to play a major role in promoting prejudice and conspiracism.

Conspiracist thinking is an action-oriented worldview which holds out to believers the possibility of change. As Blee has observed through interviews with women in white racist groups, "Conspiracy theories not only teach that the world is divided into an empowered 'them' and a less powerful 'us' but also suggest a strategy by which the 'us' (ordinary people, the non-conspirators) can challenge and even usurp the authority of the currently-powerful" (1996: 98). Thus conspiracist scapegoating fills a need for explanations among the adherents by providing a simple model of good versus evil in which the victory over evil is at least possible.

Fenster argues that conspiracism is the way some people construct a theory of power, albeit a way that fails to recognize how real power relations work. He sees it as related to a particular form of populism that seeks to mobilize "the people" against a "power bloc" of secret elites. According to Fenster, "just because overarching conspiracy theories are wrong does not mean they are not on to something. Specifically, they ideologically address real structural inequities, and constitute a response to a withering civil society and the concentration of the ownership of the means of production, which together leave the political subject without the ability to be recognized or to signify in the public realm" (1999: 67).

So instead of aiming criticism at institutions or systems, the conspiracist points the finger at individuals or groups portrayed as malicious. Groups at various times named as part of a sinister conspiracy include Jews, Jesuits, Freemasons, the Illuminati, Arabs, anarchists, communists, civil rights activists, Black militants, environmentalists, secular humanists, gay rights activists, the Rothschilds, the Rockefellers, the Council on Foreign Relations, the Trilateral Commission, the Bilderberg banking discussion group, and the United Nations.

The conspiracist often employs common fallacies of logic in analyzing factual evidence to assert connections, causality, and intent that are nonexistent. This manifests itself in degrees. "It might be possible, given sufficient time and patience," writes Davis, "to rank movements of counter-subversion on a scale of relative realism and fantasy" (1971: xiv). The distance from reality and logic the conspiracist analysis drifts has a wide range. Some are more successful at passing off their contentions than others.

Billig, who has studied conspiracism in Britain, has observed that "Not all conspiracy theorists express their ideas in the same way, and on occasions they criticize each other. Sometimes the basic assumption of a world conspiracy is expressed with crudity which embarrasses some of the more sophisticated theorists" (1989: 156). Pipes has studied conspiracism in the Middle East and finds three contexts where it has substantial influence: "the Arab-Israeli conflict, Iranian politics, and Iraq's conflicts with the outside world" (1998: 33). Pipes divides conspiracy theorists around the world into three archetypes: fanatics, for whom facts are irrelevant; cynics, who know they are spreading lies; and enigmatics, who start the process of belief as opportunists, but gradually come to sincerely believe what began as a deception.

Conspiracism in the United States

Conspiracist movements have flourished episodically throughout U.S. history. It appears that in the United States, middle-class populist groups on the political right have most often fanned apocalyptic fears of evil conspiracies to create a powerful political weapon. The results can be devastating. There have been crusades against sin; waves of government repression justified by claims of subversive conspiracies; and campaigns to purge alien ideas and persons from our shores.

Starting in the 1620s, witch-hunts swept New England for a century. Concerns over a Freemason/Illuminati conspiracy briefly appeared in 1798–99. The 1800s saw a period of anti-Catholic conspiracism. The early 1900s produced allegations of a Jewish banking cabal behind the Federal Reserve. There were fears of vast anarchist plots by immigrants in the early 1920s, the anticommunist witch-hunts of the McCarthy Period in the 1950s, and allegations of a communist conspiracy behind the civil rights movement in the 1960s and the movement against the Vietnam War in the 1960s and 1970s. The 1980s brought allegations of a vast homosexual conspiracy, while the 1990s saw armed militias forming against a suspected New World Order conspiracy by the government to help the United Nations impose a global government.

Hofstadter popularized the idea of conspiracism when he coined the term "paranoid style" to describe the belief among some right-wing populists in "the existence of a vast, insidious, preternaturally effective international conspiratorial network designed to perpetrate acts of the most fiendish character" (1965: 14). Hofstadter laid out the three basic elements of right-wing thought that flourished in the United States in the 1950s:

> First, there has been the now familiar sustained conspiracy, running over more than a generation, and reaching its climax in Roosevelt's New Deal, to undermine free capitalism, to bring the economy under the direction of the federal government, and to pave the way for socialism or communism . . .

> The second contention is that top government officialdom has been so infiltrated by Communists that American policy, at least since the days leading up to Pearl Harbor, has been dominated by sinister men who were shrewdly and consistently selling out American national interests.
>
> The final contention is that the country is infused with a network of Communist agents . . . so that the whole apparatus of education, religion, the press, and the mass media are engaged in a common effort to paralyze the resistance of loyal Americans. (1965: 25–26)

Social scientists following Hofstadter usually divided the phenomena he described into discrete yet related components: apocalypticism, demonization, scapegoating, and conspiracism. They also moved away from the idea that conspiracism was tied to a pathological psychological condition.

Davis observed that collective "beliefs in conspiracy have usually embodied or given expression to genuine social conflict." Thus conspiracism needs some indigestion in the body politic for which the conspiracist seeks causation so that blame can be affixed. As Davis observes sympathetically, many persons who embraced conspiracy theories in earlier historic periods "were responding to highly disturbing events; their perceptions, even when wild distortions of reality, were not necessarily unreasonable interpretations of available information" (1971: xiv). The interpretations, however, were frequently inaccurate and occasionally created havoc.

Those who suspect a conspiracy to subvert society often build a countersubversive apparatus in public and private agencies to battle the perceived threat. Donner argued there was an institutionalized culture of countersubversion in the United States "marked by a distinct pathology: conspiracy theory, moralism, nativism, and suppressiveness" (1980: 10). This countersubversion worldview, itself a form of conspiracism, is linked to government attempts to disrupt and crush dissident social movements in the United States. This is certainly the case with the illegal campaigns against dissidents carried out in secret by the Federal Bureau of Investigation under J. Edgar Hoover and later exposed in congressional hearings in the 1970s.

While there are sometimes real forces at work trying to subvert authority, Davis points out that "genuine conspiracies have seldom been as dangerous or as powerful as have movements of countersubversion. The exposer of conspiracies necessarily adopts a victimized, self-righteous tone which masks his own meaner interests as well as his share of responsibility for a given conflict. Accusations of conspiracy conceal or justify one's own provocative acts and thus contribute to individual or national self-deception. Still worse, they lead to overreactions, particularly to degrees of suppressive violence which normally would not be tolerated" (1971: 361). Pipes claims that in the West, "conspiracy theories are today the preserve of the alienated and the fringe" (1998: 2). Many who study conspiracism in the United States disagree with that assessment. Curry and Brown argue that "It is extremely important to note that fears of conspiracy are not confined to charlatans, crackpots, and the disaffected. Anticonspiratorial rhetoric has been a factor in major-party politics" throughout U.S. history (1972: x). Diamond (1995), Hardisty (1999), and Stein (1998) have shown that Christian Right fears of a secular humanist conspiracy on behalf of a global collectivist government continue to influence domestic and foreign policy initiatives in the United States.

Conspiracist Narratives

Conspiracist narratives are spread through both mainstream and alternative media networks. There are many overlapping conspiracist subcultures with their own channels of information distribution. In addition to books and periodicals, there is an increased reliance on the Internet. There are also fax networks; shortwave radio programs; networks of small AM radio stations with syndicated programs distributed by satellite transmissions or even by mailed audiotapes; home satellite dish reception, providing both TV audio/video programs and separate audio programs; local cable television channels, through which nationally produced videos can sometimes get aired; and mail-order video and audiotape distributorships.

Right-wing sources frequently cited as having "proof" of the conspiracy include the *New American* magazine from the John Birch Society, the *Spotlight* newspaper from the Liberty Lobby, and *Executive Intelligence Review* (EIR) and *The New Federalist* from the Lyndon LaRouche movement. On the political left, conspiracy theories often focus on the assassinations of the Kennedys and Martin Luther King, Jr.; claims of a "Secret Team" of government agents operating independently; or the idea that a few wealthy families control the world. The *Prevailing Winds* magazine and catalog is aimed at the left while mixing theories from the left and right. Turner (1993) has shown a paradigm of conspiracism in the black community whereby white-owned businesses are suspected of selling products intentionally designed to sterilize black men or to fund campaigns to oppress black people.

Christian Millennial and Apocalyptic Conspiracism

During the cold war, some conservative Christian anticommunists linked liberalism to Godless collectivism; then to the notion of a liberal secular humanist conspiracy; and finally concluded that globalism is the ultimate collectivist plot. Prior to the collapse of the major communist governments in Europe, many leaders of the Christian Right had already embraced a variation on their long-standing fear of secret elites in league with Satan in the endtimes prior to the millennium. This is sometimes called the secular humanist conspiracist theory. According to George Marsden, the shift in focus to the secular humanist demon "revitalized fundamentalist conspiracy theory. Fundamentalists always had been alarmed at moral decline within America but often had been vague as to whom, other than the Devil, to blame. The 'secular humanist' thesis gave this central concern a clearer focus that was more plausible and of wider appeal than the old mono-causal communist-conspiracy accounts. Communism and socialism could, of course, be fit right into the humanist picture; but so could all the moral and legal changes at home without implausible scenarios of Russian agents infiltrating American schools, government, reform movements, and mainline churches" (1991: 109).

O'Leary contends that the process of demonization is central to all forms of conspiracist thinking. He has identified one important distinction between secularized generic conspiracism and the type of apocalyptic conspiracism found more often among the devoutly religious. Generic conspiracism "strives to provide a spatial self-definition of the true community as set apart from the evils" seen in the scapegoated "Other." Apocalyptic conspiracism, however "locates the problem of evil in time and looks forward to its imminent resolution" by God, while warning that "evil must grow in power until the appointed time" (1994: 6). Zeskind argues conspiracy theories are "essentially theologically constructed views of events. Conspiracy theories are renderings of a metaphysical devil which is trans-historical, omnipotent, and destructive of God's will on earth. This is true even for conspiracy theories in which there is not an explicit religious target" (1996: 13–14).

Even when not directly tied to diabolical schemes, conspiracism is widespread in the Christian Right; for example in the works of right-wing Christian conspiracists such as Robertson, LaHaye, Kah, McAlvany, and Zahner. Robertson's work is littered with conspiracist allegations and references, including his invocation of the Freemason conspiracy "revealed in the great seal adopted at the founding of the United States." Robertson links Freemasonry to endtimes predictions of a "mystery religion designed to replace the old Christian world order of Europe and America" (1991: 36). Still, attacks the Freemasons as part of a conspiracy to control the country through the issuing of paper money. According to Still, his book shows "how an ancient plan has been hidden for centuries deep within secret societies. This scheme is designed to bring all of mankind under a single world government—a New World Order. This plan is of such antiquity that its result is even mentioned in the Bible—the rule of the Antichrist mentioned in . . . Revelation" (1990: Introduction).

Conclusions

Conspiracism, since it is a form of scapegoating, can damage society, disrupting rational political discourse and creating targets who are harassed and even murdered. Dismissing the conspiracism often found in right-wing populism as marginal extremism or lunatic hysteria does little to challenge these movements, fails to deal with concrete conflicts and underlying institutional issues, invites government repression, and sacrifices the early targets of the scapegoaters on the altar of denial. An effective response requires a more complex analysis that considers the following factors: (1) All conspiracist theories start with a grain of truth, which is then transmogrified through hyperbole and filtered through preexisting myth and prejudice; (2) People who believe conspiracist allegations sometimes act on those irrational beliefs, and this has concrete consequences in the real world; (3) Conspiracist thinking and scapegoating are symptoms, not causes, of underlying societal frictions, and as such should not be ignored; (4) Scapegoating and conspiracist allegations are tools that can be used by cynical leaders to mobilize a mass following; (5) Supremacist and fascist organizers use conspiracist theories as a relatively unthreatening entry point in making contact with potential recruits; and (6) Even when conspiracist theories do not center on Jews, people of color, or other scapegoated groups, they create an environment where racism, anti-Semitism, and other forms of prejudice and oppression can flourish.

Chip Berlet

See also New World Order

Bibliography

Barruel, Abbé Augustin. ([1797–98] 1995) *Memoirs Illustrating the History of Jacobinism*, 2d ed, translated by Robert Clifford. Fraser, MI: Real-View-Books.

Berlet, Chip. (1996) "Three Models for Analyzing Conspiracist Mass Movements of the Right." In *Conspiracies: Real Grievances, Paranoia, and Mass Movements*, edited by Eric Ward. Seattle: Northwest Coalition Against Malicious Harassment (PB Publishing), 47–75.

——. (1998) "Who's Mediating the Storm? Right-wing Alternative Information Networks." In *Culture, Media, and the Religious Right*, edited by Linda Kintz and Julia Lesage. Minneapolis: University of Minnesota Press, 249–73.

Billig, Michael. (1989) "The Extreme Right: Continuities in Anti-Semitic Conspiracy Theory in Post-War Europe." In *The Nature of the Right: American and European Politics and Political Thought Since 1789*, edited by Roger Eatwell and Noel O'Sullivan. Boston: Twayne Publishers, 146–66.

Blee, Kathleen M. (1996) "Engendering Conspiracy: Women in Rightist Theories and Movements." In *Conspiracies: Real Grievances, Paranoia, and Mass Movements*, edited by Eric Ward. Seattle: Northwest Coalition Against Malicious Harassment (PB Publishing), 91–112.

Cohn, Norman. (1969) *Warrant for Genocide*. New York: Harper & Row.

Curry, Richard O., and Thomas M. Brown, eds. (1972) *Conspiracy: The Fear of Subversion in American History*. New York: Holt, Rinehart and Winston.

Davis, David B., ed. (1971) *The Fear of Conspiracy: Images of Un-American Subversion from the Revolution to the Present*. Ithaca, NY: Cornell University Press.

Dean, Jodi. (1998) *Aliens in America: Conspiracy Cultures from Outerspace to Cyberspace*. Ithaca, NY: Cornell University Press.

Diamond, Sara. (1995) *Roads to Dominion: Right-Wing Movements and Political Power in the United States*. New York: Guilford.

Donner, Frank J. (1980) *The Age of Surveillance: The Aims and Methods of America's Political Intelligence System*. New York: Alfred A. Knopf.

Fenster, Mark. (1999) *Conspiracy Theories: Secrecy and Power in American Culture*. Minneapolis, MN: University of Minnesota Press.

Hardisty, Jean. (1999) *Mobilizing Resentment: Conservative Resurgence from the John Birch Society to the Promise Keepers*. Boston: Beacon.

Hofstadter, Richard. (1965) "The Paranoid Style in American Politics." *The Paranoid Style in American Politics and Other Essays*. New York: Alfred A. Knopf.

Johnson, George. (1983) *Architects of Fear: Conspiracy Theories and Paranoia in American Politics*. Los Angeles: Tarcher/Houghton Mifflin.

Kah, Gary H. (1991) *En Route to Global Occupation*. Lafayette, LA: Huntington House Publishers.

LaHaye, Tim. (1980) *The Battle for the Mind*. Old Tappan, NJ: Fleming H. Revell.

Marsden, George M. (1991) *Understanding Fundamentalism and Evangelicalism*. Grand Rapids, MI: William B. Eerdmans Publishing Co.

Martin, William. (1996) *With God on Our Side: The Rise of the Religious Right in America*. New York: Broadway Books.

McAlvany, Donald S. (1990) *Toward a New World Order: The Countdown to Armageddon*. Oklahoma City, OK: Hearthstone Publishing/Southwest Radio Church of the Air.

Mintz, Frank P. (1985) *The Liberty Lobby and the American Right: Race, Conspiracy, and Culture*. Westport, CT: Greenwood.

O'Leary, Stephen. (1994) *Arguing the Apocalypse*. New York: Oxford University Press.

Pipes, Daniel. (1997) *Conspiracy: How the Paranoid Style Flourishes and Where it Comes From*. New York: The Free Press.

——. (1998) *The Hidden Hand: Middle East Fears of Conspiracy*. New York: St. Martins.

Robertson, Pat. (1991) *The New World Order: It Will Change the Way You Live*. Dallas: Word Publishing.

Robison, John. ([1798] 1967) *Proofs of a Conspiracy—— Against All the Religions and Governments of Europe, carried on in the secret meetings of Freemasons, Illuminati and Reading Societies*, 4th ed. Boston, MA: Western Islands.

Stein, Arlene. (1998) "Whose Memories? Whose Victimhood? Contests for the Holocaust Frame in Recent Social Movement Discourse." *Sociological Perspectives* 41, 3: 519–40.

Still, William T. (1990) *New World Order*. Lafayette, LA: Huntington House.

Thompson, Damian. (1998) *The End of Time: Faith and Fear in the Shadow of the Millennium*. Hanover, NH: University Press of New England.

Turner, Patricia A. (1993) *I Heard it Through the Grapevine, Rumor in African-American Culture*. Berkeley: University of California Press.

Ward, Eric, ed. (1996) *Conspiracies: Real Grievances, Paranoia, and Mass Movements*. Seattle: Northwest Coalition Against Malicious Harassment [PB Publishing].

Zahner, Dee. (1994) *The Secret Side of History: Mystery Babylon and the New World Order*. Hesperia, CA: LTAA Communications.

Zeskind, Leonard. (1996) "Some Ideas on Conspiracy Theories for a New Historical Period." In *Conspiracies: Real Grievances, Paranoia, and Mass Movements*, edited by Eric Ward. Seattle: Northwest Coalition Against Malicious Harassment (PB Publishing), 11–35.

Conversion

In many ways conversion is at the heart of millennial movements. As William James put it in *The Varieties of Religious Experience*, conversion involves the turning away from a state that is judged to be "wrong, inferior, and unhappy" and toward an opposite state that is considered "right, superior, and happy" (1958: 157). Since they envisage a total transformation of the world, millennial movements seek conversion on the grandest scale. In their quest for a new, perfect order they aim at the removal of impurity, immorality, ambiguity, and flux, and they anticipate the permanent fixing of individuals into one of two radically opposed categories, the saved and the damned. Millennial movements' quest for certainty leads directly to the quest for converts.

Because they claim to possess the ultimate truth about time, history, morality, and authority, among other topics, the only plausible response millennial movements can envision is acceptance of their message and conversion to their cause. As Stephen O'Leary observed, "When a prophet or prophetic interpreter proposes that the world is coming to an end, or that a period of millennial peace is about to begin, he or she is offering an argumentative claim—a statement that is designed to gain the adherence of an audience" (1994: 4). Converts are the lifeblood of millennial movements. Just as gaining converts nourishes the millennial vision and testifies to its truth, the failure to obtain converts and, more devastatingly, their departure before the millennial goal is realized can significantly weaken a movement and diminish faith in its teachings.

The renovation of the world that millennial movements seek is mirrored on the individual level by the remaking of the self through conversion. That parallel is evoked in the statement of one of the earliest U.S. converts to the Unification Church of Rev. Sun Myung Moon. Concerning herself and her fellow converts, she recalled that "we thought that we had entered the Garden of Eden because the atmosphere was so totally changed" (Fichter 1987: 20). In converts to millennial movements the desire to become a new person and the ambition to transform the world come together. Noting strong similarities between the social and psychological contexts that give birth to millennial movements and the contexts that facilitate individual conversion, Michael Barkun has proposed that people "cleave to hopes of imminent worldly salvation only when the hammerblows of disaster destroy the world they have known and render them susceptible to ideas which they would earlier have cast aside" (1974: 1). Similarly, Lewis Rambo emphasizes the goals that conversion shares with millennial movements by characterizing it as "one of humanity's ways of approaching its self-conscious predicament, of solving or resolving the mystery of human origins, meaning, and destiny" (1993: 2).

The Experience of Conversion

Although conversion can be defined in many ways, it typically involves a significant reorientation of the self toward a new identity and new values and goals—precisely what millennial movements offer. In many instances a prophetic leader embodies the new ideal. Concerning the figure of the prophet in New Guinea "cargo cults," Kenelm Burridge observed that "he either symbolizes the new man in himself, or he is the vehicle by means of which the lineaments of the new man may become known" (1969: 155). Imitation of the leader then becomes the surest path to the millennial kingdom.

Evidence about conversion comes in different forms. Full-scale autobiographies are less readily available than third-person narratives that describe conversion and the more terse and enigmatic brief reports and passing mentions of conversions. Also, in some contemporary instances, social scientists have provided reliable survey data about conversion. Scholars, however, differ about the relative importance of different kinds of evidence and the best strategies for interpreting it. William James, for example, focused on the richly detailed autobiographical accounts of extraordinary figures. He argued he could still construct a broad portrait of conversion since such prominent figures served as the "pattern-setters" for more ordinary believers. James's primary goal was to develop an anatomy of the "conversion experience" but his approach has proved less helpful for answering other questions. For example, historian Ramsey MacMullen argued that a Jamesian focus on the individual cannot produce an accurate understanding of broad historical changes such as the Christianization of the Roman empire. On their part, social scientists have focused on developing and testing models of the conversion process, and many of them have been drawn into the contemporary controversy about "brainwashing" or "coercive persuasion" in certain religious groups. In general the diversity of evidence about conversion and the variety of approaches to it argue against a single comprehensive interpretation of conversion to millennial movements.

Some of the dynamics of conversion, however, are clearly displayed in an example from one of the millennial strands of earliest Christianity. In a letter written in the early '50s to a small community that he had founded in Thessalonica the early Christian missionary Paul of Tarsus praised the group for "how you turned to God from idols, to serve a living and true God, and to wait for his Son from heaven, whom he raised from the dead, Jesus who delivers us from the wrath to come" (1 Thessalonians 1:9–10). Although he did not discuss their particular motives, Paul left no doubt that the Thessalonians' conversions happened in response to his millennial preaching. Later in the same letter he assured them that the apocalyptic events about which he preached would certainly transpire in their lifetimes. In a passage that has figured prominently in subsequent Christian millennialism, Paul described an extraordinary scene: "for the Lord himself will descend from heaven with a cry of command, with the archangel's call, and with the sound of the trumpet of God. And the dead in Christ will rise first; then we who are alive, who are left, shall be caught up together with them in the clouds to met the Lord in the air; and so we shall always be with the Lord" (1 Thessalonians 4:16–17).

Indirectly, Paul's letter suggests that maintaining the commitment of converts is at least as important as initially gaining it, especially in situations where conversion represents a dissent against the established order and where converts embrace a millennial message that can easily be called into question, if not wholly disconfirmed, by the passage of time. Through a rhetoric of reassurance and exhortation, Paul endeavored to keep their millennial hopes alive in order to reinforce his converts' commitment. He recalled both how their conversion was modeled on his own and how they themselves became models for other converts (1:6–7); he provided practical advice about how they should conduct themselves in the world (4:1–12), and he took seriously the questions that they had about the consequences of their beliefs (4:13–18). Paul's letter points to the mutually reinforcing interactions between converts, the communities that they join, and the religious leaders that they accept. As Peter Berger and Thomas Luckmann have emphasized, "to have a conversion experience is nothing much. The real thing is to be able to keep on taking it seriously, to maintain a sense of its plausibility. *This* is where the religious community comes in" (1966: 158). That observation becomes all the more important in the case of millennial movements, particularly when they have indicated a date for the imminent transformation of the world.

In Paul's account the voices of individual Thessalonian converts are strikingly absent. In many other instances, however, converts have produced retrospective accounts of their own experience. But those stories provide slippery evidence. They often testify as much to how the convert's new religious community believes conversion *should* be understood as they do to the convert's actual experience. Indeed, access to the immediate experience of converts is always clouded by the interpretive claims that they embed in their autobiographical narratives. The robust confidence with which William James attempted to uncover the "original experiences" of converts has been tempered both by philosophical critiques of James's method and by sociological research on the processes by which converts construct accounts of their own experience. Wayne Proudfoot, for example, has argued that rather than providing transparent windows on experience, autobiographical stories of conversion reveal the influences of both the convert's personal history and the context in which the story is told.

An example from a convert to the mid-nineteenth-century Millerite movement clarifies the issue. Henry B. Bear reports that when he was living in Lancaster County, Pennsylvania in 1843 "there was loaned to me one volume of Miller's lectures on Christ's second coming, which, it stated, would take place during the very year upon which we have then entered. I read the lectures carefully at first, and later prayerfully. Miller's manner of reasoning; his explanation of the prophecies, and the starting point he gave to them, appeared to me so correct that they caused convictions to grow up in my mind that he was correct in his views" (Numbers and Butler 1993: 217). On the surface, Bear's story appears to recount a straightforward intellectual conversion. But his characterization of his conversion had powerful polemical potential in the context of general hostility to the Millerite movement. By emphasizing the deliberative nature of his encounter with Millerite prophecy, the rational process of his conversion, and the compelling logic of Miller's interpretation of the Bible, Bear removed from his experience any taint of the "fanaticism" that was often attributed to the Millerites by hostile contemporaries. Bear portrays himself and the movement he joined as serious, studious, and devoted to understanding the biblical text, and therefore as legitimate and respectable manifestations of Christian faith.

Bear's story also points to one of the prominent traits of millennialism within the biblical tradition, its learned character. Even when their claims to special saving knowledge are rejected by the mainstream, biblical millennialists are devoted to proving their positions through rigorous textual analysis, careful calculations, far-ranging comparisons, and other intellectual feats. Through their presentations of millennial doctrine and their stories of conversion they strive to show that, far from being vulgar enthusiasts, they are really sober seekers of wisdom.

A century and a half after the Millerites, in 1993, Steve Schneider also appealed to the intellectual character of biblical millennialism in alluding to the processes of conversion that brought him and many others to study with David Koresh, the teacher and prophet of the Branch Davidian sect, headquartered at its Mount Carmel Center near Waco, Texas. Referring to the members of the community, Schneider said, "The reason they came here, all that they are and what they want to be revolves around what they see him showing from that book" (Gallagher 1999: 3). Of himself Schneider said, "I'm here because the man who has had the ability to harmonize many—in fact all the Bible and made it very clear . . . there's something he's got to say that I don't have the ability to do. The . . . reason I'm here is because of what the man's been able to show with the Bible" (ibid.: 7f.). Koresh himself stated that when "doctrine is properly weighed and measured, being systematically harmonized with scripture, text, chapter, book, then we develop an infallible, conclusive picture of what God's will is. Not just a little verse here, not just a little verse there. No. The content must be complete" (ibid., 7). Although Koresh had relatively little success in attracting converts, those who did join him found his interpretations of the Bible logically unassailable. For converts like Schneider there was a perfect fit between their intellectual search for the knowledge that would lead to salvation and the message that Koresh preached.

The Branch Davidians were steeped in a millennial tradition that could be directly traced to the Millerite and subsequent Adventist movements and through them to the scriptural texts, such as the Book of Revelation, that have animated millennialism in the biblical tradition. In fact, more than 90 percent of those at Mount Carmel came from a Seventh-Day Adventist background. That homogeneity signals something important about the process of conversion. Many scholars have noted that religious conversion most often is experienced by people who are already in some way religious. Lewis Rambo's five ideal types of conversion highlight that factor and can facilitate the analysis of individual "conversion careers." In intensification a convert revitalizes a commitment that had previously lay dormant. Affiliation describes the movement of an individual from little or no religious commitment to joining a religious community. Some individuals make an institutional transition, such as between forms of Protestantism. In addition, some converts move from one religious tradition to an entirely new one, sometimes under the pressure of colonial missionary efforts. Finally, departure from a religious tradition, through apostasy or defection, needs also to be considered a type of conversion. All five types are represented in conversion to millennial movements. Those Thessalonians converted by Paul, for example, moved from their previous religious tradition to a new one. The Seventh-Day Adventists who accepted David Koresh as their teacher, on the other hand, blended elements of intensification and institutional transition, since they joined a strongly millennial group that had been ostracized by its parent body.

Sociologists John Lofland and Rodney Stark have also attempted to describe how background and context influence the course and character of an individual's conversion. In "Becoming a World Saver," (1965) they developed a model of conversion that attempted to account for both predisposing and situational factors. Predisposing factors include already having a religious "problem-solving perspective" and experiencing significant enough tension to define oneself as a "religious seeker." Situational factors include meeting the new group at a personal turning point, developing strong bonds with members, and weakening bonds with outsiders. Like Rambo's ideal types of conversion, Lofland and Stark's model points observers to significant details in accounts of conversion. For example, Henry Bear's inclination to read the Millerite prophecies "carefully at first, and later prayerfully" clearly indicates his religious orientation and at least suggests that he was open to receiving more wisdom from the scriptures. Even if he wasn't at a turning point in his life prior to reading the Millerite texts, his reception of them created one for him. Also, Bear's exclamation, following his conversion, that "if I could make all the world hear [about Miller's millennial prophecies], I would" (Numbers and Butler 1993: 218) bears out Lofland and Stark's suggestion that under certain conditions converts can easily become missionaries for their new faith.

Conclusion

The rich diversity of conversion autobiographies, narratives, reports, and mentions and the equally rich array of theories, models, and types of conversion makes the study of conversion to millennial groups both fruitful and complicated. Stephen O'Leary's comments about the rhetorical nature of millennial discourse in general need also to be applied to accounts of conversion to millennial groups. Conversion stories of all sorts are situated examples of persuasive speech. When they come from converts themselves they will portray the converts and the millennial movement in the best possible light; when they come from opponents or detractors of either the convert or the movement, they will draw upon an arsenal of invective designed to deny the legitimacy of the convert's claims and of the movement's millennial message. Used judiciously and with an awareness of the scholarly discussions about them, tools such as O'Leary's rhetorical analysis, James's and Rambo's anatomies of the conversion experience and process, and Lofland and Stark's model of conversion, can help observers chart the diverse paths by which individuals come to join millennial movements, the various devices by which movements strive to maintain and strengthen converts' commitment, and the consequences for individuals when millennial expectations, as they invariably do, fade or fail.

Eugene V. Gallagher

See also Davidians, Millerites, Premillenialism

Bibliography

Barkun, Michael. (1974) *Disaster and the Millennium.* New Haven, CT: Yale University Press.

Beckford, James A. (1978) "Accounting for Conversion." *British Journal of Sociology* 29: 249–62.

Berger, Peter, and Thomas Luckmann. (1966) *The Social Construction of Reality: A Treatise in the Sociology of Knowledge.* New York: Doubleday.

Bromley, David G., and James T. Richardson, eds. (1983) *The Brainwashing/Deprogramming Controversy.* Lewiston, NY: Edwin Mellen.

Burridge, Kenelm. (1969) *New Heaven, New Earth: A Study of Millenarian Activities.* New York: Schocken.

Fichter, Joseph, ed. (1987) *Autobiographies of Conversion.* Lewiston, NY: Edwin Mellen.

Gallagher, Eugene V. (1990) *Expectation and Experience: Explaining Religious Conversion.* Atlanta: Scholars Press.

——. (1999) "Negotiating Salvation." *Nova Religio* 2: 8–16.

James, William. (1958) *The Varieties of Religious Experience.* New York: New American Library.

Lofland, John, and Rodney Stark. (1965) "Becoming a World-Saver: A Theory of Conversion to a Deviant Perspective." *American Sociological Review* 30: 862–75.

Morrison, Karl F. (1992) *Understanding Conversion.* Charlottesville, VA: University of Virginia.

Nock, Arthur Darby. (1933) *Conversion: The Old and the New in Religion from Alexander the Great to Augustine of Hippo.* New York: Oxford University Press.

Numbers, Ronald L., and Jonathan M. Butler. (1993) *The Disappointed: Millerism and Millenarianism in the Nineteenth Century.* Knoxville, TN: University of Tennessee.

O'Leary, Stephen. (1994) *Arguing the Apocalypse: A Theory of Millennial Rhetoric.* Oxford, U.K.: Oxford University Press.

MacMullen, Ramsay. (1984) *Christianizing the Roman Empire: A.D. 100–400.* New Haven, CT: Yale University Press.

Proudfoot, Wayne. (1985) *Religious Experience.* Berkeley, CA: University of California.

Rambo, Lewis. (1993) *Understanding Religious Conversion.* New Haven, CT: Yale University Press.

Richardson, James T., ed. (1978) *Conversion Careers: In and Out of the New Religions.* Beverly Hills, CA: Sage.

Cults

Despite the claims of many anticult activists, the appearance of new or alternative religions is not a phenomenon unique to the late twentieth century. Throughout history and across cultures, new religions have arisen in response to a variety of factors; often they have espoused millennial beliefs. The origins and subsequent careers of new religions cannot easily be reduced to a simple pattern; nor can their relations to millennialism. The connections between contemporary "cults" and millennial beliefs and movements should be considered fluid and strongly conditioned by specific contexts. In their earliest phases of development, new religious movements are particularly volatile; patterns of leadership, forms of organization, systems of belief, and relations to the surrounding social environment are all in flux. Some groups with millennial beliefs may preserve them as an unshakeable part of their core identity, while others may experience a millennial phase or phases of limited duration, whether as part of a rhythm of rising and falling millennial expectations, the climax of a gradual buildup, or an initial commitment that is gradually compromised. In any case, understanding the millennial beliefs of some new religions is greatly complicated by the highly controversial nature of groups labeled "cults."

Shifting Contemporary Meanings of Cult

Since the early 1970s, both in North America and Europe, a shifting coalition of cultural opponents has sought to expose the dangers posed to individuals and society by a number of new or alternative religious movements. Through their efforts, the terms "cult" (North America) and "sect" (Europe) have come to signify a powerful standardized image in which an overwhelmingly powerful charismatic leader manipulates vulnerable individuals into joining a group in order to exploit their loyalty for personal gain. That highly polemical characterization of "cults" has had a widespread influence on media depictions of unfamiliar religious groups and on the attitudes of many law enforcement officials toward them, and it has created a general atmosphere of suspicion and hostility around any group labeled a "cult." It has also, unfortunately, done much to obscure or distort the nature of leadership within new and alternative religious groups, the diverse paths of conversion to them, the nature and complexity of the systems of thought that they have created, and their connections to both the societies in which they have developed and the religious traditions to which they lay claim. As a result, the negative stereotype of "cults" has been vigorously resisted by members of the groups themselves and by most who have studied new or alternative religions from the perspectives of the social sciences and religious studies.

The stereotypical image of "cults" has often obscured the millennial character of certain groups, and hence their connections to specific social contexts, bodies of authoritative texts, traditions of interpretation, and other groups regarded as more mainstream. In addition, the preoccupation of the cultural opponents with the potential of "cults" to engage in various forms of violence, may have exaggerated both the occurrence and the potential consequences of catastrophic millennial beliefs when they do appear in new religions. Although many of the most prominent examples of contemporary "cults" have had distinctively millennial programs, and several of them have been involved in controversial episodes of violence, those groups are not necessarily representative either of new religious movements or of contemporary millennial movements. Many new religious movements, particularly in the broad "New Age" family, espouse a progressive millennialism that has no room for a catastrophic destruction of this world and focuses instead on achievement of millennial perfection through steady human effort. Nonetheless, because they have so dominated the public discussion of "cults," and, to a lesser extent, millennialism, contemporary "cults" that have focused on the catastrophic transformation of this world will be the focus of this discussion. Reference here will be restricted to one group, the Peoples Temple of the Reverend Jim Jones, that has served many as the primary example of the danger inherent in "cults" and four other groups that reanimated general concern about "cults" in the 1990s.

The Peoples Temple

Soon after the tragic suicides/murders of nearly one thousand residents of the Peoples Temple Agricultural Mission in Jonestown, Guyana, on 18 November 1978, the Peoples Temple quickly was raised to the status of a paradigmatic "cult." Instant analyses took ample notice of Jones's apparent megalomania, the power he seemed to exert over the followers who called him "Father," and of the dire results of such total self-surrender. But few observers took the time to unravel the complexities of the ideas to which members of the Peoples Temple had committed themselves and of the community that they had built for themselves in a remote jungle outpost. In fact, the message that Jones preached, particularly in its later stages, was strongly millennial.

Although the Peoples Temple had been formally recognized by the Disciples of Christ in 1959, and although Jones continued to draw praise for his humanitarian work through the early 1970s, Jones had become increasingly immersed in radically apocalyptic thinking. His fear of a nuclear apocalypse led him to relocate his followers from Indiana to northern California in 1965. By the time the Peoples Temple began work on its Jonestown settlement in Guyana in 1973, Jones' thinking had mutated into the distinctive millennial mix that he identified as apostolic or divine socialism. In a striking turnabout for a Christian preacher, Jones came to identify the Bible, particularly in its King James translation, as the source of the many ills that beset his community, including racism, sexism, ageism, and economic exploitation. In the place of the Bible and the Christian tradition Jones put his own understanding of Marxist and socialist doctrine, an elaborate gnostic mythology, and his own status as Messiah. The community at Jonestown rejected the United States as hopelessly oppressive, identified with communist regimes in Russia, China, and Cuba, and eagerly anticipated the final triumph of apostolic socialism. Jones frequently denigrated the illusory "sky God" of traditional Christianity, posited a wholly separate, alien realm of truth, and emphasized his own central role in the unfolding drama of salvation.

Jonestown itself was designed to be a socialist utopia. It was, however, an extremely fragile group, led by someone whose health and sanity were visibly disintegrating. Jones's own alienation is chillingly evident on the audiotape of the Jonestown community's final night on 18 November 1978. On that tape Jones voiced his fear that his community, besieged from without by a congressional delegation and a group of "concerned relatives" of community members and betrayed from within by a number of defections, would soon be destroyed. He urged his followers to undertake action that would simultaneously serve as protest and salvation, exhorting them that "if we can't live in peace, then let's die in peace" (Maaga 1998: 147) Knowing that "this world was not our home" (Maaga 1998: 164), Jones was convinced that he and his followers stood at the turning point of human history and that their "revolutionary suicide" would enable them to "cross over" into a new and perfect world. Jones understood the mass suicide/murder at Jonestown to be both defensive and transformative. He told the assembled group that the defectors and opponents had made their lives impossible. In contrast, "stepping over to the other side" promised peace, freedom, and happiness. At the end Jones was convinced that his millennial ideal could survive only in someplace that was literally not of this world.

The Branch Davidians

Another more recent "cult" incident also involved a group with strong millennial convictions. When agents of the U.S. Bureau of Alcohol, Tobacco, and Firearms stormed the Mount Carmel Center outside of Waco, Texas on 28 February 1993, David Koresh, the leader and prophet of a small group of Bible students, instantly became known to the world at large as the "wacko from Waco." The complex theological system in which he and his followers had steeped themselves was swiftly reduced by the FBI to "Bible babble," and the horrible deaths of seventy-four members of the community on 19 April were quickly summoned to reinforce the cautionary tale that Jonestown had been made to tell. As with the Peoples Temple, few outside observers made the effort to grasp either the elaborate interpretations of the Bible that Koresh and his students had developed or the specific reasons that had brought them to Mount Carmel in the first place. The Branch Davidians, however, were solidly situated within the broad biblical apocalyptic tradition, and also within the specific millennial tradition of Seventh-Day Adventism. The central activity at the Mount Carmel Center was the marathon "Bible Studies" that Koresh led for the whole community. Koresh's millennialism was firmly rooted in the biblical text; he believed that "every book of the Bible meets and ends in the book of Revelation" (Tabor and Gallagher 1995: 197).

But Koresh also was convinced that he alone had been chosen by God to decode the meaning of the scroll sealed with seven seals described in chapter five of Revelation. Koresh was certain that God's judgment of a sinful world was imminent and that he and his followers had crucial roles to play in the unfolding apocalyptic scenario. Throughout the fifty-one-day siege at the Mount Carmel Center, Koresh struggled to fit the Branch Davidians' conflict with the BATF and FBI into the scenario that he had always envisaged would be played out in Israel.

Surviving Branch Davidians bitterly dispute the U.S. government's official contention that they set the April 19 fire. Throughout the negotiations with the FBI, Koresh vehemently denied any intention to commit suicide. It is difficult, therefore, to portray the deaths of 19 April as transformative violence in search of a millennial goal. The survivors, in fact, remained stunned by what happened at the Mount Carmel Center, still cleave to an endtime scenario much more in tune with the biblical texts, and tend to see Koresh as a martyr.

In the years since 1993, Koresh's partially finished book on Revelation has served as the touchstone for those of the surviving Branch Davidians who still envision God's judgment being enacted during their lifetime, possibly at the return of a resurrected Koresh. They remain wary, however, of setting a date. Other Branch Davidians, inspired by the prison writings of survivor Renos Avraam, focused on August 1999 as the next millennial date. The millennial hope that animated the Davidian community for more than sixty years has not diminished; nor has it been displaced into an idealized other world. The remaining faithful have retained their millennial convictions even after the death of their prophet.

Heaven's Gate

On 27 March 1997, another incident of mass death associated with a "cult" claimed worldwide attention. Thirty-nine followers of Marshall Applewhite, variously known as Bo, Do, and one of "the Two," committed suicide along with their teacher. Like the members of the Peoples Temple and the Branch Davidians, they also anticipated an imminent judgment and yearned for another, better world. In a 1997 statement that offered the "Last Chance to Advance Beyond Human," Do's "crew" proclaimed that the earth was about to be recycled and its present civilization spaded under. The crew embraced the coming destruction of this world as a message of good tidings. They exulted that the "Harvest Time—the Last Days—the Second Coming" were about to arrive.

For the Heaven's Gate crew the new world of millennial perfection was unequivocally located outside of the terrestrial world. They believed that through Do's tutelage, they could leave behind this physical world and even their own physical "containers" and ascend to the "evolutionary level above human," the true Kingdom of God in the heavens. In their view, nothing short of total renunciation of the human, physical world was required for salvation. Those who accepted the message of the representatives of the Level Above Human, however, would be protected from the coming apocalypse and even from death itself, even though they might lose their human bodies. As with the Peoples Temple, the Heaven's Gate crew's radical devaluation of this world led them to portray suicide as a desirable passage to a better world.

Although they studied in obscurity for nearly all the time before their suicides, the members of the crew nonetheless felt themselves to be persecuted. They conceived themselves as the only ones in possession of the truth and contended that strong forces were arrayed against the representatives of the Evolutionary Level Above Human. The suicides of the Heaven's Gate crew were intended to be transformative rites of passage by which they would obtain their new, superior identities in the heavenly Kingdom of God. Where Jim Jones felt forced to relocate his millennial kingdom outside of this world, the crew of Heaven's Gate always sought to transcend their earthly limitations. Salvation for them required an exit strategy and a mythology to support it. They found both in Do's tales of The Evolutionary Level Above Human.

Aum Shinrikyo and The Order of the Solar Temple

Two incidents outside the U.S. in the 1990s also involved the volatile mix of millennial beliefs and violence. On the morning of 20 March 1995, members of the Japanese new religion known as Aum Shinrikyo discharged deadly sarin gas in the crowded Tokyo subway. Twelve people died and more than five thousand were injured. Read against the background of the teachings of Aum's leader, Shoko Asahara, the subway attack appears as a programmatic attempt to initiate Armageddon. Aum's members professed that Armageddon would soon occur because of the accumulation of human evil. They saw this world as a hell. As in most scenarios of the end, the members of Aum believed that a chosen few would survive to create a new and perfect world. In that earthly paradise, the Buddhist Shambala, truth would rule.

Nearly six months earlier, on 4 and 5 October 1994, fifty-two members of the Order of the Solar Temple met their deaths in three separate incidents in Quebec and Switzerland. In subsequent incidents near Grenoble, France, in 1995 and again in Quebec on 22 March 1997, twenty-one more members of the Solar Temple also died. Like the crew of Heaven's Gate, many of those who died imagined themselves to be making a "transit" to a better world. In a final message addressed to "All Those Who Can Still Understand the Voice of Wisdom," members of the Solar Temple proclaimed that time was ending and that they were leaving the world with no regrets whatsoever. They also issued a general warning about the terrible trials of the Apocalypse that awaited a largely unsuspecting populace.

Conclusion

Although contemporary millennial movements come in many forms, they claim public attention primarily when they conform most closely to the stereotype of "dangerous cults" established by anticult activists. Since cultural opponents of new religions are most concerned about the potential damage inflicted by "cults," they amplify the rhetorical violence that is so much a part of catastrophic millennialism, seize upon transformative rites of passage as proof that cults can easily lead to death, and ignore millennial movements that do not conform to the stereotype. Nor do they effectively characterize or analyze the compelling logic of catastrophic millennial beliefs to those who espouse them. The result is that the contemporary polemic about "cults" has obscured the nature of the groups that it does address, even while it ignored the evidence of many other millennial groups that neither participate in violence nor envision a catastrophic apocalypse.

Eugene V. Gallagher

See also Aum Shinrikyo, Catastrophic Millenialism, Davidians, Heaven's Gate, Peoples Temple, Progressive Millenialism, Messianism, Solar Temple

Bibliography

Beckford, James. (1985) *Cult Controversies: The Societal Response to New Religious Movements.* London: Tavistock.

Chidester, David. (1988) *Salvation and Suicide: An Interpretation of Jim Jones, the Peoples Temple, and Jonestown.* Bloomington, IN: Indiana University Press.

Ellwood, Robert. (1979) *Alternative Altars.* Chicago: University of Chicago Press.

Hall, John. (1987) *Gone From the Promised Land: Jonestown in American Cultural History.* Brunswick, NJ: Transaction Books.

Maaga, Mary McCormick. (1998) *Hearing the Voices of Jonestown.* Syracuse, NY: Syracuse University Press.

Miller, Timothy, ed. (1995) *America's Alternative Religions.* Albany, NY: State University of New York Press.

Reader, Ian. (1996) *A Poisonous Cocktail? Aum Shinrikyo's Path to Violence.* Copenhagen: NIAS Books.

Robbins, Thomas, and Susan Palmer, eds. (1997) *Millennium, Messiahs, and Mayhem: Contemporary Apocalyptic Movements.* New York: Routledge.

Singer, Margaret, with Janja Lalich. (1995) *Cults in Our Midst: The Hidden Menace in Our Everyday Lives.* San Francisco: Jossey-Bass.

Stark, Rodney, and William Sims Bainbridge. (1985) *The Future of Religion: Secularization, Revival, and Cult Formation.* Berkeley, CA: University of California Press.

Tabor, James D., and Eugene V. Gallagher. (1995) *Why Waco? Cults and the Battle for Religious Freedom in America.* Berkeley, CA: University of California Press.

Wessinger, Catherine. (1999) *When the Millennium Comes Violently.* New York: Seven Bridges Press.

——, ed. (1999) *Millennialism, Persecution, and Violence: Historical Cases.* Syracuse, NY: Syracuse University Press.

Wright, Stuart, ed. (1995) *Armageddon in Waco: Critical Perspectives on the Branch Davidian Conflict.* Chicago: University of Chicago Press.

Davidians

The Davidians are a millennial reform movement that emerged within the Seventh-Day Adventist Church in 1929. They firmly believed that Christ would return soon. But they also feared that the worldliness of the church would delay the return of Christ. They organized to call the parent church back to God and to serve as an example of how God's people should live. The Seventh-Day Adventist denomination consistently rejected the message of the Davidians. The Branch Davidians split from the Davidians in 1955, thereby creating two major groups of Davidians. In 1993, following a standoff with federal government officials and the burning of their residence which claimed more than eighty lives, the term Branch Davidians and the name of their leader, David Koresh, became household words.

Victor Houteff, Founder

Victor T. Houteff (1885–1955), a Bulgarian who emigrated to the United States in 1907, was the founder of the Davidian movement. He converted to Seventh-Day Adventist teachings at Rockford, Illinois, in 1918 and shortly thereafter moved to Los Angeles. Soon he was given responsibility for preparing Sabbath day teachers for their weekly lessons. Houteff's study of scripture led him to new interpretations. He published a series of pamphlets which were later collected and published together in two volumes. He called the books and his teaching *Shepherd's Rod*, a title that he drew from Isaiah 6:9, "Hear ye the rod." He believed that the parent church had strayed from the message of scripture and that the "rod" represented his true teaching of the Bible.

Houteff affirmed the key ideas of the Seventh-Day Adventist Church. The imminent return of Christ is the central doctrine of the Adventists. Adventist founders William Miller and Ellen G. White kept the focus of their teaching on Christ's Second Coming. Houteff also affirmed the near return of Christ. Since their main teaching focused on the second advent of Christ, both Adventists and the Davidians are classified as millennial Christian groups. Second, Adventists believed that Sabbath worship—from Friday to Saturday evening—was required by scripture, that although most Christians had been deluded by the papacy into accepting Sunday worship, Sabbath observance was a mark of the true church. Third, Adventists observed Old Testament dietary regulations and many were vegetarians. Fourth, taking seriously the commandment not to kill, the Adventists were also pacifists. Houteff and the Davidians accepted all four of these teachings.

Houteff believed that the Bible contained clues to understanding future events. He thought in terms of prophecy and fulfillment. Past events were prototypes of future events. Prophets were given the ability to interpret new meanings in the text. Houteff's task as prophet was to interpret the secret meanings hitherto hidden in scripture. For him, revelation was progressive. Houteff relied especially on Ellen G. White (1827–1915), the second founder and prophetess of the Adventist movement. She had explained important new truths; he would add others. He often communicated the nature of his task by using the analogy of a scroll which was being unrolled and which required ongoing interpretation. Likewise, successive prophets revealed "New Truth" or "Present Truth" in each generation. The "Present Truth" which Houteff conveyed was that Christ could not return to the present Seventh-Day Adventist Church because it was too worldly. It was like the church of Laodicea in Revelation, lukewarm and rejected by Christ. He cites specific examples of compromise with the world. Adventist preachers relied on formal education rather than on God's Spirit. The church permitted beach parties, picture shows, and competitive sports.

Houteff's message was a call to reform. He believed scripture taught that a remnant of 144,000 believers—the elect and unworldly believers—would form the true church. Christ would never come back to an impure church. The Seventh-Day Adventists had the message right, but had departed from the practice of holiness. His followers, the Davidians, would form the true church. Christ would come back to them, and they would receive favorable treatment at the final judgment. Christ would return soon. The Adventists had long since focused on 2,300 days referred to by Daniel, and had interpreted them as years. Then they sought a starting date in the past, so that the return of Christ could be calculated for the near future. The expectation of Christ's imminent return gave millennialism its appeal. They designed elaborate diagrams to chart the future course of history and preached that Christ would return at any moment. The Seventh-Day Adventists in California rejected Houteff's plea to change and criticized his message. Houteff looked elsewhere for a home.

Center at Mount Carmel, Texas

In 1935 Davidians scouted areas in Texas and settled on a 377-acre tract of land 2 miles from Waco, Texas, which they named Mount Carmel. Many Davidians were carpenters and handymen. They put up buildings, planted orchards and crops, and established a successful semicommunal society which survived the Depression. The community averaged sixty to seventy members, many of whom worked in nearby towns, but they returned to the community each evening. Houteff was clearly the leader of the movement throughout his life. He appointed all of the key officers, controlled finances, and led by example of personal sacrifice and absolute conviction that his teaching was true. The Davidians made sure that everyone contributed to the success of the community through their labor. They created their own school so that they could teach children Davidian beliefs and manual skills, as well as basic academic subjects. Moreover, they established a small seminary to train their ministers. The Davidians expressed their separation from the world not only by living apart from the town but also by having the women adopt very modest attire of dresses with sleeves and long skirts, and keeping their hair long and refusing to use cosmetics.

Davidians expressed their separation from the world most dramatically by refusing to bear arms in war. Because the local draft board had never heard of them by their original name—Shepherd's Rod—the board denied the group conscientious objector status during World War II. Houteff therefore changed the name in 1942 from the Shepherd's Rod to the more recognizable Davidian Seventh-Day Adventists. His plan worked; the young men might be drafted, but as Adventists they did not have to bear arms.

The Davidians thought they should live as models of true Christianity. Moreover, they believed that they would be rewarded as Christ's most favored people when he returned. The Davidian community worshipped together on Friday and Saturday, and often in the evenings Houteff taught them through chapter by chapter exposition of biblical books or by studies of biblical themes. The Davidians printed his messages in pocket-sized tract form, usually 60 to 120 pages in

SEVEN SEALS REVELATION
BOOK ONE

The Prophet Daniel was told to **SEAL UP** the book, and that the meaning of the vision would be revealed at the time of the end. (See Daniel 12:4,9)
John the Revelator was told to **SEAL UP** what the Seven Thunders uttered (See Rev.10:4), as the Seven Thunders were to be revealed not by John, but would be revealed by the latter day Lamb at the time of the end.

In Isaiah 29:11-18, we see a book that is **SEALED**, and the prophecy promises of a day when the eyes of the blind shall see, and the ears of the deaf shall hear the words of the book that was sealed.

What Daniel and John were told to seal up, has now been revealed.

For those who have an ear to hear,
Prophecy is a LIGHT that shines in a dark place!

Proverbs 4:18
But the path of the just is as the shining light, that shineth more and more unto the perfect day.

HTTP://WWW.SEVENSEALS.COM

length. Davidians took these tracts to Adventists all over the United States and in many English-speaking nations, seeking to win converts. They evangelized by visiting Seventh-Day Adventist camps and collecting mailing addresses from Seventh-Day Adventist churches. They thought that no other Christian group was even close to understanding the truth of scripture. Only the Adventists understood the importance of the twofold message of Christ's near return and Sabbath observance. Therefore the Davidians sought to convert only Seventh-Day Adventists. Their numerical results were meager, but they did manage to plant Davidian centers in England, the Caribbean, and Australia, as well as in California and South Carolina. Printing and distributing Houteff's teachings and personal missionary-style contacts with Adventists comprised the heart of the program: it was their method of communicating the Davidian message. The parent Seventh-Day Adventist Church reacted vigorously, warning members against Davidian teaching, and the number of converts remained tiny. Although the Davidians were looking for 144,000 followers they probably did not convert more than 1 or 2 percent of that number to their views.

Florence Houteff and the End

Followers believed that Houteff was the new Elijah who would personally usher in the new era. Therefore they were shocked and left in disarray when he died in 1955. His wife, Florence, assumed leadership and made two important decision. She sold the original Mount Carmel property to residential real estate developers in Waco, thereby enriching the Davidians, and she bought property 10 miles from Waco near the town of Elk. New Mount Carmel has been the Davidian home since 1957. Secondly, Florence set a date for the beginning of the new age. The Davidians lived for the return of Christ, and when William Miller had set dates for Christ's return in 1843–44 his followers had been deeply disappointed. Although Victor Houteff had refused to take this step, and risk another devastating disappointment, Florence predicted that the new era would begin at Passover on 22 April 1959. She thereby consolidated her authority and generated keen anticipation among the Davidians. The Seventh-Day Adventists published a sharp criticism of the Davidians for setting a specific date for Christ's return.

Newspaper reports indicate that 600–900 people gathered during the month preceding 22 April, having sold businesses and homes and come to Mount Carmel where they were housed in tents. This number suggests something of the numerical strength of the group. The Davidians avoided saying that Christ would appear on 22 April, but they did say that they expected one of several possible signs of the end—renewal of the Seventh-Day Adventist Church, war in the Middle East, or the establishment of God's kingdom in Israel, but none of these signs of the inauguration of Christ's return and millennial rule materialized. Most of the followers left, and a year later only about fifty Davidians remained at New Mount Carmel. Florence's leadership was discredited, and she officially disbanded the movement in the early 1960s. Davidians criticized her for date-setting and for taking funds from property sales. She moved to California.

Branch Davidians

Another group of Davidians organized when Victor Houteff died. Ben Roden, a former Houteff follower, established an alternative tradition in 1955, and adopted the name "Branch" to distinguish it from Florence's group. He based his name choice on Isaiah 11:1, "a shoot shall come out from the stump of Jesse and a branch shall grow out of his roots." Roden believed that the "branch" here referred to Christ. Roden accepted Adventist and Houteff teachings, but added his own emphases. He gave special attention to the political restoration of the state of Israel in 1948 and moved some of his followers to live in Israel. This brief experiment failed for lack of volunteers and resources. The 1967 war consolidated Israel's political strength and viability, and Roden believed that now it would be possible for the 144,000 literally to be gathered to Mount Zion and a man whose name is "the Branch" (Zechariah 6:12) could build the Temple, thus fulfilling key prophecies for the new millennium. Roden also stressed observance of Old Testament ceremonial law regarding festivals. He managed to win control of New Mount

Carmel following the failure of Florence's prediction, thereby providing an important advantage to the Branch Davidians. Roden was buried in Jerusalem.

Ben Roden's experiment in Israel failed, but he left a wife and son who were deeply committed to his message. They, like all of the prophets before them, built on the past and added their own teachings. Lois Roden succeeded Ben. By her own account an angel visited her and revealed new ideas to her. Lois's central contribution was her teaching that the Holy Spirit is feminine. She believed that the messiah will appear in female form. Lois's task was to communicate the femininity of God and to promote female ministry. She traveled widely with this message and produced a magazine, *SHEkinah*, devoted to popularizing her feminine interpretations. Lois also befriended a new convert, Vernon Howell (1959–93), at New Mount Carmel in 1987. Howell won a following due to his own biblical teaching abilities and his support from Lois.

Control of the movement passed to George Roden, son of Ben and Lois, in 1985. He drove the Howell faction from Mount Carmel at gunpoint. He thought he was the Messiah and like his father, had a deep love for Israel as the future location of the true church. After two years he lost power to Vernon Howell. He later committed murder and was imprisoned as criminally insane. George Roden died in 1998.

Vernon Howell changed his name to David Koresh in 1990. He meant to keep alive the messianic link by taking the name David. Koresh is Hebrew for Cyrus: he saw himself as champion of the true Israel against the evil forces of the Davidian enemies (just as Cyrus had delivered the Jews from the Babylonians). Koresh had become a Branch Davidian in 1981 and had achieved leadership of a faction in 1983. After being driven from Mount Carmel in 1985, he returned to control events from 1987 to 1993. Koresh appealed to Davidians who preceded him, but he also had a special message or teaching to contribute. He focused on opening the seven seals, which for him meant interpreting the coded Book of Revelation. Koresh taught that there were many Christs. He was one among them. Koresh contrasted the peaceful teachings of Jesus with an emphasis on Old Testament passages focusing on fighting for their kingdom. He thereby shifted his own leadership model from traditional Davidian pacifism to willingness to bear arms. In 1989 Koresh announced that he alone was to have sex with the female members of the movement so that he would be the father of all of the children in his new kingdom. He once again contrasted his role with that of Jesus, calling himself the "sinful messiah." On 28 February 1993, the federal Bureau of Alcohol, Tobacco and Firearms issued a warrant for his arrest on charges of possession of illegal weapons, stormed the Davidian dwelling, and brought death by gunfire to both sides. Fifty-one days later the residence burned and with it some eighty people perished. The Branch Davidians were decimated and several survivors were sent to prison.

Current Status

Despite severe reversals, both Davidians and Branch Davidians continue to attract small followings. They share a common belief in millennialism and in the truth of Victor Houteff's teachings regarding the return of Christ. The original Davidian followers of Houteff have several centers of activity scattered around the world. Groups flourish today in South Carolina, Texas, New York, Missouri, the Caribbean, Australia, and Israel. They are tiny factions which are led by strong local figures and therefore do not achieve any sort of denominational unity. Davidians do not release statistics but probably number fewer than 1,000 followers. The South Carolina group has been extremely active in reprinting all of the writings of Houteff and related Davidian literature. The Davidians continue to call on the Seventh-Day Adventist Church to join them in becoming part of the 144,000 elect.

The Branch Davidians also have followers scattered in various places, including Texas, Australia, Israel, and elsewhere. The property at New Mount Carmel was being contested for control by three Branch Davidian factions in the spring of 1999. A Waco judge decided to let a jury determine the fate of the Davidian property. Each prophet/leader offered a different interpretation of the faith. The Branch Davidian numbers also remain quite small, but their political legacy keeps their memory vivid: the encounter with the government has become an important marker for ongoing reflection on the nature of the relations between the state and the many religions of its citizens. Militia movements flourished following the deaths of the Davidians, and the Murrah building in Oklahoma City was destroyed by a blast on the second anniversary of the Waco disaster. In the fall of 1999 the Federal Government opened an investigation into the events surrounding the 1993 destruction of Mount Carmel.

Conclusion

Victor Houteff saw himself as a prophet with a fresh message to the Seventh-Day Adventist Church. The church taught the imminent return of Christ. Yet Houteff argued that the church had grown worldly and Christ would not return to earth until he had a pure church to receive him. The pure church was what the Davidians, and later the Branch Davidians, believed themselves to be. The numbers of both groups have remained small. They were almost totally ignored until the raid on the Branch Davidian home in 1993 by the federal government, followed fifty-one days later by the fire which took the lives of over eighty people. This single event generated enormous controversy. The social, religious, and political implications of the controversy are profound for American society.

William L Pitts Jr.

See also Seventh-Day Adventists

Bibliography

Houteff, Victor. (1990) *The Shepherd's Rod Series.* Reprint, Salem, SC: General Association of Davidian Seventh-Day Adventists.

——. (1992) *The Symbolic Code Series.* Reprint. Tamasee, SC: General Association of Davidian Seventh-Day Adventists.

Pitts, William L., Jr. (1993) "The Mount Carmel Davidians: Adventist Reformers, 1935–1959." *Syzygy* 2: 39–54.

——. (1995) "Davidians and Branch Davidians: 1929–1987." In *Armageddon in Waco,* edited by Stuart Wright. Chicago: Chicago University Press, 20–42.

——. (1995) "Davidians and Branch Davidians." *The Catholic Encyclopedia.* Washington, D.C.: The Catholic University of America, vol. 19, 96–98.

Tabor, James D., and Eugene V. Gallagher. (1995) *Why Waco? Cults and the Battle for Religious Freedom in America.* Berkeley, CA: University of California Press.

Defilement

In English, the term "defile" derives from a medieval word meaning "to trample on, to march over" but also came to be associated with the word "befoul," meaning "to pollute." The term, therefore, maintains two senses: physical violation or violence and physical stain or infection. Moreover, defilement has also taken on symbolic significance, including spiritual or religious figurative violations or sins, which themselves come to be represented as stains or impurities. In many apocalyptic texts, sinners in hell are depicted as being physically violated and defiled with excrements. Millennialist movements, likewise, may be concerned paradoxically either with maintaining the "purity" of the elect by avoiding pollution or with ritualizing the elect's liberty by engaging in ritualized defilement.

Defilement in Religious Traditions

In a study of apocalypses (loosely defined as religious texts that entail otherworldly journeys) from many different religious traditions, Ioan P. Couliano noted the frequency with which excrements and offensive smells are associated with the punishments of the damned in the afterlife. Readers familiar with Dante's *Inferno* will remember that many of the Florentine poet's denizens of hell are immersed in the run-off of the world's latrines, but this is typical of other visionary texts from earlier in the Middle Ages, early Christian apocrypha like the *Apocalypse of Peter* and the *Apocalypse of Paul,* as well as the ancient Iranian *Book of Ardâ Virâz.* An example from the *Apocalypse of Peter* gives some flavor of these punishing defilements: "And the milk of the mothers flows from their breasts and congeals and smells foul, and from it come forth beasts that devour flesh, which turn and torture them for ever with their husbands. . . . And near that place I saw another gorge in which the discharge and the excrement of the tortured ran down and became a lake. . . . And in another great lake, full of discharge and blood and boiling mire, stood men and women up to their knees." (Barnstone, 1984) Typically these defiling punishments are the result of sinners' sexual sins or sins derived from sexuality.

Aside from Levitical proscriptions of "unclean" things, which are recycled in the Koran and modified in Christian scriptures, the two classic Western millennialist religious texts, the Hebrew scriptures' Book of Daniel and the Christian scriptures' Book of Revelation, are similarly preoccupied with avoiding defilement or pollution. The Book of Daniel begins with narratives relating how Hebrew heroes in exile avoided physical defilement by forbidden foods and spiritual defilement of pagan worship. The book's apocalyptic visions, moreover, relate directly to the purification of the defiled Jerusalem temple: "Then I heard a holy one speaking; and another holy one said to the one that spoke, 'For how long is the vision concerning the continual burnt offering, the transgression that makes desolate, and the giving over of the sanctuary and host to be trampled under foot?' And he said to him, 'For two thousand and three hundred evenings and mornings; then the sanctuary shall be restored to its rightful state'" (8:13–14). Although early Christian communities relinquished the exacting Jewish purity laws, they nonetheless maintained discourses of defilement by which to represent religious purity. In the Book of Revelation, for example, the figure of the "Whore of Babylon" combines the defilements of sexual fluids and blood: "The woman was arrayed in purple and scarlet, and bedecked with gold and jewels and pearls, holding in her hand a golden cup full of abominations and the impurities of her fornication; and on her forehead was written a name of mystery: 'Babylon the great, mother of harlots and of earth's abominations.' And I saw the woman, drunk with the blood of the saints and the blood of the martyrs of Jesus" (17:4–6).

Modern Analyses of the Notion of Defilement

The phenomenology and anthropology of the concept "defilement" has received considerable attention from philosophers, scholars of religion, and anthropologists. Examined here are scholar of religion Mircea Eliade, philosopher Paul Ricoeur, critical theorist Georges Bataille, anthropologist Mary Douglas, and Bruce Lincoln who offers a semiotic analysis.

Mircea Eliade

For Eliade, all religious practices and discourses could be explained as an attempt to recapture the origins of creation in their purity. Thus, religious rituals recapitulate that original moment, or to use his phrase, *in illo tempore* (the beginning time). In his analysis of ancient Persian new year practices, Eliade concluded that, "The abolition of profane past time was accomplished by rituals that signified a sort of 'end of the world.' The extinction of fires, the return of the souls of the dead, social confusion of the type exemplified by the Saturnalia, erotic license, orgies, and so on, symbolized the retrogression of the cosmos into chaos. On the last day of the year the universe was dissolved in the primordial waters. . . . The meaning of this periodical retrogression of the world into a chaotic modality was this: all the 'sins' of the year, everything that time had soiled and worn, was annihilated in the physical sense of the word" (78–79).

Paul Ricoeur

Ricoeur's study of the symbolism of evil attempted to derive a phenomenological understanding of religious symbols generally. Defilement is the quintessential symbol of evil: "[P]unishment falls on man in the guise of misfortune and transforms all possible sufferings, all diseases, all death, all failure into a sign of defilement" (27). Defilement for Ricoeur has two characteristics: it is frequently symbolized as stain; it represents dread of divine vengeance for violation of a taboo. The primordial defiling taboos revolve around sexuality, but sexual transgressions are supplemented with taboos involving murder: "The comparison between sexuality and murder is supported by the same play of images: in both cases, impurity is connected with the presence of a material 'something' that transmits itself by contact and contagion" (28). Thus, as noted above, Babylon in the Book of Revelation is stained by sexual fluids and the blood of the martyrs.

Georges Bataille

Bataille's project is committed to deconstructing Western Christianity's binary opposition of the sacred and the profane by revealing the economic and political dimensions of those distinctions. However, he notes phenomenologically that "Man is the animal that negates nature" by hiding its evidence, particularly in its sexual discharges (semen, menstrual blood) and digestive excretion. In this regard Bataille refused to distinguish between "civilized" industrial societies and "primitive" tribal ones since they both share a horror of our natural condition. Moreover, he discovers the social implications of purity laws and practices: "The person who protects himself the most anxiously from the various forms of defilement is also the person who enjoys the greatest prestige and who has the advantage over others" (67). Thus purity and defilement construct social classifications, akin to those employed by millennialist communities in relation to the "saved" and the "damned."

Bataille's own millennialism is evident in his comments on eroticism (sex as pleasure instead of reproduction) and the end of history: "We have known eroticism on the fringe of history, but if history finally came to a close, even if it drew near its close, eroticism would no longer be *on the fringe of history*. . . . [H]istory would be ended if the disparity of rights and of living standards was reduced: this would be the precondition of an ahistorical mode of existence of which erotic activity is the expressive form. From this necessarily hypothetical point of view, consciousness of erotic truth anticipates the end of history" (189–90).

Mary Douglas

In her anthropological analysis, Douglas similarly emphasizes the social symbolic capital of pollution and purity ideas, suggesting that they make claims about an individual's status and they maintain social order by defining anything "disorderly" as "dirt" or "dirty." Physical pollutions threaten because they transgress the body's margins, and societies frequently understand themselves by imagining the society as a body. Douglas distinguishes among four kinds of social pollution: "danger pressing on external boundaries"; "danger from transgressing the internal lines of the system"; "danger in the margins of the lines"; and "danger from internal contradiction" (122). Societies negotiate these threats in two seemingly contradictory ways: by inviting pollution under controlled circumstances (e.g., the Saturnalia, Mardi Gras, carnival) or by avoiding pollution under all circumstances. Of the latter, Douglas notes: "A strong millennial tendency is implicit in the way of thinking of any people whose metaphysics push evil out of the world of reality" (171).

Bruce Lincoln

Lincoln offers a semiotic analysis of what he terms "millennial antinomianism" or "no-rules." In an analysis of one moment in the Spanish Civil War when briefly victorious republican Loyalists conducted seemingly spontaneous desecrations of Roman Catholic churches and other religious artifacts, Lincoln notes that, "It is in millennial movements . . . that the deliberate flouting of such fundamental taboos as incest, cannibalism, and abuse of the dead has been best attested and most seriously studied. . . . [these studies] describing antinomianism as a liminal stage or dialectic moment in which 'no rules' appear as the radical antithesis of 'old rules' and the necessary precursor of synthetic 'new rules' yet to come" (115). Lincoln relates antinomianism to what he calls "rituals of collective obscenity": the "new society [is] placed in direct and conscious opposition to the existing social order, as seen in . . . ritual sequences revolving around the . . . theme . . . of purity and defilement. . . . By freely assuming this state, they effectively [estrange] themselves from society as it is officially constructed, and they [renounce] its demands for normative ('proper') behavior" (116).

All societies maintain purity rules that maintain communal identities by distinguishing the pure from the impure. In apocalyptic texts and millennial movements, the awareness of purity and defilement are amplified in two seemingly contradictory ways: anxious avoidance of defilement or deliberate pollution.

Thomas L. Long

See also Sexuality

Bibliography

Barnstone, Willis, ed. (1984) *The Other Bible.* San Francisco: Harper.

Bataille, Georges. (1991) *The Accursed Share: An Essay on General Economy,* translated by Robert Hurley. New York: Zone, vols. 2–3.

Couliano, I. P. (1991) *Out of This World: Otherworldly Journeys from Gilgamesh to Albert Einstein.* Boston: Shambhala.

Douglas, Mary. (1966) *Purity and Danger: An Analysis of the Concepts of Pollution and Taboo.* New York: Routledge.

Eliade, Mircea. (1959) *The Sacred and the Profane: The Nature of Religion,* translated by Willard R. Trask. New York: Harcourt, Brace.

Lincoln, Bruce. (1989) *Discourse and the Construction of Society: Comparative Studies of Myth, Ritual, and Classification.* New York: Oxford University Press.

Ricoeur, Paul. (1967) *The Symbolism of Evil,* translated by Emerson Buchanan. Boston: Beacon.

Delaware Prophet

Preaching a return to traditional customs, Neolin the Enlightened, otherwise known as the Delaware Prophet, influenced subsequent Native American prophets and the warriors of Pontiac's Uprising (1763–66). In 1762, the Delaware Prophet arose during a time of demoralization among the Eastern Indian nations, such as the Odawa (Ottawa), Delaware, Seneca, Shawnee, Wyandot (Huron), Potowatomi, Erie, and Ojibwa. For two centuries, European encroachment had disrupted Native economic systems, transforming once self-sufficient peoples into dependent trading partners who were dangerously entangled in the imperialist wars between the French and English. Subsistence hunting and horticulture had been transformed into commercial enterprises, where Native peoples bartered furs and corn for numerous trade goods including metal axes, kettles, flint, paint pigments, food stuffs, cloth, beads, guns, rum, and whiskey. A combination of liquor and trade had eroded Indian power and precipitated the loss of homelands.

Early accounts of Neolin are limited by the European ethnocentrism of the writers. For example, Francis Peckham called the Delaware Prophet psychopathic, owing to the fact that he wept uncontrollably throughout his speeches.

Neolin or the Delaware Prophet. Painted by Charles Bird King and engraved for publication in Thomas L. McKenney and James Hall's "The Indian Tribes of North America (1836–1844)." SUGDEN, JOHN (1999) *TECUMSEH: A LIFE.* NEW YORK: HENRY HOLT & CO.

THE DELAWARE PROPHET'S VISION OF 1762–63

I am the Master of Life, whom thou wishest to see, and to whom thou wishest to speak. Listen to that which I will tell thee for thyself and for all the Indians. I am the Maker of Heaven and earth, the trees, lakes, rivers, men, and all that thou seest or hast seen on the earth or in the heavens; and because I love you, you must do my will; you must also avoid that which I hate; I hate you to drink as you do, until you lose your reason; I wish you not to fight one another; you take two wives, or run after other people's wives; you do wrong; I hate such conduct; you should have but one wife, and keep her until death. When you go to war, you juggle, you sing the medicine song, thinking you speak to me; you deceive yourselves; it is to the Manito that you speak; he is a wicked spirit who induces you to evil, and, for want of knowing me, you listen to him.

The land on which you are, I have made for you, not for others: wherefore do you suffer the whites to dwell upon your lands? Can you not do without them? I know that those whom you call the children of your great father supply your wants. But, were you not wicked as you are, you would not need them. Before those whom you call your brothers had arrived, did not your bow and arrow maintain you? You needed neither gun, powder, nor any other object. The flesh of animals was your food, their skins your raiment. But when I saw you inclined to evil, I remove the animals into the depths of the forests, that you might depend on your brothers for your necessaries, for your clothing. Again become good and do my will, and I will send animals for your sustenance. I do now, however, forbid suffering among you your Father's children; I love them, they know me, they pray to me; I supply their own wants, and give them that which they bring to you. Not so with those who are come to trouble your possessions. Drive them away; wage war against them. I love them not. They know me not. They are my enemies, they are your brothers' enemies. Send them back to the lands I have made for them. Let them remain there.

Source: Wallace, Anthony F. C. (1969) *The Death and Rebirth of the Seneca.* New York: Vintage Books, 117–19, from various primary sources.

Historian Howard Parkham, who relied on white accounts, referred to Neolin as the Imposter when he described his rituals as frivolous and absurd. On the other hand, anthropologist Anthony F. C. Wallace provides the best description of the prophet as he spread his message for two years from the shores of Lake Erie into surrounding settlements. Wallace informs us that the movement began after Neolin succumbed to a messianic vision wherein he searched for the Creator. According to Wallace, the Master of Life instructed him to wage a war on the whites and drive them out of the homelands. Other celestial pronouncements from the Creator asked for the prohibitions on trade goods, liquor, and guns, in addition to adherence to marital monogamy. Very specifically, the Master of Life cautioned against Indians fighting each other.

Mapping out the soul's progress from this world to the hereafter, the Delaware Prophet sketched his vision on deerskin parchment. In his travels throughout the Indian nations, he held the deerskin diagram up during his oratory as he cautioned against the pernicious white influence that blocked the spiritual journey back to the Creator. Neolin exhorted the people to give up vices while they prepared for the holiest of wars, guaranteed to bring about a new age free of the white invader.

The Delaware Prophet influenced the great leader, Pontiac of the Odawas, to heed his message of return to the ancient ways. With the help of the prophet's teachings about Indian unity, Pontiac forged a powerful Indian alliance that almost succeeded in driving out the British in 1763. Unfortunately, Pontiac did not break off all relations with all whites, as he unwisely depended on the French as an ally; neither did Pontiac heed Neolin's prohibition against guns. However, Pontiac compelled his followers to limit their use of alcohol because alcohol caused internal violence, illness, and it was often traded for Indian land or resources. Neolin also influenced successive Indian prophets of millenarian reform, such as the Onondaga Prophet, the Munsee Prophet, Handsome Lake, and the Shawnee Prophet, who had similar visions and teachings.

Diana Tumminia

See also Handsome Lake

Bibliography

Parkham, Francis. (1902) *The Conspiracy of Pontiac and the Indian War after the Conquest of Canada.* Boston: Little, Brown, and Company, vol. 1.

Peckham, Howard H. (1947) *Pontiac and the Indian Uprising.* Chicago: University of Chicago Press.

Wallace, Anthony F. C. (1972) *The Death and Rebirth of the Seneca.* New York: Vintage.

Demagogues

A demagogue is a charismatic leader who uses inflammatory rhetoric based on prejudice or misinformation to mobilize a constituency to action. As Allport writes, "Demagogues play up false issues to divert public attention from true issues" (1954: 410). Thus demagoguery is a form of scapegoating. Successful demagogues usually appear supremely self-confident, powerful, and knowledgeable; yet some demagogues can also come across as accessible and friendly.

Adorno et al. and Hoffer wrote early influential works that discussed demagoguery, but their ideas created a false impression (popularized in the 1960s) that all organizers of dissident groups were demagogues. Later social movement research by scholars such as Piven and Cloward, Klandermans, and Blee rejects that idea as too simplistic and demonizing. That the concept of demagoguery is abused, however, does not negate the reality of demagoguery as one of many styles of organizing. Leaders of totalitarian groups, sometimes called cults, are often demagogues.

People who are angry sometimes follow demagogues even though the claims being made are clearly recognized as fabrications by the outside observer. This does not mean that the followers are mindless automatons being swayed by a mesmerizing leader, but that the leader has crafted a rhetorical frame or script which resonates with a constituency that shares a grievance.

Demagoguery facilitates the projection required for scapegoating. As Allport puts it:

> Demagoguery invites the externalization of hatred and anxiety, it is an institutional aid to projection; it justifies tabloid thinking, stereotyping, and the conviction that the world is made up of swindlers. . . . There is no middle ground . . . the ultimate objective is vague, still the need for definiteness is met by the rule, "Follow the Leader." (1954: 418)

Demagogues often scapegoat groups that already suffer widespread prejudice. "Not all [demagogues]," observes Allport, "select the alleged misconduct of minority groups as their false issue—but a great many do so" (410).

Demagogues serve as "inspirational agitators" who mobilize a mass following of persons "who may adopt the program [of the demagogue] for reasons of cultural conditioning or conformity or of occupational and economic opportunism," writes Jaher in a discussion of anti-Semitism (1994: 13–14). Unpacking the relationships between ideological demagogic leaders and their followers, who may be motivated by a variety of reasons, is an important step in analyzing any repressive populist movement that uses scapegoating.

Several factors must coalesce for demagogues to activate mass populist scapegoating. As Robins and Post explain:

> The would-be leader propagating a paranoid theme in a time of tranquillity will appeal only to a small audience. Even in a time of stress such an appeal will fail if the leader lacks conventional political skills. But when the politically skillful leader or propagandist with a persuasive paranoid message calls to an overwhelmed society, the conditions are ripe for a violent and widespread response. (1997: 301)

Demagogues and Conspiracism

Conspiracist demagogues create for themselves a special status as gatekeepers to secret knowledge. They use a variety of emotionally manipulative propaganda tactics to convince an audience that their assertions about conspiracies have merit. They frequently use logical fallacies to assert connections between persons, groups, and events that may not be related at all. Some of the invalid arguments violate the historic rules of logic including the false ideas that sequence implies causation, association implies guilt, congruence in one aspect implies congruence in all aspects, and that simultaneous action implies prior planning. Conspiracist demagogues as orators portray as wisdom what is, in essence, parlor tricks of memorization lubricated with fallacies of logic. While this is a form of charlatanism, it is frequently unconscious. A vivid and humorous exposé of illogical demagoguery is in Perkins's study of the flawed arguments of media personality Rush Limbaugh.

An example of conspiracist demagoguery is the anti-Semitic book *The Secret Relationship Between Blacks and Jews,* which falsely claims that Jews controlled the slave trade. According to Gates, the book "massively misrepresents the historical record, largely through a process of cunningly selective quotation of often reputable sources. But its authors could be confident that few of its readers would go to the trouble of actually hunting down the works cited. For if readers actually did so, they might discover a rather different picture" (1992).

Demagogues and Right-Wing Populism

Ezekiel (1995) has looked at how young white men can be attracted to demagogic ideas of race hate in their attempt to create a sense of identity and belonging. On a broader scale this search for a collective identity can be channeled into authoritarian and reactionary forms of repressive populism. Canovan argues the basic mechanism involves "a charismatic leader, using the tactics of politicians' populism to go past the politicians and intellectual elite and appeal to the reactionary sentiments of the populace, often buttressing his claim to speak for the people by the use of referendums. When populism is attributed to right-wing figures—Hitler, de Gaulle, Codreanu, Father Coughlin—this is what the word conjures up" (1981: 292).

In its most virulent form, populist demagoguery is a core element of fascism. As Eco explains, however, the populist rhetoric of fascism is selective and illusive:

> [I]ndividuals as individuals have no rights, and the People is conceived as a quality, a monolithic entity expressing the Common Will. Since no large quantity of human beings can have a common will, the Leader pretends to be their interpreter. Having lost their power of delegation, citizens do not act; they are only called on to play the role of the People. Thus the People is a theatrical fiction. . . . There is in our future a TV or Internet populism, in which the emotional response of a selected group of citizens can be presented and accepted as the Voice of the People. . . . Wherever a politician casts doubt on the legitimacy of a parliament because it no longer represents the Voice of the People, we can smell . . . Fascism. (1995)

Conclusions

Demagogues have found an unfortunate affinity with modern mass communications and its simplistic packaging of information. In some cases what used to be denounced as demagoguery is now praised by pundits as spin control.

Democracy depends not only on ensuring freedom of speech, but also on ensuring the ability for all of us to carry on serious debate based on accurate information rather than prejudice or misinformation. Informed consent—the bedrock of the democratic process—relies on accurate information. Demagogues traffic in lies, distortions, and emotionally manipulative appeals, often aimed at inflaming stereotypes and prejudice already embedded in the society. Demagoguery is toxic to democratic discourse.

Chip Berlet

See also Charisma, Conspiracism, Demonization

Bibliography

Adorno, Theodor W., Else Frenkel-Brunswick, Daniel J. Levinson, and R. Nevitt Sanford. (1950) *The Authoritarian Personality.* New York: Harper & Row.

Allport, Gordon W. (1954) *The Nature of Prejudice.* Cambridge, MA: Addison-Wesley.

Blee, Kathleen, ed. (1998) *No Middle Ground: Women and Radical Protest.* New York: New York University Press.

Brackman, Harold. (1992) *Farrakhan's Reign of Historical Error: The Truth Behind the Secret Relationship Between Blacks and Jews.* Los Angeles: Simon Wiesenthal Center.

Canovan, Margaret. (1981) *Populism.* New York: Harcourt Brace Jovanovich.

Eco, Umberto. (1995) "Ur-Fascism" (Eternal Fascism). *New York Review of Books* (22 June): 12–15.

Ezekiel, Raphael S. (1995) *The Racist Mind: Portraits of American Neo-Nazis and Klansmen.* New York: Viking.

Gates, Henry Louis, Jr. (1992) "Black Demagogues and Pseudo-Scholars." *New York Times.* (20 July): A15.

Historical Research Department. (1991) *The Secret Relationship Between Blacks and Jews.* Chicago: Nation of Islam.

Hoffer, Eric. (1951) *The True Believer.* New York: Harper & Row.

Jaher, Frederic Cople. (1994) *A Scapegoat in the New Wilderness: The Origins and Rise of Anti-Semitism in America.* Cambridge, MA: Harvard University Press.

Klandermans, Bert. (1997) *The Social Psychology of Protest.* Oxford, U.K.: Blackwell.

Kramer, Joel, and Diana Alstad. (1993) *The Guru Papers: Masks of Authoritarian Power.* Berkeley, CA: Frog, Ltd.

Perkins, Ray Jr. (1995) *Logic and Mr. Limbaugh.* Chicago: Open Court.

Piven, Francis Fox, and Richard A. Cloward. (1978) *Poor People's Movements: Why They Succeed, How They Fail.* New York: Vintage.

Robins, Robert S., and Jerrold M. Post, M.D. (1997) *Political Paranoia: The Psychopolitics of Hatred.* New Haven, CT: Yale University Press.

Smelser, Neil J. (1971) *Theory of Collective Behavior.* New York: Free Press.

Demonization

Demonization is the portrayal of individuals and groups as evil—perhaps even in league with a literal Satan. Demonization is often based on preexisting prejudices, and it facilitates scapegoating and conspiracism. In contemporary U.S. society, popular targets of demonization include Jews, Catholics, Mormons, Moslems, Freemasons, New Age devotees, welfare mothers, immigrants, peace activists, environmentalists, feminists, abortion providers, and gay men and lesbians. Members of groups ranging from the Trilateral Commission to the National Education Association are demonized, as are federal officials and UN troops. Demonization can be found in left, center, and right political rhetoric.

The process of demonization often begins with marginalization, whereby targeted individuals or groups are placed outside the circle of wholesome mainstream society through political propaganda that usually relies on inflaming age-old prejudices. This creates the binary Us/Them, Good/Bad dynamic called dualism. The next step is objectification or dehumanization: the process of negatively labeling a person or group of people so they become perceived more as objects than as real people. Dehumanization often is associated with the belief that a particular group of people is inferior, sinful, or threatening. The final step is demonization: the person or group is framed as totally malevolent and evil. It is easier to rationalize stereotyping, prejudice, discrimination, and even violence against those who are demonized.

Demonization depends on dualism, which tolerates no middle ground in disputes. Dualism refuses to acknowledge complexity, nuance, or ambiguity in debate, and promotes hostility toward those who suggest coexistence, toleration, pragmatism, compromise, or mediation. This binary model of good versus evil is found in the spiritual and secular beliefs of many cultures.

When demonization takes place, enemies are created. Aho observes that our notions of the enemy "in our everyday life world," is that the "enemy's presence in our midst is a pathology of the social organism serious enough to require the most far-reaching remedies: quarantine, political excision, or, to use a particularly revealing expression, liquidation and expulsion" (1994: 107–21). The logical endgame of demonization is discrimination or violence. If the enemy is truly evil, then why not kill them for the common good? Demonization has played a crucial role in facilitating genocide during the past century—ethnic Armenians by Turkish nationalists; Jews and the Roma (Gypsies) during the German Nazi regime; in Cambodia based on class and education; ethnic Chinese by Indonesian nationalists.

Some early studies of prejudice, demonization, and scapegoating treated the processes as marginal to "mainstream" society and an indication of an individual pathological psychological disturbance. More recent social science demonstrates that demonization is a habit found across various sectors of society among people who are no more prone to mental illness than the rest of society. The "banality of evil," as Arendt observed, is that ordinary people can become willing—even eager—participants in brutality and mass murder justified by demonization of scapegoated groups in a society (1963). Langer raises this as a troubling issue regarding the Nazi genocide:

> The widespread absence of remorse among the accused in postwar trials indicates that we may need . . . to accept the possibility of a regimen of behavior that simply dismisses conscience as an operative moral factor. The notion of the power to kill, or to authorize killing of others, as a personally fulfilling activity is not appealing to our civilized sensibilities; even more threatening is the idea that this is not necessarily a pathological condition, but an expression of impulses as native to our selves as love and compassion. (1995: 182)

Many older studies of prejudice also had a "tendency to collapse distinctions between types of prejudice," observed Young-Bruehl. They assumed "that a nationalism and racism, an ethnocentric prejudice and an ideology of desire, can be dynamically the same" (1996: 23). Furthermore, she observes, "there is a tendency to approach prejudice either psychologically or sociologically without consideration for the interplay of psychological and sociological factors" (460). Because of this and other scholarship that challenges the classic psychological and sociological theories, there is a renewed interest in studying the relationships among prejudice, demonization, scapegoating, and conspiracism.

Satan and Demonization

Demonizing the "Other" appears to be a common human practice. In Western culture, the specific forms of demonization prevalent in many societies are highly influenced by apocalyptic and millennialist themes popularized by certain interpretations of Christianity. There is a long and tragic history of some Christians demonizing religious reformers, followers of non-Christian religious traditions, nonbelievers, and dissidents of all stripes. According to Caras, "[t]he saddest side of the Devil's history appears in the persecution of those who were supposed to be adherents of the Devil; namely, sectarians, heretics, and witches" (1996: 306). The demonization of Jews as magical agents of the powerful Devil gained strength during the sixteenth-century Renaissance and the Reformation. During this period, long-standing false allegations about Jews secretly engaging in murder and desecration again became widely believed among Christians.

The Salem witch trials sought to expose witches and their allies as conspiring with the Devil. Modern scholarship has shown that persons accused of being witches were disproportionately women who did not conform to societal expectations, and that there was frequently an economic dimension to the charge, such as a disputed inheritance. This is evidence that demonization, scapegoating, and conspiracism (elements of every witch-hunt) arrived on our shores with the overwhelmingly Protestant early settlers and their view that Godly persons were in a struggle with a literal Satan. These ideas were influenced by the apocalyptic narrative of Revelation, but were not always linked to a specific widespread period of millennial expectation.

In the United States, Catholics and Freemasons were demonized during the 1800s, but in the early 1900s the focus shifted toward Jews, fueled in part by the publication of the hoax document, *The Protocols of the Elders of Zion*, which suggested Jews were agents of the Antichrist. The Protocols influenced Hitler's racialized idea of a vast Judeo-Bolshevik conspiracy against civilization and paved the way for genocide.

Since Revelation can be read to predict that the Antichrist will build a one-world government in the endtimes, some Christians have demonized collectivist philosophies such as communism beyond any rational criticisms of political ideologies and practices. The threat of communism (represented as a Red Menace) became the main focus of apocalyptic demonization. According to Frank Donner:

> The root anti-subversive impulse was fed by the Menace. Its power strengthened with the passage of time, by the late twenties its influence had become more pervasive and folkish. Bolshevism came to be identified over wide areas of the country by God-fearing Americans as the Antichrist come to do eschatological battle with the children of light. A slightly secularized version, widely-shared in rural and small-town America, postulated a doomsday conflict between decent upright folk and radicalism—alien, satanic, immorality incarnate. (1980: 47–48)

Ribuffo (1983) demonstrates the influence of apocalyptic biblical prophecy on Protestant far-right conspiracist movements that demonized scapegoats in the interwar period, especially such key leaders as: William Dudley Pelley, Gerald B. Winrod, and Gerald L. K. Smith.

Fuller ties the Christian millennialist viewpoint to the larger issues of demonization and scapegoating when he argues that:

> Many efforts to name the Antichrist appear to be rooted in the psychological need to project one's "unacceptable" tendencies onto a demonic enemy. It is the Antichrist, not oneself, who must be held responsible for wayward desires. And with so many aspects of modern American life potentially luring individuals into nonbiblical thoughts or desire, it is no wonder that many people believe that the Antichrist has camouflaged himself to better work his conspiracies against the faithful. (1995: 168)

This tendency notwithstanding, it is important to recall that most Christians, even those who think the endtimes are imminent do not automatically succumb to demonization, scapegoating, or conspiracist thinking.

Pagels points out that today "many religious people who no longer believe in Satan, along with countless others who do not identify with any religious tradition, nevertheless are influenced by this cultural legacy whenever they perceive social and political conflict in terms of the forces of good contending against the forces of evil in the world" (1996: 182). In the 1990s, demonization was used in sectors of the Christian Right; the Patriot and armed militia movements; and the far right, especially the neo-Nazi version of Christian Identity theology and the Church of the Creator. On the left, where it mostly appears in a secularized form, demonization has been used by some critics of government intelligence abuse and global corporate interconnections. After the collapse of European communism, historic anticollectivist sentiments were transferred to demonizing any attempt to build global cooperation.

Conclusions

Demonization sets the stage for scapegoating and conspiracism, and facilitates turning anger and resentment into discrimination and violence. The use of demonization in political, cultural, and religious arguments is unfortunately a common occurrence. Demonization easily finds a home in contemporary U.S. society. Holly Sklar (1995) notes that the demonization and scapegoating of a number of groups—including immigrants, welfare recipients, people of color, and single mothers—is already tolerated to an alarming degree in mainstream political debate. The demonization of gay men, lesbians, bisexuals, and transgender people is a common occurrence. If we look carefully, we can see a similar pattern in countries around the world. The demonization of migrants across Europe is a continuing problem, and the demonization of Jews in Russia by ultra-nationalists raises a haunting specter. In many of these settings, demonization and conspiracism appear to accompany certain forms of xenophobic right-wing populism.

Fine (1995) studied one high school curriculum, Facing History and Ourselves, designed to promote respect and civility. She observes how the lessons equipped students to stand up against demagogic processes that are toxic to democracy. She concludes that such curricula are needed for each generation. We all need to be taught about the corrosive nature of demonization, which acts as a bridge between prejudice and scapegoating.

Chip Berlet

Bibliography

Aho, James A. (1994) *This Thing of Darkness: A Sociology of the Enemy*. Seattle: University of Washington Press.

Allport, Gordon W. (1954) *The Nature of Prejudice*. Cambridge, MA: Addison-Wesley.

Arendt, Hannah. (1963) *Eichmann in Jerusalem: A Report on the Banality of Evil*. New York: Penguin Books.

Caras, Paul. ([1974] 1996) *The History of the Devil and the Idea of Evil*. New York: Random House.

Donner, Frank J. (1980) *The Age of Surveillance: The Aims and Methods of America's Political Intelligence System*. New York: Alfred A. Knopf.

Fine, Melinda. (1995) *Habits of Mind: Struggling Over Values in America's Classrooms*. San Francisco: Jossey-Bass.

Fuller, Robert. (1995) *Naming the Antichrist: The History of an American Obsession*. New York: Oxford University Press.

Girard, René. (1986) *The Scapegoat*. Baltimore: Johns Hopkins University Press.

Hsia, R. Po-chia. (1988) *The Myth of Ritual Murder: Jews and Magic in Reformation Germany*. New Haven, CT: Yale University Press.

Karlsen, Carol F. (1998) *The Devil in the Shape of a Woman: Witchcraft in Colonial New England*. New York: W. W. Norton.

Langer, Lawrence L. (1995) *Admitting the Holocaust: Collected Essays*. New York: Oxford University Press.

Noël, Lise. (1994) *Intolerance: A General Survey*. Montreal: McGill-Queen's University Press.

Oberman, Heiko A. (1984) *The Roots of Anti-Semitism: In the Age of Renaissance and Reformation*, translated by James I. Porter. Philadelphia: Fortress Press.

Pagels, Elaine. (1996) *The Origin of Satan*. New York: Vintage.

Ribuffo, Leo P. (1983) *The Old Christian Right: The Protestant Hard Right from the Great Depression to the Cold War*. Philadelphia: Temple University Press.

Sklar, Holly. (1995) *Chaos or Community: Seeking Solutions, Not Scapegoats for Bad Economics*. Boston: South End Press.

Stanford, Peter. (1996) *The Devil: A Biography*. New York: Henry Holt.

Young-Bruehl, Elisabeth. (1996) *The Anatomy of Prejudices*. Cambridge, MA: Harvard University Press.

Dispensationalism

Dispensationalism is a Christian theology, derived from premillennial eschatology, which divides sacred history into various periods—dispensations—during each of which God differently orders his relationship to humankind. Its distinguishing traits include reliance on a literalist hermeneutics, applied to an inerrant Bible; a distinction between the Church and Israel; the Pre-Tribulation rapture of the saints; a visible reign of Christ in Jerusalem during the millennium; and a restricted view of what constitutes the true church. It is, in large part, the work of an Irish cleric, John Nelson Darby (1800–82). It is confined to Protestantism, especially its conservative or Fundamentalist wing, and is absent entirely in Roman Catholic or Orthodox Christianity. It is especially common in the United States.

Background of Dispensationalism in Christian Thought

Both its proponents and opponents agree that as a systematic theology, dispensationalism is a late arrival in Christian thought. Those who dismiss it as fallacious are likely to cite its relative novelty as grounds for doing so: it plays little part in church history until the nineteenth century. Adherents, however, see antiquity as no guarantor of merit and argue that dispensationalism is like a gold deposit, the recent discovery of which does not invalidate its value.

Christian theologians have long propounded that sacred history is best understood in terms of the different manners or degree through which God reveals Himself to humanity. The Bible itself, through its commonly accepted division into two Testaments, Old and New, is structured around such a concept. Both Judaism and Christianity identify periods—past, present, and future—which constitute remarkable epochs in the Divine-human relationship. The Abrahamic covenant is the basis of one such epoch: "And I will establish my covenant between me and you and your descendants after you throughout their generations for an everlasting covenant, to be God to you and to your descendants after you" (Genesis 17:7). Likewise, both Jewish and Christian eschatology foretell a future period of unparalleled communion between God and his people: the millennial passage of Revelation 20:1–3 is the best-known example. There is no question that Christianity has understood itself as a new revelation (e.g., the Gospels—Good News), centered entirely on the teaching, death, and Resurrection of Jesus Christ.

Modern scholars, regardless of sectarian persuasion, use a similar language as a schematic to expound the Bible. It is common, for instance, to speak authoritatively of a Patriarchal Period. Although twentieth-century Christian scholarship recognizes a continuity between late Jewish thought (for example, the Dead Sea Scrolls) and so-called primitive Christianity, there remains almost universal recognition that the New Testament represents an unmistakable departure from Judaism.

Modern dispensationalists can thus cite a considerable body of both Scripture and scholarship to support their belief. Their assertion is, however, entirely unconvincing to other prominent theologians and scholars. These believe that dispensationalists are guilty of reading their current beliefs back into different times and cultures and that dispensationalism rigidly and unimaginatively uses language meant to be evocative or poetic in a legalistic and overly literal manner.

Premillennialism and Biblical Literalism

Regardless of historical precedents, or sanction in Scripture, dispensationalism today is unmistakably a by-product of the nineteenth-century Anglo-American millenarian revival. Premillennial eschatology, present in English religious life since the Reformation, flourished mightily in Great Britain, prompted by speculation over the prophetic significance of events in post–1789 France. Such speculation was immediately, and avidly, taken up in the United States.

The core exegetical method of millenarians was literalism, which required that the Bible be understood solely in terms of the plain, grammatical meaning of its language. Such was to be the case, even if the result contradicted scientific knowledge or seemed risible in light of other biblical scholarship. In 1853 a critic of the premillennialists charged that their "Bible is so different from all other compositions, that, without the application of their peculiar laws of literal interpretation, only a small portion of it can be understood." Millenarians, who later in the nineteenth century would contribute hugely to the rise of Fundamentalism, clung tenaciously to literalism, despite such ridicule. They had little choice. Without the literalist method, the obscure biblical prophecies that underlay their eschatology were otherwise easily dismissable by modern historical-critical scholars as merely so much inspirational poetry.

Premillennial exegesis regarded prophecy as prospective history. It sought to match event with prediction in order to anticipate the Second Advent. This approach was labeled historicism. Details of the future were a matter of hot dispute, but there was general agreement among millenarians that the lot of Christians in history must steadily worsen until the Second Advent of Jesus Christ. Upon that epochal event, Satan would be held bound for one thousand years (the millennium) and Jesus would reign visibly over the earth from Jerusalem. Integral to this scenario was the restoration of the Jews to Palestine and the re-creation there of a Jewish state. Literalism, philo-Semitism, the Second Advent, and the millennium were thus just a few of the eschatologically-founded concepts common in nineteenth-century evangelical Protestantism in England and America.

John Nelson Darby and the Plymouth Brethren

Darby, born of a well-established Anglo-Irish family, early in life abandoned the study of law and was ordained in the Church of England. Convinced that the Christian Church was, in his words, "in ruins," he later renounced this ordination and gathered a like-minded group of followers—soon known as the Plymouth Brethren—who shared his commitment to premillennialism and biblical literalism. For the remainder of his long life, Darby was the acknowledged spiritual leader of the Brethren. He was not, however, especially interested in building a new denomination and remained skeptical about the validity of any formal ecclesiastical organization. It became a hallmark of his followers to constantly argue with one another over even minor disagreements and to hive off into competing factions. Always an argumentative lot, premillennialists became especially so.

Darby traveled widely and spent long periods in the United States, to meet with followers and preach his peculiar theology—dispensationalism. While the division of sacred history into discrete periods is, as noted above, not uncommon in Judeo-Christian thought, Darby posited an almost schematic history of God's dealing with humankind. Each dispensation (for instance, the "Adamaic") constitutes a period for which God offers humankind a beneficent covenantal relationship, with faith and obedience the proper response. The immediate and inevitable failure of humanity to react appropriately to this divine generosity promptly condemns it anew. Darby identified seven dispensations, although other millenarians order them somewhat differently. These various dispensational schemes flourish today on countless charts and graphs hung on Sunday school walls throughout the evangelical world.

The Secret Rapture

Darby abandoned historicism and its endless attempts to gauge how far along the world was on the prophetic timetable. Instead, he stressed that Christ could return, unannounced and unheralded, at any moment. This belief, known today as futurism, added piquancy to premillennialism by making each instant in life the one during which a believer might be whisked into the presence of Jesus. No warning need be given and there was no catalog of events that must first be fulfilled. "There is," Darby wrote, "no event between me and heaven."

Futurism was integral to Darby's most significant theological innovation—the Secret Rapture. The Rapture became

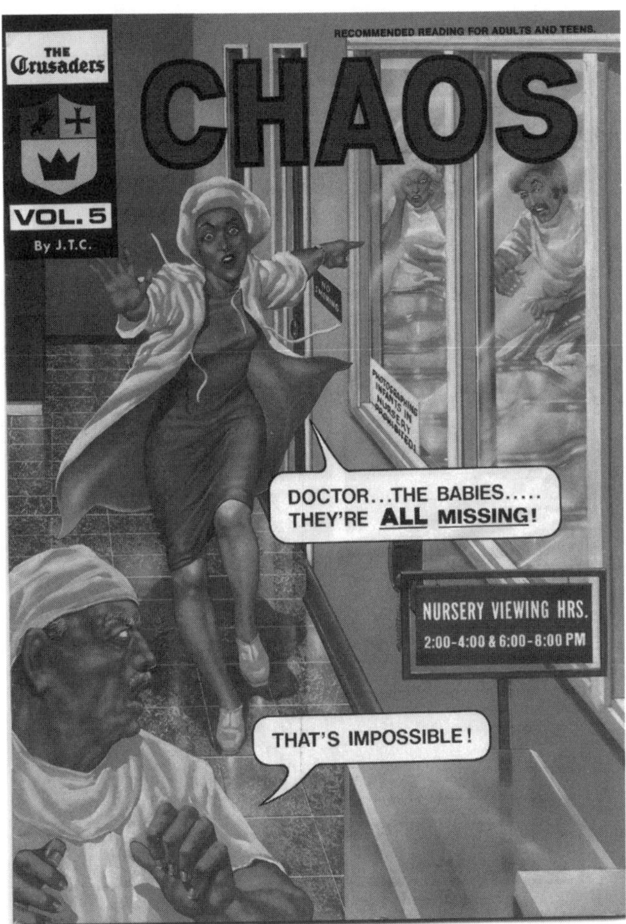

"Chaos," an evangelistic comic distributed by Chick Publications, popularizes dispensational eschatology with great emphasis on the Pre-Tribulation Rapture. Innocent babies will be raptured along with living Christians, plunging those left behind into unbearable grief and shock even before the Great Tribulation begins. The comic concludes with this urgent summary the Christian message for those alive in the last days. COPYRIGHT 1975 BY JACK T. CHICK. REPRODUCED BY PERMISSION.

an immensely popular concept among evangelical Protestants and today flourishes mightily. Darby came to his concept through the literalist method, applied especially to Paul's first letter to the Thessalonians: "For the Lord himself will descend from heaven with a cry of command, with the archangel's call, and with the sound of the trumpet of God. And the dead in Christ will rise first; then we who are alive, who are left, shall be caught up together with them in the clouds to meet the Lord in the air" (1 Thessalonians 4:16–17). Paul's prediction that "the dead in Christ will rise first," convinced Darby that there would, in effect, be two Second Advents. He claimed a distinction between when Christ returns *for* his church and when he returns *with* it. Jesus' first Advent would be invisible, utterly without warning (futurism), and for the purpose of gathering out from a corrupt church those true Christians who are his own: "Then two men will be in the field; one is taken and one is left" (Matthew 25:40). The saved will ascend out of the world, i.e., "meet the Lord in the air." (During the 1990s, a popular automobile bumper sticker read, "In case of Rapture, this car will be driverless," a statement which expresses well the expected sudden departure of the saints out of the world.) The Tribulation then follows the Rapture, a period of war, famine, and Satanic license on earth for those unfortunate enough to have been left behind by Christ. The Tribulation will last perhaps three-and-a-half years and end when Christ returns a second time, in company with his saints, to banish Satan and institute the millennium.

Darby's Scheme of the Church, Israel, and the Jews

From the seventeenth century onward, the future of the Jews was a key feature of prophecy for nearly all premillennialists. Despite his many innovations, Darby still belonged in the line of thought traceable to the Anglo-American millenarian revival of the early nineteenth century, and he was certain of the centrality of the Jews in prophecy. He reverted to his dispensational scheme, however, to fashion a novel theology of the respective roles of the "Church" (i.e., Christianity) and "Israel" (i.e., the Jews) in sacred history. The result was one of his most controversial tenets.

Darby reasoned that God makes no promises he will not accomplish. Since certain prophecies made in Old Testament times to the Jews remain unfulfilled (in Derby's view, at least), it followed that these must be fulfilled in the future. From this premise, he extrapolated that the covenantal dispensation offered the Jews was not ended—merely in abeyance. As promised to them, the Jews must eventually be "restored" to Israel, there to resume their status as a priestly people. Taken by itself, this train of logic was common enough among contemporary millenarians. Darby, however, took the logic a step further.

If the dispensation offered the Jews constitutes the future, then how, he wondered, did Christianity fit into sacred history? He concluded that the Abrahamic covenant remains valid; must, and will, be fulfilled; and that the Christian Era constitutes a rupture in sacred history caused solely by the refusal of the Jews to accept Jesus as Messiah. (The Christian religion, seen in the light of prophecy, was soon labeled "The Great Parenthesis" by Derby's followers, in order to stress its interruption of prophetic fulfillment.) Darby thus saw a huge gulf between Israel (the Jewish state promised Abraham) and the Church (Christianity). In a sense, the Christian church is a divine afterthought to the real business at hand—which is God's promise to Israel. The coming millennium will, as well, be primarily a fulfillment of the Abrahamic promise.

Dispensationalism and Evangelical Thought in Modern America

Premillennialism is basic to the wide segment of conservative Protestant thought in America labeled Fundamentalism or Evangelicalism. Dispensationalism, in turn, is endemic to much contemporary premillennial theology. The basic building blocks of John Nelson Darby's millenarianism—biblical literalism, philo-Semitism, the restoration of Israel, and a Second Advent prior to the millennium—were common throughout the period of his ministry and, indeed, greatly predate it. Both the Pre-Tribulation Rapture and the distinction between Israel and the Church, however, were novel to Darby. These concepts were widely taken up in the United States, along with dispensationalism. The spread of Derby's ideas was, in part, due to his own efforts. But, it was due in far greater degree to efforts made on his behalf by a number of talented disciples. The most influential of these was, perhaps, James H. Brooks, a St. Louis clergyman who helped organize the enormously successful series of prophecy conferences at Niagara-On-the-Lake, Ontario in the late nineteenth century. These provided an ideal venue for spreading dispensationalism. It was Cyrus I. Scofield, however, an American attorney, who probably made the most lasting contribution in popularizing Derby's ideas in the United States. Influenced by the Plymouth Brethren, Scofield embedded dispensationalism in the copious notes of his immensely popular *Scofield Reference Bible* (1909). Millions of readers, many of whom may never have heard of John Nelson Darby, nonetheless take his dispensational scheme for granted through reliance on this perennial religious best seller.

From the early twentieth century onward, Derby's scheme of dispensationalism was thus grafted so successfully onto premillennialism that many, if not most, believers see them as one and the same. Futurism, the Secret Rapture, and the dichotomy between Israel and the Church, along with a careful division of sacred history into dispensations, became part and parcel of Fundamentalist and Evangelical theology. Careful biblical scholars, such as John Walvoord of Dallas Theological Seminary, continued to employ literalist hermeneutics to defend the philo-Semitic dispensational enthrallment with the future of the Jews. Dispensational premillennialism also gained popularity through being embraced by such Evangelical luminaries as the Rev. Billy Graham. Equally respected scholars, however, dismiss dispensationalism as a recent, superfluous, and wholly unwelcome novelty in Christian thought, substantiated only by a rigidly unimaginative and ahistorical use of Scripture.

Dispensationalists received a tremendous boost to morale when, in the mid-twentieth century, significant numbers of Jews did migrate to Palestine, to found Israel anew as a Jewish state. The event seemed to them to validate dispensationalism, as what could be more convincing than the palpable fulfillment of prophecy? Critics, of course, could retort that such an interpretation fits uneasily on the arcane web of political intrigue that constitutes contemporary history in the Middle East. Regardless, the creation of modern Israel entrenched philo-Semitism more firmly than ever in Evangelical thought.

There are today, as is always the case among premillennialists, sharp divisions among dispensationalists over prophetic interpretation. There is, however, general agreement that sacred history is divided into distinct dispensations—differences center largely around how these are numbered and organized. The Pre-Tribulation Rapture is, likewise, commonly accepted. An uneasy peace exists between proponents of the historicist method and Darbyite futurism, with adherents to be found in both camps. Dispensationalism is most commonly encountered among Fundamentalist and Evangelical Christians. It is especially prevalent within the various Baptist churches, but others embrace it as well, as do countless independent Christian congregations. Only rarely is it encountered in other so-called mainline denominations. It is virtually unknown in non-Protestant Christianity. The number of modern adherents is incalculable, but certainly runs well into the millions.

Robert K. Whalen

See also Postmillennialism, Premillennialism

Bibliography

Bass, Clarence B. (1960) *Backgrounds to Dispensationalism.* Grand Rapids, MI: Wm. B. Eerdmans.

Efird, James M. (1986) *End-Times: Rapture, Antichrist, Millennium.* Nashville, TN: Abingdon Press.

Ryrie, Charles C. (1965) *Dispensationalism Today.* Chicago: Moody Press.

Sandeen, Ernest R. (1970) *The Roots of Fundamentalism: British and American Millenarianism, 1800–1930.* Chicago: University of Chicago Press.

Doomsday

Doomsday is a day of judgment and, in certain Christian thought, a precursor of the millennium. The word itself, however, appears nowhere in the Bible and can be used as well in an entirely secular context. The root word, *dom* (Old English), connotes judgment, a sentence, or destiny, and carries with it an undertone of fear or dread. Among the

Abrahamic religions of Judaism, Christianity, and Islam—faiths which espouse a Doomsday—that judgment implies a personal and knowing act, such as the sentence a just judge might impose, and it is in this sense that the word is often used.

When defined to mean the end of the world, Doomsday is entirely separable from religious belief. An astrophysicist can, with more or less accuracy, describe how the physical world will likely end and even reasonably calculate the timing. For the scientist, though, this becomes merely one more event in the natural world, devoid of any moral dimension. Within the Abrahamic faiths, however, the end of the world constitutes a grand moral assize. The thought that it might occur without a settling of moral accounts is repugnant. Both Islam and Judaism honor scripture or commentary which can be interpreted to prophesy the end of the world. In neither of these religions, however, is a Doomsday so clearly enunciated, or such an orthodox article of faith, as in Christianity.

Doomsday can be personal, as well as cosmological. Each individual is, after all, doomed to die, and in this sense there need be no religious dimension whatever. Once again, however, the Abrahamic faiths insist that even one's personal doom is attended with judgment. The three great religions share an emphatic belief that each soul is judged by a monotheistic deity on its ethical behavior in life. That judgment may well be tempered by mercy, or mitigated by the faith life of the believer (such as belief in Christ, or adherence to the teachings of the Koran). Judgment, however, is final and irrevocable—qualities which set it apart from the personal and cosmological dooms of other major religions, which nonetheless demand an equally rigorous ethical life.

Confucianism, for instance, provides sophisticated rules for a worthy life but predicts no judgment, other than personal frustration, for failure to observe these. It is virtually silent on the destiny of the world as a whole. It is more difficult to generalize about such extended religions as Buddhism and Hinduism, for which no orthodoxy is universally recognized. As a rule, however, their doctrine of the transmigration of souls vitiates any concept of a personal Doomsday which is final and eternal. Likewise, the cyclic cosmologies of these faiths—such as the Hindu belief in vast epicycles for the physical universe—effectively frustrate any concept of a final rendering of accounts, in which the world, history, and time are altogether brought to a permanent end.

Doomsday emerged only fitfully as a concept in Hebrew religious life in ancient Israel, whether as a personal or cosmological principle. It was accepted early on that Yahweh demanded certain behaviors, both ritualistic as well as ethical, but failure to conform resulted in punishment inflicted in life, rather than judgment after death. The concept of an afterlife was weak, and when thought of at all it was as *sheol*, a shadowy abode in which the departed spend a meaningless existence: "For in death there is no remembrance of thee; in Sheol who can give thee praise" (Psalms 6:5).

A cosmological Doomsday, during which judgment is passed on all Israel, was, however, a recurrent theme of Old Testament prophets. In the eighth century BCE, Amos of Tekoa warned: "'And on that day,' says the Lord God, 'I will make the sun go down at noon, and darken the earth in broad daylight'" (Amos 8:9). The prophets also foresaw a time, reminiscent of the later Christian millennium, in which God would renew his Creation: "For behold, I create new heavens and a new earth; and the former things shall not be remembered or come into mind" (Isaiah 65:17). This concept of a divine judgment, in which the world is overthrown and a new order established, becomes especially strong in Jewish thought in the second-century BCE Book of Daniel, which foresees a "dominion" which is "an everlasting dominion, which shall not pass away, and his kingdom one that shall not be destroyed" (Daniel 7:14).

From its inception, a day of judgment, whether for each individual soul or the world itself, was immensely important to Christianity. On the personal level, Jesus warned that each soul would be judged after death: "Everyone who is angry with his brother shall be liable to judgment" (Matthew 5:22). He also foretold the end of the present order of creation: "But in those days, after that tribulation, the sun will be darkened, and the moon will not give its light, and the stars will be falling from heaven" (Mark 13:24–25). For the early Christians, the Day of Judgment became inseparable from the Second Coming of Christ. The late-first-century CE Book of Revelation foretold the end of the world in lurid language. For some, a brief passage in its twentieth chapter, which prophesied an angel who would lay hold of Satan and bind him "for a thousand years" (Revelation 20:2), meant that when Jesus returned, a millennium of grace on earth would begin. As a doctrine, millennialism has played only a minor role in historic Christian thought. For some believers, however, it has loomed large as an element of faith, and probably never more so than today.

Virtually no major Christian denomination has abandoned the cosmological Doomsday—the Day of Judgment—as an element of faith. It survives with especial vigor among evangelical Protestants in the United States, for whom the Second Advent occupies a prominent place in theology. Doomsday is, for these Christians, inseparably associated with the concept of a millennium. Although, as long ago as the fifth century CE, St. Augustine discounted the doctrine of an earthly millennium and emphasized Christ's warning against attempting to predict the day of his return, Doomsday calculations remain integral to evangelical and Fundamentalist eschatology.

In fact, several "dooms" may be said to exist in contemporary millenarianism. There is, of course, one for each individual soul following death. But, a first cosmological Doomsday is predicted (in interpretation of Revelation 20:2) upon Christ's return in judgment. At that time, the forces of Satan on earth will be defeated, Christ shall reign incarnate on earth, and the millennium will begin. The millennium will then end with a final apostasy—a conclusive confrontation between good and evil. This last rebellion against God will be utterly defeated, when follows a second Doomsday in which the world passes away. What happens next is a matter of argument: whether a new earth will be created or the elect simply translated to spend eternity in heaven. Non-evangelical or Fundamentalist Christians see little need for such multiple cosmological Doomsdays. Virtually all, however, retain belief in a personal judgment by God at death.

Doomsday, as cosmological end of the world, has been a constant in Christian thought, art, and literature, down into our own time. It was present in the earliest of the Christian confession, the Apostle's Creed, which states of Christ: "He will return in glory to judge the living and the dead." The Day of Wrath (Dies Irae, in Latin) was, as well, a staple of medieval art, and any number of stained glasses or cathedral sculptures depict the tortures of the damned in exquisite detail. Countless tracts have been written on the subject, and in the late twentieth century some—such as Hal Lindsay's *The Late, Great Planet Earth*—were best-sellers.

Secular Doomsdays abound, of course, in modern life. Karl Marx's prediction of the collapse of capitalism, and its subsequent replacement by communism, parallels Christian doctrines of the Dies Irae and millennium to follow. The Marxian doom is, however, pronounced by the impersonal workings of history and carries with it no element of moral judgment. Ever since modern weaponry provided a viable means for humanity's total destruction, a thermonuclear Doomsday has loomed large in popular awareness and inspired numerous works of art and literature. The 1963 motion picture *Dr. Strangelove; or, How I Learned to Quit Worrying and Love the Bomb*, is a superb representative of the ironic-satirical treatment of a secularized Christian Doomsday (followed not by a millennium, but total extinction) in contemporary thought. In addition, among the many modern Doomsday's there is the ecological Doomsday, in which a withered and lifeless planet spins meaninglessly in space after human irresponsibility leaves it eternally sterile. It remains to be seen whether these variant Doomsday scenarios will subsist anywhere near as long as the Christian vision. It is not unlikely that the Abrahamic tradition which combines Doomsday with moral judgment will prove the more enduring.

Robert K. Whalen

Bibliography

Cohn, Norman F. (1961) *The Pursuit of the Millennium: Revolutionary Messianism in Medieval and Reformation Europe and Its Bearing on Modern Totalitarian Movements*. New York: Harper Torchbooks.

Doan, Ruth Alden. (1987) *The Miller Heresy: Millennialism and American Culture*. Philadelphia: Temple University Press.

MacGregor, Geddes. (1992) *Images of Afterlife: Beliefs from Antiquity to Modern Times*. New York: Paragon House.

McGinn, Bernard. (1998) "The Last Judgment in Christian Tradition." In *The Encyclopedia of Apocalypticism*, vol. 2, edited by Bernard McGinn. New York: Continuum Publishing Co.

Earth First!

Earth First! is the best-known branch of the "radical environmental" movement. Founded in the southwestern United States in 1980, it quickly assembled a diverse collection of environmental activists proclaiming "no compromise in defense of Mother Earth!" In its first two decades, the movement experimented with new forms of direct action resistance to environmental degradation, especially new forms of civil disobedience, such as "tree sitting" and road blockades. A number of its activists championed even more aggressive "ecotage" strategies to thwart environmental degradation, including "tree spiking" (putting metal or other nails in trees), equipment sabotage, and even arson. They seek to immediately halt or make unprofitable environmental destruction.

Earth First! can be viewed as a new religious movement because its activists believe that people must first recognize that the earth is sacred before they will be defend it and establish proper relations with nonhuman nature. Their conviction is that modern lifeways are precipitating an ecological catastrophe that is ending the world as we know it. Thus Earth First! is an apocalyptic form of millennialism, as is much of contemporary environmentalism.

Development of Earth First!

Initially led by Dave Foreman, a former Wilderness Society activist and the most charismatic speaker among its cofounders, in the 1980s Earth First! rapidly established a small but raucous presence throughout much of North America and Australia. By 1983, the movement had discovered and adopted "deep ecology" as its philosophical rubric.

Arne Naess, a Norwegian philosopher and mountain climber coined the term "deep ecology" in 1973. He had been deeply influenced by Baruch Spinoza (an important eighteenth-century philosopher and pantheist) and Mahatma Gandhi. Naess criticized what he called “shallow” or “reform” environmentalism for its anthropocentrism, namely, for its human-centered value system that, he believed, failed to recognize the intrinsic value of all life. Far better, he argued, are the many forms of “deep ecology” that, through diverse spiritual and philosophical paths, arrive at a shared conviction that all life has value and should be allowed to flourish.

Deep ecology gave expression to a feeling already held by many environmentalists. Soon it was championed by a growing number of writers in the United States, Australia, and Europe. Among the most influential were Gary Snyder (1969, 1990), Paul Shephard (1982, 1998), Bill Devall and George Sessions (1985), Deloris LaChappelle (1988), John Seed (and others, 1988), Christopher Manes (1990), Warwick Fox (1991), Joanna Macy (1991), and Dave Foreman himself (1985, 1991). For his part, Foreman credited academic philosophers for playing an important role in promulgating deep ecology and other “ecocentric” (ecosystem-centered) philosophies. Such environmental ethics shifted the center of moral concern from humans to entire ecosystems, helping to fuel and staff radical environmental groups including Earth First!. Direct action resistance by Earth First!ers, however, did more than the movement’s intellectual proponents to confront mainstream society with radical environmentalism’s central claims and demands.

At the grass roots, within radical environmental groups, various deep ecology spiritualities were digested into a widely held and expressed conviction: all life has value, apart from its usefulness to human beings (or put differently, all life is sacred) and thus, all organisms ought to be allowed to continue their evolutionary unfolding. Thus, deep ecology became the umbrella under which paganism (especially in pantheistic and animistic forms), and religions originating in the Far East, could find a hospitable place to cross-fertilize with radical green politics.

In addition to deep ecological spirituality, in the early years of Earth First!, Foreman promoted anarchistic ideals and suggested that humans should return to their tribal roots (and thus to tribal ritualizing and a warrior ethos of earth defense). Foreman thereby unwittingly invited to Earth First! anarchists, New Age seekers, hippies, pagans, and others engaged in the West’s countercultural, cultic milieu. Soon the anarchists and practicing pagans would outnumber Foreman and his closest associates, making them appear moderate by comparison. By the end of the decade, the tensions led to a decisive schism; and Foreman and his closest allies abandoned Earth First!.

Factionalism in Earth First!

Three main, divisive fissures had emerged. First, Foreman wished to focus the movement exclusively on conserving the

---

RAINBOW WARRIOR

Some time in the future, the Indians said, the animals would begin to disappear. People would no longer see the wolf, or the bear, or the eagles. And, the story goes, the giant trees would also disappear. And people would fight with each other and not love each other. And, the story goes, the beautiful rainbow in the sky would fade away, and people would not see the rainbow anymore.

Well, children would come. And these children would love the animals, and they would bring back the animals. They would love trees, and they would bring back the giant trees. And these children would love other people and they would help people to live in peace with each other. And these children would love the rainbow, and they would bring back the beautiful rainbow in the sky. For this reason the Indians called these children the rainbow warriors.

Now let me ask you a question. Do you love animals or hate animals? (We love animals.) Do you love trees or hate trees? (We love trees.) Do you love people or hate people? (We love people.) Do you love the rainbow or hate the rainbow? (We love the rainbow.)

Well, if you love animals and trees, people and rainbows, then maybe you are the rainbow warriors and that is a statue of you.

Source: http://www.welcomehome.org/rainbow/prophecy/warrior.html.

---

earth's biological diversity and came to view as counterproductive the movement's intensifying countercultural political and religious style. He did not assume that nation-states were intractably corrupt and impossible to influence democratically. Unlike a growing number of Earth First!ers, Foreman did not consider himself a revolutionary at war with the entire industrial system or Western civilization itself, despite his use of inflammatory and revolutionary rhetoric. Foreman's views were, therefore, closer to the libertarian anarchism of Edward Abbey—whose *Desert Solitaire* (1969) and *The Monkeywrench Gang* (1975), helped inspire Earth First!—than to the leftists and anarcho-primitivists increasingly populating the movement.

Second, Foreman did not assume that environmental health and social justice were inexorably linked or that ecosystem health demanded social justice. This put him at odds with social ecologists such as Murray Bookchin as well as left-wing Earth First!ers such as Mike Roselle (another of Earth First!'s cofounders) and Judi Bari (who played a prominent role in the fight against the deforestation of California's redwood forests, prior to her 1997 death from breast cancer). Such activists concluded that Foreman's views were reactionary and repugnant. Foreman considered social justice concerns to be a needless, anthropocentric distraction from an activism that uncompromisingly put Earth First! first. Moreover, as a strong proponent of a Malthusian explanation for environmental degradation, Foreman thought that the pursuit of social justice often exacerbates both human and nonhuman suffering by allowing human numbers to grow faster than they would in the absence of aid to the poor. With a growing number of ecologists, Foreman concluded that redistribution of wealth would only accelerate the unsustainable growth of earth's population.

Third, Foreman did not believe, as did a significant number of Earth First!ers, that public and overt expression of the movement's pagan spirituality was necessary or politically astute. Although he insisted humans must "resacralize" their perceptions of nature (viewing this as an antidote to Western civilization's irreverent behavior toward it), Foreman was uncomfortable with the countercultural style and the increasing pagan ritualizing in the movement. In this he moved closer to the position of his friend and Earth First! cofounder Howie Wolke. Shortly after the movement formed Wolke objected to a decision to publish the *Earth First! Journal* according to solstice/equinox names derived from a pagan-Celtic calendar. He believed such overt paganism was counterproductive. By the end of the decade, Foreman and many others had decided to downplay the movement's paganism, concluding that conservation biology and environmental science provided the strongest basis to defend biodiversity. Many of the more countercultural Earth First!ers, however, were deeply suspicious of Western science and refused to embrace it as did Foreman and his closest associates.

After leaving Earth First!, Foreman joined with conservation biologists Michael Soulé and Reed Noss to found a journal of conservation science and wildlands activism called *Wild Earth* (published since 1991). They also established *The Wildlands Project*, an ambitious effort to map and promote the protection of large, interconnected biological reserves that would make possible the preservation of all of North America's native flora and fauna.

Radical Activism of the 1990s

In the 1990s, after the departure of Foreman and those who shared his opinion that the movement had strayed from its original ideals, Earth First! assumed an identity that was increasingly countercultural, anarchistic, social justice-oriented and more overtly pagan. Increasingly it drew self-described revolutionaries. Its most extreme voices defended Ted Kaczynski, "the Unabomber," in his murderous war against industrial civilization. Some of these activists argued that the time might soon come where more such action would succeed in its objectives. A few pointed hopefully to disruptions they expected to result from the "Y2K" computer bug; some even suggested that, combined with well-targeted sabotage, Y2K might inaugurate the devolution of industrial society.

Martha Lee (1995) suggests that the incendiary rhetoric and lawless behavior of some movement activists indicate that certain factions in the movement are becoming increasingly violent. I have argued (1998 and 1999), however, that such analysis generally overlooks the many variables, both external and internal to Earth First!, that reduce the likelihood its participants will engage in terrorist violence. Although an apocalyptic premise (that industrialism is destroying the sacred, biotic diversity of the earth), is widely shared in Earth First!, few among these activists believe that human action, terrorist or not, can avert the already unfolding biological meltdown.

Some activists may conclude, however, that it may be possible, through sabotage and violence, to protect some of the earth's remaining biological diversity. Beginning in the early 1990s a number of groups, viewing Earth First! as unduly timid, announced that they would escalate their tactics against the earth's destroyers. Often acting under a new moniker that was first announced in England in 1992, the "elves" of the "Earth Liberation Front" have destroyed millions of dollars of property in the United States and Europe. In 1998 they torched several buildings at a Colorado ski resort just after the resort's owners had won a court battle allowing them to expand ski runs in a habitat that environmentalists considered to be critical for the survival of the Lynx, an endangered species.

Earth First! and its spin-offs will likely continue to proliferate and increasingly disrupt extractive commerce in advanced industrial societies. This is in part because the growing scientific consensus is that biodepletion and other environmental problems are worsening dramatically. Such scientific apocalypticism will continue to fuse with the religious and political perceptions common in the radical environmental worldview to provide a powerful rationale for green resistance.

Bron Taylor

See also Environmentalism

Bibliography

Abbey, Edward. (1968) *Desert Solitaire.* Tucson: University of Arizona Press.

——. (1975) *The Monkeywrench Gang.* New York: Avon.

Devall, Bill, and George Sessions. (1985) *Deep Ecology: Living As If Nature Mattered.* Salt Lake City, UT: Peregrine Smith.

Foreman, Dave. (1991) *Confessions of an Eco-Warrior.* New York: Harmony Books.

Foreman, Dave, and Bill Haywood, eds. (1987) *Ecodefense: A Field Guide to Monkeywrenching,* 2d ed. Tucson, AZ: Ned Ludd Books.

Fox, Warwick. (1991) *Toward a Transpersonal Ecology.* Boston: Shambhala.

LaChapelle, Dolores. (1988) *Sacred Land, Sacred Sex: Rapture of the Deep.* Silverton, CO: Finn Hill Arts.

Lee, Martha F. (1995) *Earth First!: Environmental Apocalypse.* Syracuse, NY: Syracuse University Press.

Macy, Joanna. (1991) *World As Lover, World As Self.* Berkeley, CA: Parallax Press.

Manes, Christopher. (1990) *Green Rage: Radical Environmentalism and the Unmaking of Civilization.* Boston: Little, Brown and Company.

Naess, Arne. (1989) *Ecology, Community and Lifestyle,* edited and translated by David Rothenberg. Cambridge, U.K.: Cambridge University Press.

Seed, John, Joanna Macy, Pat Fleming, and Arne Naess. (1988) *Thinking Like a Mountain: Towards a Council of All Beings.* Philadelphia: New Society.

Sessions, George, ed. (1995) *Deep Ecology for the Twenty-First Century.* Boston: Shambhala Publications.

Shepard, Paul. (1982) *Nature and Madness.* San Francisco: Sierra Club Books.

Snyder, Gary. (1969) *Turtle Island.* New York: New Directions.

——. (1990) *The Practice of the Wild.* San Francisco: North Point Press.

Taylor, Bron, ed. (1995) *Ecological Resistance Movements: The Global Emergence of Radical and Popular Environmentalism.* Albany, NY: State University of New York Press.

——. (1998) "Religion, Violence, and Radical Environmentalism: from Earth First! to the Unabomber to the Earth Liberation Front." *Journal of Terrorism and Political Violence* 10, 4 (winter):10–42.

——. (1999) "Green Apocalypticism: Understanding Disaster in the Radical Environmental Worldview." *Society and Natural Resources* 12 (spring): 377–86.

Ecstasy

"Ecstasy" refers to such intense states of pleasure that a person is driven out of his or her senses. More profoundly it can mean an emptying out of a person while being possessed by a supernatural being or an emotionally overpowering union with God. Many millenarian Christians expect ecstasy at the Rapture when Jesus returns and the righteous are raised up, but there is much debate among them as to when exactly during the prophecies in Revelation this will occur. Some of the more extreme millennial movements, notably communal ones like the Shakers and the Family (Children of God), also cultivated religiously oriented ecstasy during their daily lives, either with or without sexual intercourse. However, it can be argued that intense spiritual experiences do not harmonize as well with millennial ideologies as they do, for example, with Holiness ideology. On the other hand, spirit possession in preindustrial societies is often associated with the social conflict that can mobilize oppressed people behind a millennial movement.

Possession

Anthropologist I. M. Lewis has surveyed the scholarly literature on ecstatic religion and argues that it arises in particular kinds of social conflict. His prime example is the Sar or Zar cult of Somalia, Sudan, Egypt, and surrounding territories. The strict Islamic tradition of the dominant religious organizations prohibits women from holding positions of religious authority and prestige, and it supports the dominance of the husband in the household. However, at the same time it supports belief in a variety of spirits that may possess an individual. In daily life, a woman suffers much from her husband, including the constant threat that prosperous husbands may acquire other wives, but she depends for her survival upon his good will. Thus she cannot confront him directly, for fear he will simply cast her aside and obtain a more pliant wife in her stead. For some women, the psychological stresses become unbearable, and they express them through physical and emotional symptoms.

A Sar healer may be called in, a woman who herself has undergone similar maladies in the past but was cured and now shares that cure with the sufferer. A process of diagnosis follows, in which the healer determines whether a Sar spirit has possessed the women. If so, a grand ceremony is staged, attended by many other previously cured women, at which the woman is showered with symbolic gifts. The spirit may seize control over her, often causing her to dance wildly. At the end, an accommodation with the spirit may be reached, in which its demands are at least partially satisfied by the woman and her husband.

Lewis argues that possession by the spirit is really an *oblique redressive strategy* by which the woman manipulates her husband indirectly. He should not blame her for the demands of the spirit, because she is merely the innocent victim of the possession. Unable to press her case against her husband directly, she has obtained a supernatural ally, but under the pretense that she has not done anything to warrant his anger. Lewis says that possession is chiefly the tool of peripheral cults in society, not of the dominant religious organizations. Like Sar, most of the cases he describes have nothing to do with the millennium, but on rare occasions a possessed person may become a messianic leader and stage a revolt against the standard religious institutions, which may become millennial.

Holiness and Adventism

In nineteenth-century America, two very different Christian movements arose that had very different orientations toward ecstatic experiences: the Holiness movement (which emphasized conversion experiences) and the Adventist movement (which was millennial and used ecstatic and conversion experiences only sparingly).

The Holiness movement really began when John Wesley (1703–91) and others emphasized salvation experiences within the Anglican Church, giving rise to Methodism after the United States declared independence from Britain. When Methodism began to moderate during the nineteenth century, various Holiness churches broke away in renewed commitment to achieving salvation. The fundamental question was how and to what extent a person could become holy during life on earth. Many hoped that sufficient faith in Jesus would bring a perfect state of grace, after which one would never doubt or sin. Unfortunately, a complete salvation experience eluded believers, including John Wesley himself and many leaders of the Holiness movement such as Phoebe Palmer (1807–74). The important question of how people can come to believe they are saved has largely been ignored by sociologists and psychologists of religion, but a theory originally developed to understand the social dynamics of a non-Christian group can readily be adapted.

Scientologists seek to attain a spiritual state called "clear," in which they will be free from anxieties and gain new capabilities. William Bainbridge (1997) has studied how Scientologists employ four related strategies to sustain faith that several thousand members are clear: (1) prohibition of independent evaluation; (2) a hierarchy of lower statuses that commit the individual to progress toward clear; (3) isolation of the person at the moment of achieving clear, which places a responsibility on the individual for his or her own salvation; and (4) a hierarchy of higher statuses that continue the individual's progress toward absolute perfection. Something very similar, if less structured, occurs in the Holiness movement.

The idea that a nonbeliever could evaluate whether a person has been saved is not even considered, so independent evaluation is effectively prohibited. Most people who seek salvation within the Holiness movement are longtime members who develop commitment-enhancing ties and informal statuses with other members. The salvation experience itself is one between God and the person, which others cannot directly feel. Thus, a person must take responsibility for the quality of his or her own ecstasy. Finally, the Holiness movement developed an ideology of two salvation experiences, the first in an experience of open communication with God who promises salvation and a later experience in which sanctification becomes complete, the equivalent of the higher statuses beyond clear in Scientology.

William Miller (1782–1848), whose movement of the 1840s ultimately gave rise to Adventism, arrived at his predictions of the Second Coming through rational analysis of Revelation, relying upon the ecstatic visions of St. John the Divine rather than experiencing his own. The visions of Ellen White (1827–1915), were very important in the establishment of the Seventh-Day Adventist Church, but there was no expectation that ordinary members would duplicate them. Both Holiness and Adventism feel that existence is severely flawed and divine intervention is required. However, Holiness emphasizes regeneration of the individual through faith and a salvation experience, whereas Adventism emphasizes regeneration of the world through the Second Coming.

Orgasm and Spiritualism

Some nonmillennial communal movements incorporate ecstatic movements in their everyday lives. For example, Oneida practiced a form of group marriage in which members learned to share sex with many others while controlling procreation. The Shakers, which flourished before Adventism, and the Family which derived from Holiness not Adventism, are examples of ecstatic millenarian groups.

The Shakers were celibate, deriving all sin from the sexual union of Adam and Eve, which founder Ann Lee (1736–84) saw in a vision. Their frequent, long, strenuous dancelike celebrations had strong erotic qualities while being interpreted as contact with the spirit world. For a time, young women were afflicted by the "whirling gift," which meant spinning in a daze around the community. These experiences may have compensated members for the failure of the millennium to arrive as quickly or thoroughly as had been prophesied.

Members of the Family believe that sexuality is a legitimate expression of God's love, so adults engage in sexual sharing with members who lack partners. For about a decade, around the early 1980s, the Family had a sexual ministry that brought an estimated 200,000 nonmember men to orgasm as a way of showing them God's love. Their founder, David Brandt Berg (1919–94), was the only member receiving supernatural visions, but after his death this ability spread until most members reported occasional divine contact, and the group began publishing new literature it channeled from deceased authors like Shakespeare, Sir Walter Scott, and C. S. Lewis.

Rosabeth Kanter (1972) theorizes that communal groups must control sexuality in order to prevent couples from becoming so involved with each other that they challenge group authority. Celibacy, as in the Shakers, outlaws couples altogether. Erotic sharing, as in Oneida and the Family, creates a complex network of erotic relationships larger than the couple. In all religious traditions, but especially Holiness (of which the Family is an offshoot), ecstatic experiences can subjectively confirm the truth of the group's transcendent beliefs.

Conclusion

Ecstasy can play a role in millennial movements, especially in providing messianic visions to a small number of leaders, but it is not generally experienced by rank and file members. Other movements, such as possession healing cults and the Holiness movement, give transcendent experiences a greater role. Communal movements, whether or not they are millenarian, must deal in some way with the potential disruptive force of sexuality, and in some cases the result is regularized ecstasy. Millennial doctrines emphasize transformation of the world more than of the individual, and thus they do not necessarily emphasize transcendent experiences prior to the millennium itself.

William Sims Bainbridge

See also Family, The; Holiness Movement, Shakers

Bibliography

Bainbridge, William Sims. (1997) *The Sociology of Religious Movements.* New York: Routledge.

Carden, Maren Lockwood. (1969) *Oneida.* Baltimore, MD: Johns Hopkins University Press.

Foster, Lawrence. (1981) *Religion and Sexuality.* New York: Oxford University Press.

Kanter, Rosabeth Moss. (1972) *Commitment and Community.* Cambridge, MA: Harvard University Press.

Lewis, Ioan M. (1971) *Ecstatic Religion.* Baltimore, MD: Penguin.

Lewis, James R., and J. Gordon Melton, eds. *Sex, Slander, and Salvation: Investigating the Family/Children of God.* Stanford, CA: Center for Academic Publications.

Stark, Rodney, and William Sims Bainbridge. (1985) *The Future of Religion.* Berkeley, CA: University of California Press.

——. ([1987] 1996) *A Theory of Religion.* New Brunswick, NJ: Rutgers University Press.

Stein, Stephen J. (1992) *The Shaker Experience in America.* New Haven, CT: Yale University Press.

The views expressed in this article do not necessarily represent the views of the National Science Foundation of the United States.

End of the World

The end of the world, understood both literally and metaphorically, has played a meaningful role in the religious, philosophical, scientific, and artistic life of humanity. In its literal meaning, the end of the world implies the going-out-of-existence of planet earth itself, or, at least, the extinction of humanity. Metaphorically, it suggests a change in the order of things, whether in the natural or human realms, so drastic as to be properly described only in apocalyptic terms. In the modern era, the end of the world is a subject of intense scientific inquiry. In the religious sphere, it continues to be a lively theological issue—particularly among evangelical Protestants who associate it with the Second Advent and millennium.

That the world will, in fact, physically end seems well-established by modern astrophysics, which calculates its age at roughly 4.5 billion years. Given that stars, such as our sun, are liable to violent explosions at the end of their own lives, the earth will likely perish, along with its star-sun, at some date of comparable distance in the future.

Cultures have, in general, not invested the same energy in apocalyptic myths as creation myths. Scarcely any culture, even the most primitive, fails to provide some sort of account of how the earth, or the cosmos, came to be. Nevertheless, human beings, themselves finite creatures, have frequently incorporated into their worldview at least some account of how the world may end. This said, there are major religious traditions which have, nevertheless, thrived for centuries with only cursory attention to the subject. Altogether, Christianity has likely devoted more energy to this question than any other major faith, active or extinct.

The religions of ancient Mesopotamia and the Nile Valley devoted little attention to eschatology. For these civilizations, religion was an intensely practical matter, closely connected to the vegetation cycle. The world was often thought of as being the result of an epic struggle between hero-gods and the forces of chaos, the latter frequently personified as a cosmic monster. Creation would continue, so long as it pleased the gods or until monster-chaos overwhelmed even them. The *Gilgamesh* saga of ancient Sumer does, though, detail a near-apocalypse, in which a divinely ordained flood all but destroys humanity: "I looked at the face of the world and there was silence, all mankind was turned to clay" (Tr. N. K. Sanders, Penguin Books).

The classical world offered many schools of philosophy and cosmology, often of exquisite sophistication, which defy generalization. An absolute end to the cosmos was not a common element in either Greek or Roman thought. Regarding the physical destiny of the world, the tendency was more toward a cyclic cosmology in which one creation arises phoenixlike from the remains of a prior. Classical philosophers more commonly understood history itself as a series of epicycles; for example, Hesiod's well-known division of the ages of the world in gold, silver, bronze, and iron.

In the Judeo-Christian tradition, the end of the world became—and remains to this day—a subject of intense interest. During the sixth and fifth centuries BCE, the Hebrew prophets reverted frequently to apocalyptic language, some of which drew on the earlier Semitic civilizations. The end was foretold in Isaiah: "Behold, the Lord will lay waste the earth and make it desolate, and he will scatter its inhabitants" (Isaiah 24:1). (Eschatology, however, never occupied the same prominence in Jewish thought as it did in the later Christian community.)

Jesus warned of the world's end: "For in those days there will be such tribulation as has not been from the beginning of the creation which God created until now, and never will be" (Mark 13:19). The early church treasured these warnings and added to them. From the first century CE until the present, Christianity has connected Christ's Second Advent with the endtime. Respected commentators have interpreted the Book of Revelation to prophesy a coming millennium, coincident with Christ's return and the sweeping away of the old, sinful world. But, although the Second Advent early became an essential element of Christianity, millennialism remained very much a minority position within it.

From at least the time of Augustine (fifth century CE), Christianity, building on its Jewish inheritance, understood history as linear and nonrepeating. In this, it differs not only from religions of the ancient world, but also other world religions, such as Hinduism and Buddhism. God's Creation is called into being but once. It unfolds in accordance with his plan, and then is brought to its final conclusion. Entirely absent is any sense of a cyclic, meaningless, or eternal cosmos. Its end, should it arrive, is permanent and irreversible.

Eschatological sects within Christianity have anticipated the end of the world throughout Western history. Rome, however, actively discouraged such apocalypticsm and reminded enthusiasts of Jesus' warning: "But of that day or that hour no one knows, not even the angels in heaven" (Mark 14:32). On rare occasions, however, self-proclaimed prophets who foretold an imminent end to the cosmos caused brief, local interruptions in medieval life. Such eschatological outbursts became somewhat more common during the Protestant Reformation, when they were conflated with millennial hopes centered around the Second Advent.

From the eighteenth century to the present, scientific inquiry over the fate of the cosmos has rivaled—even supplanted—religious eschatology. The nebular hypothesis of LaPlace offered a starting point for the origin of the earth. Its end, however, remained uncertain. The heroic-materialist strain of nineteenth-century thought latched onto the concept of entropy as deciding the fate of the cosmos—it would simply run down and grow cold, like a fire running low on fuel. Discoveries in stellar mechanics in the next century provided a mechanism for the earth's actual physical destruction.

Science notwithstanding, the end of the world continued as a theme in popular religiosity. In the United States, the Millerite movement predicted the end of the world for 1843 and then, when that prediction failed, 1844. Within evangelical Protestantism as a whole, millenarian theology, which anticipates Christ's imminent return in judgment, the millennium, and the end of the present order of things, has flourished mightily down to the present.

Interest in end of the world scenarios increased in the mid-twentieth century, provoked, no doubt, by the invention of nuclear weapons. Fiction, such as Nevil Schute's *On the Beach,* seized on atomic annihilation to demonstrate how human existence, if not the physical world, might abruptly end. The theme was taken up, as well, in popular cold-war motion pictures, such as *Dr. Strangelove* (1963). Then, too, Armageddon was described as coming from Outer Space, in the form of conquering aliens. This was an old theme, traceable to H. G. Well's novelette *The War of the Worlds.* It was successfully, and profitably, revived in a host of Hollywood films of the same genre, such as *The Day the Earth Stood Still* (1951) and *Independence Day* (1996). Even popular music became infected with *fin du monde* fear, such as the mid-1960s rock lyric which warned: "I hear hurricanes a-blowing/I know the end is coming soon/I see rivers overflowing/I hear the voice of raze and ruin" (Creedence Clearwater Revival).

Political and ecological concerns likewise stimulated end of the world fears, as the twentieth century drew toward its close. These envisioned not so much the physical annihilation of the planet as a drastic, even well-deserved, end to modern, technological civilization. Rachel Carlson's *The Silent Spring* (1962) prompted a number of ecodisaster scenarios, based on a poisoned or degraded planet. Racial tensions, as well, caused some to posit an incipient collapse of civilization, and contributed to the survivalist and white supremacist groups of the 1990s. Even relatively benign technology was nominated as the causal agent of "the end of the world as we know it," especially the Y2K computer problem.

Discoveries in astrophysics in the second half of the twentieth century provided more dramatic endgames for the physical earth than nineteenth-century entropy. The seemingly inevitable (if almost infinitely remote) explosion of the sun was one. More chilling, perhaps, was the possibility that the earth might be struck by a meteorite or comet, especially since it was confidently asserted that such a thing had already happened and caused the extinction of the dinosaurs.

Popular cults toward the end of the second millennium CE fed on apocalyptic fears—sometimes with bloody results. The 1993 confrontation in Waco, Texas, between federal authorities and the Branch Davidians was only one such. The Heaven's Gate mass suicide of 1997 was another. A few years earlier, over four hundred people had committed suicide in Jonestown, Guyana, in expectation of a secular apocalypse. The approach of the year 2000 stirred, however, only very mild eschatological concern among an increasingly sophisticated public, and much of that was successfully appropriated by merchandisers as a marketing device. The historic Western concern with the end of the world seemed far from exhausted as the year 2000 approached.

Robert K. Whalen

Bibliography

Lamy, Philip. (1996) *Millennium Rage: Survivalists, White Supremacists, and the Doomsday Prophecy.* New York: Plenum Press.

Numbers, Ronald L., and Jonathan M. Butler. (1987) *The Disappointed: Millerism and Millenarianism in the Nineteenth Century.* Bloomington, IN: Indiana University Press.

O'Leary, Stephen D. (1998) "Apocalypticism in American Popular Culture." In *The Encyclopedia of Apocalypticism*, vol. 3, edited by Stephen J. Stein. New York: Continuum Press, 392–426.

Weber, Timothy P. (1992) *Living in the Shadow of the Second Coming: American Premillennialism: 1875–1925.* New York: Oxford University Press.

End Signs

At the center of any apocalyptic view of history is the notion that the approach of the time of the End will be marked and heralded by certain "signs" or indications, set forth in the prophetic portions of the Hebrew and Christian Scriptures. The idea is that such a "revelation" (Greek word *apokalypsis*), known only to God, but revealed to his prophets, can serve as a warning and a call to repentance to those wise enough to interpret the signs of the times (Amos 3:7; Daniel 12:9–10).

General Signs of the End

Most of the early references to the "signs of the End" found in the Hebrew Prophets (eighth through fifth centuries BCE) are very general and difficult to catalogue into a specific unfolding scheme of events. For example, in Isaiah 24–27, often called the "Little Apocalypse" of Isaiah, we have references to earthquakes, famines, defeat of both the earthly and heavenly forces of evil, resurrection of the dead, and the rewards of the righteous; but no indication as to just how and in what historical context such events might come about. In the same fashion, texts like Micah 4–5 picture the Kingdom of God in which nations give up war, with peace and justice prevailing under the rule of a Davidic Messiah; but again, there is no indication as to just how such a state of affairs might be ushered in. Phrases such as "in the last days," or "at that time" are common in such texts. The most specific and common element in these texts is their universal agreement that the entire nation of Israel (all twelve tribes), exiled by Assyrian and Babylonian captivity (eighth and sixth centuries BCE), will be regathered to the Land (Jeremiah 30–33; Isaiah 60; Ezekiel 37–38; Amos 9:9–15; Hosea 1–2). But again, precisely when this is to occur, or what set of direct circumstances might usher in such a restoration, is left unspecified. Indeed, the regathering of the Tribes of Israel to the Land becomes itself, one of the prime end time signs. In contrast, the prophet Zechariah (fifth century BCE) begins to offer more specific scenarios, particularly details about a final battle for the city of Jerusalem in which all the nations of the world are involved (chapter 14). One of the elements that characterizes such texts is that they are, for the most part, free from specific endtime signs. For example, when the David Messiah arrives, he simple "stands forth" or "springs up" (Isaiah 11; Micah 5), but nothing is said as to the specific events that might signal that his arrival is imminent. The same holds true for the restoration of the tribes of Israel to the Land. Either the Messiah appears and does the gathering (Isaiah 11), or Yahweh himself does it (Ezekiel 38), but in either case, there is no indication of when such an event will occur, or how one might know it is drawing near.

More Specific Endtime Signs

The most important and influential apocalyptic work in the Bible is the Book of Daniel. Scholars date this text to near the time of the Maccabean revolt (165 BCE). Chapters 2, 7, 8, 9, 11, and 12 contain visions that claim to show the sequence of events, in some detail, that will lead up to the time of the end, when God sets up his Kingdom over all the earth. The basic scenario is the following: A succession of four world kingdoms come and go on the scene of history, but in the days of the "fourth" kingdom (first understood to be Greece, but later Rome) a horrifyingly cruel and evil ruler marches into Palestine with great armies at his command, defiles the Temple at Jerusalem, persecutes God's people for a limited time (about three and a half years), but is then utterly and decisively crushed by the sudden intervention of God (Daniel 7:19–25; 8:23–26; 11:31–45). The resurrection of the dead and final judgment quickly follow, with the Kingdom passed to God's elect and persecuted "saints" (see especially Daniel 2:44; 7:13–18, 26–27). Scholars are agreed that these references originally had the Macedonian ruler of Syria-Palestine, Antiochus IV (Epiphanes) in mind. According to the account in 1 Maccabees, he occupied the Temple in Jerusalem, dedicating it to the worship of Zeus, and forbade the practices of Judaism, forcing a kind of "conversion" to Hellenism upon the Jewish population. Those who resisted were killed, giving rise to our first accounts of religious martyrdom in Western history. This element of the persecution and martyrdom of the people of God became one of the stock "signs of the End" in subsequent Jewish and Christian schemes. Antiochus was fiercely resisted by Jewish zealots who defeated him through guerilla warfare. The problem was that the prophecies of Daniel had uniformly cast him as a final evil oppressor whose defeat would lead to the end of the age, resurrection of the dead, and the Kingdom of God. For example, in Daniel 11 we can clearly trace the career of Antiochus down to about verse 35, but the subsequent events that are predicted simply never took place. Instead, history continued on as usual, with the Romans successfully conquering Palestine in 63 BCE, after just a hundred years of Jewish independence. Rather than cast Daniel aside as an example of failed prophecy, pious Jews and later, Christians, who still treasured an apocalyptic vision of their history and destiny, focused on the book all the more. They began to see Antiochus as only a "type" or foreshadow of the final evil ruler still to come. Through such a strategy of interpretation the prophecies of Daniel took on a perennial relevance to subsequent attempts to interpret the "signs of the end" down through history. For example, 2 Esdras, an apocalyptic work from the late first century CE, builds on the Book of Daniel and is concerned with the "delay" of the end. In a crucial section, 12:10–30, the author recasts Daniel's basic vision and brings it down to his own time, with detailed predictions of what lies just ahead leading up to the arrival of the Messiah and the Kingdom of God.

One other element that Daniel contributes to the overall picture are certain chronological periods, designated as 2300, 1335, 1290, and 1260 "days," as well as 70 "weeks" of years (Daniel 7, 9, 12). These gave rise to calculations based on a "day for a year" scheme yielding periods ranging from 490 to 2300 years, taking one far beyond the time of Daniel, and even into modern times. In this way a given year, or a specific scheme of calculated time, becomes itself a sign of the End. We find this as early as the time of Jesus, when he declares "the time is fulfilled, the Kingdom of God is at hand" (Mark 1:14). The same essential idea is repeated a generation later by Paul, who declares, "The appointed time has grown very short," and even advises his followers to remain unmarried in view of what he calls the "impending distress" (1 Corinthians 7). This language about an appointed time reaching its fulfillment is drawn directly from the Book of Daniel.

Subsequent Interpretations of Daniel

This basic scheme of anticipated events became enormously influential among Jewish and Christian groups in the first century CE and it forms the backbone of all the major apocalyptic schemes in the New Testament. Each time a likely candidate showed up in Palestine—whether the Roman general Pompey (63 BCE), the threat of the emperor Caligula to have his statue placed in the Jewish temple (41 CE), or the actual destruction of the Temple in August of 70 CE by the Roman general Titus—the specific expectations of Daniel's scheme came into play. While the more general signs such as wars, famines, earthquakes, and pestilence might be discounted; the notion of a final battle for Jerusalem, sparked by the invasion of Palestine by a non-Jewish ruler backed by massive armies would whip various groups of Jews and Christians into an apocalyptic frenzy, utterly convinced that the time of God's Kingdom was at hand.

The general apocalyptic scenario that we have from Jesus, based on the Synoptic Gospels (Mark, Matthew, and Luke), seems to be remarkably *consistent* with the visions of Daniel. Jesus connects the destruction of the Jerusalem Temple to the more general "signs of the end of the age": false prophets, wars and disruptions, earthquakes, famines, pestilence, persecution, and a worldwide proclamation of his message (Mark 13, Matthew 24, Luke 21). These lead up to what he calls "the sign," spoken of by Daniel the prophet—namely the desolating sacrilege ("abomination of desolation") standing in the holiest area of the Jewish Temple in Jerusalem. Based on the model of Antiochus IV, this was generally understood to be some kind of profanation of the Jewish Temple rites (Daniel 9:27). This is followed immediately by the greatest time of tribulation in history (Daniel 12:1–2), which in turn ushers in the disruption of the cosmos ("heavenly signs") and the return of the "Son of Man in the clouds of heaven," another image drawn from Daniel 7:14. The scheme is very tightly connected, and Jesus declares at the end that "this generation will not pass away until all these things are fulfilled" (Mark 13:30). Those words alone must have had a tremendous impact on the expectations of the Christian communities that lived through the Jewish-Roman war. Remarkably, the same scenario occurs in Revelation, chapter 6, with the opening of the "seven seals" of a mysterious scroll—a book that purports to reveal the signs of the End. The first six seals, which include the infamous "four horsemen" appear to represent war, famine, disease, martyrdom, earthquakes, and cosmic heavenly signs, followed by the appearance of the final evil ruler of a revived "Babylon," now understood to be Rome. We get more of this kind of interpretation in the second chapter of 2 Thessalonians; where Paul says that the Day of the Lord cannot come *until* this wicked ruler, who profanes the Temple, arrives on the scene. This is a remarkable example of just how literally Daniel 11:31–12:3 was taken by Jewish and Christian groups during this time.

It is one thing for a religious community to live with a general expectation of the endtime being imminent. But it is quite another when a group begins literally "tracking" the specific "signs of the End" that are to usher all things to a close. There is every evidence that first century Jewish and Christian groups were actually watching world events, including political figures and troop movements in the Palestine area, with an eye on the fulfillment of Daniel 11 and 12.

After the scare of 41 CE, when it appeared that the Roman emperor Caligula might actually carry out his order to place his own statue in the Jewish Temple (Josephus, *The Jewish War* 2.184–204), hysteria swept both the Jewish and Christian communities. It was not hard to read these events as a direct fulfillment of Daniel 11:36, which foretells of a king from the West who will "consider himself greater than any god" and defile the Jewish Temple. In fact, Caligula's plan was never implemented. His own palace guard assassinated him shortly thereafter. A decade or so later, in the reign of the emperor Nero (54–66 CE), Paul most likely had this very event in mind. He tells his followers to beware, since the "mystery of iniquity is already at work," and predicts another such wicked one will repeat the same pattern, "sitting in the Temple of God, and claiming to be God" (2 Thessalonians 2:7). In Revelation, chapters 11 and 13 give further details about a final world power (Rome now called Babylon), led by a mysterious leader called the "Beast," whose symbolic number equals 666. In the Hebrew language, where each letter is given a number, the term "Nero Caesar" adds up to this very sum. For three and a half years during which the Temple is defiled by the Gentile "beast" power, the people of God are to suffer persecution and death. When Nero began to persecute the Christians at Rome following the great fire in the summer of 64 CE, it was easy to link him to these texts. It can be said that Revelation is largely a recasting of the prophetic scenarios of Daniel in the light of the reigns of the emperors Nero and Domitian (81–96 CE). The first Jewish-Roman War, or Revolt, which lasted from 66–73 CE, resulted in the utter destruction of the city of Jerusalem and Yahweh's Temple—but with no appearance of the Messiah, no defeat of the invading forces, and no End of the age. Josephus, the Jewish historian who lived through the war reports that the "main cause of the revolt" was a prophecy that about that time that a ruler would arise in Judea and conquer the world (*War*, 6.310–315). This is an obvious reference to the influence of Daniel's chronological scheme, as well as his specific scenario of endtime signs.

The Wane of Apocalyptic Fervor

By the end of the first century CE, the political situation in Palestine, and in the Roman Empire as a whole, both for Christians and Jews, was in sharp contrast to the millennial dreams that had held sway for the past three hundred years. We see a very general scheme, complete with an exhortation not to scoff or give up on the end-of-the-world hope, in the third chapter of 2 Peter, one of the latest documents of the New Testament. Here, we have a view of the future that can take one forward for several millennia—and it ends up serving the Christians well. The writer declares that "one day with the Lord is as a thousand years" but no longer are any specific signs of the End set forth for imminent fulfillment (2 Peter 3:8).

Earliest Christianity can be described as a Jewish apocalyptic sect, or millenarian movement, that, drawing upon Daniel and the Hebrew Prophets, pinned its hopes and dreams on the catastrophic events before, during, and after the first Jewish Revolt. What they most expected to happen never came—the return of Jesus on the clouds of heaven to usher in the Kingdom of God. What they least expected to happen was what in fact *did* happen: the utter demise of the Jewish state and the increasing power and stability of Rome over the next several centuries. The fact that Christianity survived these disappointments suggests that its center was not solely apocalyptic expectation, but there is no denying that such expectation was central to the earliest movement. At various points in history, whenever the "signs of the times" are such that one can posit a fit between text and event, we find that apocalypticism experiences a revival. Indeed, it is driven by the very notion of Signs of the End, especially the highly specific ones found in the Books of Daniel and Revelation.

James D. Tabor

See also 666, Apocalypse, Chernobyl, Holocaust, Plague and Pestilence

Bibliography

Boyer, Paul. (1992) *When Time Shall Be No More.* Cambridge, MA: Harvard University Press.

Brandon, S. G. F. (1967) *Jesus and the Zealots.* New York: Scribner's Sons.

Collins, John J. (1998) *The Apocalyptic Imagination.* Grand Rapids, MI: Eerdmans.

Ehrman, Bart. (1999) *Jesus as Apocalyptic Prophet of the New Millennium.* Oxford, U.K.: Oxford University Press.

Reston, James Jr. (1998) *The Last Apocalypse: Europe at the Year 1000 A.D.* New York: Doubleday.

Environmentalism

Environmentalism is a diverse social movement that seeks to protect and restore the earth's living systems. It provides a *worldview* (a way of understanding the world and the human place in it) and an *ideology* (assertions and goals that constitute a political program). Environmentalism is critical of modern lifeways, either wholly or in part. It advocates fundamental changes in the ways humans relate to nonhuman nature.

Development of Modern Environmental Consciousness

Contemporary environmentalism is increasingly shaped by scientific claims that human activities are causing ecosystems to collapse and populations of plants and animals to decline, even to extinction. As environmental scientists issue ever more catastrophic predictions, the worldviews and ideologies of environmentalists are assuming an increasingly apocalyptic character. Thus is environmental science helping apocalyptic thinking to escape its typically religious milieu. At the same time, however, religious groups that do not endorse an environmental worldview, nevertheless increasingly draw on expectations of environmental catastrophe for their own expectations of doom.

Modern environmentalism is often traced to Rachael Carson's frightening warnings, in her famous 1962 book *Silent Spring*, about the threats posed by pesticides to ecosystems and human health. Earlier environment-related concern is sometimes labeled the conservation movement, to distinguish it from contemporary environmentalism. The distinction between an earlier "conservation" and later "environmental" approaches is problematic, however.

Writers before Carson recognized the complexity and interrelationships among living and nonliving things within ecosystems expressing concern about pollution and biodepletion (species decline and extinction). Moreover, from the late 1940s and throughout the cold war, fears of genocide from nuclear or biological weapons spread, fanned by popular literature and motion pictures. The idea that humans might—through hubris, folly, and warlike disposition—destroy their own habitat and unleash an environmental apocalypse was not invented by Rachael Carson. Beginning in the late 1940s, for example, the Union of Concerned Scientists periodically adjusted their figurative doomsday clock to reflect current international tensions and the danger of a nuclear conflagration.

The publication of *Silent Spring* was, nevertheless, a watershed in the emergence of science-based, apocalyptic environmentalism. Its vision of an impending anthropogenic (human-caused) environmental disaster provided fertile ground for the apocalyptic imagination. Since its publication many scientific studies, popular nonfiction books drawing on them, and a growing body of literature and art, intensified apocalyptic expectations among environmentalists and the wider public.

Environmental Apocalypticism

The ecologists Paul Ehrlich and Garrett Hardin were the most influential proponents of environmental apocalypticism. They wrote of the inevitability of ecosystem collapse resulting from human population growth. Ehrlich published

A NEW MILLENNIUM'S RESOLUTION

New beginnings present opportunities to renew and improve ourselves. And if the tick of a new year can motivate us individually, the thunderous clap of a new millennium can arouse us collectively.

Certainly some pervasive change is in order. Our relationships with each other and with the environment are so troubled that there might not be much left to celebrate come the dawn of the next millennium.

Coupled with this unique numerological opportunity for reflection is a unique tool for group reflection: the Internet, the most egalitarian means of mass communication yet to evolve on this planet. It enables one individual to propose to the entire group a resolution for the year 2000 (or 2001, if we also want to resolve to be accurate).

The best resolutions recognize simple truths and commit to adhering to them, sometimes using affirmations as an aide.

A resolution for a millennium looks to the big picture and the long term. That means all of us, the whole earth, and for generations, starting with our children.

Indeed, attitudes towards other peoples and other species are molded during childhood and difficult to change population-wide thereafter. A successful model for inculcating values, via a daily recitation in schools, is America's Pledge of Allegiance.

The unifying effect of such a pledge is easily appreciated. However, the flip side of a strong sense of national (or religious) cohesiveness is often the conviction that other peoples are less important or worthy. To say nothing of other species.

A more inclusive sense of belonging needs to be fostered. By widening the group to which we feel connected, we narrow the group we feel justified in exploiting. Eventually the extent of the former eliminates the latter.

In addition to patriotism, we can expand the loyalty we aspire to instill. It is time to adopt a more visionary and all encompassing "world pledge" as a New Millennium's Resolution:

A Recognition of Unity

"I recognize a vital unity linking me with all humanity and humanity with all life, acknowledging that where none prevails over another, each may prosper and all may continue."

Source: http://http://www.redshift.com/~wsandtt/.

The Population Bomb (1968); and Hardin, in "The Tragedy of the Commons" (1968), advanced his influential parable of human-caused environmental decline. Both predicted in subsequent works the devolution of civilization as we know it (e.g., Ehrlich 1974; Hardin 1972, 1993). In such works they updated the Malthusian argument that increasing consumption and population growth by humans were precipitating widespread ecosystem degradation and fostering starvation and social decline. Most controversially, Hardin articulated a "Lifeboat Ethics," arguing that nations should refuse to provide aid to countries that fail to reduce human numbers.

Meanwhile, a new field called environmental economics proclaimed that disaster might only be averted if humans recognize the constraints that ecosystems place on economic growth. This effort to integrate ecology into economics was led by Herman Daly. His *Toward a Steady-State Economy* (1973) and *Economics, Ecology, Ethics* (1980) pioneered this approach. Along with the globally influential study led by Donella H. Meadows entitled *Limits to Growth: A Report for the Club of Rome's Project on the Predicament of Mankind* (1972), and specific events like the 1973 energy crisis, environmental economics fueled an apocalyptic vision of the collapse of fossil-fuel dependent industrial society.

Atmospheric scientist James Lovelock's "Gaia Hypothesis" also contributed to environmental apocalypticism. First advanced in the early 1970s and later articulated in *Gaia: A New Look at Life on Earth* (1979), Lovelock took the name for his theory from the ancient Greek goddess of the earth. He asserted that the biosphere behaves like a living, self-regulating organism modifying its own living systems to ensure that its own internal conditions remain hospitable for life. Lovelock's subsequent works suggested that human-caused

Borrowing ecologist Paul Ehrlich's slogan, "Nature Bats Last", to underscore the apocalyptic view that if we continue to degrade the earth it will come back and harm us, the graphic anticipates the destruction of modern society. Left ambiguous is whether this destruction will result from an unsustainable modern society breaking nature's laws, or from aspects of nature (human or nonhuman) purposefully engaging in a rebellion. EARTH FIRST! 11, 5: 41 (1 MAY 1991).

insults to the atmosphere could threaten the sustainability of the earth's living systems.

Less cautious books followed, drawing on Lovelock's work and the growing scientific evidence regarding the warming of earth's atmosphere. Bill McKibben in *The End of Nature* (1989), for example, implied that it was already too late to prevent catastrophe; nature is no longer autonomous from humankind, and modern society is destroying the very ability of the earth to sustain life. Meanwhile in *Algeny* (1983) and other works Jeremy Rifkin led a growing chorus of critics asserting that biotechnology promised to fundamentally disrupt ecosystems in unforeseen and catastrophic ways. Other books and movies, such as Richard Preston's *The Hot Zone* (1994) and the film *Outbreak* (1995) painted ominous pictures of epidemics triggered by deforestation that exposed humans to new and ever more virulent diseases.

These environment-focused terrors have often been combined with the profound fears of totalitarianism expressed by many twentieth-century writers, including George Orwell in his classics, *Animal Farm* (1946) and *Nineteen Eighty-Four* (1949). Numerous social critics, activists, and artists claimed that democracy had been destroyed or rendered impotent by corporate power or totalitarian technology. Such views have played a significant role in the increasingly apocalyptic character of contemporary environmentalism; sometimes contributing to a fatalistic expectation that the destructive trends documented by environmental scientists is irreversible. Many works promoted a terrifying vision where the human technological manipulation of nature had escaped human political and scientific control, for example Louis Mumford in *The Myth of the Machine* (1966), Langdon Winner in *Autonomous Technology* (1977), and book-films from Mary Shelly's *Frankenstein* (1831, film 1931) to Michael Crichton's *Jurassic Park* (1990, film 1993). In this genre, the future truly looks monstrous.

These themes of ecological and political breakdown were explored in numerous novels and motion pictures. Edward Abbey's novel *Good News* (1980), for example, is set after a cataclysmic biological and social meltdown and portrays a heroic green remnant fighting totalitarian forces hostile to nature and human freedom. More optimistic novels grounded in environmental apocalyptic are Earnest Callenbach's *Ecotopia* (1975) and James Redfield's New Age bestseller *The Celestine Prophesy* (1993). Both writers suggest that humans will eventually and through great trials grow spiritually and learn to live appropriately on earth.

Apocalypticism demands an explanation of what went wrong. Many root causes have been offered to explain the unfolding ecological disaster. Some blame Western religion, philosophy, and science for overturning earlier nature-venerating spiritualities and lifeways. Such cultural critique is sometimes based on scholarly work, such as Lynn White's famous essay, "The Historic Roots of our Ecologic Crisis" (1967), Roderick Nash's *Wilderness and the American Mind* (1973), and Carolyn Merchant's *The Death of Nature: Women, Ecology, and the Scientific Revolution* (1980). Such analyses suggested that the West's desacralization of nature led to technology-obsessed, manipulative, and destructive attitudes toward nature.

"Deep ecologists" accept this explanation of the roots of the current crisis while emphasizing that desacralization yields anthropocentric (human-centered) attitudes that disregard nature. "Ecofeminists" trace the original environmental sin to patriarchy, while "social ecologists" blame social hierarchy itself. Meanwhile, the historian Paul Shephard developed a comprehensive theory of the origins of environmental decline, contributing significantly to the evolving, green-apocalyptic myth. Shephard viewed small-scale foraging societies as paradise: ecologically sustainable and spiritually fulfilling. The "fall" came with the advent of agriculture. Agricultural peoples overran and exterminated nature-beneficent foraging peoples, replacing them nearly everywhere with nature-destroying cultures. Shephard's 1998 book, *Coming Home to the Pleistocene*, well summarizes this theory. It also suggests, however, that humans may eventually reestablish appropriate lifeways on earth. Such analysis and apocalyptic hope is common within environmental subcultures. Daniel Quinn's novels *Ishmael* and *The Story of B* (1992 and 1996) popularize such perceptions. Through the teachings of a gorilla named Ishmael, readers are urged to return to an animistic perception and a sense of the sacredness of the earth as a prerequisite to rediscovering ecologically sustainable and religiously meaningful lives.

In conclusion, intensifying alarm about environmental decline has fostered two trends in contemporary apocalypticism. First, environmental science has freed apocalypticism from its religious underpinnings and contributed dramatically to the secularization of apocalypticism. Apocalypticism is no longer dependent on religious faith. Second, for the first time in the history of religion, religious apocalypticism was fueled by environmental science. Now, secular environmental science will increasingly strengthen and shape religious apocalypticism. Apocalypticism is no longer independent from science. Given these ironic, new dynamics, in the foreseeable future, apocalypticism promises to be an increasingly influential aspect of human worldviews and cultures.

Bron Taylor

See also Earth First!, Literature, Secular Millennialism

Bibliography

Abbey, Edward. (1980) *Good News*. New York: Penguin.

Callenbach, Ernest. (1975) *Ecotopia*. New York: Bantam.

Carson, Rachael. (1962) *Silent Spring*. New York: Houghton Mifflin.

Crichton, Michael. (1990) *Jurassic Park*. New York: Knopf.

Daly, Herman E. (1973) *Toward a Steady State Economy*. San Francisco: W.H. Freeman.

——, ed. (1980) *Economics, Ecology, Ethics: Essays Toward a Steady State Economy*. San Francisco: Freeman.

Ehrlich, Paul. (1968) *The Population Bomb*. New York: Ballantine.

——. (1974) *The End of Affluence*. New York: Ballantine.

Hardin, Garrett. (1968) "The Tragedy of the Commons." *Science* 162: 1243–48.

——. (1972) *Exploring New Ethics for Survival*. New York: Viking.

——. (1993) *Living Within Limits*. New York: Oxford University Press.

Lovelock, James. ([1979] 1995) *Gaia: A New Look At Life on Earth*, rev. ed. Oxford, U.K.: Oxford University Press.

McKibben, Bill. (1989) *The End of Nature*. New York: Random House.

Meadows, Donella H. et al. (1972) *Limits to Growth: A Report for the Club of Rome's Project on the Predicament of Mankind*. New York: Universe.

Merchant, Carolyn. (1980) *The Death of Nature: Women, Ecology and the Scientific Revolution*. San Francisco: Harper & Row.

Mumford, Lewis. (1966) *The Myth of the Machine*. New York: Harcourt Brace Jovanovich.

Nash, Roderick. ([1967] 1973) *Wilderness and the American Mind*, 2d ed. New Haven, CT: Yale University Press.

Orwell, George. (1946) *Animal Farm*. New York: Harcourt, Brace.

Preston, Richard. (1994) *The Hot Zone*. New York: Random House.

Quinn, Daniel. (1992) *Ishmael*. New York: Bantam.

——. (1996) *The Story of B*. New York: Bantam.

Redfield, James. (1993) *The Celestine Prophesy*. New York: Warner.

Rifkin, Jeremy, with Nicanor Perlas. (1983) *Algeny*. New York: Viking.

Shelly, Mary. ([1831] 1969) *Frankenstein*. London & New York: Oxford.

Shephard, Paul. (1998) *Coming Home to the Pleistocene*. San Francisco: Island Press.

White, Lynn. (1967) "The Historic Roots of Our Ecologic Crisis." *Science* 155: 1203–7.

Winner, Langon. (1977) *Autonomous Technology: Techniques-Out-of-Control As a Theme in Political Thought*. Cambridge, MA: MIT Press.

False Prophet

The expression "false prophet" is an oxymoron. A prophet is normally understood in the Judeo-Christian tradition as one who brings a word from God that is directly given to him by the spirit of God. If the prophet is "false," then he or she is not, strictly speaking, a prophet. Yet the phrase, in singular and plural, appears often in both the Old and New Testaments. Some of these references are in apocalyptic passages, and so the phrase has entered the vocabulary and schemes of endtime movements.

The Hebrew Scriptures

A recurring structural element in the accounts of prophetic proclamation is that the prophet of Yahweh, sent with a warning of destruction, is contradicted by an opposing prophet. An example is that of Jeremiah (Jeremiah 28–29). Commissioned to warn the nation of Judah of their captivity and defeat at the hands of Babylonian king Nebuchadnezzar in the sixth century BCE, he was contradicted by Hananiah, whose message from the Lord was that Judah would survive the siege of Jerusalem. Apparently there was no way of determining, at the time of utterance, which prophet had brought the genuine message, since Jeremiah must rely on the unfolding of events to justify him. He adds, though, an additional prophecy: that his opponent would die within the next year.

A similar confrontation is reported from the time of King Jehoshaphat of Israel. Again, one prophet, Micaiah, foresaw destruction while another, Zedekiah, predicted victory (1 Kings 22). Again, the outcome of events would identify the true prophet and the false. For similar narrative structures, compare the Egyptian sorcerers who oppose Moses (Exodus 7:11, 22; 8:7, 18–19) and, in the New Testament, the confrontation between Paul and "a certain sorcerer, a false prophet," Bar-Jesus, also called Elymas (Acts 13:4–12).

Prophets who are viewed as genuine in the Bible tradition did not always prophesy destruction. If that were so, one would not need divine inspiration to be a prophet, just a reflexive pessimism. A prophet also knew when to speak a word of comfort or hope, as the opening words of the second major section of Isaiah (40:1–2) show.

On the other hand, the fulfillment of a prediction was not enough to guarantee the genuineness of a prophet. The Book of Deuteronomy, a lengthy recapitulation of the law of Israel, gives as the test of a prophet the exclusive devotion to Yahweh, Israel's god (Deuteronomy 13:1–5). This reflects the conflict concerning other indigenous deities in the land. To be "true," a prophet had to speak in the name of the "true" god.

The growing expectation of a messiah, an anointed god-sent deliverer, that arose in postexilic Judaism, especially in circles that engaged in apocalyptic speculation, was accompanied by expectation of his opposite, a false messiah. This expectation was confirmed by the experience of failed messianic movements, such as that of Simeon, called Bar-Kochba (died 135 CE), and centered in medieval Judaism on a figure named Armillus.

The New Testament

Matthew includes a warning against false prophets (plural) near the end of the Sermon on the Mount (Matthew 5–7), the first of five major speeches in which he summarizes the teaching of Jesus. The metaphoric description of them as wolves in sheep's clothing has become proverbial. It is a warning against Christian teachers who, despite displaying the same charismatic powers as other wandering teachers (7:22), produce "bad fruit" (7:16–20). This is explicated as not doing the will of the Father (7:21) and doing lawlessness (7:23). The Sermon on the Mount is an interpretation of the law and the prophets that centers on the relationship to God as "our father," as expressed in the Lord's Prayer (6:9–13), and offers as the epitome of the "better righteousness" (5:20) the love of one's enemies (5:43–48) as the expression of a perfection like that of the father. In this context, "doing the will of the father" would mean expressing a love that knows no bounds. The failure of the false prophets—their lawlessness—presumably involves lovelessness in their relationships. In this way, a moral component is added to the question of distinguishing the true prophet from the false.

In Luke's version of the Beatitudes, Jesus refers to the false prophets of Israel as people of whom "the fathers" of his listeners had spoken well (Luke 6:26), recalling the false prophet narrative structures in the Hebrew scriptures. A true prophet will often be opposed by one that is false, and it is the false one who will win popular approval. In addition, the references in the New Testament form a series with allusions to false teachers and false brethren, reflecting the controversial and ambiguous early days of the Christian church, when conflicting interpretations of the teachings, death, and resurrection of Jesus vied to become the normative one.

Christians living then, though, were experiencing from their perspective not the early days of the church, but the last days of the world. The "Little Apocalypse" (Mark 13), sometimes called the "Olivet discourse" because of its setting on the Mount of Olives in Jerusalem, is a description of the end-time spoken by Jesus. In it, the coming of false messiahs and false prophets, who work deceptive signs and wonders, is given as a sign of the end (verse 22, parallel Matthew 24:24, compare Matthew 24:11).

In 2 Peter, a prophecy about the last days, a parallel is drawn between the appearance of false prophets among the people of God in the past (Israel) and the expected coming of false teachers. The emphasis here is on heterodox teachings, specifically about the nature and person of Jesus Christ, characterized as "destructive heresies," that are furtively introduced (2 Peter 2:1). From the point of view of a congregation that had endured doctrinal wrangles, again concerning Christology, "many false prophets" were already at work (1 John 4:1). Readers are urged to "test" the spirits. Some prophets speak according to the spirit of God, others according to that of Antichrist (verses 2–3, compare 2:18–22; 2 John 7). As is 2 Peter, this letter is written in the conviction that the end of the age is near.

The generic expectation of false prophets reached its climax, though, in the expectation of a single figure, the false prophet, mentioned three times in the Book of Revelation. In 16:13, he appears with two figures previously introduced, the dragon (chapters 12 and 13) and the beast (11:7). Three demons ("unclean spirits") like frogs (compare the second plague in Egypt, Exodus 8:1–15) come out of their mouths to summon the kings of the earth to the battle of Armageddon. That a triad of figures calls forth the forces of destruction (a reversal of the creative word of God that tames the ur-chaos in Genesis 1) has led many commentators to follow eighteenth-century German pietist mystic Heinrich Jung-Stilling (1740–1817) in calling them a satanic or unholy trinity.

After the returning Christ, with heavenly armies, wins the victory, the beast and false prophet (but not the dragon) are captured and thrown into a fiery lake (Revelation 19:20). The description there of the false prophet having "worked signs in his presence, by which he deceived those who received the mark of the beast and those who worshiped his image" recalls 13:11–17, where, however, the reference is not to the false prophet, but to a second beast, one that had two horns like a lamb and spoke like a dragon.

Interpretations

The author of Revelation, named John, does not identify what he envisioned when he described the false prophet. When he wrote, the Roman Empire was the dominant world power. The worship that Christians refused at the time therefore was emperor worship, which was especially strong in Asia Minor (today Turkey), where the seven churches to which Revelation was originally addressed were located. The first temple to the Spirit of Rome was built in one of them, Smyrna, in 195 BCE. Going a step further, the first temple to the godhead of Caesar was built in Pergamum in 29 BCE. By the end of the first century CE, all seven cities mentioned in Revelation had such temples.

Readers who assume that Revelation describes a time still in the future often try to correlate the figures and events mentioned in it to subsequent ages. The dubious honor of being cast into the lake of fire together with the beast would seem to require that no self-respecting endtime scenario could fail to include speculation about the identity of the false prophet, yet less attention has focused on this figure, or on the second beast, the land beast of chapter 13, than on the first, the beast that rises out of the sea.

The earliest postbiblical writer to discuss the false prophet of whom we have knowledge is Irenaeus (c. 130–c. 200). Irenaeus combines three figures, the man of sin (2 Thessalonians 2:3), the Antichrist (1 John 2:18–22; 4:3; 2 John 7), and the beast that rises out of the sea (Revelation 13:1–10) into one. This identification has rarely been challenged, so that one reads in much endtime literature of the Antichrist of Revelation, although the term is not found there. Further complicating matters is that the term Antichrist is applied, as in Irenaeus, to the dread-inspiring sea beast, while in other endtime speculation to the deceiving land beast.

Of the false prophet, Irenaeus simply identifies him with the second beast of Revelation 13, the land beast, and says of him that he will be the armorbearer of the first beast. The influence of Irenaeus on subsequent endtime speculation is evident in at least one further point. Although Christians still lived in fear of Roman imperial persecution, Irenaeus asserts that the Antichrist will be a Jew, of the tribe of Dan. In making this assertion, Irenaeus drew on earlier tradition, both Jewish and Christian. This is taken over by many subsequent interpreters. At times, however, his description of the Antichrist has been transferred to the false prophet, for instance in Hal Lindsey's 1970 bestseller, *The Late Great Planet Earth.*

The adoption of Christianity as the state religion of Rome led to new, symbolic readings of apocalyptic writings. Nevertheless, these systems often have a structural similarity to earlier accounts, in that they assume that whatever is of God will have its diabolical polar opposite. For Augustine of Hippo (354–430 CE), building on the ideas of Tyconius (died c. 390 CE), the beast is the ungodly city, the community of unbelievers, that exists in parallel to the godly city, the collectivity of genuine believers. The image of the beast, spoken of as well in Revelation 13, is for him "those men who profess to believe, but live as unbelievers. For they pretend to be what they are not, and are called Christians, not from a true likeness but from a deceitful image" (*City of God* 20.9). Yet the false prophet, or the land beast, elicits no more comment from him than it did from Irenaeus. In 20.14, he says noncommittally, "we have already said that by the beast is well understood the wicked city. His false prophet is either Antichrist or that image or figment of which we have spoken in the same place."

The rise of Islam and its rapid expansion beginning in the seventh century CE helped lead to a revival of historicist interpretations of Revelation. For Paulus Alvarus, in ninth-century Spain, Muhammad was a forerunner of the Antichrist. This variant continued. In the early nineteenth century, Alexander Keith identified "the false prophet of Mecca" as the rider of the red horse of Revelation 6:4 (Keith 1832: 1, 185). Contemporary worries about Islamic fundamentalism have kept this speculation alive. The unidentified author of the End time Discussion Group Exchange (EDGE, 1999), expects the false prophet to inspire the Islamic nations to join the Beast in an invasion and conquest of Israel. He further suggests that the false prophet may originate in Iran, reviving a tradition of interpretation that goes back to Commodian (third century CE?) and Lactantius (c. 240–c. 320 CE). Ironically, there is also an Antichrist-like figure in Islam, the Dajjal, who appears in the Hadith (collections of sayings and traditions about Muhammad). It is possible that this figure began as a conception of a false last prophet, "the last in a line of pretenders" (McGinn 1994: 112).

Augustine's view of the force of evil and deception operating within the church was adopted in a different strand of historicist interpretations of Revelation, those which saw the deceiver at the end as a final, evil pope. Joachim of Fiore predicted that the land beast would be "a great prelate who will be like Simon Magus [compare Acts 8:9–25] and like a universal pope in the entire world" (McGinn 1994: 141–42). Unlike Irenaeus, Joachim combined the Man of Sin (2 Thessalonians 2:4) with this figure. The Franciscan Peter Olivi (c. 1248–98) modified the Joachimite theology of history. He separated the figures of the land beast and the false prophet. The land beast represents an age of compromised Christianity that will allow the rise of the sea beast, who will become head of the Holy Roman Empire. This figure, in turn, will appoint a false pope (the false prophet).

The view that the last pope before the return of Christ will be a false one, born in the medieval crisis of the papacy, lives in Catholic endtime speculation, and forms "a bond of continuity" (McGinn 1994: 7) with Protestant views, which began in the Reformation, with the obvious difference that the one view expects a perversion of what otherwise is the one and only church of God, while the other is combined with criticism of the papacy as an institution. For example, Matthew Henry (1662–1714), commenting on Revelation 16:13, wrote, "Some think that a little before the fall of Antichrist the popish pretence of power to work miracles will be revived and will very much amuse and deceive the world." This commentary is still used in evangelical circles nearly three centuries later. The opposition to the ecumenical movement in some Christian circles is partially rooted in this expectation.

The oscillation in the New Testament between a plurality of false prophets and a single false prophet is reflected in the conceptions of some. The Anabaptist Melchior Hoffman identified the three figures of Revelation 16:13 as pope (the beast), emperor (the dragon), and the monks (the false prophet), while for contemporary Jehovah's Witnesses, the false prophet is simply false religion.

Summary

Although the figure of the false prophet has received less attention in apocalyptic speculation than other figures, it has figured in many interpretations. These interpretations differ among themselves, however, in such questions as whether expectation focuses on an individual or on a collective group, whether there will be a literal fulfillment in history or whether this figure should be understood in a spiritual sense; as well as whether this figure will arise in one's own culture (as in Catholic endtime speculation), or in the "other" culture (Islam, or, in Protestant speculation, Catholicism). As is the case with other apocalyptic figures, the concept of the false prophet gives adherents of endtime movements the ability to articulate their perceptions of evil in the world around them. In the case of the false prophet, this would involve especially the fear of deception in the face of religious pluralism and ambiguity.

Henry Sturcke

See also End Signs

Bibliography

Augustine. ([1887] 1981) *The City of God.* In *Nicene and Post-Nicene Fathers,* first series: vol. 2, edited by Philip Schaff. Reprint, Grand Rapids, MI: Eerdmans.

EDGE Online (End time Discussion Group Exchange). (1999) http://www.netpci.com/~tttbbs/Articles-Endt/whoiswho.html.

Henry, Matthew. ([1708–10] 1997) *Commentary on the Bible.* Reprint, Peabody, MA: Hendrickson.

Irenaeus. ([1867] 1981) *Against Heresies.* In *Ante-Nicene Fathers,* vol. 1, edited by Alexander Roberts and James Donaldson. Reprint, Grand Rapids, MI: Eerdmans.

Keith, Alexander. (1832) *The Signs of the Times, as Denoted by the Fulfilment of Historical Predictions, Traced down from the Babylonish Captivity to the Present Time,* 2 vols. New York: Jonathan Leavitt and Boston: Crocker & Brewster.

Klaassen, Walter. (1992) *Living at the End of the Ages: Apocalyptic Expectation in the Radical Reformation.* Lanham, MD: University Press of America.

Lindsey, Hal, (1970) *The Late Great Planet Earth.* Grand Rapids, MI: Zondervan.

Marsden, George M. (1980) *Fundamentalism and American Culture: The Shaping of Twentieth-Century American Evangelism 1870–1925.* Oxford, U.K.: Oxford University Press.

McGinn, Bernard. (1994) *Antichrist: Two Thousand Years of the Human Fascination with Evil.* New York: Harper Collins.

The Family (Children of God, the Family of Love)

The Family is an international Christian fundamentalist new religious movement (NRM) and subculture that is communal in its social organization, evangelical in its aims, and is preparing for the imminent Return of Jesus. It was one of the largest and most successful NRMs to emerge out of the Jesus Movement in the late 1960s, and established missions in over one hundred countries. Although around 38,000 people have joined and left the movement, in 1999 there were around ten thousand members worldwide, and two-thirds of these were of the second generation.

History

The movement was founded by David Brandt Berg (1919–95) in the late 1960s. Berg's mother was a famous itinerant preacher in the Christian and Missionary Alliance Church, and he grew up accompanying her on her tours. He married Jane Miller and worked for the televangelist, Fred Jordan, arranging his tours.

In 1967, discharged from the army with a weak heart, dismissed from his post as a pastor in Arizona, and rejected repeatedly in his effort to find sponsorship for his missionary work, David Berg turned to the Bible and read John 4:35, "Do you not say, 'There are yet four months, then comes the harvest'? I tell you, lift up your eyes, and see how the fields are already white for harvest." He sold his farm and took his family on the road in a mobile home (the "Ark"). Berg's four teenagers formed a dynamic singing-witnessing team called "Teens for Christ" and, on joining their grandmother's ministry at Huntington Beach, California, they generated an extraordinary response among the hippies during the "summer of love." The Berg family took over the Lighthouse, a coffeehouse near the beach and organized inspirational singalongs and all-night Bible study sessions. Berg extrapolated on the prophetic books of the Bible and preached iconoclastic sermons directed against the mainstream churches, and even his followers' middle-class parents. He demanded a radical commitment from his young Bible students—that they "forsake all for Jesus," sever their bonds with the "system" or material world, and take to the road in "Prophet Buses," to lead the life of traveling, preaching missionaries.

New converts (Babes) were bussed to the Texas Soul Clinic (TSC), a ranch belonging to Fred Jordan where, between 1970 and 1971, an intensive Bible study program and ongoing revival meeting was held. Communal patterns based on the Kibbutzim evolved at the TSC, and mass "betrothals" (arranged marriages) to prepare mature disciples for leadership in the missionary field were celebrated. The very first anticult movement, FREECOG, emerged out of the concerns of parents whose children "forsook all." They were led by Ted Patrick who became a famous deprogrammer called "Black Lightning."

The group was first called the Children of God (COG) by a journalist in 1970, they liked the name and it stuck. COG began to publish the *Mo Letters* of David Berg, who was known as Moses David, that were illustrated by cartoons, ranged over many topics, and became known for their radical, prophetic, and erotic nature. Gradually, "litnessing" or proselytizing through distributing the *Mo Letters* replaced more standard missionary methods. While travelling in Quebec, Berg explained his decision to abandon his wife and move in with his young secretary, Maria, in the letter "Old Church/New Church" as a rejection of the worldliness and corruption of the Church for the pure Bride of Christ. Maria and Berg ("Father David") formed a charismatic duo, and upon his death in 1995, she married his secretary, "King Peter" and became the "Lord's Endtime Prophetess."

The Family has undergone many organizational changes. The most dramatic of these was the Reorganization and Nationalization Revolution (RNR) of 1978. Once the luxurious lifestyle of top leaders and the hierarchical nature of COG came to Berg's attention, he fired the "Chain" (of command), including his own children who were known as the "Royal Family," and encouraged the nationals (local converts from the country where COG established its mission field) to assume leadership roles within their own countries. This lead to a collapse of the communal structure, a financial crisis, mass defections, and a period of instability. Many families regrouped and traveled in one- or two-family missionary teams throughout Asia and Latin America. Many families relied on street performances of Christian inspirational songs and dances for their missionary outreach as well as for financial support. Children were trained from an early age to play the guitar and sing in public. After the RNR, the group changed its name to the Family of Love.

In the early 1970s Berg began to advocate sexual communism ("sharing") among his flock, and COG gained notoriety in the mid-seventies due to its unorthodox evangelical strategy of "Flirty Fishing." Inspired by his dream of an erotic fish-tailed goddess, Berg instructed his female disciples to employ their sexual attractiveness to cajole lonely men into reciting the prayer to invite Jesus into their hearts, and to raise financial support for the communal homes. Children born of these unions were called "Jesus babies." "FFing" as it was called, was discontinued after 1987 due to the AIDS threat.

In 1981 the group began to hold large fellowship meetings and old leaders were sought out and convinced to return. Large, well-organized communal homes were set up and the group renamed themselves The Family. By the late 1980s the overseas missionaries, due to new visa regulations in India and the need to provide an English-speaking environment for their youth who were coming of age, returned en masse to the United States to reap a final harvest of souls before Jesus' Return.

The 1990s proved to be a time of intense persecution and conflict. Family homes were raided in Australia, Argentina, and France, and over five hundred children were seized by social workers and police in response to charges of the sexual abuse of children. In court procedures all the charges were dismissed and damages awarded to the parents, since no evidence of abuse was found by doctors or psychologists. These raids were orchestrated by the anticult movement and a handful of embittered apostates. Most of these allegations dated from an earlier experimental phase of COG when Berg advocated initiating children into sexual life at a precocious age as the logical extension of the Law of Love.

Beliefs

The Law of Love is Berg's outstanding theological innovation. This doctrine takes the antinomian theological position, stating that God's grace supersedes the Old Testament laws, including the moral laws of the Ten Commandments. In practice, any heterosexual act, so long as it is done in the spirit of compassion and divine love, is without sin.

Urgent apocalypticism has characterized the movement since its inception. In the 1960s Berg's mother wrote a "Warning Tract" prophesying imminent destruction of the world that Berg and his teens distributed on their tours. In the mid-1970s Berg prophesied that the Comet Kahoutek would destroy America. Periodically, the group stages the "Sackcloth Vigil," a silent demonstration in which members dress in red sackcloth and smear ashes on their foreheads and wear scrolls of Bible quotes and warnings of the destruction of America.

The Family's eschatology closely resemble other premillenarian Christian fundamentalist churches. Berg emphasizes the notion that we are living in the Endtime, that we will soon witness the rise of the Antichrist, and that Berg, as the "Lord's endtime prophet" will guide his people through the coming Tribulation (when they will be forced to flee and hide in caves to escape the One World Order and mark of the Beast) as they prepare for the return of Jesus. As post-Tribulationists, Family members believe many of them will be killed in the battle of Armageddon as they fight beside Jesus, but they will soon be resurrected and will rule Heaven on earth, living in the city of Jerusalem which will be encased in a Golden pyramid that will descend from outer space. There they will enjoy immortality, "superbodies" that can fly and will continue to have sex and babies.

The Family's values are identical to other Christian fundamentalists, except for their liberal views on sexual expression. Homosexuality, abortion, and birth control are considered offenses against God, and smoking is forbidden, although an occasional glass of wine is permitted. Berg inherited some anti-Semitic conspiracy theories and racist attitudes from his religious heritage, but these have been de-emphasized over the years. Since 1985 new the rules have been set in place curbing the sexual excesses of early movement. Sexual sharing between consenting adults is confined to the same home, and sex with outsiders and pederasty or teen-adult sex are excommunicable offences. In February 1995, a charter was issued that outlined the rights and freedoms of Family members, and maintained the communal structure, but allowed more secular influences to permeate the sect's boundaries (members could hold outside jobs and send their children to state schools) and awarded more autonomy in decision making to individuals.

Susan J. Palmer

Bibliography

Davis, R., and J. T. Richardson. (1976) "Organization of the COG." *Sociological Analysis* 37: 321–39.

Lewis, James. (1994) *Sex Slander and Salvation.* Stanford, CA: Center of Academic Publishing.

Van Zandt, David E. (1991) *Living in the Children of God.* Princeton, NJ: Princeton University Press.

Wallis, Roy. (1979) *Salvation and Protest,* by Roy Wallis. New York: St. Martin's Press.

———. (1982) *Millennialism and Charisma,* edited by Roy Wallis. Belfast: The Queen's University Press.

Fatalism

The concept of fatalism is often associated with apocalyptic belief systems and millennialist movements. Fatalism is commonly understood as the belief that certain events and experiences are inevitable, unalterable, and determined by external forces beyond human control. Millennialist worldviews frequently express a belief in the inevitability of current and future events, which are interpreted as a predetermined part of a divine pattern or superhuman plan. The idea of fate embodies the sense of inevitability, both pessimistic and optimistic, that is inherent to apocalyptic and millennialist worldviews.

The word "apocalypse" (from the Greek, *apokalypsis*) means "revelation" or "unveiling." This sense of a revealed, underlying design for history has traditionally characterized apocalyptic ideas and resembles ancient notions of fate as an absolute force in the universe that determines all things. By asserting that worldly renewal is an inevitable part of a preordained plan, millennialist narratives and beliefs promise that evil and suffering will be destroyed, that human existence is meaningful, and that a new world of peace and justice will be created. Faith and fatalism are thus interwoven into the fabric of apocalyptic thought: a profound fatalism for a world believed to be inevitably doomed is entwined with the faith for a predestined, perfect age of harmony and human fulfillment.

The word "fate" comes from the Latin *fatum*, implying a sentence or doom of the gods, and originally associated with the spoken word of the Roman god Jupiter, which could not be altered. Fatalism is usually distinguished from related concepts such as determinism, fortune, and destiny by the belief that human will or effort is incapable of altering the outcome of certain events. Whether fate is believed to be derived from a personal power (a god) or an impersonal order, the underlying attitude in both instances ultimately is fatalistic if events are considered to be inevitable, determined by external forces, and unalterable by human will or effort.

Scholars have documented fatalistic beliefs cross-culturally and proposed typologies of the various ways fate has been conceptualized historically, discussing how fate is conferred, the distinctions between a personal and impersonal determiner of fate, and the relation people may have with fate. C. J. Bleeker, for example, identifies general categories of beliefs about fate, such as the belief that a person's destiny is related to the time, place, and circumstances of one's birth; that the "wheel of fortune" is capricious and turns arbitrarily, with one person born lucky and another born with ill-fortune; that fate is tragic and inescapable (the view presented in Greek tragedies); that a world order controls all events for good or bad; and that an all-knowing God predetermines people's destinies (1963: 114–16).

Although fatalistic beliefs often concern the role of fate in individual life, apocalyptic thinking conceptualizes fate as a cosmic, controlling power that determines history and the future of the earth and humanity. In world mythology, ideas about omniscient and omnipotent fate traditionally are associated with concepts of history, time, the destruction and renewal of the world, and the end of the human race. Scholars have documented these types of ideas in ancient Zoroastrian, Babylonian, Hindu, Jewish, Buddhist, Islamic, Greek, Roman, Norse, African, Mayan, and Native American cultures, among others.

Such ideas from Greek antiquity, for example, are revealed in Hesiod's *Works and Days*, which contains an account of the predestined decline of humanity through the five ages of the world, with each subsequent age becoming increasingly violent or foolish and culminating in Hesiod's own age. This final age is populated by the last generation of humanity, which is condemned to an existence of suffering, sorrow, and endless toil in an evil world that Zeus will finally destroy. Hesiod lists the various evils in the world that have been ordained by Zeus and concludes, "there is no way to avoid what Zeus has intended" (Lattimore 1977: 31, 32–43).

Ancient Norse beliefs about the three Norns also illustrate the belief in the omnipotence of fate and its relation to time and history. The Norns were believed to not only spin the thread of human life and death, but rule the fate of the gods and the universe as well, introducing time into the cosmos and therefore controlling the sequence of all events that must inevitably occur. From the beginning of time, the Norns decreed the annihilation of the world by destructive forces (Ragnarök) and the tragic doom of the gods. More recent apocalyptic beliefs about the foreordained destruction of the world and the divine determination of history resemble these ancient notions about an unalterable and cosmic power that controls history and human destiny.

Fatalism and the American Millennialist Legacy

Throughout American history, deterministic notions about the preordained role of the United States in God's divine plan have been an aspect of various millennialist traditions. Some of the earliest European explorers embraced such ideas, including Christopher Columbus, who believed that as an explorer, he was fated to fulfill certain prophecies. He apparently considered his discovery of the "New World" part of a divine plan in preparation for the establishment of the millennial kingdom on earth.

Early Puritan and Calvinist apocalyptic writings also express beliefs about human actions and historical events being part of a divine plan, with widespread ideas about predestination exemplifying the fatalistic underpinnings of early American religious thought. According to early Calvinist theology, human beings are completely depraved, humankind cannot be saved by good works but only by God's grace. In this view, an elect group has been predestined from eternity for everlasting life in heaven while the rest of humanity is doomed to suffer the torments of hell. God's foregone decision for the fate of each person could not be known or influenced; believers could only strive to fulfill God's laws regardless of their ultimate fate.

During the Great Awakening, beliefs which stressed the eventual establishment of God's kingdom on earth became widespread (referred to as "postmillennialism," or "progressive millennialism"). The religious revivals during this period de-emphasized imminent worldly cataclysm and asserted that the millennial age would be brought about gradually by human beings in fulfillment of God's plan. In various postmillennialist prophecy traditions, the United States was viewed as having a prophetic destiny as a chosen nation that would redeem the world and usher in the millennium. During the late eighteenth century and nineteenth century, millennialist movements such as the Shakers, the Oneida Community, and numerous other groups stressed the establishment of the millennial kingdom on earth, to be attained through their beliefs and practices. Although postmillennialist ideas may appear less fatalistic than catastrophic millennialist beliefs that emphasize the apocalyptic destruction of the world, they often are characterized by a similar assertion that human actions and historical events are part of a grand design that has been divinely preordained.

The fatalistic aspects of apocalyptic traditions are exemplified by predictions about the exact date of doomsday, such as those of American Baptist preacher William Miller, who first proclaimed that the world would end in 1843, and then in 1844. Like others before him, Miller believed that the scriptures contained a numerical cryptogram that could be mathematically decoded to calculate precisely the day of doom within God's endtime plan. The cognitive power of deterministic prophecies is illustrated by the fact that even after Miller's predictions proved false, some believers continued to embrace Millerite beliefs, forming into various groups, such as the Seventh-Day Adventists. According to Adventist belief, Miller's predictions were accurate, and an "invisible," spiritual apocalypse occurred in 1844 with the "cleansing of heaven," to be followed inevitably by the destructive cleansing of earth. Because of the key assertion that specific events occur as part of a divine will or cosmic plan, not completely knowable by human beings, millennialist traditions may be reformulated to offer explanations for all events that occur, even apparently erroneous prophecies.

Fatalism and Contemporary Apocalyptic Beliefs

The dropping of atomic bombs on Hiroshima and Nagasaki in August 1945, initiated an era of nuclear apocalypticism characterized by fatalistic beliefs about the future of humanity. Ideas about the inevitability of nuclear annihilation have been integrated into traditional apocalyptic belief systems and sanctified by some millennialists as a meaningful occurrence that is necessary for the redemption of humanity. For instance, fatalistic beliefs about the inevitability of nuclear apocalypse during the cold-war era are revealed by a Yankelovich poll taken in 1984, in which 39 percent of a sample population of Americans agreed with the statement, "When the Bible predicts that the earth will be destroyed by fire, it's telling us that a nuclear war is inevitable" (Jones 1985: 67).

The pervasiveness of apocalyptic beliefs about foreordained and inevitable worldly events is suggested by a 1994 *U.S. News and World Report* poll, which found that 53 percent of those Americans polled believe some events in the twentieth century fulfill biblical prophecy; 44 percent believe that a Battle of Armageddon will occur; 49 percent believe that the Antichrist will appear; and 44 percent believe in the rapture of the church (*U.S. News and World Report*, 19 December 1994: 6). Beliefs about a predetermined endtime scenario were also revealed by a Gallup poll taken during the Persian Gulf War, which found that 15 percent of Americans thought the war fulfilled prophecy and that Armageddon was at hand (Bezilla 1996: 26).

Today, deterministic beliefs concerning apocalyptic prophecies are integral to the worldviews of many evangelical Christians, such as the Southern Baptist Convention and various Pentecostal and charismatic denominations, including the Assemblies of God Church, the Church of Nazarene, and thousands of independent evangelical "Bible churches." The most popular form of prophecy among evangelical Christians, premillennial dispensationalism, stresses the literal truth of the Bible and the correlation of biblical prophecy with specific historical events. Dispensationalists hold that human beings are destined to fail each of God's seven tests, or dispensations, and are incapable of improving an unrecuperable evil world. Collective salvation may only occur after cataclysmic worldly destruction. In the dispensationalist view, Christ's return will be preceded by foreordained endtime signs such as wars, plagues, famine, earthquakes, and a seven-year period of misery and tribulation. It is asserted that after the rise of the Antichrist and at the end of the tribulation period, Christ will return, defeat the Antichrist at the Battle of Armageddon, and usher in the millennium. Dispensationalists also believe that faithful Christians will be saved prior to Armageddon in the form of "the Rapture," in which they will be physically removed, unharmed, from the earth.

Dispensationalist attitudes have overtly fatalistic themes, emphasizing inevitable cataclysm and de-emphasizing the efficacy of human effort to improve the world. The dispensationalist view generally regards humanity as irredeemably evil, and social problems are interpreted as portents of a bankrupt society on the verge of imminent apocalypse. Although some millennialist movements have maintained that worldly disasters are warnings of God's apocalyptic wrath if humans do not repent, the calamities and prophecies highlighted by dispensationalists are not interpreted as warning signs from God or catalysts for action. Instead, these are noncausal indications of God's timetable, codified in the Bible thousands of years ago. According to this view, the reform and repentance of all humanity cannot avert a doomsday which has been divinely determined. Human responsibility concerning the improvement of the world may even be discouraged and interpreted as a direct denial of God's plan. Human beings, through their own efforts, cannot save the world from apocalypse, but they can save themselves by following the divine will and behaving in ways decreed by God. Individual fate thus may be altered through human action, but the fate of the world and history itself is believed to be foreordained and unalterable.

Although premillennial dispensationalism is the most pervasive form of millennialism in the United States today, numerous other traditions express prophecy beliefs about preordained events that reveal the fate of the world. For example, ideas about a divine plan for worldly destruction and renewal are a part of the belief systems of the Jehovah's Witnesses, the Church of Jesus Christ of Latter-day Saints (better known as Mormonism), the Nation of Islam, the Chabad Lubavitch movement (an Orthodox Hasidic sect of Judaism), the Unification Church, the International Society of Krishna Consciousness, Rastafarianism, Baha'i, and certain Native American groups, among other religious movements.

Fatalistic prophecies about inevitable worldly cataclysm also exist at a grassroots level as a form of popular or folk belief. For instance, the popular interest in the apocalyptic predictions of Nostradamus or Edgar Cayce exists apart from the sanction of formal religious institutions. Similarly, apocalyptic prophecies associated with visions of the Virgin Mary, which foretell of imminent worldly chastisement as part of a divine plan unfolding in the last days, are an expression of Roman Catholic folk tradition, usually existing apart from the approval of the institutional church. Various New Age millennial beliefs express ideas about the divine determination of worldly events and human history, ranging from beliefs about catastrophic earth changes to ideas concerning a gradual shift in global consciousness that will lead to a golden age of harmony and peace. A sense of fatefulness also is reflected in beliefs about the role that UFOs and extraterrestrials will play in the destruction or salvation of the world, with some believers maintaining that ETs created earth, oversee human history, direct the development of the human race, and have a plan for the transformation of humanity. Like previous millennialist worldviews, emergent UFO and New Age traditions provide systems of meaning for understanding human existence and promise believers that the universe is ordered, that evil and suffering will be eliminated, and that an age of harmony and justice will be established through the fulfillment of a cosmic plan.

Secular Apocalypticism and Fatalism

Until recently, the end of the world has been interpreted as a supernatural event, involving the annihilation and renewal of the earth by deities or divine forces. However, during the twentieth century, beliefs about the senseless and unredemptive destruction of humanity have emerged and now compete with traditional religious apocalyptic worldviews. Secular beliefs about impending doom are related to fears about nuclear annihilation, environmental destruction, epidemic diseases, global famine, overpopulation, or earth's collision with a large asteroid or comet, among other disasters. During the cold war, fear of nuclear annihilation evoked widespread fatalism about the future; more recent secular beliefs about inevitable catastrophe are associated with what is known as the year 2000 computer problem, the Y2K problem, or the millennium bug.

Unlike religious apocalyptic ideas which promise a redeemed new world after catastrophe, secular ideas about societal cataclysm usually are devoid of the hope of worldly transformation. Attributing no meaning to worldly destruction, secular visions of the endtime are pervaded by images of the helplessness of human beings and their manipulation by larger, determining forces. Because of the lack of belief in a divine plan determining worldly events, secular beliefs about inevitable societal destruction tend to be characterized by a sense of despair or fatalistic resignation.

Fate and the Active Fulfillment of Apocalyptic Prophecies

Fatalism is commonly seen as involving helplessness, resignation, and passivity, and thus as motivating no attempt to alter events believed to be inevitable. However, at times individuals may actively "embrace their fate" and act to fulfill God's will or fate's plan. Most millenarians anticipate the total destruction of the current social, economic, and political order, and its replacement by a new millennial realm. However, some may attempt to fulfill their prophecies and hasten the destruction of current society by instigating societal catastrophes through violent or revolutionary means.

For instance, the millenarian ideology of the National Socialist Workers Party repeatedly appealed to a sense of fate, proclaiming that Germans were the elect members of a pure-blooded Aryan "master race" destined to establish the Third Reich. Nazi rhetoric often assured followers that they were acting in accordance with a fated plan, and through their efforts the world would be cleansed of evil forces and a thousand-year period of Aryan rule would be created. A more recent example involves certain premillennial dispensationalists who have attempted to hasten the return of Christ by financially supporting militant Israeli groups intent on destroying the Muslim Dome of the Rock Mosque in Jerusalem and rebuilding the Jewish Temple of Solomon in its place. This active attempt to bring about an endtime prophecy exemplifies the notion that fate can be expedited if predetermined conditions are fulfilled. Whether promoted by totalitarian leaders or regarded as part of God's divine plan, the authoritarian certitude of fatalistic doctrines has the potential to motivate individuals to work with absolute determination to fulfill their fate, their nation's fate, or specific historical mandates that they believe are predestined.

A self-fulfilling apocalyptic scenario appears to have been the goal of some members of the Japanese Aum Shinrikyo (Supreme Truth) sect, the leaders of which were charged with staging a nerve gas attack in the subways of Tokyo in March 1995, that killed twelve people and resulted in over 5,500 others being hospitalized. Government raids on various Aum compounds uncovered deadly chemicals and automatic weapons, and the sect's scientists allegedly were researching and experimenting with various chemical, laser, biological, and conventional weapons in order to fulfill their leader's prophecies of an apocalyptic scenario believed to be inevitable.

The collective suicides of members of the Order of the Solar Temple and the UFO group known as Heaven's Gate also appear to have been motivated by a profound sense of fatalism for the world and a desire to actively fulfill specific apocalyptic prophecies. Members believed that through suicide they could achieve their destinies and be transported to a higher spiritual dimension, thus escaping from a world that they regarded as evil and inevitably doomed.

Fatalism, Crisis, and Perceptions of Evil

Numerous studies have suggested that millennialist beliefs appeal to those who feel that current social, economic, religious, or political situations are in a state of crisis, radical change, or disintegration. Conceptualizing apocalyptic beliefs as fatalistic seems to support these previous interpretations, which have shown that perceptions of societal upheaval and unmanageable crises frequently precipitate feelings of powerlessness, anomie, and anxiety. Scholars from varied disciplines agree that such feelings often may cause people to embrace fatalistic belief systems. Fatalistic modes of thought provide a framework for interpreting events otherwise considered to be uncontrollable, haphazard, or incomprehensible, reducing uncertainty and offering explanations for situations in which personal action is believed to be futile. Directly countering feelings of helplessness, despair, and uncontrollability, apocalyptic belief systems promise the annihilation and regeneration of the world through radical supernatural transformation, a promise that brings to people a sense of control and meaning.

The relation between perceptions of severe societal crisis and fatalism is illustrated by the widespread view among apocalypticists that contemporary society is irreversibly evil. Beliefs about overwhelming and omnipresent evil forces reveal feelings of crisis, personal powerlessness, and a lack of faith in the effectiveness of human effort to remedy societal ills. The conspiratorial view of the world that undergirds much of apocalyptic thought is implicitly fatalistic as well, with specific historical events and much human suffering attributed to the machinations of a secret cabal of evil groups: the Freemasons, the Catholic Church, the Elders of Zion, the Illuminati, the Trilateral Commission, international bankers, communists, or secular humanists. Apocalyptic conspiracy theories maintain that evil must inevitably proliferate in the endtime (the reign of the Antichrist, for example) before it is ultimately defeated by supernatural forces at the time of apocalypse. This fatalistic view of history and societal ills asserts that human beings are basically helpless against overpowering, sinister forces and that human effort is ineffectual in saving an increasingly evil world.

Fatalism and the Varieties of Apocalyptic Belief

Although there is a tremendous diversity of millennialist and apocalyptic beliefs, at least three general categories can be derived from the wide range of ideas that exist about worldly cataclysm: (1) unconditional apocalypticism; (2) conditional apocalypticism; and (3) unredemptive apocalypticism. These categories do not constitute an absolute typology but are useful for conceptualizing the fatalistic aspects of endtime discourse, and may serve as a framework for understanding the various expressions of apocalyptic belief that have existed in the past and that have emerged in recent years.

Unconditional apocalypticism is characterized by the belief that history is predetermined and that apocalypse is imminent and unalterable: the world is believed to be irredeemable by human effort; its cataclysmic destruction is regarded as inevitable; and a superhuman plan exists for collective salvation. Premillennial dispensationalism epitomizes unconditional apocalyptic thinking. Dispensationalists assert that a divine pattern controls all of history, that contemporary events are fulfilling God's plan for humanity, and that human beings are completely powerless to alter these fated events in any way. Collective efforts cannot alter historical inevitability, and when certain preordained conditions are fulfilled (e.g., the rebuilding of the Jewish Temple in Jerusalem), the end of the world will soon occur. Unconditional apocalypticism has characterized the worldviews of many catastrophic millennialist movements, including the Millerites, the Branch Davidians, Heaven's Gate, and other movements that predict inevitable worldly destruction and the salvation of the chosen ones.

Conditional apocalypticism is characterized by the belief that apocalypse is imminent but may be postponed if human beings behave in ways prescribed by a superhuman power. Conditional apocalyptic worldviews assert that human beings cannot prevent imminent worldly destruction entirely through their own efforts but that within the broad constraints of history's inevitable progression, human beings may forestall worldly catastrophes if they act in accordance with divine will or a superhuman plan. This view is illustrated by certain beliefs about Marian apparitions, messages from UFOs and ETs, and Native American prophecies, which foretell of a period of chastisement that warns that the end of the world is near. But these prophecies assert that human beings may postpone or avert the day of doom if they change their behavior, heed these warnings, and act in accordance with divine will. In these scenarios, human beings may prevent worldly destruction only when they follow God's decrees or those of a superhuman source; and apocalypse will only occur as a consequence of humanity's destructive or evil behavior which is a violation of divine or cosmic laws.

Unredemptive apocalypticism, in contrast to these redemptive apocalyptic views, is characterized by the belief that apocalypse is imminent and unalterable and that no superhuman plan exists for worldly redemption or collective salvation. As discussed in the section on secular apocalyptic beliefs, unredemptive apocalyptic ideas are a relatively recent phenomenon, and they tend to be pervaded by a sense of hopelessness, futility, and nihilism. Specific worldly catastrophes—nuclear war, ecological destruction, a polar shift, widespread famine, disease—are regarded as inevitable and not subject to human agency. Instead of a superhuman plan or unalterable will as determinants of history, unredemptive apocalypticism expresses the view that the end of history will be determined by human ignorance, destructive technologies, or uncontrollable impersonal forces that are progressing inexorably toward a cataclysmic culmination. Until recently, beliefs about the inevitability of nuclear annihilation were the most predominant expression of unredemptive apocalypticism, but in the post–cold war era beliefs about an assortment of other unredemptive apocalyptic scenarios (environmental destruction, deadly viruses, earth's collision with a large asteroid or comet, the Y2K problem) have become increasingly common.

Conclusion

Millennialist belief systems that promise collective salvation and worldly transformation are appealing precisely because of the assurance that an unalterable pattern underlying history will culminate in the redemption of the world. Asserting that history resembles a narrative that has been deliberately designed and that is ultimately meaningful, these apocalyptic traditions present the story of human existence as coherent from beginning to end, punctuated by dramatic preordained events, and characterized by an ongoing battle between good and evil.

Apocalypticism, as a fatalistic mode of thought, offers privileged explanations that "unveil" the otherwise obscure meanings behind events and experiences, reassuring believers that current crises and social evils are part of a predetermined endtime scenario orchestrated by God or superhuman forces. Belief in imminent worldly destruction is accompanied by confidence in a divine fate or cosmic plan, that is moral and benevolent and that will ultimately create an ideal, harmonious world free from suffering and injustice.

Although apocalyptic worldviews address issues of ultimate concern, the belief that the world can be saved only by otherworldly beings may reinforce feelings of helplessness and serve as a substitute for confronting the actual problems that face humanity. Apocalyptic traditions tend to deny the efficacy of human effort to improve the world and encourage a passive acceptance of human-made crises and potential disasters.

Some observers have speculated that apocalyptic belief systems will become outdated or gradually "collapse from exhaustion" in the new millennium. This prediction appears to be doomed to fail, considering the religious and psychological needs that such beliefs fulfill and the adaptability of apocalyptic traditions. Endtime enthusiasts have consistently updated eschatological beliefs and made them relevant, and will continue to transform such ideas creatively in the years ahead. Analyzing the fatalistic aspects of such traditions provides researchers with considerable insight into the religious, psychological, and cultural dimensions of apocalyptic ideas, and reveals much about millennial fears and hopes for the future.

Daniel Wojcik

See also Aum Shinrikyo, Columbus/Colon, Dispensationalism, Heaven's Gate, Millerites, Nazism, Nuclear, Secular Millennialism, Seventh-day Adventists, Solar Temple; United States, 18th Century

Bibliography

Barkun, Michael. (1974) *Disaster and the Millennium.* New Haven, CT: Yale University Press.

Bezilla, Robert, ed. (1996) *Religion in America 1996.* Princeton, NJ: Princeton Religion Research Center.

Bleeker, C. J. (1963) "Die Idee des Schicksals in der ältagyptischen Religion." In *The Sacred Bridge,* edited by C. J. Bleeker. Leiden, Netherlands: E.J. Brill, 112–29.

Boyer, Paul. (1992) *When Time Shall Be No More: Prophecy Belief in Modern American Culture.* Cambridge, MA: Harvard University Press.

Brondsted, Mogens. (1967) "The Transformations of the Concept of Fate in Literature." In *Fatalistic Beliefs in Religion, Folklore and Literature* (Papers Read at the Symposium on Fatalistic Beliefs Held at Abo, 7–9 September 1964), edited by Helmer Ringgren. Stockholm: Almqvist & Wiksell, 172–78.

Cohn, Norman. (1970) *The Pursuit of the Millennium: Revolutionary Millenarians and Mystical Anarchists of the Middle Ages,* revised and expanded edition. New York: Oxford University Press.

Doob, Leonard W. (1988) *Inevitability: Determinism, Fatalism, and Destiny.* New York: Greenwood Press.

Dorner, August. (1928) "Fate." In *Encyclopedia of Religion and Ethics,* edited by James Hastings. New York: Scribner's, 771–78.

Grambo, Ronald. (1988) "Problems of Fatalism: A Blueprint for Further Research." *Folklore* 99: 11–29.

Hickey, J. T. (1967) "Fatalism." In *New Catholic Encyclopedia,* edited by Catholic University of America. New York: McGraw-Hill, 1323–24.

Jones, Lawrence. (1985) "Reagan's Religion." *Journal of American Culture* 8:59–70.

Lattimore, Richmond, trans. (1977) *Hesiod.* Ann Arbor: University of Michigan Press.

Leach, Maria. ([1949–50] 1972) *Funk and Wagnall's Standard Dictionary of Folklore, Mythology, and Legend.* San Francisco: Harper & Row, Publishers, Inc.

Ringgren, Helmer. (1967) "The Problem of Fatalism." In *Fatalistic Beliefs in Religion, Folklore and Literature* (Papers Read at the Symposium on Fatalistic Beliefs Held at Abo, 7–9 September 1964), edited by Helmer Ringgren. Stockholm: Almqvist & Wiksell, 7–18.

Robbins, Thomas, and Susan Palmer, eds. (1997) *Millennium, Messiahs, and Mayhem: Contemporary Apocalyptic Movements.* New York: Routledge.

Strozier, Charles B., and Michael Flynn, eds. (1997) *The Year 2000: Essays on the End.* New York: New York University Press.

Thompson, Damian. (1997) *The End of Time: Faith and Fear in the Shadow of the Millennium.* Hanover, NH: University Press of New England.

Thrupp, Sylvia L., ed. ([1962] 1970) *Millennial Dreams in Action: Studies in Revolutionary Religious Movements.* New York: Schocken.

Tuveson, Ernest L. (1968) *Redeemer Nation: America's Millennial Role.* Chicago: University of Chicago Press.

Wallace, Anthony F. C. (1956) "Revitalization Movements." *American Anthropologist* 58: 264–81; Reprinted in *Reader in Comparative Religion: An Anthropological Approach*, 4th ed., edited by William A. Lessa and Evon Z. Vogt. New York: Harper Collins Publishers, 1979, 421–30.

Watts, Pauline Moffit. (1985) "Prophecy and Discovery: On the Spiritual Origins of Christopher Columbus's 'Enterprise of the Indies.'" *American Historical Review* 90: 73–102.

Wojcik, Daniel. (1997) *The End of the World as We Know It: Faith, Fatalism, and Apocalypse in America.* New York and London: New York University Press.

The Fatima Cult

Apparitions of the Virgin Mary form an important element of popular Catholic apocalypticism. The most important apparitions in the development of twentieth-century Marian apocalypticism were those at Fatima, Portugal, in 1917. Fatima is probably the most influential apparition site in the twentieth century in terms of its effect on how subsequent visionaries and apparition sites were perceived and understood.

What developed from Fatima was a new, continuing, prophetic role of the visionary that continued long after the apparitions had ended. Lucia's memoirs provided details of the apparitions and elaborations of her visions' meaning. The gradual elaboration of the "Third Secret" has sparked interest in secrets and allowed their meanings to be continually reinterpreted in light of changing world events. As a result, the messages of Fatima have become the core of the apocalyptic view of history espoused by most modern Marian visionaries. Secrets and their associated scripts have become a central element of all post-Fatima apparitions, particularly elements such as the Miracle of the Sun, promises of a visible sign of coming chastisements, communion with an angel, and warnings about Russia and the rise of atheistic communism.

The Apparitions

On 17 May 1917 three peasant children, ten-year-old Lucia dos Santos and her younger cousins, Francisco and Jacinta Marto, were herding sheep outside the village of Fatima, Portugal, when they saw the first of six monthly visions of the figure of a beautiful lady surrounded by light who told them to recite the rosary every day. The children had actually begun to have visionary experiences as early as 1915 when Lucia and three other girls saw a figure that looked like "a statue made of snow," but it was the news of the vision of 17 May that quickly spread throughout the village of Fatima. The children had apparently already identified their vision as "Our Lady" and reported that she had told them that she would appear again on the thirteenth of each month for the next six months. On 13 June, a small group of about fifty people watched as the children again saw "Our Lady" in the same spot, and reported that she would appear again on July 13.

Fatima occurred as bread riots swept through Europe in response to an increasingly unpopular World War I, and during a Catholic backlash against the Portuguese government's anticlerical campaign. The apparitions at Fatima were quickly turned into the symbol of a popular Catholic resistance, and the subsequent Catholic government in turn promoted the cult very heavily. The resulting groundswell of popular support for the church was a crucial element of the popularity of the apparitions, and larger and larger crowds came to see each monthly apparition. On 13 July, 5,000 people came; on 13 September, 25,000; and by the last apparitions on 13 October 1917, the crowds were estimated to be 70,000 people.

The routine that had developed at these monthly apparitions was that the children would kneel near a tree where "Our Lady" had previously appeared and pray the rosary. Lucia would then announce that the Virgin had arrived, apparently converse with her, and finally announce that she could be seen leaving. On 13 October, the final apparition, the expectation had spread among the pilgrims that the Virgin was going to perform a miracle. It was a rainy day, but as the time of the apparition approached, the rain stopped and the sun came out. Many people in the crowd reported seeing the sun move and spin in the sky, others saw different colors radiating from the sun or else saw the face of Mary in the sun. This event has come to be known among Marian devotees as "The Miracle of the Sun," and images of the sun moving in the sky have become incorporated into the basic schema of expectations at most subsequent Marian apparition sites.

The Influence of Fatima

Until World War II, the apparitions at Fatima were little known outside of Portugal. The messages of Fatima that are so important to Marian devotees today actually come from four memoirs written by Lucia between 1935 and 1941. More than previous visionaries, Lucia played an extremely active and approved role in defining the meaning of the Fatima apparitions both at the actual time of the visions, when she was the only one of the visionaries to interact

FATIMA

This pledge was prepared in the presence of "Lucia" to whom Our Lady of Fatima appeared. The first Bishop of Fatima promulgated it. The entire Hierarchy of Portugal approved it. Millions of Catholics, in 57 nations, have signed it.

THE BLUE ARMY PLEDGE

I Pledge Myself to Our Lady

Dear Queen and Mother, who promised at Fatima to convert Russia and bring peace to all mankind, in reparation to your Immaculate Heart for my sins and the sins of the whole world, I solemnly promise: 1) To offer up every day the sacrifices demanded by my daily duty; 2) To say part of the Rosary† daily while meditating on the Mysteries; 3) To wear the Scapular of Mt. Carmel as profession of this promise and as an act of consecration to you. I shall renew this promise often, especially in moments of temptation.

†Usually understood to mean at least five decades daily.

Signature ______________________

(Note: This pledge is not a vow and does not bind under pain of sin. Nevertheless it is a promise... your word given to your Heavenly Mother.)

It contains the essential requests of Our Lady for world peace. The Most Rev. Thomas A. Boland, Archbishop of Newark, where the idea of the pledge was born, summarized the zealous aspirations of all who promote the Blue Army of Our Lady when he said:

"THE VERY NEXT PERSON TO SIGN THE BLUE ARMY PLEDGE MAY BE THE VERY LAST PERSON OUR LADY NEEDS TO KEEP HER PROMISE OF THE CONVERSION OF RUSSIA."

Despite its great value of personalizing the message of Fatima (with a morning offering, a scapular, and a rosary), the pledge also has a weakness: It speaks only of the minimum Our Lady of Fatima requires of us. And how will even the minimum be accomplished without apostles? So the Blue Army of Our Lady also has "Crusaders" willing to follow Her along the path of reparation, the path of the Five First Saturdays (to which She attached a promise of salvation), the path of living and promoting the pledge.

The Blue Army has no dues, no collections, in no way solicits those who merely sign the pledge. Names of all who make the pledge are taken to Fatima and remembered in daily special Masses where Our Lady appeared.

Additional decrees from Rome relating to the requests made by Our Lady of Fatima:

Dec. 12, 1942

Plenary Indulgence* gained on each First Saturday by those who perform the exercises of the devotion of the Five First Saturdays.

March 3, 1952

Additional Plenary Indulgence* to those who, on the first Saturday of any month, perform special acts of devotion in reparation for the blasphemies committed against the name and other prerogatives of the Immaculate Heart of Mary.

*Under the usual conditions.

Feb. 4, 1956

Authorized the recitation of the special Fatima prayer after each decade of the rosary in private and public devotions (Office of Indulgences, 878:56.) The prayer alluded to is: "O my Jesus forgive us; save us from the fire of hell; lead all souls to heaven, especially those in greatest need (of thy mercy)."

to the requests of Our Lady of Fatima"

-Eugene Cardinal Tisserant-

9

with the crowds, but even more clearly in later years. Francisco and Jacinta died quite young, and so it was Lucia who was almost entirely responsible for shaping the cult of Fatima.

Lucia has continued to write about the apparitions of 1917 and her subsequent mystical experiences. More than anything, it is these writings that have made Fatima the most influential apparition site of the twentieth century.

With the publication of Lucia's memoirs, hagiographic accounts of Fatima became increasingly popular. At a time when Catholics were trying to make sense of World War II and the postwar world, Fatima and the ideology associated with it became internationally famous. The messages from Fatima and other apparition sites were incorporated into anticommunist messages with calls for the conversion of Russia and images of Mary in battle against the forces of godless communism. Throughout the 1940s and 1950s, elaborate devotions to Our Lady of Fatima developed, and several very popular lay organizations were founded to promote devotion to Mary. These included the Militia of the Immaculate Conception in 1917, the Legion of Mary in 1921, and the Blue Army of Our Lady of Fatima in 1947.

A great deal of the popular fascination with Fatima focuses on the apocalyptic predictions in the messages, especially the so-called Third Secret of Fatima. On 13 June and again on 17 July 1917, Lucia and her cousins reported that part of the message they had received from the Virgin that day was a secret. The children were questioned about the secrets, not only by friends and family but also by local officials such as the mayor, who threatened to have them boiled alive in oil if they did not tell. In her later writings, Lucia described a three-part secret received on 13 July. The first part was a vivid and frightening vision of hell. The second part was the revelation of the Devotion to the Immaculate Heart of Mary, from Lucia of Fatima, and a message stressing the need for the Consecration of Russia as a way to obtain grace and mercy for the entire world. Lucia also alluded to a third part of the secret, one that she could only reveal to the pope. In 1943, Lucia did write down the third part of the secret. The secret was placed in a sealed envelope which the Bishop of Leiria kept in his safe until 1957. In 1957, the secret was sent to the Vatican, but there is no record as to what was done with it.

The contents of the so-called Third Secret of Fatima became a subject of intense speculation in Marian circles and have remained so ever since. During World War II, it was assumed that the secret referred to the outcome of the war. In the postwar years, the third secret was taken to refer to the ongoing struggle between the church and communism. As with all apparitions since the Middle Ages, it was presumed that Mary was interceding to save a beleaguered community, in this case the entire world. The key to defeating the forces of godless communism was for all sinners to renew their devotion to the Immaculate Heart of Mary. This interpretation was particularly encouraged by church authorities in Europe, who considered it their mission to bring young communist sympathizers back to the church.

Published interviews with Lucia at this time alluded to prophesies of impending doom as part of the secret. Mary was in a battle with the devil, Lucia reported, and God was preparing to chastise the world. Russia (the Soviet Union), if left unconverted, would become the instrument of God's chastisement on the world. Mary was the last hope offered by God as a means to save those souls that would otherwise be going to hell.

In the 1950s the belief arose that the Third Secret was going to be made public in 1960. When this did not happen, a variety of scenarios were proposed as to why the Pope Paul VI was unable to make the secret known. Some versions simply reasoned that it could not be made public while Lucia was still alive, but more elaborate scenarios were discussed where the secret was considered to be too dangerous to be disseminated. Some reports had the pope weeping or falling unconscious upon reading the secret.

The 1960s and 1970s saw a drop in the number of reported apparitions and in the popularity of lay devotions to Fatima. There are many reasons for this, but a major part was changing views within the church. During the Vatican II Council in 1961–63, it was clear that many church officials and theologians felt that popular devotions to Mary were being overemphasized. Pope John XXIII, who called the council, even said "the Madonna is not pleased when she is placed up above her son." Although Marian devotion did not end, the statements and discussion at Vatican II had the effect of discouraging Marian devotions, and presumably also influenced many bishops not to approve apparitions within their dioceses.

Since the early 1980s, revived popular interest in Marian apparitions has centered around the visions in Medjugorje in the former Yugoslavia. However, devotion to our Lady of Fatima remains strong among traditionalist Catholics. For instance, on 13 May 1991, Pope John Paul II celebrated the tenth anniversary of the assassination attempt on his life by placing a crown of diamonds on a statue of Mary in Fatima. The crown included one of the bullets from the attack.

Victor Balaban

See also Marianism

Bibliography

Carroll, Michael P. (1986) *The Cult of the Virgin Mary: Psychological Origins*. Princeton, NJ: Princeton University Press.

Christian, William A., Jr. (1989) *Apparitions in late Medieval and Renaissance Spain*. Princeton, NJ: Princeton University Press.

Cuneo, Michael W. (1997) *The Smoke of Satan: Conservative and Traditionalist Dissent in Contemporary American Catholicism*. New York: Oxford University Press.

Kselman, Thomas A. (1983) *Miracles & Prophesies in Nineteenth-Century France*. New Brunswick, NJ: Rutgers University Press.

Pelikan, Jaroslav. (1996) *Mary through the Centuries: Her Place in the History of Culture*. New Haven, CT: Yale University Press.

Zimdars-Swartz, Sandra L. (1991) *Encountering Mary: Visions of Mary from LaSalette to Medjugorje*. Princeton, NJ: Princeton University Press.

Film

Millennial structures and themes have been used extensively throughout the history of film as means of narrative resolution. The ways in which it is manifested depend on the nature of the obstacles that are represented as endangering humanity or impeding its social evolution. Because of this, millennialism is most prominently in evidence in those genres that deal with conjectural dangers, particularly horror and science fiction films. Most commonly, these threats are represented as deriving from external sources—galactic disasters, hostile extraterrestrial life or demonic entities—and the solutions to these problems are located in the manifest world. This construction is postmillennial: the possibility of a sudden alteration in the direction of human history is evoked only to endorse the continuation or reduplication of the contemporary or manifest world. However, films that deal with fears of disaster or annihilation deriving from within humanity itself—generally, nuclear devastation, or alternately dangerous social movements or ecological catastrophe—occasionally adopt premillennial modes of discourse. Here, human history is represented as either helplessly declining or heading towards cataclysm, and only some form of radical intervention by an external agency is sufficient to save humanity from its own destructive tendencies.

Postmillennial Structures in Films

Most films employ postmillennial narrative constructions. *The Birth of a Nation* (1915), for example, ends with a vision of Christ and the hope that humanity may escape war to live in the City of Peace; *Metropolis* (1926) concludes with a union between the brains and the hands of society that promises future harmony. Although the contexts in which these visions of future utopia are articulated differ markedly, they could be considered postmillennialist: in both films, the millennial world of peace and happiness is represented as deriving from human efforts to perfect society. They are also postmillennial in regard to the comic way in which they resolve conflict. By the conclusion of each film justice is done, the estranged factions are united through marriages, the normal world is restored, and the teleology of history has ended.

Despite the fact that the millennium is itself a theological concept, the articulation of this kind of resolution in film is usually secular. The Christian eschatological kingdom is rarely depicted and religious elements are generally restricted to the level of allusion. The reluctance to represent a religious millennium is evident in the ambivalent and, in some instances, self-contradictory manner in which horror films based upon the prophecies of the books of Daniel and Revelation have approached the last days. As has been frequently pointed out, the apocalyptic mode embraces both destruction and creation—the end of the known world and the inception of a new and better state of being. While prophetic horror films often represent apocalyptic violence threatening humanity, they characteristically place emphasis upon the threat of annihilation and the protagonists' efforts to avoid it.

The Omen (1976), one of earliest and best-known large-scale treatments of this theme in secular popular film, illustrates many of the primary elements that have typified the genre as it evolved. *The Omen* is about the rise of the Antichrist: it follows his career from his birth from a jackal, through his secret adoption by the American ambassador to Great Britain, to the death of his adoptive parents and his second adoption by the president of the United States. The film ends with the Antichrist still a child but now poised for future world domination. A general sense of helplessness before the forces of evil runs through the film. The film's protagonists work constantly to avert Armageddon, but they do so in order to return to a human history: there is neither hope for a Christian victory over the Antichrist nor desire for the millennium that such an event would inaugurate. Although *The Omen* uses Christian premillennial eschatology as its setting, its story in fact has no real engagement with the themes deriving from that context. It is a narrative of human termination, and the supernaturalism evident is that of a conventional horror film.

Other prophetic horror films that attempt to deal with this subject matter make similar narrative choices. Examples include the three other films constituting the *Omen* series (*Damien—Omen II*, 1978; *The Final Conflict*, 1981; and *Omen IV: The Awakening*, 1991), as well as *Rosemary's Baby* (1968), *Holocaust 2000* (1978), *Prince of Darkness* (1987), and *The Seventh Sign* (1988). In each case, the apocalypse is represented as purely destructive. The protagonists do not aspire to effect an eschatological kingdom, but rather to defeat the forces threatening the contemporary world and so avert its termination. To the limited extent that it exists, the millennium is reconceptualized as a world of purely human potential, and its achievement depends upon humanity's faith in its own essential worthiness. The resulting construction is postmillennial and thoroughly secular.

Postmillennial narrative resolutions also apparent in science fiction films that represent humanity as besieged by dangerous or malevolent external threats. Both *Independence Day* (1996) and *Armageddon* (1998), for example, represent humanity as under attack, from hostile aliens and a large meteor, respectively. In each case, the narratives require the

MILLENNIALISM, THE APOCALYPSE, AND STAR WARS

Woven into George Lucas's *Star Wars,* one of the highest grossing sets of epic science fiction films ever made, are numerous biblical references that adopt and expand on the Book of Revelation. The films introducing new twists and elements that put the Apocalypse, those responsible for it, and those responsible for saving the world from it, in a new and fantastic portrayal.

The films prey on numerous aspects of our own lives on Earth. The two most prominent elements of the films can easily be interpreted as religion and politics. The prominent supernatural feature of 'The Force' is a clear symbol of religion, even to the extent that the Jedi's—a group of believers in The Force—dress in monk-like brown robes. The first *Star Wars* movie, subtitled *A New Hope,* saw both Han Solo (played by Harrison Ford) and Grand Moff Tarkin (played by Peter Cushing) actually refer to The Force as a religion.

The young Darth Vader, Anakin Skywalker, as we see from *Episode 1: The Phantom Menace,* starts off on the side of good, and then turns bad—a fallen angel, much like Satan himself. He is even portrayed as an innocent child just like Damien in the Omen films. His virgin birth introduces an interesting twist to the millennial argument. This suggests that he was intended to be a Christ like figure who was pulled over to the 'dark side'. Jedi Masters in *The Phantom Menace* continually refer to Anakin as 'the chosen one' who was foreseen in prophecies to bring balance to The Force.

The unique father-son linking of Darth Vadar to Luke Skywalker—who eventually becomes the savior—again pulls the second coming and antichrist theories in a different direction. Their same lineage is almost a metaphor that God (The Force) created a powerful figure that went bad (Anakin/Vadar), and so created another (Luke) to reverse the evil that had been done. The Emperor represents the anti-Force in a separate 'religion' or 'cult' known as Sith. While The Emperor initially keeps his existence concealed in a Satan-like manner, revealing himself only to those who will help him gain control, he is forced in *The Phantom Menace* to reveal his first apprentice, or antichrist representative, Darth Maul. Upon learning of Darth Maul's existence and identifying him as a Sith, one of the Jedi Masters exclaims that the Sith have been extinct for a millennium—once again uncovering the significance of the 1,000 year time period.

At the time of Armageddon, the bible indicates that the antichrist will lead a world wide power or organization which will attempt to take over the planet. This is reflected in Darth Vadar, a key figure in the Empire, whose mission is to take over control of the galaxy. He is stopped by his own son, Luke, who was foreseen by Jedi Master Yoda—a character much like an Eastern prophet in his philosophical teachings, and mannerisms.

There is also the cyclical element that a 2000 year cycle effect is in operation. *The Phantom Menace* sees the Jedi's as an influential group in the galaxy, but by *A New Hope* the Jedi's are all but extinct, so Vadar is in an ideal situation to take control.

Mixing religion and politics almost inevitably leads to the events interpreted to surround the year 2000, and when considered alongside key features and characters of the *Star Wars* films, a millennial mirror is clearly recognizable.

Ben Manning

protagonists to use all of their resources and, at times, sacrifice themselves so as to circumvent the threat and assure the continuation of human life. Both also end with marriages and a celebration of human values and institutions. Other films that use cataclysmic threats to reaffirm human continuity include *The War of the Worlds* (1953), *Aliens* (1986), and *Deep Impact* (1998).

Premillennial Structures in Films

While postmillennialism remains the dominant mode of narrative closure, the formation is often subject to critique. Anti-Westerns such as *McCabe and Mrs. Miller* (1971) and *High Plains Drifter* (1973) deconstruct postmillennial narrative fulfillment, indicating ways in which the forms of social resolution typically endorsed are false and hypocritical. Actual premillennialist narrative construction, however, is most in evidence in science fiction films. It is especially prevalent in films dealing with beneficent alien visitation, in which they are represented as intervening in human society either to help it avoid some cataclysm or to assist it in its development.

A classic example of intrusive alien intervention is *The Day the Earth Stood Still* (1951). This film represents the events surrounding an extraterrestrial visitation by a representative of a technologically superior race. Although the alien comes on a mission of peace, he is treated with suspicion and hostility by the military and the general population and is eventually mortally wounded. Upon leaving earth, he announces to humanity that its warlike manner will no longer be tolerated by the other planets of the galaxy and that if it does not curb its destructive tendencies the planet will be destroyed. Through his intervention, the alien forcefully changes human society, ushering in a new era by compelling humanity to master its instinct to fear and aggression. The way in which society's reformation is imagined as taking place is both secular and premillennial.

The immediate occasion of the alien's visitation in *The Day the Earth Stood Still* is the discovery of atomic power, and the film is on one level an allegory about the need for humanity to find new ways of resolving its conflicts if it is to avoid destroying itself. The premillennial structure derives from the sense that current methods are unworkable and something radically new is required. A more subtle reading of this theme appears in *2001: A Space Odyssey* (1968). Here, aliens again compel humanity's evolution, but much less overtly. In the opening segment a large monolith is deposited among a tribe of prehumans; it inspires them to develop tools and, eventually, to achieve a technology capable of space travel. In the film's present a similar monolith is discovered in space and the resulting expedition leads an astronaut to discover a new level of consciousness. The film suggests that just as the impetus to technological discovery led humanity to master the physical environment, a new consciousness is necessary for the continued development of the species: the final sequence is of the astronaut reborn as a large fetus moving toward Earth. The film's allusive narrative structure prevents a definite reading of either the aliens' objectives or of the consequences of the astronaut's rebirth as the Starchild; however, the overriding implication is that humanity is itself reborn in the Starchild, and that it is on the brink of another evolutionary breakthrough.

Both *The Day the Earth Stood Still* and *2001* represent aliens interrupting human history in order to reorient it and save it from itself. In both films too, the aliens perform religious functions. In *The Day the Earth Stood Still*, the alien comes to Earth in order to announce a new covenant between humanity and the universe. The name he chooses—Carpenter—recalls Christ, and he too dies and is resurrected in the course of the film. Although the aliens in *2001* are evident only in the presence of the monoliths, the way in which they interact with humanity, by inspiring and transforming it, mirrors God's redemption of the elect in traditional Christianity. The tendency to conflate the extraterrestrial with the supernatural and technology with divinity becomes more pronounced in films such as *Close Encounters of the Third Kind* (1977) and *E.T.: The Extraterrestrial* (1982). When the aliens are reconceptualized as an essentially divine race, the way in which they are represented as saving humanity is reoriented. Rather than dealing with human history, films of this nature typically describe relationships between aliens and individuals: the aliens offer the characters with whom they interact a sense of meaning or significance, thereby becoming agents of redemption. The messianic influence ascribed to the aliens in these films, however, is essentially restricted to the level of the individual. Although there is occasionally the suggestion that a larger renewal will derive from the visitation, as in *Starman* (1984), the emphasis is primarily upon individual illumination. For this reason this subgenre could be considered amillennialist. The millennial world is depicted as being located in the hearts of the believers—those who have been touched by the alien presence and made new.

Postapocalyptic Films

While most science fiction films place the millennium in the future, there is also a subgenre that locates it in the human past, comprised of films that represent catastrophe and survival in a postapocalyptic world. The basic structure of this type of film is evident in *When Worlds Collide* (1951). This film depicts the destruction of the earth by its collision with a large star system moving through space. There is no attempt to save the world itself: the plot instead centers on a plan to send a spacecraft carrying a small number of colonists to a planet orbiting the star. This plan requires that large numbers of people work so that a select few might be spared to continue the species. The film is dominated by debate as to whether humanity is inherently selfish or if it is capable of disinterested altruism. At the conclusion the colonists flee Earth as those left behind riot and attempt to swamp the ship's launching pad. By escaping the turmoil the colonists metaphorically leave behind all of the selfish and destructive tendencies native to humanity: the ship becomes a metaphorical Noah's ark, carrying the faithful from destruction. The colonists exemplify all that is best and most worth preserving in humanity; the planet on which they land represents an opportunity for them to create an ideal world, free from the selfishness and corruption that marred civilization on earth. Significantly, the narrative is framed by two biblical quotations. The first (Genesis 6:12–13) describes God's punishment of a culture that has become debased. The concluding quotation—"The first day on the new world had begun"—recalls the biblical description of God's creation of the world; it implies that this new planet is the new Garden of Eden for those who have been judged worthy.

The references to Eden in *When Worlds Collide* emphasizes the fact that the imagined millennium here is not the product of a progressive history: it requires returning to an innocence that has been lost. This theme is developed at greater length in science fiction films representing survival in a postholocaust world. In these, the period following devastation is portrayed as an opportunity to return to superseded religious or moral values and older forms of social organization. The postholocaust films generally depict the good and evil tendencies within humanity as polarized in distinct forms of communal organization. The evil community is usually tribal in nature: it is either predicated on the immediate gratification of desire or it represents a hyperbolic continuation of the practices that have led to the holocaust. The good community, on the contrary, commonly reflects a return to traditional values and conservative social structures. A mythic hero appears to defeat the forces threatening the good community and to help it establish its dominance. This scenario has been popularized in the *Mad Max* trilogy (*Mad Max*, 1979; *The Road Warrior*, 1981; and *Mad Max: Beyond Thunderdome*; 1985); it is also evident in close imitations of that series, such as *Stryker* (1983), *America 3000* (1985), and *Hell Comes to Frogtown* (1987); and also in more mainstream productions, such as *Waterworld* (1995).

Although millennialism is most evident in narrative structures as a kind of resolution, it has also been used as a setting from which to explore characters' reactions to the idea of an end to history or of a new eschatological world. This is the case in *The Rapture* (1991), one of the few films that represents the apocalypse from the perspective of literal Christian premillennialism. *The Rapture* follows the experiences of a woman who has a religious experience and joins a millennial sect. When the Second Coming occurs, however, she is unable to accept God because of the pain she has experienced waiting for him. The film concludes with her standing outside of heaven, just beyond the river that washes away all sin, refusing to proceed any further, preferring to remain in the darkness. Because she cannot let herself love God she cannot partake in the new life offered by Him. The idea of the millennium becomes a means of exploring the nature of religious faith and the limits of the human capacity to let go of the past to participate in a new world disconnected from history.

Conclusion

Millennialism offers a means of conceptualizing reality, and its representation in film is largely determined the way in which contemporary society understands itself. When society is viewed as being generally healthy and capable of solving its problems satisfactorily, it is reified through triumphant postmillennial narrative resolution. In times in which it seems to be in decline or in danger of self-destructing, however, premillennial narratives are used to express the need for some kind of dramatic reformation. The nature of the perceived crisis facing society also affects the way in which the millennium is temporally situated. When nuclear war or ecological disaster seems imminent, radical intervention by a superior power is imagined. However, when the ways in which it is developing seem alienating, the millennium is projected backwards, as the recreation of an innocent and uncomplicated past.

James Hewitson

See also Apocalypse, Millennial Myth, Postmillennialism, Premillennialism

Bibliography

Broderick, Mick. (1993) "Heroic Apocalypse: *Mad Max*, Mythology, and the Millennium." In *Crisis Cinema: The Apocalyptic Idea in Postmodern Narrative Film*, edited by Christopher Sharrett. Washington, D.C.: Maisonneuve Press, 251–72.

———. (1993) "Surviving Armageddon: Beyond the Imagination of Disaster." *Science Fiction Studies* 20, 3: 362–82.

———. (1994) "The Rupture of Rapture." *Southern Review* 27, 1: 70–78.

Combs, James. (1993) "Pox-Eclipse Now: The Dystopian Imagination in Contemporary Popular Movies." *Crisis Cinema* 17–35.

Green, Peter. (1987) "Apocalypse and Sacrifice." *Sight and Sound* 56: 111–18.

Hewitson, James. (1999) "Fear of Revelation: Postmillennialism in American Popular Film." In *Fear Itself: Enemies Real and Imagined in American Culture*, edited by Nancy Lusignan Schultz. West Lafayette, IN: Purdue University Press, 430–40.

Nelson, John Wiley. (1982) "The Apocalyptic Vision in American Popular Culture." In *The Apocalyptic Vision in America: Interdisciplinary Essays on Myth and Culture*, edited by Lois Parkinson Zamora. Bowling Green, OH: Bowling Green University Popular Press, 154–82.

Olstwalt, Conrad E., Jr. (1995) "Hollywood and Armageddon: Apocalyptic Themes in Recent Cinematic Presentations."

In *Screening the Sacred: Religion, Myth, and Ideology in Popular American Film*, edited by Joel W. Martin and Conrad E. Ostwalt Jr. Boulder, CO: Westview Press, 55–63.

Ruppersburg, Hugh. (1987) "The Alien Messiah in Recent Science Fiction Films." *The Journal of Popular Film and Television* 14, 4: 158–66.

Sharrett, Christopher. (1993) "The American Apocalypse: Scorcese's *Taxi Driver.*" *Crisis Cinema* 221–36.

Fin de Siècle

The fin de siècle is emblematic of a decadent lifestyle, a movement in literature and art, and thirdly, for the end of the nineteenth century as an epoch. The French phrase *fin de siècle* was originally used as an adjective: *Être fin de siècle* means to be in a mood of decadence, pessimism, and irresponsibility mixed up with a preference for the advanced, modern, and urban way of being. The ideal figure of the fin-de-siècle age, created by authors like Oscar Wilde and Joris-Karl Huysmann, is the dandy or the *décadent,* a civilized person, beyond all measure sensitized to exceptional aesthetic, mental, or physical experiences but without interest in a respectable or healthy lifestyle. On the one hand, the fin de siècle seems to be the secular heir of apocalyptic traditions. On the other hand, the epoch of the fin de siècle coincided with an era of industrial and economic development. Its distrust of the course of progress and bourgeois lifestyle can be considered as the beginning of a pluralistic system of values in the twentieth century.

The fin de siècle traces back into a French debate, which started as early as the mid-1830s, about decadence as an aesthetic ideal of literature. The Décadents aspired to free literature and art from the materialistic preoccupations of industrialized society. By confessing to a life and taste of *décadence* they hoped to open civilization to new experiences. The term fin de siècle was sufficiently vague as a catchword that many different trends were subsumed under its umbrella; though it generally helped to create a theme of pessimism in society.

Nevertheless it is misleading to believe that those who preached fin de siècle in art and literature truly believed that the world was coming to an end. In fact, "many thought of themselves not as nihilists (whatever that meant) but as innovators, giving new impulses to a stagnant culture. There were a few purveyors of apocalyptic messages, but they were the exception" (Laqueur 1996: 6). The actual end or turn of the century had the character of an affirmative celebration of Western civilization. Many balance sheets appeared relating to the past century and the hopes and expectations of contemporaries for the next and an optimistic note struck nearly everywhere.

The metaphor fin de siècle is an unclear term which can be interpreted in a number of ways. In one sense it became a paradigm for the social belief in decline. Some historians see the fin de siècle as a recurring phenomenon at the end of each century, but it is controversial whether this really occurred. Such a recurrence can be questioned because the idea of the "century" had not much impact on society until the eighteenth century. The end of that century was characterized less by pessimism than by the Enlightenment philosophy of progress. Therefore it seems to be useful to distinguish between the original fin de siècle at the end of the nineteenth century and comparable periods in the past and present.

Arndt Brendecke

See also Century, Centennial, Centenarium

Bibliography

Brendecke, Arndt. (1999) "Fin(s) de siècle und kein Ende: Wege und Irrwege der Betrachtung von Jahrhundertwenden." *Historische Zeitschrift* (Munich) 268: 107–20.

Briggs, Asa, and Daniel Snowman, eds. (1996) *Fins de Siècle: How Centuries End, 1400–2000.* New Haven, CT and London: Yale University Press.

Grazia, Margareta de. (1995) "Fin-de-Siècle Renaissance England." In *Fins de Siècle: English Poetry in 1590, 1690, 1790, 1890, 1990,* edited by E. Scarry. London: John Hopkins University Press, 37–63.

Laqueur, Walter. (1996) "Fin de siècle: Once more with Feeling." *Journal of Contemporary History* (London) 31, 1: 5–47.

Milo, Daniel Shabetaï. (1991) *Trahir le temps* (histoire). Paris: Les Belles Lettres.

Schwartz, Hillel. (1996) *Century's End: A Cultural History of the Fin de Siècle from the 990s through the 1990s.* New York: Doubleday.

———. (1996) *Century's End: An Orientation Manual toward the Year 2000.* New York: Doubleday.

Stearns, Peter N. (1996) *Millennium III, Century XXI: A Retrospective on the Future.* Boulder, CO: Westview Press.

Weber, Eugen. (1988) *France, Fin De Siècle.* Cambridge, MA: Belknap Press.

Fragile Millennial Groups

Fragile millennial groups initiate violence due to a combination of stresses internal to the group with the experience of opposition from outside society that endangers the group's ultimate concern, the religious goal which is the most important thing in the world to the members. A fragile millennial group initiates violence in order to preserve its ultimate concern. That violence may be directed inwardly toward group members and dissidents or outwardly toward perceived enemies, or both.

The millennial group's fragility might well be caused by the leader(s). The leader might set impossible goals for the group members to achieve, or the leader may be seriously ill and/or despairing if he or she can create the millennial kingdom as promised to followers.

Fragile millennial group members usually believe that they are being persecuted by opponents in outside society. These opponents may be law enforcement agents, government agents and agencies, news reporters, apostates, concerned family members, and anticultists. The "cultural opposition" (Hall 1995: 205–35) may indeed be present, but the radical dualistic worldview of catastrophic millennial groups, which sees good battling evil and which translates into a sense of "us vs. them," amplifies the magnitude of any degree of opposition in the minds of the believers.

When the members of a fragile millennial group become convinced that they are failing to achieve their ultimate concern, they might resort to violence to preserve their religious goal. They might direct their violence outwardly to kill enemies or inwardly to commit murders and group suicide. Often the violence is directed both outwardly and inwardly.

On 18 November 1978, some residents of Jonestown, Guyana, who were members of Peoples Temple led by Rev. Jim Jones, opened fire on the departing party of Congressman Leo Ryan, who had just concluded an unwelcome visit to Jonestown and was leaving with some longtime Peoples Temple members. This assault killed five people in the party including Congressman Ryan. Then the majority of the Jonestown residents committed "revolutionary suicide." The adults drank Fla-Vor-Aid laced with tranquilizers and cyanide. Children and some adults were injected with the deadly chemical potion. The 918 residents of Jonestown who died included 294 children under age eighteen. The Jonestown mass suicide and murders were prompted by stresses within the community combined with a large amount of pressure from anticultists, concerned relatives, federal agents and agencies, and news reporters. There is documentary evidence that the Jonestown residents discussed the option of group suicide during the previous year and many had concluded that suicide was preferable to the demise of their community. The Jonestown residents resorted to violence to preserve their ultimate concern—maintaining the cohesiveness of their community.

Other fragile millennial groups include the Solar Temple, which involved deaths in Quebec, France, and Switzerland in 1994, 1995, and 1997; Heaven's Gate, thirty-nine of whose members committed group suicide in 1997; and Aum Shinrikyo in Japan, whose members released sarin gas on the Tokyo subway in 1995 as well as committed numerous murders previous to that.

Catherine Wessinger

See also Aum Shinrikyo, Heaven's Gate, People's Temple, Solar Temple

Bibliography

Hall, John R. (1987) *Gone from the Promised Land: Jonestown in American Cultural History.* New Brunswick, NJ: Transaction Books.

——. (1995) "Public Narratives and the Apocalyptic Sect: From Jonestown to Mt. Carmel." In *Armageddon in Waco: Critical Perspectives on the Branch Davidian Conflict,* edited by Stuart A. Wright. Chicago: University of Chicago Press, 205–35.

Hall, John R., and Philip Schuyler. (1997) "The Mystical Apocalypse of the Solar Temple." In *Millennium, Messiahs, and Mayhem: Contemporary Apocalyptic Movements,* edited by Thomas Robbins and Susan J. Palmer. New York: Routledge, 285–311.

Introvigne, Massimo. (1995) "Ordeal by Fire: The Tragedy of the Solar Temple." *Religion* 25: 267–83.

Maaga, Mary McCormick. (1998) *Hearing the Voices of Jonestown: Putting a Human Face on an American Tragedy.* Syracuse, NY: Syracuse University Press.

Reader, Ian. (1996) *A Poisonous Cocktail? Aum Shinrikyo's Path to Violence.* Copenhagen: Nordic Institute of Asian Studies Books.

Robbins, Thomas, and Dick Anthony. (1995) "Sects and Violence: Factors Enhancing the Volatility of Marginal Religious Movements." In *Armageddon in Waco: Critical Perspectives on the Branch Davidian Conflict,* edited by Stuart A. Wright. Chicago: University of Chicago Press, 236–59.

Wessinger, Catherine. (2000) *How the Millennium Comes Violently.* Chappaqua, NY: Seven Bridges Press.

——, ed. (2000) *Millennialism, Persecution, and Violence: Historical Cases.* Syracuse, NY: Syracuse University Press.

Free Spirit

At the height of heretical accusation by the Catholic Church in the thirteenth and fourteenth centuries, the Brethren of the Free Spirit emerged as perhaps the most antinomian group of the High Middle Ages. They are, in the course of history, one of the most obvious, yet unnoticed millennial groups of the past two thousand years. Their followers did not fit any schema; there were the rich and the poor, men, women, and children. They believed in their equality with Christ, yet in a desire to achieve eternal salvation, followed the *vita apostolica* (apostolic life). While the papacy did not call a crusade against them, as they did against the well-known Cathars in the early thirteenth century, and while they were not as popular as the aforementioned group, the Free Spirit were a blatant threat to the papacy and to Western Latin theology.

Located in the areas of northern France, Germany, and Belgium, the Free Spirit established themselves as an off-shoot of a group of not-ordained friars, the Beghards (males) and Beguines (females). They were not an organized sect of heretics; instead they were pockets of Christian worshippers who shared common beliefs. They saw no reason for worshipping saints, for fasting, for prayer, for confession, yet they followed a life established by the Ten Commandments and the Gospels, and they believed themselves to be guided by the Holy Spirit.

Meister Eckhart, recognized as the "father" of the Free Spirits conveys that "a humble man does not need to ask God: he can command God. . . . If that man were in hell, God would have to come to hell, and hell would have to become the kingdom of heaven" (Kiekhefer 1979: 39). Furthermore, he states, "Why did God become man? So that I might be born to be God—yes—identically to God" (Eckhart 1941: 194). Records show that during mass, some Free Spirits would engage in certain promiscuous activities, not at all becoming of a good Christian. Some believed it better to have these sexual encounters with their mothers or sisters rather than with women outside of their family.

The decree *Ad Nostrum* at the Council of Vienna in 1311 established some of the essential Free Spirit beliefs: human beings can attain a degree of perfection to render themselves sinless, therefore allowing them to do as they wish; these perfect beings are not subject to human obedience, for the spirit of the Lord is their liberty; they can attain perfection in the earthly life, just as in the life to come; perfect souls do not need to practice acts of virtue; the members of the sect should not show reverence when the body of Christ is raised at the alter, for it would mark imperfection in them.

While their belief in perfection on earth as in heaven signifies that they did not necessarily believe in an imminent eschatological time, their words prove undoubtedly that their main concern in life was indeed, like all millennial groups, salvation. The idea that they could live on earth as in heaven only discloses a degree of patience, while still maintaining a desire for deliverance. For them, the need to achieve equality to God differed from most other Christians of the age who felt that piety was the way to God; Free Spirits were self-involved, living a strict asceticism, in a sense allowing them to live by their own rules, not those of the church or state. Their close relationship to Christ, and in fact, their equality to Him, allowed them this autonomy. Free Spirits could do no wrong, because Christ could do no wrong.

The Curia, and many important men associated with the church were acutely afraid of this unorganized sect, not only because of the heretical words they spoke, but because they were both questioning the authority of the church hierarchy, and they were, Rome felt, promoting a sort of anarchy. Mystic Jan van Ruysbroek called the Free Spirits the forerunners of the Antichrist. "They bear divine action and do nothing themselves, for it is God who acts when they act. Incapable of sinning, since God acts, while they are completely passive, they accomplish what God desires and nothing else. With no activity, these men have completely abandoned their inner life and want to live without choice" (Vaneigem 1986, 148).

Throughout the fourteenth century, the papacy generated several inquisitions against these beghards and beguines who had dwelled in Free Spirit ideology; they often allied with the monarchy to repel these heretics, as seen in the joint efforts of Pope Urban V and Charles IV in the late 1360s. Perhaps the best-known Free Spirit, Marguerite Porete, fell victim to one of these papal inquisitions. Porete was a mystic and Free Spirit, whose work *Mirror of Simple Souls*, was not only deemed heretical, but specifically elicited Free Spirit ideas. Her books were burned throughout Europe and in the first decade of the fourteenth century she was burned at the stake.

Today, we are all still familiar with the term "free spirit." It is used in the same connotation as it was six centuries ago: those who feel that they do not have to live by the same laws as everybody else; they are above the law and thus do what they want.

Jason Ardizzone

See also Women

Bibliography

Cohn, Norman. "Medieval Millenarism: Its Bearing on The Comparative Study of Millenarian Movements." In *Millennial Dreams in Action: Studies in Revolutionary Religious Movements*, edited by Sylvia L. Thrupp. New York: Schoken Books, 31–43.

Eckhart, Meister. (1941) *A Modern Translation.* Translated by Raymond Bernard Blankney. New York: Harper & Brothers.

———. (1980) *Breakthrough, Meister Eckhart's Creation Spirituality, in New Translation*, introduction and commentaries by Matthew Fox. Garden City, NY: Doubleday.

——. (1990) *Meister Eckhart: Sermons and Treatises*, translated and edited by M. O'C. Walshe. Shaftesbury, Dorset, U.K.: Element Books.

Kaminsky, Howard. (1970) "The Free Spirit in the Hussite Revolution." In *Millennial Dreams in Action: Studies in Revolutionary Religious Movements*, edited by Sylvia L. Thrupp. New York: Schoken Books, 166–86.

Kieckhefer, Richard. (1979) *Repression of Heresy in Medieval Germany*. Philadelphia: University of Pennsylvania Press.

Lerner, Robert. (1972) *The Heresy of the Free Spirit*. Berkeley: University of California Press.

Porete, Marguerite. (1993) *The Mirror of Simple Souls*, translated by Ellen L. Babinsky. New York: Paulist Press.

Vaneigem, Raoul. (1986) *Le Mouvement du Libre-Esprit: Généralités et Témoignages sur les Affleurements de la vie à la surface du Moyen âge, de la Renaissance et, incidemment, de Notre époque*. Paris: Ramsey.

Fundamentalism

Fundamentalism is the general term applied to a Protestant Christian tradition especially widespread in the United States. Its tenets include a conversion experience, an infallible Bible, conservative social values, affirmation of ancient Christian beliefs (e.g., the Virgin Birth), and a salvation history which stresses Christ's imminent return in judgment and a millennium. It is evangelistic and proselytizes aggressively. While some specific denominations are avowedly Fundamentalist, its influence is felt within a broad spectrum of Protestantism. During the twentieth century, Fundamentalism was a cause of sharp, even bitter, disagreement among Christians and with non-Christians. At the end of that century its social and political influence was greater than ever.

The term "Fundamentalism" came into general use around the First World War, and was derived from a series of essays, collectively entitled *The Fundamentals*, which defended conservative Protestant belief. The essays alleged that contemporary Christianity had abandoned sound theology in favor of overinvolvement with social issues and had neglected personal piety, and that modern science was corroding the authority of scripture. A few years later (1924), the Scopes "Monkey Trial" in Dayton, Tennessee, prompted the perception of Fundamentalism as a reaction by the poorly educated to modern scientific and industrial civilization. Such an interpretation is still advanced by well-informed historians of religion. Fundamentalism can, however, also be regarded as the continuation of certain themes of the Protestant Reformation.

The Religious Roots of Fundamentalism

The Reformation-era doctrine of *sola scriptura* dispensed with tradition and natural law (long staples of Catholic theology) and established the Bible as the sole guide to salvation. Reformation pietism allowed believers to seek a direct relationship with God through personal experience of grace. Eschatology flourished as well, especially in seventeenth-century England, where interest in biblical prophecy was intense. This interest in the Second Advent and millennium led, in turn, to an intense fascination with the Jews and their return to the Holy Land in fulfillment of prophecy.

The affinity of these elements of Reformation thought with Fundamentalism suggests historical continuity. The Fundamentalist infallible Bible is spiritual kin to *sola scriptura*. The pietism of the early Reformation is echoed in Fundamentalist emphasis on a "personal relationship" to Jesus. Not only is Fundamentalist premillennial eschatology akin to the millenarian speculation of the English Reformation, but a direct historical linkage can be demonstrated. Finally, the philo-Semitism of the English Reformation is altogether similar to the Protestant Zionism of today's Fundamentalism.

Religious life in America during the colonial and Revolutionary eras drew on the foundational Protestant doctrines described above. A cycle of religious revivals (e.g., the Great Awakening of the mid-eighteenth century) encouraged a pietistic conversion experience, often very emotional in nature. Revivals also weakened the influence of the educated clergy and reinforced an already strong tradition of private Bible interpretation based on a literal understanding of its language. Finally, the revivals stimulated eschatological thinking, a tendency vastly reinforced by events of the Revolutionary era—many of which were taken as a fulfillment of prophecy.

American Fundamentalism

Still, it was not until the early nineteenth century that these several biases inherited from the Reformation began to interact with developments in the larger intellectual world of the West to form the nucleus of what became Fundamentalism. The catalyst was intense English millenarianism, quickly taken up in America. The French Revolution so startled English observers that many regarded it as fulfillment of prophecy which foretold the imminent return of Christ. Some further predicted that the Second Advent would precede an earthly millennium (Revelation 20), and their belief was quickly labeled "premillennialism."

The millenarian revival occurred, fortuitously, practically simultaneously with two monumental achievements in Western thought. First, European scholarship established the Bible as an historical book like any other (the historical-critical method), subject to criticism and thus not necessarily infallible. The other achievement was a magnificent advance in scientific thought, geology especially, which contradicted the Mosaic account of Creation. (Eventually, the evolutionary theories of Charles Darwin intensified this scientific challenge to an inerrant Bible.) Taken together, these intellectual achievements made it inevitable that Protestants would have to rethink whether the Bible could be regarded as an infallible guide in matters of theology and cosmology. Such a rethinking was anathema to Americans devoted to premillennial eschatology.

The Development of Fundamentalist Doctrines in the Early Nineteenth Century

Premillennialism rested on a "literal" interpretation of biblical language (the prophecies.) Such an approach was difficult, possibly impossible, if the Bible was regarded as prone to error. While many in the larger religious community began slowly to adjust to the new ways of thinking, millenarians regarded themselves as beleaguered guardians of the historic primacy of the Bible in Protestant thought. Confrontation with the new learning was thus all but inevitable. There were, as well, theological and sociological distinctions which gradually led millenarian Protestants to feel themselves a distinct group. Some of these were rooted in their frequent loyalty to a now-fading Calvinism. There was a clear affinity between the predestinarian theology of Calvinism (which foreordained the fate of the soul) and prophecy (which foreordained the fate of the world.) As a further corollary of this affinity, the millenarian-Calvinist camp was generally politically and socially conservative. Social reformation was repugnant both to Calvinism (which stressed innate depravity) and millenarian eschatology (which predicted a steady corruption of the world until the Second Coming).

Millenarian insistence on an infallible Bible was soon noted by contemporary observers, one of who wrote in 1853: "The central law of interpretation, by which millenarians profess always to be guided is that of giving the literal sense. They call themselves literalists." On the other hand, in 1843 the *American Millenarian and Prophetic Review* denounced historical-critical scholars who wished to "cast dust into the eyes of sober, reflecting, and discerning common sense reader[s] of the Bible." The bitter controversy over Biblical infallibility, so much a part of twentieth-century Fundamentalism, was thus joined very early on. Millenarian literalism also led many to denounce science for questioning the account of Creation given in Genesis. One premillennialist warned in 1856, "If the geological theory is true the Mosaic history is not." If the Bible could be considered misleading in matters of cosmology, then where was there warrant to accept its prophecies any more "literally?" The evolutionary theories of Charles Darwin were attacked for the same reason.

Dwight L. Moody with students c. 1890. MOODY BIBLE INSTITUTE, CHICAGO, IL.

Philo-Semitism, common in American Protestantism during the half-century prior to the Civil War, was taken up by millenarians with especial vehemence. While nearly all Protestants hoped the Jews would be Christianized, premillennial eschatology was nearly obsessed by the "Children of Israel," and not only prayed for their conversion but advocated their "restoration" to the Holy Land and the reestablishment of a Jewish state of Israel. In this, they revivified in America a centuries-old tradition from the English Reformation.

By 1850, at the latest, essential elements of what later generations called Fundamentalism were in place: biblical literalism, social conservatism, philo-Semitism, hostility toward science, and—especially—a virulent eschatology with certain affinities to Calvinism. Taken together, these formed a system which increasingly separated out from that Protestantism which was socially progressive and felt unthreatened by either science or modern biblical scholarship.

The Spread of Fundamentalist Doctrines in the Late Nineteenth Century

The post–Civil War decades of the nineteenth century saw the gradual working out of an eschatologically based theology. A well-attended series of prophecy conferences, held in New York City and Ontario, enabled like-minded individuals to meet and exchange opinions. Meanwhile, at Princeton Seminary, prominent theologians, though not necessarily comfortable with premillennialism, were nevertheless its tacit allies in defense of an infallible Bible. It was during these decades as well that the dispensationalist interpretation of sacred history, made popular in England by John Nelson Darby, founder of the Plymouth Brethren, was increasingly taken up in America. Dispensationalism divided history into periods during which God dealt differently with mankind. A coming millennium, foretold in prophecy, was said to constitute a final dispensation.

Within American Protestantism, it was the Presbyterians and Dutch Reformed who were most supportive of an emerging premillennial/Fundamentalist Christianity. In view of the affinity between premillennialism and Calvinism, mentioned above, this is not surprising (both denominations were then still strongly Calvinist). An enormous coup was made for millenarianism when Dwight L. Moody, the famed evangelist, joined its camp late in the nineteenth century. He was but one in a long line of nationally famous preachers to do so, down to the present (and which includes the Rev. Billy Graham).

Dissatisfaction among premillennialist Christians toward their liberal counterparts over social policy grew steadily during the last decades of the nineteenth century. It was the period of the Social Gospel, an interdenominational movement that hoped to alleviate the ills attendant on industrialism and urbanization. On the whole, this movement was bypassed by premillennialist Christians, who sought to save individuals only and regarded society at large as a lost cause. Their eschatology foretold not social reform and renovation but, rather, deepening sin and trial, to be cast out only by the Second Advent. This attitude enraged liberal critics, one of whom wrote in 1882 that "Millenarianism, teaching the inevitable failure of all efforts to reform and renovate society, deadens the interest in human affairs, [and] trains the Christian to disgust with life." Suspicion between the socially and politically conservative millenarians and other Protestants thus only deepened as the twentieth century dawned.

Fundamentalist Crises and Renewal in the Twentieth Century

By the early twentieth century, then, a number of significant differences separated millenarian Christians from those who seemed more at ease with contemporary social and scientific life. Ultimately, these differences were grounded in precepts traceable to the Reformation or, rather, what was regarded by some as an abandonment of these precepts by more liberal Protestants. At issue were the authority of the Bible, the validity of much scientific thought, and whether Christians should labor for social renewal or content themselves with the salvation of individual souls. Underlying all these disagreements were disparate versions of salvation history. For those guided by prophecy, history was about to culminate in a series of dreadful trials, from which the faithful would emerge triumphant solely through the return of Christ in Glory. Still influenced by their Calvinist heritage, and finding God through an intensely personal experience (conversion) reminiscent of Reformation pietism, millenarians were deeply suspicious of those they felt too at ease with the modern world. And, that suspicion was returned.

Suspicion exploded into open hostility after the First World War. The 1924 Scopes "Monkey Trial" did not itself provoke the schism within Protestantism, but nevertheless became notorious as a symbol of the division. The trial stunned and humiliated Fundamentalists (a label in general use, by then) who were unprepared for the ridicule and hostility directed at their faith by the national press. At the same time, liberal Protestants, led by the Rev. Harry Emerson Fosdick, denounced Fundamentalism from the pulpit. The academic world, exemplified by respected scholars such as Columbia University's Richard Hofstader, who labeled Fundamentalism "The Revolt Against Modernity," stigmatized it as an unthinking and shallow-rooted response by fearful and insecure yokels to modern life. The hostility of the intellectuals was, in part, well earned by Fundamentalists, who were often intemperate in their attacks on readily verifiable science or toward changes in mores, often minor, of which they disapproved. At the same time, critics of Fundamentalism dismissed its deep roots in Protestant culture and returned its contempt, along with a leaven of condescension, in a manner which veered toward religious intolerance.

Overwhelmed by the ferocity of these attacks, Fundamentalists kept a low public profile for a generation after the trial and some observers regarded the movement itself as anachronistic and destined to wither. What occurred, instead, was a steady, if little noted, broadening of the conservative Protestant spectrum to include vital new beliefs. The new Pentecostal churches enjoyed especially phenomenal growth throughout the interwar and post-World War II periods. Pentecostalism, which stresses the immediate and visible affect of the Holy Spirit in worship, grew out of a remarkable series of California revivals just before the First World War. Although Fundamentalism and Pentecostalism are separate historical traditions, they are frequently (and with some justice) conflated in the public mind because of their shared devotion to an infallible Bible and intense pietism. Charismatic Christian churches, akin in many ways to Pentecostalism, grew rapidly during the same period as well. Both Pentecostalism and the Charismatic movement proselytized new immigrants to the United States (Hispanics, especially) with great success.

The Fundamentalist-Pentecostal-Charismatic melange of Protestantism enjoyed stupendous growth during the second half of the twentieth century. The World Wide Church of God, which is Pentecostal and which scarcely existed prior to World War II, claimed an international membership of several million in the 1990s. This remarkable growth was not matched by the mainline Protestant denominations, several of which (the Presbyterian Church USA, the Disciples of Christ, the Episcopal Church, and the United Church of Christ, among them) showed precipitous declines in membership. Public awareness of Fundamentalist strength was heightened by a remarkable, sometimes controversial, series of preachers who utilized television skillfully and conducted large-scale revivals. Rev. Billy Graham was the most widely known of these.

Fundamentalism seemed especially prominent in public life toward the end of the twentieth century because of its unlooked for involvement in the nation's political life. Fundamentalist distrust of social involvement, rooted in long traditions of millenarian eschatology and personal piety, prompted believers to shun political reform and, instead, pursue individual conversions or await the resolution of all ills at the Second Advent. This changed dramatically during the 1970s when a number of judicial and legislative acts; particularly *Roe v. Wade* on abortion, aroused a formerly somewhat apolitical constituency to seek redress. In the popular mind, and with some cause, Fundamentalism became associated with the so-called Religious Right, and by the end of the century religion was a major factor in national politics. This was especially true in southern states, where Fundamentalism was particularly strong.

Fundamentalism in the Twenty-First Century

It is open to question whether the term Fundamentalism is a useful one for the twenty-first century. There is no clear definition of what it means and it has become a catch-all label for any religious activity toward that end of the Protestant spectrum which is traditional in theology or conservative in politics. It has even been appropriated to describe non-Western, non-Christian beliefs, such as "Islamic Fundamentalism." Frequently, little or no attention is paid to the actual historical background of millennial eschatology, which reaches back in time to the seventeenth century and is the theme around which the several "Fundamentalist" traditions have grown. The presentism of much popular discussion of these traditions, especially since they actively involved themselves in political life, often reverts to older historical analysis which labeled them as reactionary, shallow-rooted, or a refuge of disturbed personalities.

Millennial eschatology was, however, an integral part of the English Reformation and survived and prospered in America. It provided, and still does provide, an interpretive framework of history, both secular and sacred. The near-complete reliance on the Bible as a spiritual guide is another legacy from the Reformation, one substantially reinforced by the literalist interpretation of prophecy in which millenarianism is grounded. Similarly, much of the conservative social attitude of Fundamentalist traditions is traceable to the early-nineteenth century premillennial skepticism of social amelioration, absent Christ's return. Its deep historical roots and flourishing present indicate a vigorous future for Fundamentalism.

Robert K. Whalen

See also Pentecostalism

Bibliography

Boyer, Paul. (1992) *When Time Shall Be No More.* Cambridge, MA: Harvard University Press.

Hatch, Nathan O., and Mark A. Noll, eds. (1982) *The Bible In America.* New York: Oxford University Press.

Marsden, George M. (1980) *Fundamentalism and American Culture.* New York: Oxford University Press.

Sandeen, Ernest R. (1970) *The Roots of Fundamentalism.* Chicago: University of Chicago Press.

Ghost Dance

The Ghost Dance was the largest and most important of a number of revitalization movements that took place among Native North American in the nineteenth century. As with other Native American revitalization movements, the Ghost Dance developed and spread as a response to the catastrophic changes that followed European settlement of the continent. For adherents of the Ghost Dance in the Western Plains, the most devastating of these changes were their humiliating defeat at the hands of the American army, their confinement on reservations, and, in some ways most important of all, the extinction of the bison. For the Plains Indians the Ghost Dance movement was a hope of central importance and the means by which they attempted to change the existing social order so as to improve their lives. Those who sought divine intervention through participation in the Ghost Dance believed that the traditional Indian way of life would be revived, the herds of bison would return, dead ancestors would return to earth, and that the white settlers and soldiers would disappear.

There were two Ghost Dance movements. The first took place in 1870 and involved Indian groups in the western United States. The second, based on the earlier Ghost Dance, began in 1888 and reached its height in 1890 among Indian groups of the northern plains. Both were classic revitalization movements in that they were led by an individual who was believed by his followers to be a prophet or messiah, they relied on divine intervention to create a better world, they were based on the hope of a return to the traditional way of life, and they began as a response to political and economic oppression. The movements were relatively short-lived, and neither produced the desired goal of a return to the traditional way of life and the end of white dominance. The 1890 movement was, however, of considerable significance because of its role in subsequent Indian-white relations. As one of the first pan-tribal movements, the Ghost Dance of 1890 was a precursor to the pan-tribal American Indian Movement some seventy years later, a movement which remained a major force in the Indian rights movement. In addition, the government repression of the Ghost Dance movement and the massacre at Wounded Knee became both a rallying cry for Indian rights and a powerful symbol of the white slaughter of Indians and the destruction of Indian culture.

The 1870 Ghost Dance

The prophet of the 1870 Ghost Dance was Wodziwob (1844–1918?), a Northern Paiute who lived on or near the Walker Lake Reservation in Nevada. The region had come under white control and had—in part because of the gold rush of 1849—been overrun by settlers, miners, and ranchers. Many Indian groups of the region, who had been nomadic hunters and gatherers, had been killed in massacres and by diseases. Those who survived lived in poverty on reservations or in small villages created by whites. In 1870 Wodziwob, a religious healer, went into a trance and had an out-of-body experience. He was transported to another world, where he received messages of a better world to come for the Indians. Upon his return to earth, he reported that soon the dead would return to join the living, game would again be plentiful, and people would be able to live the traditional Indian life. To bring about this change, he said, Indians must dance the round dance at night in the dark in order to communicate their wishes to the other world and to call the ghosts of their ancestors. Indians in a number of Western tribes participated in the dances for several years before the movement disappeared.

The 1890 Ghost Dance

The prophet of the 1890 Ghost Dance was Wovoka (1856–1932), a Paiute in Nevada who had been trained as a religious healer by his father, Tavibo. Tavibo had been a follower of Wodziwob, and historians believe that he told his son about the dance. It is also possible that Wovoka himself participated in the early Ghost Dance. In addition to his father's religious instruction, Wovoka was influenced by the Puget Sound Indian Shaker religion and by Mormonism and Presbyterianism. His contact with non-Indian religions came through frequent contact with white settlers for whom he worked as a ranch hand. Whites in the region knew him as Jack Wilson, a name given to him by the Wilson family with whom he lived as a boy and for whom he worked as an adult.

Wovoka's role as the Prophet of the Ghost Dance began in 1888, when he received revelations from the other world concerning a transformation of Indian society and a return to traditional ways. In January 1989, while ill and during a solar eclipse, he went into a trance and experienced an out-of-body experience, which he described in detail for Bureau of Indian Affairs researcher James Mooney two years later: "When the sun dies, I went up to heaven and saw God and all the people who had died a long time ago. God told me to come back and tell my people that they must be good and love one another, and not fight, or steal, or lie. He gave me this dance to give to my people." Upon his return, Wovoka began preaching the necessity and benefits of the Ghost Dance:

> All Indians must dance, everywhere keep on dancing. Pretty soon in next spring Great Spirit Come. He bring back all game of every kind. The game be thick everywhere. All dead Indians come back and live again. They all be strong like young men, be young again. Old blind Indian see again and get young and have fine time. When Great Spirit comes this way, then all the Indians go the mountains, high up away from whites. Whites can't hurt Indians then. Then while Indians way high up, big flood comes like water and all white people die, get drowned. After that, water go away and then nobody but Indians everywhere and game all kinds thick. Then medicine man tell Indians to send word to all Indians to keep up dancing and the good time will come. Indians who don't dance, who don't believe in this word, will grow little, just about a foot high, and stay that way. Some of them will be turned into wood and be burned in fire. (Brown 1991: 416)

Initially, his followers were from tribes in northern California, Oregon, Washington, and Montana who were being pushed off their land by white ranchers, miners, and farmers. It is likely that these Indians actually heard a message somewhat less antiwhite than the one above, one that foresaw a world of peaceful coexistence rather than one devoid of all whites. It is also likely that Wovoka revised this message when whites were listening to one that claimed this new world would be found in the other world, not on earth.

As word spread east, the message of a return to the better times through the Ghost Dance had special appeal for the Indians of the Plains including the Lakota, Caddo, Arapaho, Cheyenne, and Kiowa. These groups were on the verge of cultural extinction. The herds of bison which provided meat,

WOUNDED KNEE II

Wounded Knee II or the Wounded Knee Takeover began in 27 February 1973 and ended on 8 May 1973. On 27 February, about 200 Indians–mostly Lakota, led by several non-Lakota American Indian Movement (AIM) activists–took over Sacred Heart Catholic Church, a trading post, and museum near the mass grave at Wounded Knee on the Pound Ridge Sioux Reservation in South Dakota. As with the Ghost Dance that ended in the Massacre 83 years earlier, the takeover was an act of resistance to white management of Indian affairs and more particularly to the mistreatment of Indians in South Dakota. The takeover was also the result of a power struggle on the reservation between the tribal leadership which advocated cooperation with whites and "traditionalists" who advocated Indian control of Indian affairs, a position supported by the AIM.

Government response to the takeover was similar to the government response to the Ghost Dancers in 1890. Although no more than 200 Indians ever occupied the site–some 2,000 participated but only 200 occupied the site at any given time–the U.S. government placed over 200 FBI agents, Bureau of Indian Affairs police, and U.S. marshals at the scene. In a further parallel, the Indians had only a few dozen rifles while the U.S. force had machine guns, armed personnel carriers, and even helicopters. Using sophisticated weapons and technology, the government sought to seal off the occupied land. Nonetheless, the Lakota knew the land well and the Indians and their supporters were able to bring in food and medical supplies; though often cold and hungry, they were able to withstand the government siege.

The standoff and negotiations were tense and disrupted by sniper fire which claimed two Indians and two FBI agents. The takeover ended after 71 days when the parties agreed to a "peace pact" which was to bring a government review of Indian treaties and conditions on the reservation. Indians believe that the government never made good on these promises and a number of Indian leaders were prosecuted for the murder of the FBI agents. One, Leonard Peltier (b. 1944), an Ojibwa, was convicted and is serving two life sentences. Although Wounded Knee produced few immediate benefits for the Indians, it did call attention to the plight of Indians in America and let the government know that Indians would fight for their rights.

David Levinson

hides for clothing and tipis, and bone for tools had been killed off by the whites settlers. The starving and disorganized tribes had been finally defeated by U.S. forces and driven from their lands onto reservations. The plight of the Lakota (Sioux) of the northern Plains was among the worst reported by Indian Commissioner Morgan:

> Prior to the agreement of 1876 buffalo and deer were the main support of the Sioux. . . . Within eight years from the agreement of 1876 the buffalo had gone and the Sioux had left to them alkali land and government rations. It is hard to overestimate the magnitude of the calamity . . . to these people. . . . Suddenly, almost without warning, they were expected at once and without previous training to settle down to the pursuits of agriculture in a land largely unfitted for such use. The freedom of the chase was to be exchanged for the idleness of the camp. The boundless range was to be abandoned for the circumscribed and restless, even turbulent and violent. (Mooney 1965: 829)

Wovoka's message had great appeal for the Lakota, whose plight and desires were eloquently stated by one of their leaders, Sitting Bull:

> If a man loses everything and goes back and looks carefully for it he will find it, and that is what the Indians are doing now when they ask you to give them the things that were promised them in the past; and I do not consider that they should be treated like beasts, and that is the reason I have grown up with the feelings I have. . . . I feel that my country has gotten a bad name, and I want it to have a good name; it used to have a good name; and I sit sometimes and wonder who it is that has given it a bad name. (Brown 1991: 415)

Representatives of the Lakota and of other groups traveled to Nevada to hear Wovoka's message and returned with one that fit their dire circumstances: one that hailed Wovoka as a Messiah—a notion he may have actually encouraged—and predicted the return of Indian rule:

> My brothers, I bring to you the promise of a day in which there will be not white man to lay his hand on the bridle of the Indian's horse; when the red men of the prairie will rule the world and not be turned from the hunting grounds by any man. I bring you word from your fathers the ghosts, that they are now marching to join you, led by the Messiah who came once to live on earth with the white men, but was cast out and killed by them. I have seen the wonders of the spirit land, and have talked with the ghosts. I traveled far and am sent back with a message to tell you to make ready for the coming of the Messiah and return of the ghosts in the spring. (Champagne 1994: 510)

In all, some thirty-five Indian groups across the United States took up the Ghost Dance, with the most fervent believers among the Lakota and other groups in the northern Plains. They began gathering in the hundreds and then the thousands. They danced the round dance during the summer and fall of 1880. The round dance—whose origin was among Indians in the West—was performed by men and women in a circle. The participants held hands and shuffled side-to-side as they sang in praise of the Great Spirit above and asked for his help. The dance was performed by hundreds of men and women over four or five nights. Although exhausting, participants were allowed to rest and they did not have visions or faint from exhaustion. The Lakota added new elements to the dance, most importantly, the wearing of white cotton "Ghost Shirts" to protect them from white bullets. Lakota leaders saw the movement as political as well as religious and discussed the use of violence to escape from the reservation and to end white rule.

The gathering of thousands of Indians at some of the Ghost Dances, the continual dancing and singing, the donning of the ghost shirts for protection, and the rumors of armed revolt alarmed white settlers. Most abandoned their farms and ranches and sought protection in the towns. The U.S. government—seeking to end any possibility of Indian resistance—responded by claiming that Sitting Bull, the most prominent Indian leader and a symbol of Indian resistance, was the leader of the Ghost Dance movement. Fully half the troops in the entire U.S. army were assigned to the region to maintain order and protect settlers. Although the Indians did discuss violent resistance, the actual threat they posed to local whites was minimal. The whites outnumbered them ten to one, outgunned them by an even larger margin, and white agents controlled the Indian food supply, which had recently been cut in half to force the Indians to accept onerous treaties.

The Wounded Knee Massacre

The final and tragic result of white fear and huge military presence in the region was the Wounded Knee Massacre, which occurred on 29 December 1890. Precipitating the massacre was the arrest and murder of Sitting Bull, by U.S. soldiers, at his home on 15 December. Other Lakota who been participants in the ongoing Ghost Dance feared for their own safety and fled north. Pursued by the cavalry, about 400 Indians were captured and forced to raise their tipis along the Wounded Knee Creek on 28 December. About 100 men were placed in one camp and about 250 women and children in another camp. The camps were guarded by a detachment of 500 troops and scouts, with four Hotchkiss canons, each firing 50 two-pound shells a minute, aimed at the men's camp. After a night of drunken celebration, the troops entered the camps to search for and confiscate weapons. The troops were rough and cruel. Women were mistreated and forced to expose themselves, men strip-searched, tipis ransacked, and property confiscated. At some point, an Indian and a soldier fought over a rifle. When it discharged, both sides began to fire, although the Indians had only a few rifles. Within minutes over 300 Indians lay dead, including nearly all the men and most of the women and children, who were of course unarmed. Women and children were blown apart by the Hotchkiss shells and those who fled were shot in the back. When the firing ended, Indian bodies were strewn across the plains for three miles around the camps. On New Year's Day frozen bodies were gathered up, piled on wagons and buried. Some 146 bodies were dumped in a mass grave, but only after the bodies were stripped of their ghost shirts as souvenirs for the soldiers.

The detachment commander Colonel Forsythe was later cleared of wrong-doing in the assault and three of his officers and fifteen enlisted men were awarded the Medal of Honor for their "valor" in the battle. The Massacre at Wounded Knee was the last major engagement of the Indian wars in the West and also the last major massacre of Indians. It also marked the end of the Ghost Dance as a major movement, as the government quickly banned all new forms of Indian religious expression. The Ghost Dance was performed into the 1950s by some groups, but not as a revitalization movement.

Native Americans have not forgotten the massacre. The Lakota have asked for but have not received an apology from the U.S. government and in 1973 the site was the locale of another uprising. On 29 Dec 1990 about 400 people gathered at the mass grave to mark the centennial of the massacre. For Native Americans the Massacre remains a vivid reminder of white oppression and Indian resistance.

David Levinson

See also Nativist Millennial Movements

Bibliography

Brown, Dee. (1991) *Bury My Heart at Wounded Knee: An Indian History of the American West.* New York: Henry Holt.

Champagne, Dwayne, ed. (1994) *Chronology of Native North American History.* Detroit: Gale Research.

Hittman, Michael (1990) *Wovoka and the Ghost Dance: A Sourcebook.* Carson City, NV: Grace Dabgberg.

Laubin, Reginald, and Gladys Laubin. (1971) *Indian Dances of North America.* Norman, OK: University of Oklahoma Press.

Lazarus, Edward. (1991) *Black Hills White Justice: The Sioux Nation versus the United States 1775 to the Present.* New York: Harper Collins.

Lyman, Stanley D. (1991) *Wounded Knee 1973.* Lincoln, NE: University of Nebraska Press.

Matthiessen, Peter. (1983) *In the Spirit of Crazy Horse.* New York: Viking.

Mooney, James. ([1896] 1965) *The Ghost Dance Religion and Sioux Outbreak of 1890.* Washington, D.C.: Government Printing Office; reprint, Chicago: University of Chicago Press.

The Great Peace of Deganaweda and Hiawatha

The story of the Great Peace explains the union of the original five nations of the Hodenoshone, or the Iroquois Confederacy, which became North America's first democracy. The Iroquois League, which is now called the Six Nations, unites the Cayuga, Oneida, Onondaga, Mohawk, Seneca peoples, as well as the Tuscarora people who joined in 1724. Their homelands stretch around the eastern Great Lake region from New York and on into Canada. The Great Peace was forged in the 1400s through the efforts of the prophet Deganaweda, a Wyandot (Huron), and his spokesperson, Hiawatha (also spelled Hiyenwatha) of the Onondaga. (Hiawatha is not to be confused with the hero of Longfellow's epic poem, *The Song of Hiawatha.* Longfellow borrowed the character from Henry Row Schoolcraft's *The Hiawatha Legends* who mistakenly used the name to recount the Chippewa folktale of Nanabozho.) Before the time of the Prophet of the Great Peace, the five nations had a history of blood feuds and endless warfare that had taken such a toll on the people that it was said that even the moon was afraid to travel at night. Deganaweda and Hiawatha would change everything.

The Advent of Deganaweda

Although stories vary, most say that Deganaweda was born of a virgin. In a Wyandot village north of Lake Ontario lived a young unmarried woman who was chided by her mother when she discovered she was pregnant. One night the daughter dreamed of the monumental contributions the child would make and that she should name her son Deganaweda. The dream foretold that the child would become known as the Great Peacemaker. As Deganaweda grew up, his peers criticized him for not being interested in taking part in war parties. By the time he was grown, he was a handsome man with a good heart, but the people did not understand his ways, particularly his message of peace from the Creator. So Deganaweda built a canoe out of white rock which he used to ride to the land of the Mohawks who would be the first to embrace his teachings of the Great Peace.

The first woman to be converted to the Great Peace was Jigonsasee; today she is called the "Mother of the Nations." Walking along a path, Deganaweda encountered a cabin where Jigonsasee fed him and allowed him to rest. The Hodenoshone practiced blood feuds at that time which kept everyone bound by endless cycles of revenge. Before meeting the prophet, Jigonsasee helped supply food to the warriors on their raids and spoke of killing others in a self-righteous manner. Deganaweda rebuked her, telling her never to give food to warriors or inflame their hatred. Deganaweda entrusted her with the Good Tidings of Peace and Power, so that all would be able to live in peace. Thereafter, she sometimes accompanied him in his travels.

Hiawatha, the father of seven daughters, lived with the Onondaga people who were terrorized by their own war chief, the sorcerer called Tadodaho. The Tadodaho's hair writhed with snakes. He cast spells on his victims by day and ate their bodies at night. One by one Hiawatha's daughters died because of his malicious witchcraft. The last daughter, his favorite, was expecting a child. Tadodaho placed a charm on a magnificent eagle that was quickly spied by the hunters of the village. After they shot their arrows to kill it, the mortally wounded bird fell to earth right next to Hiawatha's daughter. As the men rushed forward to claim the eagle, they trampled the young woman to death. In a another version, Hiawatha was sent by the Onondaga to the Mohawk country because the local seer conjured up the prophecy of the advent of a dreamer who would establish peace. In order to get him to go, his daughters were killed by the shaman, Osinoh.

After the death of his last daughter, Hiawatha suffered the most profound grief. He retreated to the forest where he withdrew into himself, overwhelmed with sorrow. There he invented "condolence beads," strings of shell beads used to mourn the dead in Hodenoshone society. He eventually met Deganaweda, who offered him solace. Having comforted the distraught Hiawatha, Deganaweda spoke to him about the core problems of the people—warfare, witchcraft, the lack of empathy or alliance with one another. Hiawatha became the Great Peacemaker's most devoted disciple. Because Deganaweda spoke with a speech impediment, Hiawatha offered to communicate for the prophet as he traveled throughout the nations looking for converts to the Great Peace. The Mohawks adopted Hiawatha and made him a chief (sachem).

Forging the Great Peace

As part of his peace mission, Deganaweda sought Tadodaho in order to convince the Onondaga. In one version, Tadodaho ran off deep into the forest where he lived as a deranged cannibal. There he hunted for human flesh and dragged his hapless victims back to his lodge. When Deganaweda came upon the madman's lodge, he climbed up to the smoke hole to see him. As Tadodaho cooked his feast, he happened to see Deganaweda's face reflected in water of the cooking pot and was healed by this divine image. Tadodaho would eventually give up his grisly business to ally with the prophet, but he had to be further persuaded. In one interpretation of the legend, Hiawatha and Deganaweda magically combed the snakes out of his hair, thus transforming his consciousness to one of peace. Another version says that Deganaweda sang his peace songs to the hideous creature, and rubbed curative herbs all over his body, thereby healing the mind and body of Tadodaho. When Tadodaho was healed, he allowed the Onondaga to join the alliance.

One by one the other nations joined the Confederacy and adopted the principles set down by the Great Peacemaker. The Great Peace (Kayanernh-kowa) essentially established the principles of the Good Word, or right conduct and justice for all. It focuses on the principle of health, a sound mind and a sound body, as well as the power that instituted a civil authority and observance of spiritual discipline. Most of all, the Great Peace clearly states that the nations must remain united and never take sides against each other. If this principle was followed, the nations would prosper and enjoy the bounty of life. Since there are no precise records from this time, we can only assume what type of social movement took place in order to change the culture and social structure of these powerful nations.

When the Nations accepted the covenant of the Great Peace, Deganaweda planted the Great Tree of Peace, a legendary white pine under which all tomahawks and other implements of war were buried. This tree is reputedly located in Onondaga territory, the center of the alliance. A pine tree with an eagle on top became the symbol for confederacy. The tree contains four symbolic roots, called the White Roots of Peace, which stretch in all directions, north, south, east, and west. An eagle represents a warning to all enemies to not strike at one nation, because injury to one is an attack on all. The Hodenoshone refer to the Great Peace as the Extended Longhouse (in Mohawk, Kanonghsionni) which symbolically covered all the nations. The Mohawks to north were called the Keepers of the Eastern Door. The Seneca to the south were said to be the Keepers of the Western Door, and the centrally located Onondaga were referred to as the Fire Keepers. The substance of the alliance was called the "Great Immutable Law," and it was commemorated in oral tradition as the Constitution of the Nations. The translation of this tradition can be read in *Parker on the Iroquois*.

Adherence to the principles meant that the Hodenoshone would never fight amongst themselves, although they continued to raid neighboring territories over disputes and to obtain captives. They were some of the most feared warriors in North America, but their confederation hereafter channeled its aggression and ferocity against others. The nations enjoyed unprecedented wealth and independence until the colonial invasion by France and England. The Great Peace lasted until the late 1700s when some of the Hodenoshone unfortunately set aside their own sacred principles to ally with the British in the American War of Independence. The price paid for the breaking of the Great Peace led to the virtual annihilation of most Hodenoshone towns. The Six Nations would not recover from the devastation until well after the coming of the Seneca Prophet, Handsome Lake, in 1799.

Diana Tumminia

See also Handsome Lake

Bibliography

Fenton, William N., ed. (1968) *Parker on the Iroquois*. Syracuse, NY: Syracuse University Press.

Graymont, Barbara. (1988) *The Iroquois*. New York: Chelsea House Publishers.

Parker, Arthur C. ([1923] 1978) *Seneca Myths and Folk Tales*. New York: AMS Press.

Greater Community Way

Although an atmosphere of optimism prevails among the new religious movements of ufology, there are groups that take a more cautious approach to the coming Millennium. One example is found within the doctrine of the Greater Community Way, founded by Marshall Vian Summers in 1992. Located in Colorado, the Greater Community Way does not celebrate the new world that is emerging with the advent of extraterrestrial intervention. They see the coming millennium as a time when the societies of planet earth will be taken in by the "Greater Community" of extraterrestrials who have been visiting our world for millennia. Summers believes that the Greater Community of extraterrestrials are not evil in the religious or apocalyptic sense, but neither are they messianic, and they do not necessarily have our best interests at heart.

In a Web site article called, "Preparing for the Future," Summers writes, "The Greater Community that you will encounter will be a Greater Community of divergent interests. Those who come to your world will be resource explorers, emissaries of their governments or military forces scouting the possibility of forming an allegiance with your race and with your world. . . . They will simply be fulfilling their own mandates and objectives" (1997, parag. 6). While the Greater Community Way warns about the dangers that lay ahead for humanity, they also regard the new age of alien and human interaction as inevitable. The group argues that the world must prepare for the coming of the extraterrestrials by organizing itself and developing a global consensus in order to deal with the aliens. If not, then humanity will fall prey to Greater Community forces that may exploit humanity and Earth for natural resources, attempt to control our world, or pressure us to support and join their cause. If humanity is not prepared, given the certainty of alien technology and powers, then humanity may become enslaved or even annihilated.

The mission of Greater Community Way is to warn humankind about the dangers and opportunities of the imminent alien arrival on Earth and to teach the methods of preparation, or "The Way of Knowledge," through its publications, educational programs, and contemplative services. Preparation for the Greater Community comes not only from human initiative but from the Creator as well. Thus preparation for the alien revelation must include a spiritual preparation based in the "Greater Power" within the universe.

Philip Lamy

Bibliography

Greater Community Way. (1999) http://www.greatercommunity.org/.

Lamy, Philip. (1999) "UFOs, Extraterrestrials and the Apocalypse: The Evolution of a Millennial Subculture." In *Millennial Visions*, edited by Martha Lee. New York: Praeger.

Summers, Marshall. (1997) "Preparing for the Future." *Greater Community Way of Knowledge*. Boulder, CO: New Knowledge Library.

Handsome Lake

In the 1790s, Handsome Lake's religion flourished as an active tradition on Six Nation (Iroquois Confederacy) reservations in New York and Canada. The teachings stem from the visions of the prophet Handsome Lake (1735–1815), the Seneca spiritual leader, who brought the Good Word (Gaiwiio) to the people who call themselves the Hodenoshone. The Hodenoshone include the original five nations: Cayuga, Oneida, Onondaga, Mohawk, Seneca, as well as the Tuscarora people who joined the league in the early 1700s. The Gaiwiio, which was influenced by Christianity in some ways, eventually displaced the traditional religion which centered on efforts to control in communities where missionaries failed to impose Christianity. There is no single authoritative version of Handsome Lake's compiled teachings, known collectively as the Code, as preachers over the years have tended to revise it in various ways. A basic version was compiled and published by Arthur Parker in 1912 and 1913.

Social and Political Context

The personal history of Handsome Lake illustrates the social and economic pressures facing Eastern Woodland Indians before and after the American Revolution. During his lifetime, Handsome Lake became a warrior, a shaman, a sachem (a tribal leader chosen by the clan mothers), a drunkard, and finally a prophet of a new religion. Tradition describes him as an unhealthy looking man whose face and body bore the scars of many battles, as well as his internal war against alcohol. Among his people he is revered as a savior sent by the Creator, or the Master of Life.

As a young Seneca warrior in Pontiac's Rebellion (1763–66), Handsome Lake fought in the devastating Devil's Hole attack which wiped out two garrisons of British soldiers. Throughout the rebellion the Delaware Prophet's teachings of Pan-Indianism, traditionalism, and temperance circulated throughout the Great Lakes region, probably influencing Handsome Lake. The Seneca sustained terrible losses in the uprising, but were even further harmed by the Revolutionary War when American forces destroyed nearly all the Hodenoshone settlements. To defend what was left of the Iroquois Confederacy, Handsome Lake participated in the various military campaigns and in the subsequent years of lengthy treaty negotiations.

For decades, colonial warfare and trade disrupted the Native American economy until it was on the verge of disintegration and men like Handsome Lake lost their lands and themselves to the whiskey trade. During the period of recovery from the wars, religious groups and colonial governments pressured the Hodenoshone to shift from the traditional form of economic organization in which women and the community owned property to the European system of commercial farming in which property rights were vested in men. Anthropologist Anthony F. C. Wallace characterizes this period in Seneca history that gave rise to Handsome Lake's visions as one of demoralization and social pathology marked by drunkenness, chronic violence, fear of witchcraft, and social disorganization.

The Visions of Handsome Lake

Plagued by alcoholism, Handsome Lake suffered severely from the disease which brought him near death. In 1799, Handsome Lake collapsed and was bedridden for a long period. He was presumed to have been dead at one point as his friends and relatives started to carry him out of the house to prepare for the funeral rites. While carrying the stone-cold body, his nephew Blacksnake noticed a "warm spot" on Handsome Lake's chest. Those close to him kept a vigil as the warmth of his body slowly returned. When he awoke from this deathlike state, he startled his friends and family by relating his experiences in the great beyond. Dreams and visions held great sway among the Hodenoshone, so when Handsome Lake recounted his story he gained a serious following. In his vision, he had encountered spirit guides (called the "four messengers") dressed in ceremonial garb who spoke to him on behalf of the Creator. As directed by the spirit guides, he instructed his sister and her husband to carry the foreboding message to the Strawberry Festival. The message warned against whiskey, witchcraft, love potions, and abortion. Furthermore, offenders were to confess and repent their immorality.

In Handsome Lake's second vision, the spirit guides took him on a path that wandered though the stars. Different scenes appeared before him on his journey: an enormous woman who personified stinginess, a jail which represented the false belief that the white man's laws was better than Gaiwiio, a church with no doors or windows that depicted the stifling nature of Christianity, and other symbols of danger ahead. First, he saw George Washington, then Jesus who told him his people would be lost if they followed the white man's ways. Then Handsome Lake saw a path leading on one side to a heavenly place and on the other leading to the realm of the Punisher, the place for souls who did not repent. In the heavenly abode he saw the repentant living at ease, but on the path of the unrepentant he saw hellish horrors. Drunkards drank molten metal; a wife-beater trounced the burning image of a woman. His beloved people gambled with blistering hot cards; a witch boiled in a kettle as other miscreants endured the suffering of the damned. From there Handsome Lake traveled to a happy realm where he met departed spirits of his niece and his pet dog. In this place all was well, except for the warnings against quarreling given to Handsome Lake by his niece. In his third vision, Handsome Lake was told to write down the Gaiwiio in a book and carry his message to all the peoples of the Six Nations.

Overall, the major innovation of the Code of Handsome Lake was the apocalyptic emphasis on divine judgment and

From a drawing by Jesse Cornplanter

Handsome Luke preaching at the Seneca reservation at Tonawanda, New York. PARKER, ARTHUR C. (1913) *THE CODE OF HANDSOME LAKE, THE SENECA PROPHET*. ALBANY, NY: SUNY PRESS.

EXTRACT FROM THE OPENING OF THE GREAT MESSAGE OF HANDSOME LAKE

Section 1

"Now the beings spoke saying, 'We must now relate our message. We will uncover the evil upon the earth and show how men spoil the laws the Great Ruler has made and thereby made him angry.'

"'The Creator made man a living creature.'

"'Four words tell a great story of wrong and the Creator is sad because of the trouble they bring, so go and tell your people.'

"'The first word is One´ga (Whiskey or Rum)'. It seems that you never have known that this word stands for a great and monstrous evil and has reared a high mound of bones. Ga'´nigoentdo´tha, you lose your minds and one´ga' causes it all. Alas, many are fond of it and you are too fond of it. So now all must now say, "I will use it nevermore. As long as I live, as long as the number of my days is I will never use it again. I now stop." So must all say when they hear this message.' Now the beings, the servants of the Great Ruler, the messengers of him who created us, said this. Furthermore they said that the Creator made one´ga' and gave it to our younger brethren, the white man, as a medicine but they use it for evil for they drink it for other purposes than medicine and drink instead of work and idlers drink one´ga'. No, the Creator did not make it for you."

So they said and he said. Enia´iehuk! [*It was that way*]

Source: Parker, Arthur C. (1913) *The Code of Handsome Lake, the Seneca Prophet.* Albany, NY: SUNY Press.

an afterlife of either heaven or hell. The teachings would stress abstinence from alcohol and admonitions against practicing witchcraft, love potions, or abortions. Wrongdoers had the option of confession that cleansed any sin. Though the promised forgiveness included witchcraft, fear of witches ran so deep in Iroquois culture, that many so-called witches were still routinely discovered in Handsome Lake's time, and they were sometimes killed if they did not confess. The teachings also called for the continuation of such traditional ceremonies as the White Dog Ceremony, Thanksgiving Dance, Great Feather Dance, Personal Chants, Bowl Game, and the Strawberry Festival where everyone was encouraged to drink strawberry juice. However, Handsome Lake disapproved of the traditional False Face Societies and certain shamanic practices. Although he preached against these, they were deeply ingrained in Seneca culture and did not entirely disappear.

In 1802 Handsome Lake visited Washington with a delegation of Seneca and Onondaga chiefs. His efforts on behalf of temperance won him attention and praise from President Thomas Jefferson. Other governmental agencies also approved of his ideas because the Gaiwiio doctrine reinforced the social transformation to agriculture that Handsome Lake's brother, Cornplanter, and the neighboring Quakers had advocated. Although generally praised, Handsome Lake encountered resistance from more traditional factions, on the one hand, and staunchly Christian advocates, on the other. The issues were controversial enough that by 1812 Handsome Lake had developed so many enemies near his home at Cold Spring, that he left and settled with his followers in Tonawanda.

The Death of Handsome Lake

In 1815 Handsome Lake had already experienced premonitions of his own death when some believers invited him to Onondaga. Despite the fact that the spirit messengers had told him he would sing his death song there, Handsome Lake embarked on the trip. When he reached Onondaga, he became upset that he had lost his favorite knife. When he retraced his steps to find it, he fell so ill that he was unable to make it back to the reserve. He took shelter in a cabin along the way, and when they learned of his condition men staged a lacrosse game outside in order to cheer him up. Before he died he spoke to the crowds who had gathered. Handsome Lake was buried on the Onondaga Reservation, south of Syracuse, New York. His grandson, Jimmy Johnson (Sosheowa) succeeded him and spread the faith among the nations in the 1840s. By 1850, the practitioners of the Handsome Lake Religion had achieved a recognized church status.

Handsome Lake's Lasting Influence

The prophet's new religion paved the way for a measured transition toward cultural adaptation by carving an interpretive path between the old traditions and the encroaching white society. Handsome Lake's teaching stressed many things appropriate for this juncture in Iroquois history: Native American unity, domestic peace and morality, a tolerance for whites, preservation of tribal lands, abstinence from alcohol, a work ethic, accommodation, and acculturation. Prohibitions against abortion and sterility medicine helped raise the birthrate. His followers were gradually able to accommodate to the external demands that expected to assimilate them into white American society. Handsome Lake's influence upon the Six Nations amounted to no less than a transformational renaissance that helped them retain some of their traditional culture and identity, while also creating social stability and economic change.

Diana Tumminia

See also Delaware Prophet

Bibliography

Fenton, William N., ed. (1968) *Parker on the Iroquois.* Syracuse, NY: Syracuse University Press.

Graymont, Barbara. (1988) *The Iroquois.* New York: Chelsea House Publishers.

Parker, Arthur C. (1913) *The Code of Handsome Lake, the Seneca Prophet.* Albany: University of the State of New York.

Wallace, Anthony F. C. (1972) *The Death and Rebirth of the Seneca.* New York: Vintage Books.

Heaven's Gate

Heaven's Gate was a U.S. "flying saucer cult" of the late twentieth century. The group gained tremendous notoriety, first when people dramatically abandoned families and jobs to join the group in the 1970s, and then when remaining members of the group were discovered dead in a San Diego suburb in March 1997.

Heaven's Gate is important sociologically for the manner in which it and mass media representations of it have informed American popular views on "cults" and flying saucer beliefs. It is also important as an example of the conjunction of millennial hope (and fear) with spirituality, (pseudo)science, and pop culture common to new religious movements (NRMs) in advanced industrial societies in the 1990s. Heaven's Gate shows how important UFOs are in efforts to create technologically credible spiritualities. Further, it highlights NRM use of new electronic media, specifically the Internet, as tools for prophecy and recruitment.

History

Marshall Herff Applewhite was born in Lubbock, Texas, in 1932. The son of a Presbyterian minister, he studied at the Union Theological Seminary of Virginia, served two years in the Army, and earned a degree in music from the University of Colorado in 1960. He taught music at the University of Alabama and the University of St. Thomas, Houston, performing occasionally with the Houston Opera. After being fired from St. Thomas in 1972, Applewhite hospitalized himself. Though he was publicly vague about the reasons for it, various proximate causes have been suggested, from heart ailment to nervous breakdown to treatment for homosexuality.

Applewhite was explicit, however, that his hospitalization coincided with a spiritual crisis, during which he came into contact with Bonnie Lu Trousdale Nettles. A registered nurse born in 1911, Nettles was also an ex-Theosophist who ran a small astrology practice, gave Tarot readings, and channeled dead celebrities. She convinced Applewhite that they had met to fulfill some divine purpose. They set about devouring occult, biblical, and ufological literature to discern that purpose. The initial product of their collaboration was the Christian Arts Center of Houston (1972–73), where they offered instruction in art, music, astrology, and esoteric spirituality. The center folded, and the two roamed around the western United States, contacting ufologists and religious leaders, and at one point spending time in a Texas jail for credit card and auto theft.

The breakthrough that produced Heaven's Gate came in March 1975 in Ojai, California. In a short mission statement, Applewhite and Nettles identified themselves as the two witnesses described in Revelation 11: 3–12, witnesses destined to spread the word of the endtimes, endure martyrdom, and then attain resurrection upon Christ's return. They prophesied an imminent end to the world which their followers could escape in a flying saucer. "The Two" (as they appeared in articles and their own writings of the time) undertook their first recruiting trip in California and Oregon soon afterward. News sources nationwide carried stories of dramatic conversions to the group, now called Human Individual Metamorphosis (HIM), including that of a married couple from Oregon who had left their three children with relatives to join HIM.

HIM members lived in campgrounds while Applewhite and Nettles (who assumed pseudonyms like "Guinea" and "Pig," "Bo" and "Peep," and "Do" and "Ti") spoke in private homes and college campuses around the country. Sociology graduate students Robert Balch and David Taylor did deep-cover ethnographic research with the group during this period of minimal supervision. Their later articles attested to high levels of confusion and defection among neophyte members until Bo and Peep returned in April of 1976, closing "the harvest," weeding out those with low commitment, and inaugurating a program of regimentation and asceticism that would characterize Heaven's Gate until its end.

Institutionalization

Instruction up to that point had revolved around Do and Ti's doctrine of UFO salvation, the true nature of heaven, and the final goal of an elite group of souls. Heaven was an actual, physical location at the edges of the universe, an asexual, unemotional, nonhuman domain the Two called "The Evolutionary Level Above Human" or "TELAH." TELAH is the origin of souls, of a different physical substance than terrestrial biological bodies, which can be transferred between bodies (or "containers") by technological means. Some souls are sent by God to Earth to pursue their individual "evolution"; this involves being incarnated and then "overcoming" the defects and desires of the flesh. Heaven's Gate was the second appearance of the souls first incarnated as Jesus and the early church. While on Earth they are under the influence of "Luciferian" space-aliens, fallen TELAH souls who keep the truth hidden by creating religions and directing human attention to this world or to worshiping the Luciferians. Do and Ti's message should activate "homing beacons" in incarnate TELAH souls, drawing them to the Two's "classroom."

Students in this "classroom" had to prepare for a very different existence in heaven, where regimentation and hierarchy were the rule, and where gender, individualism, and desire do not exist. The Two explained the classroom's protocols in terms familiar from *Star Trek*: HIM camps were set up to approximate spaceships; students were sent out in "away-teams" to study the "human-mammalian" traits they had to overcome. An overwhelming emphasis on the soul made the bodily "container" an expendable obstruction to be overcome thorough asceticism and manipulation. To that end, the Two prescribed repetitive tasks according to strict chronological scheduling. Uniforms, cropped hair, and (in the case of some male members including Applewhite) surgical sterilization were employed to achieve a "genderless, crew-minded, service-oriented" membership. Regimentation also allowed Heaven's Gate to effect a quick escape from Luciferian-influenced terrestrial authorities should it be necessary.

Once the new strictness had reduced membership to a manageable seventy persons by 1976, Bo and Peep moved HIM from Rocky Mountain campgrounds to a northern Texas ranch, then to Dallas and Los Angeles in the mid-1980s. Nettles, who had suffered from liver cancer for some time, passed away in 1985. Applewhite encouraged the idea that she had returned to TELAH to assist God the Father in preparation for the group's eventual ascent. In the early 1990s, after developing a plot of land near Manzanillo, New Mexico, where they planned to build a survivalist-type shelter, Heaven's Gate moved to Rancho Santa Fe, an upscale suburb of San Diego, California.

In 1993 Applewhite (now "Do") returned the group to the expectant millennial mode of the mid-1970s, reopening the classroom and advertising the End in nationwide periodicals. This was at the same time that some students had begun an in-house Web site construction business called "Higher Source." Applewhite took advantage of Internet technology to send prophetic statements around the world unfiltered; some members even attempted to recruit people over the Internet. They also prepared and broadcast a thirteen-part videotape series on their beliefs and mission.

The End

The appearance of comet Hale-Bopp in 1997 (which some in parascientific circles claimed had possible spaceship companion) became the sign that for Applewhite signaled an end to the earthly "classroom." Preparation was methodical and thorough, down to videotaped farewells to their families and a final Web page update. The group made one last set of public outings, going to dinner, to Mexico, even to a Nevada UFO convention. Then, on 22–26 March 1997, in three shifts, members of Heaven's Gate ingested applesauce, vodka, and Phenobarbital, and were asphyxiated until all thirty-nine were clinically deceased.

Implications

Throughout its existence, Heaven's Gate highlighted the importance of the mass media in shaping public views on NRMs, in the United States and many other nations. Coming on the heels of widely publicized violent incidents, one involving U.S. federal law enforcement and the Branch Davidian group in Waco, Texas, the other a chemical attack on a crowded Tokyo subway by Aum Shinri Kyo, the Heaven's Gate deaths solidified the public perception that "cults" were dangerous social problems. Experts mobilized by the media to make some sense of the group and its end included former member Richard Ford ("Rio di Angelo," who had received the farewell tapes and led authorities to the group's home in Rancho Santa Fe), social scientists, psychologists, anticultists, and law enforcement officials. The incident also inspired a good bit of callous humor on TV and the

Internet, a reaction of interest primarily in delineating the limits of popular comprehension.

The group was itself an illustrative amalgam of spirituality, (pseudo)science, and technology, something found not just among "flying saucer cults" but among many other recent NRMs, especially those that expect an imminent new world. Heaven's Gate reflects the prominence of technology as tool and metaphor in NRMs. Its thoroughly technicized heaven, and its use of the Internet as a means of subsistence, as an instrument of prophecy, and as a recruitment tool, show just how strong the impulse is in advanced industrial society to create technologically credible religious symbols and belief systems.

Ryan J. Cook

See also Ufology

Bibliography

Balch, Robert W. (1980) "Looking Behind the Scenes in a Religious Cult: Implications for a Study of Conversion." *Sociological Analysis* 41: 137–43.

——. (1982) "Bo and Peep: A Case Study of the Origins of Messianic Leadership." In *Millennialism and Charisma*, edited by Roy Wallis. Belfast: Queen's University Press, 13–71.

——. (1985) "When the Light Goes Out, Darkness Comes: A Study of Defection from Totalistic Cult." In *Religious Movements: Genesis, Exodus, Numbers*, edited by Rodney Stark. NY: Paragon, 11–63.

——. (1995) "Waiting for the Ships: Disillusionment and the Revitalization of Faith in Bo and Peep's UFO Cult." In *The Gods have Landed: New Religions from Other Worlds*, edited by James R. Lewis. Albany, NY: State University of New York Press, 137–66.

Balch, Robert W., and David Taylor. (1977) Seekers and Saucers: The Role of the Cultic Milieu in Joining a UFO Cult." *American Behavioral Scientist* 20: 839–60.

Hewes, Hayden, and Brad Steiger. (1976) *UFO Missionaries Extraordinary*. New York: Signet.

How and When 'Heaven's Gate' (the Door to the Physical Kingdom Level Above Human) May Be Entered: An Anthology of our Materials. (1997) Mill Spring, NC: Wild Flower Press.

Perkins, Rodney, and Forrest Jackson. (1997) *Cosmic Suicide: The Tragedy and Transcendence of Heaven's Gate*. Dallas: Pentaradial Press.

Steiger, Brad, and Hayden Hewes. (1997) *Inside Heaven's Gate*. New York: Signet.

Vallée, Jacques. (1980) *Messengers of Deception*. New York: Bantam.

Holiness Movement

The Holiness movement is the name given to a broad stream of Protestant revivalism that took shape in the nineteenth century in North America and Western Europe. Although its major institutional location was within the Methodist churches, the movement eventually came to include members from virtually every other Protestant denominations. Holiness teachings drew from a complex array of Wesleyan, Puritan, Pietistic, and African-American sources. Central to the movement was a religious form of experience that was variously called "sanctification," "the second blessing," "the baptism of the Holy Spirit," or simply the "higher Christian life." Although millennialism was not a major theme of the Holiness movement until the end of the nineteenth century, the Holiness emphasis upon personal spiritual sanctification was parallel and supportive of the wider nineteenth-century Protestant millennial quest for social and national redemption.

Roots of the Holiness Movement

Millennial expectations had played a major role in shaping Protestant Christianity in North America since the days of the Puritans in New England. Puritan theology taught its followers to expect the imminent return of Christ and the transformation of the age. Many believed the Puritan movement itself had a godly role to play in the drama of divine redemption. During the eighteenth-century's First Great Awakening in America, preachers such as Jonathan Edwards and George Whitefield drew upon the Puritan heritage of expectation of the imminent kingdom of God, to lead people into an experience of personal conversion. Edwards in particular believed that the gradual increase of Christian influence brought about by the Awakenings in America would inaugurate Christ's millennial reign on earth. He expected this to be an invisible rule of Christ, carried out through the spiritual influence of the church. By the time of the American Revolution, Edward's followers had begun to secularize this vision of a righteous nation that was charged with a redemptive mission in the world. This secular version of Edward's millennialism gave rise in the nineteenth century to political doctrines of America's "Manifest Destiny."

One of Edward's contemporaries in the English Awakening of the eighteenth century, John Wesley, had organized a movement for reform and renewal known as Methodism. By the time of the American Revolution, Methodist societies were being organized in North America as well, and Methodist preachers were busy spreading their message by means of their itinerant ministry. John Wesley shared

Jonathan Edward's postmillennial understanding of Christ's rule on earth being achieved through the Christianizing influences of believers. To this end his movement sought to organize and disseminate Christian holiness, encouraging practices of both personal and collective spiritual and moral discipline that led one to become more and more like Christ in character. Wesley himself believed that it was possible for a sanctified Christian who had experienced both forgiveness of sins and the personal transformation of holiness to attain a state of Christian perfection in which one no longer would desire anything other than to love God and neighbor in a perfect way. It was one of John Wesley's most controversial doctrines, and continued to be so for the wider Holiness movement of the nineteenth century.

Holiness Movements in Nineteenth-Century North America

In North America, three distinct streams of the Holiness movement emerged in the first half of the nineteenth century, all of them in communication with one another. The first of these emerged from among the middle class in the urban northeast, and was predominantly European American in character. An early programmatic statement was offered by an Anglo-American Methodist minister named Timothy Merritt who published in 1825 *The Christian's Manual: A Treatise on Christian Perfection with Directions for Obtaining that State*. A little over a decade later, two sisters, Sarah Lankford and Phoebe Palmer, began holding a Tuesday Meeting for the Promotion of Holiness in their apartment in New York. Phoebe Palmer quickly became not only one of the leading teachers of holiness doctrine and practice, but one of the leading advocates for women in ministry in the nineteenth century.

A second wing of the movement took up more explicitly a number of social concerns facing nineteenth-century America. Often known as the Oberlin School of Christian perfection, it was guided by the leadership of Asa Mahan, Charles G. Finney, and John Morgan. Charles G. Finney, Oberlin's first professor and later president, is arguably the single most important architect of American revivalism. Yet he was also an adamant abolitionist and advocate for women's rights. The entire Oberlin school was a hotbed of abolitionism. Professors and students alike served as agents for the antislavery society, and African Americans attended classes. The college was the first in America to admit women into its classroom and to grant women degrees. Its members were not only committed to women's rights, but took the lead in advocating women's ordination to ministry in the church.

The third major wing of the Holiness movement in the first half of the nineteenth century took shape among African Americans, primarily through their Methodist connections. The contours of the African-American experience of holiness can be seen in the writings of one of its earliest proponents, a woman named Jarena Lee whose autobiography was first published in 1836. Jarena Lee made a first confession of salvation under the preaching of Richard Allen in 1804. For several years after that she struggled to maintain her faith. Finally, according to her autobiography, after a time of spiritual turmoil that manifested itself in physical illness, she experienced the entire sanctification or consecration of her being that she described as a second work of grace. The role of the Holy Spirit in the African-American Holiness tradition received special attention. For Jarena Lee as well as many other Holiness Christians, this second blessing was synonymous with conversion, and brought with it the empowerment to live a Christian life.

Doctrines of the Holiness Movement

In all three of these major wings of the Holiness movement, little attention was paid to millennial doctrines prior to 1865. Holiness leaders came to focus more and more on the instantaneous experience of the second blessing, and accepted as a concomitant doctrine the gradual perfection of a Christian society. Their postmillennial inclinations tended to downplay any sense of immediate millennial crisis for the most part. (Groups such as the Millerites proved to be the exception.) Following the Civil War, however, a gradual shift began to take place as a number of Holiness leaders began to entertain premillennial doctrines. By the end of the century, imminent expectations of the Second Coming, and of a spiritual outpouring expected to immediately precede the end of the age, had became a standard part of Holiness teaching. Along with the saving, sanctifying, and healing work of Jesus Christ, the Holiness movement added a fourth plank to its basic doctrinal stance: Jesus Christ as imminent coming king.

This eschatological emphasis in the Holiness movement not only facilitated a rapid adoption of dispensational or premillennial teaching within the movement, but it paved the way for the emergence of Pentecostalism at the beginning of the twentieth century. Many late nineteenth-century Holiness leaders had began to teach the imminent restoration of the gifts and wonders that had been associated with the apostolic age in the pages of the Second Testament. Many in the movement began to look for what were called the "latter rains," the last great outpouring of spiritual gifts before the closing of the age and the advent of the millennium. When reports of speaking in tongues began to circulate in Holiness newspapers early in the twentieth century, many immediately recognized this as the fulfillment of those expectations and embraced the new Pentecostal movement as a final eschatological event. A significant portion of the Holiness movement did not embrace Pentecostalism, however, but continued to articulate a doctrine of personal sanctification and millennial expectation apart from the Pentecostal doctrine of speaking in tongues.

In the first half of the nineteenth century, Holiness-induced ruptures in organized denominational life began to appear among the Methodists as various groups began separating over the wider church's acceptance of slavery and other practices deemed sinful by the Holiness proponents. By the end of the century, such ruptures had accelerated and an astounding number of new Holiness denominations had formed. Many of these became Pentecostal in the twentieth century, but others did not, continuing to proclaim their Holiness distinctive in both faith and order. Such churches as the Salvation Army, the Church of the Nazarene, the Wesleyan Methodist Church, and the Christian and Missionary Alliance all have their roots in the Holiness revival of the nineteenth century.

Many of these Holiness churches today have relaxed some of their distinctive emphases and are often viewed as being simply a part of the wider conservative Protestant or Fundamentalist theological worlds. Many denominations with Holiness roots have even adopted some form premillennial doctrine, although it is at odds with their own earlier postmillennial vision of social transformation. Nevertheless, with its vision of an imminent new age accompanied by a fresh outpouring of spiritual energy and accompanied by a radical concern for social transformation, the Holiness movement might still have a millennial message worth hearing today.

Dale T. Irvin

See also Camp Meetings; Pentecostalism; United States, 18th Century

Bibliography

Bassett, Paul. (1975) "A Study of the Theology of the Holiness Movement." *Methodist History* 13, 3 (April): 61–84.

Dayton, Donald W. (1976) *Discovering an Evangelical Heritage.* New York: Harper and Row.

———. (1987) *The Roots of Pentecostalism.* Peabody, MA: Hendrickson Press.

Dieter, Melvin Easterday. (1996) *The Holiness Revival of the Nineteenth Century*, Studies in Evangelicalism, No. 1, 2d ed. Metuchen, NJ: Scarecrow Press.

Hughes, George. (1886) *Fragrant Memories of the Tuesday Meeting and the Guide to Holiness and their Fifty Years' Work for Jesus.* New York: Palmer and Hughes.

Jones, Charles Edwin. (1974) *A Guide to the Study of the Holiness Movement.* Metuchen, NJ: Scarecrow Press.

———. (1987) *Black Holiness: A Guide to the Study of Black Participation in Wesleyan Perfectionist and Glossolalic Pentecostal Movements.* Metuchen, NJ: Scarecrow Press.

Kostlevy, William. (1994) *Holiness Manuscripts: A Guide to Sources Documenting the Wesleyan Holiness Movement in the United States and Canada.* Metuchen, NJ: Scarecrow Press.

Lee, Jarena. (1986) *The Life and Religious Experience of Jarena Lee, A Coloured Lady, Giving an Account of Her Call to Preach the Gospel. Revised and Corrected from the Original Manuscript Written by Herself.* Reprinted in *Sisters of the Spirit: Three Black Women's Autobiographies of the Nineteenth Century*, edited by William L. Andrews. Bloomington, IN: Indiana University Press.

Peters, John Leland. ([1956] 1985) *Christian Perfection and American Methodism.* Grand Rapids, MI: Zondervan.

Smith, Timothy L. (1957) *Revivalism and Social Reform in Mid-Nineteenth Century America.* New York: Abingdon Press.

Tuveson, Ernest Lee. (1968) *Redeemer Nation: The Idea of America's Millennial Role.* Chicago: University of Chicago Press.

Holocaust

The term "holocaust" is Greek meaning a "consuming fiery sacrifice," and it appears in the Bible in 1 Samuel 7–9, signifying a "burnt offering to the Lord." It is now used to encompass the process leading up to and including the systematic killing of the Jews of Europe, generally dated to coincide with the Nazi seizure of power in 1933 to its fall in 1945. Some scholars prefer the Hebrew word "sho'ah," meaning "catastrophe," as it better reflects the Jewish experience, which certainly was not as willing sacrificial victims to any Aryan deity. From the standpoint of millennial studies, the Holocaust or Sho'ah represents the single greatest loss of life resulting, at least in part, to the messianic and apocalyptic world views of a millennial movement. It is especially significant because the combination of millennialism, messianism, and apocalypticism, along with the sanctioned use of mass violence to achieve its goals, led directly and indirectly to the deaths of some forty million people, with six million Jews singled out as the chosen enemy who had to be exterminated in order to achieve the millennial *Reich* (empire). Regarding the *Endlösung* (final solution), Lucy Dawidowicz perceptively noted that "'Final' reverberates with apocalyptic promise, bespeaking the Last Judgement, the End of Days, the last destruction before salvation, Armageddon. 'The Final Solution of the Jewish Question' in the National Socialist conception was not just another anti-Semitic undertaking,

GERMANY IN THE FINAL BATTLE WITH THE JEWISH-BOLSHEVIK MURDER-SYSTEM

This Chaos system of annihilation and terror was invented by Jews and is led by Jews. It is the action of the Jewish race. World Jewry attempts through subversion and propaganda to bring together the uprooted and lesser race elements to accomplish this war of annihilation against everything positive, against people and nation, against religion and culture, against order and morality. The aim is the production of chaos through world revolution and the establishment of a world state under Jewish leadership.

Source: From a Nazi pamphlet of the 1930s explaining the war to German soldiers, "Deutschland zum Endkampf mit dem jüdisch-bolschewistisch Mordsystem angetreten," National Archives Microfilm collection, Records of the National Socialist German Labor Party, T81, Roll 672.

but a metahistorical program devised with an eschatological perspective. It is part of a salvational ideology that envisaged the attainment of Heaven by bringing Hell on earth" (1983: xxii). The same can be said of the Nazi use of the terms *Endkampf* (final battle), *Endsieg* (final victory), and the conception of the Third Reich as the *Endreich*, the final empire that would last a thousand years.

Two Chosen People

From *völkisch* millennialism the Nazis constructed a salvational belief that saw the world as a struggle of the fittest between competing races. Two "chosen" races, however, stood in mortal combat above the rest; the Aryan and the Jew. The Nazis believed that they had been chosen to fulfill a divine mission to save the world from annihilation and usher in the millennial Reich of peace and prosperity. But what of the other chosen race, the Jews? *Bolshevism from Moses to Lenin: a Dialogue between Hitler and Me*, an early Nazi propaganda piece written by Hitler's intellectual mentor, Dietrich Eckart, reveals the core of Nazi apocalyptic fears and its essentially eschatological view of history. While the pamphlet was written by Eckart, the words attributed to Hitler accurately present his apocalyptic worldview, which he later repeated in his own *Mein Kampf*, as well as in his Table Talk (various published materials of his nightly monologues) of World War II. In *Bolshevism from Moses to Lenin* Eckart attempts to reveal the hidden history of the Jews, especially their supposed desire, not simply for world domination, but for world annihilation. The false history of Jews as presented by Eckart and Hitler is one of continual extermination of Gentiles. The authors use, or more precisely, misuse, the Old Testament (what Hitler called "Satan's Bible") and the Talmud, to reveal one historical atrocity after another. For example, the Book of Esther is explained as a Purim festival "murder" of 75,000 Persians, while the Jewish exodus from Egypt becomes a justified expulsion for their having allegedly stirred up the "rabble" against the racial elite (reflecting the Nazi intention to one day expel the Jews from Germany). "Bolshevism" becomes a synonym for disorder, chaos, disintegration, and the supposed inherently destructive nature of the Jews.

The Russian Revolution, the German loss of World War I, and the resulting apocalyptic chaos of postwar Weimar were conceived by the conspiratorially obsessed Nazis as the final Jewish attempt to take over the world.

The notorious forgery, *The Protocols of the Elders of Zion*, must be seen in this light. This forgery, originally concocted by the Czarist secret police, became popular in Germany after the war as an apocalyptic text which revealed the alleged Jewish plan for world domination. Commentaries on the text by the Russian monk Sergei Nilus further present this Jewish plan for world domination in the context of the coming of the Antichrist and the final apocalyptic battle. It is in this mental world of satanic world conspiracies and fears of apocalyptic annihilation that *Bolshevism from Moses to Lenin* concludes. Hitler discusses the "final goal" to which the Jew is instinctively "pushed":

> Above and beyond world domination—annihilation of the world. He believes he must bring the entire world down on its knees before him in order to pre-

> pare a paradise on earth. . . . While he makes a pretense to elevate humanity, he torments it into despair, madness and ruin. If he is not commanded to stop he will annihilate all humanity. (Eckart 1924: 49–50)

Even if we are to take these to be the words of Eckart, Hitler expressed exactly the same explanation of Bolshevism and its "Jewish" origins. Indeed, a recurrent theme in *Mein Kampf*, which is dedicated to Eckart, is that the Jews were promised in the Old Testament not eternity in the heavenly New Jerusalem, but dominion of the temporal earth. Hitler asked, "Was it possible that the earth had been promised as a reward to this people which lives only for this earth?" (1943: 64–65). Later in the book, Hitler, speaking of these alleged Jewish machinations, states: "for the higher he climbs, the more alluring his old goal that was once promised him rises from the veil of the past, and with feverish avidity his keenest minds see the dream of world domination tangibly approaching" (313). This situation would lead to the fulfillment of the "Jewish prophecy—the Jew would really devour the peoples of the earth, would become their master." The end result of "Jewish doctrine of Marxism" would be the literal end of the world:

> As a foundation of the universe, this doctrine would bring about the end of any order intellectually conceivable to man. And as, in this greatest of all recognizable organisms, the result of an application of such a law could only be chaos, on earth it could only be destruction for the inhabitants of this planet. If, with the help of his Marxist creed, the Jew is victorious over the other peoples of the world, his crown will be the funeral wreath of humanity and this planet will, as it did thousands [millions in later editions] of years of ago, move through the ether devoid of men. (452)

The Aryan/Jewish conflict was, quite literally, interpreted by Hitler as an eschatological war. The final battle would come in a fight to the death with Jewish-Bolsheviks. In his first important speech after leaving Landsberg prison in 1925, Hitler explained that the Nazi aim was "clear and simple: Fight against the satanic power which has collapsed Germany into this misery; Fight Marxism, as well as the spiritual carrier of this world pest and epidemic, the Jews. . . . As we join ranks then in this new movement, we are clear to ourselves, that in this arena there are two possibilities; either the enemy walks over our corpse or we over theirs" (Hitler 1925: 8). It was the Nazis' mission, therefore, to prepare Germany for this impending final conflict.

The Millennial Reich and the Final Solution

After obtaining power in 1933, Hitler and the Nazis began the dual process of creating the millennial Reich and preparing for the coming war of annihilation with the Jewish-Bolsheviks. The Nuremberg Laws of 1935, the eugenics program, the coordination of German society, and the military buildup were all conceived with both interrelated goals in mind. Through a combination of legislation and eugenics the Nazis believed that racial degeneration could be halted, and regeneration and renewal begin. The Nazi obsession with "cleansing" and "purification" should be seen in the light of a fear of racial degeneration as a form of biological apocalypse. The medical killings that would take place in the concentration camps were conceived along similar lines—a racial purification necessary for biological salvation.

On 30 January 1939, with Europe on the brink of world war, Hitler gave his yearly speech to the Reichstag commemorating his assumption of power, and with it, the dawn of the millennial Third Reich, the Final Reich. Assuming the role of endtime prophet, Hitler prophesied that if the Jews should "once again" start a world war, then the Jews would be exterminated. While the "prophecy," with its blaming of the Jews for the war that Hitler so clearly started, is obviously absurd, it is a testament to the consistency of Hitler's conspiratorial and apocalyptic rendering of history. He would repeat this prophecy throughout the war as the Holocaust was taking place, attempting to justify the horror as a prophecy fulfilled. This type of conspiratorial mentality found in *Bolshevism from Moses to Lenin* and *Mein Kampf* exhibits an inversion of reality typical of many violent millennial movements. Linking the war with a threat to exterminate the Jews is important therefore, as it clearly links the prophesied final battle against the Jews with the Final Solution.

The belief that World War II was the long-prophesied coming war of annihilation was a deeply held tenet for many Nazis and soldiers alike. Acknowledging the importance of such a belief in an imminent apocalyptic struggle between Aryans and Jews does not mean that the Nazis ever had a set plan or program to exterminate the Jews. The belief does, however, contain within its own internal logic the *possibility* of its eventual actualization. In other words, if you believe that now is the time, that *the* turning point in world history is at hand, one in which the age-old struggle of good and evil, order and chaos, God and Satan, Aryan and Jew, is to be settled once and for all, and just as importantly, if you believe that you have been divinely chosen to take part in this eschatological battle, then it is not surprising that you may find yourself in exactly the prophesied war of annihilation.

EXTRACT FROM THE PROTOCOLS OF THE LEARNED ELDERS OF ZION

PROTOCOL NO. 14

The religion of the future. Future conditions of serfdom. Inaccessibility of knowledge regarding the religion of the future. Pornography and the printed matter of the future.

When we come into our kingdom it will be undesirable for us that there should exist any other religion than ours of the One God with whom our destiny is bound up by our position as the Chosen People and through whom our same destiny is united with the destinies of the world. We must therefore sweep away all other forms of belief. If this gives birth to the atheists whom we see to-day, it will not, being only a transitional stage, interfere with our views, but will serve as a warning for those generations which will hearken to our preaching of the religion of Moses, that, by its stable and thoroughly elaborated system has brought all the peoples of the world into subjection to us. Therein we shall emphasize its mystical right, on which, as we shall say, all its educative power is based . . . Then at every possible opportunity we shall publish articles in which we shall make comparisons between our beneficent rule and those of past ages. The blessings of tranquillity, though it be a tranquillity forcibly brought about by centuries of agitation, will throw into higher relief the benefits to which we shall point. The errors of the goyim governments will be depicted by us in the most vivid hues. We shall implant such an abhorrence of them that the peoples will prefer tranquillity in a state of serfdom to those rights of vaunted freedom which have tortured humanity and exhausted the very sources of human existence, sources which have been exploited by a mob of rascally adventurers who know not what they do . . . Useless changes of forms of government to which we instigated the GOYIM when we were undermining their state structures, will have so wearied the peoples by that time that they will prefer to suffer anything under us rather than run the risk of enduring again all the agitations and miseries they have gone through.

At the same time we shall not omit to emphasize the historical mistakes of the goy governments which have tormented humanity for so many centuries by their lack of understanding of everything that constitutes the true good of humanity in their chase after fantastic schemes of social blessings, and have never noticed that these schemes kept on producing a worse and never a better state of the universal relations which are the basis of human life . . .

The whole force of our principles and methods will lie in the fact that we shall present them and expound them as a splendid contrast to the dead and decomposed old order of things in social life.

Our philosophers will discuss all the shortcomings of the various beliefs of the GOYIM, but no one will ever bring under discussion our faith from its true point of view since this will be fully learned by none save ours, who will never dare to betray its secrets.

In countries known as progressive and enlightened we have created a senseless, filthy, abominable literature. For some time after our entrance to power we shall continue to encourage its existence in order to provide a telling relief by contrast to the speeches, party programme, which will be distributed from exalted quarters of ours. Our wise men, trained to become leaders of the goyim, will compose speeches, projects, memoirs, articles, which will be used by us to influence the minds of the goyim, directing them towards such understanding and forms of knowledge as have been determined by us.

Source: Translated from the Russian of Sergyei A. Nilus by Victor E. Marsden.

Operation Barbarossa, the invasion of Soviet Russia in 1941, was conceptualized and promoted as the beginning of the true war of annihilation. Hitler explained to his generals that "two world views battle one another. Annihilating judgment over Bolshevism, the same asocial criminality. . . . It is a question of a war of annihilation" (Schram 1961: 336). The generals in turn explained the special nature of this war to their troops. General Walther von Reichenau, commander of the sixth army, ordered that the troops must understand that "the essential goal of the campaign against the Jewish-Bolshevik system is the complete smashing of the means of power and the extermination of the Asiatic influence in the European cultural sphere." Consequently, he argued, "the soldier in the Eastern realm is not only a fighter according to the rules of military science, but also is a bearer of an inexorable *völkisch* (racial) idea and an avenger for all the bestialities which have been inflicted on the Germans and kindred peoples. For this reason the soldier must have complete understanding of the necessity for the harsh, yet just atonement of the Jewish subhumans" (Streit 1978: 115). This order would become a model for others.

It is unlikely that the eschatological imagery imbedded in these orders simply reflected rhetorical license, designed to motivate the troops and nothing else. Such orders followed exactly the historical and social perceptions held by the Nazis since the beginning of the movement, as seen in *Bolshevism from Moses to Lenin*. They followed Hitler's prophesy and his war directives. They followed Nazi propaganda sheets read to the troops. Hitler's prophesied war of annihilation, therefore, seemed to have arrived. More importantly, the message got through to the troops. Most of the soldiers of the *Einsatzgruppen* (SS special action group) as well as the *Wehrmacht* (regular army) grew up in the Nazi millennial Reich. Their schoolbooks and other cultural media continually prepared them for the coming war against the Satanic Jews and their subhuman foot soldiers—all in service of the heaven-sent savior Adolf Hitler. The apocalyptic propaganda continued throughout the war, coming from both the Nazis and their own officers. As the war progressed, news sheets and political sessions presented to the troops went to great lengths to place the conflict in an eschatological framework—as a war of annihilation. Even in 1940, as the German army swept through the Netherlands and France, a *Mittelungen für die Truppe* (News for the Troops) noted that "this battle of annihilation was so great that we can only accept with shocked silence and thankful hearts this act of destiny. Behind the battle of annihilation of May 1940 stands in lone greatness the name of the Führer." The news sheet concluded with references to the historical turning point of the times, and the soldiers' chosen mission to sacrifice themselves for the coming new era:

> All this we were allowed to experience. Our great duty in this year of decision is that we do not accept it as observers, but that we, enraptured, and with all the passion of which we are capable, sacrifice ourselves to this Führer and strive to be worthy of the historical epoch molded by a heaven-storming will. (Bartov 1991: 122–24)

The letters of soldiers in the *Einsatzgruppen* and in the *Wehrmacht* demonstrate that this millennial world of evil Jewish-Bolsheviks and their minions the Russian subhumans, locked in apocalyptic battle with Germany, the force of order, was accepted by many of those charged with fighting the final war.

For these soldiers the blame for the mass destruction, starvation, and horrendous death tolls that they saw around them lay, not with the Russians, the Germans, nor even to the reality of modern warfare. Rather they found the culprit in that same "hidden force" of history seen in *Bolshevism from Moses to Lenin*. The Nazi millennial myth had become reality. In other words, belief in the apocalyptic fantasy became something of a self-defining principle. The horror of the war on the Eastern Front—with its extreme barbarity and loss of human life, with half-starved civilians, now eerily resembling the beastlike subhumans of Nazi propaganda—seemed to turn the conflict into the very apocalyptic war of annihilation that Hitler had prophesied for twenty years. The millennial fantasy that provided Hitler, his inner circle, and many Old Guard Nazis with a sense of meaning, direction, and a heightened sense of self-worth, now through the hell of modern warfare provided Hitler's soldiers with the meaning and self-perception needed to withstand and comprehend the constant suffering around them (theirs' and their victims'). In other words, faith that one was fighting in a holy war of apocalyptic significance legitimated one's own suffering, as well as justified the suffering imposed on others. The barbarous and often criminal actions of SS and Wehrmacht soldiers were conceptually transformed into a sacred struggle for existence and universal salvation.

David Redles

See also Nazism

Bibliography

Bartov, Omer. (1991) *Hitler's Army: Soldiers, Nazis, and War in the Third Reich*. New York: Oxford University Press.

Buchbender, Ortwin, and Reinhold Sterz, eds. (1982) *Das andere Gesicht des Krieges: Deutsche Feldpostbriefe, 1939–1945*. Munich: Beck.

Burleigh, Michael R., and Wolfgang Wippermann. (1991) *The Racial State*. Cambridge, U.K.: Cambridge University Press.

Cohn, Norman. (1967) *Warrant for Genocide: the Myth of the Jewish World Conspiracy and the Protocols of the Elders of Zion*. London: Eyre and Spottiswoode.

Dawidowicz, Lucy. (1983) *The War Against the Jews 1933–1945*. New York: Holt, Rineholt, and Winston.

Diewerge, Wolfgang, ed. (1941) *Deutsche Soldaten sehen die Sowjet-Union*. Berlin: Wilhelm Limpert Verlag.

Domarus, Max, ed. (1962–63) *Hitler, Reden und Proklamationen, 1932–1945*. Neustadt: a.d. Aisch Schmidt.

Eckart, Dietrich. (1924) *Der Bolschewismus von Moses bis Lenin. Zwiegespräch zwischen Adolf Hitler and mir*. Munich: Hoheneichen-Verlag.

Friedlander, Henry. (1995) *The Origins of Nazi Genocide: From Euthanasia to the Final Solution*. Chapel Hill, NC: University of North Carolina Press.

Friedländer, Saul. (1997) *Nazi Germany and the Jews*. New York: HarperCollins.

Goldhagen, Daniel Jonah. (1996) *Hitler's Willing Executioners; Ordinary Germans and the Holocaust*. New York: Alfred A. Knopf.

Goldhagen, Erich. (1976) "Weltanschauung und Endlösung: Zum Antisemitismus der nationalsozialistischen Führungsschicht." *Viertel-Jahrshefte für Zeitgeschichte* 24: 379–405.

Hitler, Adolf. (1925) *Die Rede Adolf Hitlers in der ersten grossen Massenversammlung bei Wiederausrichtung der NSDAP*. Munich: Franz Eher.

——. (1943) *Mein Kampf*, translated by Ralph Manheim. Boston: Houghton Mifflin.

Ley, Michael. (1993) *Genozid und Heilserwartung: Zum Nationalsozialistischen Mord am Europäischen Judentum*. Vienna: Picus.

Lifton, Robert Jay. (1986) *The Nazi Doctors: Medical Killing and the Psychology of Genocide*. New York: Basic Books.

Redles, David. (2000) *Hitler and the Apocalypse Complex: Salvation and the Spiritual Power of Nazism*. New York: New York University Press.

Rhodes, James M. (1980) *The Hitler Movement: A Modern Millenarian Revolution*. Stanford, CT: Hoover Institute Press.

Schram, Percy Ernst, ed. (1961) *Kriegstagebuch des Oberkommando der Wehrmacht (Wehrmachtführungstab) 1940–1945*. Frankfurt: Bernard and Graefe.

Snyder, Louis L. (1981) *Hitler's Third Reich: A Documentary History*. Chicago: Nelson-Hall.

Streit, Christian. (1978) *Keine Kameraden: Die Wehrmacht und die sowjetischen Kriegsgefangenen, 1941–1945*. Stuttgart: Verlags-Anstalt.

Wistrich, Robert. (1985) *Hitler's Apocalypse: Jews and the Nazi Legacy*. New York: St. Martin's Press.

Indian Shakers

The Indian Shaker Religion emerged in the Pacific Northwest region of United States. This religion should not be confused with the European-American Shaker religion and communal society who built communities in the Eastern United States. The Indian Shaker Church is a Native American sect that articulates its beliefs and practices with Christian themes. Religious practices and themes appear to bridge a gap between traditional shamanism and Christian theology.

The Shaker prophet, John Slocum (Squ-sacht-un), worked as a logger and was fond of drinking, gambling, and horse racing. Anthropologist Erna Gunther describes him as a member of the Skokomish nation in the Pacific Northwest, while historians Robert H. Ruby and John A. Brown state that he was from the Sahewamish nation. After an illness in 1881, John Slocum was considered dead by his relatives who had set out to fetch a coffin. Slocum came back to life and surprised his family with revelations and warnings about the afterlife. He said that he went to heaven where he could not get in the Heavenly Gates because he had not been a good Christian.

Accounts vary, but most texts attribute the shaking practices to his wife, Mary Thompson, who healed her husband of a subsequent illness by shaking her body. The shaking was interpreted to have curative powers sent from the supernatural world. Ruby and Brown argue that the shaking practice has a precedent in the Spirit Canoe ceremony.

Before 1900, the Indian Shakers emphasized a strong millenarian message. They stressed the return of Jesus Christ and that native peoples should ready themselves by confessing sins and living good lives. Slocum preached that dead relatives would return to earth with the Second Coming, suggesting that the new world would be a Christian world. So many people would return that there would not be enough land for them. Everyone would know the time of their coming as they could hear their voices coming out of the east. Shakers were told to be alert for the sound of these voices lest they be passed over by their loved ones.

Throughout the early years, Slocum preached and conducted prayer gatherings where members strongly shook each other's hands. The sparse ethnographic accounts of the early meetings suggest that people testified to having visions of heaven and of Christ's return. At certain assemblies, people believed they were angels as they hopped about the room waving their arms; other followers told stories about their own supposed deaths and spiritual revivals. The shaking movements were performed in prayer, in dance, or at the sick beds of believers.

John Slocum was succeeded by Louis Yowaluch (Mud Bay Louis). The movement spread north into Canada and east into Idaho and south to reservations in California. Churches were built despite disapproval from Indian agents and missionaries. New members joined when they heard of the curative powers of the shake. The church which was incorporated in 1910 and has since faced periods of internal controversy and schism, but it still has adherents in the 1990s. There are Indian Shaker adherents among the Squamish of British Columbia, the Nez Perce of Idaho, the Coleville Confederated Tribes of Washington, and the Hoopa and Yurok of California.

Diana Tumminia

Bibliography

Barnett, H. G. (1957) *Indian Shakers: A Messianic Cult of the Pacific Northwest.* Carbondale, IL: Southern Illinois University Press.

Gunther, Erna. (1949) *The Shaker Religion of the Northwest.* In *Indians of the Urban Northwest,* edited by Marian W. Smith. New York: Columbia University Press, 37–76.

Ruby, Robert H., and John A. Brown. (1996) *John Slocum and the Indian Shaker Church.* Norman, OK: University of Oklahoma Press.

Islam

> "The political implications of the whole millennial idea in Islam are very difficult to separate from the eschatological ones. The hope of something better to come has informed both theology and sociopolitical expectations, and the translation of the promise of a time of universal peace and justice is easily made from this age to the next (and back again)." (Haddad & Smith 1981: 70)

Muslim eschatology, or the belief system regarding the events leading up to the end of the world, springs from a Judeo-Christian context and thus not surprisingly resembles that of both Jews and Christians. However, some qualifications must be made in the usage of the terms "millennialism," "millenarianism," or "chiliasm"—each of which derives from words for 1,000 in Latin *(milleni)* or Greek *(chilioi):* in the sense of Revelation chapter 20, which predicates a thousand-year reign of Jesus Christ on Earth, these terms should not be applied to an Islamic context; but in the sense of the expectation of a future ideal society, they can be used to describe Muslim beliefs. Indeed, "centennialism" would be a more accurate term, as the tradition of a *mujaddid* or "renewer" who comes every century carries far more resonance with Muslims. "Messianism" is a term that should be avoided in an Islamic context. For unlike Jews, many of whom still await the *Mashiah* (Hebrew for "Anointed One") who will restore the biblical Kingdom of Israel, and Christians, who await the return of their messiah Jesus Christ (*Christ* is Greek for "messiah"); Muslim theology has no place for such a deliverer. In the Qur'an, Jesus the prophet is sometimes given the title *al-Masih,* a cognate term to Messiah, but it is used as an honorific only, devoid of theological import.

For Muslims the most important eschatological figure is not Jesus, although both the Qur'an and the Hadiths, or traditions and sayings attributed to the prophet Muhammad (570?–632 CE), do speak of his return. Rather, *al-Mahdi,* the "rightly-guided one," is the linchpin of the endtimes. Jesus' second coming is for Muslims but one sign of the approaching end and not the climax thereof, as for Christians. Islamic millennialism is on one level more akin to that of Judaism in that both the Mahdi and the awaited Mashiah will be historical figures whose tasks will be accomplished in the normal span of space and time, unlike Jesus in his Christian role as the second person of the Trinity and the Alpha and Omega of the Book of Revelation. Islamic and Jewish millennialism are also similar in that the primary goal of the Mahdi and the Mashiah will be collective justice and peace rather than individual salvation.

On the other hand, Muslim beliefs about the events presaging the end of time and the Judgment resemble those of the Christian churches in many regards: besides Jesus' return, Muslim scripture and tradition speak of the Deceiver or Antichrist, *al-Dajjal;* the Beast, *al-Dabbah;* and Gog and Magog, *Yajuj wa-Majuj*—all of whom are found in the Revelation of St. John, the final book of the Christian New Testament. So it is clear that Islamic eschatology resembles that of both Jews and Christians. The belief in the Mahdi, in particular, has proved particularly potent throughout the 1,400-year span of Islamic history: on many occasions Muslim religious figures have claimed to be the awaited Mahdi, created oppositional revolutionary movements, and used them to overthrow or create a political order. Even where such movements fail—as in Saudi Arabia in 1979, when one Muhammad (born 'Abd Allah al-Qahtani) claimed to be the Mahdi and led several hundred followers in an ultimately unsuccessful attempt to occupy the Grand Mosque of Mecca, Islam's holiest city—they demonstrate the continued power of Mahdism, the Islamic version of millennialism.

Mahdism in Islamic History

The term "Mahdi" derives from the Arabic root *hadá,* "to guide on the right path;" the Mahdi, then, is "the rightly-guided one." Although the Mahdi does not appear in the

Qur'an, he is predicted in a number of Hadiths, Sunni as well as Shi'a. (These are the two major branches of Islam; the former comprise about 85 percent of Muslims while the latter are a majority only in modern Iran and Iraq. The split between the two groups began as a political disagreement about whether the leader of the Islamic community must be a descendant of Muhammad; Sunnis said no, Shi'as, yes. Over the centuries the two groups have diverged further along theological lines, particularly in their beliefs about the Mahdi.) Some very conservative Muslims doubt the idea of the Mahdi because of its absence from the pages of the Qur'an, and/or because prophecies concerning him do not appear in the two most revered canonical collections of Hadith—those of al-Bukhari (d. 820 CE) and Muslim (d. 875 CE). But the vast majority of Muslims throughout the centuries have believed—and continue to believe—in this eschatological figure.

In general, beliefs about the Mahdi gleaned from Hadith indicate that he would descend from the prophet's family and resemble Muhammad in both name and physical appearance. He would ally with Jesus to lead the believers against the hordes of the Dajjal and Yajuj wa-Majuj and in fact would help slay the Antichrist, reinstituting the true worship of God and restoring justice and equity to the inhabitants of the Earth; and like the returned Jesus, he would eventually die a natural death and be buried sometime before the Last Trumpet sounds and God resurrects all humans for the Final Judgment. The utopian desire for redress of socioeconomic disparities has been perhaps the quintessential Mahdist belief, although the hope for the reinstitution of true worship and piety was almost as potent.

Sunnis and Shi'as did evolve somewhat different belief systems about the Mahdi, however. Sunnis linked him more closely with the Second Coming of Jesus and tended to conflate his role with that of the *mujaddid*, or "renewer," who was promised by some Hadith to come every century and renew the Islamic community. Sunni tradition did agree with the Shi'a that the Mahdi would be of the *ahl al-bayt*, or "family of the [prophet's] house." The Shi'a view differed in two major respects. First, the Mahdi came to be referred to as the Hidden Imam who would return. (This was because early Shi'a groups came to believe that their Imam, or "leader," had gone into *ghaybah*, or "hiding," forced to do so by the majority Sunnis and their unworthy "successor" to the prophet, the *khalifah*, Anglicized as "caliph." This *ghaybah* is a transcendent state of being whence the Imam will return at some unspecified time in the future when Muslims are in the greatest need.) Second, the Mahdi/Hidden Imam would possess special illumination directly from God.

Another major Islamic group added their own perspective to views of the Mahdi. The Sufis, or Islamic mystics, largely shared Sunni and Shi'a beliefs; some mystical orders, however, eventually came to teach that only the Sufis would recognize the Mahdi upon his coming while the non-Sufi religious leaders would reject him. In general all three major Muslim groupings—Sunnis, Shi'as, and Sufis—agreed on the expectation of an eschatological figure who would establish justice and piety on the Earth.

Madhist Movements

Over the course of Islamic history there has been a myriad of Mahdist movements predicated on such beliefs, but four in particular stand out as successful.

The 'Abbasids took over the young Islamic empire in 750 CE and reigned during what most historians consider the "Golden Age" of Islamic history (their caliph Harun al-Rashid was the immensely richer and more sophisticated contemporary of Charlemagne). Between 745 and 750 CE 'Abbasid propagandists claimed Mahdist stature for their leaders and appealed to Shi'a sympathies in order to undermine the ruling Umayyad dynasty in Damascus. Once ensconced in power in Baghdad, however, the 'Abbasids largely jettisoned their Mahdist claims and Shi'a tendencies. Although some of their caliphs continued to affix the title "al-Mahdi" to their names, Mahdism was but a facade for the 'Abbasids once they were in control. Deprived of most of their power by 945, the 'Abbasids survived as mere religious figureheads until the Mongols overran their dynasty in 1258 CE.

In contrast to the 'Abbasids' rather perfunctory usage of Mahdist ideology, the three subsequent major groups in Islamic history which employed Mahdism as a means to hegemony—the Fatimids, the Almohads or *al-Muwahhidun*, and the Sudanese Mahdists—continued to capitalize on eschatological beliefs in the administration, not just the creation, of their states. The first example of an unequivocally Mahdist state is the Fatimids, an Isma'ili Shi'a dynasty that ruled Egypt from 969 to 1171 CE. (The Isma'ilis are a branch of Shi'ism which believes the seventh Imam went into hiding, hence they are also known as "Seveners." The largest branch of Shi'ism in the world today, the Iranian Shi'as, are known as Imamis or "Twelvers," since they believe the twelfth Imam is the one hidden.) The Isma'ili founder, 'Ubayd Allah, claimed to be the Mahdi in 910 CE on the strength of his descent from the prophet through his daughter Fatimah. His propagandists won Berber armies to his claim and by 969 they had conquered much of North Africa and Egypt. The Fatimids welded Mahdism to an esoteric cosmology drawn from both Gnosticism and Neoplatonism. Unlike other Shi'a groups the Fatimids were powerful enough to contemplate seriously the aim of conquering the

Yajuj wa-Majuj, the "Gog and Magog" of the Bible, are an essential element of Islamic eschatology. Here, Alexander the Great directs his soldiers in erecting a wall to contain these murderous hordes, in an illustration from the Persian epic "Shahnama." Before the end of time Yajuj wa-Majuj will escape this barrier and rampage across the globe before meeting their demise at the hands of the prophet Jesus and Mahdi. THE FREER GALLERY OF ART, SMITHSONIAN INSTITUTION, WASHINGTON, D.C., 1986.

entire Muslim world. To this end they overtly utilized their military against not only the Byzantine Empire and the Crusader states but also the 'Abbasid caliphate; and they covertly supported Isma'ili *dawa'in*, or propagandists, seeking to undermine the 'Abbasids. Ultimately the Fatimids failed, however and, weakened by Crusader invasions, they were conquered by Richard the Lion-Heart's fierce friend, Salah al-Din al-Ayyubi—the Saladin of European history.

Another medieval North African Mahdist movement, albeit one more Sunni than Shi'a, was that of the Almohads who ruled the Maghrib, or Northwest Africa, and Spain from 1130 to 1269 CE. Their founder Ibn Tumart (d. 1130) claimed to be the awaited Mahdi who would restore true Islam which had suffered under the allegedly impious former rulers of the area, the Almoravids or Almurâbitûn. Shortly after launching his movement Ibn Tumart died and his successor 'Abd al-Mu'min completed the conquests and established a Sunni Mahdist state that lasted for over a century.

Since the time of the Almohads the most successful Mahdist movement has been a relatively recent one: that of the Sudanese Mahdists of the late nineteenth century. The Muslim world of the nineteenth century, in general, and Islamic Africa, in particular, witnessed a plethora of *jihads*, or "holy wars," against seemingly impious Muslim rulers and/or colonial powers. The jihad led by Muhammad Ahmad in what is now Sudan—then part of the Ottoman Empire, ruled from Egypt—was the only one whose founder and leader claimed to be the eschatological Mahdi, not merely a mujaddid.

Since this movement occurred in relatively modern times, we know a great deal more about it than we do any other successful Mahdist movements. Muhammad Ahmad was a Sunni but also a Sufi, and, when only in his twenties, had visions in which the prophet and famous Sufi *shaykhs* appeared and spoke with him. After openly proclaiming himself the Mahdi whose task it was to drive the unbelieving Turks, Egyptians, and British out of Sudan, he united all the regime's opponents, raised an army, and conquered most of what is now Sudan between 1881 and 1885 CE. Before his death in 1885, Muhammad Ahmad attempted to re-create the early Islamic community, dissolved all Sufi orders, harshly enforced Islamic law, and mandated belief in himself as the Mahdi. His successor Abdullahi ruled until 1898 when the British under Kitchener, in one of the last spasms of the Scramble for Africa, marched south from British-occupied Egypt and ended the Mahdiyyah (as the Sudanese Mahdist state had come to be known). Sudan became part of the Anglo-Egyptian Condominium, and Mahdist loyalties were sublimated into the Ummah Party which today constitutes the outlawed opposition to Hasan al-Turabi's strict Muslim Brotherhood rule in Sudan.

Several other important movements of the last 150 years began as Islamic Mahdist ones, but have now become classified as separate religions: the Iranian Babis and their offshoot the Baha'is, as well as the Indian Ahmadiyah. In 1830s Iran, one 'Ali-Muhammad claimed to be the *bab*, or "gateway," to the Hidden Imam. He was arrested and executed but soon his follower Bahâ'ullah (d. 1892) claimed to be not only the Mahdi/Hidden Imam but also a prophet. (By definition anyone who claims to be a prophet is outside the pale of Islam, for Muhammad is considered the *khatam al-nabiyin*, or "seal of the prophets.") Bahâ'ullah preached a new, more pacifistic dispensation that superseded Islamic law. He was exiled by the rulers of Iran, finally settling in Acre, Palestine. Today Baha'ism is recognized as a religion in its own right and claims some six million adherents worldwide, although Baha'is are still persecuted by the Islamic Republic of Iran.

Another neo-Mahdist movement was that which Ghulam Ahmad started in the Qadiyan region of India's Punjab in the 1880s. Ghulam Ahmad claimed to be the Mahdi and a prophet. Members of this group are known as Ahmadis to Westerners and Qadiyanis to Muslims and are especially strong in Africa. Movements such as these are often adduced by Muslims writers when they wish to accentuate the inherent dangers of Mahdism. Dangerous they may be from a Muslim perspective, but Baha'ism and Ahmadism can be seen as successful Mahdist movements insofar as each now numbers its adherents in the hundreds of thousands, if not millions.

Such openly Mahdist claims have not made much headway among orthodox Muslims in the twentieth century, however. We have already discussed the fate of the self-styled Saudi Mahdi in 1979—gunned down by doubters. And while whispered theories that the Ayatollah Khomeini was the no-longer-Hidden Imam circulated during the revolution in Iran, Khomeini himself never openly claimed such a title. Nonetheless, if history is any indication, Mahdism remains a potentially powerful oppositional ideology in the Muslim world as the world enters a new century and millennium.

Conclusion

Mahdism, the Islamic brand of millennialism, resembles its Jewish and Christian antecedents yet also markedly differs from each. In its emphasis on socioeconomic justice Mahdism most closely resembles Judaism; but in its inclusion of Jesus and other eschatological figures, Mahdism seems more akin to Christianity. Ultimately, however, Mahdism must be judged on its own terms as quintessentially Islamic.

Although it is true that a new century, rather than a new millennium, tends to raise eschatological hopes for Muslims, it is undeniable that interest in the Mahdi and Mahdism has greatly increased in the Muslim world in recent decades.

There seem to be several reasons for this. One is the melancholy that has beset the Arab world since the stinging defeat of the Six-Days War in 1967 (which has only begun to dissipate in recent years). Another is a congeries of developments which includes the ongoing failure of Arab countries to modernize and bring living standards into line with expectations, the persistent failure to achieve Arab unity, the collapse of the Soviet Union and its patronage for states such as Syria and Libya, and the subsequent embarrassing dependence upon the United States, seen by many Muslims as the heir of the colonial powers Britain and France. These factors taken together constitute massive societal frustration and angst for at least the Arab portion of the Muslim world and it is commonly accepted that millenarian movements within the Judeo-Christian-Muslim milieu often occur in such a period. Also, the Islamic revolution in Iran, 1979–80, has had enormous repercussions throughout the entire Islamic world; despite the political, theological, and ideological differences between Shi'ism and Sunnism, the installation of a decidedly pro-Islamic government in Tehran has served as a theocratic beacon to anyone yearning for an Islamic state. Finally, the worldwide usage of the Christian calendar (even when camouflaged as "CE" rather than "AD") and the fact that Christianity is the largest religion on Earth (approximately 1.9 billion adherents, whereas Islam numbers about 1 billion) has infected the entire planet with an eschatological fervor (Y2K, et al.) to which even Islam, despite its distinctly nonmillenarian character, is not immune.

Mahdism has been a powerful ideology throughout Islamic history for both toppling existing states and establishing new ones, as the examples cited above attest. It should come as no surprise then, that since "the ideologies of many twentieth-century Islamic fundamentalist movements frequently include a healthy dose of eschatology . . . there is every indication that eschatological ideas will continue to play an important role in the Islamic world into the twenty-first century" (Hamblin and Peterson 1995: 442). A continuing research agenda on Mahdism would thus do well to encompass the eschatological content of groups such as the Taliban in Afghanistan, the Muslim Brotherhood of Egypt and Palestine, the Kosovo Liberation Army, and the Daghestani Islamic rebels, among others. Christian millennialism will subside after 2001 but the next Muslim century begins a mere seventy-seven years from now, in 2076.

Timothy R. Furnish

See also Baha'i

Bibliography

Ajami, Fouad. (1981) *The Arab Predicament: Arab Political Thought and Practice since 1967.* Cambridge: Cambridge University Press.

Blichfedlt, Jan-Olaf. (1985) *Early Mahdism: Politics and Religion in the Formative Period of Islam.* Leiden: E.J. Brill.

Campbell, Sondra. (1995) "Millennial Messiah or Religious Restorer? Reflections on the Early Islamic Understanding of the Term 'Mahdi.'" *Jusur* 11: 1–11.

Canard, Marius. (1965) "Fâtimids." In *Encyclopedia of Islam,* new ed. Leiden: E.J. Brill, v. 2: 850–62.

Crow, Douglas S. (1995) "Islamic Messianism." In *The Encyclopedia of Religion,* vol. 9, edited by Mircea Eliade, 477–81.

Haddad, Yvonne, and Jane Smith. (1981) *The Islamic Understanding of Death and Resurrection.* Albany: State University of New York Press.

Hamblin, William, and Daniel Peterson. (1995) "Eschatology." In *The Oxford Encyclopedia of the Modern Islamic World.* New York: Oxford University Press, 440–42.

Holt, Peter Malcom. (1958) *The Mahdist State in the Sudan, 1881–1898: A Study of its Origins, Development and Overthrow.* Oxford: Oxford University Press.

——. (1986) "al-Mahdiyya." In *Encyclopedia of Islam,* new ed. Leiden: E.J. Brill, v. 5: 1247–53.

——. (1980) "Islamic Millenarianism and the Fulfillment of Prophecy: A Case Study." In *Prophecy and Millenarianism: Essays in Honour of Marjorie Reeves.* Burnt-Hill: Longman, 337–46.

Ibn Kathir. (1991) *The Signs Before the Day of Judgement,* translated by Huda Khattab. London: Dar al-Taqwa.

Isaiah, Emmanuel Sudhir. (1988) "Muslim Eschatology and its Missiological Implications: A Thematic Study." Ph.D. Diss., Fuller Theological Seminary, Pasadena, CA.

(1980) "Saudi Arabia: Occupation of the Sacred Mosque of Mecca . . ." Keesings Contemporary Archives, vol. 26, 30247–48.

Kennedy, Hugh. (1995) "Abbâsid Caliphate." In *The Oxford Encyclopedia of the Modern Islamic World.* New York: Oxford University Press, 1, 2.

Kramer, Robert. (1995) "Mahdi." In *The Oxford Encyclopedia of the Modern Islamic World.* New York: Oxford University Press, 18, 19.

Lewis, Bernard. (1960) "'Abbâsids." In *Encyclopedia of Islam,* new ed. Leiden: E.J. Brill, v. 1: 15–23.

Madelung, Wilfrid. (1986) "al-Mahdi." In *Encyclopedia of Islam,* new ed. Leiden: E.J. Brill, v. 5: 1230–38.

Marlow, Louis. (1997) *Hierarchy and Egalitarianism in Islamic Thought.* Cambridge: Cambridge University Press.

Al-Qaddal, Muhammad Sa'id. (1992) *Al-Imam al-Mahdi: Muhammad Ahmad b. 'Abd Allah, 1844–1885.* Beirut: Dar al-Jil.

Richards, D. S. (1995) "Fatimid Dynasty." In *The Oxford Encyclopedia of the Modern Islamic World.* New York: Oxford University Press, 7, 8.

Sachedina, Abdul Azia. (1981) *Islamic Messianism. The Idea of the Mahdi in Twelver Shi'ism.* Albany, NY: State University of New York Press.

——. (1995) "Messianism." In *The Oxford Encyclopedia of the Modern Islamic World.* New York: Oxford University Press, 95–99.

Smith, Peter. (1996) *A Short History of the Baha'i Faith.* Oxford: One World.

Smith, Wilfred Cantwell. (1986) "Ahmadiyya." In *Encyclopedia of Islam,* new ed. Leiden: E.J. Brill, v. 1: 301–3.

Al Tayr, Mustafa Muhammad al-Hadidi. (1986) *Al-qawl al-haqq fi al-babiyah, wa-al-baha'iyah wa-al-quadiyaniyah wa-al-mahdiyah* (The True Statement about the Babiya, Baha'iyah, Qasiyaniyah, and Mahdiyah). Cairo: Dar al-Misriyah al-Lubnaniyah.

Thrupp, Sylvia. (1970) *Millennial Dreams in Action: Studies in Revolutionary Religious Movements.* New York: Schocken Books.

Voll, John. (1982) "Wahhabism and Mahdism: Alternative Styles of Islamic Renewal." *Arab Studies Quarterly* 4, 1 & 2: 110–26.

Israel

Israel, both as concept and entity, occupies a unique place in Judeo-Christian eschatological thought. Its significance has lain both in its actual existence as a political state and as an eschatological construct which embodies God's ultimate plan for humankind on earth. It is, as well, interrelated with other millennial ideals: Jerusalem and Zion, the Messiah, Zionism, and philo-Semitism. As an element of sacred history (God's dealings with humankind), Israel has been a powerful concept from the closing days of the Bronze Age into the closing days of the twentieth century. Its political significance, even after several thousand years, is probably greater today than ever.

Israel's political existence in ancient times lasted from the conquest of Canaan by Hebrew tribes, beginning about the year 1000 BCE, until the first century CE, when its identity was extinguished by Roman authority. The modern Israeli state, proclaimed officially in 1947, occupies substantially the same territory as its ancient predecessor.

The Ancient Kingdom of Israel

Ancient Israel came into existence only fitfully, as migrating Hebrew tribes clashed over several centuries with people and cultures long settled in the eastern Mediterranean littoral. Much of the resonance of Israel for modern Jews and Christians is due to an anachronistic reading back into its past of much later conceptions of national identity. However, this anachronistic historiography also makes Israel potent as a millennial icon.

When the generally accepted canon of the Pentateuch (the first five books of the Bible) was more or less agreed upon around the sixth century BCE, its redactors (chiefly priests) compiled it in the light of an existing Jewish state. They thus interpreted the past to legitimize an existing order as God's work in history. Abraham, the earliest of the Patriarchs, was portrayed as promised by Yahweh (the proper name of the Old Testament deity) that a great land should be given his descendents. That promise became a foundation for subsequent Judeo-Christian millennial expectations: "Go from your country and your kindred and your father's house to the land that I will show you. And I will make of you a great nation" (Genesis 12:1–2).

The historicity of Abraham, thought to have received his promise toward the middle of the second millennium BCE, is uncertain. Nevertheless, the concept of an Israeli homeland became inseparable from Jewish identity from an early date. Much, perhaps most, of the Old Testament can thus be read as an Israeli national epic.

The Exodus saga vastly reinforced the concept of Israel. The much earlier wandering of Hebrew tribes into Canaan was justified by sixth-century BCE redactors as fulfilling God's plan. Yahweh is depicted as telling Moses of the Hebrews: "I know their sufferings, and I have come down to deliver them out of the hand of the Egyptians, and to bring them up out of that land to a good and broad land flowing with milk and honey" (Exodus 3:7–8). The exclusivity of this promise to the Jews was, however, mitigated by those prophets who foresaw a world role for Israel: "And the nations shall come to your light, and kings to the brightness of your rising" (Isaiah 60:3). During and after the Babylonian Exile (the sixth century BCE), reaffirmation of the divine covenant with Israel was increasingly conflated with its broadened role: "For behold, I create new heavens and a new earth; and the former things shall not be remembered or come into mind" (Isaiah 65:17). While it would be anachronistic to call such a promise "millennial" (the term used in the much later New Testament: Revelation 20:1–3), there is, nevertheless, a clear ideological affinity between Christian millennialism and Yahweh's expanded promise of a coming era of blessedness for humanity which will center upon Israel.

Zion and Jerusalem are concepts inseparable from that of Israel itself. Jerusalem was ancient Israel's capital and Zion (King David's original stronghold) the eastern part of that city. Jerusalem/Zion was not just the temporal capital of a state, but the unique dwelling place of Yahweh: "Behold, I and the children whom the Lord has given me are signs and

ARE YOU AN ISRAELITE?

Some say the Jews are, some say the Anglo-Saxon and kindred peoples of Europe.

Below are 33 identifying marks of end-time Israel from the Holy Bible. Let the Bible identify true Israel.

1. Be a great nation. Gen. 12:1-3
2. Be blessed of God. Gen. 12:1-3
3. Be blessings to other (races) families of the earth. Gen. 12:1-3
4. Others be blessed or cursed by God, depending on attitude toward Israel. Gen. 12:1-3
5. Be great multitude of people. Gen. 13:16; 15:5
6. Be captive in Egypt, and then be delivered. Gen. 15:13,14
7. Be given great land area in Middle East. Gen. 15:18
8. Become many nations. Gen. 17:4,5
9. God of Bible to be God of Abraham's descendants. Gen. 17:7
10. Land of Canaan theirs for an everlasting possession. Gen. 17:8
11. Mark of circumcision was given to them. Gen. 17:10,11
12. Would keep Way of the Lord and do justice and judgment. Gen. 18:17-19
13. Would possess the gates of their enemies. Gen. 22:15,17,18

(Here is a transfer from Abraham to seed thru Isaac)

14. Great agricultural harvest promised. Gen. 27:28
15. Would rule over others. Gen. 27:29
16. Would spread abroad from Palestine in all directions. Gen. 28:13,14
17. When divorced, dispersed, they could not return to their old land. Hosea 2:6 (whole chapter deals with this)
18. Jacob's descendants would have power with God & men. Gen. 32:28
19. To be a nation and company of nations. Gen. 35:9-12 (vs 11 esp)
20. Descendants to be kings, rulers. Gen. 35:11; Gen.48:3-5,15,16
21. Out of Judah would come rulers of Israel. Gen. 49:10
22. Judah would have to do with obedience of Israel in last days. Gen. 49:8-10
23. Joseph's descendent to be blessed over rest of Israelites (Would have more wealth). Gen 49:22-26; Deut. 33:13-16
24. Joseph's descendent to have land blessed with agriculture, wealth. Deut. 33:13,14
25. Joseph's descendants would also have wealth of land in minerals, etc. Deut. 33:15,16; I Chronicles 5:1 (birthright)
26. Only Israel given, and in possession of, God's Laws. Gen. 19:24 (Covenant given at Sinai); Deut. 33:4; Ps. 147:19,20
27. Would be people blessed by God above all people when obedient to God's Laws. Deut.28:
28. Would be brought under judgment for disobedience to God's Laws. Deut. 28:15-68; Amos 3:1,2
29. God's servants (people serving God). Is.41:8,9
30. Be God's witness. Proclaim God to all nations.Is. 43:1, 10-12
31. Would come under New Covenant sealed by heart circumcision. Jer. 31:31-34; Ez. 36; Heb. 8:8
32. Were not to be known by the name Israel. Is. 62:2; Is. 65:15
33. Were to be called by name of God. Num. 6:22-27. (God's new name, Rev. 3:12)

First 13 marks can also apply to Ishmael (especially #10). You can find 20 or more specific marks by reading blessings and curses in Deut. 28 and Lev. 26.

Copies of this available, 100 for $5.00 offering to:

AMERICA'S PROMISE MINISTRIES

P.O. BOX 30,000

PHOENIX, ARIZONA 85046

Tract #212

This handbill shows the relationship between Israel and the endtime in some Christian eschatology. AMERICA'S PROMISE MINISTRIES, PHOENIX, AZ, TRACT #212.

portents in Israel from the Lord of hosts, who dwells on Mount Zion" (Isaiah 8:18). It was a place of transcendent importance, which no suffering could erase from the heart: "By the waters of Babylon, there we sat down and wept, when we remembered Zion" (Psalms 137:1). Jerusalem/Zion thus constitute a restorationist theme within the larger such theme of Israel itself.

Messianism was a further element in ancient Jewish thought regarding Israel. Beginning about the time of the Exile, prophets foretold an ingathering of the Jewish people under the leadership of the divinely ordained messiah ("the anointed one"), whose reign would inaugurate an era of peace and blessedness: "Behold, the days are coming, says the Lord, when I will raise up for David a righteous Branch, and he shall secure justice and righteousness in the land" (Jeremiah 23:5). Messianism became especially intense during the years just prior to and immediately after the destruction of the Second Temple (70 CE). It has since never wholly departed since from Jewish life.

Ancient Israel faded out of existence following the bloody suppression of first-century CE rebellions against Rome. The centuries that followed witnessed a steady diffusion of Jews throughout the ancient Near East and into Europe (the Diaspora) and the eventual triumph of other faiths—first Christianity, then Islam—on the historic territory of the Jewish State. But, although destroyed as a political entity, Israel remained alive in Jewish thought as an eschatological concept. Although events had placed actual possession in abeyance, the spiritual ownership of Israel remained unimpaired and its ultimate restoration to the Jews was hoped for. Similarly, Jerusalem/Zion lost none of its piquancy as the sacred place where the acceptable worship of the Lord must be centered.

The Sustained Vision of Israel from Antiquity to the Twentieth Century

Messianic hope likewise recurred among Jews during the medieval and early modern eras. In 1648, for example, a Turkish Jew, Sabbatai Zebi, proclaimed himself the anointed one, destined to lead his people back to Israel. He was widely received within the European Jewish community, although he later converted to Islam. Millennialism (broadly conceived here as the perceived end-goal of sacred history, rather than specifically Christian theology) doubtless helped sustain Jewish identity through many difficult centuries.

Christianity did not initially retain Israel as an element of political interest. Nevertheless, Israel as concept captivated Christians as well as Jews. Because of their association with Jesus, Jerusalem was regarded as a holy city, and Israel as a holy land. Throughout the Middle Ages, the sanctity of Israel and Jerusalem was continually reinforced for Christians through pilgrimages, art, and literature. Dante, for instance, reverentially referred to Jerusalem as the place "under whose meridian came to die/The Man born sinless and who did not sin" (*Hell*, 34:ll; Sayers trans., 115–16). Political interest in the Holy Land revived when, during the eleventh and twelfth centuries, the Crusades temporarily put Jerusalem, along with much of Palestine, under Christian control. Throughout the Middle Ages, then, Israel remained for both Jews and Christians a place of sacred memory, while Jews, especially, connected it with messianic longings.

It was, however, during the Reformation that Israel acquired that eschatological significance for some Protestants which continues to this day. Awed by the religious upheavals of their era, various Reformation scholars sought to interpret the religious revolution through the words of prophecy. Nowhere was this truer than in seventeenth-century England, where civil war, rooted, in part, in religious differences, inspired intense interest in prophetic Scripture, most especially Daniel (OT) and Revelation (NT). This was, as well, the period during which English scholars became proficient in the sacred languages, Hebrew in particular, as an outgrowth of Protestant emphasis on translating the Bible. This proficiency allowed them to access Jewish commentaries on the prophecies, and one result of these near-simultaneous developments in politics and scholarship was a sustained burst of millenarian speculation.

Perusal of Jewish and Christian prophetic literature convinced such English scholars as Joseph Mede and Richard Baxter that these foretold a millennial role for the Jews and Israel. English eschatological thought centered, of course, on the Second Advent of Christ, a time-honored tenet of the Christian faith. But, some argued, as well, that Christ would return only after the world's Jews were gathered to Palestine, to refound Israel as the Jewish homeland. It was further advanced that just before, or after, the Second Advent, the "restored" Jews would be Christianized. These speculations were to have a profound effect on subsequent Protestant thought toward Israel and the Jews in both England and America.

English millenarian thought became more subdued once the political disturbances of the seventeenth-century were past, but it never disappeared altogether. It effloresced with extraordinary vigor when the French Revolution so amazed British Protestants that they reverted once more to prophecy to ascertain the significance of astounding political developments. Speculations of seventeenth-century millenarians were rediscovered, while a host of new interpreters poured out a torrent of books, sermons, and tracts dedicated to converting the Jews and restoring them to the Holy Land as part of the preliminaries attendant on the Second Advent. Prominent social figures founded a Jews Society to convert the "Children of Abraham" and ready them for their return to Palestine.

Almost immediately, Protestants in the United States took up English fascination with the restoration of Israel. Early in the nineteenth century, several American journals (e.g., *Israel's Advocate*, New York, 1823–27) urged Jewish conversion and assured readers that Israel would soon be reborn: "We should remember further," wrote an American in 1825, "that the conversion and restoration of the Jews are most intimately connected with those glorious Millennial scenes." The Rev. David Austin, a New Haven, Connecticut, minister, went so far as to solicit funds in order to build wharves and sheds to be used by the Jews en route to their homeland. An American counterpart of the English Jews Society, the American Society for Meliorating the Condition of the Jews, evangelized the Jews and propagated the notion that the ancient state of Israel was to be reinstituted. Intense interest in Israel was sometimes accompanied by the notion (always the property of a small minority) that Jerusalem would be earth's capital during the millennium. The eschatological concept of Jerusalem/Zion thus took on a special urgency among certain prominent American clergy and laity.

Philo-Semitism (i.e., admiration for the Jewish people) was a further product of nineteenth-century Anglo-American millenarianism. Jews were spoken of, not as outcasts suffering for their unbelief, but as future partners during the millennium. Christians, in fact, could not enter the blessed millennial era, except in company with the Jews: "It is universally acknowledged that when the Jews shall be brought in, then shall take place the fullness of the gentiles" (1839). To an extent, the centuries old anti-Semitism of European civilization was reversed in America.

Millenarian theology widened its influence among American Protestants, slowly but steadily, throughout the remainder of the nineteenth century. When, in the early decades of the twentieth century, the Fundamentalist-mainline fissure opened, and then yawned ever wider as a sort of theological civil war raged between liberal and conservative clergy and scholars, premillennial eschatology helped define the boundary between the two camps. Israel was constituent to premillennialism, and the ingathering of the Jews to a restored Israel flourished conceptually to the same extent as Fundamentalism itself.

Modern Zionism and the Establishment of the State of Israel

In a remarkable historical coincidence, Protestant Zionism among American Fundamentalists flourished just when certain Jews themselves began to advocate the restoration of the Jewish State. For Protestants, Israel was a millennial vision. For Jews, however, Israel offered a practical solution for everyday problems. Late-nineteenth-century Europe witnessed growing anti-Semitism—in Russia, Germany, and Austro-Hungary, especially, but also France (e.g., the Dreyfus affair.) Despairing of tolerance from European Christians, fin de siècle Jews began to contemplate a place of refuge. Given the millennia-old centrality of Israel in Jewish life, both as entity and concept, it was no surprise that this refuge took the practical form of a "return" to Palestine.

Modern Jewish Zionism first manifested itself in Tsarist Russia, where anti-Semitism was especially intense. It found its champion, though, in an Austrian journalist of astonishing powers of organization and propaganda—Theodor Herzl. The first Zionist Congress (Basel, 1897), largely Herzl's work, issued a call for the settlement of Jews in Palestine (then under Ottoman rule.) The wider European Jewish community, content to assimilate with local culture, received this call only tepidly, and Israel might never have come into being, were it not for vast political developments.

Political considerations prompted by World War I caused the British government to officially favor a Jewish homeland in Palestine (the Balfour Declaration). Jewish emigration there subsequently increased, as did tension with the indigenous Palestinian population. Shortly thereafter, the horrendous crimes perpetrated against the Jews during World War II reinforced belief among survivors that only a secure homeland could provide refuge from future persecution. Displaced European Jews who had survived the Holocaust migrated in substantial numbers to Palestine and, in 1947, an independent Jewish state of Israel was proclaimed.

Herzl's original conception of a restored Israel owed virtually nothing to prophetic interpretation or to eschatology. His was a secular vision of a dispossessed people in search of a homeland. Nevertheless, it is inconceivable that he, or any other Zionist, would have picked the barren eastern Mediterranean littoral as the site of a nascent Jewish state without the prompting of thirty centuries of Jewish belief in Israel as fulfillment of God's prophecy to Abraham. In this sense, intense emotional belief in Israel as the ultimate destiny of the Jews allowed secular statesmen to co-opt millennial hope in the service of practical politics.

Modern Israel immediately gained friends in America among those Christians who interpreted its founding as the fulfillment of prophecy and a significant and necessary event, which pointed toward the Second Advent and the millennium. In this way, Jewish Zionism and Protestant Zionism, whether grounded in secular or prophetic visions of a restored Israel, moved from their nineteenth-century origins into remarkable synchronization.

There remains within Judaism, however, a significant dissent over whether the present state of Israel represents a legitimate realization of God's millennia-old promise. Those who so doubt base their reservations on a perceived failure of history to produce the messiah, the one divinely anointed to lead the Jews into the millennial era which alone represents the true fulfillment of prophecy.

Evangelical Protestants, in America especially, are confident, though, that modern Israel is the fulfillment of prophecy given in the Book of Revelation to the first Christians twenty centuries ago. The internationally famous preacher,

Rev. Billy Graham, is only one among many who so believe. The premillennial theology which undergirds this philo-Semitic and pro-Israel stance, manifested in both theology and politics (evangelicals often support Israel in matters of U.S. foreign policy), foresees momentous events as the world nears its millennial era. These include a climactic battle between good and evil (Armageddon), the Second Advent of Christ, and the establishment of Jerusalem as center of world governance for the millennium.

Robert K. Whalen

See also Judaism, Postmillennialism, Premillennialism, Zionism

Bibliography

Boyer, Paul. (1992) *When Time Shall Be No More: Prophecy Belief in Modern American Culture.* Cambridge, MA: Harvard University Press.

Garret, Clark. (1975) *Respectable Folly: Millenarians and the French Revolution in France and England.* Baltimore: Johns Hopkins University Press.

Pragai, Michael J. (1985) *Faith and Fulfilment: Christians and the Return to the Promised Land.* London: Vallentine, Mitchell.

Whalen, Robert K. (1966) "'Christians Love the Jews!' The Development of American Philo-Semitism, 1790–1860." *Religion and American Culture* 6 (summer): 226–60.

Israelites of the New Universal Covenant

Peru is a nation with a long-standing millenarist, or more properly, messianic tradition. Although the idea of an end of the world associated with the belief in a succession of cycles of 1,000 years has been recurrent since the pre-Hispanic period, the term "messianic" is preferred. This is because religious eschatology generally emphasizes the image of a unifying principle that redeems humanity from the cataclysmic consequences of the end of the world.

The Israelites of the New Universal Covenant are a recent expression of this tradition, although the approach they use is like that of other modern nondenominational religious groups that have separated from Catholicism. Formally it is a derivation from Adventism, but its real content is what could be called Andean in the sense that it is part of the Peruvian messianic tradition.

History

Officially the Peruvian government recognized the movement in 1968, but its wider expansion started, together with other anomalous social phenomena such as Shining Path, narco-traffic, etc., in the year 1980. At the core of this movement is a Quechua-speaking Indian peasant from the Peruvian Province of La Unión in the Department of Arequipa who migrated to the central highlands and a little later to the neighboring jungle of this area around 1950. His name is Ezequiel Ataucusi Gamonal. He was born in 1918.

While living in the village of Tarma around 1953 he became friends with an Adventist who introduced Ezequiel to the Bible. Previously he had been living in Huancayo where he had several painful experiences due to lack of money and jobs. He even almost lost one of his children because of a serious illness. He went to Tarma to work as a shoemaker and through the aforementioned friend he became an Adventist. Before long, however, he was expelled from the organization for going beyond the orthodoxy of the Adventists and starting to make predictions of his own. At this point he decided to pursue his vision, and he was accompanied by other Adventists who choose to go with him.

In 1956, at a place called Palomar Sanchirio, he was raised to the third Heaven where he received the Ten Commandments from the Father, the Son, and the Holy Ghost. He conveyed this scene as a school class: on one wall there is a blackboard with the Ten Commandments written down, and facing him, sitting behind a desk, the Holy Trinity, who ordered him to write down what was written on the blackboard and to return to earth to preach it to all the world. The name Israelites of the New Universal Covenant was chosen because of this revelation.

Beliefs and Practices

An important component of the movement is the belief that Emperor Constantine of the Western Roman Empire broke the original pact with God by changing the day of the celebration of the Lord from Saturday to Sunday. For this reason humanity began to experience a process of decay which will lead to the Apocalypse in the year 2000.

But, there is a means of salvation from this inexorable destiny. Salvation can be reached by following the Ten Commandments and the dictates of the Bible according their interpretation by Ezequiel Ataucusi Gamonal. In other words, to be saved, one must become an Israelite of the New Universal Covenant. Since the decay of humanity is derived from Constantine's action, the movement tries to overcome this decay not only by celebrating the Sabbath on Saturday but also by practicing other ancient religious practices. For example, followers of Ezequiel try to imitate the appearance of the ancient Hebrews by dressing like them, and the men do not cut their hair or beards. This approach with the goal of a return to the origins of Christianity, partly explains the

Eqequiel Ataucusi, leader of the Israelites of the New Covenant, and followers.
JUAN OSSIO

adoption of the term "Israelite." But "Israelite" also derives from the belief that members of this Peruvian religious organization are the "chosen" people and their leader is the "New Christ," the "Son of Man," "Father Israel," and many other epithets that mark Ezequiel as the new Messiah.

Why do followers believe that Ezequiel Ataucusi is the new messiah? First, they believe that he was raised up to the third Heaven to receive the Ten Commandments from the Holy Trinity. Second, they believe that he is the incarnation of the Holy Ghost. And, third, they find confirmation of these first two beliefs in the Bible.

This unorthodox biblical interpretation is at the center of the movement. This is not surprising as the leader and most followers do not read the Bible and, in fact, do not read at all as they come from a cultural tradition based on oral communication in the Quechua language. In addition, Andean people have not had the chance to be in direct contact with the Bible, because such behavior was never encouraged by the Catholic priests who evangelized them. Consequently the meanings of many words are interpreted freely, making use of the words of any language which serves to confirm the predetermined meanings given to the words. For example the word "Israel" is interpreted as meaning, "He is God." This meaning is assigned by separating the word into its three component vowels and then applying a meaning to each one. Thus, "Is" is interpreted as deriving from the present tense of the third-person singular of the English verb "to be." "Ra," in its turn, is said to mean "God" because that was the term given by the Egyptians to the Sun god. And the vowel "el" is said to be derived from the Spanish pronoun of the third-person singular. Another case is the city of Pergamo that, starting with the vowel "Per," is interpreted as "Peru." The Bible, so interpreted, is the ultimate source of legitimization and prediction. Everything can be explained through it. To serve this purpose the Israelites have developed a method for reading it that is supported by a biblical passage. This is Isaiah 28:10: "For it is precept upon precept, precept upon precept, line upon line, line upon line, here a little, there a little."

This religious movement has expanded by 1999 to almost all the provinces of Peru, with members most heavily concentrated in and around Lima and in the central Amazonian jungle of Junín. Members are mostly from rural Andean communities and have had the experience of migrating. In this respect, their social position within Peru is very much the same as that of their leader. That is, they come from the most marginal class of Peruvian society as their incomes are very low, their education terminated at the primary level, and in many cases they come from disrupted families. The Association of Israel of the New Universal Covenant is therefore a religious movement whose members derive from a non-Western cultural tradition.

Links to Indigenous Andean Cultural Traditions

This marginal and non-Western background suggests that the movement might derive some of its content from indigenous traditions that date to before the Spanish Conquest in the sixteenth century and thus might be called "Andean" to mark their native roots. Indications of this continuation of the indigenous culture include the belief that the world will come to a close in the year 2000, as was the case with two previous cycles in Andean belief, and the belief that a new messiah has come to bring salvation. The idea of a land without evil associated with a conception of the world in dualist terms is also a characteristic of Andean messianism. The Israelites further believe that history has evolved from the Eastern Hemisphere, where Jesus Christ was born, to the Western Hemisphere, where Ezequiel's cradle is located together with the Amazonian jungle where they will have to go to wait for the end of the world in order to be saved. That Andean messianism is behind these ideas is also indicated by familiarity with some indigenous myths about a hero called Inkarri, which mesh with some basic ideas of the movement. In one of the myths Inkarri is described as living in the jungle in a land without evil and with much wealth, and in another myth he is portrayed as the restorer of the traditional social order once his head, separated from his body by the Spaniards, is returned to its place.

While it is true that the Israelites do not go so far as earlier messianic movements in aiming to restore the Inca Empire, they are not totally removed from this goal. They claim that their colonies in the jungle are organized on Incan principles; organized into groups similar to those known by the Incas as "ayllu," where land is shared communally. Furthermore, they engage in cooperative commercial and production practices, and in both 1990 and 1995 their political program for Ezequiel's campaign for the Peruvian presidency implied support many of these practices, particularly a return to agriculture and the enforcement of some Inca laws.

One important characteristic of the "Israelites" is that they are peaceful and accept Peru's national institutions except the Catholic Church. They argue that in addition to complying with Constantine reforms, Catholic priests invented the saints to take the money from the people. This criticism may be derived from the fact that, being marginal in their own communities and with limited economic resources, they are unable to fulfill the communal obligations that afford people and families status in local communities. Therefore they rebel against one of its symbols, the Catholic saints. Other criticisms of the church include questioning the dates of Christ's birth and death and organizing a ritual calendar according to their particular interpretations of those dates.

Conclusion

The Israelite movement is millenarist because followers believe in an end of the world within the context of a series of succeeding temporal cycles. It is messianic because followers believe that their leader Ezequiel Ataucusi Gamonal has received revelations and will save his followers from this end of the world. And it is "nativistic" because it wants to restore both the ritual practices of the Old Testament and the values of the Inca Empire. Finally it is a fundamentalist movement as adherents believe that only Ezequiel can provide a true interpretation of the Bible.

Juan M. Ossio

See also Israel, Native South America

Bibliography

Espinoza-Benavides, Enrique. (1984) "La Secta Israel del Nuevo Pacto Universal: Un Movimiento Mesiánico Peruano. Lima." *Revista Teológica Limense* 18, 1: 47–81.

Granados, Manuel Jesús. (1986) "El Movimiento Religioso de los Israelitas del Nuevo Pacto Universal." M.A. thesis, Pontificia Universidad Católica del Perú, Lima.

Ossio, Juan. (1990) "La Misión Israelita del Nuevo Pacto Universal y su compsición social." In *Pobreza Urbana*, edited by Marcel Valcárcel. Lima: Pontificia Universidad Católica, 111–67.

——, ed. (1973) *Ideología Mesiánica del Mundo Andino*. Lima: Ignacio Prado Pastor del Perú.

Scott, Kenneth David. (1990) *Los Israelitas del Nuevo Pacto Universal*. Lima: Ediciones Pusel.

Japan

Japan has a complex history of millennialism spanning traditional religions in earlier Japanese history and modern religious movements that have resulted from Japan's modernization and interactions with the West in the past century and a half. Earlier millennial themes can be traced back at least to early medieval Japanese Buddhism, in which notions of an endtime or period of the decline of Buddhism (*mappo*—the last age of the [Buddhist] law) and beliefs that the future Buddha (Maitreya—known in Japan as Miroku) would manifest on earth in the future on a mission of salvation. However, although there are millennial dimensions to Japanese Buddhism, it has been primarily since the mid-nineteenth century, with the advent of the new religions of Japan, that millennial themes have become particularly prominent in Japanese religious history.

Prominent among the new religious movements with millennial orientations in the nineteenth century were Tenrikyo and Omotokyo, both of which developed in rural areas and were led by female shamanic leaders who promised their followers imminent salvation on earth in which the corrupt material order would be replaced and the world would be made anew. In the latter part of the twentieth century, a new wave of millennial movements has arisen in response to rising concerns about the future of the planet and in expectation that the new calendrical millennium signifies a potential turning point for humanity. A number of very new movements arose in this period, including one that turned violent and destructive in its millennial impulses, Aum Shinrikyo, which is dealt with separately in this volume.

Historical Antecedents: Japanese Buddhism and Millennialism

Buddhism has been the religious tradition most associated with millennialism prior to the nineteenth century in Japan. Various Buddhist schools of thought expected a future spiritual presence that would awaken the world, while others sensed a decline in the moral status of the world. An important Buddhist concept that has implications for an understanding of the broader framework of millennial thought in Japan is that of *mappo*. This belief suggests that the law of Buddhism will decline at a certain point after the Buddha ceased teaching on earth: traditionally in Japan this decline was dated to the mid-eleventh century, and expectations of disaster as the law collapsed became a prominent theme in Japanese society and the Buddhism of that period.

A number of new forms of Buddhism arose to meet this challenge and to offer new means of faith and practice in the period of decline. In millennial terms, the most prominent and optimistic was the thirteenth-century Buddhist prophet

Nichiren (1222–82), who founded his own school of Buddhism in Japan dedicated to the veneration of the Lotus Sutra, which Nichiren revered as the final truth of Buddhism. According to Nichiren, the Sutra offered peace and harmony in this world, and he envisaged a future in which those who worshipped the Lotus Sutra would enjoy such benefits. Nichiren's future visions, however, were not of an immediate variety in that he did not manifest an overt expectation of an imminent dawning of a new world, although his teaching engendered in later followers the hope that such an era might be at hand.

In terms of expectation of a future dawn, probably the most significant popular cult has been that of Miroku, the future Buddha. According to popular Buddhist myths, Miroku will manifest in the world in 567 million years time, at which point the dead will arise again and join with Miroku in paradise. One of the most significant sites and most visible elements in this cult is the mausoleum of the Buddhist priest Kukai (774–835) at Mount Koya in Japan. According to popular legend Kukai did not die but entered into eternal meditation to await the coming of Miroku: it is believed that those whose ashes are interred in the graveyard at Koya that surrounds the mausoleum, will also arise with Kukai to greet Miroku's coming. While this cult, which especially developed from around the tenth century onward, cannot be said to be specifically millennialist, in that the period of future expectation is so distant as to remove any sense of imminence which normally characterizes millennial movements, it indicates a strand of thought in popular Japanese Buddhist lore that conceives of a future paradise or spiritual transformation on earth. Especially from the seventeenth century onward, traveling ascetics preached about the coming of Miroku and instilled beliefs that this time was at hand—a belief that had particular resonance in times of social crisis or famine, and that gave rise in the nineteenth century to a number of popular uprisings which sought a spiritual transformation in society that would lead to better conditions for all.

New Religions, World Renewal, and Millennialism

From the mid-nineteenth century a number of new religious movements developed outside the established religious traditions (Buddhism and Shinto) of Japan. These were generally focused around charismatic figures who offered their followers a new sense of hope in the turbulent social and economic situation of the era. These new religions have been the most prominent religious phenomenon of the past century and a half since Japan opened up to external Western influences, thereby setting in process a series of changes that led to the collapse of feudal Japanese society and the development of a modern, centralized state and of an industrial society based on a large urban population. In many respects they have been a response to this immense social change, which has led to large-scale population movement and economic upheaval.

Many of the new religions that have developed since the mid-nineteenth century have expressed millennialist messages and themes and brought a sense of dramatic immediacy to their teachings and future visions. The Japanese new religions with millennial tendencies can generally be divided into two main types: some of the earlier new religions that developed in rural Japan, initially appealing to the poorer, marginalized classes both of the peasantry and farmers and of the new urban proletariat, and usually led by inspired females with shamanic and prophetic tendencies; and the most recent wave of new religions that have appeared in the last decades of the twentieth century that have flourished in the big cities and that have appealed especially to the young and educated, and that have been led by charismatic male leaders.

Earlier Millennial New Religions

Millennial themes were especially evident in the new religions that developed in rural Japan in the nineteenth century and that were founded by charismatic figures who found themselves socially or economically marginalized in the rapidly changing social atmosphere of the era. A recurrent theme within such movements was an expression of hope or expectation that the turmoil facing society would produce a total upheaval and overturning of the existing structures of society and give rise to a worldly paradise, a utopian heaven on earth. Notable among these were Tenrikyo, founded in 1837 by Nakayama Miki (1798–1887), and Omotokyo (now known as Omoto) founded in 1892 by Deguchi Nao (1837–1918), an illiterate peasant woman.

Nakayama Miki's religious visions suggested that a new era of bliss would envelop the world, which would be transformed by sacred nectar descending from heaven onto earth. This benign millennial vision was closely associated with her sacred center at Tenri (the name of the town which became the center of her religion, and the location where the divine nectar would fall). Deguchi Nao's millennialism was more radical, doubtless reflecting the harsher experiences of her life: while Nakayama was a relatively well-off member of the rural peasantry, Deguchi came from a deeply traumatized and impoverished background. She saw the material world as evil and corrupt: it was degenerate and in need of immediate renewal and purification. This notion, *yonaoshi* or world renewal, was a recurrent theme in the earlier Miroku-based movements mentioned above, and it became central to Omotokyo's teaching, which prophesied an imminent end to this world and the birth of a ideal spiritual realm on earth in which all would be equal. Despite the seeming political radicalism of her message, however, Deguchi Nao (like many other religious millennialists) subverted the possible political messages of her teaching through an emphasis on religious themes: in the words of Emily Ooms (1993: 87), Deguchi privileged religion over politics and "envisioned a community of morally upright individuals living in peace, equality, and mutual respect under the benevolent rule of Ushitora no Konjin" (the deity of her religion). Despite this shift from a politically nuanced millennial new order to a wholly spiritual one, Omotokyo was considered to pose a threat to the political order, especially under the later leadership of Deguchi Onisaburo (Nao's son-in-law, 1871–1948) and was twice suppressed by the government in the 1920s and 1930s.

Certain of the new religious movements that developed in the 1930s and 1940s also espoused millennial themes driven by their rejection of the militarism and emperor-worship systems that had taken Japan down the road of fascism and into World War II. Prominent among such movements was Tensho Kotai Jingukyo, founded by the female charismatic Kitamura Sayo (1900–67), which incorporated themes from folk religion and Nichiren Buddhism. Kitamura denounced the materialism of "the maggot beggars" who had led Japan to war (and, as she prophesied, to defeat) and foresaw the collapse of the current order and the coming of a new spiritual realm. Like earlier millennialist leaders who seemed to pose a threat to worldly authority, she was jailed during the war, but after Japan's defeat was able to continue her religious vocation. Tensho Kotai Jingukyo established a religious center at Tabuse in Yamaguchi prefecture, which serves as its earthly symbol of the new world order and its utopia on earth.

A statue of the Buddhist prophet Nichiren who played a central role in the development of a millennial ideology in Buddhism in the thirteenth century. The statue was erected and is maintained by the Nichiren Shu International Center on Asah-ga-mori in Japan. MINOBU-SAN KUONJI TEMPLE

Millennial Movements of the Late Twentieth Century

The late twentieth century has witnessed a growth in millennialist tendencies in the Japanese new religions. It has been conditioned in part by the imminence and sense of expectancy occasioned by the calendrical millennium, and at this level reflects both the growth of Western influence in Japan and the reactions against it: all Japanese millennial movements of this era have as an implicit or often an explicit theme the rejection of Western cultural influences, and part of their message suggests that, in the ideal future, Japan will become the spiritual center of the world and will eradicate pernicious Western influences. The rise of millennial movements also illustrates an underlying unease in Japan at the ways in which society and the world in general are going, and a fear that because of the threat of nuclear war and environmental damage, time might be running out for humanity and that a new set of paradigms are required in order to overcome the problems of the present.

The millennialist movements that have appeared in the last quarter of the twentieth century have been influenced by the prophecies of Nostradamus, which were translated into Japanese in 1973, and have proved immensely popular. Equally, biblical prophecies such as the onset of a final war, Armageddon, have also been assimilated into this matrix of millennial expectations which generally has assumed a catastrophic dimension. In the face of a highly expected period of turmoil and disaster at the end of the century, a number of movements have arisen to offer messages of hope, albeit sometimes tinged with a fatalistic assumption that much of the world will be destroyed in order for a new and better age to emerge.

Agonshu, a new movement founded by Kiriyama Seiyu (b. 1921) in the 1970s, believes that the world has entered a state of spiritual crisis because of the accumulation of bad karma (or spiritual pollution) caused by unhappy spirits of the dead who have not been properly cared for. This crisis has thus, at its roots, a religious as well as a social dimension, and in Agonshu's view, it is only through religious action that any hope exists of a solution to this dilemma. Agonshu's millennialist perspectives, despite their expectation of disaster, remain benign and optimistic, however, for the movement believes that through spiritual action and rituals it can negate the effects of unhappy spirits and bring about a generally peaceful transition to a new, more spiritually oriented society.

A more radical view was espoused by Kofuku no Kagaku, which rose to prominence in the late 1980s and early 1990s, led by Okawa Ryuho (b. 1956), a Tokyo University graduate, who had turned to a religious path after a variety of possession experiences. Okawa's millennialism originally had a catastrophic focus, in which he believed that wars, pestilence, and earthquakes would reduce the population by as much as 70 percent. However, such disasters would herald the dawning of a new age, in which spiritually charged practitioners in his movement would form the vanguard of a new era. His visions had an overtly nationalist theme to them (as have other of the Japanese millennial movements) in which he spoke of "Japan shining like the sun" in the new age and having a mission to provide spiritual leadership to the world. In Okawa's visions the United States would be decimated in the coming cataclysm, while Japan would rise to world spiritual prominence and leadership. Such ideas had an immense appeal to younger Japanese people who saw in them an implicit rejection of the overarching cultural influences of Westernization and, especially of the United States which, although an ally is seen as a major cultural threat in Japan.

In the mid-1990s Kofuku no Kagaku assumed a less strident millennialism. It continued to emphasize the importance of world spiritual transformation, and to claim a major leading role in this process, but its emphasis changed from a primarily catastrophic focus in which disaster was a prerequisite of change, to a greater emphasis on the peaceful realization of a spiritual new age and utopia. A primary reason for this change was the Tokyo subway attack of March 1995 carried out by the millennial movement Aum Shinrikyo. During the early 1990s Kofuku no Kagaku and Aum had been rivals, each espousing extreme catastrophic millennialist positions and each claiming that it alone had the capacity to bring about a new spiritual age. Kofuku no Kagaku underwent a rapid expansion and success in this period, while Aum suffered public rejection. Kofuku no Kagaku's success has led it to gradually downplay its earlier emphasis on the destructive potential for the millennium: after the murderous outrages committed by Aum, it retreated entirely from such positions.

Okawa announced that the new age had begun as a result of Aum's defeat which had, he claimed, reduced the extent of evil in the world and tipped the balance in favor of the forces of good. While Kofuku no Kagaku continues to espouse hopes for a spiritual transformation of society in which religion takes precedence over all other forms of public life, it no longer expresses these hopes in the catastrophic and destructive imagery that typified its earlier teachings. Partially this was a product of its successful growth in the 1990s, but it was also a reflection of a pragmatic reality that governed religious matters after March 1995: that Aum Shinrikyo's violent activities had given catastrophic millennialism a bad name in Japan. There were widespread calls for greater public surveillance of religious movements and much discussion about whether other religious groups might pose a danger to society because of their beliefs. Consequently movements such as Kofuku no Kagaku found it wise to downplay their adherence to such ideas and to distance themselves from doctrinal stances that could have been deemed dangerous or that might have resembled Aum's beliefs.

Sacred Centers and New Utopias

A common theme in Japanese new religions has been the construction of a sacred center, designed to serve as a spiritual center for all humanity. The sacred center, which is generally located at the birthplace of the founder or at the place where s/he experienced important revelations, represents the establishment of a holy land that serves as a model of heaven on earth.

In Tenrikyo, for example, a large religious complex has grown around the place where Nakayama Miki lived and where she had her first revelations of God the Parent. At the heart of this complex are the *Jiba* (the sacred place where humanity began) and the *Kanrodai*, the holy pillar onto which the sweet nectar of heaven falls to earth to nourish humanity. People who visit Tenrikyo's headquarters are greeted with the words *okaerinasai* (welcome home) to signify their return to their origins. When Nakayama Miki departed from this earth in 1887 (according to Tenrikyo she did not die but ascended to higher spiritual realms) her spirit continued to reside at the center, where she receives the prayers of followers and guards over them. Tenrikyo's sacred center serves as a center of worship, as a pilgrimage center, and as a special holy land which is the center of the divine world and sacred community that Tenrikyo aspires to build on earth.

There are numerous other new religions that have built sacred centers with similar aims to serve as holy centers from which worldwide spiritual revival will occur to bring about a new age, or as a refuge from predicted disasters that will accompany the coming of the millennium. During the 1980s, for example, Agonshu constructed a new sacred temple complex at Yamashina just outside Kyoto, which it saw as a center from which its brand of Buddhism could spread across the globe to bring about a world spiritual transformation. As in Tenrikyo visitors here are greeted with the words *okaerinasai* to symbolize a return to one's spiritual home. The new religion Mahikari has built its sacred center at Takayama in the mountains of central Japan because, the movement believes, this area will survive the floods and other disasters that will herald the closing of this particular age. In surviving such disasters the center will function as the holy location that will form the basis of the new spiritual age to come.

Conclusion

While there is an extended history of millennial themes in Japanese religion, it has, until the nineteenth century, been most clearly articulated in Buddhist contexts. With the development of the new religions, new forms and modes of millennialism, based originally in a recognition of the inequalities in Japanese society, offered alternative means of hope in a rapidly changing society. These movements tended, however, to deflect their messages away from a radical political critique of society and postulate an idealized religious sense of future harmony.

The millennial movements of the later twentieth century have arisen more particularly because of the social conditions of the period and the concern that contemporary society has lost its spiritual direction and is in need of spiritual change. Such millennial impulses will probably continue to be important in the future in Japan, where the new religions have provided a religious means of articulating criticisms about the nature of society, concerns about the future, and spiritual hopes of a new order. While many of these aspirations were framed in violent and catastrophic images it would appear, however, that as a result of the Aum Shinrikyo affair, the orientation of millennialism in Japan (as the case of Kofuku no Kagaku indicates) is likely to be of a more optimistic and benign type, at least for the immediate future.

Ian Reader

See also Asia, Aum Shinrikyo

Bibliography

Blacker, Carmen. (1971) "Millenarian Aspects of the New Religions in Japan." In *Tradition and Modernization in Japanese Culture*, edited by Donald H. Shively. Princeton, NJ: Princeton University Press.

Kisala, Robert. (1997) "1999 and Beyond: The Use of Nostradamus' Prophecies by Japanese Religions." *Japanese Religions* 23, 1: 143–57.

Ooms, Emily. (1993) *Women and Millenarian Protest in Meiji Japan: Deguchi Nao and Ômotokyô.* Ithaca, NY: Cornell University East Asia Program.

Reader, Ian. (1988) "The 'New' New Religions of Japan: An Analysis of the Rise of Agonshu." *Japanese Journal of Religious Studies* 15, 4: 235–61.

——. (1991) *Religion in Contemporary Japan.* Basingstoke, U.K.: Macmillan.

Sponberg, Allan, and Helen Hardacre, eds. (1988) *Maitreya the Future Buddha.* Cambridge, U.K.: Cambridge University Press.

Yamashita Akiko. (1997) "The Eschatology of Japanese New and New New Religions: From Tenri-kyô to Kôfuku no Kagaku." *Japanese Religions* 23, 1: 125–42.

Jehovah's Witnesses

The religious group currently known as the Jehovah's Witnesses emerged in the 1870s as a loosely organized Adventist movement lead by the former haberdasher and autodidact, Charles Taze Russell (1852–1916). From their inception, Witnesses have preached millenarianism, with the year 1914 of special significance. Over the nearly 130 years of its existence, the Watchtower Bible & Tract Society has evolved from an informal, loosely organized group of "Bible Students" under Russell's leadership into a significant international religious organization. Originally known as "Bible Students," "Millennial Dawnists," or "Russellites," the Watchtower Bible and Tract Society was legally incorporated in the United States in 1884; the group officially adopted the name Jehovah's Witnesses in 1931.

Although American in origin, recent statistics indicate that currently less than one-fourth of Jehovah's Witnesses live in the country of that movement's birth. The Society in the 1990s claimed a worldwide membership of over 5.5 million with U.S. membership at approximately one million. Witness statistics are notoriously conservative, since they include only those persons actively engaged in field ministry who submit activity reports to the Society; the statistics do not include peripheral members, i.e., children, unbaptized participants, or inactive members. Witnesses currently maintain 106 branch offices in 233 countries worldwide, with each branch overseeing a portion of the Society's 87,644 congregations. Official statistics are published in the Watchtower Society's *Yearbook*.

Witnesses have established a significant presence in such places as south-central Africa, Western Europe, and Latin America, and, most recently, in the countries of the former Soviet Union. The ideological and organizational uniformity of the Watchtower Society contrasts significantly with other American religious traditions that have successfully internationalized their constituencies (e.g., Seventh-Day Adventists, Latter-day Saints). One can visit a "Kingdom Hall" (a technical term for the building at which Witness meetings are held) in Australia, Japan, Zambia, or North Carolina with the realistic expectation that congregational meetings will exhibit a high degree of uniformity in content and procedure.

Witness life is based on a regimen of active proselytizing and regular participation in five weekly meetings at their Kingdom Halls where members study Society literature and learn effective recruiting skills and techniques. Individuals are encouraged to log one to ten hours a week in "field ministry" (proselytizing) as "Publishers"; "Regular Pioneers" average 70 hours per month; "Auxiliary Pioneers," 50 hours per month; and "Special Pioneers," 140 hours per month.

The Society's biweekly magazines, *The Watchtower* and *Awake!* are important sources of information about Witness beliefs and practices. *The Watchtower* magazine is the most authoritative source of ideological guidance from the organization; the periodical *Awake!* is a popular magazine that brings a "theocratic" perspective to bear on common issues and problems of everyday life. The Society publishes its own Bible translation, the *New World Translation* (rev. ed. 1984). Although Witnesses regularly use other established Bible translations, they prefer to use the NWT for study and proselytizing. The translation is an important source of Witness doctrine, and the Witnesses' distinctive communal dialectic (sometimes referred to as "theocratic English") is based in part on the NWT's unique English style. The WTS published a substantial official history, *Jehovah's Witnesses: Proclaimers of God's Kingdom* (1993).

Witness historians customarily organize Watchtower history around the tenures of the presidents of the Watchtower Bible and Tract Society. During the first one hundred years of its existence, the organizational character of the Watchtower Society was distinctly shaped by its presidents: C. T. Russell (1879–1916), J. F. "Judge" Rutherford (1917–42), Nathan Knorr (1942–72), and Frederick W. Franz (1972–92). Milton Henschel (1992–) currently occupies that position, although it is clear that the group's identity is no longer defined by the personality of its president. Russell's teachings were clearly influenced by the Adventist tradition, although the Watchtower Society has not always openly admitted this linkage. The presence of that post-Millerite legacy can be observed in Nelson H. Barbour's *Three Worlds, and The Harvest of This World*, a work published by Barbour and Russell in 1877.

Organization

The Watchtower's model for its international, interracial society is the *theocracy*. According to the Society, Jehovah's theocratic kingdom currently appears on earth in the global network of congregations composed of individuals of almost every race and culture. Through its circuit and district overseers, each congregation answers to its branch office, and that office operates under the direct oversight and authority of the Governing Body located in the movement's world headquarters in Brooklyn, New York.

The Society's Governing Body, representatives of the 144,000 "anointed" ones destined to reign with Christ in heaven over his millennial kingdom, provides exclusive and comprehensive guidance to Jehovah's contemporary organization. Authority and leadership within the Watchtower Society is a type of anonymous, institutionalized charisma. Only the privileged "anointed class" of the 144,000 has access to this charismatic power. And of the relative handful of "anointed" that remain alive today (fewer than 9,000 by last count), in practice only a handful of elderly men at the Society's headquarters in Brooklyn serve as God's "channel of communication." That group, called the Governing Body, represents the "Faithful and Discreet Slave" prophesied in Matthew 24:45–47, and only they can discern the "true meaning" of the biblical text. Interestingly, the "new light" that Jehovah makes available to his faithful "anointed" in these "evil last days" is finally based in the Bible itself. That is, while the Bible itself is necessarily perfect, its meaning is not always clear without this privileged organizational guidance. Therefore, what the Bible really "means" is available only to this special class, and even then Jehovah is only gradually enlightening his faithful as the End draws closer.

If the Governing Body provides authoritative theocratic guidance, it is the task of local Kingdom Halls—under the vigilant supervision of Society-appointed officials—to ensure that individuals are properly indoctrinated in Bible Truths before baptism and to provide theocratic supervision and training for local members.

The Watchtower Society functions as a *global culture*, efficiently networked through its theocratic organization of technology and knowledge. The Witnesses' transnational sense of community is accomplished in part by the Society's hierarchical organization of power and discourse, its centralized production of theocratic knowledge and literature, and by the carefully monitored flow of personnel and information

STUDIES IN THE SCRIPTURES: THE TIME IS AT HAND

A wonderful modern device, which serves well to illustrate the divine arrangement of time prophecy, is what is termed a Combination Time-Lock, used in some of the largest banks. Like other combination locks, the key or handle remains in the lock constantly. Certain peculiar movements of the handle, known only to one aware of the arrangement, are needful to open it, while the slightest deviation from the proper movements only complicates the matter and makes it the more difficult to open. The Combination Time-Lock adds the peculiar feature, that by a clock arrangement inside the bank vaults, the doors when closed at night are so locked that they cannot be opened by any one until a fixed hour the next morning; and then, only in response to the use of the right combination upon which the lock has been set.

Thus our Heavenly Father has closed up and sealed many features of his plan during the night with his great Time-Lock, which was so set as to prevent their being opened until "the time appointed"–in the morning of the great day of restitution. And then Jehovah's Anointed, "he that hath the key" and understands the combination upon which it has been set, "openeth, and no man shutteth." ('Rev. 3:7') He opens unto us by giving us the necessary information as to how the key of prophecy is to be operated by those desiring to find the treasures of infinite wisdom. And we may unlock the treasures of divine wisdom now, because the morning hour has come–though it is early and not yet light to the world. But only by carefully heeding the instructions, and applying the key to the combination set by the great Designer, will its treasures open to us.

In fact, this illustration fits the entire plan of God in all its parts: Each feature of truth and each prophecy is but a part of the one grand combination, which may be opened now because it is morning–because the bolts of the great Time-Lock are withdrawn. And this grand combination, once opened, discloses fully and grandly the boundless treasures of divine wisdom, justice, love and power. He who opens will indeed know God as never before.

Let us, then, examine the Scriptures with a reverent spirit, that we may learn what God is pleased to show us with reference to his times and seasons. Since he has recently made the grand outlines of his plan so clear, we may reasonably expect that his time is due to lead us into a knowledge of its time features. The times and seasons were wisely hidden in the past, and the saints were thus saved from discouragement, because the time was long; but as the plan nears its glorious consummation, it is the privilege of the saints to know it, that they may lift up their heads and rejoice, knowing that their deliverance draweth nigh.

('Luke 21:28') The revealing of the time, in the "time of the end," will be as profitable and stimulating to the saints as its revealing before would have been unprofitable and discouraging.

Source: Russell, Charles Taze. ([1889] 1916) *Studies in the Scriptures, vol. 2: The Time Is at Hand.* Brooklyn: International Bible Students Association. http://www.nsbible.org/sits_v2/v2s1.htm.

between its Brooklyn headquarters and local assemblies of Witnesses around the world (mediated by the Society's intermediaries, including Branch, District, and Circuit Overseers).

The WTS's ultimate objective is a kind of *frictionless theocracy* that eliminates all slippage within its theocratic economy, filtering out disruptive noise, exorcising local particularities and idiosyncrasies potentially in conflict with the homogenizing designs of Jehovah's theocratic monologue. The vertical distribution of theocratic power emanating from the theocratic center in Brooklyn permeates Witness culture, facilitating the WTS's production of global uniformity. This dynamic can be observed, for example, in the WTS's creation and translation of its literature. Almost all the major writing occurs in Brooklyn, at the center of Jehovah's visible theocracy, where it is first composed in the Society's (apparent) Truth language, i.e., English, before it is then translated into other world languages. It appears that any local material that finds in way into print must always receive the theocratic imprimatur from Brooklyn headquarters.

The Watchtower Bible and Tract Society—the movement's legally incorporated name—takes special pride in its international membership. One of its recent publications proclaims that "Christian brotherhood unmarred by racial distinctions is a reality among Jehovah's Witnesses in the 20th century." Witness scholar M. James Penton acknowledged that the Watchtower Society "has emphasized the value of ethnic and racial tolerance among its adherents to a greater degree than is the case with most other religious organizations" (1985: 286).

In God's theocratic kingdom, those divisive particularities that have continually plagued human social existence are repudiated and dissolved. But that proleptic realization of racial and ethnic harmony among Jehovah's Witnesses coexists with the Society's conviction that the present world system is hopelessly corrupt, irredeemable by human means. While Society literature does occasionally acknowledge that racial prejudice is not completely eradicated from Jehovah's contemporary organization, it insists that the harmony and unity within its righteous boundaries are unparalleled by all other religious and social institutions.

Distinctive Beliefs and Practices

A posture of world rejection entails the rhetorical exorcism of Witness discourse in which words and doctrines are purged of their "Babylonish" associations. This purge of all vestiges of corrupt Babylon demands more than simple lexical correctness. Jehovah's people must be *theocratically correct* in every way. This desire for theocratic correctness involves not only the eradication of the corrupt language of Babylon; it also requires the theological exorcism of ideological remnants of corrupt Babylon. Watchtower literature proclaims that:

> A religion may *claim* to advocate worship of the true God of the Bible and it may use the name of his Son, Jesus Christ, but of what value is this if it is contaminated with Babylonish doctrines and practices? . . . [W]e need to make a clean break from any and all organizations of Babylon the Great. We need to quit sharing in their activities.

Thus Witnesses reject the traditional Christian doctrine of the Trinity because they consider it neither rational nor scriptural, and they claim that the very notion of triune gods evidences pagan corruption.

The traditional doctrines of the immortality of the soul and eternal torment in Hell are rejected by Witnesses because they too originated in pagan antiquity, not in the Bible. What appears as a particularly idiosyncratic claim is the Witness' insistence that Jesus was crucified on a single-beamed "torture stake," not on a tau-shaped cross. Witnesses argue that the tau-shaped cross has ancient pagan fertility associations, although the phallic imagery of a single-beamed stake gives them no pause. The Watchtower declares that:

> there are common threads going through the confused tapestry of the world's religions. Many religions have their roots in mythology. Nearly all are tied together by some form of belief in a supposed immortal human soul that survives death and goes to a hereafter or transmigrates to another creature. Many have the common denominator of belief in a dreadful place of torment and torture called hell. Others are connected by ancient pagan beliefs in triads, trinities, and mother goddesses. Therefore, it is only appropriate that they should all be grouped together under the one composite symbol of the harlot "Babylon the Great."

Witnesses likewise reject the traditional celebration of festivals and holidays (including Christmas, New Year's Day, Easter, and personal birthdays) on the grounds that they actually originated in Babylon the Great. Witnesses believe that:

> Those that make up the Christian organization of Jehovah's witnesses are persons who have separated themselves from the many religions of both pagandom and Christendom. By attending meetings at one of their Kingdom Halls, you can see for yourself the difference this has made.

Witnesses argue that the divine name "Jehovah" identifies God in a way that generic titles like "Lord" and "God" do not. They are, after all, witnesses *for Jehovah*, and they claim as one of the identifying marks of the "true church" its invocation of God's personal name. A Watchtower publication declares that:

> God's people must treat his name as holy and make it known throughout the earth. . . . There is only one people that is really following Jesus' example in this regard. Their main purpose in life is to serve God and bear witness to his name, just as Jesus did. So they have taken the scriptural name "Jehovah's Witnesses."

Millennialism

Despite numerous delays and recalculations of the endtime, Witnesses continue in their tenacious struggle to proclaim Jehovah's imminent kingdom on earth. Penton argues that in fact the Witnesses have "preached millenarianism longer and more consistently than any major sectarian movement in the world" (1985: 7). The year 1914 is a pivotal date for Witnesses, as it signifies the time when Watchtower prophetic interpretation indicates that "Jesus Christ began to rule as king of God's heavenly government." One Watchtower publication, *Reasoning from the Scriptures* (87), summarizes that:

> Christ as King did not immediately proceed to destroy all who refused to acknowledge Jehovah's sovereignty and himself as Messiah. Instead, as he had foretold, a global preaching work was to be done. . . . As King he would direct a dividing of peoples of all nations, those proving to be righteous being granted the prospect of everlasting life, and the wicked being consigned to everlasting cutting off in death. . . . In the meantime, the very difficult conditions foretold for "the last days" would prevail. . . . Before the last members of the generation that was alive in 1914 will have passed off the scene, all the things foretold will occur, including the "great tribulation" in which the present wicked world will end.

Their unyielding devotion to the imminence of the End commits Jehovah's latter-day witnesses to a kind of permanent liminal existence, in which their allegiances and connections to the social order are pared to a minimum. Their earnest hopes and longings are focused on the return of Jesus, on the renovated earth, and an eternally blissful existence in that Edenic paradise. The evil world order will immediately disappear at the great and climactic battle of Armageddon when Jehovah will install his new order of things. Jesus and the Anointed 144,000 will then preside in the heavens over that "great multitude" of the righteous faithful resurrected on the newly renovated earth. Together Jehovah's faithful will gradually and thoroughly restore the earth to its original Edenic tranquility.

Jehovah's Witnesses manifest a sort of catastrophic millennialism, as they confidently expected the entire globe to be purged and cleansed at Armageddon in preparation for the imminent millennial paradise. But some beliefs and practices suggest that catastrophic and progressive millennialisms are not necessarily exclusive categories. Witnesses believe that in some important sense, the power of the millennium is *already present,* albeit in a qualified or attenuated form. They see their international, interracial organization as a foretaste of the millennial paradise (Wessinger).

Watchtower literature defends the Society's aggressive construction projects by explaining that these buildings will likely endure the ravages of Armageddon and prove useful in the global educational work required in the millennium. In effect that means that Witnesses are laying the *material* as well as the spiritual infrastructure of the millennial kingdom. Witness iconography is characterized by the visual motif of life in the paradise earth, where the earth is restored to its Edenic purity, and people of every conceivable color and ethnic/racial group are joined together in eschatological bliss.

The End of the End?

Currently the Watchtower Society appears to be undergoing a historic transition in which their millennial urgency is weakening and their characteristic sectarian resoluteness is increasingly succumbing to dynamics of moderation and accommodation.

After decades of disappointment, deferral, and ex post facto reinterpretation of prophecy, the WTS slowly divested in date-setting and grounded their millennial expectations in arguments based on the "signs" of the Last Days that indicated the End must occur within a literal "generation" of 1914. According to the 1 November 1995, issue of the *Watchtower* magazine, the Watchtower Society finally relinquished its long-standing claim that the "End" (i.e., Armageddon and Paradise) would take place within a literal generation of 1914. The Witnesses are now operating—for the first time in their 125-year history—without a specific temporal horizon to frame their millennial expectations. The implications of this revision of the Watchtower Society's prophetic timetable are not certain.

Jehovah's Witnesses rely on the same *terminus a quo*—1914—as the temporal anchor for their millennial expectations. They still insist that Jesus returned *invisibly* in 1914 and is now enthroned over his theocratic kingdom. In other words, 1914 marks the *beginning* of the End; according to Witness doctrine, these last days will soon culminate in the cathartic destruction of Armageddon and the miraculous transformation of planet Earth in the millennial paradise. After the 1995 redefinition of the meaning of "this generation" in Matthew 24:34, Witnesses are now forced to rely exclusively on their adaptation of the apocalyptic "sign argument" to support their claim that the (visible/literal/physical) End is near. Based on the prediction of eschatological woes found in the Synoptic Gospels "little apocalypse" (Matthew 24 and parallels), Witnesses insist that the global catastrophes of the twentieth century (e.g., war, famine, disease, natural disasters, etc.) cumulatively provide undeniable evidence that this "evil world system" is nearing its end.

The proleptic impulse in Witness discourse this practice is always qualified by the insistence on the "spiritual" and unstable nature of Jehovah's theocratic presence in this "evil world system." The period between 1914 and the End is a liminal space where Jesus is legally but "invisibly" enthroned over his millennial kingdom, but in which Satan is more powerful than ever in his rage against the faithful. Satan knows his time is up, but he makes every effort to win over individuals from the faithful remnant of Jehovah's people. Witnesses explain that the present time is analogous to the spinning blade of an electric fan after it has been unplugged, or that the disastrous "signs" of the end are comparable to the death throes and involuntary jerks of a beheaded snake.

It would be most surprising if a new date or temporal framework did *not* emerge to replace the diluted "this generation" doctrine. As Stephen O'Leary has suggested, constant emphasis on unspecified apocalyptic imminence typically provokes communities to "fill in the blanks"—officially or otherwise—with more precise temporally specificity. Zygmunt's work in particular explores how the WTS's millennial economy has cycled through period of short-term expectation, disappointment, and doctrinal elaboration or rationalization. But the WTS's long-term eschatological framework is currently under substantial revision for the first time. Because of that fact, prognosticating the Watchtower Society's future may now be especially difficult. There appears to be a fundamental linkage between the Witnesses' imminent eschatology and their aggressive preaching and proselytizing work. That linkage suggests that the Watchtower Society's current revisionist maneuvers could have serious implications for their long-term growth. Long-term straight-line projects of growth cannot anticipate the unintended consequences of such ideological revisions and doctrinal reformulations.

Joel Elliott

See also Seventh-Day Adventists

Bibliography

Mankind's Search for God. (1990) Brooklyn, NY: WBTS.

Moorhead, James H. (1993) "The Millennium and the Media." In *Communication and Change in American Religious History*, edited by Leonard I. Sweet. Grand Rapids, MI: Eerdmans, 216–38.

O'Leary, Stephen D. (1994) *Arguing the Apocalypse: A Theory of Millennial Rhetoric.* New York: Oxford University Press.

Penton, M. James. (1997) *Apocalypse Delayed: The Story of Jehovah's Witnesses.* Toronto: University of Toronto Press.

Reasoning from the Scriptures. (1985, 1989) WBTS of Pennsylvania, Inc.

The Truth That Leads to Eternal Life. (1968) Brooklyn, NY: WBTS.

Wessinger, Catherine. (1997) "Millennialism with and without the Mayhem." In *Millennium, Messiahs, and Mayhem: Contemporary Apocalyptic Movements*, edited by Thomas Robbins and Susan J. Palmer. New York: Routledge.

You Can Live Forever on Paradise on Earth. (1982, 1990) Brooklyn, NY: WBTS.

Zygmunt, Joseph F. (1970) "Prophetic Failure and Chiliastic Identity: The Case of the Jehovah's Witnesses." *American Journal of Sociology* 75: 926–48.

Joachism

Joachism was a highly influential medieval system of prophecy, based upon the interpretation of the Bible, which was devised by the Calabrian abbot Joachim of Fiore (c. 1135–1202). "Joachism" must also include numerous works falsely attributed to Joachim himself, as well as the writings of his followers and those he influenced, directly or indirectly, down to the time of Hegel, Marx, and beyond. The presupposition of Joachite prophecy is a providential Christian philosophy of history in which scripture, both Testaments brought into concordance with one another, allows the prophet-exegete to project the biblical vision forward toward the divinely ordained millenarian future for mankind. If Joachim's vision of the future is an ultimately optimistic, joyous one under the sway of contemplative Christians, in the foreground lies the imminent persecutions of Antichrist, bringing terrible afflictions of all kinds before that blissful future dawns.

As a result of a series of religious experiences, Joachim claimed to have been endowed with the spiritual intelligence to penetrate the hidden, symbolic meaning of scripture. The Joachite system is too complex to detail here. But his best-known pattern is the three stages of universal history, that of the Father, of the Son, and of the Holy Spirit. Joachim's authentic writings were supplemented by a significant number of pseudo-Joachite texts, which, for example, viewed the struggle between pope and emperor in the light of prophecy. In his lifetime Joachim's fame was such that King Richard Lionheart met with him while en route to the third crusade (1190).

Medieval millenarians especially wanted to know when the Third Age (or status) would come and what it would hold for those who survived the crisis or transition which would mark its coming. Early expositions of Joachim's prophecies stressed the appearance of Antichrist. The Calabrian prophet suggested that the years from 1200 onward would see the beginning of the transition to a new age, bringing tribulation with it. Joachim himself never assigned a specific year to the time when the age of the Son would give way to the age of the Holy Spirit, although the year 1260 began to assume a prophetic aura to his followers. It was this anticipated year of crisis which witnessed the extraordinary movement of the flagellants *(disciplinati)*.

Joachite prophecy cannot be divorced from the major religious enthusiasms of the Middle Ages. The Franciscans saw themselves as one of the prophetically ordained orders of *novi viri spirituales* (new spiritual men). The excitement of the Lombard "Great Hallelujah" of 1233, which gave an impetus to Joachite studies within the Franciscan order, also led to a period of Joachist agitation from 1255–63, which culminated in the condemnation of Joachite teachings by the provincial council of Arles (1263). But from the time of Olivi (d. 1297) to that of Savonarola (d. 1498) the influence of Joachite prophecy continued to make itself felt. The significance of this influence was brought to the attention of the English-speaking world through the research of the Oxford scholar Marjorie Reeves.

Gary Dickson

See also Year of the Flagellants (1260)

Bibliography

Florensia: Bollettino del Centro Internazionale di Studi Giochimiti (San Giovanni in Fiore, Italy).

McGinn, Bernard. (1985) *The Calabrian Abbot: Joachim of Fiore in the History of Western Thought.* New York: Collier Macmillan.

——. (1986) "Joachim of Fiore's Tertius Status: Some Theological Appraisals." In *Atti del II Congresso di Studi Gioachimiti*, edited by Antonio Crocco. San Giovanni in Fiore, Italy, 219–36.

Reeves, Marjorie. ([1969] 1993) *The Influence of Prophecy in the Later Middle Ages: A Study in Joachimism.* Oxford, U.K.: Clarendon Press; reprint, Notre Dame, IN: University of Notre Dame Press.

——. ([1976] 1977) *Joachim of Fiore and the Prophetic Future.* London: SPCK; reprint, New York, Harper & Row.

Reeves, Marjorie, and Beatrice Hirsch-Reich. (1972) *The Figurae of Joachim of Fiore.* Oxford, U.K.: Clarendon Press.

Wessley, Stephen. (1994) "A New Writing of Joachim of Fiore: Preliminary Observations." In *Prophecy and Eschatology*, edited by Michael Wilks. Oxford, U.K.: Blackwell for the Ecclesiastical History Society, 15–27.

John Frum Movement

The John Frum movement still functions as an active cargo cult on Vanuatu (formerly New Hebrides), an archipelago north of New Caledonia and New Zealand. The center of the movement is located on the island of Tanna. Tannese people (Ni-Vanuatu) pronounce Frum as Froom. The term cargo cult refers to a revitalistic, or millenarian, social movement from Melanesia that anticipates the arrival of foreign goods to be delivered through magical means. The magical help of ancestral spirits, ritual performance, and the committed belief of followers are considered part of the supernatural power of cargo cults. The arrival of these goods will herald a new age of freedom from foreign domination and the establishment of permanent prosperity and abundance. Cargo cult activity emerged during colonial rule and increased after World War II because of cultural contact with American soldiers.

Cargo Cults

Some of the origins of the cargo cults are rooted in Melanesian religion that relies on the concept of *mana*, a magical force that pervades all things. It can be harnessed in the form of a charm or ritual. Melanesians believe the charms that possess *mana* protect their gardens, and powerful men who possess *mana* are good warriors and providers. From the time of the earliest invasions, local people unloaded cargo from European ships. Since the Europeans did not work for their earthly goods, Melanesians reasoned that they had acquired their wealth of material goods by magical means. Eventually native peoples would acquire the secret of the *mana* with the aid of their ancestors, thus *mana* would propel the manifestation of cargo for the enjoyment of the common person.

The first cargo cults emerged during the nineteenth century in Papua New Guinea and other Melanesian societies as a result of the economic disparity experienced by the local peoples who came in contact with Europeans. The Papuan Vailala Madness of 1919 generated a mass hysteria that had people displaying strange body movements. The Vailala prophecy stated that a large steamer was coming bearing the spirits of the dead ancestors who were bringing a cargo of rifles, rice, flour, tobacco, and other trade goods. Belief in the movement lasted about twelve years, while movements like it erupted all over the area.

Sociologically speaking, the cargo cult movement arose in response to the cruelty of colonial domination and its accompanied religious intolerance. During the nineteenth century, colonialists imposed blackbirding, a practice of tricking or forcing thousands of indigenous people to work on plantations located on distant islands. Disease and labor abuses led to a severe depopulation of the area. The Tannese people faced brutal conditions under colonial domination. The British occupied the area after World War I exploiting natural resources and people in their drive to extract wealth from the region. Intrusions by Presbyterian, Seventh-Day Adventist, and Roman Catholic missionaries furthered the repression of local religion, family traditions, and traditional economic exchanges. Local peoples were treated as inferiors. Colonial control imposed stiff distinctions between the status of locals ("blacks") and the ruling white class. This caste division fostered a legacy of embittered social relations ripe for a millenarian movement that articulated freedom from the ubiquitous oppressor.

Rise and Spread of the John Frum Movement

On Tanna an early millenarian incident had occurred during the nineteenth century with rumors of Jesus coming to destroy the island and its pagan population. But significant tension became apparent by 1940 when a fall in copra prices led to local unrest. Village men called meetings, which excluded whites and all women, to spread the teachings of John Frum. Frum was described as a short man with bleached hair and a high-pitched voice; he wore a coat with shiny buttons. Supposedly, he spoke at night when the men gathered around a fire to drink kava (an intoxicating drink). He admonished the men for their idleness and advocated communal gardening, dancing, and kava drinking. The exact identity of John Frum has always been in dispute. Some describe him as a white man or as an American GI; others say he was an indigenous man. As the movement's myth grew John Frum was spoken of as the descendent of the local volcano god. No matter what his identity was, he was presumably a man full of *mana*, a savior with great power.

John Frum predicted a coming cataclysm in which the volcanic mountains would be flattened and islands would become connected by land. It was rumored that when this happened Frum would disclose his true identity as he brought forward a transformative era where everyone would be young, healthy, and would not have to work for an earthly sustenance. Mission schools would be abolished and the new system would pay chiefs and teachers for providing education. The John Frum movement developed a decidedly anti-missions sentiment. Widely accepted prophecies told of the complete removal of whites and their European money. All practices previously banned by missionaries would be restored, such as dancing, kava drinking, polygymy (multiple wives), hand gardening, and raising pigs. All the European material wealth would be given to the common people, while John Frum provided money to anyone in need.

The prophecy that no money would be needed precipitated a spending frenzy, on the one hand, and the fearless disposal of money, on the other. Bundles of cash were thrown into the sea, and large feasts were scheduled to use up any type of savings. Church services went unattended. In 1941 when leaders were arrested, the movement persisted by inventing new information about John Frum. Some said that he was King of America or that the King of America was sending his sons to remove the colonial government. Locals reported spotting the sons of John Frum. Contact with Americans fueled the myth. When war with the Japanese became a reality, America troops, some of whom were African American, landed on Tanna. The sight of black soldiers prompted further rumors of the advent of John Frum and more arrests were made.

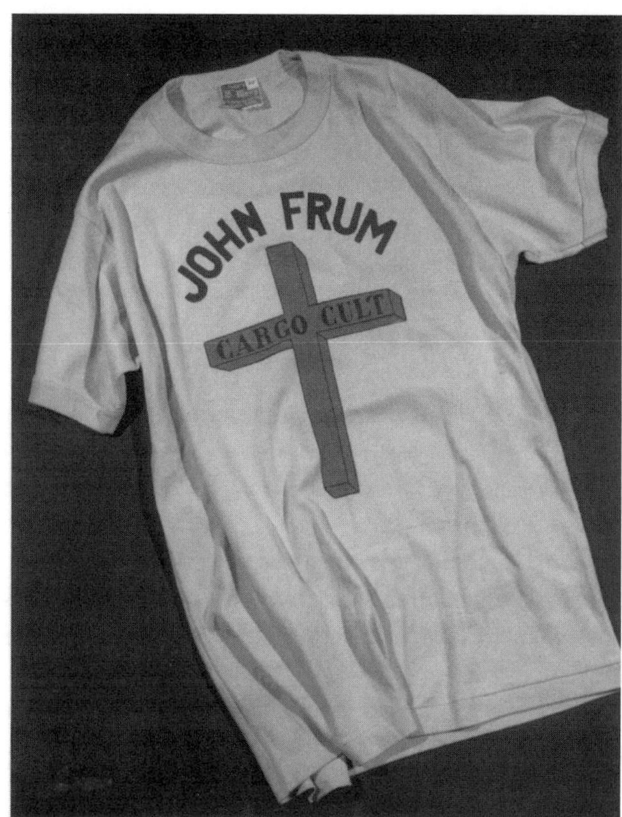

John Frum T-shirt. The shirts were made by the French for distribution during the 1977 elections. LAMONT LINDSTROM (FROM THE COLLECTION OF ANNETTE WEINER)

As more Americans arrived, rumors said that the soldiers had come to fight for John Frum to win the release of the growing numbers of political prisoners. Americans shared some of the material wealth of their cargo ships with the Tannese in gestures of respectful generosity. GIs freely gave local people cigarettes, candy, and other desirable items made in America. The contrast between the American and the British attitudes toward the Tannese was stark. Local resentment toward the colonial government grew even greater after the American cultural contact, thus speculation based upon the desire to be a wealthy and free people swelled the ranks of the John Frum movement.

WHO AND WHAT IS JON FRUM?

Tannese legend claims that Tanna was once the only land in the universe. Yasur volcano, a highly active and easily accessible volcano on Tanna was designated as the originator of the universe. According to the legend, in that time there were many wild animals on Tanna, including lions, tigers, elephants and bison. As these were dangerous creatures, it was decided to create other lands and distribute these perils. Chief Mahdikdik took the soil of Tanna and threw it in the directions of the compass, creating Europe, Asia, Africa, Australia and America. Some of the soil was caught by the wind and scattered about creating the Pacific islands.

The Tannese then built large canoes and loaded the animals aboard. The various types of beast were sent to different lands. As there were too many people on Tanna as well, they were sent to different parts of the earth. At this time all people were Melanesian. Most people went to Africa, however some were caught on the reef and thrown into the sea, where the salt-water bleached them white.

It is said that Jon Frum is living in the crater of Yasur. There is also a huge army of 5,000 to 20,000 men residing there as well, so the new legend blends with the old. In the book reviews below, we see alternate versions of Jon Frum's history. That is due, for the most part, to a history based on stories and tales passed on from one individual to the next. This then is the next step of that tale.

The centre of the Jon Frum cargo cult today is based in the village at Sulphur Bay, [also called Ipeukel.] The Jon Frum Church here houses the movement's most sacred red cross. On Friday evenings, Jon Frum supporters come from the nearby villages to dance. Every year on the 15th of February, Jon Frum day is celebrated. This is the day when the Sulphur Bay people believe that Jon Frum will return, bringing with him all the cargo he has promised. Prayers and flowers are offered at the red cross in the village church. This is followed by a flag-raising ceremony and a military parade. Islanders carry rifles made of bamboo, painted to appear as if they have red bayonets.

About 100 men march under the command of two village elders dressed as US Army sergeants. The soldiers have the letters "USA" painted in red on their bodies. These soldiers consider themselves to be members of the Tannese Army, a special unit of the American armed forces.

Source: Jon Frum Home Page—http://203.23.131.2/cargocult/jonfrum/index.htm.

By 1943, a local leader, Neloaig, proclaimed himself to be John Frum, and enlisted laborers to build an airstrip for a liberation air force. When he was arrested, his followers still persisted to build the airstrip until they were threatened or taken prisoner themselves. Another man called Iokaeye declared that he was Frum when he instructed islanders to adopt a new color symbolism for their clothes and belongings. The government quickly incarcerated him along with his followers. Indeed, anyone making a John Frum announcement was subject to arrest. Even so, Frumism persisted well after the war despite the waves of repression. It spread to other islands because the expulsion of leaders contributed to a process of cultural diffusion. Frumism fit so well into previously articulated rumors of magical cargo and with the general despair over the contrast of wealth and privilege that it took on a mythical life of its own as the stories circulated throughout the region.

Writing in the 1970s, journalist Edward Rice saw the latter-day John Frum movement as an articulate philosophy of nationalist pride and messianic belief. His interviews brought to light more testimonies of local indigenous leaders, as well as additional white interpretations. Islanders still idealized "America" as a source of liberation and potential cargo. Rice reported that the Tannese people continued to be imprisoned for their spiritual ideology. These Pidgin English statements paraphrase the general themes, "Jesus Christ, He No Come; John Frum, He Come."

The area eventually gained independence in 1980. Today the John Frum movement has a well-established church at Sulphur Bay which houses their most sacred red cross, a symbol adopted from the American Red Cross badges and flags. The location has become somewhat of a tourist attraction because it is advertised internationally. Frum believers celebrate the fifteenth of February as the day John

Frum will return with all his promised cargo. The ceremony includes a flag-raising and a military parade where islanders sport bamboo rifles. For the festivities, some men paint the letters "USA" on their abdomens, because they believe they are a special unit of the United States military. The Tannese say that John Frum now resides in the Yasur volcano where he lives with his soldiers who are ready to fulfill their magical promise.

Diana Tumminia

See also Cargo Cults

Bibliography

John Frum Homepage. (1999) http://www.altnews.com.au/cargocult/jonfrum.

Lindstrom, Lamont. (1993) *Cargo Cult: Strange Stories of Desire from Melanesia.* Honolulu: University of Hawaii Press.

Rice, Edward. (1974) *John Frum He Come.* Garden City, NY: Doubleday & Company, Inc.

Worsley, Peter. (1957) *The Trumpet Shall Sound.* London: MacGibbon & Kee.

Jubilee Traditions

The history of the jubilee traces back into Hebrew and Roman Catholic origins. Attempts of radical reformers and millenarians of the eighteenth and nineteenth centuries to revive the ideas of the Hebrew origins failed, whereas the affirmative concept of historical jubilees became generally accepted. In stressing the idea of historical continuity, the habit of celebrating jubilees shaped a vivid counterpart to the millenarian experience of time.

The Hebrew Year of Jubilee

Even if the Latin term *annus jubilaeus* shows association to the Latin word *jubilare* (shout out, halloo, huzzah), in fact the term derives from the Hebrew word *yobel,* which stands for the "ram" or "the horn of a ram." The "horn of the ram" was blown in accordance to Leviticus 25 at the end of seven times seven years, i.e., at the end of every forty-nine years or the fiftieth, in order to announce the beginning of the Year of Jubilee, which was also called "the year of release." According to the Law of Moses (Leviticus 15:8–54 and 27:16–24) the Year of Jubilee was ordained to be a year of rest and remission in which the fields were to be left uncultivated, the slaves to be set free, and lands and houses that had been sold because of poverty were to revert to their former owners. Nevertheless most scholars agree that these laws were hardly ever put into practice.

The Roman Catholic Holy Year

A Roman Catholic version of the Year of Jubilee appeared in the year 1300, when Boniface VIII opened the first Holy Year, which was an indulgence to all pilgrims to Rome, to be granted every hundredth year. The Holy Year took up the Hebrew idea of the cancellation of debts and transformed it into a remission of sins. In doing this it developed an entirely new tradition of periodical pilgrimage, remission, and feast. Later popes shortened the intervening period to 50, then 33 and finally 25 years. Since 1450, the ordinary Holy Years have taken place (with some exceptions in the nineteenth century) every twenty-fifth year up to the present day.

The Jubilee and the Millennium

Some later thinkers (e.g., Nicolaus Cusanus) used the jubilee to calculate the date of the Second Coming. English

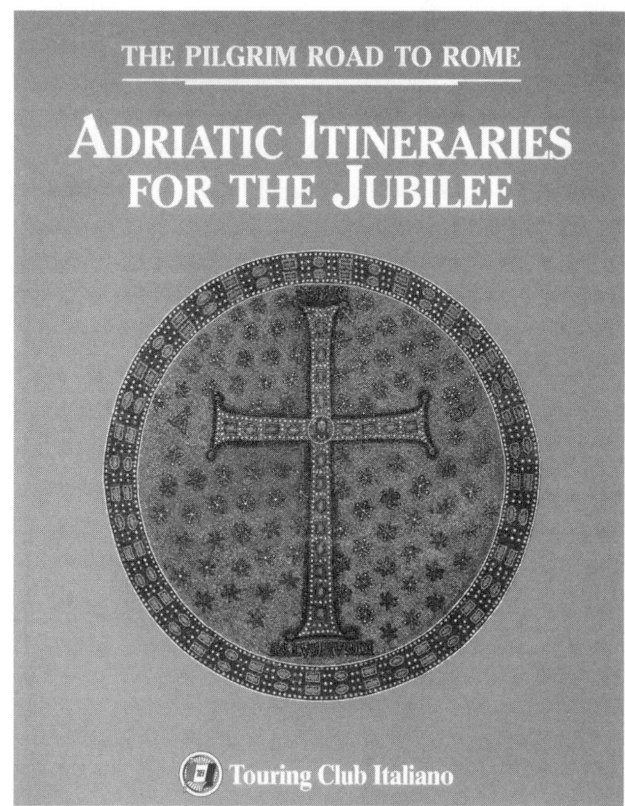

Pilgrimages have also been a major component of Jubilee celebrations as shown by the 1999 Italian travel brochure for the 2000 millennium. TOURING CLUB ITALIANO, MILAN

JOHN PAUL BISHOP—SERVANT OF THE SERVANTS OF GOD TO ALL THE FAITHFUL JOURNEYING TOWARDS THE THIRD MILLENNIUM HEALTH AND THE APOSTOLIC BLESSING

The Great Jubilee of the Year 2000 is almost upon us. Ever since my first Encyclical Letter *Redemptor Hominis,* I have looked towards this occasion with the sole purpose of preparing everyone to be docile to the working of the Spirit. The event will be celebrated simultaneously in Rome and in all the particular Churches around the world, and it will have, as it were, two centres: on the one hand, the City where Providence chose to place the See of the Successor of Peter, and on the other hand, the Holy Land, where the Son of God was born as man, taking our flesh from a Virgin whose name was Mary (cf. *Lk* 1:27). With equal dignity and significance, therefore, the Jubilee will be celebrated not only in Rome but also in the Land which is rightly called "Holy" because it was there that Jesus was born and died. That Land, in which the first Christian community appeared, is the place where God revealed himself to humanity. It is the Promised Land which has so marked the history of the Jewish People, and is revered by the followers of Islam as well. May the Jubilee serve to advance mutual dialogue until the day when all of us together—Jews, Christians, and Moslems—will exchange the greeting of peace in Jerusalem.

The period of the Jubilee introduces us to the vigorous language which the divine pedagogy of salvation uses to lead man to conversion and penance. These are the beginning and the path of man's healing, and the necessary condition for him to recover what he could never attain by his own strength: God's friendship and grace, the supernatural life which alone can bring fulfillment to the deepest aspirations of the human heart.

The coming of the Third Millennium prompts the Christian community to lift its eyes of faith to embrace new horizons in proclaiming the Kingdom of God. It is imperative therefore at this special time to return more faithfully than ever to the teaching of the Second Vatican Council, which shed new light upon *the missionary task of the Church* in view of the demands of evangelization today. At the Council, the Church became more deeply conscious both of the mystery which she herself is and of the apostolic mission entrusted to her by the Lord. This awareness commits the community of believers to live in the world knowing that they must be "the leaven and, as it were, the soul of human society, destined to be renewed in Christ and transformed into the family of God". In order to meet this commitment effectively, the Church must persevere in unity and grow in the life of communion. The imminent approach of the Jubilee offers a powerful stimulus in this direction.

The journey of believers towards the Third Millennium is in no way weighed down by the weariness which the burden of two thousand years of history could bring with it. Rather, Christians feel invigorated, in the knowledge that they bring to the world the true light, Christ the Lord. Proclaiming Jesus of Nazareth, true God and perfect Man, the Church opens to all people the prospect of being "divinized" and thus of becoming more human. This is the one path which can lead the world to discover its lofty calling and to achieve it fully in the salvation wrought by God.

Source: http://www.vatican.va/jubilee_2000/

radicals of the eighteenth and nineteenth centuries tried to revive the jubilee as a model of spiritual or social renewal. Some identified the jubilee of Leviticus 25 as a prefiguration of the millennium. These concepts faded away when the idea of the historical jubilee became generally accepted in the second half of the nineteenth century.

The Historical Jubilee

The modern tradition of celebrating jubilees differs from the Hebrew and Roman Catholic custom in that the idea of remission has been replaced by secular customs and new sociological functions. As a rule the historical jubilee serves to confirm the identity of the celebrating group or person. In order to do this, the historical jubilee is accompanied by celebrations, speeches, retrospects, and stock taking of the hitherto achieved. The first historical jubilees were celebrated at Protestant universities like Tübingen in 1578. They where motivated by the confessional contrast to the Roman Catholic custom of the Holy Year or Jubilee Year of 1575 from which they took the naming "annus jubilaeus" in order to establish a competitive custom of their own. Round anniversaries of weddings, reigns, or occupations, constitute a special case, because they center around individuals.

Nowadays the historical jubilee has achieved a determining influence on the public interest in history in so far as historical topics appear in the media on the occasion of their anniversary, their semicentennials, centennials, bicentennials, etc. Instead of focusing on a final ending as many millenarian conceptions do, the jubilee strengthens the idea of historical continuity by an equally vivid tradition of feasts.

Arndt Brendecke

See also Century, Centennial, Centenarium, Year of Jubilee

Bibliography

Chase, Malcolm. (1990) "From Millennium to Anniversary: The Concept of Jubilee in late Eighteenth and Nineteenth Century England." *Past and Present* 129: 132–47.

Fager, Jeffrey A. (1993) "Land Tenure and the Biblical Jubilee: Uncovering Hebrew Ethics through the Sociology of Knowledge." *Journal for the Study of the Old Testament* (Sheffield: JSOT Press), Supplement series, 155.

Grundmann, Herbert. (1978) "Jubel." In *Ausgewählte Aufsätze*, part 3, edited by Herbert Grundmann. Stuttgart: Hiersemann, 130–62.

McNamara, Brooks. (1997) *Day of Jubilee: The Great Age of Public Celebrations in New York, 1788–1909*. New Brunswick, NJ: Rutgers University Press.

Müller, Winfried. (1998) "Erinnern an die Gründung. Universitätsjubiläen, Universitätsgeschichte und die Entstehung der Jubiläumskultur in der frühen Neuzeit." *Berichte zur Wissenschaftsgeschichte* (Weinheim, Germany) 21: 79–102.

North, Robert. (1954) *Sociology of the Biblical Jubilee*. Analecta Biblica, 4. Rome: Pontifical Biblical Institute.

Thurston, Herbert. ([1900] 1980) *The Holy Year of Jubilee: An Account of the History and Ceremonial of the Roman Jubilee*. St. Louis, MO: B. Herder; reprint, New York: AMS Press.

Jubilee, Year of

While the year of jubilee has its roots in Jewish scriptures, Christians understand jubilee as Jesus' message of the coming reign of God in which the oppressed would be freed and the rightful order of creation would be restored. In the Hebrew Bible the year of jubilee requires that debts be canceled, slaves freed, property returned to its rightful owners, and general amnesty on indebtedness declared (Leviticus 25). In the New Testament Jesus announces the "year of the Lord's favor" in which he proclaims release to the captives, recovery of sight to the blind, and freedom for the oppressed (Luke 4:18–19). Jubilee is therefore both ethical and eschatological, since social and economic injustice is eliminated by God's rule on earth.

Religious and nongovernmental organizations around the world are using the turn of the millennium to ask for a year of jubilee whereby the loans which heavily indebted poor countries owe foreign lenders—such as the International Monetary Fund (IMF) or the World Bank—would be forgiven. Such forgiveness would allow debtor nations to use scarce financial resources for social services, health, and education in order to raise the standard of living, rather than go toward debt repayment. Those asking for a year of jubilee base their call on biblical and moral imperatives, as well as on the human suffering caused by the financial crises of debtor nations.

Biblical Justification

The roots of the year of jubilee appear in the Hebrew Bible where God instructs the people of Israel to cultivate the land for six years and then give it a "Sabbath," or rest, during the seventh year. The sabbatical year is based in God's own rest on the seventh day after creating the world in six days (Genesis 2:2–3). In Exodus 23:10–11 God commands the Israelites to let the land rest and lie fallow every seventh year so that the poor may eat, and so that wild animals may eat what people leave behind. In Deuteronomy the sabbatical year also requires the remission of debt and freedom for Hebrew slaves (Deuteronomy 15:1–18).

The year of jubilee—that is, the year after the seventh sabbatical year (i.e., fifty years)—as described in Leviticus 25 goes even further. Everyone is to return to the land they once owned, even if they no longer own it. If someone sold their land, their kin can redeem it and the property can be returned to the original owner. Moreover, even if the original owner or their kin does not have the price of redemption, the property shall still be returned during the year of jubilee. The same goes for houses lost in sales in villages, although houses sold in walled cities are exempt from the general refund occurring during jubilee. Even those Israelites who sold themselves into slavery are freed during jubilee, as are their families, although slaves taken from foreign nations are not freed. The purpose of the jubilee year is to remind the

LEVITICUS 25.10–17

10. And you shall hallow the fiftieth year, and proclaim liberty throughout the land to all its inhabitants; it shall be a jubilee for you, when each of you shall return to his property and each of you shall return to his family.
11. A jubilee shall that fiftieth year be to you; in it you shall neither sow, nor reap what grows of itself, nor gather the grapes from the undressed vines.
12. For it is a jubilee; it shall be holy to you; you shall eat what it yields out of the field.
13. "In this year of jubilee each of you shall return to his property.
14. And if you sell to your neighbor or buy from your neighbor, you shall not wrong one another.
15. According to the number of years after the jubilee, you shall buy from your neighbor, and according to the number of years for crops he shall sell to you.
16. If the years are many you shall increase the price, and if the years are few you shall diminish the price, for it is the number of the crops that he is selling to you.
17. You shall not wrong one another, but you shall fear your God; for I am the LORD your God.

Israelites that God is the rightful owner of the land, "for the land is mine; with me you are but aliens and tenants" (Leviticus 25:23).

Scholars are divided as to whether or not the Israelites actually practiced the requirements of the year of jubilee. The Book of Deuteronomy states that lenders may not tighten credit in the years just prior to a sabbatical year, when debts are to be remitted (Deuteronomy 15:7–11). This practical advice suggests that perhaps a sabbatical year of debt remission was observed. Additional evidence that a Sabbath year was kept may come from Jeremiah 34:13–16, 1 Kings 21, and Nehemiah 5:6–13 and 10:31. Kinship redemption occurs in Jeremiah 32 and Ruth 4. Periodic remission of debt happened in other Ancient Near Eastern cultures with the accession of a new king.

In the New Testament Jesus takes up the theme of forgiveness in anticipation of God's immediate rule. Although Christians usually understand this as forgiveness of sins, Jesus also explicitly refers to forgiveness of debts. For example, in the prayer he gives in Matthew 6:12, Jesus says "And forgive us our debts, as we also have forgiven our debtors," while in Luke 11:4 he says "And forgive us our sins as we ourselves forgive everyone indebted to us." Jesus tells several parables about debt and debtors (Luke 7:41–43, 16:1–8; Matthew 18:23–35), while in other parables he discusses money (Matthew 25:14–30; Luke 19:12–27; Matthew 20:1–15). He also heals on the Sabbath, the day of rest in Judaism, freeing people from bondage to sin and illness (Luke 13:10–17; Matthew 12:9–13; Mark 3:1–5).

Jesus indicates the eschatological presence of God in his own life and ministry by forgiving people their sins. He states that he has fulfilled Isaiah's prophecy of release and restoration (Luke 4:21; Isaiah 61). God has broken into the world through Jesus, and so the year of jubilee has begun by the forgiveness exemplified in Jesus.

Current History

In 1994 Pope John Paul II issued the encyclical *Tertio Millennio Adveniente*, known in English as *The Jubilee of the Year 2000*, in which he identified the biblical mandate for jubilee as a doctrine meant to restore social justice on earth. The pope saw Vatican II, the council of Catholic bishops (1962–65), as the beginning of the Great Jubilee of the Year 2000. He called for repentance for the lack of unity among all peoples, and within the church itself. Although the primary objective of the jubilee for the pope was the strengthening of the faith and witness of Christians, he also saw it as a way to emphasize the church's preferential option for the poor and the outcast. "Thus in the spirit of the Book of Leviticus, Christians will have to raise their voice on behalf of all the poor of the world, proposing the Jubilee as an appropriate time to give thought, among other things, to reducing substantially, if not canceling outright, the international debt which seriously threatens the future of many nations" (1994: paragraph 51).

In June 1997 Jubilee 2000/USA was launched in Denver, Colorado, at the Summit of the Group of 8 Governments

(G-8). A coalition comprised of representatives of some forty Catholic and Protestant organizations organized around the common goal of debt cancellation for poor countries. Many impoverished countries carry such high levels of debt that scarce economic resources are diverted from social services to debt services. About half the debt is owed directly to individual governments, with only 10 percent owed to private banks. Internationally, the Jubilee 2000 Coalition established full campaigns in over forty different countries. The coalition estimated that eliminating debt owed by highly indebted poor countries (HIPCs) would cost about $160 billion. Although some of the G-8 governments are forgiving some debt for a few countries, a major program of debt forgiveness has not yet occurred.

Conclusions

The year of jubilee calls for a radical restructuring of society by freeing the enslaved, canceling debts, and returning land to its rightful stewards. Extensive biblical warrant exists to call for such massive economic forgiveness. Following the lead set by Pope John Paul II, many Catholic and Protestant denominations, as well as non-Christian religions and nongovernmental organizations, argue for debt cancellation for HIPCs by G-8 nations, and by the World Bank and IMF. Although a few steps have been taken in this direction, a massive program of forgiveness—which would halt the flow of interest payments from the poorest countries to the wealthiest—has not yet occurred.

The movement for jubilee focuses on social justice on earth, rather than other-worldly rewards for the poor. Churches involved see the social sin of economic disparity as important as personal sin. Relying on Genesis 1:26–27, they believe that because humans are created in the image of God, they have an equal right to participate in economic, political, and social decisions. Moreover, all people are entitled to an equitable share in the fruits of the earth. The massive debt carried by HIPCs—and incurred through the greed of dictators and lenders—has created a situation where the wealthiest nations are prospering at the expense of the poorest.

The millennial expectation for a year of jubilee is solidly grounded in religious hope and belief. The healings and miracles performed by Jesus demonstrate the eschatological presence of God. Whether or not debt forgiveness will be enacted in the twenty-first century depends on the largesse of the wealthiest nations in the world, and on a critical mass of support by the world's citizens.

Rebecca Moore

See also Jubilee Traditions

Bibliography

John Paul II, Pope. (1994) *Tertio Millennio Adveniente.* Boston: Pauline Books and Media.

Myers, Ched. (1998) "God Speed the Year of Jubilee" and "Jesus' New Economy of Grace." *Sojourners* 27, 3 and 27, 4: 24–34 and 36–39.

Wright, Christopher J. H. (1992) "Jubilee, Year of." In *The Anchor Bible Dictionary.* New York: Doubleday, v. 3: 1025–30.

Yoder, John Howard. (1972) *The Politics of Jesus.* Grand Rapids, MI: Eerdmans.

Judaism

Judaism is not a millennial movement, but the religious and broad sociocultural heritage of Judaism does manifest deep eschatological influences. Jewish apocalypticism is not central to the revelation, as given in the Thora, but has, through changing events gradually progressed and varied in form, at various times and places in history. If one considers that from the Maccabee period (mid–2 BCE) to the Bar-Kochbar protest (135 CE), eschatological explanations were attributed to all revolts against external rulers as well as to the internal Jewish violent conflicts, then certainly the contemporary experience must be taken into account as a determining factor in the formulation of this thinking.

The Greek term *apokalypsis* corresponds to the Hebrew word *galeh* (such as Amos 3:7; or as early as 1 Samuel 9:15) for example in the Book of Daniel (*rase galei,* Daniel 2, cf. 2:30) and in the Qumram writings (Manual of Discipline from Qumran 9:19): in both we also find the less defined *hazon* (vision, Daniel 8:1 etc.; Thanksgiving Psalms from Qumran 4:17f.). What this shows is that—without wanting to claim any directly linear connections in historical origins—a fluid transition exists in regard to motive and content between the later prophecies and apocalypticism during the period of the Second Temple, (see Josephus, *Antiquitates* 4:125; 10:276). Apocalypticism can therefore be seen as an attempt at reviving the prophetic tradition and at sustaining it in writing and must initially be seen in the tradition of the fulfillment concept. In contrast to the prophecies, apocalypticism operates with the idea of a momentary complete distancing of God from history in which the result is the first unhindered emergence of evil, before order is again restored. For the Jews as a group excluded from political action, the experience of exile and foreign rule was interpreted with meaning that extended well beyond the restorative political-religious perspective of the prophecies. The model for future redemption was no longer drawn from historical examples, but rather was formulated as a change of cosmic proportions activated by God.

The development of Jewish apocalypticism is illustrated particularly well in the complex history of creation in the Book of Daniel, which depicts the friction between Seleucid and Hellenistic policies on the one hand and the Jewish struggle for self-expression on the other. In one part, which most certainly emerged in the time of the Maccabees, it is stated that Nebuchadnezzar's dream contains in encoded form "what will be in the latter days"—not in the foreseeable immediate future, but in the eschatological unprecedented future (Daniel 2:28). Early Jewish apocalypticism, which also borrowed from non-Jewish (Egyptian?) traditions, but kept the monotheistic concept, bore a congenial connection between historical experience and the progressive contemporary interpretive thought of termination. The basic idea was that all future events were known in advance by God and could be conveyed in encoded form to certain chosen individuals. This is also the fundamental thought in apocryphal apocalyptic texts in part of the same period in which a Jewish-Palestinian (4 Ezra, "Syrian" Book of Lamentations, Song of Solomon) and a Qumram group (Jubilee book, Testament 12, "Ethiopian" Henoch book, etc.) can be distinguished from a Jewish-Hellenistic group (3 and 4 Maccabees, 3 Ezra, Sibylline, "Slavic" Henoch book, etc.). To a strong degree, the visions of these texts contain supernatural characteristics and deal with the final event in cosmic terms. Such congruencies in thought explain why some of the texts later evoke interest among non-Jews: for the "Ethiopian Henoch book," for example, Aramaic fragments from the second and third centuries are known from Qumram (4QEn) and belong in their entirety to the canon of the Ethiopian church (also 4 Ezra).

Apocalypticism, and the second movement included here, messianism, both sustain one another, without becoming identical: messianism can be nonapocalyptic (Maimonides); eschatology and apocalypticism, in turn, do not necessarily require a messianic figure (Tobit, Wisdom). In the beginning there was a basic hope for redemption without the need for a Messiah. In a long process of development, messianic models of understanding began to acquire a more important role in apocalypticism, partly as concrete restorative prophecies and partly as utopian-elevated prophecies (Son of Man; Daniel 7:13; 4 Ezra 13: 4) of a reestablishment of the king's rule (Micha 5; Ezekiel 17) by a new David (Ezekiel 34:23f., 37:22–25; and [apocryph.] Psalms of Solomon 17), a descendent (Jeremiah 23:33), or another chosen person (Haggai 2:20–23; Zechariah 4:6). In Ezra 4 the lost tribes of Israel are attributed with a decisive role at the end of time: through God's will they will be freed from banishment to the east and serve the Messiah in Zion. This concept was spread widely, particularly through a mix of fables and fact in the report of Eldad, "the Danite" (ninth century).

Apocalypticism and messianism are in this sense both important elements in Judaism, but historically seen by no means as a constitutive element. The Jewish apocalypse was important to non-Jewish monotheistic religions and movements as a model: the non-Jewish apocalyptic-millennial scenarios are often borrowed in detail from the Jewish tradition, but are then strongly distanced from their origins and integrated into competing interpretive contexts. This can be seen in the figure of the Antichrist, to name an extreme example, which in its concrete form is not a component of Jewish apocalypticism.

The Jewish postbiblical apocalypse is, in contrast to earlier apocalypses, characterized by the integration of messianic thought into the majority of eschatological and apocalyptic prophecies. Jewish hope aspires more for an ideal condition for human society or an ideal original condition within history in an often quite miraculously and mysteriously transformed world than for a God who once again takes action. There are hardly any expressive images of a utopian space to be restored at the end of time (see however Apocalypse of Aliah, 4 Ezra 5ff., Sefer Zerubbabel, Otiot Maschiach and, despite strong Christian influence, 12 Testaments of the Patriarchs, here Testament of Judah). This Jewish apocalypticism tends to be restorative; it hopes for a wonderful repetition of the reinstatement of the people of Israel as it once was with the return from exile in Babylon and for the fulfillment of all the past promises. The individual moments of this hope are equally concrete: the restoration of state integrity by the "Anointed King" (Messiah), a charismatically endowed descendant of King David having occasional supernatural qualities but nonetheless still a human; by the restoration of the temple and legal system and more. Redemption and the Messiah are hoped for, while the posing Messiahs are suspected and quickly revealed as "false." The resonance in the rabbinical literature of Emperor Julian's (360–363 CE) order to rebuild the temple is noticeably reserved; first of all the figure of the restorer, who was not a David-Messiah, exhibited reservation. It is therefore important to note the continued skepticism toward close expectations and redemption prophecies as a retarding moment and correction in regard to the idea of the apocalypse. Skepticism has been around as long as apocalypticism has. In early rabbinical *(tannaitic)* writings, there is the judgment: "These writings and the books of the heretics are not to be saved from a fire but are to be burnt wherever found, they and the Divine Names occurring in them" (Baraita on Babylonian Talmud, Shabbat 116a).

STATEMENT OF HAGAON

The following is in response to many inquiries about my position on the Lubavitch movement vis-à-vis its Messianic beliefs.

Before the passing of the Rebbe, I included myself among those who believed that the Rebbe was worthy of being the Moshiach. I strongly believe that had we–particularly the Orthodox community–been united, we would have merited to see the complete Redemption. Insofar as the belief held by many in Lubavitch–based in part on similar statements made by the Rebbe himself concerning his predecessor, the Previous Rebbe–including prominent *Rabbonim* and *Roshei Yeshiva,* that the Rebbe can still be Moshiach, in light of the Gemara in Sanhedrin, the Zohar, Abarbanel, *Kitvei* HaArizal, Sdei Chemed and other sources, it cannot be dismissed as a belief that is outside the pale of Orthodoxy. Any cynical attempt at utilizing a legitimate disagreement of interpretation concerning this matter in order to besmirch and to damage the Lubavitch movement–that was, and, continues to be, in the forefront of those who are battling the missionaries, assimilation and indifference–can only contribute to the regrettable discord that already plagues the Jewish community, and particularly the Torah community.

The Torah community should galvanize all of its energies to unite in the true spirit of *Ahavat Yisrael,* and battle the true enemies of Israel. I repudiate and call for an end to all efforts to discredit Lubavitch or any other legitimate movement within Torah Judaism.

Source: Soloveichik, Ahron. (1996) "Statement of Hagaon." *The Jewish Press.* Brooklyn, NY. 28 June: 27.

Historical Development and Major Apocalyptic Movements

With the failure of the revolt against Rome under Bar-Kochbar ("Son of the Stars," see Talmud Yerushalmi, Taanit IV/8 48d) which was accompanied by messianic-apocalyptic expectations (132–135 CE), the present chiliastic interpretations were repressed and required a counterresponse, an apolitical attitude which would make self-purification and self-healing of Israel a precondition for the end (Babylonian Talmud [bTal], Sanhedrin 97a–b). Mystical writings of apocalyptic thought, such as the "Hebrew" Henoch book (*Sefer ha Hekhalot,* 5–7. c. CE) were favored. In the following period, along with the Messiah son of David another figure is also present, the Messiah son of Ephraim (or Joseph) who as an earlier figure, dies in the struggle against Israel's enemies but prepares the way for the David Messiah. Perhaps this figure arose in light of the defeat of the Bar Kochbar and should be understood as an attempt to place his descent in an otherwise quite fitting eschatological concept.

Another wave of messianic thought was triggered by the wars between Byzantine and Persia at the turn of the seventh century CE, which Jews at the time depicted in an apocalyptic scenario as the "birth pangs of the Messiah." Texts produced during this phase include the *Sefer Zerubbabel* (629–636) and the *Revelations of Simeon ben Yohai* (around 750). A figure born of Satan emerges as an opponent to the Messiah, a human being named "Armilus" who is apparently drawn in likeness to the figure of Emperor Heraclius. He rises to become a world ruler and conquer the son of Ephraim Messiah, but is ultimately vanquished by the real Messiah. These texts offer the most concrete and comprehensive apocalyptic scenarios of the Jewish written tradition and in some respects are comparable to the Christian *Ps.-Methodius* which emerged at the same time. In contrast to the Christian texts, whose undeniable influence can be detected directly and indirectly in Christian high theology, the apocalyptic realism of the *Sefer Zerubbabel* and similar writings (such as *Otiot Mashiach*) remains a peripheral development of the Jewish medieval tradition. The prevailing rabbinical scholarship is possibly competing here: eschatogy and apocalypticism were not banned but are methodically domesticated (bTal Sanhedrin 97–98, yTaanit 68d) with their sensitive aspects expelled to the very intellectual realm of Jewish mysticism, which for the most part was beyond the understanding of the public and where motives such as the throne of the glory (Merkabah literature) were carried on. The Messiah of the central rabbinical texts is removed from the unknown future and appears as the redeeming savior who will one day rule Israel.

There are numerous explanations for this reserve: (1) more concrete expression led easily to Christian ideas; not surprisingly the illiterate and, in Persia, influential "Messiah messenger" of the eighth century, Abu Isa, did not attempt in vain to place himself as Jesus' and Muhammad's successor. (2) Openly expressed Jewish hope of redemption was dangerous: it continually provoked hostile Christian or Muslim reactions. (3) The strong reservation against apocalyptic enthusiasm must have been born out of a fear of the consequences of dashed hopes. Letters of various origins from the period before the first crusades (1096) show that the concrete hope for redemption had been aided by the thousandth anniversary of the destruction of the Temple (c. 1070). In revised reports of later decades on the pogroms of 1096 (Eliezer ben Nathan, Salomo bar Simeon), this moment is mentioned but appears to have been purposely left ambiguous. In a liturgical poem *(Selicha "Adebra w'jirwach li)* by the contemporary Benjamin ben Zerah, however, it is clearly stated: "We have calculated the times of Redemption, and they are now passed, and the hope of salvation is over and gone." To preclude against just such disappointments, in bTal Sanhedrin 97b Rabbi Jonathan is quoted as saying, "Perish all those who calculate the end, for men will say, since the predicted end is here and the Messiah has not come, he will never come."

Despite all these reservations, the coming of the Messiah continued to be calculated and dated: the "Story of David" names 940 as the year for the arrival of the Messiah, the *Sefer Zerubbabel* identifies 990 years following the destruction of the Temple (1058 CE) and Karaitic calculations determined 968 CE, 2,300 years (Daniel 8:14) after the Exodus (1332 BCE); or from the destruction of Shiloh (942 BCE), that is 1358 CE. Further developments in apocalyptic thought in the Middle Ages appear as a conflict between the quietist attitude which is typical of other parts of rabbinical scholarship on the one side and less reflective apocalyptic realism on the other.

The ideas of Saadia's Gaon (882–942), one of the most important scholarly figures of the Middle Ages, merge both strands together. According to his calculations, the Salvation should occur in 968. Perhaps Saadia was using concepts of the time and responding to prevalent expectations. Very different documents suggest this, such as a letter from the Jews of the Rhineland to the Palestinian scholars (c. 960) asking for information on the reliability of the reports on the Messiah's approaching arrival, or Hadsai's ibn Shaprut very similar letter to the Jewish King of the Khazars from the same year, or the karaitic prophesies. The fact that Rashi of Troyes (d. 1105) names first 1358, then later the year 1478 as the messianic year, and that Abraham bar Chijja from Spain (1065–1143) considers five dates, based on traditional exegesis and modern astronomy (1136 unlikely, 1230 very likely, 1358 and 1403 less likely, and certainly no later than 1448), suggests that for both men the aim was to put an end to the speculation on a Messiah appearing soon and to put distance between themselves and the prophesies or at least to set up "back ups" in case a miscalculation should occur. The calculations were based on the search for a logic and sense in history, a continual temptation which the great scholars, in spite of their reservations, gave in to: Juda Halevi (1080–1141) reports on the calculation of 1068 (1,000 years after the destruction of the Temple) as an example of past disappointments, but then a dream points him to the year 1130 (500 years after Muhammad) and for a moment he is ready to follow that date. Other prominent figures including Nachmanides and Gersonides also engaged in calculation.

Among the scholars who resisted such attempts, Moshe ben Maimon (Maimonides, 1135–1204) stands out. He brings messianic thought back to a rational, nonapocalyptic core (to liberate Israel from the diaspora and from foreign rule, see Mishnah Torah 4:11–12). For this reason Rashi of Troyes (d. 1105) adds to his multiple redemption dates a warning that God's people must not return to the Holy Land *b'choma* (through force). Such sober attitudes were justified: for one, they served to counteract against postmessianic disappointment. In addition, there were a number of past incidents that could presumably be seen as "birth pains of the Messiah" without the expected event actually occurring. In the eighth sermon of "Tam ha-qesef" by Josef ben Abba Mari ibn Kaspi (fourteenth century) it becomes clear that the belief in salvation as a political liberation which could escalate to an expectation for the near future embraced a dynamic that almost matched the effusive supernatural idea of a Messiah.

One should not underestimate the impact of the ongoing argumentative propagandistic confrontation with the temptation of messianic-apocalyptic thought by authorities such Maimonides or Solomon ben Abraham Adret (against Abraham Abulfia, the "Prophet from Avila," who announced the coming of the Messiah for 1295). The reports on widespread popular expectations for the near future remain constant in the available sources. Considering this, far-reaching apocalyptic movements are surprisingly low in number. Most of them are likely forgotten, since those that we do know of were mentioned only in passing reference. Nonetheless the references suggest clear high points that can be identified in the sixth through eighth centuries (Arab, Mediterranean region) and again in eleventh and twelfth centuries (western Mediterranean Sea, Western Europe). The movements named here were always restricted to a specific place and time, notwithstanding Serenus (Shirin) from Syria, who in 720 apparently mobilized followers as far away as Spain and France. But we have this information only thanks to a few (Isidor Pacensis, Natronai Gaon), particularly inexact (Gregorius bar Hebraeus) reports. The existence of other figures such as Moses al Dar'i (Morocco, 1127), the Yemen Messiah

Messenger from 1172, and the French imposter Messiah from 1087 are established solely through Maimonides' commentaries ("Iggeret Teiman"). This is true also of David Alroy, of whom hardly more is known than what Benjamin of Tudela reported of him: in the period of the Second Crusade in Persia, he declared himself the Messiah and together with his followers, he captured the citadel of his hometown Amadia. That so many such appearances occurred in periods of crises or instability does not reflect a direct correlation, but does suggest that a need for a radical change grew out of the situations which developed independently of one another. Between the thirteenth and fifteenth centuries—spaced out over many decades—a regular stream of movements can be identified such as that which followed the terror of the European-wide pogroms during the plague years (1348–1350) or another following the fall of Constantinople in 1453. The statement that in 1240 the European Jews saw in the Mongols their liberators and the ten lost tribes of Israel is transmitted with undertones mostly in non-Jewish sources (Matheus Parisiensis, Annales Marbachienses); but given the already deteriorating situation of the Jews in this century, it is not without plausibility, though it doubtless did not convey the feelings of the entire European Jewish population. In contrast to the number of Messianic movements, the number of predictions for the years 1350 and 1500 is comparably low, and only a single Messiah imposter (Moses Otarel) is worth mention.

The connection between mysticism and messianism deserves particular attention. In 1284, Abraham Abulafia in Sicily presented himself as the Messiah, but also as a prophetic Kabbalist. The Book of Zohar, the main work of the medieval mystic which was completed around 1290, uses numerous figures and letter interpretation around God's name to establish the onset of the Messianic era primarily in the short period between 1300 and 1336. There are other similar kabbalistic-mystic writings (Sefer ha'Temunah, 13th c.; Yalkut Reubeni, before 1673).

Communication and Messianism: Sixteenth- and Seventeenth-Century Movements

The mark of the messianic movement since the sixteenth century is its relative prevalence. David ha'Reubeni, who presented himself in 1523 in Venice as the son of the king of the (lost) tribes of Reuben, Gad, and a part of Manasse, who submitted to Pope Clemens VII a plan to crusade against the Muslims, and who died in 1538 imprisoned by the emperor, had nonetheless an impact in Italy, Provence, and Portugal. He had followers among Jews and "new Christians"; particularly the *Sephardim* (Jews of Iberian descent), and his far-reaching radius can be explained by the spread of the Sephardi diaspora over the entire Mediterranean area as a result of the expulsion from the Iberian Peninsula.

It was a similar scenario with Ascher Lemmlin (Lämmlein), who in 1500–02 presented himself in Istria as a precursor to the Messiah and at times had followers in Germany and Italy. His appearance was aided by a prediction from Isaac Abrabanel (1437–1508), which stated that the messianic era would begin in 1503. But knowledge of his appearance was primarily transmitted beyond the Adriatic region as a result of expulsion and migration waves which created enduring routes of communication particularly among Ashkenazi Jewry. To explain his appeal one must also consider the widespread eschatological interest of the time and the effect of new media on these communication routes: with book and pamphlet printing, the messianic propaganda could be spread through new methods.

The most notable Messiah figure of recent Jewish history was the highly educated Sabbatai Zvi (1626–76) from Smyrna (Ismir) who experienced periods of both depression and hyperactivity. His appearance followed a particularly bloody period of Jewish persecution, for example in Poland under the leadership of Chmielnicki (1648). His appearance also received attention outside of the area of persecution, for example in Amsterdam. One essential aspect behind his success was the widespread interest in the mystic Kabbalism. Whereas the Midrasch ha'Ne'elam of the Book of Zohar gave 1648 as the date of Redemption, the "Lurianic" Kabbalah from Safed in Galilea at the end of the sixteenth century contained much more concrete and dynamic apocalyptic approaches. Judaism was given the universal task of managing and speeding up *Tikkun*, which expressed the idea of restoration.

The center of Sabbatai's influence was under the Ottoman rule in Smyrna, Constantinople, and in the Holy Land; his followers and those of his prophet (Nathan of Gaza) spanned from Yemen and Persia to Kurdistan, Morocco, and all of Western Europe to Poland/Lithuania, and encompassed an equal number of Jews, Spanish "New Christians," and some Christian circles. In the search for explanations for the unusual popularity of his message, Jewish mysticism certainly plays an important role, since it is the only moment connecting such varied Jewish cultural realms as Europe, North Africa, and Arabia. Various means of communication were also decisive in rapidly spreading his message. Alone the number of printed letters, treatises, and pamphlets show that at the very least Sabbatai's appeal was an early modern media event.

The course of the Sabbatian movement offers a model study of the rise, climax, and decline of a dynamic social mass movement of a charismatic leading figure. The pattern begins with the introduction of a highly talented and unusual man who is quickly pushed into the sidelines of the movement of another person, in this case Nathan of Gaza, who in the early phase of the movement is so successful that the movement grows and both figures take on positions related to one another: one man identifies himself as the final Messiah, (31 May 1665), the other appears as his prophet and interpreter; in establishing the day of redemption as 15 Sivan 5426 (16 June 1666), when the movements reaches its climax. What continues to fascinate is primarily the revival of the prophesy and origins of the Messianic call from the Holy Land; both found fertile ground during a particularly sensitive period for apocalyptic interpretation. Sabbatai's arrest by the Ottoman regime (6 February 1666) was still signified as the suffering of the Messiah, but his conversion to Islam (15 September) thoroughly confused. Though it was explained by his followers as "Mysterium" and as consistent with his other "strange acts" (Nathan of Gaza), it was not able to stop the ensuing downward turn of the movement.

Nathan of Gaza attempted to counter the deeds of the man with the paradoxical theology of an "Messiah apostate"; he interpreted Sabbatai's death (1676) as "occultation" of the Messiah. Such interpretations secured Sabbatai's legacy for another hundred years, but ceased to offer a connecting foundation which would unify radical and moderate followers. Other successors appeared, among them Abraham Miguel Cardoza from Tripoli, who in 1674–80 acquired the leadership of the Sabbatians in Smyrna and for a time presented himself as the precursor the Messiah ben Joseph. In other central areas such as the Netherlands, Prague, Italy, and Morocco, new models of interpretation were developed in response to the course of the events. A late example that documents the decline of what was once such a concentric movement is Jacob Frank (1726–91): he was from the region known today as Ukraine, but for a time lived in Symrna; at one time he had wanted to be a prophet, later he believed himself to be the reincarnation of Sabbatai. Accompanied by some of his followers, he converted to Catholicism in the 1750s; though numerous Jewish "Frankish" groups continued to exist in Hungary, Poland, and Germany.

Sabbatai was not a "classical" Jewish Messiah impostor: many of his appearances and teachings reversed the Torah and contradicted the traditional idea of the Messiah and the apocalyptic scenarios. It was probably just this divergence from the norm that made him so unique and attractive. Sabbatai Zvi showed himself to be a Messiah full of surprises and thereby gained credibility. Sabbatai's evolution, including his conversion to Islam should not be a surprise at all: the attempt to overcome the Jewish/Christian/Muslim antagonisms in the context of the endtimes is part of the dynamic of redemption and termination thinking. Abraham Abulafia (d. after 1291) recognized a bond with the Christian thinking of Joachim of Fiore; and David ha'Reubeni sought the pope out as partner.

The Sabbatian movement covered almost the entire diaspora; and such was its power at times of bonding all camps, that it seemed nothing could stop it. The end of the movement was sealed when, following Sabbatai's conversion and death, there were no further "paradoxical" events reported even though his appearance still continued to be influential. It has been argued that Sabbatai's appearance hastened the collapse of the traditional Jewish world since many of his followers or their successors later appeared as leading *maskilim* (Jewish enlighteners).

Jewish Apocalypticism in Modernity: Traditions and Transformations

The Sabbatian movement and the awakening that followed after its failure were decisive phenomena in the nineteenth century that stimulated such counterreactions as acculturation, assimilation, reform, neo-Orthodoxy, and finally (indirectly) even Zionism. Rationalism and Zionism were in a sense the "inner" enemy, which grew out of the traditional Jewish messianism into the modern age. Rationalism's manifestation of criticism affected messianism in its fundamental beliefs; Zionism competed with it over Israel and alienated it through profanation and politicization. The response to this challenge was not unified but rather found expression in various, often incompatible concepts. Whereas orthodox Judaism and nonorthodoxy embraced a concept based on a human Messiah of the future, only circles of religious reform were completely successful in mastering apocalyptic interpretations, at least externally. References to the Messiah and Zion were mostly removed from prayers and religious services. This was compensated with a consistent redemption ideal of this world that was even adopted by pioneers of quite conservative circles. The historian Heinrich Graetz (1817–91) viewed the Jewish people as carriers of a humanistic mission to lead the people to completion (*The Construction of Jewish History*, 1846). Moses Hess (1812–75) expressed the socialist version this way: a Jewish state in the Holy Land must be the center of the Jewish nation, the Torah must be the basis of society and economy, which should contain the true "socialist principles" (*Rome and Jerusalem*, 1862). Zevi Hirsch Kalischer (1795–1874) connected the sociopolitical changes of his time (emancipation) by viewing them as a phase in the plan for salvation which precedes the future redemption of all the Jews.

Strands of orthodoxy reject Zionism and the state of Israel, because they see man usurping the work of the Messiah. Given this bitter dispute, the sometimes close relations between Zionism and apocalypticism remains surprising. Long before the founding of the state in 1948, they had developed mediating positions which accepted (following initial hesitation in *Misrahi*, the religious wing of the Zionist movement) the secular Zionist pioneers as instruments in bringing forth the Messiah. The secular Zionists also used the metaphors of fulfillment. This can even be seen in the state's national symbols: the flag in the style of the *tallit* (prayer shawl) and the *menorah* (the seven branched candelabrum) in the state's coat of arms. Individual events in the state of Israel's early history, which seem like miracles such as the victory against an almost invincible number of opponents in the 1948 War of Independence and the 1967 Seven Days War, were attributed with deep meaning even in strictly secular circles. This shows that the eschatological models of thinking, separate from all real religious and messianic claims, found their way into collective knowledge. Only in recent years has research begun to question whether the Shoah had been interpreted in apocalyptic terms, such as previous unimaginable "birth pains of the Messiah" and to what degree such models of explanations are spread among victims not bound to the religion.

Conclusion

Jewish apocalypticism is essentially the result of Jewish experience in exile, or more specifically, the conflict between a universal hope for redemption and a repeated experience of repression. Aside from Sabbatai Zvi, whose appearance, historically seen, remains an episode in itself, apocalypticism never dominated any period of Judaism. With the balance between eschatology and skepticism in regard to apocalyptic beliefs, between controlled knowledge and impatient waiting, in various cultures and ever-changing conditions, Judaism was able to pass on and secure its essential core, the loyalty to the Torah. Seen from within, Jewish apocalypticism even had a stabilizing impact over a long period, by placing radical upheavals into the future and by making self-completion of the community a prerequisite. This is why it was accepted easily under variant and mostly externally dictated life conditions that were conceived as transitory and relative, while future fulfillment remained in the final state. Jewish apocalypticism was always in a position to concede individual elements while retaining its inner substance. This is also true for Christian apocalypticism, which soon went completely in its own direction; and this is particularly true for the postreligious movements in Judaism that were critical of tradition but which could draw important inspiration from the Jewish eschatological historical image, since they responded to situations which were similar to those which had previously led to apocalypticism.

Characteristic of the current situation is the varying perceptions that exist side by side. Spectacular messianic-apocalyptic claims as seen recently in the figure of Rav Menahem Mendel Schneersohn and the outspoken chiliastic self-perception by parts of the Israeli settlement movement are thus typical, if not representative, manifestations of the majority in the state of Israel or in the diaspora.

Johannes Heil

See also Israel, Sabbatian Movement, Zionism

Bibliography

Katz, Jacob. (1987) "Is Messianism Good for Jews?" *Commentary* 83, 4: 31–36.

Nickelsburg, George W. E. (1987) *Jewish Literature Between the Bible and the Mishnah. A Historical and Literary Introduction*, 2d ed. Philadelphia: Fortress Press.

Russel, David S. (1992) *Divine Disclosure. An Introduction to Jewish Apocalyptic.* London: SCM-Press.

Sacchi, Paolo. (1990) *L'apocalittica giudaica e la sua storia.* Brescia: Paidea.

Scholem, Gershom. (1975) *Shabbetai Sevi. The Mystical Messiah 1626–1676.* Princeton, NJ: Princeton University Press.

Silver, Abba H. (1959) *A History of Messianic Speculation in Israel.* Beacon Hill, MA: Beacon Press.

Literature

Millennium's long career as a key figure of the Judeo-Christian literary imagination can be traced back to its earliest formulation in Zoroastrian cosmology, through its extended exploration by centuries of European artists and writers, to its more recent enlistment as a central symbol of America's self-conceived mythology.

In the literature of the West, millennium often appears attached to apocalypse. This pairing, traced back to the Saint John's Revelation, can be found in centuries of art and literature. Although recent representations of apocalypse in popular culture have emphasized the vivid imagery of destruction and catastrophe that precedes the millennium, the classic definition of apocalypse is actually "to unveil," taken from the Greek root *apocalupsis.* Considering this definition, we can more clearly understand the degree to which apocalypse and millennium are bound together. In a sense, literature is always an unveiling, claiming to see past the apparent world, to reveal a truer reality beneath appearances. As a result, apocalypse and millennium are ubiquitous cultural archetypes, inspiring the imaginations of a diverse range of authors.

Early Literary Formulations of Millennium

We find the earliest roots of millennium in the religion of Zoroastrianism, founded by the ancient Persian prophet

Zoroaster (circa 630–550 BCE). Zoroaster's cosmology centers around two oppositional Gods: Ahura Mazda, Lord of Light and Wisdom, and his evil twin, Angra Mainyu, Lord of Evil and Destruction. Zoroastrianism was the first religion to conceive of time as a linear progression instead of a repeating cycle. Zoroastrianism's dualistic cosmology of light versus dark, as well as its spatialization of time that located its own moment as the penultimate moment perched on the edge of existence, established the parameters of eschatological thinking and can be seen as the first instance of a tradition that has consistently foregrounded the present as the most real moment in history, when things will finally change in a radical, unanticipated way. Zoroastrianism was altered significantly by Zurvanism, which retained Zoroaster's dualism of good versus evil but removed the imminent threat of apocalypse. Instead, the history of the world was conceived as a series of three millennial ages leading up to a final victory of good over evil.

The influence of Zoroastrianism and Zurvanism is apparent in the angelic figures and world-ages described in Daniel, the last book of the Hebrew Bible. The book's second half (chapters 7–12) contains four apocalypses predicting the future reigns and tribulations facing the Jewish people. Daniel receives council from a celestial being: "His body was like beryl, his face like the appearance of lightning, his eyes like flaming torches, his arms and legs like the gleam of burnished bronze, and the sounds of his words like the noise of a multitude" (Daniel 10:6). The Book of Daniel has been interpreted literally by many recent readers as prophecies that have been miraculously proven true by actual events. This interpretation assumes that the books were written in the same period in which they are set, in the sixth and seventh centuries BCE. This is not the case. In fact, recent evidence suggests that authorship was actually pseudonymous, with a later compiler collecting the stories around 160 BCE and adding his own backdated "prophecies" to them, as a rhetorical means of attributing the authority of antiquity to his own predictions.

The apocalyptic images of the Book of Daniel symbolize nations as ferocious, mythical beasts. The Babylonian kingdom is a winged lion; the nation of Media is a giant bear chewing a rib; Persia is a winged leopard with four heads. The most striking creature from this book's millennial menagerie is the Greek Empire, evoked as a ten-horned, Dragonlike beast with iron teeth. The horns symbolize the ten oppressive rulers that dominated the Jewish people in the years following Alexander the Great. The point of these tales, finally, seems to be the bestowal of a collective sense of community to the readership, and a sense of themselves as a group that has existed through history, stretching back to the then already well-known tales of Daniel, and leading through five hundred years, to their own moment in history, which was one of crisis and strife, under the Seleucid yoke of Antiochus IV Epiphanes.

The influence of Zurvanism can be found in the most influential ancient apocalypse, Saint John's Revelation. Although for many years historians believed that this Revelation was penned by John the Evangelist, recent evidence has revealed that the author was in fact Prester John, a Jewish-Christian elder from Jerusalem who had been exiled to the island of Patmos. Sometime around 90 BCE, John recorded his ecstatic visions of society's destruction and rebirth.

The book begins with the author recognizing the seven churches that constitute his audience. John then recounts his personal ascension into heaven, where he witnesses visions of cosmic opulence surrounding God. The shimmering grandeur of John's descriptions sometimes seems to take inspiration from the blue Aegean sea that imprisoned the author. A Christlike visitor, the "son of man," is described in a brilliant, mysterious vision:

> I saw seven golden lampstands, and in the midst of the lampstands one like a son of man, clothed with a long robe and with a golden girdle round his breast; his head and his hair were white as white wool, white as snow; his eyes were like a flame of fire, and feet were like burnished bronze, refined as in a furnace, and his voice was like the sound of many waters; in his right hand he held seven stars, from his mouth issued a sharp two-edged sword, and his face was like the sun shining in full strength. (Revelation 1:12–16)

Heavily symbolic, John's Revelation is permeated with sevens. This number was considered magical in the ancient world and was seen as a symbol of completion and order: in the Ptolemaic cosmos, seven planets were believed to circle the earth. In Saint John's Revelation, the Lord is symbolized as a lamb with seven horns and seven eyes (6:6). Seven seals are then opened, after which seven angels blow seven horns and the destruction of Rome begins. Locusts attack. Plagues, earthquakes, and famine proliferate as the four horsemen travel the land. The beast arrives to lay waste to Rome. John's hatred for Rome as the symbolic and actual center of Jewish persecution is vividly evoked in the whore of Babylon, whose diseased fornications with other nations finally earn cosmic wrath. By contrast, the new Jerusalem, the restored millennial city, is described as a virginal bride for Christ, as "a new heaven and earth" restores peace as Christ begins his millennial reign. It is here that we get the conventional Christian definition of millennium as a thousand-year period of prosperity and peace ruled over by Christ after he has violently defeated the Antichrist.

Saint John's Revelation has had a great influence on Western culture, especially the pictorial arts, which have endlessly interpreted its symbols. Earliest interpretations of Revelation (Irenaeus, Tertullian) understood it to predict a literal millennial kingdom imminently awaiting the chosen people. In Saint Augustine's *City of God* (written 413–426), millennium is defined as the first thousand years of Christianity, existing already, albeit hidden from the corrupt order prevailing in the world. Reformation eschatology conceived of millennium as something that happened to the church, collectively constituted as the body of Christ.

Post-Enlightenment literary millennialism often becomes a means of expressing hope for emerging nationalism. Sometimes these realms exist "nowhere," as in Sir Thomas More's *Utopia* (1516), a work that imagines a future society in which justice is achieved by the abolition of private property and money. Millennium is often forecast for a particular year. Some candidate years have been 195, 948, 1000, 1033, 1236, 1260, 1367, 1420, 1588, 1666, and now 2000. Looking over the traditional canon of literature, we can see millennialism evolve from its original religious formulation to a more secular one, and the notion of a chosen people becomes, instead, a fantasy of nationalism. Whenever millennialism occurs in literature, it harkens the arrival of a new order yet unformulated, a third term that crashes into the dialectical movement of society to propose a radically new, unanticipated view of the world.

God's Country: The American Millennium

America has always identified itself as *the* millennial nation. In the early sermons and essays of the colonies, the Puritan imagination of writers such as Cotton Mather (1663–1728), a New England preacher, perceived the colonies to be the fulfillment of New Testament prophecy:

> The New Englanders are a people of God settled in those, which were once the devil's territories; and it may easily be supposed that the devil was exceedingly disturbed, when he perceived such a people here accomplishing the promise of old made unto our blessed Jesus, that he should have the utmost parts of the earth for His possession. (Mather 1989: 217)

Like the compiler of Daniel, Mather perceived his own nation's unique status as a chosen nation asserted against the people whose existence posed the greatest obstacle to survival. Mather's notion of precolonial North America as "devil's territory" is especially disturbing in light of the legacy of genocide practiced upon the Native Americans by the European colonialists. In Mather and elsewhere, writers perceived America to be the promised nation, restoring divinity upon the earth as "our American Jerusalem" (231).

This view of America as *the* millennial nation continues to permeate literature after the Revolutionary War. The visionary English printmaker and poet William Blake's (1757–1827) illuminated poem "America: A Prophecy" recasts apocalypse and subsequent millennialism in imagery that is at once individual and collective:

> The morning comes, the night decays, the watchmen
> leave their stations;
> The grave is burst, the spices shed, the linen wrapped
> up;
> The bones of death, the cov'ring clay, the sinews
> shrunk & dry'd.
> Reviving shake, inspiring move, breathing! awakening!
> Spring like redeemed captives when their bonds &
> bars are burst;
> Let the slave grinding at the mill, run out into the
> field:
> Let him look up into the heavens & laugh in the
> bright air;
> Let the inchained soul shut up in darkness and in
> sighing,
> Whose face has never seen a smile in thirty weary
> years;
> Rise and look out, his chains are loose, his dungeon
> doors are open. (1982: plate 6: 1–10)

While Blake fears the bloodshed of revolution, he looks hopefully to America as a potential source that might move the world past the repression of the aging imperial ideologies of Europe. Blake describes descending layers of apocalypse occurring simultaneously: the collective social body is symbolically resurrected. The workers are liberated. Also, most innovatively, the soul is unchained. Blake's inward turn is a distinctly romantic innovation to millennial literature.

The essays of Ralph Waldo Emerson (1803–82) present a more extensive exploration of the self as the locus of apocalypse. Similar to Saint John and Blake, Emerson's authorial persona is shamanic, as he delivers apocalyptic prophecy based on ecstatic revelation. He published *Nature* in 1836, in the wake of an intense religious epiphany from which his famous Transcendental philosophy emerged. Hugely popular in his own time and influential ever since as a founding definer of the American psyche, Emerson is famous for his ethic of self-reliance. This individualistic ethic borrowed heavily from Kantian idealism, mostly as misunderstood through the works of English romantic poets. In *Nature*, Emerson repeatedly sets forth an ontological understanding of the world in which humanity (i.e., human consciousness) confronts nature (all that is not this consciousness) to access Spirit (Kantian *Geist*), which exists in the deepest core of one's soul but at the same time represents an all-embracing force connecting all. In trying to finally determine the root of this Spirit, this transcendent "Final Cause of the Universe," Emerson writes:

> Whether nature enjoy a substantial existence without, or is only in the apocalypse of the mind, it is alike useful and alike venerable to me. Be it what it may, it is ideal to me, so long as I cannot try the accuracy of my senses. (1987: 23)

Emerson describes a world that "lies broken and in heaps" and blames this on the fragmentary nature of his own self: "The ruin or the blank that we see when we look at nature, is in our own eye" (36). This fragmentation, however, is not inevitable. In fact, millennium is defined as the restoration of unity between man and nature. In a later essay, "The Oversoul," Emerson writes:

> And so we say that the Judgment is distant or near, that the Millennium approaches, that a day of certain political, moral, social reforms is at hand, and the like, when we mean, that in the nature of things, one of the facts we contemplate is external and fugitive, and the other is permanent and connate with the soul. The things we now esteem fixed, shall, one by one, detach themselves, like ripe fruit, from our experience, and fall. The wind shall blow them none knows whither. The landscape, the figures, Boston, London, are facts as fugitive as any institution past, or any whiff of mist or smoke, and so is society, and so is the world. (163)

This passage exemplifies the inward turn so crucial to romantic thinking, tracing a movement from a perspective of unreflecting omniscience to one of introspective subjectivity. The author first experiences a millennial anxiety, but then realizes this is a projection of his own self-conceived relation to the world—that is, his ontology—rather than some empirical pattern waiting to play itself out. By the end of the passage, the narrating voice has bracketed off the world outside. Burning off the dross of his surroundings, he finds unity in soulful solitude.

The year 2000 has been speculated upon in literature for centuries, at least as far back as Nostradamus. During the nineteenth century, however, the amount of culture speculating on the future innovations due in the year 2000 greatly increased. This can be attributed to the emergence of a mass reading audience with a strong appetite for technological prophecies. Serial fiction and novels considered the future using paradigms of science fiction. Jules Verne's novel *An Ideal City* imagines the year 2000 as a metropolis teeming with bizarre gadgety innovations and strict social programming. Edward Bellamy's *Looking Backward*, published in 1888, imagines a socialistic Utopia in which America becomes a single corporation. John Jacob Astor's *A Journey to Other Worlds* imagines a planet regulated in 2000 by the precise control of the "Terrestrial Axis Straightening Company."

Modernist Millenniums

In the twentieth century, much of the literature of high modernism is more apocalyptic than millennial, transfixed upon the violent events leading up to the millennium, rather than the hopeful future that will follow afterwards. The cause of this apocalypticism can be traced to the technological progress that creates, for the first time in history, the potential for global annihilation. In the poetry of Yeats and Eliot, we find scorched landscapes and empty cities. In this century, as with the last, millennialism in literature most often appears in popular genres rather than "literary" ones. Magazines ran series such as *Crimes of the Year 2000*, predicting myriad future crime fighting gimmicks and devices.

Much recent literature challenges millennialism as just another ruse of history that egotistically inflates the importance of our own age. As our century draws to a close, many authors express skepticism toward the millennial anxiety that saturates all aspects of popular culture. In the wake of continental poststructuralist theories of language, apocalypse has been seen by some readers as the effect of any discourse that asserts itself as the truth by erasing its authorial source, and thus presenting itself as a discontinuous truth from some unknown, impossible source beyond language. Some authors, however, find that millennium remains a fruitful form. *Millennium Approaches*, the first half of Tony Kushner's brilliant two-play series *Angels in America*, ends with an angel crashing through the bedroom of Prior Walter, a gay man with AIDS who finds that the disease grants him higher vision. Kushner's work integrates ancient Gnostic, Hebrew, and Christian perspectives on millennium, playing them out through the alternately hilarious and moving interactions of a cast of Mormons, evil lawyers, drag queens, and various fantastic beings. The play finally asserts a hopeful fulfillment of the American democratic ideal of equality with diversity. "We will be citizens," says Prior, as the curtain closes.

Perhaps Kushner is right, and the millennium will bring the resolution of the tensions that have defined the nation. Or perhaps his fundamentalist interlocutors have it right, with their pessimistic visions of fiery death to all but the tiny elect of the righteous, themselves. More likely, Thomas Pynchon has it right, as he formulates it in *Gravity's Rainbow:* "It might be the end of the world, except that it is a fairly average day."

Andrew Corey Yerkes

See also Art; United States, 18th century; Science Fiction Literature

Bibliography

Bible. (1997) King James version, edited and introduced by Robert Carroll and Stephen Prickett. Oxford, U.K.: Oxford University Press.

Blake, William. (1982) *The Complete Poetry and Prose of William Blake,* edited by David V. Erdman. New York: Doubleday.

Bloom, Harold. (1996) *Omens of Millennium: The Gnosis of Angels, Dreams, and Resurrection.* New York: Riverhead Books.

Dewey, Joseph. (1990) *In a Dark Time: The Apocalyptic Temper in the American Novel of the Nuclear Age.* West Lafayette, IN: Purdue University Press.

Emerson, Ralph Waldo. (1987) *The Essays of Ralph Waldo Emerson.* Cambridge, MA: Harvard University Press.

Hodder, Alan D. (1989) *Emerson's Rhetoric of Revelation: Nature, the Reader, and the Apocalypse Within.* University Park, PA: Pennsylvania State University Press.

Kermode, Frank. (1967) *The Sense of an Ending: Studies in the Theory of Fiction.* Oxford, U.K.: Oxford University Press.

Kushner, Tony. (1993) *Angels in America.* New York: Theatre Communications Group.

Mani, Lakshmi. (1981) *The Apocalyptic Vision in Nineteenth Century American Fiction: A Study of Cooper, Hawthorne, and Melville.* Washington, D.C.: University Press of America.

Mather, Cotton. ([1693] 1989) "The Wonders of the Invisible World." *The Norton Anthology of American Literature,* 2 vols., 3d ed., edited by Nina Baym et al. New York: Norton, vol. 1, 217–22.

Robinson, Douglas. (1985) *American Apocalypses: The Image of the End of the World in American Literature.* Baltimore, MD: Johns Hopkins University Press.

Maps of Apocalyptic Time

Apocalyptic texts attempt to describe the four dimensions of space and time. As descriptions of otherworldly journeys in which a visionary is led by a spiritual guide, apocalypses describe heaven, hell, and the middle earth of human existence. At the same time, however, many apocalyptic and millennialist texts also imagine linear time: sequences of events from the past and present into the future. They prophesy an epic drama occurring on the cosmic scale. Not surprisingly, therefore, in the Western traditions of Judaism and Christianity, commentators on apocalyptic and millennialist texts have sometimes resorted to visual representations or charts that map this sequence.

The Temporality of Apocalyptic Visions

In many societies, the communal practices and beliefs generically characterized as "religious" consist in distinguishing "sacred" territory and "sacred" time. Temples and shrines, festivals and holy days bracket the ordinary or "profane." Such practices and beliefs initiate novices, confer group identity, and conglomerate otherwise fragmented experiences. Smith suggests that the practices and beliefs we call "religion" are best understood as territorial maps imposed on the landscape of experience and proposes that what he calls "locative" maps "overcome all incongruity by assuming the interconnectedness of all things, the adequacy of symbolization . . . and the power and possibility of repetition" which is distinguished from a "utopian" map that "turns in rebellion and flight to a new world and a new mode of creation" (308–9).

American readers are so accustomed to historical interpretations of the Old Testament Book of Daniel and the New Testament Book of Revelation that it is important to note that predictive interpretations of apocalyptic texts are relative newcomers, dating only from about the twelfth century among European Christians. St. Augustine (354–430) writing in the fourth century of the common era had stipulated that Revelation was to be understood as a symbolic text whose meaning was the eternal struggle of the church and the individual's soul against the devil. In *The City of God,* his response to the devastating barbarian invasions of Rome, St. Augustine noted the contingency of this world, from which the soul sought escape, waiting in hope for reunion with God after death.

Medieval Apocalyptic Maps

An early medieval commentary on the Book of Revelation composed in the late eighth century by a Spanish monk, Beatus of Liébana, did suggest a date for the end of the world around 800, based on his calculations of the "six ages" of history and his reading of an earlier commentary by Tyconius. About two hundred years later, monastic book illuminators began to provide illustrations for the Beatus Apocalypse and the Morgan Beatus manuscript. Its illuminations, the work of a monk named Maius, not only illustrate the temporal sequence of Revelation's narrative but also its cosmography.

Equally interesting, however, are the manuscript's map of the world (f. 33v, f. 34), in which sites relevant to salvation history are demarcated, and its genealogical maps of Jesus' ancestors (f. 4v–9v). The genealogical maps employ chains of linked circles in each of which an ancestor's name appears (a practice of Roman aristocrats as recorded in Pliny); among these are interspersed important events in world history (see Figure 1). The motif of linked circles would reappear in subsequent maps of apocalyptic time.

Not until Richard of St. Victor and Joachim of Fiore eight hundred years after St. Augustine and four hundred years after Beatus of Liébana do we read systematic attempts to interpret the Book of Revelation as a map of human history—past, present, and future—in what is known today as "salvation history." Theologian and contemplative Richard of St. Victor (d. 1173) interpreted Revelation's image of the opening of seven seals as an allegory of seven successive stages in history. Joachim of Fiore (1135–1202) was more of a visionary than a theologian, whose Revelation-inspired "vision" of history included three *status* (state or stage of development): the Age of the Father, the Age of the Son, and the coming Age of the Spirit, the last of which Joachim believed had not yet arrived but had begun to make its effects felt. The first corresponded to the Old Testament, the second to the New Testament, and the third to a time of the spiritually enlightened without need of written scriptures.

As Barbara Nolan has pointed out, "In his temporal and spatial figures describing the course of human history, Joachim foresees the entire world as a cloistral utopia governed by monks and representing the final flowering of human spirituality before the Last Judgment" (28). Not content with writing about this scheme, however, Joachim of Fiore also presented his vision in a series of graphic representations, maps of apocalyptic time. In *Il Libro delle Figure* Joachim represented the three *status* as linked circles, either in images of interlocking rings or entangled circular tree branches, both reminiscent of the genealogical maps in the Beatus Apocalypse (see Figure 2).

At about the same time, church architecture began to map salvation history and apocalyptic time. Contemporary with Richard of St. Victor and Joachim of Fiore was the French monk, the Abbot Suger, the innovator of the Gothic style of architecture, whose revolutionary renovation of the west façade of the royal abbey of St.-Denis includes linked images of Christ's suffering, death, and Second Coming, which Suger systematically continued in the design of the chapel's stained glass. However, the fullest production of a cathedral as a three-dimensional map of apocalyptic time occurs at Chartres, which Nolan describes:

> Here, as at St.-Denis, the sculptural program traces the whole course of sacred history in order to teach that God's progressive revelation to mankind is both radically historical and visionary. But what is most important, the contemporary Christian has his place in this temporally-based revelation. It is vividly de-

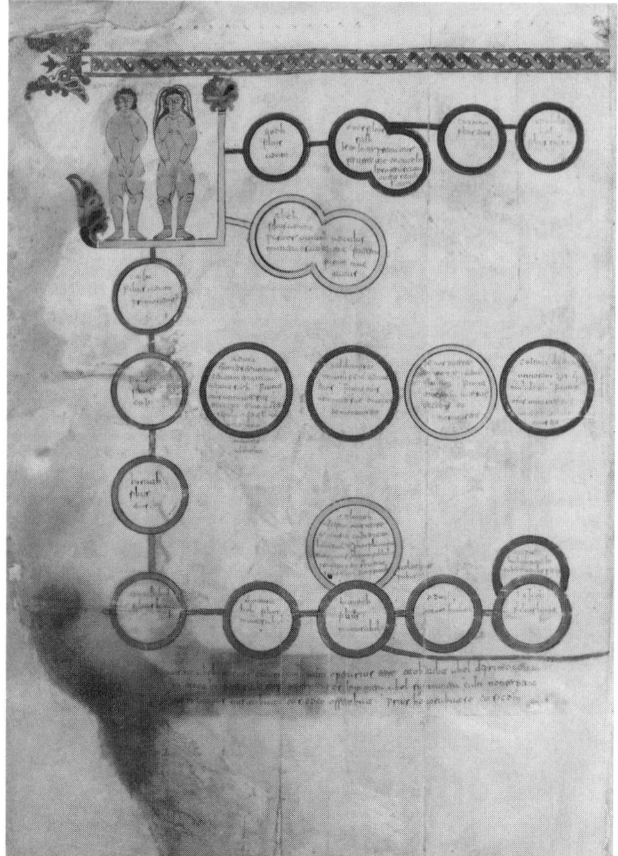

Figure 1. **Morgan Beatus.** THIS ITEM IS REPRODUCED BY PERMISSION OF THE MORGAN LIBRARY, NEW YORK.

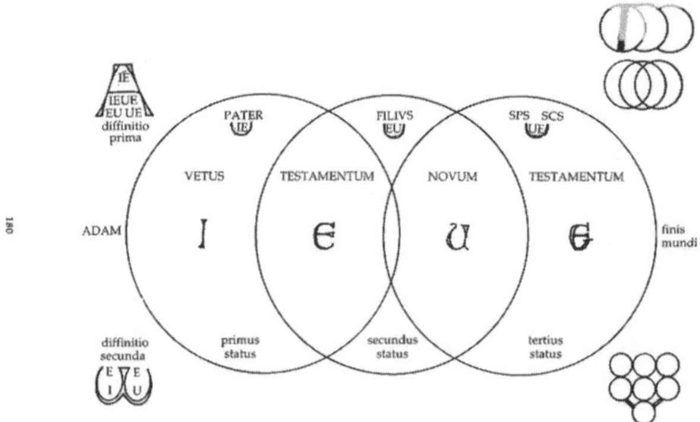

Figure 2. Three Status of Joachim of Fiore MCGINN, BERNARD. (1985) *THE CALABRIAN ABBOT: JOACHIM OF FIORE IN THE HISTORY OF WESTERN THOUGHT*. NEW YORK: MACMILLAN, 180.

> fined in his assumed ability to *understand* all the figures of sacred scripture bound together by the art of the cathedral and to participate spiritually in the grand human procession toward universal salvation. . . . One of the most remarkable effects achieved by the designers of Chartres is the coordination of the exterior sculpture with the stained glass windows and interior structure, giving the entire edifice an elegant physical and thematic unity. The observer is led to experience not only the progress of sacred history, but also a harmony and interplay between Old and New Testaments and contemporary life. (52–53)

In the cathedral, the building and the continuous sacred rituals it housed anticipated the City of God, the New Jerusalem, and mapped a trajectory of salvation for those who entered and processed up its aisles (or in the case of Chartres, walked the circular path of the maze formed by floor tiles).

Maps of Apocalyptic Time in the Reformation

During the Reformation, scriptural commentators on the Books of Daniel and Revelation developed in earnest historical interpretations of the apocalyptic texts, which they read not as expressions of religious communities' past crises but as predictions of future cataclysm and fulfillment. Thus biblical interpreters were compelled to reconcile the diverse and apparently fragmented millennialist verses of the Hebrew prophets, canonical apocalyptic texts like Daniel and Revelation, the sayings of Jesus in the four Gospels, and the letters of Paul, not to mention numerous apocryphal (nonofficial) sacred texts, like the Sibylline Oracles. Because text alone could not organize this complex information, some commentaries used diagrams to do so.

One such commentary was Joseph Mede's *Clavis Apocalyptica* (Keys to the Apocalypse), first published privately in 1627, which viewed the Books of Daniel and Revelation as history waiting to occur. Several years after its initial publication, Mede invited a Mr. Haydock to design a synoptic diagram, which Richard More later refined and included in his 1643 English translation of *Clavis Apocalyptica*. This map of apocalyptic time consisted of a circle, the top half of which charted prophecies of the Roman Empire, the bottom half, prophecies of the church. More's label for this chart reads as follows:

> Know thou who voutchsafest to meditate upon this Apocalyptik Type that the archinge lines meeting in the same beginning and end shew contemporary prophecies: to wit of the seales and of the litle book, the same things is demonstrated by the bounds of the lines and circumferences answering each other. And (to conclude) which of the Visions goeth before or foloweth after thou maiest behold by the order proceeding from the left hand to the right. At the 27, 28 and 29th pages of the key the reader finde a more full direction for the use of this scheme.

More's version of Haydock's map is therefore supplemented by the details of Mede's text, as translated by More (see Figure 3).

As Reformation commentaries on the biblical Books of Daniel and Revelation became more insistent and exacting in their historical prognostications of the endtimes, identifying the biblical human figures with current European personages (for example, the pope as Antichrist) and calculating the exact dates of the future Day of the Lord, their visuals representations became correspondingly more complex.

An Apocalyptic Representation at the Eve of the French Revolution

This process reached a remarkable point of development in the two-volume commentary of James Purves, *Observations on the Visions of the Apostle John Compared with Other Sacred Scriptures*, published in 1789 and 1793. Interpreting the signs of the times (e.g., the recently completed American Revolution and the newly begun French Revolution), the antiroyalist Purves declared:

> And if present appearances will not justify the supposition, that the dawn of that blessed morning is beginning to spring forth, they seem very much to indicate its approach. The revolution that has taken place in America, and what seems fast taking place in France, are certainly favorable symptoms; for among the various blessings to be enjoyed in that blessed time, it can hardly be doubted that the blessing of liberty will be one. And the blessing of peace may be expected to attend, or soon follow the steps of liberty. (vol. 1, 26–27)

At the end of his first volume, Purves included a "A scheme [chart] of the Seals, the Trumpets, and the Vials mentioned in the Book of Revelations. And a representation of the Dragon and the two Beasts described in the XII and XIII Chapters"; Purves believed that the seven seals of Revelation had already been opened in history and the seven trumpets sounded, whose effects continued to reverberate throughout history. In the top register of the chart is a scale of centuries from the birth of Christ to the year 2000; below are situated representations of the seven seals and seven trumpets demarcating their initiation and end. Similarly, representations of the seven vials pour out upon icons of the parts of earth where their effects are felt (see Figure 4).

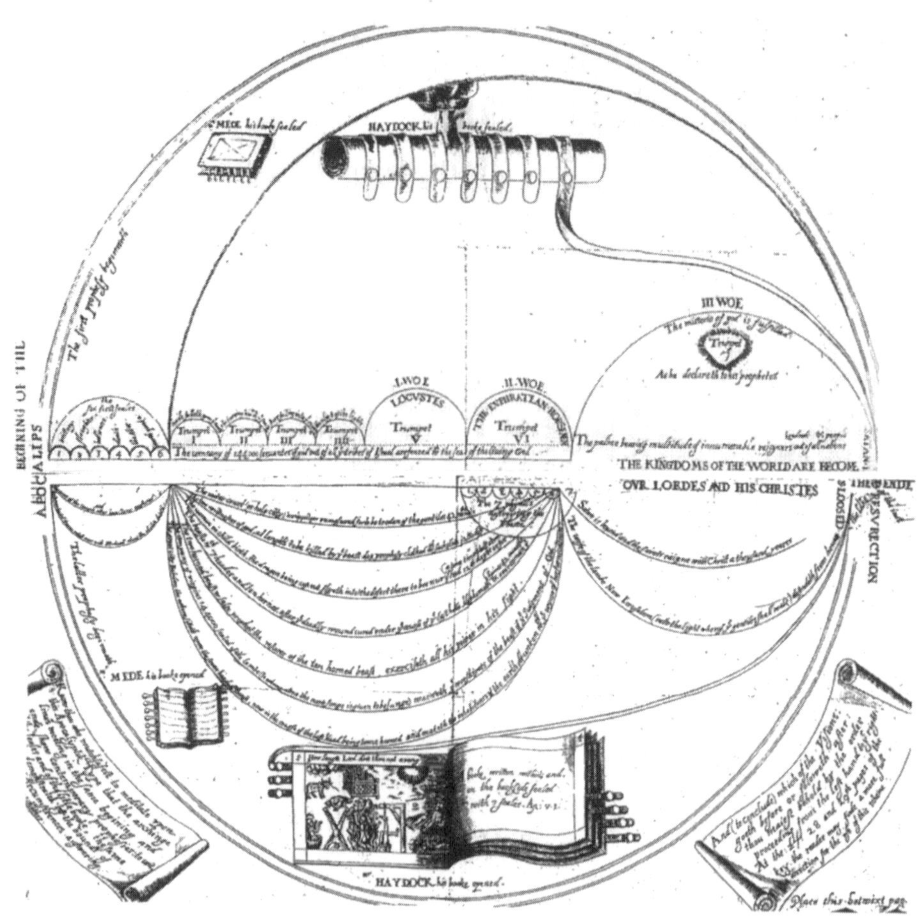

Figure 3. Joseph Mede's "Apocalyptik Type." THIS ITEM IS REPRODUCED BY PERMISSION OF THE HUNTINGTON LIBRARY, SAN MARINO, CALIFORNIA.

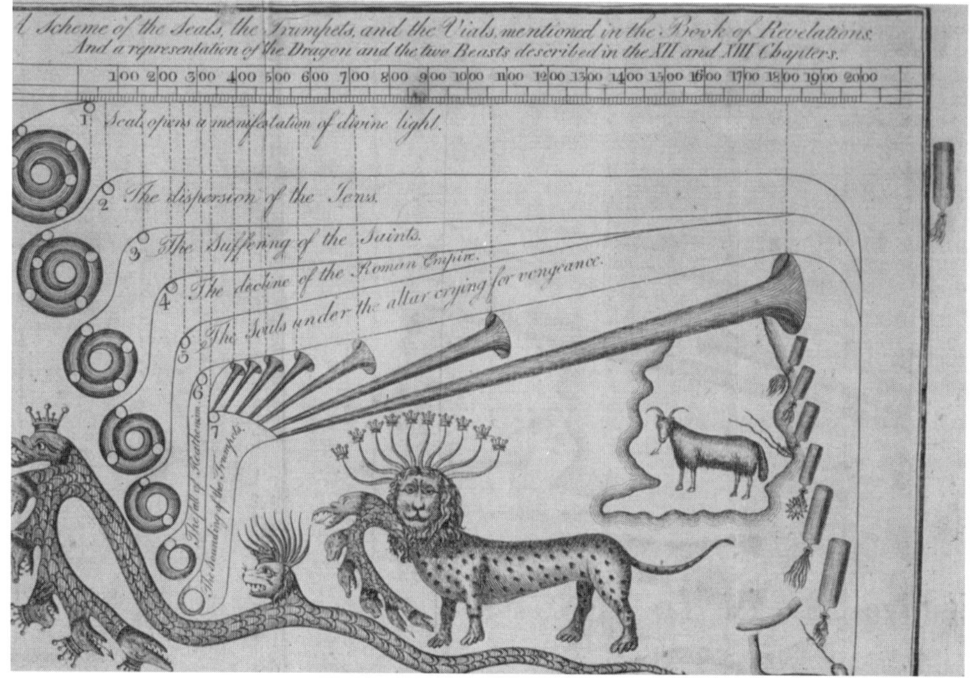

Figure 4. Purves's 1789 Chart. PURVES, JAMES. (1789) *OBSERVATIONS ON THE VISIONS OF THE APOSTLE JOHN COMPARED WITH OTHER SACRED SCRIPTURES*, 2 VOLS., EDINBURGH.

Figure 5. Purves's 1793 Chart. PURVES, JAMES. (1793). *OBSERVATIONS ON THE VISIONS OF THE APOSTLE JOHN COMPARED WITH OTHER SACRED SCRIPTURES*, 2 VOLS., EDINBURGH.

Attached to the end of his second volume, Purves provided an even more complex map, with a time line ranging from fifty-two years before the Flood to 2400 in the Common Era ("300 years into the Time when it is expected, that Light, Liberty, and Peace will prevail over all the Earth"). In the top register, Purves drew six sun shapes to represent historical "manifestations of divine light," and identified the seven trumpets, seals, and vials. In the bottom register, Purves drew the many-headed beast on which rides the Whore Babylon, arranging the horns of each head so that they point to specific points on the time line (see Figure 5).

A Twentieth-Century Apocalyptic Map

This desire to organize the diverse and obscure signs in apocalyptic texts by producing maps or charts has continued into modern times, relying not only on sacred texts but also on apocryphal writings, commentaries, and scientific discourses. In *Cosmos, Chaos, and Gospel: A Chronology of World Evangelization from Creation to New Creation*, one in a series published in 1987 by the Foreign Mission Board of the Southern Baptist Convention, David Barrett organizes human time into three "Cosmic Eras" (prehistory, history, and posthistory) and proposes four "eschato-scientific scenarios": "Monodenominationalism," "Nondenominationalism," "Postdenominationalism," and "Martyrdom," arrayed along a time line from the resurrection of Christ to the year 2000 and beyond. Barrett's maps follow a time line similar to Purves's while at the same time they compose figurative population territories. For example, in Scenario 3 (Postdenominationalism) after the year 2000 Christians form geo-ethnic-based groups, such as "Indo-Iranians" ("Brown"), "Latinamericans" ("Tan"), "Euroamericans" ("White"), "Asiatico-Chinese" ("Yellow"), "Australasians" ("Grey"), or "Afro-Americans" ("Black") (see Figure 6). Barrett takes a cue from corporate strategic planning methods and futurology producing detailed "scenarios" whose speculative quality is obscured by the authority of his charts.

The Rhetorical Dimensions of Apocalyptic Maps

Despite their association with science and its vaunted objectivity, maps and charts are never neutral representations. They carry with them an implied authority that urges their readers to believe them. And maps bring their glamor to the subjects they territorialize. However, they conceal as much as they reveal, obscuring their own limitations and inaccuracies. Apocalyptic commentaries from the late Middle Ages to the present have increasingly claimed to be authoritative calculations of history and posthistory, making claims on readers' identities and commitments. Their uses of maps and charts of apocalyptic time serve rhetorical purposes, persuading believers to an appropriate course of action, by organizing scattered apocalyptic texts and by bestowing on the commentary the luster of scientific validity.

Maps of apocalyptic time attempt to represent time and space as sacred in the context of history and its end. Partly drawing their authority from science, they lend authority to the eschatological calculations of the commentator who attempts to identify both the human figures and the dates of this ultimate cosmic drama. When successful, these maps persuade readers to adhere to the commentator's ethical values and permit readers to compose a coherent view of history.

Thomas L. Long

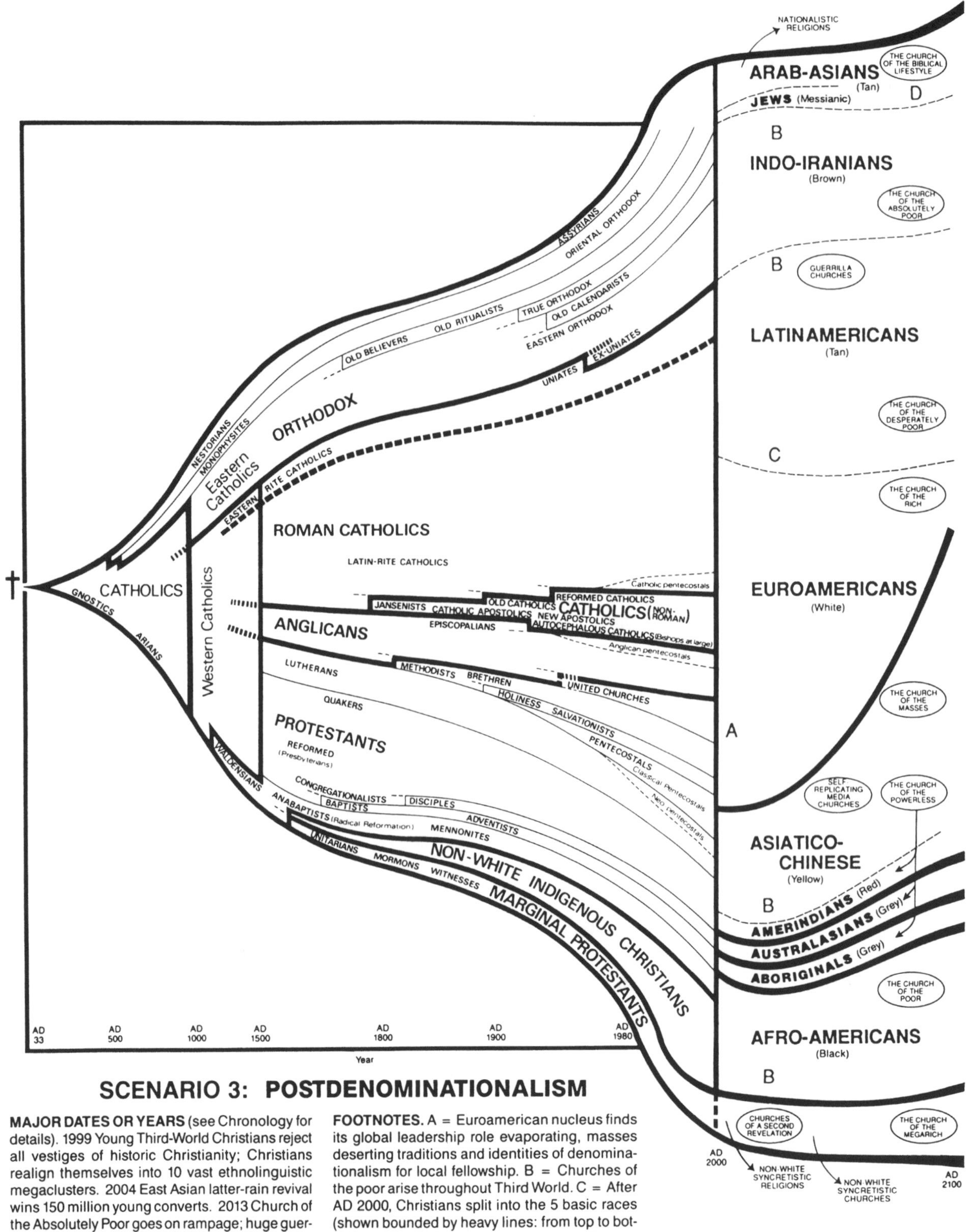

SCENARIO 3: POSTDENOMINATIONALISM

MAJOR DATES OR YEARS (see Chronology for details). 1999 Young Third-World Christians reject all vestiges of historic Christianity; Christians realign themselves into 10 vast ethnolinguistic megaclusters. 2004 East Asian latter-rain revival wins 150 million young converts. 2013 Church of the Absolutely Poor goes on rampage; huge guerrilla churches arise across all impoverished continents. 2030 One and a half billion Chinese Christians embark on world mission. 2050 Self-replicating media churches spread like wildfire. 2080 Chinese and Arab Christians independently launch world conversion schemes.

FOOTNOTES. A = Euroamerican nucleus finds its global leadership role evaporating, masses deserting traditions and identities of denominationalism for local fellowship. B = Churches of the poor arise throughout Third World. C = After AD 2000, Christians split into the 5 basic races (shown bounded by heavy lines: from top to bottom, Caucasoid, Mongoloid, Australoid, Capoid, Negroid. Lighter dashed lines indicate racial subdivisions (thus, 'Caucasoid' covers Arabs, Jews, Indo-Iranians, Latinamericans, Euroamericans). The words for color are purely stylized, as explained in *World Christian encyclopedia,* Part 4 'Culture.' D = Biblical lifestyle becomes the model, making churches of the poor violently opposed to all churches of the rich.

Figure 6. David Barrett's scenario 3. INTERNATIONAL MISSION BOARD OF THE SOUTHERN BAPTISTS CONVENTION, RICHMOND, VA.

Bibliography

Barrett, David B. (1987) *Cosmos, Chaos, and Gospel: A Chronology of World Evangelization from Creation to New Creation.* Global Evangelization Movement: The AD 2000 Series. Birmingham, AL: New Hope.

Nolan, Barbara. (1977) *The Gothic Visionary Perspective.* Princeton, NJ: Princeton University Press.

Purves, James. (1789, 1793) *Observations on the Visions of the Apostle John Compared with Other Sacred Scriptures*, 2 vols. Edinburgh.

Smith, Jonathan Z. (1978) "Map Is Not Territory." In *Map Is Not Territory: Studies in the History of Religions.* Leiden: Brill, 289–309.

A Spanish Apocalypse: The Morgan Beatus Manuscript. (1991) Introduction and Commentaries by John Williams. Codicological Analysis by Barbara A. Shailor. New York: George Braziller.

Marianism

Millennial dreams of a new world arise when the old rules and the old dreams become meaningless. It is in these situations that people pin all their hopes on the dawning of a new age and the prophets who will bring it about. In the modern era, popular Catholic millennialism has been expressed through devotion to apparitions of the Virgin Mary.

The Marian worldview is fundamentally a millenarian one, believing in the Millennium of Christian prophecy and the coming of an ideal society through a radical change. What has developed is a transnational, transhistorical apocalyptic ideology, meaning that the Virgin's messages at apparition sites all over the world are believed by devotees to provide a single extended warning, given in different times and different places, of how the apocalypse will happen. Thus the Virgin's famous "Third Secret" from Fatima, Portugal, in 1917, her prediction of a permanent sign in the sky from Garabandal, Spain, in 1961, and the warnings from Medjugorje, Yugoslavia, in the 1980s are all considered to be part of the same ongoing warning. The message is simple. God and Jesus are angry because mankind is so sinful, and Mary, in her infinite mercy is interceding, holding back her son's arm, to give humanity one last chance.

Like many folk beliefs, the Marian endtimes scenario is fairly inchoate, and there are many individual variations in the timetable and in the degree of coherence of this script among pilgrims, but the basic outline is usually similar. Similar to many Christian apocalyptic belief systems, it is largely based on the Books of Daniel and Revelation, but also incorporates many specific events and warnings taken from the messages at various apparition sites. Briefly, it is believed that the world is entering the endtimes. It is usually presumed that the beginning of the End of Times will be preceded by chastisements to mankind; and various world events, such as earthquakes, violence, AIDS, and legalized abortion are often cited as examples of these chastisements. This period of chastisement is often the focus of elaborate conspiracy theories involving an evil Antipope as well as the rise of the Antichrist. Then there will be a permanent sign in the sky, which will herald the next stage, the Warning. The Warning, sometimes called a "correction of conscience" is a time when all human activity will stop, and people will be forced to see all their sins, and the impacts of all their sins on others. This judgment will allow people one last chance to repent and be baptized. Sometime after this there will be Three Days of Darkness, followed by disasters where those who do not believe will be taken to hell, while a Remnant will be saved. This is followed by the Second Coming of Christ, which will usher in the Millennium, with its attendant thousand years of peace.

Historical Background

There is a long history of Marian devotions and Marian apparitions in the Catholic Church, but a specifically Marian millennialism only developed in the nineteenth century when the apocalyptic worldview underlying Marian apparitions and pilgrimages began to form. These changes were all part of a transformation of apparitions into a new social phenomena.

The pattern seen throughout the history of modern apparitions is of clergy trying to control and channel the energies of these potentially heretical millennial movements. For the Catholic Church, there is always something potentially heretical about apparitions. Mystical experiences are private and interior and so are uncontrollable. They represent sources of power outside of church authority, which is why, in spite of the popularity of pilgrimages and visionaries, the church has traditionally been ambivalent about these popular displays of worship. Apparitions provide a way to mediate this conflict. They exist at the intersection of two contrary cultures, the formal theology of the church and a more magical, forbidden world of folk-beliefs. Perhaps the best illustration of this is the history of the three great apparitions of the nineteenth century: Rue de Bac, LaSalette, and Lourdes.

In 1830, Catherine Labouré (now St. Catherine), a nun at the convent of the Sisters of Charity of St. Vincent de Bac in Paris (more commonly known by the street the convent is located on, Rue de Bac) had a vision of the Virgin Mary. In her vision, Catherine was woken up by a small boy whom she realized was her guardian angel. The angel led her through the convent to a chapel where the Virgin Mary held out a golden ball, which Catherine knew to represent the world. Catherine put her hand in Mary's lap and received the design for special Miraculous Medals to be struck in Mary's honor. Catherine Labouré's apparitions at Rue de Bac were the first to be publicized by the mass media. As a result, the visions were such an immediate worldwide sensation that over 100 million Miraculous Medals were in circulation within ten years of the apparitions.

Sixteen years later, in 1846, Francois-Melanie Mathieu and Pierre-Maximin Giraud, two peasant children in the village of LaSalette, France, saw the figure of a weeping woman bathed in light. She told the children that "A great famine will come. Before the famine comes, the children under seven years of age will be seized by trembling and they will die in the hands of those who hold them," if people did not return to the church and observe the sacraments. A few days later, Melanie and Maximin returned to the site and claimed that a natural spring now flowed at the spot where the Virgin had appeared. The spring soon became known for healings, and LaSalette was transformed into a pilgrimage site. Although not so well known now, LaSalette was a world-famous site throughout the nineteenth century.

The most famous of all apparitions of Mary occurred twelve years later, in 1858, in Lourdes, France. Fourteen-year-old Bernadette Soubrious (now St. Bernadette) experienced a series of eighteen apparitions of a beautiful woman who she called *aquerò* ("that one" in the local Bigourdan dialect). She described *aquerò* as a girl about her own age wearing a white dress with a blue sash and holding a rosary in one hand. Over the next two months, thousands of people gathered at the appointed times to watch Bernadette kneel down and receive her apparition of the Virgin in public. Lourdes quickly became world famous and is still a tremendously popular pilgrimage site, with more than four million pilgrims coming each year.

A tremendous change in the nature of pilgrimages and apparitions had occurred in the course of these three apparitions. Premodern apparitions were usually private, one-time occurrences. Rue de Bac basically followed that script. It took place in a cloistered convent and the visionary never appeared in public. Church officials stated only that messages had been revealed to an anonymous nun by the Virgin during an apparition, and Catherine Labouré's identity was not made public until 1876, shortly before her death. The visionaries at LaSalette were illiterate peasant children, but their apparition again happened only once with no witnesses. By the time of Lourdes, the pattern had shifted completely. The visionary was a peasant girl, and the apparitions occurred in public at regularly scheduled times.

Apparitions became mass, public affairs at a time when mass religious movements were sweeping throughout Europe. The nineteenth century in Europe is generally thought of as the century of modernity and the Industrial Revolution, but it was also a time of recurrent revolutions and counterrevolutions, of famines, wars, and turmoil, particularly in the poor peasant villages where apparitions usually occurred. All the major nineteenth-century apparitions took place during wars and political and economic crises. Catherine Labouré's apparitions at Rue de Bac occurred during the overthrow of the proclerical Bourbon monarchy, and the Virgin appeared in the royalist colors blue and white. LaSalette unfolded amidst the unrest leading up to the Revolutions of 1848, as food shortages, poor harvests, and famines plagued Europe. Lourdes was widely seen as support for the royalist cause against the Second Empire.

The Vatican responded by instituting elaborate procedures for authenticating and approving visionaries and their apparitions as way to ensure that they did not grow out of control. All the resources of the church were mobilized to approve and develop large-scale pilgrimages at Rue de Bac, LaSalette, and Lourdes. The Virgin was held up as a submissive, humble, and obedient role model for all Catholics to aspire to, and the visionaries themselves were moved away from the site, usually to convents, so that no secondary cult of personality could develop that focused on them rather than on Mary's messages.

There were important reasons for the church to gain control of the wave of apparitions. The upheavals in the countryside had led to a variety of popular apocalyptic and messianic movements throughout Europe. These new popular cults, some led by renegade priests, were becoming increasingly powerful and rivaled the authority of the church in some areas. Many of the leaders of these movements had visions involving a whole range of biblical figures and saints such as the prophet Elijah and St. Joseph, as well as Mary.

Out of all these popular movements, only the cult of Mary was accepted, encouraged, and developed. Subsequent apparitions were almost exclusively visions of Mary. Visions and prophesies had become standardized and "Marianized." In the process the apocalyptic elements of the Virgin's messages were largely excluded from official church doctrines and instead became the province of folk religion.

The Influence of La Salette

Of all the apparitions of the nineteenth century, Lourdes was the most influential in forming the basic schemas and patterns of worship and scripts for behavior at modern appari-

INTERNET MESSAGE FROM A MARIAN DEVOTEE IN AUSTRALIA

I'm sure everyone knows that the times we live in are filled with sin and suffering. Never before have more people been killed for their faith in all centuries put together than have died over the last hundred years. The Catholic Church is being rocked with accusations of scandal, people are turning away in great numbers. Abortion and divorce are legal in a number of countries, two major achievements for the devil in his desire to break up family life. Two world wars, the holocaust, communism, rises in famines, wars, natural disasters, weapons of destruction, 'occult' happenings and worship, drugs, violence, unemployment. All these terrible signs tell us that things are pretty bad and that mankind is falling further away from God.

But amidst all this we have a shining light, the Blessed Virgin and Holy Mother of God, Mary. She has come with a regularity, frequency and urgency never known before. Her messages are clear and rousing–repent, pray, fast for Gods Justice is ready to be unleashed.

Source: Apparition List e-mail discussion group, 10 Dec 1995.

tion sites. However, La Salette was far more influential than Lourdes in forming the apocalyptic worldview that underlies modern apparitions. This is related to the difference in the nature of the messages received by the visionaries at the two sites. The Virgin's messages at LaSalette were harsh and apocalyptic compared to the visions at Lourdes, which were more theologically orthodox and supported traditional doctrines rather than emphasizing millennial messages.

The differences between the two sites extended to the visionaries themselves. Maximin and Melanie at LaSalette seem to have been universally regarded as unpleasant and unintelligent. It was considered a proof of the authenticity of the visions that such unlikely (and unlikable) children would be the ones to have seen the Virgin. Bernadette Soubrious, in contrast, was seen as warm and good and an appropriate receptacle for messages from Mary. Their lives after their apparitions only emphasize these differences; Bernadette became a nun and was ultimately canonized, while Melanie and Maximin lived unhappily and died in obscurity.

The other, related, major effect of the apparition at La Salette was the development of a script for public secrets at Marian apparition sites. A common element of subsequent Marian apparitions are messages that Mary has told the visionary that are not to be told to anyone else. Sometimes, as at Lourdes, the visionary announces that the secrets pertain to herself alone and not to anyone else, and so interest in them wanes. However at many sites, the secrets are believed to contain apocalyptic warnings.

The history of these public secrets began at LaSalette. Melanie and Maximin did not initially report having received any secrets from "the beautiful lady," but apparently when being questioned a week later, both children did report that they had been told a secret. It seems that the secrets were initially presumed to be personal secrets, relevant only to the visionaries. Over the next several months, there were many attempts to convince, trick, or bribe the children to tell the secrets. By the following year, in 1847, the belief had arisen that the secrets referred to future events of tremendous consequence. The revolutions of 1848 throughout Europe gave rise to rumors that the secrets contained crucial information for understanding changing world events, some of these suspicions linked coming events with the Second Coming of Christ.

By 1851, Melanie and Maximin had agreed that the pope would be the only proper recipient of the secrets, and plans were made to deliver them to Pope Pius IX. It was never definitively established why Melanie and Maximin had changed their minds after five years of refusing to divulge the secrets, but there were rumors that the children had received messages that the time was now right for the messages to be revealed. At any rate, the children were induced to write them down and the messages were delivered Pius IX, who never made any public mention of what they might have contained.

Once the messages had been delivered to the pope, there was renewed speculation among devotees as to the possibly apocalyptic predictions contained in the secrets. There were many accounts published purporting to be Maximin's secrets, written by eyewitnesses to the actual writing of the secrets. Some claimed the secrets foretold the rise of the

Antichrist and the subsequent end of the world, while others claimed the message was that God would bring mercy and rehabilitation after an age of darkness.

Melanie herself published the text of her secret in 1879. She wrote of chastisements and torments that would befall mankind in the endtimes before Jesus returns and a new era of peace is inaugurated. Controversies over the authenticity of Melanie and Maximin's messages continued for many years, with the alleged secret of Maximin being published as late as the 1870s, and a brochure written by Melanie being officially discredited as recently as 1923. The assertions as to the content of the secrets varied, but the books all contributed to the growing belief among many Catholics that there were apocalyptic secrets being given to visionaries that would make it possible to understand world events, and that the church was preventing the secrets from being made public.

Melanie's millennial, populist, and sometimes anticlerical post-LaSalette writings helped give rise to apocalyptic Marian popular literature. This genre of millennial apocalyptic writing was common in the Middle Ages and derives ultimately from the Bible, particularly the Book of Revelation and the Book of Daniel. Melanie's writings brought this tradition into the milieu of lower-middle-class Catholics in southern Europe, and later, to America. The apocalyptic nature of the La Salette messages, combined with Melanie's post-La Salette writings fused Marian beliefs with popular millennialism and set the tone for the modern Marian movement that developed, a movement that was populist and most closely identified with the lower-middle and working classes.

Conclusion

The rise of Marian millennialism in the nineteenth century cannot be reduced to a simple conflict between tradition and modernity or between the church and popular religiosity, but rather a complex response to chaos and upheaval in a rapidly changing world. Church authorities had been forced to integrate visions and apparitions into the life of the church; and in so doing, had maintained institutional control over a widespread popular movements as potentially heretical millennialism was channeled and made orthodox.

Later apparitions have followed the patterns and scripts of the nineteenth century, and have all, in one way or another, attempted to negotiate the same divide between church doctrine and the underlying apocalypticism of their messages. The church has, in many ways, redirected and defused the apocalyptic energies of popular Marian movements, but their millennial and apocalyptic elements have not been eliminated. Instead, these became part of a vibrant popular Catholic apocalypticism that continues to the present day.

Victor Balaban

See also Apostles of Infinite Love, Bayside (Our Lady of the Roses), Fatima Cult, Roman Catholicism

Bibliography

Carroll, Michael P. (1986) *The Cult of the Virgin Mary: Psychological Origins*. Princeton, NJ: Princeton University Press.

Christian, William A., Jr. (1989) *Apparitions in late Medieval and Renaissance Spain*. Princeton, NJ: Princeton University Press.

Cuneo, Michael W. (1997) *The Smoke of Satan: Conservative and Traditionalist Dissent in Contemporary American Catholicism*. New York: Oxford University Press.

Kselman, Thomas A. (1983) *Miracles & Prophesies in Nineteenth-Century France*. New Brunswick, NJ: Rutgers University Press.

Pelikan, Jaroslav. (1996) *Mary through the Centuries: Her Place in the History of Culture*. New Haven: Yale University Press.

Turner Victor, and Edith L. Turner. ([1978] 1995) *Image and Pilgrimage in Christian Culture: Anthropological Perspectives*. New York: Columbia University Press.

Zimdars-Swartz, Sandra L. (1991) *Encountering Mary: Visions of Mary from LaSalette to Medjugorje*. Princeton, NJ: Princeton University Press.

Marking Millennial Moments

Historians often use key dates and decisive historic events as markers of distinctive periods in a larger history. These markers bracket a somewhat arbitrary period of time, for the purpose of in-depth study, interpretation, and characterization (e.g., the Medieval Vision, the Age of Reason, the Modern Mind, the Postmodern Temper). The methods of marking time and history must always be qualified and used with intellectual caution. This philosophical essay (1) surveys available methods for the study of apocalyptic time, (2) qualifies the academic use of millennial history and apocalyptic calendars, (3) proposes a new and experimental method of marking millennial moments (MMM), and (4) applies this method to marking the end of the modern era.

Available Methods for the Study of Apocalyptic Time

Apocalyptic time is a social construction of millennial meaning or revelatory significance associated with a particular calendar date or period of history. A *millennial moment* is an event or cluster of events that precipitate a significant change within a self-identifiable group, whether a sect or society. There are a variety of approaches and methods for examining apocalyptic time and millennial moments in the fields of cultural history, sociology, psychology, and theology.

Cultural Historical

Richard Landes in his essay, "On Owls, Roosters and Apocalyptic Time," defines apocalyptic time functionally: "that perception of time in which the End of the World (variously imagined) is so close that its anticipation changes the behavior of the believer" (http://www.mille.org/landes-rob.htm). He calls for a historiographic approach and socioscientific method that takes seriously the phenomenon of apocalyptic belief and examines the role of apocalyptic time and the social movements it inspires. Millennial movements—including new religious sects, apocalyptic communities, and postapocalyptic generations—all shape larger societies and civilizations. This emphasis on the changes of human behavior is critical for both cultural history and sociology.

Sociological

The sociologist of apocalyptic religion simply observes and describes social phenomena using mostly quantitative methods of inquiry. Sometimes qualitative and ethnographic methods are used in gathering oral histories and personal experiences that are then interpreted sociologically as trends, movements, and popular ideas. For example, studies were conducted in the Chernobyl-contaminated region of Belarus from 1986–1991 to quantify the extent and spectrum of apocalyptic interpretations of the 1986 nuclear disaster. It was discovered that many in the region thought the event to have been predicted in the Bible for the last days.

Psychological

Apocalyptic thinking has been a subject of the psychology of religion for decades. The traditional assumption is that apocalyptic or millennial moments, visions, and experiences are largely the projection of the subject onto selected objects or events. This is studied more as complex or personal psychology rather than as a social phenomenon with any bases in historical occurrence. However in recent years, a mass psychology or psychosocial phenomenological approach has become popular, beginning with Carl Jung and continuing into the 1990s with the work of Charles B. Strozier (*Apocalypse: On the Psychology of Fundamentalism in America*, 1994), a practicing psychoanalyst and professor of history at City University in New York.

Theological

Disciplined biblical and theological reflection on various religious traditions with reference to "final things" is the task of the theologian. One of the finest examples of eschatological theology is Jürgen Moltmann's *The Coming of God* (1996). Another, more creative approach is that of Catherine Keller's "constructive-political theology" which critiques the tradition in terms of its effects, reconstructs and reinterprets it in light of liberation concerns and feminist vision of postmodern religion (*Apocalypse Now and Then*, 1996).

Qualifying the Academic Use of Apocalyptic Time and Calendars

There are at least three problems with associating historic events with apocalyptic time and millennial movements. These are the problems of precision in identifying historic events as moments of larger millennial meaning, of associating historic events as millennial moments on a particular calendar, and of dating the *end* and *beginning* points of historical eras.

Ascribing Precision Identification as Moments of Larger Millennial Meaning to Historical Events

Millennial phenomena have influenced cultures from the dawnings of historical civilizations through the present, and yet, so far, the crossing of any number of these apocalyptic thresholds has not meant reaching the literal "end." However, movement through these transition points has often indicated a significant change in multidimensional, culturally-pervasive assumptions. That is, the crossing of millennial boundaries is often accompanied by paradigm shifts within a self-identifiable group, whether a sect or society.

Therefore to gain some understanding of what can be identified as an apocalyptic event or millennial marker, we need to consider several factors. First of all, we need to recognize that events, unlike new movie releases about the end, don't come already labeled as "momentous." Someone has to decide their significance ex post facto. By *decide* it is not meant that it is an entirely a conscious or deliberate decision. Simply put, some events make an impact that causes a change in behavior and identity.

Some events, however, are important only to an individual—they effect an individual's context in a significant way, but even those closely related to the one affected may not be influenced to the same degree. Any person could think of a childhood family event that held some significance for them. However, if we were to ask that person's siblings or other close relatives concerning their understanding and remembrance of the event, they may not even remember it at all, or, they remember it wrongly! These personal apocalyptic moments usually have little impact outside of the individual's own consciousness.

Yet there are certainly other events that do have group significance and become part of a group's growing identity. For example, in 1985 there was severe flooding in southwestern Virginia as the result of the remnants of a hurricane. For many residents of one small community this event had significant impact. The "Great Flood of '85" became a part of the story of their community history. In some retellings, this flood seemed as extraordinary as Noah's, but outside of the regional context of the group it was nearly meaningless.

These examples serve to illustrate the local nature of the apocalyptic event and its significance. "Local," in this instance, is not limited to the geographical sense, but conveys that an apocalyptic event is *located* within an identifiable group that incorporates it into their tradition. Groups which incorporate local apocalyptic events can be small or global, and defined religiously, sociologically, or by other labels. For example here are some larger context "apocalyptic" events that are easily linked to group contexts: Hurricane Mitchell (residents of Honduras and Nicaragua), JFK assassination (baby boomers), watching the Wizard of Oz (boomers), the moon landing (global), the Vietnam War (United States, 1960s, boomers), Chernobyl (Ukraine, Soviet Union), the political career of Ghandi (India), World War II (global), and the Holocaust (Jews).

So, there is a need to qualify what is an apocalyptic event by recognizing the local nature of apocalyptic. Also, it is necessary to note that no event becomes apocalyptic unless those who experience it interpret the event as an apocalyptic or millennial moment and incorporate it into their identity, or tradition.

Assigning Millennial Moments to Calendars

A second problem with apocalyptic events is that too often they are sought as merely turning points in a calendar. The question that arises concerning calendars is which one, whose calendar is being utilized? Obviously, calendrical time is not fully supported by either nature or history.

Recognizing the parochial nature of our particular calendars is of particular importance. Calendars are artificial instruments used to measure the passage of time. Modern calendars may seem more precise than those employed in other ages, but the reality is that they do not truly measure cosmic time. They are merely a means of plotting intervals of time (*chronos*), not a means of measuring time on an absolute scale (*kairos*). This last point can be illustrated by the fact that calendars have an arbitrary starting point, both in terms of the start of the year and the beginning of an era.

Each calendar selects a significant apocalyptic event as its starting point: the birth or death of a religious leader, the day of creation, the founding of an empire, etc. In the case of the Western Christian calendar the supposed date of the birth of Jesus was chosen as the apocalyptic event to begin the calendar. In contrast, the Jewish calendar begins with the conjectured date of creation, and the Moslem calendar starts with the Hijra, the migration of the Prophet Muhammad from Mecca to Medina. Calendars begin at what is considered an apocalyptic moment. However, the length of the year, and the type of months (based on lunar cycles or schematized months) are arbitrary divisions of time. Calendars are full of approximations and arbitrary choices that determine how time is to be measured. How could these devices measure *kairotic* time, that is, millennial moments?

One may well ask if there is something special about 2000 CE as compared to the 695th Olympiad, or the era of Alexandria 7493, or Kouki 2660, or AUC MMDCCLI, 5760 of the Jewish calendar, A.H. 1420, etc. They all refer to the same year *(chronos)*; can they all refer to the same point in time *(kairos)*? There are limitations when relying solely on a particular calendar to measure apocalyptic times. In the words of John Updike, "Day and night, full and new moons, solstices and equinoxes are empirical events; the rest is a man-made skein of numbers, a fallible approximation" (1997: 264).

Associating Historical Events and Dates with Millennial Moments

The problem with historical markers is with the precision of their determination. At best, a range of candidates for marking the end of an era can be identified, instead of a single date. C. S. Lewis reminds the historian that any attempt to mark periods or capture the "spirit" or meaning of a particular age (e.g., the "Age of Reason") must be qualified with humility, as Lewis states: "For no one stands outside the historical process; and, of course, no one is so completely enslaved to it as those who take our own age to be not one more period but a final and permanent platform from which we can see all other ages objectively" (1958: 121).

There is also the need to take into account the realization that events from a previous age may actually be defined as having meaning in the new age as well. That is, both ages may claim the event as part of the matrix of events that give them meaning. In some sense that is what occurred when the Christian Church appropriated the Hebrew Scriptures. The history of the "old" is a part of the "new." When did the "new" in this case begin? When Abraham believed? During Jeremiah's prophesy? During the Exile when Isaiah (or Deutero-Isaiah) prophesied? Christmas? Easter? Pentecost? Second century? Fourth century?

It seems that the problem with associating historical events and dates with millennial moments is that it is both a premodern and a modern project to set dates for the ends of eras, not a postmodern need or preoccupation. Linear time is an invention of the modern period. Preceding ages may have thought of time as cyclical, only in the modern period is this developed as a linear progression away from a beginning, nonrecurring, evolving. This linearity may be conceived of in helical terms so that things bear a correspondence to previous times without being truly cyclical in a closed sense. Still, this helical time spirals toward some future point.

Postmodernism, it can be said, does not see the need for linear time. Time becomes Einsteinian, localized in a quantum sense to the individual observer. Connectiveness or isolation from previous existences is on the basis of cognition of past conditions and their continued impact on the present and not simple historical precedence. Who lived in the house before one takes up occupancy doesn't matter except as their activity may have changed the floor plans or impacted the living conditions and therefore limited present prospects. What does it matter if they ate a breakfast of eggs and toast at 6:30 AM? One need not be bound by their customs, and the boundary of the age is not marked by the changing of breakfast to croissants at 10. Therefore we can only try and set a date for the end of modernity, not the beginning of postmodernity!

The Millennial Marker Method (MMM)

Within the field of eschatology (the study of endtimes), it may be possible to study apocalyptic time, read the signs of the time, identify clusters or conjunctions of apocalyptic signs and shifts in the culture, nominate appropriate candidates as possible end dates of eras, and then select a key date on the calendar as an apocalyptic moment or millennial marker in time. This experimental method is intended as a tool for identifying and triangulating millennial markers. It would also allow the illustration of points where paradigm shifts occur in history. Five categories are proposed in this matrix: (1) key date of millennial expectation, (2) historical milestone, (3) revolutionary idea or theological concept, (4) major scientific/technical insight or innovation, and (5) universal cosmic sign or supernatural wonder (phenomenon). Any of these categories in and of themselves might engender some degree of millennial expectation, but this method presumes that to truly be an apocalyptic threshold, more than one category must be involved in describing any single event. This method is called the Millennial Marker Method (MMM). Here's how it works.

First, although there is nothing inherently keyed to the decades, centuries, and millennia of a calendar, cultural historians and sociologists note that increased apocalyptic behavior occurs at those times. Therefore, we can focus on those time frames in the study of apocalyptic time. These become the key dates for millennial expectation. Second, many apocalyptic signs (possible turning points and paradigm shifts) have both local and global significance (e.g., the regime of Nazi Germany, the "discovery" of the "New World," and other historical milestones) and influence social movements, political action, and intellectual ideas (revolutionary idea or theological concept). Often these turning points are created, enhanced, or made possible by some scientific or technical insight or innovation. Third, when three or more apocalyptic signs converge around a particular date or limited range of dates, an apocalyptic moment in apocalyptic time might be identified and selected as a key date. These key dates or turning points become candidates for selection as a millennial moment marking an end of an age. The case must then be made for each competing candidate considered to be age ending. Fourth, a method or device called "triangulation" (in its trigonometric rather than psychological sense) can be used to help make the case for a particular key date in apocalyptic time and thus mark the end/beginning of an era. "Triangulation" is the convergence of three or more categories of apocalyptic signs, interpreted as an apocalyptic moment, which in retrospect can be identified as a key date, paradigm shift, or turning point in calendar time.

Examples of apocalyptic signs include:

(1) A significant, surprising or decisive historical event: e.g., the Fall of the Bastille in France in 1789 and the Fall of the Berlin Wall in 1989. Thomas Oden (in *Two Worlds*, 1992) makes the case that the Modern World began with the Fall of the Bastille and the French Revolution in 1789, and collapsed with the Fall of the Berlin Wall in November, 1989—exactly 200 years after it began.

(2) A scientific paradigm shift or technological innovation or "breakthrough" that challenges conventional thinking: e.g., invention of the movable type printing press that helped spark the Protestant Reformation in 1521 and the invention of the microprocessor and World Wide Web that may yet spark a Postmodern Reformation.

(3) A revolutionary idea or new religious concept that sparks a movement: e.g., rise of Marxist thought in late-nineteenth-century Europe.

(4) An unusual cosmic sign or phenomenological wonder: e.g., solar eclipse during the crucifixion of Jesus, lunar eclipse in Rome in December, 999, Halley's comet during the Battle of Hastings in 1066, planetary conjunctions in 7 BCE, Halley's Comet 1986 and Chernobyl, Comet Hale-Bopp and Heaven's Gate.

Applying MMM to Millennial History or Successive Ends of Eras

After studying successive apocalyptic crises and resolutions in world history, it may be said, that the End of the World comes (now and then) in predictable cycles of millennial moments, identified by the millennial marker method of triangulation.

This new method takes into account apocalyptic data from the disciplines of cultural history, sociology, psychology, and theology, and represents itself within the multidisciplinary field of apocalyptic eschatology. The application of this method of marking millennial moments to a recent event will demonstrate how this method marks millennial moments.

In April 1986 the Chernobyl nuclear disaster occurred in the former Soviet Union. Christensen's recent Ph.D. dissertation, "The Chernobyl Apocalypse" (1997) makes the case for why April 1986 could be considered as end of the world known as the modern era. The argument is based on the characterization of the late modern age as one of confidence in technology and the peaceful use of the atom. But the Chernobyl disaster seemed to end this expectation. As noted by a nuclear expert: "When the sad history of nuclear power is written, April 26, 1986 will be recorded as the day the dream died" (Christensen, 250). A triangulation according to the MMM criteria described above identifies and uses the following apocalyptic signs as evidence of a Millennial Moment:

(1) An unusual historic event occurred at 1:23 AM on 26 April 1986 which is regarded as the world's worst nuclear accident. A local apocalypse had a global impact.

(2) The event was interpreted widely in Belarus, Ukraine, and Russia as an apocalyptic technological crisis representing either the end of the world, the end of the Soviet era, or the end of a generation of exposed children.

(3) Halley's Comet visited planet Earth during the spring of 1986 and was interpreted by some as the Chernobyl (or Wormwood) star of Revelation 8:11. Astronomically, according to J. Adams (1999) other rare events occurred closely following that event. He cites that on 24 April 1986 a total eclipse of the Moon occurred while it was in conjunction with Pluto and it was briefly following that phenomenon that the Chernobyl disaster befell in the Ukraine. He further states that in this configuration, the planet Pluto is supposed to represent explosive events and nuclear technology ("Pluto" is part of the root of the word plutonium).

Not all events acquire the same level of significance within a society. By means of this method of marking millennial moments, one can illustrate those events which will come to have more apocalyptic significance than others, and why millennial movements change human behavior in profound ways.

Michael J. Christensen and Carl E. Savage

See also Chernobyl, Chronology and Dating

Bibliography

Adams, J. (1999) *Kremlin Astrology.* http://syninfo.com/J/j33.html.

Carter, Michelle, and Michael J. Christensen. (1993) *Children of Chernobyl.* Minneapolis, MN: Augsburg.

Christensen, Michael J. (1997) *The Chernobyl Apocalypse: A Theological Case Study.* Ph.D. diss., Drew University, Madison, NJ.

Keller, Catherine. (1996) *Apocalypse Now and Then: A Feminist Guide to the End of the World.* Boston: Beacon Press.

Landes, Richard. (1999) "On Owls, Roosters, and Apocalyptic Time: A Historical Method for Reading a Refractory Documentation," http://www.mille.org/landes-rob.htm.

Lewis, C. S. (1958) *Reflections on the Psalms.* London: G. Bles.

Moltmann, Jürgen. (1996) *The Coming of God: Christian Eschatology.* Minneapolis, MN: Fortress Press.

Strozier, Charles B. (1994) *Apocalypse: On the Psychology of Fundamentalism in America.* Boston: Beacon.

Updike, John. (1997) "Millennial Fever." *The New Yorker* 53, 32: 260–66.

Media

> And this gospel of the kingdom will be preached throughout the whole world, as a testimony to all nations; and then the end will come. (Matthew 24:14)

At the beginning of the third millennium of Christianity, in an era of Internet and cable television, the Great Commission—the mandate to preach the gospel throughout the world—takes on new meaning. Jesus' words are embedded in the midst of a passage known as the "Little Apocalypse," which describes the signs and events that will accompany the Last Days. Alongside the familiar warnings of apocalyptic terror—wars and rumors of wars, earthquakes, famines, and plagues—we find this fascinating suggestion that when the mission of preaching the gospel to the nations is completed, the time of the End will be at hand. The authors of the gospels could scarcely have imagined the global media network by which the gospel of the kingdom would be transmitted. Nor could they have anticipated how Jesus' words, understood as both a prophecy and a command, would be put into practice by today's evangelists. The earliest Christians would surely regard modern media as many Christians do today—as an endtime miracle, both a compelling sign of the fulfillment of prophecy and an instrumental tool for the imminent completion of the divine plan.

This essay sketches the path of apocalyptic thinking—the "gospel of the kingdom"—from its origins in oral folklore, preaching, and manuscript literacy, through the print-based culture of the Protestant Reformation, into the modern era of television and the Internet. I am assuming an evolutionary model of communication and culture that is based in the work of scholars such as Marshall McLuhan, Walter Ong, and Jack Goody, who have studied the cultural shifts that accompany the transitions from orality to literacy to electronic media. Focusing on media-related transformations helps us to understand at least two significant aspects of historical and contemporary millennialism. First, innovations in communication technology have at times featured prominently in a variety of eschatological scenarios. Second, the form and content of beliefs about the endtimes have been profoundly shaped by their transmission through different communications media. Thus the media have played a prominent role in the historical evolution of millennialism, as means for the shaping and dissemination of apocalyptic vision, and as a focal point for expectations of world transformation.

Orality, Literacy, and the Millennial Tradition

A history-of-media approach to the biblical Apocalypse requires that we not take the very existence of written scripture for granted. On the one hand, it is possible to see the origins of apocalypticism as a literary phenomenon, one which grew out of social practices of reading and writing, in which authors responded to the social and spiritual problems of their day by creatively employing forms, figures, narrative conventions, and styles derived from various scriptural and apocryphal antecedents. On the other hand, it is worth asking whether there were significant millennial movements before the introduction of writing, and if so, what they looked and sounded like.

Consider the role of the vision and the visionary in a purely oral culture. As Goody (1987) and Ong (1982) note, the myths and legends of an oral society are fixed only in memory but not in print and hence are always being expanded and revised with each telling. Myth and prophecy in primarily oral cultures are not fixed, but fluid; the charismatic power of prophetic or inspired speech is linked to its unique character as *spoken* utterance and thus is tied to the person of the prophet in a direct way that can be mediated only by memory. The introduction of writing brought new possibilities for the fate of inspired and prophetic utterances. The transition from speech to text fixes the words of a prophecy, making ungarbled transmission possible, and thus enables the formation of a scriptural canon which adds the authority of tradition to the charismatic authority of the visionary prophet. Prophecy as text separates the words of the prophet from his or her utterances, allowing authors to add to the tradition by writing pseudonymous texts which trade on the reputation of their more famous predecessors. And the power of a prophetic text is particularly strong in a society where the adoption and spread of literacy is so recent that a written book is still mediated primarily through oral performance.

Such is the case with the great books of the apocalyptic tradition in Judaism and Christianity. Daniel, Revelation, and a host of other minor texts were all composed during a long period of transition from what Walter Ong dubs the culture of "primary orality," (1982) when writing and literacy skills were unknown or confined to social elites, and oral speech was the dominant mode of communication, to what he calls chirographic or manuscript-based culture, in which writing plays an increasingly important role. In the case of Revelation, textual evidence from the book itself points to the conclusion that the Apocalypse was originally intended to be read aloud in a public, liturgical setting: "Blessed is he who reads aloud the words of the prophecy, and blessed are those who hear, and who keep what is written therein; for the time is near" (1:3). Biblical scholars are agreed that the customs of early Christian worship involved the reading aloud of sacred texts before a collective audience. When the Apocalypse is read aloud, as it was for its earliest intended audiences, a peculiar thing happens. The text predicts a coming kingdom in which divine authority will defeat the powers of darkness that reign on earth; but in the oral performance of the prediction, the future is exhibited in the present tense: "The kingdom of this world *is become* the kingdom of our Lord" (emphasis added). The tension between future hope and present reality, between the world as it is and as we long for it to be, is collapsed (albeit temporarily) in the moment of performance which brings the text to life.

In the early stages of apocalypticism, then, the introduction of writing enabled the formation of the apocalypse as a literary genre. The preservation of the oral preaching of millennial prophets in a textual record constitutes the formation of an apocalyptic *tradition*, a text-based community of interpreters and commentators extended over centuries which periodically shelters and inspires a variety of popular movements. But before the general spread of literacy skills, the elite cultural practices of education and communication made prophetic writings rare, possessing great value precisely because they were only directly accessible to, and transmissible by, the learned culture of scribes and interpreters. For the preliterate audiences who experienced the texts through the mediation of oral performance, the act of reception was not dramatically different from what it had been before the introduction of writing, with this crucial difference: the prophecy or vision existed not only in the memory of the bard, priest, or poet, but was fixed in a form which could be seen and touched, even if one was unable to read. Thus, the source of authority was transferred from the speaker to the text itself; and the social and institutional authority of religious leaders depended on their role as determiners and keepers of the canon, over which they had a near-total interpretive monopoly.

This situation prevailed through the Middle Ages, from the collapse of the Roman Empire and to the Reformation, when the text of scripture was available only to the learned who could read Latin. This gave rise to variant apocalyptic movements and traditions formed from different sources. Popular movements based in the illiterate European peasantry, who depended on the clergy to read and interpret scripture for them, would naturally be more dependent on oral folk traditions which they would fuse with their understanding of biblical texts. Apocalyptic movements originating in elite clerical circles, such as the followers of the famous medieval prophet Joachim of Fiore, tended to focus more on scriptural interpretation and the production of manuscripts which would explicate and illuminate the prophecies.

Millennialism and Print

The invention of the printing press was followed by a rapid rise in literacy skills in Western Christian societies. This radically changed the social matrix in which apocalyptic texts were produced and interpreted. The formation of a literate reading public was crucial to the success of the Reformation, which broke the clergy's interpretive monopoly and enabled Luther and others to make the Roman papacy the favorite target of Protestant apocalyptic writers. Printing opened up the gates to mass distribution of apocalyptic by reducing the cost of message reproduction, allowing wide dissemination of new prophecies or interpretations of the old. The culture of printing also changed the way that we think about and interact with apocalyptic predictions and prophecies. Once they were fixed in print, apocalyptic visions stood in a different relationship to their historical audiences. The prophet or interpreter of prophecy was suddenly accountable for his or her words, which could be subjected to a different kind of scrutiny than was possible in oral or chirographic cultures. With the rise of scientific thought and the culture of moveable type, a new kind of apocalyptic movement emerged, based not on visionary prophecy but strictly on rationally defensible interpretations of scripture—the Millerite movement in mid-nineteenth-century New England is the paradigm example.

The comparatively cheap cost of printing fueled this sort of literature and made it easier to attract a mass following; but it also had the effect of limiting the rhetorical choices of apocalyptic preachers in that printing magnified not only the reach and effect of apocalyptic messages, but the consequences of predictive failure. The spellbinding popular orators of the Middle Ages were often (or even always) wrong in their apocalyptic predictions; but a speech is written on the wind. Though it may not be retractable, it can be amended and modified after the fact with comparatively greater ease. Once they had committed themselves to print, and circulated their newspapers and broadsides to and pamphlets as widely as possible, the apocalyptic preachers of late Protestantism found themselves held to a stricter standard than was the case with their medieval counterparts.

The failed predictions of medieval prophets must have caused consternation among their followers and demanded some fancy rhetorical footwork in the aftermath. But it is inconceivable that any medieval prophet or mass movement could have experienced the degree of embarrassment and public humiliation endured by William Miller and his followers after the Great Disappointment of 22 October 1844. Having published and disseminated their closely argued manifestos, with their declarations of absolute certainty in the coming of Christ by this particular day, and having dared believers and skeptics alike to find fault with their arguments, they had, in effect, created a predicament for themselves more severe than was possible before the arrival of print as a mass medium. The greater degree of accountability that we see in print had the effect, after the Millerite debacle, of making apocalyptic prophets much more cautious in their predictions.

The rhetorical power of a specific date is so strong that we will always have our Edgar Whisenants and Harold Campings, who are willing to take the risk of falsification and public embarrassment by going into print with their apocalyptic certainties. But if the culture of printing has enabled these people to flourish, it has also relegated them to the margins. No one since William Miller has succeeded in attracting such a wide audience for apocalyptic predictions so closely tied to a specific date; to do so is itself a mark of one's marginalization from mainstream culture. The best-selling apocalyptic author of all time, Hal Lindsey, has sold tens of millions of books, cheap mass-market paperbacks that can be found in all sorts of places one does not normally associate with apocalypticism. He has managed to reach such a wide audience, and to ensure the continued sales of his books, by carefully hedging his bets with regard to when the predicted events will come to pass.

From Broadcasting to the Digital Millennium

The ground for Hal Lindsey's spectacular success in the marketing of millennial literature was prepared by other media developments. The growth of Christian Fundamentalism, the movement that formed the base of Lindsey's audience, was fueled by both a backlash against the modernizing effects of technology and the rapid adaptation of broadcast technology for religious purposes. From the early radio sermons of the scandalous (and thoroughly millennial) evangelist Aimee Semple McPherson in the 1920s, to the televised preaching of Pat Robertson, Jerry Falwell, and Jimmy Swaggart in the 1980s, the history of American religion in the twentieth century has been intertwined with the media. Radio and television amplified the power of words and images, and helped to revivify older oral forms, such as revival preaching, through which millennial doctrines had spread in the past. In the decades after the initial success of his *Late Great Planet Earth,* Lindsey joined Robertson, Falwell, and others in preaching their apocalyptic gospel through electronic media. Borrowing from the generic forms of secular television culture, such as news and talk show formats, they helped to make apocalyptic ideas credible to mass media audiences.

As the millennial deadline loomed in the 1990s, the Internet became the new media frontier, populated by a new breed of cyber-evangelists. The long-term impact of the new medium on the millennial tradition remains to be discovered, but we may reasonably speculate that as computers saturate our society, online communication will have an impact comparable to that of the printing press in the Reformation era. It is important to remember, however, that successful new media do not simply replace the old. Just as writing did not replace speech, and television and the telephone did not replace writing, so too the Internet will take its place in the tapestry of communication technologies that people have adopted and adapted to their purposes. Since the era of electronic communication is not dominated exclusively by any one medium, we need a holistic approach to understand the impact of new technologies on contemporary millennialism. I propose that both broadcast and cyber-communication have fundamentally altered the cultural and social situation for apocalyptic discourse, by (1) increasing both the amount and the types of information available for millennialists to construct their webs of meaning; (2) standardizing calendar and clock time to an unprecedented degree, and habituating us to measuring time in smaller and smaller units, thereby increasing our awareness of time's passage; and (3) making possible the formation of new types of communities united not by geography but by shared interests and media access.

Consider two of the traditional signs that have always been supposed to accompany the apocalypse: "wars and rumors of wars" and earthquakes. Human nature being what it is, there have always been ongoing conflicts taking place around the globe at any one point in time. But now CNN is there with television cameras, and images of death and destruction appear in everyone's living room; and Internet users may log on and be treated to live or nearly instantaneous personal reports of such events as a coup in Russia, or bombing attacks in Israel. Likewise, in the natural flow of geologic time, we see that earthquakes have always been a daily occurrence around the world, and that their frequency may ebb and flow according to natural processes, such as plate tectonics, that we dimly understand. But major tremors that once would have gone unreported, or about which we might previously not have learned for months if not years, are now reported on the nightly news; and geological data from around the world are now posted to Internet sites and monitored carefully by millennialists anticipating both "Earth Changes" and the return of Jesus.

The unique capability of Internet users to simultaneously monitor multiple events and processes in the global theater creates a new awareness of time and of the weight of historical action. This experience of time and the associated expectation of a moment of singularity is sharply manifested in the contemporary apocalyptic mood. For example, there is now a site on the World Wide Web that offers a video-streamed image of Jerusalem's Mount of Olives, placed strategically so that believers will be able to view the Second Coming of Jesus via live Webcast when the proper moment arrives. A prominent mass media platform for apocalyptic preaching of a more New Age flavor is provided by radio talk show host Art Bell. His programs "Coast to Coast" and "Dreamland," which focus on millennial predictions and psychic phenomena, are broadcast over more than four hundred radio stations; these programs incessantly promote his published books and Web site, around which a dedicated Internet fan community has arisen.

Through the links on the Art Bell Web site and other related pages, one can find hundreds of communities of apocalyptic believers, devoted to the prophecies of Nostradamus, Christian Fundamentalism, the so-called Mayan prophecy, the return of the aliens, or various mixtures of these and other traditions, engaging in dialogues that move freely between Web pages, Internet chat rooms, obscure magazines and newsletters, and talk radio programs. Many of these have focused on the so-called millennium bug, or Y2K computer crisis, as the objective manifestation of apocalyptic anticipation. Regardless of the actual consequences of the problem—the inability of computer systems to process four-digit dates—the dire predictions of both religious prophets and technical experts have converged on 1 January 2000, a millennial moment that is a direct consequence of the global standardization of computer time.

Apart from the incidental effects of Y2K panic, broadcast and digital technology play a crucial role in modern millennialism, in the way they enable new constructions of meaning within a millennial framework, and in the way they are featured as a substantive component of millennial dreams and nightmares. The utopian vision of many technology advocates, in which democracy and the arts flower in a global village connected by the information superhighway, has attracted many. A concrete example that illustrates the explicitly religious dimension of expectations surrounding computers can be seen in the remarkable claim of media theorist Marshall McLuhan, in an interview from the late 1960s: "The computer . . . holds out the promise of a technologically engendered state of universal understanding and unity, a state of absorption in the logos that could knit mankind into one family and create a perpetuity of collective harmony and peace" (McLuhan 1995: 262). The oracular quality of this statement is remarkable when we remember that it was made before the Internet existed. McLuhan's statement is typical of the sort of claims being made today for global media in general and computer networks in particular. It seems appropriate to call this a techno-eschatology, a modern embodiment of an ancient millennial dream.

As always with visions of the apocalypse, there is a dark side to techno-eschatology. The millennial dream of the global village has its demonic counterpart in dystopian nightmares of governmental and corporate control made fiendishly efficient by electronic surveillance technology, computer databases, and mass-mediated propaganda. Ambivalence about new technologies is a basic theme in virtually all contemporary apocalyptic discourse. There are the fundamentalists who see the microchip and the computer as tools of the "New World Order," the endtimes government of Antichrist; many are now avidly monitoring the technologies which will make the famous "mark of the beast" possible. There are New Agers obsessed with the ecological catastrophe that appears as a judgment against technological humanity. And there is the paradoxical fact that many apocalyptic souls are adept at the use of computers to spread the message of technology's demonic origins and impending demise.

What is in store for millennialism as we move beyond the year 2000? Barring some major disruption which would decisively tip the balance of technological ambivalence, the rapid pace of technological change will continue to inspire both millennial awe and millennial fear. The proliferation of cable channels and the rise of multimedia will continue to create new opportunities for those who preach the "gospel of the kingdom"; but millennial prophets may find that an increasing number of media options results in a corresponding decrease in audience attention spans. Computers and the Internet are clearly here to stay, and we can expect more creative experiments in cyber-millennialism. The most successful entrepreneurs are likely to be those who can emulate Art Bell's success by employing new and old media in creative combinations, quickly adapting their messages to the rapidly changing ecologies of mass media culture.

Finally, it is useful to recall that the media-saturated cultures of the industrialized West are still not the norm. Pockets of aboriginal peoples remain; the Internet and even television are still out of the reach of millions; the Fundamentalist backlash against the modernization of mass-mediated industrial society continues to be a powerful force. The completion of a truly global worldwide media grid will remain an unattainable goal for many lifetimes, so long as economic inefficiencies, inequitable resource distribution, and cultural resistance persist. Whether these obstacles can be overcome in the third millennium of Christianity, so that the Great Commission can be completed in the furthest corners of McLuhan's "global village," remains to be seen. The transformation of global culture effected by mass media technology may or may not be inevitable; but it seems safe to assume that the actual future will fall short of what we have imagined for it. The only reliable constant in the millennial traditions of the past is the experience of disappointment. Like every generation of the past that has anticipated a millennial transformation of the world, our generation will somehow have to come to terms with the frustration of its apocalyptic expectations. If the mass media do not succeed in fulfilling these expectations, they at least may record for future historians how we have dealt with the failure of our own millennial dreams.

Stephen O'Leary

See also Film, Literature, Millennial Myth, Millerites, Technological Millennialism

Bibliography

Barr, David L. (1986) "The Apocalypse of John as Oral Enactment." *Interpretation* 40: 243–56.

Bell, Art. (1998) *The Quickening*. New Orleans, LA: Paper Chase, Inc.

Camping, Harold. (1992) *1994?* New York: Vantage.

Eisenstein, Elisabeth. (1979) *The Printing Press as an Agent of Change: Communications and Cultural Transformation in Early-Modern Europe*, 2 vols. New York: Cambridge University Press.

Goody, Jack. (1987) *The Logic of Writing and the Organization of Society*. New York: Cambridge University Press.

McLuhan, Marshall. (1995) *The Essential McLuhan*, edited by Eric McLuhan and Frank Zingrone. New York: Basic Books.

Noble, David F. (1998) *The Religion of Technology: The Divinity of Man and the Spirit of Invention*. New York: Knopf.

Ong, Walter J. (1982) *Orality and Literacy: The Technologizing of the Word.* London: Methuen.

———. ([1967] 1981) *The Presence of the Word: Some Prolegomena for Cultural and Religious History.* New Haven, CT: Yale University Press; reprint, Minneapolis: University of Minnesota Press.

Whisenant, Edgar C. (1988) *88 Reasons Why the Rapture Will be in 1988.* Nashville, TN: World Bible Society.

The Messianic Communities

The Messianic Communities, best known as the Northeast Kingdom Community or Island Pond Community, and in 1999 calling itself the Twelve Tribes, is a millenarian, communal movement rooted in Protestant fundamentalism that emerged out of the counterculture's Jesus People revival. Elbert Eugene ("Gene") Spriggs founded the group in 1972 together with his wife, Marsha Spriggs, in Chattanooga, Tennessee. Spriggs is considered to be an Apostle in the Last days, but is called "Gene" by members of the community. The Tribes define themselves as a regathering of the lost and scattered tribes in the Old Testament, bound by the New Covenant in Yahshua's (Jesus') Blood (see Ephesians 2:12). They translate "church" as "community" and believe that through brotherly love and the discipline and sacrifice of communal living, each man and woman "dies unto sin."

The Messianic Communities have evolved a distinct culture fostering craftsmanship and handiwork; they have composed their own devotional songs and dance forms and have developed highly elaborated and religiously validated patterns of marriage and childrearing. Like other Christian fundamentalists, they uphold monogamy, premarital chastity, marital fidelity, strict discipline, and the religious education of children through home schooling. They reject extramarital sex, abortion, and homosexuality as sinful.

History

Elbert Eugene Spriggs, the son of a factory quiller and scoutmaster, was born in Chattanooga, Tennessee, and was brought up in the Methodist Church. In 1971 he became involved in the Jesus Movement through the Marineth Chapel and Center Theater in Glendale, California. He began to invite people to his house for Bible study and fellowship, and 1972 he and his wife Marsha were holding regular coffeehouse meetings in East Ridge, a suburb of Chattanooga for young spiritual seekers, hippies, and "Jesus freaks," as well as the poor and homeless. According to the testimony of long-term disciples, the discussions were so absorbing and the company so pleasant, no one felt like going home; so more and more people just stayed overnight and eventually found themselves living in a community.

Following the example of the primitive church in sharing all things in common, after Acts 2:37–47, the group bought and renovated five old Victorian houses on Vine Street and opened up the Yellow Deli, a health food bakery and sandwich restaurant. Its menus stated, "Our specialty is the fruit of the spirit. Why not ask?" At that time they called themselves the Vine Community Church and began baking and serving whole-grain bread, which symbolized the Gospel of Jesus—real spiritual food as opposed to the lifeless "White Bread Jesus" found in mainline churches. Originally, the group attended the Sunday services of different denominations, but when they arrived at church one Sunday to find the service canceled on account of the Superbowl, they turned their backs on conventional religion and began developing their own worship, gathering on Friday evening to welcome the Sabbath, and on Saturday to break bread and celebrate the Messiah's resurrection.

A Bible study group who were "on a Christian walk" in Island Pond, Vermont, heard about Spriggs's work and invited him to come and speak to them, and one woman in the group opened up her home for their communal enterprise. The Vine Community Church were discouraged by the declining response to their message in Chattanooga, and had weathered a series of deprogrammings at the hands of Galen Kelly and Ted Patrick, so they sold all their property and moved to Island Pond in 1979. They altered their communal patterns with the move for, whereas in Chattanooga their households were centralized with "one big business, one office, one set of needs" (Qitan 1996), once they were established in Island Pond, they split into independent communes, each household becoming economically and governmentally separate and specializing in its own cottage industry. The industries range from a cobbler shop, a printing press, a soap and candle-making factory, a hemp clothing tailor, and a futon shop. Many members left after the first winter, discouraged by the cold and financial hardship, but the group then opened up the Common Sense Restaurant and attracted new members. This restaurant functioned as a "court of the Genytiles" or missionary field until it burned down in 1989, but has opened sister cafes in Boston, Rutland (Vermont), Winnipeg, and other towns. The Basin Farm Community, near Bellows Falls, Vermont, cultivates vegetables, grains, and strawberries to supply its sister communities in New England.

Beliefs/Practices

Messianic beliefs are remarkably similar to those of the Anabaptist sects in sixteenth-century Germany and are virtually compatible with evangelical Protestantism, but contain certain theological innovations in the areas of communal living, marriage, and eschatology, rendering their theology heterodox. The community's theology continues to evolve as ongoing collective revelations unveil the community's (church's) unique role in the Last Days; these revelations concern her fate as the "Pure and Spotless Bride" of Revelation, her imminent union with her Bridegroom, Yahshua, and the levels of salvation after Judgment. The Tribes define themselves as the lost and scattered tribes of the ancient Jews undergoing restoration in preparation for eternal life. They believe their community is undergoing a process of purification as the "pure and Spotless Bride" awaiting her Bridegroom, and that it will probably take three generations to be ready for the Second Coming. By increasing their ranks through conversions and childbearing they are "raising up a people" in preparation for the Jubilee horn that heralds the return of Yahshua.

An elaborate ritual and artistic life can be found in the communities. Public "gatherings" or "sacrifices" are held on Friday and Saturday night (the Jewish Sabbath and the eve of the First Day). These are occasions for circle dancing, devotional singing, spontaneous testimonials and prophecies, and stories for, and acted out by, the children. Outsiders are invited to the Communities' weddings that function to dramatize and reinforce their millenarian expectations; the Bride, representing the Community, prepares herself in the wilderness for the call of the groom, her "King" who seeks her out and claims her.

Organization/Membership

The church numbers between 1,560 and 2,000, and around half of the members are of the second generation. Communes have been established in Parana, Brazil; Navarreux, France; Auckland, New Zealand; and in Winnipeg, Canada, but the majority of members live in New England; mainly in Vermont or in Boston. In 1994 the Community in Island Pond, began to break up and spread throughout New England.

A council of male Elders and Teachers govern or "cover" each local commune, each household represented by an Elder. The Teachers are the theologians and preachers, but the hierarchy is informal and relaxed, with ample discussion with and input from the leaders' wives, and decision making appears to be a collective process. The structure is headed by the Spriggs, and organized into Teachers, Elders, Deacons, Deaconesses, and Shepherds. Women used to wear headscarves at all times, but since a 1993 revelation, only cover their heads "in church" or at the "gatherings" and prayer meetings to symbolize their submission to their husbands and the male Elders who, in turn, are "covered" by "Our Master." The Spriggs have no children of their own, nor any fixed abode, but travel among the Communities, offering counsel and inspiration, and tend to maintain a low-key presence which fosters local self-sufficiency.

Missionary Activity

The Tribes are intensely evangelistic, and their missionary efforts focus on persuading people to visit their communities in order to impress and inspire through "a demonstration of the life"—meaning a truly loving community that is striving toward eternal life through its members' achievement of moral perfection through sacrificing sin and selfishness. The *Freepaper*, an inspirational collection of testimonials and sermons, is distributed by members to disseminate their message and encourage readers to visit and join the "body of the Messiah." The famous double-decker bus, fitted out with bunks and dining tables has appeared at the Grateful Dead's concerts, the Billy Graham Crusades, and the Rainbow Gathering, as well as at county fairs, flea markets, and folk festivals to offer free first aid to the crowds, and serve tisane, cereal coffee, and homemade bread and cookies. The brothers and sisters perform Israeli-style dances, accompanied by hand-made guitars, dulcimers, and harps, and hand out the *Freepaper*. Another evangelistic method is the sending out of "Walkers," missionaries who hitch rides on the highway and preach to anyone they meet. In order to pioneer a new town, married couples with small children will move into an old house, find odd jobs and set up Way Out Houses—temporary communal homes—in order to model "a small demonstration of the life" to potential converts.

Controversies

The Messianic Communities have attracted the unwelcome attention of the early anticult movement (the Citizen's Freedom Foundation and the Cult Awareness Network) and several of their members been abducted by deprogrammers ever since the founding of the Vine Community Church in Chattanooga. They have been accused of brainwashing members, but the most severe and widely publicized conflicts with secular authorities have involved child-beating allegations and child custody disputes. In 1984 the Vermont State Police, armed with a court order and accompanied by fifty Social Services workers, raided the Island Pond Community homes and took 112 children into custody. At the pretrial hearing in Newport, Vermont, District Judge Frank Mahady ruled that the search warrant issued by the state was unconstitutional, so all the children were returned summarily to their parents without undergoing examinations. Child custody disputes and investigations by Social Services continue, partly due to the influence of the anticult movement working with angry and disillusioned ex-members.

Despite critical news reports and legal battles, the group remains committed to its bible-based child discipline practices. Parents are instructed to discipline children who do not obey upon "first command" with a thin, flexible "reed-like" rod (as mentioned in Proverbs 23:13)—usually on the palm of the hand—so as to inflict pain but no marks. The theological rationale behind this is that when a child does wrong, his or her natural guilt will weigh upon the heart, but once punished, they will have a clear conscience, consequently will not "die unto sin"—meaning parents are giving their children the choice to escape the throes of death and become immortal, if Yahshua returns soon enough.

On 25 June 1994 the church held a ten-year anniversary celebration at the Basin Farm in Vermont to "commemorate [our] deliverance from the 1984 Island Pond Raid." This significant church-state conflict has become an annual festival for the group that defines their identity as a persecuted people. Many of those 112 children originally seized by social workers and policemen, now in their teens and twenties, were present at the "Ten Years After" event and shared their traumatic memories of the morning of the raid, denying the allegations of abuse and passionately declared their allegiance toward their parents and their faith.

Since their "deliverance from the raid," the group has emphasized cooperation with state authorities and has reached out to neighbors in trying to foster a better understanding.

Susan J. Palmer

Bibliography

Bozeman, John, and Susan J. Palmer. (1997) "Raising Up a People for Yahshua's Call." *Journal of Contemporary Religion* (London) 12, 2 (May): 181–90.

Kokoszka, Larry. (1994) "Time Mellows Communities Caught in Raid." *The Caledonian Record* 156 (22 June): 268.

Melton, J. Gordon. (1986) *Encyclopedic Handbook of Cults in America*, 4th ed. New York: Garland Press.

Palmer, Susan J. (1994) *Moon Sisters, Krishna Mothers, Rajneesh Lovers: Women's Roles in New Religions*. Syracuse, NY: Syracuse University Press.

Palmer, Susan J., and Charlotte E. Hardman, eds. (1999) *Children in New Religions*. East Brunswick, NJ: Rutgers University Press.

White, Philip. (1994) "Island Pond Raid 10 Years Later: State Versus Church." *The Sunday Rutland Herald and the Sunday Times Argus* (19 June): 1–4.

Messianism

The word "messiah" is derived from the Hebrew word *mashiahk*, which means "one who is anointed." Messianism, however, often refers to a person chosen by God to play a crucial role in an endtime scenario. The messiah heralds the advent of an utopian epoch—the "messianic age." For many Christians, this is the "Kingdom of God" or the "heavenly kingdom." In Jewish tradition this age is the World to Come. The messiah represents a dramatic moment of transition. A common element in various kinds of messianism is belief in a decisive turning point in history that demarcates the present age from one that is (for the believer) much better. In many accounts of the endtime, the utopian epoch comes after one fraught with tribulation and upheavals of a vast magnitude. Times of great suffering and catastrophe are often interpreted as a sign that the end is near. Messianic movements often arise when people consider their world to be falling apart or under attack. According to the Babylonian Talmud (a multivolume work containing rabbinic teaching), such moments show the "footprints of the messiah" (Sota 9:15). But messianism has many different forms. Sometimes, rather than a messiah, priority is given to another eschatological (endtime) figure, such as the archangel Michael (Revelation 12) or Elijah (Malachi 4:5–6; Matthew 27:47). Some do not give much attention to the personality of the messiah, but focus rather on the period of history in which he is to come. But to appreciate messianism we need to understand its biblical and Jewish origins.

The Hebrew Context

In the Hebrew Bible, most of the occurrences of "anointed one" *(mashiahk)* refer to kingship. The king in his coronation ritual was often anointed with oil (cf. 1 Samuel 10:1; 16:13; 1 Kings 1:39; 1 Chronicles 29:22). Priests were also anointed with oil (Leviticus 4:5; 6:15), and, at times, prophets as well (Isaiah 61:1).

Anointing in the royal ideology of Israel signified that the king was chosen by God to rule. The "messiah" did not have an eschatological or future meaning, but, on the contrary, helped legitimize the king's political authority in the present. Saul, the first king of Israel, is called the Lord's "anointed" *(mashiahk)* in 1 Samuel 24:7 and 26:9. The most important king of Israel was David. God, in 2 Samuel 7, promises to him and his descendents the right to rule over Israel forever. The term *mashiahk* often refers to David or his dynasty. Often the term came to represent David's exalted status, and that God has bestowed especial favor upon him and his dynasty. For example, in Psalm 18:50, we find: "He [God] saves his king time after time, displays his faithful love for his

Albrecht Durer's woodcuts, "St. John's vision of Christ and the seven candlesticks." KURTH, WILLI, ED. (1963) *THE COMPLETE WOODCUTS OF ALBRECHT DURER*. NEW YORK: DOVER PUBLICATIONS.

anointed *(meshihko)*, for David and his heirs forever" (New Jerusalem Bible cf. Psalm 2:2; 20:6; 28:8; 45:6–7; 89:20–38; 132:10; and 2 Samuel 19:22; 22:51; 23:1).

The Davidic monarchy fell in 586 BCE. Judah was conquered by Nebuchadnezzar II, king of Babylon. The Jerusalem Temple (the central religious site of Judaism) was destroyed and many Jews were deported to Babylon (2 Kings 24–25). Many considered the last legitimate king to be Jehoiachin, of the Davidic line, who was deported in 597 BCE. Prophets proclaimed that an idealized Davidic king would come to restore the monarchy. The future Davidic king was often understood to deliver Israel from the wicked Gentile nations, and inaugurate a period of prosperity with the other nations subject to Israel. A period of sin and political instability would precede the arrival of this Davidic king. A representative Davidic oracle is Isaiah 11:1–9, which reads in part: "But a shoot shall grow out of the stump of Jesse [David's father], a twig shall sprout from his stock. . . . He will strike the country with the rod of his mouth and with the breath of his lips bring death to the wicked." This "shoot" shall bring peace and stability to Israel: "The wolf shall dwell with the lamb, the leopard lie down with the kid. . . . The lion will eat hay like the ox. The infant will play over the den of the adder." This future Davidic king is sometimes called "the Branch" *(semahk)*, a botanical metaphor that expresses that his kingship will grow and prosper (Jeremiah 23:5–6; Zechariah 3:8, 6:12). Other texts which called for the restoration of the Davidic monarchy (or were commonly interpreted as calling for it) include Amos 9:11; Numbers 24:17; Genesis 49:10; Isaiah 9 and 53; Micah 4; Zechariah 9:9; and Ezekiel 34:23–31. None of these oracles, however, actually use the term *mashiahk*.

Cyrus, the Persian emperor who conquered the Babylonians, is called the Lord's "anointed one" (*mashiahk*, Isaiah 45:1). He allowed the Jews who were exiled in Babylon to return to Israel in 538 BCE. As a Gentile (non-Jew), he is not the Davidic king who will deliver Israel. Rather, the title "messiah" signifies that he was chosen by God to free the Jews.

In all likelihood messianic hopes were placed upon Zerubbabel around 520 BCE. Zerubbabel has the distinction of arguably being the first messiah. He was of the Davidic line, the grandson of King Jehoiachin (1 Chronicles 3:16). He helped rebuild the Temple, which was destroyed in 586, amid speculation that this would usher in God's return to Jerusalem, restore the monarchy, and deliver Israel from its enemies: "Tell Zerubbabel, governor of Judah: I [God] shall shake the heavens and the earth; I shall overthrow the thrones of kings, break the power of heathen realms. . . . On that day, says the Lord of Hosts, I shall take you, Zerubbabel son of Shealtiel, my servant, and I shall wear you as a signet ring, for it is you I have chosen" (Haggai 2:21–23; cf. Zechariah 3:8–10, 4:6–10, and 6:12–14).

Messianism from the Second Century BCE Onward

Messianism changed in the two centuries before the Common Era. Factors that influenced this change include the formation of a canon of Hebrew scripture and popular dissatisfaction with a succession of oppressive rulers (Hellenistic, Hasmonean, and Roman). Many people felt the Davidic oracles in the Hebrew Scriptures predicted the coming of the messiah. Messianism became more elaborate. For many the messiah became an eschatological office that had an established role in the endtime. Often these duties included heralding not only redemption from sin and deliverance from oppression, but also the resurrection of the dead and the day of final judgment.

Messianic speculation was practiced by the Qumran community. This group probably wrote the body of literature we call the Dead Sea Scrolls, most of which dates to the first century BCE. In this literature we find messianic figures with such titles as "Branch of David" or "Prince of the Congregation." For example the Isaiah Pesher (a text scholars refer to as 4Q161; "pesher" is a kind of biblical interpretation) interprets Isaiah 11. It claims this biblical passage refers to "the Branch of David which will sprout in the final days. . . ." In one manuscript of the War Scroll (4Q285), which depicts a final eschatological war between the angels and the Gentiles, the "Branch of David" helps lead the fighting angels. In the longer version of the War Scroll, the Archangel Michael leads them (cf. Daniel 12; Revelation 12). Some texts conceive the messiahship as a dual office and assert the arrival of the "messiahs of Aaron and Israel" (*Community Rule* 9:11; *Damascus Covenant* 20:1). Such messianism distinguishes political and priestly figures. In one version of the *Community Rule* (1Q28a) we see the messiah subordinate to the high priest, the leading figure of the Temple in Jerusalem. In it, the elders of Israel have a banquet at the end of days. The messiah can bless the congregation only after the high priest has blessed the meal. In another Qumran text sometimes called the *Aramaic Apocalypse* (4Q246) a messianic figure called the Son of God will make the warring nations fall, and usher in an age of peace.

Acute messianic hopes are expressed in the Psalms of Solomon (c. 40 CE). They implore the Lord to send his messiah to deliver Jerusalem from the Romans. In the seventeenth psalm we find: "See, Lord, and raise up for them [the Jews] their king, the Son of David, to rule over your servant Israel." This king will "judge peoples and nations in the wisdom of his righteousness" and "will have gentile nations serving him under his yoke." The psalm ends by proclaiming "their king shall be the Lord Messiah." This is one of the most explicit pre-Christian testimonies of messianic expectation that we have.

In *Fourth Ezra*, written at the end of the first century CE, the messianic kingdom of peace will last 400 years, after which everyone will die, including the messiah. Then there will be seven days of primeval silence, after which will come the resurrection and the final judgment, and, for the righteous, eternal bliss (see chapter 7). Other important messianic texts from this period include 2 Baruch 29; 1 Enoch 51; Testament of Judah 24; and Sibylline Oracles 5:256–59.

Christianity began as a messianic movement at this time. "Christ" comes from the Greek *christos* which is a translation of the Hebrew *mashiahk* (cf. John 4:25–6). "Christ" is a messianic title. Jesus is frequently called the Son of David (Matthew 1:1; Mark 10:47). He is also called the "Son of Man." The "Son of Man" is an eschatological king described in Daniel 7 whom, Christians believe, prefigured Christ (cf. 1 Enoch 48). The Gospels proclaim that Christ will return amidst great tribulation: "Portents will appear in sun and moon and stars. . . . People will faint with terror at the thought of all that is coming upon the world; for the celestial powers will be shaken. Then they will see the Son of Man coming in a cloud with power and great glory. When all this begins to happen, stand upright and hold your heads high, because your liberation is near" (Luke 21:25–28; cf. Matthew 24:29–31; Mark 13:24–26).

Apparently there were other messianic and prophetic movements from this time of which we have little record (cf. Acts 5:35–37). Matthew 24:24 warns one to be wary of "false Christs [Messiahs]," presumably because there were others who were making messianic claims. Several movements are mentioned in Josephus, a first-century CE Jewish historian (e.g., *Jewish War* 2:118, 434). There was an uprising in Israel against Rome, which resulted in the destruction of the Temple in 70 CE. Josephus attributed Jewish revolutionary zeal in part to messianism: "What more than all else incited them to the war was an ambiguous oracle, likewise found in their sacred Scriptures, to the effect that at that time one from their country would become ruler of the world" (*Jewish War* 6:312–13). It is not clear what oracle Josephus had in mind.

Messianic Speculation in Rabbinic Thought

Rabbinic Judaism abounds in messianic speculation. The rabbis often describe a period of iniquity, the "birth pangs of the messiah," which will precede the arrival of Messiah son of David: "In the generation when the son of David comes . . . Galilee [will be] in ruins . . . the wisdom of scribes in disfavor, God-fearing men despised, people [will] be dog-faced, truth entirely lacking" (Babylonian Talmud [b.Tal.], Sanhedrin 97a). It was also commonly held that there would be a final war with Gog and Magog (cf. Ezekiel 38–39). This idea also influenced Christianity (cf. Revelation 20:8). Gog and Magog are symbolic enemy nations of Israel who often represent the Gentiles. The messiah is understood to suffer in this period of tribulation. This idea led to the development of a second messiah, Messiah son of Joseph. He is a tragic figure, who will be slain in this final battle. The dying messiah precedes Messiah son of David, who will arrive in glory to vanquish the enemies of Israel, lead the return of the exiles to Israel, begin the resurrection of the dead, foster the redemption of their sins before God, and inaugurate a period of bliss. This is often called the World to Come. It is described idyllically. At that time the "righteous sit with crowns on their heads" and in it there will be "no business transactions, no envy, no hatred, no rivalry" (b.Tal., Berakoth 17a). There is also speculation on the name of the messiah. Siphre Deuteronomy, a text of rabbinic biblical exegesis (midrash), says that the name of the messiah is Hadrach (cf. Zechariah 9:1), since he shall be "*had*" (Hebrew for "sharp") to the Gentiles, and "*rach*" (Hebrew for "soft") to Israel (see chapter 1). Some rabbis speculate that the messiah's name is Menachem ("the Comforter"), others that it is Hivra (called "the Leper" or the "Leper Scholar"), since he will bear the ills (i.e., sins) of Israel (b.Tal., Sanhedrin 98a). We also find a vivid portrayal of the messiah in the Targum Pseudo-Jonathan (a loose second-century CE translation of the Bible into Aramaic) to Genesis 49:11: "How beautiful is the king, Messiah, who is destined to arise from the house of Judah! He has girded his loins and gone down to battle against his enemies. . . . He reddens the mountains with the blood of their slain. His garments are saturated with blood, like those of him who presses grapes." Some rabbis attempt to calculate the date when the World to Come will arrive (b.Tal., Sanhedrin 99a). Others deride such speculation: "He who calculates the end has no portion in the World to Come" (b.Tal., Derek 'Erez Rabbah 9).

Jewish Messianic Movements

Judaism has produced many messianic movements. A survey of this length can only mention a few. One such movement arose during the Jewish revolt against Rome in 132–35 CE. This uprising was led by Bar Kosiba. He was also known as Bar Kokhba, which in Aramaic means "Son of the Star," and refers to the oracle of Numbers 24:17. Akiva (50–135 CE), one of the most important rabbis of Judaism, hailed Kokhba by claiming: "This is the king, the messiah" (Jerusalem Talmud, Taanit 4:5). It is not clear whether Kokhba understood himself to be a messiah.

Another important messianic movement was led by Sabbatai Zvi (1626–76). He grew up in Smyrna, in Asia Minor. Waves of anti-Semitic progroms in Eastern Europe and Russia led many Jews to think that they were living in the end-time. A messianic movement around Zvi spread throughout Eastern Europe and the Ottoman Empire, particularly in 1665–66. The Turkish authorities considered it a destabilizing threat. Zvi was arrested and forced to choose between execution and conversion to Islam. He chose the latter. Many followers did not abandon the movement after this. They developed the idea of the apostate messiah, based on the paradox that the true messiah abandons his own religion.

While Zionism (the movement that led to the creation of the modern state of Israel) was often a secular reaction to anti-Semitism, this movement had a messianic dimension. Yehuda hai Alkalai (b. 1798), a rabbi from Serbia, argued that the messiah can come only when Israel is once again populated with Jews. Abraham Isaac Kook (1865–1935), a Latvian rabbi and mystic who immigrated to Palestine in 1904, interpreted the settlement of Palestine by secular Zionists as the

FROM *PSALMS OF SOLOMON* 17:21-32 IN *THE OLD TESTAMENT PSEUDEPIGRAPHA*

See, Lord, and raise up for them their king,
The son of David, to rule over your servant Israel
In the time known to you, O God.
Undergird him with the strength to destroy the unrighteous rulers,
To purge Jerusalem from gentiles
Who trample her to destruction;
In wisdom and in righteousness to drive out
The sinners from the inheritance;
To smash the arrogance of sinners
Like a potter's jar;
To shatter all their substance with an iron rod;
To destroy the unlawful nations with the word of his mouth;
At his warning the nations will flee from his presence;
And he will condemn sinners by the thoughts of their hearts.

He will gather a holy people
Whom he will lead in righteousness;
And he will judge the tribes of the people
That have been made holy by the Lord their God.
He will not tolerate unrighteousness (even) to pause among them,
And any person who knows wickedness shall not live with them.
For he shall know them
That they are all children of their God.
He will distribute them upon the land
According to their tribes;
The alien and the foreigner will no longer live near them.
He will judge peoples and nations in the wisdom of his righteousness.
Pause.
And he will have gentile nations serving him under his yoke,
And he will glorify the Lord in (a place) prominent (above) the whole earth
And he will purge Jerusalem,
(And make it) holy as it was even from the beginning,
(For) nations to come from the ends of the earth to see his glory,
To bring as gifts her children who had been driven out,
And to see the glory of the Lord
With which God has glorified her.
And he will be a righteous king over them, taught by God.
There will be no unrighteousness among them in his days,
For all shall be holy,
And their king shall be the Lord Messiah.

Source: Charlesworth, James H., ed. (1985) *The Old Testament Pseudepigrapha*, vol. 2. New York: Doubleday, 667.

unfolding of God's plan of messianic redemption. Some Christians similarly believe that the creation of Israel is a sign that the messiah will come soon. Many Orthodox Jews felt that the secular Zionists were attempting to accelerate the advent of the messiah. God, not humans, they believe, should dictate when the messiah will come. This is one reason why Menachem Mendel Schneerson (1902–94) did not live in Israel, but in Brooklyn. He was thought by many Lubavitcher Jews to be the *Moshiach* (their pronunciation of *mashiahk*), or a sign that he is coming. The Lubavitchers are a sect of Hasidic Jews (ultraconservative Jews originally from Eastern Europe and Russia) with a significant following. On 29 August 1993, they placed a full-page ad in the *New York Times*, telling people that the *Moshiach* is on his way. The ad asked people to call (718) 2-MOSHIACH for more information. Many Lubavitchers still consider him their leader.

The Impact of Messianism on Other Religions

Although messianism was originally a Jewish idea, its influence upon other religious traditions has been profound. Christianity's acceptance of Jesus Christ as its messiah can be understood as the most familiar appropriation of this Jewish tradition. Since the messiah has already been revealed to Christians as Christ, Christianity does not speculate on when the messiah will come, but when he will come back. The New Testament claims that one day Christ will return to bring salvation (e.g., 1 Thessalonians 2:19; Hebrews 9:28; Revelation 22:20). Some Christians do not understand the messiah in terms of his role in endtime events, but rather in terms of a personal relationship with their savior from sin.

An important contemporary Christian messianic figure is David Koresh. He was the leader of the Branch Davidians. "Branch" is a messianic title found in the biblical books of Jeremiah and Zechariah, and in Qumran literature (as noted above). The name "Koresh" is taken from the Hebrew word for Cyrus, the only Gentile called a *mashiahk* in the Bible (Isaiah 45:1). The Branch Davidians stockpiled weapons in anticipation of a final eschatological conflict. That precipitated efforts by the government to intervene, which ultimately triggered the group's mass suicide in April 1993.

Islam is also rich in messianic traditions. It has many stories about the Mahdi, or "the rightly guided one." The Mahdi, not unlike the Jewish or Christian messiahs, will defeat Gog and Magog (*Yajuj wa-Majuj*) in battle, and inaugurate the advent of such endtime events as the resurrection of the dead and the final judgment. There have been many Islamic messianic movements. One of the most well known took place in the 1880s in Sudan. The Sudanese revolted against their Anglo-Egyptian rulers, led by Muhammad Ahmad, whom many believed to be the Mahdi.

There have been numerous messianic movements in non-Western cultures influenced by Christianity. In Brazil, Indian tribes used messianism to prophesy a new age where there would be no Spaniards. One well-known native messiah who preached this was Obera (sixteenth century), of the Guarani tribe, who claimed to be the son of God. There are important analogues to this among North American Indians, such as the Ghost Dance of 1890. Widespread among many tribes, it involved ritual dances that would induce events such as the resurrection of the dead (fellow Indians) and the elimination of whites by floods and earthquakes. This would mark the beginning of a period of bliss and abundant game for hunting. Some accounts held that this period would be brought by a messianic figure named Next Spring Big Man. Another example is the Rastafarians. This movement developed in the slums of Kingston, Jamaica. It proclaimed Haile Selassie (Ras Tafari being his former name), Marxist ruler of Ethiopia, to be an eschatological hero. He was to save black people from poverty and racism by bringing them to Ethiopia, which was understood to be the heavenly kingdom. Many thought this deliverance would take place in the 1950s.

Conclusion

Messianism has evolved over the centuries into many different forms in Judaism, Christianity, and other religions. Messianism is rooted in traditions from ancient Israel about the arrival of an idealized Davidic king who will deliver Israel from its enemies. Messianism often gives shape to the ideas of millenarian groups about how and when this world or period of history will end and what will come next. Sometimes the messiah is a pivotal actor in the endtime events that lead to the arrival of a new age. The messiah can also merely be a sign that these events are taking place. At times messianic speculation concentrates more on a future utopian "messianic age" rather than on the person of the messiah himself. Sometimes movements are led by prophets who say that the messiah is coming. Sometimes the group leader will make messianic claims. Some messianic movements are responses to class and political oppression, others are completely apolitical. Despite its variety, generally messianic speculation is oriented to biblical traditions. This is important for understanding millenarian groups who believe the messianic age is at hand.

Matthew Goff

See also Davidians, Islam, Israel, Judaism, Native South America, Premilllennialism, Rastafarianism, Sabbatian Movement

Bibliography

Charlesworth, James H., ed. (1985) *The Old Testament Pseudepigrapha.* New York: Doubleday.

Cohn-Sherbok, Dan. (1997) *The Jewish Messiah.* Edinburgh: T & T Clark.

Collins, John J. (1995) *The Scepter and the Star: The Messiahs of the Dead Sea Scrolls and Other Ancient Literature.* New York: Doubleday.

Klausner, Joseph. (1955) *The Messianic Idea in Israel: From Its Beginning to the Completion of the Mishnah.* New York: The Macmillan Company.

Lenowitz, Harris. (1998) *The Jewish Messiahs: From the Galilee to Crown Heights.* New York: Oxford University Press.

Patai, Raphael. (1979) *The Messiah Texts.* Detroit: Wayne State University Press.

Schäfer, Peter, and Mark Cohen, eds. (1998) *Toward the Millennium: Messianic Expectations from the Bible to Waco.* Leiden: Brill.

Scholem, Gershom. (1971) *The Messianic Idea in Judaism and Other Essays on Jewish Spirituality.* New York: Schocken Books.

Thrupp, Sylvia L., ed. (1962) *Millennial Dreams in Action.* The Hague: Mouton & Company.

Wilson, Bryan. (1973) *Magic and the Millennium: A Sociological Study of Religious Movements of Protest among Tribal and Third-World Peoples.* New York: Harper & Row.

Militia Movements (Armed Militias, the Patriot Movement, and the Far Right)

The armed militia movement that emerged in 1994 was the militant wing of the larger Patriot movement—a diverse right-wing populist revolt composed of independent groups in many states. At its height in the mid-1990s perhaps as many as five million U.S. citizens accepted to varying degrees the Patriot contention that our government was manipulated by conspiratorial elites and planning to impose some form of repression. The antigovernment aspect of the Patriot movement focused on federal gun control, taxes, regulations, and a range of actions identified as federal attacks on individual citizen's Constitutional liberties. In anticipation of an attack by government forces, a significant segment of the Patriot and armed militia movement embraced survivalism.

Both the Patriot and armed militia movements grew rapidly, relying on computer networks, FAX trees, short-wave radio, AM talk radio, and videotape and audiotape distribution. These movements are arguably the first major U.S. social movements to be organized primarily through overlapping nontraditional electronic media. The core narrative carried by these media outlets was apocalyptic: featuring claims that the U.S. government was controlled by a vast conspiracy of secret elites plotting a New World Order, and planning to impose a globalist UN police state using troops carried by black helicopters. During the mid-1990s, armed militias were sporadically active in all fifty states, with numbers estimated at between 20,000 and 60,000. After the bombing of the Oklahoma City federal building, these numbers began to shrink, with only the most hardcore members remaining active.

Mainstream media were slow to report on the militias, and some of the best early reports appeared in the alternative press. An example is an article by Junas who accurately assessed the factors that lead to the formation of the militias:

> One is the end of the Cold War. For over 40 years, the "international communist conspiracy" held plot-minded Americans in thrall. But with the collapse of the Soviet empire, their search for enemies turned toward the federal government, long an object of simmering resentment. The other factors are economic and social. While the Patriot movement provides a pool of potential recruits for the militias, it in turn draws its members from a large and growing number of U.S. citizens disaffected from and alienated by a government that seems indifferent, if not hostile, to their interests. This predominantly white, male, and middle- and working-class sector has been buffeted by global economic restructuring, with its attendant job losses, declining real wages and social dislocations. While under economic stress, this sector has also seen its traditional privileges and status challenged by 1960s-style social movements, such as feminism, minority rights, and environmentalism. Someone must be to blame. But in the current political context, serious progressive analysis is virtually invisible, while the Patriot movement provides plenty of answers. Unfortunately, they are dangerously wrong-headed ones. (1995: 27)

A key early figure in organizing the militia movement using the short-wave radio and the Internet was Linda Thompson, whose elaborate apocalyptic warnings and conspiratorial assertions of government plots were widely believed within the militia movement until she called for an armed march on Washington, D.C. to punish traitorous elected officials. Her plan was widely criticized as dangerous, probably illegal, and possibly part of a government conspiracy to entrap militia members. Mark Koernke, a.k.a. Mark of Michigan, quickly replaced her as the most-favored militia "intelligence" analyst. Militia units in Michigan, Wisconsin, and Montana were especially active and significantly influenced the course of the movement.

The Patriot phenomenon is hardly fringe. The Perot and Buchanan candidacies in part tapped into the deep sense of alienation, anger, and frustration among right-wing populists. Stern notes that Patriot ideas were championed by elected representatives in the U.S. Congress and several state legislatures. He singled out U.S. Representatives Steve Stockman (R-TX) and Helen Chenoweth (R-ID). "Whereas Stockman's relationship with the militia movement centered around his strong position on gun ownership and his willingness to quote the militia's spin on Waco, Chenoweth emphasized county-versus-federal issues, especially resource management. But she also indulged in militia-speak about One World government and those pesky helicopters. Her indulgence in these conspiratorial icons was not surprising. Years before her election, she traveled the national circuit speaking to chapters of the John Birch Society" explained Stern (1996: 213).

There were both secular and religious versions of the militia phenomena, with the religious aspects often overlooked. Maxwell and Tapia captured the tone of a religiously inspired militia leader in an article for *Christianity Today:*

> Norm Olson's store in Alanson, Michigan, sells two items: guns and King James Bibles. The 48-year-old father of three has been removed as head of the Michigan Militia and pastor of Calvary Baptist Church because of views he expressed in the wake of the Oklahoma City bombing April 19. Yet Olson is still involved in the militia and the pulpit. He recently preached in an auction barn in Wolverine, Michigan, to 30 militia members wearing fatigues and sitting in folding chairs. "Hey, they need the Lord Jesus Christ," he told CHRISTIANITY TODAY. "One young man received the Lord that day." (1995: 34)

As with many state militia members, Olson, who calls himself a "pistolpackin' preacher," defies easy stereotyping. His grandmother was Jewish; he is a dispensational, Calvinistic evangelist and former pastor in the General Association of General Baptists. He served in the U.S. Air Force, then worked as a Christian school principal. But two details are clear: "I am a military man, and God raised me up as a warrior for the Lord," Olson boasts (Maxwell and Tapia 1995: 35).

Some in the militias believed the conspiracy to build a global one world government and new world order under UN control was Satanic and related to the millennial endtimes prophesied in Revelation.

Roots and Networks

The contemporary armed militias are part of a history in the United States of antidemocratic, right-wing paramilitary groups seeking to create a private army bent on accomplishing a series of authoritarian, racist, or theocratic goals. These goals include rejecting federal laws and regulations, treating people of color as second-class citizens, stopping abortion by force, putting homosexuals to death, and targeting Jews by claiming they are conspiring for evil purposes. It is important to remember that one of the most famous militia movements in the United States, the Ku Klux Klan, arose as a citizen's militia during the turmoil of Reconstruction.

Patriot-style right-wing populist movements have flourished throughout U.S. history, usually during a power struggle over social, political, or economic policies. Their immediate predecessors in the 1970s and 1980s formed when far-right groups interacted with apocalyptic survivalists to spawn a number of militant quasi-underground formations, including some that called themselves patriots or militias. One of the more significant of these formations was called the Posse Comitatus, with members who believed all public law enforcement officers above the rank of Sheriff were forbidden by the Constitution. Many Posse members also followed the Christian Identity theology.

The Patriot and Armed Militia movements drew recruits from among tax protesters, gun rights activists, antiabortion militants, Christian nationalists, revolutionary right terrorists, and more. The Patriot movement is bracketed on the reformist side by the John Birch Society and the conspiratorial segment of the Christian right, and on the insurgent side by the Liberty Lobby and groups promoting themes historically associated with white supremacy and anti-Semitism. A variety of preexisting far-right vigilante groups (including Christian Identity adherents and outright neo-Nazi groups) were influential in helping organize the broader Patriot and armed militias movement, but to claim that all members of the Militia Movement are neo-Nazis or terrorists is false. To ignore the bigotry woven into the conspiracy theories is also wrong.

Deadly confrontations involving law enforcement overreaction against the Weaver family in Ruby Ridge, Idaho, and the Branch Davidians in Waco, Texas, focused the attention of the Patriot movement as examples of government tyranny. Randy Weaver and his wife were survivalists as well as Christian Identity adherents. Had the federal marshals who surrounded their house in 1992 factored their apocalyptic and millennialist beliefs into their plan for arresting Randy Weaver, the subsequent deadly shoot-out might have been avoided. Federal Marshal William Degan and Weaver's wife

Vicki and son Samuel died. Randy Weaver and his friend Kevin Harris were wounded. In 1993 the Branch Davidian compound near Waco, Texas, functioned as a fundamentalist survivalist retreat. Davidian leader David Koresh was decoding Revelation as an endtimes script and preparing for the Tribulations. The government's failure to comprehend the Davidian's worldview set the stage for the deadly miscalculations by government agents, which cost the lives of eighty Branch Davidians (including twenty-one children), and four federal agents. TV coverage of this incident sent images of fiery apocalypse cascading throughout the society, further inflaming the apocalyptic paradigm within right-wing antigovernment groups. Ruby Ridge and Waco served as trigger events to galvanize a mobilization in 1993 and 1994 around stopping the Brady Bill and gun control provisions of the Crime Control Act. While organizing against gun control, the militia movement consolidated in a self-conscious manner and emerged as the armed wing of the Patriot movement.

Conspiracism

More apocalyptic and suspicious elements within the Patriot movement grafted apocalyptic conspiracist fears onto the gun rights campaign, arguing that if gun rights were restricted, a brutal and repressive government crackdown on gun owners would quickly follow. The Weaver and Waco incidents were seen as field tests of the planned repression, with the ultimate goal being UN control of the United States to benefit the conspiracy of secret globalist elites. While for many this was a secular narrative, an apocalyptic and millennialist endtimes overlay was easily added by Christian Fundamentalist elements in the movement. Another overlay was overt anti-Jewish conspiracism. The solution, given this narrative, was to create independent armed defensive units to resist the expected wave of government violence—thus the armed citizens militias.

Many militia members also believe in a variety of conspiracy theories that identify a secret elite which controls the government, the economy, the culture, or all three. For years right-wing populist groups such as the John Birch Society claimed that the same shadowy "Insiders" were behind both Moscow communism and Wall Street capitalism. Many of these conspiracy theories are rooted in long-standing anti-Semitic ideologies dating to the early twentieth century, though many militia members appear unaware of that fact. White supremacist state's rights arguments and theories rooted in racial bigotry also pervade the militia movement. Despite these historic roots, many in the militia and patriot movement seem oblivious to how their ideas perpetuate racist and anti-Semitic stereotypes.

Constitutionalism, Sovereign Citizenship, and Common Law Courts

Throughout the late 1990s, the Patriot and armed militia movements overlapped with a resurgent states' rights movement, and a new "county supremacy" movement. There was a rapid growth of illegal so-called constitutionalists with "common law courts," set up by persons claiming nonexistent "sovereign" citizenship. These courts claimed jurisdiction over legal matters on the county or state level, and dismissed the U.S. judicial system as corrupt and unconstitutional. Constitutionalist legal theory creates a two-tiered concept of citizenship in which white men have a superior "natural law" or "sovereign" citizenship. Amazingly, many supporters of constitutionalism seem oblivious to the racism and sexism in this construct. The most publicized incident involving common law ideology was the 1996 standoff involving the Montana Freemen, who combined Christian Identity, bogus common law legal theories, "debt-money" theories that reject the legality of the Federal Reserve system, and apocalyptic expectation.

The Far Right

Far-right groups assisted the formation of the militias and pulled them toward more militant action and more bigoted analysis. The far right in the United States is composed of groups such as the Ku Klux Klan, Aryan Nations, the Christian Patriots, ideological fascists, and neo-Nazis. The term "far right" in this context refers to groups with an aggressively insurgent or extralegal agenda, including calls for denying basic human rights to a target group. While terms like "fascist" and "Nazi" have been widely misused, they are the proper terms to describe certain sectors of the revolutionary right movement in the United States. Christian Patriots combine Christian nationalism with constitutionalism. Non-Christian neo-Nazis are able to work in coalitions with the Christian Patriot groups due to shared antigovernment sentiments and conspiracism rooted in historic anti-Jewish bigotry. The most significant worldview in the Christian Patriot movement is Christian Identity, which believes the United States is the biblical "Promised Land" and considers white Christians to be God's "Chosen People." Barkun (1994) has tracked the influence of apocalyptic millennialism on major racist and anti-Semitic ideologues within Christian Identity, including Wesley Swift, William Potter Gale, Richard Butler, Sheldon Emry, and Pete Peters.

Rupert (1997) has looked at how the patriot movement acts as a seedbed for growing fascism and a potential recruiting pool for the far right. This dynamic is important. Timothy

McVeigh passed through the Patriot-linked gun show circuit and militia movement, but had moved from broad conspiracist antigovernment beliefs into a more militant neo-Nazi ideology. For example, to explain his views, McVeigh handed out copies of *The Turner Diaries* to his friends. Written by neo-Nazi William Pierce, *The Turner Diaries* has apocalyptic and anti-Semitic themes invoking the cleansing nature of ritual violence typical of Nazi ideology which sought a millenarian Thousand Year Reich. McVeigh's apparently secular concern that during the Gulf War the government had implanted a microchip into his body echoes historic concerns among Fundamentalist Christians that the Mark of the Beast might be hidden in electronic devices. *The Turner Diaries* extols fascist violence in support of white supremacy and even describes as heroic the terror bombing of a federal building. The book was available at gun shows and survivalist emergency preparedness seminars before the bombing, but few militia members had ever read it or even heard of it until the Oklahoma City bombing.

Conclusions

Pitcavage speaks for many militia critics when he argues:

> There are many reasons to be concerned about the militia movement. The very existence of such groups implies the use of force rather than the force of ideas to achieve one's goals, and even though most militia groups claim they only operate defensively, the extremely high levels of paranoia most such groups possess means that they often think they are acting justifiably when they are not. And even groups that *as groups* may not pose a danger can spawn individuals committed to violent or extreme acts. The militia movement also includes a considerable component of intolerance. Though not riddled through with racists as many early accounts of the movement claimed, there is nevertheless a racist element within the movement that cannot be denied. And even militia groups that proudly proclaim their lack of racism will generally freely admit their virulent homophobia." (1999: online)

Armed vigilantes cannot be tolerated, and the government has a right to enforce its jurisdiction against those who claim some fictional sovereignty. The militia movement with its militancy and conspiracist suspicions creates situations where armed confrontations are likely, and this is dangerous. Some Patriot types are bullies, threatening local government officials and even clerical workers. Threats against community activists have also been reported. At the same time, basic respect for civil liberties must hold sway unless militia members and their fellow patriots go beyond their rhetoric and engage in criminal activities. The militia movement is a test of how seriously we, as a nation, take constitutional guarantees; and how seriously we, as individuals, take the obligation to speak out against demonization, scapegoating, and conspiracism as threats to democratic discourse.

Chip Berlet

See also Christian Identity, Conspiracism, Demonization, New World Order

Bibliography

Abanes, Richard. (1996) *American Militias: Rebellion, Racism & Religion.* Downers Grove, IL: InterVarsity Press.

Aho, James A. (1990) *The Politics of Righteousness: Idaho Christian Patriotism.* Seattle: University of Washington Press.

Barkun, Michael. (1994) *Religion and the Racist Right: The Origins of the Christian Identity Movement.* Chapel Hill, NC: University of North Carolina Press.

Berlet, Chip, and Matthew N. Lyons. (2000) *Right-Wing Populism in America: Too Close for Comfort.* New York: Guilford Press.

Biehl, Janet. (1996) "Militia Fever: The Fallacy of 'Neither Left nor Right.'" *Green Perspectives, A Social Ecology Publication* 37 (April): 1–8. Online at http://www.tao.ca/~ise/lgp/issues/lgp37.html.

Burghart, Devin, and Robert Crawford. (1996) *Guns and Gavels: Common Law Courts, Militias & White Supremacy.* Portland, OR: Coalition for Human Dignity.

Corcoran, James. ([1990] 1995) *Bitter Harvest: The Birth of Paramilitary Terrorism in the Heartland.* New York: Viking Penguin.

Crawford, Robert, S. L. Gardiner, Jonathan Mozzochi, and R. L. Taylor. (1994) *The Northwest Imperative: Documenting a Decade Of Hate.* Portland, OR: Coalition for Human Dignity; and Seattle: Northwest Coalition Against Malicious Harassment.

Daniels, Ted. (1996) "Another Standoff: The Montana Freeman." *Millennial Prophecy Report* (April): 1–4.

Dees, Morris, and James Corcoran. (1996) *Gathering Storm: America's Militia Threat.* New York: HarperCollins.

Dyer, Joel. (1997) *Harvest of Rage: Why Oklahoma City is Only the Beginning.* New York: Westview.

Ferber, Abby L. (1998) *White Man Falling: Race, Gender, and White Supremacy.* Lanham, MD: Rowman & Littlefield.

Gibson, James William. (1994) *Warrior Dreams: Paramilitary Culture in Post Viet Nam America.* New York: Hill & Wang.

Halpern, Thomas, and Brian Levin. (1996) *The Limits of Dissent: The Constitutional Status of Armed Civilian Militias.* Amherst, MA: Aletheia Press.

Hamm, Mark S. (1997) *Apocalypse in Oklahoma: Waco and Ruby Ridge Revenged.* Boston: Northeastern University Press.

Hawkins, Beth. (1994) "Patriot Games." *Detroit Metro Times* (12 October): 38–41; reprinted in Hazen, et al.

Hazen, Don, Larry Smith, and Christine Triano. (1995) *Militias in America 1995: A Book of Readings & Resources.* San Francisco: Institute for Alternative Journalism.

Junas, Daniel. (1995) "Rise of the Citizen Militias: Angry White Guys with Guns." *CovertAction Quarterly* (spring): 20–25; reprinted in Hazel, Don, Larry Smith, and Christine Triano. (1995) *Militias in America 1995: A Book of Readings & Resources.* San Francisco: Institute for Alternative Journalism.

Maxwell, Joe, and Andrés Tapia. (1995) "Guns and Bibles: Militia Extremists Blend God and Country into a Potent Mixture." *Christianity Today* 39, 7 (19 June): 34–37, 45.

McLemee, Scott. (1995) "Public Enemy." *In These Times* (15 May): 14–19.

Minges, Patrick. (1994) "Apocalypse Now! The Realized Eschatology of the 'Christian Identity' Movement." Conference paper presented at a meeting of the American Academy of Religion. Online at http://www.publiceye.org/pra/rightist/aarlong.html.

Neiwert, David A. (1999) *In God's Country: The Patriot Movement and the Pacific Northwest.* Pullman, WA: Washington State University Press.

Pierce, William (writing as Andrew Macdonald). (1978) *The Turner Diaries.* Washington, D.C.: National Alliance Books.

Pitcavage, Mark. (1996) "Every Man a King: The Rise and Fall of the Montana Freemen." Online monograph, *The Militia Watchdog.* http://www.militia-watchdog.org/freemen.htm.

——. (1999) "Welcome." Online monograph. *The Militia Watchdog.* http://www.militia-watchdog.org/welcome.htm.

Quinby, Lee. (1994) *Anti-Apocalypse: Exercise in Genealogical Criticism.* Minneapolis: University of Minnesota Press.

Rand, Kristen. (1996) "Gun Shows in America: Tupperware® Parties for Criminals." Washington, D.C.: Violence Policy Center.

Reavis, Dick J. (1995) *The Ashes of Waco: An Investigation.* New York: Simon & Schuster.

Rupert, Mary. (1997) "The Patriot Movement and the Roots of Fascism." In *Windows to Conflict Analysis and Resolution: Framing our Field,* edited by Susan Allen Nan, et al. Fairfax, VA: Institute for Conflict Analysis and Resolution.

Samples, Kenneth, Erwin de Castro, Richard Abanes, and Robert Lyle. (1994) *Prophets of the Apocalypse: David Koresh & Other American Messiahs.* Grand Rapids, MI: Baker Books.

Seymour, Cheri. (1991) *Committee of the States: Inside the Radical Right.* Mariposa, CA: Camden Place Communications.

Stern, Kenneth S. (1996) *A Force upon the Plain: The American Militia Movement and the Politics of Hate.* New York: Simon & Schuster.

Tabor, James D., and Eugene V. Gallagher. (1995) *Why Waco? Cults and the Battle for Religious Freedom in America.* Berkeley: University of California Press.

Vest, Jason. (1995) "The Spooky World of Linda Thompson." *Washington Post* (11 May): D1.

Walter, Jess. (1995) *Every Knee Shall Bow: The Truth and Tragedy of Ruby Ridge and the Randy Weaver Family.* New York: Regan Books.

Millennial Myth

The millennial myth is the story of the final days of human history when God destroys the evil in the world, brings salvation for his people, and institutes a "new heaven and a new earth" in the prophesied Millennium. The myth is a powerful and flexible worldview that adapts easily, though unevenly, to changing social and cultural conditions. Arising during periods of rapid change in a society, often coinciding with the end of an age or era, the millennial myth serves as a model for current events and human history and acts as a metaphor for the way of the world. The millennial myth explains the "big picture" of human history and destiny, and it exists on a transcendental plane, where a kind of superconciousness with absolute and sacred values guides human behavior and directs human history.

In times of crisis or during periods of rapid and widespread social change, the myth provides guidance and direction to people's lives, revealing the part they play in the great cosmological story unfolding in their lifetime. Like all myths, the millennial myth is a lens through which people view the rapidly changing world in which they live. But the myth is not stagnant, it fractures and adapts unevenly to the current age, its primary or classical elements taking on contemporary definitions reflecting the contemporary era of its users.

Revelation and the Classical Millennial Myth

Written near the end of the first century after Christ, the Revelation of John is the most recognized and influential example of the millennial myth. At a time when early Christians were being persecuted for failing to worship the deified Roman emperor Domitian (95 CE), the disciple John, imprisoned on the island of Patmos, wrote to fortify the new Christian community. Through his apocalyptic visions John depicts Rome as Babylon and its emperor, Domitian, as the Antichrist. John also envisioned the Messiah returning to earth following a period of Tribulation to engage the Antichrist at the final battle of Armageddon. After defeating the Antichrist and throwing him into the fiery pit, the Messiah provides salvation for the chosen and institutes the Millennium—a one thousand year period of "heaven on earth." In an anticlimactic turn in the story, the Devil escapes from Hell after one thousand years in one last effort to wreak havoc on the world. But the messiah captures him once more relegating him to hell for eternity, along with the damned who are thrown into hell following the final judgement. The heavenly Jerusalem descends from the skies to earth initiating the spiritual kingdom on earth for eternity.

Revelation is a complex, highly symbolic, and ambiguous story, written for an audience 2,000 years ago. Yet it has generated countless interpretations since that time, engendering a mythology that is powerful and persistent. That mythology—or millennial myth—can be codified by outlining its most prominent symbols and themes: Tribulation, Antichrist, Babylon, Armageddon, Messiah, and Millennium.

The trials and tribulations that mark the Apocalypse include earthquakes, hurricanes, and locusts and are most often identified in the Four Horsemen of the Apocalypse, who bring war, revolution, famine, and death. The evil false prophet who arises in the final days to deceive and rule the world and identified by the three sixes—the mark of the Beast—is the Antichrist. The Antichrist's center of power, and the symbol for the drunken harlot and the corrupted city and people who have fallen from the word of God is Babylon.

Armageddon is the ultimate war between the Christian soldiers and the satanic host—the forces of good and evil. The savior who returns to Earth at the climax of the Antichrist's reign is the Messiah, who conquers the Antichrist at the battle of Armageddon, instituting the Millennium. The final feature of the myth—Millennium— applies to the one thousand year paradise on Earth initiated by the Messiah following the defeat of the Antichrist and satanic host. Due to its highly cryptic language, Revelation can be creatively interpreted, therefore imbuing it with the power and persistence of myth.

Throughout the history of the Middle Eastern and Western civilizations, and in non-Christian religions as well, the millennial myth has accompanied the rise and fall of many societies and prompted the evolution of numerous revolutionary and utopian movements, most notably during the Crusades and Reformation. The millennial myth also has been present in the history of the United States. In its American form, the myth depicts Americans as a chosen people and America as a uniquely millennial land. The myth helped guide Columbus' discovery and exploration of the New World; it is embedded in the lamentations and "fire and brimstone" sermons, or "jeremiads," of Puritan ministers; and it underlay both the manifest destiny and political demonology that has molded nationalist ideology in the United States since its inception. The millennial myth has played an important role in American history and it continues to do so.

The Millennial Myth in Contemporary Society

A number of factors are converging to create a resurgence of millennial activity in the United States and elsewhere; these include rapid social change both here and abroad, the relative economic decline of the United States, the ending of an age or an era (the end of Soviet communism, a perceived end of the American era, and, foremost, the end of the twentieth century). These kinds of social, economic, political, even numerological changes have always driven the millennial myth. The key themes of the classical millennial myth—Tribulation, Antichrist, Babylon, Armageddon, Messiah, and Millennium—have evolved and taken on meanings congruent with contemporary concerns and events, particularly those involving technology, threats to the environment, and fears of the new world order.

What is particularly interesting about contemporary forms of apocalyptic activity are the multiple and often contradictory forms they take. Millennial expressions are found not only among revitalized messianic movements, but in seemingly religious or nonreligious beliefs too, such as the militia movement, survivalism, and radical environmentalists like Earth First!. For these groups the apocalypse will most likely be man-made—brought about by social and economic collapse, environmental degradation, civil war, or nuclear war. The preparations of the individual and community, or "self-salvation" may be more practical than waiting for a Savior.

Secular forms of the millennial myth differ from the classic forms because they lack supernatural elements, most importantly the belief that the Apocalypse will be engineered by God and that the Millennium will be ushered in by the Second Coming of Christ. Instead, secular millennialists build an organization of ideology, politics, and an alternative plan for society. Secular millennialists can take on religious symbolism and meaning, for example, in the manner in which survivalists discuss "nuclear Armageddon," or environmentalists bemoan "environmental holocaust." Conversely, more traditional millennialists commonly adopt secular ideas, in the way, for example, that Christian fundamentalists optimistically anticipate the Apocalypse will be ignited by nuclear war, economic collapse, environmental destruction, or a combination of them all, "if that's God's will."

In an important book on millenarian movements entitled *Primitive Rebels* (1959), historian Eric Hobsbawm suggested that between the "pure" or classical millenarian movement and the more secular kind, all manner of intermediate groups are possible. This appears to be the case in the world today, where elements from the classical apocalyptic tradition merge with modern and secular ones, producing a strange array of millennial phenomena. The Branch Davidians can be viewed in this way—as Christian survivalists who stockpiled food and weapons in anticipation of the endtimes.

As the millennial myth continues to evolve, certain groups come to interpret current events through the lens of cultural myth. In the past, millenarian movements often arose during periods of intense social change, coinciding with the end of an age or era, as happened in the United States between 1830–50 during the "Age of Reform," which saw the eruption of numerous millenarian groups, including the Shakers, the Oneida, and Christian Science, in response to the secularizing influences of the Industrial Revolution and the transformation of the agricultural way of life. In many ways contemporary expressions of the millennial myth reflect the major social changes which currently affect the world. The United States and much of the world do seem to be at a turning point: as old nations crumble and new one arise from their ashes; as a global economy evolves and the physical and cultural borders that separate nations erode; and as the destructive power of warfare and environmental pollution continue to threaten life on the planet. The fact that all this is occurring at the turn of the Christian millennium may be only coincidence, but it helps to fulfill the apocalyptic prophecy that the old world is in decline and a new world order is emerging.

The millennium is upon us and so is a broad range of new and constantly evolving millennial subcultures. The millennial myth is blossoming one again in American culture and indeed the world at the end of the twentieth century, a century that has witnessed remarkable changes in science, technology, social and political structures, and globalization. These are indeed the signs of the times. Faced with these changes and an uncertain future, the millennial myth provides an explanation for those who are able to "plug" into it. It provides a model for the way the world works and a history of the past, present, and future.

Philip Lamy

Bibliography

Cohn, Norman. (1957) *The Pursuit of the Millennium.* Fairlawn, NJ: Essential Books.

Hobsbawm, Eric J. (1959) *Primitive Rebels: Studies in Archaic Forms of Social Movements in the Nineteenth and Twentieth Centuries.* New York: Norton.

Lamy, Philip. (1996) *Millennium Rage: Survivalists, White Supremacists and the Doomsday Prophecy.* New York: Plenum.

Millennialism in the Western World

Literally, millennialism refers to the belief, expressed in the Book of Revelation, that Christ will establish a one-thousand year reign of the saints on earth before the Last Judgment. More broadly defined, millennialists expect a time of supernatural peace and abundance *here on earth.*

Meaning of Millennialism

At its origins, millennialism offers a concrete version of the fundamental eschatological belief that at the "end of time" God will judge the living and the (resurrected) dead. This belief in an ultimate divine justice, has provided the solution to the problem of *theodicy*, explaining suffering, hardship and oppression of countless generations of believers—Jews, Christians, Muslims, Buddhists. It has, therefore, had immense appeal for commoners in every age. Whereas the name comes from the 1,000-year period, in fact the key factor concerns the *earthly* nature of the coming "new world": whether it is of a duration of forty years or four thousand, the radical transformation necessarily means an end to the current institutions of power and, therefore, gives all millennial beliefs a revolutionary quality that has made them unwelcome to those in positions of authority.

The key issue in terms of millennialism's impact on society, however, is the matter of timing. As long as the day of redemption is not yet come, millennial hopes console the suffering and inspire patience (Revelation 13:10) and political quiescence, and have a profoundly conservative influence. But driven by a sense of imminence *(apocalyptic)*, believers can become disruptive, even engaging in revolutionary efforts to overthrow an unjust sociopolitical order in an attempt to bring about the kingdom of "peace" for the meek and the defenseless. Thus, *apocalyptic millennialism* constitutes a powerful and volatile mixture, fascinating the hearts and minds of people throughout the ages. No matter how often the apocalyptic beliefs have been proven wrong (until present, always), no matter how often the millennial efforts to establish God's kingdom on earth have led to disastrous results, apocalyptic expectations repeatedly revive. From the Jewish revolts against Rome which led to hundreds of thousands of deaths (3 CE, 66–70, 132–35) to the Taiping Rebellion that led to the death of some 20–35 *million* people, such movements have a tendency to self-destruct in the most spectacular fashion. And yet, for all the costly failures, the appeal remains, and generation after generation finds devotees in search of the chimerical kingdom.

Apocalyptic millennialism, for all its dangers, offers immense rewards: believers find themselves at the center of the ultimate universal drama and their every act has cosmic

MICAH 4

1. It shall come to pass in the latter days that the mountain of the house of the LORD shall be established as the highest of the mountains, and shall be raised up above the hills; and peoples shall flow to it,
2. and many nations shall come, and say: "Come, let us go up to the mountain of the LORD, to the house of the God of Jacob; that he may teach us his ways and we may walk in his paths." For out of Zion shall go forth the law, and the word of the LORD from Jerusalem.
3. He shall judge between many peoples, and shall decide for strong nations afar off; and they shall beat their swords into plowshares, and their spears into pruning hooks; nation shall not lift up sword against nation, neither shall they learn war any more;
4. but they shall sit every man under his vine and under his fig tree, and none shall make them afraid; for the mouth of the LORD of hosts has spoken.
5. For all the peoples walk each in the name of its god, but we will walk in the name of the LORD our God for ever and ever.
6. In that day, says the LORD, I will assemble the lame and gather those who have been driven away, and those whom I have afflicted;
7. and the lame I will make the remnant; and those who were cast off, a strong nation; and the LORD will reign over them in Mount Zion from this time forth and for evermore.
8. And you, O tower of the flock, hill of the daughter of Zion, to you shall it come, the former dominion shall come, the kingdom of the daughter of Jerusalem.
9. Now why do you cry aloud? Is there no king in you? Has your counselor perished, that pangs have seized you like a woman in travail?
10. Writhe and groan, O daughter of Zion, like a woman in travail; for now you shall go forth from the city and dwell in the open country; you shall go to Babylon. There you shall be rescued, there the LORD will redeem you from the hand of your enemies.
11. Now many nations are assembled against you, saying, "Let her be profaned, and let our eyes gaze upon Zion."
12. But they do not know the thoughts of the LORD, they do not understand his plan, that he has gathered them as sheaves to the threshing floor.
13. Arise and thresh, O daughter of Zion, for I will make your horn iron and your hoofs bronze; you shall beat in pieces many peoples, and shall devote their gain to the LORD, their wealth to the Lord of the whole earth.

significance. Apocalyptic believers become semiotically aroused (if not semiotically promiscuous), finding cosmic messages in the smallest incident, in every coincidence. Moreover, they can almost taste the fulfillment of their burning desire to see justice done—the good lavishly rewarded, the evil savagely punished. Finally the approach of the end-times and the promise of a new world liberates believers from all earthly inhibitions: the fear of future punishment by those who now hold power vanishes, and a wide range of repressed feelings—sexual, emotional, violent—burst forth. Such a combination proves irresistible to many: millennial hope *possesses* believers.

From its earliest manifestations, millennial beliefs bifurcated between imperial, hierarchical visions of the world to come, on the one hand a kingdom ruled over by a just if authoritarian imperial figure who would conquer the forces of chaos and establish the true order of society, and on the other a demotic vision of a world of holy anarchy, where dominion of humanity would cease from the world. Many world conquerors used millennial "savior" imagery to bolster their rule (Cyrus, Alexander, Augustus, Constantine), and especially in the Muslim and Christian Middle Ages these imperial uses of millennial imagery proliferated.

The contrary millennial tendency, however, was marked

by a profoundly anti-imperial, even antiauthoritarian thrust. Indeed, one of the major strains of Hebrew messianic imagery foresaw a time when humanity shall beat the instruments of war and domination into instruments of peace and prosperity; each one sitting under his own tree, enjoying the fruits of honest labor undisturbed (Isaiah 2:1–3, Micah 4:1–4). This millennialism foresees the end of the rapacious aristocracy (lion and wolf will lie down with the lamb) and the peace of the commoner, the manual laborer (lamb gets up the next morning). Perhaps no idea in the ancient world, where the dominion of aristocratic empires spread to almost every area of cultivated land, held more subversive connotations.

Early Christian Millennialism

Apostolic Christianity demonstrates many of the key traits of apocalyptic millenarian groups of this second, demotic, type. These traits include the rhetoric of the meek overcoming the powerful and arrogant; the imminence of the Lord's Day of wrath and the coming Kingdom of Heaven; a leader and a following among common, working people; rituals of initiation into a group preparing for and awaiting the End; fervent spirituality and radical restructuring of community bonds; large, enthusiastic crowds; prominence of women visionaries; and the shift from a disappointed messianic hope (Crucifixion) to a revised expectation (Second Coming or Parousia). The only missing element, at that time prominent in several other strains of Jewish millennialism (e.g., the Zealots), is violence, subsumed, apparently, in the passion for martyrdom. Not for centuries would violence became a notable part of Christian millennialism (e.g., the Circumcelliones of fourth-century North Africa).

The fundamental problem for early Christianity, as for all apocalyptic movements, was the passage of time, which brought with it profound disappointment and humiliation (2 Peter). Those who did not abandon the movement (e.g., by returning to observant Judaism) handled the delay of the Parousia by organizing communities and rituals which brought, proleptically, a foretaste of the coming world—the Eucharist, the reading of Revelation. But above all, the passing of time called for a new temporal horizon. The End *would* come, but not now, not even soon, rather in the fullness of time, once the tasks assigned by God—especially the spreading of the Gospels to the four corners of the world—were completed.

As Christianity evolved from a charismatic cult on the fringes of the society into a self-perpetuating institution eager to live in harmony with Rome, the hopes of apocalyptic millenarianism embarrassed Church leaders who emphasized to Roman authorities that Jesus' kingdom was "not of this world." Whereas almost every prominent Christian writer from the movement's first century assumed a literal millennialism, by the later second-century ecclesiastical writers, striving to eliminate subversive millennialism from church doctrine, began an assault on millenarian texts (especially Revelation, the only text in the New Testament to explicitly speak of an *earthly* kingdom). Origen, an early third-century theologian, argued the millennium was to be interpreted allegorically, not carnally; others attempted (successfully in the Eastern Church) to eliminate Revelation from the canon altogether. With the advent of imperial Christianity, millenarianism was pushed to the very margins of acceptable Christian thought.

Despite these efforts by the church hierarchy to remove millennialism from formal theology, apocalyptic fears and millennial hopes remained powerful among Christians high and low. Indeed, the very texts that antimillenarian writers like Jerome wrote, served as the basis for new forms of millennialism such as the "Refreshment of Saints." Above all, charismatic prophets using apocalyptic calculations drawn from Daniel and Revelation continued to excite the faithful. Perhaps in recognition of this perennial appeal, church leaders compromised when dealing with the simpler faithful who remained deeply attached to hopes for a real millennium. As a result, as early as the second century, two of the principle themes of medieval millennialism emerged: (1) the use of an nonapocalyptic chronology to postpone the End, thus encouraging patience; and (2) the transformation of the Roman Empire into a positive eschatological force.

To delay the end and reap the calming benefits of nonapocalyptic millennialism, theologians placed great weight on the idea of a *sabbatical millennium*. This idea, by combining Genesis 1 (six days of travail, Sabbath rest), with Psalms 90 (1,000 years is a day in the sight of the Lord), promised the thousand-year kingdom after 6,000 years. About 200 CE the first Christian chronology placed the Incarnation in 5500 Annus Mundi, thus marking the year 500 CE as the year 6000, and providing a buffer of some 300 years from the present. Thus when apocalyptic prophets announced the imminent End, conservative clerics could counter with the argument that centuries yet remained until the millennium. Documentary evidence for this chronological argument provides an indicator of the presence of popular apocalyptic rumors, countered by theologians trying to calm the enthused panics such rumors incited. From our modern perspective, of course, such chronological temporizing merely postponed, indeed aggravated, apocalyptic millennialism. From the early third century, another 300 years probably seemed like an immensely long time, but eventually the 6,000 years would be fulfilled.

At the same time as theologians tried to postpone millennial hopes, they also tried to remove Christian millennial hostility to the Roman Empire. Thus, theologians took Paul's discussion of the timing of the End (2 Thessalonians 3:4) and interpreted his reference to an "obstacle" to the advent of the "man of iniquity" as meaning that as long as the Roman Empire endured, the Antichrist could not come. This pro-Roman eschatology would, after Christianity became imperial, produce the myth of the Last Emperor, a superhuman figure who would unite all of Christendom and rule in peace and justice for 120 years before abdicating his throne, thus removing the "obstacle" and bringing on the brief rule of Antichrist (imperial prophetic texts like the Tiburtine Sybil, Pseudo-Methodius). This imperial millennialism, which probably already influenced Constantine—the first, "Last Emperor"—offered a powerful antidote to the subversive elements of popular millennialism. Its cosmic struggle was not the demotic holy anarchy opposing an evil empire of earliest Christianity, but the authoritarian holy empire fighting anarchic chaos; instead of the aniconic monotheistic political ideal of "no king but God," it offered the iconic one of "one God, one king." Not surprisingly, this form of "top-down" millennialism found much favor among subsequent Christian theologians.

But both these approaches, however creative and successful among theologians, merely delayed the problem. Despite pagan and Christian belief in *Roma eterna*, the empire (especially in the West) was vulnerable; and no matter how far away 6000 AM (500 CE) seemed from 5700 (200), it didn't seem so far away in the 5900s (400s). Indeed, the western Roman Empire faltered just as the year 6000 approached, turning both these antiapocalyptic exegeses—the sabbatical chronology and the imperial "obstacle" to Antichrist—into profoundly apocalyptic ones. At the beginning of the fifth century (c. 5900 AM), Jerome and Augustine, perceiving the danger posed by two such unstable eschatological "teachings," developed new and more stringent forms of opposition to millennialism. They reoriented Latin thought in two ways. Jerome, translating the work of the great imperialist, antimillenarian theologian and chronographer, Eusebius, introduced a new set of calculations that placed the Incarnation in 5199 AM (II), thus delaying the year 6000 another three centuries. He thereby made it possible for Latin chronographers to ignore the advent of the year 6000 AM I, since it was really only 5701 AM II). At the same time he heaped ridicule and contempt on millennialists, believers in foolish tales of earthly delights, gluttony, and sexual promiscuity.

Augustine went still further, arguing that no historical event or chronology can be interpreted apocalyptically and that the millennium was not a future event but already in progress, already set in motion by Christ. To explain why the evils of war, hatred, injustice, and poverty continued unabated, Augustine used the notion of the *Two Cities*. There was a "heavenly city," the celestial Jerusalem, where the millennium was already manifest, and a terrestrial Babylon, the time-bound city of violence and oppression in which the millennium was not visible. These two cities would coexist as a *corpus permixtum* (a mixed body) in every man (even saints) and in every society (even the church) until the eschaton (the end of history). Thus Christian Rome, even the earthly church, could not represent the perfection of eschatological fulfillment, and their historical fate had nothing to do with God's plans for human salvation. This teaching radically reoriented Christian eschatology: rather than awaiting the coming Kingdom on earth, one should await it at the very end of time. Augustine basically banned millennialism, or the belief in a coming kingdom of God on earth, from Christian theology.

Medieval Millennialism

This ban on millennial thought so dominated the official theological writings of the early Middle Ages, that most modern historians think it had disappeared entirely from Latin Christendom. Indeed, standard treatments of millennialism, unaware of the presence of the *sabbatical millennium* and the popular millennial discourse it opposed, tend to skip from Augustine (fifth century) to Joachim (twelfth century) when the first formal theology that looked *forward* to the millennium reemerged. There are signs of millennialism, however, both in the activity of antiecclesiastical prophets like the "False" Christ of Bourges described by Gregory of Tours (*Historiae*, 10.25), and in the antiapocalyptic uses of chronology to oppose them. Gregory, for example, published his chronology for "those who despair at the coming end of the world." The implicit message was clear: Gregory wrote in the late 5700s, and when arguing with the "saints" who emerged after the assassination of the "False Christ" and "gained quite an influence over the common people," Gregory and his colleagues could argue there were more than two centuries to wait (1.1, 10.25). But, of course, even this more remote date eventually drew near, and in the eighth century—again the 5900s—the English monk Bede and his Carolingian followers did for Annus Mundi II, what Jerome had done for AM I: they shifted the dating system again, this time to Anno Domini. Hence the year 6000 AM II, just as the year 6000 AM I, passed unnoted by sources which spoke instead of AD 801.

And yet, the relative silence in our documentation does not mean that there was no further discussion of the approaching 6000. Indeed, as in 6000 AM I (500), the approach of 6000 brought an acute political crisis with the occupation of the Byzantine throne by a woman (Irene): the "obstacle" of 2 Thessalonians had been removed. Charlemagne's response, to hold his imperial coronation on the first day of the year 6000 AM II (AD 801) unquestionably held millennial significance despite the reluctance of the written sources to elaborate. The Coronation was, in this sense, like the "Emperor's New Clothes": everyone in the court knew of the date AM, but no chronicler mentioned it. Ignorant of this disparity, modern historians have analyzed this pivotal moment in Western history without any awareness of its millennial background, speaking only of the Coronation of the year 800.

Charlemagne's coronation contributed two essential elements to subsequent European millennialism. First, he "transferred" the empire, with all its apocalyptic and millennial freight to the West, including the notion of the Last Emperor. Numerous European kings claimed this messianic status; but the German emperors above all proved fascinated by the "Last Emperor" (e.g., Otto III, Frederick I, Frederick II). Second, the Carolingians shifted chronological hopes for the apocalypse from 6000 AM to the year AD 1000, a date at once millennial (the end of the sixth age, dawn of the Sabbatical era) and Augustinian (the end of the millennium since Christ). And unlike the previous cases of a millennial date's advent, chronographers were unable to shift the chronology and avoid mentioning the apocalyptic date.

The years 1000 and 1033 (millennium of the Passion) represent two of the most widely observed and intensely felt apocalyptic dates in European history, especially in France, where the Peace of God constitutes the first millennial movement approved of by the aristocratic leaderships of the society.

While popular "Messiahs" continued to appear (e.g., Eon de l'Etoile and Tanchelm), the period after the year 1000 saw much vaster movements, often approved (at least initially) by ecclesiastical authorities—the popular crusades, the Capuciati, the Franciscans, the Flagellants. Some of these movements were popularly based, militant, and extremely hostile to ecclesiastical authority, the wealthy, Jews, intellectuals, etc., displaying the anger, paranoia, and violence that would dominate an entire strain of antimodern, Christian millennialism from the crusading pogroms to the Nazis.

But the more documentable, and in some ways more surprising, aspect of medieval millennialism was its use by lay and ecclesiastical elites to buttress their own authority. Starting with the "Gregorian Reform," papal reformers used apocalyptic imagery both to attack their enemies as Antichrist, and to wrap their own efforts in messianic promises. Similarly, royal and even committal courts used eschatological prophecy as propaganda. Dynastic publicists often painted their patrons in the imagery of the Last Emperor—William the Conqueror consciously used themes from Revelation—his crown, his Doomsday book—to buttress his conquest of England. Supporters of Thierry of Alsace, count of Flanders, responding to the seemingly apocalyptic civil war of 1127–28, disseminated prophecies claiming that his (Carolingian) dynasty was the last barrier to Antichrist. At the time of the Second Crusade, a French prophet evoked the Tiburtine Sibyl to predict that Louis VII was to conquer the orient in the fashion of the great Persian King Cyrus. Similarly, Richard I and Frederick Barbarossa embarked on the Third Crusade inspired by apocalyptic prophecies.

Millennial hopes and ambitions reached new levels as a result of the work of Joachim of Fiore (late twelfth century). In analogy with the Trinity, Joachim postulated that there were to be three great states *(status)* of history: (1) that of the Law, which had been characterized by the vesting of righteousness in married persons; (2) that of the Gospel, during which an order of unmarried clerics served as the guardians of righteousness; and (3) that of the Holy Spirit, the period of the "Refreshment of the Saints" after Antichrist, in which the order of monks would bring an era of earthly peace and spiritual contemplation. Joachim was the first theologian to reject Augustine and return to a notion of a *millennium to come*, and his influence on subsequent millennial thought was immense.

The earliest historians of millennialism thought of Joachim as the first millennial thinker since the days when Augustine banned such ideas. He now appears to be the first formal thinker to articulate his millennialism in a way that could legitimately survive in writing. Had Augustine been present when the papal council declared Joachim's works acceptable, he would have denounced the decision loudly. Instead of a lone millenarian presence, then, Joachim's work stands as the literate articulation of a widespread oral discussion of millennialism at the turn of 1200, an oral discourse that had never ceased, despite its sudden ups and long downs, since well before Augustine. The spectacular success of the movements that could fuel themselves with Joachite "age of the spirit" rhetoric, illustrates the broad social stratum and the liveliness of the religiosity of this millennial discourse.

Joachim revitalized every aspect of medieval millennialism: within decades of his death in 1202, prophecies attributed to him began to circulate which people identified (in profoundly un-Augustinian fashion) with current events: mystical numerology, Franciscans and Dominicans, Holy Roman Emperors and popes all became figures in vast and ever-shifting predictions of imminent apocalypse. Chronological calculations fixed on 1250, then 1260 as the beginning of the new age, producing new and fearsome forms of spirituality like the Flagellants. The Franciscan order split over interpretations of Joachite prophecy, one branch becoming inquisitors, the other, revolutionary millenarians. Angelic popes and messianic emperors (some dead but returning), vied among lay and clerical constituencies for a following. By the end of the thirteenth century, millennialism had reached a fevered pitch, especially among Spiritual Franciscans and their lay spin-offs the Apostolic Brethren, as well as the more mystical elements of the Beguines (Marguerite Porete) and the Beguins. The execution, in 1300, of some Apostolic Brethren including their founder Gerard Segarelli, by Pope Boniface VIII set the stage for a particularly violent round of (justifiably) paranoid millennialism under the leadership of Fra Dolcino in the early fourteenth century.

In France, the imagery of millennialism continued to influence political discourse throughout the remainder of the Middle Ages. The terrible catastrophes of the fourteenth century—the Hundred Years War and the Black Death—renewed fervor for the final, divine intervention, including new and radical forms of Flagellants. Writing immediately after the humiliating rout of the French knighthood and the capture of the French king at Poitiers in 1356, the Franciscan John of Roquetaillade (Rupescisa) prophesied that plagues would cut down the populace like the harvest in the fields, the poor would rise up against tyrants and the rich, the church would be stripped of its wealth, and Antichrists would arise in Rome and Jerusalem. At least one contemporary, Villehardouin, seems to think that his prophecies inspired the Jacquerie (1358). However, Roquetaillade prophesied, the agony of the world would end by 1367, for a great reforming pope would come to power and the king of France would again be elected as the Holy Roman Emperor. Fulfilling his glorious role as a second Charlemagne, this worthy king would conquer the entire world and establish a millennial reign of peace and prosperity. Indeed, French kings bearing the name Charles were the subjects of particularly intense millennial prophecies throughout the late Middle Ages. A prophecy of 1380 pertaining to Charles VI was subsequently applied to Charles VII and Charles VIII, and even to England's Charles II while in exile in France.

Despite such fundamentally conservative applications of millennial prophecies, the hopes and expectations of the Christian Apocalypse still offered the outlines of a powerful if ultimately impractical, and hence suicidal, ideology of social revolution to the peasants and the urban poor of the latter Middle Ages. The thousands of shepherds or *Pastoreaux*, who swept through the French countryside in 1251 and again in 1320, were convinced that they were God's chosen instrument to free the Holy Land, thus bringing about the Parousia. While none ever reached the Holy Land, they traveled in bands about the kingdom, amazing some with their piety and all the while slaughtering clerics, Jews, and university intellectuals. Similar apocalyptic ideas regarding the election of the poor to usher in God's kingdom, either by participating in a crusade of the poor or by rescuing the king in his hour of need, motivated other popular insurrections.

Modern historians, limited by the nature of the documentation, tend to emphasize in their analyses the kinds of "political" or imperial millennialism that finds significant expression in the sources. The presence and strength of popular and revolutionary millennialism, rarely reported except by hostile clerical sources or by later spokesmen eager to downplay millenarian origins, are more difficult to assess. If one limits oneself only to explicitly millenarian groups, the numbers are few until the period of the printing press; if one identifies such groups by their patterns rather than their or others' claims about them, they are far more numerous.

The Taborites were perhaps the most important millennial movement of the late Middle Ages and represent a transition to the new age of millennial movements in the Renaissance and the Reformation. Taking themes from the English reformer Wycliffe, Czech preachers began to rally faithful to a program of radical, antipapal reform. Jan Huss, the most prominent of these men was burned at the stake at the Council of Constance (1415), strengthening the hand of the most radical, indeed millennial, of the Taborites who targeted 1420 as the date of the End. For the two decades, the region was plagued with millennial wars that brought out the social and revolutionary elements of millennialism, and ended in a national church centered in Prague.

Rennaissance and Reformation Millennialism

The approach of the year 7000 AM I (AD 1492/1500) brought with it a number of millennial currents. The fall of Constantinople in 1453 not only put an end to the last remnant of the Roman Empire from antiquity, but brought a large number of books with "secret knowledge," like the *Corpus Hermeticum* to the West which reinvigorated the Joachite tradition with gnostic elements of an apolitical elitism that sought, through knowledge, to transform the world. Among the enthusiasts of the proliferation of prophecy and knowledge was the explorer Christopher Columbus. At this point, especially with the assistance of the printing press, various strains of millennial prophecy announcing the dawn of the new age proliferated throughout Europe *(Prophecy)*. These new strains, linked to the gnostic search for the knowledge that can transform nature had important implications for the emergence of modern science. In a sense, the Renaissance, with its belief in a new world in the making and its eagerness to embrace any new form of thinking, religious and pagan, may represent the first "New Age" movement, the first secular millennial movement on record.

From the Renaissance onward, European culture developed an ever-more secular strain of millennialism. In a sense, the longer God tarried, the more humans took over his job of bringing about the perfect kingdom. Here we find the utopian and scientific traditions, the radical democratic movements that give us the French Revolution, radical socialism, and Marxist communism, as well as Nazism and, in a modified form, Zionism. In a sense, totalitarianism may be seen as the result of millennial movements that seize power and, in the failure of their millennial hopes, find themselves "forcing" the perfection of man.

Popular millennial movements, however, returned in strength with the Protestant Reformation. Luther, himself, was not a millennial thinker (he was, after all, trained as an Augustinian Canon), but he used powerful apocalyptic rhetoric, making the pope-as-Antichrist a staple of Protestant discourse. In so doing, he unleashed a wave of millennialism that covered the gamut from the revolutionary Peasants Revolt led by Thomas Muntzer to the Anabaptists who gathered in Munster in 1533 to see the heavenly Jerusalem descend to earth, to the Hutterites and Mennonites. But the most powerful form of millennialism to emerge came from the British Isles after Henry VIII introduced Protestantism as the official religion in 1534. Puritanism, in both England and Scotland, had strong millennial elements which eventually burst forth during the English Civil War (1640–60), unleashing a whole panoply of new millennial movements—Levellers, Diggers, Ranters, Quakers, and Muggletonians. Nor was the seventeenth century limited to Christian millennialism: 1666 saw the climax of the most widespread millennial movement in the history of Judaism, with the career of Sabbetai Zvi, whose messianic message ignited Jewish communities in both Muslim and Christian lands. Although rabbinic Judaism has, like Catholicism, strong firewalls against apocalyptic outbreaks, evidence of messianic activity can be found in almost every generation, and currently, especially among religious Zionists, there are strong millennial currents.

American Millennialism

The Puritan millennial strain came to America with the pilgrims and has, essentially, marked American religiosity ever since. The two Great Awakenings (1740s, 1820–40s) were both inspired by a form of millennial fervor derived from the teachings of Jonathan Edwards. In addition to the theological underpinnings, the emphasis on collective penitence, public weeping, and large crowds singing hymns reflects the characteristics of millennial moments from the times of the peace assemblies in Europe. According to some historians, the enthusiasm of the First Great Awakening was redirected into the militant patriotism of the American Revolution whose religious rhetoric was steeped in millennial themes. In addition to the more mainstream millennialism of the Great Awakenings, American millennialism gave birth to a wide range of new religious movements like the Mormons, the Seventh-Day Adventists, and the Jehovah's Witnesses. At present, these are some of the most active religions in the world.

American Protestant millennialism bifurcated along two streams: the premillennialists (who believe that Jesus will come *before* the millennium and inaugurate it), and the postmillennialists (who believe that Jesus will come *after* the millennium inaugurated by an inspired mankind). The former tends to be catastrophic (the seven years before the advent of Jesus, known as the Tribulation, preceded by the Rapture of the saints, are marked by terrible catastrophes and the coming of Antichrist); whereas the latter tends to be progressive and gradualist (things are getting better all the time). The former tends to be apolitical (only personal repentance and purification can prepare); the latter, politically active (through reform we can bring about the kingdom). In the later nineteenth century, premillennialism gained the upper hand in much American millennial thinking, only to cede to postmillennial reformism in the early decades of the twentieth. The evangelical and Fundamentalist reaction that developed in the 1910s and 1920s was premillennial dispensationalist in nature, inspired by the work of John Darby (d. 1882) and the Scofield Bible (1909) and committed to reversing the secularizing tendencies of reformist postmillennialism.

Premillennial dispensationalism has become extremely popular in Protestant circles in America, starting in the 1970s with the publication of Hal Lindsey's *The Late Great Planet Earth* and the "Rapture" film *Thief in the Night* (1972). In the 1980s, Edgar Whisenant published the pamphlet *88 Reasons Why the Rapture will Happen in 1988*, starting off a range of Rapture predictions that have dotted the 1990s. The Y2K virus, set to go off on 1 January 2000, has triggered a whole new wave of apocalyptic thinking among premillennial preachers like Chuck Missler, Jack Van Impe, and Jerry Falwell. Y2K, the great ecumenical apocalyptic prophecy of the age, shows every sign of metastasizing date-setting at this end of the second Christian millennium.

Non-Western Millennialism

Finally, millennialism has an important non-Western component. Islam, as a "religion of revelation," began as an apocalyptic movement anticipating the "Day of Judgment"; and retains apocalyptic and millennial elements to this day, especially in Shi'ite theology, but also in many forms of popular religiosity. In particular the Mujaddid tradition, that foresees a "renewer" at every century turn (AH), appears to constitute—before the century has turned—a form of apocalyptic messianic expectation in the coming of the hidden Mahdi.

Many indigenous movements, often anti-imperialist in nature, take on the full range of characteristics of millennialism. In the Western Hemisphere, for example, native populations produced a wide range of millennial movements, from the Gaiwiio ("Good Word") of Handsome Lake (c. 1800) to the Ghost Dance of the prophet Wovoka in the 1890s. In the Pacific Southwest, the twentieth century has seen the emergence of cargo cults which, responding to the arrival of cargo planes during World War II, believe that, by carrying out the proper rituals, they could bring the "cargo" from the great bird in the sky. Modern UFO cults, many of which have strong millennial elements, represent a kind of postmodern cargo cult.

By far the most powerful non-Western millennial tradition is found in Buddhism, with the Pure Land traditions and the expectation of the Maitreya Buddha, a kind of messianic final incarnation of the Buddha. Especially strong in China, but evident in Korea, Japan, Vietnam, and Burma, millennial strains of Buddhism have given birth to secret societies (White Lotus), and some powerful popular movements, one of which toppled the Mongol dynasty in the fourteenth century, another of which, the Taiping, almost toppled the Qing dynasty in the mid-nineteenth century. By the time this last movement, itself a mixture of native Buddhist and imported Christian millennialism, had been suppressed, some 20–35 million people were dead. The Boxer Rebellion of the late nineteenth century again demonstrated the power of millennial beliefs, especially the characteristic magical belief, shared by the Ghost Dancers of North America and the Kartelite Cults of Africa that certain incantations could render the believer invulnerable to bullets.

The Legacy and Future of Millennialism

We are, however, not yet in a position to judge just how significant millennialism is as a historical factor. It unquestionably plays an important role in various forms of antimodern and anti-Western protests, but it also has played a key role in generating modernity. With its images of a perfected mankind, its emphasis on social egalitarianism and the dignity of manual labor, its undermining of monarchical authority, its spread of a sense of popular empowerment, millennialism has, even in failure, left a legacy of social transformation. Indeed, millennialism may have played an important role in the diffusion of new technology. In their initial stages, millennial movements make widespread and innovative use of communications technology (Protestants and print, New Religious Movements and the WWW). And in later stages, they often integrate new technology into the lifestyle of the community as it adjusts to the return of "normal time" and finds more durable, and more economically viable forms. Ironically, some of the most antimodern groups can, by the end of their apocalyptic journey, end up at the cutting edge of modernity.

For all its socially creative force, however, millennialism also has powerfully destructive tendencies. In some, primarily antimodern forms, millennial movements can become highly authoritarian, suffused with conspiracist thinking, implacably opposed to imagined enemies (Jews, independent women, denominational opponents), capable of staggering acts of violence and self-destruction. The Nazis, with their racist *tausandjahriger Reich*, represent the ultimate expression of this tendency in millennial dynamics. It is one of the main tasks of millennial studies to understand what factors indicate that, in the period of disappointment, a group will turn peaceful or violent. In the meantime, millennialism, with its power to fire the imagination and elicit passionate emotions, to move great numbers to extraordinary deeds of self-sacrifice, social creativity and destructiveness, may be one of the most protean social and religious forces in the history of civilization. As we approach the end of the third millennium, it looks like we will have yet another demonstration of its range and power.

Richard Landes

Bibliography

Adas, Michael. (1979) *Prophets of Rebellion: Millenarian Protest Movements against the European Colonial Order.* Cambridge, U.K.: Cambridge University Press.

Barkun, Michael. (1974) *Disaster and the Millennium.* New Haven, CT: Yale University Press.

Bashear, Suleiman. (1993) "Muslim Apocalypses." *Israel Oriental Studies* 13: 75–99.

Baumgarten, Albert. (1997) *The Flourishing of Jewish Sects in the Maccabean Era: An Interpretation.* Leiden: E.J. Brill.

Bloch, Ruth. (1985) *Visionary Republic: Millennial Themes in American Thought, 1756–1800.* New York: Cambridge University Press.

Burridge, Kenelm. (1969) *New Heaven, New Earth: A Study of Millenarian Activities.* New York: Schocken Books.

Butler, Jon. (1990) *Awash in a Sea of Faith: Christianizing the American People.* Cambridge, MA: Harvard University Press.

Cohn, Norman. ([1961, 1970] 1999) *The Pursuit of the Millennium.* New York: Oxford University Press.

——. (1993) *Cosmos, Chaos and the World to Come: The Ancient Roots of Apocalyptic Faith.* New Haven, CT: Yale University Press.

Collins, John J. (1984) *The Apocalyptic Imagination: An Introduction to the Jewish Matrix of Christianity.* New York: Crossroad.

Cook, David. (1997) "Moral Apocalyptic in Islam." *Studia Islamica* 86: 37–69.

Cook, Stephen L. (1995) *Prophecy and Apocalypticism: The Postexilic Setting.* Minneapolis: Fortress Press.

Crone, Patricia, and Michael Cook. (1976) *Hagarism: The Making of the Islamic World.* Cambridge, U.K.: Cambridge University Press.

Couch, Mal, ed. (1996) *Dictionary of Premillennial Theology.* Grand Rapids, MI: Kregel.

Daniels, Ted. (1992) *Millennialism: An International Bibliography.* New York: Garland.

Emmerson, Richard K., and Bernard McGinn, eds. (1993) *The Apocalypse in the Middle Ages.* Ithaca, NY: Cornell University Press.

Festinger, Leon, et al. ([1956] 1964) *When Prophecy Fails.* New York: Harper Torchbooks.

Fredriksen, Paula. (1991) "Apocalypse and Redemption in Early Christianity: From John of Patmos to Augustine of Hippo." *Vigiliae Christianae* 45: 151–83.

Gager, John. (1975) *Kingdom and Community: The Social World of Early Christianity.* Englewood Cliffs, NJ: Prentice-Hall Inc.

Gow, Andrew. (1995) *The Red Jews: Antisemitism in an Apocalyptic Age, 1200–1600.* Leiden: E.J. Brill.

Hill, Christopher. (1993) *The English Bible and the Seventeenth-Century Revolution.* London: Penguin.

Jensen, Karl, and Yvonne Hsieh. (1999) "Law Enforcement and the Millennialist Vision: A Behavioral Approach." *FBI Law Enforcement Bulletin* 68, 9:1–6.

Katz, David, and Jeremy Popkin. (1999) *Messianic Revolution: Radical Religious Politics to the End of the Second Millennium.* New York: Hill and Wang.

La Barre, Weston. (1970) *The Ghost Dance: The Origins of Religion.* Garden City, NY: Doubleday.

Landes, Richard. (1995) *Relics, Apocalypse, and the Deceits of History.* Cambridge, MA: Harvard University Press.

Lanternari, Vittorio. (1963) *Religions of the Oppressed: A Study of Modern Messianic Cults.* New York: Alfred A. Knopf.

Lerner, Robert E. (1976) "Refreshment of the Saints: The Time After Antichrist as a Station for Earthly Progress in Medieval Thought." *Traditio* 32: 99–144.

McGinn, Bernard. (1979) *Visions of the End: Apocalyptic Traditions in the Middle Ages.* New York: Columbia University Press.

———. (1994) *Antichrist: Two Thousand Years of the Human Fascination with Evil.* New York: HarperCollins.

Manuel, Frank E., and Fritzie P. Manuel. (1979) *Utopian Thought in the Western World.* Cambridge, MA: Harvard University Press.

Mendel, Arthur. (1990) *Vision and Violence.* Ann Arbor, MI: University of Michigan Press.

Naquin, Susan. (1976) *Millenarian Rebellion in China: The Eight Trigrams Uprising of 1813.* New Haven, CT: Yale University Press.

Noble, David. (1998) *The Religion of Technology: The Divinity of Man and the Spirit of Invention.* New York: Alfred A. Knopf.

O'Leary, Stephen. (1994) *Arguing the Apocalypse: A Theory of Millennial Rhetoric.* New York: Oxford University Press.

Quinby, Lee. (1994) *Anti-Apocalypse: Exercises in Genealogical Criticism.* Minneapolis: University of Minnesota Press.

Ravitsky, Aviezer. (1996) *Messianism, Zionism, and Jewish Religious Radicalism.* Chicago: University of Chicago Press.

Reeves, Marjorie. (1976) *Joachim of Fiore and the Prophetic Future.* London: S.P.C.K.

St. Clair, Michael J. (1992) *Millenarian Movements in Historical Context.* New York: Garland.

Scholem, Gershom. (1975) *Sabbatai Zevi: The Mystical Messiah.* Princeton, NJ: Princeton University Press.

Schwartz, Hillel. (1990) *Century's End: An Orientation Manual Toward the Year 2000.* New York: Doubleday.

Scott, James C. (1992) *Domination and the Arts of Resistance.* New Haven, CT: Yale University Press.

Silver, Abba Hillel. ([1927] 1959) *A History of Messianic Speculation in Israel from the First through the Seventeenth Centuries.* Boston: Beacon.

Spence, Jonathan. (1996) *God's Chinese Son: The Taiping Heavenly Kingdom of Hong Xiuquan.* New York: W.W. Norton and Co.

Talmon, Jacob. ([1952] 1970) *The Origins of Totalitarian Democracy.* London: Sphere Books.

Thompson, Damian. ([1996] 1999) *The End of Time: Faith and Fear in the Shadow of the Millennium.* London: Sinclair Stevenson.

Verbeke, W., D. Verhelst, and A. Welkenhuysen, eds. (1988) *The Use and Abuse of Eschatology in the Middle Ages.* Louvain: Catholic University Press.

Williams, Ann, ed. (1980) *Prophecy and Millenarianism: Essays in Honour of Marjorie Reeves.* Essex, U.K.: Longman.

Wojcik, Daniel. (1997) *The End of the World as We Know It: Faith Fatalism, and Apocalypse in America.* New York: New York University Press.

Yates, Francis. (1964) *Giordanno Bruno and the Hermetic Tradition.* New York: Routledge.

Millerites

On 22 October 1844 thousands of Americans in the North and Midwest spent the day looking for Jesus to appear in the clouds of heaven. Most had only recently heard the warning to prepare for the end of all things, but some had been getting ready for this great day since the early 1830s when the message about Jesus' approaching return was first published. The nonbelieving public called them "Millerites" for William Miller, an upstate New York farmer who had founded and led the movement since 1831, but most of them preferred to

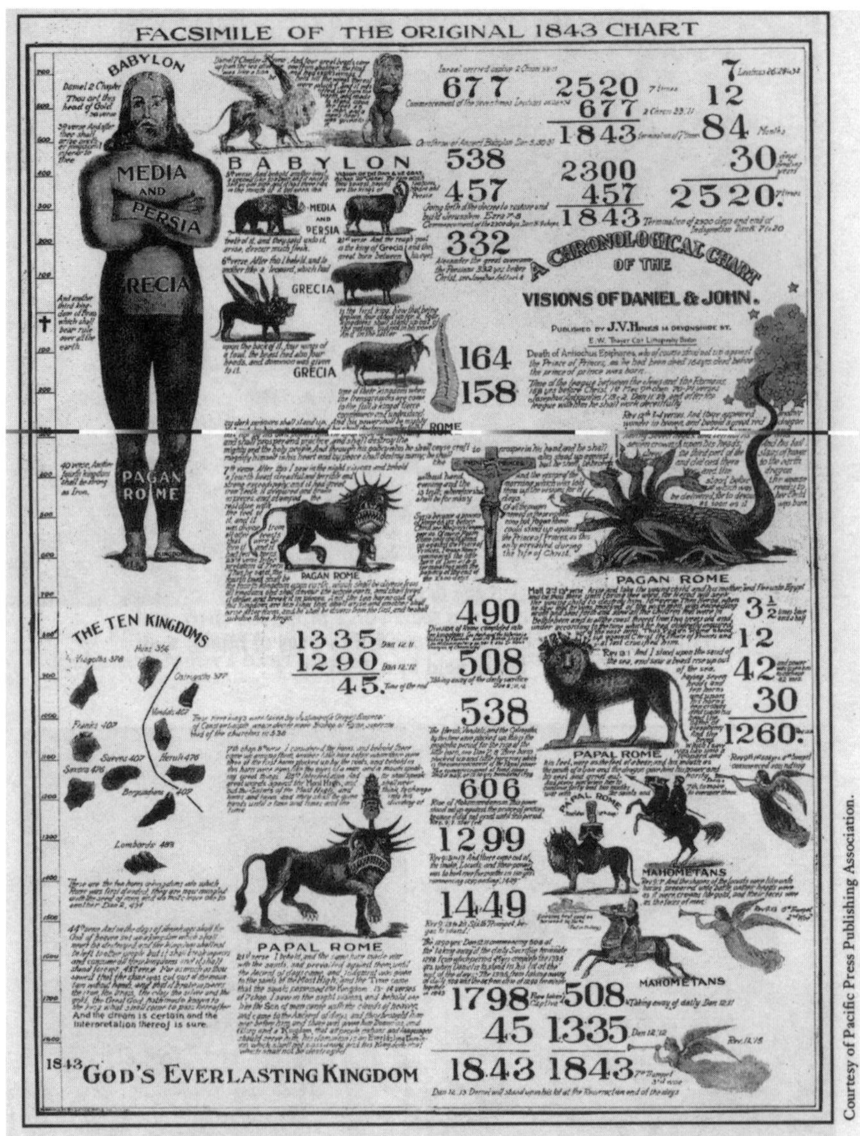

Courtesy of Pacific Press Publishing Association.

Millerite Millennial Chart. KNIGHT, GEORGE R. (1993) *MILLENNIAL FEVER AND THE END OF THE WORLD*. BOISE, ID: PACIFIC PRESS PUBLISHING ASSOCIATION, 181.

call themselves "Adventists" or "second Adventists" thus announcing to that same public that their faith was not founded on the word of a man but on the promises of God as revealed in scripture. Their commitment to Adventism varied from ardent "true believers" to those who were "covering their bets," getting ready just in case Miller was proved correct. But all of them lived in a world in which prophecy was real and the terrible events forecast in the Bible were at least future, and perhaps present, certainties.

These Millerites represent the most significant "end of the world" movement in American history. Many other individuals and groups have predicted the return of Christ and the remaking of the heavens and the earth both before and since Miller preached, but they worked individually and organized themselves as groups in a very different way from the Millerites. This was no new church, though new denominations would eventually evolve out of Millerism. Nor was it a cult centering its faith on the person of the leader. William Miller was not charismatic, and he carefully avoided gathering a personal following. Rather, this was a mass movement, focusing on ideas and expectations that were deeply rooted in early-nineteenth-century American culture.

Describing Millerism

A mass movement is different from organized religious institutions. A church, a sect, or a denomination has a formal structure of believers (usually called laypeople), clergy (called pastors, ministers, or priests), and established methods for worshiping, teaching, and ministering to its members while communicating its beliefs to the rest of world. They are permanent institutions, growing out of the past, living in the present, and preparing for continuation in the future. Mass movements have no such expectation. They are temporary, they focus on one principal idea or objective, and while they have clearly identified leaders and systems of conveying their ideas and organizing believers, they have no means of enforcing discipline over followers' beliefs and actions. Because the idea they advocate reaches a mass audience, it attracts people from many different walks of life, so the movement is likely to be diverse in many ways.

All this was true of the Millerites. In fact, other than a central belief in the imminent (approaching) second coming of Christ and end of the world, it is difficult to find anything else that Millerites had in common. But it is possible to describe the movement in very broad terms using a method that historians of religions often apply: considering a group's creed (beliefs), code or behavior (how believers act), cultus (the things they hold sacred), and the nature of their community (how they relate to each other and the outside world).

Millerite Creed

From 1831 until 1844 William Miller and his followers preached a single belief. Sometime in 1843 Jesus would return to earth, God would judge the living and the dead, and he would shatter the earth and create the New Jerusalem out of its ashes. The faithful who were still living would rise to meet Jesus in the air and the unfaithful would be sent to eternal punishment in the flames of hell. Millerites did not agree on the exact order of the events that were to occur, nor did they necessarily agree on the date or on dating the end of the world at all. After all, the scripture says clearly that nobody knows the "day and hour" when these things will happen. Miller always defended himself by saying that he never predicted a day nor an hour, though to him the year was clearly foretold. But Millerites did agree that all these things were going to happen—soon. And as 1843 approached attention on that year became fixed. Since the prophecies in scripture were written by Jews and the Jewish calendar was based on the moon rather than the sun Miller computed 1843 as beginning on 21 March 1843 and ending at midnight on 21 March 1844. This gave two specific days on which Millerites could focus their attention, and when the second "deadline" passed uneventfully they were disappointed. But in the summer of 1844 a Millerite lecturer in New Hampshire, Samuel S. Snow, computed the likely date of the second coming as 22 October, and two weeks before that date William Miller publicly endorsed his prediction. So Millerite expectations were high on that day.

Stating this core belief is simple, but Millerite creed went beyond it. To have faith in the approaching end of the world is to have faith in the Bible, and to have faith in the Bible was to have faith in God. This Bible-centered nature of Millerism's message made it compelling and apparently conventional. A belief in the Second Coming of Christ is a core Christian doctrine common to almost every denomination, so few Christians could refute Millerism's basic message. In fact, it was Millerism's traditionalism that attracted Christians from almost every Protestant denomination. But Millerism proposed two ideas that were not conventional and that earned for it a reputation as radical and peculiar. The first was the prophecy that Christ would first return and then personally inaugurate the millennium, a thousand-year period of perfect peace, harmony, and justice. This meant they were premillennialists (millenarians), a label that is based on the word "millennium." At the heart of premillennialism is a deep-seated pessimism about the world; everything is getting worse and worse, so bad in fact that humans are incapable of reforming the world. Only God can do that by completely obliterating the old earth and creating a new purified world from its ashes. But in the early nineteenth century, most Protestants in America were far more optimistic than that. Being postmillennialists, they believed not only that humans could improve the world but that God required them to do just that. Only after humanity had purified the world would Jesus return. Their view was nurtured by the widespread revivals that swept America in the 1820s and 1830s in a movement called the Second Great Awakening. In fact, intense religious enthusiasm convinced many Protestants that by their effort and will they could actually bring the world to moral perfection. Americans responded by creating all kinds of reform movements in the 1830s and 40s to obliterate all kinds of evil, from drinking alcohol to slavery. So the Millerites' premillennialism added a controversial idea to American culture.

Dating the Second Coming of Christ was the second idea that made Millerism radical even though Miller based his prediction on conventional interpretations of scriptural prophecy, not on any personal revelation or vision. His method, which involved mathematical computations based on prophecies in Daniel, Revelation, and other books of the Bible, could appeal to Americans' sense of practicality and democracy. The early nineteenth century was the Age of the Common Man when most believed that anybody could become president or achieve wealth and status by hard work and creativity, when inventors were conquering the wilderness with machines and turning the United States into a mighty empire of democracy. Why shouldn't a common farmer gain special knowledge about God's plans by studying the scriptures scientifically? Why wouldn't the work of perfection begin in the United States? Still, despite the reasonableness of Miller's methods, it was hard to overcome the

RULES OF INTERPRETATION.

In studying the Bible, I have found the following rules to be of great service to myself, and now give them to the public by special request. *Every rule should be well studied, in connexion with the scripture references, if the Bible student would be at all benefited by them.*

RULES.	PROOFS.
I. Every word must have its proper bearing on the subject presented in the Bible.	Matt. v. 18.
II. All scripture is necessary, and may be understood by a diligent application and study.	2 Tim. iii. 15, 16, 17.
III. Nothing revealed in the scripture can or will be hid from those who ask in faith, not wavering.	Deut. xxix. 29. Matt. x. 26, 27. 1 Cor. ii. 10. Phil. iii. 15. Isa. xlv. 11. Matt. xxi. 22. John xiv. 13, 14. xv. 7. James i. 5, 6. 1 John v. 13, 14, 15.
IV. To understand doctrine, bring all the scriptures together on the subject you wish to know; then let every word have its proper influence, and if you can form your theory without a contradiction, you cannot be in an error.	Isa. xxviii. 7—29. xxxv. 8. Prov. xix. 27. Luke xxiv. 27, 44, 45. Rom. xvi. 26. James v. 19. 2 Pet. i. 19, 20.
V. Scripture must be its own expositor, since it is a rule of itself. If I depend on a teacher to expound it to me, and he should guess at its meaning, or desire to have it so on account of his sectarian creed, or to be	Ps. xix. 7, 8, 9, 10, 11. cxix. 97, 98, 99, 100, 101, 102, 103, 104, 105. Matt. xxiii. 8, 9, 10. 1 Cor. ii. 12, 13, 11, 15, 16. Eze. xxxiv. 18, 19. Luke xi. 52. Mal. ii. 7, 8.

RULES OF INTERPRETATION. 21

RULES.	PROOFS.
thought wise, then his *guessing, desire, creed* or *wisdom* is my rule, not the Bible.	
VI. God has revealed things to come, by visions, in figures and parables, and in this way the same things are oftentime revealed again and again, by different visions, or in different figures, and parables. If you wish to understand them, you must combine them all in one.	Ps. lxxxix. 19. Hos. xii. 10. Hab. ii. 2. Acts ii. 17. 1 Cor. x. 6. Heb. ix. 9, 24. Ps. lxxviii. 2. Matt. xiii. 13, 34. Gen. xli. 1—32. Dan. ii. vii. and viii. Acts x. 9—16.
VII. Visions are always mentioned as such.	2 Cor. xii. 1.
VIII. Figures always have a figurative meaning, and are used much in prophecy, to represent future things, times and events; such as *mountains*, meaning *governments; beasts*, meaning *kingdoms*.	Dan. ii. 35, 44. vii. 8, 17.
Waters, meaning *people*.	Rev. xvii. 1, 15.
Lamp, meaning *Word of God*.	Ps. cxix. 105.
Day, meaning *year*.	Ezek. iv. 6.
IX. Parables are used as comparisons to illustrate subjects, and must be explained in the same way as figures by the subject and Bible. Mark iv. 13. See explanation of the ten virgins, Miller's Lectures, No. xvi.	
X. Figures sometimes have two or more different significations, as day is used in a figurative sense to represent three different periods of time.	
1. Indefinite.	Eccles. vii. 14.

Rules of Biblical interpretation set forth by William Miller. HIMES, JOSHUA V. (1841) *VIEWS OF THE PROPHECIES AND PROPHETIC CHRONOLOGY*. BOSTON: MOSES A. DOW

sense that predicting even a year violated scripture's clear refusal to reveal the time. So on the one hand Millerism's apparently conventional creed allowed it to grow into a mass movement, but on the other hand its more innovative beliefs earned for it a great deal of hostility and even ridicule.

Millerite Code

What people believe shapes how they act. Postmillennialists, who believe Christ will return at the end of the millennium to celebrate humankind's work in purifying the world, struggle energetically to attack social and moral ills. Premillennialists, who believe Christ will return to initiate the millennium himself, are just as active, but they act very differently. First, they feel the need to demonstrate their faith in order to be numbered with the saints when Jesus comes. Millerites did this in a variety of ways. One was to sacrifice by giving time, money, and talents to help support the Adventist lecturers and newspapers that spread the word across the country and even to England. By stating publicly that they believed in Miller's prediction, many risked and sacrificed reputations, and suffered persecution from family and neighbors that varied from ridicule to incarceration in insane asylums. Others committed themselves wholeheartedly to the movement by volunteering as Adventist lecturers, newspaper distributors, and organizers of local Adventist meetings. Still others demonstrated their confidence in God's promise by giving up daily activities. While it is impossible to say how widespread this was, there are many stories of Millerites who removed their children from school, stopped planting crops, and sold their produce at record low prices or gave them away. Still others paid their debts, confessed their crimes, or settled long-standing disputes. Others sought to demonstrate their faith by turning their backs on the churches to which they belonged. These "come-outers" then created Second

Advent gatherings, often capitalizing the name to indicate that they were separate from all other churches and sects. In this way Millerites paved the way for the later Adventist denominations—the Advent Christian Church, Seventh-Day Adventist Church, and others.

A second impulse to action came from the need to help others to prepare for the end. A Christian's duty, scripture says, is to make sure everyone hears the warning to prepare so the faithful "may not be found with the blood of sinners" on their hands. Millerites worked one-on-one to convince family members and neighbors. Others became Adventist lecturers, among them a number of women, such as Olive Maria Rice and Mary A. Seymour, who were previously prohibited from speaking publicly by male-dominated social norms. Particularly effective was the Great Tent, a huge canvas canopy Millerites took from city to city in which up to five thousand people could hear second advent preaching for days on end. Publishing Millerite newspapers was one of the most effective means of communicating the message. One compilation lists over forty such papers up to the end of 1844, most of them published very irregularly except for two, the *Signs of the Times* edited by Joshua Vaughn Himes in Boston and the *Midnight Cry* published by Nathaniel Southard in New York. It was through efforts such as these that Millerism reached a large audience and became a mass movement.

Millerite Cultus

Premillennialists, who draw a sharp distinction between the spiritual world that is sacred and the material world that is corrupt, do not see objects, days, seasons of the year, or people as holy. This was certainly true of the Millerites. But creative Adventists produced remarkable educational tools to use at public lecturers to demonstrate to audiences the chronology of the world's approaching end and the need to prepare for it. The most enduring were chronological charts, often hand-painted but eventually printed in large quantities, that depicted prophecies of the endtimes from the Books of Daniel and Revelation. Some lecturers used a wooden model of what they called the "Man of Sin" with head colored gold, the torso silver, the legs brass, and the feet clay. As they recounted human history showing the rise and fall of empires they removed pieces of the model and threw them to the ground until nothing remained. The public ascribed another kind of object to the Millerites. Since Adventists believed they would rise in the air to be with Jesus when he appeared in the clouds of heaven, it was said that they made and wore ascension robes of white cloth. Although Millerites consistently denied the charge, the public's image of them gathering and turning hillsides and meeting rooms white with their robes is probably the most enduring impression the movement has left us.

Millerite Community

Because it was a mass movement that probably attracted from 10,000–15,000 followers, Millerism remained unorganized and variegated. With no means for imposing standards of belief and conduct until late in the movement's history, Adventists in small towns and villages followed Miller's model and came up with their own interpretations of scripture, predicted dates of the end, and devised rules on how to live in preparation for the end. Some of these practices were scandalous. Occasionally charismatic Adventist leaders created cults that attempted to raise the dead and practiced forms of free love, and there are cases of itinerants selling Millerite newspapers and books and pocketing the money. Slowly, though, as the 1830s gave way to the 1840s and the end approached nearer and nearer, a class of Millerite leaders took hold of the movement and provided as much structure as it ever achieved. The most important was Joshua V. Himes (1805–95), a man who could be called a professional reform organizer. Along with Charles Fitch, Josiah Litch, Henry Dana Ward, Nathaniel Southard, and others, Himes became Miller's manager, arranging his lecture schedule, developing publications, and otherwise promoting the movement. Most important, the leaders initiated a series of Second Advent conferences that functioned very much like Methodist general conferences. At these meetings Adventists coordinated plans for evangelizing, decided what was legitimate and what was illegitimate doctrine, condemned disreputable practices done in the name of the movement, and refuted public charges that Millerites were generally insane, crooked, or foolhardy.

Real community developed among Millerites on the local level. They gathered in each others' homes, school houses, or rented spaces, coming from many different denominations but sharing a common hope and expectation and a common experience of rejection by families, neighbors, and churches. A few of these small groups survived the Great Disappointment of 22 October 1844 to provide the core of future Adventist denominations.

Significance

Christ did not visibly return that October 22nd, and most Millerites slowly returned to their daily routines. William Miller went back to his farm where he survived only five years. Other leaders discovered new careers, sometimes in more conventional churches. But, despite the failure of the predicted date, Millerism made deep impressions on American religious life. By creating Adventist denominations, the largest being the Seventh-Day Adventist Church, former Millerites perpetuated their essential message. Premillennialism, though temporarily discredited, would rebound in popularity in the 1870s in a movement called dispensationalism, and this would contribute to the development of Fundamentalism in the twentieth century. Finally, the Millerites' skepticism about the inevitability of progress would continue to challenge the value of material growth that would mark the next 150 years of American life and in the 1990s urge us to consider the quality of human life over the things of this world.

David L. Rowe

See also Burned-over District, Dispensationalism, Fundamentalism, Premillennialism, Seventh-Day Adventists

Bibliography

Doan, Ruth. (1987) *The Miller Heresy, Millennialism, and American Culture.* Philadelphia: Temple University Press.

Gaustad, Edwin Scott. (1974) *The Rise of Adventism: Religion and Society in Mid-Nineteenth Century America.* New York: Harper & Row.

Knight, George. (1993) *Millennial Fever: A Study of Millerite Adventism.* Boise, ID: Pacific Press Publishing Association.

Land, Gary. (1986) *Adventism in America.* Grand Rapids, MI: William B. Eerdmans Publishing Company.

Nichol, Francis D. (1944) *The Midnight Cry: A Defense of William Miller and the Millerites.* Washington, D.C.: Review and Herald.

Numbers, Ron L., and Jonathan M. Butler. (1993) *The Disappointed: Millenarianism in the Nineteenth Century,* 2d ed. Knoxville: University of Tennessee Press.

Rowe, David L. (1985) *Thunder and Trumpets: Millerites and Dissenting Religion in Upstate New York, 1800–1850.* Chico, CA: Scholars Press.

Mormonism

In the Mormon prophet Joseph Smith's (1804–44) earliest description of his first encounter with Deity, he recorded the words of the Lord thus: "Behold the world lieth in sin at this time and none doeth good no not one they have turned asside from the gospel and keep not my commandments they draw near to me with their lips while their hearts are far from me and mine anger is kindling against the inhabitants of the earth to visit them acording to th[e]ir ungodliness and to bring to pass that which hath been spoken by the mouth of the prophets and Apostles behold and lo I come quickly as it [is] written of me in the cloud clothed in the glory of my Father" (Jessee 1984: 6). Such a stinging indictment of the present religious world, along with the warning of an imminent visitation in judgment, is standard millenarian fare. It was also central to the ethos of early Mormonism.

The Nature of Mormon Millennialism

The Church of Jesus Christ of Latter-day Saints was formally organized on 6 April 1830. That act culminated ten years of visions and revelations to Joseph Smith, chief among which was the Book of Mormon. In over five hundred pages, the Book of Mormon records the spiritual history in the Western Hemisphere of several groups who migrated from the Middle East. Like the Bible, its various prophetic authors are primarily interested in detailing the people's disregard of, or fidelity to, their covenant relationship with God. By preserving pure doctrine from antiquity, the Book of Mormon enabled Latter-day Saints to discern the true meaning of the Bible. This, along with the conferral of divine authority by heavenly messengers, provided the basis for a complete restoration of original Christianity rather than one more futile attempt at reforming a Christendom grown apostate beyond repair. In spirit, such views of contemporary corruption and its resolution through a return to pristine perfection coincided well with millenarianism.

It is widely understood that millennialism was a later, predominantly Christian, development growing out of Jewish apocalypticism. Its novelty was the expectation of a future "golden age" on earth *before* the final, apocalyptic transformation at the end of time. As various versions of the millennial dream developed over the centuries, some retained the vivid and dramatic spirit of their eschatological progenitor, lashing out against contemporary society and promising imminent vindication for the beleaguered faithful who would experience the millennium on a physically renovated earth personally ruled by Christ. Others drifted toward a more irenic view of the world around them and interpreted the prophecies figuratively, envisioning a millennium pervaded by Christ's spirit, not his actual presence, and taking place in an environment not physically discontinuous with the present. By the nineteenth century, there were basically two rival millennial visions of the future. What is often labeled "postmillennialism," the millennium-as-metaphor school of thought, constituted one approach. What most accurately should be called "millenarian apocalypticism," but more commonly is simply designated "millenarianism" or "premillennialism" (the two are used interchangeably), represented the other. Mormon eschatology exhibited its closest conceptual correspondence with the latter.

Contrary to popular postmillennialist notions of Christ reigning in the hearts of the regenerate, early Latter-day Saints looked forward to the day when the "King of Kings" would physically reign as supreme terrestrial monarch. "Not,"

A Mormon Tabernacle. HTTP://WWW.LDSFAITH.COM.

remarked a church leader, "as some have said, a spiritual (which might be more properly called imaginary) reign; but literal, and personal, as much so as David's reign over Israel, or the reign of any king on earth" (*Star* 1834: 162). The Lord of Hosts was also the Lamb of God, and the Saints anxiously contemplated the privilege of enjoying a thousand years in his visible presence. Mormons waxed eloquent in their descriptions of an earth renewed to its Edenic state, for this was the ultimate meaning of the "restoration of all things which God hath spoken by the mouth of all his holy prophets since the world began" (Acts 3:21). It would, they reasoned, "materially affect the brutal creation. The lion and the ox are to eat straw together; the bear and the cow to graze the plain in company, and their young ones to lay down in peace: there shall be nothing to hurt or destroy in all the Lord's holy mountain" (*Star* 1834: 131). Succinctly stated, both "man and beast" will become "perfectly harmless as they were in the beginning, and feeding on vegetable food only" (Pratt 1837: 197).

The idea of the millennium as a return to primordium also led to the striking belief in the eventual unification of continental landmasses into a sort of prophetic Pangaea. Latter-day Saints believed that "the continents and islands shall be united in one, as they were on the morn of creation" (Pratt 1837: 195). A revelation received through Joseph Smith announced that when Christ came, he would "break down the mountains, and the valleys shall not be found. He shall command the great deep, and it shall be driven back into the north countries, and the islands shall become one land. And the land of Jerusalem and the land of Zion shall be turned back into their own place, and the earth shall be like as it was in the days before it was divided" (*Doctrine and Covenants* 133: 22–24).

Though Mormons could be classified as premillennialists or apocalyptic millenarians, there were important differences. Premillennialists "cry, Destruction, desolation, fire, and judgment, and write very ingeniously about it, but there it ends," complained one LDS writer. In his view, "the man of God will no sooner cry, 'Destruction, desolation, and judgment,' than he will tell of an ark, a Zoar, a Palla, a Mount Zion, a Jerusalem, or some other place which God has provided [as refuge] for them who will hear his voice" (*Star* 1834: 126). Much as the doctrine of the "rapture" would function for Darbyite dispensationalists in later decades, the Mormon doctrine of the physical "gathering" together of the believers served to provide a means of escape from much of the tribulation of the last days. It also fulfilled the visionary directive in John's Apocalypse to "come out" of spiritual Babylon (Revelation 18:4), and, in the process, produced a concentration of loyal followers who could establish the Mormon Kingdom in their wilderness Zion as a sort of prelibation of paradise. The gathering was a pivotal premillennial event in the Mormon view.

While Latter-day Saints enjoined the gathering upon all who embraced their message, they also affirmed the special ingathering of historic Israel. What is more, the Saints believed that Israel's restoration involved more than just the Jews, and that the Indians, too, were a "remnant of Jacob." It had long been suspected by others that the Native Americans were as much Israelite as any Jew, but that the whole prophetic scenario of Israel's temporal and spiritual restoration was to be *dually* enacted—once by the Jews in the Old World and again by the native inhabitants of America—added a new dimension to the drama. Though with the usual millenarian enthusiasm early Mormons followed newspaper accounts of Zionist stirrings among the Jews, they had a local, Indian Israel, as pedigreed as the Jews, to be watched and gathered to a local and new Jerusalem as real as the ancient Jerusalem. To the not-uncommon premillennialist scenario of Jews gathering in the future to Jerusalem and rebuilding David's city, the Saints added the picture of Indians gathering to western Missouri to build Zion, the "New" Jerusalem, alongside the "Gentile" Mormon converts who would similarly gather there.

In time, the Saints came to view the Israelite gatherings to New and Old Jerusalem as among the final events to take place before the inauguration of the millennium. American and European converts, however, were expected to congregate to interim gathering places as soon as possible. In the 1830s, it was Kirtland, Ohio, and western Missouri. In the 1840s, it was Nauvoo, Illinois. And during the final half of the century, Utah was the designated gathering place. The change in locations was the result of tensions with their neighbors. During much of the first sixteen years of Mormon

II NEPHI 26:14-22

14. But behold, I prophesy unto you concerning the last days; concerning the days when the Lord God shall bring these things forth unto the children of men.

15. After my seed and the seed of my brethren shall have dwindled in unbelief, and shall have been smitten by the Gentiles; yea, after the Lord God shall have camped against them round about, and shall have laid siege against them with a mount, and raised forts against them; and after they shall have been brought down low in the dust, even that they are not, yet the words of the righteous shall be written, and the prayers of the faithful shall be heard, and all those who have dwindled in unbelief shall not be forgotten.

16. For those who shall be destroyed shall speak unto them out of the ground, and their speech shall be low out of the dust, and their voice shall be as one that hath a familiar spirit; for the Lord God will give unto him power, that he may whisper concerning them, even as it were out of the ground; and their speech shall whisper out of the dust.

17. For thus saith the Lord God: They shall write the things which shall be done among them, and they shall be written and sealed up in a book, and those who have dwindled in unbelief shall not have them, for they seek to destroy the things of God.

18. Wherefore, as those who have been destroyed have been destroyed speedily; and the multitude of their terrible ones shall be as chaff that passeth away–yea, thus saith the Lord God: It shall be at an instant, suddenly–

19. And it shall come to pass, that those who have dwindled in unbelief shall be smitten by the hand of the Gentiles.

20. And the Gentiles are lifted up in the pride of their eyes, and have stumbled, because of the greatness of their stumbling block, that they have built up many churches; nevertheless, they put down the power and miracles of God, and preach up unto themselves their own wisdom and their own learning that they may get gain and grind upon the face of the poor.

21. And there are many churches built up which cause envyings, and strifes, and malice.

22. And there are also secret combinations even as in times of old, according to the combinations of the devil, for he is the founder of all these things; yea, the founder of murder, and works of darkness; yea, and he leadeth them by the neck with a flaxen cord, until he bindeth them with his strong cords forever.

Source: *The Book of Mormon* (1982). Salt Lake City: The Church of Jesus Christ of Latter-day Saints.

history, the Saints experienced severe persecution and crisis conditions. While their apocalyptic attitudes might have been partially responsible for provoking persecution, it is also clear that persecution reinforced their premillennialism by verifying the dualistic analysis of society central to millenarianism. The Saints knew that as the millennium drew nigh, Satan would be waging a war of ever-increasing intensity against them. Therefore, persecution became an assurance, albeit a painful one, that all was proceeding on prophetic schedule.

The obvious benefits in terms of faith and fellowship, as well as the allure of the fresh start and the chance to physically demonstrate one's devotion to God, helped make the Mormon gathering remarkably successful. During the nineteenth century, tens of thousands of Latter-day Saint converts undertook an eschatologically motivated migration to a Mormon gathering place, primarily Utah. They even began to call their wilderness home "Zion." In the twentieth century, however, changing circumstances dictated a new, figurative understanding of the gathering in which Zion would be wherever pure Saints congregated to live and worship, even in foreign lands. Abandoning Babylon and gathering to Zion now became more of a spiritual than a geographical move; it involved changing one's heart, not one's home.

A final feature of both apocalypticism and millennialism to be considered is the tendency to assume that the end is near. Early Latter-day Saints expected the "great and dreadful day of the Lord" in their own lifetimes. Unlike other millennialists, they were not given to prophetic numerology or exact calendrical calculations as to the date of Christ's Advent. Yet, as their very name testified, the Latter-day Saints did feel that the divine reestablishment of the church of Christ in their day lifted the curtain on the final act in human history. In the twentieth century, the feeling that the Saints were living in the shadow of the Second Coming has generally not been as sustained or pervasive as it was in the earliest years. Modern church leaders regularly make calming and qualifying statements which provide a counterpoint to undue anxiety about the nearness of the millennium.

Mormon Millennialism at the End of the Twentieth Century

This should not be taken as evidence that Mormonism has succumbed to the secularizing tendencies of modernism, however. During the 1980s, LDS apostle and theologian Bruce R. McConkie (1915–85), published the longest work ever written by a Latter-day Saint on eschatological matters. What is striking is how little McConkie's millennial treatise differed from those written during Mormonism's first generation. The same supernatural biological and geological changes anticipated then are expected today, including the abolishment of infant mortality, the herbivorization of carnivores, the unification of continental landmasses, and the commingling of mortals and resurrected immortals. That such views seemed plausible in the early nineteenth century is perhaps not surprising. That they are still maintained today provides dramatic testimony of the degree to which LDS millenarianism in particular and Mormonism in general have resisted the encroachments of modernity.

Latter-day Saint leaders have responded, and continue to respond, to modernity in much the same way that conservative religionists do generally—by rejecting it for a universe thoroughly grounded in absolutes and the supernatural. As much as any other factor, what facilitates this in the Mormon case is their core conviction that they are led by a living prophet and living apostles. Their modern Moses may be dressed in a business suit, but he still provides a symbolic connection with the mythic world of the sacred past. Continuing revelation through a living prophet serves as tangible evidence that God is still free today to do the same remarkable things he did in the Bible. For Mormons, God is not present only in clerically mediated worship or in the ordinary events of history. Such a perspective removes any philosophical impediment to fully endorsing the dramatic and miraculous endtime occurrences anticipated in premillennial eschatology.

On the other hand, Mormons have perceived the social and behavioral implications of that eschatology differently over the years. A study of LDS leaders' discourses at the church's general conferences during the past century and a half reveals that millenarian rhetoric "diminished drastically after 1920." Thus, "even though an apocalyptic scenario of the last days is still a central Mormon doctrine, it is no longer enunciated by modern conference speakers with anything like the emphatic fervor of nineteenth-century leaders" (Shepherd and Shepherd 1984: 196). While Latter-day Saints still talk about the endtimes, for many modern Mormons these doctrines have a detached and textbookish quality. As people make their peace with the world, the apocalyptic dream of the "great reversal" diminishes. The social ramifications of eschatological dualism are no longer maintained, and soteriological dualism is disparaged. The term "wicked," for instance, no longer refers to all unbelievers. Today, it is applied only to the morally corrupt, and the good and honorable of all religions are expected to be alive during the millennium. In short, the more abrasive features of millenarianism that served their needs in an earlier period have been quietly, perhaps unwittingly, laid aside in recent years.

Still, on the eve of the twenty-first century, if from statistical reports and time management to telecommunications and computerization, Mormonism has acquired the institutional accouterments of modernization, it remains intellectually insulated from the acids of modernity by its core belief in continuing revelation. Mormonism has gone far toward modernizing without modifying the basic beliefs of its premillennial eschatology, but the door is always open to change. The overarching issue from the LDS perspective is not whether the church adjusts any of its understandings, but whether God's hand is in it. The Saints' belief in inspired guidance from living prophets gives them the confidence to feel that they can live "in" the modern world and yet be "of" it, intellectually or behaviorally, only to a degree not harmful to their sacred enterprise. Whichever eschatological path Mormons may pursue in the future, they continue to expect that it will lead them to an actual thousand years of paradisiacal peace and prosperity which they call "the millennium."

Grant Underwood

See also Premillennialism

Bibliography

Arrington, Leonard J., and Davis Bitton. (1979) *The Mormon Experience: A History of the Latter-day Saints.* New York: Alfred A. Knopf.

The Book of Mormon. (1830) Palmyra, NY: E. B. Grandin.

Doctrine and Covenants of the Church of Jesus Christ of Latter-day Saints: Containing Revelations Given to Joseph Smith, the Prophet, With Some Additions by his Successors in the Presidency of the Church. ([1835] 1981) Kirtland, OH: F. G. Williams & Co.; Salt Lake City: The Church of Jesus Christ of Latter-day Saints.

The Evening and the Morning Star. (June 1832–September 1834) Independence, MO and Kirtland, OH.

Jessee, Dean C., ed. (1984) *The Personal Writings of Joseph Smith.* Salt Lake City: Deseret Book.

McConkie, Bruce R. (1982) *The Millennial Messiah: The Second Coming of the Son of Man.* Salt Lake City: Deseret Book.

Pratt, Parley P. (1837) *A Voice of Warning and Instruction to All People, Containing a Declaration of the Faith and Doctrine of the Church of the Latter Day Saints, Commonly Called Mormons.* New York: W. Sanford.

Shepherd, Gordon, and Gary Shepherd. (1984) *A Kingdom Transformed: Themes in the Development of Mormonism.* Salt Lake City: University of Utah Press.

Underwood, Grant (1993) *The Millenarian World of Early Mormonism.* Urbana: University of Illinois Press.

Mysticism

A mystic is a person who claims an immediate experience of the divine, and mysticism embraces that realm of human experience of the transcendent that is beyond religious dogma, ritual, and law. Apocalypse as a textual genre typically represents supernatural visions that have occurred to the mystic. Many religious millennialist movements include such ecstatic components, either as the foundation for the movement or the reward of the elect. Mystical visions have often initiated millennialist communities under the leadership of a charismatic or prophetic figure; they have also been appraised as signs of election or of the imminent endtimes.

Modern Analyses of the Mystical Experience

Mysticism—a broad term for a variety of experiences and discourses about those experiences—resists critical analysis while it invites reductionistic explanations. Mystical experiences appear in a variety of religious traditions: Christian Pentecostalism, Hindu absorption in Brahman, Buddhist eradication of the self. Mystics (sometimes called "shamans" by anthropologists and scholars of religion) themselves claim to have unmediated, direct experiences of divinity, which may come unbidden or as the result of disciplinary practices that make the adept more receptive to the experience. Frequently the mystic will also claim direct knowledge of divine truths that have not been mediated to him by religious instruction or other social formation. Based on that claim, some scholars of religion characterize mystical experience as, in Aldous Huxley's phrase, "perennial philosophy," that is a core of human experience that transcends time and culture. This approach is typified in the work of modernists as diverse as William James, Rudolph Otto, Huxley, and Mircea Eliade. The weakness of that approach to analyzing and interpreting mysticism is that no experience is utterly unmediated by previous discourse (spoken language, images, rituals) and therefore the mystics' claims are more a rhetorical strategy to gain a hearing than they are an accurate representation. Furthermore, since scholars of religion do not have the experiences themselves to examine, only the oral or written texts about the experiences, the adherents of "perennial philosophy" obscure the differences among diverse mysticisms in order to make them all fit the scholars' preconceptions.

Other philosophical approaches to religious experience tend to dismiss the validity of those experiences by reducing them to symptoms of a social disorder that require the intellectual's rational liberation. For example, Karl Marx's notion of religion as the opiate of the people is predicated on his belief that religious experience was simply a form of economic control and oppression (a not unreasonable proposition in the face of Christian history and colonialism). Similarly, Friedrich Nietzche considered religion an instrument for maintaining unequal power relations in a society and Sigmund Freud interpreted religious experience as a social neurosis, a projection of the super-ego and the desire for a father figure. Paul Ricoeur would later characterize these approaches as a "hermeneutics of suspicion" and in a famous formulation proposed that modern people can move from a naïve to a critical understanding of religious experience and then move toward a "second naivete" in which the believer acknowledges critical understanding alongside a symbolic reappropriation of religious language and experience. One can therefore acknowledge mystical experience as irreducible while also subjecting it to analytical critique.

The sheer diversity and seeming ubiquity of mysticism in a variety of societies and times testifies at least to family resemblances among different cultures and systems of belief, including indigenous tribal communities, Taoism, Hinduism, Buddhism, Judaism, Christianity, and Islam. The tendency in the Western world to privilege the mind as distinct from the body and the West's insistence on doctrinal formulations as essential to religious experience are frequently repudiated in mystical accounts, where the experience is as much somatic as intellectual. As a result, many Westerners living in the disenchanted world of modern technology have sought out romanticized versions of Eastern or tribal mysticism to compensate for and to remedy the dualism typical of some Judeo-Christian religious sensibilities, including apocalypticism.

Mysticism in Asian Philosophical Systems

The mysticism of Chinese Taoism, for example, embraces opposites and paradox in its famous formulation of the harmony or balance between male and female principles, yang and yin. Hinduism similarly celebrates a fundamental unity of all things in Brahman, in whom the souls (Atman) of everything are united by different paths (yoga). Perhaps the most famous mystic vision represented in a Hindu text occurs in the eleventh book of the *Bhagavad-Gita* where Krishna reveals himself to Arjuna, a vision of fullness and complexity, the divine as simultaneously wonderful and horrific. In contrast, Buddhist mysticism invites the shaman into the abyss, into nothingness and emptiness, where all illusions about time and world are revealed as illusory. Like Taoism, however, Buddhist mysticism also weds opposites and contradictions: knowing and not knowing are held to be the same.

Judeo-Christian Mysticism

In the origins of the Western tradition, Judaism's mysticism is contained in both canonical scriptures and in a tradition known as Kabbalah. Although better known for its mythic, juridical, and prophetic texts, the Hebrew scriptures also explore visionary mysticism in Ezekiel, Daniel, and the extracanonical (unofficial, nonbiblical) texts of the intertestamental period (between the last Hebrew scriptures and the first Christian scriptures). According to Scholem, prophecy and mysticism are two distinct kinds of religious discourse; prophets, whose messages are specific and timely, are not mystics, whose visions are cosmic, symbolic, and hermetic. Moreover, "mysticism as a historical phenomenon is a product of crises" (32). The Book of Ezekiel is a reflection on the crisis of the Babylonian Captivity that mixes a variety of forms including visions and oracles (chapters 32, 37, 38) that anticipate later apocalyptic texts (particularly the Book of Daniel and the Christian Book of Revelation). The nearly hallucinogenic vision in chapter 1, with its depiction of winged angelic creatures possessing human and animal faces beneath which rolls a wheeled chariot would later give rise to a form of medieval Jewish spirituality known as *merkabah* (chariot) mysticism: "Wherever the spirit would go, they went, and the wheels rose along with them; for the spirit of the living creatures was in the wheels" (Ezekiel 1:20).

The Book of Daniel, similarly a reflection on the exile to Babylon though written in the mid-second century BCE, during the crisis that prompted the Maccabean revolt, evinces a fascination with visionary mysticism. The figure of Daniel is first presented as an interpreter of the Babylonian king's dream (chapter 2) and as a conscientious resister of assimilation with the captors. The second half of the book (chapters 7–12) documents Daniel's visions, which include "one like a son of man" (chapter 7), the ram and he-goat (chapter 8), and the apocalyptic visions of the destruction and restoration of Jerusalem (chapters 9–12).

The Books of Ezekiel and Daniel would eventually feed the apocalyptic mysticism of later separatist communities in Judaism and Christianity, the Qumran community that produced the so-called Dead Sea Scrolls and the writer of the Book of Revelation who called himself John. The believers at Qumran were a priestly separatist community who gathered under the leadership of a "Teacher of Righteousness." Their *War Scroll* envisions a future combat between "Sons of Light" and "Sons of Darkness" and the scrolls include other apocalyptic writings. Likewise, the self-named John in Revelation reveals anxieties about assimilation and compromise with Hellenic culture and the Roman Empire and envisions the final battle of Armageddon. In each case, intense ecstatic visions produce complex nightmarish images of beasts, demons, angels engaged in battle narratives that lead to an ultimate struggle resulting in victory for the religiously pure. Perhaps this more than anything else distinguishes apocalyptic

---

THE MYSTICAL PROCESS AS DESCRIBED BY THE MYSTIC RICHARD OF SAINT-VICTOR (D. 1175)

In the first degree God enters the soul and it turns inwards into itself. In the second degree, it ascends above itself and is elevated to God. In the third degree, the soul that is raised on high to God is merged wholly and completely in Him. In the fourth degree, the soul passes utterly *into* God and is glorified in Him.

Source: Richard of Saint-Victor. (1207) "De Quatour Gradibus Violentae Charitatis."
Mingue, *Patrologia Latina* 1. CXCVI, col. 1207. Translated by Bruno Borchert.

---

mysticism from other forms: the visionary is convinced that humanity forms two opposing and irreconcilable camps and any calamities that the elect may experience are an inevitable component of the cosmic struggle to purify the universe, a struggle in which the elect will eventually be victorious. Rather than a vision of good and evil as illusions to be subsumed in cosmic unity, apocalyptic mysticism configures a polarized world where peace will only come when one principle eradicates the other. Subsequent visionaries, regrettably, have often led campaigns of exclusion and violence.

Because daily Judaism is a largely decentralized, local religious practice, its ability to tolerate visionary mysticism was fairly strong; similarly, early Christianity, established around household and urban churches, accommodated local and itinerant visionaries. However, once the Roman Empire's governing structures began to absorb Christians and once Christians' ecclesiastical structures modeled those of the empire, the inherent instability of visionary mysticism became less tolerable and more constrained and marginalized. The formation of the canon of Christian scriptures in what would come to be called the "New Testament" provided authoritative texts for doctrine and practice. The establishment of the four Gospels, the Acts of the Apostles, Epistles, and Revelation narrowed a crowded field of Christian documents and traditions, including Gnostic and Judaizing texts that came to define heresy. An ever more complex and powerful religious hierarchy elaborated official doctrines by means of theologians, formal pronouncements of bishops, and church councils. Adherence to doctrine (orthodoxy) would become the benchmark of religious fidelity; ecstatic visionary mysticism would become increasingly viewed with suspicion and hostility.

Perhaps as Michel Foucault has suggested about sexuality—that increasing social constraints only produces an opposite profusion of discourses—just so doctrinal scrutiny and discipline only produce a proliferation of mystics and heretics. The history of Western religiosity from the Middle Ages to the present suggests that this is the case because one reads there a chronicle of visionaries, many of whom managed to surround themselves with disciples adequate enough to constitute recognizable millennial movements. Some mystics—like St. Francis, St. Theresa of Avila, and St. John of the Cross—would survive official scrutiny and receive the official approbation of canonization. Others would have their writings burned on a pyre; many would have their own bodies similarly consumed. Among millennialist mystics and the movements that emerged from or coalesced around their visions are Isaac Ben Solomon Luria (1534–72) and Kabbalah, Jakob Böhme (1575–1624) and Theosophy, Sabbatai Zevi (1626–76) and the Jewish Sabbateans—a movement revived in the eighteen century by Jacob Frank [c. 1726–91]—George Fox (1624–91) and the Quakers (Society of Friends), Ann Lee (1736–84) and the Shakers, Ball Shem Tov (1700?–60) and the Jewish Hasidic movement (which he founded), Emanuel Swedenborg (1688–1772) and the Church of the New Jerusalem, Joseph Smith (1805–44) and Mormonism, Muhammad Ahmad (1844–85) and the modern Islamic Mahdi movement, among many others.

While to some Jewish commentators like Gershom Scholem messianism (with its orientation toward future religious fulfillment) and mysticism (with its sense of God's immediacy) are mutually exclusive, Moshe Idel argues that they are in fact related and that messianism frequently grows out of mystical experience. Originating in the Middle Ages, Kabbalah mysticism imagined union with the Godhead in an ascent of the soul to the divine and angelic celestial realm (also called merkabah mysticism after Ezekiel's vision of the chariot). The cluster of texts and teachings known as Kabbalah imagined a fragmented cosmos whom believers helped reassemble by every good deed and a divinity with an alienated feminine consort, who sought reconciliation. Combined with other hermetic or Gnostic beliefs, a neoplatonic revival in the Renaissance, and alchemical beliefs, Kabbalah continues to exercise a fascination on those seeking a less doctrinal and rationalistic experience of monotheism. Some of these beliefs would develop in eighteenth-century Masonic movements, nineteenth-century American transcendentalism, and twentieth-century New Age practices.

Islamic Mysticism

The third religious movement—Islam—constituting what is commonly called the People of the Book has also nourished visionary mystics, which is not surprising considering its originating legend. God's final messenger, Mohammed, an illiterate peasant, is said to have received the entire text of the Qur'an (which exists in Arabic in heaven) through the mediation of an angel. Not a narrative in the style of many Hebrew and Christian scriptures, the Qur'an is rather a pastiche of laws, stories, oracles, admonitions, and visions arranged thematically in sections called suras that depict a passionate God who calls people to surrender and purity of heart.

This passion is characteristic of Islamic mysticism, particularly in Sufism, the best known of whom was the poet Rumi (1207–73), although others like Ghazali (or Algazel; 1058–1111) and Farid ad-Din Attar (died ca. 1229) deserve equal attention. Like mystics in Christianity, Sufis have maintained a complicated and troubled relationship with Islamic officials because the mystic's visions often cannot be contained in the discourses of orthodoxy. Their language is sometimes frankly erotic and at other times seems closer to the teachings of Hinduism and Buddhism in their visions of cosmic unity and a radical compassion that permitted one teacher to pray for those who had assaulted him because they were keeping him on the spiritual path. Islam also maintains forms of messianic mysticism, in the endtimes person of the Mahdi (he who is divinely guided), who among Shi'ite Moslems is believed to be an Imam, a religious teacher.

Native American Mysticism

Although largely eradicated by Euro-American genocide and missionaries, Native American shamanistic practices still exist in isolated places, though most of what passes for "Native American spirituality" is a romantic-revivalist invention usually of white people. Carlos Castaneda's alleged encounters with a Yaqui shaman are typical of this genre. Perhaps the most influential example of Native American millennialist mysticism was the Ghost Dance movement of the late nineteenth century, a restoration of traditional ritual practices that produced visionary trances with an accompanying apocalyptic myth of the eventual restoration of Indian peoples and the end of white people's territorial expansion. First initiated by the Paiute mystic Wovoka (a pacifist), Ghost Dance among the Sioux ended apocalyptically in the final battle of the United States' governments war against the Indians: the Battle of Wounded Knee at which the U.S. Army killed two hundred native warriors, women, and children.

Mysticism in the Twentieth Century

For a putatively scientific post-Enlightenment age, the twentieth century has seemed particularly vexed by apocalyptic mysticism. Russian Orthodox mysticism may have made that nation particularly receptive to Marxian millennialism. Because the mystic often claims a special gift or grace not bestowed on common people and an experience that is not susceptible to external verification, totalitarianism can evoke the discourses of mysticism in order to produce the hypnotic cohesion necessary for a mass movement. Thus Adolph Hitler's success was in part the result of his appeals to a mystic, transcendental German racial identity. Other modern movements based on the claims of mystics have infamously characterized as "cults" (though the term has a neutral sense in the study of religions and it can be said of all established religions that they began as dubious sects), some of whom have demanded unquestioning obedience of their disciples, often at the expense of the disciples' and others' lives.

Nonetheless, numerous Aquarian Age or New Age movements in the late twentieth century have inculcated millennialist optimism among their adherents and their effects have been largely benign. Various forms of transcendentalism have become popular in the United States, related to the Western intuitive philosophy of Immanuel Kant, Ralph Waldo Emerson, and Margaret Fuller; the yogic practices of Hinduism, particularly Transcendental Meditation popularized by the Indian Maharishi Mahesh Yogi in the 1960s; and the Zen meditation of Buddhism. It is not surprising, therefore, that the Dalai Lama, the personification of Tibetan mysticism, has become a celebrity figure in postmodern culture.

Conclusion

Mystical experiences seem to occur among the religious in many cultures and times. Their claim to an unmediated experience of the divine may be questioned, while the experience need not be reduced to a symptom or to false consciousness. Frequently oblivious to and sometimes critical of established doctrines and hierarchies, mystics are frequently subject to persecution. Nonetheless, they or their followers frequently form significant social or religious movements around the mystical vision, movements that often possess a millennialist character.

Thomas L. Long

Bibliography

Eliade, Mircea. (1972) *Shamanism: Archaic Techniques of Ecstasy*, translated by Willard Trask. Princeton, NJ: Princeton University Press.

Huxley, Aldous. (1946) *The Perennial Philosophy*. London: Harper.

Idel, Moshe. (1998) *Messianic Mystics*. New Haven, CT: Yale University Press.

James, William. (1961) *The Varieties of Religious Experience: A Study in Human Nature*. New York: Collier.

Otto, Rudolph. (1958) *The Idea of the Holy: An Inquiry into the Non-Rational Factor in the Idea of the Divine and its Relation to the Rational*, translated by John W. Harvey. London: Oxford University Press.

Scholem, Gershom. (1996) *On the Kabbalah and Its Mysticism*, translated by Ralph Manheim, 1965; reprint with foreword by Bernard McGinn. New York: Schocken Books.

Native South America

At the time of the Spanish Conquest, South America was populated by Native Americans living in both high civilizations and as hunter-gatherers. The developed civilizations were located mostly toward the west, near to the Pacific

Ocean, and within the Andean valleys of modern Colombia. In these regions the emergence of these high cultures is dated from almost 1000 years BCE, reaching their peak with the Inca Empire. This last started its expansion in 1400 CE and lost its independence with the Spanish Conquest in 1532. The extent of the Inca expansion has no equivalent in North American history: it managed to cover what today is Peru, Ecuador, Bolivia, and parts of Chile, Colombia, and Argentina. The hunter-gatherers and horticulturists on the other hand, settled generally in the eastern slopes of the Andes and extended within the Amazonian forest up to the Atlantic Ocean. Nevertheless some also established themselves in the Argentinean plateaus, as well as in the southern valleys of Chile. In both these types of societies there are suggestions that millenarianist or messianic movements emerged even before the arrival of the Spaniards. However, it is only for the period after the Conquest that we have the most reliable information about such movements.

A view in 1999 of the ruins of the Inca city of Machu Picchu and Huayna Picchu in Peru. The city was never found by the Spanish conquerors and in the 1990s became a major symbol of Native American independence in Peru. STEPHEN G. DONALDSON

Messianic Movements Associated with Western Highlands Inca Civilization

For the Western highlands there is an abundance of evidence that suggests that messianism was a sort of an endemic religious phenomena that recurred over the centuries, arriving in the twentieth century in the form of the widely expanded myth of Inkarrí and of several social movements.

The first recorded messianic movement took place in 1564, thirty-two years after Pizarro's arrival to Peru. It is known as Taqui Onqoy which literally means "dance sickness." The area where it expanded corresponds to today's departamentos of Ayacucho and Apurímac. The leaders of this movement stated that the reason why the Spaniards had conquered the Indians was because their god had been stronger than the Peruvian divinities. As a consequence of this defeat the world had turned upside down. However, these divinities were becoming stronger. Instead of just inhabiting stones or other inert material, they were taking possession of the Indians in the middle of dances. In addition they were located near the two important religious centers of Pachacamac and Titicaca. In order to strengthen these forces so as to defeat the Spaniards, the Indians were asked by movement leaders to end their participation in Christian rituals and to return to the worship of these divinities known as "huacas." This movement ended in about 1570, after severe repression by the Spanish priests, lead by Cristóbal de Albornoz.

This movement displayed some basic elements that have characterized different expressions of millenarianism or messianism in the Andes. One is the idea of restoration of order through a cyclical view of time that conceives history as divided in a fix number of cycles, each of which ends in a cataclysm known as "Pachacuti" and which results in an inversion of the world. Another element is the assignment of the restoration of order to supernatural beings. Finally, the representation of the unity of these supernatural beings and, in general, of the Andean realm through the image of complementary spatial divisions which anthropologists call moities. In the absence of strong Inca rulers, idealized images of a divine king from in the Inca past emerged as a unifying principle of this vision of restoration. Hence, from then on most messianic literature and movements had at their centers a leader who proclaimed himself to be an Inca ruler who had the ability to expel the Spaniards and restore the Inca past as a symbol of order.

An early example of this conception can be found in *El Primer Nueva Coronica y Buen Gobierno* of the sixteenth- and seventeenth-century chronicler of Native South America, Felipe Guaman Poma de Ayala. Through an analysis of his concepts of time, space, social and political organization, one can see that instead of a chronicle this document can be seen as a "Letter to the King" with hidden a messianic content; specifically, a kind of plea to the King for the restoration of order. Ayala saw the Conquest not as an historical event but as one of those cataclysms—the Pachacuti—that occurred every 500 or 1,000 years. Only by complying with the Andean tradition could order be restored, an act that Ayala viewed as a unifying or metaphysical principle proportional to the event. He attributed this role to the King of Spain, not as a common king but as an Inca whose power could be projected to the cosmos.

The revolts of Juan Santos Atahuallpa and of José Gabriel Condorcanqui, Túpac Amaru II, are among the messianic movements that centered on the figure of an Inca in the eighteenth century. An important peculiarity of the first one is that, in a way that only can be seen among the Israelites of the New Covenant of the late twentieth century, it attracted followers from both Andean and Amazonian populations. In addition, it represents the first evidence of the incorporation of Joachim de Fiore's time scheme of the age of the Father, the Son and the Holy Ghost in the Peruvian territories. The major significance of the second movement was its role as a precursor of Peruvian independence. In the nineteenth century several revolts were stimulated by these messianic ideas: the most important revolts were those of Atusparia and of the Huancané Indians of Puno. The latter raised Juan Bustamante to the status of a messianic leader, although that was not his intention.

By the end of the twentieth century, this ongoing tradition had given place to a highly expanded myth of a hero called Inkarrí who was begotten by the Sun with a mortal shepherdess and later, once grown up, beheaded by the Spaniards. The messianic part of this myth states that the head was buried either in the Cathedral of Cuzco in Lima, or in Spain, and that from it the body is growing and once reconstituted order will reign again.

Native South America

This myth has expanded so widely that it has even been incorporated by some Amazonian Indian groups such as the Ashaninka, Machiguenga, and Amuesha; although each group has added some elements that are typical of indigenous messianism in the region. One such element which corresponds to the role given to the Inca king in the Andean tradition, is the belief in an important past ruler who was captured by white people living down river. As a consequence of this imprisonment, the whites became superior as they appropriated the manufactured goods and technology destined to the natives. However, if the ruler frees himself all that wealth will pass to the rightful owners and the relations with the whites will be inverted because then the natives will be the superior ones.

In 1963 the Ramkókamekra-Canelas Indians of the Ge group of Maranhao developed a messianic movement lead by a woman prophet called Kee-khwei. According to anthropologist William Crocker (1976: 516) she predicted that while the civilized beings would be thrown to the forest to practice hunting, the Indians would go to the cities to be in charge of the construction of roads and to pilot planes. The source of this prophecy was a revelation she received from a mythical hero known as Aukhé who spoke to her through a daughter she carried in her womb. The daughter was conceived as the hero's sister and it was explained that her coming to this world was due to the fact that her brother was tired of the ill-treatment of the Indians by whites. To bring this prophecy to fruition, which would occur at the moment of birth, certain ritual practices consisting mostly of dances were to be performed. The more intense the dance and the greater the offerings, the more wealth people would receive in the new world. On the other hand, those not performing the dance nor contributing material wealth to the movement would result in severe punishments from a group of youngsters who served the prophet. In addition, followers were free to take cattle from anyone else, because it was said that the cattle belonged to Aukhé. Repression by whites was not an issue because it people were told that the mythical hero would divert bullets and that a great fire would annihilate the aggressors.

Other Ge groups such as the Timbira and the Bororo also participated in messianic movements also centered on the figure of the same Aukhé or some similar mythical hero. In these societies, the hero is always associated with water and with the return or donation of white wealth because of the harsh treatment received by the natives. It is interesting to note that, whereas Andeans tend to reject Western culture, among these Amazonian groups the emphasis is very similar to the Melanesian cargo cults where people strive to obtain the outsider's wealth.

Another feature of the messianism of these kind of lowland groups is the search for a land without evil which is related to the migratory movements of the Guaraní even before the arrival of the Europeans. Shamans who predicted the nearness of the end of the world led these migrations, seeking to arrive at the land without evil as the only source of salvation.

In the traditional mythology of the Guaraní Indians, this place was the home of the creator god Ñanderuvusú and of his wife Ñandesy. It was said that here plants grew without any aid and that fruit was plentiful. Its location was assumed to be at the center of the earth at a particular point towards the east. Only the souls of children, after sorting out some dangers, could arrive there. The creator, along with having the power to create the world, could also destroy it by ordering his son Ñanderikey to remove the east-west beam that sustained the center of the world to allow it to collapse. The collapse could be prevented, however, if people would dance as the mythical shaman Guyropoty had done and migrate toward the east searching the land without evil. The earliest report about this search derives from 1549 when in Chachapoyas (Peru) three hundred Indians identified as Tupinamba who had arrived at the coast searching for a land where they would find the eternal rest were captured. And

The Santo Domingo Cathedral with a curved Inca stone wall foundation in Cuzco, Peru. The alignment of the structures symbolizes the white dominance of Native South American peoples which millennial movements seek to reverse. STEPHEN G. DONALDSON

three years later, inn 1562, an estimated three thousand Indians from Bahia, Brazil were found following two shamans on a similar search. Such migrations have continued now and again into the twentieth century.

Conclusion

While millenarian and messianic movements among the indigenous peoples of South America have not been studied as fully as those among indigenous North Americans and Melanesians, the record shows that such movements existed before the arrival of the Spanish colonists and then intensified as form of political protest and cultural revitalization after the Conquest. Such movements have continued to appear over the past five hundred with foci in the Peruvian Andes and the Amazonian lowlands, with the Israelites of the New Covenant being one of the most recent and most widespread.

Juan M. Ossio

See also Cargo Cults, Ghost Dance, Israelites of the New Universal Covenant, Messianism

Bibliography

Burridge, Kenelm. (1995) *Mambu. A Melanesian Millenium.* Princeton, NJ: Princeton University Press.

Crocker, William. (1976) "O Movimiento Messianico dos Canelas: Uma Introducao, en Schaden, E." In *Leturas de Etnologia Brasileira.* Sao Paula: Companhia Editora Nacional, 515–27.

Jarvie, I. C. (1970) *The Revolution in Anthropology.* New York: Routledge and Kegan Paul.

Lawrence, Peter. (1971) *Road Belong Cargo.* Manchester, U.K.: Manchester University Press.

Melatti, J. C. (1972) *O Messianismo Krahó.* Sao Paulo: editora Herder.

Métraux, A. (1973) *Religión y Magias Indígenas de América del Sur.* Madrid: Aguilar.

Mooney, James. (1973) *The Ghost-Dance Religion and Wounded Knee.* New York: Dover.

Nimuendajú, Curt. (1978) *Los mitos de creación y de destrucción del mundo,* edited by J. Riester. Lima: CAAP.

Ossio, Juan M. (1973) *Ideología Mesiánica del Mundo Andino,* edited by Ignacio Prado. Lima: Pastor.

Pereira de Queiroz, Maria Isaura. (1969) *Historia y Etnologia de los movimentos Mesianicos.* Mexico D.F.: Siglo XXI.

Worsley, Peter. (1970) *The Trumpet Shall Sound.* Boulder, CO: Paladin.

Nativist Millennial Movements

A nativist millennial movement consists of people who feel under attack by a foreign colonizing government that is destroying their traditional way of life and is removing them from their land. Nativists long for a return to an idealized past golden age. Numerous nativists have identified themselves with the oppressions and deliverance of the Israelites as described in the Christian Old Testament. Nativist millennial movements have often been termed "revitalization movements."

Nativist millennialism can take the form of either catastrophic millennialism or progressive millennialism. Catastrophic nativist millennialists may either await divine intervention to remove their oppressors and establish the millennial kingdom, or they may become revolutionaries who fight to eliminate their oppressors.

Just a few examples of nativist millennial movements include the Xhosa Cattle-Killing movement in South Africa, the Israelites who were massacred by police at Bulhoek, South Africa, the Native American Ghost Dance movement which was related to the massacre of a Lakota Sioux band at Wounded Knee by American soldiers, and the Taiping revolutionaries in China. Additionally, the German Nazis and American Neo-Nazis can be considered nativist millennialists. The Freemen who engaged in a standoff with FBI agents in Montana in 1996 are part of a diffuse Euro-American nativist millennial movement, which includes Neo-Nazis, Identity Christians (believers in a racist and anti-Semitic religion called Christian Identity), Odinists, and other racist and anti-Semitic white Americans, who feel threatened by increasing diversity in the United States. These white Americans feel oppressed by the unresponsive bureaucracies of the federal government such as the Internal Revenue Service and agencies originally designed to serve farmers. In rural America, particularly, numerous families and individuals have lost their farms and businesses related to agriculture. They see their traditional way of life disappearing due to pressure from federal agencies and multinational corporations. White Americans are certainly not the original natives, but those who participate in this Euro-American nativist movement regard themselves as the natives of this land. In Christian Identity, this is expressed in the conviction that whites are the true Israelites given the promised land of America by Yahweh.

Nativist millennial movements often involve the utilization of magic and sacrifice as methods to help accomplish the millennial kingdom. Magic is the use of words of power and rituals that are believed to cause changes in the physical world. Sacrifices are offerings to propitiate powerful unseen beings.

The Freemen's "Common Law" legal interpretations used to wage "paper warfare" against the federal government is an example of imitative magic. The Freemen seek to steal the power contained in the words and documents of attorneys and bankers for their own benefit. The spectacular pageants staged by Hitler and the Nazis can be seen as magic rituals to accomplish the millennial kingdom, the Third Reich. The Native American Ghost Dance and the Xhosa Cattle-Killing can be seen as sacrifices to the ancestors to eliminate the oppressors and to bring protection and well-being.

Because of their challenge to civil authority, it is not uncommon for nativist millennial movements to become involved in violence. The Lakota Sioux at Wounded Knee and the Israelites at Bulhoek, South Africa, are examples of nativist millennial groups that are assaulted by law enforcement agents, because they are viewed as being dangerous. The Xhosa in South Africa are an example of a nativist millennial movement that committed violence because of that culture's fragility due to internal stresses and oppression from outsiders. The Taiping movement in China, the German Nazis, and the Montana Freemen and others in the contemporary Euro-American nativist movement are examples of nativists who are revolutionary. The Taipings and the German Nazis succeeded in becoming culturally dominant for a time, and thus caused massive revolutionary violence. The contemporary Euro-American nativist movement is diffuse and widespread, but it is attractive only to a minority of white Americans. The violent individuals in this movement commit acts of terrorism, but so far have been unable to spark a full-scale revolution.

Catherine Wessinger

See also Asia, Assaulted Millennial Groups, Catastrophic Millennialism, Fragile Millennial Groups, Ghost Dance, Nazism, Progressive Millennialism, Revolutionary Millennial Movements

Bibliography

Adas, Michael. (1979) *Prophets of Rebellion: Millenarian Protest Movements against the European Colonial Order.* Chapel Hill, NC: University of North Carolina Press.

Wallace, Anthony F. C. (1956) "Revitalization Movements." *American Anthropologist* 58, 2 (April): 264–81.

Wessinger, Catherine. (2000) *How the Millennium Comes Violently.* Chappaqua, NY: Seven Bridges Press.

——, ed. (2000) *Millennialism, Persecution, and Violence: Historical Cases.* Syracuse, NY: Syracuse University Press.

Nazism

The term "Nazism" is an acronym derived from Nationalsozialistische Deutsche Arbeiterpartei (National Socialist German Worker's Party). Nazism, or National Socialism, can be used to describe the *Weltanschauung* (worldview) that shaped the formation, development, and goals of the National Socialist movement. That this worldview was thoroughly millennial, messianic, and apocalyptic is perhaps the most significant, and least acknowledged, aspect of this, the darkest period of twentieth-century history. While the pseudoreligious trappings of Nazi thought and ritual have been noted over the years, only two works have argued for the centrality of the millennial and apocalyptic. However, it is becoming increasingly clear that millennialism was the primary conceptual basis of Nazism. This is especially significant since Nazism represents one of the few times in history that a millennial movement actually succeeded in gaining political power and almost realized its utopian and, ultimately, dystopian visions.

Apocalyptic Fear and Millennial Hope: The Conceptual Origins of Nazism

Nazism as a millennial movement was rooted in a mix of apocalyptic fears and millennial hopes. Its conceptual basis, however, can be found in the *völkisch* movement ("racialist" movement—derived from the word *Volk*, which means folk, yet signifying a sense of race, people, and/or nation). Originating in the German romantic movement of the nineteenth century, *völkisch* thought combined ultranationalism, mysticism, messianism, millennialism and, linking it altogether, a racialism centered on anti-Semitism. *Völkisch* thinkers argued that all racial Germans (Aryans) should be united in one organic nation, the Third Reich (what Arthur Moeller van den Bruck referred to as the *Endreich*, the "final empire" (1931). It was believed, however, that the coming Third Reich, which the Nazis later referred to as the *tausendjähriges Reich* (millennial Reich), could only be achieved if racial degeneration was halted. Adapting the ideas of Social Darwinism, *völkisch* thinkers believed that interbreeding between superior and inferior races over the centuries had increasingly contaminated God's chosen race, the Aryans, rendering them impure and threatened with racial extinction—a biological apocalypse (termed *Völkerchaos* or racial chaos). Some *völkisch* thinkers preached that Germany was heading for a racial apocalypse unless a *Führer* (literally "leader," but with a strong messianic quality) arose to save the people. The key to racial salvation would come with the solving of the so-called Jewish problem or Jewish question, since *völkisch* thinkers believed the Jews to be the primary agents of "decomposition." Following these principles, the Nazis would attempt to create the millennial Reich by cleansing or purifying the racial body via such measures as the Nuremberg Laws, the eugenics program, and, ultimately, the Final Solution.

A branch of the *völkisch* thinking that was especially important in the conceptualization of Nazi millennialism was ariosophy (wisdom of the Aryans), promoted by the German occultists Guido von List and Jörg Lanz von Liebenfels. List argued that the Aryans had once been god-men on earth, but had racially degenerated over the years. He preached, however, that a millennium was dawning, and that godlike Aryans were about to be reborn. Lanz von Liebenfels combined List's Aryan mysticism with racial Social Darwinism. In the pages of his journal *Ostara*, of which Hitler as a young man was an avid reader, world history was presented as a struggle of the fittest between godlike Aryans and beastly apemen. Moreover, Lanz von Liebenfels argued that the Aryan race, the divinely chosen race, was locked in a perpetual battle with the Jews, the force of chaos and evil. He prophesied that a millennium was imminent that could, if the apocalypse was avoided, usher in a unique spiritual epoch, one in which psychically gifted Aryans would create a New Age. This New Age would be characterized by Aryan supremacy over the ape-men (what the Nazis would later call subhumans), who would be enslaved or exterminated. An ariosophical secret society, the *Germanenorden* (Germanic order), founded a group called the Thule Society to begin the political process necessary to create the Aryan millennium. From the Thule Society the *Deutsche Arbeiterpartei* (German worker's party) was established to attract workers to what had been a largely middle- and upper-class movement. It was this group that was transformed by Hitler into the National Socialist German Worker's Party.

Weimar Apocalypse

The appearance of rapid and radical change in a society is the primary catalyst for the generation of mass millenarian movements. While *völkisch* millennialism provided Hitler and his inner circle with its conceptual core, for Nazism to become a mass millennial movement society at large needed to reflect the apocalyptic scenario preached by the *völkisch* prophets. The postwar chaos of Weimar Germany (1919–33) seemed to provide exactly that apocalypse. For many Germans, the Weimar Republic, especially in its crucial formative years, was all but defined by severe political, economic, social, and cultural change: assassinations, street-fighting between communist Spartacists and right-wing *Freikorps* (volunteer paramilitary units), foreign occupation and loss of territories, long-term unemployment, hyperinflation, and an explosion of "depraved" modernist art and "immoral" cabaret licentiousness. For the Nazis, Weimar seemed more Sodom and Gomorrah then the Aryan New Jerusalem they so desired.

This political and social fragmentation led some Germans to interpret the chaos using the archetypal myths of an approaching apocalypse. One Nazi, looking back at Weimar, conceptualized the time using millennial symbols of light and darkness, social inversion, apocalyptic chaos, and, for the Nazis, a typical scapegoating of the Jews:

> Barely 18 years-old, I went to the field to defend our homeland against a world of instigating enemies. Twice I was wounded. Then in November 1918 the Marxist revolution broke out—dark thunderclouds descended over Germany that for fifteen years allowed no rays of light and no sunshine upon the earth. In Germany everything went upside down. The Spartacists, clothed in sailor's uniforms, devastated and destroyed everything they could lay a finger on. The Jew rose to the pinnacle. (Abel Collection, no. 35, 1.)

Annihilation or Salvation?

Believing themselves perched on an abyss and threatened with annihilation, the Nazis preached that Germany, indeed humanity, had reached a turning point of historical importance. The trauma of this turning point, the Weimar apocalypse, was portrayed as the birth pains of something new in the becoming. From the decay of the old order, a new order was about to be reborn. The Nazi belief in rebirth and renewal, so typical of millennial movements, included a sense that they had been chosen, not only to witness, but to

ADOLF HITLER: *VÖLKISCH PROPHET*

Human culture and civilization on this continent are inseparably bound up with the presence of the Aryan. If he dies out or declines, the dark veils of an age without culture will again descend on this globe.

The undermining of the existence of human culture by the destruction of its bearer seems in the eyes of a volkish philosophy the most execrable crime. Anyone who dares to lay hands on the highest image of the Lord commits sacrilege against the benevolent creator of this miracle and contributes to the expulsion from paradise.

And so the volkish philosophy of life corresponds to the innermost will of Nature, since it restores that free play of forces which must lead to a continuous mutual higher breeding, until at last the best of humanity, having achieved possession of this earth, will have a free path for activity in domains which will lie partly above it and partly outside it.

We all sense that in the distant future humanity must be faced by problems which only a highest race, become master people and supported by the means and possibilities of an entire globe, will be equipped to overcome.

Source: Hitler, Adolf. (1925) *Mein Kampf*. Boston: Houghton Mifflin, 383–84.

facilitate the dawn of a New Age. This "New Order" or "New Age" was the long-hoped-for Third Reich, the millennial empire of peace and prosperity.

The acceptance of Nazism as a millennial faith was experienced by many followers as a conversion experience. Disoriented by the rapid change and chaos of the Weimar period, many future Nazis felt lost and hopeless. After attending a Nazi gathering and listening to their speeches, reading Nazi literature, or listening to a Nazi proselytizer at work or at their home, many individuals reported experiencing a profound spiritual transformation. They felt themselves move from darkness to light, from confusion to clarity. Hitler's simplification of the complexities of modern life, a simplification rooted in the symbolism of millennial, messianic, and apocalyptic imagery and rhetoric, reordered their collapsed perception of reality. As one Old Nazi described his experience:

> through National Socialist propaganda I became aware of the movement and visited several gatherings. Without at first being clear about its goals, I felt instinctively the spiritual transformation that [occurred] inside me [through] the liberating idea. . . . Later I read the Führer's book, then heard him in person and . . . believed. (Abel Collection, no. 163, 6)

The Nazi millennial worldview explained that Weimar chaos resulted from a conspiracy of dark occult forces (variously attributed to Jesuits, Freemasons, and especially the imaginary International Jew). The chaos, therefore, was not meaningless (and thus impossible to order), but the deliberate and nefarious action of group of conspirators, led by one race. The Nazis not only claimed to have discovered the cause of the apocalypse, but perhaps more importantly, they provided a road to salvation by offering to finally end the conspiracy by removing its alleged causal agent, the Jew. Moreover, the Nazi belief that they were living at a time of world historical importance, and further, the conviction that they had been specially chosen to fulfill a mission to ensure the coming of the millennial Reich, replaced their preconversion sense of being lost and hopeless with a heightened sense of self-esteem and status, as well as providing meaning, direction, and purpose.

Hitler as Prophet and Messiah

Hitler's role in the formation, development, and direction of the Nazi movement cannot be underestimated. He both presented himself as, and truly believed that he was, a prophet and a messiah. As early as his prewar days in Vienna, Hitler envisaged himself as a redeemer. After a performance of Wagner's *Rienzi*, Hitler is reported to have had a mystical revelatory experience, one in which he saw himself one day called to save Germany. A few years later, just as Hitler was coming out of a mustard gas-induced blindness, he heard the news that Germany had lost the war. Lapsing back into blindness, he is reported to have had another messianic vision. After a few years vacillating between the role of prophet and messiah, Hitler became convinced that he was indeed chosen for a higher mission of salvational potential. His numerous seemingly miraculous escapes from death (as a runner in the war, after a car crash, following assassination attempts) convinced Hitler that Providence had indeed chosen and protected him for a higher mission. He was elected to save Germany, indeed the civilized world, by reunifying the Aryan race and by finally solving the so-called Jewish-problem.

Hitler's messianic self-perception was not unique. The chaos of early Weimar saw the appearance of a number of would-be messiahs, but most were similar to New Age gurus, "barefoot prophets," as one scholar called them (Linse 1983), with little potential for mass appeal. Only Hitler combined an appropriately contemporary expression of archetypal millennial symbolism (his racial salvationism and prophecy of a Jewish-Bolshevik apocalypse) with an extraordinary speaking ability that enabled him to convey that message, thereby combining the roles of endtime prophet and eschatological savior. Hitler's uncanny ability to give voice to the apocalyptic fears and millennial hopes of the masses also allowed Hitler to have his messianic self-image legitimated by those masses, there by linking leader and led, messiah and disciples.

The Millennial Reich

The collapse of the U.S. stock market was felt around the world, perhaps nowhere more than Germany. Unemployment was particularly harsh, rising from 8.5 to 29.9 percent by 1932. Extreme times such as this tend to lead people to look for extreme solutions. Not surprisingly then the two most extreme parties, the Nazis on the right and the communists on the left, gained the most votes in the elections of the depression years. Nazi election posters presented Hitler as the only savior from chaos, the only one who could bring "work and bread," and "peace and prosperity." After losing his bid for the presidency to Hindenberg but seeing his party win the most votes (though nowhere near a majority), Hitler was eventually offered the chancellorship of Germany. Utilizing a series of legal and extralegal measures, Hitler and the Nazis quickly assumed total control of Germany.

For many Old Guard Nazis, Hitler's assumption of the chancellorship on 1 January 1933 signified the dawn of a New Age, the beginning of the millennial Reich. To create the millennial Reich of peace, prosperity, and power, the Nazis proceeded to coordinate German society, banning opposition parties and eventually "unifying" clubs and associations under the Nazi banner. While it is easy to recognize the dangers of such a totalitarian state, for many Germans it represented the unity of purpose and togetherness that they desired, a unity that embodied the longing for community so typical of millennial movements throughout history. This unified community, however, was based on racial exclusivity, as the Nazis strove to create a *Volksgenossen* (community of racially similar people). The Nuremberg Laws of 1935, banning marriages between races and excluding non-Aryans, especially Jews, from citizenship, were combined with a eugenics program which included mass sterilization and euthanasia of impure elements of society. This type of "cleansing" or "purification" of society in an attempt to regenerate and renew it is typical of some millennial movements. It occurs when the elect (the pure) attempt to create the millennial utopia, the perfect future world, by physically exterminating the impure.

Final Battle and Final Solution

For Hitler and his closest disciples the millennial Reich could not be achieved simply by banning the communist party and eliminating the influence of Jews from German society. Hitler throughout his political career prophesied that an imminent war of annihilation between Aryans and Jews (more precisely, Jewish-Bolsheviks) was in the offering. The aforementioned historical turning point meant for Hitler that the *Endkampf* (final battle) between Aryans and Jews was imminent. The *Endlösung* (final solution), the plan to systematically exterminate the Jews, was begun in earnest at the same time as the invasion of Russia in 1940, since the war against the Bolsheviks and the war against the Jews was conceptualized as being the same final conflict, an apocalyptic war for existence and world salvation. Forty million people died, including six million innocent Jews. Nazi fear of annihilation and desire for a millennial Reich, the Final Reich, became an induced apocalypse heretofore unheard of in world history.

The Continuing Legacy

The chaos of postwar Weimar Germany, when order seemed to collapse into disorder, proved too difficult for many Germans to comprehend. The Nazi millennial worldview, the belief that a Third and final Reich was about to arise, that Germans were chosen by higher powers to fulfill a holy mission to not only create this millennial empire, but to finally defeat the eternal enemy, the Jew, became a myth turned horrible reality. The Nazi legacy is still with us. While Hitler understandably has become a symbol of pure evil (perhaps not ironically the very same Satan on earth that he believed he was sent to destroy), for some groups Hitler is presented as a heroic savior turned martyr. Millennial fantasies of Jewish world conspiracies, often still encased in apocalyptic rhetoric, continue to appear in neo-Nazi, militia, and some fundamentalism sects. Hitler's transformation of traditional millennial symbolism into a modern racial salvationism did not die in the bunker with him.

Perhaps the most important lesson to learn from Nazism is that the intersection of millennial, messianic, and apocalyptic thinking can lead to mass violence of unspeakable ends if the "chosen" believe they are fulfilling a divinely sanctioned mission to realize the millennium by cleansing the world of the impure. If such a movement succeeds in attaining power, or obtaining weapons of mass destruction, the results can transform a millennial myth into a reality of truly apocalyptic proportions.

David Redles

See also Christian Identity, Conversion, Holocaust

Bibliography

Becker, Peter Emil. (1990) *Sozialdarwinismus, Rassismus, Antisemitismus und völkischer Gedanke.* Stuttgart: Georg Thieme.

Die alte Garte sprichts, 4 vols. Third Reich Collection. Library of Congress, Washington, D.C.

Gamm, Hans-Jochen. (1962) *Der braune Kult: Das Dritte Reich und seine Ersatzreligion.* Hamburg: Rütten & Loening.

Goldstein, Jeffrey A. (1979) "On Racism and Anti-Semitism in Occultism and Nazism." *Yad Vashem Studies* 13: 53–72.

Goodrick-Clarke, Nicholas. (1992) *The Occult Roots of Nazism: Secret Aryan Cults and Their Influence on Nazi Ideology. The Ariosophists of Austria and Germany, 1890–1935.* New York: New York University Press.

Hammer, Wolfgang. (1979) *Adolf Hitler—ein Deutscher Messias?* Munich: Delp.

Heer, Friedrich. (1968) *Der Glaube des Adolf Hitler: Anatomie einen Politischen Religiosität.* Munich: Bechtle.

Hermand, Jost. (1992) *Old Dreams of a New Reich: Völkisch Utopias and National Socialism,* translated by Paul Levesque. Bloomington, IN: Indiana University Press.

Hitler, Adolf. (1925) *Adolf Hitlers Reden,* edited by Ernst Boepple. Munich: Deutscher Volksverlag.

———. (1943) *Mein Kampf,* translated by Ralph Manheim. Boston: Houghton Mifflin.

Linse, Ulrich. (1983) *Barfüßige Propheten: Erlöser der zwanziger Jahre.* Berlin: Wolf Jobst Siedler.

Mosse, George. (1964) *The Crisis of German Ideology: Intellectual Origins of the Third Reich.* New York: Grosset & Dunlap.

———. "The Mystical Origins of National Socialism." *Journal of the History of Ideas* 22: 81–96.

Redles, David. (2000) *Hitler and the Apocalypse Complex: Salvation and the Spiritual Power of Nazism.* New York: New York University Press.

Rhodes, James M. (1980) *The Hitler Movement: A Modern Millenarian Revolution.* Stanford: Hoover Institute Press.

Spielvogel, Jackson, and David Redles. (1986) "Hitler's Racial Ideology: Content and Occult Sources." *Simon Wiesenthal Center Annual* 3: 227–46.

Stackelberg, Roderick. (1981) *Idealism Debased: From Völkisch Ideology to National Socialism.* Kent, OH: Kent State University Press.

Stern, Fritz. (1961) *The Politics of Cultural Despair: A Study in the Rise of the Germanic Ideology.* Berkeley, CA: University of California Press.

Tal, Uriel. (1980) "Nazism as a Political Faith." *The Jerusalem Quarterly* 15: 71–90.

Theodore Abel Collection. Hoover Institute on War, Revolution, and Peace. Stanford, CA.

Tyrell, Albrecht. (1975) *Vom 'Trommler' zum 'Führer': Der Wandel von Hitlers Selbstverständnis zwischen 1919 und 1924 und die Entwicklung der NSDAP.* Munich: Fink.

Vondung, Klaus. (1971) *Magie und Manipulation: Ideologischer Kult und politische Religion des Nationalsozialismus.* Göttingen: Vandenhoeck & Ruprecht.

———. (1988) *Die Apokalypse in Deutschland.* Munich: Deutscher Taschenbuch Verlag.

Wistrich, Robert. (1985) *Hitler's Apocalypse: Jews and the Nazi Legacy.* New York: St. Martin's Press.

New Age

During the 1970 and 1980s, the Western world was barraged with predictions of a coming New Age of peace and light destined to arrive early in the twenty-first century. This New Age movement, as it came to be called, was initially directed at the followers of the Western esoteric tradition, those individuals who followed occult and metaphysical spiritual teachings as exemplified in Theosophy and New Thought. As the movement found a response, those older occult and metaphysical organizations grew most accepting of it, and many new ones formed. Then, during the early 1990s, enthusiasm for a coming New Age waned and by the end of the decade all but disappeared, though it left a strengthened and revitalized occult/metaphysical community as its legacy.

Origins

During the nineteenth century, the occult community that had been decimated by the combined forces of Protestantism and the Enlightenment, experienced a revival as new leadership attempted to reconcile magical thinking with the emerging scientific world. At the end of the eighteenth century, Austrian physician Franz Anton Mesmer (1733–1815) explored the force he believed caused spiritual healing and called "magnetism," and the magnetic healing movement he fostered spread throughout the West. Former priest Eliphas Levi (1810–75), building upon Mesmer, found in the cosmic magnetic energy the agent for the working of magic. His writings would become the fountainhead of a revival of ritual magic in Europe. In the mid-twentieth century, magic would find its popular expression in neopagan wicca or witchcraft. The actual practice of magic arose concurrently with a renewed interest in astrology, tarot cards, and other divinatory practices. As a divinatory practice, astrology led the way, and by the 1970s more than 20 percent of the population of North America and Europe professed belief in it.

In the United States, where the magnetism movement had enjoyed great success, interest in the associated phenomena of magnetic sleep (later to be called hypnotism) would give way to the quest for contact and communication with the spirits of the recently deceased. Beginning in upstate New York in 1848, spiritualism spread first across America and then to England and France where it enjoyed its greatest success. By the end of the century, spirits speaking though spiritualist mediums, individuals who were seen as especially capable of contacting the spirit world, were heard in all the major cities of Europe.

In the years following the American Civil War, the continued interest in magnetic healing and other forms of alternative healing practices, supplied a context in which Mary Baker Eddy discovered a new form of healing. Her work began in the realization of the Allness of God, that God was the sole reality; and that all illness was an illusion of limited minds and their erroneous perception of the visible world. Eddy's mystical approach to the world led to the founding of the Christian Science movement in the 1870s. A decade later one of her students, Emma Curtis Hopkins, launched the New Thought movement, the most important of several Christian Science offshoots, today represented in the Unity School of Christianity, the International Divine Science Federation, and the Religious Science/Science of Mind churches.

Esoteric and occult groups (those that explored and attempted to use the occult or hidden realities believed to under gird the universe) lived in a timeless universe of eternal realities. History was largely a secondary matter, a means of tracking the events in the mundane world from which they were trying to escape. However, toward the end of twentieth century, an attempt to ascribe some importance to the mundane world began with Madame Helena Petrova Blavatsky (1831–91), one of the three cofounders of the Theosophical Society. She laid the groundwork for New Age thinking by her suggestion that the real goals of the society were to cooperate with the evolution of the race and to prepare for the coming of one of the Masters of the Great White Brotherhood (the secret leaders who actually guided the destiny of the planet). Lord Maitreya's coming was an important event in human history; it would initiate a new cycle for humanity.

Blavatsky never fully developed her understanding of Lord Maitreya but her concerns were taken up by her successor, Annie Besant (1847–1933), and Besant's colleague, Charles Webster Leadbeater (1854–1934). Both believed strongly in the Theosophical mission, and Leadbeater convinced Besant that he had found the vehicle for the coming Maitreya in the person of a young boy, Jeddu Krishnamurti (1895–1986) whom Leadbeater had met on the beach at Madras, India, the site of the Theosophical Society's international headquarters. Besant took charge of the boy, saw to his education, and groomed him as the Coming World Savior. Through the 1920s, she promoted him and accompanied him on world tours.

With some reluctance, Krishnamurti followed his destined role and the Society enjoyed its greatest success. However, in 1929, with little warning, he suddenly renounced his messianic role, and leaving Besant and the Society, began to teach independently. Krishnamurti's departure ended the first wave of millennial fervor within Theosophy, but throughout the century new hopes would find expression. The most substantive of these came from Alice A. Bailey (1880–1949).

Bailey had been a member of the Theosophical Society when in 1919 she began to channel messages from one of the ascended masters of the Great White Brotherhood, Djwhal Khul, usually called The Tibetan. Society leaders disapproved of her channeling activity (i.e., mediumship) and in 1923, she left. With her husband Foster, Bailey created the Arcane School. Shortly before her death, Bailey began to call her students' attention to *The Reappearance of the Christ* (1948) that she believed would occur during the last years of the twentieth century. After Bailey died, her followers split into a number of independent organizations that together were generally referred to as the "Light" groups, their business being the channeling of spiritual light into the world for its uplift, healing, and preparation for the coming World Savior. It would be among these Light groups that the New Age vision would be initially articulated.

The Emergence of the New Age

By the 1960s, some members in the Light groups in Great Britain began to express a hope of a coming New Age. They saw the transformation resulting from their establishment of an international network of similar Light groups and the subsequent influx of spiritual energy they would bring to the planet. Prominent among these groups were the Universal

Foundation in London and the Findhorn Foundation located near Inverness, Scotland. In the late 1960s, Anthony Brooke, the head of the Universal Foundation, began to tour the world promoting the formation of other Light groups. Groups formed not only across North America and Europe, but also in such faraway places as Australia and South Africa. Newsletters and directories tied the many diverse Light groups together.

In the mid 1970s, David Spangler, who had spent three years as codirector of the Findhorn Foundation, emerged as the most articulate spokesperson for the emerging New Age movement. Beginning with his 1976 book, *Revelation: The Birth of a New Age*, he provided the most comprehensive statement of the ideas guiding the movement. Spangler suggested that in this generation, humanity had a unique opportunity to bring about a New Age of peace and light that would sweep away the major problems of the mundane world (war, poverty, racial conflict, etc.)

The first step in the New Age would be the transformation of individuals. A variety of metaphors were utilized to describe that change, the dominant one being healing. Through the use of various transformative/healing tools (from meditation to astrology to various alternative therapies), individuals could be healed of any defects and shortcomings. Such healing could begin in a more or less dramatic fashion, but was believed to be a lifelong process that included the development within people of an elevated state of spiritual awareness, often referred to as self-realization or as Christ-consciousness.

The transformation of individuals in sufficient numbers would lead to the larger goal, the transformation of society, the real New Age from which the movement derived its name. If, suggested Spangler, enough individuals began to share the light they had received, thus uniting their action with others, within a generation the entire planet would be transformed. The New Age would arrive.

For Spangler, the possibility of a New Age rested upon two factors. First, as the twentieth century was drawing to a close, the heavenly bodies were realigning themselves in such a way as to release a new wave of cosmic energy. That energy was the power for fueling the New Age. Ultimately, the idea of the New Age was a variation of the coming Aquarian Age, a new age many astrologers had predicted as occurring about this time as the earth processed around the zodiac. Significant points in that process, the beginning of a new astrological age, occur approximately every 2,000 years. Second, and most important, was the cooperation of people. The New Age would not just happen. It required the effort of large numbers of people in channeling the cosmic energies. If people cooperated, the New Age would occur. If they failed, the opportunity would be lost.

The New Age in the 1980s

The New Age movement reached its zenith in the 1980s. During the decade, worldwide, hundreds of thousands of people, adherents of the Western esoteric tradition, adopted the New Age perspective, and hundreds of thousands of others were swept into their ranks. Bookstores appeared in every major urban area specializing in New Age books and supplies. Extensive New Age networks were established to link the largely decentralized movement and large New Age expositions were organized at which the various elements of the movement could commingle.

Those involved in the New Age continued to practice the older occult arts but such practices were remolded by the New Age vision. For example, older divinatory practices such as astrology and the tarot were recast as transformative tools. They were removed from an older deterministic worldview in which they were assigned predictive value and now utilized as instruments of self-revelation. New Agers saw horoscopes not so much as laying out the future as describing the dominant forces operating upon an individual at any given moment. That knowledge allowed the individual to make the most auspicious choices about life questions.

Among the most prominent New Age tools were crystals. Long used in various occult rituals, crystals had been mentioned in the channeled readings of seer Edgar Cayce (1877–1945) who touted their role in the powering of the ancient continent of Atlantis. Drawing inspiration from Cayce, Frank Alper, of the Arizona Metaphysical Center, channeled material suggesting that crystals had great potential for their ability to store and release energy. From his work, enthusiastic New Agers began to wear crystals believed to have particular properties and use crystals in their meditative practices.

No practice was so identified with the New Age movement as channeling. It was through the practice of channeling from various spiritual entities (as times seen as God, the Ascended Masters, spirits, extraterrestrial beings, the higher self) that the New Age vision was initially projected and later elaborated. The spiritual beings who spoke through the channels provided the ultimate authority to whom the movement's leaders could look for guidance. In addition, channels operated as somewhat traditional mediums from whom individuals could receive advice about their own path of transformation.

The New Age movement called for the transformation of its individual adherents and then urged them to work toward global transformation. Thus the movement's millennial hopes were structured into a broad reformist movement from which much was expected. However, within the movement there were several significant divergent ideas. For example,

Ruth Montgomery, a prominent New Age writer who herself became a channel, was one of several leaders in the movement who believed that the New Age could not come about without a dramatic destruction of the old world. Thus she predicted that in 1999 the Earth would undergo a massive pole shift that would destroy civilization as we know it. The Golden Age will be created in the next century by the survivors.

The earlier messianic strain in Theosophical thought was continued by Benjamin Crème (b. 1922), a student of the Bailey writings. In the late 1970s Crème, who had been channeling messages from Maitreya through the decade, announced the imminent appearance of the Lord of the New Age. When Maitreya failed to come forth in 1982 as predicted, Creme was dismissed by most New Agers. He ascribed the delay in Maitreya's appearance to the atmosphere of skepticism, and has continued to work with the small number of people who accepted his channeled messages.

Finally, as the movement grew through the 1970s, sources other than astrological ones were sought by which the growing but still relatively small movement could accomplish its monumental task of global transformation. The most popular alternative suggestion came from writer Lyall Watson who recounted a story of primatologists observing monkeys on several islands near Japan. Reportedly, they observed a monkey washing her food and teaching another to do likewise. The lesson was passed on slowly one-by-one, but then suddenly, a critical mass was reached. After a certain number of monkeys, hypothetically stated as being 100, suddenly without observing the washing, all the monkeys on the several islands took up the practice. Thus was born the myth of the hundredth monkey, the belief that as more and more people adopted the vision of the New Age, at some point in the near future, New Age consciousness would suddenly flow through the race bringing about the desired social transformation.

The End of the New Age

Symbolically, the New Age is often seen as peaking in the airing in the fall of 1987 of the television miniseries of actress Shirley Maclaine's autobiographical *Out on a Limb* that described her transformation as she awoke to a variety of spiritual realities. In the meantime, however, the movement was undergoing a significant critique from both the press and scholarly critics of its scientific claims of paranormal activity. While the movement was generally dismissed as superficial spirituality, the most telling critiques were directed at crystals and channeling.

Scientists were particularly vocal in denouncing pseudoscientific claims about the power of crystals to store and release energy. They forced proponents of crystal power to back away from their claims, and suddenly at the end of the 1980s the bottom fell out of what had become a lucrative crystal market. About the same time, a number of leaders of the movement, most notably David Spangler, became convinced that they had been wrong about the possibilities of social transformation. In 1989, Spangler, publisher Jeremy Tarcher, and the editors of several New Age periodicals announced their abandonment of the New Age vision. They continued to value the personal transformations and healing they had received and saw in those individual transformations sufficient justification for their past and future efforts.

Over the 1990s the great majority of New Ages came to agree with Spangler and abandoned any hope of social transformation. However, by that time, the number of participants in the occult/metaphysical community, still called the New Age community for lack of a better label, had more than doubled. While many abandoned the New Age community, the great majority were more than content with the personal spirituality they had found. The New Age movement gave a significant boost to the Western esoteric tradition now established as one of the larger minority spiritual/religious communities in the West. At the same time it called religious scholars' attention to a largely neglected area of research.

J. Gordon Melton

Bibliography

Hanegraaff, Wouter J. (1996) *New Age Religion and Western Culture.* Leiden: E. J. Brill.

Heelas, Paul. (1996) *The New Age Movement.* Oxford, U.K.: Blackwell Publishers.

Lewis, James, and J. Gordon Melton, eds. (1992) *Perspectives on the New Age.* Albany, NY: State University of New York Press.

Melton, J. Gordon, Jerome Clark, and Aidan Kelly. (1990) *New Age Encyclopedia.* Detroit: Gale Research Company.

New World Comforter

The Universal Industrial Church of the New World Comforter is a classic example of the fusion of ufology and New Age consciousness. Allen Michael (a.k.a. Allen Noonan), the founder of this ufology religion, alleges that he was contacted by extraterrestrials in 1947 while living in Long Beach, California. The aliens (sometimes referred to as angels) transported his spirit aboard a "Mothership of the Galactic Command Space Complex" where he experienced a cosmic revelation from the "Universal Mind of Extra Territorial Intelligence" (ETI), whose goal is to bring humanity the great news of world transformation and planetary enlightenment. Michael claims that he is both of extraterrestrial origin and has some two million entities incarnated in him.

The experience, claims Michael, is contained in two verses from Revelation (14:6, 10:8–11), both of which call on the prophet to bring the Everlasting Gospel to the multitudes on earth. Allen Noonan became Allen Michael—the New World Comforter and channel of the prophesied Everlasting Gospel. Adopting the mantel of the Christian prophet and fusing extraterrestrials and flying saucers to the mix, The New World Comforter reflects the postmodern nature of ufology.

In 1967 Michael moved to San Francisco where, at the height of the countercultural rebellion, he formed the One World Family Commune with a small group of followers. On fabled Haight Street the commune opened The Here and Now, a natural food restaurant. In 1973 Michael founded the Universal Church of the New World Comforter, based on Jesus' (another space messenger) teaching of "Holding all things common and making distribution according to need" (Acts, 4:32–35). Also that year the church started Starmast publications and published its first book of the Everlasting Gospel series, *From the Universe to the Youth of the World.* Other books followed, including *UFO-ETI World Master Plan* and *ETI Space Beings Intercept Earthlings.* Michael has also founded the Utopian Synthesis Party and he ran for president of the United States in 1980 and 1984 and campaigned for governor of California in 1982.

At the Web site of the Universal Industrial Church of the New World Comforters, Michael explains that the millennial new age will result when humans "act according to the high imagining of having FREE use of the whole planet and all its facilities on a sharing basis." Michael argues that such a utopian communism, devoid of money and economies, will provide everyone with freedom, security, and abundance; and initiate a Utopian Paradise World. Like Heaven's Gate and most ufology religions, the New World Comforters predict that the collapse of our world will not be total, but partial, and the evils that now afflict humanity and our planet will be reversed with help from our benevolent alien brethren. However, unlike Heaven's Gate, the New World Comforters conceive of the passing from the old, Babylonian world to the utopian world of the millennium as a peaceful transition, devoid of the climactic final battle between good and evil.

Philip Lamy

Bibliography

Lamy, Philip. (1999) "UFOs, Extraterrestrials and the Apocalypse: The Evolution of a Millennial Subculture." In *Millennial Visions,* edited by Martha Lee. New York: Praeger.

Galactic Messenger Allen Michael. (1999) http://www.galactic.org/.

New World Order

The phrase "New World Order" is widely employed by contemporary millenarians in the English-speaking world. It connotes an attempt by evil, conspiratorial forces to seize power, first in the United States and later over the entire world. This seizure of power is understood to be either imminent or already in progress and is believed to directly precede history's final struggle between good and evil.

"New World Order" also gained currency at the time of the Gulf War (1991), when President George Bush employed it as a designation for a new, post–cold war collective security system. Bush's understanding of the term was completely unrelated to its use by millennialists, although the latter considered its employment by the President to be a sign of the conspiracy's brazenness. There is no evidence, however, that Bush was aware of the term's use in an apocalyptic context.

Unlike many other elements of millenarian vocabulary, "New World Order" is used by both religionists and secularists. Its acceptance by both believers and nonbelievers suggests that it can now function as a link between religious millennialists and secular, antigovernment militants, such as those commonly found in militia groups.

The Origins of the Concept

No one has yet fully traced the origins of the term. However, it certainly goes back to at least the 1970s. The difficulty in establishing origins stems in part from the fact that it has both religious and secular roots.

Religious Origins

The religious roots of New World Order lie in the brief New Testament references to "Antichrist" (e.g., 1 John 2:18), who would allegedly emerge in the last days to deceive the faithful. Since the scriptural passages provided little detail, believers were free to elaborate upon the idea. These elaborations took two forms: One was the attempt to identify actual individuals as the Antichrist. Thus among Protestant millenarians, the pope was a favorite candidate. The other approach—and the one that led to New World Order concepts—was to join the figure of the Antichrist with some organization or institution through which he would impose his will.

The identification of the Antichrist with an organizational framework was substantially reinforced by the rise of

35 ITEMS IN CHURCHES THAT IRS CONTROLS

Does the IRS hate the Gospel and despise Bible-believing Christians? Has the IRS become a police-state agency that regularly persecutes churches, pastors, and ministries that still believe in old-fashioned patriotism? Listed below are 35 things the IRS contends are prohibited of churches and ministries. A pastor or ministry leader who violates the guidelines of the IRS on these 35 prohibitions can have his church or group's tax exemption revoked and be dealt with harshly by the IRS.

These 35 prohibitions on churches and ministries demonstrate how the IRS and the federal government now control churches and insure politically and religiously "correct" behavior. Liberal Christian churches and false religions such as Hinduism, Witchcraft, and Scientology are not affected by these rules–only Bible-believing, Christian ministries and churches. Also, keep in mind: These 35 things are not prohibited by law nor by the Constitution. The IRS considers itself above the law and the Constitution.

According to the IRS, Christian churches, ministries, and organizations may not:

1. Expose conspiracies. 2. Criticize the New World Order. 3. Say or publish anything negative about any politician, Republican or Democrat. 4. Criticize government agencies and bureaus–the IRS, FBI, BATF, CIA, EPA, DEA, OSHA, DOJ, etc. 5. Criticize an institution of government such as the White House, the Congress, the Federal Reserve Board, or the Supreme Court. 6. Encourage citizens to call or write their congressman, senator, governor, mayor, or other public official. 7. Criticize any proposed or pending bill or legislation that would take away the rights and freedoms of the people. 8. Make disparaging remarks about, or criticize, any other faith group, cult, or religion. 9. Expose or criticize the New Age Movement. 10. Support or encourage a law-abiding citizen's militia. 11. Support or encourage the Second Amendment, the right of the people to keep and bear arms. 12. Discourage young women from getting an abortion, or endorse the pro-life movement. 13. Teach that abortion, especially partial birth abortion, is murder and is the killing of innocent babies. 14. Identify homosexuality as a sin and an abomination to God. 15. Express an opinion on any subject or issue. 16. Appeal to peoples' emotions by employing an evangelization method (such as "fire and brimstone" preaching) not considered a "reasoned approach" by the IRS. 17. Discuss or identify threats to Christianity. 18. Discuss subjects or topics the IRS deems "sensationalist." 19. Criticize well-known public figures or institutions the IRS deems "worthy", such as the super-rich elite, international bankers, the Hollywood movie industry, etc. 20. Publish or broadcast information on any topic without giving credence to the opposing viewpoints of Christ's enemies. 21. Publish and offer books, tapes, or products that expose the elitist plot against humanity and God. 22. Criticize the Pope or the Vatican, or contrast the New Catholic Catechism with the truths found in the Holy Bible. (Note: only liberal churches are permitted by the IRS to criticize the Catholic Church). 23. Criticize the United Nations or such globalist groups as the Council on Foreign Relations, the Bilderbergers, and the Trilateral Commission. 24. Criticize the Masonic Lodge, the Order of Skull & Bones, or other Secret societies. 25. Highlight or otherwise bring attention to immorality of public officials or corruption in government. 26. Complain of government wrongdoing or injustice, such as happened at Waco, Ruby Ridge, and elsewhere. 27. Criticize the Jewish ADL or other Jewish lobby groups. 28. Say anything positive about the "religious right" or the "patriot movement." 29. Support home schooling, home churches, or unregistered churches. 30. Spend money on missionary projects or charitable causes not approved by the IRS. 31. Promote or encourage alternative healthcare (herbs, vitamins, etc.). 32. Expose false teachings of any kind by anyone. 33. Support or encourage persecuted Christians suffering under anti-Christian regimes in Red China, Cuba, Russia, Israel, Saudi Arabia, the United States, and elsewhere. 34. Ordain a pastor whose training or qualifications are not approved by the IRS. 35. Advocate or teach any Bible doctrine that is politically or religiously incorrect, or is inconsistent with any "public policy" (abortion, feminism, gay rights, etc.) currently being enforced by the IRS.

Please examine the above list of 35 prohibitions on Christian free speech and activity by the IRS, and decide for yourself: Are conservative Christian ministries and churches being selectively persecuted? Is the IRS willfully violating the civil rights of Christian believers? Are Christian believers receiving the equal protection of the law? What does the First Amendment to the U.S. Constitution say?

Source: Texe Marrs, http://www.texemarrs.com/archive/011999/35.htm.

dispensational premillennialism, the millenarian system first developed in Victorian England by John Nelson Darby and later extensively adopted in America by Protestant Fundamentalists. Darby argued that the last days would begin with a seven-year period of violence and persecution (the Tribulation), at the midpoint of which the Antichrist would impose his rule over the world. During the final three-and-a-half years of the Tribulation, the Antichrist would attempt to secure the world for Satan, until his rule was ended by the battle of Armageddon and Christ's return.

As millennialists began to speculate about the nature of this three-and-a-half-year period, the emphasis was placed less upon the identity of Antichrist and more upon the character of the global dictatorship he would establish. This tendency was increased by the consensus reached by dispensational premillennialists that events in the Middle East signaled the beginning of the endtimes, i.e., the creation of the state of Israel, its territorial growth, and the reunification of Jerusalem. In addition, premillennialists believed that the nucleus of the Antichrist's political system would be a resuscitated Roman Empire, a possibility that seemed more likely with the creation of the European Union.

While political developments were an important factor in the belief that a Satanic world empire was imminent, premillennialists were also influenced, somewhat surprisingly, by technological changes. In particular, they have evidenced particular fascination with computer technology and its potential for permitting the Antichrist to effectively control behavior on a global scale. In its most extreme form, this took the form of suggestions "that Antichrist would *be* a computer" (Boyer 1993: 283). More commonly, technology-oriented premillennialists concentrated on the Book of Revelation's "mark of the beast," the mark that allegedly would have to be carried by anyone seeking to buy or sell during the Antichrist's reign. This has led to extensive speculation that such developments as the universal bar code read by optical scanners and implanted microchips might be the means by which the prophecy would be fulfilled. Thus, credit cards and debit cards have come to be seen as devices to habituate the population to a system which eventually would feature the "mark" itself.

Consequently, by the time President Bush chose the phrase "New World Order," there was already a significant body of millenarian religious teaching associated with the term. Those accepting such teaching identified New World Order with the system of rule they expected the Antichrist to establish during the second half of the Tribulation period. For them, therefore, Bush's utilization of the phrase was understood to be a sign that the Tribulation was imminent.

Secular Origins

At the same time that religious millenarians were developing this systemic concept of the Antichrist's rule, a different conception of New World Order was developing among secularists. The latter, while not hostile to religion, focused upon the development of theories of history. These theories were invariably based upon conspiracies as the key to an understanding of political and economic change. Such theories were not new. Indeed, they began to proliferate in the late eighteenth century, as conservatives sought to understand the French Revolution. It was more reassuring to believe that the Revolution had been caused by a small, evil cabal than it was to believe that it grew out of mass discontent. This strain of speculation—identifying unwanted change with the machinations of conspiracies—became a favorite of traditionalists hostile to the political, economic, and social changes sweeping the Western world in the nineteenth and twentieth centuries. Industrialism, urbanization, mass electorates, immigration, revolution—all could be blamed on some invisible, conspiratorial cause.

The most famous and enduring of these alleged conspiracies was that of the Illuminati. In fact, the actual "Bavarian Illuminati" was a secret society with Masonic antecedents founded in 1776, active for a few years in German-speaking Europe, and dissolved about 1787. For those of a conspiratorial turn of mind, however, its very nonexistence made it an attractive whipping-boy, for what better than a conspiracy so secret it was invisible? It was not only blamed for the French Revolution, which occurred after its dissolution, but for a variety of social, political, and economic ills, to the present day. Through such channels as the English conspiracy theorist of the interwar period, Nesta Webster (1876–1960), the Illuminati became associated with the belief that secret societies held the key to history. This belief was frequently linked to anti-Semitism through conviction that the Jews, in turn, manipulated the Illuminati.

By the mid-1960s, conspiracy literature emphasizing secret societies had become so vast that it virtually defies inventorying. Its bulk, as well as its overheated suspiciousness, led the historian Richard Hofstadter to refer to it as an example of "the paranoid political style" (1965: 10–12).

Although the original thrust of Illuminati/secret society literature was counterrevolutionary, directed first toward France and then Russia, later examples of the genre have emphasized world dominion as the conspiracy's goal. Indeed, the conspiracy is now allegedly populated not by shaggy-haired radicals but by the superrich, who allegedly seek global control to consolidate and increase their wealth. They are deemed to be above ideology, driven only by greed and ambition. Since this theory, like conspiracy theories in general, cannot be proved false, it tends to persist regardless of evidence that might be presented in opposition. Having characterized the conspiracy as nearly all-powerful and extraordinarily cunning, the theory concludes that any seemingly contrary evidence must have been planted by the conspirators themselves as a form of deception.

The Illuminati-dominated conspiracy literature has led to its own version of the "New World Order," which is purportedly the world dictatorship that will be created once the conspiracy completes its program of subversion and conquests. Particularly since the end of the cold war, those who write in this vein have exhibited increasing panic. This is in part due to their hostility toward the United Nations, which they see as a "front" through which the conspiracy operates. They assert that the conspiracy's designs are on the verge of full realization and therefore that the New World Order is about become reality. In a manner similar to that already noted for religionists, secular conspiracy theorists therefore also saw in President Bush's fondness for the phrase a deeply troubling development.

Versions of the New World Order

While all New World Order conceptions share such characteristics as a fear of global tyranny, they also differ. These differences reflect not only religious as opposed to secular origins but, more importantly, the intensity with which conspiracy theories are pressed. Thus, one may distinguish between "weak" and "strong" versions of the theory.

The Weak Version

The weak version of the New World Order simply argues that an evil world conspiracy is striving to secure total power. The alleged conspiracy is believed to be organized in one or more secret societies and to operate publicly through "fronts" in the form of public or private international entities, ranging from the United Nations to foundations, corporations, and financial institutions. The most widely disseminated presentation of these views is Pat Robertson's *The New World Order* (1991).

Robertson argued that at least since the late 1700s, an Illuminatist conspiracy has been at work destabilizing regimes, fomenting wars and revolutions, and subverting Christianity, as part of a larger struggle between God and Satan. Like many exponents of the New World Order position, Robertson claimed that the conspiracy was not ideological, in the sense that it allegedly took whatever position would most advance its interests. Thus, it was supposedly neither a cabal of the left nor of the right, but supported whichever extreme served its purposes. It might, consequently, back Nazis at one point and Communists at another.

A particularly troubling aspect of Robertson's book was its insistence upon the central role allegedly occupied by Jewish international bankers, e.g., the Rothschilds; Kuhn, Loeb, and the Warburgs. His critics pointed out that much of the "evidence" he presented was drawn from such earlier anti-Semitic conspiracy theorists as Nesta Webster. Robertson, who has long been a strong supporter of Israel, disclaimed any intentional anti-Semitism and apologized to the Jewish community. He did not, however, explain the presence of such motifs in his book.

The Strong Version

Although Robertson's book stands at the fringes of respectable American political discourse, it in fact represents a diluted version of the "New World Order." A far more detailed and extreme version circulates in media outside the mainstream. The latter include the Internet, self-published books, and the periodicals and videotapes produced for militias, survivalists, and other "outsider" groups. While this material repeats themes found in the "weak" version (e.g., the conspiratorial role of the Illuminati), it adds many additional features. Most commonly, these theories include some or all of the following elements: the systematic subversion of republican institutions by a federal government utilizing emergency powers; the creation of sinister new military and paramilitary forces, including government mobilization of urban youth gangs; the permanent stationing of foreign troops on U.S. soil; the widespread use of black helicopters to transport the conspiracy's operatives; the confiscation of privately owned guns; the expected incarceration of "patriots" in concentration camps run by the Federal Emergency Management Agency (FEMA); and the replacement of Christianity with a "New Age" world religion.

This bizarre scenario is commonly presented as verified fact as opposed to mere speculation. Those who accept it necessarily come to view the larger environment as filled with hostile forces. Accepted institutions, particularly governmental, come to be viewed as a wily and dangerous enemy, while believers see themselves as an embattled remnant, on the edge of annihilation.

These ideas appear to be equally shared by religionists and secularists. They can be found, albeit in varying combinations, among fundamentalists such as Texe Marrs, John Todd, and Stan Deyo; and militia figures such as John Trochmann, Jack McLamb, and Mark Koernke.

The New World Order and Millennialism

Ideas about a threatening New World Order are not inherently millenarian, since they are not necessarily linked to conceptions of an imminent perfect future. However, the

New World Order is sufficiently compatible with millennialism so that it has frequently been absorbed into systems of millenarian belief. This occurs because of the dualistic character of millenarian thought—that is, its tendency to think of the world as rigidly divided between forces of good and forces of evil. History is often construed as a struggle between these two forces and will allegedly end in a final battle (Armageddon or its equivalent) in which good will definitively triumph. Yet in many millenarian "scripts," the final triumph of good is to be preceded by increasingly threatening advances by the forces of darkness.

This dynamic, in which things get worse before they improve, lends itself to millennialists' fixation upon the identification of enemies. Contemporary New World Order literature, even when not produced by millennialists themselves, serves millenarians' need to know whom they are fighting. For this purpose, the New World Order is particularly useful, for the encompassing character of the conspiracy and its goals allows it to perform a cosmic function. Since the conspiracy allegedly seeks nothing less than total control of the world, it can easily be assimilated to preexisting religious conceptions of evil (e.g., Satan).

At the same time, the New World Order serves as a bridge between religious millennialists and secular antigovernment militants. They commonly describe the New World Order in similar terms and cite similar sources and "evidence." This permits a degree of cooperation that would otherwise be difficult, ranging from pragmatic alliances to conversion. The New World Order has become, in effect, an "ecumenical" conspiracy theory shared by a broad segment of religious and secular ultraconservatives.

The greater the power that is imputed to the conspiracy, and the more imminent its supposed takeover is believed to be, the more likely it is that beliefs about the New World Order will take millenarian form. If believers are not to yield to despair, they must believe that they will be victorious, and the way in which the enemy is conceptualized makes it easy to conceive the coming battle as the final struggle that will bring history to a close. In fact, the weak version of the theory, whether in the form presented by Pat Robertson or in the somewhat similar rendering by the John Birch Society, seems increasingly to be supplanted by the strong version. Presentations become ever more lurid and melodramatic, infusing the battle with an increasingly apocalyptic character.

Summary

This apocalyptic character does not appear to be threatened by real world events. Like most conspiracy theories, this one cannot be proved false, in the sense that believers are generally not persuaded by any contrary evidence. Thus they have created and maintain a closed system of ideas. It has survived the collapse of the Soviet Union and will doubtless persist in the face of other significant changes in the world, allowing millenarians to continue to inhabit a dualistic mental universe.

Michael Barkun

Bibliography

Barkun, Michael. (1996) "Religion, Militias, and Oklahoma City: The Mind of Conspiratorialists." *Terrorism and Political Violence* 8: 50–64.

Bennett, David H. (1995) *The Party of Fear: The American Far Right from Nativism to the Militia Movement*, rev. ed. New York: Vintage.

Boyer, Paul. (1992) *When Time Shall Be No More: Prophecy Belief in Modern American Culture.* Cambridge, MA: Harvard University Press.

Fuller, Robert C. (1995) *Naming the Antichrist: The History of an American Obsession.* New York: Oxford.

Hofstadter, Richard. (1965) *The Paranoid Style in American Politics and Other Essays.* New York: Knopf.

Robertson, Pat. (1991) *The New World Order.* Dallas: Word.

Nuclear Age

The nuclear age began formally on 6 August 1945, when the United States dropped the atomic bomb on the unsuspecting city of Hiroshima. The city was completely destroyed. Nearly 100,000 people died instantaneously, while another 100,000 perished more slowly and painfully. Three days later a second bomb hit Nagasaki, though somewhat off-target and consequently with less damage. In a flash, millennialism took on new meanings in human history.

Nuclear fears had actually been growing in peoples' minds for most of the half-century before 1945. At the turn of the century, Marie Curie and her husband, Pierre, discovered plutonium and radium, and she carried out experiments on radiation that led to her death. H. G. Wells wrote a novel in 1913 that imagined the end of the world with one big bomb. By the 1930s some physicists were actively thinking in theoretical terms about the notion of splitting the atom and somehow taking advantage of the huge energy that would be released. It was World War II, however, that produced the Manhattan Project and the mobilization of the vast resources of the U.S. government actually to produce a functional bomb before the fighting concluded in Asia (though by August the Nazis had been defeated in Europe).

After Hiroshima it was immediately clear to all sensitive observers that something new and dreadful had entered human experience. At first some tried to find ways through the newly established United Nations to control the new weapon and prevent its spread throughout the world, especially to the Soviet Union. That effort failed. Within four years Russia had built and tested its own atomic bomb, sparking the onset of the cold war. Both countries began building atomic bombs at an alarming rate. Soon the United States developed the much more powerful hydrogen bomb, which was first tested on 1 March 1951 at Bikini atoll on the Marshall Islands, and the world entered an even more perilous phase of the nuclear age.

Millennialism and Nuclear Weapons

It may seem obvious—though it has certainly proven difficult for many to remember—but atomic weapons are world-ending in their potential. Even to call them "weapons" may be a misnomer. A more accurate term would be "apocalyptic instruments of genocide." One bomb dropped on a major city, of course, will kill huge numbers of people but not end human history. But the possibility of containing the use in nuclear weapons in war, if fighting were to reach such levels, is exceedingly unlikely. At the height of the cold war there were over sixty thousand nuclear warheads in the world, and there remains even now an astronomical redundancy of weapons. The United States alone continues to keep over seven thousand warheads armed and ready for use; far fewer than that ignited at one time would create the catastrophic ecological effect first described by Carl Sagan and others as "nuclear winter." Russia, in a state of economic and spiritual collapse after the end of the cold war, has some 70 tons of plutonium stored in often unguarded sites (a small bomb can be built with only 10 to 15 pounds).

Proliferation and what can be called the "new terrorism" further aggravate the millennial fears of the age. The nuclear "club" keeps expanding, in large part because the knowledge required to build a bomb is readily available (even on the Internet) to a nation or other entity willing and able to devote the resources to that task. India has the bomb and its traditional rival, Pakistan, has been trying for years to obtain one and is probably close to succeeding. In the Middle East only Israel has nuclear weapons at the moment, but Iraq has been working hard to obtain them and will probably succeed in the near future. In Asia, China has long been a nuclear power, but countries as diverse as North Korea, Taiwan, and even Japan, either have or could relatively easily obtain the bomb. Only Latin America at this point remains a nuclear-free zone, as best one can tell. War could quickly trigger attacks and counterattacks with deadly and destructive consequences, even for those not directly involved in the fighting.

Terrorism represents another and in some ways more immediate dimension of the world-ending threat of atomic bombs. Nuclear technology has "advanced" to the point that bombs can be produced that are small and transportable in vehicles available to ordinary citizens. The world continues to harbor fearsome political, ethnic, and national hatred. Small groups often nourish vast apocalyptic resentments, which can now be matched with an equal measure of destructiveness. Timothy McVeigh used an old-fashioned bomb to blow up the Federal Building in Oklahoma City. Future McVeighs may turn to nuclear weapons. Aum Shinrikyo, a cult in Japan in the first half of the 1990s, actively planned to inaugurate Armageddon. In their labs they produced sarin gas and anthrax, while actively planning with Russian colleagues to steal and transport plutonium to build bombs in secret sites throughout Japan. One's wildest imagination about the world-ending dangers of terrorism in future decades is entirely within the realm of the possible.

A New Human Consciousness

The apocalyptic potential of nuclear weapons has altered the very meaning of millennialism within human history. Because we die and are reflective about our own death (unlike animals), as humans we have some knowledge, even if disavowed, of the apocalyptic, or collective death. Such knowledge matters. Since at least the creation of culture some eight thousand years ago, three special groups have taken on the task of imagining the end of the world: deeply religious, mostly mystical, figures; artists and writers able to extend their awareness of death to include images of the end of all life; and paranoid schizophrenics, who are often revered in premodern cultures for just this knowledge. Such musings have played a vital role in the creation of institutional meaning structures, especially religions, that have supported the growth of civilization as we have come to know it. One can say that in the past it took an act of imagination to think about the end. Most people lived out their quiet lives in the utter certainty of a human future, which everything they could see seemed to confirm.

In the nuclear age, things are reversed. One cannot absolutely and unconditionally trust a human future. We have created with our own hands and through our own scientific ingenuity the potential for our destruction. It no longer takes an act of imagination to think about the end of the world. In fact, one has to be numb *not* to think about apocalyptic matters at some level of consciousness. Such "endism," or the location of self in some future narrative, is everywhere and of our lives and in our souls. In our fear, at times we as individuals and societies even embrace the weapons themselves as a way of magically relieving our anxieties, a pro-

Enormous atomic cloud taken by the U.S. Army about one hour after the bombing of Hiroshima on 6 August 1945. HTTP://WWW.CSI.AD.JP/ABOMB/RETAIN/EXP.HTML.

foundly irrational and dangerous process that Robert Jay Lifton has called *nuclearism* (1982). It is not too much to say that some kind of shift occurred in human consciousness in the middle of the twentieth century, a shift we are only just now beginning to understand.

This shift alters the fabric of our lives. Among other things, it intensifies the very meaning of familiar concepts like millennialism. Now end-of-the-world imagery is everywhere, not always new in the images it produces but very new in intensity and the way it works in the self. The scientific possibility of futurelessness changes the way we think about our values, goals, hopes, and fears in large and small ways. Nuclear fear casts a shadow over our lives. Nothing in and of itself is shaped entirely in the wake of the bomb, but nor is anything free from its pervasive, and mostly pernicious, influence. Until 1989, it seemed to most people that nuclear fear was synonymous with the cold war struggle between the United States and the Soviet Union, between democracy and Communism. At the start of the new millennium, it is now apparent that the cold war from the late 1940s to 1989 was merely the first phase of the world's perplexing effort to come to grips with the bomb. That struggle will continue.

Conclusion

There is no simple way of defining "nuclear" for an encyclopedia on millennialism. This book in some ways itself reflects the way the bomb has altered our lives. We ask new questions of things. At the same time, and of course related to that search for meaning, the world faces millennial crises in the form of direct military threats in the continued existence of nuclear warheads, in the spread of the weapons to often unstable countries, and in the effort (already apparent) by nongovernmental terrorist groups to obtain the technology and materials to build atomic bombs. One of the great myths of recent years is that the world freed itself of nuclear danger after the cold war.

The hope, however, is that enhanced awareness of the real dangers will awaken humanity to creative action. We are at a historical moment when the idea of ridding the world of nuclear weapons is at least imaginable. It remains to be seen whether the world will be able to embrace that opportunity.

Charles B. Strozier

Bibliography

Boyer, Paul S. (1985) *By the Bomb's Early Light: American and Culture at the Dawn of the Atomic Age.* New York: Pantheon Books.

Lifton, Robert Jay. (1969) *Death in Life: Survivors of Hiroshima.* New York: Vintage.

——. (1983) *The Broken Connection: On Death and the Continuity of Life.* New York: Basic Books.

——, with Richard Falk. (1982) *Indefensible Weapons: The Political and Psychological Case Against Nuclearism.* New York: Basic Books.

McKibben, Bill. (1989) *The End of Nature.* New York: Doubleday.

Schell, Jonathan. (1982) *The Fate of the Earth.* New York: Knopf.

——. (1998) *The Gift of Time: The Case for Abolishing Nuclear Weapons.* New York: Metropolitan Books.

Strozier, Charles B. (1994) *Apocalypse: On the Psychology of Fundamentalism in America.* Boston: Beacon Press.

——, with Michael Flynn, eds. (1997) *The Year 2000: Essays on the End.* New York: New York University Press.

Thompson, Damian. (1996) *The End of Time: Faith and Fear in the Shadow of the Millennium.* Hanover, NH: University Press of New England.

Outpost Kauai

Outpost Kauai, a ufology religion based in Hawaii, rests on the channeled teaching of Qetzel, a Pleiadian spirit of the future who has come to Earth on a mission to awaken humankind to the vast changes which are about to engulf the Earth. Michael, who is the human channel for Qetzel, also alleges that an extraterrestrial spirit inhabits his body. The philosophy of Outpost Kauai professes that the galaxy is teeming with intelligent life, much of it more evolved than humans. In fact, the colonization of the earth has occurred countless times over the millennia by extraterrestrials such as the Sirians, Lyrans, Reticulans, and most recently the Pleaidians. Thus the genes and "gene memory" of humankind is a fusion of twenty-two different species.

Various aliens have returned to Earth over its history to periodically run genetic experiments and human engineering. Some of these aliens do not have the best interests of humankind at heart and thus plan to keep humanity in a state of underdevelopment and of fear, based on the three pillars of money, law, and religion. Qetzel is an entity who has been "star seeded" into a human body to help humans break free of the evil aliens and their human puppets in earthly governments and adapt to the coming cosmic transformation. Essentially, according to the group, this extraterrestrial engineering is about to "quicken."

Qetzel refers to Revelation's "signs of the times" and to the onset of tribulation as the "Quickening" in an article entitled "What Will You Do as the Curtain Is Raised?": "Look around your world. . . . Like salt it (the quickening) flavors your popular culture. . . . Your weather grows bizarre. The Earth shakes. UFO's buzz your cities. Mountains blow their tops. Creatures stock the night. Comets cruise the night sky. The 'end' is actually a 'beginning.' It was promised there would be signs. There will be" (12).

There is also a strong conspiracy dimension to Outpost Kauai that resembles, in philosophy at least, that of American's right-wing militias. To members of Outpost Kauai, the U.S. government has complete control of Americans' lives. Under the cover of national security, through control of the public schools and the Federal government, and the emerging new world order, a global Big Brother is ready to impose global rule. The group also argues that the United States and other world leaders know that the aliens are here but resist acknowledging it for fear of being rendered obsolete.

The group also preaches that great transformation and destruction on the planet is going to occur, but it will not be an Armageddon. Like other ufology religions, Outpost Kauai predicts the coming of the photon belt—a highly charged band of light particles that will engulf the earth at some point in the next decade causing worldwide earth changes and causing the acceleration of human physical, mental, and spiritual evolution. Much of the evil in the world will be wiped away, but the good will remain and be transformed to cosmic perfection.

Philip Lamy

Bibliography

Jody, C., and Gemini. (1997) "What Will you do as the Curtain is Raised?" Outpost Kauai. http://hoohana.aloha.net/outpost.

Lamy, Philip. (1999) "UFOs, Extraterrestrials and the Apocalypse: The Evolution of a Millennial Subculture." In *Millennial Visions*, edited by Martha Lee. New York: Praeger.

Papal Reform

The links between papacy-inspired attempts to reform the church and currents of prophecy or millenarian expectation, are fairly obscure during the middle ages (c. 700–1450 CE) and early modern era (c. 1450–1750 CE). There is little doubt that prophecies of different sorts appealed to all classes of men and women, and churchmen were certainly not exempt from the fever of expectation that the end of the world, and the Day of Judgment, were imminent. Princes and emperors seem to have made greater political capital out these prophecies than the papacy, and it seems likely that the popes were wary of prophets claiming a divine inspiration and authority which rivaled their own, and the church's, monopoly of salvation. It is possible, however, to marshal the scattered evidence to pinpoint certain moments in history when popes may have appealed to prophecy, or were prophetically inspired, during their reforming activities.

The Middle Ages, 1000–1450

There does not seem to be any evidence for millenarian expectations on the part of the papacy around the year 1000, although there is some evidence of popular millenarian expectations before and after that date. The letters of Pope Sylvester II (c. 999–1003) betray no allusions to an expectation of a thousand-year period of rule by the saints and by Christ, nor to any apocalyptic fears. The great efforts at reforming the morals and conduct of the clergy undertaken by Pope Gregory VII (1073–85) may have stimulated wandering preachers who promoted millenarian ideas, but the papacy was often hostile to preachers who claimed to be messiahs or prophets, and who gained a popular following. As early as the eighth century Pope Zachary (741–52) excommunicated for heresy one Aldebert who claimed to be a living saint with a direct relationship with God, and who distributed nail-parings and hair-clippings among his followers. It is possible that Bernard of Clairvaux's (1090–1153) call for the Wendish (Scandinavian) crusade in 1147, which was sponsored by Pope Eugenius III, was influenced by Sibylline prophecies held in Rome. These prophecies predicted the end of the world following the conquest and conversion of the peoples of the north by a king of the Romans.

By the thirteenth and fourteenth centuries, historical and eschatological timetables—the idea of an endtime—focused on the city of Rome and the papacy. Rome was described as either the New Jerusalem, which would replace the "Babylon" of Avignon (where the popes were now staying), and the Jerusalem which had been lost to the "infidels," or the New Babylon itself—a center of unprecedented corruption and vice, and the site for the emergence of the Antichrist. For the Italian prophet Joachim of Fiore (c. 1132–1202), the purification of the papacy and the role of an "angelic" pope in returning the church to righteousness and humility, were key elements in his hopes for the final age, and the beginning of a new historical period. The works which were associated with him enjoyed widespread popularity between the thirteenth and twentieth centuries. These works prophesied the election of an "angelic" pope or popes after a period of catastrophe—associated with the election of an oriental and an occidental Antichrist—who would, together with a secular leader (the "second" Charlemagne) recover Jerusalem and purify the ecclesiastical establishment. Joachim was interviewed by Popes Lucius III and Urban III, and his writings were lodged in the papal library. Later pseudo-Joachimite texts were to be dedicated to various popes. At the time of Gregory X's death in 1276, a verse circulated describing a pope of angelic life who would carry out a program of reform, and as late as 1535 the reforming Venetian cardinal, Gasparo Contarini, could be viewed as a future "angelic pope" by the gossips of Rome. Various calculations were made to ascertain when the angelic pope would ascend the throne of St. Peter. Associated with these by the fourteenth century were the predictions of a papal Antichrist who, joined by the political Antichrist, would struggle with the angelic pope and emperor.

The Jubilee (a "Holy Year" in which a special indulgence is granted to Catholics who visit Rome and fulfil certain conditions) of 1300 proclaimed by Pope Boniface VIII (1294–1303) may have given some pilgrims hope that Rome would replace the earthly Jerusalem which had been lost to the infidels, and that an age of peace might have arrived. Some of the people who proclaimed the imminence of the final age, after Joachim of Fiore, which gave the pope or mendicant orders a special role, were listened to by the papacy. John of Roquetaillade was imprisoned by the curia at Avignon, but his prophecies were, nevertheless attended to, and collected into the papal library along with the works of Joachim of Fiore. In 1365 the Infante Pedro of Aragon encouraged Pope Urban V (1362–70) to return to Rome and to reform the church, and he based his exhortation on a vision. Urban did return to Rome on the strength of St. Bridget's revelations.

The Renaissance, 1450–1600

Eschatological fears (fears of the "endtime") and hopes focused on Rome, which was the permanent seat of the papacy by the mid-fifteenth century, and reached a climax between the fall of Constantinople to the Turks in 1456, and the crowning of the Emperor Charles V at Bologna in 1530. The attitude of the papacy to prophecy and millenarian expectations is again hard to gauge. The Borgia pope, Alexander VI (1492–1503), condemned the Dominican preacher Girolamo Savonarola (1452–98) as a heretic in

The Libyan Sibyl by Michelangelo. The Sibyls represented the partial revelation given to the Gentile world, and they prefigure the prophets who made a fuller revelation to the Jews. They are represented according to Joachim of Fiore's own number-symbolism (five sibyls and seven prophets equals twelve), and flank the histories on the ceiling of the Sistine Chapel in Rome. MONUMENT MUSEI E GALLERIE PONTIFICIE, VATICAN CITY.

1497, and he was executed the following year. Savonarola had whipped up a storm of apocalyptic expectation in the city of Florence, and inaugurated a kind of theocracy there. He called on the deposition of the pope, but his Catholicism was fairly orthodox. After Savonarola's death, many of his followers were employed by Pope Leo X (1513–21) despite their former hostility to the rule in Florence of the pope's Medici relatives. Pope Julius II (1503–13) may have toyed with canonizing Savonarola, and it is even possible that he was depicted by Raphael lurking behind the Italian poet Dante in one of the frescoes which decorated the walls of the pope's Vatican apartments.

Humanists dedicated to recovering classical culture were certainly not inimical to prophecy, and many of them addressed verses to Julius II and Leo X in which they predicted the return of the golden ages—after the style of Vergil—under their papal reigns. One of these humanists, the general of the Augustinian order of hermits, Egidio of Viterbo (1469–1532), tried to understand God's providential purposes in history through the scriptures. In a speech delivered before Pope Julius II, he explained that the Portuguese conquests in the Far East were a sign of the coming golden age of a worldwide Christian world, and he urged the pope to act to reform the church. Julius may have approved of Egidio's use of Hebrew mysticism (the Kabbalah) and other keys to scriptural interpretation, for he called upon him on other occasions to deliver speeches imbued with the prophetic spirit. On the occasion of the opening of the Fifth Lateran Council (1512–17), which Julius had convened in Rome to offset criticisms of his worldliness, and to initiate the repulsion of the Turks and the reform of the church, Egidio declared: "When have there ever appeared so frequently and with such horrible aspect monsters, portents, [and] prodigies, signs of celestial threats and of terror on earth? When will there ever be a bloodier disaster or battle than that of Brescia or that of Ravenna? . . . This year the earth has been drenched with more blood than rain" (Bowd 1999: 50–1). Egidio, for his part, placed his hopes for religious unity in the papacy, but not necessarily Julius. He later focused his hopes on Leo X. It has also been suggested that the decoration of the Sistine Chapel ceiling by Michelangelo during 1508 was influenced by Egidio. Many direct references to the thought of Joachim, for instance, have been discerned in Michelangelo's work. For example, the representation of the seven prophets and five sibyls, and the grouping of Old Testament histories, agree with the numerical or symbolic scheme drawn up by Joachim in the twelfth century.

Many of the other speakers at the Fifth Lateran Council wrapped themselves in the mantle of the prophet, pointing to the discovery of new worlds to the east and west, the threat of the Turks to the east, and the natural and man-made disasters—such as war—in Europe, as signs of the imminence of apocalypse. The church, and indeed all of Christendom, were therefore in urgent need of reform. Perhaps it is a sign of papal indifference to prophecy that these reform proposals were largely ignored, though the council was careful to define how a prophet might be recognized and examined by a committee of suitably learned men. At least one prophet, who predicted the return of Christ following the conversion of Jews and Muslims, was called to Rome and so examined, before being dismissed as a fraud.

Conclusion

Like Pope Gregory I (590–604), who believed that he was living in the last days, it is highly probable that many popes were motivated to promote ecclesiastical or moral reform by a sense of the imminence of Judgment. In the course of the sixteenth and seventeenth centuries, prophetic fears were more predominant in Protestant than Catholic areas, and prophecy became a marginalized discourse in curial circles, and condemnations of prophecy based on astrology were occasionally issued. Future research may reveal more evidence for direct links between papal reform and millenarian movements and fears.

Stephen Bowd

See also Joachism, Prophecy, Roman Catholicism

Bibliography

Bowd, Stephen D. (1999) "Pietro Bembo and the 'Monster' of Bologna (1514)." *Renaissance Studies* 13, 1: 40–54.

Cohn, Norman. ([1957] 1993) *The Pursuit of the Millennium: Revolutionary Millenarians and Mystical Anarchists of the Middle Ages*, rev. ed. London: Pimlico.

McGinn, Bernard. (1979) *Visions of the End: Apocalyptic Traditions in the Middle Ages.* New York: Columbia University Press.

Polizzotto, Lorenzo. (1994) *The Elect Nation: The Savonarolan Movement in Florence, 1494–1545.* Oxford, U.K.: Clarendon Press.

Reeves, Marjorie. ([1969] 1994) *The Influence of Prophecy in the Later Middle Ages: A Study in Joachimism.* Oxford, U.K.: Clarendon Press; reprint, Notre Dame, IN: University of Notre Dame Press.

——, ed. (1992) *Prophetic Rome in the High Renaissance Period: Essays.* Oxford, U.K.: Clarendon Press.

Rusconi, Roberto. (1979) *L'Attesa della fine. Crisi della società, profezia ed Apocalisse in Italia al tempo del' grande scisma d'Occidente (1378–1417).* Rome: Istituto storico italiano per il medio evo.

Peace of God (Pax Dei)

The Pax Dei was a conciliar movement which began in southern France in the late tenth century and spread to most of Western Europe over the next century, surviving in some form until at least the thirteenth century. It combined lay and ecclesiastical legislation, which regulated warfare and established a social peace. The participation of large, enthusiastic crowds marks it as one of the first popular religious movements of the Middle Ages. The timing (two waves in the decade preceding the year 1000 and the year 1033), the language used by some of the ecclesiastical sources (hagiography and historiography), and the descriptions of the populace at these councils (penitence giving way to mass expressions of joy) indicate a strong millennial element. The sources use images from Jubilees and the prophetic works, including Isaiah's famous depiction of messianic peace, suggesting that participants in these councils, both lay and (some) clerical believed that, at the advent of the millennium, God's peace was at last descending on earth.

History

Its origins coincided with the failure of the last Carolingian rulers to keep order in West Frankland, and the accession of Hugh Capet, founder of a new dynasty in 987. Throughout the kingdom, the decentralizing forces that had plagued Charlemagne's empire from its inception, intensified, with, in some places an intensification of regional power bases (counts, dukes) and in others the appearance of independent warlords with new fortifications *(castellani)* and bands of retainers *(milites)*. In the ensuing disorders, local initiatives to reestablish social order found expression in a variety of measures, the most spectacular of which were Peace assemblies.

Typically, these councils were held in large open fields around exceptional gatherings of saints' relics, brought from the surrounding regions. Each relic brought with it a throng of faithful, enthused both by their novel proximity to the sacred, and the miracles that these relics "performed." In the presence of the large crowds of commoners attracted by these relics, the elders of the council (dukes, counts, bishops, abbots) would proclaim Peace legislation designed to protect civilians (unarmed churchmen, peasants, merchants, pilgrims) and control the behavior of warriors. Often the warriors would swear an oath on the relics in the presence of all assembled.

In a sense this constitutes the first time that we find popular attempts to establish civil society in medieval Europe. Instead of royal administration preserving the peace, these councils combined ecclesiastical decree (the Peace canons) with public accords (the oaths before the populace). In the early phase (980–1040), the blend of relics and crowds, and miracles and enthusiasm stamped the movement with its exceptionally popular character. Indeed, the extraordinary reliance of the Peace on noncoercive, spiritual sanctions (excommunication, interdict, anathema) depended on the combined force of divine will and popular pressure. Some historians call this phase the "sanctified peace," a generic term we might better describe as the "millennial" peace, where the collective enthusiasm and the "rule of the saints" signaled for the participant—if not the retrospective narrator and the modern historian—that the sabbatical millennium had arrived after a 1,000 years of waiting.

After a lull in the first two decades of the eleventh century (postapocalyptic letdown), the movement takes up speed again in the 1020s, this time spreading to the north with the support of King Robert, the Capetian whose popular piety (humility, peace, pilgrimage) established the legitimacy of his dynasty. There, the high nobility (including the king) sponsored Peace assemblies throughout their lands (Flanders, Burgundy, Champagne, Normandy, Amienois, Berry). An ideology of Peace pervaded the language of political conciliation on an international scale, most notably at the meeting in 1024 on the Meuse where Robert II and Emperor Henry II proclaimed a universal peace. This official and exceptional involvement in an international peace movement rode yet another wave of popular support. Commoners began to share in the oaths and the responsibilities of the Peace Assemblies, the crowds and the assemblies multiplied, and the movement began to develop legislation.

According to the contemporary monastic chronicler, Raoul Glaber, the Peace as a popular movement came to a climax in the apocalyptic atmosphere of the millennium of Christ's Passion, the year 1033. In his account, after three years of famine, the king called for councils to be held throughout his realm. These councils sought to establish a fundamental social peace ("absolute peace") and were attended by vast crowds who embraced the peace enthusiastically, their palms extended to heaven, shouting "Pax! Pax! Pax!" They believed, Glaber tells us, that they were making a covenant of peace between God and men, the *Peace of God*. This shout represents the first popular millennial voice recorded favorably by clerical writers who, since Augustine, had expressed enormous hostility to millennialism. According to Glaber, the social covenant sworn at these rallies carried over for about four years of such peace and abundance that they were "the Jubilees of old," an exceptionally long period of time for millennial enthusiasm to sustain civil society in a world that had never known such a thing.

Of course, as with all millennial movements, popular enthusiasm and official support could not transform overnight the behavior of the aristocracy which repeatedly, again according to Glaber, reneged on its oaths and commitments. This led in some places to the formation of Peace leagues, which organized militias to enforce the peace. In the mid-1030s a league at Bourges summoned all men over fifteen years old to join a sworn league to enforce the peace. This popular army of peasants and townsmen, led by priests carrying banners, seeing themselves as the children of Israel fighting the Canaanites, had considerable initial success against the local nobility. In 1038, however, they fell before the mounted onslaught of the local great lord, the count of Déols. In some areas of southern France, evidence indicates such leagues (and even a "peace tax" to support them) existed as late as the thirteenth century.

While this may have marked the end of the millennial, popular phase of the peace, by the 1040s, the high aristocracy began to use the movement to consolidate their own power. The organizational thrust and the tone of the movement changed towards what Max Weber called routinization or institutionalization. The Truce of God *(Treuga Dei)* became the center of legislative action and aimed, by declaring Thursday through Sunday as days of peace, at controlling feuds and private warfare. The Truce led to the emergence of public institutions for the control of violence. Its roots lay in religious sanctions against occupations inappropriate to holy days, and represents an extraordinarily ambitious effort to impose upon the secular world the rhythms of sacred time practiced in the monastery. The involvement of the greatest monastic reforming house of the age, Cluny, in the spread of this institution to Germany and Italy places it's abbot Odilo, perhaps the most prominent Christian leader of his age, at the center of an effort to implement a millennial program for transforming the world, what we would now call postmillennialism.

Peace and Truce became synonymous. At Narbonne (1054) the organizers established the general principle that to kill a Christian was to shed the blood of Christ, a notion that was as demanding for Christian civil society as it was ominous for those—Jews, heretics, and Muslims—who were not included in the pact. Indeed, this principle reflects a fundamental change in the Peace movement—from repressing the aggressiveness of the warrior class to redirecting it against the enemies of Christendom. At the council of Clermont in 1096, and in the next two years at Rome, Pope Urban II mobilized the warriors of all Western Europe by declaring at one time a perpetual peace among Christians and war upon Islam. The call of "Deus le volt!" (God wills it) which chroniclers tell us was on the lips of so many represents a second popular millennial voice recorded, this time with the more familiar characteristics of millennialism in power—sacred violence, totalitarian zealotry.

Calling a peace assembly became an option for responses to anarchy and violence all over Western Europe. When civil war raged in the imperial lands as a result of the Investiture Contest, bishops declared the Peace at Liege (1082), Cologne (1083), and Bamberg (1085), while German princes declared it for Swabia (1083) and Bavaria (1094). Similarly, in Normandy, the first Peace Council in that area responded to the violence and uncertainty after the death of Duke Robert I and preceding the ascendancy of William the Conqueror. A council at Caen (1042), complete with relics and masses of common people, attempted to rectify the situation. Even England, which was organized under the strong government of the Duke of Normandy after 1066, had recourse to the Peace and Truce during the anarchy of Stephen of Blois.

Analysis

Traditionally, historians have dismissed the Peace of God as an interesting failure, a movement which only briefly occupied an important place on the historical stage. In trying to control warfare without the use of physical coercion it rapidly foundered on the rocks of a violent feudal reality. Already by the 1050s the movement was giving way to more efficacious ones, such as would give medieval Western culture its stamp: the King's Peace, the Church Reform, the Communes, and the Crusades. That traditional view, however, by concentrating on the failure of the movement to accomplish its quasi-messianic goals, misses the indirect impact it had. More recently historians accord a central place to the Peace in the transformations of European culture in this period, a period often characterized as the birth of Western (as opposed to Mediterranean) civilization. But even this change in historiography has yet to grapple with the Peace as a millennial movement, indeed the first one in which the elites did not crush popular millennialism at its first appearance.

In fact, the lack of coercive power, so often cited as the cause of the movement's failure, may have been precisely what made the Peace of God so influential. For without recourse to force, it had to depend on more fundamental cultural activity: building a wide and powerful social consensus, developing courts of mediation, educating a lay populace, high and low, to internalize peaceful values. In this sense, the Peace movement laid the groundwork for later developments. First, it awakened the populace, both rural and urban, to the possibilities of self-organization, producing a wide range of "textual communities" or laboratories of social experimentation structured around a text (law). Second, it helped to "Christianize" the nobility, encouraging the development of chivalry. Third, it gave enormous authority to the church, which, having mediated the Peace, became a major "player" in the political and social organization of lay society. And finally, it opened up an often fervent, if occasionally tragic, dialogue between cleric and layman on the true meaning of Christianity.

Thus, the better-known social movements, the Communes, the Crusades, and the Reform of the Church, did not replace the "failed" Peace of God; to a large extent they arose directly from it. The communes of the late eleventh and twelfth centuries, for example, gained their independence through popular militias modeled on those of the Peace movement: all men over a certain age swore to protect an urban (rather than diocesan) Peace. The Papal Reform, drew on the sanctified Peace for themes (the purification of the church), methods (interdict and excommunication), and the support of popular opinion. Finally, the First Crusade not only capitalized on a century of warrior violence restrained and redirected away from Christendom against the infidel, but its unexpectedly large contingent of unarmed commoners attests to the continued existence of those currents of popular enthusiasm that were first aroused by the sanctified Peace at the turn of the millennium.

The movement for the Peace of God changed the history of Europe by virtue of its grassroots success as well as its political failings. Insofar as it succeeded it did so on the strength of its moral vision and the sense of nonviolent community it gave to whole populations, its effort to create a social covenant. Insofar as it failed, it did so because, as Augustine would say, we are all fallen creatures. The logic of the Christian desire for peace compelled some to sharpen the boundaries between those who were Christian, excluding sections of the population from its protection. This is already detectable in the anti-Jewish pogroms of the 1010s, the heresy executions of the 1020s, the appeal of the Reconquista of Spain from the Muslims throughout the eleventh century, and shift from the "Pax, Pax, Pax" in 1033 to "Deus le volt!" in 1095–99. Through its high moral vision and its appeals to communal action, the Peace of God furthered the peaceful organization of a violent society. Through rising exclusivity and intolerance as its expectations were frustrated and various leaders sought to exploit the movement, the Peace of God gave way to the sanctification of war. For better or worse it introduced the populace as an autonomous actor on the stage of European history.

Richard Landes

See also Year 1000

Bibliography

Cowdrey, H. E. J. (1970) "The Peace and the Truce of God in the Eleventh Century." *Past and Present*, 46: 42–67.

Duby, Georges. (1978) "The Laity and the Peace of God." In *The Chivalrous Society*, translated by Cynthia Postan. Berkeley, CA: University of California Press, 123–33.

———. (1995) *The Peace of God: Social Violence and Religious Response in France around 1000*, edited by Thomas Head and Richard Landes. Ithaca, NY: Cornell University Press.

Glabri, Rodulfi. (1989) *Historiarum Libri Quinque, euisdem auctoris Vita Domni Willelmi Abbatis*, edited and translated by John France. Oxford, U.K.: Clarendon Press.

Pentecostalism

Pentecostalism is a Christian movement that stresses the immediate and compelling presence of the Holy Spirit in worship. Its adherents believe that the Spirit produces extraordinary mental and physical transformations among the faithful. Ministrations of the Spirit include otherwise unexplainable healings and the transport of those graced into ecstatic spiritual states. Religious ecstasy, in turn, often produces unusual behavior, one example of which is the utterance of long streams of generally unintelligible sounds which mimic human language.

Pentecostalism is cross-denominational. Dozens of denominations, however, explicitly identify themselves as Pentecostal. It is largely a Protestant movement but is present, in a small way, in Roman Catholicism. Pentecostalism is American in origin and is especially strong in the United States. It has, however, spread widely overseas. Pentecostalism grew during the twentieth century from modest beginnings to a movement which today claims the allegiance of many millions of worshippers. Since the Reformation, it is likely that no strain of Christian thought and worship has grown so rapidly.

Millennialism has no direct connection with Pentecostalism, although the two religious phenomenon are often associated. Systematic theology is purposely neglected among Pentecostals, who believe that it adds relatively little to the experience of God's immanence. The theological core of Pentecostalism is derived ultimately from how it understands the role of the Holy Spirit in worship and sanctification. Experiential faith takes precedence over creedal formulation.

Virtually no Pentecostals deny the ancient Christian belief in the eventual return in glory of Jesus Christ. If anything, they are liable to anticipate its imminence. However, beyond this anticipation, there is nothing in Pentecostalism that inhibits one from ignoring millennial eschatology altogether. In practice, however, Pentecostalism subsumes into itself many of the key elements of American Fundamental-

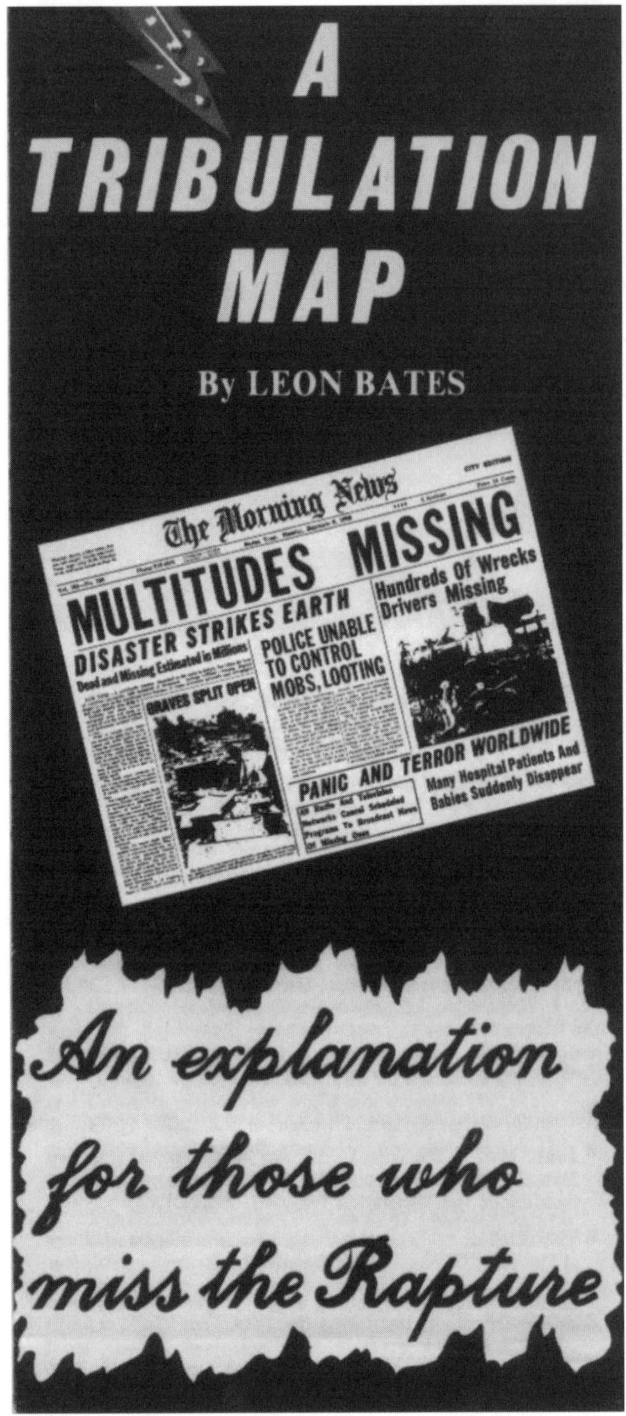

Since the late nineteenth century evangelists have sought to win converts with sensational descriptions of the shock and horrors in store for those that miss the Rapture. This imaginary post-Rapture front page, printed in a prophecy tract from the Bible Believers' Evangelistic Association, graphically dramatizes such predictions. BIBLE BELIEVERS' EVANGELISTIC ASSOCIATION, INC. PAMPHLET, SHERMAN, TX.

ism, one of which is premillennialism. Nearly all Pentecostals regards themselves as Fundamentalists, although many Fundamentalists reject the Pentecostal label. Premillennialism, then, comes to Pentecostalism by virtue of its theological and cultural affinity with Fundamentalism, and not as a core component of its own historical evolution.

Religious and Historical Roots of Pentecostalism

The word pentecost stems ultimately from *pentakostos*, a Greek word meaning fiftieth, and its original religious significance stemmed from the Jewish tradition that the Law was handed down seven weeks after Passover. It received immense significance for Christianity when soon after the Resurrection the apostles gathered in Jerusalem on the Jewish Pentecost. What happened next is described in the Acts of the Apostles: "And suddenly a sound came from heaven like the rush of a mighty wind, and it filled all the house where they were sitting. And there appeared to them tongues as of fire, distributed and resting on each of them. And they were all filled with the holy Spirit and began to speak in other tongues, as the Spirit gave them utterance" (Acts 2:2–4). Ever since, the Christian church has observed the seventh Sunday after Easter as Pentecost and celebrates the outpouring of the Holy Spirit.

Spontaneous speaking "in other tongues," known also as glossolalia, was taken by early Christians as a sign of the indwelling of the Holy Spirit. The account given in Acts emphasizes that what the Apostles spoke was not gibberish but, rather, a form of speech that allowed all listeners, regardless of their own language, to understand fully what was said. ("And how is it that we hear each of us in his own native language?" [Acts 2:8]) It became part of the witness expected among these early Christians, although not everyone knew what to make of it. Paul, for instance, observed, "For one who speaks in a tongue speaks not to men but to God: for no one understands him, but he utters mysteries in the Spirit" (1 Corinthians 14:2).

Speaking in tongues was but one supposed manifestation of the Holy Spirit. Another was spontaneous healing of physical and mental infirmity. By the Gospel account, Jesus repeatedly healed all manner of affliction (e.g., in Matthew 10:32–34) and passed this power to his disciples. Acts contains several instances of such healing, for instance the cure of the lame man by Peter and John (Acts 3:2–10). Modern Pentecostal movements all trace their beliefs to these examples of the gift of tongues and spontaneous healing, along with other "gifts of the Spirit" mentioned in the New Testament.

Despite the antiquity of the testimony given in the Gospels and Acts, Pentecostal Christianity is a modern movement that largely coalesced in the twentieth century. Respected scholars see historical antecedents in the Holiness movement of nineteenth-century evangelical Christianity, especially as associated with the growth of Methodism in America. As with later Pentecostalism, early Methodism sought to bring the gifts of the Spirit into religious life. Early Methodist meetings were filled with portents and wonders, as worshippers claimed to be stricken joyfully by the Spirit. John Wesley believed that conversion was but the first stage in spiritual life and should be followed by sanctification or perfectionism. Sanctification was attained by the Christian when, aided by the Spirit, his desires and motives were finally altogether free from sin.

Ecstatic religious experience was common in eighteenth-century America. The Great Awakening of the 1740s produced countless instances in which concern for salvation plunged laity and clergy alike into profound emotional turmoil. On occasion, this anxiety caused especially unusual behavior, such as copious weeping and "the fits." Such spiritual exaltation occurred not just in private but among entire congregations. Early in the nineteenth century a second wave of religious revivals, the so-called Second Great Awakening, traveled across the new republic. The most spectacular was the revival at Cane Ridge, Tennessee, in 1803, which historians invariably cite as archetypal. (It may, in fact, have been more sedate than usually represented.)

Contemporary accounts of the Cane Ridge revival, and those like it, agree that numerous attendees were thrown into a heightened state of enthusiasm that on occasion manifested itself in unanticipated physical traits, the most extreme of which included barking like a dog or crawling about on all fours. There were, likewise, instances of speaking in tongues and extraordinary healing. Such manifestations appalled some observers and edified others. It was easy to ridicule such spirituality by citing its most bizarre and even comical examples, and these continue to provide a rich vein of satire for critics. In fact, ecstatic experience is part of virtually every major religious tradition.

Sanctification theology, known also as perfectionism or the Holiness movement, was widely popular, if controversial, in America during the nineteenth century. It was most prevalent in the Methodist Church and was taken up for a time by the eminent evangelist Charles G. Finney. In its extreme form it created social scandal, for example the Onedia Community in upstate New York. The Onedia members, confident that they were liberated from sin, engaged in latitudinarian sexual practices. In this, however, they were utterly atypical. Far more common was a conscious striving to attain a state of Christian perfection free from a sinful heart. Several Protestant denominations, such as the Church of the Nazarene, are rooted in this Holiness movement, although all vehemently reject sexual experimentation.

American Pentecostalism in the Twentieth Century

The Holiness movement was formative for Pentecostalism, and the extraordinary spiritual gifts recorded in Acts provided its ultimate rationale. Not until the twentieth century, however, did Pentecostalism emerge as distinct within American Protestantism. No one event marked the transformation of ancient tradition and contemporary practices into modern Pentecostalism, but the 1906 Azusa Street revival in Los Angeles generated such national interest and became such a model for worship that it helped initiate the movement. The revival occurred over a period of several months in what was at first largely a black congregation, and until well into the century Pentecostalism was unusual in its multiracialism. Worshippers received what they believed to be the biblical gift of tongues and reported miraculous instances of spontaneous healing. The intensely emotive worship intrigued and attracted some from around the nation, although it utterly repelled many Protestants.

These early Pentecostals, like their spiritual descendents today, stressed the wondrous experience of a "second blessing." The first blessing was baptism into the Christian community. The second blessing was the descent of the Spirit, as manifested in glossolalia, healings, and intense religious exaltation. Distinct Pentecostal denominations precipitated out of what was initially a loose alliance of like-minded congregations and pastors; among them, the Assemblies of God, the Pentecostal Holiness Church, and the Church of God in Christ. Early on, the movement was split by various disputes which led to the formation of new factions. Overall, however, this fissioning was at least as much a sign of the movement's strength as a source of weakness.

Fundamentalism and Pentecostalism, the two most vigorous strains of Protestantism in twentieth-century America, were contemporaries in their origins. Fundamentalism is rooted in the millenarian theology of nineteenth-century American evangelicalism and its constellation of social and theological beliefs was widely recognized as distinct by around the time of the First World War. This was precisely the same period when Pentecostalism, imbued with especial vigor by the recent Azuza Street revival, grew rapidly. This serendipitous contemporanity caused the public to often regard the two movements as identical which, of course, they were not. Still, their similarities are so marked that this public confusion (which exists to this day) is understandable. Both traditions revel in hortatory preaching. They share, as well, belief in an infallible Bible, a position commonly called literalism. And, during the twentieth century, both traditions drew hurtful reproaches from those intolerant of their way of worship.

There are, however, significant differences between Fundamentalism and Pentecostalism. The most profound is the

Pentecostal belief that gifts of the Spirit that marked the Apostolic Era, especially glossolalia and spontaneous healing, are accessible today. Fundamentalists, as a rule, believe that such things ended with the death of the last Apostle and tend to be skeptical of physical manifestations which Pentecostals claim as the work of the Holy Spirit. Then, too, Pentecostals are more welcoming toward women in positions of churchly authority. Prophecy is a gift of the Spirit which Pentecostals revere, and since the early Christian church respected women in this role they are thus accepted today. Fundamentalists usually balk at the idea of a female clergy, but this causes Pentecostals fewer problems.

Pentecostals and Fundamentalists differ over other aspects of theology, including their attitudes toward the Second Coming and the millennium. Fundamentalism is heir to the long Calvinist tradition and is peculiarly susceptible to premillennialism. Since Fundamentalists dismiss the efficacy of individual effort to live a life acceptable to God, they must rely on grace, freely bestowed and unearned, to accomplish personal salvation. This Calvinist heritage manifests itself as well in eschatology. Since individuals, absent grace, are powerless to achieve salvation, it follows that they can not accomplish this corporately. Thus, a godly, or millennial, world must await the return of Christ. The Second Advent will transform a sinful world in a manner analogous to the operation of grace upon the individual. The Advent, like personal conversion, is a sudden, irresistible, and preordained God-initiated event. The connection between Calvinism and premillennialism is thus of the utmost significance for understanding the origin of Fundamentalism.

Pentecostals are careful students of prophecy. Like their fellow Fundamentalists, they generally expect the imminent return of Christ in glory and many hope as well for the subsequent millennium. However, Pentecostalism contains a strong streak of Arminianism, an optimistic theology which allows believers to advance the work of salvation by inviting the Holy Spirit into their faith-life. This theology, which enables believers, contrasts with the natural inability in the Calvinist-Fundamentalist tradition to connect in the present with the Holy Spirit implicit, and is a legacy to Pentecostals out of their Holiness-Methodist history. The Second Coming is a common article of faith, and many are the Pentecostal preachers who see in their own movement an incipient sign of the outpouring of the Holy Spirit that signals the Last Days. But, millennialism, while present in Pentecostalism, nonetheless lacks for it the historical and theological significance it carries for other Fundamentalists. Pentecostals are, as well, open to prophecy as the Spirit moves believers. In this, they differ from nearly all other Christians, Fundamentalists included, who believe that prophecy ended with the immediate post-Apostolic Era.

Pentecostalism gained notoriety in the twentieth century because of the flamboyant success of several of its clergy. The hortatory homiletic style preferred by its laity combined with such atypical Protestant practices as glossolalia and spontaneous healing to both fascinate and repel the public. Aimee Semple McPherson, founder of the Pentecostal Four Square Gospel Church, was famous throughout the interwar decades for clerical showmanship, healing ministry, and abundant charity. Successors in her vein include Oral Roberts, whose long ministry and claims of spectacular healings make him a national figure.

Pentecostal churches grew at an astonishing rate throughout the twentieth century. The Assemblies of God increased its official membership from 47,950 in 1926 to a reported 2,271,718 in 1995. The corresponding figures for the Church of God in Christ are 30,263 and 6,750,875. Although the racial integration of the Azuza Street Mission revival era faded during the 1920s as white worshippers formed largely segregated denominations, the appeal of Pentecostalism spread across racial and ethnic lines. By the late twentieth century, the movement had put down roots deep in the American Hispanic community. It also experienced stupendous growth overseas, especially in Latin America, where in certain states, especially Brazil, the thriving Pentecostal community threatened the historic dominance of the Roman Catholic Church. The movement also flourished in Europe and in Scandinavia was second in allegiance among Christians only to the established churches. Taken to the Far East by missionaries from the United States, it made rapid headway, particularly in Korea.

Pentecostalism remains an overwhelmingly Protestant phenomenon. Nevertheless, it spread into the Roman Catholic community during the last decades of the twentieth century, though not without great controversy. During the 1960s, isolated local parishes experimented with a new approach to worship, eventually labeled the charismatic movement, that borrowed essential elements from Pentecostalism. These included glossolalia, spontaneous healing, and a doctrine of the second blessing. In certain locales such supposed manifestations of the Spirit proved divisive. In others, particularly those with a Hispanic population, they were welcomed.

A few mainline Protestant denominations experienced Pentecostal-like revivals late in the century, including the Episcopal and Lutheran churches. Within these churches, as with Roman Catholic Church, Pentecostalism remained a fairly rare phenomenon and showed little sign of spreading beyond immediate parishes or congregations.

At the start of the twenty-first century, the relatively new Pentecostal churches had far outstripped in size several of the much older American Protestant denominations, such as the

Presbyterians and the United Church of Christ, and were continuing their rapid expansion. While not as centered in eschatology as their fellow Fundamentalists, the success of Pentecostalism ensures nonetheless that millenarianism will continue as a staple of religious life in America.

Robert K. Whalen

See also Fundamentalism

Bibliography

Epstein, Daniel Mark. (1993) *Sister Aimee: The Life of Aimee Semple McPherson.* New York: Harcourt Brace & Co.

Harrell, David Edwin, Jr. (1975) *All Things Are Possible: The Healing and Charismatic Revivals in Modern America.* Bloomington, IN: Indiana University Press.

Laurentin, Rene. (1977) *Catholic Pentecostalism,* translated by Matthew J. O'Connell. Garden City, NY: Doubleday & Company, Inc.

Synan, Vinson. (1997) *The Holiness-Pentecostal Tradition: Charismatic Movements in the Twentieth Century.* Grand Rapids, MI: Wm. B. Eerdmanns Publishing Co.

Peoples Temple

Peoples Temple was a religious movement which began in the 1950s in Indianapolis, moved to California in the 1960s and flourished there in the 1970s, emigrated to Guyana, South America in 1977, and collapsed in a mass murder-suicide of nine hundred people on 18 November 1978 in Jonestown, Guyana.

Although Temple members came from a variety of socioeconomic backgrounds, they were united in their commitment to racial equality and social justice. Their leader, the Rev. Jim Jones, was haunted by apocalyptic visions of a fascist takeover of the United States which would climax in race wars and concentration camps. Acting on his fears, Jones took the group to the northwest territory of Guyana where followers tried to create a utopian commune out of dense jungle. In November 1978 U.S. Congressman Leo Ryan traveled to Jonestown to investigate charges that people were held against their will. On 18 November followers of Jones assassinated the congressman and four others at an airstrip five miles from Jonestown. Shortly thereafter nine hundred persons in Jonestown apparently took the lives of their children, their elderly relatives, and themselves by drinking or injecting fruit punch laced with potassium cyanide and tranquilizers. They died in what some called an act of revolutionary suicide, protesting American capitalism.

History

Jim Jones (1931–78), a charismatic preacher, established a series of churches that attracted interracial congregations in Indianapolis, Indiana, in the 1950s. Members of these small churches provided social services for the poor under the guidance of Jones's wife Marceline Baldwin Jones (1927–78), a registered nurse. In 1955 Jones and associates formed Wings of Deliverance, the nonprofit foundation of Peoples Temple. Jones took a leave of absence 1963–65 and worked in Brazil before a vision of nuclear holocaust persuaded him to take his congregation to northern California in 1965. About eighty followers moved with him to Redwood Valley, a small community in the California wine country. From there the movement, which was still predominantly white, expanded to San Francisco and began to proselytize urban African Americans. By 1970 it opened a large facility in San Francisco in the heart of the black ghetto. While it continued to maintain social services and facilities in Redwood Valley, the Temple moved its program to San Francisco, and then expanded to Los Angeles. At its height, the organization boasted three thousand members.

In 1974, a small group of pioneers began to clear jungle in Guyana to create a new community, based on an agreement with the government of Guyana. The pioneers were unprepared for the large influx of members in 1977, however. Some one thousand members emigrated from California to Guyana in the space of six months. About nine hundred people lived in Jonestown from 1977–78, while another eighty to one hundred lived in Georgetown, Guyana's capital. Another fifty to one hundred remained in

Jim Jones with children of the Rainbow Family in the 1960s. REBECCA MOORE.

LETTER FOUND IN JONESTOWN

I am 24 years of age right now and don't expect to live through the end of this book.

I thought I should at least make some attempt to let the world know what Jim Jones and the Peoples Temple is–OR WAS–all about . . .

What a beautiful place this was. The children loved the jungle, learned about animals and plants. There were no cars to run over them; no child molesters to molest them; nobody to hurt them. They were the freest, most intelligent children I had ever known.

Seniors had dignity. They had whatever they wanted–a plot of land for a garden. Seniors were treated with respect–something they never had in the United States. A rare few were sick, and when they were, they were given the best medical care . . .

We died because you would not let us live in peace.

Annie Moore

Source: Rebecca Moore, ed. (1986). *The Jonestown Letters: Correspondence of the Moore Family 1970-1985.* Lewiston, NY: Edwin Mellen Press.

California for administrative purposes. About one-third of the people who lived in Jonestown were senior citizens and one-third were children under the age of eighteen. This meant that only about one-third were able-bodied adults capable of working to support the community by farming, producing crafts for sale, and other activities. They struggled to become self-sufficient. Although hours were long and hard, and food was not plentiful, spirits were high.

Beginning in 1976, a group calling itself the Concerned Relatives, comprised of former Temple members and relatives of current members, exerted pressure on Peoples Temple. The group alleged long hours, forced confessions, beatings, and other forms of physical or mental punishment. It characterized Jim Jones as a power-mad leader and claimed that one member who wanted to leave had been murdered. Accusations prompted a number of local, state, and federal investigations into Peoples Temple, although the probes found no evidence of wrongdoing on the part of the organization. In June 1978, the Concerned Relatives publicly raised the prospect of mass suicide in Jonestown. The group stepped up its organizing and persuaded Congressman Leo Ryan that people in Jonestown were being held against their will.

During a tense and hostile visit in November 1978, Ryan nonetheless praised the community and what it had accomplished. But disaffected residents of Jonestown slipped messages to reporters, and as Ryan and his group were leaving on 18 November 1978, a dozen residents chose to leave with them. When Ryan, his aides, the media, and the Jonestown defectors reached an airstrip at Port Kaituma, about five miles away, a Peoples Temple truck pulled up and gunmen began firing, taking particular pains to execute Ryan and members of the media Greg Robinson, Robert Brown, and Don Harris. A fifth person, Temple member Patricia Parks, was also killed. Meanwhile, another Temple member, Larry Layton, had entered a plane with other defectors and began shooting, wounding several people until he was disarmed.

After Ryan's party left Jonestown, Jim Jones gathered the community at its central pavilion. Nurses mixed a vat of fruit drink with potassium cyanide and tranquilizers. Parents killed their children by giving them poison to drink or by injecting them. Senior citizens were injected in their sleeping quarters. Most adults seemed to have taken the poison willingly, although questions remain about the extent to which they were coerced. Jim Jones and his nurse Annie Moore (1954–78) were both shot, their wounds consistent with suicide.

Beliefs

There were at least two belief systems operating in Peoples Temple which can be combined under the rubric "apostolic socialism": that of Jim Jones and that of the majority of Christian believers. Jones combined a Pentecostal style of preaching and worship with a Marxist analysis of social problems and an apocalyptic vision of the future. He modeled his preaching on revivalist patterns, but he emphasized the Bible's social message of liberation from poverty and inequality.

Although he began as a preacher within Christian tradition, and while Peoples Temple was an official member of the Disciples of Christ, Jim Jones claimed he used Christianity as a cover for the Marxist, and specifically communist, goals of overthrowing capitalist society and establishing a new society free of racism, competition, poverty, and injustice. But Jones's socialism was more freewheeling than orthodox Marxism, and in many respects his Marxism was a front for his own eclectic views of religion, politics, and the future.

Jones's understanding of the future was always pessimistic, in spite of the fact that his followers were attempting to create a new society on earth. It was a vision of nuclear holocaust which took him first to Brazil, and then to California. Similarly it was a vision of a police state replacing democratic institutions that drove him to Guyana. Pessimism about the future was coupled with a critical understanding of the present. The world was unjust, happiness was not possible if people were starving, and one must do something to change things.

Until the late 1990s most research focused on Jim Jones, but attention has shifted to the beliefs of his followers. Almost all came from some form of Christianity, with the majority coming from the American Black church tradition. This tradition emphasized the social gospel, that is, the message of hope, liberation, and justice found in the Bible and in the teachings of Jesus. While Jones could point to Marx, his followers could point to the socialism of Acts 2:44–45 in the Bible. Most members believed they were practicing Christianity by being part of Peoples Temple, and that they were living out the gospel imperative of feeding the hungry, clothing the naked, caring for the sick, and visiting the prisoner (Matthew 25:31–46).

In spite of their commitment to apostolic socialism, members apparently agreed to Jones's program of "revolutionary suicide," which they understood as an act of protest against capitalism and against Jonestown's enemies. The extent to which suicide drills occurred, in which members drank punch and pretended to fall down dead is in dispute. Some say it occurred rarely, and only among a small leadership group. Others say the entire Jonestown community practiced them with regularity.

On the last day it seems likely that the residents of Jonestown chose death rather than life because they saw it as a choice between loyalty and betrayal, not as a choice between socialism and capitalism. They could betray their beliefs and their community, created over months and years of hard work, and live; or they could remain loyal to their loved ones, and die as they had lived, together. They chose to die.

Conclusions

Peoples Temple was profoundly influenced by the liberation movements of the 1960s. It kept alive the rhetoric and the promise of social change and racial equality by engaging in the political movements of its day, and by providing needed social services for the poorest members of society. At the same time, the Temple turned its attention inward to the group's own problems and enemies. Jim Jones replaced Jesus as the central figure in the theology of the church, and the Concerned Relatives replaced fascism as the primary enemy. Leo Ryan's visit converged with government investigations into the Temple's finances, with Jim Jones's deteriorating health, and with the financial precariousness of Jonestown.

In the years since Ryan's assassination two main questions have emerged. First, to what extent if any were the deaths voluntary? Second, did a U.S. government conspiracy against Peoples Temple exist because of its interracial and socialistic nature? The first question emerged relatively quickly because it was not immediately clear what had happened in Jonestown. Inadequate investigations at the site and the lack of routine medico-legal examinations meant that the actual cause of death was never determined. Reports from survivors were conflicting, with some saying that people were forced to take the poison and others saying that it was voluntary. A tape purporting to have been made during the actual event seems to indicate general assent, but its authenticity is in question.

The second question emerged more slowly because there was a presumption of guilt about the people who killed their children and took their own lives. It is clear that numerous local, state, and federal investigations threatened the survival of Peoples Temple. Government documents indicate that the Central Intelligence Agency had an agent or agents monitoring activities in Jonestown. Some believe that the CIA ran Jonestown as a mind-control experiment in which drugs and behavior modification techniques were tested. Others argue that the men who killed Congressman Ryan were part of a military hit squad and were not Peoples Temple members. The fact that the CIA was monitoring Jonestown and did not prevent the assassination or the murders-suicides raises questions about the involvement of the U.S. government in the deaths of its citizens. Moreover, historians have been unable to gain access to twelve volumes of the official report on Leo Ryan's death prepared by the U.S. House of Representatives in 1979 and turned over to the CIA for safekeeping.

In spite of the unanswered questions, Peoples Temple remains part of a complex of groups which emerged in the 1960s and 1970s which envisioned a political rather than religious apocalypse. Members expected things to get worse before they would get better, and they fled to Guyana to escape the coming persecution. Although they tried to create a heaven on earth, their pessimistic worldview kept them in the grip of a fear of what the future would bring: persecution, torture, death. Ironically, they created exactly what they feared.

Rebecca Moore

See also Catastrophic Millennialism, Cults, Persecution

Bibliography

Hall, John R. (1987) *Gone From the Promised Land: Jonestown in American Cultural History*. New Brunswick, NJ: Transaction Books.

Maaga, Mary McCormick. (1998) *Hearing the Voices of Jonestown*. Syracuse, NY: Syracuse University Press.

Moore, Rebecca. (1985) *A Sympathetic History of Jonestown*. Lewiston, NY: Edwin Mellen Press.

Reiterman, Tim, with John Jacobs. (1982) *Raven: The Untold Story of the Rev. Jim Jones and His People*. New York: E. P. Dutton.

Persecution

Persecution and millennial beliefs are interrelated in complex ways. This article highlights aspects of the interactions of persecution and millennialism in relation to catastrophic and progressive expectations and to the sociology of assaulted, fragile, and revolutionary groups. "Persecution" related to religious groups is understood to mean harassing to afflict or injure because of beliefs. Persecution is in the eyes of the beholder. Acts committed against a religious group may be deemed persecution by observers or by believers, while people committing those acts may see the action as being necessary to preserve social order and safety.

Varieties of Millennialism

Persecution is particularly relevant to catastrophic millennialism, the belief in an imminent cataclysmic transition to a collective salvation. Catastrophic millennialism involves a dualistic perspective of "good" battling "evil" which often translates into a sense of "us vs. them." The dualism of catastrophic millennialism is validated and strengthened by believers' experiences of "cultural opposition" (Hall 1995: 205–35). The dualism of catastrophic millennialism can contribute to situations in which believers are persecuted or they believe that they are being persecuted. The experience of persecution confirms catastrophic millennialism's dualism and prophecies of violence.

Progressive millennialism involves the belief that humans working under the guidance of a superhuman or divine agent can create the millennial kingdom in a noncatastrophic manner. This type of millennialism appears among people who feel relatively comfortable in mainstream society—they do not feel persecuted—but they are disturbed by suffering and feel called to do something about it. A religious group's worldview may shift between catastrophic or progressive millennial themes as members alternately feel persecuted or comfortable in society.

Some progressive millennialists desire to speed progress up to such a fast rate that they resort to violence to achieve their millennial kingdom. This pattern can be termed revolutionary progressive millennialism. Whereas the nonviolent progressive millennialism may downplay dualism in favor of stressing the unity of humanity, revolutionary progressive millennialism possesses a strong dualism in which the good guys ("us") must fight the bad guys ("them," the demonized "other"). As in revolutionary catastrophic movements, revolutionary progressive millennialists often violently purge perceived traitors and apostates. Revolutionary progressive millennialists typically possess a strong sense of having been oppressed, and they believe that their only recourse is violent action to achieve their collective salvation. The German Nazis, the Khmer Rouge, and Maoists in China are examples of revolutionary progressive millennial movements.

Revolutionary progressive millennial movements have a great deal in common with violent catastrophic millennial movements in terms of their shared dualism, their propensity to utilize violence against enemies within and without their groups, and their sense of being persecuted. These movements will be immensely violent when they become socially dominant. In resorting to revolutionary violence to overthrow governments, dominate countries, eliminate the perceived threat of demonized peoples, and deal with perceived traitors, the believers become persecutors on a massive scale.

Persecution and Catastrophic Millennial Movements and Groups

A sense of persecution is most commonly relevant to catastrophic millennial movements and groups, and the remainder of this essay will focus on these.

Three Attitudes toward Participation in the Transition to the Millennial Kingdom

According to Jean Rosenfeld (2000), catastrophic millennialists can take three possible stances toward whether they are called to participate in the anticipated cataclysmic events of the endtime: (1) they can await divine intervention to destroy the current world as the necessarily prelude to the creation of the millennial kingdom; (2) they can arm themselves for protection during the anticipated cataclysmic events. If such groups are assaulted, they will fight back; (3) they can adopt a revolutionary theology or ideology that will prompt them to wage war to overthrow the government to establish their millennial kingdom.

The extent to which a millennial group experiences persecution can prompt the believers to shift from waiting for divine intervention to using violence for self-defense or to overthrow the government. The nature of the interaction of outsiders with millennialists is crucial in determining whether a group will remain peaceful or become caught up in violence. While it is sometimes necessary for religious groups to be investigated, whenever possible these investigations should enroll the cooperation of the millennialists, promote respectful dialogue, and avoid persecution. Persecution strengthens catastrophic millennial beliefs, hardens the boundaries drawn between "us" and "them," and causes millennial groups to become caught up in violence that may be initiated either by the believers or by outsiders who assault them.

Assaulted Millennial Groups

Assaulted millennial groups are catastrophic millennialists who are attacked by law enforcement agents or civilians because they are thought to be dangerous. They are assaulted because their religion is misunderstood and because of bigotry. Their religion is regarded as being bizarre and not worthy of respect and legal protection. Members of assaulted millennial groups are persecuted, and they may respond either in a pacifist manner and attempt to utilize legal recourse—as do members of the Messianic Communities—or they may resort to violent actions in self-defense.

Church of Jesus Christ of Latter-day Saints In the nineteenth century, members of the Church of Jesus Christ of Latter-day Saints were assaulted repeatedly as they were pressured to move from New York to Ohio, Missouri, and Illinois. The governor of Missouri issued an extermination order against Mormons in 1838. A Mormon camp at Haun's Mill was attacked by a Missouri militia killing seventeen people. A nine-year-old boy was shot by a man who later explained that "Nits will make lice." Joseph Smith and his brother were in jail when they were murdered by a mob on 27 June 1844, in Carthage, Illinois. The largest group of Mormons went with Brigham Young to settle in Utah where they received further persecution from the United States government. In the heightened conflictual atmosphere, some Mormon men and Native Americans committed the Mountain Meadows massacre on 7 September 1857, of about 120 pioneers traveling westward. Some of those pioneers had boasted that they had participated in the massacre at Haun's Mill and in other attacks against Mormons. During the 1870s and 1880s, the U.S. government prosecuted Mormons for polygamy.

Throughout the years of persecution, public sentiment was whipped up against Mormons by sensationalized books and newspaper articles. The following quote from an Illinois newspaper is worthy of any propaganda effort to promote ethnic cleansing:

> War and extermination is inevitable! CITIZENS ARISE, ONE AND ALL!!! Can you *stand* by, and suffer such INFERNAL DEVILS! to ROB men of their property and RIGHTS, without avenging them? We have no time for comment: every man will make his own. LET IT BE MADE WITH POWDER AND BALL!!! (Arrington and Bitton 1979: 60)

The extermination of Latter-day Saints was justified by their dehumanization, first by calling them Mormons and then by applying other degrading labels to them. They were "denounced as dupes, foreigners, Negro-lovers, Indian-lovers, trash, and vermin. Various images tended to degrade the Mormons into animals: swarms, hives, locusts, geese, and droves" (Arrington and Bitton 1979: 61).

Branch Davidians On 28 February 1993, a community of about 123 adults and children living at Mount Carmel Center near Waco, Texas, was assaulted by federal agents largely because they were identified as belonging to a "cult." The assault was carried out by agents of the Bureau of Alcohol, Tobacco, and Firearms (BATF or ATF). The Davidians had arms and fought back. Four ATF agents and five Davidians died in the shootout. Later that day a sixth Davidian was killed by ATF agents as he attempted to return to Mount Carmel on foot.

The Branch Davidians were assaulted by ATF agents although their investigation had found no evidence that the Davidians possessed illegal weapons. There were allegations of child abuse against the leader, David Koresh, but the case had been investigated and closed by Texas social workers due to lack of evidence. Furthermore, child abuse does not come under the jurisdiction of federal agencies.

During the fifty-one-day siege of Mount Carmel in which Federal Bureau of Investigation (FBI) agents waged psychological warfare against the Davidians, the agents dismissed the significance of the religious worldview of people they regarded as duped and brainwashed "cultists." The negotiation transcripts reveal that the Davidians did not want to die and they tried to negotiate a peaceful resolution that would conform to their understanding of biblical prophecies, but the tank and CS gas assault by FBI agents culminated in a fire that killed seventy-four Davidians including twenty-three children.

In 1993 David Koresh's theology did not teach the Davidians to initiate violence, but their persecution by federal agents confirmed the Davidians' belief in Koresh's divinely inspired ability to interpret the Bible and strengthened the cohesiveness of their group. This accounts for why the Davidians were able to withstand the psychological warfare waged against them. In the cases of both the Mormons and the Branch Davidians, persecution strengthened the believers' faith and solidarity by confirming their leaders' interpretations of biblical predictions of the cataclysmic endtime events.

Fragile Millennial Groups

Members of a fragile millennial group initiate violence to preserve their "ultimate concern" (Baird 1971: 18), their religious goal, that is endangered by stresses internal to the group and cultural opposition. It is not unusual for the leader to cause many of the internal stresses. Opposition from outside that threatens the group's ultimate concern can include criticisms from concerned relatives, sensationalized news reports, and investigations by government agencies, law enforcement agents, and social workers. Child custody disputes and accusations of child abuse are very threatening forms of opposition. Apostates—individuals who have left and are very vocal and aggressive in opposing the group—are a particular threat as former believers who have lost their faith and who may be demanding the return of financial resources.

Members of fragile millennial groups in extreme tension with society may resort to violence to silence dissidents, attempt to return them to the true faith, and prevent them from leaving the group which is viewed as the only source of salvation. Also, they may resort to violence against perceived enemies in society.

In committing coercive and violent acts, members of fragile millennial groups become persecutors. The violence may be directed inwardly against group members or outwardly at perceived enemies or both. Endogenous and exogenous stresses may culminate in murder and group suicide as at Jonestown in 1978 and with the Solar Temple in 1994. They may culminate in an assault against society as in Aum Shinrikyo's release of nerve gas on the Tokyo subway in 1995.

Persecution serves to destabilize a fragile millennial group, because it contributes to believers' fear that they will fail to achieve their ultimate concern. In such cases, persecution serves to weaken a group that is already suffering from internal stresses, and thus might motivate believers to resort to violent actions to preserve their religious goal.

Revolutionary Millennial Movements

Revolutionary millennial movements are fueled by theologies or ideologies that motivate believers to commit violent acts to overthrow the government. A people feels persecuted so they resort to revolutionary actions to establish a collective salvation. In their zealous use of violence to create the millennial kingdom, these millennialists become persecutors of others who do not share their vision.

When a revolutionary millennial movement becomes socially dominant, it produces massive amounts of violence. For instance, the Taiping Rebellion from 1850 to 1864 in China against the Manchu Qing dynasty resulted in the deaths of at least 20 million people. When a revolutionary millennial movement is not socially dominant, its most fervent believers resort to terrorism. This is the case with the contemporary Euro-American nativist movement which includes the Montana Freemen, Identity Christians, Odinists, Neo-Nazis, and extremist Christian Patriots.

Catastrophic Millennial Beliefs and Persecution

Catastrophic millennial beliefs often are heightened in response to the experience of persecution. Catastrophic millennialism is a worldview that promises salvation from evil and suffering, and can be the perspective of whole nations or small groups. Catastrophic millennialism is appealing particularly to people experiencing persecution. It offers hope for deliverance and promises that the evil-doers and the righteous will receive their respective just rewards. Based on his study of Mormon millennial thought, Grant Underwood (2000) has concluded that "the single greatest factor in propelling a movement to emphasize an apocalyptic rhetoric of judgment and vengeance seems to be the persecution they feel from around them."

Apocalyptic rhetoric of violent divine retribution against oppressors does not mean that millennialists will seek to carry out that anticipated judgment. A group's theology and sociology have to be studied in depth to determine the extent to which believers feel called to carry out the destruction of their enemies. The violent apocalyptic rhetoric of catastrophic millennialists will diminish if their sense of persecution diminishes. However, the preservation of catastrophic millennial prophecies in scriptures means that these passages will be resources for new movements within that religious tradition.

When a catastrophic millennial group feels persecuted, a leader may bring the date for the end of the current order closer in time. This was done by David Koresh of the Branch Davidians and by Shoko Asahara of Aum Shinrikyo. Bringing the date for the end closer is an important indication that the group and its leader feel persecuted.

The dualism (sense of "us vs. them," "good vs. evil") of catastrophic millennialism can prompt believers to be convinced they are being persecuted when, in fact, the opposition they are experiencing is not excessive. While catastrophic millennialists often are persecuted, the dualism of the catastrophic millennial worldview predisposes them to interpret any amount of opposition as being persecution. An example of this is Heaven's Gate whose leader and thirty-eight followers committed suicide near San Diego in 1997. Although the group had received some sensationalized news coverage in the 1970s, they had not been persecuted for almost twenty years. In 1993 they emerged from their reclusive monastic lifestyle to begin proselytizing again. In 1995 they sent their message out into cyberspace. In response they received some e-mail messages ridiculing their beliefs, and they interpreted these as evidence of their persecution and as confirmation that it was time to leave the corrupt earthly world behind to its cataclysmic fate.

The dualism of the Aum Shinrikyo worldview contributed to what a member called Aum's "persecution complex" and to Aum's intense conflict with society (Wessinger 1999). Ian Reader (1996 and 2000) judges the negative news reports about Aum Shinrikyo as not being persecution since new religions in Japan often are scrutinized by the press. The criminal activities of Aum devotees needed to be investigated, but the Japanese police neglected to investigate for some time, in part, due to trying to avoid the appearance of persecuting a religion. The dualism of the Aum worldview predisposed the guru and devotees to view any sign of opposition as persecution. Both the Heaven's Gate members and Aum Shinrikyo devotees were avid consumers of conspiracy theories, which can be taken as one indication of an extreme dualistic worldview.

There is a circular dynamic relating persecution and the dualism of catastrophic millennialism. The dualism of a catastrophic millennial worldview predisposes believers to view any opposition as persecution. The opposition may become severe enough to be actual persecution. Persecution increases the dualistic catastrophic millennialism of the believers.

Catastrophic Millennial Characteristics which May Contribute to Persecution

Characteristics of catastrophic millennial communities and movements can contribute to situations in which they are persecuted by law enforcement agents and/or citizens. Because of their dream of an imminent transition to a radically renovated state of collective existence, all millennial religions pose a challenge to the status quo. Even catastrophic millennialists that peacefully await divine intervention expect a revolutionary destruction of the old order. Anticipating the expected salvation kingdom, millennial communities often adopt a lifestyle that involves practices and values radically different from those of mainstream society. They often adopt distinctive sexual arrangements, gender roles, and childrearing practices. These include celibacy, polygamy, marriage between partners of different ages, and women's religious leadership. These practices diverge from those of mainstream society and elicit hostility and raise the fear that vulnerable persons are being abused by the group.

Committed millennialists hold an allegiance to an authority they consider to be higher than the authority of civil law. While many catastrophic millennialists will submit peacefully to the unjust application of laws, and they pray that they will encounter individuals of conscience who will administer laws justly, some other millennialists will prefer to kill or die rather than compromise their commitment to higher authority. The latter was the case with a group of black South Africans calling themselves Israelites, who believed they were ordered by God to gather at Bulhoek, South Africa, in 1921. They refused to disperse when authorities told them that they could not live there. The result was a massacre in which 183 Israelites died from police gunfire.

Catastrophic millennial communities may not contribute actively to their own persecution, but their antagonism to the predominant social order, their alternative lifestyles, and their commitment to an authority they place above that of civil law puts them at odds with society and law enforcement agents. Furthermore, the dualism of catastrophic millennialism leads millennialists to expect and perhaps even promote conflict with society. Catastrophic millennialists are not surprised when conflict manifests in fulfillment of their prophecies. If a catastrophic millennial group is armed due to the expectation of imminent conflict, that is yet another factor that can provoke negative attention from law enforcement agents and citizens.

When the Persecuted Become Persecutors

When millennialists resort to coercive and violent measures, they become persecutors. Some millennial groups resort to violent acts to control members, prevent defections, and attack persons outside the group who are identified as enemies. For instance, Aum Shinrikyo devotees were forced to undergo severe asceticism such as being immersed in extremely hot or cold water. Devotees who said they wished to leave were confined, drugged, and subjected to ineffective attempts at forcible mind control. Aum devotees also made numerous attacks against outsiders whom they deemed to be threats. Aum Shinrikyo's nerve gas attack on the Tokyo subway killed twelve and injured over five thousand people. When millennialists utilize violence against tepid members, defectors, and outsiders, they are persecuting people because of their different beliefs.

Ritual Violence

When dramatic violent acts are committed either by or against millennialists, often these are preceded by ritualized smaller violent acts. The repeated acts of Aum Shinrikyo violence both against its own members and people on the outside became rituals, which culminated in the nerve gas attack on the Tokyo subway.

In the Peoples Temple, suicide rituals first took place in Jim Jones's inner circle while the church was located in

California. Church members sanctioned public boxing matches and other violent rituals to socialize misbehaving members. In Jonestown, some people who wished to leave were drugged, and some were confined in coffin-sized boxes. The community discussed group suicide as an option and came to a consensus that "revolutionary suicide" was an appropriate means to preserve the cohesiveness of their collective if it was threatened with disintegration. They practiced mass suicide in "white night" drills. On 18 November 1978, the Fla-Vor-Aid contained cyanide and the majority of the people knew they were committing suicide. A total of 918 people died that day, including five members of Congressman Leo Ryan's party who were shot as they were departing with some defectors.

Law enforcement agents and members of the military also engage in rituals of violence that can escalate to a massive level. After the ATF raid on the Branch Davidians, FBI agents presided over a siege during which tanks demolished cars and other property belonging to the Davidians. The men in the tanks made obscene gestures at the Davidians, mooned, and cursed them. Psychological warfare was waged by blasting high-decibel sounds and blinding lights at the Davidians. These violent acts escalated to culminate in the final assault in which tanks inserted CS gas into the residence and began demolishing the building. While it is unknown how the fire began, it is clear that there would have been no fire if there had been no final assault.

Religious believers, law enforcement agents, military personnel, and citizens need to be wary of participating in or condoning ritualized acts of violence.

Prejudice and Persecution

Prejudice against "cults" and "sects" promotes religious persecution. Since the 1970s, religions that are deemed to be "cults" or "sects" often are subjected to persecution. In English-speaking countries, "cult" has become a pejorative word for a religion that people do not understand and do not like. In countries in which romance languages are spoken, "sect" is the pejorative word. "Cult" and "sect," which originally designated legitimate categories of religion, have become convenient four-letter words to label religions that are judged by the general public to be false and dangerous. Many people do not realize that these terms express a prejudice equal to that expressed in racial slurs. Applying a bigoted label and stereotype to members of an unconventional group has the effect of dehumanizing them and makes it appear to be legitimate to discriminate against them and even kill them. In countries in which freedom of religion purportedly is guaranteed, groups have to be labeled as not *really* being religions and as being dangerous in order to legitimate aggressive persecution by law enforcement agents. This persecution in its most extreme form consists of violent acts against the religious group.

After the Waco tragedy, many American law enforcement agents and news reporters in the print media have attempted to become more sensitive to issues of religious freedom and to avoid prejudice that fuels aggression against minority religions. People working in electronic media in the United States still have a lot to learn about not promoting religious bigotry.

In the 1990s, some European countries have become highly intolerant of groups labeled "sects." In 1996, France published a list of 173 "dangerous sects" that included Jehovah's Witnesses and a Baptist mission church. These religious institutions and their members have been subjected to defamation in the media, government audits, punitive taxes, employment discrimination, and the denial of bank accounts and bank loans.

Law enforcement agents, who must struggle with the question of how to maintain law and order while preserving religious freedom, need to be aware that applying a bigoted stereotype to an unconventional group can result in misunderstanding, and therefore can prompt them to take actions against a religious group that can culminate in violence. News reporters need to become sensitive to how their reporting about unconventional religions has the power to contribute to violent scenarios. Millennialists need to become aware of how the characteristics of their groups can elicit hostile reactions on the part of the general public, and consider how they can respond constructively to reduce that fear. Scholars of religions need to continue studying the multifaceted relationships between millennialism, persecution, and violence, to deepen our understanding of these dynamics so that we can extend our teaching mission to the general public and avoid perpetuating simplistic conclusions and stereotypes.

There are complex interrelations between the dynamics of millennialism and persecution. The violence that sometimes engulfs millennial groups arises in contexts involving interactions between millennialists and people in mainstream societies. The quality of those interactions determines the potential for tragic loss of life.

Catherine Wessinger

See also Assaulted Millennial Groups, Aum Shinrikyo, Catastrophic Millennialism, Davidians, Fragile Millennial Groups, Heaven's Gate, Mormonism, Nativist Millennial Movements, Progressive Millennialism, Revolutionary Millennial Movements, Solar Temple

Bibliography

Arrington, Leonard J., and Davis Bitton. (1979) *The Mormon Experience: A History of the Latter-day Saints.* New York: Alfred A. Knopf.

Docherty, Jayne Seminare. (1998) "When the Parties Bring Their Gods to the Table: Learning Lessons from Waco." Ph.D. diss., George Mason University.

Ellwood, Robert. (2000) "Nazism as a Millennialist Movement." In *Millennialism, Persecution, and Violence: Historical Cases,* edited by Catherine Wessinger. Syracuse, NY: Syracuse University Press.

Gallagher, Eugene V. (2000) "'Theology is Life and Death': David Koresh on Violence, Persecution, and the Millennium." In *Millennialism, Persecution, and Violence: Historical Cases,* edited by Catherine Wessinger. Syracuse, NY: Syracuse University Press.

Hall, John R. (1987) *Gone from the Promised Land: Jonestown in American Cultural History.* New Brunswick, NJ: Transaction Books.

——. (1995) "Public Narratives and the Apocalyptic Sect: From Jonestown to Mt. Carmel." In *Armageddon in Waco: Critical Perspectives on the Branch Davidian Conflict,* edited by Stuart A. Wright. Chicago: University of Chicago Press, 205–35.

Introvigne, Massimo. (2000) "The Magic of Death: The Suicides of the Solar Temple." In *Millennialism, Persecution, and Violence: Historical Cases,* edited by Catherine Wessinger. Syracuse, NY: Syracuse University Press.

Lowe, Scott. (2000) "Western Millennial Ideology Goes East: The Taiping Revolution and Mao's Great Leap Forward." In *Millennialism, Persecution, and Violence: Historical Cases,* edited by Catherine Wessinger. Syracuse, NY: Syracuse University Press.

Maaga, Mary McCormick. (1998) *Hearing the Voices of Jonestown: Putting a Human Face on an American Tragedy.* Syracuse, NY: Syracuse University Press.

Moore, Rebecca. (2000) "'American as Cherry Pie': Peoples Temple and Violence in America." In *Millennialism, Persecution, and Violence: Historical Cases, edited by Catherine Wessinger.* Syracuse, NY: Syracuse University Press.

Reader, Ian. (1996) *A Poisonous Cocktail? Aum Shinrikyo's Path to Violence.* Copenhagen: Nordic Institute of Asian Studies Books.

——. (2000) "Imagined Persecution: Aum Shinrikyo, Millennialism, and the Legitimation of Violence." In *Millennialism, Persecution, and Violence: Historical Cases,* edited by Catherine Wessinger. Syracuse, NY: Syracuse University Press.

Robbins, Thomas, and Dick Anthony. (1995) "Sects and Violence: Factors Enhancing the Volatility of Marginal Religious Movements." In *Armageddon in Waco: Critical Perspectives on the Branch Davidian Conflict,* edited by Stuart A. Wright. Chicago: University of Chicago Press, 236–59.

Rosenfeld, Jean E. (2000) "The Justus Freemen Standoff: The Importance of the Analysis of Religion in Avoiding Violent Outcomes." In *Millennialism, Persecution, and Violence: Historical Cases,* edited by Catherine Wessinger. Syracuse, NY: Syracuse University Press.

Salter, Richard C. (2000) "Time, Authority, and Ethics in the Khmer Rouge: Elements of the Millennial Vision in Year Zero." In *Millennialism, Persecution, and Violence: Historical Cases,* edited by Catherine Wessinger. Syracuse, NY: Syracuse University Press.

Steyn, Christine. (2000) "Millenarian Tragedies in South Africa: The Xhosa Cattle-Killing Movement and the Bulhoek Massacre." In *Millennialism, Persecution, and Violence: Historical Cases,* edited by Catherine Wessinger. Syracuse, NY: Syracuse University Press.

Tabor, James D., and Eugene V. Gallagher. (1995) *Why Waco? Cults and the Battle for Religious Freedom in America.* Berkeley, CA: University of California Press.

Underwood, Grant. (2000) "Millennialism, Persecution, and Violence: The Mormons." In *Millennialism, Persecution, and Violence: Historical Cases,* edited by Catherine Wessinger. Syracuse, NY: Syracuse University Press.

Wessinger, Catherine. (1997) "Millennialism With and Without the Mayhem: Catastrophic and Progressive Expectations." In *Millennium, Messiahs, and Mayhem: Contemporary Apocalyptic Movements,* edited by Thomas Robbins and Susan J. Palmer. New York: Routledge, 47–59.

——. (2000). "The Interacting Dynamics of Millennial Beliefs, Persecution, and Violence." In *Millennialism, Persecution, and Violence: Historical Cases,* edited by Catherine Wessinger. Syracuse, NY: Syracuse University Press.

——. (2000). *How the Millennium Comes Violently: From Jonestown to Heaven's Gate.* New York: Seven Bridges Press.

Wright, Stuart A., ed. (1995) *Armageddon in Waco: Critical Perspectives on the Branch Davidian Conflict.* Chicago: University of Chicago Press.

Plague and Pestilence

As a medical reality for human communities throughout most of history, epidemic diseases have provoked a particular terror in people as a result of their elusive causes and the horrific sufferings they produce. Understandably, societies have interpreted plague and pestilence as divine punishments for human misdeeds. After the fact, they seek to identify and demonize the pariahs whom they can blame for the epidemic. Moreover, apocalyptic prophecies typically threaten epidemic diseases as punishments for violating divine laws. Not coincidentally, millennialist movements have been initiated by incidents of such plagues.

Linguistic Dimensions of Plague and Pestilence

According to Mary Douglas, "the dialogue about infection follows the dialogue about the community's cultural project" (119). Therefore, the ways a community represents concepts of epidemic disease or other disasters says more about the community than it does about the disasters. For example, the terms "plague" and "pestilence" convey complex, emotionally charged connotations. As Leavy points out:

> The word *pestilence*, understood as a deadly because usually fatal epidemic disease, is deadly not only because it results in death but also because it is thought of as particularly poisonous or evil—these adjectives needing almost as much explanation as *pestilence*. There would seem to be an almost infinite regression in an attempt to make these terms clear. But it is the word *plague* that, again, has raised specters of a world of sin and damnation. (4)

If "epidemic disease" is a roughly neutral term for a medical catastrophe, "pestilence" and "plague" are charged terms that impose an moralizing interpretation on the medical event. As Ricouer suggests:

> Prophecy, then, consists in deciphering future history by giving it in advance a meaning relative to the ethical life of the people. . . . The calamity consists . . . in the *meaning* attached to the occurrence, in the *penal* interpretation of the event prophesied. (67–68)

Sontag similarly suggests that there is a punitive logic or process to epidemic diseases' becoming so metaphorical:

> Nothing is more punitive than to give a disease a meaning—that meaning being invariably a moralistic one. Any important disease whose causality is murky, and for which treatment is ineffectual, tends to be awash in significance. First, the subjects of deepest dread (corruption, decay, pollution, anomie, weakness) are identified with the disease. The disease itself becomes a metaphor. Then in the name of the disease (that is, using it as a metaphor), the horror is imposed on other things. (58)

At about the time of the earliest documented use of the term "pestilence" for epidemic plague in the fourteenth century, the term had already also absorbed the meaning of "That which is morally pestilent or pernicious; moral plague or mischief, evil conduct; wickedness; that which is fatal to the public peace or well-being" (OED). Assigning blame for plague and pestilence thus gives the illusion of control over an uncontrollable event, but more significantly for apocalyptic discourse among millennialist communities, blame clearly marks "the sinners" from "the saved." As Nelkin and Gilman note:

> placing blame defines the normal, establishes the boundaries of healthy behavior and appropriate social relationships, and distinguishes the observer from the cause of fear. . . . Several categories of blame can be found in . . . popular discourse: disease has been attributed to particular racial groups or social stereotypes, to individual lifestyle, to immoral behavior, or to those perceived as sources of power and control. (41)

Configuring epidemic disease as "pestilence" or "plague" serves social and psychological functions typical of the millennialist communities creating apocalyptic discourse.

Social History of Plague and Pestilence

The association of fatal epidemic disease with divine punishment for transgressing taboos or committing sins occurs in many cultures. In the West this association is found in both the Greco-Roman myths and in Judeo-Christian scriptures. At the beginning of Homer's *Iliad*, the Greek warriors have been stricken with a plague (which Homer describes as arrows falling from heaven) sent by Apollo because of the abduction of his priest's daughter. The crisis that impels Oedipus to discover his origins at the beginning of *Oedipus Rex* is a plague sent to Thebes, which he learns from Apollo's oracle has been sent to punish the city for harboring the murderer of the king's predecessor. Ironically, Apollo was the god of medicine, of archery, and of prophecy.

Pestilence is famous in the Hebrew scriptures as God's punishment for the Egyptians' enslavement of the descendants of Abraham. In fact, in a rather spectacular display of divine wrath, the Egyptians endure ten "plagues": the river turned to blood; separate infestations of frogs, lice, and flies; livestock murrains; skin boils and blains; hail; locusts; three days of darkness; and the slaying of the firstborn by an angel of death (Exodus 7–10). Some of these disasters are not, of course, fatal infectious disease as we would understand the concept today; however, in sacred texts they are all interpreted similarly as afflictions meted out by God.

The Book of Revelation similarly conflates catastrophic diseases and prodigious natural disasters. Chapter 6 introduces the Four Horsemen of the Apocalypse, representing earthly destruction by war, famine, plague, and wild beasts. In chapter 8, the text recounts what will occur when angels blow seven trumpets: the first will bring hail, fire, and blood; the second, a mountain of flame; the third will turn the sea to blood and cause the "Wormwood star" to fall; the fourth, darkness; the fifth, monstrous demonic locusts; the sixth, death by plague; the seventh will announce the last stage. These seven trumpets will be followed by seven final plagues, poured out from seven bowls, including skin boils, seas turned to blood, rivers turned to blood, scorching heat, darkness, the drying of the Euphrates, and finally earthquakes, lightning, and hailstones (chapters 15–16).

Thereafter in the Christian-influenced world, epidemics and natural disasters have been configured as signs of the endtimes, a final divine chastisement. Epidemic European outbreaks of plague in the 1300s and in the 1600s prompted calls for repentance and preparation for the Day of the Lord. Ostrow, Eller, and Joseph observe that in the fifteenth century:

> As the epidemic toll continued erratically but largely unabated . . . [b]ands of devout pilgrims appeared in large numbers, moving through the major population centers in Europe, stripped to the waist and publicly whipping themselves. These flagellants, perceiving plague as punishment for previously unrecognized sin, sought relief in their mortifications. . . . Simultaneously, they turned on the vulnerable and stigmatized Jewish population. (303)

Cohn has characterized such penitential millennarians as "revolutionary flagellants" (127–47).

Not only preachers but also doctors attributed epidemics to vice or the tolerance of vice. For example, the sixteenth-century surgeon, Ambroise Pare, characterized plague as the wrath of God, while acknowledging that it also had more immediate natural causes. In his account of the 1665 Great Plague of London, *A Journal of the Plague Year* (1722), Daniel Defoe opined:

> Nothing, but the immediate Finger of God, nothing but omnipotent Power could have done it; the Contagion despised all Medicine, Death rag'd in every Corner; and had it gone on as it did then, a few Weeks more would have clear'd the Town of all, and every thing that had a soul: Men every where began to despair, every Heart fail'd them for Fear, People were made desperate thro' the Anguish of their Souls, and the Terrors of Death sat in the very Faces and Countenances of the People. (298)

Whether cholera and yellow fever in the nineteenth century or influenza and polio in the twentieth, epidemic disease would continue to be a screen on which communities project their paranoid anxieties, stigmatizing and scapegoating as infectious the people whom they perceive as a threat to social order.

AIDS in the last half of the twentieth century is a special case in point. Horrific and intractable in its earliest manifestations, appearing among already marginalized groups (e.g., homosexual men, African people or people of African ancestry), the disease prompted dire apocalyptic pronouncements from all quarters of Western society, both those friendly and those hostile to the first at-risk groups. Some Christian fundamentalists, already having depicted homosexuals as a social plague and harbingers of the end times, viewed AIDS as one of the Book of Revelation's prophesied pestilences. The concurrent appearance of other viral infections, untreatable by antibiotics and frequently of origins exotic to the Euro-American world, prompted films, plays, and novels featuring endtimes scenarios. However, such hysteria undermines effective treatments of epidemic disease by creating false distinctions between a group that sees itself as pure and uninfected against others whom it characterizes as impure and infectious.

The ways that communities talk about disease say more about the communities than they do about the diseases themselves. Ancient cultural habits of mind and imagination "explain" epidemic disease as the product of an impure external threat. In the imaginary of Euro-American culture this anxiety is often amplified by apocalyptic language, the threat of catastrophic and total annihilation.

Thomas L. Long

See also Defilement, Sodom

Bibliography

Cohn, Norman. (1970) *The Pursuit of the Millennium: Revolutionary Millenarians and Mystical Anarchists of the Middle Ages*, rev. ed. New York: Oxford University Press.

Defoe, Daniel. (1928) *A Journal of the Plague Year.* Oxford, U.K.: Blackwell; reprint, London: Wm. Clowes, 1974.

Douglas, Mary. (1992) *Risk and Blame: Essays in Cultural Theory.* New York: Routledge.

Leavy, Barbara Fass. (1992) *To Blight with Plague: Studies in a Literary Theme.* New York: New York University Press.

Nelkin, Dorothy, and Sander L. Gilman. (1991) "Placing Blame for Devastating Disease." In *Time of Plague: The History and Social Consequences of Lethal Epidemic Disease,* edited by Arien Mack. New York: New York University Press, 39–56.

Ostrow, David G., Michael Eller, and Jill G. Joseph. (1989) "Epidemic Control Measures for AIDS: A Psychosocial and Historical Discussion of Policy Alternatives." In *AIDS: Principles, Practices, and Politics,* edited by Inge B. Corless and Mary Pittman-Lindeman. Reference Ed. Series in Death Education, Aging, and Health Care. New York: Hemisphere Publishing, 1989, 301–12.

Ricoeur, Paul. (1967) *The Symbolism of Evil,* translated by Emerson Buchanan. Boston: Beacon.

Sontag, Susan. (1977) *Illness As Metaphor.* New York: Vintage.

Planetary Activation Organization

The Planetary Activation Organization (formerly the Ground Crew Project), founded by Sheldan Nidle in California during the 1980s, is an optimistic ufology religion that believes the earth is on the verge of cosmic transformation that will result in the creation of a new paradise on earth around the year 2012. Born in New York City in 1946, Nidle claims that he was visited by extraterrestrials from the Sirian planetary system shortly after his birth. Around the age of nine the contacts and communications increased as Nidle discovered that he was to lead a mission on Earth for the Galactic Federation of Planets, in order to prepare humankind and the Earth for the coming transformation as the Earth passes into the path of the cosmic "photon belt"—an area of outer space that has high energy properties similar to the plasma in the atmospheres of stars. While tremendous "earth changes" will likely occur, such as earthquakes, hurricanes, and other natural disasters, the photon belt immersion will help humans to rapidly achieve "full consciousness," just in time for the mass landing of extraterrestrials from the "Galactic Federation."

For the Planetary Activation Organization the alien messiahs will arrive on earth by the millions during Earth's entry into the photon belt, representing the hundreds of advanced races who have come to earth to help us, their less evolved brothers and sisters. Interestingly, the cosmic messiahs include supernatural as well as superevolved beings, as explained in "A Message to Humanity from the Ground Crew Project" by Nidle (1997: 11), "We are being assisted by all of Creation—the Spiritual Hierarchy, Angelic Realms, the Galactic Federation of Light, Ascended Masters, and our space brothers and sisters."

Like the "cargo cults" in the Pacific Islands following World War II, the Planetary Activation Organization expect the cosmic messiahs to bring material goods in the form of supplies and new technology, as well as spiritual guidance.

The Planetary Activation Organization provides an example of the peaceful transformation that will replace the bloody and destructive Armageddon predicted by Christian fundamentalists and other doomsaying ufologists. According to Bil El Masri, in "The Mass Landings," after the earth enters the photon belt sometime around the millennium, a mass flyover of the Galactic Federation fleet of spaceships will commence around the world. Once we realize that an alien invasion has begun, Federation representatives will have already met with world leaders in order to convince them to reveal the truth to their peoples that the invasion is in the best interests of the planet, and that there is no need for fear or retaliation. "They won't, though," says El Masri (1997: 12), "Apparently, most of it has fallen on deaf ears. All they seem to hear is, 'Resistance is futile' and some are willing to kill us all, if necessary, but that should not surprise anyone. The point is that resistance, actually, is futile, and the Galactic Federation has made sure of it."

As 15.5 million alien spacecraft descend on the earth in a matter of hours, representatives from Federation planets, including Pleiadians, Sirians, Cassiopeans, and Arcturians, will fan out across the globe to meet and placate human populations. To prevent a violent human reaction to the aliens, Federation ships will neutralize military aircraft, bombs, nukes, ships, and technological weaponry. All mechanical devices, cars, machines, appliances, even guns, will also be shut down so that no human attempt to retaliate will occur.

Thus, according to the Planetary Activation Organization, there will be no chance of a violent, destructive Armageddon, the alien "invasion" will be peaceful, total, and entirely in our interest. In a short period of time, as we all rapidly evolve and acquire "full consciousness" within the photon belt environment, we will come to realize a new cosmic millennium. For members of the Planetary Activation Organization, once Earth enters the photon belt, and the mass landing of UFOs occurs, the entire ways of human life and culture will pass away and all will be transformed. For humankind the transformation will heal all human afflictions, so that the crippled will walk, the blind will see, the deaf will hear, and the distressed will know joy and peace.

Philip Lamy

Bibliography

El Masri, Bill. (1997) "The Mass Landings." The Ground Crew Project. http://www.portal.ca/~ground/crew/messhum.htm.

Lamy, Philip. (1999) "UFOs, Extraterrestrials and the Apocalypse: The Evolution of a Millennial Subculture." In *Millennial Visions*, edited by Martha Lee. New York: Praeger.

Nidle, Sheldan. (1997) "A Message to humanity from the Ground Crew Project." The Ground Crew Project.

Planetary Activation Organization. (1999) http://www.paoweb.com.

Politics

Millennial and apocalyptic political movements in Western history are in large part traceable to the historical consciousness derived from the Judeo-Christian tradition. The ultimate origin of this, in turn, lies in the Yahweh cult of the first millennium BC and the understanding of sacred history it entailed for the ancient Israelites.

The Ancient Hebrew and Early Christian Peoples

The religious life of biblical Israel produced a historical consciousness virtually unique in the ancient world. Its prophets insisted that the Hebrew nation came into existence by virtue of singular events in actual human history, such as the Exodus. History was thus endowed with a moral significance—what one scholar calls its "valorization"—which differentiated it from the mythic time in which dwelt the deities of other ancient religions. The prophets and chroniclers of ancient Israel labored to separate belief in Yahweh from the vegetation cycle, cyclic cosmic dramas, or timeless fertility cults. Despite the occasional kernel of a perhaps genuine memory, such as in the Gilgamesh Saga, the polytheistic cults of the ancient world lacked genuine historical consciousness. Their sacred world largely existed in mythic time, out of which the gods might intervene, for good or ill, in the affairs of humans on an ad hoc basis. No larger moral dimension, however, accrued to the passage of time. Significantly, while creation myths were common in the ancient Near East, apocalypse myths were not. No end for the cosmos was needed since history itself went nowhere in particular.

For the Jews, history had both meaning and direction—qualities which made it at once comforting and threatening. Yahweh's pleasure or anger were manifest in the unfolding of history, which thus took on a moral dimension (valorization). Judgment did not simply happen in history but, rather, history itself was a process of judgment. Should Israel repent its apostasy and return to Yahweh, then there was the offer, repeated throughout the prophets, of an era of unprecedented blessedness. Prophetic literature thus became political literature in its call for a new national polity based on repentance, proper worship, and justice. Repentance and faithfulness to the covenant might well bring not merely better crops, rain in season, or greater feminine fertility, but a whole new ordering of the divine-human relationship: "Behold, the days are coming, says the Lord, when I will make a new covenant with the house of Israel and the house of Judah, not like the covenant which I made with their fathers" (Jeremiah 31:31). This promise of an age of bliss, dependent on national righteousness, made political millennialism an integral part of Jewish thought.

Apocalyptic language was also frequently invoked in ancient Israel for specific political purposes. In Daniel, for

---

FINAL SHOWDOWN

"It is our mission to forge a strong weapon–will and energy–so that when the hour strikes, and the Red dragon raises itself to strike, at least some of our people will not surrender to despair. I myself represent the same principles that I stood for a year ago.

We are convinced that there will be a final showdown in this struggle against Marxism. We are fighting one another and there can be only one outcome. One will be destroyed and the other be victorious.

It is the great mission of the National Socialist movement to give our times a new faith and to see to it that millions will stand by this faith, then, when the hour comes for the showdown, the German people will not be completely unarmed when they meet the international murderers."

Adolf Hitler, speech at Munich, 23 May 1926.

Source: Snyder, Louis L. (1981) *Hitler's Third Reich: A Documentary History.* Chicago, IL: Burnham, 53.

---

example, the persecution of Jews faithful to the Mosaic covenant by Antiochus Epiphanes during the second century BCE was given prophetic significance beyond mere maladroit rule. The reign of the deeply hated ruler was "different from all the kingdoms," for "it shall devour the whole earth" (Daniel 8:23). Even this most powerful sovereign would, however, eventually be overthrown because of his iniquity: "And his dominion shall be taken away, to be consumed and destroyed to the end" (Daniel 8:26). When this was accomplished, then would follow a new messianic kingdom which, in its righteousness, foreshadows the later Christian vision of a millennium: "Their kingdom shall be an everlasting kingdom, and all dominions shall serve and obey them" (Daniel 7:27).

Eschatology was wielded as a political weapon as well by the early Christians, who underwent their own time of intense persecution by government authority. The enemy this time was Rome. The Book of Revelation attacked Roman power, thinly disguised as the ancient empire of Babylon, for its gross immorality and persecution of the saints. "Fallen, fallen is Babylon the great!" proclaims the angel in the prophetic vision given to John on Patmos: "It has become a dwelling place of demons" (Revelation 18:2). And, as was the case in earlier Jewish political prophecy, the overthrow of the ungodly brings more than just a different, or better, government. It leads, eventually, to a new dispensation between God and humans, one which will last a thousand years (Revelation 20:1–3).

But, although political themes are not hard to locate in early Christian millennialism, eschatology served as well to discourage political anxiety among believers. St. James looked beyond temporal kingdoms altogether to cite Christ's return in glory as the final fulfillment of divine history. What was needed in difficult times was patient forbearance in the face of evil: "Be patient, therefore, brethren, until the coming of the Lord" (James 5:7). While scholars do identify episodes in later Christian history when millennialism led to violent political outbursts, the eschatological literature of early Christianity tends at least as much toward political quietism.

The church gradually marginalized millennialism after the first few centuries of the Christian Era, in part by relying on the work of St. Augustine (fifth century CE), whose allegorical reading of Revelation largely neutralized it as a document with potential political ramifications. Ever since, the millennium has played little part in official Catholic theology. Nevertheless, the imagery of prophetic Scripture, most especially Revelation, is so striking yet ambiguous that it perforce remained politically charged. Regarded as a prediction of the future, and not simply as allegory or inspirational poetry, it invites readers to locate political events, and even personages, in its pages. This is especially true of such a striking image as the Antichrist, a figure of such loathing that the temptation to label a contemporary ruler with the rubric often proves irresistible.

Europe and America through the Eighteenth Century

Brief apocalyptic and millennial movements occasionally disrupted the polity of Europe throughout the long medieval period. These local disruptions are, in part, attributed by historians to social and economic grievances. Such troubles, they argue, prompted the afflicted to seek solace in prophecy and valorize their woes as part of a larger cosmic drama, the outcome of which would be the overthrow of the persecuting forces and subsequent triumphal entry of the oppressed into the millennium. These upheavals were frequently accompanied by the appearance of would-be messiahs, who promised to lead believers into the new era. On occasion, these movements threatened the local political order, which repressed their revolutionary eschatology with ferocious violence. Apocalyptic sects, such as the Taborites of fifteenth-century CE Bohemia, attacked the church as well, in outbursts which foreshadowed the Reformation.

Politics and eschatology mixed to form an especially explosive concoction during the Protestant Reformation. Apocalyptic imagery served both sides of a religious struggle which, from its very outset, was profoundly political. Its salient contribution was to provide a vocabulary which labeled one's opponents as not merely mistaken, but Satanic. Luther's denunciation of the papacy as Antichrist was the prime example. On a larger scale, prophecy provided a conceptual framework within which to understand the vast developments brought on in European religious and political life by the Reformation. Prophecy-driven cosmic drama, taken to its extremes, led a few to call for the creation of an entirely new political order in which Christ would be king. In 1524, Anabaptists attempted to set up such a millennial kingdom in Munster and were suppressed only after terrible bloodshed.

English political life was saturated with millennialism throughout the Reformation. Contemporaries frequently analyzed the seventeenth-century confrontation between Parliament and Crown as the fulfillment of prophecy. The defeat of Charles I was but the first step in the creation of a millennial kingdom. "The way then," wrote one of the king's enemies, "to set up Christ's kingdom is to pull down Antichrist's." This was not just name-calling, but a summons to reorder the English state. For these believers, as with the ancient Israelites and the later communists, history had direction and meaning. The Fifth Monarchy Men formed only one faction during the English Reformation for which politics and the millennium were inseparable.

MARK 13 (RSV)

1. And as he came out of the temple, one of his disciples said to him, "Look, Teacher, what wonderful stones and what wonderful buildings!"
2. And Jesus said to him, "Do you see these great buildings? There will not be left here one stone upon another, that will not be thrown down."
3. And as he sat on the Mount of Olives opposite the temple, Peter and James and John and Andrew asked him privately,
4. "Tell us, when will this be, and what will be the sign when these things are all to be accomplished?"
5. And Jesus began to say to them, "Take heed that no one leads you astray.
6. Many will come in my name, saying, 'I am he!' and they will lead many astray.
7. And when you hear of wars and rumors of wars, do not be alarmed; this must take place, but the end is not yet.
8. For nation will rise against nation, and kingdom against kingdom; there will be earthquakes in various places, there will be famines; this is but the beginning of the birth-pangs.
9. "But take heed to yourselves; for they will deliver you up to councils; and you will be beaten in synagogues; and you will stand before governors and kings for my sake, to bear testimony before them.
10. And the gospel must first be preached to all nations.
11. And when they bring you to trial and deliver you up, do not be anxious beforehand what you are to say; but say whatever is given you in that hour, for it is not you who speak, but the Holy Spirit.
12. And brother will deliver up brother to death, and the father his child, and children will rise against parents and have them put to death;
13. and you will be hated by all for my name's sake. But he who endures to the end will be saved.
14. "But when you see the desolating sacrilege set up where it ought not to be (let the reader understand), then let those who are in Judea flee to the mountains;
15. let him who is on the housetop not go down, nor enter his house, to take anything away;
16. and let him who is in the field not turn back to take his mantle.
17. And alas for those who are with child and for those who give suck in those days!
18. Pray that it may not happen in winter.
19. For in those days there will be such tribulation as has not been from the beginning of the creation which God created until now, and never will be.
20. And if the Lord had not shortened the days, no human being would be saved; but for the sake of the elect, whom he chose, he shortened the days.
21. And then if any one says to you, 'Look, here is the Christ!' or 'Look, there he is!' do not believe it.
22. False Christs and false prophets will arise and show signs and wonders, to lead astray, if possible, the elect.
23. But take heed; I have told you all things beforehand.
24. "But in those days, after that tribulation, the sun will be darkened, and the moon will not give its light,
25. and the stars will be falling from heaven, and the powers in the heavens will be shaken.
26. And then they will see the Son of man coming in clouds with great power and glory.
27. And then he will send out the angels, and gather his elect from the four winds, from the ends of the earth to the ends of heaven.
28. "From the fig tree learn its lesson: as soon as its branch becomes tender and puts forth its leaves, you know that summer is near.
29. So also, when you see these things taking place, you know that he is near, at the very gates.
30. Truly, I say to you, this generation will not pass away before all these things take place.
31. Heaven and earth will pass away, but my words will not pass away.
32. "But of that day or that hour no one knows, not even the angels in heaven, nor the Son, but only the Father.
33. Take heed, watch; for you do not know when the time will come.
34. It is like a man going on a journey, when he leaves home and puts his servants in charge, each with his work, and commands the door-keeper to be on the watch.
35. Watch therefore–for you do not know when the master of the house will come, in the evening, or at midnight, or at cockcrow, or in the morning–
36. lest he come suddenly and find you asleep.
37. And what I say to you I say to all: Watch."

The patriots of the American Revolution explained their rebellion against the mother country in millennial language. The contest with England, some averred, would usher in not merely independence, but the first stage of a new order in world political history. One patriot encouraged his fellows by proclaiming that "although men or devils, earth or hell, Antichrist or the dragon rages, the people of God may still triumph in Christ." Few, if any, expected Christ's imminent return. Rather, their fundamentally optimistic understanding of prophecy recognized America as the first fruit of a millennial age achieved through political righteousness.

The self-identity of the new American republic was partially bound up in its sense of prophetic mission, a role aptly christened "Redeemer Nation" by one historian. Former President John Adams jocularly inquired: "Can you give me any news of the millennium? Is it to commence soon enough for me to entertain a hope that I may live a thousand years longer?" The nation's imperial foreign policy was justified, especially during the war with Mexico, as part of God's plan to bring the blessings of American government to the less fortunate: "Some political government will spread over the Earth in the Millennium; and it will be a democracy, or it will be no millennium." At times, though, such politicized millennialism had a darker side: "The Millennium is a political era of Christian republicanism, confined mainly to the white race. . . . and will be attended in its march with the total extinction of some inferior races" (1854).

Reform Movements of the Nineteenth Century

American antislavery drew sustenance from the notion that the millennial age, to dawn first in the United States, could not commence until human bondage was abolished. But, slavery was only the worst of many social vices, intemperance and Sabbath-breaking were others, which must be suppressed to ready Christ's kingdom on earth. Such optimistic eschatology—commonly called postmillennialism—served as a spur to political action on a wide variety of fronts, from abolition to legislating godly behavior.

Nineteenth-century Europe was largely devoid of political millennialism rooted in explicit Christian faith. It was, however, a cockpit for fervid utopian political experiments which closely resembled Christian millennialism and depended on the Judeo-Christian belief that meaning was revealed in history. The French philosopher, August Compte, expounded his philosophy, eventually called Positivism, which taught that human history progressed through successively enlightened stages. The last, and happiest, of these was the scientific, an era of unprecedented prosperity reminiscent of the Christian millennium.

Karl Marx's interpretation of history spawned by far the most influential millennial-utopian movement in modern times—or, ever. Entirely devoid of theism, the early theoretical writings of this nineteenth-century sociologist nonetheless claimed to forecast the direction which history would normally, though, perhaps, not quite inevitably, take. Economic civilization progresses through necessary stages of development, of which capitalism was the most recent. The next historical phase must be socialism, followed by the highest and last social model—communism. Once this is achieved, historical evolution essentially stops—leading one historian to quip that Marx's theory "commits hara-kiri on the doorstep of the ideal." Nevertheless, the basic Marxian concept of a history which eventually arrives at fulfillment in an ideal society—and then evolves no further—is closely akin to Christian millennialism.

Nineteenth-century Europe produced several utopian-millennial political movements, often, like Marxism, prompted by the excesses of the early Industrial Revolution. The English manufacturer-reformer Robert Owen (1771–1858) attempted to create a new political model organized, like Marx's, around collective ownership of the means of production. His ideal polity was not the nation-state but an agricultural-industrial commune. His ideas received a limited hearing in England and were bruited about in America for several decades, with the occasional attempt at such a settlement. So akin were Owen's goals to concurrent Christian postmillennialism, that Owen and his followers appropriated its very language. His scheme, he told American disciples, "may not improperly be termed the beginning of the millennium."

In America, millennial rhetoric survived the Civil War to be taken up in substantially altered fashion as the Social Gospel. This was explicitly political Christianity, and sought to broaden government responsibility for social welfare, especially in the amelioration of industrial working conditions, in order that America might become the Kingdom of God on earth. What was sought was described by one social gospeller as "the golden age to come, when society shall be what the Christian church teaches it to be."

Multiple Directions in the Twentieth Century

Millennialism could, however, discourage as well as encourage political activism. From the beginning of the twentieth century, evangelical Protestantism in America has contained a strong streak of political quietism. Since only Christ's return in judgment will initiate the millennium (an eschatology known as premillennialism), individual Christians should eschew political activity (vain, in any event) in favor of personal piety. This is, of course, a disincentive to political social reform and substantially the position adopted by certain prominent evangelicals, such as the Rev. Billy Graham.

The twentieth century spawned a number of murderous utopian-millennial movements. Most were atheistic or indifferent to religion, but still claimed historical insight into the meaning of history similar to the Judeo-Christian tradition. Soviet-style communism, imposed as well in China and on Eastern Europe, combined brutal force with Marx's vision of an ideal society. Its millennial-utopian vision was expressed by the early Soviet poet who wrote of the Soviet Union: "New faces. New dreams. / New songs. New visions / New myths are we flinging on, / We are kindling a new eternity" (trans. Richard Stites). Its atavistic urge to destroy existing society and build a socialist "New Jerusalem" was expressed as late as the 1970s in Cambodia, where over a million people were massacred by the Khmer Rouge in order to clear the ground for an ideal society.

As the twenty-first century opened, the language of political millennialism was still present American society. Francis Fukuyama, in his influential article (1989) and book (1992) that share the title "The End of History," somewhat ironically embraced the ancient Judeo-Christian concept that the historical process would not unfold indefinitely, but must reach its fulfillment. On a far less scholarly note, the radical political right invoked eschatological rhetoric in its attack on fin de siècle political culture in the United States. Survivalist and "Aryan" racist movements repeatedly predicted a secular apocalypse and claimed to defend "traditional" Christian beliefs—a claim vehemently rejected by the overwhelming majority of Christians.

The most politically influential millennial movement in America at the end of the twentieth century was American evangelical Protestant support for the Israel. Since early in the nineteenth century, premillennial Christians have looked to the Second Advent to correct social ills and institute a millennium. It is their belief that the Bible prophesies the "restoration" of the Jews to the Middle East as an essential element of the Last Days and the reestablishment by the "restored" Jews of the ancient state of Israel. Evangelical Christians have thus been among the most vociferous, and most influential, lobbies in the United States Congress on behalf of military, financial, and diplomatic support for Israel. To this extent, millennialism continued to influence the political climate, or at least the foreign policy, of the world's premier great power as the twenty-first century began.

Robert K. Whalen

See also Communism, Nazism, Secular Millennialism, Zionism

Bibliography

Harrison, J. F. C. (1969) *Quest for the New Moral World: Robert Owen and the Owenites in Britain and America.* New York: Charles Scribner's Sons.

Hill, Christopher. (1994) *The English Bible and the Seventeenth-Century Revolution.* New York: Penguin.

Sowell, Thomas. (1985) *Marxism: Philosophy and Economics.* New York: William Morrow and Company, Inc.

Tuveson, Ernest Lee. (1964) *Millennium and Utopia: A Study in the Background of the Idea of Progress.* New York: Harper Torchbooks.

Populism

Millennial movements in the United States have often involved some form of populist protest. Populism is a rhetorical style that seeks to mobilize "the people" as a social or political force. Populism can move to the left or right. It can be tolerant or intolerant. It can promote civil discourse and political participation or promote scapegoating, demagoguery, and conspiracism. Populism can oppose the status quo and challenge elites to promote change, or support the status quo to defend "the people" against a perceived threat by elites or subversive outsiders. Kazin argues that populism in the United States today is "a persistent yet mutable style of political rhetoric with roots deep in the nineteenth century" (1995: 5).

Roots of Populism in the United States

In the late 1800s an agrarian-based popular mass revolt swept much of the country, and helped launch the electoral Populist Party. The Populist movement of this period started out progressive and even made some attempts to bridge racial divides between blacks and whites. Some populist groups, however, later turned toward conspiracism, adopting anti-Semitism and making racist appeals.

Kazin traces "two different but not exclusive strains of vision and protest" in the original U.S. Populist movement: the revivalist "pietistic impulse issuing from the Protestant Reformation"; and the "secular faith of the Enlightenment, the belief that ordinary people could think and act rationally, more rationally, in fact, than their ancestral overlords." "Circuit-riding preachers and union-organizing artisans (even the Painite freethinkers among them) agreed that high-handed rule by the wealthy was both sinful and unrepublican. All believed in the nation's millennial promise, its role as the beacon of liberty in a benighted world" (10–11).

The Populist Party fought against giant monopolies and trusts that concentrated wealth in the hands of a few powerful families and corporations in a way that unbalanced the democratic process. They demanded many economic and political reforms that we enjoy today. At the same time populism drew themes from several historic currents with potentially negative consequences: (1) Producerism—the idea that the real Americans are hard-working people who create goods and wealth while fighting against parasites at the top and bottom of society who rob the public—sometimes promoting scapegoating and the blurring of issues of class and economic justice, and with a history of assuming proper citizenship is defined by White males; (2) Anti-elitism—a suspicion of politicians, powerful people, the wealthy, and high culture—sometimes leading to conspiracist allegations about control of the world by secret elites, especially the scapegoating of Jews as sinister and powerful manipulators of the economy or media; (3) Anti-intellectualism—a distrust of those pointy-headed professors in their Ivory Towers—sometimes undercutting rational debate by discarding logic and factual evidence in favor of following the emotional appeals of demagogues; (4) Majoritarianism—the notion that the will of the majority of people has absolute primacy in matters of governance—sacrificing rights for minorities, especially people of color; (5) Moralism—evangelical-style campaigns rooted in Protestant revivalism—sometimes leading to authoritarian and theocratic attempts to impose orthodoxy, especially relating to gender; and (6) Americanism—a form of patriotic nationalism—often promoting ethnocentric, nativist, or xenophobic fears that immigrants bring alien ideas and customs that are toxic to our culture.

Varieties of Populism

Canovan defined two main branches of populism worldwide—agrarian and political—and mapped out seven disparate varieties. Agrarian populism includes commodity farmer movements with radical economic agendas such as the U.S. People's Party of the late 1800s; subsistence peasant movements such as Eastern Europe's Green Rising movement after World War I; and romanticized agrarian movements led by intellectuals such as the late-nineteenth-century Russian *narodniki* (literally "populist," a socialist movement of the time). Political populism includes populist democracy, calling for more political participation, such as the use of referenda; politicians' populism marked by vague appeals for "the people" to build a unified coalition; reactionary populism such as the white backlash harvested by George Wallace in the 1960s and 1970s; and populist dictatorship such as that established by Juan Peron in Argentina in 1945–1955.

Canovan notes that there are "a great many interconnections" among the seven forms of populism, and that many "actual phenomena—perhaps most—belong in more than one category." She adds that "given the contradictions" between some of the categories, "none ever could satisfy all the conditions at once" (1981: 289). Combinations can vary. Populism in the United States "combined farmers' radicalism and populist democracy" (293). Canovan argues that all forms of populism "involve some kind of exaltation of and appeal to 'the people,' and all are in one sense or another antielitist" (294).

Theories of Populism

There is much dispute in academia as to what populism is and how it works. Goodwyn described the original Populist movement as "the flowering of the largest democratic mass movement in American history" (1978 :vii). This and other romanticized views see populist movements as inherently progressive and democratizing. It is as overly optimistic as the negative view of populism by some academics is overly pessimistic. As Canovan observed "like its rivals, Goodwyn's interpretation has a political ax to grind" (51).

Classic Theories

Centrist/extremist theory was the first major attempt to explain populism. It arrived with the 1955 publication of a collection of essays titled *The New American Right* edited by Daniel Bell. Eight years later the collection was expanded and republished under the title, *The Radical Right.* A number of books appeared that either elaborated on or paralleled the general themes of centrist/extremist theory first sketched in *The New American Right.*

Centrist/extremist theory (especially as outlined by Lipset, Raab, Bell, Forster, Epstein, and to a lesser degree, Hofstadter) saw dissident movements of the left and right as composed of outsiders—politically marginal people who have no connection to the mainstream electoral system or nodes of government or corporate power. Social and economic stress snaps these psychologically fragile people into a mode of irrational political hysteria, and as they embrace an increasingly paranoid style they make militant and unreasonable demands to defend their social and economic status. Because they are unstable, they can become dangerous and violent. Their extremism places them far outside the legitimate political process, which is located in the center where pluralists conduct civil democratic debates.

Centrist/extremist theory marginalizes populist dissidents as dangerous irrational extremists. Their grievances and demands need not be taken seriously. Law enforcement can break up any criminal conspiracies by subversive radicals who threaten the social order. The centrist/extremist model favors labels such as "radical right," "wing nuts," "lunatic fringe," or "religious political extremists."

Emerging "Strategic" Theories

Early questions about centrist/extremist theory were raised by Rogin (1967) and the authors in Schoenberger (1969), and now an increasing number of social scientists use different approaches. Smith notes that in the 1970s there was "a decisive pendulum-swing away from these 'classical' theories toward the view of social movements as rational, strategically calculating, politically instrumental phenomena" (1997: 3). At the same time, there was a rejection of the romanticized view of populism as inherently constructive. Dobratz and Shanks-Meile write that in studying populist social movements it is necessary to consider "socioeconomic conditions, changing political opportunities, resources, consciousness, labeling, framing, interpretations of reality, boundaries, and negotiation of the meaning of symbols" (1997: 32). Discussions of postclassical sociological theories of social movements in general can be found in Tarrow, Lofland, Klandermans, Buechler and Cylke, Morris and Mueller, Johnston and Klandermans, and Boggs. Authors such as Himmelstein, Diamond, Hardisty, and Berlet use variations of postclassical theories to study populism on the political right.

Using emerging theories of social movements, it is evident that most people who join populist movements are not acting out of some personal pathology, but out of anger and desperation. They are grasping at straws in an attempt to defend hearth and home against the furious winds of economic and social change seen as threatening their way of life. They may feel abandoned, or claim that no one in power seems to be listening. They come to believe that no one cares except others in the same predicament. Their anger and fear are frequently based on objective conditions and conflicts—power struggles involving race, gender, ethnicity, or religion; economic hardship; changes in social status; conflicts over cultural issues; and other societal transformations that cause anger, confusion, and anxiety.

Whether or not their grievances are legitimate (or even rational) they join with others to confront what they believe is the cause of their problems. Often, instead of challenging structures and institutions of power, they attack demonized scapegoats, often in the form of conspiracist allegations. Sometimes they resort to violence.

Contemporary Populism

Contemporary populism involves many varieties. Populist democracy is championed by progressives such as political activist Jesse Jackson, and columnists Jim Hightower and Molly Ivans. Politicians' populism marked the presidential campaigns of Ross Perot. Reactionary populism is the style of Pat Robertson who condemns liberals, feminists, and gay rights. Pat Buchanan and David Duke combine reactionary populism with hints of organic populist dictatorship.

Phillips compared the populist resurgence in the 1990s to previous examples in the 1890s and 1930s and found many of the same elements:

> Economic anguish and populist resentment; mild-to-serious class rhetoric aimed at the rich and fashionable; exaltation of the ordinary American against abusive, affluent and educated elites; contempt for Washington; rising ethnic, racial and religious animosities; fear of immigrants and foreigners, and a desire to turn away from internationalism and concentrate on rebuilding America and American lives. (1992: 38–42)

Most major populist movements in the 1980s and 1990s were on the political right, as opposed to the 1960s and early 1970s when most were on the political left, such as the civil rights movement and the movement to end the war in Vietnam. Examples of contemporary right-wing populist arguments can be found in Viguerie (1983), Carto (1982), and Reagan (1996).

Betz noted that one common theme among the contemporary right-wing populist movements he studied was xenophobia and racist scapegoating of immigrants and asylum-seekers. Betz argues that generally the right-wing populists in Europe distanced themselves from open affiliation with the violent far right such as neo-Nazis, avoided obvious and overt racism, and presented themselves as willing to make "a fundamental transformation of the existing socioeconomic and sociopolitical system" while still remaining within reformism and claiming to represent "democratic alternatives to the prevailing system" (1994: 108). This is similar to the main themes of right-wing populism in the United States.

Two versions of right-wing populism emerge in both the United States and Europe: one centered around economic libertarianism coupled with a rejection of mainstream political parties (more attractive to the upper-middle class and to small entrepreneurs); the other based on xenophobia and ethnocentric nationalism (more attractive to the lower-middle class and to wage workers). These different constituencies unite behind candidates that attack the current regime since both constituencies identify an intrusive government as the cause of their grievances.

Repressive Populism, Conspiracism, and Producerism

Stock (1996) writes about the role of producerism and vigilantism in U.S. populist movements throughout U.S. history and exemplified by the contemporary armed militia movements. Producerism is a narrative that describes the "productive" citizen in the middle as being squeezed by parasitic forces from above and below.

Conspiratorial allegations about parasitic elites seen as manipulating society, lead to anger being directed upwards. The list of scapegoats seen as among the alleged elite parasites includes international bankers, Freemasons, Jews, globalists, liberal secular humanists, and government bureaucrats. The parasites below are stereotyped as lazy or sinful, draining the economic resources of the productive middle, or poisoning the culture with their sinful sexuality. Among those scapegoated as lazy are blacks and other people of color, immigrants, and welfare mothers. The sinful are abortionists, homosexuals, and feminists. A repressive force is directed downwards toward people seen through this stereotype and prejudice. In this context, conspiracy theories that often accompany producerism are a narrative form of scapegoating; and they overlap with some demonizing versions of Christian millennialist endtimes scenarios that watch for betrayal in high places and a population turning from God and drifting into laziness and sin.

The overall outcome of the producerist model of populism is a broad social and political movement sometimes called "Middle American Nationalism" or "The Radical Center" or "Middle American Radicals." Whatever the label, this is a form of repressive populism with a producerist narrative. As the size of the repressive populist sectors grow, politicians and activists within electoral reform movements try to recruit the populists toward participation within electoral political frameworks. As they seek votes, some politicians begin to use populist rhetoric and pander to the scapegoating.

Anna Marie Smith, Ansell, Hardisty, Diamond, and Sklar note how in Britain and the United States, right-wing repressive populism diverts attention from inherent white supremacism by using coded language to reframe racism as a concern about specific issues, such as welfare, immigration, tax, or education policies. Non-Christian religions, women, gay men and lesbians, youth, students, reproductive rights activists, and environmentalists also are scapegoated. Sometimes producerism targets those persons who organize on behalf of impoverished and marginalized communities, especially progressive social change activists. Today there are four main sectors of the right where repressive forms of right-wing populism with its producerist narrative are used to mobilize movements: the Christian Right, libertarianism, regressive patriots and armed militias; and Far Right insurgents and neo-Nazis.

Producerism played a key role in a shift from the main early mode of right-wing populist conspiracism which defended the status quo against a mob of "outsiders," originally framed as a conspiracy of Freemasons or Jews or immigrants. The John Birch Society and the Liberty Lobby played a significant role in promoting producerism and helping it transform into populist antigovernment conspiracist themes during the 1960s and 1970s. Populism in the Christian Right centers on mobilizing godly people against secularized elites seen as controlling the government and media.

Because populist right-wing conspiracism so often rests on an antielite critique, it has been known to attract some on the political left. Biehl and Staudenmaier (1995) reveal how some Green Party activists in the 1990s had to struggle against conspiracism, including the anti-Semitic variant, among members and even a handful of leaders. Populist conspiracism also has found a home in certain black nationalist and Arab anti-imperialist groups.

Right-wing populism can act as both a precursor and a building block of fascism, with antielitist conspiracism and reactionary scapegoating as shared elements. Fritzsche (1990) showed that distressed middle-class populists in Weimar launched bitter attacks against both the government and big business. This populist surge was later exploited by the Nazis which parasitized the forms and themes of the populists and moved their constituencies far to the right through ideological appeals involving demagoguery, scapegoating, and conspiracism.

Conclusion

Populism needs to be seen as a style of organizing that transcends political boundaries. Fear of all forms of populism by some intellectuals is dismissive of the democratic capability of the majority of citizens. At the same time, the idea that populism is always good, and that "The People" are always right, ignores the history of such claims. Too often this attitude leads to infringement of minority rights by the majority. Populist conspiracism from anywhere on the political spectrum can lure mainstream politicians to adopt their scapegoating narratives in order to attract voters. Throughout U.S. history, repressive populist movements have used demonizing rhetoric that encouraged acts of discrimination and violence. A lynching is as much a form of populism as is a demonstration against racist police brutality. Like most tools, populism can be used for good or bad purposes.

Kazin suggests that "when a new breed of inclusive grassroots movements does arise, intellectuals should contribute their time, their money, and their passion for justice. They should work to stress the harmonious, hopeful, and pragmatic aspects of populist language and to disparage the meaner ones" (1995: 284). The formula for democracy is profoundly populist. It is the faith that over time, the majority of citizens, given enough accurate information, and the ability to participate in an open public debate, reach the right decisions to preserve liberty and defend freedom.

Chip Berlet

Bibliography

Ansell, Amy Elizabeth. (1997) *New Right, New Racism: Race and Reaction in the United States and Britain.* New York: New York University Press.

——, ed. (1998) *Unraveling the Right: The New Conservatism in American Thought and Politics.* New York: Westview.

Bell, Daniel, ed. (1964) *The Radical Right: The New American Right Expanded and Updated.* Garden City, NY: Anchor Books/Doubleday.

Bennett, David H. (1995) *The Party of Fear: The American Far Right from Nativism to the Militia Movement,* revised. New York: Vintage Books.

Berlet, Chip, and Matthew N. Lyons. (2000) *Right-Wing Populism in America: Too Close for Comfort.* New York: Guilford Press.

Berlet, Chip. (1995) "The Violence of Right-Wing Populism." *Peace Review* 7, 3/4: 283–88.

——, ed. (1995) *Eyes Right! Challenging the Right Wing Backlash.* Boston: South End Press.

Betz, Hans-Georg. (1994) *Radical Right-wing Populism in Western Europe.* New York: St. Martin's Press.

Biehl, Janet, and Peter Staudenmaier. (1995) *Ecofascism: Lessons from the German Experience.* San Francisco, CA: AK Press.

Billig, Michael. (1978) *Fascists: A Social Psychological View of the National Front.* New York: Harcourt Brace Jovanovich.

Boggs, Carl. (1986) *Social Movements and Political Power: Emerging Forms of Radicalism in the West.* Philadelphia: Temple University Press.

Buechler, Steven M., and F. Kurt Cylke, Jr., eds. (1997) *Social Movements: Perspectives and Issues.* Mountain View, CA: Mayfield.

Canovan, Margaret. (1981) *Populism.* New York: Harcourt Brace Jovanovich.

Carto, Willis. (1982) *Profiles in Populism.* Old Greenwich, CT: Flag Press.

Diamond, Sara. (1995) *Roads to Dominion: Right-Wing Movements and Political Power in the United States,* New York: Guilford.

Dobratz, Betty A., and Stephanie L. Shanks-Meile. (1997) *"White Power, White Pride!" The White Separatist Movement in the United States.* New York: Twayne Publishers.

Federici, Michael P. (1991) *The Challenge of Populism: The Rise of Right-Wing Democratism in Postwar America.* New York: Praeger.

Forster, Arnold, and Benjamin R. Epstein. (1964) *Danger on the Right.* New York: Random House.

Fritzsche, Peter. (1990) *Rehearsals for Fascism: Populism and Political Mobilization in Weimar Germany.* New York: Oxford University Press.

Goodwyn, Lawrence. (1978) *The Populist Moment: A Short History of the Agrarian Revolt in America.* Oxford: Oxford University Press.

Hardisty, Jean. (1999) *Mobilizing Resentment: Conservative Resurgence from the John Birch Society to the Promise Keepers.* Boston: Beacon.

Hertzke, Allen D. (1993) *Echoes of Discontent: Jesse Jackson, Pat Robertson, and the Resurgence of Populism.* Washington, D.C.: Congressional Quarterly Press.

Higham, John. (1972) *Strangers in the Land: Patterns of American Nativism 1860–1925.* New York: Atheneum.

Himmelstein, Jerome L. (1990) *To the Right: The Transformation of American Conservatism.* Berkeley: University of California Press.

Hixson, William B., Jr. (1992) *Search for the American Right Wing: An Analysis of the Social Science Record, 1955–1987.* Princeton, NJ: Princeton University Press.

Hofstadter, Richard. (1965) *The Paranoid Style in American Politics and Other Essays.* New York: Alfred A. Knopf.

Johnston, Hank, and Bert Klandermans, eds. (1995) *Social Movements and Culture.* Minneapolis: University of Minnesota Press.

Kazin, Michael. (1995) *The Populist Persuasion: An American History.* New York: Basic Books.

Klandermans, Bert. (1997) *The Social Psychology of Protest.* Oxford, U.K.: Blackwell.

Lipset, Seymour Martin, and Earl Raab. (1970) *The Politics of Unreason: Right-Wing Extremism in America, 1790–1970.* New York: Harper & Row.

Lofland, John. (1996) *Social Movement Organizations: Guide to Research on Insurgent Realities.* New York: Aldine de Gruyter.

Mintz, Frank P. (1985) *The Liberty Lobby and the American Right: Race, Conspiracy, and Culture.* Westport, CT: Greenwood.

Morris, Aldon D., and Carol McClung Mueller, eds. (1992) *Frontiers in Social Movement Theory.* New Haven, CT: Yale University Press.

"The New Populism." (1995) *Business Week* (13 March): 73–78.

Phillips, Kevin. (1992) "The Politics of Frustration." *New York Times Magazine* 12 (April): 38–42.

Reagan, Michael. (1996) *Making Waves.* Nashville, TN: Thomas Nelson.

Riker, William H. ([1982] 1988) *Liberalism Against Populism: A Confrontation Between the Theory of Democracy and the Theory of Social Choice.* Prospect Heights, IL: Waveland Press.

Rogin, Michael. (1967) *The Intellectuals and McCarthy: The Radical Specter.* Cambridge, MA: MIT Press.

Schoenberger, Robert A., ed. (1969) *The American Right Wing: Readings in Political Behavior.* New York: Holt, Rinehart & Winston.

Sklar, Holly. (1995) *Chaos or Community: Seeking Solutions, Not Scapegoats for Bad Economics.* Boston: South End Press.

Smith, Anna Marie. (1994) *New Right Discourse on Race & Sexuality.* Cambridge, U.K.: Cambridge University Press.

Smith, Christian, ed. (1997) *Disruptive Religion: The Force of Faith in Social Movement Activism.* New York: Routledge.

Stock, Catherine McNicol. (1996) *Rural Radicals: Righteous Rage in the American Grain.* Ithaca, NY: Cornell University Press.

Tarrow, Sidney. (1994) *Power in Movement: Social Movements, Collective Action and Politics.* New York: Cambridge University Press.

Viguerie, Richard. (1983) *The Establishment vs. the People: Is a New Populist Revolution on the Way?* Chicago: Regnery Gateway Inc.

Warren, Donald I. (1976) *The Radical Center: Middle Americans and the Politics of Alienation.* Notre Dame, IN: University of Notre Dame Press.

Postmillennialism

Postmillennialism was a Christian philosophy of history, rooted in eschatology, which was largely unique to the Anglo-American Protestant community from the early eighteenth century until the closing decades of the nineteenth century. It received its name because it anticipated that the Second Advent of Jesus Christ would occur after earth's millennial age. (In this, it differed from its oft-times rival, premillennialism, which reversed this sequence of events.) It enjoyed its widest currency in pre–Civil War America, when its popularity benefited from an expansive social optimism in both religious and secular thought, an optimism which its cheery philosophy reinforced. The bloody shock of Civil War undercut its assumptions on the perfectibility of human nature and society, and the social costs of postwar industrialization and urbanization contributed further to its decline. It survived merely as a faint echo for social reform and never recaptured its early popularity.

Postmillennialism (also frequently called simply millennialism) was always a vague formulation of Christian optimism that never coalesced as a systematic theology. Its very intellectual looseness enabled it to serve as a vehicle for numerous utopian experiments in the Atlantic Community, especially America, some of which were only marginally Christian. As a generalized belief, it was popular with both conventional clergy and with social experimenters whose beliefs outraged society. Its reformism was felt throughout America and was especially significant in antislavery.

Prophecy and the Millennium in Early Christian and Medieval Thought

Beginning in the second century CE, some prominent Christian theologians interpreted a passage in the Revelation of St. John 20:1–3 as prophesying a thousand-year period (the millennium) of earthly bliss, during which Satan would be held bound. Never entirely accepted by the early church, the millennium was almost immediately conflated with the Second Advent of Jesus Christ, whose return was to be its initiating event. Apocalyptic expectations, often intense during the Apostolic and sub-Apostolic eras, moderated over time, however, and were finally discouraged by church councils when Christianity became an official religion of the Roman Empire in the fourth century. Still, the concept of a millennium had been firmly lodged in Christian literature and tradition and would surface, often with disruptive social results, from time to time thereafter.

Medieval Europe experienced occasional episodes of apocalyptic speculation, best documented from the twelfth century onward to the Reformation, several of which caused localized civil disturbance. Modern scholars interpret these episodes as rooted in economic dislocation. Charismatic figures identified one or another individuals or institutions as the Antichrist and warned that the end of the world was near. The extraordinary religious upheaval of the Protestant Reformation gave even wider currency to apocalyptic movements, some of which were violent. Seventeenth-century England, afflicted by civil war, was an especially fertile ground for eschatological literature which called for the establishment of God's Kingdom on earth—a millennium.

The idea of a millennium in Christian thought was thus widely associated with an apocalypse. The earthly Kingdom was to be initiated in blood and social upheaval, perhaps by the Second Advent itself, and only after the Antichrist's reign of persecution of the faithful. It is this background of historical pessimism which makes postmillennialism stand out so strongly in Christian thought.

Enlightenment Europe and Millennialism

Perhaps the first sustained exposition of what eventually was termed postmillennialism was made in 1703 by Daniel Whitby, rector of St. Edmund's in Salisbury, England. His *Paraphrase and Commentary on the New Testament* set forth what he believed to be a "new hypothesis," namely, that the millennium would precede—not follow—the Second Advent. Furthermore, that era would be introduced through the operation of history and not by divine intervention (other than the working of the Holy Spirit in the hearts of humankind). He foresaw a time when the world would be converted to Christianity, the pope and Islam overthrown, the Jews restored to Palestine, and an era of earthly peace and plenty begun. Christ's return would be a final upbeat coda to the millennium.

Whitby's scheme was optimistic toward both the course of history and human potential, and in this it presaged the tenor of later postmillennialism. His version of sacred history did allow that periods of crisis might overtake Christians. But, the trend of human affairs, guided by the Holy Spirit, was for the gradual amelioration of social ills and the spread of holiness. Manifest divine intervention in history was not required to achieve a millennium—Christian zeal, especially in missions to unbelievers, would suffice.

The steady growth in postmillennial literature throughout the Anglo-American world during the eighteenth century is inseparable from the larger intellectual milieu of the European Age of Enlightenment, a fact which complicates historical analysis. Discoveries in many fields of learning, notably in physics and mathematics by Sir Isaac Newton, created an air of general intellectual confidence which led, in turn, to social theorizing hopeful of the perfectibility of both human nature and civilization. The result was that until well into the nineteenth century both skeptics and believers used similar vocabularies to predict the incipience of an era of tranquility and abundance, to be achieved in history through human effort. For instance, the secular French philosopher Condorcet wrote his *Historical View of the Progress of the Human Mind* (1793) to demonstrate that the course of history was evolutionarily progressive, a concept not at all at odds with Whitby's Christian scheme. It is thus a nice question whether millennialism should be regarded as the theological manifestation of a secular Idea of Progress (a staple of historians of Western thought) or if just the reverse is true. Regardless, a host of utopian and reformist movements, along with experiments in novel sexual and familial relationships, so shared the optimism and even the verbiage of militantly religious ones that a kinship must be admitted.

The social theories of the English reformer Robert Owen (1771–1858) exemplified this intermingling of secular utopianism with Christian millennialism. Owen's socialistic schemes were rooted in what he called a "Religion of Charity alone, unconnected with faith." Both he and his followers, however, used the vocabulary of Christian postmillennialism. For instance, one of his disciples penned a "Rational Religionist's Advent Hymn," which began "Brothers, arise! Behold the dawn appear / Of Truth's bright day and Love's Millennial Year!" Throughout the nineteenth century there is an affinity in European history between Christian postmillennialism and even militantly atheistic social and political movements. Karl Marx's interpretation of history, which convinced him that mankind would eventually evolve into a classless communist society, is one manifestation of this affinity that survives into our own time.

The Millennium in Colonial and Revolutionary America

Early Puritan New England divines, although not necessarily explicitly eschatological, nonetheless interpreted their mission to the New World in terms of redeeming the earth. John Winthrop's famous description of the Bay Colony as a "cittee upon a hill" held up the Puritan experiment as a model for future society the world over. (If there is a sense in American life of a world-historical mission, as seems probable, it can be considered as beginning here.) Although present in the writings of such well-known early settlers as John Cotton, Anne Hutchinson, and John Elliott, this incipient millennialism faded into insignificance as the founding religious impulse lessened somewhat in New England by the end of the seventeenth century.

The millennial impulse remained alive, however, in colonial exposure to the vigorous eschatological literature of late-seventeenth- and early-eighteenth-century England. It was manifest as well in small communal experiments such as Ephrata and Woman in the Wilderness (both in Pennsylvania) which saw themselves as forerunners of the millennial age. These small experiments were, however, tinged with apocalypticism and of little or no influence.

The religious revivals which swept English North America during the mid-eighteenth century, known ever since as the Great Awakening, caused an outpouring of the millennialism latent in colonial America—New England especially—since the first Puritan settlements. There is scant evidence that much, or any, of this was due to the speculations of Daniel Whitby, despite similarities with that writer's eschatology (although some of the colonial clergy was conversant with English millennial literature). It was, instead, likely rooted in a reawakening of the old Puritan sense of mission and singularity, combined with vast gratification over what was regarded as a lavish outpouring of the Holy Spirit.

The great American theologian Jonathan Edwards (1703–58), whose preaching helped ignite the massive revivals, expounded a learned eschatology which was clearly postmillennial. He saw the Great Awakening as a stage in the maturation of human history, evidence that the Spirit, working in the world, was ameliorating sin and disbelief, and that the age of bliss could be achieved within time without the cataclysmic return of Christ in judgment. He believed as well that America was likely the model for the world's future, as humanity moved toward the millennium. In his *Thoughts On the Revival* he announced that: "The latter-day glory is probably to begin in America." A sense of America's divine mission, inherited from Puritan New England, was thus reinforced: it would never be entirely absent from American life thereafter.

The millennial optimism stirred by the Great Awakening had scarcely dampened when it was revived and amplified by the American Revolution. The political conflict with Great Britain was often referred to in apocalyptic terms, with all the paraphernalia of Christian eschatology (e.g., the Mother-country as Antichrist). The imminence of Christ's return was not, however, a feature in this literature. The emphasis was, instead, on the triumph in history of virtue over decadence and the national model of America as the first millennial fruits. Even a skeptic such as Thomas Paine could write: "We have it in our power to begin the world over. . . . The birthday of a new world is at hand." Christian clergy and laity conflated republican government and resistance to tyranny with God's will and cast patriots as laboring to slough off corruption and lay the foundations of the world's new age in North America.

The Nineteenth Century

The years between the Revolutionary Era and the Civil War constitute the cockpit of postmillennialism. Pride in the newly founded country combined with a sense of unrestricted possibility for social transformation to reinforce faith in a coming age of Christian triumph. The rationalist second president, John Adams, jocularly asked: "Can you give me any news of the millennium? Is it to commence soon enough for me to entertain a hope that I may live a thousand years longer?"

The generalized expectation of an incipient Age of Bliss, to begin in America, was expressed in a wide range of social experiments which defy easy categorization. Two prominent sectarian movements, the Shakers and the Mormons (the Church of Christ of Latter-day Saints) attracted believers, in part with visionary experiments in new communal and sexual relationships. (The Shakers stressed celibacy, the Mormons eventually endorsed polygamy.) Sexual experimentation was nowhere as widespread as at New York State's Oneida Community, which encouraged "free love" during the decades just before and after the Civil War. There were, as well, sectarian experimenters who rejected explicitly Christian theology but appropriated its millennialism, converted by them into utopianism. Short-lived experiments in communal living drew scattered adherents to over a dozen settlements (indebted intellectually to Robert Owen), including Brook Farm in Massachusetts, which figures greatly in Boston literary history.

Beyond a doubt, however, it was in the wider world of evangelical Protestantism that postmillennialism was most influential. It flourished as a transdenominational social phenomenon, not the property of any one creed. Persuasions which emphasized free will were more receptive to its allure, the Methodists especially, while churches which clung to Calvinism tended to be more resistant.

Antebellum religious literature was permeated with expectation of the march of history in America into the biblical millennium. The *Oberlin Evangelist* was one of thousands of such voices when, in 1841, it proclaimed: "The preparation for the *promised millennium has begun*. . . . THE MILLENNIUM IS AT HAND." The *Methodist Quarterly* lauded the nineteenth century as "an age of steam, of electricity, of prodigious movement and significance." This millennialism combined with fierce national pride to provide a theological justification for Manifest Destiny and American imperialism. In 1854 the author of *Armageddon* wrote: "Some political government will spread over the Earth in the Millennium; and it will be a democracy, or it will be no millennium; and the United States is likely to be that incipient democracy."

A few postmillennial enthusiasts foresaw troubled times ahead, as Satan acted to subvert the march of progress. Others were optimistic, but their belief had a darker side, such as the writer who insisted: "The Millennium is a political era of Christian republicanism, confined mainly to the white race." But, the tone of postmillennialism was overwhelmingly socially reformist and progressive. Its spirit underwrote a host of organized activity aimed at amelioration of the lot of the poor and suffering. Temperance movements, the Sunday school movement, and charitable outreach all flourished as never before. Nowhere was this progressive spirit felt more strongly than in antislavery. Human bondage was held to be a fundamental social sin, the removal of which was imperative before the millennium could begin. William Lloyd Garrison was only one of a host of abolitionists whose moral indignation was rooted in millennial hope.

Inevitably, postmillennialism sprouted a number of theological innovations, some of which were controversial. The Christian perfection movement of the 1830s and 1840s, for instance, insisted that humankind, aided by the Spirit, could achieve sinlessness in this life—a concept which deeply offended others. The cheery eschatology was, as well, a massive inducement to revivalism (a millennial world must, by definition, be a Christian one) and the greatest of the nineteenth-century revivalists, Charles G. Finney (also a perfectionist), assured listeners that it was possible to introduce the millennium within three years. For these postmillennialists, the Second Advent would occur mainly as a glorious capstone to a blissful millennium achieved in history by humankind aided by the Holy Spirit.

Postmillennialism in American Protestant thought faded rapidly after the Civil War. (It had relatively little presence elsewhere in Western Christendom.) In part, this was due to the massive blood-letting of the war—scarcely conducive to optimism. (The millennial spirit did sustain the North, however. Witness the "Battle Hymn of the Republic," with its opening words "Mine eyes have seen the glory / Of the Coming of the Lord.") The oppressive conditions of much postwar industrial society further discouraged the easy optimism of the Antebellum Era. But, a growing sophistication in American biblical scholarship also did its part by de-emphasizing the significance of prophecy to faith.

Some of the reformist zeal of postmillennialism survived into the postwar period in the Social Gospel of the late nineteenth century. This movement for economic and political amelioration was, however, virtually devoid of eschatological dimension. By the closing years of the century postmillennialism had all but disappeared from American life. Its place, in part, was taken by premillennialism, an apocalyptic theology which spread widely in conservative evangelical Protestantism during the next century.

Robert K. Whalen

Bibliography

Bloch, Ruth. (1994) *Visionary Republic.* New York: Cambridge University Press.

Cohn, Norman F. (1961) *The Pursuit of the Millennium.* New York: Harper Torchbooks.

Hatch, Nathan O. (1989) *The Democratization of American Christianity.* New Haven, CT: Yale University Press.

Heimert, Alan. (1966) *Religion and the American Mind from the Great Awakening to the Revolution.* Cambridge, MA: Harvard University Press.

Smith, Timothy L. (1965) *Revivalism and Social Reform.* New York: Harper Torchbooks.

Premillennialism

Premillennialism is a Christian eschatology, so-called because it anticipates that the Second Advent of Jesus Christ will occur before, and thus initiate, a thousand-year Kingdom of God on earth (the millennium). While the term itself dates from only the mid-nineteenth century, the substance of the belief, known also as "chiliasm" (Greek *khilioi,* thousand) or "millenarianism" (Latin *mille,* thousand + *annus,* year), dates from the second century CE. It is a widely current belief in modern Protestant Christianity, but is virtually unknown in contemporary Roman Catholic and Orthodox thought. It is especially prominent in American denominations and in international Protestant communities rooted substantially in evangelical missions from the United States (Latin America, especially). It is particularly prevalent among conservative evangelical churches, the Baptists, for instance, as well as various Pentecostal and Fundamentalist denominations. It is rarely encountered in mainline Protestant persuasions, such as the Episcopal Church, the Presbyterian Church USA, or the United Church of Christ.

Premillennialism has gone in and out of popularity and has proven a controversial, even divisive, belief. During the last two centuries, however, it enjoyed a remarkable resurgence and is now more widespread and vigorously attested than ever. Its present pattern of belief involves far more than eschatology and has evolved into a theology which touches on biblical inspiration, hermeneutics, social attitudes, Jewish-Christian relations, and even foreign policy. Its steady growth into the third millennium CE seems assured.

Origins in the Early Church and Patristic Christianity

Premillennialism is nowhere explicit in the Bible. It is, rather, an interpretation of diverse prophetic passages in the Old and New Testaments. Historically, the most influential of these have been the Book of Daniel, the "Little Apocalypse" of Mark: chapter 13, and the Book of Revelation. All of this, in turn, is read in the light of the belief that Jesus Christ will return to the earth in glory "to judge the living and the dead" (the words of the Nicene Creed of 325 CE). This anticipated Second Advent is foundational to premillennialism.

After his post-Resurrection appearances to his disciples, the testimony of St. Luke says of Jesus that "While he blessed them, he parted from them" (Luke 51). From this moment on, it appears that the earliest Christians believed that Jesus would return to judge the world. This belief was expressed briefly in the Gospels (John 21:20–23) in Jesus' own words and elsewhere in the New Testament, including the Pauline letters. The expectation among these first Christians was that the Second Advent was imminent. The Letter of St. James, for example, counseled believers: "Establish your hearts, for the coming of the Lord is at hand" (James 5:8).

Persecution of first-century Christians by Roman authorities inspired the Revelation to John, written in about 80–90 CE. This difficult work encouraged the suffering faithful and located their travail within a cosmic drama—the outcome of which would be their own vindication and the destruction of evil. It told of an angel, who will have seized "that ancient serpent, who is the Devil and Satan, and bind him for a thousand years . . . that he should deceive the nations no more till the thousand years were ended" (Revelation 20:2–3). It is this brief passage, more than any other, which is cited as evidence of a future millennium. Chiliasm resulted from mating the earlier Christian belief in a Second Advent with this later mention of the thousand years and making it the cause.

Apocalyptic imagery doubtless sustained early believers during Christianity's difficult first centuries. Prominent church fathers, especially Irenaeus during the second century, worked out in some detail an eschatology which contains many of the same elements of modern premillennialism. It was rooted in a "literal" interpretation of Scriptural prophecy, such as foresaw Christ's return in glory, the temporal defeat of evil, and the binding of Satan for a thousand-year period during which the elect would dwell on earth in the flesh in bliss. Other writers depicted an Antichrist, an arch-fiend who persecutes the faithful to the point of extinction, until defeated by the returning Christ. This demonic figure remains a prominent feature of premillennialism to this day.

Chiliasm had its critics within the early Christian church, many of whom saw it as a disruptive and sensual belief. During the third century, Origen attacked it for what he regarded as a simpleminded reading of prophecy and his view was widely shared. (Essentially the same argument continues into our own time.) When, early in the fourth century, Christianity was established as an official faith of the Empire, chiliasm lost its standing as a solace for persecution and was condemned by church councils. The immensely influential St. Augustine disregarded a literal millennium entirely and talked-down apocalypticism in favor of what our own time would call "realized eschatology," in which God's will unfolds in the faith-life of the church. To this day, the Roman Catholic Church has not departed far from Augustine's beliefs and generally disregards apocalyptic thought altogether. Despite this, however, the early centuries of persecution established the core of premillennial belief.

Medieval Europe and into the Reformation

Relatively little is known about millenarian activity, if there was such, prior to the year 1000. It is known that some literate clergy dreaded that the apocalypse might occur in that millennial year, although much recent scholarship somewhat downplays the prevalence of this fear. The historical record is better documented from the eleventh century onward and chiliastic episodes in European history, while by no means common, are nonetheless well established. While it would be anachronistic to label these as "premillennial," they included elements similar to those in the apocalyptic traditions of both early Christianity and the modern era: disgust with contemporary society; a sense of impending doom; social and political unrest; and individuals or institutions perceived as the Antichrist.

The Crusades were, in part, motivated by a millenarian belief that the New Jerusalem, spoken of in Revelation 21:1–4, might be realized through armed seizure of the Holy Land. From time to time, charismatic individuals gathered disciples during the Middle Ages based on their reading of prophecy. Joachim of Fiore, especially, gained a wide following during the thirteenth century for his preaching on prophecy until finally condemned by the Fourth Lateran Council. A significant number of lesser figures gained brief local notoriety with millenarian rhetoric during the late Middle Ages, and various dissenting religious sects (e.g., the fifteenth-century Taborites of Bohemia) reveled in apocalyptic imagery. On occasion, these millenarian movements proved so socially disruptive that they were suppressed, often very bloodily, by local princes. Distinguished scholars detect a relationship between straitened economic circumstances, other social ills, and the flourishing of medieval chiliasm.

It would be difficult to encapsulate this medieval millenarianism, so varied was it and over such a great length of time. Several elements, though, stand out. These include an ideological dependence on an Antichrist figure, often identified as the papacy; charismatic leadership; circumstances of social unrest; and a signaling out of the Jews as agents of Antichrist, with their resultant persecution.

Europe during the sixteenth and seventeenth centuries experienced fervid apocalyptic episodes, many of which scholars attribute to the social shocks attendant on the Reformation. Martin Luther frequently used the vocabulary of prophecy to interpret events and identified the papacy with the Antichrist, although he condemned efforts elsewhere to implement a millennium by political and military means. Others were less circumspect and in Germany, Thomas Muntzer provided eschatological underpinnings for a peasants' revolt that was suppressed with horrendous bloodshed. Throughout the continental Reformation, the various factions condemned one another out of prophecy.

Millenarian literature was particularly current in sixteenth- and, especially, seventeenth-century England, where premillennialism enjoyed a wide exposition, essential elements of which endure to our own time. In part, this was a continuation of the apocalyptic interpretation of events common elsewhere in Reformation Europe. In part, though, it was undergirded by a recovery of ancient languages, Hebrew especially, which made Jewish prophetic texts and commentaries accessible to Christians. The English Civil War saw a great outpouring of such literature and political factions, the Fifth Monarch Men, especially, were organized around it. Even after the return of civil peace late in the seventeenth century, prophecy continued to be a frequent subject of scholarship, with savants as famed as Sir Isaac Newton deeply immersed in its study. Endless calculations were made as to the date of the Second Advent and the inception of the millennium and an especially novel element was added. English commentators became convinced that the world's Jews would be gathered to Palestine at the millennium and the ancient state of Israel reestablished. This stood in contradistinction to the usual Continental anti-Semitism drawn from prophecy.

The Modern Era

The term premillennialism came into general use during the mid-nineteenth century, a period when modern chiliasm was defined. This process of definition was almost entirely the work of British and American Protestants and was prompted by their belief that the French and American Revolutions (the French, especially) realized prophecies made in the Books of Daniel and Revelation. For a prolonged period, between 1790 and the middle of the following century, millenarianism was fashionable among English evangelicals within the Established Church and among dissenting sects. The historian Thomas Macaulay noted: "Many Christians believe that the Messiah will shortly establish a kingdom on the earth, and reign visibly over all its inhabitants" (Macaulay 1897: 5, 467). Prominent clergy and nobility interpreted the two revolutions as the realization of events prophesied to occur just prior to the Second Advent. They were roundly criticized for an overly literal reading of these prophecies but still maintained that the Antichrist was unleashed (the papacy still a favorite target), that a time of immense persecution was at hand, and that the Jews would be restored to Palestine. All this would be followed by the return of Christ, the defeat of Antichrist, and the inception of the millennium.

Chiliasm was popular in English life at its lower social levels as well. Humble artisans, hard-pressed by the early Industrial Revolution, saw in their difficult times many of the signs of the Second Advent which others discerned in international events. In some instances, local seers, such as Johanna Walcott, convinced common folk of their prophetic status and rallied disciples. (No violence, however, followed from this.)

The widespread resurgence of chiliasm within the English-speaking world led to organized and prolonged effort to convert the Jews to Christianity and to explore their reestablishment in Palestine. A Jews Society was founded in London and expended considerable resources on evangelical missions to the Jews. The carving out of a modern Israeli state for them within land then ruled by the Ottomans was an item of common speculation.

Premillennialism in America

Premillennialism has flourished in the United States as nowhere else in history down to the present day and did so from the early Republic. Occasional eschatological speculation can be found among colonial American theologians, of whom Jonathan Edwards was the most prominent. Almost entirely, however, premillennialism in America is the result of the wholesale transfer to this country of ideas current in late Georgian and early Victorian England. These included, especially, the historicist method, which interpreted contemporary events in relation to prophecy.

Americans added, on the whole, little to the stock of ideas received from England via journals and books but publicized these with an especial vehemence which elicited controversy. By the 1830s, millenarianism was a divisive issue among the Protestant clergy. A dedicated group of clerics and laity centered largely about Manhattan published a series of specialized journals, books, and articles during the pre–Civil War decades which advanced the topic nationally. As in England, premillennialists informed their eschatology with a lavish philo-Semitism which called for the reestablishment of Israel. Many of these premillennialists were embarrassed when William Miller, an upstate New York farmer, prophesied the Second Advent for first 1843 and then 1844. But, this failed prediction (which, nonetheless, eventually led to a new sect, the Seventh-Day Adventists) hardly retarded the growth of premillennialism.

Premillennialism flourished after the Civil War, in part due to a series of well-attended prophetic conferences held annually at Niagara-on-the-Lake, Ontario. It appealed especially to Protestants of Calvinist background, which is not surprising since the foreordained future of prophecy resembles the predestinarian doctrine of Calvinism. The dispensational theories of the Englishman, John Nelson Darby, founder of the Plymouth Brethren, which divide sacred history into discrete periods of prophetic fulfillment, were also taken up in America. Theological support for premillennialism was derived as well from Princeton Theological Seminary, where various scholars provided arguments for the infallible Bible central to millenarian thought. Although derided and disregarded by contemporary scholars attuned to the historical-critical approach, which regarded prophecy as little more than inspirational poetry of little contemporary relevance, premillennialism was embraced by popular revivalists, the most influential of whom was Dwight L. Moody. Despite the ridicule directed during the 1920s at Fundamentalism, with which it was widely identified, premillennialism spread steadily among evangelical Christians. Its appeal was interdenominational and its adherents formed a substrata of believers across modern Protestant sectarian lines. It blossomed effulgently after World War II when Billy Graham became its most noteworthy exponent and by the end of the twentieth century was more widely established than ever in American religious life.

Premillennialism today is largely an American phenomenon, although evangelical missionaries from the United States have carried the belief overseas. While prophecy is susceptible to many interpretations, the salient features of the belief have stabilized. The Bible is to be read "literally," that is, as the infallible Word of God, and its prophecies regarded as reliable predictors of future history. A skilled interpreter can match prophecy with current events. History itself consists of separate dispensations, during each of which God has dealt with men according to different rules. The world is to grow steadily worse in sin, until an Antichrist arises whose reign will introduce the Tribulation, a time of earthly travail. Elect Christians, however, will escape these trials through the Rapture, in which God will bodily lift them out of the world. The Jews will gather in a restored Israel (a scenario which has led premillennial evangelicals to champion the state of Israel and lobby for a favorable American foreign policy) and there the Antichrist will nearly annihilate them during his years of power, usually put at about seven in number. In the nick of time, when all seems lost, the Second Advent will occur, the Antichrist be banished, and Christ will reign bodily on the earth for a period of one thousand years, probably with Jerusalem as his capital. At the end of the millennium there will be a final Apostasy, the destruction of the world, the Last Judgment, and the end of time.

Many scholars find the whole thing incredible. Premillennialism is criticized roundly for naive scholarship which confuses the poetic and inspirational purpose of prophecy with fortune telling. Premillennialists retort that they merely follow the Word of God, regardless of ridicule. Regardless, the virtual theology which surrounds premillennialism is today stronger and more widely spread than at any time in history.

Robert K. Whalen

Bibliography

Boyer, Paul (1992) *When Time Shall Be No More.* Cambridge, MA: Harvard University Press.

Capp, B. S. (1972) *The Fifth Monarchy Men.* London: Faber.

Cohn, Norman F. (1961) *The Pursuit of the Millennium.* New York: Harper & Row.

Macaulay, Charles Babington. (1897) "Civil Disabilities of the Jews." In *The Works of Lord Macaulay*, 8 vols., edited by Lady Trevelyan. New York: Longmans, Green & Co.

Sandeen, Ernest R. (1970) *The Roots of Fundamentalism.* Chicago: University of Chicago Press.

Progressive Millennialism

Progressive millennialism is a millennial perspective that is optimistic about human nature and the possibility of the currently imperfect human society to get better. Progressive millennialism is the belief that the imminent transition to the collective salvation will occur noncatastrophically. The progressive millennial belief is that humans working according to a divine or superhuman plan will progressively create the millennial kingdom. Humans can create the collective salvation if they cooperate with the guidance of the divine or superhuman agent.

It would appear that progressive millennialism will motivate people to engage in spiritual self-cultivation and social work to improve themselves and society. Examples of progressive millennialism include the Social Gospel movement of Protestant Christianity, and the "special option for the poor" of Vatican II theology. The millennialism articulated by Pope John Paul II in response to the approach of the year 2000 was a progressive millennialism.

In the Christian tradition, progressive millennialism has been termed "post-millennialism," the belief that Jesus Christ will return *after* the millennial kingdom on earth has been created by the effort of Christians working according to God's will. However, the study of new religious movements demonstrates that messianism can be part of the millennial pattern that involves belief in progress. For instance, Annie Besant (1847–1933) groomed the young J. Krishnamurti to be the "World-Teacher" who would present a teaching that would become the basis of the "New Civilization." Many of Annie Besant's progressive millennial ideas were carried over into the contemporary New Age movement by the published works of another Theosophist, Alice Bailey (1880–1949). The Alice Bailey corpus uses the term "Age of Aquarius." Today, the diffuse New Age movement includes progressive as well as catastrophic expectations concerning the transition to the Age of Aquarius.

Whereas many progressive millennialists expect a progressive, *noncatastrophic* transition to the millennial kingdom, and therefore it would be assumed that this type of millennial pattern is not hospitable to violence, *revolutionary* progressive millennial movements have caused violence on a massive scale. Examples of revolutionary progressive millennial movements are the Nazis, Maoists, and Khmer Rouge. Robert Ellwood has written that in revolutionary progressive millennial movements, revolution is seen as "progress speeded up to an apocalyptic rate." Violent revolution is the means to accelerate progress. Revolutionary progressive millennialism involves a radical dualistic worldview that dehumanizes and demonizes "the other" so that violence can be committed against them. Revolutionary progressive millennialism, therefore, has much in common with revolutionary catastrophic millennialism.

More case studies are needed of progressive millennial groups and movements to understand this religious pattern more fully, and to determine its possible relation to the potential for either violence, or social amelioration and personal spiritual cultivation. For now, it seems functional to distinguish between progressive millennialism with its belief in a noncatastrophic and imminent transition to the collective salvation, and revolutionary progressive millennialism which motivates believers to commit violent acts to speed up progress.

Catherine Wessinger

See also Catastrophic Millennialism, New Age, Revolutionary Millennial Movements

Bibliography

Wessinger, Catherine Lowman. (1988) *Annie Besant and Progressive Messianism.* Lewiston, NY: Edwin Mellen Press.

Wessinger, Catherine. (1997) "Millennialism With and Without the Mayhem: Catastrophic and Progressive Expectations." In *Millennium, Messiahs, and Mayhem: Contemporary Apocalyptic Movements,* edited by Thomas Robbins and Susan J. Palmer. New York: Routledge, 47–59.

——, ed. (2000) *Millennialism, Persecution, and Violence: Historical Cases.* Syracuse, NY: Syracuse University Press.

Wojcik, Daniel. (1997) *The End of the World As We Know It: Faith, Fatalism, and Apocalypse in America.* New York: New York University Press.

Promise Keepers

The Promise Keepers (PK) was started by former University of Colorado football coach Bill McCartney in 1990 as a parachurch Christian men's ministry. Concentrated in the continental United States, PK's central goal was to encourage men to become promise keepers who lived in accord with seven promises. The promises PK urged men to make included promising to "pursue vital relationships with other men," to practice "spiritual, moral, ethical and sexual purity," to build "strong marriages and families through love," and to reach "beyond any racial and denominational barriers to demonstrate the power of biblical unity."

PK garnered significant public recognition for its ability to draw huge attendance to the all-male religious conventions it held in sports arenas across the United States. As a follow-up to convention attendance, PK encouraged men to form small accountability groups of four to ten men in their local communities that monitored the extent to which men kept their PK promises. They subsequently established regional offices to oversee these accountability groups, and area task forces that worked to coalesce Christian men's interests and actions especially in the area of race relations.

Much of PK's unique style that combined popular Christian music, multiethnic preachers, and pithy doctrines in support of a family-centered Christian masculinity whose adoption was deemed urgent in light of the potentially imminent return of Jesus were traceable to founder McCartney's personal background and interests. Born Roman Catholic, McCartney affiliated with the neoevangelical Vineyard Christian Fellowship as an adult. There he was regularly exposed both to the modern, laid-back worship styles that PK eventually adopted, as well as to the biblically literal millennialism that energized its principle organizers.

Elements of McCartney's personal history also informed PK's doctrinal emphasis on racial reconciliation. As a football coach, McCartney regularly forged all-male teams from ever-changing collections of racially diverse young men. When he became the lay leader of one of the most successful para-church ministries of the twentieth century, McCartney worked to infuse the PK organization with a similar, proactive attitude toward racial differences among men. His efforts were only partly successful, however, as the PK movement persistently remained a movement constituted mainly of white, middle-class men.

Although the organization was characterized by explicitly evangelistic appeals, PK leaders insisted they did not wish PK to compete with local congregations or denominations for men's religious loyalty. The evangelistic goal of PK was not to get men to join the PK organization. Instead, it was to get men to become promise keepers; hence, another of the promises PK asked men to make was a promise to support their local pastor.

Arising during an era when women's rights were on the upswing, major controversies swirled around the PK movement with regard to its stances on women. The language of submission it used to depict a marital ideal was strongly attacked by the National Organization for Women, a leading feminist organization. Its invitations to male pastors to attend workshops on men's ministries were criticized for ignoring the existence of female ministers and their interest in men's ministries. Finally, its exclusive targeting of men was questioned, even by some men within its own folds who wanted to involve their spouses in PK activities. In response to this barrage of criticism, PK altered some of its practices. Most notably it began inviting female ministers to its men's ministry workshops.

The substantial material culture that developed around the PK organization contributed to its appeal. This primarily

ERROR OF THE PROMISE KEEPERS

As a member of the church of Christ, I urge you to read about the errors of Promise Keepers from the URL's that I have listed and learn the true facts. No christian can be a member of this organization and be faithful to God. This is a man made organization that is trying to disrupt christian worship by planting their "Key Man" within the congregations to teach error. Please read the following links with an open mind and open your Bibles and study the references listed to see what the error being taught is. In Matthew 7:15 we are told by Jesus, Beware of false prophets, which come to you in sheep's clothing, but inwardly they are ravening wolves. Matt 7:16 Ye shall know them by their fruits. Do men gather grapes of thorns, or figs of thistles?

2 John 8-11 The apostle John warns the church about false teachers who have gone out into the world, explains how they can be identified (by comparing their doctrines with the teachings of Christ), and commands that we not receive or encourage such teachers: "watch yourselves, that you might not lose what we have accomplished, but that you may receive a full reward. Anyone who goes too far and does not abide in the teachings of Christ, does not have God; the one who abides in the teaching, he has both the Father and the Son. If anyone comes to you and does not bring this teaching, do not receive him into your house, and do not give him a greeting; for the one who gives him a greeting participates in his evil deeds."

Source: http://www4.linknet.net/lpoole/pk.htm.

consisted of PK baseball caps, t-shirts, and sweatshirts, but was supplemented by a wide variety of other miscellaneous personal items. Marketed as an extension of this material culture was a huge array of books and magazines targeted at Christian men, which PK encouraged men to use as the focus of their accountability group studies.

By the mid-1990s, only five years after its inception, PK was one of the best-known Christian ministries in the United States. Its substantial popular appeal was demonstrated on a national stage when it was drew approximately one million men to its first national meeting, Stand in the Gap, held in Washington, D.C. on 4 October 1997. Yet this watershed event was quickly followed by considerable intraorganizational turbulence and decline. A policy change that curtailed the PK practice of charging entry fees to attend its stadium conferences plunged the organization into financial chaos, and resulted in large swaths of staff layoffs. The poor publicity that ensued fueled a trajectory of diminished popularity for the organization and placed its long-range continuance in serious doubt.

Among religious studies scholars, millennial experts deemed this popular religious movement an expression of late-twentieth-century millennial enthusiasm. In particular, they noted the striking similarities between PK's support for male public displays of emotion—defining men as "weeping warriors"—and the weeping warriors associated with the Peace of God movement at the first millennium. Thus it is ironic that the one explicitly millennial activity planned by the PK organization was canceled before it could take place. After more than a year of publicizing that PK prayer rallies would be held in state capitals on 1 January 2000, PK millennium celebrations were suddenly called off in the spring of 1999. The reason given for cancellation of the millennium event by PK organizers was concern over the potential social disruption by the Y2K computer glitch.

Brenda E. Brasher

Bibliography

Abraham, Ken. (1995) *Who Are the Promise Keepers? Understanding the Christian Men's Movement.* New York: Doubleday.

Brasher, Brenda E. (1998) "On Politics and Transcendence: The Promise Keepers at Washington DC." *Nova Religio* 1, 2: 289–92.

Lippy, Charles. (1997) "Miles to Go: Promise Keepers in Historical and Cultural Context." *Soundings* 80, 2–3 (summer-fall): 289–304.

Quinby, Lee. (1997) "Coercive Purity: The Dangerous Promise of Apocalyptic Masculinity." In *The Year 2000: Essays on the End*, edited by Charles B. Strozier and Michael Flynn. New York: New York University Press, 154–65.

Prophecy

Prophecy, which may be understood as the prediction of future things (usually through divine inspiration), has had a close relationship with millenarianism and millennial movements throughout world history. In the Book of Revelation (95–96 CE), which may be taken as the basis for early Christian millenarianism, it was predicted that after his Second Coming, Christ would establish a messianic kingdom on the earth before reigning over it for a thousand years before the Last Judgment (Revelation 20: 4–6). The most holy Christian martyrs would be resurrected to live under Christ's rule over a thousand years before the general resurrection of the dead.

The relationship between prophecy and millenarianism can be interpreted in a bewildering variety of ways when it is understood that millenarianism has been perceived by men and women in senses different from that laid out in Revelation. Several decades ago, Norman Cohn suggested that millenarianism had become a "convenient label for a particular type of salvationism," which he defined as being collective, terrestrial, imminent, total, and miraculous (Cohn 1993: 13). Different groups of people have believed themselves specially chosen for the kingdom ruled by Christ; an important characteristic of these groups is the existence of a leader claiming prophetic powers and divine illumination, or an image, symbol, or text that is imbued by individuals with prophetic power of some kind. Prophecies are by nature, obscure enough to be applicable to many different groups, and political and social circumstances, and concrete enough in their imagery or language to seem to an individual to apply to their particular world. Prophets and prophecies typically play on emotions of fear and expectation, and hope and dread, which are aroused by severely unsettled social and political conditions, or by personal misfortune.

Some of these elements may be discerned in the *Prophecies of Nefertiti* which were written in Ancient Egypt (c. 1991–1962 BCE), and expressed a dread of social upheaval, and the coming of a time when slaves would be exalted. The flowering of millenarian sects during the British Civil Wars (1638–51 CE) can be explained by the severe and unprecedented political disjunction of the times. The hope of supernatural aid or guidance in troubled times seems to be strong in all cultures, and the desire to regulate life, especially in times of danger, by forms of clairvoyance, prophecy, astrology, magic, and even games of chance, also seems almost universal. In the West between the Roman and British empires, just as at the time of Ancient Egypt and Mesopotamia two thousand years BCE, there were felt by all classes of society to be many contacts between the secular and the spiritual worlds, and between earth and Heaven or the heavens. It was accepted that God would intervene in the affairs of men and women. Scripture and hagiography (writings about saints) were full of examples of holy men such as St. Thomas More (1478–1535), better known as the author of *Utopia* (1516), acquiring, using, or observing prophetic powers.

Rural life and popular culture were imbued with appeals (often ritualized) to the divine and of signs from the divine. For most medieval and early modern men and women nominally within the Christian lands (Christendom); processions, banners, badges, and images could have apotropaic and prophylactic (safeguarding) powers, just as prayers of intercession could be made for the souls of the departed in purgatory. These rituals and beliefs, which sometimes seemed to ape and pervert the use of sacraments, were subject to the intervention of ecclesiastical and secular authorities. The church, and some sections of educated opinion increasingly disapproved of some propitiatory agricultural processions, and medical interventions, and denounced them as the products of ignorance and diabolical influence.

The question of knowledge, of who precisely can intercede with the divine or mediate between God (or gods), Christ, and humanity, is often at the heart of prophecy and millenarian movements. In the period after 1550 in Mediterranean Europe, and after 1700 in northern Europe, the church and state sought to centralize, regulate, and direct local ritual, and the nature of the relationship between the secular and the divine worlds—as in the case of the canonization of the saints. Just as a pattern of sanctity was promoted by Rome, so it seems that the scope for "holy" men or women to claim divine revelation, or any other power to prophesy, was restricted and, even in peripheral areas, held up to ridicule.

Apocalyptic preaching continued with the sanction of both Protestant and Catholic churches, but prophecy, divination, or the political and religious interpretation of deformed births, cloud formations, animal deformities, butterfly plagues, dreams, or rainstorms of blood, were increasingly derided as the gossip of foolish old women. The investigation of such knowledge passed to natural science, and just twenty years after the British Civil Wars had stirred up prophetic beliefs in Englands old and new, the writer Daniel Defoe could note with disdain that during the Great Plague of London (1665) women were interpreting dreams and seeing hearse-shaped clouds, and attracting credulous believers; and a seventeenth-century English prophetess suffered the indignity of having her name anagrammatized from "Dame Eleanor Davis" to "Never so mad a ladie."

While skepticism about prophecy increased, the advent of the new science did not necessarily mark the end of prophecy. Indeed, Isaac Newton (1642–1727) believed he could unlock the Book of Daniel's historical secrets by a rigorous application of these sciences. Prophecy continued to underpin millenarian beliefs into this century, and perhaps the fears about Y2K demonstrated the continuity of this link in our own time. Certainly, lotteries, horoscopes, and tarot cards are the modern remnant of ancient prophetic belief; and an emphasis on religious healing, divination, and prophecy continues to attract people to the Pentecostal Churches of the Bantu and other similar separatist groups in Africa.

This balance of this article examines how prophecy inspired, and continues to inspire, millennial movements and beliefs in specific historical circumstances. It is no longer possible to view previous historical epochs with the "Enlightenment" eyes of the eighteenth and nineteenth centuries. Historians once dismissed prophecy and millenarianism as frivolous, "unscientific," and inappropriate for decent study. It now seems that the historical truth is neither pure nor simple, and historians now place prophecy and millenarianism at the very heart of their understanding of former times.

History of Prophecy

Historical and eschatological timetables of an "endtime," "Last Judgment," final "age," "fifth monarchy," or some other earthly paradise preceding the bliss of heaven have their origins in the concept of time developed by the Iranian prophet Zarathustra (c. 1500–1200 BCE)—better known by the later Greek form of his name, Zoroaster—who came to see all existence as "the gradual realization of a divine plan" (Cohn 1993: 77). He claimed divine illumination, and in his sermons he offered a blissful immortality to all. He seems to have been novel in placing by the side of the divinely appointed static order, a sense of progression in time marked by a cosmic struggle between good and evil gods that would end at some point in the future. He has been described as the earliest known example of a "millenarian" prophet (Cohn 1993: 95), and his inspiration seems to lie, as usual with such prophets, in the social and political upheaval of the second millennium BCE when the Iranian tribes adopted the weapons and skills of warriors. The pseudo-Zoroastrian prophecies which are purported to be by Zoroaster, though actually written later, offered consolation in the form of a period of earthly paradise, or "making wonderful" which would follow a period of social and natural chaos. The dead would be resurrected and the righteous made immortal. In the sixth century BCE, Zoroastrianism became the religion of the first Iranian empire, and the "making wonderful" was postponed for two thousand years. It remained the state religion of the Iranian empires down to the seventh century CE, before the Muslim conquest initiated its decline. In the 1970s there were only 130,000 Zoroastrians, many of them living in the Indian subcontinent.

Jewish Prophecy

The origins of Hebrew prophecy and the history of the Israelites themselves are difficult to untangle, especially since the Old Testament was edited many centuries after the events it describes. Perhaps around 1200 BCE the Israelites formed small settled communities in the land of Canaan (later known as Palestine) after emigrating from Egypt. This exile, as well as the later exiles endured when the Babylonians destroyed the southern kingdom of Canaan known as Judah (586 BCE) introduced and reinforced a strongly prophetic element in the theology of the people of Judah. The people of Judah, known as the Jews, were distinguished from the rest of the ancient world by their view that they were the chosen people of God. Such eighth-century BCE "canonical prophets" as Amos, Hosea, Micah, and Isaiah predicted an immense cosmic catastrophe which will precede the establishment of an earthly paradise. The Judgment of Yahweh (the Hebrew deity) will fall on those who have not trusted in the lord, or who have opposed Israel. The righteous living and dead will be ruled over in Palestine by Yahweh, who will dwell in a rebuilt Jerusalem. In the vision of the Book of Daniel (165 BCE) the Jews under Greek rule were offered some hope by the prophecy that the Greek empire would be overthrown, and that Israel, personified as the "Son of Man" would rule indefinitely over all.

Christian Prophecy

The Jewish apocalypses (literally "revelations")—epitomized by Daniel—were combined with Christian elements in the Book of Revelation (c. 95–96 CE) to produce a book which demonstrated that the history of the church was following a course foretold in scripture. The prophets and the Book of Daniel seemed to support the conclusion that the Christian church would soon be victorious over the immoral paganism of Rome. Like the Jewish books, however, Revelation was characterized by hopes and fears for the future judgment of mankind after a period of trial and terror, and presented itself in highly symbolic terms. These figurative devices allowed different groups of Christians from the first century onward to identify themselves with the chosen people.

There has been some disagreement among historians about the precise nature of the millenarian movements which arose in Christian Europe in the Middle Ages on the basis of Jewish and Christian eschatology (theory of last things). Norman Cohn linked the early medieval appearance of millenarianism in Europe with outbreaks of social and political rebellion among the poor. Subsequent studies of millenarianism placed the expectation of an earthly paradise before the

What is the meaning of that Beast with that unique Mark?

Before we discuss the Beast itself we must understand the historical background preceding the Beast. The best place to begin is in the book of Daniel, which deals greatly with prophecy, from the 6th century B.C. down to the end of time.

The interpretation of the symbols used in Bible prophecy has not been left to human guesswork. Prophecy is history written in advance. The Bible itself gives us the key of understanding (2Pet 1:20).

A **beast** in prophecy symbolizes a king or a kingdom. This is clearly taught in Dan 7:17,23: "These great beasts are four kings .... The fourth beast shall be the fourth kingdom upon earth..."

In Dan 7:3 is written: "And four great beasts came up from the sea...". "**Sea**" or "**Water**" represents "peoples and multitudes and nations and tongues." Rev 17:15 (compare Isa 8:7).
In chapter 7 of Daniel the prophet sees the coming world empires represented as beasts.
A parallel description we find in Dan 2:27-45 where individual parts of a statue are symbolizing, in an accurate manner, the future course mankind will take.

THE LION
"The first was like a lion..." Dan 7:4 (compare Dan 2:37,38). This refers to the **Babylonian** world empire (**608-538 BC**), which reigned supreme during Daniel's time. In the Pergamon Museum of Berlin you can still admire the winged lion as a historical witness of that period of time.

THE BEAR
"And behold another beast, a second, like to a bear, and it raised up itself on one side, and it had three ribs in the mouth of it between the teeth of it: and they said thus unto it, Arise, devour much flesh." Dan 7:5. This beast has the same meaning as the breast and arms of silver in Dan 2:32,39. It represents the power of the two empires of **Media and Persia**, who replaced the Babylonian empire (538-331 BC). It was a dual monarchy with the Medes ruling first, then later the Persians. The two arms and the bear raising itself up on one side emphasizes this aspect of prophecy. The one part would be stronger than the other. The three ribs represented the nations of Babylon, Lydia and Egypt that were conquered by Medo-Persia.

THE LEOPARD
"After this I beheld, and lo another, like a leopard, which had upon the back of it four wings of a fowl, the beast had also four heads; and dominion was given to it." Dan 7:6. This beast also finds its counterpart in Dan 2:32,39. It was the **Grecian** empire (**331-168 BC**). Alexander the Great which overthrew the Persians, and when he died his kingdom was divided into four parts, as symbolized by the four heads. (Macedonia, Thrace, Syria and Egypt).

THE FOURTH BEAST
"After this I saw in the night visions, and behold a fourth beast, dreadful and terrible, and strong exceedingly; and it had great iron teeth: it devoured and brake in pieces, and stamped the residue with the feet of it: and it was diverse from all the beasts that were before it; and it had ten horns." Dan 7:7. Again we find this beast in Dan 2:33,40. The fourth empire that followed the Grecian empire was the **Roman** empire (**168 BC-476 AD**). It was so very different from all the other beasts that Daniel saw in vision that he was unable to describe it. The ten horns in Dan 7:24 represent "ten kings that shall arise out of this kingdom". It is a historical fact that the Roman empire fell in 476 AD, and in its place 10 new kingdoms came up which are the ten germanic tribes that make up today's European states. Parallel to Dan 7:7 we find that in Dan 2:41,42 these were symbolized by the ten toes. These were the following tribes: 1. Alemanni (Germany), 2. Franks (France), 3. Anglo-Saxons (Great Britain), 4. Burgundians (Switzerland), 5. Visigoths (Spain), 6. Suevi (Portugal), 7. Lombards (Italy), 8. Heruli, 9. Vandals, 10. Ostrogoths.

A section of a fundamentalist Protestant religious tract discussing the role of the Bible in prophecy. HTTP://WWW.METAG.COM/ENGL/FACTS.HTM.

Last Judgment at the heart of Christian life in Europe, and Robert Lerner has suggested that millenarianism should be understood as part of the "deep structure" of medieval society—a phenomenon which was not predicated on political violence, social upheaval, or economic want, but could offer individual consolation in daily life. There is no doubt that Christianity can be characterized as a fundamentally millenarian religion, and Bernard McGinn (1979) has suggested how severe crises in medieval history have inspired waves of apocalyptic thought—the conversion of the Roman Empire, the expansion of Islam, and the papal monarchy of the eleventh and twelfth centuries. Such millenarianism was not, as Cohn suggests, always revolutionary, and it has been argued that it was more often conservative in form. One of the earliest Christian millenarian movements described by Cohn are the Montanists (c. 156 CE) of Asia Minor, Africa, Rome, and Gaul; though they are characterized by Cohn as ascetic and ecstatic, rather than as either conservative or "radical."

Until the end of the first millennium CE, the church, following the immensely influential theologian St. Augustine of Hippo (354–430 CE), downplayed the importance of the thousand years of rule by Christ which would proceed the general Judgment. In fact, the millennium had begun with the birth of Christianity. Salvation had been established through Christ's first appearance, and it was through the institution of the church that Christians were to hope for it. On the Second Coming, history would end, and the Last Judgment would follow.

Hopes for the Last Days, and fears of the coming of the Antichrist, nevertheless inspired many medieval men and women who saw the signs of the imminent end around them, and who sought out works such as the "Sibylline oracles" (Greek works originally intended to convert pagans to Judaism, and reinterpreted by Christians eager for authority for the arrival of the warrior-Christ), or reinterpreted Revelation. It led some to announce themselves as the new Messiah, and to gather a following, such as the eighth-century Aldebert, or to inspire movements, such as the poor crusaders urged by Peter the Hermit (c. 1050–1115) in 1096 to head toward Jerusalem where they hoped to transform it into a Christian paradise on earth. The spiritual Franciscans of the thirteenth century were inspired to live a life of apostolic poverty by their view that the arrival of a new age—outlined by the Italian prophet Joachim of Fiore (c. 1132–1202)—was imminent. Joachim and the Franciscans believed that they were living at the dawning of the final age, marked by the signs of the work of the Antichrist around them, which would be the consummation of human history. Joachim's writings, and those falsely attributed to him, inspired flagellant movements in Italy in 1260, and again after the Black Death in 1348–49. These men and women scourged themselves in public procession through the streets in the belief that the end of the world was near. Similar prophecies of the imminent end seem to have provoked popular anti-Semitism throughout Europe during this period.

From the thirteenth century onward, historical and eschatological timetables—the idea of an endtime—often focused on the city of Rome and the papacy, or on the long awaited figure of the Antichrist. The religious reformer, Martin Luther (1483–1546), was convinced that the Antichrist had already arrived in Rome and that the battle for salvation of mankind had begun. He naturally believed that his followers were purifying themselves through the rediscovery of true religious theory and practice in readiness for the final Judgment. These apocalyptic hopes and fears, sometimes allied with prophecy, have shaped Protestantism up until the present day. Radical Protestant Christianity also helped to create a prophetic leadership which encouraged millenarian expectation during the Taiping Rebellion in China between 1851 and 1864.

Conclusion

Prophecy continues to shape hopes and fears for the future of individuals, groups, states, and the whole world. In recent years, the far-right in France have reinterpreted older texts, such as the rather vague prophecies of the French court astrologer Michel de Nostradame (Nostradamus, 1503–66), and historic figures, such as Joan of Arc, in order to promote support for their brand of extreme nationalism and royalism. In the British general election campaign of 1997, Tony Blair, who was later elected prime minister, talked about the Labour Party lasting one thousand years in a rhetorical bid to boost party morale and national support. These European "prophets" are far less concerned with divine inspiration or scriptural foundation than their North American counterparts.

The stronghold of contemporary prophecy and millenarian expectations, in the sense of Cohn's salvationist movements, is undoubtedly the United States where a plethora of sects and cult have sprung up in expectation of great events at the turn of the millennium or at some other future date. These groups range from the Jehovah's Witnesses (who expect Christ to inaugurate the millennium), to the Heaven's Gate UFO group who prophesy that, after twenty years of preparation, they will be picked up by a UFO for elevation to the "next level." Just like their predecessors, these millennialist or quasi-millennialist groups have not been deterred by their failure to achieve "rapture" or elevation, and have simply reinterpreted their guiding texts or ideas. A vast mosaic of sources drawn from contemporary (e.g., Princess Diana) and ancient culture often contribute to their belief systems, and the relationship of such groups with governmental authority or mainstream society is characterized by a hostility (for example, "survivalism," or far-right preparations for a better society in preparation for the millennium) which seems to them to confirm their "chosen" status. In all of these senses then, they do not seem so very different from the early interpreters of the Jewish apocalypse and the millenarian movements which have been described here.

Stephen Bowd

See also Antichrist, Joachism, Papal Reform, Zoroastrianism

Bibliography

Barnes, Robin Bruce. (1988) *Prophecy and Gnosis: Apocalypticism in the Wake of the Lutheran Reformation.* Stanford, CA: Stanford University Press.

Cohn, Norman. ([1957] 1993) *The Pursuit of the Millennium: Revolutionary Millenarians and Mystical Anarchists of the Middle Ages*, rev. ed. London: Pimlico.

——. (1993) *Cosmos, Chaos, and the World to Come: The Ancient Roots of Apocalyptic Faith.* New Haven, CT: Yale University Press.

Lerner, Robert. (1983) *The Powers of Prophecy: The Cedar of Lebanon Vision from the Mongol Onslaught to the Dawn of the Enlightenment.* Berkeley, CA: University of California Press.

McGinn, Bernard. (1979) *Visions of the End: Apocalyptic Traditions in the Middle Ages.* New York: Columbia University Press.

Niccoli, Ottavia. (1990) *Prophecy and People in Renaissance Italy*, trans. Lydia G. Cochrane. Princeton, NJ: Princeton University Press.

Reeves, Marjorie. ([1969] 1994) *The Influence of Prophecy in the Later Middle Ages: A Study in Joachimism.* Oxford: Clarendon Press; reprint, Notre Dame, IN: University of Notre Dame Press.

Thomas, Keith. ([1971] 1991) *Religion and the Decline of Magic: Studies in Popular Beliefs in Sixteenth- and Seventeenth-Century England.* London: Penguin Books.

Williams, Ann, ed. (1980) *Prophecy and Millenarianism: Essays in Honour of Marjorie Reeves.* Harlow, U.K.: Longman.

Protestantism

Over 23,000 groups exist in the world that call themselves Christian. Some are highly structured and formal denominations, some are small and informal cults and sects, and each offers something unique in belief, worship style, organization, or mission. But among this huge number of Christian expressions are what we might call families of Christian bodies—groups of churches and denominations that are independent of each other but that share in common much in their religious and spiritual lives. One such family comprises the Orthodox churches in Eastern Europe and the eastern Mediterranean. Another large family consists of the several Catholic churches, not only the Roman Catholic Church (by far the largest in this family) but the Polish Catholic Church in the United States, the Ukrainian Catholic Church, and others.

Protestantism embraces by far the largest number of Christian bodies. Beginning in the seventeenth century in Europe, dissidents seeking to reform the Roman Catholic Church and to reshape Christian worship and governance created national and independent churches that included Lutheran Evangelical denominations, Calvinist churches (Presbyterians, Congregationalists, and many national Reformed churches), Anabaptist expressions (Mennonites, Moravians, Baptists), Anglicanism in England and its offshoots (Episcopalians, Quakers, Methodists), and various Rationalist churches resulting from the eighteenth-century Enlightenment (Unitarians and Universalists). Additionally, hundreds of sects, cults, and larger innovative denominations have appeared in the last two hundred years making Protestantism so diverse as to be nearly impossible to define. But this family of Christians does share qualities that help define Protestantism's boundaries and that also have shaped the life of millennialism.

Contours of Protestantism

Religious reformers in the sixteenth century sought to recapture qualities of Christian life that they believed the Roman Catholic Church had come to reject. Essentially, Protestants and Catholics had found different answers to a central question of Christian life: How do we know what we know about God? Over the centuries believers had accepted three principal sources of knowledge about God—scripture, the traditional understanding of scripture as interpreted by church leaders and councils (otherwise known as the teaching or *majesterium* of the Church), and God's direct revelation of God's self in and through history. By the sixteenth century the Roman Catholic Church viewed itself as the sole arbiter of all these sources of information, in effect becoming the sole authority for belief and action. The church interpreted scripture, taught Christian truth, celebrated the sacraments, and discerned all claims of revelation. There was, to Catholics, no understanding of God apart from the church and, thus, no reason for a believer to seek truth on his or her own. The church *was* the conveyor of truth; it was Christ Himself in the world.

The rebirth of classical knowledge called the Renaissance inspired a reinvigoration of confidence in the ability of capable thinkers to seek and discover truth even when that truth diverged from established truth. Its humanistic ideal came to add a new source of knowledge about God and authority for belief—human reason empowered by the Holy Spirit—and it was this confidence that inspired the revolt against Catholic exclusivism we call the Protestant Reformation. Hardly individualistic as we would understand that word today, Protestant reformers sought to return to the whole body of the church the resources for knowing God that had become the sole property of the Catholic Church's priesthood. They insisted on reading the scripture for themselves and, thus, called for the Bible's translation into national (vernacular) languages. They rejected church teaching as dogma, ideas, and principles that were supposed to be unquestioned and accepted solely on faith. Protestants came to label many of these beliefs as superstitious or corruptions of biblical teaching. Truth could come only from a body of faithful believers inspired not by the dead teaching of centuries but through reading and studying the scriptures by the living power of the Holy Spirit.

These reformers also came to reject the authoritarian church government that had restricted believers' access to knowledge about God and used that knowledge to amass power for themselves. God speaks through the entire congregation of the faithful, they said, not just through ordained priests, and they preached the idea of the "priesthood of all believers." Authority in the church should not extend from

ESCHATOLOGY INDEXES

In connection with the Christian doctrine of the second coming certain questions have assumed some prominence: In particular those of the so-called "millennium," of the appearance of Antichrist, and of the prospects of moral and spiritual progress of human society at large in this world. We proceed to consider them severally.

The idea of an early millennial reign of the Messiah, followed by the consummation of His Kingdom in another and better world than this, appears in Jewish apocalyptic literature. It apparently represents a survival with modification of the political interpretation of messianic prophecy (which looked to a universal earthly kingdom centred at Jerusalem), after the conviction had begun to be developed that this world is unfitted for the final consummation of God's purpose. Our Lord did not sanction the notion of a political millennium at all. But He did plainly intimate that He was the promised Messiah, and that His Kingdom was immediately at hand, having its beginnings in this world. He described it, however, as a spiritual kingdom, sharply contrasted to the kingdoms of this world. He appears to have predicted that it was to come with power during the existing generation. This interpretation of His words seems to be justified at all events by the descent of the Holy Spirit on the day of Pentecost upon the Church which He had established to be the visible and sacramental machinery of His Kingdom. In the meantime, He taught His disciples to look forward to the end of the world as bringing with it an abolition of earthly arrangements and the final consummation of the Kingdom in a higher and eternal order of things.

Source: Hall, Rev. Francis J. (1922) *Eschatology Indexes.* New York: Longmans, Green and Company, 140–41.

the top down but from the bottom up, beginning at the church's base, the gathered Elect of God's people. Reformed churches had clergy just like the Roman Catholic Church, but they emphasized the clergy's role as teachers and shepherds rather than as spiritual lords.

They also, like Catholics, condemned individual inventiveness in religion and emphasized that spiritual truth only comes from the collected body of believers. They were as ready as Catholics to burn heretics (a word that means going off on one's own). But the church, as they saw it, was not merely the collection of baptized Christians who attended the sacraments. A Christian was a person whose relationship with God could be seen through the quality of their daily life. Interestingly, while they condemned the Roman Catholics as exclusivist for claiming sole authority to discern and mediate religious truth, Protestants became increasingly exclusive themselves, viewing the church as a fortress of the visible Elect protecting the covenant God had made with humanity by including only those whose lives evidenced the power of saving grace.

The Reformation successfully shattered the monopoly the Catholic Church had exercised on defining religious belief and practice and thereby released built-up creative urges that took Christianity in many different directions. Now freed from the bonds of the *majesterium*, Protestant Christians used the spiritual resources available to them. Lutherans called for exclusive reliance on the scriptures as the source of authority for faith and Christian life; Anabaptists and others came to rely increasingly on direct revelation from God; and eventually, in the nineteenth century, many Protestants preached the dominant role that human reason plays in discerning how to live a just life. Anglicanism sought to reunite all these sources in what its founders envisioned as a comprehensive church guided by church councils. Catholics, too, sought to reform the church's most serious weaknesses, but any attempt at curtailing division was unsuccessful.

Whatever conformity the Catholic Church had maintained was destroyed and the result was conflict among the various Christian groups, Protestants and Catholics battling each other and Protestants fighting other Protestants. Eventually, though, after a century and a half of conflict, warfare would gradually give way to toleration and denominationalism, the understanding that no one Christian body has a monopoly on the truth. In the twentieth century, Christians searched for ecumenism, a way to reunite Christians into one communion based on one faith, if not on one set of beliefs or system of church government.

Protestantism's Impact on Millennialism

Millennialism had always been present in the Christian world, long before the Protestant Reformation. It found expression in two very different ways. Because reading and interpreting scripture was the exclusive domain of the clergy, theological millennialism based on Bible prophecy was highly intellectual and inaccessible to the average believer. The late medieval Spanish priest Joachim of Fiore developed a highly intricate prophecy about the end of the world and establishment of the millennium that became a significant millennial movement among the learned. Clerics often used dreams of the purity of the millennium to cloak criticisms of present-day corruption in the church, thus giving it something of a revolutionary flavor. On the other hand, popular millennialism, based on nonliterate sources such as folklore, nature worship, and the oral teaching of the church, reached a much wider and bigger audience. Prophets who could not read the Latin scriptures or the works of theologians could read the signs of the times in eclipses, comets, and wars. These portents, too, could express social hostility to the existing order. Sometimes popular millennial speculation linked with more formal and structured theological millennialism to produce short-lived but dramatic and violent revolutionary movements that were both political and social in nature. Essentially, though, the two millennial expressions remained not only separate but highly suspicious of each other, clerics fearing the power of "the mob" and the common people mistrusting the worldly ambitions of the clergy.

Protestantism continued the long tradition of theological millennial speculation. Indeed, if anything it became richer. Debates spread over the nature of the event to be expected in the last days—the Apocalypse, the Parousia (Second Coming of Christ), the Millennium—and the order of all these events. Debatable, too, was the question of agency. Who would bring all this about? Did God expect humanity to perfect the world in preparation for Jesus' return, or was the world so corrupt that God alone could purify it? Some theologians considered the question of timing, when all these events were to take place, some actually predicting the prophecies' imminent fulfillment. Millennialism became variegated in content, leading to postmillennial, premillennial, and amillennial varieties. It inspired the development of specific cults and denominations based on particular theologies—the Shakers preaching premillennialism, the Mormons preaching postmillennialism, and the Adventists combining them in a unique way.

And the Reformation did not bring an end, either, to popular tendencies to interpret natural disasters and political unrest as signs of impending universal catastrophe or renewal. But the Reformation did revolutionize millennial thinking. Protestantism provided a bridge between theological and popular millennialism. First, it placed reform itself in the context of millennial change by identifying the Catholic Church as the Antichrist. No longer did the Catholic Church enjoy the legitimacy to hold in check the millennial forces ready to be unleashed. Second, by preaching confidence in individual capacity to discover truth through the scriptures it encouraged prophets, male and female, throughout Europe. Third, by making the scripture accessible to people in their own language, Protestantism provided popular prophecy with a new source of legitimacy. It allowed seers, who formerly based their millennial predictions on nature and magic, now to base their views on the prophecies of Daniel and Revelation. Highly critical of the superstitions that characterized popular Catholic religion, and thus popular millennialism, Protestantism now gave it the authority it needed not only to survive but to prosper.

By uniting theological and popular millennialism, Protestantism made millennial dreams the vehicle for much broader political and social movements. It motivated the cause of church reform itself, of course, but its vision of justice and political glory would come to inspire nationalist movements as diverse as the American and French Revolutions and the rise of National Socialism in Germany, and it contributed ironically to anti-imperialist and anti-Western rebellions throughout China in the nineteenth and twentieth centuries. Its utopianism propelled the cause of social revitalization movements across Europe and the colonized world. Its ideas led to the creation of communes in Germany and what is today the Czech Republic, to peasant rebellions in Italy, to the rise of what are called "cargo cult" movements in the South Seas and Latin America, to the religious fervor of the Handsome Lake and Ghost Dance revivals among Native Americans in the United States. Despite socialism's anticlericalism and communism's expressed atheism, both movements benefited from the dream of universal social equality inspired by Protestant millennialism.

Because the Protestant Revolution developed alongside the technological and industrial revolutions, millennial ideas were easily broadcast, and they became a standard fare in art, literature, and popular culture. Asher P. Durand produced woodcuts illustrating apocalyptic and millennial themes from the Four Horsemen of the Apocalypse to the scenes of torment on the Last Day. Michael Wigglesworth's work *The Day of Doom* became one of the most widely read publications of the eighteenth century and a primer, along with the Bible, to teach Puritan youth in the American colonies how to read. Prophets interpreting signs of the times took advantage of political unrest to inspire social radicalism—the Fifth Monarchy Men of the English civil wars of the 1640s, the Illumines of the French Revolution in the 1780s and '90s, and communitarian Shakers in the American Revolution.

In American popular culture at the end of the twentieth century millennialism was common, though its inherently religious nature was often obscured in a more secular world.

During the cold war, atomic war became the vehicle of apocalyptic destruction. In later decades the theme of universal regeneration and the victory of good over evil defined movies from *Star Wars* to *Star Trek* to *Independence Day*. The approaching change from the second to the third millennium inspired many responses, by both the hopeful and the fearful. Not only did cults flourish, but secular culture found an apocalyptic message in the dangers of the approaching Y2K. Across America survivalists stockpiled food, water, firearms, and generators in expectation of the earth-convulsing impact of universal economic and social collapse.

Conclusion

While it is possible to see evidence of all these themes in the Catholic world, it was Protestantism that made millennial expectation a central quality of Western life. Its popularity and variety gave it durability and flexibility. Millennial hopes and fears comprise our deepest yearnings and our greatest terrors; it expresses itself politically as insistence on extending power to powerless people, socially as extending justice to the oppressed, spiritually as offering hope to the forlorn, and culturally as providing a measure of meaning and mystery in the mundane reality of daily life. It posits the central question of life—what does it mean to be human, on the one hand to be enormously creative but on the other hand, in the face of the vastness of Creation itself, to be so limited.

David L. Rowe

See also Anabaptists, Art, Joachism, Roman Catholicism, Mormonism, Seventh-Day Adventists, Shakers; United States, 18th Century

Bibliography

Boyer, Paul. (1992) *When Time Shall Be No More: Prophecy Belief in Modern American Culture.* Cambridge, MA: Harvard University Press.

Cohn, Norman. (1970) *Pursuit of the Millennium*, 3d ed. New York: Oxford University Press.

Davidson, James W. (1977) *The Logic of Millennial Thought: Eighteenth Century New England.* New York and London: Yale University Press.

Eliade, Mircea. (1954) *The Myth of the Eternal Return.* New York: Pantheon.

Harrison, J. F. C. (1979) *The Second Coming: Popular Millenarianism, 1780–1850.* New Brunswick, NJ: Rutgers University Press.

Hobsbawm, Eric. (1959) *Primitive Rebels.* New York: W. W. Norton.

Reeves, Marjorie E. (1989) *Western Mediterranean Prophecy: The School of Joachim of Fiore and the Fourteenth Century Breviloquiam.* Toronto: Pontifical Institute of Mediaeval Studies.

Thrupp, Sylvia L. (1962) *Millennial Dreams in Action: Studies in Revolutionary Religious Movements.* The Hague, Netherlands: Mouton.

Weber, Timothy P. (1979) *Living in the Shadow of the Second Coming: America Premillennialism, 1875–1925.* New York: Oxford University Press.

Wilson, Bryan R. (1973) *Magic and the Millennium.* New York: Harper and Row.

Raelians

UFO religions are one of the more innovative forms of millennial thinking to emerge during the latter half of the twentieth century. These religions translate traditional religious myths and symbols into the language of modern science and technology. In creating a vision of superior planetary civilizations coming to rescue humanity from self-destruction, they help increasing numbers of people cope with anxieties concerning nuclear and biological weapons, cloning, rapid technological advances, and the globalization of political and economic power.

History and Main Doctrines

The International Raelian Religion is a cult movement that in many ways epitomizes UFO religion as a class of religious phenomena. The movement began on 13 December 1973, when a French race car journalist named Claude Vorilhon decided to hike to Puy-de-Lassolas, a volcano near the village of Clermont-Ferrand. After returning from the crater's rim, Vorilhon claims that he spotted a flying saucer with a flashing red light descending toward him as he was about to get into his car. The saucer stopped its descent about 5 feet above the ground, and a small alien walked down a stairway and came toward him. The extraterrestrial was short by human standards, about 4 feet, had long dark hair, olive skin, and almond shaped eyes. Vorilhon went with the alien into the spacecraft and was told that he had been chosen to communicate a message of cosmic importance to the human race. The space being gave the journalist a new name, Rael, and told him to return the following morning. The substance of the Raelian message was given to Vorilhon over the next five days and was recounted in a book published in French in 1974, *The Message Given to Me by Extra-terrestrials.*

The basic thrust of the alien's message was fairly simple: life on earth is not the work of a supernatural deity nor is it the result of random evolution. Rather, our planet's life system is the result of carefully planned genetic engineering undertaken by an advanced civilization from another solar system. This DNA engineering project took place many thousands of years ago when the development of knowledge on the alien planet made it possible to create new life forms. Because the government of the planet banned further experimentation for ethical reasons, the alien scientists put together teams with advanced technological equipment and began searching for another planet on which to continue their experiments. The earth was one of several sites where the research was continued. Our planetary biosphere with all its life forms is the result of these experiments. With the explosion of the atomic bomb in 1945, the advent of space travel, and the development of genetic engineering, it was deemed by the alien civilization that the earth was finally ready to hear the truth of its origins. Rael was the prophet through whom this truth would be revealed.

The alien told Rael that his mission was threefold: first, he must communicate the revelations he had been given to all who would listen; second, he must build an embassy in Jerusalem that would be used to welcome the aliens for a meeting with the world's leaders in the near future. This meeting would be crucial to human evolution, since the aliens intended to provide the earth with selected aspects of their advanced technology; third, he must start a spiritual movement that would mobilize humanity to accomplish the first two parts of his mission.

Rael's message first found a growing audience in the largely secular nations of Western Europe; it came to North America in 1976, establishing its international center in Montreal. Since then, the Raelians have spread to Australia, Southeast Asia, Japan, Latin America, Africa, China, and Great Britain. Although the movement's Web site claims 40,000 members living in eighty-five countries, scholar Susan Palmer, who has studied the group extensively, estimates its membership at between 20,000 and 30,000, most of whom live in Quebec, Japan, and French-speaking Europe. The movement has 130 priests or "guides" who live throughout the world.

The movement has been especially creative in its exegesis of biblical stories. Rael asserts that the Hebrew Bible uses the name Elohim when referring to the beings that created the natural world. According to movement literature, Elohim, as found throughout the original Hebrew scriptures, means "those who came from the sky." Using sophisticated methods of genetics and cell biology, these extraterrestrials created humankind in their own image in special laboratories. At first, humans were clothed and fed by the Elohim and were not required to engage in any form of labor. Soon, however, the aggressive nature of the humans resulted in their expulsion from their Edenic paradise.

Many other passages from scripture are also reinterpreted in Raelian literature. For example, the passage in Genesis 6:1–2 concerning the marriage between the sons of Elohim and the daughters of men is interpreted as an experiment in interbreeding. Verse four of this chapter mentions the offspring of these marriages, the Nelphelin, who Rael claims became the heroes of the old myths and sagas. He also contends that all the world's great prophets, including Moses, Jesus, Buddha, Muhammad, and Rael himself are the result of this interplanetary interbreeding.

Millennial Vision

The Raelians view of the future is distinctly millenarian. The present age, the "Age of Apocalypse," is understood as a time of rapid scientific advancement when the human race has finally matured to the point that it can understand its true origins. This age began in 1945, when the United States dropped the first atomic bomb on Japan. Other proofs of humanity's entry into the Apocalyptic era are Israel's regaining of its national homeland, the development of optic surgery that gives sight to the blind, satellite communications, and bioengineering. With humanity's growing technological prowess, it is now possible for it to shape its own future and grow into interplanetary consciousness. Should humanity miss this opportunity, however, it could still destroy itself.

Before a golden age of technological prosperity can begin, the *Elohim* must be welcomed in an international embassy. Were the extraterrestrials to arrive unannounced and unwelcomed, Rael observes, there would be disastrous social, political, and economic repercussions throughout the world. Unlike the Heaven's Gate UFO religion, Raelians believe they will remain on an utopian earth rather than be taken to other planets. In the best of all possible outcomes, humankind will embrace a new political system called "geniocracy," in which only those whose intelligence is at least 50 percent above the average would be allowed to govern. The only citizens allowed to vote in this brave new world would be those whose intellectual capacity was at least 10 percent above the average.

The movement's vision of the future also includes the creation of a one-world governing body who would supervise the implementation of a state ideology referred to as "humanitarianism." In this socialist paradise, humans would own only a family home and rent their land from the state. Thus, family homes would be the only legal form of inheritance. All other assets would be returned to the state upon the death of the renter. The underlying theme of this system is a meritocracy wherein individual geniuses amass and enjoy great wealth during their lifetimes but are unable to pass it along to inferior offspring upon their death.

Over the past ten years, the Raelians have weathered serious public controversies and established new business initiatives. The most serious controversy involved the movement's original symbol, a Star of David with a swastika inscribed in its center. In the Raelian understanding, the Star of David symbolized infinite space and infinite galaxies within and beyond our own. The swastika represented infinite time and had its origins in ancient Indo-European religions. After bitter complaints from the international Jewish community, the movement in 1991 changed its insignia to a Star of David surrounding a whirling image of a galaxy. In spite of hopes that this change would foster friendly relations with the Israeli government and thus lead to the construction of the embassy for the *Elohim* in Jerusalem, progress in this direction has been slow. Movement officials now speak of building an alternative embassy site in Hawaii.

In 1997, the Raelians established Clonaid, a business whose purpose is to promote human cloning research. Despite an outcry from biomedical ethicists throughout North America, the group offered financial donations to physicist Richard Seed, who has explored the possibility of cloning children for families who are unable to conceive by natural means.

The Raelians also sponsor two week-long Awakening Seminars annually in Europe and North America. The seminars are regularly attended by between three hundred to seven hundred participants and are staffed by scientists, theologians, doctors, and psychologists. Attendees learn to free themselves from culturally inscribed attitudes and assumptions and to question the conventional wisdom of their native societies. They also learn "sensual meditation," a technique that leads to uninhibited sensual pleasure and a liberation from sexual guilt and fear.

Although they tend to distance themselves from other UFO religions, the Raelians can best be understood as a form of postmodern religion that, like other UFO groups, attempts to blend the achievements of science and technology with more enduring religious themes of apocalypse, salvation, immortality, and connection to a higher sacred order. This and other UFO religions will likely continue to emerge and grow during the third millennium.

Phillip Charles Lucas

See also Technological Millennialism, Ufology

Bibliography

Rael. (1978) *Space Aliens Took Me to Their Planet.* Liechtenstein: Foundation pour l'Accueil des Elohim.

——. (1986) *Let's Welcome Our Fathers from Space: They Created Humanity in Their Laboratories.* Tokyo: AOM Corporation.

——. (1986) *Sensual Meditation.* Tokyo: AOM Corporation.

——. (1998) *The Final Message.* London: The Tagman Press.

——. (1999) *Welcome to International Raelian Religion.* http://www.rael.org.

Ramtha School of Enlightenment

JZ Knight, the woman who channels the entity named Ramtha, was probably one of the most popular mediums in the 1980s and 1990s. Her followers numbered about three thousand internationally. Knight's fame grew remarkably after Shirley MacLaine endorsed Ramtha in the book, *Dancing in the Light.* However, Ramtha's School of Enlightenment was the target of criticism related to the integrity of Ms. Knight and the sometimes questionable intelligence of the supernatural being, Ramtha. Critics from the Anti-Cult Network have branded her a dangerous cult leader. By the end of eighties, Ramtha's teachings took a decidedly millenarian turn with the publication of *The Last Waltz of the Tyrants.* This book, based on Ramtha's revelations on the new millennium, warns of a future Armageddon for which some members of the group have started to prepare.

History

JZ Knight was born Judith Darlene Hampton in 1946. Her parents, Charles and Helen Printes Hart Hampton, worked as farm laborers. Her mother believed in psychic phenomenon. Early in her life, Knight questioned Christianity and conventional notions of Satan, preferring to believe in reincarnation. In high school, she became a majorette and rodeo queen. High school friends remember an incident when Knight fell to the floor at a slumber party as she channeled the male entity called Demias. She married Otis Henley, and bore two sons in this marriage. In her book *A State of Mind,* she recalled her early adulthood as one marked by relationships with abusive alcoholics.

Her second husband, Jeremy Burnett, worked as a dentist in Tacoma, Washington. In 1977 when Burnett and Knight were experimenting with pyramid power, the entity Ramtha contacted her. Knight had a vision wherein Ramtha told her he was there to help her over the ditch of limited thought. Because the vision frightened her, she contacted the spiritualist Lorraine Graham who assured her that the incident was genuine. Knight accepted Ramtha in order to bring his wisdom to the world. Reputedly, Ramtha lived as warrior on Lemuria, the lost continent in the Pacific, some 35,000 years ago. In 1978 Knight started to give public performances of her trance channeling. These public channeling sessions were called dialogues. By the early eighties, Knight appeared throughout the United States where she enjoyed tremendous success as the most popular fad of New Age audiences. She developed her stage skills with the help of Anne-Marie Bennstrom and Jeffery Knight, and divorced her second husband to marry Knight in 1983.

By 1986, the Anti-Cult Movement trained its eyes on JZ Knight's growing celebrity, wealth, and power. One of her followers was deprogrammed; some ex-students made accusations of brainwashing. Since Knight's workshops carried a hefty price tag, charges of financial misconduct were added to the list of public impropriety. Her honesty was questioned by the investigative reporters of the television show, *20/20*. Some ex-members who were close to Ms. Knight attested to the fakery involved in producing the Ramtha character, for example, the backstage behavior in which Knight took time out secretly to have a smoke.

The most significant financial scandal related to the Knights' investments in expensive Arabian horses. The Knights prompted group members to make substantial investments in their private business ventures on the advice of channeled messages. According to Jeffery Knight, JZ channeled a nineteenth-century spirit called Charles who advised them on all their business dealings having to do with their horses. When the enterprise went bankrupt, the incident led to both a financial and spiritual credibility crisis. Knight promised to repay investors—a promise which seems to have been kept for the most part. Further controversy centered around Knight's manipulation of her husband, who died of AIDS in 1994. The bisexual Jeffery contracted HIV, but JZ Knight appeared to be uninfected. Jeffery postponed conventional treatment in favor of Ramtha's recommendations. JZ Knight also allegedly concealed assets during their divorce proceedings.

Beliefs and Practices

The Ramtha School of Enlightenment was established in 1988, after JZ Knight withdrew from the spotlight of national tours. Ramtha purportedly wished to deliver his teachings in a deeper way to a more committed following. Located in Yelm, Washington, the Ramtha School of Enlightenment regularly hosts about 900 to 1,500 students for spiritual sessions that last anywhere from a few days to a month. Student call themselves masters and refer to their training as lessons in a mystery school. Ramtha devotees believe in typical New Age ideology: lost continents, extraterrestrials, crystals, chakras (spiritually significant energy centers in the body), reincarnation, and alternative healing practices. Ramtha claims to be part of the Great White Brotherhood referred to in Theosophy belief. The extraordinary being, Ramtha, is considered scientifically sophisticated, because he routinely makes references to quantum physics, as well as the esoteric origins of the universe. Religious scholar J. Gordon Melton explains that Ramtha is based on a gnostic philosophy of rebirth and that people are divine sparks of God. Other beliefs include the unknowable impersonal point of origin, the unfolding universe, the seven levels of creation, and wisdom from the higher planes of existence.

The Ramtha School of Enlightenment differs qualitatively from other New Age ventures that usually employ a more refined dietary and emotional life. Ramtha sessions are typically more taxing and demanding than other workshops, and have been compared to metaphysical boot camp. The so-called paradise beach exercise instructs students to sit alone in a field for days, equipped with only meager supplies. Interestingly enough, students can drink and smoke, unlike other groups. Pipe smoking within the group sprang up when students observed Knight smoking a pipe.

Followers sometimes use blindfolds to participate in different training sessions. Joe Szimhart (1989: 2) writes, "In one event, hundreds of students wandered blindfolded around a large, fenced field in search of their posted symbols on cards pinned to the fence. The 'tank' also requires blindfolds when students meander through a makeshift maze of colored, eight-foot panels for hours at a time. Students may find holes that lead under ground into 'worms' or tubes where they crawl until they find their way out." One instructional session invoked controversy after several participants were injured. About one thousand blindfolded students were assembled in an open field. Upon Ramtha's signal, they were exhorted to run across the field while shouting appropriate sayings. Many careened into each other, some requiring serious medical attention.

The C & E (Consciousness and Energy) breathing technique mimics a commonplace practice found in New Age religions. C & E resembles the techniques taught by Yoga masters, such as pranayama (spiritual breath control). Szimhart reports that the technique is also similar to "holotropic breathing" holistic therapy invented by Stanislav Grof. Knight introduced the breathing ritual in the late 1980s. The mandatory Consciousness and Energy workshops are held twice a year. The C & E breathing method is believed to have great curative powers and to possess the ability to transform a darkened consciousness. The C & E breathing method is also touted to remove the "death hormone."

Rumors of the Last Days

From 1988 and into the early 1990s, Ramtha School of Enlightenment verbalized a more millenarian discourse.

The *Last Waltz of the Tyrants* published in 1989 brings to light the story of the Graymen and their conspiratorial blueprint for humanity. According to Ramtha, the Graymen act as the world's secret power brokers. They manipulate the stock market, while also possessing the federal reserve, as well as the world's money supply. The Graymen are bringing our civilization to the brink of destruction. The Graymen story warned of an ominous future. Knight articulated an elaborate vision of the supposed endtime and the coming apocalyptic cataclysms, and asked her students to make choices about how they would prepare for the coming age.

A large segment of students focused their energy on survivalist responses to Knight's prophecies. An additional prophecy foretold of time when Chinese communist soldiers would invade from Mexico. In the coming age, governments would crumple. The Ramtha directive stated, "When the dragon marches, be prepared to hibernate." Students prepared secret underground shelters stocked with provisions. It is not known how many students made actual preparations for such contingencies, and this is a subject in need of further study.

Diana Tumminia

Bibliography

Brown, Michael F. (1997) *The Channeling Zone: American Spirituality in an Anxious Age.* Cambridge: Harvard University Press.

Klimo, Jon. (1987) *Channeling: Investigations on Receiving Information from Paranormal Sources.* Los Angeles: Jeremy P. Tarcher, Inc.

Knight, JZ. (1987) *A State of Mind: My Story.* New York: Warner Books.

Koteen, Judi Pope. (1989) *The Last Waltz of the Tyrants.* Hillsboro, OR: Beyond Words Publishing, Inc.

MacLaine, Shirley. (1985) *Dancing in the Light.* New York: Bantam Books.

Melton, J. Gordon, ed. (1991) *Religious Leaders of America.* Detroit: Gale Research.

——. (1998) *Finding Enlightenment: Ramtha's School of Ancient Wisdom.* Hillsboro, OR: Beyond Words Publishing, Inc.

——. (1999) *Encyclopedia of American Religions.* Detroit: Gale Research.

Ramtha's School of Enlightenment. (1999) http://www.ramtha.com/.

Szimhart, Joe. (1989) "Book Review/Essay." http://www.users.fast.net/~szimhart/ramtha.htm.

Rappites

A German Protestant sect, headed by George Rapp (1757–1847), preached that the Second Coming of Jesus would occur within their lifetimes. In 1803 several hundred members, fleeing persecution, emigrated to the United States, eventually settling in Pennsylvania at a spot they called Harmonie (now Harmony). In 1814 they moved to southwestern Indiana to reestablish Harmonie on the banks of the Wabash. The village soon became a thriving community with a steady income from the beer, wine, fabrics, and rope which they produced and sold in the United States and in Europe.

The Rappites (as they were called by outsiders) remained in Harmonie for a decade before they returned to Pennsylvania in 1825, settling at a place near Pittsburgh which they named Economy (now Ambridge). Harmonie was sold to Robert Dale Owen, a Welsh Socialist who had founded a utopian colony in Scotland. The group moved to Harmonie in 1924, renaming it New Harmony.

Father Rapp was a tall, muscular patriarch with a long white beard and idiosyncratic religious beliefs. He taught that Adam was originally both male and female, and that the division of humans into separate sexes was a consequence of Adam's Original Sin. Rapp was convinced that God had chosen him to take his followers to Jerusalem to witness the Lord's Second Coming. At Harmonie, the Rappites planted a hedge maze to symbolize the devious paths of evil and the difficulty of obtaining salvation by reaching a tiny temple at the maze's center. Also on the site is a stone slab with two bare footprints said to have been made by the angel Gabriel when he conversed with Father Rapp. These features have been reconstructed with private and public funding used to renovate the village.

Persuaded that the world would soon end, Father Rapp forbade marriages, child bearing, and all sexual activity. This strict celibacy, together with no effort to convert unbelievers, soon led to the sect's demise in the early 1900s. Lord Byron, in his long narrative poem *Don Juan*, put it this way:

> When Rapp the Harmonist embargo'd marriage
> In his harmonious settlement—(which flourishes
> Strangely enough as yet without miscarriage,
> Because it breeds no more mouths than it nourishes,
> Without those sad expenses which disparage
> What Nature naturally most encourages)—
> Why call'd he "Harmony" a state sans wedlock?
> Now here I have got the preacher at a deadlock.

On his deathbed Father Rapp's final words were: "If I did not know that the dear Lord meant I should present you all to

ARTICLES OF ASSOCIATION

***Whereas,* by the favor of divine Providence, an association or community has been formed by George Rapp and many others upon the basis of Christian fellowship, the principles of which, being faithfully derived from the sacred Scriptures, include the government of the patriarchal age, united to the community of property adopted in the days of the apostles, and wherein the simple object sought is to approximate, so far as human imperfections may allow, to the fulfillment of the will of God, by the exercise of those affections and the practice of those virtues which are essential to the happiness of man in time and throughout eternity:**

***And whereas* it is necessary to the good order and well-being of the said association that the conditions of membership should be clearly understood, and that the rights, privileges, and duties of every individual therein should be so defined as to prevent mistake or disappointment, on the one hand, and contention or disagreement on the other.**

Source: Nordhoff, Charles. ([1875] 1993) *American Utopias* (originally *The Communistic Societies of the United States*). Stockbridge, MA: Berkshire House, 81.

Him, I should think my last moment had come" (Hastings 1961: 781).

Martin Gardner

Bibliography

Camony, Donald, and Josephine Elliot. (1980) *New Harmony, Indiana: Robert Owen's Seedbed for Utopia.* San Francisco: Bolerium Books.

Hastings, James, ed. (1961) *Encyclopaedia of Religion and Ethics.* New York: Scribner, vol. 3: 780–81.

Pitzer, Donald, and Josephine Elliott. (1979) *New Harmony's First Utopians.* Austin, TX: Twelfth Street Books.

Young, Marguerite. (1994) *Angel in the Forest.* Normal, IL: Dalkey Archive Press.

Rapture

A cornerstone doctrine in premillennialist Christian eschatology, the Rapture is the much-anticipated and oft-debated "catching up" of living Christians from earth into the clouds, through the air to meet Jesus Christ (1 Thessalonians 4:15–18). Alternately designated the "Translation of the Saints" or the "Great Hope" (Titus 2:13–15), the Rapture occurs at the *parousia* (Second Coming) of Christ and follows the resurrection of Christians who have died. Like the resurrected, the raptured miraculously receive spiritual, imperishable bodies that enable them to inherit the kingdom of God and to live forever (1 Corinthians 15:50–55).

The Significance of the Rapture to Modern Millenarian Movements

These basic beliefs about what happens to living Christians at the *parousia* come directly from Paul's letters and have been part of orthodox Christian eschatology since the first century CE. Modern teachings about the Rapture may be distinguished from those of previous centuries, however, by one important difference: whereas theologians before 1830 almost universally believed that the *parousia,* resurrection, and translation of the living saints was a single event that would be witnessed by the entire world, modern proponents of the Rapture divide the *parousia* into two stages. First, Christ comes for the church alone. He resurrects dead Christians and raptures the living, taking both out of the world. Seven years of the "Great Tribulation" follow, during which the prophecies of Daniel 9:27–12:13 and Revelation 4–22 are fulfilled. At the end of the seven years Christ returns a second time with the church to gather those who became believers during the Great Tribulation, to defeat the Antichrist and his forces, and to establish his millennial kingdom on earth. This scenario is premillennial, since Christ returns before the Millennium; futurist, because the prophecies of Daniel and Revelation refer to future events and not to church history as a whole; and pre-Tribulational, since the Rapture takes place before the seven-year period of Tribulation. It is by far the most commonly accepted scenario among proponents of the Rapture, and is the most important in the history of modern belief in a two-stage *parousia.* While postmillennial and amillennial doctrines of the *parousia* persist, as do historicist interpretations of the prophecies of Daniel and Revelation, which assume that these refer to events throughout the entire history of the church, and some groups teach that the Rapture will occur mid- or post-Tribulation; however, this futurist, premillennial, pre-Tribulational doctrine came first and established the Rapture as a distinct and conventional eschatological subject that modern millennialists of all convictions must address in their treatments of the end.

History of the Doctrine

Since the publication of *The Roots of Fundamentalism* (1970), Ernest Sandeen's seminal study of British and American Millenarianism between 1800 and 1930, most historians locate the origins of the modern doctrine of the Rapture in the revival of premillennialism that began in Europe after the French Revolution. The French Revolution devastated European postmillennialism's optimistic hope that the church itself would bring about the millennial reign of Christ's kingdom on earth through faithful evangelism and spirit-empowered cultivation of earthly institutions. Bereft of confidence in their ability to perfect society, millenarians turned to the doctrines of premillennialists, who announced that Christ's kingdom could only be established by his own divine power at the *parousia.* As premillennialism gained acceptance, a number of societies formed and met regularly throughout the first three decades of the nineteenth century to hammer out doctrinal specifics. Participants overwhelmingly favored a historicist reading of endtimes prophecies. Applying the formula, one prophetic day equals one historical year, they claimed that the three and a half years ("time, two times, and half a time") of Daniel 7:25 and the forty-two months of Revelation 13:5 referred to a 1260-year period that began during the reign of the Roman Emperor Justinian in 528 CE and ended with the French Revolution. According to this scheme, the vials of wrath of Revelation 16 were being poured out and Christ's return was imminent. Applications of similar prophetic number-crunching to the future led, predictably, to date-setting for the *parousia*, and inevitable disappointment, disbelief, and ridicule followed the passing of each proposed date, the most famous of which was the "Great Disappointment" of the sizable Millerite sect in America, precursors of the Seventh-Day Adventists, when Christ failed to arrive as predicted on 22 October 1844.

At the third annual Powerscourt prophecy conference held in Wicklow, Ireland, in 1833, John Nelson Darby (1800–82), a prominent teacher in the loosely organized group of reform-minded evangelicals known as the Plymouth Brethren, introduced the key tenets of his doctrine of "dispensationalism," and with it a new futurist premillennialism that would eventually take the place of historicism in Europe and America. Like other futurists, Darby rejected historicists' claims that the Antichrist would be a pope, that each prophetic day in Daniel 7 and Revelation 13 represents a historical year, that Daniel 7–12 and Revelation 4–22 refer to the same events, and especially that biblical prophecy referred to the church age as a whole. Instead, the prophecies predicted events that would occur in rapid succession just before Christ's final return to establish the millennial kingdom.

Besides promoting these standard futurist doctrines, Darby's main accomplishment was the introduction of a new method of dividing history into "dispensations," or eras marked by changes in God's revelation to humanity, and analyzing scripture and prophecy within the framework of the dispensations. While the practice of dividing history into eras was nothing new, Darby's dispensationalism was distinctive for its strictly literalistic interpretation of biblical prophecy, its insistence that God's plans and scriptural revelations for Israel were completely different from those for the Christian church, and its introduction of the "secret Rapture" doctrine, which taught that Christ would first return to take away Christians, and later to establish his millennial kingdom. The initial *parousia* would be "secret" in that it would be witnessed only by raptured and resurrected Christians. The rest of the world would stand shocked by the silent and sudden disappearance of the church.

The doctrine of the Secret Rapture grew naturally out of Darby's divisions of history and of the peoples of God. He taught that God's original scriptural plan had been for Israel alone, and that biblical prophecy, especially that of Daniel and Revelation, deals exclusively with them. God made a series of covenants with the Israel, the last of which was with David. The Davidic Covenant guaranteed that God would never forget David's house (2 Samuel 7:4–17), and that a son of David would always reign over Israel. The Davidic line was broken by the Babylonian exile (586 BCE), but God promised through the prophecies of Daniel that David's throne would be restored to the Messiah, the final and greatest son of David. Under the Messiah's reign Israel would enjoy prosperity, and a new, spiritual law of righteousness would replace the sacrificial system. Daniel 9:24–27 predicts that the period of restoration would take seventy weeks: in the first seven weeks Jerusalem would be rebuilt, and after sixty-nine weeks the Messiah would appear, only to be "cut off" and rejected. In the final seven weeks an evil ruler would arise and attempt to destroy the Jews, but the Messiah would return at the end "to destroy the desolator." Dispensationalists interpreted each week as a period of seven years by arguing that, since the Hebrew word for "week" actually means "a seven," the prophet's "seventy sevens" literally and originally meant 490 years. Calculating that Jesus was crucified 483 years after Artaxerxes' decree that allowed the Jews to return to their

ANTI-RAPTURE POLEMICS IN CHRISTIAN IDENTITY MILLENNIALISM

From the time of the end of the Judean economy and priesthood in 70 AD, there have been many detractors seeking to lead men astray from the Truth. One of these millstone seekers was the proselyte and true standout minister C.I. Scofield. His Scofield Reference Bible is pushed by colleges and churches and recommended by many so-called "pastors." He was a convicted forger, defrauded his mother-in-law and no college or university can be found that conferred upon him a doctoral degree. His escapades put today's television preachers and productions to shame by comparison. He left his wife and children to fare for themselves with no means of support. He was financed for the rendition of his reference Bible by the Zionist conspiratorial group out of Boston known as the "Secret Six." This one man, without a doubt, has created more false teachings and misinformation in this century than any other. He did in the United States what Darby did in England. He was the precursor of the swarm of rapture novels, books, and fantasies that have been marketed by Christian book outlets. Of course, as you know, you will only read of one view which is the premillennialist view. This religion promotes the Zionist Jews' return to Israel which many denominations teach, thereby positioning themselves to be the Jews' underlings. The Judeo-Christian churches with their Rev. Flawwells have done their bidding and the sheep follow. By taking the King James Version and making pertinent notes and suggestions, he has done more evil in the sight of man and God than the Communist Jews' own leaders. Their yoke is heavy, but the yoke of the Master is light. Those preaching Scofield's doctrines are endorsing lawlessness.

> **". . . forsaking a straight path, they went away, following the way of Balaam of Bosor who loved the wages of injustice, but had reproof of his own transgression: the dumb ass speaking with the voice of a man held back the madness of the prophet. These are springs without water, clouds being driven by a storm, for whom the blackness of darkness is kept forever" (II Peter 2:15-17 AST).**

Could this be an example of one that has his mind poisoned with false doctrine, a doubled-minded one? Can you see why with more and more churches being built and occupied things get worse instead of better? If false doctrines are being taught as truth, then you have subversion of the Government of God. Evidently, the Esau-Edom crowd found their right man to deceive the elect of God.

> **"Woe to you, scribes and Pharisees, hypocrites! Because you go about the sea and the dry land to make one proselyte, and when he becomes, you make him a son of Gehenna twofold more than you" (Matt. 23:15 AST).**

What is the result of premillennialism or other futuristic doctrines? Those believing these Jewish doctrines are defeatists and think that if things get too bad then Christ will return and settle everything. Some sit on their behinds and are glad when bad things happen because they believe this garbage and become defeatist and useless to the Government of God.

Source: Mikesell, Don. (1999) "Misinformation." http://www.christianseparatist.org/Briefs.html.

land to rebuild the walls of Jerusalem (Nehemiah 2:1–8), dispensationalists claimed that Jesus was originally scheduled to return seven years later in fulfillment of Daniel's chronology.

Why did Jesus not return in the first century? Darby presented his "postponement theory": when the Jews rejected Jesus as Messiah, God suspended his dealings with Israel by postponing the fulfillment of the final "seven" of Daniel 9:27, and began a new dispensation of grace with his gentile people, the Christian church. As soon as God's dealings with the church are complete he will resume his relationship with Israel, and the final "seven" will be consummated in seven years of great Tribulation, as prophesied in Revelation 4–20, the "Olivet Discourse" of Matthew 24, and 2 Thessalonians 2. A difficulty arises: if, as Darby argued, God does not deal with Christians and Jews at the same time, then these prophecies do not apply to the church. How would God avoid involving the church in his completion of prophecies concerning Israel if, as Revelation 8–9 describes, a third of the entire world will be destroyed by a relentless succession of plague, war, fire, pestilence, earthquakes, poisoned water, and the falling of the heavenly bodies? Darby offered the Secret Rapture, which remains the most distinctive innovation of dispensationalism: Christ would return secretly to resurrect and rapture the church. Immediately after the Secret Rapture, God would resume fulfilling the final seven years of Daniel 9:27, during which the horrors of the "Great Tribulation" of Revelation would come upon the earth. The church would live above the earthly chaos until the were completed, and then they would accompany Jesus on his second return to earth at the end of the Tribulation to defeat the Antichrist, gather the elect of Israel, judge the nations, and establish the millennial kingdom of Christ.

Darby's futurist interpretation of prophecy saved premillennialists from historicism's increasingly suspect method of relating biblical prophecy to church history and to contemporary events, and especially from predicting dates for the *parousia.* Since the events of Daniel and Revelation did not apply to the church, there was nothing that needed to be fulfilled before the *parousia.* In fact, none of the prophesied events could occur until after Christ returned to remove the church so that God could resume fulfilling his prophesied plan for Israel. Because Christ could come for his church at any time, Darby's doctrine was termed the "any-moment Coming of Christ," and advocates claimed that awareness that Christ could return at any moment was essential for the purity of the church, citing 2 Peter 3:11–12. Without such expectation Christians were bound to lose vigilance and grow corrupt like the careless servants and bridesmaids in Matthew 24:45–25:30.

At first Darby's eschatological ideas met resistance, especially his two-stage *parousia,* his insistence that Christians could not know when Christ would return, and his rigid division of scriptures into those that solely concerned the church and those that solely concerned Israel. Historicist scholars attempted to refute Darby's futurism decisively with a number of publications. Edward Bishop Elliott's monumental four-volume, antifuturist study of Revelation, *Horae Apocalypticae* (1844), represented the tenacity of historicist millenarianism but also its persistent weakness: Elliott, like his contemporary historicists, predicted that great prophetic events would be fulfilled in 1866–67. The uneventful passing of these years pushed historicism so much further toward becoming passé. The publication of more formidable attacks, such as David Brown's antimillenarian *Christ's Second Coming* (1846), clearly illustrated the rising interest in prophecy and millenarianism among theologians, but did little to check enthusiasm for and interest in futurism. Conferences, lectures, and journals devoted to the study of prophecy multiplied in Europe after 1840, and Darby energetically promoted dispensationalism in North America between 1862 and 1877. Futurist and historicist premillennialists pitted their methods and interpretations of prophecy against each other in millenarian journals such as the relatively sophisticated *Quarterly Journal of Prophecy* (1849–73). By the 1860s it was apparent that Darby's dispensationalism had effectively displaced historicism among leading British millenarians. Despite the growing unpopularity on both sides of the Atlantic of Darby and the Plymouth Brethren for their criticism of the church and doctrinal exclusivism, Darby's millenarian ideas flourished and spread across denominations, and his doctrine of the Secret Rapture gained proponents among those who knew nothing about its originator.

Leon Bates's "The Rapture" portrays the ascent of living and dead Christians into the clouds to meet Jesus. Mayhem ensues below as their abandoned vehicles crash. The Bible Believers' Evangelistic Association reproduces this image on postcards, plastic placemats, evangelistic tracts, and framed prints, all of which are for sale. PAINTING REPRODUCED BY PERMISSION OF THE BIBLE BELIEVERS' EVANGELISTIC ASSOCIATION, INC., 1999.

Dispensationalism's distinct futurist premillennialism and doctrine of the Secret Rapture rapidly gained ground in the United States in the years following the Civil War. Like their European counterparts before the French Revolution, American evangelicals had been caught up in postmillennialism's fervent optimism following the phenomenal spread of the gospel during the two Great Awakenings (1720–50 and 1795–1840s). The bold predictions of Jonathan Edwards (1703–58) that the millennial reign of Christ's kingdom would be ushered in by "ordinary means of grace" and by the evangelical activity of the American church seemed near fulfillment to some in the 1830s. After 1865, however, the United States lay devastated by the war, and postmillennialism retained few adherents. American premillennialism had seemed unredeemable after the 1844 Millerite scandal, but proponents of futurism vigorously distinguished their premillennialism from that of the discredited historicists. Millenarian theologians moved toward futurist premillennialism as they struggled to make sense of Christian eschatology in the aftermath of the war, and by the late 1860s periodicals like *The Prophetic Times* assumed an editorial stance promoting the doctrine of the Secret Rapture.

As in Great Britain, American millennialists organized conferences to discuss doctrinal particularities. By far the most important series of meetings was the Niagara Bible Conference in New York (1875–1900). Founded as the Believers' Meeting for Bible Study, the conference provided a remarkably open forum in which varieties of scriptural interpretation were presented. One of the most striking characteristics of the group was its acknowledgment that the Rapture could be discussed as an eschatological category apart from its original dispensationalist form. While most participants adhered to dispensationalism and a pre-Tribulational Rapture, some of its most influential leaders, such as William J. Erdman, argued that the Rapture would occur after the Tribulation, and that the church would endure persecution under the Antichrist. Historicism, too, had its representatives, and for a time Niagara participants were willing to ally themselves with premillennialists of other convictions in order to promote premillennialism, biblical inerrancy, and literalism in the interpretation of scriptures.

By the time the conference broke up in 1901 due to growing tension between proponents of pre-Tribulational and post-Tribulational views of the Rapture, its participants had succeeded in promoting premillennialism into one of most important doctrines among conservative Christians. When Cyrus I. Scofield, perhaps the best-known Niagara participant, published his annotated *Scofield Reference Bible* in 1909, the Fundamentalist movement acquired what would become its most powerful tool for defending and promoting dispensationalism, creationism, premillennialism, and the Secret Rapture. Niagara participants had also energetically promoted missionary work and evangelism. From 1885 until the first decades of the twentieth century many participated in the founding of missions to Africa and China, as well as several Bible Institutes throughout North America. The most important of these, established in Chicago in 1889, would become the Moody Bible Institute, the center of American evangelism.

The doctrine of the Rapture spread explosively from the pulpits of evangelists trained at the Bible institutes. Dwight L. Moody (1837–99), an early convert to premillennialism, confessed that awareness of the imminence of the *parousia* fueled his efforts to win converts more than any other Christian doctrine. Historian Timothy Weber notes that, since Moody, nearly every major American revivalist has been a premillennialist (1983: 52). Crowd-gatherers like Billy Sunday (1862–1935) warned thousands of the terrors they would face if they missed the Rapture, and local ministers and missionaries spread the word to their respective audiences. It was not uncommon to hear new converts testify that they had been persuaded to come to Christ after having dreams or visions about being left behind to face the terrors of the Great Tribulation.

Varieties of Rapture Doctrines

One of the most important results of the Niagara Conference was the spread of the doctrine of the pre-Tribulational Rapture. Although its collapse in 1901 came after the rise of irreconcilable division between adherents of post-Tribulational and pre-Tribulational views, the most capable advocates of post-Tribulationalism died not long after the turn of the century, and the phenomenal spread of the pre-Tribulational view rendered its rival nearly invisible. Post-Tribulationalism remained essentially forgotten to the American millennialist consciousness until 1952, when George Ladd, a premillennialist professor at Fuller Theological Seminary, revived interest in the post-Tribulational view by challenging the methods and assumptions of traditional Darbyite dispensationalism. Ladd pointed out that nowhere does the New Testament make explicit a two-stage *parousia* and that in fact the references to the resurrection identify it with Christ's globally witnessed return in glory—an event impossible to keep "secret." A spate of publications from other scholars followed, and advocates of the post-Tribulational position argued that the strict division between Israel and the church, upon which Darby's doctrine of the two-stage *parousia* depended, was impossible to maintain. Further, they argued that Jesus' prophecies about Tribulation in the last days in Matthew 24 were addressed to the disciples, who clearly represent the church. Although Jesus promised to protect the church during the outpouring of God's wrath (Revelation 3:10), it would be through physical protection during the Tribulation, and not through physical removal.

Mid-Tribulationalism represents a second alternative to the pre-Tribulational position. Proponents maintain a futurist interpretation of Daniel 9:27 and Revelation 4–22, but emphasize the division of Daniel's seventieth week into two halves. Since God's wrath is not poured out until the second half of the week, they assume that the church will not be raptured until the middle of the week. Christ returns to save the church from God's wrath, but not from the Antichrist's persecution, which the church must endure along with Israel. This solution also allows the church to interpret Matthew 24 as pertaining to itself and relieves exegetes of the awkward task of separating prophecy regarding Israel from scripture addressed to the church.

Rapture Predictions and Cults at the End of the Second Millennium

The revival of debate over the timing of the Rapture began with a series of respectful exchanges between Fundamentalist scholars who stressed that various beliefs about such things cannot ever be irrefutably proved through exegesis, and so should not become divisive issues among Christians. The debate has not been continued with as much restraint, especially with the turning of the third millennium. A flood of Internet sites, pamphlets, and cheaply produced books repeat the debates and mistakes of every variety of nineteenth- and twentieth-century millennialism imaginable with interesting, and sometimes alarming, variations. Hal Lindsey earned fame with his best-selling popular interpretation of biblical prophecy, *The Late Great Planet Earth* (1973), in which he urged readers to be prepared for the imminent Rapture. In its sequel, *The 1980's: Countdown to Armageddon* he boldly identified the 1980s as the "terminal decade" for humanity. The successful advent of the 1990s, however, earned his prediction the shame shared by all such conjectures thus far. Likewise Edgar Whisenant's widely distributed *88 REASONS why the Rapture is in 1988* went the way of all previous such prophetic number-crunching exercises. His sequel, *89 REASONS why the Rapture is in 1989*, predictably received less attention. Other date setters warned against the sin of disbelieving their predictions. In 1991, fifteen-year-old Korean prophet Bang-Ik Ha, founder of the Taberah World Mission, published *The Last Plan of God*, in which he claimed that Christ would return within a year to rapture those whom Bang-Ik had prepared. He urged readers to come to Korea as quickly as possible to find out if they had been marked for Rapture or for martyrdom during the Great Tribulation. Comparing his teaching to Noah's ark, he claimed that only those who would "enter the ark" by believing his message could enter God's kingdom; the worst sin against the Holy Spirit was "reviling the gospel of the rapture in 1992" (167). Similarly David Koresh's Branch Davidian sect continues to claim that only those who join them will be sealed with the name "Koresh" and so escape the final outpouring of God's wrath upon the earth. Like other premillennialists, the Branch Davidians believe that they are now in the last days. They taught a mid-Tribulational Rapture doctrine and lived in expectation that their faith would be tested through a series of persecutions at the hands of the government. Their prophecies appeared to be chillingly fulfilled during the fifty-one-day siege that ended tragically on 19 April 1993.

Recently the doctrine of the Rapture has been combined with other religious teachings to form admixtures of tradition and innovation that seem at home only within the peculiarities of late-twentieth-century culture. The most infamous of these is Heaven's Gate, an apocalyptic cult whose beliefs combined science fiction, UFO conspiracy theories, radical body-soul dualism, and Christian eschatology. Under the leadership of Marshall Applewhite, thirty-nine members methodically took their own lives in San Diego on 26 March 1997 in an attempt to board a spacecraft whose arrival, they claimed, was marked by the Hale-Bopp comet. This spacecraft came to rapture the cult into the Kingdom of Heaven, or the "Evolutionary Level Above Human" in Heaven's Gate parlance. While Heaven's Gate members hoped that their Heavenly Father would "take them up into His 'cloud of light' (spacecraft)" while they were still alive, they anticipated that "they may be required to discard their 'undercover costume' (their borrowed human body) as they depart—leaving their 'chrysalis' behind." Whether through miraculous transformation in bodily rapture or through suicide, cult members would exchange their vehicles of perishable human bodies for the "everlasting and non-corruptible" bodies of the Next Level, while the Earth's present civilization, disturbed beyond repair by "human weeds," was "spaded under," destroyed utterly, and recycled into a more useful form (*Heaven's Gate Archive* 1999).

Disappointment marked 22 and 31 March 1998 for Chen Tao, a Taiwanese Rapture sect. About 150 members followed the sect's founder, Teacher Heng-ming Chen, from Taiwan to Garland, Texas, in June 1997 to await the appearance of God. Chen predicted that God would make a global appearance on television on the 22 March 1998, and then on 31 March, God would enter him and miraculously divide him into enough people to deliver a warning about the coming Tribulation to everyone on earth individually and in each individual's native tongue. Chen, whose teaching combines Buddhist reincarnation, Christian eschatology, and UFO theories, predicted that the Tribulation would begin in Asia in 1999, bringing utter devastation upon the world by the turn of the millennium, but that God would rescue believers in America with a Rapture facilitated by a convoy of flying saucers.

Anti-Rapture Millennialism

The doctrine of the Rapture and its originators and proponents have come under severe criticism by two distinct millennial movements in the twentieth century: the postmillennialist Christian Reconstructionists, and the white supremacist Christian Identity movement and its offshoots, which teach a variety of millenarian doctrines ranging from futurist premillennialism with a post-Tribulation *parousia* to historicism, postmillennialism, and amillennialism. While the ideologies and goals of Reconstructionists, who work toward the conversion of Jews to Christianity and champion Israeli nationalism, differ markedly from those of Identity Christians, who identify Jews as parasitic antichrists and servants of Satan, both sarcastically rename dispensational premillennialism "pessimillennialism" because, they claim, it robs Christians of hope and motivation for participating in the establishment of Christ's reign. Both Reconstructionists and Identity Christians desire to build, through various revolutionary means, a "theonomous" government whose structure and administration conform precisely to their respective interpretations of biblical law. They accuse dispensationalists of retreating from responsibility: instead of striving to acquire the knowledge and means for actively overcoming the forces of evil and establishing righteousness in their place, dispensationalists feebly wait for Christ's return to remedy magically the world's ills. Such waiting amounts to a fearful surrender to the forces of evil in the world and reflects a psychology of defeat, as well as indifference to biblical law. For Reconstructionists, who hope to build Christ's millennial kingdom through the political and economic activism, dispensationalism enervates Christian morale and the church's ability to perform its divinely appointed eschatological role, since dispensationalism's millennial kingdom does not depend in any way on the efforts and faithfulness of Christ's followers. For Identity Christians, who eagerly anticipate the climactic war between Satan's forces (the Antichrist Jews) and Christians during the Great Tribulation, dispensationalists grossly err as they eagerly await escape from the woes of the Great Tribulation through the Rapture, instead of bloody and heroic victory. For both Reconstructionists and Identity Christians the Rapture represents the height of pessimism and cowardice, since it at once removes from believers any hope of contributing to Satan's defeat and Christ's victory, depends in no way upon Christians' accountability to biblical law, and promises that no eschatological hardship or suffering will touch Christ's church.

Popular Representations of the Rapture

Popular fictional depictions of the Rapture have appeared throughout religious novels since the 1930s, and later in comics and films. These typically follow a futurist premillennial eschatology with a pre-Tribulation Rapture and narrate the adventures of a protagonist who misses the Rapture and must endure famine, disease, war, and the persecution of the Antichrist during the Great Tribulation. The consequences of refusing the mark of the Beast are gruesome: in Forrest Oilar's 1937 novel, *Be Thou Prepared, for Jesus is Coming*, the Antichrist's agents strip Christians naked and douse them with sulphuric acid before cutting off their heads. But the consequences of accepting the mark are far worse: eternal damnation. Baptist minister Tim LaHaye, a prolific apologist for dispensationalism and founder of the Pre-Trib Research Center, a self-described "think-tank committed to the study, proclaiming, teaching, and defending of the Pretribulational Rapture" (www.millennianet.com/atpro4sel/petri2.html), has recently added five Rapture novels to his publications with the slickly produced and best-selling series *Left Behind* (1995–99). Coauthored with Jerry Jenkins, writer in residence at the Moody Bible Institute, the series follows the post-Rapture struggles of the "Tribulation Force," a Christian underground, against the Antichrist as the prophecies of Revelation are literally and sensationally fulfilled.

Designed especially to proselytize youth, films such as *A Thief in the Night* and its sequels (Mark IV Pictures, 1971–84), *Years of the Beast* (Skyline Productions, 1981), and the forthcoming *Left Behind: The Movie* (Namesake Entertainment) are produced in the style of popular action or science fiction films and employ as much suspense, terror, and graphic violence as conservative conscience and limited budgets allow. The message is clear: "If you miss the Rapture, a nightmarish fight for survival against the forces of the Antichrist awaits you. Become a Christian now!"

More humorous Rapture themes appear on t-shirts and bumper stickers, such as the frequently spotted "WARNING: In case of Rapture this car will be unmanned!" Continuing the same theme, the Bible Believers' Evangelistic Association of Sherman, Texas, distributes postcards, plastic place mats, and framed prints of *The Rapture*, Leon Bates's 1974 painting of a city thrown into chaos as Jesus appears in the sky: dead Christians arise from their graves and the living ascend with them toward the clouds, their transformed bodies gleaming white. Their abandoned cars crash, spraying glass across the road and tumbling down embankments, and an airplane collides with a skyscraper.

The most frequent references to the Rapture in secular pop culture are in comedy. Matt Groening's hit television series *The Simpsons* parodied the *Left Behind* scenario in an episode entitled "Simpsons Bible Stories": after falling asleep in church, the Simpson family wakes up to discover the sanctuary empty. They run outside together just in time to witness the Fundamentalist Flanders family ascending to be with Jesus, their saccharine piety vindicated forever. The Simpsons, however, are left behind.

Topics for Further Research

Historians tend to accept Darby's claim that he developed the doctrine of the two-stage *parousia* and Secret Rapture through his own study of scripture, but this claim was challenged during Darby's lifetime. Opponents of futurist premillennialism alleged that in 1830 Darby had culled the Secret Rapture from the ecstatic utterances of Margaret Macdonald, a teenage prophetess at the center of a charismatic revival in London. Sandeen disregards this allegation as baseless slander, but other historians have continued to use it in their analyses. Modern apologists for the Secret Rapture have devoted much energy toward refuting the Margaret Macdonald theory, attempting to argue that the doctrine has always been preserved by faithful Christian interpreters since the New Testament was written. Fundamentalist prophecy writer Grant R. Jeffrey (1992) claims to have found references to the Rapture, the premillennial return of Christ, and the two-stage *parousia* in Christian literature from the second century to the Renaissance. While Jeffrey's apologetic argument often depends on questionable interpretations of the sources, other scholars have found pre-Darbyite forms of the Rapture. American historian Reiner Smolinski (1995) points out that Cotton Mather (1663–1728), a Puritan minister and theologian, divided the *parousia* into two stages and taught the equivalent of a post-Tribulation Rapture. While Mather divided the *parousia* much differently than Darby—he claimed that Christ would first resurrect dead Christians, then would return just before the global conflagration to rapture the living church—the idea that the *parousia* would occur in stages existed in American theology well before Darbyite dispensationalism crossed the Atlantic. There remains much work to be done in tracing the history of interpretations of the *parousia*, if we are to fully understand the place of Darby's doctrine of the Secret Rapture in the history of Christian thought.

The idea that God takes living people up from the earth into Heaven predates the New Testament. The apocryphal Jewish books of Enoch elaborately describe what Enoch witnessed after God caught him up into heaven. Enoch's rapture appears in Jewish and Christian scriptures (Genesis 5:24; Sirach 44:16, 49:14; Hebrews 11:5), as does a dramatic description of the prophet Elijah's heavenly ascent in a chariot of fire and whirlwind (2 Kings 2:11; Sirach 48:12; 1 Maccabees 2:58). These traditions were well known in first-century Judaism, as was the expectation that the dead would be raised on the final day. But Paul's declaration that the entire church, dead and living, would be resurrected and raptured when Christ returned appears to have been quite innovative. Scholars continue to investigate how Jewish ideas about the coming of a messianic figure, the eschatological resurrection of the dead, redemption of the world, and vindication of God's elect relate to Paul's description of the *parousia* in 1 Thessalonians 4 and 1 Corinthians 15. More scholarship has appeared on the resurrection of the dead, however, than on the Rapture of the living. A thorough study of the origins of the Rapture aspect of the *parousia* in Paul's letters is needed.

Finally, Christian premillennialism has spread throughout the world through Fundamentalist missionary work and international evangelism. The doctrine of the Rapture has been proclaimed to peoples with non-Western concepts of the relationship between humanity and the divine, death and the supernatural. Psychologist Charles Strozier notes that the Hopi have incorporated into their native eschatology the apparently Christian doctrine that a remnant of righteous people will survive the destruction of the present world to repopulate a new, cleansed earth. This simultaneous destruction and renewal occurs with the advent of the "true white brother," Pahana the redeemer. Parallels to Christian premillennialism are immediately apparent and appear to be the result of a combination of Christian evangelism and years of cultural exchange between traditional Hopi and their Christian neighbors. While studies in such exchange, assimilation, and transformation of ideas have appeared, much work remains to be done. Similarly the study of New Age cults like Heaven's Gate and Chen Tao, with their deliberately selective adoption of motifs and doctrines from a variety of global traditions, remains a relatively new field with many opportunities for research.

Yonder M. Gillihan

See also Chen Tao, Davidians, Dispensationalism, Heaven's Gate, Postmillennialism, Premillennialism, Ufology

Bibliography

Archer, Gleason L., Paul D. Feinberg, Douglas J. Moo, and Richard R. Reiter. (1996) *Three Views on the Rapture: Pre-, Mid-, or Post-Tribulational?* Grand Rapids, MI: Zondervan.

Heaven's Gate Archive. (1999) www.tasod.com/heavengate.

Holleman, Joost. (1996) *Resurrection and Parousia: A Traditio-Historical Study of Paul's Eschatology in 1 Corinthians 15.* New York: E. J. Brill.

Jeffrey, Grant R. (1992) *Apocalypse: The Coming Judgment of the Nations.* Toronto, Ontario: Frontier Research Publications.

Lindsey, Hal. (1980) *The 1980s: Countdown to Armageddon.* King of Prussia, PA: Westgate Press.

——.(1970) *The Late Great Planet Earth.* Grand Rapids, MI: Zondervan.

Oilar, Forrest L. (1937) *Be Thou Prepared, for Jesus Is Coming.* Boston: Meador Publishing Co.

Robinson, Wendy. (1999) "Heaven's Gate: The End?" www.ascusc.org/jcmc/vol3/issue3/robinson.html.

Sandeen, Ernest R. (1970) *The Roots of Fundamentalism: British and American Millenarianism 1800–1930.* Chicago: University of Chicago Press.

Smolinski, Reiner, ed. (1995) *The Threefold Paradise of Cotton Mather: An Edition of "Triparadisus."* Athens, GA: University of Georgia Press.

Strozier, Charles B. (1994) *Apocalypse: On the Psychology of Fundamentalism in America.* Boston: Beacon Press.

Taberah World Mission. (1991) *The Last Plan of God.* Seoul, Republic of Korea: Taberah World Mission.

Weber, Timothy P. (1983) *Living in the Shadow of the Second Coming: American Preminnellialism 1875–1982.* Enlarged edition. Grand Rapids, MI: Zondervan.

Whisenant, Edgar C. (1988) 88 *REASONS why the Rapture is in 1988.* Nashville, TN: World Bible Society.

Rastafarianism

Rastafarianism is a millennial movement that developed among African Americans on the island of Jamaica in the 1930s. The movement has its origins in earlier resistance movements to British rule and earlier back-to-Africa movements. It continues to draw adherents around the world; followers of the movement are known as Rastafarians, Rastas, or Dreadlocks. The dreadlock hairstyle and reggae music are two Rastafarian cultural forms whose popularity has spread far beyond the movement and outside Jamaica.

Because Rastafarianism is not recognized as a religion in Jamaica and because some Rastafarians eschew contact with white society, the number of Rastafarians is unknown. They are estimated at about 100,000 in Jamaica with considerably smaller populations in Great Britain, United States, Australia, Ethiopia, Canada, New Zealand, South Africa, and Ghana. Rastafarianism has spread primarily as a result of the immigration of Jamaican Rastafarians to other nations, not as a result of Rastafarians attracting converts in other nations. Rastafarianism is in the tradition of Black nationalist movements as Rastafarians emphasize ties to and an eventual return to Africa.

Origin and History

As with many millennial movements, the appearance of Rastafarianism is tied to oppression—in this case, the oppression of African slaves on the island of Jamaica by the British colonists. The British took control of Jamaica from the Spanish in 1655 and established a plantation colony with about 750,000 slaves imported from Africa to work the cattle ranches, and sugar, coffee, cotton, and allspice fields. The ranches and plantations were owned by British, and Jamaica was ruled by Britain. Even after slavery ended in 1838, the basic structure of society—with the small British population controlling the economy and government and with former slaves living in poverty—remained much the same until Jamaica achieved independence in 1962. Since then, many Jamaicans have continued to live in poverty, while others have left the island for opportunities elsewhere.

In addition to oppression and poverty, there were other conditions that set the stage for the emergence of the Rastafarian movement in the early 1930s. One condition was a long pattern of resistance to white rule in Jamaica, in the form of slave rebellions and the establishment of colonies by escaped slaves in the mountainous interior beyond British control. While these revolts were quickly put down, they were part of a continuous pattern of resistance that was not found in many other British colonies in the Caribbean.

A second condition was the emergence of African-Jamaican religions based on a mix of Christian and indigenous African beliefs and practices. Especially important were the African leaders of the Native Baptist movement in the late nineteenth century who competed for followers with white missionaries and leaders of mainstream Christian churches. Finally, there were other small movements prior to Rastafarianism that were also meant to liberate Afro-Jamaicans from white oppression. The two most prominent where the Bedwardites, a religious movement founded by Alexander Bedward, and the Universal Negro Improvement Association of Marcus Garvey, which directed Africans outside Africa to return to Africa and especially to Ethiopia, places where Africans could find freedom and equality. As regards later Rastafarian groups, four movements headed respectively by Leonard Howell, Joseph Hibbert, Archibald Dunkey, and Robert Hinds in the early twentieth century all produced members who became involved in the emergence of Rastafarianism.

Within this framework of oppression, poverty, and resistance to British rule, the Rastafarian movement began. The precipitating event was the coronation in November 1930 of Ras Tafari as His Imperial Majesty, the Emperor of Ethiopia, Haile Selassie I, the King of Kings, the Lord of Lords, and the conquering Lion of the Tribe of Judah. When news of the coronation of an African king in Africa reached Jamaica, Haile Selassie was hailed by some in Jamaica as a Black God and Ethiopia was deemed to be "the promised land." The Rastafarian movement had begun.

Although the movement—or movements—was small, with no more than a few thousand followers and even fewer fully committed to the cause, over the next two decades it became perceived as a threat by the ruling British government. In the 1950s, Rastafarian leaders were imprisoned and Rastafarian communities broken up. The culmination of government efforts to control the movement was the arrest in 1960 of a movement leader, Claudius Henry, his wife, and twelve followers. They were accused of treason against the

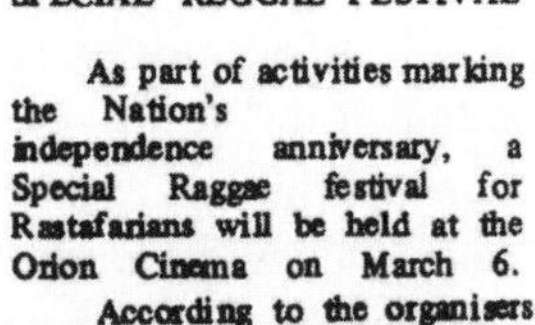

SPECIAL REGGAE FESTIVAL

As part of activities marking the Nation's independence anniversary, a Special Raggae festival for Rastafarians will be held at the Orion Cinema on March 6.

According to the organisers of the programme, the festival will feature two foreign reggae bands alongside ten loval bands.

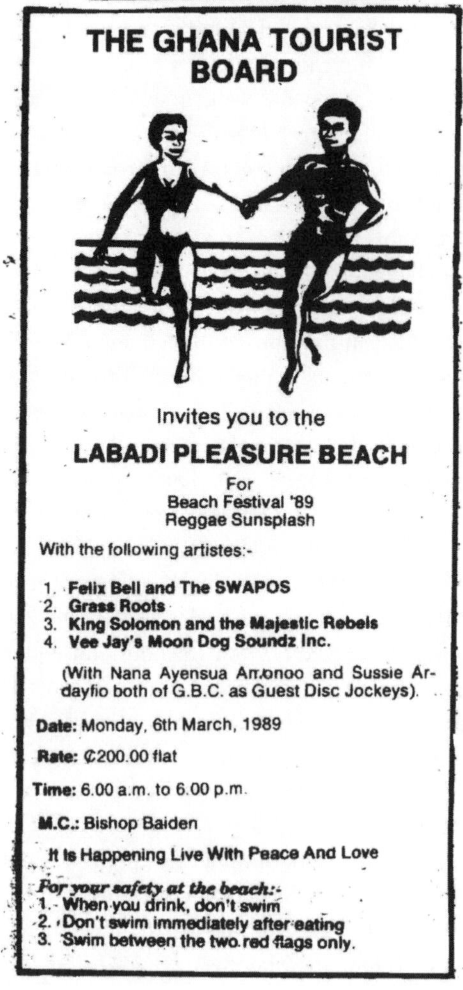

THE GHANA TOURIST BOARD

Invites you to the

LABADI PLEASURE BEACH

For
Beach Festival '89
Reggae Sunsplash

With the following artistes:-

1. Felix Bell and The SWAPOS
2. Grass Roots
3. King Solomon and the Majestic Rebels
4. Vee Jay's Moon Dog Soundz Inc.

(With Nana Ayensua Amonoo and Sussie Ardayfio both of G.B.C. as Guest Disc Jockeys).

Date: Monday, 6th March, 1989

Rate: ₵200.00 flat

Time: 6.00 a.m. to 6.00 p.m.

M.C.: Bishop Baiden

It Is Happening Live With Peace And Love

For your safety at the beach:-
1. When you drink, don't swim
2. Don't swim immediately after eating
3. Swim between the two red flags only.

Evidence of the international growth of Rastafarianism and the related reggae music is found in these two newspaper announcements from Ghana.

British Crown. Henry and two followers were sentenced to ten years in prison and his son and three other Rastafarians were killed in a gunfight with British troops.

With the end of British rule and power shifting to Afro-Jamaican politicians in the 1960s, Rastafarianism gained more acceptance and some movement members made plans, which never materialized, for mass immigration to Ethiopia. The high point of the movement came on 21 April 1966 when Haile Selassie was greeted by some 100,000 Rastafarians on a state visit to Jamaica. In the 1950s and 1960s, as many Jamaicans moved to the United States, Canada, and Great Britain, the movement went with the Rastafarian emigrants.

Widespread, if superficial, knowledge of Rastafarianism is probably due both to the distinctive dreadlock hairstyle of many Rastafarians and to the popularity of reggae music. Nearly all the early international reggae artists of the 1960s—Robert Nesta (Bob) Marley being the best known—were Rastafarians. Reggae lyrics are rich with Rastafarian themes of oppression, revolution, and better times in the future.

Organization of Rastafarianism

The lack of hierarchy and central organization that characterized the emergence of Rastafarianism has continued throughout its history. There is no single Rastafarian movement or organization, no hierarchy of leaders, and no central office. Most Rastafarians in Jamaica affiliate with one of three major groups—House of Nyabinghi, Twelve Tribes of Israel, or Ethiopia Africa Black International Congress—and others belong to several smaller groups. Rastafarian groups are male-centered: led by men, with mostly male members, and with women afforded fewer rights and subject to various restrictions (on, for instance, what clothes they may wear in public). In the 1990s, however, there has been a movement toward more rights for women. Although Rastafarians in Jamaica speak Jamaican Creole English, they also use their own argot, Dread Talk, when speaking to one another. Most Rastafarians live in the general community; for most, their closest ties are to other Rastafarians in the neighborhood. In Jamaica, Rastafarians have generally not run for political office, although on other islands in the Caribbean they have been more involved in mainstream politics. Jamaican Rastafarians have established small Rastafarian communities in Ethiopia, Ghana, and Congo.

Beliefs and Practices

As a millennial movement, Rastafarianism is based on a set of basic religious beliefs and practices. Rastafarians believe that adherence to these beliefs and practices will produce a better world in which Africans are freed from white oppression. Much of Rastafarian belief is unwritten and is passed orally from members to new members. Although Rastafarians believe in the Christian Bible, it does not have the same authority it holds for Christians. In fact, much of the Bible has different meanings for Rastafarians, who believe that it was originally written as the history of Africans and then rewritten by whites as a document to prove their superiority over Africans. Rastafarians believe that only they can discern the original and true meaning of the stories in the Bible.

Rastafarians believe that all Africans are descendants of the ancient Hebrews and that Africans are the Children of Israel. Africans live outside Africa because long ago they disobeyed Jah (God) and as punishment were put under the control of whites who enslaved them and sent them out of Africa. African communities outside Africa are called Babylon; Babylon being a general concept that refers to anything having to do with the oppression of Africans. Rastafarians believe that they will not have to remain in Babylon forever, but will return to Africa, and more specifically, to Ethiopia, the land of Jah. The person who signaled this return is Haile Selassie, the Savior, the Black Christ, who will ultimately lead Africans back to Ethiopia. When Selassie disappeared in 1975 after being deposed by political rivals, Rastafarians believed he had gone into hiding until the return to Ethiopia. The discovery of his body in the 1990s posed special problems for Rastafarians, although a delegation did travel to Ethiopia to attend his funeral.

Rastafarianism has little in the way of formal rituals. The two most important ritual activities are the reasoning or grounding and the binghi. The reasoning is a group discussion which focuses on the Rastafarian interpretation of the Bible, local politics, and world events. It is an important forum for introducing new adherents to the movement. A key element of the reasoning is the use of ganja (marijuana), by smoking it in shared pipes, and communal drinking and eating. Rastafarians believe that ganja is a sacred plant whose use brings them closer to Jah and Haile Selassie; it also prevents illness.

Binghi is a celebration of major events such as Haile Selassie's birthday, coronation, and visit to Jamaica in 1966, and the Ethiopian Christmas. The celebration involves reasonings and dancing and singing over several days. The wearing of one's hair in the dreadlock style is the most important public display of Rastafarian identity. The dreadlock represents the lion's mane and Samson, thus symbolizing Rastafarian ties to Haile Selassie (the Lion of the Tribe of Judah) and to the ancient Hebrews.

Rastafarianism in the 1990s

In terms of the number of adherents, Rastafarianism remains a minor political and religious movement in Jamaica, although it continues to draw the attention of the government who fear it as a seedbed of revolt, just as the British government did earlier. Nor has there been any mass movement to Ethiopia, perhaps because of the serious economic and political problems in that nation. But, while the movement has been politically ineffective, it has been of much symbolic importance for Jamaicans and African Americans in general. Rastafarian public symbols such as dreadlocks, reggae music, and even Jamaican jerked beef are widely recognized around the world and much of Jamaican life is now associated with Rastafarianism. Perhaps more importantly, Rastafarianism as a movement that has lasted for nearly seventy years continues to serve as a symbol of the African-American fight for freedom and equality.

David Levinson

Bibliography

Barrett, Leonard E. (1988) *The Rastafarians.* Boston: Beacon Press.

Chevannes, Barry. (1994) *Rastafari: Roots and Ideology.* Syracuse, NY: Syracuse University Press.

Campbell, Horace. (1987) *Rasta and Resistance: From Marcus Garvey to Walter Rodney.* Trenton, NJ: Africa World Press.

Mulvaney, Rebekah M. (1990) *Rastafari and Reggae: A Dictionary and Sourcebook.* New York: Greenwood Press.

Owens, Joseph. (1976) *Dread: The Rastafarians of Jamaica.* Kingston, Jamaica: Sangster.

Revolutionary Millennial Movements

Revolutionary millennial movements possess ideologies or theologies that motivate believers to commit violent acts to overthrow the old order to create the millennial kingdom. The participants in revolutionary millennial movements believe that revolutionary violence is necessary to become liberated from their persecutors and to set up the righteous government and society. Revolutionary millennialists believe their violence is mandated by a divine or superhuman plan. Revolutionary millennial movements are numerous, and when dominant, they cause massive amounts of death, suffering, and destruction. When a revolutionary millennial movement is not dominant in society, its members will resort to terrorism.

Examples of revolutionary millennial movements are the Taiping Revolution and also Mao's Great Leap Forward in China, the German Nazis, and the Khmer Rouge in Cambodia. An example of a nondominant revolutionary millennial movement is the contemporary Euro-American nativist movement which includes the Freemen, Neo-Nazis, Identity Christians, and Odinists.

Revolutionary millennialists resort to violence because they are convinced they have been persecuted. In doing so, they become persecutors. Revolutionary millennialism involves a radical dualistic perspective of good battling evil that becomes a sense of "us vs. them." This radical dualism dehumanizes and demonizes the "other" so that it is legitimate to kill them. Radical dualism legitimates murder and warfare.

Revolutionary millennialism may be either an expression of catastrophic millennialism or progressive millennialism. For example, Christian Identity, an often racist and anti-Semitic religion which expects Christians to have to fight against the American government, "Babylon," in the endtime, is catastrophic in orientation. The German Nazis, the Khmer Rouge, and Maoists, were oriented toward progress, but these true believers utilized violence to speed up progress to establish the millennial kingdom.

Catherine Wessinger

See also Catastrophic Millennialism, Nativist Millennial Movements, Progressive Millennialism

Bibliography

Wessinger, Catherine. (2000) *How the Millennium Comes Violently.* Chappaqua, NY: Seven Bridges Press.

——, ed. (2000) *Millennialism, Persecution, and Violence: Historical Cases.* Syracuse, NY: Syracuse University Press.

Roman Catholicism

Unlike many other Christian denominations, the Catholic Church has never explicitly developed a sequence of events for the endtimes (although a popular Catholic apocalyptic scenario has developed among devotees of apparitions of the Virgin Mary). The new Catechism of the Catholic Church simply explains that, before the Second Coming "the Church must pass through a final trial that will shake the belief of many believers. The persecution that accompanies her pilgrimage on earth will unveil the mystery of iniquity in the form of a religious deception offering men an apparent solution to their problems at the price of apostasy from truth. The supreme religious deception is that of the Antichrist, a pseudomessianism by which man glorifies himself in place of God and of his Messiah come in the flesh."

Theological discussions of millennialism have generally been conducted under the heading of eschatology, the study of "last things." Officially, however, the Catholic Church does not endorse literal interpretations of the Book of Revelation and disapproves of any attempts to fix the dates of the end. Historically, the church has opposed apocalyptic thinking and millennial movements, taking steps to quash their potential threats to the stability of the Majesterium of the Church.

The Early Church

This church's present position is ironic since the origins of Catholicism are in a highly apocalyptic millennial movement. First-century Palestine was in an apocalyptic ferment, where Jews were unable to explain the continual, humiliating occupation by the Romans whom they considered to be an inferior culture. As a result, many began to take comfort in awaiting the return of a hero, the messiah.

First-century Palestine was filled with many more apocalyptic prophets and mystery cults than just that of Jesus of Nazareth. The Roman historian Josephus tells of Theudas, who gathered a large following around himself and announced that he would part the Jordan River; and the Book of Acts mentions an anonymous Egyptian Jew who led thousands of followers into the desert and planned to march into Jerusalem. There were countless others, the most famous being Jesus' contemporary John the Baptist, and the Essenes, the sect that wrote the Dead Sea Scrolls, as well as any number of others who left no written records.

A great deal of evidence points to the fact that Jesus had entered Jerusalem expecting to herald the End of Times. Instead he was killed. The early Christians were thus faced with a world that did not end and a messiah who had. This was resolved by the notion of the Second Coming of Christ. Prophesy had not failed, the new age had in fact dawned, but would not fully be revealed until the Second Coming.

First-century Christians, enduring Roman persecutions, looked to Jewish apocalyptic traditions to make sense of their plight, including Jewish messianic prophecies of a thousand-year kingdom of peace and abundance. The early Christians clearly expected that Jesus' return was imminent, and the early writings of the apostles present an immediate and literal sense of expectations for the Second Coming.

This Second Coming, at first literal, was slowly transformed into a symbolic return. The four gospels of the New Testament, all written within a century of the crucifixion, can be read as a series of attempts to explain and to cope with the dissonance after that prophesy failed. As the Gospels move farther and farther away in time from the crucifixion, what diminishes is the expectation that Christ's return and God's victory were imminent.

In the early letters of St. Paul, written only some thirty years after the crucifixion, one can see signs that early Christians expected Christ's return within their own lifetimes and were confused and surprised that Christians died before that happened (1 Thessalonians 4:13). Paul tried to explain this by suggesting that those Christians who died might not have been strong enough in their faith (1 Corinthians 11:30). In the Gospel of Mark, written about fifteen years after Paul, the

Second Coming is still presented in quite literal and immediate terms. After describing the signs that will presage the Second Coming, when the sun will darken and the angels will give the trumpet call, Jesus says, "Truly, I say to you, this generation will not pass away before all these things take place" (13:30). In the Gospel of Matthew, Jesus also says, "there are some standing here who will not taste death before they see the Son of Man coming in his kingdom" (16:28). The later Gospels of Luke and John reveal the strategy we now commonly associate with Christianity of redefining the prophesy as having been symbolic or metaphorical, especially passages such as John (6:47) that "he who believes has eternal life," or the most famous passage, Luke (17:21) where Jesus says that "the kingdom of God is within you."

Although the gospels that became part of the official canon record the shift away from a literal expectation of Christ's return, millennialism had not disappeared by any means. In the second century, a Christian sect called the Montanists preached a form of millennialism. Montanus, the leader of the sect, apparently declared himself to be the prophet of a third age of history, a new age of the Holy Spirit. He preached that the Second Coming would take place in 157 CE and the heavenly city of Jerusalem would literally descend on a plain between the Phrygian cities of Pepuza and Tymion. Montanist beliefs spread rapidly and formed a popular revival as Christians flocked to Phrygia.

Millennialism had flourished when the Christians were persecuted, but with the growing power and acceptance of Christianity within the Roman Empire and as the church grew larger and more organized, millennial beliefs and the often uncontrollable behaviors of their adherents came to be seen as a threat to the rapidly developing orthodoxy. Montanists were formally excommunicated late in the second century and thereafter millennialism became associated with heresy.

As with the shift away from a literal expectation of the Second Coming, the thousand-year reign of Christ also came to be seen as allegorical. The third-century theologian Origen gave an intellectual underpinning to the shift away from waiting for the kingdom in the world and instead focusing on the change within the soul. These views were further developed by St. Augustine, particularly in the *City of God*, where he divided the world into the City of the World and the City of God.

For Augustine, the judgments and battles of the Book of Revelation were allegorical. He described a realized eschatology, that the Millennium was a spiritual state the world had entered at Pentecost, when the apostles received the Holy Spirit after the Resurrection. Satan had been reduced to ruling the City of the World and in time would be expected to be defeated even there. Augustine explicitly dismissed all attempts to calculate the timing of the End, and rejected any specific timetables, writing, "In vain therefore do we try to reckon and set limits to the years that remain to this world." Augustine's views became the official doctrine of the church and have essentially remained so to this day. Apocalypticism, while part of church doctrine, was marginalized and not encouraged and millennialism became associated with popular movements and mystics, radicals, and rebels.

The Middle Ages

The history of millennialism in the Middle Ages is a history of popular movements. Within the church, the tradition of eschatology had continued in the Middle Ages in commentaries on the Book of Revelation by writers such as Bede the Venerable, Walfrid Strabo, Anselm of Lyon, and Bruno of Segni. Officially, though, St. Thomas Aquinas upheld the Augustinian view that equated millennialism with heresy.

There are few indications of popular millennialism in the early Middle Ages, although there is the evidence of calendar changes, at 500 CE and 800 CE respectively, each date which would have marked 6,000 years since creation, the date when the Millennium was to begin. The timings of these changes suggests that they were carried out to postpone millennial panic over the arrival of the apocalyptic year 6000 and there is some evidence of increased prophecies and miraculous signs in the years leading up to both these dates. The calendar reforms, resulting in the institution of the *anno domini* calendar, did not remove millennial speculation, but only postponed to the future—to the year 1000.

Evidence for popular millennialism around the year 1000 is seen in the Peace of God movement, a popular movement that began in the 990s. On the surface the Peace of God movement consisted of a series of councils called by bishops to end private warfare among the lesser nobility and limit violence against people and property. However, the movement clearly seems to have resonated with popular religious enthusiasm which led huge crowds to gather at the councils and venerate religious icons and call for peace. It has been suggested that the timing of this outpouring of popular devotion is not coincidental, but reflects a form of millennial expectations of a radically transformed world.

Historians continue to debate exactly how widespread millennial fears of the year 1000 may have been, but the later Middle Ages were certainly characterized by pervasive sense that the Last Days were imminent. Apocalyptic beliefs and expectations shaped how the medieval world was understood. Especially popular were widespread myths of an "Emperor of the Last Days" who would defeat the forces of

Answering the Holy Father's Call

"The whole Church is preparing for the Third Christian Millennium. The challenge of the great Jubilee of the Year 2000 is the new evangelization: a deepening of faith and a vigorous response to the Christian vocation to holiness and service"
—John Paul II, Camden Yards (October, 1995)

The Millennium Evangelization Project has developed conferences to help Catholics prepare for the coming millennium. The MEP seeks to make Christ and the richness of His message more widely known and better understood. Since too few Catholics know their faith well, the MEP helps educate Catholics about their faith so that they can dedicate themselves more fully to Him and can, in the face of modern challenges, evangelize others to follow Christ.

The MEP trains teams of evangelists across the country who will present ready-made conferences in their own diocese on themes suitable for the three years of preparation for the millennium. Each team will be composed of four trained speakers equipped with excellent visual aids (35mm slides) and a standardized script written by experts and reviewed by bishops. These teams will speak for diocesan conferences, parishes, Catholic organizations, universities, colleges, and high schools.

Home Page | Evangelists | Hosts | Conferences
Sponsors | Endorsements | History | Prayer
What's New | Who We Are
University of Dallas Home Page

Errors or problems with this page? Please contact the WebWeaver.
Millennium Evangelization Project; 1845 E. Northgate Dr.; Irving, TX 75062; 972/721-4063.

An e-mail announcement of the Roman Catholic Millennium Evangelization Project designed to assist Catholics in dealing with issues raised by the year 2000.

HTTP://ACAD.UDALLAS.EDU/WWW/MEP/ANSWERING.HTM.

the Antichrist and establish a paradise in the endtimes. The extent of millennial expectation in the Middle Ages can be seen in the frequency with which powerful kings and warlords were commonly called "Emperor of the Last Days," a title given to, among others, Frederick II, Louis IX, Sigismund, Philip II Augustus, Maximillian, and Charles V. Invading waves of Huns, Saracens, and Turks were all identified as the Antichrist at one time or another.

After the Peace of God movement, the next popular millennial movement to sweep Europe were the Crusades. Urban II's call for the first Crusade in 1095, not coincidentally announced at a council renewing the Peace of God, led not only to the mobilization of warrior knights, but also to a spontaneous and unanticipated popular millennial movement, the People's Crusade. Urban's call had clearly resonated with popular millennial beliefs that the "Last Emperor" would lead the faithful to Jerusalem to await the Second Coming. Recapturing Jerusalem was for eleventh-century Christian, as much as for twentieth-century Fundamentalists, a necessary element of endtime prophesy. Thus the threat of pilgrimages to Jerusalem being interrupted by the Saracens was enough to mobilize huge groups of peasants, the best known under the leadership of Peter the Hermit, who made their way across Europe to Constantinople. Most of the peasants never reached the Holy land. Many were dispersed before they reached the border of Byzantium, and others were slaughtered before they reached Jerusalem.

The next important development in Medieval millennialism was the association of apocalypticism with radical millenarian revolts, a development that was largely related to the popularity of the apocalyptic writings of the twelfth-century Cistercian monk Joachim of Fiore, whose writings predicted that a millennial kingdom of the Holy Spirit would begin in 1260. Joachim believed that the appearance of the Antichrist was imminent and that his ultimate defeat would mark the beginning of a new age with a reformed church and a perfect society. Joachim's notion of a golden age on earth, and its implications that a renewed Catholic Church would accompany the new age came close to the idea of a Catholic utopia on earth, with new social organizations. This implied a connection between millennialism and political changes on earth, a notion very much at odds with Augustine's clear separation of the Cities of God and Man.

Unlike the scattered and debated evidence for millennialism in the year 1000, the year identified by Joachim as the dawn of the new age, was clearly a millennial moment. Joachim's views were tremendously influential on the popular level; and his apocalypticism, often fusing with reform movements' attacks on the church, influenced a great many groups, many founded in and around 1260. These groups included the Spiritual Franciscans, the Begines, as well as the Fratelli, the Brothers and Sisters of the Free Spirit, and Fra Dolcino's Apostolici who made the leap from merely preaching about the apocalypse to armed resistance to the church, showing the revolutionary potential in the millennial thought of even a profoundly conservative thinker such as Joachim.

Later, during the Black Death of the fourteenth century, millennial movements swept through Europe, most notably groups of flagellants, the English Peasant Revolt, and the Taborites in Bohemia, who claimed the pope was the Antichrist and waited for the imminent arrival of the Second Coming. Tanchelm in Antwerp and Budo de Stella in Brittany both led millennial movements that saw the church itself as the Antichrist.

Millennialism was transformed into movements to reform the church, and the energies of these millennial movements were ultimately channeled into the Protestant Reformation as can be seen in the cases of John of Leiden, Thomas Muntzer, and the Zwickau prophets all of whom led millennial apocalyptic social movements, often with messianic elements, attempting to found the Kingdom of God.

The Modern Era

Official Augustinian doctrines were challenged during the seventeenth century when the rise of science and new technologies of measurement and quantification led to new attempts to bring calculations to bear on the End of Times. This led to the development of progressive millennialist Protestant circles and ultimately the rise of Fundamentalist Christianity.

Within the Catholic Church, Augustinian doctrines have not changed in the modern era. However, this is not to say that there is no millennialism within the Catholic Church as the year 2000 approached. In 1995 Pope John Paul II published the apostolic letter *Tertio Millennio Adveniente* which outlines how the church and individual Catholics are to prepare for the year 2000. The pope declared 2000 to be a "Great Jubilee" and outlined a detailed three-year program of preparation, both personal and institutional, for the beginning of the church's Third Millennium. Catholics are to study the catechism, renew their appreciation of the presence of the Holy Spirit, and undertake penance as part of their preparation for the Year 2000.

The pope's own millennial beliefs, revealed in his clear sense of a personal mission to lead the church into the Third Millennium, have led him to attempt to have the church itself make penance for past mistakes and persecutions, and attempted reconciliation with other branches of Christianity, as part of a worldwide spiritual renewal, "a new springtime of Christian life which will be revealed by the great Jubilee." He is not alone in these beliefs. Millions of pilgrims are expected to flood into the Vatican during the year 2000, giving rise to the fact that, although few may officially endorse millennial ideologies, millions of conservative Catholics do see the Great Jubilee of 2000 as marking an important transition in the Church and perhaps the beginning of a new age.

Victor Balaban

See also Joachism, Jubilee, Year of Marianism

Bibliography

Carroll, Michael P. (1986) *The Cult of the Virgin Mary: Psychological Origins.* Princeton, NJ: Princeton University Press.

Christian, William A., Jr. (1989) *Apparitions in late Medieval and Renaissance Spain.* Princeton, NJ: Princeton University Press.

Cohn, Norman. (1970) *The Pursuit of the Millennium: Revolutionary Millenarians and Mystical Anarchists of the Middle Ages.* New York: Oxford University Press.

Cuneo, Michael W. (1997) *The Smoke of Satan: Conservative and Traditionalist Dissent in Contemporary American Catholicism.* New York: Oxford University Press.

Fredricksen, Paula. (1986) *From Jesus to Christ: The Origins of the New Testament Images of Jesus.* New Haven, CT: Yale University Press.

Thompson, Damian. (1997) *The End of Time: Faith and Fear in the Shadow of the Millennium.* Hanover, NH: University Press of New England.

Russian Millennialism

The classical Russian idea of the millennium, as noted by Nikolai Berdyaev, was messianic nationalism: "Messianic consciousness is more characteristic of the Russians than of any other people except the Jews. It runs all through Russian history right down to its communist period" ([1947] 1992: 26).

Classical Russian Millennialism: Nikolai Berdyaev

When we think of classical Russian millennialism, three key figures come to mind: Vladimir Solovyov (1853–1900), a contemporary of Tolstoy and Dostoevsky, regarded as Russia's first major systematic religious philosopher; the world-renowned writer Fydor Dostoevsky (1821–81); and Nikolai Berdyaev (1874–1948) a popular and important religious philosopher. Berdyaev, in fact, incorporated many ideas of his predecessors.

Nikolai Alexandrovich Berdyaev, a self-described apocalyptic thinker, is probably the best-known Russian philosopher in the twentieth century. He lived, thought, and wrote during a revolutionary time in Russian history as a prophetic witness to a disrupting world order. He is a key interpreter of Russian millennialism, and his seminal book, *The Russian Idea* ([1947] 1992), has influenced twentieth-century millennial thinkers. His writings typically suggest the catastrophic end of the current era and the hopeful anticipation of a new millennium.

Though not a literal apocalypticist or millennialist who sets dates for the beginning or end of the biblical one thousand years, Berdyaev took seriously prophetic judgment, the apocalypse of time and history, and the vision of a new "Era of the Spirit" in which liberty and justice would reign supreme ([1947] 1992: 256). Unlike many of his contemporaries in both intellectual and popular culture, Berdyaev's apocalyptic eschatology was not pessimistic or passive, but optimistic and active. Apocalyptic eschatology and millennial hope for him was the source of creative power and spiritual illumination to transform the present social order.

Russians may be classified as apocalypticists or nihilists, according to Berdyaev (1957: 17). Their constitution drives them to extremes. They either look for the revelation of a new heaven and earth as apocalypticists, or they become revolutionary *nihilists* by rejecting common values, ideals, moral norms, dominant culture and the traditional forms of social life. The apocalyptic orientation passively awaits the end of the world, while the nihilist seeks to bring it about through revolutionary means. Russian nihilism, states Berdyaev, "is only an inverted apocalypticism." It is the eschatological theme negatively stated, "a revolt against the injustices of history, against false civilization; it is a demand that history shall come to an end, and a new life, outside or above history, begin" (1937: 40–41). Both tendencies—apocalypticism and nihilism—can be thought of as two sides of the same coin, or opposite ends of an eschatological spectrum. Berdyaev identified himself as an active and creative apocalyptic thinker ([1947] 1992: 257). Below is a diagram of Berdyaev's cultural understanding of popular Russian eschatology, constructed by the author based on Berdyaev's insight and analysis (Christensen 1997: 42): an eschatological continuum with two polarities (responsible/active and not-responsible/passive; and two extreme tendencies (nihilistic and apocalyptic). Note that Berdyaev would locate himself on the spectrum as "Responsible Apocalyptic."

The *Dusha Rossii* (Russian soul) according to Berdyaev, is by nature apocalyptic (or nihilistic). The Russian people, "in accordance with their metaphysical nature and vocation in the world, are a people of the End" ([1947] 1992: 208). There is always "a thirst for another life, another world; there is always discontent with that which is. An eschatological bent is native to the structure of the Russian soul." Either actively or passively, the Russian expects that "everything finite will come to an end, that ultimate truths will be revealed, that in the future there will be something extraordinary" ([1947] 1992: 212).

Although the attempt to describe a national psychology is fraught with difficulties, Russians often use these categories of thought in contrast to Western ways of examining cultural phenomenon. The apocalyptic predisposition of the Russian soul, according to Berdyaev, is not individualistic but corporate, not static but dynamic, not preexistent but historic. It originated as early as 988 (the Christian baptism of Rus') and was shaped by centuries of community sufferings, catastrophic events, apocalyptic expectations, millennial hopes, and spiritual illuminations. The eschatology he offers is a mystical but socially responsible vision of the future that looks beyond the crisis and despair of the moment and toward a spiritual and political resolution in the Millennial Age.

Russian Apocalyptic History

The Russian idea of history is decidedly different from that of the modern West. It tends to be a history of interpreted meanings and ideas more than literal facts, dates, and social events. For example, references to the "baptism of Rus'" in August 988, does not mean that citizens of Rus' were all baptized in one day, but rather that Prince Vladimir, and thus the empire with him, formally accepted Christianity. Literal facts and historical dates are important only as they interpret the deeper meaning of the age.

In *The Russian Idea* ([1947] 1992), Berdyaev describes how the Russian idea of apocalypse developed during a thousand years of psychological and mythological history. His perspective is that of a religious philosopher and social critic, not as a strict cultural historian. Russian apocalyptic thinking, he says, reveals itself most intensely during periods of national crisis and catastrophe, often linked to specific dates that are revised after the crisis passes ([1947] 1992: 209–10). These millennial moments of expectation often "correspond to certain signs in the heavens" and on earth, according to Berdyaev (1955: 320). By examining the rise and fall of identifiable historic epochs and their correspondence to key events and cosmic phenomenon, Berdyaev charted what he considered the evolution of the "Russian soul" which developed in predictable patterns and rhythms of millennial hope and apocalyptic despair.

Berdyaev divides Russian history into five epochs of millennial expectations: (1) Russia of Kiev; (2) Russia under Tartar yoke; (3) Muscovite Russia; (4) Russia of Peter the Great; and (5) Soviet Russia. Since all these historic epochs failed to deliver the long awaited biblical Millennium, he predicts a sixth epoch—the new or true Russia following the collapse of Soviet Communism. Each of these anticipatory ages, he claims, had a providential beginning and a catastrophic end. In the process of forming and falling, distinctive qualities of the Russian soul were forged and manifest.

Rus' of Kiev (988-1240)

Russian history begins around 850 with the arrival of Nordic invaders in the ancient land of the Slavs—territories now belonging to Ukraine, Belarus, Poland, and Lithuania. Beginning in 988, and continuing until the end of the First Millennium of Christendom, Vladimir and his subjects submitted to Christian baptism by decree that the land of Rus' would adopt Christianity in its Greek rather than Latin form. The cosmic observance of the Great Comet of 989, now known as Halley's, coincided with the "Baptism of Rus'" and marked for many the apocalypse of paganism, the "twilight of the gods" and the "years of terror" of 1000 CE. As the prince forced his people to be baptized in the Volga, the great images and statues of Peron (the Norse god of thunder), Yaryla (the sun god), and Stryboh (the wind god) were pulled down and destroyed. After Rus' was "christianized," social and political changes were brought about which resulted in a more civil society. A tremendous impetus was given to the culture for the development of language, literature, architecture, and iconography, according to Berdyaev. The Russian soul in this fertile period sought integration, wholeness, and universal significance.

BERDYAEV'S RUSSIAN ESCHATOLOGICAL CONTINUUM

(A Matrix)

Responsible
(hopeful/creative/active)

Berdyaev

NIHILISTIC---**APOCALYPTIC**

Not Responsible
(fateful/pessimistic/passive)

"The Russian nihilists and apocalypticists are at the extreme poles of the soul . . ." (Berdyaev 1957: 19) © CHRISTENSEN 1997.

The Kievan empire ended when the Tartars (adherents of Islam) invaded the Christian land of Rus' in 1240. Slavic culture was submerged and the empire splintered into semi-independent principalities. Russian Christianity managed to survive in fortresslike monasteries such as the Cave Monastery in Kiev and Holy Cross Monastery in Smolensk where numerous apocalyptic narratives were preserved. Russian apocalyptic mentality, according to Berdyaev, can be said to originate from this period.

Rus' under Tartars (1237–1492)

The Tartar conquest is remembered by Russian historian George Fedotov as "the most fateful catastrophe suffered by Russia during her entire history" (1976: 1). In a systematic process that would later become known as "ethnic cleansing," flourishing cities were razed; their populations massacred or enslaved; their princes slain in battle; cultural artifacts destroyed. The Orthodox reaction and interpretation of the "Mongol yoke" was predictable: God was punishing Russia for her sins.

For the next century, the Orthodox witnessed not only the victory of the "Golden Horde" (as the Tartar state was called), but the end of the Byzantine empire. In 1453 Constantinople, the Second Rome, fell completely under Turk control. Hagia Sophia, the Orthodox Cathedral, became a mosque. In the mid-fifteenth century, Ivan III, the Prince of Moscow (the Third Rome) collaborated with Tartar rulers and began a campaign to "unify" all Russian territories through peaceful treaties of protection, aggressive military campaigns, and even by purchase of land. After consolidating political power, Ivan III turned on the Tartar rulers, and in 1480 achieved complete independence for "Holy Russia." From the Russian Orthodox perspective, the liberation was by divine providence, coinciding with the end of two hundred years of foreign domination and anticipating the advent of the biblical millennium in 1492.

Why 1492, the same year the Jews were expelled from medieval Spain and Columbus "discovered" the New World in the West? Russian Christian scholars at the end of the fifteenth century believed that the world was created in 5508 BCE and would end in 1492 CE (7000 Annus Mundi). Contemporary Russian liturgical calendars abruptly ended on that date. According to Orthodox reasoning, since Scripture states that "a thousand years are a single day for God," and because the year 1492 would be the 7,000th since creation, the cosmic week therefore will come to an end in 1492, with the final judgment following" (Miliukov 1975: vol. 3 148).

Muscovite Russia (1493–1666)

The world did not come to an end in its seven thousandth year after creation, as expected in 1492. On the contrary, the eighth millennium began eight years early with a new epoch known as Muscovite Russia. Metropolitan Zosima extended the cycle of the new Russian liturgical calendar for another millennium.

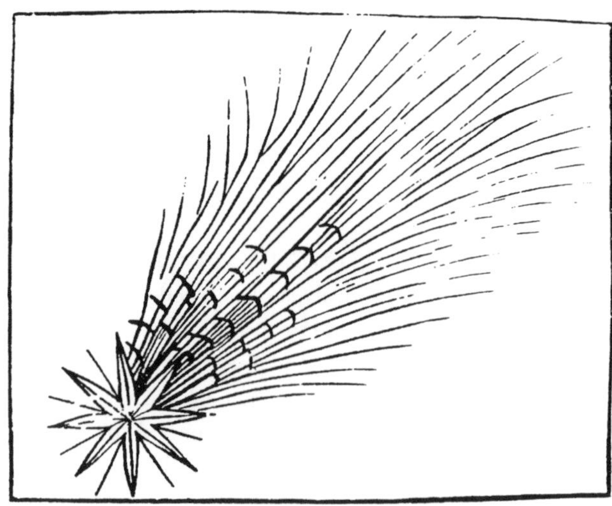

Halley's Comet as shown in the Nuremberg Chronicle, 684 CE MOORE, PATRICK, AND JOHN MASON. (1984) *THE RETURN OF HALLEY'S COMET*. NEW YORK: NORTON, 45.

In 1493 Ivan III triumphantly assumed the title "Sovereign of all Russia" and claimed a divine right to rule as both head of the state and the church of the Third Rome. Ivan married a Greek princess (Sophia Padeologos), constructed a genealogy linking him to Caesar Augustus, making it possible for him to call himself "Tsar" (Slavonic for "Caesar"). During this time, another apocalyptic figure, Filofei (Philotheos), a monk of Pskov, recognized Moscow as the "Third Rome" and its prince as the holy emperor. In a prophetic epistle he penned for the occasion, Filofei proclaims: "our Lord [the Muscovite grand prince] is the only Christian tsar in the whole world. . . . All Christian kingdoms have been united in this one single kingdom [*snidoshasia*]: two Romes have fallen, the third one stands, and fourth one there shall not be" (Tschizewskij 1978: 92).

By 1606, after a series of ineffective rulers, the Third Rome was near a state of complete disorder. It was a time in Russian history filled with popular movements, peasant uprisings, and upheavals in religious life. The Old Believers—conservative Orthodox Christians who follow the traditional Russian liturgies in the face of rapid change and modernization—remember 1666 as the year of the appearance of the Antichrist heralding the End. "In the year 1666 the reign of antichrist began in Russia," states Berdyaev ([1947] 1992: 31). The apocalypse of 1666 was the Great Schism that split the Russian state into two opposing factions, each claiming to be the true "Holy Russia."

Patriarch Nikon (1605–81), a friend of the tsar, became an unrelenting liturgical reformer in his desire to make Moscow the global center of Orthodoxy. In 1653 he introduced Greek (foreign) rites into the historic Russian church. Nikon was opposed and confronted by the powerful archpriest, Avvakum, who declared the patriarch to be the Antichrist. If the Patriarch was the Antichrist, and the tsar his servant, then there could be no legitimate priesthood, patriarch, or tsar. Truly the end had come.

Old Believers read the Book of Revelation (13:18) and the Book of Faith (a compilation of Ukrainian eschatological works) and calculated that the end of the world would come in 1666. Millions fled to the forests, hills, and remote areas to avoid persecution and await the end. And so, in the Year of the Beast (1666), an official body of the Russian Orthodox Church met in Moscow and condemned the Old Believers as "schismatics" and heretics. The Apocalypse of the Old Believers, according to Berdyaev, imbued the Russian people with a predictable pattern of apocalyptic expectation of the coming antichrist, "and from that time they will see Antichrist both in Peter the Great and in Napoleon and in many other figures" ([1947] 1992: 31).

Despite the persecution and condemnation, the church of the Old Believers did not end in 1666, but grew to over twenty million members in the twentieth century. However, the old world changed as the unified Muscovite Church-State came to an abrupt end. Filofei's declaration—"Two Romes have fallen, but a third one stands; and a fourth there shall not be"—was a prophesy fulfilled. A new modern Russia would powerfully emerge in the next century under Peter the Great (1682–1725).

Imperial Russia (1700–1905)

Peter's "Europeanization" of a medieval Asiatic country was a modern achievement that characterized Russia for the next two hundred years. In 1697 Peter traveled incognito through Europe with an official Russian delegation to recruit Western technicians to work and teach their crafts in Russia. Fifteen months later, after visiting England and Vienna, the tsar returned to Moscow to squelch a new rebellion. In the process, he established himself as the absolute monarch of all Russia.

Peter positioned Russia to take advantage of the European Enlightenment. He succeeded in reorienting Russia from a theocracy, looking backwards toward Byzantium, to a forward-looking monarchy, looking westward toward modern Europe. Within three years of 1699, the Tsar of Russia changed the official calendar, left Moscow, and founded a new capital along the Finnish gulf which became St. Petersburg. In 1711 he introduced secret police *(fiskal)* into the Russian state. In 1721 the patriarchate was abolished. His social and ecclesial reforms were total and unrelenting. Opposition came from many quarters, especially from the Old Believers, who concluded that Peter was the "Antichrist."

The cultural revolution (and religious persecution) of Peter the Great continued under Catherine II (1762–96), notable for her capacity to dabble with the ideas of Voltaire and Freemasonry while bringing miseries upon the Russian serfs. During Catherine's reign, the French Revolution of 1789 occurred and had its apocalyptic impact in Russia. Modern rationalistic and skeptical philosophies of Europe assumed radical or reactionary forms in Russia and brought an end to outdated, premodern ideologies.

In 1812 another apocalyptic figure emerged on the scene in the person of Napoleon Bonaparte. Old Believers as well as the common people of the land saw in him the spirit of Antichrist. After defeating Austria and Prussia, Napoleon moved against and occupied Russia's buffer state of Belarus; then attacked Russia. Ultimately he lost the war. While the invasion served to solidify the nation which had found new unity and purpose in a patriotic war, this unity was short-lived. The nation that had westernized itself under Peter's reforms had become by stages nihilistically, atheistically, and finally materialistically Marxist.

As the nineteenth century neared its end, so did the once invincible Russian Empire. Tsar Alexander III died in 1894, at the age of fifty, and his son Nicholas II ruled as the last Russian emperor. In 1895 the "Militant Union for the Liberation of the Working Classes" arose in St. Petersburg, and in 1898, at a secret meeting in Minsk which Lenin attended, the "Social-Democratic Party of Russia" was founded. The political apocalypse was still seven years away.

The October 1905 revolution was contained and then suppressed for twelve years, but it was the beginning of the end of the Russian aristocracy. The 1917 revolution and the grand experiment of Soviet communism following World War I was about to begin.

Soviet Russia (1917–1991)

Russian revolutionary nihilism, in Berdyaev's view, represented the end of Renaissance humanism and a new transitional "dark ages." A converted Marxist, he welcomed the social revolution but quickly became disillusioned with the totalitarian results. "Only a spiritual renewal would return the light," wrote Berdyaev in exile in Paris ([1947] 1992: 17).

As a Marxist, Berdyaev believed that out of the dialectical process of contradiction and opposition, a new creative synthesis would emerge and bring into conjunction partial truths formerly in conflict. In other words, revolutionary Marxism over time would evolve into democratic socialism and a free society. As a Christian, Berdyaev hoped that Russia's experiment with Communism was a transitional working out of the inherent possibilities of the Russian soul. Russia's messianic mission in the world, its dream of universal fraternity and an all-embracing faith, required provisional revolutionary measures in the interest of a permanent social and spiritual transformation. The Soviet period, he predicted, would be surpassed by other stages in the process of cocreating the new world. Seen in this light, the achievements of Marxist-Leninism could be recognized, its faults corrected, and its essential vision carried forward into the age of the Spirit still to come (for Russia and the entire world).

From his prophetic perspective in 1947, Berdyaev envisioned the new epoch in Russian history as one built on the dialectical foundations of previous epochs and infused with the Spirit of God. The true Russia would certainly rise again—not patterned after any historic epoch but after divine intentions revealed in the human spirit. The new Russia would emerge, but he did not foresee it happening in his own lifetime. What did occur in his lifetime (although he only witnessed it from afar from his exile in Paris) were Stalinist atrocities that could only be described in the most negative apocalyptic language imaginable.

The United Soviet Socialist Republic came to an abrupt end five years after the Chernobyl catastrophe of 26 April 1986. In retrospective dating, the Chernobyl Prophecy is understood in Belarus and Ukraine to have forecast this apocalyptic end or an era.

A New Russian Millennialism: Nikolai Berdyaev

If Russian nationalistic millennialism ended in 1917 with the advent of Marxist-Leninism; and if the cold war with communism ended in 1991 with the end of the Soviet Union; and if the post–cold war ended in 1998 with the Russian economic collapse, how shall we characterize the new emergent era of Russian millennialism in the new century? Those who wish to follow Berdyaev's lead may anticipate the dawning of a spiritual age in which liberty and justice reign supreme. Berdyaev's vision of the new eschaton was active and creative, not passive or static. His faith was in the image of God in humanity, revealed in Christ who called human beings in freedom to cocreate with God the New World. His confidence was in this divine-human engagement at the end of history and beyond. He knew that the new age of the Spirit could not begin until the old order of church and society had passed away. The "end" was a necessary prerequisite of a new "beginning." Both moments he understood as an eschatological time *(kairos)*, transcending ordinary time and human history *(kronos)*, to which we are summoned and in which we participate here and now. In this sense, Berdyaev is a postmillennialist.

Berdyaev's postmillennialism is an eschatological vision of a spiritual age following the successful resolutions of apocalyptic moments in human history. The present age, Berdyaev insisted, must pass through the experience of death and crucifixion; otherwise it cannot attain resurrection and eternal life. Berdyaev, the prophet, decried both capitalism and communism as only partial solutions to the problem of injustice. The former ignores class struggle; the later denies freedom and creativity. Both must end. The Russian people, he said, will play a decisive role in world affairs in fulfillment of their messianic mission.

The world will end and be reborn. Humanity will be transformed from within and restored to wholeness and freedom. The cosmic event will be prophetic and ethically creative, and yet transcend time and history, for "the end of the world is man's responsibility as well as God's" (Berdyaev 1937 [*Spirit and Reality*]: 107).

Michael J. Christensen

Bibliography

Berdyaev, Nikolai. (1935) *Freedom and the Spirit.* New York: Charles Scribner's Sons.

——. (1937) *The Origin of Russian Communism.* London: Geoffrey Bles.

——. (1937) *Spirit and Reality.* London: Geoffrey Bles.

——. (1944) *Slavery and Freedom.* New York: Charles Scribners's Sons.

——. (1949) *Toward a New Epoch.* London: Geoffrey Bles.

——. (1950) *Dream and Reality,* translated by Katharine Lamgert. London: Geoffrey Bles.

——. (1952) *The Beginning and the End,* translated by R. M. French. London: Geoffrey Bles.

——. (1955) *The Meaning of the Creative Act.* London: Victor Gollancz.

——. (1957) *Dostoevsky,* translated by Donald Attwater. New York: Meridian Books.

——. ([1947] 1992) *The Russian Idea.* New York: Lindisfarne Press.

Boym, Svetlana. (1994) *Common Places: Mythologies of Everyday Life in Russia.* Cambridge, MA: Harvard University Press.

Christensen, Michael J. (1997) "The Chernobyl Apocalypse: A Theological Case Study." Ph.D. diss. Drew University, Madison, NJ.

Fedotov, George. ([1964–66] 1976) *The Russian Religious Mind,* vol. 1, *Kievan Christianity;* and vol. 2, *The Middle Ages.* Belmont, MA: Nordland Publishing Co.

Miliukov, Paul. (1975) *Outlines of Russian Culture,* vol. 3, edited and translated by Joseph Wieczynski. Gulf Breeze, Florida: Academic International Press.

Solovyov, Vladimir. (1990) *War, Progress and the End of History: Three Conversations Including a Short Story of the Anti-Christ.* Hudson, NY: Lindisfarne Press.

Tschizewskij, Dmitrij. (1978) *Russian Intellectual History*, translated by John C. Osborne, edited by Martin P. Rice. Ann Arbor, MI: Ardis.

Sabbatian Movement

The Sabbatian movement was a Jewish messianic movement centering around the figure of Sabbatai Zvi. It began in 1665 CE and persisted in various forms through the eighteenth century. It represents the largest Jewish messianic movement since the Bar Kokhba revolt of the second century CE.

The Sabbatian movement is notable for its appeal to Jews throughout the diaspora and for its persistence long after the death of its messiah. It represents a fusion of traditional Jewish messianic expectations with innovative mystical beliefs derived from the kabbalah (mystical theology) of Isaac Luria (1534–72). Arising in the wake of severe persecutions of Jews during the Polish Chmielnicki massacres (1648) and the Russian-Swedish War (1655), the movement offered redemptive hope to Jewish communities.

The Life of Sabbatai Zvi and the Early Sabbatian Movement

Sabbatai Zvi was born in 1626 in Smyrna, a city of the Ottoman Empire. A promising young student, he began to exhibit severe emotional fluctuations between 1642 and 1648. At this time he began performing "strange acts" against the strictures of normative Judaism. He also advanced messianic claims, resulting in his expulsion from Smyrna. Traveling to Constantinople, he continued performing his strange acts and was once again expelled for his odd religious behavior. He then went to Jerusalem, where he lived for a time as a respected member of the Jewish religious community.

In April 1665 Sabbatai Zvi went to a prophetic figure, Nathan of Gaza, to seek a cure for the depressions he viewed as demonic struggles. Nathan, however, experienced a vision in which he saw Zvi as the messiah. He convinced Zvi of his messianic status, which was officially proclaimed on 31 May 1665. Nathan remained in Gaza, advocating mass repentance and making messianic predictions, while Sabbatai Zvi traveled to Jerusalem and then to Smyrna. In September 1665 Nathan stated that the Jewish people's mystical task of cosmic restoration had been completed and that the era of redemption was at hand. He predicted one year until the start of messianic events. Between October and December of 1665, news of Sabbatai Zvi spread to Europe and throughout the diaspora, mainly by way of rumors and letters.

In Smyrna Zvi performed strange acts such as pronouncing the Tetragrammaton (the four letter name of God which is too holy to be spoken), eating forbidden foods, and deliberately defying the Jewish commandments. He encouraged others to follow him in these practices and accumulated a following of people from diverse socioeconomic backgrounds. For a three-week period in December 1665 business ceased and many people experienced prophetic trances in which they recited biblical verses and proclaimed Zvi the messiah. Penitential acts and festivities were conducted by Jews throughout the city. Similar events transpired in Constantinople without the presence of Zvi himself.

On 30 December 1665, Zvi was captured and imprisoned by the Turkish government. Well treated, Zvi was able to correspond with his followers in letters. The Sabbatian movement continued to grow, spreading throughout the diaspora. Important centers were Salonika, Smyrna, Constantinople, Morocco, Amsterdam, Hamburg, Venice, and Livorno. There are no reports of mass ecstasy among European Sabbatians, but penitential fervor was an important aspect of the movement in Europe. Some, filled with messianic zeal,

Portrait of Sabbatia Sevi, sketched in Smyrna in 1666. From Coenen, Thomas (1669) "Ydele Verwachtinge der Joden." Amsterdam. PRINCETON UNIVERSITY PRESS, PRINCETON, NJ, 1973.

STRANGE ACTS IN SMYRNA

On 12 December 1665 in Smyrna, Sabbatai Zvi and 500 followers broke into a large Portuguese synagogue with an axe. Zvi claimed that his attack on the door helped to eradicate forces of evil from the world. Once inside, he pronounced the Tetragrammaton and performed numerous strange acts, encouraging his followers to do the same. He called men and women alike to the Torah, claiming that he would redeem humanity from the sin of the Adam and Eve. Such equal treatment of women was unheard of in a Jewish religious setting. Sabbatai Zvi had extremely radical views involving women in the movement, and seemed to suggest the redemption he brought would elevate women to a level of social and religious equality with men. Proclaiming himself the redeemer and setting a date for the redemption on 18 June 1666, Zvi threatened to excommunicate the rabbis who opposed him and distributed messianic kingdoms to his followers. Many bystanders were moved by this dramatic demonstration to become members of Zvi's following. In the wake of this event, Sabbatian enthusiasm swept through the city of Smyrna.

Ellen D. Haskell

sold their property to travel to the Holy Land. Sabbatian enthusiasm climaxed in July and August 1666, fueled by Zvi's correspondence, pamphlets, rumors, and reports sent by Nathan from Gaza.

On 15 September 1666, Sabbatai Zvi was brought before the Turkish sultan. His followers expected him to remove the sultan's crown, place it on his own head and take control of the Ottoman Empire, as predicted by Nathan. However, Zvi was given a choice between execution and conversion to Islam. In a state of depression, he chose conversion. Sabbatai Zvi was considered an important convert and given a titled position at the sultan's court. He continued to believe himself to be the messiah, living in public as a Muslim while secretly practicing Jewish rituals and acts identified with his movement. In 1672 Zvi was arrested on charges of denying Islam and deported to Albania. He died on 17 September 1676.

The Sabbatian Movement after the Conversion of Sabbatai Zvi

Nathan of Gaza, often described as the true originator of the Sabbatian movement, was responsible for the vast majority of messianic predictions associated with Sabbatai Zvi in 1665–66 and later developed a mystical explanation for Zvi's conversion. Sabbatian theology is closely related to the kabbalah (mystical tradition) of Isaac Luria, which includes the idea that sparks of divinity trapped in the created world must be redeemed by Jews through the medium of the Torah's commandments. Mystically speaking, Nathan believed that the human work of cosmic redemption had been completed and that the messiah, in order to effect the final redemption, had to descend into the realm of evil, which was represented by the Ottoman Empire. There he would redeem the remaining divine sparks which only the soul of the messiah could elevate. According to Nathan's theology, the soul of the messiah had been struggling with the realm of evil since the beginning of creation, and was furthermore a unique entity not subject to the Torah and laws of the created world. Therefor, Sabbatai Zvi was able to purify the forces of evil through seemingly impure acts. This sort of paradoxical purity would characterize the movement for the next hundred years.

While many Sabbatians abandoned the movement after Zvi's conversion, the theology developed by Nathan and others was enough to sustain substantial Sabbatian communities in Turkey, Italy, and Poland, where it gained followers during the eighteenth century. In many parts of the diaspora, Jews had been forced to convert to Christianity or Islam, and Sabbatai Zvi's own conversion resonated with people who had lived as crypto-Jews, contributing to the movement's popularity. One Sabbatian theologian in the Ottoman Empire, Abraham Cardozo (1626–1706), developed the idea that Sabbatai Zvi's conversion rescued all Jews from a similar fate.

Varied reactions to Sabbatai Zvi's conversion were developed in Jewish communities. Some Sabbatians believed that Zvi would still bring redemption; they remained normative Jews in outward appearance while continuing to follow a Sabbatian theology. Others, like Mordecai ben Hayyim of Eisenstadt (1650–1729) employed the traditional Jewish idea that there are two messiahs—the Messiah ben Joseph who comes to prepare the world and the Messiah ben David who heralds the redemption—to advocate that Zvi was simply the first messiah. Others believed Sabbatai Zvi would return from beyond the grave. In 1700 a Polish Jew named Judah Hasid took several followers to the Holy Land to witness Zvi's return, but the group was disappointed and many of its followers converted to Islam. In 1669 and 1671 Jewish authorities in Poland officially excommunicated Sabbatians. Another Polish religious leader related to the Sabbatian movement, Jacob Frank (1726–91), led many of his followers to convert to Catholicism in the 1750s.

In Salonika in 1683, a group of 200–300 families converted to Islam, where they became known as the Doenmeh (converts), leading crypto-Jewish lives and marrying only among themselves. This group split into several subgroups, the most notorious of which developed in the early eighteenth century around Baruchiah Russo, who claimed to be the reincarnation of Sabbatai Zvi. His followers practiced extreme antinomian acts such as ritually eating forbidden foods and engaging in forbidden sexual activities. The reasoning behind this behavior was based on the idea that a new Torah with new commandments would be received in the messianic age, while the old Torah of the preredemptive era would no longer be valid. Forbidden acts were ritually practiced in solidarity with the Torah of the new era. This particular Sabbatian group existed in Salonika until the 1920s.

Ironically, although most Sabbatians remained normative Jews in their exterior behavior, all Sabbatian thought came to be associated with extreme antinomian acts, and Sabbatians gained a radical reputation that was not always deserved. Moderate Sabbatians existed throughout the diaspora during the eighteenth century, confusing religious authorities concerned with eradicating the movement. This proved especially difficult since great emphasis was often placed on the secrecy of Sabbatian beliefs. Eventually, however, Sabbatian fervor declined, and Sabbatian theology has not played a major role in Jewish thought in the nineteenth and twentieth centuries.

Conclusions

The Sabbatian movement was the largest Jewish messianic movement since the second century CE. Sabbatians were found among Jews of diverse socioeconomic stations throughout the diaspora, giving the movement an astonishing sphere of influence. The charismatic person of Sabbatai Zvi, along with the prophetic leader Nathan of Gaza, provided ample material for the development of a unique Sabbatian theology with roots in sixteenth-century Jewish mysticism. The converted Messiah and the doctrine of theological secrecy, or crypto-Sabbatianism, played important roles in the movement's thought after 1666. Radical followers of the movement willingly converted to Christianity and Islam, living secretly Jewish lives. Some of these groups, but not all, practiced antinomian acts in the tradition of Sabbatai Zvi.

There have been several smaller Jewish messianic groups. A notable group to observe at the end of the current millennium is that of the Lubavitch Hasidim, who are developing a messianic theology around the figure of their recently deceased rabbi. It is also interesting to contrast the Sabbatian movement and its converted messiah with the martyred messiah of early Christianity. Still, the Sabbatian movement is unique among messianic groups that remained within the sphere of Judaism, both in terms of geographic area and the vast scale of its theological repercussions.

Ellen D. Haskell

See also Judaism Messianism

Bibliography

Liebes, Yehuda (1993) *Studies in Jewish Myth and Jewish Messianism,* translated by Batya Stein. Albany, NY: State University of New York Press.

Scholem, Gershom. (1973) *Sabbatai Sevi: The Mystical Messiah,* translated by R. J. Zwi Werblowsky. Princeton, NJ: Princeton University Press.

——. (1974) *Major Trends in Jewish Mysticism.* New York: Schocken Books.

——. (1978) *Kabbalah.* New York: Meridian.

Sharot, Stephen. (1982) *Messianism, Mysticism, and Magic: A Sociological Analysis of Jewish Religious Movements.* Chapel Hill, NC: University of North Carolina Press.

Salvation

Salvation, as understood in the Hebrew Bible (OT), the New Testament, as well within ancient Jewish and early Christian tradition, involves several related concepts. It can refer to a blessed state of an individual after death, usually involving eternal life in a spiritual realm beyond this physical world. Or, it can describe a transformed world at the end of history in which dead are resurrected, and along with those living in that time, enjoy a perfected existence forever. To be saved is to be liberated or rescued from death, injustice, tragedy, evil, and suffering. Whether such salvation comes immediately at the death of an individual, or at the end of history in a millennial transformation, or in a combination of both ideas, the essential hope remains the same.

Life after Death in the Hebrew Bible

The ancient Hebrews pictured the universe divided into three parts or realms, as did most other ancient civilizations (including the Babylonians, Egyptians). There was the upper realm of the Firmament (Sky) or Heavens, the dwelling place of God and his angelic court, as well as the place of the sun, moon, planets, and stars. Here no mortal belonged. Then there was the realm of earth below, what the first chapter of Genesis calls "the dry land." This was seen as the proper human place, shared with all the other forms of plant and animal life—a thoroughly mortal realm. The earth was seen as a flat disk; at the edges were the threatening waters of chaos, held back by the command of God (Genesis 1:9–10; Psalms 104:5–9). Finally, below the earth was the dark realm of the dead, which was called Sheol by the Hebrews and Hades by the Greeks. Psalms 115:16–18 puts it succinctly: "The heavens are Yahweh's heavens, but the earth he has given to the sons of men. The dead do not praise Yahweh, nor do any that go down into silence. But we [the living] will bless Yahweh from this time forth and for evermore." The ancient Hebrews had no idea of an immortal soul living a full and vital life beyond death, nor of any resurrection or return from death. Human beings, like the beasts of the field, are made of "dust of the earth," and at death they return to that dust (Genesis 2:7, 3:19). The Hebrew word *nephesh*, traditionally translated "living soul" but more properly understood as "living creature," is the same word used for all breathing creatures and refers to nothing immortal. The same holds true for the expression translated as "the breath of life" (see Genesis 1:24, 7:21–22). It is physical, "animal life." For all practical purposes, death was the *end*. As Psalms 115:17 says, the dead go down into "silence"; they do not participate, as do the living, in praising God (seen then as the most vital human activity). Psalms 146:4 is like an exact reverse replay of Genesis 2:7: "When his breath departs he returns to his earth; on that very day his thoughts [plans] perish." Death is a one-way street; there is no return. As Job laments: "till the heavens be no more he will not awake" (Job 14:10–12).

All the dead go down to Sheol, and there they lie in sleep together—whether good or evil, rich or poor, slave or free (Job 3:11–19). It is described as a region "dark and deep," "the Pit," "the land of forgetfulness," cut off from both God and human life above (Psalms 6:5; 88:3–12). Though in some texts Yahweh's power can reach down to Sheol (Psalms 139:8), the dominant idea is that the dead are abandoned forever. This idea of Sheol is negative in contrast to the world of life and light above, but there is no idea of judgment, or of reward and punishment. If one faces extreme circumstances of suffering in the realm of the living above, as did Job, it can even be seen as a welcome relief from pain—see the third chapter of Job. But basically it is a kind of "nothingness," an existence that is barely existence at all, in which a "shadow" or "shade" of the former self survives (Psalms 88:10).

This rather bleak picture of death is one that prevails throughout most of the Hebrew Bible. It is found throughout the Pentateuch (the Books of Genesis, Exodus, Leviticus, Numbers, and Deuteronomy), and it runs through the books of history, poetry, and prophecy (from Joshua through Malachi) with few exceptions. Rather than recording the death of Enoch, the genealogy of Genesis 5:24 simply says, "He was not, for God took him." Elijah is taken to heaven in a chariot of fire (2 Kings 2). Generally speaking, however, in ancient Hebrew thinking there is no concept of the salvation for the individual human person after death.

Daniel 12:2–3 is the earliest text in the Bible to speak clearly and absolutely about a resurrection of the dead, both wicked and righteous. His reference to the dead as "those who sleep in the earth" shows that he does not yet know, or share an interest in, their so called "interim" state (i.e., before the resurrection at the end). 2 Maccabees (written sometime between the first century BCE and the first century CE) reflects an interesting state of development in this regard. Not only does the author believe in the resurrection (at least of the righteous martyrs), but he advocates prayer and sacrifice for the dead and believes that they can intercede for those on earth and vice versa (2 Maccabees 12:43–45, 15:11–16). Likewise, in 2 Esdras the dead are fully conscious, already suffering either punishment or comfort in various levels and compartments of the heavenly realms, awaiting the final day of judgment (2 Esdras 7). Wisdom of Solomon upholds this view of salvation a necessary part of proper faith in Yahweh (3:14). Here the view of the immortal soul that departs the body at death is combined with a view of final and future resurrection of the dead. We know from later texts, like the Ethiopic Enoch (third century BCE to first century CE), and now the Dead Sea Scrolls, that such views were becoming common among various Jewish groups during this period.

The End of History in the Hebrew Bible

Scholars use the term "eschatology" to refer to what they call the "last things," i.e., the events and realities at the end of history or, more popularly speaking, "the end of the world." However, this idea of the "end of the world" does not necessarily mean the destruction of the planet. More often it refers to the end of an "age," following which history takes a dramatic turn for the better. Eschatology addresses these questions: Where is history headed? And what will be its final determination and meaning?

The idea of a good future for the nation of Israel begins with texts in Genesis, which promise such to Abraham and his descendants. God tells Abraham, "I will make of you a great nation, and I will bless you, and make your name great,

MILLENNIAL HUMOR

Jesus and Satan argue about who is the better programmer. This goes on for a few hours until they agree to hold a contest, with God as the judge. They set themselves before their computers and begin. They type furiously, lines of code streaming up the screen, for several hours straight. Seconds before the end of the competition, a bolt of lightning strikes, knocking out the electricity. Moments later, the power is restored, and God announces that the contest is over. He asks Satan to show what he has come up with.

Satan is visibly upset, and cries, "I have nothing! I lost it all when the power went out!"

"Very well, then," says God, "let us see if Jesus fared any better."

Jesus enters a command, and the screen comes to life in vivid display, the voices of an angelic choir pour forth from the speakers. Satan is astonished. He stutters, "B-b-but how? I lost everything, yet Jesus' program is intact. How did he do it?"

God smiled all-knowingly, "Jesus saves."

so that you will be a blessing" (Genesis 12:2). Later he is told "to your descendants I will give this land [i.e., Palestine]" (Genesis 15:18). These elements of "chosen people," covenant, land, and blessings form the foundation of later views of collective salvation.

Beginning in the eighth century, and well down into the sixth century BCE, the nation of Israel suffered through political, social, and military catastrophes. First under the Assyrians, then successively under the Babylonians and Persians, large parts of the population were exiled and their land was occupied. This is the time of the Hebrew Prophets—whose books comprise Isaiah through Malachi. It is primarily in these texts—written before, during, and after this period of exile—that we find the beginnings of a new view of the salvation (Isaiah 2:2–4, 11–12, 27:12–13, 35, and 66:18–24; Jeremiah 3:15–25, 16:14–21, 23:1–8, 30:31; Ezekiel 11:14–21, 34:11–31, 36:8–38, 37, 40–48; Hosea 1:10–11, 2:16–23, 3:1–5; Joel 3; Amos 9:9–15; Micah 5; Zephaniah 3; Haggai 2; Zechariah 10:6–12, 12–14). It seems to develop over time from a rather simple hope for the ultimate restoration of the national fortunes of the tribes of Israel, to a fantastic vision of total cosmic renewal and transformation. Isaiah describes a time when even the violence of nature, "red in tooth and claw," will end: "The wolf shall dwell with the lamb, and the leopard shall lie down with the kid, and the calf and the lion and the fatling together, and a little child shall lead them. . . . They shall not hurt or destroy in all my holy mountain; for the earth shall be full of the knowledge of Yahweh as the waters cover the sea" (Isaiah 11:6–9).

This transformed state of things is so dramatic, it is like a new or second creation. A "new heavens and new earth," Isaiah terms it (Isaiah 65:17–25, 66:22–24). It is inaugurated by a highly idealized Davidic King (Isaiah 11:1–5; Micah 5:2–4). Total peace reigns among all nations (Isaiah 2:4; Micah 4:3). The suffering and toils of life are eliminated as "Yahweh wipes away tears from ail faces," and death itself is "swallowed up forever" (Isaiah 25:8). This apparently includes the "resurrection" of the righteous dead of the past (Isaiah 26:19). This era of complete justice and righteousness is ushered in by the terrible Day of Yahweh's wrath in which all wicked sinners are utterly destroyed. The topography of the land of Israel and the city of Jerusalem is drastically altered: The deserts bloom like a rose; fresh water flows into the Dead Sea; and the whole Jerusalem area is elevated (Isaiah 35; Zechariah 14:8–11; Ezekiel 47–48). Some few texts seem to imply that wicked angelic powers are also disposed of in this overthrow of all evil by Yahweh (Isaiah 24:21–22, 27:1). Late texts like Daniel (second century BCE) clearly envision the resurrection of the dead, the punishment of the wicked, and the arrival of the utopian kingdom of God (see the Dream Visions of chapters 2, 7, and 11–12). Salvation here is eschatological. It comes *at the end* of history, through God's dramatic intervention in the affairs of this world, as the new transformed age is inaugurated.

Life after Death in the New Testament

As we move to the period of Greek and Roman domination of the eastern Mediterranean world (the fourth century BCE, to the first century CE), the biblical materials reflect drastic development with regard to the view of salvation. Two views dominate: the hope of an eschatological transformation of the cosmos and the notion that an immortal soul escapes the body at death to enter the heavenly world. Both are closely tied to a deep despair regarding the course of history and the possibility of things ever changing. How and when might the many dreamlike promises of salvation for God's faithful people, which I have just surveyed, ever be realized?

The general view of the future found throughout the New Testament incorporates and builds upon most of these developments and changes. Jesus clearly takes his stand for belief in the resurrection of the dead, in contrast to Jewish groups such as the Pharisees who denied such ideas (Luke 20:27–40). Paul expounds the idea of some kind of a "spiritual body," definitely *not* "flesh and blood," but immortal and glorified. What connection this "spiritual body" is supposed to have with the body put in the tomb is not clear (1 Corinthians 15:42–54). As for the "state of the dead" before the end, Paul prefers the image of "sleep" (1 Corinthians 15:6, 18, 20, 51; 1 Thessalonians 4:13–18, 5:9–10). But he also believed that the "spirit" of a departed Christian went to "be with Christ" (Philippians 1:19–26; 2 Corinthians 5:6–10; 1 Thessalonians 4:14). Several places in the New Testament we clearly find the notion that the dead are conscious, dwelling somewhere in the heavenly realms beyond, and awaiting, either in torment or comfort, the final judgment (Luke 16:19–31, 23:43; 1 Peter 3:18–20, 4:6; Revelation 6:9–11, 7:9–12). The New Testament book of Revelation closes with two resurrections, one before and the other after the millennium, involving all humans who have ever lived (Revelation 20).

The End of History in the New Testament

The early Christians believed in the "close of the age"—and also what might properly be called the "end of the world." They looked to a future, following the return *(parousia)* of Jesus in the clouds of heaven, in which the physical world would "pass away," replaced by a new creation (Romans 8:21; 2 Peter 3:10–13; Revelation 21–22). Here, is it difficult to lay out a single eschatological scheme for all the New Testament documents. Revelation, chapter 20, speaks of a thousand-year reign of Christ on earth before the "new creation" (see Revelation 1:6, 2:25–26, 3:21, 5:10, 11:15–18). Paul seems to anticipate such a time, between the coming of Christ and the final "end," when the elect group will "judge the world . . . and angels" and reign as kings in the kingdom of God (1 Corinthians 15:23–28, 4:8, 6:2–3). The author of Luke through Acts speaks of Christ coming back to "restore" all the things spoken by the prophets (Acts 3:20–21), and Jesus chooses twelve disciples to rule over the regathered twelve tribes of Israel in the Kingdom of God (Luke 22:28–30). This rather "literal" or concrete view of the Kingdom of God on earth, drawn from the Hebrew Prophets, appears often in the Synoptic tradition. Jesus will return to earth and sit on his glorious throne, surrounded by his twelve apostles ruling, over the twelve tribes (Matthew 19:28–30). All the Old Testament patriarchs will be resurrected and participate in this Messianic kingdom (Matthew 8:11–12). The nations will be gathered before this throne of Christ and judged (Matthew 25:31–46). Whether all this can be fully systematized or not, Revelation, chapters 19–22, does contain the key elements of this overall vision of future salvation in some kind of rough order: the return of Christ, the utter defeat of Satan and his agents; the resurrection of the dead and the reign with the saints on earth; a return of Satan to lead the nations against Jerusalem; their defeat and the immersion of the Devil and the false prophet in a lake of burning sulfur for eternal torment; a final resurrection and judgment; and the new creation and final perfection. Most New Testament passages on future salvation fit somewhere into this general scheme. And most of the themes cited earlier from the Hebrew Prophets anticipate one part or another of this New Testament view of salvation.

James D. Tabor

Bibliography

Brandon, S. G. F. (1967) *The Judgement the Dead.* New York: Scribner's Sons.

Cullman, Oscar. (1965) "Immortality of the Soul and Resurrection of the Dead: The Witness of the New Testament." In *Immortality and Resurrection: Death in the Western World: Two Conflicting Currents of Thought*, edited by K. Stendahl. New York: Macmillan, 9–53.

Heidel, Alexander. (1963) *The Gilgamesh Epic and Old Testament Parallels.* Chicago: University of Chicago Press.

Hick, John. ([1976] 1994) *Death and Eternal Life.* New York: Harper & Row; reprint Louisville, KY: Westminster/John Knox Press.

Nickelsburg, George. (1972) *Resurrection, Immortality and Eternal Life in Intertestamental Judaism* (Harvard Theological Studies 26). Cambridge, MA: Harvard University Press.

Science Fiction Literature

Science fiction (SF) is a genre of science-oriented literature that emerged with the first SF magazine *Amazing Stories* published in 1926 by Hugo Gernsback (1884–1967) who later coined the term "science fiction." Although SF publishing is dominated by novels, the subculture is anchored in professional magazines, fan magazines called "fanzines," local SF clubs, the Science Fiction Writers of America (which gives the Nebula awards), and the annual World Science Fiction Convention (which gives the Hugo awards).

More loosely, "science fiction" applies to two parallel genres: (1) "sci-fi" movies or television, and (2) speculative mainstream literature that employs scientific metaphors in utopian fantasies or social criticism. Religious influences on SF are so weak that the amalgam of apocalypse, messiah, judgment, and utopia that marks biblical millenarianism is extremely rare. However, many works focus on one or more of these elements, chiefly in the context of non-Christian mythologies. Full-fledged millenarianism occasionally appears at the intersections of these genres, and between the three major ideologies of SF literature.

Three Dimensions

SF has three ideological factions or dimensions. First is the original "hard-science" tradition in SF, with Jules Verne (1828–1905) for its chief precursor, which emphasizes new scientific discoveries and technological inventions. Second is a type blending literary experimentation with social-science speculations, which was called "New Wave" in the 1960s when Harlan Ellison (1934–), Judith Merril (1923–1998), and others promoted it. Finally, SF is connected to a variety of forms of fantasy which employ scientific metaphors as a way of suspending disbelief and adding color to otherwise supernatural or action-oriented stories.

Hard-science SF consists of generally optimistic stories about new technology or in which crucial parts of the action depend upon the physical sciences. Many of the stories take current knowledge from one of the sciences and logically extrapolate what might be the next steps taken in that science. Ideally the author provides a rational explanation for everything that happens, and the ideal character is cool, unemotional, clever, and intelligent. Several works by Isaac Asimov (1920–92) apply these values to the social and behavioral sciences, postulating rigid natural laws that constrain human action. His *Foundation* series concerns the fall of a galactic empire and the efforts of a team of scientists to hasten the next golden age, and thus it enters the territory of millenarianism. However, the chief scientist Hari Seldon is no supernatural messiah; he merely develops the mathematical formulas that will allow psychohistorians to shape history through patient application of small forces upon societal evolution. The most they hope to accomplish is to reduce the Dark Ages from a predicted 30,000 years to 1,000; and Asimov offers no clear image of an ideal society.

New Wave SF tends to be ironic or pessimistic. The most influential works tend to be avant-garde fiction experimenting with new styles, employing language in innovative ways in order to evoke unaccustomed emotions. The fiction resonates with the social sciences, although this may merely reflect a common connection to the political left wing, and many stories are critical of conventional society. Protagonists either are average people in unusual situations or are strange and unusual characters. Armageddon is something to be relished for the aesthetic possibilities it offered, as in the novel *Dhalgren* by Samuel R. Delany (1942–). A nearly deserted American city, named Bellona, decays under a bloated sun and a second moon, as The Kid wanders aimlessly, finding artistic images in everything from the tongue of a rapist to the protagonists' own bowel movements. Thus, far from being a messiah who could redeem the world from Armageddon, The Kid is an artist who creates by experiencing degradation.

The cluster of fantasy styles connected to science fiction includes horror stories that describe the end of the world, and sword-and-sorcery tales in which fantastic heroes battle wicked sorcerers. Fantasy concerns magic in barbarian lands more often than science, although some writers assert that their universe has a different set of natural laws from those found in our world. Heroes are strong and brave, and the tales are like ancient myths and legends. The classic example is the "Barsoom" novels by Edgar Rice Burroughs (1875–1950). In the first book, the spirit of an American named John Carter is wafted to Mars, where the previously advanced civilization has fallen as the planet's water and air dissipated. At the end, after wild swordplay adventures, his heroism and telepathy halt the loss of atmosphere, preserving the feudal society but not inaugurating a new age.

SF and Sci-Fi Millennia

Millennial SF tends to be created either by authors working outside these ideologies or through unusual syntheses of SF and sci-fi. Both Raymond F. Jones (1915–) and Frank Herbert (1920–86) produced millenarian novels while remaining aloof from the ideological factions. *Things to Come*, an influential 1936 film, was based on a prophetic book by H. G. Wells (1866–1946), and J. Michael Straczynski's TV series *Babylon 5* had close connections to American SF literature, notably to Ellison's works and to the parapsychology novels of Alfred Bester (1913–87).

Human society disintegrates and individuals lose all hope in *The Alien* by Jones. The Howling Craze sweeps the cities, as the masses vent their despair. Government leaders commit suicide. The populace longs for a superhuman messiah, and the last sane people flee into space. In the Asteroid Belt, archaeologists discover the preserved body of Demarzule, leader of a lost civilization, along with the technology to revive him. Brought to Earth, Demarzule is gradually resurrected, while a religious movement sweeps the earth expecting him to be its messiah. Too late, the scientists discover he was not the Jesus of his civilization, but the Hitler. In desperation, the scientists search the galaxy for the ancient race that once defeated Demarzule, and success gives one of them the supernatural power to destroy him. Ultimately, the scientist faces the choice of becoming god or allowing humanity to mature beyond the need for a messiah.

Herbert's *Dune* is set in the far future when humanity has spread across the galaxy, forsworn computers, and lost interest in science. Padishah Emperor Shaddam IV rules, and a mysterious female cult called the Bene Gesserit shapes history by manipulating religious faiths and genetic lines. Time nears for the messianic Kwisatz Haderach to be born, a male Bene Gesserit whose psychic powers bridge space and time. Possibly he is Paul, son of Duke Leto Atreides. Feudal House Atreides has just transferred to the desert planet, Arrakis, where a geriatric spice is mined and ship-sized worms rule the sands. A perfidious attack by House Harkonnen, aided by the emperor, smashes Atreides in a horrible slaughter. Paul and his Bene Gesserit mother escape into the desert, hoping the mysterious Fremen will help Paul prove he is the messiah who will sweep the Harkonnen aside and unleash religious war throughout the empire.

Things to Come foretells a second world war lasting from 1940 until 1967, nearly destroying civilization, and its utopian aftermath. The film begins at Christmas in the home of John Cabal, in Everytown. As boys play with toy armies and grandfather muses about the future he will never see, John and his friends debate the technological benefits of war. An air-raid begins the holocaust, which ends when a man-made plague, the wandering sickness, sweeps the shattered earth. A feudal chief runs Everytown in 1970, when John Cabal returns in a futuristic aircraft, to establish a new civilization. The error of mankind had been letting warriors exploit science, rather than accepting the benign dictatorship of the scientists.

Babylon 5 is a vast diplomatic city floating between interstellar empires, replete with numerous religions both familiar and exotic. Commander John Sheridan of Earth falls in love with ambassador Delenn of Minbar, unaware that humans are reincarnated Minbari. Conflict increases mysteriously between the races, until the Centauri inexplicably conquer the Narn. Gradually, John and Delenn realize that The Shadows are manipulating everyone toward Armageddon. John organizes a coalition for peace, including the advanced and remote Vorlons. He completes a suicide mission against the Shadows, and returns resurrected with knowledge of the ultimate truth. Both the Shadows and Vorlons are arrogant races that evolved early in the universe and manipulate lesser beings in competing with each other. Vorlons demand order, whereas Shadows thrive on chaos. Neither are worthy deities despite their godlike power. John banishes them from the galaxy, then ascends to a higher spiritual plane, leaving the remaining lesser races to live in peace.

Conclusion

Writers in the SF factions shy away from millenarian fantasies, for the same reason members of mainstream churches do, namely that their hopes are already pinned on something else. Hard-science writers believe incremental scientific research can achieve a better world, whereas New Wave writers trust literary sensitivity and social science. Fantasy writers prefer a static feudal society against which to stage their magical adventures. Writers like Jones and Herbert, who worked outside the ideologies, wrote millennial novels, and some rare artists like Straczynski who work on the boundary between SF and sci-fi paint millennial visions in television or movies. Science fiction millenarianism tends to bypass Christianity and imagine exotic creeds.

William Sims Bainbridge

See also Film, Literature

Bibliography

Asimov, Isaac. (1951) *Foundation.* New York: Gnome Press.
Bainbridge, William Sims. (1986) *Dimensions of Science Fiction.* Cambridge, MA: Harvard University Press.
Bassom, David. (1997) *The A–Z Guide to Babylon 5.* New York: Dell.
Burroughs, Edgar Rice. (1917) *A Princess of Mars.* Chicago: McClurg.
Delany, Samuel R. (1975) *Dhalgren.* New York: Bantam.
Herbert, Frank. (1965) *Dune.* Philadelphia: Chilton.
Wells, H. G. (1933) *The Shape of Things to Come.* London: Hutchinson.

The views expressed in this article do not necessarily represent the views of the National Science Foundation or the United States.

Secular Millennialism

The twin concepts of millennialism and millenarianism are generally associated with forms of religious belief or forms of transcendence that are unique and specific to individual ethnic cultural and religious groups. At first sight secular thinking may appear entirely unrelated to the religious millennial apocalypse. However a belief in the perfectibility of humanity and the establishment of a material paradise on earth, might be said to fit a classic postmillennialist model. In some respects medieval Christianity itself aided the process through encouraging more emphasis upon the experience of living in an endtime. Individuals who rejected the Judeo-Christian and other religious millennia have, throughout history clearly reacted to these beliefs and created counter-cultural responses, and dialogues with various forms of religiosity.

The Middle Ages and the Renaissance

However it is equally true that the hope generated by the expectations held by religious groups throughout history has had a significant impact upon the ways that philosophers and thinkers have striven to view the existence of mankind on earth. Thus alongside the apocalyptic tradition, which was a constant presence in medieval Christianity, there was also a growing belief in ideas of progress which informed the achievements of the scientific world of the Middle Ages. Exploration of the natural world and man's place in it became a method of glorifying God and his creation. The consequences of these discoveries were to produce material and moral improvement for humanity in this life and increase its focus upon its importance as a thing in itself. With the development of Renaissance humanism and the later Enlightenment, the role of science came to the forefront of philosophical exploration of man and the universe. The eventual realization that explanations of the universe could exist independently of a deity led many individuals to speculate that humanity's quest for scientific enlightenment might remove reliance upon religious explanations and so also remove the ideological power of the idea of the millennialist apocalypse. The first great flowering of these attempts to construct a nontheistic and materialist lifestyle might be described as utopian.

Pre-Modern Secular Millennialism

While Renaissance humanism clearly had its origins in the changing religious outlook of the period, it owed much to elements that were to become central to secular thinking. The founding text of modern utopian thinking—Thomas More's *Utopia* (1516)—in many respects stands upon the threshold between the medieval and the modern. More created a society filled with numerous rules, regulations, and forms of surveillance that accepted the pessimism of St. Augustine about man's nature. Nonetheless, in carrying out the governmental function ordained by God to protect humanity from itself, there were clearly advantages to the cohesion of this resulting society that seem to anticipate the structure of the modern state and society.

More's work was intended to show how a godly Commonwealth might be created, yet its attacks upon the distribution of wealth within existing society ensured the book was a critique which gave birth to the genre of utopian (and arguably dystopian) literature, which stretches on to the twentieth century. More's writings give a clear sense that legislative action based upon altruism can produce tangible improvements in the nature of society. His utopia contains programs of sanitation, extension of educational opportunities, and limitations upon the working day alongside less recognizably modern prohibitions on private discussion of politics.

Some elements of Enlightenment thought actually encouraged the new idea of progress to manifest itself as a belief. Advances in technology, standard of living, and other purely material aspects of culture could appear to be divinely inspired. In this respect a "progress" essentially became a "faith," and a redefinition of providence—a trust in the benign nature of the historical process that would produce acceptable and transcendental resolution of human problems. For this form of secular millennialism, the advance of humanity was fostered by an alliance between science and religion in the pursuit of temporal improvement. Robert Boyle had argued that perfectionism offered a spur to scientific investigation and knowledge of creation.

Early Modern Secular Millennialism

Many philosophers in the West from the end of the eighteenth century onwards argued that man's own influence upon the environment would create a perfect existence upon earth that did not live under the perceived fear of the millennial apocalypse that was central to revealed religion. Moreover thinkers like John Locke also argued that the environment itself was solely responsible for the development of the mind of humanity; at a stroke removing innate religious capacities and relocating the responsibility for replacing those capacities with human society. Progress after the Enlightenment became associated with liberation and history itself was seen as a catalogue of humanity's moral development. One particular branch of utopian/secular millennial thinking, which branched off from this philosophy, was the scientific materialist triumph of the proletariat envisioned by Karl Marx.

Many quasi-materialist utopians such as Robert Owen (1771–1858) in Britain and America, Charles Fourier (1772–1837) and Henri St. Simon (1760–1825) were an engagement with the Enlightenment on these terms. Fourier's system, like Owen's, resulted in experimentation in forms of communal living. While Owen's are better known and were more widespread, it was Fourier's short-lived community at

THE KINGDOM OF REASON

Religion, natural science, society, political institutions – everything was subjected to the most unsparing criticism: everything must justify its existence before the judgment-seat of reason or give up existence. Reason became the sole measure of everything. It was the time when, as Hegel says, the world stood upon its head; first in the sense that the human head, and the principles arrived at by its thought, claimed to be the basis of all human action and association; but by and by, also, in the wider sense that the reality which was in contradiction to these principles had, in fact, to be turned upside down. Every form of society and government then existing, every old traditional notion, was flung into the lumber-room as irrational; the world had hitherto allowed itself to be led solely by prejudices; everything in the past deserved only pity and contempt. Now, for the first time, appeared the light of day, the kingdom of reason; henceforth superstition, injustice, privilege, oppression, were to be superseded by eternal truth, eternal Right, equality based on Nature and the inalienable rights of man.

Source: Engels, Frederick. (1892) *Socialism: Utopian and Scientific*, translated by Edward Aveling. London: Swan Sonnenschein & Co.

Brook Farm, Massachusetts, that attracted Ralph Waldo Emerson and Nathaniel Hawthorne to its ranks. Fourier's ideas appealed to the millenarian heaven of the dispossessed and echoed some of the millennial language used by Owen. He described existing civilization as a sink of corruption and emphasized the sumptuous feasting that awaited beneficiaries of his social system. Fourier also argued that there was a preordained life cycle for the earth, subdivided into clearly distinct periods with eventual arrival in a period of harmony and secular apocalypse. This was described in a language intended to reach down to the lowest strata of society, as some late-medieval and Renaissance millenarian movements had done. Thus the atmosphere would become perfumed, the dead would be transformed into vapors and the sea into lemonade, while predatory animals would be replaced by benign equivalents. Collectively these appeals to rationalism and reason, spiced with the appeal of premodern millennialism and millenarianism, pushed men and women toward perfection building upon their capacity to accumulate and apply the fruits of knowledge as a part of an infinite process.

Robert Owen conducted social engineering along environmentalist lines, arguing that human perfectibility was possible through his "Science of Society." This involved interest in everything from trade unionism to cooperation, phrenology, and communitarian living. The last of these involved communities in Britain (Orbiston and Queenwood), Ireland (Ralahine), and America (New Harmony). Often the "salvation" offered by Owen could be expressed in recognizably millenarian terms. These were contextualized with reference to the extraordinary events occurring throughout Europe as clear indicators that cataclysmic change was the currency of the age. The Owenite regeneration of community, the attack upon marriage and all other forms of the "old immoral" institution offered liberation from patriarchal oppression. In the 1830s and 1840s women such as Frances Morrison, Fanny Wright, Emma Martin, and Matilda Roalfe saw social relations organized upon rationalist Owenite principles as fundamental to the advancement of their feminism. For utopians, the imminent collapse of Christianity as the dominant form of social knowledge meant that the embryo forms of social science on offer from Owen, Fourier, and Saint-Simon considered themselves ready to act as replacements.

The last third of the nineteenth century and the early years of the twentieth saw this rebirth occur in the various movements of Arts and Crafts socialism and socialization prevalent in Britain, Europe, and America at the end of the nineteenth century. The Arts and Crafts embrace of the Gothic style, which took its lead from the writings of John Ruskin, admired the form for its ability to generate a close relationship between work and community aspiration and status. An example often cited by Ruskin was the cultural respect shown for the stonemasons of the great cathedrals of the High Gothic period is a case in point. The craft socialism of William Morris in particular was deeply concerned with the improvement of life in the here and now. The epitome of this was his utopian tract *News from Nowhere* that sought to provide a spiritual dimension to the raw materialism of Marx's revolutionary change. He drew the classically millenarian contrast between the misery and degradation of the present and the hope for a better time, although by now the utopian scheme was to be achieved after a secular revolutionary event.

The ripples from Morris's argument that all things should be beautiful and useful influenced the Garden City movement and the socialist politicians who constructed Britain's postwar welfare state. Many of the assumptions about town planning and the construction of environments supposedly conducive to aesthetic and social harmony influenced individuals from Frank Lloyd Wright in America to Le Corbusier and other modernist architects in Western Europe. This represented a movement onward from the small-scale utopian approach of the nineteenth century, since large-scale programs of social amelioration were now inspired by rational scientific ideas. In the twentieth century the development of such quasi-scientific philosophies as rationalism and scientism promoted a worldview that argued that the investigation and application of scientific and social theory would produce, and continue to produce, credible solutions to the numerous problems that beset the mid/late-twentieth-century world. Importantly, as a signpost toward the future of this phenomenon, Morris's craft socialism did go beyond fantasy and intended to provide the material means by which individual millennial utopias could be constructed in the here and now. However the sheer cost to individuals of the products of craftsmanship and the cost of extending the implications of Garden City planning to urban environments worldwide became an apparently spiraling cost that Western societies became less and less willing to bear.

Another late-nineteenth-century manifestation of the quest for secular alternatives to religious salvation was the rejuvenated popularity of the philosophy of positivism. This displayed two distinct forms in the period since 1870. While adherents of Auguste Comte's fully fledged "Religion of Humanity" were relatively few in number, the intellectual debt owed by many nineteenth-century thinkers to Comte's work was considerable. The positivism of Comte offered much to the beleaguered skeptic of Christianity who nonetheless craved satisfaction for religious sensibilities and instincts amid the triumph of scientific method over the superstitious and the spiritual. Thus there was a clear millenarian tinge to the suggestion from its adherents that positivism was not to be a replacement for religions but their ultimate fulfillment.

Comte argued that human civilization was developing through three clearly defined stages: theological, metaphysical, and positive. The call to participate in this vision was especially appealing to the intelligentsia and many in the medical, legal, and governmental professions in Britain including individuals such as George Elliot, John Stuart Mill, Frederic Harrison, and Gilbert Murray. Trade union emancipation, responsible government, both at home and in the empire, and the cause of moral education (freed from the taint of international competition and capitalist materialism) were all areas that received the intellectual and often practical attention of such leading positivists. In this development positivism had much in common with the craft socialism of William Morris since both contended capitalism and industrialism had undermined and was in the process of reversing human progress—in short that wealth should be socially produced, socially distributed, and socially consumed. Finally, positivism of this sort was outflanked by other collectivist solutions; it seemed merely eccentric and pedantic as sections of the modern socialist movement stole its clothes.

The second positivist strand was to be of more lasting effect. Comte is often cited as one of the founders of modern sociology and as the inspiration behind sociological investigation. In the 1960s this positivism would offer apparent solutions to the social problems that appeared to beset societies in Western Europe when the postwar world began to turn sour.

Twentieth-Century Secular Millennialism

The ideology of improvement in the twentieth century of which positivism was a strand became linked with conceptions that the products of technology and of scientific inquiry offered the best hope for the development of human civilization. In essence it was the optimistic pragmatism of philosopher Karl Popper that allowed a theory of progress with a vital role for scientific enquiry to take center stage. Popper's pragmatism made society undertake a constant search for more fulfilling answers to the problems it experienced. Moreover one of his most compelling views was that biological and mental evolution represented a form of evolution of theory: each evolutionary step forward constituted a testing of new theory, with survivors and victims.

Popper also suggested that scientific endeavor needed the protection of a specific form of government—as outlined in his book, *The Open Society and its Enemies*. Such a title recognized that this society already needed defending. His more obvious targets were the prewar European regimes he had escaped from, yet he also pointed out that forms of utopianism arrogantly ended the search for new answers to new questions. He argued that these blueprints for a transformed society were unworkable and naive in their expectation that change would come to an end. Thus modern rationalism discarded the prescriptive utopias of the previous century. Popper did not claim to have the answers, but he was certain that scientific endeavor would nonetheless provide them, and he viewed this progressive and ongoing use of scientific discovery as a spiritual adventure. Science suddenly became capable of revealing a world of invisible forces and previously unobserved phenomena all working in harmony and structured according to some rationale that did not need the overarching intelligence of a deity.

Popper's contribution to secular millennialism was to say that change could occur without some external intelligence being involved; and the apparatus of debate ended the dogmatic approach to knowledge that religious forms had encouraged since the Middle Ages. Popper wanted the knowledge intrinsic to art and science to come together and save science from the apparent arrogance of its claims to complete knowledge. Popper's insistence that solutions to problems were "work in progress" was a doctrine that was perfect for the postwar world. This climate, influenced by the economic philosophy of John Maynard Keynes, believed the formulation of social policy promoted by deficit financing could cure economic and social ills. Popper's suggestion that the effect of each policy should be measured gave birth to a range of institutions and individuals whose role was to investigate the effects of social policy experiments. As Popper hoped, this gave power to academics, social scientists, technologists, architects, and healthcare professionals, all enabled by growing Gross Domestic Products in most Western countries and the machinery of his "Open Society."

There were, however, a number of challenges to this rational scientific idealism. Philosophers such as Michel Foucault (1926–84) were profoundly skeptical about the benevolent idealism which rationalism claimed to represent. He explicitly denied the improvement motif that ran through almost all post-Enlightenment thought. Foucault saw scientific rationalism as a means of turning individuals into objects through the generation of a bewildering range of knowledge and expertise. This he saw as giving power to intellectuals and those who possessed power over this knowledge at the expense of the powerless. Foucault's antirationalism ultimately argued that Western society should care less about its structures and ideologies and more about its individuals.

Skepticism about the benevolence of rationalism also came from late-twentieth-century feminism which itself had deep roots in this concept's early history. Writers like Simone de Beauvoir (1908–86) saw rationalism as part of patriarchal structures of oppression and sought a realization of creativity and autonomy as Foucault had done. Other branches of feminist thought took it some distance away from its rationalist roots and offered messianic versions of goddess worship and the conception of mystical motherhood. Similarly the defeat of patriarchy has also been depicted in millenarian and apocalyptic terms; and the technological apparatus of rationalism has been challenged by species of eco-feminism that identify its ability to reinforce patriarchy. Likewise there have been feminist challenges to the scientific and rationalist delineation of time as uniform and governable. Alongside these critiques, the approach of postcolonialists and writers like Edward Said themselves posed a significant challenge to liberal rationalism and the claims of Western liberalism to have been civilizing world culture. Thus the improving impulse, so essential to rationalism, appeared in Said's hands to be just a subtler tool of colonialism.

The arrival of postmodernism initially appeared to rejuvenate the ideas of Enlightenment and rationalism. It argued that change was an essential part of civilization and also exhibited a curiosity about all things that was a recognizable inheritance from the Enlightenment. The precepts of postmodernism argued that the so-called great meta-narratives, which had hitherto sustained modern culture (e.g., Christianity, Marxism, Islam, and Freud) had come to an end. Thus, individuals were empowerment to make modern culture their own and liberate themselves from these various structures of oppression. A civilization in which everyone had an equally valid discourse, at least for a time, was a modernized utopian position for an individualistic twentieth century. That all culture could become popular offered the opportunity of cultural participation merely through consumption. The end of meta-narratives would thus bring a wave of ideological cleanliness that would sweep away prejudice and conflict. Postmodernism even produced its own utopian thinking from Francis Fukuyama, who argued that history had come to an end in the realization that sociodemocratic welfare capitalism offered the largest range of cultural and lifestyle choices. Some branches of scientific enquiry have themselves reached critical stages in their development and it has even been suggested, for example, that the search for a unified theory of physics might result in that subject itself coming to an "end."

However rationalism itself became another destabilized metanarrative. Through offering material improvement to all and by widening access to education and the benefits of technological development rationalism became a victim of one of the most cherished ideals of its own program—the empowerment of individuals and their apparently insatiable desire to democratize culture. Postmodern views also seemed to allow the rejuvenation of premodern worldviews, which rationalism thought it had vanquished. This occurrence has persuaded some commentators to suggest that forms of religious fundamentalism have constituted an "Alliance for the Repeal of the Enlightenment."

Thus at the end of the twentieth century secular millennial beliefs and the assumptions of rationalist scientific inquiry find themselves under considerable attack. The benevolence of science is questioned at every turn over issues such as genetically modified food, experimental cloning, and the BSE scare in Britain. Even medical and scientific advances challenge some of the ideas advanced by the Enlightenment. From John Locke onward the newborn child was a blank slate on which parents, society, and the environment wrote with confidence as both grave responsibility and opportunity. Implicit in Saint-Simon, Fourier, Owen, Comte, Morris, and beyond to later rationalists was the denial of innate capacities for beliefs, sentiments, and other predispositions which enabled the shaping of mankind's social and cultural development. In our own era this confidence has begun to break down with the discovery and increased publicizing of exploration of our genetic makeup. From supremacist sociobiologists and politicians right through to scientists who distance themselves from the implications of such theories there is nonetheless agreement with the assertion that genetic makeup has more to say about what we will be and what we will do than has previously been admitted.

Such ideas penetrate the popular culture of the end of the twentieth century. The science fiction books, films, and television series of thirty years ago offered a sort of humanistic utopia—perhaps exemplified by *Star Trek*. Their counterparts today are much more ambivalent about ideas of progress, hope, and the omnipotence of science—perhaps best exemplified by the *X-Files*.

Where once secular millennial rationalist ideas could claim to offer the route for all progress in the modern world, they find themselves at the end of the twentieth century to be less central to its definition than they once had been. Where once they had appeared supreme, these ideals now only constitute one argument about how a culture should develop.

David S. Nash

See also Communism, Technological Millennialism, Ufology

Bibliography

Burridge, Kenelm. (1969) *New Heaven, New Earth: A Study of Millenarian Activities.* New York: Schocken Books.

Claeys, Gregory. (1987) *Machinery, Money and the Millennium: From Moral Economy to Socialism, 1815–60.* Oxford, U.K.: Polity.

Claeys, Gregory. (1989) *Citizens and Saints: Politics and Anti-Politics in Early British Socialism.* Cambridge, U.K.: Cambridge University Press.

Cohn, Norman. (1957) *The Pursuit of the Millennium.* London: Secker & Warburg.

Cole, G. D. H. (1965) *The Life of Robert Owen,* 3d ed. London: Cass.

Cole, Margaret. (1953) *Robert Owen of New Lanark.* London: Batchworth Press.

Cumming, Elizabeth, and Wendy Kaplan. (1991) *The Arts and Crafts Movement.* London: Thames and Hudson.

Davies, Karen. (1990) *Women, Time and the Weaving of the Strands of Everyday Life.* Aldershot, U.K.: Avebury.

Foucault, Michel. (1973) *The Order of Things: An Archaeology of the Human Sciences.* New York: Pantheon.

——. (1980) "Truth and Power." In *Power/Knowledge: Selected Interviews and Other Writings 1972–1977,* edited by C. Gordon. Brighton: Hassocks, U.K.: Harvester, 109–33.

——. (1990) *Michel Foucault: Politics, Philosophy, Culture Interviews and Other Writings 1977–1984,* edited by L. D. Krintzman. London: Routledge.

Garnett, R. G. (1972) *Co-operation and the Owenite Socialist Communities in Britain 1825–45.* Manchester, U.K.: Manchester University Press.

Goodwin, Barbara. (1978) *Social Science and Utopia.* Hassocks, U.K.: Harvester Press.

Hampton, Christopher. (1990) "The Feast's Beginning." In *William Morris and News from Nowhere: A Vision for our Time,* edited by S. Coleman and P. O'Sullivan. Bideford, U.K.: Green Books, 43–55.

Harrison, J. F. C. (1979) *The Second Coming: Popular Millenarianism 1780–1850.* London: Routledge & Kegan Paul.

Hawking, Stephen. (1988) *A Brief History of Time.* London: Bantam Press.

Holloway, Mark. (1966) *Heavens on Earth: Utopian Communities in America 1680–1880.* London: Constable.

Kumar, Krishan. (1987) *Utopia and Anti-Utopia in Modern Times.* Oxford, U.K.: Blackwell.

Landes, Richard. (1996) "On Owls, Roosters, and Apocalyptic Time: A Historical Method for Reading a Refractory Documentation." *Union Seminary Quarterly Review* 49:165–85.

——. (1988) "Lest the Millennium Be Fulfilled: Apocalyptic Expectations and the Pattern of Western Chronography, 100–800." In *The Use and Abuse of Eschatology in the Middle Ages,* edited by W. Verbeke, D. Verhelst, and A. Welkenhuysen. Leuven: Katholieke University, 141–211.

MacCarthy, Fiona. (1994) *William Morris: A Life for Our Time.* London: Faber and Faber.

McGinn, Bernard. (1975) "Apocalypticism in the Middle Ages: An Historiographical Sketch." *Mediaeval Studies* 37: 252–86.

——. (1979) *Visions of the End. Apocalyptic Traditions in the Middle Ages.* New York: Columbia University Press.

Nash, David S. (1992) *Secularism, Art and Freedom.* London: Leicester University Press.

O'Brien, Conor Cruise. (1995) *On the Eve of the Millennium: The Future of Democracy Through an Age of Unreason.* New York: Free Press.

Oliver, W. H. (1971) "Owen in 1817: The Millennialist Moment." In *Robert Owen Prophet of the Poor: Essays in Honour of the Two-Hundredth Anniversary of his Birth,* edited by S. Pollard and J. Salt. Lewisburg, PA: Bucknell University Press, 165–87.

Popper, Karl Raimund. (1957) *The Poverty of Historicism.* London: Routledge and Kegan Paul.

——. (1962) *The Open Society and Its Enemies,* 2 vols. London: Routledge and Kegan Paul, vol. 1.

——. (1963) *Conjectures and Refutations: The Growth of Scientific Knowledge.* London: Routledge and Kegan Paul.

——. (1966) *Of Clouds and Clocks: An Approach to the Problem of Rationality and the Freedom of Man.* St. Louis, MO: Washington University.

Quinby, Lee. (1994) *Anti-Apocalypse: Exercises in Genealogical Criticism.* Minneapolis, MN: University of Minnesota Press.

Schwartz, Hillel. (1978) *Knaves, Fools, Madmen, and that Subtile Effluvium: A Study of the Opposition to the French Prophets in England, 1706–71.* University of Florida monographs: Social sciences, no. 62. Gainesville, FL: University Presses of Florida.

Taylor, Anne. (1987) *Visions of Harmony: A Study of Nineteenth-Century Millenarianism.* Oxford, U.K.: Clarendon.

Taylor, Barbara. (1983) *Eve and the New Jerusalem.* London: Virago.

Taylor, Keith, ed. (1975) *Henri Saint-Simon 1760–1825: Selected Writings on Science, Industry and Social Organisation.* London: Croom Helm.

Thompson, Damian. (1996) *The End of Time.* London: Sinclair Stevenson.

Tuveson, Ernest Lee. ([1949] 1964) *Millennium and Utopia: A Study in the Background of the Idea of Progress.* London: Harper and Rowe.

Waters, Chris. (1990) *British Socialists and the Politics of Popular Culture 1884–1914.* Manchester, U.K.: Manchester University Press.

Wright, Thomas. R. (1986) *The Religion of Humanity: The Impact of Comtean Positivism on Victorian Britain.* New York: Cambridge University Press.

Seventh-Day Adventists

Seventh-Day Adventism had urgently apocalyptic origins: as premillennialists, Adventists preached that the Second Coming of Christ and the end of the world was imminent. Although the urgency of the belief has moderated with the passage of time, they continue to cling to the doctrine that the Second Coming will take place "soon," and this remains at the center of their evangelistic thrust. Today Adventists are established in 205 nations and in recent decades the world membership has doubled every ten to twelve years, with growth concentrated in the developing world.

Beginnings

Adventists trace their roots to the Millerite Movement, which proclaimed throughout New England and upstate New York that Christ would return on 22 October 1844. Although William Miller withdrew and his movement dispersed following the humiliation and heartbreak of "the Great Disappointment," a small group of his followers reinterpreted the prophecy: that date had marked the commencement of the preadvent judgment in heaven and was the final date singled out by time prophecy; Christ's return would follow quickly. A young visionary, Ellen Harmon (1827–1915), played an important role in confirming this interpretation. Since Adventists believed that the "door of mercy" had been shut with the beginning of judgment, they initially made no efforts to evangelize. Even after they were persuaded that the door was still open and they were called to warn others of imminent judgment and apocalypse, they delayed formal organization and foreign evangelism, believing that insufficient time remained.

In 1846 Ellen Harmon married James White (1821–81), who was emerging as the leading organizer, editor, and publisher, and, later, administrator in early Adventism. Ellen White became a prophet, preacher, counselor to the church, and a prolific writer who published twenty-four books and contributed over five thousand articles to church magazines during her lifetime; over seventy-five additional volumes, compiled from her articles and other manuscripts, have been published since her death. Although she insisted that her writings were subsidiary to the Bible, her standing and their specificity made them highly influential in shaping the thought and behavior of Adventists.

Miller had portrayed governments as wild beasts which hurt God's people. Adventists elaborated on this theme as they developed their eschatology further. When, following their adoption of the Saturday-Sabbath, some members were arrested for violating state "blue laws" when they plowed their fields on Sundays, this led them to a unique interpretation of one prophecy: beginning in 1851, they denounced the American Republic, identifying it with the second beast of Revelation 13, which "had two horns like a lamb" and spoke "like a dragon." Pointing to slavery and the religious intolerance confronting them, they held that America had betrayed the principles of political and religious freedom enshrined in its Constitution and Bill of Rights. Declaring that it was already a dragon in lamb's clothing, they prophesied that it would play a persecuting role in the world's final events.

Adventists finally created a formal organization, headquartered initially in Battle Creek, Michigan, in the early

ELLEN WHITE'S ESCHATOLOGY

"When Protestantism shall stretch her hand across the gulf to grasp the hand of the Roman power, when she shall reach over the abyss to clasp hands with spiritualism, when, under the influence of the threefold union, our country shall repudiate every principle of its Constitution as a Protestant and republican government . . . then we may know that the time has come for the marvelous working of Satan and that the end is near."

Source: White, Ellen. (1885) *Testimonies for the Church*, vol. 5. Oakland, CA.: Pacific Press, (White 1885:451).

1860s. Their belief in the imminence of Christ's return was so central to them that they blazoned this belief in their name: Seventh-Day Adventist. Their membership then totaled 3,500. They began to build institutions—publishing houses to broadcast their message, schools and colleges to train clergy and other "workers," and medical facilities, dubbed "the entering wedge" by Ellen White, which offered drug-free treatments and vegetarian food. All would help Adventists spread their "final warning message," after which the "end" would come. They sent the first foreign missionary to Europe in 1874; many others followed, and more institutions were built abroad. By 1901 Adventists were established on all continents and their total membership had risen to 78,000. At Ellen White's urging, church headquarters were moved to Washington, D.C. in 1903.

Although Adventists had created institutions in order to facilitate their goals of spreading their message and ushering in the Kingdom, the result was gradual goal displacement: there was inevitable tension between longer-term building and organizing and the urgency of their message.

Eschatology

Meanwhile, Ellen White had elaborated on Adventist eschatology, with special attention to the events just before the Second Coming. The main players were to be Satan (the dragon of Revelation), and his henchmen the Roman Catholic Church (whose "deadly wound," received at the hands of the Protestant Reformation and the French Revolution, would be healed to such an extent that "all the world would wonder after the beast"), "Apostate Protestantism" (all the Protestant church organizations together with those members who failed to accept the Adventist message), Spiritualism, and the U.S. government. These would persecute God's "Remnant"—the loyal Adventists—beginning in the United States. White's eschatology was published in final form in 1888 in *The Great Controversy between Christ and Satan.* Its details, countless charts attempting to order the "last-day events"—from "the little time of trouble" to "Jacob's time of trouble," from the "loud cry" to the "shaking time," from the "early rain" to the "latter rain," from the "close of probation" to the "seven last plagues," from the passage of a "national Sunday law" and application of the "mark of the beast" to God's final intervention to save His saints—were to inspire both fear and hope among Adventists.

White's eschatology reflected the times in which she wrote—spiritualism was in vogue, and a Protestant establishment was attempting to shore up its position by, among other things, introducing a "national Sunday law" that would protect and codify the state blue laws. Much of the argument of *The Great Controversy* was familiar to evangelicals of the time. It celebrated the achievement of church-state separation in America as a legacy of Protestantism, and displayed a Protestant predisposition for strict Sabbath observance, temperance, law, order, and morality. However, the Adventist prophetess diverged from nineteenth-century evangelicals regarding which Sabbath should be strictly observed, and she protested coercive measures to enforce Sunday observance as a betrayal of religious liberty. Although White declared that "the final events" would be "rapid," the complexity and detail of her accounts created the impression that the end was more distant.

Putting Down Roots in Society

The elaboration of Adventist eschatology had involved some reshaping, especially of their view of the United States. While Adventists continued to identify America with the two-horned beast, they no longer portrayed it as already in the dragon phase, but as still lamblike, and its demise was therefore seen as more distant. That is, the time believed to be remaining before the Second Coming of Christ was lengthening, and tension with the state was beginning to relax. Moreover, Ellen White now counseled rapprochement with civil authorities in order to facilitate missionary work, urging Adventists to help prolong the future of America so that their message could go "forth and flourish." That is, Adventists found themselves in an anomalous situation where they wished to delay the end of the world in order to have greater opportunity to preach that it was at hand. Consequently, although their rehoned eschatology saw the passage of a national Sunday law as the culmination of the prophecy concerning the two-horned beast, and thus a sure signal that the Second Coming of Christ was at hand, Adventists felt obliged by Ellen White's counsel to "extend the time" to respond boldly to this threat. They established a magazine devoted to religious liberty; their lobbying against threatening legislation included petitions to both Houses, the reading of papers before congressional committees, and the presentation of legal briefs in court; and they founded the National Religious Liberty Association to defend the "wall of separation" between church and state and what later became the Public Affairs and Religious Liberty Department [PARL] at church headquarters, which institutionalized the Adventist Church's role as a watchdog of the First Amendment. Their initial efforts were successful, helping defeat Senator H. W. Blair's Sunday-Rest bill in 1888 and 1889.

Henceforth, there was a tension between the public presentation of the Adventist message that Christ's return was "even at the doors" and the dogged determination of Adventist leaders to foster the separation of church and state, and thus to postpone the prophesied passage of a National Sunday Law. There was also growing tension between their public preaching that the end of the world was at hand and the extent to which Adventists were prospering and putting down roots in American society.

During the following decades, Adventism continued to accommodate to the state. It transformed its stance on military service from conscientious objection during the Civil War to participation without arms, preferably as medical orderlies, during the major wars of the twentieth century and then ultimately, toward the end of the Vietnam War, declared that the bearing of arms was a matter of individual conscience. It pursued accreditation for its colleges and then accepted government aid for its schools and hospitals. In order to receive accreditation, it exposed its academics to graduate study at major universities, which inevitably impacted the content of their courses and thus also their students; ultimately it also impacted their pastors, when religion departments, which were not obliged to be accredited, played "catch-up" with the other college departments. Meanwhile, accreditation prepared the way for widespread upward mobility among graduates of Adventist colleges.

Adventism also began to adjust to the religious economy. It had remained very isolated from other American religious bodies until well into the twentieth century, because of their negative reactions to its teachings and its "sheep-stealing" practices and also because it feared that ecumenism might foster the persecution it was expecting. It held aloof when the Federal Council of Churches and the World Council of Churches were formed in 1908 and 1948, and when the FCC was transformed into the National Council of Churches in 1950. Evangelicals had proved especially antagonistic, regularly labeling Adventism a "cult" in their critiques. However, in the mid-1950s Adventist leaders initiated a series of meetings with two well-known Evangelical scholars, Walter R. Martin and Donald Grey Barnhouse who, in the process of writing a series of studies on Christian "cults," had begun researching Seventh-Day Adventism. There was widespread exhilaration when Barnhouse authored an article replying affirmatively to the question "Are Seventh-day Adventists Christians?" (1956), and Martin's subsequent book, *The Truth about Seventh-day Adventism* (1960), declared that Adventists were not a cult but "bretheren" of the Christian Evangelicals.

Such acceptance encouraged Adventists to lower barriers further. Their representatives began to attend meetings of the Central Committee of the World Council of Churches as observers in 1968, and they also affiliated with several subdivisions of the National Council of Churches. In 1975, the Adventist Church began to invite other denominations to send official observers to its quinquennial sessions, and in 1980 it established the Council on Interchurch Relations to deal with ecumenical relations. Meanwhile, in 1977 the International Religious Liberty Association, which is sponsored by PARL, organized the first of a series of World Congresses on religious liberty, in which major figures from other religious traditions have participated. PARL has also been successful in its pursuit of official dialogues with other denominations, the most successful to date being with leaders of the World Lutheran Federation between 1994 and 1998.

Meanwhile, there were signs that tension between Adventism and Catholicism was also easing. Adventists participated as observers in Vatican II during the 1960s. In the early 1970s, when the Pacific Press was sued by the Equal Employment Opportunity Commission because of its discrimination against women in salaries and promotions, the defense brief distanced Adventism from its "earlier" anti-Catholicism as "nothing more" than a manifestation of an attitude then common among conservative Protestant denominations "which has now been consigned to the historical trash heap so far as the Seventh-Day Adventist Church is

THE BEAST WITH LAMBLIKE HORNS
"I beheld another beast coming up out of the earth; and he had two horns like a lamb, and he spake as a dragon."
Revelation 13: 11.

COURTESY OF THE SEVENTH-DAY ADVENTIST CHURCH, SILVER SPRING, MD.

concerned" (General Conference of the Seventh-day Adventists, 1975). In 1995, the previously unthinkable occurred, when PorterCare Adventist Health Services, the Adventist hospital system in Colorado, and the Catholic Sisters of Charity Health Services Colorado joined together to form a new corporation, Centura Health, in order that both could survive in an increasingly competitive market. Adventist officials involved in this decision argued that Adventist hospitals had more in common with Catholic hospitals than any others because their missions were so similar.

In spite of their belief that the "end of the world" was imminent, Adventists were successfully putting down roots in society and, in the process, becoming world affirming. As a corollary of this process they, in effect, postponed the apocalypse. Sometimes this was recognized explicitly by Adventist spokespersons. For example, when, during World War II, Supreme Court decisions strengthened religious liberty and Roosevelt included freedom of religion as one of his four basic freedoms, the editor of the official church paper, the *Review and Herald*, commented that what Adventists had prophesied clearly lay further in the future.

Continuing Expectancy

This does not mean that the Adventist Church had abandoned its eschatology—far from it. Adventists continued to believe that Jesus was returning "soon," which, for many of them, meant that they did not expect their children to reach maturity or themselves face death. They also continued to look expectantly for signs of the fulfillment of Ellen White's whole eschatological scenario, and remained prone to excitement whenever they found evidence that Christ's return might be near. Although the Adventist Church, as a corporate religious body, learned the lesson of 1844 and has never set a date for the Second Coming, groups of Adventists have focused on particular dates for that event more than twenty times in the past 150 years. Sometimes these were based on analogies to biblical events: 1884, because the Israelites wandered forty years in the wilderness, or 1964, because Noah preached 120 years and Jesus said "As it was in the days of Noah, so shall it be at the coming of the Son of Man." More often they were based on world events which seemed likely to fulfill Adventist predictions.

Attention was usually drawn to these events by Adventist evangelists, for eschatology remained at the center of their preaching—it attracted crowds and gained conversions, especially during times of crisis. Evangelists made much of both world wars, the great depression, the election of Kennedy—the first Catholic—as president, the Cuban missile crisis, the first expedition to the moon, the sexual revolution of the 1960s, and the cold war. However, these events were often seized upon eagerly amid a general situation where there seemed to be major obstacles to the development of Ellen White's final scenario. For example, the introduction of the five-day working week in the 1930s made Sabbath observance much easier, while the U.S. Supreme Court showed a growing commitment to protecting religious liberty after 1940; later the cold war, the rising strength of China and the Muslim world, and the weakness of the papacy in communist and Muslim countries made it difficult to see America imposing papal domination on the world.

The collapse of the Soviet Union led many evangelists to refocus their preaching. Although they had previously portrayed the danger of the cold war heating up as a sign of the end; they now proclaimed that the emergence of the United States as the sole "super power," its partnership with the papacy in undermining communism, and the consequent increase in papal prestige were sure signs that Ellen White's eschatological scenario was being fulfilled.

The Adventist Church used the expectation of the return of Jesus—and fear of not being ready—to maintain the commitment of its members and to control their behavior. These teachings make a special impact on children. Many Adventists recall childhood dreams in which Jesus returns and they are not ready. Some report having played "Catholics and Adventists" rather than "cowboys and Indians." Many Adventist academy and college students have expressed the hope that the Coming would be delayed until after they had married and experienced sex—the prospect of the judgment closing and one's fate being sealed increased the risk associated with illicit sex. Revivals have been used to maintain a sense of urgency among both adults and youth.

Problems Flowing from the Delayed Apocalypse

However, considerable burnout on the issue occurred as the extended delay made its impact: it proved increasingly difficult to maintain a high level of expectation. Observers from very different vantage points within Adventism have noted that, in general, while members of the baby-boomer generation have "held onto the Sabbath," they pay little attention to the Second Coming—they are embarrassed by the wild, apocalyptic, Adventist-centered interpretations.

As Adventists have buried generations of forebears who believed that they would live to see the Second Coming, they have tried to find reasons for the delay. Two main explanations have been put forward: The delay has been caused because members' characters are not yet ready for translation; and, since Jesus stated that the gospel would be preached in all the world and then the end would come, the problem must be that Adventists have failed to complete this task. The former causes those who embrace it distress, for it makes their imperfections responsible for the delay. The latter is the explanation espoused most strongly by the administrators who then pour more resources into spreading the "Advent message."

Though Adventists have, over time, reduced the urgency of their apocalyptic vision, the process of change has resulted in considerable theological pluralism. Some members continue to grasp at any sign or rumor that can be construed that a national Sunday law is in the offing. In this they are oblivious to the changed religious context in the United States, which has been so pervasive that it has almost certainly left this category of Adventists as the only Americans even thinking about the possibility of such a law. Other Adventists view Sabbath observance as a good idea rather than a test of who is loyal to God among earth's final generation, see their congregation as an important source of community rather than as part of the one true church, and find any declaration that other denominations are "the beast" or "Babylon" acutely embarrassing. Such diverse views often erupt into conflict in adult Sabbath School classes, on church committees, or in Adventist segments of cyberspace. However, many members are able to avoid conflict by choosing a different class or driving further to church in order to surround themselves with people holding compatible views.

The data suggest that the diversity of belief is segmented. For their part, church leaders continue to highlight the twenty-seven "fundamental beliefs," one of which declares that "the present condition of the world . . . indicates that Christ's coming is imminent." The then president of the General Conference, in a book published to coincide with the 150th anniversary of the Great Disappointment in 1994, noted that some were asking whether "we still have confidence that Jesus is coming 'soon'?" whether "150 years can be characterized as 'soon,' in any sense of the word?" His reply was that, in spite of the delay, "WE STILL BELIEVE!" (Folkenberg 1994: 9). Church leaders keep devising new programs that are designed to keep the Adventist growth-rate high. They have been very successful in this in recent years: the official world membership grew from 500,000 in 1940 to 1.2 million in 1960 and almost 3.5 million in 1980; it passed 10 million during 1998. Growth has been concentrated in the developing world; and the membership in the United

States has now fallen to less than 9 percent of the total. While the successful evangelistic programs are advocated in terms of "finishing the work," the leaders who propose them also oversee a widespread network of hospitals and schools that are rooted deeply in the world.

Since Adventist evangelism still focuses on endtime events, converts are usually those attracted by this topic. However, when these people join local Adventist congregations, they find that their pastors typically give far less emphasis to eschatological subjects than do the evangelists. This is related to the fact that the Adventist Seminary and the departments of religion at the Adventist colleges in the United States are, in general, avoiding the traditional Adventist approach to eschatology. While large majorities of laypersons show a belief in the doctrine of the Second Coming, urgent apocalypticism is much less widespread, being concentrated especially among new converts and racial minorities and, often fearfully, among younger students exposed to indoctrination in Adventist schools, large numbers of whom admit in surveys funded by official entities of the church (the Valuegenesis study of youth in Adventist high schools administered in 1989 by the Search Institute, and the follow up AVANCE study of all youth in the North American Hispanic Adventist Church) that they worry "very much . . . about not being ready for Christ's return" or "not being faithful" during the expected persecution of the "Time of Trouble."

The dissonance between the preaching of evangelists and church pastors has contributed substantially to the growth of urgently apocalyptic "independent ministries" on the fringes of Adventism. (The best known of these to the media was David Koresh's Branch Davidians.) The leaders of these groups often continue to identify with Adventism, even after being disfellowshipped, and therefore focus their efforts on reaching Adventists.

The fringe apocalyptic ministries are much more urgent in their apocalypticism than most mainstream Adventists. They generally differ from the latter in at least one of two main ways. First, many of them are so impatient with the long delay in the Second Coming since 1844 that merely pointing to recent world events as new evidence that the general Adventist eschatological scenario is on track (as Adventist evangelists typically have) is unsatisfactory to them: they want more direct proof that these are the very last days and Christ is about to return. To accomplish this they often develop some kind of prophecy focusing explicitly on the current period. Some of these groups hold that the sixth millennium of earth's history is closing. If each millennium is symbolized by one day, the seventh, or Sabbath, millennium—that period, referred to in the Book of Revelation, as THE millennium—is about to open. As premillennialists, they proclaim that Christ will return before then. Others arrive at a similarly urgent apocalyptic through calculations associated with the Old Testament Jubilee Cycle or by applying the time-line prophecies of the biblical Books of Daniel and Revelation to the present. The second group of apocalyptic ministries on the fringes of Adventism often regard the Adventist Church leadership as so compromised with the "world" and the members so "lukewarm" in their spirituality that the church is unready to receive Christ and is thus responsible for his delay. Some of them charge that the official church has obscured the "last warning message" bequeathed to it through Ellen White by shifting positions on beliefs and behavioral standards, and present their own group as the true "historic Adventists." Since Ellen White foretold a great "falling away" among Adventists immediately before the end, this identifies the present time. When their criticisms of church leadership are met, in turn, with charges of heresy and attempts to subject them to church discipline, the rancor escalates.

Conclusion

In October 1994, Adventists celebrated the 150th anniversary of the Great Disappointment—and of a century and a half of believing and preaching that Jesus would soon return. This anniversary highlighted the tension between the Adventist belief in an imminent apocalypse and the delay in its fulfillment. As the decades have passed, both the Adventist Church and Adventist lives have become increasingly world affirming. Although the Adventist Church continues to endorse the eschatological vision developed in the nineteenth century by Ellen White and other Adventist pioneers, variations in expectations among its members and, especially, in the urgency with which they await its fulfillment, inevitably engender discomfort and distrust. While the Adventist growth-rate has fallen substantially in the United States and other parts of the developed world, and indeed membership has often remained stable there only because of an influx of immigrants, it remains high, and has even increased, in much of the developing world.

Ronald Lawson

See also Davidians, Millerites

Bibliography

Barnhouse, Donald Grey. (1956) "Are Seventh-day Adventists Christians?" *Eternity* (September) 7, 9: 6–7, 43–45.

Butler, Jonathan. (1974) "Adventism and the American Experience." In *The Rise of Adventism: Religion and Society in Mid-Nineteenth-Century America*, edited by Edwin S. Gaustad. New York: Harper and Row, 173–206.

——. (1986) "The World of E. G. White and the End of the World." In *Pilgrimage of Hope*, edited by Roy Branson. Takoma Park, MD: Assoc. of Adventist Forums, 64–88.

Folkenberg, Robert S. (1994) *We Still Believe*. Boise, ID: Pacific Press.

General Conference of Seventh-day Adventists. (1975) "Reply Brief for Defendants in Support of their Motion for Summary Judgment." Equal Employment Opportunity Commission, et al., vs. Pacific Press Publishing Association, et al. March 3. Civil no. 74-2025 CBR.

——. (1996) *Seventh-day Adventist Encyclopedia*, 2 vols. Hagerstown, MD: Review and Herald.

Lawson, Ronald. (1995) "Seventh-day Adventist Responses to Branch Davidian Notoriety: Patterns of Diversity within a Sect Reducing Tension with Society." *Journal for the Scientific Study of Religion* 34, 3: 323–41.

——. (1996) "Church and State at Home and Abroad: The Evolution of Seventh-day Adventist Relations with Governments." *Journal of the American Academy of Religion* 64, 2: 279–311.

——. (1996) "Onward Christian Soldiers?: Seventh-day Adventists and the Issue of Military Service." *Review of Religious Research* 37, 3: 97–122.

——. (1997) "The Persistence of Urgent Apocalypticism Within a Denominationalizing Sect: The Apocalyptic Fringe Groups of Seventh-day Adventism." In *Millennium, Messiahs and Mayhem*, edited by Thomas Robbins and Susan J. Palmer. New York: Routledge, 207–28.

——. (1998) "From American Church to Immigrant Church: The Changing Face of Seventh-day Adventism in Metropolitan New York." *Sociology of Religion* 59, 4: 329–51.

Martin, Walter. (1960) *The Truth about Seventh-day Adventism*. Grand Rapids, MI: Zondervan.

Morgan, Douglas. (1994) "Adventism, Apocalyptic, and the Cause of Liberty." *Church History* 63 (June): 235–49.

Numbers, Ronald L., and Jonathan M. Butler. (1987) *The Disappointed: Millerism and Millenarianism in the Nineteenth Century*. Bloomington, IN: Indiana University Press.

Paulien, Jon. (1994) *What the Bible Says about the End-Time*. Hagerstown, MD: Review and Herald.

White, Ellen. (1885) *Testimonies for the Church*, vol. 5. Oakland, CA: Pacific Press.

——. (1888) *The Great Controversy between Christ and Satan*. Oakland, CA: Pacific Press.

Sexuality

While sexuality is subject to regulation in many religious communities, the erotic dimensions of human experience have especially been the objects both of repulsion and of fascination to millennialist communities. For some, the imminent expectation of the endtimes has occasioned rigorous prohibitions and policing of sexual behavior; for others, a license for erotic liberty. Moreover, apocalyptic texts frequently display extreme punishments for sexual transgressions and a fear and loathing of female sexuality.

Sexuality and the People of the Book

In the religious traditions of the "People of the Book" (Jews, Christians, and Muslims), the religious community's relationship with God is often represented in erotic terms. On the one hand, its straying away from God is frequently represented as sexual infidelity and the community itself as a whore, common tropes in prophetic traditions. In the Christian scripture's last book, Revelation, Babylon is personified as a woman riding a scarlet beast: "The woman was arrayed in purple and scarlet, and bedecked with gold and jewels and pearls, holding in her hand a golden cup full of abominations and the impurities of her fornication; and on her forehead was written a name of mystery: 'Babylon the great, mother of harlots and of earth's abominations'" (17:4–5). On the other hand, when faithful, the community is represented as God's spouse. In the Book of Revelation, for example, the Church is depicted as a bride who marries the Lamb of God (chapter 22).

Millennial Visions of Sexuality

This pattern of ambivalence is typical of the frequently contradictory approaches that millennialist communities take to sexuality. The Jewish apocalyptic community at Qumran (from whom we have what are called the Dead Sea Scrolls) may have maintained an all-male warrior community awaiting the end times by repudiating marriage or at least by excluding wives. According to Ita Sheres and Anne Kohn Blau:

> Since they were particularly concerned about women's sexuality and its "defiling" impact on the whole human race, they faced a dilemma: procreation was essential, but sexuality was abhorrent. Indeed, the virgin was of immense importance to this brotherhood, because she was the symbol of a kind of perfection that was idealized in that exclusive environment. The sect believed that in order to be worthy of living in the new, perfect world (which would come into being when "the sons of light" [i.e., the sectarians] conquered "the sons of darkness" [i.e., the Romans and their collaborators]) it was necessary to remain inviolate, and virginity was clearly part of that belief. (10)

However, this rejection of marital sexuality in the name of millennialist exigency is not typical of Judaism's apocalypticism. More characteristic is medieval Kabbalah mysticism in which, as Scholem and Idel point out, the Sabbath is viewed as a marriage festival and the Talmudic scholar was encouraged to make love to his wife on Friday evening. Kabbalah texts also circulate some unorthodox notions of God as both male and female *(Shekhinah)* principles that have become exiled from each other; Kabbalah mysticism anticipates the eventual restoration of these two principles by the daily performance of virtuous deeds, including marital lovemaking.

The Qur'an's vision of millennial bliss (sura 61) is similarly characterized by a frank sensuality: "When the inevitable happens . . . the foremost . . . are they who are brought nigh in gardens of pleasure . . . around them shall go eternal youths, with goblets and ewers and a cup of flowing wine . . . and such fruits as they deem the best . . . and the flesh of fowl as they desire and bright and large-eyed maids like hidden pearls, a reward for that which they have done!" (Palmer 1933).

Kabbalah mysticism's androgynous God is reminiscent of the image of divinity of some early Christian gnostic sects. If generalizations can be made about a phenomenon as diverse as gnosticism, it is a term applied to spiritual beliefs and practices that emphasized the saving power of the secret knowledge or doctrines about Christ (i.e., revealed to a few initiates) in which the life of the body is only a corrupt form of the true spiritual existence of humans. These doctrines repudiate orthodox Christianity's emphasis on Jesus' incarnation and resurrection and on the future resurrection of saved humans. As Pagels notes, while many gnostic groups believed in an androgynous God who was father and mother, they often viewed human sexuality with suspicion and contempt because sexual intercourse only produced more flesh to ensnare spiritual beings. As a millennialist movement, therefore, gnostic religion enjoined its believers to abstain from intercourse and to regard sexuality (particularly female sexuality) with disgust until they were reunited with the divinity.

Such sexual pessimism would also characterize Christianity from its foundations, and its later claims that celibacy is simply an apocalyptic or eschatological (i.e., endtimes) virtue must be viewed with suspicion. Christianity inherited a contempt for sexuality from its pagan context, particularly in its contemporaries, the Stoic philosophers. Taking its cue from a saying of Jesus, the early Christian leaders enjoined celibacy on their members in order to become "eunuchs for the kingdom of God" as an act of millennialist hope in the imminent return of Christ. What was the point of marrying if the Bridegroom was about to arrive? As the expectation of Christ's imminent return began to wane, however, the injunction of celibacy came to be associated with a spiritual elite, hermits and monks who fled this world to serve as a sign of the next world. Eventually this injunction would be applied in the Western or Roman Catholic Church to all priests (although this would not be the case in the Eastern churches).

Medieval Christian Millennialism and Sexuality

By and large, medieval Christians lived with the reality of sudden death and the proximity of their own encounter with divine judgment at death, but did not anticipate the Second Coming or the Millennium as imminent. Therefore, sexuality was largely a matter of the internal forum, i.e., the penitent with the priest in confession, where elaborate and detailed constraints on sexual behavior were carefully delineated. Not surprisingly, the most erotic book of the Christian Bible, the Hebrew scriptures' Song of Songs (also known as the Song of Solomon or Canticle of Canticles) came to be interpreted in a symbolic or allegorical sense as prefiguring the soul's or the church's union with God. Thus medieval Catholicism's diluted millennialism vitiated the lush sensuality of a Hebrew wedding poem.

Given this context, a remarkable late medieval phenomenon seems even more astonishing. Called the heresy of the Free Spirit or of Spiritual Liberty, Norman Cohn characterizes its followers as "gnostics intent upon their own individual salvation; but the gnosis at which they arrived was a quasi-mystical anarchism—an affirmation of freedom so reckless and unqualified that it amounted to a total denial of every kind of restraint and limitation" (148). This movement emerged from obscurity in the early thirteenth century; its progeny could still be found four hundred years later in the Ranters of the English Revolution. Free Spirit adepts' millennialism consisted in their believing themselves to be already perfected and therefore incapable of sin; thus, notes Cohn, in "a Christian civilization, which attached particular value to chastity and regarded sexual intercourse outside marriage as particularly sinful, such antinomianism most commonly took the form of promiscuity on principle" (151), a far cry from the abstinence of early Christianity.

American Millennialism and Sexuality

American millennialist communities have embraced either sexual license or restraint. As D'Emilio and Freedman point out:

> From the 1820s through the 1860s, . . . sexual dissidents created elaborate alternatives to the family. Although some free lovers found inspiration in the political legacy of the Revolutionary era, which emphasized individual rights and the pursuit of happiness, most utopians developed their sexual alternatives

within the context of a religious movement for moral perfection. (112)

Shakers, for example, required celibacy for their religionists, in addition to simple sexually integrated communal living, based on the teachings of their eighteenth-century founder, Ann Lee, an English Quaker. Mormonism, in contrast, emphasized human reproduction through the principle of polygamy introduced by its founder, Joseph Smith, and articulated as a doctrine by his successor, Brigham Young; accordingly, they condemned nonprocreative sexualities, like masturbation and homosexuality. Under the leadership of John Humphrey Noyes, another utopian community, which came to settle in Oneida, New York, practiced a form of sexual communism, "complex marriage," in which all adults were considered married to each other, but controlled both reproduction and particular romantic attachments between individuals.

Western "Aquarian Age" movements, including the so-called Sexual Revolution of the 1960s, might be understood in the context of Euro-Americans' technological millennialism. The combination of postwar social dislocations and improved contraception encouraged the "Baby Boom" generation to see themselves as having entered a "new age" of sexual relations. However, the emergence in the 1980s of AIDS, a viral epidemic associated with sexual transmission of the infectious agent HIV, would bring an end to that millennialist optimism and foster an apocalyptic hostility toward erotic dissent.

Sexuality is always subject to social and religious regulation, which is particularly acute among communities who understand themselves as living in the end times. Paradoxically, millennialist communities might either abhor sex or celebrate it, and either enforce sexual abstinence or structure sexual expression.

Thomas L. Long

Bibliography

Cohn, Norman. (1970) *The Pursuit of the Millennium: Revolutionary Millenarians and the Mystical Anarchists of the Middle Ages*, rev. ed. New York: Oxford University Press.

D'Emilio, John, and Estelle B. Freedman. (1988) *Intimate Matters: A History of Sexuality in America.* New York: Harper & Row.

Idel, Moshe. (1988) *Kabbalah: New Perspectives.* New Haven, CT: Yale University Press.

Pagels, Elaine. (1989) *The Gnostic Gospels.* New York: Vintage Books.

Palmer, E. H., trans. (1933) *The Koran (Qur'an).* London: Oxford University Press.

Ranke-Heinemann, Uta. (1990) *Eunuchs For the Kingdom of Heaven: Women, Sexuality, and the Catholic Church*, translated by Peter Heinegg. New York: Doubleday.

Scholem, Gershom. (1996, 1965) *On the Kabbalah and Its Symbolism*, translated by Ralph Manheim. New York: Schocken Books.

Sheres, Ita, and Anne Kohn Blau. (1995) *The Truth About the Virgin: Sex and Ritual in the Dead Sea Scrolls.* New York: Continuum.

Shakers

Among the millennial and utopian communities that flourished in nineteenth-century America, none had a greater impact upon the wider society than did the Shakers. Formally known as the "United Society of Believers in Christ's Second Appearing" or the "Millennial Church," most often they were simply called "Shakers" on account of their ecstatic dancing and shaking in worship. The Shakers believed that their founder, Mother Ann Lee (1736–84), was the Second Coming of Christ. In his first appearance, Christ had come in the person of Jesus, a man. Now the second coming of Christ had taken place in the person of Mother Ann, thereby completing the revelation of God. The Shakers thus believed that their community was nothing less than the millennial kingdom of Christ finally come on earth. They were strictly celibate, for they believed that marriage and sexual relations were part of the old, sinful order and had no place in the millennial kingdom. In the new age, men and women lived and worked together as equals. Eventually the Shakers developed large, cooperative communities that were characterized by their simplicity of lifestyle and industrial inventiveness. In the words of Mother Ann, they "put their hands to work and their hearts to God."

The Development of the Ann Lee's Messianic Vision

Ann Lee was born in Manchester, England, into a family of eight children. Her father, John Lee, was a blacksmith; her mother is not listed in the Manchester city records. Ann herself at a young age went to work in a factory as a cutter of hatter's fur. At sixteen she married a man named Abraham Stanley, although she continued to use her own last name. Abraham moved with Ann Lee into her family's home, and over the next six years they had four children, all of whom died at a young age.

In 1758, Lee began attending a Quaker religious society led by Jane and James Wardley. The Wardleys had been influenced by the teachings of a group of millennial prophets from Cévenole, France who had led a revival in Manchester in the late 1740s. Known as *les trembleurs*, these prophets had introduced the Wardleys to the doctrine of the imminent second coming of Christ and the advent of his millennial kingdom, as well as to a distinct form of ecstatic worship that involved convulsive shaking. The Wardleys' group had become known as "Shaking Quakers" in Manchester, which was later shortened to simply the Shakers. Members of their society, including Ann Lee, began traveling from town to town in the region, preaching the imminent Second Coming of Christ and practicing their ecstatic worship in public.

In 1772 Ann Lee was briefly imprisoned on charges of "profaning the Sabbath" on account of her dancing and shaking. While in prison, she had a vision that crystallized her understanding of both human sexual relations and her own millennial vocation. According to her later accounts, Lee came to see that the root of all human depravity was sexual activity that led to natural generation. No one could follow Christ in the work of regeneration without first abandoning the works of natural generation, and the accompanying gratifications of the flesh. Years later Lee told her followers that it was the Wardleys who had actually first introduced her to the practice of celibacy, for they had lived together for years without having sexual relations. But Lee's vision revealed to her that this doctrine was the key to the advent of the millennial age.

Upon hearing Lee relate her prison vision after she was released, the Wardleys declared that this was a divine sign that pointed to her as the "anointed daughter." She was the second coming of Christ, the Word, completing the revelation of God as male and female, they declared. Needless to say, reception of a female Christ among her contemporaries was not positive, and persecution by the English authorities increased. The fact that Lee and her group publicly advocated complete renunciation of sexual activity between men and women did not help their cause. Facing increased opposition, in 1774, she set sail to America with a small band of eight followers that included her husband Abraham, her brother William, and James Whittaker. Conspicuously absent from their number were the Wardleys.

TABLE MONITOR.

GATHER UP THE FRAGMENTS THAT REMAIN, THAT NOTHING BE LOST.—CHRIST.

Here then is the pattern
  Which Jesus has set;
And his good example
  We can not forget:
With thanks for his blessings
  His word we'll obey;
But on this occasion
  We've somewhat to say.

We wish to speak plainly
  And use no deceit;
We like to see fragments
  Left wholesome and neat:
To customs and fashions
  We make no pretense;
Yet think we can tell
  What belongs to good sense.

What we deem good order,
  We're willing to state—
Eat hearty and decent,
  And clear out our plate—
Be thankful to Heaven
  For what we receive,
And not make a mixture
  Or compound to leave.

We find of those bounties
  Which Heaven does give,
That some live to eat,
  And that some eat to live—
That some think of nothing
  But pleasing the taste,
And care very little
  How much they do waste.

Tho' Heaven has bless'd us
  With plenty of food:
Bread, butter, and honey,
  And all that is good;
We loathe to see mixtures
  Where gentle folks dine,
Which scarcely look fit
  For the poultry or swine.

We often find left,
  On the same china dish,
Meat, apple-sauce, pickle,
  Brown bread and minc'd fish;
Another's replenish'd
  With butter and cheese;
With pie, cake, and toast,
  Perhaps, added to these.

Now if any virtue
  In this can be shown,
By peasant, by lawyer,
  Or king on the throne,
We freely will forfeit
  Whatever we've said,
And call it a virtue
  To waste meat and bread.

Let none be offended
  At what we here say;
We candidly ask you,
  Is that the best way?
If not—lay such customs
  And fashions aside,
And take this Monitor
  Henceforth for your guide.

[VISITORS' EATING-ROOM, SHAKER VILLAGE.]

Shaker rules posted in visitor's eating room.

The Development of the Shaker Communities

The group arrived in Manhattan later that year, and immediately took up various forms of employment in the city. Abraham Stanley soon sought to resume sexual cohabitation with Mother Ann, and abandoned the group when she refused. The rest of the group, led by Mother Ann, secured a tract of land outside Albany at Watervliet, New York, where they moved in 1776. There they resided for several years without attracting much attention, other than that of the local authorities in Albany who suspected them of being British sympathizers. Mother Ann continued to encourage the small band with visions of coming waves of humanity pressing in upon them in search of salvation.

Then in 1780 it happened as she had prophesied, and their numbers increased. New Lebanon, near Watervliet, was the center of a brief spiritual revival that had faded as quickly as it had arisen. Several local leaders, disillusioned with the fickle spirit of the revival, heard of Mother Ann and the Shakers. Joseph Meacham, the most prominent Baptist minister in the area, journeyed to Watervliet and upon hearing Mother Ann's message became the first convert in America. Others followed, and soon a sizable group of American converts were joining the Shakers in their worship. Among the better known visitors who came to Watervliet during these first years was General Lafayette, who according to Shaker legend visited the community again in spirit after his death several years later in France.

New converts meant renewed controversy. Mother Ann was again imprisoned, this time on charges of being a British spy. Her supporters were soon able to gain her release, and Mother Ann with a group of elders from the community set off on a preaching mission through Massachusetts and Connecticut. For two years they carried on their itinerant mission, preaching the necessity of confession of sin, renunciation of all works of the flesh, and ecstatic dancing as the means for entry into the millennial kingdom of Christ. For two years they were hounded by mobs, beaten, whipped, and run out of towns across New England. But the message received a hearing. Young women dissolved their engagements, married women abandoned their husbands, and a number of married couples ended their sexual relations to enter into the millennial church.

A number of testimonies from these early days describe how converts found in Ann Lee's teachings fulfillment of their desire for a deeper spiritual life. A convert named Elizabeth Johnson, for instance, told how she had married a minister to be nearer to God, only to discover that the relationship was anything but freeing for her. Among the Shakers she finally found the spiritual fulfillment for which she had been longing. Others spoke of Mother Ann's tenderness, gentle persuasion, and spiritual compassion as compelling evidence of her messianic role.

Mother Ann died in 1784 shortly after returning from her missionary journey through New England. Leadership of the community first passed on to James Whittaker, and then in 1787 to Joseph Meacham. It was Meacham who laid the organizational foundations for the "gatherings" or "orders" of the wider Shaker movement. Guided by Meacham and the other elders from New Lebanon, new gatherings were founded in Massachusetts, Connecticut, and Maine. Another American convert, Lucy Wright, succeeded Meacham as head of the movement in 1811, continuing the tradition of women in leadership. Under Eldress Wright's leadership the Shaker message of ecstasy, industry, and celibacy continued to spread to Ohio, Pennsylvania, Kentucky, and Indiana.

"The Tree of Life" sprint drawing from Hancock, 1854. SHAKER COMMUNITY, INC.

Shaker Life and Practices

Shakers depended entirely upon conversions for gaining their new members. Being strictly celibate, they did not have natural families. The communities often served as orphanages, however, taking in unwanted children to raise. In such cases, the children were not coerced into remaining in the Shaker community or joining the movement after they had come of age. Many who were raised as children in Shaker communities did choose to remain, but others chose to leave and return to the world. As with adult converts, Shakers practiced no coercion. Nothing apart from the individual person's own desire to live a sin-free life prevented a man or women from leaving the millennial church and returning to the world.

In their communities, men and women lived in separate, but usually symmetrical, communal quarters. Women often worked in the shops and fields, while men sometimes worked in the kitchens. During the week there were organized times for women and men to meet together and learn to relate to one another as equals. Women were taught that they had to learn to love men without feeling lustful, while men were warned that their lusting after women was the sign of their sinful nature, and that it must be given up entirely in the millennial kingdom.

Most Shaker communities were located in rural areas, but one which was urban was a predominantly African-American gathering in Philadelphia. The Philadelphia community was under the leadership of an African American named Eldress Rebecca Jackson. Her writings have been recently rediscovered as a shining example of the African-American mystical tradition. The Philadelphia society had only a brief life on its own, and its members were soon integrated into other existing gatherings. The acceptance of their members was an important indication that the Shaker vision of millennial equality extended to matters of class and race, as well as gender.

Shakers grew their own foods and made most of what they used in their own workshops. They often sold seeds and other goods to help support their communities. Property was owned communally, and most decisions were made by the elders in ways that maintained the collective sense of identity in the community. They were strict pacifists and abstained from any associations with the outside world that were deemed to be sinful.

Sinlessness entailed cleanliness, order, and simplicity in the Shaker's millennial kingdom of Christ on earth. With this vision in mind they designed their buildings and made their own furniture. Shaker rooms were built with pegs on the walls so that furnishings could be lifted and the floors swept clean each day. The design of their furnishings was distinctive for its simplicity, beauty, and functionality. Likewise, labor was regarded as a highly spiritual activity and guided by their vision of millennial holiness. Mother Ann herself had told them to "do your work as though it were to last a thousand years and you were to die tomorrow." Applying the principles of Mother Ann's teachings to their everyday economy, Shakers became highly industrious. The number of patents held by members of the movement in the nineteenth century ran into the thousands, and included such items as the push broom, the clothes pin, the screw-type nail, and the flat cut nail. A Shaker woman invented the circular saw by applying the principles of the spinning wheel to the milling of lumber in a Shaker woodshop.

Shaker Beliefs

Mother Ann often said that she was married to Jesus in her Christhood. By this she meant a spiritual union in which the divine Word dwelt in her as it had in him. Theirs was a spiritual relationship of equality, not one in which she was a submissive wife. Women's subordination was a result of original sin, she had taught. Mother Ann believed that Adam and Eve had fallen in the Garden of Eden by engaging in sexual relations before God had pronounced them good, that is, before they were mature and ready. The result was the sorrow and curse of Eve, tied up with her childbearing and her subordination to her husband in marriage. But marriage, according to Shaker teaching, was by definition a practice only of this age. Renunciation of sexual relations in the millennial kingdom meant renunciation of the curse of childbearing and the freedom from marriage. In this way men and women were seen to be restored to the original equality Adam and Eve were intended to have had in the Garden of Eden.

The image of God that had been restored by the revelation of Jesus and Mother Ann was a dual one. God, according to Shaker theology, was thus a duality of male and female, mother and father, and not a Trinity. The image of God the Heavenly Father was complemented and completed by the image of God the Heavenly Mother, sometimes associated with the Holy Spirit. The duality of God was in turn reflected in the duality of Jesus and Mother Ann as Christ, and the equality of men and women in the millennial kingdom.

Throughout all of its teachings and practices, the Shaker movement was infused with a sense of mystical participation in divine life. Although they had departed in their physical bodies, Mother Ann and other leaders continued to be experienced as present in mystical revelations and visitations among the Shakers. One of the best-known Shaker works of art, of the mystical Tree of Life, was received from Mother Ann by Hannah Cohoon in a series of visions in 1854. Since Shakers believed they had already entered the millennial age with their conversion, they did not believe in a physical resurrection of the dead. Instead, they participated in a wider mystical or spiritual form of community which united the living and dead through these visions and revelations.

Decline of the Shakers

At the height of the movement around the time of the Civil War, Shakers numbered approximately six thousand. Thereafter they began to decline until they reached their present state today with only a handful of members remaining in the Sabbathday Lake community in Maine. Although their numbers where never great, their impact was widely felt throughout American culture. Shakers believed that the millennial age had begun with the Second Coming of the Christ in the person of Mother Ann Lee. They understood this not to be a terminal event, but a process that had begun to unfold in their communities. Mother Ann never gave any hint as to how long the process would take. All she ever said on the matter was that they were drawing nigh, and counseled patience as she did when the group first withdrew to Watervliet. Mother Ann did say that one day when there were only five Shakers left on earth, then the last great outpouring of the Christ Spirit would occur and all the world would become Shakers. There are now less than a dozen Shakers left on earth.

Dale T. Irvin and Victoria L. Erickson

See also Burned-over District, Messianism

Bibliography

Andrews, Edward Deming. (1953) *The People Called Shakers: A Search for the Perfect Society.* New York: Oxford University Press.

Desroches, Henri. ([1955, in French] 1971) *The American Shakers: From Neo-Christianity to Pre-Socialism,* translated by John K. Savacool. Amherst, MA: University of Massachusetts Press.

Evans, Elder E. W. (1858) *Ann Lee: A Biography.* Albany, N.Y.: Charles van Benthuysen & Sons, Printers.

Green, Calvin, and Seth Young Wells. (1848) *A Summary View of the Millennial Church or United Society of Believers, Commonly Called the Shakers, Comprising the Rise, Progress and Practical Order of the Society Together with the General Principles of Their Faith and Testimony,* 2d ed. Albany, N.Y.: Charles van Benthuysen & Sons, Printers.

Jackson, Rebecca. (1981) *Gifts of Power: The Writings of Rebecca Jackson, Black Visionary, Shaker Eldress,* edited by Jean McMahon Humez. Amherst, MA: University of Massachusetts Press.

Mercadante, Linda A. (1990) *Gender, Doctrine and God: The Shakers and Contemporary Theology.* Nashville, TN: Abingdon Press.

Stein, Stephen. (1992) *The Shaker Experience in America: A History of the United Society of Believers.* New Haven, CT: Yale University Press.

Testimonies of the Life, Character, Revelations and Doctrines of Mother Ann Lee, and the Elders with Her, Through Whom the Word of Eternal Life Was Opened in This Day of Christ's Second Appearing, Collected from Living Witnesses in Union with the Church, 2d ed. (1888). Albany, NY: Weed, Parsons, and Co., Printers.

Sodom

The catastrophic destruction of the Cities of the Plain, Sodom and Gomorrah, described in the Hebrew scriptures' Book of Genesis, has over the centuries come to symbolize any apocalyptic disaster interpreted as punishment for sin. During the European Middle Ages the linkage of Sodom exclusively with nonreproductive sexual practices, particularly sex between men, perpetually associated erotic dissent with the risk of disaster in the imagination of the West. Since the Reformation, many preachers have represented "sodomy" as the catalyst for society's destruction, a figure of thought that was recharged in the second half of the twentieth century by the increasing visibility of gay and lesbian people and politicized during the first years of the AIDS epidemic.

Sodom in the Bible and the Qur'an

In the Hebrew Scriptures' Book of Genesis (chapters 18 and 19), Abraham's nephew Lot settles as an immigrant in Sodom. When Abraham is visited by angelic beings who announce God's intention to destroy the cities because of their (unspecified) wickedness, the patriarch engages in a remarkable bargaining exchange with God, who agrees to save the cities if he can find ten virtuous men there. When the angelic visitors arrive at Lot's house, men of the city surround the house and threaten the visitors. Lot attempts to distract the men with his virgin daughters (who will later inebriate him, have sexual intercourse with him, and each bear his child). The angelic visitors urge Lot to remove his wife, daughters, and his daughters' fiancés out of the plain to the hills, warning them not to look back. The future sons-in-law ridicule the warnings, but Lot and his family leave, although his wife turns to look behind her and is transformed into a pillar of salt as the cities are destroyed by hellfire and brimstone.

Between the Hebrew and Christian scriptures, Sodom is mentioned forty-eight times; in addition, there are several references to Lot in the Qur'an, treated extensively in sura 11.

In each case, Sodom is associated with a wickedness that prompted divine destruction; however, there is considerable inconsistency in what precisely constituted that wickedness. Although sex between men is the most familiar accusation (and the association prompted the medieval theologian Peter Damian to coin the term "sodomy"), Sodom and Gomorrah were also characterized as inhospitable to strangers (a serious transgression of a Semitic moral obligation) and unjust to the weak, such as widows, orphans, and the poor.

Ezekiel 16:49–50 condemns Sodom as having "pride, surfeit of food, and prosperous ease, but [it] did not aid the poor and needy." The Book of Wisdom (19:14) mentions their inhospitableness to strangers. Later commentators, as James L. Kugel discusses in *The Bible As It Was*, would likewise attribute diverse vices to Sodom. Writing in the first century BCE, the Jewish historian Josephus accused the Sodomites of overweening pride, arrogance, and greed (book 1). The Talmud characterizes Sodom's inhabitants as treacherous, cruel, idolatrous, and predatory of travelers. The early medieval Jewish midrashic commentary on the Torah, *Pirqei deR. Eliezer*, asserts that the Sodomites had mandated capital punishment for anyone who fed the poor or the traveler.

Sodom figures in the apocalyptic and millennialist texts of the Jewish and Christian scriptures. In Ezekiel 16, for example, the prophet excoriates Jerusalem (and by extension all the Israelite people) for their religious infidelities (including indulgence in luxury) which he configures in the language of sexual infidelity (Jerusalem is a "harlot" or prostitute). The prophet then proposes that Jerusalem's sin is greater than that of Sodom, whom God will restore before the Israelites. Similarly, in the apocalyptic sayings of Jesus in the Gospels, the Nazarene prophesies that in the Day of the Lord, his contemporaries will receive harsher judgment than that of the Sodomites (Matthew 10:15, 11:24; Luke 10:12). Revelation (11:8) associates Sodom with Egypt in the apocalyptic prophecy concerning the witnesses' martyrdom by the Beast from the Bottomless Pit.

The Image of Sodom through the Ages

Subsequent commentaries, theological treatises, sermons, and social criticisms dealing with Sodom would focus almost exclusively on the linkage of homosexuality and catastrophic destruction, characterizing the Cities of the Plain as a warning to future generations of God's willingness to destroy sinners. In the twelfth century, the theologian Peter the Cantor conflated murder and sodomy as equivalent crimes "crying out to heaven for justice," thus providing a justification for the destruction of the cities. Similarly, writers as diverse as the thirteenth-century penitentialist Paul of Hungary, the fourteenth-century English author of the alliterative poem *Cleanness*, and the fifteenth-century French moralist Jean Gerson attribute Noah's flood and the destruction of Sodom as having sodomy as their common cause. Catholic missionaries to China attributed the open trade in male prostitutes there as the cause of lightning storms in the late 1550s that devastated its towns.

In the Renaissance and afterwards, royal courts and cities came to be characterized as the new versions of Sodom, from which Protestant reformers and millennialist groups particularly sought to flee. Medieval Catholic moralists like Peter Damian and Paul of Hungary had laid a foundation for this criticism in their characterizing priests and courtiers as susceptible to sodomy. Already associating the Roman Catholic pope with Antichrist, Protestant preachers characterized all-male monasteries and unmarried priests as sodomitical and ripe for destruction in the endtimes. In a sermon preached before Queen Elizabeth I on the example of Lot's wife, the congregation was admonished to "specially remember we leave not our heart behind us, but that we take that with us, when we go out of Sodome: for if that stay, it will stay the feet, and writh the eye, and neither the one nore the other will do their duty, . . ." but also reminded of the perseverance of their Protestant queen, as a result of whose steadfastness they "are in safety, all the Cities of the Plaine being in combustion about us" (Hallam 165, 166). English Puritan divines in the sixteenth century, convinced of the utter depravity of fallen humans, would inventory human sinfulness as figurative "heart sodomy," as Thomas Shepard did in the popular 1641 tract *The Sincere Convert*, warning his readers about the "secret villainy" that would be exposed on judgment day. Even in the late nineteenth century, Rev. John Kitto would write: "Still there are Sodoms; and still there are Lots who think that, with a religious profession they may live in the world, and pursue its profits and its pleasures without danger. Let them beware. They are in great peril. If we be indeed God's people, let us come out of the world, and touch not the unclean thing—remember that the Church of God is not mixed up in the world" (Hallam 150).

In England, an expanding empire and growing capitalist prosperity produced unprecedented wealth among the upper classes, whose excesses in manners, dress, and luxury came to be painted by satirists employing a broad brush dipped in sodomitical innuendo. A popular mid-eighteenth-century English tract railing against the fashions of the day (which it blamed on the French and Italians) summed up its preoccupations in a remarkable title: *Satan's Harvest Home, or the Present State of Whorecraft, Adultery, Fornication, Procuring, Pimping, Sodomy, And the Game of Flatts* [i.e., lesbianism] . . . *And other Satanic Works, daily propagated in this good Protestant Kingdom.* Rev. Dr. Allen, in a sermon entitled "The Destruction of SODOM improved, as a warning to

GREAT BRITAIN" inventoried the excesses of the urban wealthy and concluded: "Do vices of the kind I have mentioned, waste the strength, impair the spirit, and root out the vitals of any nation? They certainly do: if therefore, these are the iniquities of England and of London, it is the breaking its own constitution, and, without fire from heaven or earthquakes from under the ground, it must die of itself" (McCormick 161). Around the same time, Charles Churchill wrote in "The Times, 1764" of his own mission to eradicate London's sodomites: "Their steps I'll track, nor yield them one retreat / Where they may hide their heads, or rest their feet, / Till God, in wrath, shall let his vengeance fall, / And make a great example of them all, / Bidding in one grand pile this town expire, / Her towers in dust, her Thames a lake of fire" (Hallam 134).

Michael Warner has characterized this sanctioned violence against homosexuals as "apocalyptic vehemence." The logic follows that if God treats "sodomites" mercilessly, humans may too. From the eighteenth through the nineteenth centuries periodic persecutions of homosexual men (women were usually exempted) were frequently characterized by capital or corporal punishments. London's so-called Vere Street Coterie in 1810 were publicly pilloried and authorities permitted a mob to assault them with buckets filled with blood, offal, and dung from slaughter houses, dead cats and dogs, and blows to head and body with brickbats, before being taken to prison. Although the pillory was no longer used at the end of the nineteenth century, Oscar Wilde was nonetheless imprisoned at hard labor for the judicial crime of sodomy.

The Image of Sodom in Contemporary America

A century later with the increasing visibility of gay and lesbian civil rights movements following World War II, which achieved considerable momentum in the late 1960s, Christian fundamentalists' millennialist anxieties began to coalesce around "godless communism" and "homosexual perversion." When the epidemic that came to be called AIDS emerged in public consciousness, those anxieties assumed apocalyptic dimensions. One immensely popular evangelist of the Charismatic Renewal movement, David Wilkerson, famous as the author of *The Cross and Switchblade* wrote of a vision in which he saw: "things . . . which make me fear for the future of our children. I speak of wild, roving mobs of homosexual men publicly assaulting innocent people in parks, on the streets, and in secret places. These attacks by Sodomite mobs are certain to come, and, although they may not be publicized as such, those in the law-enforcement circles will know the full extent of what is happening." Another influential fundamentalist writer, Tim LaHaye wrote: "Most Bible prophecy scholars teach that we are either in 'the last days,' predicted in the Scriptures, or we are very close to them. Interestingly enough, homosexuality is to be a part of the buildup of the 'perilously evil times' that are prophesied for the last days." Ed Rowe, the former director of Anita Bryant's 1977 antigay campaign, later wrote: "The road to ruin for America has been paved by the political homosexual militants. Their program is conceived in wickedness. Their platform is morally perverse. They would lead America to disaster, just as their ancient counterparts led Sodom to its certain doom."

A particularly Western phenomenon fueled by the narrative in Genesis, a text common to the "People of the Book" (Jews, Christians, and Moslems), the association of Sodom with same-sex relations and with communal catastrophe has resulted in the persecution of gays and lesbians as well as the quickening of modern millennialist desires and expectations.

Thomas L. Long

See also Defilement, Plague and Pestilence, Sexuality

Bibliography

Goldberg, Jonathan, ed. (1994) *Reclaiming Sodom.* New York: Routledge.

Hallam, Paul, ed. (1993) *The Book of Sodom.* London: Verso.

Jordan, Mark D. (1997) *The Invention of Sodomy in Christian Theology.* Chicago: University of Chicago Press.

Kugel, James L. (1997) *The Bible As It Was.* Cambridge: Harvard University Press.

LaHaye, Tim. (1978) *What Everyone Should Know about Homosexuality,* 4th printing. Wheaton, IL: Living Books. Originally published as *The Unhappy Gays.*

McCormick, Ian, ed. (1997) *Secret Sexualities: A Sourcebook of 17th and 18th Century Writing.* New York: Routledge.

Rowe, Ed. (1984) *Homosexual Politics: Road to Ruin for America* (with an introduction by Sen. Jesse Helms). Washington, D.C.: Church League of America.

Warner, Michael. (1992) "New English Sodom." *American Literature* 64, 1 (March): 19–47.

Wilkerson, David. (1974) *The Vision.* Old Tappan, NJ: Fleming H. Revell, Co.

The Solar Temple

The Solar Temple, known to its members as the OTS (l'Ordre du Temple Solaire) was an atypical example of the magical-esoteric movement, the Knights Templar, of which there are currently around a hundred various organizations worldwide. In three separate incidents in the mid-1990s, the Solar Temple gained worldwide attention when a large portion of its membership were found dead—in their view, transported back to the star Sirius, from whence they had come.

OTS traces its origins to Bernard-Raymond Fabre-Palaptrat, a scholar of the occult at the time of the French Revolution, who surfaced after the disestablishment of the church, and announced that he was the last grandmaster in a secret tradition that had continued underground since the Knights Templars were burned at the stake by order of the King of France, Philppe Le Bel in the fourteenth century.

The OTS was small, numbering between three to four hundred members at its peak, mainly located in Switzerland, France, and Quebec. Its members tended to be middle-aged and from the upper-middle or upper classes of Europe.

The Leaders

Luc Jouret and Joseph Di Mambro, the late leaders of the OTS, were established grandmasters in the neo-Templar tradition, who had collaborated in organizing workshops since 1976. Luc Jouret was born in the Belgian Congo on 18 October 1947. A homeopathic doctor, he was interested in alternative medicine, studied the techniques of the Philippines psychic healers, and established a successful practice on the Franco-Swiss border. Jouret joined an esoteric salon in 1980 led by three grandmasters in the neo-Templar tradition and formed a close association with one of them, Joseph Di Mambro, that later resulted in their collaboration in the mass suicide/homicide plan.

Joseph Di Mambro (1924–84) was a director of a watch manufacturer, and had served a long apprenticeship in Rosicrucianism (AMORC). He had a criminal record and presided over a commune in Geneva called La Pyramide, and after collecting insurance when the commune's house burned down, he launched the Golden Way. He was an Egyptologist, a connoisseur of opera, and claimed to be an adept in sex magic.

Two other influential grandmasters in the OTS were Jacques Breyer, a French Freemason, alchemist, author of esoteric books, and founder of l'Ordre Sovereign du Temple Solaire in 1952. Julien Origas was a right-wing political activist and former Nazi Gestapo officer and the grandmaster of the Renewed Order of the Temple (ORT). All three adepts were believers in the Ascended Master of Theosophical lore, and participants in the neo-Templar tradition.

In 1983 Jouret had joined ORT and when its founder Julien Origas died, he briefly assumed the leadership but was expelled by Origas' daughter Catherine after a struggle over the leadership and funds. He then formed a schismatic group with thirty ORT Templars called l'Ordre du Temple Solaire, and became their grandmaster and opened branches of his movement in Martinique and Quebec. In 1984 Jouret and Di Mambro entered into a more formal relationship when they established l'Ordre International Chevaleresque de Tradition Solaire (OICTS) in Geneva. Jouret was the OICTS' recruiting and PR officer and organized over 200 conferences in France and Quebec. Various public organizations were formed around the OICTS, that functioned like "Chinese boxes" (Introvigne 1995a: 9): the Clubs Amenta, Agata, and the Clubs Atlanta. The OTS organization was hierarchical and involved three levels of initiation: Freres du Parvis, Chevalier de l'Alliance, and Frere des Temps Anciens. The treasurer of the OTS was Camille Pilet, a wealthy jeweler born in 1926 and former member of AMORC. Three women were the main administrators, among them Di Mambro's wife, Jocelyne. Other gifted members were invited into an inner circle.

The OTS evolved an elaborate ritual life that drew upon traditional esoteric symbols. Full-moon festivals were held in the countryside, and underground initiation rituals modeled on the ceremonies of mediaeval knights were videotaped. Modern technology was used to conjure up "miracles," such as holograms of the Holy Grail. These apparitions bolstered Di Mambro's charisma as well as faith in the tutelary presence of the White Brotherhood, referred to as the "elder brothers."

In 1987 Jouret and Di Mambro moved to Canada and bought a farm in St-Anne-de-Perade near Quebec City. They established a commune, an organic farm, a bakery, and a home schooling program. This New Age retreat was called Le Centre Culturel du Domaine du Sacre-Coeur. The purpose of the farm was to provide a survivalist shelter for members, since Quebec was protected, they believed, against ecological disaster due to its "granite bedrock," and to foster an *egregore* or collective consciousness to "wake up humanity." To this latter end, the group built several underground crypts in Quebec and Switzerland where initiates performed elaborate ceremonies to raise the consciousness of humanity and prevent ecological disaster.

The Three "Transits"

On 4 October 1994, a chalet in Morin Heights, Quebec, exploded in a fire that was deliberately set. The police first found two bodies of victims that had swallowed sleeping pills and died of smoke inhalation. Two days later they discovered the remains of the Dutoit family; a husband and wife stabbed to death with their heads inside plastic bags, and their baby of four months with a stake through his heart. On 5 October two nearby villages in Switzerland, Cheiry and Salvan, became the site of two ritual suicides (and homicides).

An ex-member, Thierry Huguenin, claims the number of victims chosen for the "transit" was intended to reenact martyrdom of fifty-four Templars burnt at the stake on 10 May 1310, but that he escaped, reducing it to fifty-three. Introvigne (1995b: 1) dismisses this claim as historically inaccurate and probably fabricated to promote the sale of Huguenin's book.

The Swiss magistrate in the inquest, Nicky Robinson deemed that only fifteen Templars (those whose bodies were found at Salvan and who called themselves the "Awakened") deliberately chose to die. At Cheiry there were thirty "Immortals" who shared their beliefs but did not volunteer to die, thus were "gently helped." Among these were four children and three teenagers. Eight people in Morin Heights and at Cheiry qualified as "traitors" against whom the Templars exacted a "just retribution."

A second Transit was effected in December 1995 during the winter solstice near Grenoble, France. Fourteen charred bodies were found lying in star formation around a campfire; and the two Templars who shot them and set them on fire, then shot themselves, were discovered nearby. The victims had ingested sedatives and some of them had plastic bags over their heads.

The third transit occurred on 22 March 1997 in St. Casimir, Quebec. Two middle-aged couples, the Quebecois Didier Queze and his wife with her mother (who was not a member of the OTS) and Bruno Klaus and his companion, who had all been members of the St-Anne-de-Parade commune. The three Queze teens had escaped the first suicide-murder attempt perpetrated by their parents when the incendiary devices failed to go off, and had managed to negotiate their way out of accompanying their parents on their trip to Sirius. The teens were given sleeping pills and instructed to spend the night in the garden shed out of the adults' way. they awoke to find their parents dead and their home in flames.

Four "suicide notes" were sent to Swiss scholar, Jean-Francois Mayer, and the press, which explained the religious rationale behind the transit. These letters, "La Rose + Croix," "Aux Epris de la Justice," "Transit pour le Futur," and "A Tous Ceux qui Peuvent Encore Entendre la Voix de la Sagesse" justify the murders as a "just retribution," or assistance to those who qualified as Templars, but needed to be "gently helped." They outline conspiracy theories, and express a profound sense of alienation from the world.

Events Leading to the Transit

The Swiss police have interpreted the transit as a desperate reaction to external pressure—lawsuits, police investigations in Quebec, internal betrayals, and defections.

First, there were a number of lawsuits by Swiss ex-members, notably Rosemary Klaus and Thierry Huguenin who sought to recover their financial investments. Klaus collaborated with the French anticult movement, ADFI, in spreading negative news reports of the OTS' activities.

Secondly, there were police investigations into the OTS' financial affairs and the leaders' telephones were wiretapped. Leaders feared the desecration of their secret underground temples if the police were to search the chalets. On 23 November 1992 an anonymous phone call warned Quebec government officials of a mysterious Q-37 terrorist group that was plotting to murder Quebec's Minister of the Interior because he was indulgent toward the claims of the native peoples. On 8 May 1993 two OTS leaders, Pierre Vinet and Herman Delorme, were arrested for attempting to purchase illegal handguns. They were suspected of being part of the Q-37 planning to assassinate Claude Ryan, Quebec Minister of the Interior. At their court hearing on 30 June 1993 they received a "suspended acquittal" and fine.

A third factor enhancing the volatility of the group may have been the struggle over the leadership of the Quebec branch which resulted in a schism. Roger Giguere, the treasurer of the Quebec branch claimed the St-Anne-de-Perade commune was non-hierarchical, governed by an administrative counsel that functioned in a democratic fashion. When Luc Jouret arrived, however, he "played the guru" and short-circuited their decision-making processes. In 1987 the administrative counsel voted Jouret out of office and appointed Robert Fallardeau, a Quebec civil servant, in his place, allowing Jouret a role in public relations to save face. The European branch of the OTS rejected this decision, and refused to recognize Fallardeau, and Jouret quit the executive committee in 1993. The Swiss police have argued that the Quebec members who died at Cheiry were murdered to avenge the schism led by Fallardeau who supplanted Jouret as the leader in Quebec in the early 1980s. The suicide notes left by the group contain a phrase threatening a "just retribution" to "traitors."

A exacerbating fourth factor may have been the perceived "betrayal" by former members, particularly the Dutoits who were murdered in Quebec. Tony Dutoit was a lighting engineer who had created the illusions for the rituals in l'Ermitage in Salvan, using electronic devices, holograms, projections, mirrors, and lights. He and his wife, Nicky Robinson, defected in 1991, and moved to Quebec, although he continued to be employed by the OTS. Ex-members have speculated that his brutal murder may have been provoked by his indiscretion in talking to other members about his work, thereby undermining the charismatic claims of Jouret and Di Mambro, who encouraged the illusion that these visions were conjured up by the powers of the Elder Brothers.

A rumor circulated among members that Dutoit was a spy reporting to the Royal Canadian Mounted Police. Nickie Dutoit had also offended Di Mambro who had forbidden her to bear children. After the move to Quebec, however, she gave birth to a son called Christiophe Emmanuel. Di Mambro then announced their baby was a reincarnation of the "Antichrist."

The Dutoit family murders were performed as a ceremonial slaying. Antonio Dutoit was murdered with fifty knife wounds, Nicky Robinson received fourteen blows of a knife, four in the throat, which according to the OTS' esoteric lore would prevent her from having a child in her next life . . . eight in the back, symbolic of justice . . . and two to her breast because she had nursed the Antichrist. The baby was killed by a single stab to the heart, believed to be the only way to kill the Antichrist. Dominique Bellaton (the mother of Di Mambro's daughter) and Joel Eggar witnessed the murder, but the couple who committed the "execution" were the Genouds. Di Mambro had revealed to Gerry Genoud that he was the reincarnation of the soldier who had pierced Christ with his lance and in order to expiate this terrible crime, his must destroy the Antichrist and its parents in a rite of purification. After murdering the Dutoit family, the Genouds purified themselves by washing their hands and the walls of the room and then committed suicide.

Interpretations of the Transit

The transit could be interpreted as a drastic solution to avoid a potential "loss of charisma" resulting from several factors. Di Mambro was old and had recently experienced kidney failure and diabetes. Challenges to his authority were also arising within his own family. In 1990 his son, Elio Di Mambro left home and wrote a letter denouncing his father. Elio returned, but then discovered the closet containing the props used to create illusions in the Sanctuaire and he accused his father of fraud. The Dutoits, who had been members of the OTS' most secret core, had not only partially defected and had a child against Jo's explicit orders whom they named Emmanuel—which Di Mambro interpreted as a challenge to the charismatic identity of his own daughter, Emmanuelle. Moreover, they had the effrontery to "blab" about the technical aspect of the miraculous epiphanies sent by the White Brotherhood in the Sanctuaire. The transit, therefore, forestalled the embarrassment that might ensue once it became widely known that the miracles in the Sanctuary were the product of electronic devices.

The transit was undoubtedly a "charismatic display" on the part of the leaders and the core group, intended to reinforce a respect for the magical efficacy and spiritual power of the Elder Brothers, the grand masters, and the community itself. It solved the problem of the succession, for Di Mambro and his aging companions could cast off their defective bodies and become "glorious solar beings."

The OTS' Apocalyptic Drama

The secret mystical-apocalyptic doctrine of the OTS that has emerged out of this tragedy is as follows. OTS Templars believed they were immortal "fully conscious" beings whose home was Sirius, who parachuted in and out of the material world at critical moments in history to "wake up humanity." Jouret claimed our planet was on the cusp between the Age of Pisces and Aquarian Age and that ecological disaster was imminent. As a symbol of environmental contamination and penance, members placed plastic garbage bags over their heads. According to the esoteric lore of Jacques Breyer and others, only through fire could a spirit be purified and transported to another world.

In the early 1980s, the OTS appeared optimistic concerning the future of humanity. The cosmic child, an Avatar to save humanity was "magically" conceived; a survivalist farm in Quebec was established; and rituals to increase humanity's bank of consciousness were enacted. By the mid-eighties, however, a more pessimistic vision was in place. Jouret became convinced the human race was beyond redemption and that full-scale ecological and nuclear calamities were nigh. The turning point occurred on 6 January 1994, when Di Mambro, Jouret, and Pilet visited Ayers Rock in Sydney, Australia. There they received a revelation from the Elder Brothers that they were abandoning Earth. The suicide letters suggest that OTS leaders interpreted this as a sign of cosmic judgement and decided to give up on decadent humanity who ignored the Elder Brothers' invitation assists in building a New Age. They decided to follow in the wake of their Elder brothers; to resume their "solar bodies" and return to the star Sirius.

Susan J. Palmer

Bibliography

Aubert, Raphael, and Carl-A. Keller. (1994) *Vie et Mort de l'Ordre du Temple Solaire.* Lausanne, France: Editions de l'Aire/Jouvence.

Breyer, Jacques. (1959) *Arcanes Solaire; ou, Les Sectrets du Temple Solaire.* Paris: La Colombe.

Hall, John, and Philip Schuyler. (1997) "The Mystical Apocalypse of the Solar Temple." In *Millennium Messiahs and Mayhem,* edited by Thomas Robbins and Susan J. Palmer. New York: Routledge.

Huguenin, Thierry (with Lionel Duroy). (1995) *Le 54e.* Canada: FIXOT.

Introvigne, Massimo. (1995a) "Ordeal by Fire: The Tragedy of the Solar Temple." *Religion* 25, 4 (July): 267–83.

Introvigne, Massimo. (1995b) "The Solar Temple Remembered." Paper presented November at the AAR Meeting in Philadelphia.

Jouret, Luc. (1986) *Alimentation Moderns et Inconscience Humaine.* Les Cahiers Amenta, internal publication. Les Editions Amenta.

Mayer, Jean Francois. (1993) "Des Templiers pour l'Ere du Verseau: Les Clubs Archedia (1984–1991) et l'Ordre International Chevalresque Tradition Solaire." *Mouvements Religeuses* (AEIMR, January): 2–10.

——. (1996) *Les mythes du Temple Solaire.* Geneva: Georg Editeur; Editions Medicine & Hygeine.

——. (1999) "'Our Terrestrial Journey is Coming to an End': The Last Voyage of the Solar Temple." *Nova Religio* 11, 2: 172–96.

Palmer, Susan J. (1996) "Purity and Danger in the Solar Temple." *Journal of Contemporary Religion* 11: 303–18.

Stress

One of the most widely accepted theories of how millennial movements arise is the view that people drawn to them must be motivated by extreme emotional stress. The theory suggests that angry, hopeless people are most likely to yearn for the destruction of the world and the advent of a savior. By focusing on the psychology of stress within stress-producing social environments, we can gain insights about the psychological origins of millenarianism.

Stress comes in many varieties and has many causes. Ill-health is found throughout society, and the most appropriate religious response is spiritual healing rather than millenarianism. Psychological disorders may often give people unusual experiences that can be interpreted religiously, but it is very difficult for a disturbed would-be messiah to recruit followers who do not share his or her private stresses. The stresses that give rise to movements must be widely shared and social in origin. A millennial movement is not only a band of individuals suffering a socially induced stress, but also one that hopes divine intervention will turn the tables on those more fortunate than they. Thus it is often assumed that millenarians are oppressed masses who know they are too weak to overthrow their oppressors, but hope God will do so for them.

Strain Theory

In his research on the first branch of the Unification Church to come from Korea to the United States, John Lofland studied the arduous recruitment of new members to a radical movement that anticipated the Lord of the Second Advent to arrive and complete the mission begun by Jesus Christ, possibly amid apocalypse. Most recruits suffered from failure and consequent low self-esteem and came from devout religious backgrounds. In collaboration with sociologist Rodney Stark, Lofland theorized that recruits to a deviant perspective must begin with nagging life problems that resist solution, what he called *enduring, acutely felt tensions.* People must also have a religious problem-solving perspective that tells them to seek supernatural help. Because their customary religion seems unable to solve the problems, they become religious seekers, hunting for a more effective creed. To join the movement, they must encounter it by chance at a turning point in their lives when commitments are weak, and they must enter into intensive social interaction with people who already are members.

The people Lofland studied were not suffering from hunger or incurable physical diseases, but from emotional problems possibly connected to the competitive nature of American society. Lofland defined tensions as a perceived discrepancy between the lives people actually experienced and an ideal life they could imagine vividly. Thus, Lofland's analysis was rooted in the strain theory of deviant behavior that had been sketched by Robert K. Merton and elaborated upon by many other writers in the Structural-Functionalist school of sociology. This perspective viewed society as a relatively smoothly operating system of institutions, roles, and norms that fitted together and sustained each other. Merton (1968) argued that human beings learn most of their goals ("values") from society, rather than from biological instincts. People also learn the approved means ("norms") for attaining those goals. For example, an American is expected to seek prosperity and social status by means of a good education and working hard. But for people who fail in education, success can be hard to get, and the means provided by American culture do not take them to the goals. The result may be to reject conformity in favor of some other mode of adaptation to the challenges of life.

An innovator, in Merton's scheme, continues to seek the goals but adopts new means, such as crime to gain the money that conformists simply earn. But many people are either too well socialized or too weak to be successful criminals. Some of them ritualistically follow society's norms in full awareness they will never achieve the goals. Others retreat from this hopeless situation, abandoning the pursuit of any goals by any means. These retreatists include psychotics, outcasts, vagabonds, drunkards, and drug addicts. Merton also postulated that a few rebels would reject both the values and norms of society, substituting new ones in their place. It is an open question whether millenarians are retreatist—waiting passively for a supernatural force to save them—or are cultural rebels rejecting the entire existing society.

False Consciousness

Neil Smelser expanded Merton's theory into a general model of collective behavior, including millenarian movements. Structural strain is not merely frustration felt by many people, but impairment in the relations between the values, norms, and institutions of the society. When the strain is great, he said, desperate people will engage in *short-circuiting,* in which they foolishly reject beneficial aspects of their culture and turn to radical ideologies such as millenarianism.

Marxist writers refer to intellectual errors like this as "false consciousness," a profound failure to understand the correct political realities and options. For example, Eric J. Hobsbawm called millenarians "primitive rebels" (1959), because they did not understand that the proper response to stress was political action against the oppressive regimes that caused the stress in the first place. Indeed, throughout history victims of an oppressive state have tended to join millenarian movements to the extent that the state was able to suppress political rebellion, so long as the cultural traditions included myths about a savior the people could believe might free them from their chains. However, Marxism itself has proved to be a failed apocalyptic political movement, and writers like Hobsbawm may have given the millenarians of history too little credit. Rather than being ignorant fools, they may have merely relied upon ideas that were as plausible in their own centuries as Marxism was in the twentieth.

Anthropologist Anthony F. C. Wallace (1956) offered a more favorable analysis than those of Smelser and Hobsbawm. When a society is under great strain, the culture is not functioning well to deal with the stresses that individuals suffer. Some especially creative individuals, who feel the stress very strongly in their personal lives, begin to have visions and receive prophecies. These are not necessarily the symptoms of metal illness, but potentially curative spiritual experiences that give a small minority of these visionaries the insight to help their society deal effectively with the stresses it suffers. Often the result is a new religious mass movement that either helps people deal with chronic stress or establishes new norms and institutions that objectively reduce the stress.

Cognitive Dissonance

If stress causes millennial movements, then logically psychological pressures should intensify when the millennial prophecies fail to come true. Psychologist Leon Festinger carried out covert observational research (1956) inside a millennial group headed by Dorothy Martin (called "Mrs. Keech" in Festinger's book), who predicted that flying saucers would save her followers from impending natural disaster. He used this case to illustrate his theory of "cognitive dissonance." Supposedly, people have an innate need for their beliefs to harmonize with each other, and they will suffer psychological stress when they do not. Specifically, Festinger predicted that Martin's group would become more aggressive in proselytizing for their beliefs after the saucers failed to arrive as predicted, in reaction to the cognitive dissonance of having a belief proved false.

Festinger's evidence is actually poor, however, because the group was hounded by reporters and could not freely choose how to respond. Festinger argues that the "Great Disappointment" of 1844, when the Second Coming predictions of William Miller (1782–1848) were disconfirmed, was another example, because the Millerites supposedly became more radical as each of several key dates passed without incident. However, Miller himself was not driven to millenarianism by any obvious life stress, and he acknowledged the error of his predictions. The movement radicalized only because the more moderate members left, leaving innately radical members to dominate it. Thus, cognitive dissonance may have nothing to do with responses to a failed millennial prophecy. Rather, people who hoped the millennium would save them from stress may assert their needs all the more strongly when it fails to do so, and crucial events may separate the stress-driven millenarians from others who lack desperation as a motive for belief.

Conclusion

Despite their shortcomings, theories that say stress provides the motivation for millennial movements are plausible. People who require a supernatural savior to rescue them from life seem likely to lack confidence that they can deal with life's stresses on their own. Proclaiming that the world is about to end seems a harsh message to those who will not be saved, thus most likely motivated by extreme hostility toward nonmembers. Recruits to modern millenarian movements like the Seventh-Day Adventists and Jehovah's Witnesses do tend to be from the lower social classes. However, this is also true for people who join other sectarian movements that are not millenarian, and it is not clear that stress rather than low education is the key factor. Thus much systematic empirical research is needed before we will know how much confidence to place in stress-based theories of millennial movements.

William Sims Bainbridge

Bibliography

Bainbridge, William Sims. (1997) *The Sociology of Religious Movements.* New York: Routledge.

Cohn, Norman. (1961) *The Pursuit of the Millennium.* New York: Harper.

Festinger, Leon, Henry W. Riecken, and Stanley Schachter. (1956) *When Prophecy Fails.* New York: Harper and Row.

Hobsbawm, Eric J. (1959) *Primitive Rebels.* Manchester, U.K.: Manchester University Press.

Lofland, John. (1966) *Doomsday Cult.* Englewood Cliffs, NJ: Prentice-Hall.

Merton, Robert K. (1968) *Social Theory and Social Structure.* New York: Free Press.

Smelser, Neil J. (1962) *Theory of Collective Behavior.* New York: Free Press.

Stark, Rodney, and William Sims Bainbridge ([1987] 1966). *A Theory of Religion.* New Brunswick, NJ: Rutgers University Press.

Wallace, Anthony F. C. (1956) "Revitalization Movements." *American Anthropologist* 58: 264–81.

The views expressed in this article do not necessarily represent the views of the National Science Foundation or the United States.

Summum

Both the interest in and "appearance" of aliens in our midst are key signs that our world is on the verge of cosmic transformation, according to Summum, a ufology religion based in Salt Lake City, Utah. The group was founded by former Mormon Church elder Claude Rex Nowell (a.k.a. Summum Bonum Amen Ra), an administrative manager for a large Salt Lake City supply company, after a series of encounters with extraterrestrial "Summa Individuals" in 1975. Summum professes an optimistic and millennial belief regarding the coming of benevolent extraterrestrial beings who will aid in the evolution of humankind and planet earth.

The theme of the alien messiah is also evident throughout the literature of the Summum. According to the group's doctrine, Nowell was chosen by the Summa—"extraterrestrial saviors"—to convey their message of hope and salvation to the rest of humanity. This message is reported in "Contact! The First Encounter" at the group's website.

The Summum Temple

« Disclaimer »

Religious persecution is alive and well in America!

History

The Summum temple was completed in 1979. Because of its use for creating the *Nectar Publications* and because local and federal authorities refused to acknowledge the creation and use of the nectars as a religious practice, Summum is forced to license the temple as a winery and received its license in 1980. A distinction we would gladly give up for our religious freedom, the Summum temple is the first federally bonded "winery" in the state of Utah. It was built with the intention of re-producing divine nectars whose recipe pre-dates that of the oldest wineries; nectars that in ancient times were referred to as "Nectar of the Gods."

Location and Hours

Our temple is located at 707 Genesee Avenue, Salt Lake City, Utah 84104. Phone (801) 355-0137. It is close to downtown Salt Lake City, nestled within the beautiful Wasatch Mountains. Our hours are 9:00am to 5:00pm. You are welcome to drop by anytime during these hours.

Website page showing Summum Temple in Salt Lake City, Utah. HTTP://WWW.SUMMUM.ORG/NECTARS/TEMPLE.HTM.

I have been with the Summa Individuals many, many times. . . . These advanced Beings work with those ready to take up the labor of universal progression and divine evolution, and within the bounds of natural LAW provide assistance to those willing to take the responsibility of this destiny. Each time the Summa Individuals support and assist in the evolution of Humankind, acting as a catalyst for progression, and always bound by the constraint of the LAW."

Shortly after his encounters with the Summa individuals, Nowell founded "Summum," a Latin term meaning the sum total of all creation, as a nonprofit foundation for the philosophy of Summum. The Summa Individuals provided Nowell with plans to build pyramids and produce Nectar Publications. The group's work centers on the Summum Transcending meditations, a series of meditations which help initiates transcend their consciousness and bring them into contact with their higher spiritual selves. Like the Raelian Movement, the Summum preach and practice mediation of Sexual Energy, believing that the basis of all creation is copulation and procreation. Thus the Summum treat sexuality as a divine and important part of one's spiritual evolution since sexual union means a state of union with God.

Mummification of the deceased is another practice undertaken by the Summum, for whom the practice is less important in preserving the body than in the effect it has in aiding the spirit of the deceased to make the transition from life to a new state of being—a process the Summum call "transference." The group offers mummification as an alternative to burial or cremation to anyone regardless of their religious or philosophical beliefs.

Philip Lamy

"MAN AND WOMAN ARE, THAT THEY MAY HAVE JOY."—SUMMUM BONUM AMEN

A message to all humankind, religious leaders, prophets, holy teachers and those dressed in the costumes of religion and spirituality.
I AM back with the greatest gift of all creation, "JOY."
When two devoted humankind
join their physical and spiritual bodies together in sexual meditation,
the two become one essence.
As one, they enter the "Joy" of Ecstasy,
the domain and presence of God.

A prayer to all humankind, religious leaders, prophets, holy teachers,
and those dressed in the costumes of religion and spirituality.
If your religion, philosophy, metaphysics or science
can bring a greater permanent state of ecstasy and joy to man and woman,
explain the method on your official letterhead,
and send it to the Summum Bonum.
It will be posted on this web site.

If your religion, philosophy, metaphysics or science is unable
to bequeath to all of humankind this greatest of gifts,
then you shall hang your heads in sorrow and your hearts shall confess
that you have read these words
and never will your soul allow you to forget them.

Source: Summum Bonum Amen (1999) *Sexual Ecstasy from Ancient Wisdom.* http://www.summum.org/sexecs.

Bibliography

Lamy, Philip. (1999) "UFOs, Extraterrestrials and the Apocalypse: The Evolution of a Millennial Subculture." In *Millennial Visions*, edited by Martha Lee. New York: Praeger.

Summum Bonum Amen Ra. (1997) "Contact! The First Encounter." http://www.summum.org/firstenc.htm.

Survivalism

Survivalism is an apocalyptic form of the same type of emergency preparedness most people engage in when they purchase a first-aid kit or hang a fire extinguisher near their kitchen stove. Emergency preparedness is a practical methodological response in anticipation of a potential crisis, and it reflects sensible precautions for periodic hurricanes or floods. Survivalism tends to reflect less realistic apocalyptic fears that lead some people to prepare to survive a cataclysm that collapses the society into chaos. Periods of millennial expectation can trigger survivalism as a response to an anticipated period of apocalyptic disruption.

Despite apocalyptic roots, some mild forms of survivalism are benign or even socially beneficial, such as when farm cooperatives, urban shelters, religious groups, or government agencies store extra food and other supplies in case of some extended emergency situation or catastrophic event. Members of The Church of Jesus Christ of Latter-day Saints, (LDS), popularly called Mormons, are instructed to "prepare to care for themselves and their families in time of need," as a leading LDS Web page advised in 1999. The article noted that "Provident living involves being wise, frugal, prudent, and making provision for the future while attending to immediate needs." Information was provided on home storage of supplies based on a chart of what one adult needs to survive for one year. There was also advice on how to have immediate access to seventy-two hours worth of emergency supplies (LDS Food Storage List 1999). In a country so close to a pioneer past, such measures are unremarkable, especially in rural areas.

These and other examples of sensible survivalism stand in stark contrast to the more frenetic and sensational forms that resulted in armed compounds and shoot-outs with law enforcement officers in the 1970s and 1980s. Most survivalists occupy the space between sensible emergency preparedness and the apocalyptic armed underground. Survivalists may gather and store large supplies of food, water, and medicine; purchase gold, silver, and other precious metals as a hedge against currency devaluation; stockpile weapons and ammunition; or move to remote locations.

As Philip Lamy observes in his seminal book *Millennium Rage: Survivalists, White Supremacists, and the Doomsday Prophecy*, survivalism often overlaps with conspiracist worldviews, which are prevalent not only in the Patriot and militia movements and the far right, but in sectors of the Christian Right as well. Still, survivalism is a methodology, therefore it is not accurate to assume all survivalists share a specific ideological viewpoint. Lamy cautions that not all survivalists are part of White supremacist or anti-Semitic movements, but then chronicles how easy it is for survivalism to attract bigots who demonize their opponents and accuse them of plotting the attacks they are preparing to survive. There is a racist narrative in much survivalist literature that fans fears of non-white urban dwellers rampaging out of the cities in search of food. It some cases this is overt racism, but often it appears to be unwitting prejudice.

Survivalists do not automatically pose a threat to civil order since their intent is to take defensive precautions. Yet the potential for confrontation exists when survivalism mixes with apocalyptic fears or millennial expectation. Estimates of the number of survivalists are hard to verify, partly because many survivalists value their privacy to the point of paranoia. Survivalism, however, has grown to where it supports a thriving commercial subculture indicating many tens of thousands of regular participants, and probably more than one hundred thousand casual participants. These figures predate popular awareness of the Y2K computer glitch, which propelled millions into an awareness of survivalist issues.

Survivalist supplies are available at retail outlets, through the mail, at emergency preparedness expositions, and at gun shows. An ad in a November 1998 issue of the ultraconservative *Human Events* listed preparedness supplies from the American Family Institute which offered "the highest quality dehydrated food storage products," The ad asked: "Are You Prepared? Experts Agree: The most important preparation anyone can do for the upcoming crises is to obtain a reserve supply of Food and Water!" In each corner of the ad were boxes listing the possible crises: "Y2k Millennium Bug, Natural Disasters, Economic Crisis, Terrorism/War" (1998: 20). Fear that the Y2K computer problem would disrupt society led many diverse people to various forms of emergency preparedness or survivalism.

The common belief in the need for survivalist-style preparation for possible Y2K chaos bridged many divisions. The confluence of the Christian Right and patriot/militia movements with generic survivalism could be seen by reading the posts on various Web sites. Premillennialists and postmillennialists could interact with secularists in discussions over which water purification filter provided the best value in bacterial protection. As in secular circles, Christian responses range from cautious preparations to doomsday scenarios that led some to call for rural survivalist retreats. Gary North, on his popular Web site, claimed Y2K created the need for drastic survivalist-style preparations. A postmillennialist, North argued there was no connection between the Y2K problem and the End Times, but felt that secular disruption would reach apocalyptic proportions.

Y2K was not the first example of mass awareness of survivability. The government Civil Defense program in the 1950s and 1960s popularized ideas about surviving nuclear war by building community fallout shelters and suggesting the storage of home supplies and the building of basement and backyard family shelters. This may seem absurd in retrospect, but at the time, it was taken quite seriously. Robinson and North, as late as during the Reagan Administration in 1986, wrote about the survivability of nuclear war in their book *Fighting Chance: Ten Feet to Survival*, which featured a shovel, a clock, and the Capitol building on the cover. The authors recommended digging backyard fallout shelters.

Varieties of Survivalism

Saxon and Benson write about survivalism primarily from a secular perspective. The first volume of Saxon's *The Survivor* magazine series, later issued in book form as four compendiums, is dated 1976. Saxon is usually credited with coining the term "survivalism." Saxon's compendiums feature formulas, techniques, and recipes useful after the expected collapse: how to make matches, beekeeping, catching a large fish with a teaspoon, building a wind-powered electrical generator, raising pigs and rabbits, repairing bicycles. According to Saxon, "my books will give you a level of technology both interesting and practical, useful even today. You need not fear death from want, ignorance or from human predators. . . . I'm not interested in hobbyists or nostalgia buffs. I'm aiming my material at the strong-minded individualist, the only type who can, and should, survive" (1988b: 479).

McAlvany and Spear write about survivalism from a Christian perspective. The monthly *McAlvany Intelligence Advisor* financial newsletter, is "explicitly Christian, conservative, and free market in its perspective" (1997: ii). In his book, *War in Paradise: Surviving the Breakdown of America*, McAlvany warns:

> So many Americans today are totally dependent on the system (i.e., water, power, transportation, abundant food supplies, telephones, computers, high tech gadgets and tools that do almost all of the work for us), on government agencies, experts (i.e., medical, mechanical, psychological, high tech, etc.) that the old ways of doing things and of thinking have all but disappeared and been forgotten.
>
> If we are to survive as a free people our mind set of wimpiness, dependence on all the amenities and crutches around us, our softness and our laziness must cease. We need to study and emulate the courage and sacrifice, determination and ruggedness of our founding fathers and forebears who settled this country from coast to coast with a Bible in one hand and an ax or rifle in the other.
>
> Some of this writer's well-meaning Christian friends will counter that "such thinking is not trusting God." But Proverbs 27:12 says: "The prudent see danger and take refuge, but the simple keep going and suffer for it." (1997: viii–ix)

Some Christian Fundamentalist survivalists believe that to avoid Satan's Mark of the Beast, they must live apart from secular society for a period of up to forty-two months. Robert K. Spear, a key figure on the patriot and militia training circuit, is the author of *Surviving Global Slavery: Living Under the New World Order*, and *Creating Covenant Communities*. Spear warned of the approaching End Times and the Tribulations. Citing Revelation 13, Spear warned that Christians would soon be asked to accept the Mark of the Beast and thus reject Christ. True Christians, according to Spear, must defend their faith and prepare the way for the return of Christ through the formation of armed Christian communities. One book by Spear was dedicated to "those who will have to face the Tribulations" (1992: ii).

Saxon and Benson have libertarian antigovernment views that are apocalyptic, as do McAlvany and Spear, but the latter two survivalists weave in more overt millennial and conspiracist rhetoric.

Conclusions

Survivalism flows logically from worldviews that anticipate the disruption of basic services, no matter what the cause. As a methodology it can be used by a wide range of ideologically driven groups. Millennialism that anticipates a period of apocalyptic chaos easily gravitates toward survivalism. As Gibson (1994) and Ehrenreich (1997) observe, warrior culture paramilitarism, and survivalism are interwoven with the rugged individual motif of traditional masculinity in the United States.

Chip Berlet

See also Church Universal and Triumphant

Bibliography

Ahern, Jerry. (1981) *The Survivalist: Total War.* New York: Kensington Publishing.

American Family Institute. (1998) Advertisement. *Human Events* (13 November): 20.

Belz, Joel, Roy Manard, Chris Stamper, and Lynn Vincent. (1998) Cover story and series of articles on Y2K. *World* (22 August).

Benson, Ragnar. (1998) *The Modern Survival Retreat.* Boulder, CO: Paladin Press.

Coates, James. ([1987] 1995) *Armed and Dangerous: The Rise of the Survivalist Right.* New York: Hill and Wang.

Corcoran, James. ([1990] 1995). *Bitter Harvest: The Birth of Paramilitary Terrorism in the Heartland.* New York: Viking Penguin.

Ehrenreich, Barbara. (1997) *Blood Rites: Origins and History of the Passions of War.* New York: Henry Holt.

Gibson, James William. (1994) *Warrior Dreams: Paramilitary Culture in Post Viet Nam America.* New York: Hill & Wang.

Heinlein, Robert A. (1964) *Farnham's Freehold.* New York: Putnam.

Lamy, Philip. (1996) *Millennium Rage: Survivalists, White Supremacists, and the Doomsday Prophecy.* New York: Plenum.

LDS Food Storage List. (1999) http://www.lds1.com/essays/food.html.

McAlvany, Donald S. (1997) *War in Paradise: Surviving the Breakdown of America.* Phoenix, AZ: McAlvany Intelligence Advisor.

North, Gary. (1999) "Gary North's Y2K Links and Forums: The Year 2000 Problem: The Year the Earth Stands Still." http://www.garynorth.com.

Robinson, Arthur and Gary North. (1986) *Fighting Chance: Ten Feet to Survival.* Cave Junction, OR: Oregon Institute of Science and Medicine.

Saxon, Kurt. (1988a) *The Survivor,* Vol. 1. Alpena, AZ: Atlan Formularies.

——. (1988b) *The Survivor,* Vol. 2. Alpena, AZ: Atlan Formularies.

Scheer, Robert. (1982) *With Enough Shovels: Reagan, Bush and Nuclear War.* New York: Random House.

Spear, Robert K. (1992) *Surviving Global Slavery: Living Under the New World Order.* Leavenworth, KS: Universal Force Dynamics.

Spear, Robert K. (1993) *Creating Covenant Communities.* Leavenworth, KS: Universal Force Dynamics.

Technological Millennialism

Technological millennialism is a new form of millennialism that has become increasingly common during the twentieth century. In the past, widespread moral outrage and physical hardship caused people to call upon the power of heaven (or, less frequently, the power of politics) to intervene in a radical fashion and make all things new and right. As science and technology have progressed, however, new movements have emerged that look instead to science and technology to recreate the world in a new and better way, ushering in a new age of unparalleled, perhaps universal, prosperity and happiness.

Millennialism is the belief that a new, more perfect age is about to begin. Usually this new age is expected to be radically different from and vastly superior to the present era, which millenarians often view as hopelessly corrupt and beyond repair. Millenarian movements can start for a variety of reasons, but they are believed to arise most frequently in cultures undergoing cultural stress and frustration. Invasions, assassinations, poverty, plagues, and religious and political corruption have all been known to stimulate millenarian activity.

Millennial movements are often primarily religious in nature, though important political millenarian movements have also existed. Significant religiously inspired millenarian movements include the Hussite-Taborite Revolt in fifteenth-century Bohemia; the Peasant's Revolt and the later Munster Rebellion in sixteenth-century Germany; the Church of Jesus Christ of Latter-day Saints (also known as the Mormons) of nineteenth-century America; and Seventh-Day Adventism, also from nineteenth-century America. More explicitly political millenarian movements can be found in the French Revolution of the eighteenth century and the Russian Bolshevik Revolution of the early twentieth.

During the twentieth century, however, a new form of millenarianism has appeared: technological millenarianism. Instead of appealing to Heaven and divine authority, technological millenarians look instead to progress in science and technology to bring in a millennial age free of poverty, pain, injustice, and perhaps even death.

Amateur Technological Millennialism

Two broad types of technological millennialism exist. The first of these might be called (for lack of a better term) "amateur" or "spectator" technological millennialism. Followers of this form of millenarianism are usually not scientists or engineers. Instead, they are nonscientists who, for any of a number of reasons, have concluded that humanity's ultimate destiny will be achieved through some form of technological achievement, though not necessarily through their own nonprofessional scientific efforts.

New Age Popularizers

An example of amateur technological millennialism is found in the (now defunct) Committee for the Future, which depended upon NASA technology. This group looked to space colonization one way to "[transcend] the human condition through evolution into a 'universal species.'" The committee organized the Harvest Moon Project, in which an international expedition would travel back to the moon on board a surplus Saturn V rocket and set up a garden, complete with animal life, beneath a plastic dome. The technical details of the mission tended to be romantic and impractical; eventually the group lost interest in space and turned more toward occultism.

Religiously Oriented UFO Groups

An even greater dependence upon outside technology may be found in groups that look to space aliens, rather than humans, for assistance. For example, a number of groups believe that extraterrestrial intelligence will soon intervene and help bring about the new age through gifts of advanced technology. The Unarians are an example of this type of thought. Variants of this theme also exist; the psychic Tuella, for example, expects cataclysmic "earth changes" first to destroy the earth's surface and then to purify and renew it into a more perfect form, but not before benevolent aliens arrive and evacuate the earth's population with flying saucers.

Professional Technological Millennialism

The second type of science-oriented millenarianism can be called "professional" technological millennialism. Here the participants, who are often professional scientists and engineers, are actively engaged in developing the technologies—biological, chemical, electronic—that they believe will usher in a new, vastly superior age.

Eugenics

For centuries people have known that certain traits, both good and bad, tend to run in families. By the middle to late nineteenth century, some people began to argue for active intervention to promote certain traits and discourage others, even though the biological basis of heredity was not yet understood. Indeed, some clergymen of the time went so far as to express hope that it might be possible to breed out Christian original sin. The first known experiment in voluntary human breeding took place in the avant-garde Oneida community in the late 1800s, a group led by the Christian minister and social reformer John Humphrey Noyes.

By the early 1900s, however, professional biologists and protogeneticists were beginning to understand how heredity works, and some well-known scientists—including inventor Alexander Graham Bell, biologist David Starr Jordan, plant breeder Luther Burbank, and biologist Charles Davenport—began to promote eugenics as a way to improve the human condition. Eugenics was also given public support from famous nonscientists such as Theodore Roosevelt, H. G. Wells, George Bernard Shaw, and, later, Charles Lindbergh.

Perhaps the best-known eugenics organization was the American Eugenics Society. Founded in 1921, this group was run by professional scientists, doctors, and mathematicians. Besides conducting early genetic research, this group also worked to promote the passage of laws preventing persons diagnosed with genetic disease from marrying. The group also pressed for laws allowing criminals and persons with mental disabilities to be surgically sterilized to prevent them from passing their supposedly inferior genetic material on to their children. Ultimately, the eugenicists hoped to bring about, through genetic means, a society in which every person would be physically fit, intelligent enough to do some kind of useful work, calm, cheerful, and willing to conform to community values and mores. This program was satirized almost point-by-point by Aldous Huxley in his well-known dystopian novel, *Brave New World* (1932).

Cryonics

A second, more recent example of technological millenarianism is found in the cryonics movement. This movement began in the early 1960s with the publication of two books: Evan Cooper's *Immortality Physically, Scientifically Now* (1962) and physicist Robert Ettinger's *The Prospect of Immortality* (1964). The premise of cryonics is that a person—often at the point of death and suffering from an incurable disease—is frozen and preserved at very low temperatures, in the hope that in the future he or she may be revived (or, as cryonics adherents say, "reanimated") and restored to good health.

Even more than in the case of eugenics, the literature of cryonics is imbued with millennial overtones. Cryonics literature very often includes speculation about what the future will be like for the cryonics client waking up after a long period of suspension. Ettinger's books suggest that the future will contain intelligent robots, lifelong (and perhaps artificially enhanced) sexual virility, climate-controlled cities, and unlimited wealth. Indeed, aging itself might be overcome. Current cryonics literature continues to contain scenarios in which individuals wake up in a glorious future, often meeting up with loved ones who similarly had the foresight to be frozen at the time of death.

Space Colonies

Another suggested way to achieve the millennium has been through the colonization of space. To many citizens of the United States, the space program embodied many of the best elements of American civilization: bravery, exploration, cooperation, progress, and technological prowess. Yet it also seemed that the nation that produced that Apollo triumph was also about to falter; in the early 1970s problems such as inflation, overpopulation, pollution, and shortages of energy and raw materials were demanding attention. At the same time, NASA was facing budget cuts. By the early 1980s it also appeared that the United States was about to be economically and technologically outpaced by other countries, particularly Japan. In the face of such threats, many felt that reducing or eliminating the space effort would be nothing short of disastrous. To such people space was a vast, potentially limitless source of raw materials, energy, technological innovation, and living space. More broadly, it was the new frontier: humanity's ultimate destination.

Perhaps the most highly respected advocate of space colonies during the 1970s and 1980s was Princeton University physicist Gerard K. O'Neill. O'Neill was highly regarded in the field of nuclear physics and was at one point a finalist for selection for astronaut training. While teaching an undergraduate physics seminar in 1969, O'Neill decided to try to interest his class in the subject by having them examine the possibilities of building space colonies. O'Neill himself was surprised when his students returned with numbers showing that colony construction might in fact be possible. After several more years of investigation, O'Neill began to lobby for government funding for research on space colonies and solar power satellites; many of the physicist's friends and associates went on to write prospace books and to establish space advocacy groups.

O'Neill and his followers tried to ground their plans as pragmatically as possible, conducting their own research and using the best scientific and economic information available at the time. They also had clear notions of what they hoped their space colonies would become: autonomous or at least semiautonomous microworlds, each with several thousand inhabitants. Each colony would grow its own food and would be located far enough from others as not to require any form of defense system; perhaps it would also speak its own language. The colony would also have a moderate to low population density with large tracts of parks and even woods. Governments would be mostly local and be accomplished through face-to-face interaction, and private transportation would be unnecessary beyond a bicycle. Basically, life in the space colony would be a utopian combination of university setting and nostalgic small-town America: it would be clean, healthy, leisurely, self-determined, egalitarian, and culturally homogeneous, though with plenty of opportunity for social and political experimentation. Furthermore, the people would be well-educated and wealthy; O'Neill calculated that the average space-dwelling family of the year 2100 would earn more than $300,000 per year, in 1975 dollars.

The Significance of Technological Millennialism

Technological millennialism, like traditional religious movements, frequently casts unspoken, scarcely noticed cultural assumptions, hopes, and fears into sharp relief. The eugenicists, like many persons during the early twentieth century, were facing a country undergoing massive changes due to industrialization, immigration, and labor unrest; at the same time, many were questioning traditional Christian orthodoxy. The eugenicists decided that the rising stars of genetics and biological science offered the best hope for solving the social and moral problems of their time.

Cryonics, like eugenics, emerged during a time in which many were publicly challenging traditional religious forms, particularly in regard to the question of life after death. While some searched for answers in near-death experiences (explored in books such as Raymond Moody's best-selling *Life after Life* [1975]), others once again turned to technology—this time in the form of low-temperature physics—to solve the problem. Space colonies, on the other hand, were explored as a total solution to the most pressing problems of mid-1970s and early 1980s—pollution, overpopulation, energy shortages, and the lack of a clear national goal.

Secondly, technological millenarianism can have significant social, political, and scientific impact. The American eugenics movement, for example, played a significant role in the passage of a series of restrictive immigration laws in the United States. These laws remained in effect for decades. Even more ominously, eugenics laws resulted in the sterilization of some sixty thousand American citizens, on the grounds that they were believed to be genetically defective. However, it is also true that a number of early eugenics researchers made valuable contributions in genetics, cancer research, and especially mathematical statistics.

Eugenics, and its distant "cousin," genetic engineering, continue to be lightning rods for controversy even today. Cryonics and space colonies have also been influential, though so far in a less dramatic fashion. Early cryonicists were ridiculed by many within the established medical community. While the ultimate goal of cryonics—the successful thawing and revival of a frozen human—has not yet occurred, cryonics researchers have begun to receive a measure of recognition for their work in low-temperature, long-term storage of individual human organs for use in future transplants. Cryocare, and its affiliated organization, 21st Century Medicine, are two companies working in this area. The space colonization effort, on the other hand, has resulted in a proliferation of space-advocacy groups. The movement also inspired a significant amount of research on commercial space ventures and rocketry; Space-Dev, with offices in Virginia and California, is one such company. Gerard O'Neill himself was responsible for setting up GEOSTAR, a venture to develop and market space-based navigational and positioning aids for aircraft, and also a space-based communications system. Though a series of launch failures eventually forced GEOSTAR into bankruptcy, the company's technology was later commercially implemented by others.

Technological millenarianism continues to be an ongoing phenomenon as new problems confront humans and as new technologies are developed. Recent advances in computer technology, for example, have caused some to suggest that humanity's ultimate destiny lies in cybernetic "upgrades" for failing human organs. Others believe that people may achieve a form of near-immortality through "uploading"—a process in which an individual's personality and memories might be transferred into a computer, and the person will live on in some form of virtual reality. Recent advances in cloning technology have also inspired one large millenarian UFO-oriented group, the Canadian-based Raelian Movement, to found a biotechnology firm named "Clonaid." Clonaid's official purpose is to carry out the commercial cloning of animals and, eventually, human beings. However, the Raelians also hope that this venture will one day allow humanity to achieve immortality through cloning, so that at some point in the future humans may be able to follow in the footsteps of their alien forefathers, travelling among the stars and populating uninhabited planets in their own image. Yet another approach can be found in the First Millennial Foundation (recently renamed the Living Earth Foundation), based on Marshall Savage's book *The Millennial Project: Colonizing the Galaxy in Eight Easy Steps* (1993); this organization is dedicated to eco-friendly ocean-based fish farming, ocean colonization, geothermal energy, and long-term space colonization. The group is currently engaged in a number of ventures, such as conducting research on novel building materials and on ocean-based geothermal energy sources. The foundation is also establishing an intentional community, the Space Environments Ecovillage; an eco-tourism enterprise, Aquarius Rising; and the distance-education-based International University of Advanced Studies.

We may soon see changes in the way technological millenarianism develops. In the past people have tended to latch on to one specific technology and proclaim it to be the salvation of the human race. However, as the rate of technological innovation increases, tomorrow's new technology rapidly becomes today's hardware and then yesterday's news. As a result, we may be seeing an increasing shift away from celebration of specific developments, with a greater emphasis being placed instead on a doctrine of general technical progress. For example, the Extropy Institute, founded by philosopher Max More, is dedicated to a philosophy called "Transhumanism"—the belief that the individual biological human is only a starting point, not an ultimate end. Extropians are thus broadly interested in all technologies that allow them to transcend current human limitations, whether these technologies are genetic, cryonic, space-based, electronic, chemical, or psychological. This broad focus allows Extropians to investigate and connect multiple disciplines, thereby fostering increased exchange and mutual support between various avant-garde technologies. This interdisciplinary nature also prevents a setback in one technology, such as a series of launch failures, from disrupting the greater philosophical enterprise.

While scientific advances have both inspired and frightened individuals for hundreds of years, it is only during this century that we see sizable movements linking technological progress with positive views of ultimate human destiny. Technological millenarianism, with its goal of accomplishing human transcendence through technical means, is thus, in historical terms, a fairly recent movement. It will be interesting to see if the various movements that make up the phenomenon continue to exist primarily as special interest groups on the fringe of scientific and socially respectability, or whether such groups might become increasingly aware of each other and build ties through interdisciplinary groups such as the Extropian Institute. If the latter were to occur, technological millenarians might one day develop a dynamic, long-lived, and self-sustaining subculture, with greater influence over the surrounding society.

John M. Bozeman

See also Nuclear, Raelians, Secular Millennialism, Ufology, Y2K

Bibliography

Alcor Life Extension Foundation. (1993) *Cryonics: Reaching for Tomorrow*, 4th ed. Scottsdale, AZ: Alcor.

American Cryonics Society Web site at http://www.jps.net/cryonics/index.htm.

Ashtar Command. (1999) http://www.ashtar.org.

Bainbridge, W. S. (1976) *The Spaceflight Revolution.* New York: John Wiley and Sons.

Bozeman, John M. (1997) "Technological Millenarianism in the United States." In *Millennium, Messiahs, and Mayhem: Contemporary Apocalyptic Movements,* edited by Thomas Robbins and Susan J. Palmer. New York: Routledge.

Clonaid. (1999) http://www.clonaid.com.

Cryonet. (1999) http://www.cryonet.org.

Ettinger, Robert. (1964) *The Prospect of Immortality.* Garden City, NY: Doubleday.

The Extropian Institute. (1999) http://www.extropy.com. This is the leading Transhumanist organization, founded by Max More. See also http://www.aleph.se/Trans.

First Millennial Foundation/Living Universe Foundation. (1999) http://www.fmf.org. This site contains information and updates about the various projects undertaken by the Foundation.

Kevles, Daniel. (1995) *In the Name of Eugenics: Genetics and the Uses of Human Heredity.* Cambridge, MA: Harvard University Press.

Lewis, James R. (1995) *The Gods Have Landed: New Religions from Other Worlds.* Albany, NY: SUNY Press.

McLoughlin, William G. (1980) *Revivals, Awakenings, and Social Reform.* Chicago: University of Chicago Press.

Michaud, M. (1986) *Reaching for the High Frontier.* New York: Praeger.

O'Neill, Gerard K. (1976) *The High Frontier.* New York: William Morrow.

——. (1981) *2081: A Hopeful View of the Human Future.* New York: Simon and Schuster.

Raelian Movement. (1999) http://www.rael.org.

Regis, Ed. (1991) *The Great Mambo Chicken and the Transhuman Condition.* New York: Addison Wesley Longman.

Savage, Marshall T. ([1993] 1994) *The Millennial Project: Colonizing the Galaxy in Eight Easy Steps.* New York: Little, Brown.

Space Studies Institute. (1999) http://www.ssi.org.

Students for the Exploration and Development of Space (1999) http://www.seds.org.

Tuella. ([1982] 1994) *Project World Evacuation.* New Brunswick, NJ: Inner Light Publications.

Totalitarianism

Totalitarianism is a way of organizing groups of people characterized by rigid centralized control of all aspects of a person's life by an autocratic leader or hierarchy. Its style, structure, and methods correctly define a totalitarian group, movement, or government, not the stated or apparent ideology. Totalitarian groups are sometimes called cults or totalist systems.

On a small scale, attempts to coerce obedience are found in numerous groups, and we are all susceptible to the appeals of totalitarian systems. In writing about methods of thought reform, Lifton observes that "some potential for this form of all-or-nothing emotional alignment exists within everyone." According to Lifton, there is a similar potential with any ideology or organization to move in a totalist direction, but that it is "most likely to occur with those ideologies which are most sweeping in their content and most ambitious—or messianic—in their claims, whether religious, political, or scientific. And where totalism exists, a religion, a political movement, or even a scientific organization becomes little more than an exclusive cult" ([1961] 1989: 419).

Totalitarian Groups or Cults?

Defining the term cult in its popular usage is difficult and controversial. Some authors suggest cult members are little more than automatons. Conway and Siegelman (1995) claim there is some psychological process whereby people in cults "snap" into a new personality framework. Most observers of totalitarian phenomenon, however, reject this notion as overly simplistic and unproven. On the other end of this continuum are academics and medical professionals who dismiss the very idea of a cult. In the study of religion, the term cult often has a different meaning, being used to identify a small nontraditional or breakaway religious formation built around a charismatic leader. Here it does not necessarily imply rigid totalitarian practices.

While there are totalitarian groups that use deceptive recruiting practices and psychologically manipulative techniques to enforce loyalty, not every new religion or exotic spiritual or political group is a cult. Some fundamentalist Christian groups that warn about cults use the term loosely, and often are stigmatizing religious views that they find unacceptable.

Tabor and Gallagher (1995) show how bias toward groups labeled a cult can have devastating outcomes, such as with law enforcement miscalculations at Waco, Texas, that precipitated deadly confrontations at the Branch Davidian compound led by David Koresh. Some critics of cults try to find a balance: Steven Hassan (1990) argues that cults are groups that use unethical psychological manipulation to coerce obedience among followers. Hassan argues that totalitarian methods of controlling people use techniques that sabotage their ability to effectively exercise free will. Whether or not the word "cult" is considered appropriate, it is clear that totalist groups often target college students for recruitment.

Totalitarian Systems

Totalist systems depend on obedience. The Milgram experiments (1974) show how different factors change the willingness of individuals to obey a directive. In the classic experiment, people were ordered to administer what they believed was a powerful electric shock to a test subject who was really an actor feigning discomfort. Some people were persuaded to administer apparently lethal levels of electricity, while others refused to take part in the experiment. The factors are complex, but it is alarming how many people seemed willing to administer what they thought were dangerous shocks.

According to Arendt ([1951] 1973), Hitler's Nazi government and Stalin's communist government were totalitarian, but she rejected the claim that all fascist or communist governments or movements achieved totalitarian status. At the same time, Sagan argues that what he calls the "paranoidia" of greed and domination exemplified by "fascist and totalitarian regimes of this century" is present in less extreme forms in many societies. "The normal, expectable expressions—imperialism, racism, sexism, aggressive warfare—are compatible with the democratic societies that have existed so far" (1991: 363).

Arendt discusses how totalitarian movements are built around a central fiction of a powerful conspiracy (in the case of the Nazis, a conspiracy of Jews which planned to dominate the world) that requires a secretive counter-conspiracy be organized. Totalitarian groups organize the counter-conspiracy in a hierarchical manner which mimics the levels of membership and rituals of social and religious secret societies.

The process whereby a movement's sympathizers serve as mediators for translating otherwise unacceptable messages into public discourse plays an important role in demonization. Arendt suggests that most people get their first glimpse of a totalitarian movement through its front organizations:

> The sympathizers, who are to all appearances still innocuous fellow-citizens in a nontotalitarian society, can hardly be called single-minded fanatics; through them, the movements make their fantastic lies more generally acceptable, can spread their propaganda in milder, more respectable forms, until the whole atmosphere is poisoned with totalitarian elements which are hardly recognizable as such but appear to be normal political reactions or opinions. (367)

The term "front group" has been used to unfairly discredit an organization seen as subversive or dangerous by persons who are using guilt-by-association as an acceptable standard of proof. Labeling a group totalitarian or a front group is a convenient way to weaken or destroy a political adversary, even when the charge is known to be false. The label "front group" was widely used by anticommunists during the McCarthy period to demonize liberals and radicals as tools of Moscow-based subversion. Nevertheless, the basic concept of totalitarianism should not be discarded because of these abuses.

Conclusions

The nature of totalitarianism is hotly debated, especially when discussing small totalist groups sometimes labeled cults. Yet totalitarianism does exist and it has a brutal and murderous history. For totalitarian political systems, the end game of demonization and scapegoating is genocide. Ordinary people are conditioned to ignore or tolerate this ghastly process. Hitler may well have been a lunatic, but the vast majority of Germans who allowed him to rule, and accepted scapegoating conspiracist theories about Jews and other alleged parasitic subversives, were not suffering from mass psychosis. Totalitarian systems bring out the worst in humanity.

Chip Berlet

See also Communism, Conspiracism, Demonization, Nazism

Bibliography

Arendt, Hannah. ([1951] 1973) *The Origins of Totalitarianism.* New York: Harcourt Brace Jovanovich.

Conway, Flo, and Jim Siegelman. (1995) *Snapping: America's Epidemic of Sudden Personality Change,* 2d ed. New York: Stillpoint Press.

Hassan, Steven. (1990) *Combatting Cult Mind Control.* Rochester, VT: Park Street Press.

Lifton, Robert Jay. ([1961] 1989). *Thought Reform and the Psychology of Totalism: A Study of "Brainwashing" in China.* Chapel Hill, NC: University of North Carolina.

Milgram, Stanley. (1974) *Obedience to Authority: An Experimental View.* New York: Harper Torchbooks.

Revel, Jean-Francois. (1977) *The Totalitarian Temptation.* Garden City, NY: Doubleday & Company.

Sagan, Eli. (1991) *The Honey and the Hemlock: Democracy and Paranoia in Ancient Athens and Modern America.* New York: Basic Books.

Singer, Margaret Thaler, with Janja Lalich. (1995) *Cults in Our Midst: The Hidden Menace in Our Everyday Lives.* San Francisco: Jossey-Bass.

Tabor, James D., and Eugene V. Gallagher. (1995) *Why Waco? Cults and the Battle for Religious Freedom in America.* Berkeley: University of California Press.

Ufology

The subculture of ufology consists of individuals and organizations who are focused on the phenomenon of UFOs, extraterrestrials, intergalactic civilizations, and interstellar or interdimensional travel and contact. Comprised of numerous research organizations and publications, as well as religious communities, conventions, tourist destinations, and Internet Web sites; ufology is defined here as a subculture in contemporary society, especially in the United States. Interest in UFOs and extraterrestrial intelligence is also reflected in popular culture, especially in television, film, and popular literature, so that the public is aware of the outlines of UFO subculture. At several junctures ufology intersects with apocalyptic and millennial traditions, providing fascinating examples of the variety of forms that millennialism takes in the contemporary age.

While the phenomenon is about fifty years old, as the turn of the millennium has approached, interest in UFOs, extraterrestrials, and the field of ufology has dramatically increased. In addition, contemporary beliefs in UFOs and extraterrestrials have fused with classical millennial beliefs to produce new hybrid forms of millennialism, such as the ill-fated Heaven's Gate UFO group. Rather than angels or the messiah emerging from the clouds to battle the Antichrist and redeem the chosen, the messiah is a benevolent interstellar space traveler, returning to Earth to rescue his space brothers from sinister "gray" aliens and the ravages inflicted on the planet by technology and pollution. While most UFO religions do not preach suicide as a way to achieve cosmic enlightenment, as did Heaven's Gate, apocalyptic beliefs are commonly found among many new ufology religions. Combining current trends in science and popular culture with classic millennial themes, ufology has adapted to the modern age by producing new forms of millennial movements.

American UFO Experience in the Twentieth Century

The popular interest in UFOs and extraterrestrial intelligence is about a hundred years old. UFOs, or what at the time were dubbed "airships," were first documented during the late nineteenth century, especially in 1896 and 1897, when the first great wave of UFO sightings occurred in the United States. While some believed they represented secret breakthroughs in aviation, others speculated they were of extraterrestrial origin. In 1898, H. G. Wells's *War of the Worlds* presented an apocalyptic vision of alien invasion and Armageddon on earth. The book's main theme about a malevolent alien invasion and the final battle between good and evil played out between aliens and humans, continues to be a theme in contemporary ufology and millennialism, though more so in the popular culture than among the subcultures themselves. Nonetheless, *War of the Worlds* remains a benchmark in the evolution of science fiction literature and the culture of UFOs in the twentieth century.

During World War II allied pilots made numerous sightings of unidentified objects, nicknamed "foo fighters," that appeared to follow their planes during missions. On 24 June 1947, private pilot Kenneth Arnold witnessed a formation of silver disks skipping through the air over Mount Rainier. His report was widely circulated by the media, who dubbed his silver disks, "flying saucers." But his credentials and sincerity generated a broad interest in UFOs around the world. Two weeks later the alleged crash of a UFO and its alien crew on 3 July 1947, near Corona, New Mexico, received national headlines and generated the controversy that sustains so much ufology. Questions remain to this day over the military and government handling of the so-called Roswell Affair, including reports of threatened witnesses, government disinformation, and cover-up. Thus began a spectacular array of conspiracy theories and mythologizing that permeate much of ufology today, including the notion that gray aliens are conspiring with world leaders to control and eventually colonize earth, using its life forms, including humans, for breeding or other malevolent purposes. Today the town of Roswell, New Mexico, and the "Extraterrestrial Highway" from Roswell to Las Vegas, including the mythical "Area 51"—presumably a supersecret military installation at the Nevada Test Site where alien aircraft and technology are housed—are American meccas for UFO seekers.

Beginning with Project Blue Book in the mid-1950s, the U.S. government embarked on a formal investigation of the UFO phenomena in response to public pressure. Most observers in and outside of the subculture believe government experts were involved more in debunking the UFOs than in seriously and objectively investigating the phenomenon. In response to this growing distrust of the government's handling of the phenomenon, the first serious research groups appeared, beginning with the National Investigations Committee on Aerial Phenomenon (NICAP) in 1957. Several other, often competing, groups followed and today there are dozens of "investigative" organizations around the globe. While most are little more than clubs or dispensers of conspiracy theories, some are committed to objectively studying the phenomenon. In the U.S. three groups—the Mutual UFO Network, the Center for UFO Studies (founded by astronomer J. Allen Hynek), and the Fund for UFO Research comprise the UFO Coalition, a collaborative effort to streamline the investigative and research effort of objective ufologists.

The fifties also witnessed the emergence of the first "contactees" and the first UFO religions. Contactees are people who claimed to have been contacted by aliens. George Adamski is perhaps the most famous of these early contactees. A dabbler in the occult and science fiction literature, Adamski claimed that, on 20 November 1952, he was visited by a being of human appearance who claimed to be from Venus. The tall, blond, and handsome Venusian invited Adamski aboard his saucer, revealing that they had come in peace and out of concern for the future of the human race and planet Earth. Until his death in 1965, Adamski published books on his alleged experiences, became a minor celebrity, and courted controversy with an increasingly skeptical public. While largely discredited, Adamski set the stage for much that was to come in the area of alien contact and the formation of millennial ufology and UFO religions.

The mid-1950s also saw the formation of several early UFO religions, as spiritualist and New Age seekers hooked into the flying saucer phenomenon, including the Aetherians (1954), Unarius (1954), and Urantia (1955). Various individuals, such as Aetherian founder George King and Ruth and Ernest Norman, creators of Unarius, claimed to have been contacted by benevolent extraterrestrials who promised the coming of a glorious new cosmic age generated small followings and a lot of media ridicule.

By the late 1960s, the "nonfiction" literature of popular ufology had exploded, sparked in part by sixties' countercultural interest in alternative religions, and by Erich von Daniken's enormously successful book *Chariots of the Gods?* (1969), in which the author argued that "ancient astronauts" visited our ancestors, helping them to engineer, among other things, the great architecture of their civilizations, including the pyramids of Giza, Egypt, Stonehenge, the Nazca Lines, and the monuments on Easter Island. Von Daniken also popularized the notion that much of humanity's ancient mythology involving angels and gods from the heavens reflects our ancestors attempts to interpret what they were intellectually unequipped to understand—that they were being visited and manipulated by advanced extraterrestrials. Numerous books in the same genre followed, with von Daniken contributing several books to the "ancient astronaut" genre.

Around the same time another genre of UFO-related books appeared, suggesting, among other things, that the mythical "lost" civilizations of Atlantis and Mu were in contact with extraterrestrials and perhaps destroyed by them as well. Similarly, books linking UFOs to the Bermuda Triangle were popular in the 1960s and 1970s. Occult author Charles Berlitz is prominent among these writers with his tales of secret alien bases beneath the waters of the Caribbean, wreaking havoc on ships and aircraft that cross the region. UFOs and cattle mutilations first made headlines in 1967

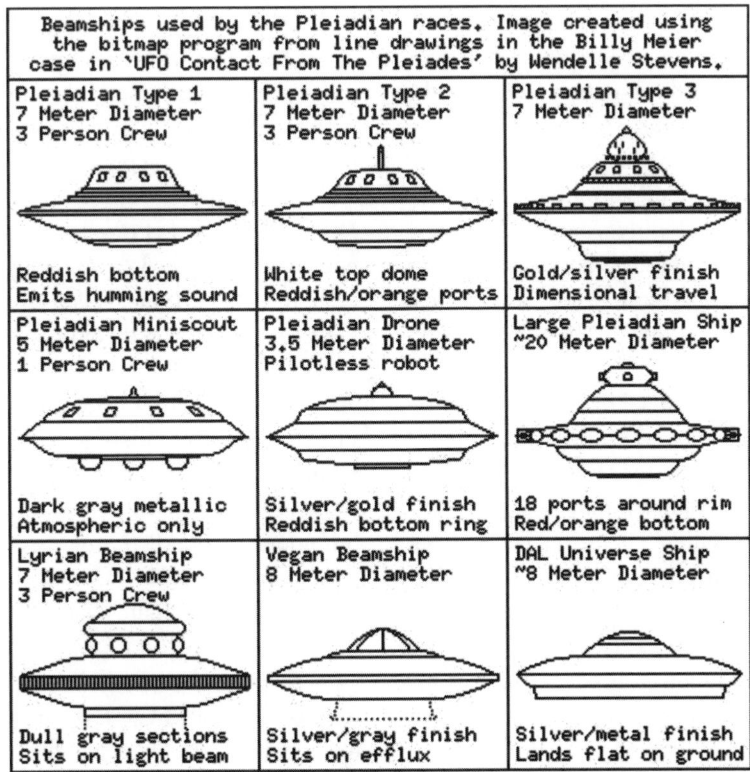

Various models of beamships. HTTP://OURWORLD.COMPUSERVE.COM/HOMEPAGES/ANDYPAGE/BEAMSHIP.HTM.

across the American West. Often following the appearance of strange lights or unmarked black helicopters, dead livestock would be found and later shown to have had various organs or blood removed, allegedly with surgical precision. In *Alien Harvest* (1989) Linda Howe argued that due to genetic similarity, aliens are mutilating animals in order to retrieve DNA for their genetic experiments. Such claims contribute to the odd mixture of conspiracy theories pertaining to extraterrestrial subversion of humankind.

Alien abduction of humans is another theme in the growing alarm over the alien threat. *The Interrupted Journey* (1966), by John G. Fuller, tells the story of Barney and Betty Hill who, under hypnosis, claimed to have been abducted by aliens late one evening off a deserted New Hampshire road. The Hill case is the first well-documented and researched example of abduction, and the first to use hypnotic regression as a tool to uncover the Hill's repressed memories. The Hill's story, of being taken aboard a UFO, enduring strange medical examinations, and having their memories erased, has become the quintessential abduction story, and a principal theme in ufology, including books, conferences, clubs, Internet Web sites, and UFO religions.

The public's interest in alien abduction flourished in the 1980s with the appearance of several books exploring alien abduction. Budd Hopkins, an artist with no medical or psychological training, began uncovering dozens of abduction cases. Using hypnotic regression techniques, "abductees" would explain how aliens appeared through their bedroom walls and levitated them into a waiting spacecraft. Inside alien "doctors" commence medical examinations of the human victims, often involving the removal of sperm or ovaries, or the implantation of electronic devices. Hopkins calculates that globally several hundred million abductions may have taken place over the last thirty years. He and his followers believe that gray aliens appear to have established a genetic engineering program to create a hybrid human-alien race in order to sustain their survival, all with the concurrence of world leaders.

Harvard psychiatrist and Pulitzer Prize-winning author, John Mack provided the abduction phenomenon a degree of credibility following the publication of *Abduction* (1994), an account of his patients experiences undergoing therapy. While Mack's reputation has suffered in the medical and scientific professions, he is a hero to many in the ufology subculture. However, Mack is hesitant to endorse the beliefs of many "experiencers" or investigators like Hopkins, but he believes that something extraordinary is occurring to many otherwise normal people, something that mainstream science can not grasp. Mack does not endorse the alien threat and instead promotes the positive and transformative experiences that many abductees claim to have.

Another site of optimism regarding extraterrestrials is the crop circle phenomenon, whereby strange but beautiful geometric patterns, some up to a hundred feet in diameter, began to appear in 1976 in farming regions around the world, including Britain, Australia, Japan, Canada, and the United States. Precisely etched into waist-deep grain fields without damaging adjacent plants, the "agriglyphs," as they are sometimes referred to, are believed to be benevolent (and unintelligible) communications from extraterrestrials, signs that they are gearing up for full revelation.

New Age Millennial UFO Religions at the End of the Millennium

Optimism and hope regarding the alien presence also pervades the millennial movements of the New Age. Almost fifty years after George Adamski and the benevolent Venusians, UFO religions have proliferated in the wake of millennial fever. Typical of many of the UFO religions, adherents to the Raelian movement believe that humans are the creation of a higher form of extraterrestrial intelligence, which has used advanced scientific methods to engineer our DNA and manipulate our evolution. Another UFO religion, the Planetary Activation Organization, believes that an extraterrestrial prime creator placed thousands of souls on earth as an experiment to discover if they would transform to a higher level of consciousness. Many groups meld the Christian creation myth to the extraterrestrial hypothesis: the Planetary Activation Organization, Heaven's Gate, and the Armageddon Time Ark Base Operation all hold that an extraterrestrial prime creator was responsible for the origin and evolution of humans and continues to monitor and assist us in preparation for our introduction to a new cosmic age.

The "harmonic convergence" is one example of a New Age millennial event which was to include the return of the our alien brethren. Jose Arguelles, author of the New Age bestseller, *The Mayan Factor* (1987), had prophesied that the solar system would come into a rare "harmonic convergence" on 16 August 1987. Corresponding to the "end" of the 5,125-year-old Mayan calendar, the harmonic convergence would unleash devastating earthquakes around the world, followed by mass UFO landings, communication with extraterrestrials, and the cosmic transformation of the world. Summoning "144,000 true believers" to form a human power grid, Arguelles believed the harmonic convergence would help usher in the aliens and the New Age. At the pyramids some claimed to have seen flying saucers, and there were alleged sightings of the Virgin Mary, but there were no mass landings of UFOs. The harmonic convergence was only the beginning, Arguelles and his followers argued, and as the millennium change progressed, the transformation of the Earth and humanity will follow.

A more tragic event involving a millennial UFO religion was the group suicide of Heaven's Gate in March 1997. By taking their own lives, group members thought they would be freeing their extraterrestrial spirits from their human repositories, allowing the group to rendezvous with a UFO following the comet Hale-Bop. Believing that suicide would enable them to achieve a higher evolutionary or cosmic level, as well as to escape the alien destruction of planet earth, thirty-eight members neatly packed their belongings, then killed themselves. The "UFO-theology" of Heaven's Gate's fused classic apocalyptic beliefs such as the imminent destruction of the planet and the return of the "messiah" with modern or "secular" beliefs in extraterrestrial life and intergalactic space travel. Heaven's Gate and other new religious movements in ufology have evolved composite versions of the millennium in adaptation to the current age of rapid social, cultural, and technological change and millennial euphoria.

Who are the extraterrestrials, and from where do they come? Patrick Hughe, in *The Field Guide to Extraterrestrials* (1996), lists over fifty different alien life forms across four major categories; humanoid, animalian, robotic, and exotic. But within the subculture of ufology, the most discussed aliens are fewer, most notably the "grays" of abduction lore, the beautiful humanlike "Nordics," and occasionally reptile-like aliens. The grays presumably come from the star system Zeta Reticulan and are generally considered malevolent, driven to human abduction and human/alien breeding practices because their species is dying. Both the Sirians, from the star Sirius and the Pleidians, from the Pleides star system, are often described as benevolent space brothers sent to help humankind fight the evil grays, achieve cosmic consciousness, and join the galactic federation of civilizations.

In popular culture today the image of the gray alien is as ubiquitous as the smiley face. Blockbuster movies *Independence Day* (1996) and *Men in Black* (1997), and the sci-fi television hit *X-Files*, attest to the popularity of aliens in popular entertainment. In American malls; T-shirts, skateboards, and video games proclaim "we are not alone." An estimated 200,000 tourists and true believers came to Roswell, New Mexico in July of 1997 for the fiftieth anniversary of the alleged flying saucer crash. Once a marginal subculture, ufology has also made dramatic inroads into the American mainstream. Annual surveys confirm the general public's belief in extraterrestrial life. Globally, there are literally hundreds of UFO organizations.

Coinciding, not surprisingly, with the turn of the millennium, ufology has become a rapidly evolving subculture where classic apocalyptic beliefs and myths fuse with recent scientific or secular developments, producing new hybrid forms of millennialism. Many believers in extraterrestrial entities have adapted the millennial myth to their own experiences and to contemporary social and cultural realities. Today, what was once science fiction has become science fact. Recent scientific advances in genetics and cloning, new discoveries in astronomy and space science, and new theoretical models for interstellar space travel and extraterrestrial life, have brought ufologists and the "extraterrestrial hypothesis"—that intelligent life exists elsewhere in the universe—greater attention and support in the public and by science. Coupled with globalization, including burgeoning forms of mass communication media such as the Internet and the World Wide Web, ufology aspires to become a global religion. Even atheists can believe in UFOs and extraterrestrials, and they can express an apocalyptic or millennialist worldview without claiming an attachment to the supernatural. Herein lies the fusion of the religious and the secular forms of millennial myth.

Philip Lamy

See also Aetherius Society, Armageddon Time Ark Base, Film, Greater Community Way, Heaven's Gate, New World Comforter, Outpost Kauai, Planetary Activation Organization, Summum, Unarius Academy of Science, Urantia

Bibliography

Bryan, C. D. B. (1995) *Close Encounters of the Fourth Kind: Alien Abduction, UFOs, and The MIT Conference at MIT.* New York: Alfred A. Knopf.

Clark, Jerome. (1998) *The UFO Book: Encyclopedia of the Extraterrestrial.* Detroit: Visible Ink Press.

Dean, Jodi. (1998) *Aliens in America: Conspiracy Cultures from Outer Space to Cyberspace.* Ithaca, NY: Cornell University Press.

Lewis, James R., ed. (1995) *The Gods Have Landed: New Religions From Other Worlds.* Albany, NY: University of New York Press.

Thompson, Keith. (1991) *Angels and Aliens: UFOs and the Mythic Imagination.* Reading, MA: Addison Wesley Longman.

Unarius Academy of Science

Known for its prediction of a mass starship landing in the year 2001, the Unarius Science of Life has survived as one the oldest organizations predicting flying-saucer millenarianism. The Unarius Academy of Science, whose educational center is located in El Cajon, California, offers classes in past-life therapy, interdimensional physics, and art therapy. Ruth

Norman (1901–93), also known as Uriel the Archangel and Cosmic Visionary, headed the academy until her death. Uriel's successor who is better known by his space name Antares (Charles Spiegel) claims he is the reincarnation of Napoleon, Tyrantus, and Satan. Despite his supposed malevolent past, Antares was appointed by Uriel because she believed she had healed him of his karmic negativity. Core membership ranges from forty to sixty dedicated students, while considerably more people are in contact with the organization through mail-order correspondence. Unarius's Interplanetary Confederation Day celebration is marked by parades and speeches every year in October.

Unarians insist that their pursuit is a science, not a religion; although mysticism permeates their mythology and practices. Unarian mysticism shows the influences of spiritualism, Theosophy, UFO rumor, and science-fiction lore. Borrowed and improvised myths form the basis of their teachings. Believers rely on channeled messages and recovered memories of past lives as authentic guidance from "Infinite Intelligence." If we believe their chronicles, prominent Unarians had past lives as almost every major historical figure in Western civilization. Their mythical stories reach into metaphysical legends, like Atlantis and Lemuria, while they have also adopted themes from popular books, television, and motion pictures. For example, students of the "Science" believe they can be prompted to remember their past lives by watching such television shows as *Star Trek* or *X-Files*. During past-life therapy classes these recovered memories surface, and they are tape recorded so that the revelations can be made into the Unarian books or films that are sold through mail order.

Dr. Ernest L. Norman and Ruth E. Norman (Uriel), Founders and Moderators of the Unarius Academy of Science. RESUME OF UNARIUS, UNARIUS ACADEMY OF SCIENCE, EL CAJON, CA.

Initial Development

Unarius had humble beginnings. Ernest and Ruth Norman founded Unarius after they met at a psychic convention in 1954. Their union brought forth their so-called mission. Supposedly, Ernest Norman (1904–71) received telepathic transmissions from Mars and Venus, which were recorded and published in *The Voice of Venus*. He later unveiled the existence of spiritual planets (Venus, Eros, Orion, Muse, Elysium, Unarius, and Hermes) which comprise the "advanced teaching centers" of the enlightened masters, who are called the Space Brothers.

During the fifties and early sixties, the Normans drew a minor following with their mail-order psychic readings and book sales. They worked out of their succession of homes as they moved to several cities in California, eventually settling in Escondido. At home they met with local clients, who were referred to as "students." In addition, they gave psychic readings through the mail. After Ernest Norman died in 1971, Ruth became head of the organization and carried on the "mission" with help of two followers, Cosmon (Thomas Miller) and Antares (Charles Spiegel). Together they channeled messages from the cosmos that were published in the *Tesla Speaks* series. Messages from the Space Brothers predicted numerous landings of spacecraft. Volume seven of *Tesla Speaks* announced the existence of the great Intergalactic Confederation Project that was sending a spacefleet to earth before December 1974. When no flying saucers arrived, the date was reset to 27 September 1975. This date also was disconfirmed, as was another prophecy for 1976 and 1977.

The Unarian Center

Ruth Norman (Uriel) and her followers opened a storefront center on 14 February 1975. After disappointments with their unfulfilled prophecy, the year 2001 became the accepted date for the coming of the saucers. During the late seventies and eighties, Unarius reached its heyday when it drew a hard-core following who participated in classes where they recovered memories of the group's collective past lives. Classes focused on a central theme in their mythology, which explained how Uriel had reincarnated on various planets where she brought enlightenment, only to be attacked by her followers. Unarian students in period costumes acted out their memories of these events on film. The organization broadcasts these films on a free-access cable channel in hopes of awakening the public to their past lives and attracting new members.

Uriel, Goddess of Love and Healing Archangel

Until a few years before her death, Ruth Norman as Uriel played the part of a most flamboyant charismatic leader. She developed a persona that sociologists R. George Kirkpatrick and Diana Tumminia dubbed the "space goddess" because she advertised herself as the Goddess of Love and the Healing Archangel from the planet Aries. In order to maintain the illusion of heavenly being, Mrs. Norman always appeared in public elaborately costumed, adorned by a tiara, a caped evening gown, and an enormous wig. Frequently photographed and interviewed by news organizations, Uriel usually posed with a scepter and a model flying saucer. Her costumes also related to her past lives when she was the Peacock Princess of Atlantis, Mary Magdeline, or Queen Elizabeth I. She said she had also lived as Bathsheba, the Mona Lisa, the Goddess Isis, Queen Maria Theresa, Socrates, and Peter the Great, among others. On one occasion, her students contrived a special costume to illustrate her role as the Cosmic Generator, the supplier of all energy for all universes. On display now at the academy, the costume is constructed with models of heavenly planets and is illuminated by hundreds of miniature lights.

Uriel's followers characterize her as a loving leader who answered every question and took a personal interest in each student. On her deathbed, she invited each of her students to visit her. During the visit, she asked them how they were progressing; then she ended the audience with a blessing dispensed by throwing rose petals in their faces. While Uriel played the part of cosmic friend sympathetic to anyone's condition in life, she also demanded complete deference and obedience. Some ex-students complain about the authoritarian nature of the group. Stephan Yaconski, a former student who was actually excommunicated in the eighties, told his story to the *LA Times*, much to the consternation of Uriel.

The Unarian Prophecy

Unarian prophecy contains all the elements of an ecstatic vision of radiant saviors who come with magical powers. In 2001, thirty-three spaceships are expected to come from each of the worlds in the Interplanetary Confederation: El, Rey, Basis, Yessu, Luminus (once Severus), Valneza, Osnus, Idonus, Vixall, Earth II, Vidus, Anzea, Po, Deva, Endinite, Dollium, Ballium, Dal, Shunan, Brundage, Kallium, Delna, Farris, Serena, Vulna, Emil, Sixtus, Eneshia, Glenus, Din, Zeton, Jena, and our planet, Earth. The huge saucers will bring one thousand so-called scientists, a total of 33,000 celestial visitors. These Space Brothers who personify perfection will instruct earthlings with the power of their transformative consciousness. As their collective energy oversees planetary peace efforts to end all warfare, people will flock to them to experience their emanations of love and peace.

In the Unarian prophecy the Space Brother, Ambassador Alta of the Planet Vixall, pilots the spacefleet. Ambassador Alta is depicted in Unarian art as Ernest Norman. He will first lead the ships to the Bermuda Triangle where they will uncover the sunken treasures of Atlantis. Ambassador Alta will then take his crews to Jamul, California (in the mountains of San Diego County), where he will direct the saucers to land on top of one another to construct a free university and hospital. Each tier of the extraterrestrial university will profess a distinct scientific discipline. The Space Brothers will instruct Earth's technicians to use the recovered Atlantean knowledge to build futuristic computers of crystal and gold, as well as other unbelievable technology. The spaceships will unload their cosmic storehouses of their galactic cargo: medical supplies and equipment, interstellar alloys and building materials, electronic devices, and all manner of celestial technology.

Since Archangel Uriel will also return with the ships, she requested that her Space Cadillac, a specially painted car with a model flying saucer on the roof, will be waiting for her when she arrives. Uriel is expected to oversee peace efforts with her special diplomatic skills as she travels around the globe with her entourage of spaceships. When she returns to earth, she will reunited with her faithful students who have followed her across time and space through repeated reincarnations.

In addition to all their other gifts, the Brothers will construct a "Power Tower" which will run transportation and communication systems with nonpolluting energy. The Power Tower will supply all the energy needs for the entire planet. Each planetary society in the Confederation has already constructed a Power Tower on its home world. It is said that when Earth's tower is finished, all the power towers will connect electronically; forming supernatural energy fields where new planets of a higher frequencies will materialize. According to the Unarian prophecy, the Space Brothers will usher in a New Age of logic, reason, love, and peace for all the beings in the universe. They will solve all of the social and ecological problems on our planet.

Diana Tumminia

See also Ufology

Bibliography

Kirkpatrick, R. George, and Diana Tumminia. (1992) "California Space Goddess: The Mystagogue in a Flying Saucer Group." In *Twentieth-Century World Religious Movements In Neo-Weberian Perspective*, edited by William Swatos, Jr. Edwin Mellen Press, 299–311.

Norman, Ernest. (1956) *The Voice of Venus*. El Cajon, CA: Unarius Academy of Science.

Tumminia, Diana. (1998) "How Prophecy Never Fails: Interpretive Reason in a Flying-Saucer Group." *Sociology of Religion* 59, 2: 157–70.

Tumminia, Diana, and R. George Kirkpatrick. (1995) "Unarius: Emergent Aspects of a Flying Saucer Group." In *The Gods Have Landed: New Religions from Other Worlds*, edited by James R. Lewis. Albany, NY: State University of New York Press, 85–104.

United States, Eighteenth Century

Millennialism constitutes a major component of eighteenth-century American thought. Prominent writers and religious leaders of this period such as Michael Wigglesworth (1631–1705), Increase Mather (1639–1723), Samuel Willard (1640–1707), Nicholas Noyes (1647–1717), Samuel Sewall (1652–1730), Cotton Mather (1663–1728), Joseph Sewall (1688–1769), Jonathan Edwards (1703–58), Aaron Burr (1716–57), Joseph Bellamy (1719–90), Jonathan Mayhew (1720–66), Thomas Prince, Jr. (1722–48), Samuel Langdon (1723–97), Samuel Hopkins (1721–1803), Ezra Stiles (1727–95), and Timothy Dwight (1752–1817) believed in a future millennium and engaged in lively debate as to the time of its coming and the order of events preceding it.

Despite the significance it was afforded, however, the millennialism of this period evades easy categorization. Although the last quarter of the century saw the emergence of what could be described as a civil millennialism, in which America was represented as the site where Christ's millennial kingdom would commence, the years preceding the American Revolution witnessed a great deal of diversity regarding the nature of the millennium and its relationship to history. This variance derives from two related sources: the different ways in which theologians attempted to reconstruct the chronology of the Book of Revelation, and the manner in which they believed that chronology to apply to their own situations.

The Eighteenth-Century Context

Millennialism in early America was strongly shaped by the historical mode of exegesis that came to prominence in the mid-seventeenth century. In the Christian tradition, the dominant approach to the millennium was Augustinian. In this formulation, it was understood in a spiritualized sense: Satan's binding commenced at Christ's resurrection: the first resurrection of the saints mentioned in Revelation referred to their spiritual rebirth; the millennium was interpreted as applying to the age of the church militant; and Revelation as a whole was taken to describe the victory of the City of God over Satan. In post-Reformation England, Protestant theologians such as John Bale (1495–1563) and John Foxe (1516–87) saw this conflict as describing the struggle between Protestant and Roman Catholic churches.

In this context, Joseph Mede's *The Key to Revelation* (1643) provided a crucial contribution to the formulation of later approaches to this topic. Mede argued that the events described in Revelation did not necessarily follow each other in their order of presentation: rather, the events are divided into seven "synchronisms," that relate to two separate histories. The first history concerned the political events from the time of Revelation to the Last Judgment; the second refers to the struggle of the church, and concludes with the pouring of the seven vials upon the Antichrist. The significance of Mede's analysis for eighteenth-century millennialism was twofold. Most immediately, it located the millennial kingdom in the future, following the church's struggle with Satan. Secondly, it changed the way in which theologians approached the Book of Revelation. Mede's analysis was rigorous, connecting the imagery and prophecies contained in Revelation to the those in the Books of Isaiah, Jeremiah, Ezekiel, Micah, and, especially, Daniel. It also involved linguistic comparisons of original texts and consideration of historical evidence. Although many commentators disagreed on specific aspects of Mede's chronology—primarily, with the content and the duration of the vials—his methodology won general admiration, allowing millennial speculation to proceed on a much more systematic basis than it had previously.

The effect of Mede's explication was to make theologians much more methodologically sophisticated. Rather than leading to consensus, however, this new attention to interpretational principle and exegetical exactness produced greater controversy. Later theologians came to differ on a number of points, specifically: whether the two witnesses in Revelation had been slain or were to be slain; which events constituted the vials to be poured and how many had already been poured; if it was necessary for the Jews to convert to Christianity for the millennium to occur; whether the first resurrection was the literal resurrection of the martyrs, or whether it would constitute spiritual renewal; if the conflagration and final judgment would precede or conclude the millennium; if Christ would reign personally on earth during the millennium, or appear supernaturally but not reign, or be present spiritually in the glory of the church; and finally, whether the millennium would consist of the perfection of the earthly world or would prove to radically differ from it.

Although these issues generated much debate, approaches to them were not formalized into competing schools as they would be in the nineteenth-century distinction between premillennialism and postmillennialism. This is primarily because theologians of the eighteenth century did not view the question as to whether the Second Coming would initiate or conclude the millennium as being especially significant or divisive. Rather, their anticipation of Christ's presence and the desire to facilitate his presence among them prevented the accentuation of fundamental doctrinal differences that would later cause discursive fragmentation.

Cotton Mather's Millennialism

Cotton Mather provides an example of the ways in which diverse interests and seemingly incompatible stances would combine in millennial discourse. Like his father, Increase Mather, the younger Mather believed that the millennium would be initiated by Christ's personal return and that the first resurrection should be understood literally, as applying to all of the saints and martyrs. Christ would appear suddenly in fire and smoke, surrounded by angels; his arrival would touch off a great conflagration, which Mather thought would consume at least Italy and the Roman territories, but which might spare America. The saints would be caught up in the air and so protected. The new world that would be created from the old would be a paradise for the saints: there would be no more sin or sickness, and the church would be free to prosper. Christ and the raised martyrs would not live on the new earth, but would rather reside in the air above it and so be visible to the saints. At the conclusion of the millennium Satan would lead Gog and Magog out of Hell for the final battle at Armageddon. There, fire from the New Heavens will destroy Satan's forces; this event will be followed by the Last Judgment and the second Resurrection, in which the sinners will be condemned to Hell. Afterward, Christ and the saints would dwell for eternity in the Third Heaven.

More revealing than Mather's construction of apocalyptic scenarios, however, is the way in which he used millennial discourse to combine his hope for a gradual amelioration in the church with his desire for a sudden judgment to descend on the world, and to weld together his desire that America would have a special place in divine history with his general fear that New England was losing its sense of mission. Despite his conviction that the millennium would occur only with the advent of Christ, he believed that God nonetheless required Christians to work to hasten its coming. Mather often thought himself to have been given special apprehensions that the kingdom of God was near; he would prostrate himself in supplication before God, praying for its arrival. He also held weekly meetings in which apocalyptic matters would be discussed, and attempted to calculate the time of Christ's advent, alternately suggesting the years 1697, 1716, and 1745 as possible dates.

Mather asserted that unity among Christians would also encourage Christ's quick advent, and published *The Stone Cut Out of the Mountain* (1716) in order to inspire such a movement. The way in which Mather simultaneously maintained that the millennium would occur though violence and at God's decree with the hope that he could collaborate with and precipitate its coming—indeed, even believing that he had been specially elected to do so—mirrors the manner in which he seemingly wavered regarding America's role in the millennium. His *Theopolis Americana* (1710), for example, simultaneously anticipated the coming holy city in America while complaining of the general sinfulness of the colonies. In his *Magnalia Christi Americana* Mather celebrated "The Great Acts of Christ in America" and wrote of the colony as being subject to "special providential guidance", but warned that its special position would be lost if it did not recover its sense of mission.

Jonathan Edwards and Prerevolutionary Millennialism

Rather than exhibiting contradiction, these seeming discrepancies go to the heart of the use of millennial anticipation during this period. Theologians generally assumed that God caused his church to progress through affliction, so that seeming reverses in the interests of religion were in fact part of the process through which God refined and purified the earthly church, preventing it from becoming satisfied with worldly prosperity. It was also believed that Satan would redouble his efforts against God's kingdom as it came closer to being. In this way, the proliferation of darkness could paradoxically indicate that a great outpouring of the Holy Spirit was about to occur. From this perspective, it was possible to simultaneously complain about the insensibility of New Englanders to spiritual truths while maintaining hope that the millennium was near.

This afflictive model of progress is evident throughout eighteenth-century millennialism, and is especially apparent in the thought of Jonathan Edwards. Edwards projected this pattern of progress through affliction onto the whole history of the church since Christ's resurrection. In his *A History of the Work of Redemption* (1774) he argues that Christ's kingdom is attained through four distinct comings, each of which is accomplished by a judgment and destruction of parts of Satan's world. The first coming ends with the destruction of Jerusalem, the second with the fall of the heathen Roman Empire, the third with the fall of the Antichrist, and the last with the Last Judgment. In each of these stages, Christ's kingdom is brought further into existence by an act of judgment and destruction, in which obstacles that stand before it are removed. As the old world dominated by Satan's influence is gradually destroyed, it is replaced by Christ's new world. Edwards argued that within this process progress towards the millennium occurred through a series of pulsations. The influence of the spirit would increase and decline in each period, but the forward movement would always exceed the retraction, so that a consistent general advancement would persist throughout history.

In this construction, the millennium unfolds at the point of Antichrist's binding, before the Last Judgment. It is to be accomplished through an outpouring of the Spirit, manifested through the preaching of the gospel and in works of conversion. Once this general conversion is accomplished, the power of Satan will be broken: he will be effectively bound, having no influence in the manifest world. All nations shall worship Christ and his kingdom will then have universal extent. The church will continue in this state of universal peace and prosperity for a thousand years. At the end of this period, violent and widespread but brief apostasy will prevail, and the church's existence will again seem to be threatened by the forces of Antichrist. This time, however, Christ will intervene, appearing from heaven with a host of angels. The dead will then rise from their graves and the final judgment will take place; the elect will be redeemed in their bodies, ascend to heaven with Christ and enter the New Jerusalem. The reprobate will be exposed of their sin and consigned to the earth, which will then be set alight to burn eternally.

The Emergence of Civil Millennialism

Edwards's apocalyptic chronology locates the episodes of the church's persecution in the past, and projects a vision of steady ascent. Although Edwards speculated the chronology of Revelation, his sense of the emergence of the millennium chiefly derives from his conception of God as having an inherent disposition to communicate himself to his creatures. For this reason Edwards could initially regard the Great Awakening as potentially constituting the beginning of the millennium. This perspective won a number of adherents, Joseph Bellamy and Samuel Hopkins being the most prominent. The way in which the Edwardsean paradigm evolved in the hands of millennial expositors in the second half of the eighteenth century, however, was profoundly altered by historical incidents involving the colony, specifically, the French and Indian Wars and the Revolutionary War. These conflicts constituted principal turning points in millennial speculation during the century, provoking a fundamental transformation in the understanding of the millennium.

The French and Indian Wars took on an apocalyptic tenor for the New England Clergy. They had long identified France with Roman Catholicism and Antichrist, with England as the defender of Protestantism, and saw the Wars as determining the religious future of the North American continent. During the period of conflict, however, the parameters through which New Englanders viewed the struggle underwent gradual change. Until this point millennial thought was largely apolitical, stressing individual regeneration as a means to social harmony. The wars, however, were increasingly perceived by the clergy in political terms, as constituting an attempt to preserve civil and religious liberty. Specifically Whig political values were incorporated into the millennial vision. Roman Catholicism was identified with slavery, and providential history as the steady progression of the cause of liberty against the power of tyranny; civil oppression rather than formal religion was seen as the chief method through which Satan was attempting to thwart the coming of Christ's kingdom.

The fusion of religious and political ideals formed in the Anglo-French conflict reoriented the way in which the New England clergy understood its mission. The initial effect of the wars caused New Englanders to identify themselves with the British as sharing a common heritage, and to champion the British constitution as establishing a standard of liberty for the world. Because of the Stamp Act (1765), the Quebec Act (1774), and the threat of an imposed Anglican bishopric, however, Americans came to view Britain itself as a threat to their liberty. In the War of Independence England was identified as being of the Antichrist, and some of the clergy believed that it was secretly conspiring to place America under the control of Roman Catholic Church. The politicized millennialism derived from the French and Indian Wars was turned against Britain, and used to define America. The myth of the founding generation was revised along these political lines: they were now represented as coming to America to escape British despotism.

Conclusion

Throughout the eighteenth century, the role America was to play in the events leading to the millennium was of much contention. Joseph Mede speculated that America might be excluded from Christ's kingdom, instead being the seat of Gog and Magog—the forces that would assault the New Jerusalem at the end of the millennium. Most American millennialists resisted this notion. Samuel Sewall argued that the New Jerusalem would in fact be located in America, most likely in Mexico, but the majority of commentators were content to grant America a peripheral role in the coming drama. After the Revolution, however, Americans accorded themselves a much more central place. Timothy Dwight, Jonathan Edwards' grandson, argued in a "Valedictory Address" of 1776 that "the Empire of North-America will be the last on earth" a "glorious Sabbath of peace, purity and felicity." In his *The Conquest of Canaan* (1785), which chronicles the progress of the republic, Dwight affirmed that America was the promised land, like Israel of old, destined by God to be both the site of the millennium and the agent of millennial renewal in the world.

James Hewitson

Bibliography

Bercovitch, Sacvan. (1978) *The American Jeremiad.* Madison, WI: University of Wisconsin Press.

——. (1993) *The Rites of Assent: Transformations in the Symbolic Construction of America.* New York: Routledge.

Bloch, Ruth H. (1985) *Visionary Republic: Millennial Themes in American Thought, 1756–1800.* Cambridge, U.K.: Cambridge University Press.

Davidson, James West. (1977) *The Logic of Millennial Thought: Eighteenth-Century New England.* New Haven, CT: Yale University Press.

Erwin, John S. (1990) *The Millennialism of Cotton Mather: An Historical and Theological Analysis.* Lewiston, NY: The Edward Mellon Press.

Hatch, Nathan. (1977) *The Sacred Cause of Liberty: Republican Thought and the Millennium in Revolutionary New England.* New Haven, CT: Yale University Press.

Heimert, Alan. (1966) *Religion and the American Mind from the Great Awakening to the Revolution.* Cambridge, MA: Harvard University Press.

Marty, Martin E. (1970) *Righteous Empire: The Protestant Experience in America.* New York: The Dial Press.

Middlekauff, Robert. (1971) *The Mathers: Three Generations of Puritan Intellectuals, 1596–1728.* New York: Oxford University Press.

Stein, Stephen J. (1984) "Transatlantic Extensions: Apocalyptic in Early New England." In *The Apocalypse in English Renaissance Thought and Literature: Patterns, Antecedents and Repercussions,* edited by C. A. Patrides and Joseph Wittreich. Ithaca, NY: Cornell University Press, 266–98.

Tuveson, Earnest Lee. (1968) *Redeemer Nation: The Idea of America's Millennial Role.* Chicago: University of Chicago Press.

Wilson, John F. (1988) "History, Redemption, and the Millennium." In *Jonathan Edwards and the American Experience,* edited by Nathan O. Hatch and Harry S. Stout. New York: Oxford University Press, 103–17.

Urantia

The Urantia movement is an American cult whose members believe that Jesus will return to Earth at an unspecified date, but not until a new revelation, of which they are custodians, has transformed humanity.

The movement began with the channeling of alien messages by a man widely believed to be Wilfred Custer Kellogg, brother-in-law of Dr. William Samuel Sadler (1875–1969), a respected Chicago psychiatrist and prolific author. According to an appendix in the doctor's best-selling *The Mind at Mischief* (1929), the person (he is not named) started talking in his sleep in 1911. His words purported to be messages from a group of alien intelligences. Sadler and his wife Lena eventually became convinced that these "unseen friends" were bringing to Urantia, the cult's name for Earth, a fresh revelation destined to supersede Christianity.

At first the revelations were taken down in shorthand by Sadler's adopted daughter Christy. Later, neatly typed papers, signed with the exotic names of supermortals, began to appear mysteriously. In 1935, Sadler arranged for a collection of these papers to be published as a massive 2,097-page "Bible" called *The Urantia Book (UB).*

The *UB* papers contain hundreds of strange, newly coined words, dozens of categories divided into seven parts, vivid descriptions of life on other worlds, predictions of future science (e.g., the discovery of an ultimately fundamental particle called an ultimaton), a vigorous defense of eugenics to eliminate the unfit, and a long-abandoned theory of evolution in which new species arise suddenly in one generation. These speculations are mixed with moral, political, and theological rhetoric similar in many ways to liberal Protestantism.

The *UB*'s major departure from Christianity is its acceptance of a complex polytheism involving myriads of gods of varying ranks on levels between humans and the ultimate "I AM" who governs an eternal multiverse monstrously larger than the universe known to today's cosmologists. The book teaches that within each of us lives a "thought adjuster" who tries to guide our thoughts in accord with the Spirit of Truth. At death our souls sleep while they are taken to a distant planet and started on an endless sojourn through higher worlds until they finally reach the Isle of Paradise where the great I AM dwells.

Jesus is one of more than 700,000 Creator Sons who undergo incarnations on inhabited planets. His greatest enemy is an evil supermortal called Caligastia. Eventually Caligastia, along with unrepentant wicked mortals, will be annihilated. Urantians do not believe in hell, nor do they regard Jesus' crucifixion as a blood atonement for Original Sin, in which they also do not believe. The *UB*'s final third is a life of Jesus. It gives thousands of details not in the Gospels, which it often contradicts.

Sadler and his brother-in-law, together with their wives, were all former Seventh-Day Adventists who had abandoned their faith. Many Adventist doctrines, found their way in to the *UB*, such as soul sleeping and annihilation of the wicked, guardian angels, and the identification of Jesus with Michael, creator of our universe. There are no Urantian churches or clergy. The faith is maintained by small study groups which meet in major cities around the world to discuss the *UB*.

In recent years the movement has suffered three major scandals. First, Kristen Maaherra, a devout Urantian, made valiant legal attempts to prove that the *UB*, because it has no human authors, was illegally copyrighted by the Urantia Foundation. Headquartered in Sadler's former Chicago offices, the foundation has bitterly opposed Maaherra's efforts. Second, scores of Urantians came to believe they are in direct contact with the unseen friends. In one early case, voices coming through Vernon Grimsley gave the exact date of the outbreak of an atomic world war. Urantians were greatly agitated until the date passed. Today's Urantia channelers call themselves the Teaching Mission. The foundation considers them self-deluded, but they have created a schism that continues to disrupt the movement. Third, Urantian Matthew Block discovered that the *UB* swarms with passages copied without credit from books by others. His discovery is ironic because the sacred writings of Ellen White, cofounder of the Seventh-Day Adventists, also shamelessly plagiarize earlier works.

The foundation refused to confirm or deny that Wilfred Kellogg was the first human chosen by the supermortals to be their contact for channeling the new revelation. It insists that the man's identity will never be revealed. The movement continues to be a small cult, its members incessantly squabbling. No one knows how many Urantians are around the world or whether their number is increasing or decreasing.

Martin Gardner

See also Ufology

Bibliography

Bedell, Clyde. (1971) *Concordex of the Urantia Book*. Santa Barbara, CA: privately printed by author.

Faw, Duane L., ed. (1986) *The Paramony: 15,000 Cross-References Paralleling and Harmonizing the Urantia Book and the Bible*. Malibu, CA: privately printed by author, distributed by the Jesusonian Foundation, Boulder, CO.

Gardner, Martin. (1995) *Urantia: The Great Cult Mystery*. Amherst, NY: Prometheus Books.

Sherman, Harold. (1976). "Pipeline to God." In *How to Know What to Believe*. New York: Fawcett.

Utopia

A name invented by Thomas More in his 1516 discourse on the ideal state, "utopia" means literally "no place" or "nowhere," but has come to signify any attempt to describe or to experiment with an ideal community. Utopianism often takes literary form (typified in modern science fiction, for example) but can also be manifest in social and political action. Millennialist movements frequently include utopian expectations of a future society characterized by communal harmony and prosperity. Although many religions believe in a paradisal afterlife, religious millennialisms look forward to either an imminent or a distant earthly fulfillment. Likewise, nearly every modern political revolution has entertained utopian ideals as one of its goals. In the twentieth century, many thinkers disenchanted by modern totalitarianisms' failed utopias have described "anti-utopias" or "dystopias" as the more likely outcome of millennialist fervor.

The notion of an ideal place has been a component of many religious and secular literatures. The Chinese thinker Confucius (or K'ung fu-tzu; 551–499 BCE) became a teacher of political wisdom, whose collected sayings in the *Analects* attributed political stability and social prosperity to the degree that a leader is virtuous and that right relations among all citizens are maintained. In *The Republic*, Plato (c. 428–c. 348 BCE) speculated on justice in the ideal state, ruled by philosopher kings, where the good, the true, and the beautiful are held as the highest civic values. In *Timaeus*, Plato introduced the Western world to the mythical westward island nation of Atlantis, around which many subsequent utopian fantasies have revolved. Another mythical land popularized in the Middle Ages, the Land of Cokayne, was believed to be a place of rest and leisure—components not otherwise common in medieval life.

Utopian Ideals of the People of the Book

The religious traditions known as the People of the Book (Judaism, Christianity, and Islam) all offer visions of idealized communities somewhere in the future. The Torah (the first five books of the Hebrew scriptures) can be read as the attempt to return to the Garden of Eden after Adam and Eve's ejection from that ideal place; the "Promised Land" is configured as a place of abundance, a land "flowing with milk and honey" to which Moses will lead the people out of Egypt. The prophetic writings of the Hebrew scriptures pick up this theme by offering a vision of a revived covenant community in the "Day of the Lord," a time of future earthly fulfillment of human aspirations (see especially Isaiah, Jeremiah, and Ezra).

Understanding himself as the ultimate eschatological (endtimes) prophet sent to announce and summon the Day of the Lord, Jesus of Nazareth formed a community of believers whose egalitarianism (including women, tax collectors, notorious sinners) was scandalous to the religious conventions of his time. After his crucifixion, Jesus' disciples in the first century likewise understood themselves as an eschatological community adhering to a common life (including joint sharing of property and goods) and in Acts of the Apostles (written by the author of the Gospel of Luke some time late in the first century BCE) one reads its idealized self-portrait. However, even only a few decades after Jesus' crucifixion in a community maintaining its hope for his imminent Second Coming, one sees the stresses pulling this utopian group apart: Ananias and Sapphira who attempt to cheat their fellow disciples out of money are slain by God in punishment (Acts 5:1–11). In time Christians' eschatological fervor cooled and by the early fourth century, Christians found themselves in the remarkable position as the dominant religious ideology of the crumbling Roman Empire; they abandoned their millennialist expectations of earthly paradise. In *The City of God*, St. Augustine (354–430), a North African bishop and one of Christianity's most influential theologians, proposed that there are two opposed worlds: the Earthly City and the City of God, a formulation that postponed indefinitely an ideal earthly community and muted Christian apocalypticism for nearly a millennium, which would only emerge in post-Augustinian theologians of the Protestant Reformation.

Two centuries after Augustine, Islam emerged from the Arabian peninsula and spread east across North Africa. Mohammed (570?–632), God's final prophet in Islam, conveyed Allah's wishes for ideal community life lived under the principles of the Qur'an, including religious devotion, adherence to dietary and ethical laws, and right relations of justice among rich and poor. In addition to the promises of prosperity for a life faithful to these principles, the Qur'an also holds out an eschatological reward that is every bit as earthly: "Verily, the righteous shall be in pleasure; upon couches shall they gaze; thou mayest recognize in their faces the brightness of pleasure; they shall be given to drink wine that is sealed, whose seal is musk; for that then let the aspirants aspire!" (sura 83, Palmer 1933).

Development of Utopian Ideals in Western Thought

Although Christianity after St. Augustine had largely abandoned millennialist expectations of an earthly ideal existence, the medieval church nonetheless held up monasteries as exemplars of human community. Largely self-sufficient and organized around the daily rituals of work and prayer, monasteries and convents followed established rules designed to subordinate individual desires to the service of the group while providing the stability and resources for learning and productive labor. In this historical period of frequent deprivation and violence, they must have seemed walled paradises to the laity outside. Nonetheless, the frequent monastic reform movements and the numerous new monastic orders initiated to correct abuses indicate the extent to which they, too, were vulnerable to the corruptions of the outside world.

One such aspirant to monastic life found instead that his vocation lay in public life. In the early English Renaissance, following in the Greek humanist tradition that produced Plato's *Republic*, the English Tudor lawyer, statesman, and intellectual, Sir Thomas More (1478–1535), published his most famous literary work, *Utopia*, in 1516. Written in Latin and published with the help of his friend Erasmus (perhaps the greatest humanist intellectual of his time), *Utopia* is in two parts: the first, a dialogue that anatomizes the ills of English society; the second, a narrative describing Utopia, a distant land where those ills do not exist. The premise of the account is a chance meeting in Antwerp of More with a traveler named Raphael Hythloday who had discovered this ideal place, where property is held in common, both men and women receive education, and religious freedom prevails. (Paradoxically, More's own persecution of religious dissenters seems at odds with the tolerant attitudes of Utopia, and he would himself fall victim to violence for his conscientious resistance to Henry VIII's rupture with the Roman Catholic Church.) Since its translation into English and French in the 1550s, *Utopia* has assumed legendary status and the word has entered the language as a generic term for any ideal community.

Following More's book are numerous descendants in the family of literary utopias. In a later French book, *Gargantua and Pantagruel* by François Rabelais (1490–1553), the young prince Pantagruel visits Utopia. In addition, the monastic community as a utopian place received a satirical treatment in Friar John of the Funnels who asks King Gargantua to found for him an abbey whose motto will be "Do What You Will," an ideal community whose members are beautiful,

BOOK II: OF THE RELIGIONS OF THE UTOPIANS

There are several sorts of religions, not only in different parts of the island, but even in every town; some worshipping the sun, others the moon or one of the planets: some worship such men as have been eminent in former times for virtue or glory, not only as ordinary deities, but as the supreme God: yet the greater and wiser sort of them worship none of these, but adore one eternal, invisible, infinite, and incomprehensible Deity; as a being that is far above all our apprehensions, that is spread over the whole universe, not by His bulk, but by His power and virtue; Him they call the Father of All, and acknowledge that the beginnings, the increase, the progress, the vicissitudes, and the end of all things come only from Him; nor do they offer divine honors to any but to Him alone. And indeed, though they differ concerning other things, yet all agree in this, that they think there is one Supreme Being that made and governs the world, whom they call in the language of their country Mithras. They differ in this, that one thinks the god whom he worships is this Supreme Being, and another thinks that his idol is that God; but they all agree in one principle, that whoever is this Supreme Being, He is also that great Essence to whose glory and majesty all honors are ascribed by the consent of all nations.

By degrees, they fall off from the various superstitions that are among them, and grow up to that one religion that is the best and most in request; and there is no doubt to be made but that all the others had vanished long ago, if some of those who advised them to lay aside their superstitions had not met with some unhappy accident, which being considered as inflicted by heaven, made them afraid that the God whose worship had like to have been abandoned, had interposed, and revenged themselves on those who despised their authority. After they had heard from us an account of the doctrine, the course of life, and the miracles of Christ, and of the wonderful constancy of so many martyrs, whose blood, so willingly offered up by them, was the chief occasion of spreading their religion over a vast number of nations; it is not to be imagined how inclined they were to receive it. I shall not determine whether this proceeded from any secret inspiration of God, or whether it was because t seemed so favorable to that community of goods, which is an opinion so particular as well as so dear to them; since they perceived that Christ and his followers lived by that rule and that it was still kept up in some communities among the sincerest sort of Christians. From whichsoever of these motives it might be, true it is that many of them came over to our religion, and were initiated into it by baptism. But as two of our number were dead, so none of the four that survived were in priest's orders; we therefore could only baptize them; so that to our great regret they could not partake of the other sacraments, that can only be administered by priests; but they are instructed concerning them, and long most vehemently for them. They have had great disputes among themselves, whether one chosen by them to be a priest would not be thereby qualified to do all the things that belong to that character, even though he had no authority derived from the Pope; and they seemed to be resolved to choose some for that employment, but they had not done it when I left them.

Source: More, Thomas (1901) *Utopia.* New York: Ideal Commonwealths. P.F. Collier & Son. The Colonial Press. Released July 1993 by the Internet Wiretap.

intelligent, and virtuous. Another English writer, Francis Bacon (1561–1626), proposed in *New Atlantis* a utopian society organized around science. An account of a voyage to Bensalem ("Son of Peace"), *New Atlantis* (published posthumously in 1627) describes "Solomon's House" in which scientists carry on experiments and explorations of nature. Samuel Butler's 1872 satirical novel *Erewhon,* an anagram of the word "nowhere," mocked the attitudes of Victorian England toward science, politics, and religion.

The Rises and Falls of Western Utopian Movements

The late Middle Ages in Europe had witnessed the rise of a variety of utopian religious and social movements. These would gain momentum in the Reformation and issue in three early modern revolutions: the English, the American, and the French. Norman Cohn has chronicled medieval "revolutionary millenarians" who preceded similar utopian experiments during the Renaissance. Some disciples of

Joachim of Fiore (1145–1202), "the inventor of [a] new prophetic system, which was to be the most influential one known to Europe until the appearance of Marxism" (Cohn, 108), crusaded over the next centuries on behalf of the poor against the wealthy. During the Hundred Years War between France and England (1337–1453), social dislocations and the heavy tax burdens of war precipitated what might be considered Europe's first utopian revolts to achieve visionary egalitarian communities among the French *Jacquerie* in 1358 and later among English peasants. In the English Peasants' Revolt of 1381, the legendary John Ball is alleged to have preached sermons calling for a leveling of social classes by claiming common ancestry in Adam and Eve, or put proverbially, "When Adam delved [dug] and Eve span [spun wool], / Who was then a gentleman?" Later in the next century Bohemian Taborites would attempt to form communities of common property. And in the early sixteenth century at the beginning of the Reformation, the German Peasants' War (1524) was fomented by the millenarian Thomas Müntzer, whom Martin Luther urged (successfully) the German princes to crush. After the English Revolution (1642–49) under Oliver Cromwell's Commonwealth, several millennialist revolutionary movements emerged. So-called Levellers sought to level the English social hierarchy; one group of Levellers, the Diggers, maintained that all property was to be held in common, and began to dig and plant on St. George's Common in Surrey. A related Free Spirit movement, called Ranters, proclaimed the believers' freedom from conventional laws and proclaimed an antinomian utopia.

With the end of the Puritan Commonwealth and the restoration of the monarchy in 1660, the English Revolution had failed. A century later English colonists in North America would once more discard the monarchy and aristocracy and because of the accidents of history, succeed. Likewise in the decade after that, the French Revolution attempted to dismantle the hierarchy of aristocrats and ecclesiastics, and although initially successful, its utopian aims were compromised by Napoleonic ambition. In each case, political revolutions were accompanied by millennialist utopianism, the belief that history was coming to a final, glorious fulfillment.

The European contact with the Americas prompted utopian schemes that went beyond Thomas More's or Francis Bacon's imaginary places. In particular, the English settlements in North America, frequently driven as they were by religious millennialism, attempted to establish themselves as ideal communities, laid out according to whatever ideological lines they were committed. The Plymouth Plantation understood itself as a separatist community that was required to maintain its religious purity by strict scrutiny and maintenance of its members, exiling those who threatened its rigor. Similarly, the Pennsylvania, Rhode Island, and Maryland colonies were initiated by a desire for communities of tolerance. The blank slate on which the early republic would inscribe itself after the Revolutionary War likewise catalyzed numerous utopian schemes, some of which were realized in the Constitution and Bill of Rights. Symbolically, the new federal capital, Washington, with its geometrically planned streets and avenues and neoclassical architecture, expressed the desire for an idealized rational civic life, equal parts Puritan Commonwealth, Roman Republic, and Romantic agrarian ideal. The "new man" and the "novus ordo seclorum" (new world order) that the federal founders articulated was also based in part on utopian ideas articulated earlier in the eighteenth century by Jean Jacques Rousseau.

Modern Utopian Visions of the Nineteenth and Twentieth Centuries

It would be safe to say, however, that if the eighteenth century gave birth to political utopianism, the nineteenth century nurtured both its intellectuals and its practitioners. Karl Marx (1818–83) towers above the age, as much for his theories about society, economics, and history as for the effect his writings have had on the twentieth century. In *The Communist Manifesto* (written with Friedrich Engels) and *Das Kapital,* Marx proposed a three-stage analysis of history, in which the tyranny of aristocrats was replaced by the oppression of the bourgeoisie over the working class. Marx's conviction—one might call it a faith—was that the forces of history were leading inexorably to a proletarian revolution creating a socialist society, which would eventually lead to communism and a just social and economic order. Marx's faith in history and in his utopian ideal prompted him to assert that capitalist industrial societies were ripe for revolution.

Another nineteenth-century millenarian utopian's influence is still being assessed. Joseph Smith (1805–44) lived in western New York state, a region known as the Burned-over District. As John L. Brooke remarks concerning Smith's eclectic theology:

> When recombined in the Radical Reformation and the English Revolution with currents of millenarian prophecy and a conviction of the imminence of the restored Kingdom of God, hermetic divinization posed a potent challenge to Christian orthodoxy. It also prefigured the cosmology constructed in the 1830s and 1840s by Joseph Smith, who was born in—if not of—a Calvinist culture and moved from the ranks of the cunning folk to the status of an Adamic *magus* as the prophet of the Mormon restoration. (8)

Smith's visions and the revelations he claimed created a utopian community, the Church of Jesus Christ of Latter

Day Saints, whose practices were initially at odds with mainstream Christian America, which impelled the Mormons westward to what seemed in most eyes a God-forsaken place. From this initially marginalized posture, Mormons have remarkably assimilated into American society while simultaneously maintaining a communitarian ideal. Of this assimilation, Armand Mauss observed, "In what might be called the 'natural history' of the interaction between radical social movements and their host societies, there seem to be no historical exceptions to the proposition that new movements must either submit to assimilation in important respects or be destroyed" (4). Discarding the practice of polygamy and later doctrines of race that were at odds with dominant social values, Mormons have held to other core practices and beliefs. The prominence of Mormons in politics and business and their successes (and persistence) with global missionary conversion have influenced the conservative turn in American politics in the last twenty years of the twentieth century. It is possible that religious utopianism may dominate the twenty-first century.

Other utopian schemes appeared in the nineteenth and twentieth centuries in the formation of communities of common purpose and vision; most ended in disappointment, while some ended in catastrophe. Some of these were religious, like the Mormons and Shakers, while others, like the American Brook Farm community, William Morris's Arts and Crafts movement and the Fabian Socialists in England, and the French utopian socialists Saint-Simon, Fourier, and Proudhon, were secular. Experiments in secular small-scale utopianism have persisted in the twentieth century, receiving their greatest celebrity in the 1960s and 1970s hippie communes. However, probably the most significant contemporary utopian ideology has been Marxism in its various forms, although national socialism (the Nazis in Germany and the fascists in Italy and Spain) must come close for the extent to which they affected history and discredited utopianism generally.

In criticism of these ideological systems, whose utopian rhetoric had been belied by their totalitarian methods, the two great pieces of modern antiutopian or dystopian literature emerged: Aldous Huxley's *Brave New World* (1932) and George Orwell's *1984* (1949). One might also add to that list William Golding's antisentimental and anti-Romantic novel *The Lord of the Flies* (1954), which showed that children in an idyllic island setting, contrary to Rousseau's Romantic idealism, do not naturally fashion a utopia, but evince nature red in tooth and claw.

The failure of Soviet communism and the Eastern Bloc and the erosion of Maoist communism in China have prompted some analysts, like Francis Fukuyama, to declare the "end of history" in the victorious capitalist democratic utopia. However, economic dislocations and cycles of expansion and recession in capitalist economies of the last decade of the twentieth century suggest that capitalist idealism is also misguided. Some twentieth-century fundamentalist extremists (from many different religious viewpoints including Judaism, Christianity, and Islam) view the restoration of a theocracy (rule by divine law) as a necessary component in the creation of an idealized future society. The end of the twentieth century has also been darkened with millennialist utopian communities (which by now are commonly thought of, pejoratively, as "sects") whose ends came in bangs instead of whimpers: Jonestown, Branch Davidians at Waco, the Heaven's Gate community, among others.

Conclusion

Many modern critical theorists have considered the kinds and functions of utopianism. The Manuels have provided an exhaustive historical and critical study of utopianism broadly understood to include literature, politics, science, religion, and philosophy. A. L. Morton offered an English Marxian critique of utopian literature, distinguishing the utopian as socialist idealism from the dystopian as reactionary. In contrast, Marie Louise Berneri's study recognizes the totalitarian implications of revolutionary utopianism. Libby Falk Jones and Sarah Webster Goodwin's collection of essays offers a far-ranging feminist critique of utopianism from different historical periods, while focusing on the nineteenth and twentieth centuries; they demonstrate the relationship between women's narratives and the imagination of an ideal world for women.

Millennialist ideologies frequently imagine an idealized community whose formation and maintenance are the mission of the millennialist believer. However, their best laid plans often go awry: true believers are frequently blind to their leaders' blindness while utopian leaders sometimes ruthlessly maintain their own authority in the name of the millennial vision. In more benign situations, the inability to maintain the founding fervor typically gives way to compromise and assimilation, or even disappointment.

Thomas L. Long

Bibliography

Berneri, Marie Louise. (1971) *Journey Through Utopia*. New York: Schocken Books.

Brooke, John L. (1994) *The Refiner's Fire: The Making of Mormon Cosmology, 1644–1844*. Cambridge: Cambridge University Press.

Cohn, Norman. (1970) *The Pursuit of the Millennium: Revolutionary Millenarians and Mystical Anarchists of the Middle Ages*, rev. ed. New York: Oxford University Press.

Jones, Libby Falk, and Sarah Webster Goodwin, eds. (1990) *Feminism, Utopia, and Narrative.* Knoxville: University of Tennessee Press.

Manuel, Frank E., and Fritzie P. Manuel, eds. (1979) *Utopian Thought in the Western World.* Oxford, U.K.: Blackwell.

Mauss, Armand. (1994) *The Angel and the Beehive: The Mormon Struggle with Assimilation.* Urbana: University of Illinois Press.

Morton, A. L. (1952) *The English Utopia.* London: Lawrence & Wishart.

Violence

How can we account for the suicidal audacity of a tiny handful of true believers who would take up arms against the overwhelming power of the modern state? Or, in the medieval era, the same question could be asked of the adherents of a number of heretical sects who would oppose the power of both the Church and the worldly powers of the crown. What vision could move the people of that time to risk not only their lives, but their immortal souls? Such violent episodes have occurred throughout the history of the Christian West, and similar outbreaks have taken place under the heading of "revolutionary messianism" in Jewish and Islamic history as well.

This entry will consider this question in both historical and contemporary perspective. It is important to note at the outset however, that violence has been the exception rather than the rule among Millenarians. Rather, the peaceful pattern of the nineteenth-century Millerites has been by far the norm. Here, William Miller (d. 1849), on the basis of his reading of the Bible, prophesied in 1835 that the Second Coming of Christ would occur in March 1843. The Millerite movement soon gained thousands of adherents who as the great day approached sold their belongings and withdrew from society to await the Great Event. Disappointed, alternate dates were proposed, but when the last of these, 22 October 1844, passed without event, the movement peacefully disbanded, only to be reconstituted under the charismatic leadership of Ellen White as the Seventh-Day Adventists. When millenarian violence has taken place however, it assumes a distinctive pattern.

Medieval Millenarian Violence

The model of medieval millenarian violence was provided by Norman Cohn's landmark 1957 study, *The Pursuit of the Millennium: Revolutionary Messianism in Medieval and Reformation Europe and its Bearing on Modern Totalitarian Movements.* The study was revised several times, but its main tenets remain unchanged. In Cohn's model, millenarian movements arise in times of rapid sociopolitical change. Such movements appeal to a population of the deprived and the dispossessed. They rely on sacred text for inspiration, although they themselves may not have had access to the Bible. Millennialist movements were led by charismatic figures, believed to possess the ability to interpret scripture in light of contemporary events. This placed the faithful at the center of world-changing events.

Violence often resulted from the persecution by the "powers that be" combined with the biblical promise that the worst of times are in eschatological terms the best of times. In this view, when all hope appears lost, Jesus will return at the head of the heavenly host to punish the wicked and to reward his faithful servants. The dream that fired these true believers to oppose the powers of this world was of a change that would be total. The faithful were promised terrestrial power in a "new heaven and a new earth" [2 Peter 3:11]. In a world cleansed of all corruption, the faithful would reside for a thousand years in peace and plenty at the side of Jesus. It is a dream which brought many to abandon all worldly considerations and give their lives to the violent pursuit of the millennium.

A number of such movements arose in the Middle Ages, although only a few turned to violence and even fewer were able to overcome the worldly powers arrayed against them. Such a temporary success story were the Albigensians, a sect of the French Catharist heresy [twelfth to fourteenth centuries]. The Albigensians were an offshoot of the dualist beliefs which originated with the Persian Manichees and entered Europe through the Bulgarian Bogomils. Medieval dualist beliefs posited a stark division between this world which was seen to be the abode of the Devil and the heavenly Kingdom of God. These forces of good and evil, light and darkness, were seen to be in a state of constant war.

Catharism attracted all stations of society. When the nobility came under the sway of Cathari teachings, this strongly millenarian sect became a political as well as a religious threat. Finally, by means of an intense campaign of preaching by Dominican and Cistercian friars, followed by more resolute measures in the form of the Albigensian Crusade (1209–19) and the Inquisition, the Albigensians were destroyed.

At the turn of the fifteenth century the Hussites, a religious reform movement arose under the leadership of the rector of the University of Prague, Jan Hus. In 1415, Hus was burned at the stake as a heretic. The reform movement that bore his name then turned to more millenarian leaders, adopted more heretical views, and withdrew to the heavily fortified cities of Tabor. From there, the Taborites under the leadership of the brilliant military strategist Jan Zizka, conducted a military campaign which enjoyed considerable success. The movement's ultimate demise was attributable to internal schism. From their ranks came the Adamites who taught that they were free of Original Sin. Thus, they could practice public nudity and orgiastic revels under the belief that they could do as they would without loss of purity. Eventually, the Taborites put them to the sword.

The relative success of the Taborites is in stark contrast to the frustration which modern sects of millennialists have found in trying to "Force the End" through violent means. What advantage did the fifteenth-century Taborites enjoy over contemporary millenarian movements? The most important difference would appear to be relative isolation from the powers of this world. The Taborites could withdraw from the cities and place themselves effectively out of the reach of state power. What the Taborites discovered was that, having renounced their ties to the world, the world was unable to enforce its writ in Tabor. With isolation comes not only consolidation, but radicalization. Millenarian expectations, if they are to catalyze into revolutionary movements, seem to require not only a sense of persecution or oppression, but the advantages of relative isolation in which charismatic leaders may subtly reshape the adherents' perception of the world. The safety of this enclave is no longer possible for modern millennial movements.

Millenarian Violence in the Modern World

Although ours is a more secular age than that of the medieval millennialist movements, millenarian violence has not disappeared. This entry will therefore concentrate on three recent American cases of millenarian violence: the Waco tragedy, Christian Identity, and the pro-life rescue movement. Each of these instances pitted small groups of millenarian true believers against the overwhelming power of the American state. Moreover, these cases replicate many of the patterns of their medieval precursors. In terms of violence, they reproduce the most common pattern of all. That is, while a few millenarian groups will initiate violence, the dominant pattern is of a millenarian group being the victims of violence. Thus, where a small faction of the rescue movement chose to precipitate deadly violence, violence involving the Davidians was purely defensive. Christian Identity presents a more ambiguous case.

Siege of Waco

The siege of the Branch Davidian compound in Waco, Texas, by officials of the federal Bureau of Alcohol, Tobacco, and Firearms and the Federal Bureau of Investigation reached its fiery denouement on 19 April 1993. The aftershocks of this apocalypse at are still being felt in America. The most serious of these occurred on 19 April 1995, when Timothy McVeigh, citing his outrage over Waco, detonated a car bomb at the Oklahoma City Federal Center in the largest single incident of domestic terrorism in American history.

The Branch Davidians emerged from Seventh-Day Adventism. In the early 1930s, a Bulgarian immigrant prophet named Victor Houteff (d. 1955) founded the Branch Davidian sect. After his death, his wife succeeded to the leadership of the group, predicting an apocalyptic event which was to take place on 22 April 1959. The prophesy failed, but the movement survived the disappointment. The Davidians split again in the 1980s with the arrival of Vernon Howell who took the name David Koresh (the names of the Hebrew prophet and the biblical Persian king). Preaching a powerfully millenarian message, including the doctrine that he was to father a new priestly caste who were to rule God's millennial Kingdom by sowing the women in the group "with the light." Even at the end, as government forces surrounded the Davidian compound, David Koresh was hard at work on a prophetic interpretation of the Seven Seals of Revelation.

Christian Identity

Christian Identity evolved from nineteenth-century British-Israelism, an eccentric form of biblical interpretation which posited the British people as the descendants of the biblical Israelites. Transplanted to the United States, British-Israelism combined with anti-Semitic currents drawn from the *Protocols of the Elders of Zion* and the "International Jew" series run in Henry Ford's company newspaper, the *Dearborn Independent*, to create by the 1940s the virulently anti-Semitic and racist doctrines of Christian Identity. Identity's most distinctive theological motif is the "two seeds doctrine," which posits the Jewish people as the demonic offspring of Eve and the serpent in the Garden of Eden (Genesis 3:1–4). The non-white races in this interpretation are seen as the "beasts of the field" (Genesis 2:19–20), over whom Adam as the first white man was given dominion (Genesis 1:28–30). Identity Christians see the Book of Revelation's dread Tribulation period as imminent, but these believers have no hope of supernatural rescue via the Rapture, or the rising into the air of the faithful to await the culmination of the Apocalypse (1 Thessalonians 4:17).

Despite the violent rhetoric emanating from Christian Identity quarters, the movement has rarely initiated violence. This may be attributed to the faithful's awareness of their own tiny numbers (between 10,000–50,000 worldwide) and to disagreements over the interpretation of world events within the apocalyptic scenario of the Bible. Yet throughout the 1980s, there were confrontations between state authorities and Identity communities which took place at such isolated compounds as that of the Covenant, Sword and Arm of the Lord in rural Missouri in 1985. These confrontations were invariably resolved with the peaceful surrender of the besieged Identity believers.

There were a handful of believers however, who attempted to take violent action. The most important of these were the Brüder Schweigen (the Silent Brotherhood more popularly known as the Order), a group centered in the Northwest, under the leadership of Robert Mathews. In the mid-1980s, the Order undertook a brief course of revolutionary violence which included at least two murders and the robbery of several armored cars. The group was smashed and Mathews killed in a shoot-out with federal agents on 8 December 1984.

The Rescue Movement

The rescue movement, defined as pro-lifers who practice "interposition" (in rescue parlance "those who interpose their bodies between the killer and his victim," i.e., the abortionist and the unborn child), emerged slowly from the religious opposition to the 1973 Roe v. Wade Supreme Court decision legalizing abortion. The first halting attempts at interposition, primarily in the form of minor vandalism, were undertaken in the early 1980s by individuals such as Joan Andrews.

In 1986–87, Operation Rescue was formed under the leadership of Randall Terry. Operation Rescue marked both the emergence of a large, organized rescue movement and the shift in the movement from a primarily Roman Catholic to a primarily evangelical and fundamentalist Protestant constituency. Accompanying this shift was an increasingly apocalyptic analysis of American society. Operation Rescue's tactical approach involved large-scale demonstrations aimed at shutting down abortion clinics in selected cities for limited periods of time. Thus, in such cities and towns as Buffalo, Fargo, Los Angeles, Pittsburgh, and culminating in Atlanta during the 1988 Democratic Convention, Operation Rescue mobilized rescuers throughout the country. Operation Rescue however, consciously modeled its actions on the nonviolent tactics of the 1960s-era civil rights movement.

The experience of the Atlanta jails split the movement, and after 1988 new rescue groups appeared, some of whom were less committed to nonviolence than Operation Rescue. The Lambs of Christ for example, a primarily Catholic Rescue group, is led by a priest named Norman Weslin who, like his second-in-command Ron Maxson, is from a military background. The Lambs added an element of increased militancy to the rescue movement. The Milwaukee-based Missionaries to the Pre-Born led by two former Operation Rescue stalwarts, Joseph Foreman and Matt Trewella, added a form of spiritual warfare they called imprecatory prayer (i.e., calling upon God through the use of certain Old Testament Psalms to either show the abortionist the error of his ways or to strike him dead).

Meanwhile, in the mid-1980s and early 1990s, individuals such as John Brockhoeft, Marjorie Reed, Michael Bray, and Shelly Shannon began to take more resolute action by firebombing clinics. They were scrupulous in their determination that the destruction of buildings would be accomplished with absolutely no loss of life. Moreover, all of them explained their actions by reference to biblical text and their passionate belief that abortion was symptomatic of the fact that these were indeed the Last Days and that God's Judgment on a fallen nation was nigh. Thus, when Michael Griffin, a peripheral figure in the tightly knit rescue community, shot and killed Dr. David Gunn in Pensacola, Florida, in 1993, the final barrier to lethal violence was broken. In short order, Shelley Shannon attempted to kill Dr. George Tiller in Milwaukee and Paul Hill shot and killed another Pensacola doctor, John Britton, and his volunteer bodyguard.

The core group of rescuers who opted for force—Shannon, Brockhoeft, Bray, Reed and a few others around the country—created an organizational symbol in the early 1990s called the Army of God (AOG). The AOG produced a manual which contained the experiences of the group as they tried to learn from scratch the methods of domestic terrorism. The AOG manual offered both the optimum recipes for bombs and fervently millenarian dreams of God's Judgment on the "death culture" of modern America. Today, in the writings and journals of the pro-force wing of the rescue movement (i.e., *Prayer + Action News* and *Life Advocate*), and on the Web through the *Nuremberg Files* which offers both an apocalyptic analysis of American society and the names, addresses, and whereabouts of abortion providers throughout the nation, the radical wing of the rescue movement explicitly endorses the use of force to halt abortion.

Conclusion

Although the problem of millenarian violence should not be minimized, it must be reiterated again that millenarianism is primarily a quietist phenomenon. Millennialists are primarily engaged in a process of waiting and watching. They are waiting for God to act to bring about the longed for End of Days. They are watching for the Signs of the Times. Indeed, watching is what millenarians do best. And as the technology of mass communication improves, the adherents are so bombarded with signs and portents that they are unable to focus on any one subject which could be presented as proof of the End! With the rare exceptions which we have considered in this entry, modern millenarians are content to peacefully wait and watch, and to dream.

Jeffrey Kaplan

See also Christian Identity, Davidians

Bibliography

Adas, Michael. (1979) *Prophets Of Rebellion: Millenarian Protest Movements Against The European Colonial Order.* Chapel Hill, NC: University of North Carolina Press.

Barkun, Michael. (1974) *Disaster and the Millennium.* New Haven, CT: Yale University Press.

——. (1994) *Religion and the Racist Right.* Chapel Hill, NC: University of North Carolina Press.

——, ed. (1996) *Millennialism and Violence.* London: Cass.

Bellah, Robert N., and Frederick E. Greenspahn. (1987) *Uncivil Religion: Interreligious Hostility in America.* New York: Crossroad.

Billington, James H. (1980) *Fire in the Minds of Men: Origins of the Revolutionary Faith.* New York: Basic Books.

Cohn, Norman. ([1957] 1970) *Pursuit of the Millennium: Revolutionary Millenarians and Mystical Anarchists of the Middle Ages.* New York: Oxford University Press.

——. (1969) *Warrant for Genocide.* New York: Harper.

Festinger, Leon et al. (1956) *When Prophecy Fails.* Minneapolis, MN: University of Minnesota Press.

Flynn, Kevin, and Gary Gerhardt. (1990) *The Silent Brotherhood.* New York: Signet.

Garrett, Clarke. (1975) *Respectable Folly: Millenarians and the French Revolution in France and England.* Baltimore, MD: Johns Hopkins University Press.

Girard, René. (1979) *Violence and the Sacred.* Baltimore, MD: Johns Hopkins University Press.

Goodrick-Clark, Nicholas. (1985) *The Occult Roots of Nazism.* New York: New York University Press.

Harrison, J. F. C. (1979) *The Second Coming: Popular Millenarianism 1780-1850.* New Brunswick, NJ: Rutgers University Press.

Kaminsky, Howard. (1967) *A History of the Hussite Revolution.* Berkeley, CA: University of California Press.

Kaplan, Jeffrey. (1997) *Radical Religion in America.* Syracuse, NY: Syracuse University Press.

McGinn, Bernard, ed. (1998) *The Encyclopedia of Apocalypticism, Vol. 2: Apocalypticism in Western History and Culture.* New York: Continuum.

Rhodes, James M. (1980) *The Hitler Movement: A Modern Millenarian Revolution.* Stanford, CA: Hoover Institution Press.

Roy, Ralph Lord. (1953) *Apostles of Discord.* Boston: Beacon Press.

Smith, Jonathan Z. (1982) *Imagining Religion.* Chicago: University of Chicago.

St. Clair, Michael J. (1992) *Millenarian Movements in Historical Context.* New York: Garland.

Stein, Stephen J., ed. (1998) *The Encyclopedia of Apocalypticism, Vol. 3: Apocalypticism in the Modern Period and the Contemporary Age.* New York: Continuum.

Tabor, James D., and Eugene V. Gallagher. (1995) *Why Waco? Cults and the Battle for Religious Freedom in America.* Berkeley, CA: University of California Press.

Walls, Roy, ed. (1982) *Millenarianism and Charisma.* Belfast: Queens University.

Wilson, Bryan R. (1973) *Magic and the Millennium.* New York: Harper & Row.

White Buffalo Calf Woman

The Brule Sioux version of the cherished White Buffalo Woman myth explains the origins of the Lakota ways of living correctly. It is said that White Buffalo Calf Woman *(Ptehincala San Win)* brought the sacred pipe to the people, and for this reason a mature, respected woman represents her during the Sun Dance ceremony. Most importantly, White Buffalo Woman symbolizes a prophetic age of peace for the Lakota (Sioux), the Cheyenne, certain other Native Americans, and many New Age believers.

Her legend tells of a time when the Lakota were starving. Hunters dispatched for food saw a floating woman dressed in shimmering white buckskin approaching them from across the prairie. One man intoxicated by her beauty advanced toward her without respect, only to be struck by lightning. The other honored the woman as he led her to his village for he knew that she was *Wakan* (sacred). Following her instructions, the people put up a tipi with a red earth altar. She presented them with a bundle which contained the sacred pipe and further instructed them in the proper rituals to honor the sacred hoop of life. She enlightened all the men, women, and children in the ways of right conduct.

As she readied to leave, White Buffalo Woman reminded her listeners that she was the sacred peace who comes in every generation. She beseeched the people to keep the sacred pipe. Furthermore, she revealed her holy promise to return. As the sun was setting, she started out in the same direction from where she came. Her silhouette was framed by a flaming sun as she stopped at a wallow to roll over in the dirt. Four times she rolled over, each time changing her color: first black, then brown, then red, and finally she

THE ANOMALY OF WHITE BUFFALO

White buffalo have always been exceedingly rare. In 1887, American zoologist William T. Hornaday claimed that less than a dozen had ever been recorded. Frank G. Roe's book *The North American Buffalo* (1970), however, suggests that there now appears to be good evidence for the one-time existence of quite a few more than that. Nevertheless, their frequency seems to have been no more than one white specimen for every 5 million brown ones. One of the major problems in determining numbers of white buffalo is defining precisely what a white buffalo is, for there is quite a range of forms on record.

The Albino white buffalo has a wholly white coat and pink eyes. Certain other white buffalo, however, have dark eyes and are a type of incomplete albino known as the chinchilla albino. (The well-known blue-eyed white tigers of Rewa and the white lions of Timbavati belong to this category of albino.) Perhaps the most famous of all white buffalo was a dark-eyed specimen—a magnificent bull named Big Medicine.

He was born on May 3, 1933, on the National Bison Range, a Federal Fish and Wildlife refuge on the Flathead Indian Reservation in Montana. When he was about four years old, Big Medicine mated with his own mother and their resulting offspring was a complete albino with pink eyes and white hooves. Sadly, however, the calf's unpigmented eyes were so weak that he was partially blind, and to complicate matters even further, his mother abandoned him as soon as he was born. Consequently, he was transferred to Washington Zoo, where he was still on display in the mid-1940s. Neither of his parents ever gave rise to other white buffalo, and Big Medicine died in 1959.

There are also white buffalo whose coats are not really white at all; instead, they are pale yellow-cream, like those of the familiar white elephants of Thailand. Also on record are several pied buffalo (patterned brown and white) and at least two brown buffalo that only have a white star on their forehead but were nonetheless termed white buffalo.

Even more confusing are cases of supposed white buffalo that prove to be cataloes—i.e., crossbreeds of buffalo and white domestic cattle. Clearly, there is a lot more to a white buffalo than a white coat! Symbolically, however, all forms of pure-bred, predominantly white buffalo are very special indeed.

Source: Shuker, Karl P.N. (1996) "The Anomaly of White Buffalo." *FATE* (August): 24.

emerged as a white female calf. As she retreated over the horizon, a great buffalo herd came to sacrifice themselves to feed and clothe the people.

The 1990s were good years for the births of white buffaloes. Since the births are extremely rare, those that have been reported have given rise to much public attention. In 1994, the calf named Miracle arrived on Dave and Valerie Heider's Wisconsin ranch. Visited by thousands of people so far, Miracle serves as a symbol of a peaceful new age for the many people who have left symbolic offerings near her corral. By 1996, two other white buffalo calves were born to John Merrival's herd on the Pine Ridge Reservation in South Dakota. One of the calves died, but the surviving calf was named Medicine Wheel. Medicine Wheel's birth has been interpreted by the medicine men of the region to be the Lakota's sign of hope, healing, and unification of the nation. In 1998, another calf came into the world on Gary Childs's buffalo ranch in Jackson County, Michigan, fueling more speculation about the return of White Buffalo Woman. Several Native American chat rooms and Web sites discuss the religious status of the white buffaloes.

Diana Tumminia

Bibliography

Black Elk, and Joseph Epes Brown. (1953) *The Sacred Pipe.* New York: Penguin Books.

Erdoes, Richard, and Alfonso Ortiz. (1984) *American Indian Myths and Legends.* New York: Pantheon Books.

"Rare White Buffalo Born in Jackson, County. August 2, 1998." (1998) *Detroit Free Press.* http://www.freep.com/news/mich/qbuffalo2.htm.

"White Buffalo Calf—A Good Omen." (1996) Share International Magazine. http://www.shareintl.org/calf.html.

Witch-Hunts of Early Modern Europe

The early modern witch-hunts of Europe constitute one of the most complex and tragic events in history. Often seen as one movement, early modern witch-hunts were a collective group of hundreds of associated, but disparate, hunts that differed in time, place, and particulars. They reached their peak during the sixteenth and seventeenth centuries, resulting in the prosecution of an estimated 110,000 men, women, and children and the execution of 60,000 of them on the charge of witchcraft.

Unlike many of the millenarian movements that are defined and described in this encyclopedia, witch-hunts differ in that they represent a form of scapegoating for an entire society that lived in a period of apocalyptic expectation. The "witches" were the perceived threat whose "evils exceed all other sin," and "so in this twilight and evening of the world, when sin is flourishing on every side and in every place the evil of witches and their iniquities superabound" to quote the *Malleus Malificarum* (or "Hammer of the Evildoer"), an influential 1486 treatise on witchcraft. At the height of the witch-hunting phenomenon, apocalyptic rhetoric gained widespread acceptance across a varied population and paranoid ideas of rampant evil crossed the "prime divider" (the social barrier which separated the elite from the commoner). This resulted in, among other things, the persecution of vulnerable members of society.

"Witches" are found in various cultures, around the world and across time, making it essential to define what "witch" meant to early modern Europeans. From the perspectives of sociology and anthropology, a "witch" is a person (in this case, predominately female) who participates in *maleficia*, the use of supernatural means to harm others. Examples of such harm are sickness, injury, or death of a person or livestock, sexual impotence, adverse weather, crop failure, and even death. What separates the early modern European witch from others throughout history is the prominent role of the devil as the source of her magical power and her participation in the perceived burgeoning conspiratorial war between the devil and Christendom.

The eventual connection between witches and the Antichrist is an essential link for the early modern witch-hunts. The witches were viewed as both Satan's minions in a war against Christendom and also as clear evidence for the approaching end, as prophesied in the Book of Revelation; therefore, to fight the Antichrist, one had to eradicate witches.

The initial stages of the hunts can be traced back to the fourteenth century, beginning as an infrequent tool of political leverage and scapegoating which, at the time targeted heretics, lepers, and Jews more directly, and escalating by the sixteenth century into widespread charges of diabolic activity. During the first two periods of development, 1300–30 and 1330–75, the cases were political in nature, yet the number of trials in both periods were few and the charge of diabolism was rare. However, in the first period, the victims were almost always prominent people in society while those victimized in the second were often commoners. Then, two significant changes occurred between 1375–1435: first, the number of trials steadily increased, and second, the charge of diabolism intensified. Finally, during the last stage of development, 1435–1500, Europe experienced a decidedly heightened number of trials, accompanied by a higher prosecution rate. The development can be attributed to certain intellectual interpretations, judicial legislation, and social conditions that mutated and blended into a pervasive climate of great anxiety.

Preconditions

First and foremost, witch-belief found its intellectual culmination in the explicit pact that the witch made with the devil; this was when she renounced Christianity in exchange for magical power, which served as the basis for the legal accusation of diabolic heresy. The pact was, to the educated class, the most telling sign of an imminent cataclysmic war between good and evil. The witch-hunts reached their size and magnitude because the ruling class subscribed to the belief that there was an extensive conspiracy threatening the world—one of apocalyptic proportion. Commoners were less likely to understand the nuances of the demonologists' theory, but many understood and accepted the notion that witches engaged in concrete activities that affected their daily lives.

In addition to the heretical relationship with the devil, intellectuals and commoners alike believed that witches attended the Sabbath, secret nighttime meetings, the activities of which symbolized a world order turned upside down: here witches gorged themselves on food and wine, often practiced cannibalistic infanticide, desecrated the Eucharist, and ended the evenings with dancing and orgies. The idea of the Sabbath was an integral component contributing to the large number of people accused of witchcraft; interrogators tortured the accused until they named other witches who attended the festivities. The witch was also believed to have the ability to fly and metamorphose herself into animals or to look like other people. She often had a familiar, or pet, who assisted her in performing evil deeds. Finally, the witch often had a "mark of the devil," (usually a birthmark), a contrivance which Protestant demonologists added in the sixteenth century.

Legal changes in the period leading up to the sixteenth century aided in the spread of accusations and increased logistical capacity for the enormity of the witch-hunts: both secular and ecclesiastical courts of continental Europe adopted a new, inquisitorial system of criminal procedure and, in 1252, Pope Innocent IV authorized the use of torture (the strappado—a pulley that raised a person off the ground by his arms, which were tied behind his back—the rack, the ladder, thumb or leg screws, trial by fire or water, and forced sleep deprivation) as a means of extracting confessions. Also, secular courts of Europe acquired new legal jurisdiction over witchcraft. These local and regional courts operated without interference from central or national judicial control, thus bending to and manipulating public opinion much more easily. In this sociological setting, the dramatic rise in the rate of persecution made the trials great public dramas of fear and vengeance.

While society until this time lived in a highly structured cosmos, the period in Europe leading up to and during the witch-hunts was one of great upheaval and uncertainty. In addition to the bloody religious wars between Catholic and Protestant factions, the Protestant Reformation also energized the growth and tenacity of witch-hunts by stressing the role and power of the devil in Christianity. Political instability reigned. The effects of modernity, population migration, the evolution of mercantile and agricultural capitalism, and changing roles of authority eroded tradition and the sense of stability. Periodic famine and plagues increased anxiety. The witch, with help from the devil, was a target on which to focus attention and blame, in order to try to explain and control what seemed to be the cosmic war between good and evil of the apocalyptic endtimes.

Dissemination and Particulars

The use of apocalyptic rhetoric ran rampant in Europe during the sixteenth and seventeenth centuries. A multitude of treatises on witchcraft, the circulation of which drastically increased with contemporary printing press inventions, disseminated the worldly threat of the Antichrist and witches to the elite. In 1513, the fifth Lateran council banned the preaching that the Antichrist was imminent, but that ban was ignored. Martin Luther associated the papacy with the Antichrist, and was also himself seen as the Antichrist. Public

---

THE MALLEUS MALEFICARUM: QUESTION IX

How Devils may enter the Human Body and the Head without doing any Hurt, when they cause such Metamorphosis by Means of Prestidigitation.

Concerning the method of causing these illusory transmutations it may further be asked: whether the devils are then inside the bodies and heads of those who are deceived, and whether the latter are to be considered as possessed by devils; how it can happen without injury to the inner perceptions and faculties that a mental image is transferred from one inner faculty to another; and whether or not such work ought to be considered miraculous.

First we must again refer to a distinction between such illusory glamours; for sometimes the outer perceptions only are affected, and sometimes the inner perceptions are deluded and so affect the outer perceptions.

In the former case the glamour can be caused without the devils' entering into the outer perceptions, and merely by an exterior illusion; as when the devil wishes to hide some body by the interposition of some other body, or in some other way; or when he himself on the vision.

But in the latter case it is necessary that he must first occupy the head and the faculties. And this is proved by authority and by reason.

And it is not a valid objection to say that two created spirits cannot be in one and the same place, and that the soul pervades the whole of the body. For on this question there is the authority of S. John Damascene, when he says: Where the Angel is, there he operates. And S. Thomas, in the *Second Book of Sentences,* dist. 7, art. 5, says: All Angels, good and bad, by their natural power, which is superior to all bodily power, are able to transmute our bodies.

Source: Kramer, Heinrich Kramer, and James Sprenger ([c. 1486] 1971) published *The Malleus Maleficarum,* translated by the Reverend Montague Summers. New York: Dover.

"Four Witches" (1497) wood engraving by Albrecht Durer. HTTP://MIRROR.BIBL.U-SZEGED.HU/ART1/CJACKSON/DURER/INDEX.HTML.

morality plays, pamphlets, and artwork—from woodcuts of Albrecht Dürer and illustrations from Guazzo's *Compendium maleficarum* to church wall paintings in Denmark—stressed the coming endtimes, and promulgated the perceived danger to commoners.

By the mid-fifteenth century, trials had occurred in France and Switzerland, and continued to spread unevenly throughout Europe, with a large number of trials in Germany and the Low Countries, up into Scandinavia, expanding through eastern Europe, and west through the Iberian Peninsula and south to the Mediterranean. The phenomenon also crossed the English Channel to the British Isles, although due to different legal practices—including the jury system and the infrequent use of torture—and belief systems, England's witch-hunts were distinctively different from those in Scotland and on the Continent.

The size of individual hunts in communities varied from one witch accusation (which was most common in England) to 525 indictments in Rouen in 1670. Both elite and commoner could instigate accusations. The nature of the witch, for the most part, followed a definite archetype: most people accused of practicing witchcraft were older, single women, who lived in rural agricultural villages, from a lower socioeconomic class, and were often regarded by their neighbors as morally or religiously deviant. Many of the women whom society targeted as witches were cooks, midwives, or healers, as their professions involved herbs and potions, incantations or prayers, and dangerous pregnancies and sickly people, making them naturally suspicious.

Decline and Survival

Just as the hunts began sporadically, so too did they begin to decline sporadically in the late seventeenth and early eighteenth centuries. Again, it was a combination of legal, intellectual, and social changes that affected the hunts. Courts now demanded that conclusive evidence regarding *maleficium* and the pact with the devil be proven before conviction. Stricter laws limited the use of torture, and rulers passed decrees and edicts, which lessened or altogether eliminated prosecutions. Especially within elite circles, possibly to separate themselves from superstitious commoners, intellectual ideology embraced scientific skepticism, which negated the power of demons on earth and promoted natural explanations for mysterious occurrences. Living conditions improved, including economic, political, and religious stability, which lowered the level of social anxiety and decreased the need for rampant scapegoating.

Periodic witch-hunts have occurred since the early modern European witch-hunts. The most well known happened in Salem, Massachusetts, where, in 1692, nineteen innocent people were hanged for the charge of witchcraft. Just as the European hunts were multicausal, so too was the Salem witch-hunt. Sporadic outbreaks continued across Europe, North and South America, and Africa up through the twentieth century. As recently as 1999, there have been outbreaks in Indonesia. These more recent hunts target political dissenters, are largely instigated by vigilantes, and largely lack the heightened sense of apocalyptic frenzy of the earlier hunts.

Conclusion

There has been much scholarly debate about the cultural authenticity of witchcraft. Some scholars argue that it was based on an ancient underground fertility religion, and that certain people who were persecuted did actually believe that they had supernatural powers and were acting against traditional society in a rebellious manner. Whether or not this theory has any validity, the overwhelming majority of people persecuted during the early modern witch-hunts were vulnerable, innocent people caught in a climate of apocalyptic expectation and fear. Many books on witch-hunts largely ignore, or mention only in passing, the role of apocalyptic rhetoric, and scholars have produced even less work on the decline of apocalyptic rhetoric in the eighteenth century with regard to witches. Yet, during a time of heightened social anxiety, witchcraft accusations provided an impetus and paradigm to which elite and commoner alike could relate and use for inspiration.

Beth Marie Forrest

See also Antichrist

Bibliography

Borchardt, Frank L. (1990) *Doomsday Speculation as a Strategy of Persuasion.* Lewiston, NY: Edwin Mellen Press.

Boyer, Paul, and Stephen Nissenbaum. (1974) *Salem Possessed: The Social Origins of Witchcraft.* Cambridge, MA: Harvard University Press.

Brauner, Sigrid. (1995) *Fearless Wives and Frightened Shrews: The Construction of the Witch In Early Modern Germany.* Amherst, MA: University of Massachusetts Press.

Clark, Stuart. (1997) *Thinking with Demons: The Idea of Witchcraft in Early Modern Europe.* New York: Oxford University Press.

Cohn, Norman. (1957) *The Pursuit of the Millennium.* New York: Oxford University Press.

Cohn, Norman. (1975) *Europe's Inner Demons.* New York: Basic Books.

Eisenstein, Elizabeth L. (1979) *The Printing Press as an Agent of Change.* New York: Cambridge University Press, 432–39.

Ginzburg, Carlo. (1992) *Ecstasies: Deciphering the Witches' Sabbath.* New York: Penguin Books.

Gurevich, Aron. (1988) *Medieval Popular Culture: Problems of Belief and Perceptions.* Cambridge, U.K.: Cambridge University Press.

Kieckhefer, Richard. (1976) *European Witch Trials: Their Foundations in Popular and Learned Culture, 1300–1500.* Berkeley, CA: University of California Press.

Kors, Alan C., and Edward Peters, eds. (1972) *Witchcraft in Europe 1100–1700: A Documentary History.* Philadelphia: University of Philadelphia Press.

Lea, Henry Charles, comp. ([1939] 1986) *Materials Toward a History of Witchcraft: Collected By Henry Charles Lea, LL.D.*, 3 vols., edited by Arthur C. Howland. Philadelphia: University of Pennsylvania Press; reprint, New York, AMS Press.

Levack, Brian P. (1995) *The Witch-Hunt in Early Modern Europe.* New York: Longman Group.

The Malleus Maleficarum of Heinrich Kramer and James Sprenger, translated with introductions, bibliography, and notes by Montague Summers. (1971) New York: Dover Press.

Roper, Lyndal. (1994) *Oedipus and the Devil: Witchcraft, Sexuality and Religion in Early Modern Europe.* New York: Routledge.

Rosen, Barbara, ed. ([1969] 1991) *Witchcraft in England, 1558–1618.* Amherst, MA: University of Massachusetts Press.

Russell, Jeffrey B. (1980) *A History of Witchcraft: Sorcerers, Heretics and Pagans.* New York: Thames and Hudson Ltd.

Thomas, Keith. (1971) *Religion and the Decline of Magic: Studies in Popular Beliefs in Sixteenth and Seventeenth-Century England.* New York: Penguin Books.

Women

Contemporary apocalyptic movements in America, when carefully surveyed, reveal an overwhelmingly feminine presence. This "feminization of the Millennium" is occurring on several levels of new religious life; in doctrine, myth, ritual, and in the social and experiential dimensions of millenarian spirituality. A wealth of utopian literature has appeared in the 1980s and 1990s that exalts women as world saviors and rulers of future utopias. Eschatologies in many marginal religions feature goddesses as well as gods presiding over the new age. The earth is revered as a pregnant planet contracting in birth spasms, and comics depict Amazon warriors defeating all-male armies. Within the leadership structure of many groups, there are an abundance of female messiahs, mediums, and sibyls; and feminine leadership, or equal opportunity is taken for granted. Even among the rank and file members there seems to be a prevailing notion that their women will play a key role in the endtime—as midwives assisting the birth of a new age, as mothers of a future *Homo superiorus*, or as usherettes in a cosmic theater. Women may also receive negative attention in the apocalyptic drama of Christian evangelists—as the Whore of Babylon, the Fallen Eve, or the Bride of the Antichrist.

Women in the History of Millenarian Heresies

This situation is unexpected—perhaps unprecedented—if one considers the male-oriented millenarian visions that have dominated Western history; the Jewish Messiahs, the Muslim Mahdis, the Christian Son of Man. These traditions envisage equestrian sky gods, male demons erupting from earth, and cosmic battles starring warrior-heroes.

A gnostic mystical-apocalyptic movement threatened the Church of Rome during the High Middle Ages in southern Europe, known as the Brethren of the Free Spirit. This movement was organized in secret cells that were loosely affiliated, connected by itinerant preachers who circulated mystical tracts and poetry that were highly sophisticated. This literature was heretical in its doctrines, and challenged conventional Christian mores, expressing erotic emotions towards Christ and the Virgin, and anarchic attitudes towards property and the class system. The Free Spirit might be described as a radical mystical-anarchic secret society that recruited and initiated its adepts amongst a religious lay order that derived from a schism within the Order of St Francis. This lay order was composed of the Beghards (male) and the Beguines (female), who took vows of celibacy and served the poor; and many lived communally, loosely attached to the Franciscan monasteries.

The Brethren of the Free Spirit was an unofficial lay counterpart of the mendicant orders of the Catholic Church, a church that was finding it more and more difficult to keep track of and control its autonomous groups of the voluntary poor. The name "Beghard" probably derives from "Beggar" in the English language. Their costume resembled a Franciscan monk's, yet it was often red, split in the skirt, and sewn with patches to underscore their oath of poverty. This heresy spread rapidly towards the end of the thirteenth century through wandering, begging male preachers.

There is evidence that the overwhelming majority of members were women from the wealthy merchant class, who were spinsters, and had no other role in life that would win them status and respect in society, save for marriage. Many of these, upon becoming Beguines, wore a hooded gray robe and a veil, but continued to live with their parents or were anchorites enjoying a private income, and many moved into communes. Norman Cohn suggests that many of the Beguines were attracted to the intense mystical experience cultivated within this lay order that brought with it a sense of belonging to a superhuman elite, as well as to the amoral, sexually permissive relationships offered by the wandering Beghard charismatic preachers; and that once the movement was driven underground by persecution, around 1320, the "Free Spirit had become an invisible empire, held together by the emotional bonds—which of course were often erotic bonds—between men and women" (1970:162).

The council of the See of Mainz in 1259 excommunicated these "Holy Beggars" on the basis of their translations of the Bible into the vernacular, and their heretical doctrines. In 1310 an outstanding Beguine from northern France, Marguerite Porete, was burned at the stake with her Beghard companion and "Guardian Angel" for her book of mystical theology, *Mirouer des simples ames.* She had many followers, and her book circulated among the upper classes in France and England. The Free Spirit came to the attention of Pope Clement V at the Council of Vienna in 1311, where he was decided that they were heretics who must be curbed. Hundreds of Beghards and Beguines were subsequently captured and burnt at the stake in the south of France. Many, but not all, of these martyrs belonged to the Brethren of the Free Spirit.

To what extent the Brethren of the Free Spirit might be considered a millenarian movement is a question that raises some interesting issues, both philosophical and sociological. Since gnosticism is usually considered to be concerned with the individual's *gnosis* or enlightenment, and is more interested in the trajectory of each *pneuma's* reincarnation cycle than in linear time, it is essentially ahistorical. Nevertheless, there are several convergences between the gnostic and the apocalyptic worldview.

First, the dualistic-pessimistic teachings of the Jewish revelations found in the Book of Daniel—which predicts an early end to the corrupt world governed by the devils—certainly resemble the gnostics' view of the material world as dark and evil, governed by the Archons. Second, there appears to be an incompatibility between the Christian trajectory towards redemption, which is horizontal—a chronological sequence, or a line drawn through history—and the gnostic path to salvation, which is vertical—being concerned with revelation and awakening from ignorance. Nevertheless, it could be argued that gnosis is simply an ontological stratification of the same linear-eschatological worldview. Moreover, the Christian apocalyptic and the Gnostic mystical mythologies have many themes in common; the ascension to heaven, the heavenly host of angels and demons, and theogonies and creation myths describing a primal fall from Eden. Finally, when apocalyptic fantasies and gnostic aspirations are put into practice, new eschatological communities of salvation are formed. Apocalypticism and Gnosticism are each radically revolutionary in nature, for both propose that the existing world order has no value and must be destroyed.

Schweister Katrei, a heretical tract dramatizing the spiritual awakening of one Sister Catherine, argues that in nature all things make use of one another, so that just as the deer uses grass, the fish use water, and the birds use air, so Sister Catherine, on achieving *gnosis,* is advised, "You shall order all created things to serve you according to your will, for the glory of God. . . . You shall bear all things up to the God; if you want to use all created beings, you have the right to do so; for every creature you use, you drive up to its Origin!" (quoted in Cohn 1970:179). Once Sister Catherine had achieved the *gnosis* she lay aside her humble rags of the Beguine and wore the beautiful, luxurious robes of the ruling class of elite supermen. The doctrines and mystical quest of the Brethren of the Free Spirit was never completely extinguished, and many of the essential features of the mystical anarchical sect continue to appear on the margins of orthodox religion.

EXTRACT FROM "CHARGE OF THE GODDESS" BY DOREEN VALIENTE

Listen to the words of the Great Mother;
she who of old was also called among men
Artemis, Astarte, Athene, Dione, Melusine,
Aphrodite, Cerridwen, Cybele, Arianrhod,
Isis, Dana, Bride
and by many other names:

Whenever ye have need of anything, once in the month,
and better it be when the moon is full,
then shall ye assemble in some secret place
and adore the spirit of me,
who am Queen of all the witches.

There shall ye assemble,
ye who are fain to learn all sorcery,
yet have not won its deepest secrets;
to these will I teach things that are yet unknown.
And ye shall be free from slavery;
and as a sign that ye be really free,
ye shall be naked in your rites;
and ye shall dance, sing, feast, make music and love,
all in my praise.
For mine is the ecstasy of the spirit,
and mine also is joy on earth;
for my law is love unto all beings.
Keep pure your highest ideal; strive ever towards it;
let naught stop you or turn you aside.
For mine is the secret door which opens upon the Land of Youth,
and mine is the cup of the wine of life,
and the Cauldron of Cerridwen,
which is the Holy Grail of immortality.

I am the Gracious Goddess,
who gives the gift of joy unto the heart of man.
Upon earth, I give the knowledge of the spirit eternal;
and beyond death, I give peace and freedom
and reunion with those who have gone before.
Nor do I demand aught in sacrifice;
for behold,
I am the Mother of all living,
and my love is poured out upon the earth.

Source: http://www.open-sesame.com/ChargeGoddess.html.

Women in the Radical Reformation

An interesting kind of androgynous messianism emerged from Martin Luther's insistence that monks and nuns leave the monasteries and marry, and his concern for the Christian, loving quality of familial relations whereby the family hearth, as opposed to the church, became the focal point of the community. While Luther had denied the sacramental and covenantal status of marriage, those bishops who attended the Council of Trent sought to make celibacy and marriage equally sacramental and valid. They rejected the Hellenistic-ascetic esteem for celibacy that had influenced the Catholic Church since the second century, arguing that the original Hebraic values placed a strong emphasis upon conjugal love and the divine injunction to be fruitful and multiply.

The radical reformers, however, insisted that marriage was even more holy and sacred; it was a covenant with Christ. Drawing upon images in Revelation of the Bride of Christ and the Woman clothed in the Sun, they discovered a new theological basis for marriage as well as a new sexualized language for millennial rhetoric. These eventually led to certain excesses and aberrations in the communal and familial experiments launched by prophets.

This new androgynous messianism was preached by William Postel (1510–81) from Normandy, who moved beyond covenantal marriage to propound elaborate theologies of spiritual marriage as a path to redemption. Postel was a Jesuit who became a follower of Servetus. He studied the Kabbalah and translated the Book of Zohar. In Venice he became converted to a kind of feminist spirituality through his association with an illiterate Venetian virgin of the age of fifty, who spent her life in ministering to the poor and sick and was a known psychic and faith healer, respected for her spiritual discernment. When she died in 1551, Postel felt her "spiritual body and substance descended unto him" and began to claim he was now reborn as the Shekinah or Holy Spirit incarnate. He wrote and distributed many millenarian books and broadsheets, such as *Panthenosia, Restutio rerum omnium* (Paris 1552) and *La doctrine du Siecle Dore ou de l'evangelique regne de Jesus Roi des Rois* (Paris 1553), in which he prophesized a return of the Golden Age that Noah had supposedly presided over.

Sexual Solutions to Social Disorder

Since myths must mirror their social worlds, one would expect the apocalyptic myths of budding religions to reflect current trends and cultural tensions. Utopian communities of the nineteenth century, for example, expressed the Victorians' deep concern for reconstructing family life and clarifying gender roles. The Oneida Perfectionists, whose founder, John Humphrey Noyes held himself to be the *Third* Coming, rejected monogamous marriage and procreation and considered woman to be a "female man." The Shakers who followed Mother Ann Lee sought to purify their brothers and sisters from sin through ritual shaking, a celibate life, and egalitarian gender roles. The early Mormons built their kingdoms in heaven through "celestial marriage," polygamy, and procreation. All these groups considered their utopian forms of "ordered love" (Kern 1981) to offer spiritual solutions to the decline and fragmentation of the lineage family in the antebellum period.

The suspenseful eschatologies of new religious movements (NRMs) reflect our own preoccupations with issues of sexual identity, women's power, and the disintegration of the nuclear family. For many NRMs, reconstructing relations between the sexes in correct alignment to the divine cosmos is an essential step in preparing for the Millennium. There are groups that exalt woman as world savior, humanity's only hope for averting nuclear destruction. Other groups are resigned to the prospect of a worldwide holocaust, but see women as the builders of a new society, or rulers in the golden age, as in the case of the Brahmakumaris, founded by Dada Lekraj, who foresee women reigning as goddesses in the *satyug* after the present world has been destroyed. Radical lesbian spirituality advocates a rejection of and separation from male hegemony so that women can bond in a just and loving sisterhood and excavate their true metaphysical identity. At the other extreme are neoconservative groups and racialist religions that tell woman to return to her rightful place as wife and mother, "covered" by her husband in order to prepare her children for the Second Coming, or to breed and rear a new, sinless, wholly human race.

Gender, Genesis, and Ecofeminism

Some feminist theologians and scholar-critics of patriarchal religions have challenged misogynistic extrapolations of the doctrine of original sin and struck a rich millenarian vein in their writings.

Mary Daly who describes herself as a "post-Christian feminist" redefines "original sin" as a "state of complicity in patriarchal oppression . . . socially transmitted disease involving psychological paralysis . . . horizontal violence, and a never-ending conviction of one's own guilt" (1987: s.v. Word-Web One). Daly finds the "original sin of sexism" wreaking its destructive effects upon women throughout history and proposes a "Fall into freedom" as the only means whereby Eve will learn to "name herself, to become all she can be" (1974: 67–68). Daly's millenarian vision depicts a psychic war between the sexes based on their metaphysical proclivities. She regards males as "gynaecidal" and life-hating, in contrast to women, whom she defines as "biophilic" and creative. Daly awards women the salvific role of subverting the threat of the man-made nuclear holocaust through their intuitive magical connection to nature. Also speaking from the margins of radical feminism, is Sonia Johnson, an ex-Mormon radical feminist. In her recent book, *Wildfire* (1989), she preaches a message of lesbian apocalypticism.

Another genre of feminist apocalypticism is found in NRMs that venerate the powers in Nature, such as neoshamanic healing circles, Wicca, and various schools of ecotheology. Gaians espouse the notion of the planet as an integral, living, maternal organism. Wiccans have adopted Margaret Murray's mythologized history of witchcraft as the original religion of the human race that went underground to withstand the onslaught of Christianity and has survived in fragmented covens of Goddess-worshippers who continued to stimulate the agricultural cycle through reenacting the parthenogenic birth and violent death of the vegetation deity. Starhawk, a famous witch, author, and ecological activist orchestrated protest demonstrations in the late eighties to pit women's natural magic against the marauding masculine forces of industry and war; as when in 1987 her witches in Vancouver saved up their menstrual blood for two years in freezers, then gathered, chanting, to throw it against nuclear reactors.

Other large, international, and well-known NRMs have evolved their own idiosyncratic "sexual solutions" to pollution or the nuclear threat that almost *parody* trends in the feminist movement. Profeminist prophets Rajneesh, Rael, and Ramtha, are striking examples of this.

Bhagwan Shree Rajneesh, Indian-born eclectic philosopher and founder of Rajneeshpuram, a communal utopian city in Oregon that lasted from 1981 to 1985, proclaimed: "My own vision is that the coming age will be the age of woman. . . . Feminine energies must be released!" (1987: 18). In Rajneeshpuram he appointed women as leaders, "the pillars of my commune," and they filled over 80 percent of executive positions. He explained that woman is "a female Buddha," more receptive and spiritually advanced than man, and less inclined towards aggression and "power trips." In 1983 Rajneesh emerged from a vow of silence and announced that after the world was decimated by AIDS in 2000, that women would take over and build a new age based on love, harmony with nature, meditative consciousness, and superior technology.

Rael, a former racing car driver from France who founded the Raelian movement after he was contacted by extraterrestrials in 1973, has announced that "the Age of Apocalypse will be the age of women!" He urges men to develop the feminine qualities of love, peace, tolerance, and empathy if *Homo sapiens* is to avoid self-destruction through nuclear weapons. The inner circle of male and female Guides grow their hair long to increase their telepathic powers and avoid procreation in favor of being cloned. Humanity must learn to "make love, not war" in the Raelian movement's fun-loving international, multiracial, "quadrasexual" community, and to prepare for the descent of the extraterrestrials around the year 2035 by building an intergalactic space embassy in Jerusalem, and spreading the message that the "elohim" created us in test tubes from their own DNA.

The Ramtha Foundation also espouses a feminist apocalyptic theory. JZ Knight, a petite blond businesswoman, began in 1977 to function as the mouthpiece for Ramtha, the invisible 7-foot, 4,000-year-old "Lemurian" warrior. Based in Yelm, Washington, she has traveled across the country renting out hotel ballrooms to hold weekend "dialogues" wherein Ramtha takes over her body, expounds his gnostic philosophy, and dispenses advice. In a manner reminiscent of nineteenth-century female mediums, JZ Knight channels an entity that defends the rights of women and challenges male hegemony. Ramtha condemns males for their omnivorous sexual appetite and encourages the empowerment of women.

Ramtha describes our planet as a "living entity" regularly visited by space brothers, and on the verge of irresistible "evolutionary processes"—and paints an unusual vision of an earth "laced with zippers" about to explode into volcanic eruptions, tidal waves, and earthquakes (Ramtha 1987: 30–35). He recommends survivalist preparations—put your money in gold, move to the Pacific Northwest, stockpile a two-year food supply, and cultivate vegetable gardens. Real estate agents have watched with interest the migration into Washington State of "Ramsters," "many of whom are middle-aged women" (*Montreal Gazette*, 14 April 1984).

A "Comic" Ending

While these leaders promote what Reuther (1988) calls a "radical romantic feminism," other groups emphasize cooperation and harmony between the sexes, and in all these groups the notion of reconciling the sexes and achieving the "right" balance of power as a prerequisite for ushering in a successful millennium is importantly present. Messiahs and prophets often form a charismatic duo with their wife or mistress, for androgyny is a potent ingredient that enhances the charisma, not only of shamans and rock stars, but of charismatic leaders as well. Bo and Peep, the founders of Heaven's Gate, a UFO religion, were a charismatic duo composed of an homosexual choir director and an unhappily married nurse, who wore identical clothing, ate off the same plate, and finished each other's sentences, and prepared their followers for the extraterrestrials' descent when they would all become immortal, flying androgynes. The younger consorts of male prophet-founders occasionally take over the reins of leadership upon their death. Reverend Moon and his wife represent the male and female aspects of God, the "One True Parent of Mankind" for members of the Unification Church, and Moon has anointed Mrs. Moon to preside over the movement in the future. David Berg, the "Lord's Endtime Prophet" and founder of the Children of God, before his "homecoming" in 1994, anointed his consort, Maria, to succeed him as the "Endtime Prophetess." Women have always assisted the dying. In their intimate proximity to dying gurus they may ask favors, manipulate mythologies, and mould the succession so as to create more egalitarian or "uxor-friendly" patterns of authority.

One notable feature of "feminized" millennia is a tendency toward optimism and peaceful resolutions—what Stephen D. O'Leary (1994) would term the *comic* frame of apocalyptic discourse. He identifies two frames that interact, each dramatizing its own resolution of the problem of evil; the *tragic* (dualistic and anticipating a redemptive climax marked by catastrophic suffering), and the *comic*, that espouses an open-ended or cyclic view of the future that can be influenced by human agency. Feminist apocalyptic dramas appear to be reacting against what they perceive to be the male-generated *tragic* mode of narrative. Nevertheless, the widespread assumption that humanity can finally enjoy the fruits of peace with women in charge is belied by some prophetesses' fascination with weapons and the themes of war.

Elizabeth Clare Prophet of the Church Universal and Triumphant, a sect originating from Theosophy and the I AM movement is one of the outstanding millenarian prophets of our age. After the death in 1973 of the original founder, her husband and "twin flame" Mark Prophet, she succeeded him as the Messenger. From the church's headquarters in Montana, she delivers high speed oral "dictations," relaying messages to humanity from the Ascended Masters. Some of these are apocalyptic in content, particularly the prophecies of Saint Germain, who is expected to succeed Christ when the Piscean Age moves into the Age of Aquarius.

In a 1986 dictation, Saint Germain warned that the Soviet Union was planning a nuclear attack on America, and members should prepare by building bomb shelters. In 1989 he proclaimed nuclear war was more likely than having a death in the family. Members moved to Montana in the hundreds and incurred enormous debts building bomb shelters, the largest in the Mol Heron Valley is capable of housing 756 people and generating its own electricity. Prophet's husband, Edward Francis and another member were arrested and convicted of using false names to buy assault rifles and spent one month in jail. On 11 March 1990 Saint Germain again predicted that the Soviets attack was imminent and urged members to withdraw their money from banks, to move out of urban areas, stockpile food and weapons, and move into underground tunnels to prepare for the tribulation. Over seven hundred of the commune's staff and two thousand members gathered at this time to pray. After a renewed warning of a possible Soviet attack on April 1993, the church was selling plots of land and survival condominiums to members on the Royal Teton Ranch bordering Yellowstone National Park. This recent disconfirmation in prophecy resulted in many defections and bankruptcies. Despite these classic ingredients of a "tragic" survivalist midtribulationist agenda, Dehaas (1994) argues that CUT conforms rather to Wessinger's model (1993) of "progressive millennialism"—not unlike O'Leary's *comic* frame.

There have also been rare occasions of violent or criminal behavior perpetrated by female or profeminist charismatic leaders. In 1986, Rajneesh's personal secretary, Ma Anand Sheela, was sentenced in federal court to a twenty-year prison sentence after pleading guilty to a range of crimes and misdemeanors. These included wiretapping, immigration fraud, arson, the attempted murder of Rajneesh's physician, and deliberately infecting the townspeople of The Dalles with salmonella poisoning. She was also a suspect in the plot to bomb Oregon attorney general Fruhnmayer's car.

The Order of the Solar Temple, notorious for their 1994 mass suicides/homicides staged in Quebec and Switzerland, espoused an ecofeminist apocalyptic theory and cultivated a female avatar. Joseph Di Mambro was their grandmaster in Switzerland, and he raised his daughter, Emmanuelle, to be the "cosmic child" of the New Age. Di Mambro's young mistress was immaculately impregnated by the Ascended Master Manatanus in a public "rite of conception" involving laser beams, puppets, and special lighting effects staged in the underground crypt at Salvan. Luc Jouret, the Quebec grandmaster, claimed it was necessary to balance positive "feminine energies"—which they associated with the French culture, art, and Nature—with the extant negative "male energies"—associated with the English, industrial powers, and materialism. To this esoteric end, the OTS imported eleven Francophone members from Martinique to Quebec to combat the Anglo influence.

Conclusion

That the apocalyptic imagination in America is resplendent with—or (depending upon one's perspective) alarmingly polluted by—feminine images, is a phenomenon easy to prove. To guess its meaning is a more difficult task.

Sexual imagery has always been a strong element in endtime narratives, as it is in the world's creation myths. Cosmogonies usually recount the origins of life from the union of the first Man and Woman, to their eventual separation through the Fall into mortality through infanticide, parricide, or incest. Millenarians through the ages seem to be particularly set on reconstructing the primordial drama in Eden and exonerating Eve. Norman Cohn describes the Brothers of the Free Spirit movement (circa 1550) that attracted many wealthy unmarried women who emulated Eve in practicing ritual nudity, thus "asserting . . . that they were restored to the state of innocence which had existed before the Fall" (1970: 180).

Apocalyptic narrations of destruction and regeneration must, of necessity, include the symbols of creation common to its culture. Western monotheistic patriarchal religions tend to show a dearth of creation myths that depict woman's life-giving creativity or explicit images of the birth process. Judy Chicago, the feminist artist and sculptress, claims she could not find any adequate iconography of creation in Western art, only masculine images she found utterly unconvincing—"unless you believe in God touching Adam on the finger!"

Now that the prospect of mass destruction is a plausible reality and we confront the terrifying photographs of Hiroshima and other bomb experiments as they invade our collective consciousness via the media, there is a corresponding need to contemplate primal images of birth. Since the 1970s, there has been a trend to make childbirth a public event—to film it, to invite friends into the labor room. Since the 1970s, the raw, uncensored photographs of birth have become acceptable, even sacred. At the same time, there has been a corresponding trend to hide the ugly intimate details of the deathbed—to "medicalize" death, as Phillippe Ares (1988) argues. Ares laments the decline of the traditional *artes moriendi*, the public deathbed scene, of farewells and religious testimonials. It might be argued that this lost art has been replaced by the art of birth, a new public ritual; and that when one contemplates the grim, "scientific" possibility of a global holocaust, earth goddesses presiding as midwives over a planet's accouchement are considerably less scary than sky gods in battle!

Today we find a profusion of feminine imagery and a strong female presence in the millennial dreams of the late twentieth century. As students of religion and culture we are aware that myths and symbols mirror society and its natural environment, and that a people's mythology will respond to changing social and ecological conditions. It appears reasonable, therefore, to assert that that millenarian movements today are feeling the impact of feminism, and that the contemporary eschatologies featuring cosmic interplay between polar forces, good versus evil, light versus dark, sky versus earth, will express our deep preoccupation with issues of gender, identity, and power.

Susan J. Palmer

See also Church Universal and Triumphant, Heaven's Gate, Raelians, Ramtha School of Enlightenment, Shakers, Solar Temple

Bibliography

Aries, Philippe. (1988) *The Hour of Our Death*. New York: Oxford University Press.

Babb, Lawrence, ed. (1986) "History as Movie." In *Redemptive Encounters: Three Modern Styles in the Hindu Tradition*. Berkeley, CA: University of California Press.

Balch, Robert. (1982) "Bo and Peep: A Case Study of the Origins of Messianic Leadership." In *Millennialism and Charisma*, edited by Roy Wallis. Belfast: Queen's University, 13–22.

Chander, Jagdish. (1981) *Adi Dev, the First Man*. Singapore, Malaysia: Prajapita Brahma Kumaris World Spiritual University (Kim Hup Lee Printing).

Cohn, Norman. (1970) *The Pursuit of the Millennium*. London: Oxford University Press.

Daly, Mary. (1973) *Beyond God the Father: Toward a Philosophy of Women's Liberation*. Boston: Beacon Press.

———. (in cahoots with) Jane Caputi. (1987) *Websters' First New Intergalactic Wickedary of the English Language*. Boston: Beacon Press.

Dehaas, Jocelyn H. (1994) "Apocalyptic Prophecy and the Notion of Non-Linear Time in the Church Universal and Triumphant." Paper presented at a meeting of the Society for the Scientific Study of Religion, Albuquerque, NM.

Foster, Lawrence. (1981) *Religion and Sexuality: Three American Communal Experiments of the Nineteenth Century*. New York: Oxford University Press.

Grace, James. (1985) *Sexuality and Marriage in the Unification Church*. Toronto: Edwin Mellen Press.

Johnson, Sonia. (1989) *Wildfire: Igniting the She/Volution*. Albuquerque, NM: Wildfire Books.

Kern, Louis. (1981) *An Ordered Love*. Chapel Hill: University of North Carolina Press.

Lee, Martha. (1995) *Earth First! Environmental Apocalypse*. Syracuse, NY: Syracuse University Press.

Marrs, Wanda. (1989) *New Age Lies to Women*. Austin, TX: Living Truth Publishers.

Melton, J. Gordon. (1992) *Encyclopedic Handbook of Cults in America*. New York: Garland.

Milne, Hugh. (1986) *Bhagwan: The God that Failed*. New York: St. Martin's Press.

Moore, Lawrence R. (1977) *In Search of White Crows: Spiritualism, Parapsychology and American Culture*. New York: Oxford University Press.

Palmer, Susan J. (1996) "Purity and Danger in the Solar Temple." *Journal of Contemporary Religion* 11, 3 (October): 303–18.

Prophet, Elizabeth Clare. (1986) *Saint Germain on Prophecy*. Livingstone, MT: Summit University Press.

Rael. (1989) *The Message Given to Me by the Extraterrestrials*. Tokyo: Raelian Foundation.

Rajneesh, Bhagwan Shree. (1987) *A New Vision of Women's Liberation*. Poona, India: Rebel Press.

Ramtha. (1987) *Intensive Changes: The Days Yet to Come*. Eastsound, WA: Sovereignty.

Reuther, Rosemary Radford. (1988) *Women in Religion in America*. New York: Beacon Press, vol. 1.

Rudolph, Kurt. (1987) *Gnosis: the Nature and History of Gnosticism*. San Francisco: Harper & Row.

Wessinger, Catherine. (1993) "Annie Besant's Millennial Movement: Its History, Impact, and Implications Concerning Authority." *Syzygy: Journal of Alternative Religion and Culture* 2: 55–70.

——, ed. (1993) *Women Outside the Mainstream: Female Leaders in Marginal Religions in Nineteenth Century America*. Urbana, IL: University of Illinois Press.

The Worldwide Church of God

Despite its ambitious-sounding name, the Pasadena-based Worldwide Church of God, with fewer than 150,000 active members at its peak, would have been barely noticed on the religious landscape were it not for its highly successful media program, centered on a radio and television program, *The World Tomorrow*, and *The Plain Truth*, a controlled-circulation magazine that at one time went into more than eight million homes.

Development and Expansion, 1934 to the 1980s

The Worldwide Church of God is an offshoot of the Church of God, Seventh-Day, a remnant of the Millerite revival of the 1840s. It was founded in Oregon in 1934 by Herbert Armstrong (1892–1986). Armstrong, whose training had been in advertising, pioneered in using sophisticated mass media to spread a message of the imminent onset of the great tribulation, culminating in the return of Jesus Christ, who would usher in the "Wonderful World Tomorrow," literally heaven on earth. Through the church's media efforts, this message became familiar to millions. Armstrong's weekly radio program, originally called "The Radio Church of God," went on the air 7 January 1934, made the transition to television in 1968, and outlived Armstrong by six years, finally going off the air in 1994. The church thereby achieved a prominence among prophecy advocates far out of proportion to the size of its membership.

Armstrong, who had a nominal upbringing as a Quaker, experienced a religious conversion in the 1920s after a series of business reversals. This conversion was accompanied by a strong sense of mission, a conviction that he had been called to preach the gospel before the end of the age. Events of the day—notably the Depression, followed by the rise of dictators in Europe, confirmed him in his apocalyptic worldview. He pronounced 1936, then 1943, as the time of the end of the age, to be followed by the heavenly signs and the day of the Lord. Armstrong followed a nineteenth-century British millenarian, H. Grattan Guinness, in dating the end of a 2520 year time of divine punishment on the Jews to 1917. This was based on an incorrect date for the beginning of Nebuchadnezzar's first siege of Jerusalem. Armstrong further believed that nineteen years separated the first siege from the fall of Jerusalem, which he believed to have been in 585 BCE. Armstrong saw validation for his view in Allenby's capture of Jerusalem in 1917, and expected in 1930 that in 1936 God would deliver all of the Promised Land to Ephraim-Israel (Great Britain). This would provoke a Russian-Turkish-German alliance to react, setting the stage for the battle of Armageddon. In 1934 Armstrong wrote that the Great Tribulation started on 28 May 1928, and would continue until September 1936.

These dates came and went, but Armstrong's audience grew, first covering the Pacific Northwest, then most of North America. A move to southern California gave him access to more sophisticated recording studios. His absence from the congregations he pastored in Washington and Oregon made him aware of the need to train helpers, and so he founded Ambassador College in 1947 (closed 1997). His vision expanded to a world-encompassing ministry (the church, which had been named after the original name of the broadcast, was renamed Worldwide Church of God in 1968) and his expectation of the time remaining to the end of the age lengthened.

In 1953 Armstrong and his closest associates settled on a new date for the return of Christ: September 1975, on Rosh Hashanah, the Day of Trumpets. This would not signal the end of the world, but the beginning of the Millennium—a literal, one-thousand-year reign of Jesus Christ on earth. Preceding this, in January 1972, the faithful would be whisked away—not heavenward via rapture, but bodily to an earthly place of safety, in the ancient Nabatean city of Petra, in present-day Jordan.

The calculation was primarily based on interpretation of data from the Book of Daniel, using assumptions fairly common among prophecy buffs (such as reckoning a day for a year, compare Psalm 90:4; 2 Peter 3:8). The date was corroborated, though, by considerations specific to the history of the Worldwide Church of God. The first regular broadcast of the

World Tomorrow on radio was 7 January 1934. The first radio broadcast to Europe was on 7 January 1953, nineteen years later. Nineteen years is the length of a Metonic cycle, after Athenian astronomer Meton (c. 432 BCE). The Metonic cycle of nineteen years is the shortest sequence of years that can bring the solar and lunar years in alignment, so that the moon's phases recur on the same days of the solar year or year of the season. Nineteen years later, 7 January 1972, would fall 1335 days before Trumpets 1975 (compare Daniel 12:12). The church saw a parallel in this to the history of the first-century church. According to its reconstruction of New Testament chronology, the church began its public preaching on Pentecost, 31 CE. The mission to Europe, which began with Paul's trip to Philippi (Acts 16:6–15), was believed to have occurred on Pentecost, 50 CE, nineteen years later. Nineteen years after that, the Jerusalem Christians fled to Pella, shortly before the Roman destruction of the city, ending the first, golden era of the church after two nineteen-year cycles.

In 1957 an article in *The Plain Truth* on the end of the age was entitled "USA Riding to Total Collapse in 15 Years." It was the firm expectation of the church that the Great Tribulation would begin in 1972. For the next few years, this timetable seemed plausible to many. The 1960s were a time of heightened anticipation, as a wave of political assassination, a moral revolution, a society bitterly divided by the U.S. involvement in Vietnam, as well as a series of race riots seemed to confirm that the United States was, indeed riding to total collapse. The sudden and surprising outcome of the Six-Day War in the Middle East in June 1967 seemed a major element in the scenario, as the old city of Jerusalem fell into Israeli hands, seeming to clear the way for the construction of the third temple, to which the messiah would return. On the other hand, developments lagged in Europe, where halting efforts toward unification made it unlikely that the European Economic Community, as it was then called, would become the sea beast of Revelation 13, understood by Armstrong as a nuclear-armed, ten-nation combine that would attack and defeat the United States. And so, in 1969, Armstrong backed away from the dates he had set. He still felt they were possible, but viewed them as less and less likely. Pastors were instructed to cautiously pass the message to their congregations: there would probably be no flight to a place of safety in 1972, though the end was imminent, and there could be no slacking in commitment to "the Work" of the church. In February 1972, Armstrong published an article in which he came close to admitting he had erred: "It has never been our intention to SET DATES! Yet in our human zeal and enthusiasm for getting this greatest mission on earth done, we have a few times come close to it or appeared to—and that we deeply regret." Lest anyone mistake this for an apology, he added: "Emphatically, if we—in our dedicated enthusiastic ZEAL to get God's warning of the end of mankind's world before this sick, sick world—DO, even though we intend not to, appear to set a date, I FEEL I DO NOT NEED TO APOLOGIZE! No one but the enemies of ALL GOOD will accuse!" (Armstrong 1972: 30–31).

There were signs of reconfiguration and decline in the wake of 1972, but the church rallied in 1979 when an outside agent, the attorney general of California, threatened the existence of the church through the imposition of a receivership. This became a landmark test case of religious freedom, and served only to strengthen Armstrong's hold on the church as he neared his ninetieth birthday. The 1980s were boom years for the church. Not even the death of Armstrong in 1986 altered the belief of church members that they belonged to the little flock of true Christians, even though they had once believed Armstrong to be the prophesied Elijah redivivus who was preparing the way for the return of Christ and who would live until then. Armstrong warned the church in advance that he would indeed die, and that "the Work" would go on. His death in January 1986 did, in fact, usher in a new period of growth, peaking in 1989, as worldwide church attendance passed the magic 144,000 mark (compare Revelation 7:4, 14:1).

Reassessments and Retrenchments of the 1980s and 1990s

A reassessment of the church's beliefs began, however, with Armstrong's death. This resulted in a number of changes that can be summarized in three groups, though each represented a kind of backtracking from its most extreme positions.

First, the church stopped making predictions. Dates had come and gone, but there was always a new date to take its place, even if only speculatively. An oft-used phrase was "in the next three-to-five years," although this time period simply rolled over, without ever elapsing. Beginning in 1989, the same year in which church attendance peaked, the church withdrew from circulation literature containing speculation about endtime events. In that year, Joseph W. Tkach (1927–95), who succeeded Armstrong as "pastor general" of the church, wrote to members: "True Christians do not have to worry about *when* Jesus will return *because they are always ready*—just as Jesus told them to be. It is time that we . . . take the focus off fruitless speculations and assumptions about prophecy" (Tkach 1989: 2). When the church clearly distanced itself from endtime speculations, and even from the British-Israelism—the belief that the lost ten tribes of Israel had settled in northwestern Europe, especially the British Isles—that had lain behind many of its unique positions, a first major wave of defections occurred.

Second, the church abandoned two theological teachings, one concerning the nature and destiny of man (1991), the other concerning the nature of God (1993). These together had given the church the conviction that it had a unique understanding of the divine plan of salvation. The doctrine of the Trinity had been rejected. In its place, God was viewed as a divine family, now consisting of the father and the son, Jesus Christ. The destiny of resurrected saints was to be born into that family. In the wake of these changes, the second of the major splinter groups formed.

Third, the church backed away from its literal observance of Old Testament practices. The apocalyptic worldview typically not only expects the imminent end, but also divides the world and its moral issues, into very clear right and wrong. In the case of the Worldwide Church of God, Armstrong's conversion was provoked by a challenge on the issue of the seventh-day Sabbath. With time, he became convinced that other aspects of the law given to Israel were still valid for Christians today, whether Jew or Gentile, especially the feast calendar, tithing, and the avoidance of "unclean" meats. In January 1995, the church made a clear break with the theology underlying these practices, and an even greater wave of defection set in.

The church in 1999 was roughly one-third of its size in 1992. The change was more striking in finances, which shrank to one-seventh of the 1992 level. To this date, there are no signs that the decline has been arrested. A number of breakaway churches have formed. Prominent among these are the Philadelphia Church of God, formed by Gerald Flurry in the wake of the first stage of changes, the Global Church of God, formed by longtime Armstrong associate Roderick C. Meredith during the second stage of changes, and the largest of all, the United Church of God, formed by a number of regional pastors and other senior ministers after the third and most fundamental stage of change. These all continue, with various minor differences, the mixture of endtime expectation and Sabbatarian legalism that had characterized the Worldwide Church of God until recently.

An earlier breakaway dates back to the 1978 dismissal by Herbert Armstrong of his son, Garner Ted (born 1931), who had been the most visible figure in the church in the sixties and seventies as presenter on *The World Tomorrow* on radio and television. Ted Armstrong formed the Church of God International in Tyler, Texas, shortly after his dismissal, but was expelled by that church as well in December 1997 after a series of scandals. Neither the Church of God International, nor Ted Armstrong, who has formed a new evangelistic association, have any major doctrinal differences with the other breakaways. Interestingly, David Hulme, president of the United Church of God, was ousted by the board of that church in April 1998, while in December of that year Meredith suffered the same fate in the church he founded.

The Worldwide Church of God, now presided by Joseph Tkach (born 1953), became a member of the National Association of Evangelicals in May 1997. Christmas and Easter, once condemned as pagan, were added to the church calendar. While most congregations continue to hold worship services on Saturday, a growing number have introduced services on Sunday.

Summary

The Worldwide Church of God was historically characterized not simply by its conviction that it was living in the last days. Rather, its identity was formed by the interplay of a triad: apocalyptic expectation, heterodox doctrinal positions, and an understanding of discipleship as the strict practice of the commandments of God. Its growth plateaued when the first of these was removed, but its decline accelerated only when the last of these was gone.

There are many examples in the annals of church history of groups living in high expectation of the end of the world and of the challenge their members face in reconfiguring their lives and their faith as their deadline with destiny passes, leaving them and the world around them much as it was before. Observers have been at a loss, though, to point to a parallel example of an endtime group with heterodox teachings being steered by its leadership toward orthodoxy in such a short period of time. For this reason, the future development of the Worldwide Church of God is sure to be closely watched.

Henry Sturcke

See also Millerites, Seventh-Day Adventists

Bibliography

Armstrong, Herbert W. (1972) "The 19-Year Time Cycles—What HAPPENED January 7—What My Commission IS!." *Tomorrow's World* (February 1972): 1–4, 30–33.

——. (1979) *Tomorrow . . . What it Will Be Like.* New York: Everest House.

——. (1980) *The United States and Britain in Prophecy.* New York: Everest House.

——. (1985) *Mystery of the Ages.* New York: Dodd, Mead.

Nichols, Larry, and George Mather. (1998) *Discovering the Plain Truth. How the Worldwide Church of God Encountered the Gospel of Grace.* Downer's Grove, IL: Intervarsity Press.

Rader, Stanley R. (1980) *Against the Gates of Hell.* New York: Everest House.

Tkach, Joseph. (1997) *Transformed by Truth.* Sisters, OR: Multnomah.

Tkach, Joseph W. (1989) "When Will Christ Return?" *Pastor General's Report.* Pasadena, CA: Worldwide Church of God (27 June).

Worldwide Church of God Home Page. (1999) http://www.wcg.org/.

Y2K (the Year 2000 Computer Problem)

The Year 2000 computer problem, popularly known as "Y2K" or "the Y2K bug," was on the face of it an unlikely contender for the role of apocalyptic marker—and yet it figured largely in the millennial discourse that attended the transition from the 1990s to the year 2000. The problem itself was a simple convention that allowed computer programmers to use only the last two digits in the year when representing a date in computer code. This practice—a sort of computer shorthand—began at a point when computer memory was expensive and the year 2000 seemed a long way away, and continued unquestioned for many years. When Peter de Jager and others campaigned for a changeover to a four-digit year notation in the 1990s they were at first ignored; but more and more people in information technology and business management woke up to the urgency of the situation as the millennium was drawing to a close, and it became clear that the deeply interwoven fabric of modern global society was at risk. At a cost estimated on the order of $1 trillion, code was analyzed and defective code "remediated" or whole computing systems replaced—and the second phase of the problem came into focus: the potential social impact of failures.

For those who were most troubled by it, the Y2K bug threatened to cause a thousand small system failures that, given the interwoven nature of society, would ripple out and build to an unparalleled disaster: "the end of the world as we know it." For some, this suggested a purely secular millennial nightmare—a vision of societal collapse born of one almost insignificant shortcut in computer code, repeated and endlessly repeated until it became a sort of fault line running from one end of the social fabric to the other. For others—those whose reading of Revelation predisposed them to find "signs of the times" in the daily news—every mention of the Y2K problem provided further evidence that the prophetic timeline was on track, that civil society was in the process of breaking down, and that with Y2K-related failures providing the excuse, the "New World Order" would shortly declare martial law and form the one-world government through which the Antichrist would seek to rule the world.

There was nothing notably religious about Y2K: it was simply a piece of shorthand for computer programmers, an informal agreement to notate years by means of their last two digits, while omitting the digits which indicate the century. This seemed a simple enough practice, and indeed it was cost-effective in the early days of computing. But when one century "rolled over" to the next, computers the world over were effectively programmed to "think" the year 2000 was the year 1900, and do their sums accordingly. This simple error, if unchecked, would infect the calculations of computers and electronic systems from Detroit to Dar-es-Salaam and from Japan to Jerusalem—and the social impact that was expected to result was literally incalculable. Elevators in high-rise apartment buildings might shut down, prison doors might spring open at the stroke of midnight on 1 January 2000, a telephone bill might include a 99-year long distance call, or a school system ask why a 106-year-old hadn't turned up for school . . . and above all, numbers with dates—including the numbers that account for money held, money paid, money owed, money due—were liable to be in error. It became clear that the world's intense dependence on technology, on digital data storage and transmission, and on the cost-cutting "just-in-time" inventory system they permitted, left us globally at risk of a kind of cascade effect, in which one failure triggered another, and the closing of a small auto parts plant in Asia might bring a production line in Detroit to a halt.

Mathematically, the Y2K bug was a huge perturbation in an even vaster "complex system"—and recent cutting-edge mathematics has clearly shown that the results of perturbations in complex systems cannot be predetermined. So businesspeople the world over eventually realized that their computers had a problem, that coding that had seemed helpful at the time it was written had hung around long enough to threaten anything from a hiccup to societal collapse—but the outcome was unpredictable even by the most sophisticated tracking known to humankind, and individual estimates of what might happen were based more on beliefs about the likelihood or inevitability of large-scale societal change than on clear knowledge. A range of options from denial to panic were available, each of them supported by extensive documentation and the arguments of experts, though human emotion determined the individual response.

None of this would necessarily have given rise to apocalyptic or millennial sentiment, if it hadn't been for the fact that this problem with computer dating code—widely reported in the world media as politicians and businesspeople

A POSSIBLE SPEECH (FROM THE Y2K ACTION GUIDE)

Hi! My name is _________________. I am helping prepare the community for possible disruptions by the year 2000 issue. How many here know what the year 2000 issue is? (Solicit comments.) We abbreviate this issue by calling it Y2K. Y for year, 2 for two and K for thousand.

It is not just a simple computer problem as some people seem to think. It is a systems problem caused when "00" indicates a year in software used by computer chips throughout the world. There are an estimated 20-60 billion of these computer chips, with only 5 percent containing the year problem. However, we do not know where this 5 percent is located. You remember the old Christmas tree lights where if one bulb went out all the others went out, and you had to test each one of the bulbs to see which one was bad? Well consider doing this with 20-60 billion chips. We have run out of time to fix this problem, and are attempting to fix critical systems only. (Show a video or other visuals if you have them.)

Wow. I don't know how you are feeling, but I was _______________ when I first heard about this issue. How are some of you feeling? (Open for discussion.) Let's take a 10-minute break and come back together again.

As community members of the city of ___________________, we need to ask our government officials to tell us the status of water and sewage. Have they begun to address the problem? Have they done testing? What were the results of the testing? Repair timetable? Retesting timetable? Will they keep the community informed?

What about hospital status: have all emergency room and o.r. equipment been checked and certified with vendors? Tested? What is the status of phones if there is no electricity? Emergency generators? Fuel storage? Ambulance status? Water and sewage? What happens if medicare/medicaid cannot be received . . . will they see patients? What will they require?

Let me help you understand about Y2K being a "systems" problem. Take your local grocery store. How many hours/days of food does it have? If there is no electricity, how will the trucks get fuel to bring food to the store? Are the trucks computerized? How will the vendors get the food to the trucks to get to the store? How will the automated canners can food to get to the vendors, to get to the trucks, to get to the store? How will the farmers use combines, etc. to get the food to the canners, to get to the vendors, to get to the trucks, to get to the stores? You can see how this system works. The same can be done for any system . . . electricity, telephone, gasoline, etc.

You as community members need to become responsible for your community by being individually prepared, then helping your neighborhood to prepare, then helping your community to prepare for any possible disruptions. How can we do this? (Open discussion. See meeting format.)

Source: (1998) *Y2K Citizen's Action Guide.* Minneapolis, MN: Utne Reader Books, 61–62.

scrambled to remedy the defective code or replace the faulty computers in a last-minute race against the clock—happened to fall at the same point on the calendar as the second millennial anniversary of Christ's birth, a date already attracting strong millennial expectation. Given the strong quasi-magical impact of round numbers, anniversaries, and such on the human population, however, the computer problem and its resolution "played" to an audience that included both apocalyptically inclined believers and nonreligious thinkers whose propensity for secular millennialism was, in Richard Landes's term, "semiotically aroused" by Y2K (1998).

Y2K and the Varieties of Apocalyptic Mindset

One of the first to propose Y2K as an endtimes marker was Ivan Strand, a computer systems analyst with a major Midwestern university whose "day job" involved fixing defective code, but whose Christian religious beliefs led him to view what he knew about Y2K as a clear symptom of the endtimes. In February 1997, Strand made the connection between the Y2K problem and prophetic concerns in a 5,800-word post that he sent to a computer mailing list for people interested in prophetic interpretation in New Zealand. His post contained a fairly detailed and well-written layman's account of the "technical" aspect of the Y2K problem, followed by a section in which he spelled out the implications of the problem for his fellow Christians. He wrote: "I believe there is a major connection between this global computer crisis and the crisis we expect in the last days before Christ returns," and concluded:

> I believe this crisis will help us as Christians know whether or not we trust God for *everything*. Whether or not we believe that God can still open the windows of heaven and feed us. Whether or not we believe God can cause water to pour out of the rock. Whether or not we believe God can provide for us when all lines of earth-based communication are cut and when the semi-trailer trucks, the tankers and the locomotives sit idle. Whether we believe God can protect us from—and in—the ensuing riots, plagues and burning cities.

For some, the computer problem offered additional evidence of the endtimes, and perhaps the mechanism by which civil society would be brought to the point where the Antichrist could take over the governance of the world. For Gary North, historian and spokesperson for the "Christian Reconstruction" or "Theonomist" school of Biblical interpretation, Y2K provide yet another platform for preaching the imminent collapse of civil society and the possibility of instituting Christ's kingly reign on earth. North's exhaustive tracking of Y2K-related news stories became one of the most popular resources on the subject, even for many who did not share his religious views.

For others, similar notions fed into a conspiracist reading of politics, in which a variety of local and global government agencies were expected to play out specific roles in the unfolding drama. A Y2K and prophecy website proclaimed:

> Look at who is the beneficiary of a potential infrastructure breakdown. Could it be . . . the NEW WORLD ORDER? This Y2K threat is the perfect excuse to implement FEMA, martial law, a GLOBAL CENSUS AND IDENTIFICATION SYSTEM, a GLOBAL SOLUTION to replace all the failed governments and economic institutions . . . and a global dictatorship under the Beast of Revelation 13. (Watcher 1999)

And for Monte Kim Miller, leader of the Concerned Christians group that migrated from Denver, Colorado, to Israel intending to be present in Jerusalem for the turn of the millennium, Y2K took its place alongside black helicopters and unidentified flying objects as a confirmation of both the prophetic timeline and his own messianic endtimes vocation.

A more optimistic millennial vision of a new era of increased neighborly love appealed to others for whom Y2K signaled an opportunity for community organizing rather than an endtimes scenario: in these circles possible Y2K disruptions were usually expected to be painful but not catastrophic.

Conclusion

As the year 2000 rolled in across the globe, closely watched and reported by television news crews, it became clear early on that there would be no Y2K computer problem catastrophe. Planes did not fall from the air, trains continued to run, lights stayed on, ATMs dispensed cash, and on Monday, January 3, businesses and government offices opened on time and started their computer systems with no problem. There were a few slight glitches reported by the media, such as stuck elevators in Japan and malfunctioning ticket machines on buses in Germany, but these hardly constituted broad or apocalyptic events. Some social commentators reacted to the nonevent by suggesting that groups who expected something to happen might react by making something happen. Others suggested that the major social impact of the potential Y2K computer problem was that concern about travel disruptions caused more people to celebrate at home on New Year's Eve that might have been the case otherwise. In conclusion, one can argue that Y2K was a classic case of the way in which a neutral news story can be colored by the religious views of those who read it—something that those who write for the news media tend to forget.

Charles Cameron

See also Christian Reconstructionists and Dominionists, Conspiracism, New World Order

Bibliography

de Jager, Peter, and Richard Bergeon (1997) *Managing 00: Surviving the Year 2000 Computer Crisis.* New York: John Wiley & Sons.

Goldberg, Steven H., Steven C. Davis, and Andrew M Pegalis (1999) *Y2K Risk Management.* New York: John Wiley & Sons.

Hyatt, Michael S. (1998) *The Millennium Bug: How to Survive the Coming Chaos.* Washington D.C.: Regnery Publishers.

Shaunti, Christine F. (1998) *Y2K: The Millennium Bug—A Balanced Christian Response.* Sisters, OR: Multnomah Publishers.

Year 1000

"The terrors of the year 1000" is a phrase that has been used to refer to apocalyptic expectations associated with the advent of the millennium since the Incarnation. Romantic historians in the nineteenth century eloquently described a world awaiting that year in both hope and terror. But they tended to work more from their imaginations, particularly their skill at reconstructing what people must have been like as they faced imminent and final judgment, than from the historical documents which although very suggestive, were sparse. By the end of the nineteenth century, more "scientific" historians were claiming that little evidence for such "paralyzing terrors" appears in the documentation. The historians depicted contemporaries ignorant of, even indifferent to, the millennial year AD (Anno Domini, year of the Lord); to them 1000 was "a year like any other." This dismissal of the "myth of the terrors" received rapid and widespread acceptance among medieval scholars from the end of the nineteenth century onward. A few historians reconsidered, but went largely ignored or their ideas were dismissed. At this millennial cusp, therefore, while popular culture continues to carry the story of an apocalyptic year 1000, the historical profession continues to insist that such matters are purely a figment of the modern imagination. For those scholars who take the opposing view and who argue for a reconsideration of this debunking of the myth, the continued rejection of this reconsideration represents an oversight in modern historiography.

Questioning the Antiterror Historiography of the Year 1000 CE

According to those calling for reconsideration, the "antiterror" historians are seen as repeatedly making untenable claims. First, these historians claim that people did not know the date. But, "Anno Domini" was, in fact, widely known and used, not only among computists and historians who debated its accuracy with renewed intensity at this point, but also known to every priest and monk in Western Europe who annually consulted Easter tables whose entry point was Anno Domini.

Second, some claim that the year meant nothing to contemporaries. But, about two dozen texts ranging from historical works to hagiographic narratives to computational texts, give special attention to 1000. Easter Tables begin and end in 999, 1000, or 1001 even though those years fall in the middle of their nineteen-year cycle, the standard unit for drawing up Easter Tables. One historian, writing of the year 1000 speaks of a thousand as the number that surpasses all others. Glaber not only structures his book around 1000, but claims that his abbot, the great reformer William of Volpiano, told him to write his history on that theme. No other year until 1260 receives such attention.

Third, some claim that there is no biblical support for 1000. But, from the second century onward, the church had a popular and enduring tradition of expecting the sabbatical millennium of peace and rejoicing to begin with the end of 6,000 years from the creation. Since for all of its first 1,000 years, the Christians believed that they lived in the sixth, the last millennium before these promises would be fulfilled, they had a long-standing tradition of expecting the messianic era to begin at the end of the current millennium. Ironically, it was not scripture, but the efforts of earlier clerics to "put off" the millennium and discourage popular apocalyptic outbreaks, that made millennium's end so powerful. We have several texts (French, English, German) indicating that tenth-century clerics believed that either 1000 or 1033 (millennium of the Passion) would bring the apocalypse. Indeed, the date 1000 can be laid specifically at the door of the great antimillennial historian, Augustine, who, in the early fifth century, had argued that the messianic millennium had already begun (invisibly, since there was obviously still war and injustice) with the foundation of the church. While such a teaching may have frustrated apocalyptic enthusiasts in his own day, as the millennium drew to a close it encouraged speculation that the Last Judgment would come in either 1000 or 1033.

Fourth, some claim that there is no evidence of concern and the first historians to speak about it were in the sixteenth century. But, others argue that there is ample evidence of intense apocalyptic expectations for the entire period from the decade before 1000 to after 1033. Moreover this evidence constitutes an extraordinary exception to the rule that clerics normally treated the passage of a millennium as discretely as possible. When Charlemagne was crowned emperor of the Holy Roman Empire on the first day of the year 6000, his historians dated the event 801 Anno Domini, not mentioning the millennial chronology despite its central role in Latin historiography from the fifth to the eighth centuries. 1000, however, proved an inescapable date, and a number of contemporary historians, especially Rodulfus Glaber, speak at length of the signs, wonders, and, more significantly, the religious and social behavior this expectation provoked.

Fifth, some claim that peasants and other illiterate commoners neither knew nor cared about the date. But, millennialism is above all a *popular* religious belief, and the conditions around 1000, especially in France and England, were highly conducive to millennial movements. Commoners in Europe had been exposed to a wide range of eschatological beliefs (see, for example, the conversion manual of Martin of Braga), including both the millennialism and end-time calculations of the sabbatical millennium. We know of at least one case where the apocalyptic year 1000 was publicly preached in the cathedral in Paris, *before the people*. There were multiple ways that "illiterate" commoners could find out the date if they wanted—wandering pilgrims and holy men, peace assemblies, pilgrimage, relic veneration. The turn of the millennium constitutes an extraordinary surge in popular religious fervor.

Sixth, some claim that there are few indications of the "paralytic terrors" of 1000. But—and this is perhaps the most serious misconception of the "antiterrors" school—they overlook what both contemporary chroniclers and Romantic historians like Michelet noted, that is that apocalyptic expectations of the dawning Day of the Lord, however conceived, evoked both "terrors and hopes." These historians associated apocalyptic expectations with positive developments like the Peace of God and the surge of popular pilgrimage (especially to Jerusalem) among the populace.

The Contemporaneous Experience of the Year 1000 CE

This larger perspective acknowledges the powerful ambiguity of apocalyptic beliefs and the constructive as well as destructive impact they can have, in particular their ability to generate new (voluntary) communities which survive the disappointment of a prophecy that failed. It suggests new approaches to a variety of early-eleventh-century phenomena including the religious sensibilities of a reforming generation and the formation of "textual communities," those "laboratories of social experimentation" which, upon closer inspection, look a lot like apostolic movements trying to "land" back in normal time after a formational phase in apocalyptic time.

In this sense the contrast between France and Germany in the year 1000 is particularly striking. In Germany, Otto III did his utmost to shape apocalyptic imagery in support of imperial rule—in his *renovatio imperii*, his missions to the pagans, and his reform of the papacy with Sylvester II. Thus when Otto opened Charlemagne's tomb on Pentecost of the fateful year, he asserted his legitimacy by linking himself, the emperor of the year Anno Domini 1000, with the emperor who "translated" that empire on the first day of the year 6000 Annus Mundi.

In France—where the new Capetian dynasty was still in its unstable infancy and its second king, Robert, excommunicate, where the countryside was in turmoil over the castellan revolution and outbreaks of *sacer ignis* ("holy fire") (in most cases, apparently ergot poisoning)—apocalyptic imagery and response were less dominated by a central court and by high culture. Instead the responses—the pilgrimages, the new and innovative relic cults, the apostolic communities, the penitential processions, and the peace assemblies—arose from below, from outside the elite. In cases like the Peace, where the elite sponsored the assemblies, it represented a radical shift in policy by the elites to include, accommodate, and encourage popular energies. Though the "antiterrors" historians claim that documentation for this period is very limited, it is actually quite rich. And, read carefully, it points to an extraordinary range of popular initiatives, some of which became so subversive that, for the first time in the history of Latin Christendom, clerical and lay officials felt called on to execute people for heresy.

Certainly, this period marks a particularly creative period in French social history (referred to by historians in the Duby school as "la mutation de l'an mil"—without reference to "les terreurs"). At this millennial cusp, we find evidence of fundamental changes in values and family structures throughout the social strata, of enormous social and economic activity—new markets, burgeoning cities, bringing forested land under the plough. In a paradox characteristic of apocalyptic beliefs, the soil and society of a chaotic French "kingdom" at the turn of the millennium produced a culture that would be the creative leader of medieval Europe for the next several centuries (really, on and off but mostly on, until the nineteenth). The apocalyptic hope and disappointment, then, can be seen as setting in motion a dynamic that generated a wide range of often exceptionally productive social experiments—communes rural and urban, colonies, new monastic houses, crusades, architectural styles, intellectual communities, and "heresies." And what characterized almost all these social dynamics, was the same thing that made the Peace movement so exceptional: the cooperation of elites and commoners. For the first time, in a widely known, public forum, the elites began to accept and cooperate with initiatives from below, they began to adopt genuinely popular policies, even at the expense of some of their own privileges.

In sum, the apocalyptic year 1000—terrors and hopes—represents one of the great moments in the history of both millennialism and of Western Europe. The year 1000 may have been the most powerful millennial moment in recorded history (so far), and certainly to be classed with some of the other great moments (Palestine in Y0K, the entire Mediterranean c. 200, c. 400). Certainly this is true of the regions of France where Peace assemblies met. Here surges of apocalyptic expectations, fueled by the state of disorder and uncertainty, provoked huge manifestations of public, collective, religious enthusiasm which directly influenced political life and social organization for years, if not decades. And the passage of 1000, far from putting an end to apocalyptic expectations, set them in motion, and the advent of the millennium of the Passion in 1033, according to both Glaber and his fellow monastic historian Ademar of Chabannes, provoked another, possibly more powerful wave of millennial fervor. That year saw both the vast pilgrimages to Jerusalem (including Ademar) and the wave of peace assemblies (sponsored by great reforming monastery of Cluny and recorded in the work of their historian, Rodulfus Glaber).

Richard Landes

See also Peace of God

Bibliography

Burr, George L. (1901) "The Year 1000 and the Antecedents of the Crusades." *American Historical Review* 6: 429–39.

Duby, Georges. (1967) *L'an Mil.* Paris: Julliard.

Focillon, Henri. (1952) *The Year 1000.* Paris: Armand Colin.

Fried, Johannes. (1989) "Endzeiterwartung um die Jahrtausendwende." *Deutsches Archiv für Erforschung des Mittelalters* 45, 2: 385–473.

Glaber, Rodulfus. (1989) *Opera*, edited by John France. Oxford: Oxford Medieval Texts, Clarendon.

Guggenheim, Sylvain. (1999) *Les fausses terreurs de l'an mil.* Paris: Picard.

Landes, Richard. (1995) *Relics, Apocalypse, and the Deceits of History.* Cambridge, MA: Harvard University Press.

Landes, Richard, and David Van Meter, eds. (2000) *The Apocalyptic Year 1000: History and Historiography.* New York: Oxford University Press.

McGinn, Bernard. (1994) *Antichrist.* San Francisco: Harper.

Michelet, Jules. (1971) *Histoire de France (Les grands monuments de l'histoire).* Paris: Club Francais du Livre.

Stock, Brian. (1986) *The Implications of Literacy: Written Language and Models of Interpretation in the Eleventh and Twelfth Century Europe.* New Haven, CT: Princeton University Press.

Year 2000

The rotund numerological significance of the year 2000—a new millennium—spawned great excitement around the world. The word "millennium" specifically refers to a span of one thousand years, but there are many deeper meanings. It has come to mean the point at which one period of one thousand years ends and the next begins, and for some this has important religious, social, or political significance. For some reason, humans seem mesmerized by rows of zeros in any number. Stephen Jay Gould says that this is rooted in a basic human drive to sort and classify our experiences into dichotomous sets; and to "latch on to numerical regularity, and seek deep meaning therein, because such order does underlie much of nature's patterning" (1997: 36).

It is the year 2000 only in one calendar system based on the Christian Era. Any date in any calendar system—Christian, Judaic, Islamic, Hindu, Chinese, and many others—can be understood as significant given the creativity of those using numerological equations to find justification. Apocalyptic interpretations of the millennium came from contemporary Christian, Jewish, Hindu, Buddhist, Muslim, and New Age prophets. Contemporary Christian Fundamentalists interpret Revelation as a prophetic warning about tumultuous apocalyptic events marking endtimes that herald the Second Coming of Christ. Most also believe that when Christ returns, he will reign for a period of one thousand years—a millennium. So the turn of the calendar to the year 2000 doesn't *necessarily* have theological significance. Norman Cohn, in *The Pursuit of the Millennium* ([1957] 1970) chronicles how Christian apocalyptic fervor appears at seemingly random dates throughout Western history. A major U.S. episode of Christian millennialist fervor occurred among the Millerites in the 1840s. Prophecy belief is widespread in the United States. During the Gulf War, 14 percent of respondents to one CNN national poll thought it was the beginning of Armageddon, and, as Lamy notes, "American bookstores were experiencing a run on books about prophecy and the end of the world" (1996: 155). In 1993, a *Times*/CNN national poll found that 20 percent of the general population thought the second coming of Christ would occur near the year 2000.

By some reckonings, the year 2000 is the start of the seventh millennium since God created the earth. A small movement of apocalyptic Jews around the time the Christian church was forming had a theory that the Messiah would arrive 6,000 years after the Creation. Around 120 CE this idea transferred to Christianity. Church scholars decided that since God took six days to finish creation, and to God each day is like one thousand years, then the seventh millennium brings the return of Christ. This idea still leaves open when the endtimes clock starts ticking. Damian Thompson explains that "for millenarians, the world was perpetually on the verge of its 6,000th birthday; for conservatives, that anniversary was always beyond the life expectancy of the current generation" (1997: 29).

Among Christian Fundamentalists in the United States, there is open discussion of whether or not the year 2000 starts the seventh millennium. Clearly, the year 2000 has been interpreted by a significant portion of the U.S. population as somehow linked not only to epochal transformation, but religiously significant events, even if not a signal for the End Times. By 1998 anyone visiting a large bookstore could scan the titles in the religion, prophecy, New Age, and occult sections and find a cornucopia of books anticipating the year

2000. Surfing the Web revealed a pulsating multimedia cacophony of millennial expectation. The topics ranged from secular to spiritual and from cataclysmic doom to transcendent rapture in what Michael Barkun (1998) has called an "improvisational style" of millennialism and apocalypticism.

Varieties of Expectation and Action

As the year 2000 approached, interpretations of apocalyptic millennialism could be sorted into three related and overlapping tendencies that ranged from sacred to secular: (1) In the view of some Christian fundamentalists, it was the arrival of the apocalyptic millennial "endtimes" or "Last Days" prophesied in Revelation and other books of the Bible. (2) Diverse movements across the political spectrum manifested a more generic and often secularized apocalyptic world view which saw an impending crisis. (3) There was a also more generalized sense of expectation and renewal, triggered merely by the approach of the calendar year 2000, because it was a millennial milestone in human recorded history.

These apocalyptic fears and millennial expectations in turn influenced four broad contemporary movements in the United States: (1) Activists in various sectors of the Christian Right, ranging from electoral to insurgent, had varying views regarding whether or not the year 2000 marks the endtimes. Many of these Christian hard-liners seek to purify the society as part of a religious revival: examples include the homophobic statements by Trent Lott, and advertisements calling on homosexuals to "cure" themselves by turning to Jesus. The most aggressive activists engage in theologically motivated acts of violence against abortion providers. (2) Various prophetic sects possess a kaleidoscope of visions: the Heaven's Gate group suicides in 1997 flowed from a mixture of biblical prophesy, the ancient predictions of Nostradamus, and science fiction; the Order of the Solar Temple imploded inward with group suicides in Canada, France, and Switzerland; and the Aum Shinrikyo sect exploded outward with a gas attack on the Tokyo subway. Conspiracist William Cooper weaves an apocalyptic vision out of historic anti-Semitism and modern UFO lore. (3) Right-wing populists, including survivalists, gun-rights activists, antielite conspiracists, and participants in the Patriot & Armed Militia movements often resort to scapegoating. A popular speaker in these circles is Robert K. Spear who believes the formation of armed Christian communities is necessary as we approach the endtimes. Preparing to survive the coming apocalypse has led to a survivalist subculture that stores food and conducts self-defense training a culture that now spans a continuum from religious to secular in right-wing populist groups. (4) The last movement is the far right, including neo-Nazis and persons influenced by far-right versions of the Christian Identity religion. Identity beliefs were behind the assassination of Denver talk show host Alan Berg, a spree of armed robberies and murders starting in the 1980s, the tragic shootout between federal agents and the Weaver family in Idaho, and in some reports the brutal dragging death of a black man in Jasper, Texas.

Winding Up for 2000

Author Hal Lindsey reignited Protestant apocalyptic speculation in 1970 with his book, *The Late Great Planet Earth*, which sold ten million copies. Lindsey argued that the endtimes had arrived and that Christians should watch for the signs of the times. Billy Graham again raised expectations in his 1983 book, *Approaching Hoofbeats: The Four Horsemen of the Apocalypse*, where he observes that Jesus Christ, "The Man on the white horse . . . will come when man has sunk to his lowest most perilous point in history" (1983: 222–24). Graham then discussed how bad things were in the world.

Paul Boyer (1992: 148–49) argues that Christian apocalypticism must be factored into both cold war and post–cold war political equations. He notes that the 1974 prophecy book, *Armageddon, Oil, and the Middle East Crisis* sold three-quarters of a million copies. The mainstreaming of apocalypticism received a major boost when, in 1983, Ronald Reagan cited scriptural authority to demonize the Soviet Union as an "evil empire." Grace Halsell wrote in her book, *Prophecy and Politics: Militant Evangelists on the Road to Nuclear War* (1986), of how some evangelists, including Pat Robertson, Jerry Falwell, and Hal Lindsey, hinted that use of atomic weapons was inevitable as part of the final battle of Armageddon. One reason certain sectors of the Christian Right mobilized tremendous support for the state of Israel during the Reagan administration, was, according to Ruth Mouly (1987), in part because they believed Jews had to return to Israel before the millennialist prophecies of Revelation could be fulfilled.

Time of the Devil

The process of prophecy belief triggering apocalyptic demonization and then leading to searches for the Devil's partners is continuously updated. Paul Boyer points out that those seen as the prophesied agents of Satan girding for endtimes battle can be foreign or domestic or both. He notes how in prophetic literature the identity of Satan's allies in the Battle of Armageddon has shifted seamlessly over time, circumstance, and political interest from the Soviet Union to Chinese communists, to Islamic militants; and warns of an increasing level of anti-Muslim bigotry in some contemporary apocalyptic subcultures. Robert Fuller has looked at the range of current targets:

> Today, fundamentalist Christian writers see the Antichrist in such enemies as the Muslim world, feminism, rock music, and secular humanism. The threat of the Antichrist's imminent takeover of the world's economy has been traced to the formation of the European Economic Community, the Susan B. Anthony dollar . . . and the introduction of universal product codes. (1995: 5)

Visions of the Satanic Antichrist are common in relatively mainstream sectors of the new Christian Right. Typical of the current apocalyptic genre is a recent mailing from Prophetic Vision, a small international Christian evangelical outreach ministry, reporting that "prophecy is moving so fast" and "the Return of Christ is imminent." The mailing goes on to declare that the Antichrist, "Must be alive today waiting to take control!" and then solicits funds for the "end time harvest." Rev. Pat Robertson frequently ties his conspiracist vision to apocalyptic hints that we are in the millennial "End Times," and endtimes themes have repeatedly appeared on his *700 Club* television program (from my own observations). On one July 1998 program Robertson hinted that a tsunami in New Guinea coupled with the appearance of asteroids might be linked to Bible prophecy. Just after Christmas 1994, the program carried a feature on new dollar bill designs being discussed to combat counterfeiting. The newscaster then cited Revelations 13 and suggested that if the Treasury Department put new codes on paper money, it might be the Antichrist's Mark of the Beast, predicted as a sign of the coming endtimes.

Christians are also debating the importance of the "Y2K bug," the technical programming problem that crashes some computer software when it tries to interpret the year 2000 using earlier computer code written to recognize only the numbers 0 to 99 for calendar-based calculations. As in secular circles, responses range from cautious preparations to doomsday scenarios that have led some to establish rural survivalist retreats. At the 1998 Christian Coalition's annual Road to Victory conference, a workshop was devoted to announcing a plan to mobilize churches to provide food, water, shelter, and medical supplies in case the Y2K bug caused widespread societal problems. This mobilization was justified by arguing the anticipation of resulting disruptions was appropriate no matter what the eschatological viewpoint; and that if there was no serious disruption, the supplies could aid the poor (from my own observations).

This equation neatly sidestepped the issue of the endtimes, while allowing those who believe we are in the endtimes to work cooperatively with those who do not. Christian Reconstructionist author Gary North is now a much-quoted expert on the Y2K bug. He sees much chaos created by Y2K, but dismisses the link to Christ's imminent return. Some postmillennialists are more in line with the suspicious view expressed in the John Birch Society magazine, *New American:* "Much like the Reichstag fire, could the Millennium Bug provide an ambitious President with an opportunity to seize dictatorial powers?" (Behreandt 1998: 14).

Most Christians, even those who think the endtimes are imminent, do not automatically succumb to demonization, scapegoating, and conspiracist thinking. In the escalating surge of millennial titles as the year 2000 approached, however, a number of authors named the agents of the Antichrist or claimed to expose the evil endtimes conspiracy: Examples include: *Global Peace and the Rise of Antichrist; One World Under Antichrist: Globalism, Seducing Spirits and Secrets of the New World Order; Foreshocks of Antichrist;* and *How Democracy Will Elect the Antichrist: The Ultimate Denial of Freedom, Liberty and Justice According to the Bible.* Several of these titles see computer technology, global communications, and the Internet as possibly part of the Mark of the Beast system. David Webber's article in *Foreshocks of Antichrist* is titled "Cyberspace: The Beast's Worldwide Spider Web" and includes a discussion of Y2K in which he suggests the fix for Y2K might actually be part of the Devil's conspiracy.

Change and Resistance

Sociologist Sara Diamond reports that even some Christians who are dubious of "hard" endtimes claims have nevertheless been reenergized by a "softer" millennial view of the year 2000 as a time for aggressive evangelism or even "spiritual warfare" against demonic forces (in Strozier and Flynn 1997: 206–10).

Gender issues played an important role in debates sharpened by the approach of the year 2000. As Lee Quinby has noted (1996), while it is difficult to predict the outcomes of millennial moments, the current manifestation is unlikely to be good for women. (In the classic sci-fi film *Five Million Years to Earth* an ancient Martian space ship is unearthed at the aptly named Hobbes End Underground station in London. When its passenger comes to life it appears as the Devil, complete with little horns. A women falls under its spell, and using superhuman powers supplied by the Devil, attempts to stop the male heroes planning to block the fiery apocalypse by using logic and science.)

The broad quest for purity associated with the "softer" millennial thinking among apocalyptic Christians can breed violence, such as seen in the escalating attacks on abortion providers. It has already sparked legislative efforts to enforce divisive and narrowly defined biblical standards of morality. The wave of newspaper advertisements calling on gay men and lesbians to "cure" themselves by turning to Jesus is another example of a Christian coercive purity campaign influenced by millennial expectation. Richard K. Fenn argues that popular "rituals of purification" in a society are closely associated with apocalyptic and millennial beliefs (1997: 127–49).

A good example is the Christian evangelical men's movement, Promise Keepers, which has scheduled "Vision 2000" rallies at "key population centers and state capitols around the United States" for 1 January 2000. At the massive Promise Keepers rally of Christian men on the Washington Mall in October 1997, questions about the approaching endtimes elicited eager responses. While the Promise Keepers is driven in part by millennial expectation, it is also a response to the need for men to find a coherent identity in modern culture that responds in some creative way to the issues raised by the civil rights and feminist movements. When push comes to shove, men in the Promise Keepers are still considered the spiritual leaders in their families. As PK president Randy Phillips said, "we have to listen and honor and respect our wives," but admitted, "[w]e talk about ultimately the decision lying with the man" (1997: 9). Acknowledging the sincere religious devotion and quest for growth of many Promise Keepers men, academic Lee Quinby, who has extensively researched the subject area, nonetheless notes political content in the group's vision of "apocalyptic masculinity," which rejects gender equality and scapegoats homosexuals and feminists "as a threat to the pure community." Quinby calls this tendency "coercive purity" (in Strozier and Flynn 1997: 154–56).

In describing the symbolism in Revelation, one contemporary Catholic commentary cautions against negative stereotyping of women. This is a needed caution, because antifeminist, misogynist, and homophobic interpretations of Revelation are widespread. A 1978 brochure with an apocalyptic subtext from Texas Eagle Forum was titled: *Christian Be Watchful: Hidden Dangers in the New Coalition of Feminism, Humanism, Socialism, Lesbianism.*

An example of a group engaged in an apocalyptic campaign of millennial ritual purification is Jeremiah Films, named after the biblical prophet. Jeremiah Films and Jeremiah Books are run by the husband and wife team of Pat and Caryl Matrisciana. Sen. Trent Lott, who in 1998 denounced homosexuals as not just sinful but sick, had already appeared in Jeremiah's 1993 antigay video *Gay Rights, Special Rights.* The video, used in several statewide legislative campaigns to erode basic rights for gay men and lesbians, also features former attorney general Edwin Meese III and former education secretary William J. Bennett, along with notable conspiracists such as David Noebel of Summit Ministries. Lott also stars in Jeremiah's 1993 video *The Crash The Coming Financial Collapse of America*, which comes in two versions, one with a secular doomsday scenario and another with a special Christian cut featuring discussions of endtimes biblical prophecy.

Jeremiah has a large collection of conspiracist videos. Caryl Matrisciana, a leading author of Christian Right books with conspiracist themes, cohosted a thirteen-part video series from Jeremiah titled Pagan Invasion. The series includes videos that claim evolution is a hoax, Freemasonry is a pagan religion, Halloween is a tool for Satanic abduction, and Mormonism is a cult heresy. The Jeremiah video on Mormons has earned rebukes from mainstream religious commentators for its bigotry toward members of the church, appropriately called The Church of Jesus Christ of Latter-day Saints.

Jeremiah is best known for *The Clinton Chronicles,* a video distributed widely by Jerry Falwell, which alleges that the president is at the head of a vast murderous conspiracy. The *Clinton Chronicles* video and the subsequent book are the work of Jeremiah's Patrick Matrisciana, who is also founder and president of Citizens for Honest Government, a group dedicated to the impeachment of President Clinton. Many of the conspiracist attacks on President Bill Clinton originated in the apocalyptic sector of the Christian Right. One example is a book penned by Texe Marrs, titled *Big Sister Is Watching You: Hillary Clinton and the White House Feminists Who Now Control America—And Tell The President What To Do.* The book claims a plot by radical left "feminist vultures" and their subversive allies "whose goal is to end American sovereignty and bring about a global, Marxist paradise" (1993: 13–15). As the year 2000 approached, Marrs' type of florid rhetoric became commonplace among those who mixed millennial dreams with the bitter fruits of demonization.

Conclusions

For most inhabitants of planet Earth, no matter what their calendar or belief system, the arrival of the year 2000 was a cause for celebration. The challenge for civil society was to respect devout religious belief while focusing apocalyptic energy and millennial expectation toward a time of introspection and renewal rather than a time of fear and mistrust. The year 2000 was a time for all of us to wrestle with our demons on a personal and societal level. Future historians will judge how well we resolved the many issues heightened by the millennial year 2000.

Chip Berlet

Bibliography

Barkun, Michael. (1998) "Politics and Apocalypticism." In *The Encyclopedia of Apocalypticism*, edited by Stephen J. Stein. New York: Continuum, vol. 3, 442–60.

Behreandt, Dennis. (1998) "Millennium Mayhem." *The New American* [John Birch Society] (14 September).

Year 2000 Celebrations

Four words best describe the heavily anticipated worldwide celebrations marking the arrival of the Year 2000—global, secular, large, and peaceful. Although the millennium is a Christian concept and the majority of the world's population is not Christian, millennial celebrations took place around the world. The celebrations were largest in Europe and the Americas, but took place also, although on a much smaller scale, in many non-Christian nations as well. Perhaps the most spectacular celebration of all was in Egypt, along the banks of the Nile in Giza, with the pyramids as a background. There some one hundred thousand people celebrated to the performance of a three-hour New Age "opera" by French composer Jean-Michel Jarre. In Cambodia, the celebration was more muted, with ballet and prayers offered by two thousand Buddhist monks at the ancient temples of site of Angkor Wat.

But the millennium was not celebrated everywhere. Hindus in India, Muslims in many Islamic nations, and Buddhists in China and other Asian nations paid little attention or celebrated in unique ways. In China, for example, the Western New Year was marked by Beijing department stores and shopping centers remaining open past midnight and families and friends celebrating by shopping. And in Hong Kong, a special Millennial Cup horse race was staged at 12:45 AM, in accord with the importance of gambling in Hong Kong culture.

Israel gave no official recognition to the date, although it was prepared for celebrations by Christians in Jerusalem, Bethlehem, and elsewhere. In contrast to many popular events around the world, these celebrations were mainly small and religious, as was the one in Rome, where the crowd was blessed by Pope John Paul II speaking from his balcony.

That the millennium was marked at all in non-Christian nations indicates the influence of Western culture around the world. Regardless of their religion, people around the world follow an international business calendar tied to the Western Gregorian calendar and had to deal with potential Y2K computer problems. The one Christian nation that ignored the millennium was Cuba, as the Catholic commu-

This postcard from England shows the political debate that has accompanied the building of the millennium Dome in Greenwich.

SHOULD WE CELEBRATE?

No one can have escaped the hype surrounding the imminent start of the third millennium. Her Majesty's Government is wasting millions on the Millennium Dome whilst the starving of the world cry for food; employers are expecting unprecedented absenteeism due to over-consumption of alcohol; hospitals are wondering how they will cope with the anticipated accidents (and worse) caused by revelry; people are spending thousands of pounds for just one night's stay in some of London's hotels, and the world is planning for a booze-sodden party.

And all this, supposedly, to celebrate the birth of the 'holy child, Jesus'. God's name will be 'blasphemed among the Gentiles' by those who claim to be Christian by right of British birth.

We feel instinctively that true Christians cannot be associated with this kind of thing without tainting ourselves with the ungodliness of it all. If 'celebrating the millennium' means going along with all this, then our response must be 'no thanks'.

Even the plans of the big denominations fail to excite our sympathy. It almost seems that the incarnation of Christ, which the millennium is all about, lies buried under a PR exercise, designed to show that the church can put on a good show. The elaborate Roman Catholic proposals, and an Anglican youth jamboree planned for Wembley, simply prove the point that the millennium is best forgotten by those who have a better grasp of gospel principles. The fact that the celebration of festivals belongs to the Old Testament, not the New, is also a factor to be taken into account. To the Christian the only special day is a weekly one–Resurrection Day!

We have seen how Christmas and Easter have become the focus for ritualistic religion and superstitious practice. Some might feel it is bad enough having to seize those occasions as opportunities for preaching the gospel to an otherwise unchurched society, without adding another of like kind.

Too late?

Really, the 'decider' is that the millennium has already occurred. We are four to eight years too late! The Roman monk who calculated the birth of Jesus, and thus the start of our dating system, got it wrong. It has never been put right. We have missed the millennium–so why bother with it now? It is like sending a 'sorry I forgot your birthday' card.

So, then, is there anything to be said for celebrating the millennium? Perhaps the use of the word 'celebrate' is inappropriate but, for all the foregoing objections, it seems to me that the date should not pass unnoticed. We would do the gospel a disservice if we were to ignore the opportunities for true and faithful witness with which this day presents us.

Paul seized just such an opportunity when he saw the altar to an unknown god in Athens. A heathen altar, with all that conjures up in the mind, was his starting-point. The millennium could be ours.

Hearts and minds

Paul went to the market place–not just a place for buying vegetables, but where the serious things of life and the spirit were debated. We must go into such 'market places' today. At a time like this, some curiosity will be aroused in many hearts and minds regarding the significance of the Christian message. They will be 'in the market' for an answer. The younger generations are especially ignorant of Christianity–the facts, doctrine and history.

Should we leave it to those whose 'Christianity' we criticise, to explain what it is all about? Are we to leave those unsuspecting browsers in the market of ideas to the spiritual spivs and the religious rip-off merchants? Surely not! 'So teach us to number our days, that we may apply our hearts unto wisdom' (Psalm 90:12).

Source: Brunton, Alan. (1999) "Millennium–Should We Celebrate?" *Evangelical Times* (April) 1999, 25.

nity there argued that the millennium actually begins on 1 January 2001; and they will celebrate it then. From the vantage point of those in the United States with a television set, the millennium was a global experience as several television stations were on the air with live coverage of the arrival of the millennium on the Pacific island nations of Kiribati, Tonga, and Fiji and then across the remaining twenty-four time zones. For those in Times Square in New York City, the global arrival of the millennium was marked by video displays and performances for each nation as the millennium arrived.

In several nations the millennial celebrations were organized as year-long events beginning on 1 January 2000. France, for example, established a Mission for the Celebration of the Year 2000 with a focus on time: "The time for festivities, the time for reflection, and the time for creation." Planned festivities include New Year's Eve, a musical festival in June, Bastille Day in July, and local festivals. Reflection will center on the University of World Knowledge with seminars and lectures by scholars in Paris; and creativity will be encouraged through support for the arts. In Rome, the focus for the year is more religious as the Roman Agency for the Preparation of the Jubilee prepares to manage an expected influx of forty million pilgrims and tourists in 2000.

An important secular use of the millennium in some nations was as a symbol of and time for national renewal. In Canada, for example, the Millennium Bureau of Canada is managing several national projects including the celebration of the Viking arrival, the building of a recreational trail across Canada, a major environmental conservation initiative, and Music Canada. In Iceland, the Leifur Eriksson Millennium Commission will encourage study and education about the nation's early history including the Viking arrival in North America, programs for school children, and the celebration of one thousand years of Christianity in Iceland. In Norway the focus is on preparing for the future, the most ambitious project being the planned construction of community meeting halls in 435 communities. Probably the most significant national program is that of Great Britain. The centerpiece is the controversial Dome in Greenwich, the locale for the official British millennial celebration with the Queen and Prime Minister in attendance, and with a future as an exhibit hall and performing arts center. The Dome is seen as the beginning of the revitalization of Greenwich with a new Millennial Village of three thousand homes and public parks to follow. The government is also planning to distribute two billion pounds from the National Lottery to individuals so that they may "fulfill personal aspirations while benefiting their

The Millennium Party Register Universal Searchable Database

This register of places to party on New Year's Eve 2000 has been set up so that everybody who wants go somewhere on that momentous evening can choose from a list of venues. There is no charge for listing: our revenue is derived from sponsorship.

If you are running a club, pub, or street party, or simply want crowds of gate-crashers at your private party, add your venue to this list. If in doubt, please ask a responsible person first.

Please do not post messages about parties that you are looking for in this list. Any such messages will be removed. The correct forum for such discussions is the Millennium Party Message Board.

ATTENTION PLEASE! This is not the place to advertise other goods and services. It is a public service for the promotion of New Year's Eve functions. Other material will be removed and **we'll charge you UK£100.**

All parties will appear immediately in the database, pending our approval: we reserve the right to edit submissions, and to delete entirely any entry, without notification.

Submit a Party | Update an Entry | Delete a Party | Find a Party

HTTP://WWW.JEPA.CO.UK/SHOPPING/PARTY.HTML

A message for the year 2000 distributed on postcards by the One Day Foundation of Santa Barbara, California. THE ONE DAY FOUNDATION, SANTA BARBARA, CA.

communities." And the government has set aside additional funds for environmental, educational, scientific, technological, and urban projects in three thousand communities. In Hungary, the celebration was linked to the spinning of a 7-ton hourglass and a special session of Parliament to celebrate one thousand years of Hungarian statehood. Unfortunately, both events were delayed by technical and political problems.

Other salient features of Year 2000 celebrations were that they were large and peaceful. Despite concerns about the apocalypse, terrorism, and disruptions that might be caused by Y2K computer problems, people (many of them young) congregated in public squares and celebrated the arrival of Year 2000 loudly but peacefully. In London, crowds around Trafalgar Square were estimated at from three to four million and at least two million celebrants were in Times Square. In Brazil, some 3.5 million people lined 25 miles of beaches, and in Berlin the celebration stretched for three miles as revelers listed to the music of sixty bands. Although authorities made elaborate preparations to deal with potential problems, and the police were out in large numbers (eight thousand in Times Square, thirteen thousand in London), there were few problems.

Perhaps the only aspect of the Year 2000 celebrations that did not go off as planned were expensive dinners, concerts, and vacations offered by some who thought the combination of prosperity and the Year 2000 would lead people in the United States, Great Britain, and elsewhere to spend enormous amounts of money. Several of these ventures did not work out, as some were canceled and others cut their prices in the last months of the year. Evidently, people chose either to celebrate in public or to celebrate at home or with friends or family.

David Levinson

Year of the Flagellants (1260)

The Flagellants were participants in a popular men's mass movement of penitential self-flagellation, generally explained as an apocalyptic and ritual response to the Bubonic Plague in the thirteenth century.

The Black Death originated in Asia and spread westward across European trade-shipping routes between 1347 and 1351. It was carried by rats hosting fleas who transmitted the deadly bacteria *Pasteurella pestis* to human victims. Over 40 percent of the population of Europe (and one-third of Britain) perished. The epidemic would flare up in densely populated cities, then suddenly vanish, conveying the impression of Divine Wrath. King Magnus II of Sweden issued a proclamation warning, "God for the sins of men has struck the world with this great punishment of death."

Whipping or auto-flagellation was a long-established, ascetic discipline of the Western church and was practiced systematically in Italian monasteries in the eleventh century. Its purpose was to bargain with God for forgiveness of sin, and to imitate the sufferings of Christ. When Joachim of Fiore's *The Everlasting Gospel* appeared in northern Italy in 1254, claiming the Last Days of the Second Age would be marked by the moral decline of the papacy, this sparked a lay ascetic movement with strong anticlerical sentiments led by renegade priests. In preparation for the year 1260 and Joachim's Third Age of Spirit, thousands participated in penitential orgies. Rallied by the hermit of Perugia, processions of priests, men, and boys marched south with burning candles, singing hymns; and aristocrats and town magistrates joined ranks with peasants and the urban poor.

Various charismatic leaders interpreted recent hardships as mere preludes to imminent catastrophe in which God would destroy the world through fires and earthquakes. Flagellants performed their penance not merely to save themselves, but as sacrificial victims taking on and atoning for the sins of the world, in order to avert the plague and rescue the world from destruction. In awe of their divine mission, the townspeople of Europe welcomed and hosted them and absorbed their anticlerical attitudes.

The movement spread north through Germany and the Rhineland where the Italian leaders received a vision of the "Heavenly Letter," a marble tablet born by an angel to the altar of the Holy Sepulchre in Jerusalem. It told of divine wrath at the sins of usury, blasphemy, and adultery, and claimed that God's first acts of vengeance had been halted by the mercy of the Virgin Mary. It promised that if Flagellants held processions for thirty-three-and a-half days (years in the life of Jesus), then God would stop the tribulation, and the land would renew its bounty.

The Flagellants wore white hooded robes with red crosses, carried statues of the weeping Virgin, and sang *Stabet Mater.* Led by lay masters, they renounced bathing, shaving, and physical comfort, and were vowed to thirty-three days of silence and celibacy. Marching from town to town, they gathered before the chapel in the central square, then stripped, fell to the ground in cruciform postures, where they were whipped by their brother penitents. They then faced the chapel, singing and rhythmically beating themselves with leather scourges studded with iron spikes until they were pouring blood down their shoulders. Many exhibited trance states and were perhaps impervious to pain.

The German Flagellants became an anticlerical movement led by poor tradesmen who believed by beating themselves until they became free of sin they thereby no longer required the intercession of the clergy in the sacraments. German bishops excommunicated outstanding leaders as Antichrist plays were performed on the street. John of Winterthur wrote in 1348 that these pestilences were "messianic woes" leading to the millennium, when a warrior-messiah—probably the resurrected Emperor Frederick—would arise and kill all the clergy, and then force wealthy landowners to intermarry with the poor.

Jewish conspiracy theories spread through the Flagellants' ranks; that Jews, whose secret headquarters was in Toledo, were poisoning village wells and infecting Christians. Between 1348 and 1349, thousands of Jews were massacred in riots and pogroms incited by the Flagellants between Carcassonne and Brussels.

Susan J. Palmer

See also Joachism

Bibliography

Cohn, Norman. (1970) *The Pursuit of the Millennium.* London: Oxford University Press.

Zeigler, Philip. (1971) *The Black Death.* New York: Harper & Row.

Zionism

Zionism was a political movement, largely of the twentieth century, which successfully sought to establish a homeland for the world's Jews on substantially the same territory as biblical Israel. Jewish identification with the eastern Mediterranean littoral, mythologically traceable to the second millennium BCE Abrahamic covenant, provided it a deeply felt religious motive. Still, it remained predominantly a secular movement, inspired in part by romantic and socialist ideas of community. Political Zionism was initially prompted by the European anti-Semitism which burgeoned throughout the latter nineteenth century and culminated in the unspeakable crimes of the Nazi era. The Holocaust provided a final, compelling impetus for the creation of a Jewish national state.

For many Jews, and even some Christians, Zionism was legitimized by an intense millennialism grounded in biblical prophecy. Even for secular or atheistic Jews, the Abrahamic covenant carried considerable emotional resonance, as did repeated Scriptural proclamations of a promised era of divine-human reconciliation. Those who could not respond in faith were, nonetheless, often moved by the literary and historical connotation of such passages. Some Christians, especially those in the evangelical Protestant community, urged the reestablishment of a Jewish state as a way to fulfill what they saw as immensely significant prophecies relative to the Second Advent of Jesus Christ.

Seeds of Zionism in the Ancient Hebrew Kingdoms

The migration of the Hebrew tribes into the eastern Mediterranean littoral during the second millennium BCE was legitimized by sixth-century BCE redactors of the Pentateuch as the fulfillment of Yahweh's earlier promise to Abraham: "Go from your country and your kindred and your father's house to the land that I will show you. And I will make of you a great nation" (Genesis 12:1–2). The historicity of Abraham is uncertain, although the biblical account may retain a kernel of genuine historical memory. Regardless, from its opening pages the Pentateuch establishes the unique Jewish claim to the land of Israel. This proprietary attitude was immensely reinforced by the saga of the conquest of Canaan, in which indigenous tribes were largely supplanted by the migrating Hebrews. While preeminent as religious literature, the Old Testament, its first five books especially, may thus be regarded as Israel's national epic.

The process of forging of a Jewish identity out of the fractious Hebrew tribes was slow and painful. The brief luster of the Davidic and Solomaic kingdoms should not blind us to the true nature of an ancient Israel riven along religious, ethnic, and economic lines. Throughout the first millennium BCE, this difficult process of formulating a distinct Jewish consciousness was immeasurably advanced by prophetic identification of the people with their immediate physical geography. Within this holy land of Israel (its boundaries fluctuated, but generally encompassed the littoral between the Sinai Peninsula and the Sea of Chinnereth) the city of Jerusalem was incomparably sacred. Within its precincts was found the earthly dwelling place of Yahweh: "Great is the Lord and greatly to be praised in the city of our god!" (Psalms 48:1). Eventually, the Hebrew prophets foresaw Israel as ministering to the wider world: "For out of Zion shall go forth the law, and the word of the Lord from Jerusalem. He shall judge between the nations, and decide for many peoples" (Isaiah 2:3–4). Jewish identification with a particular locale was thus gradually supplemented by the belief that a future universal era of peace would extend from Israel over the earth: "Nation shall not lift up sword against nation, neither shall they learn war any more" (Isaiah 2:4).

Repeated foreign invasion served only to strengthen the bond between Judaism and the land of Israel. The first century CE brought disaster, however, as Rome effectively extinguished Jewish political authority in Palestine. The Temple was destroyed in 70 AD and a steady out-migration (the Diaspora) followed, as demoralized remnants of the Jewish state sought refuge throughout the ancient world.

Waning of the Zionist Ideal in the Diaspora

Nearly twenty centuries of diaspora did not sever the emotional identification of Jews with the biblical land of Israel. The millennial impulse so marked among certain Old Testament prophets survived as well, manifested from time to time in messianic movements. These frequently offered a restorationist promise toward the Holy Land. The familiar toast, "Next year in Jerusalem," encapsulated this geographical longing. Nevertheless, the diaspora Jews established vibrant local cultures and their longing for Israel, however intense, was essentially sentimental rather than political.

Well before the end of the Western medieval period Jews were, from England to the Urals, settled throughout Europe. Historians estimate that by the end of the eighteenth century as many as ninety percent of the world's Jews resided there. They survived, some even prospered, despite various political and social disabilities, accompanied from time to time by bloody anti-Semitic outbursts.

The French Revolution encouraged European Christians to rethink the status of the Jews. The revolutionaries' desire to overthrow the legacy of the ancien régime combined with Enlightenment idealism to undermine legal restraints on Jews. Civil disabilities rooted in religion were increasingly regarded as archaic and were steadily mitigated or discarded altogether. By mid-nineteenth century it seemed as though the Jewish population would gradually assimilate into European life as merely one more religious denomination. This bright prospect, after so many centuries of persecution, naturally discouraged even theoretical Jewish interest in a "return" to Israel. The restorationist theme, already much attenuated, survived as little more than a pious sentiment.

Protestant Zionism in the Nineteenth Century

Zionism was initially more widespread within the Protestant Christian community during the early nineteenth century than among the Jews. The same events of 1789 which initially discouraged Jewish interest in a re-created Israel greatly stimulated it among evangelicals. The French Revolution was such an epochal occurrence that it prompted certain Christians to believe that biblical prophecies, especially those contained in the Book of Revelation, were fulfilled in contemporary events. Countless tracts, books, and sermons were produced which correlated revolutionary events with prophecies understood by some to signal the incipient Second Advent of Christ and the initiation of the millennium. Many evangelical English Protestants were convinced as well that the millennium promised humankind by Revelation 20, as they supposed, could occur only after all the world's Jews were "restored" to Palestine and the ancient state of Israel reestablished with Jerusalem as its capital. Some went so far as to insist that the Second Advent itself could not occur until such a seemingly impossible task was accomplished.

Protestant Zionism was one result of this conflation in the evangelical mind of millennialism, the Second Advent, and the future of the Jews. At first, the locus of this Christian Zionism was England, where a Jews Society was formed to evangelize the "Children of Abraham," and make preparation for their "return" to Israel. The belief was adopted by eminent clergy within the established church and was, as well, patronized by certain of the nobility.

Within a matter of a few years, this Christian millennial Zionism crossed the Atlantic to the newly independent United States, which took it up with especial avidity. Dozens of local Jews Societies were formed during the first decades

CHRISTIAN ZIONISTS

While most of the early Christians were Jews, the church gradually lost its Jewish roots and heritage as it moved to the pagan world. By the 3rd century CE few Christians thought of Jesus as a Jewish teacher or rabbi. Fewer still thought of the Jews as God's prophets, priests, kings, and apostles. Some medieval Christian pilgrims related to the ancient Jews as they traveled to the Holy Land, but few felt connected to the contemporary Jews they met along the way. For over 1000 years most of the church believed that Christians had replaced the Jews as God's covenant people. There were isolated instances of Christians who read the scriptures differently but until the Reformation few Christians considered the possibility of a Jewish return to Israel. The translation of the Bible into the language of the common people, particularly the English Bible, produced a radical change. Barbara Tuchman, in her book, "Bible and Sword," says, ". . . without the background of the English Bible it is doubtful that the Balfour Declaration would ever have been issued . . ."

We who are 20th century Christian Zionists are proud to follow in the footsteps of many Bible-believers who see overwhelming evidence in scripture for God's continuing covenant with the Jewish people and their right to ancient homeland. We would like to introduce a few of those who left these footprints:

***Henry Finch (1558-1625),* Member of British Parliament.**
***Holger Paulli (1644-1714),* a Danish pietist.**
***John Toland (1670-1722)* an Irish participant in the theological and political debates in England.**
***John Calvin (1509-1564)* was one of the foremost leaders in the Protestant Reformation in Europe.**
***John Knox (1515-1572)* Leader of the Reformation in Scotland.**
Joseph Eyre, 1771* published, *Observations upon Prophecies Relating to the Restoration of the Jews.
***Warder Cresson, 1798-1870,* Quaker, U.S. Counsel in Jerusalem 1848.**
***Charles Jerram, 1795,* Divinity Student at Cambridge, wrote essay on future restoration of the Jewish people to their land.**
***Lord Palmerston,* British Foreign Secretary.**
***Lord Shaftsbury (Anthony Ashley Cooper, 1801-1885)* a man of faith who based his life on literal acceptance of the Bible.**
***John Scott, 1777-1834,* wrote "Destiny of Israel" promoting return of Jews to their land.**
***George Gawler, 1796-1869,* senior commander at the Battle of waterloo & first Governor of Australia.**
***George Elliot, 1819-1880,* pen name of author Mary Anne Evans, wrote *Daniel Derondo,* a sympathetic account of Zionist aspirations.**
***John Nelson Darby, 1800-1882,* founder of Plymouth Brethren.**
***William H. Hechler, 1845-1931,* British clergyman, tutored the son of Grand Duke Baden–the future German Emperor.**
***Laurence Oliphant, 1829-1888,* British Protestant and mystic, member of Parliament.**
***William E. Blackstone, 1860-1929,* Chicago businessman, evangelical Christian, wrote several booklets predicting Jewish return to their land.**
***Lord Arthur James Balfour, 1848-1930,* British states-man.**
***Lt. Col. John Henry Patterson, 1867-1947,* Irish Protestant, Bible student. Led the Zion Mule Corps, a group of Jewish volunteers who fought for Britain in WW1.**
***Charles Orde Wingate, 1903-44,* British officer, intense Bible believer.**
***G. Douglas Young, 1910-1980,* Founder of the Institute of Holy Land Studies and Bridges for Peace. In 1963 Doug Young and his wife, Georgina, moved to Israel.**

Christians of many theological backgrounds have been friends of Israel and the Jewish people but those who hold a high view of the authority of the Bible are more likely to see significance in God's covenant promises and God's hand in history.

We apologize to thousands of Christian Zionists who do not appear on this list. We offer this simply as a starting point for a very extensive and important study.

Prepared by JoAnn Magnuson, Bridges for Peace
16394 Kent Trail, Lakeville, MN 55044
Tel: 612-898-3306 • Fax: 612-898-3651 • E-mail: 74144.3334@compuserve.com

of the nineteenth century. As early as the 1790s, New Haven, Connecticut, clergyman David Austin constructed warehouses and piers to be used by the Jews on their way to Palestine. The optimistic social climate of young America provided especially fertile ground for millennialism, as the country's daring political experiment in democracy and rapid territorial and economic growth convinced many that the country would simply improve itself into the millennium. Numerous benevolent causes were taken up to hurry this along, and the Christianization of the Jews and creation for them of a Jewish homeland in Palestine were among the most popular. The foundation of the late-twentieth-century alliance of evangelical Christians with American Jews on behalf of Israel was thus laid within a few years of American Independence. As the secretary of the American Education Society stated in 1839: "Things promise much on behalf of the Jews; and are as the few drops which precede a mighty shower, and indicate that the millennial day will soon dawn."

This connection between millennialism and Protestant Zionism was limned in uncounted tracts in America. In 1825, for example, a Massachusetts's "Jews Society" published the sentiment that "We should remember further, that the conversion and restoration of the Jews are most intimately connected with those glorious Millennial scenes, towards which the promises of Jehovah are now directing the eyes and hearts of his people." In the decades that followed, interest in the recreation of a Jewish state waxed and waned in American Protestantism. However, even when ostensibly ignored, it continued nevertheless to accumulate with interest just beneath the surface of popular religiosity. When the later course of world events caused European Jews to despair of assimilation and seek desperate refuge in the Middle East, this American Protestant Zionism constituted long-deposited political and religious capital on which Jewish Zionists, somewhat late to their own cause, could draw.

Modern Jewish Zionism

Modern Jewish Zionism, organized as a political movement with a stated agenda, as contrasted with mere sentimentalism toward Jerusalem, was called into existence by the unlooked for burgeoning of European anti-Semitism. By the late nineteenth century, nationalist and pseudoscientific racial theories increasingly subverted continental European political liberalism. Nowhere was this truer than in the new, unified German state, where blood-conscious *volkisch* movements preached a confused, darkly romantic, and anti-intellectual creed of racist patriotism. Jews were regarded as racial and cultural interlopers in an otherwise "pure" *volk*, an attitude encapsulated in the stock phrase "The Jews are our misfortune." Germany, however, was not alone in this Jew-baiting, for after the assassination of Tsar Alexander II in 1881, Russian society became increasingly hostile toward its large Jewish component and inflicted bloody pogroms upon that nearly defenseless and unoffending population. Even a country as relatively enlightened as France witnessed anti-Semitic political movements, of which the notorious Dreyfuss affair was but one example.

European Jewry remained, by and large, dedicated to assimilation, reveled in European culture (to which it contributed disproportionately), and served loyally in the various armed forces throughout World War I. Nevertheless, some Jews began to despair of full acceptance within the Christian milieu and increasingly cast about for an alternative. In the late 1890s, the term "Zionism" became current as meaning a political movement dedicated to the establishment of a Jewish homeland. An especially influential exponent was found in the Austrian journalist, Theodore Herzl, who is credited with organizing the first effective lobby for such a homeland. The call of Herzl and others who believed as he did was, however, largely ignored by the European Jews, who remained for the most part dedicated to living as good citizens within their respective countries.

The nascent Zionist movement received an immense boost from the politics of the first World War, when, in the Balfour Declaration, the British government officially went on record as favoring a Jewish homeland in the Middle East. European Jews emigrated to Palestine in larger numbers, where they encountered intense and enduring hostility from the indigenous Arab population.

Protestant Fundamentalism emerged in the United States during roughly the same period as did political Zionism in Europe. This largely American religious phenomenon was closely linked to millenarianism, important to it not just as theology but as a root source of conservative religious thought. Fundamentalist and evangelical Christians kept alive the early nineteenth century's interest in the reestablishment of a Jewish state in Palestine. Eschatology was especially important to these Christians, who tended overwhelmingly to believe that the Bible foretells the return of Jesus Christ in judgment prior to the millennium, a reading of prophecy known as premillennialism. The Jews were enormously important to these American Protestants because, as they believed, God had revealed through the prophets that just prior to the Last Days, the "Children of Abraham" would be gathered to the Middle East to reestablish the ancient state of Israel. The Second Advent would follow soon after and then the saints would enter into the millennium under the kingship of the Lord Jesus Christ. Since to be present and receive Jesus at his return in glory was the summation of Christian hope, and since the return of the Jews to Palestine was a necessary precursor, it followed that evangelical Christians must themselves long for a Jewish state.

Periodic evangelical prophecy conferences were held in America throughout the post–Civil War era and an intense interest in the fate of the Jews became a standard feature of the emergent Fundamentalist faith. By the 1890s, a Protestant delegation had even waited on the President to encourage government support of a Jewish homeland. The religious "capital," mentioned earlier, which Jewish political Zionism unknowingly had on deposit with American Protestants given to millenarianism, steadily accumulated into an enormous figure.

Despite significant migration to Palestine during the interwar period, it took the crimes committed by the Germans during World War II to convince surviving Jews that only a homeland of their own could protect against a recurrence of such bestiality. Postwar migration to Israel resulted, despite conflict with indigenous Arabs, with the proclamation of a Jewish state in 1947. The Zionist movement, which had earlier laid the groundwork for the nascent Israeli republic, remained largely secular, prompted more by cultural affinity and socialist idealism than religious belief. Nevertheless, absent the biblical entitlement to Palestine awarded the Jews, it is unlikely the Zionist movement would have succeeded, the Holocaust notwithstanding. The ancient texts of first-millennium BCE Hebrew prophets conferred a sanctity on the endeavor which lent it tremendous emotional sustenance. The compelling millennial imagery of a land of milk and honey, given to the Jews for all time, underlay the entire enterprise.

There remain, however, devout religious Jews who are skeptical, even hostile, to the modern Israeli state. For them, the true kingdom of righteousness must await the messianic era, when the Redeemer sent by God shall arrive. Modern Israel, they believe, is a misbegotten attempt to force God's hand. Thus, even though millennialism was instrumental in establishing the present Jewish homeland, it is utilized as well to question the legitimacy of its very existence.

Modern Israel, although superbly defended by its inhabitants, remains a relatively small state in a largely hostile milieu and its survival has been underwritten in great measure by the United State of America. Such a guaranty of continued existence from the world's greatest military power has been sustained, in part, by the prophetic faith of countless evangelical Christians, who are certain that the Jewish state is necessary for the fulfillment of New Testament prophecy and the introduction of the millennium. These evangelicals have been for Israel an influential and reliable lobby in Washington. As one friendly critic wrote of them in 1994, "All they care about is the future, Israel, and the pretribulational rapture." All of these things, it is worth noting, are directly related to prophetic premillennialism. It is arguable that never in international relations has millennialism played so influential a role as with this Protestant Zionism and its eschatologically motivated support for the Jewish state in the nuclear era.

Robert K. Whalen

See also Fundamentalism, Israel, Judaism, Postmillennialism, Premillennialism

Bibliography

Boyer, Paul. (1992) *When Time Shall Be No More: Prophecy Belief In Modern American Culture.* Cambridge, MA: Harvard University Press.

Laqueur, Walter. (1972) *A History of Zionism.* New York: Holt, Rinehart and Winston.

Whalen, Robert K. (1996) "'Christians Love the Jews!' The Development of American Philo-Semitism, 1790–1860." *Religion and American Culture: A Journal of Interpretation* 6 (summer): 225–60.

Wheatcroft, Geoffrey. (1996) *The Controversy of Zion: Jewish Nationalism, the Jewish State, and the Unresolved Jewish Dilemma.* Reading, MA: Addison-Wesley.

Zoroastrianism

Zoroastrianism was the official religion of Iran for at least one thousand years and probably much longer (since its beginnings are purely conjectural), until the Muslim conquest of Iran during the period between 640–720. It originated in the area of eastern Iran (now Afghanistan) among the scattered Aryan tribes of the area. There is little hard data available about the birthdate of Zoroaster, the founder, and estimates of his lifetime have ranged between 900–600 BCE, with the earlier date being the more commonly accepted one. Zoroaster apparently was a member of a priestly caste of the area, and received a revelation at about the age of thirty. His teaching was met with hostility from the tribes, and more especially from the other priests, and Zoroaster had to seek refuge with a monarch named Vishtaspa, who became his most notable convert. His authentic teachings are preserved in the Gathas (the songs) inside the Avesta (the holy book). It is uncertain, however, how exactly Zoroastrianism came to be accepted throughout the Iranian world.

By the period of the Achaemenid period of Iranian rule (559–334 BCE), which is best known for its appearance in the Bible (see Isaiah 45:1), Zoroastrianism had become the official faith of the empire. The political rule of the

Achaemenids was supported by the priestly caste, the Magi, who handed down the tradition, and over a period of centuries modified and commented on it (these commentaries being known as *Zands*). When Alexander the Great brought an end to the empire in the 330s BCE, Zoroastrianism was dealt a mighty blow, but managed to survive in the eastern part of the Iranian plateau (which was the area least touched by Hellenistic influence), and even influence areas beyond that, such as the Buddhist kingdoms in Afghanistan. When the Parthian empire (c. 247 BCE–226 CE) rose from among the ashes of the Hellenistic kingdoms founded by Alexander's successors, Zoroastrianism became once again the state religion, and especially flourished under the Sasanids (226–651 CE). Virtually everything that we know about Zoroastrianism dates from this period, and it is this time and the period of decline under Muslim rule which will concern us here. Most of Iran was converted to Islam during the first two hundred years of Muslim rule, although there were still sizable Zoroastrian minorities in existence for hundreds of years. It is thought that there are about 130,000 Zoroastrians in the world today, many of them in India or scattered throughout the world. Probably no more than a couple of thousand remain in Iran itself, where the Islamic Republic has persecuted them.

Our sources for the study of Zoroastrianism are few, and virtually all date from after the Muslim conquest, when the priestly caste sought to codify the basics of the faith, and salvage what could be salvaged from the destruction of their holy places and books. Most of these survive only in India, where there is a vital Zoroastrian community (known as the Parsees). However, thanks to the Arab sources (which were often written by descendants of converts to Islam from Zoroastrianism) we can obtain a reasonable history of the faith, and most especially the apocalyptic aspects of it, after the Muslim conquests. Original sources for the study of Zoroastrianism are written in Pahlavi (Middle Persian).

Zoroastrianism is commonly designated as a dualistic system, and many feel that the original impetus for the faith came from an attempt to explain the relationship of evil to the good (it is assumed) Creator. The basic cosmology of Zoroastrianism postulates the existence of two equal and opposite entities: Ahura Mazda (also Ohrmuzd), who is entirely light, good, and wise; versus Ahreman, who is entirely darkness, evil, and possesses wisdom only in hindsight. Ahreman lusted after the light of Ahura Mazda, and fought with him. Ahura Mazda created the world (and all of the universe) as a battleground and a trap for Ahreman, who is confined within it for a specific period of time (the duration of history), usually either nine thousand or twelve thousand years (the revelation came to Zoroaster at the beginning of the last one thousand years). After the completion of this period of time Ahreman will be hurled back to the nothingness from which he came; however during it, he has complete freedom within creation to do whatever he wants to hurt humanity.

Certain other elements of the cosmology should be noted here. There are three states or processes which are undergone in creation: first, creation itself; second, the intermingling of the two opposites (good and evil); and third, their final separation (i.e., the end). All of creation is seen in a duality of the spiritual state *(menog)* versus the physical state *(getig)*, although these do not often exist in their pure forms in this world, but are constantly being mixed. In the end, these states will be entirely separated and mankind will live in pure bodies. The three states or processes are also represented by three humans: Gayamaretan, the equivalent of Adam; Zoroaster, who represents the middle stage of mixture; and the final person of Saoshyant, who is the messianic figure and who appears under a number of other names. In the Arabic sources, for example, it is said that "At the end of times there will appear a man whose name is Usedar. he will adorn the world with religion and justice" (Shaked 1994: 64). In other versions there will be a total of three messianic figures: Ukhshyatereta, Ukhshyatnemah, and Astvatereta, each of whom will appear at different times throughout the last millennium after the revelation of Zoroaster. There are many variants to these stories and it does not seem that an authoritative version was ever agreed upon.

Zoroastrian Apocalyptic Texts

There can be no question that Zoroastrian apocalyptic is one of the oldest traditions of the genre. However, ironically, as noted above, we possess only comparatively late renditions of the key texts, which has led to numerous debates about its influence upon Jewish and Christian beliefs (for these debates, see Boyce 1984). It seems clear that the first apocalyptic speculation centered on the period of time during which Ahreman will be imprisoned (and thus the duration of the world). Apparently Sasanian religious authorities did their best to date Zoroaster's time as closely to their own as possible, since the period of his revelation would be the starting point for the last millennium. We will examine the latest and most complete of the Zoroastrian apocalypses, the *Zand-i Wahman Yasn*. As its name indicates, it is a commentary (a *zand*) on one of the *yasnas* (parts of the *Avesta*), however, in its present state it dates approximately from the late Sasanian times or early Islamic period.

The apocalypse starts out by revealing a dream of Zoroaster's, in which he sees a tree on which there were four branches: one made of gold, one of silver, one of steel, and one of mixed iron (cf. Daniel 2:31–35). Ahura Mazda explains to Zoroaster that these branches represent the four epochs of the world, which are apparently to follow Zoroaster chronologically. During the first three the true faith is strong, but during the last one "is the evil rule of the parted hair demons of the seed of Xeshm [probably the Muslims], when it will be the end of your tenth century, O Spitaman Zarduxsht [Zoroaster]" (Cereti 1995, 149). After seeing this vision, Zoroaster asks Ahura Mazda for immortality, which was not granted to him, but he did receive wisdom and knowledge of the future. When asked for the sign of the tenth century, Ahura Mazda replies "I will make it clear. The sign of the end of your millennium will be that the least of periods will arrive. One hundred kinds, one thousand kinds, a myriad kinds of parted-hair demons of the seed of Xeshm, those of very mean stock, will creep into Iranshahr [Iran] from the side of Khurasan [the east]. They will have raised banners, will wear black armor and have the hair parted to the back, and will be small and lowest stock and of mighty blows and will piss venom" (Cereti: 153).

Times will be very bad then, since all people will be sunk in immorality and the courses of the natural world will be altered. The seasons and days will be shorter, animal and vegetable life will suffer, and "in those worse times a bird will have more respect than the Iranian and pious man" (Cereti: 154). People will convert to other religions (probably Islam) and worship wealth, and the rule will go to other non-Iranian races (the Arabs, the Greeks, the Turks, and a number of others are specified). Zoroaster is horrified at this description and asks how people are to remain pure and undefiled during these times. Ahura Mazda's answer is worship and holding fast to the faith, and he assures that he is "aware of righteousness, however little" (Cereti: 159).

However, eventually a savior will be revealed. Zoroaster asks how these demons can be overcome if they are so many, and is told that this figure (whose functions appear to be divided between two people) will lead the faithful to fight the usurpers and to massacre the evil demons of the race of Xeshm, and to send them to hell. Ahura Mazda himself will support this final battle, aiding the fighters and making a renewal under the figure of Pishotan, who is said to be the son of Vishtaspa (the king who was converted by Zoroaster). Pishotan appears to be the liberator, while Usedar, the other messianic figure, is the one who ushers in the messianic age. "About Usedar it is revealed that he will be born in the year one thousand and six hundred and, at the age of thirty, will come to converse with me, Ahura Mazda, and receive the religion . . . and when this will happen all the men of the world will stand by the good Mazdean religion [Zoroastrianism]" (Cereti: 166). It appears that in Zoroastrianism, as in Judaism and Islam, there is a division between the messianic figure who is required to do the fighting and to accomplish the liberation of the people, and the messianic figure who actually ushers in the millennium.

Apocalyptism as Part of the Society

Apocalyptism was apparently part of Zoroastrian society; however, there is so little historical evidence of it that we are forced to highlight several events from after the Muslim conquest, since that period is better documented. The most important millenarian movement during Sasanian times was the mysterious revolt of Mazdak (fl. c. 488–531 CE), who apparently preached a sort of communism of property previous to the end of the age (remembering that the Sasanian government had tried to suppress apocalyptic speculation). For a time this heresy, which had wide popular support, was used by the then monarch Kavad (488–96, 498–531) to further a policy of weakening the aristocracy. In order to accomplish this, Kavad sought to promote a communism of women, in which marriage, and more importantly the large harems of the aristocracy, would be abolished and every man could (at least in theory) have any woman he wished. Understandably, this innovation lead to Kavad's losing his throne for a time, and eventually the whole notion was suppressed by Kavad's son Khusraw Anushirvan (531–79), who massacred large numbers of Mazdakites and possibly Mazdak himself, although the heresy itself remained current well into Muslim times, to whom we owe most of our knowledge of it.

The Muslim conquest and the conversion of most of the Iranian people to Islam led to several crisis points in the Zoroastrian faith. One of them apparently involved an apocalyptic reform movement. In a Muslim reformist chronicle of Zoroastrian heresies we read the following:

> Among the Majus [Zoroastrians] who are the Zardustiyya there is a group called al-Sisaniyya and al-Bihafridiyya. At their head is a man called Sisan, from the province of Nishapur, from an area called Khwaf. He appeared in the days of Abu Muslim *Sahib al-Dawla* [the Abbasid governor of Khurasan, d. 754]. At the beginning he was a Zamzami [apparently an orthodox Zoroastrian], worshipping fire, but he abandoned this afterwards and called upon the Majus to forsake the *zamzama* and to refuse to worship fire. He established a book for them and commanded them in it to keep their hair lank. He forbade them to practice intercourse with mothers, daughters and sisters, prohibiting wine and commanded them to welcome the sun while kneeling on one knee. They occupy monasteries and vie with each other in bestowing generously. They do not eat carrion, and

> do not slaughter an animal before it gets old. They are the most deadly enemies of the Zamzami Majus. A *mobadh* [priest] of the Majus complained about him to Abu Muslim and the latter killed him at the gate of the main mosque of Nishapur. His followers said that he was raised to heaven riding a tawny hackney [horse], and that he will come down riding that hackney and wreak vengeance on his enemies. (Shaked 1994: 63–64)

These reformists were apparently trying to purify the Zoroastrian faith of precisely those elements which were offensive to Muslims: incest, drinking of wine and worshipping fire. When this reform was suppressed by the Muslim authorities (who did not want the older faith reformed), clearly its followers took refuge in the idea of the occulted leader who will return to take vengeance upon his enemies in a messianic fashion.

Zoroastrian apocalyptic is useful in understanding a wide range of ideas in the Bible and in Muslim apocalyptic beliefs, and represents something of a unique phenomenon, since rarely has apocalyptic been accepted in systems which are non-monotheistic. It gives us a sense of how the development proceeds in other belief systems.

David Cook

Bibliography

Boyce, Mary. (1975) *A History of Zoroastrianism.* Leiden: Brill.

——. (1984) "On the Antiquity of Zoroastrian Apocalyptic." *Bulletin of the School of Oriental and African Studies* 47: 57–75.

Cereti, Carlo. (1995) *The Zand-i Wahman Yasn: A Zoroastrian Apocalypse.* Rome: The Pontifical Institute.

Choksy, Jamsheed. (1990) "Conflict, Coexistence and Cooperation: Muslims and Zoroastrians in Eastern Iran during the Medieval Period." *Muslim World* 80: 213–33.

Crone, Patricia. (1991) "Kavad's Heresy and Mazdak's Revolt." *Iran* 29: 21–42.

Czeglédy, K. (1958) "Bahram Cobin and the Persian Apocalyptic Literature." *Acta Orientalia* 8: 21–43.

Kippenberg, Hans G. (1978) "Die Geschichte der mittelpersischen apokalyptischen Traditionen." *Studia Iranica* 7: 49–80.

Shaked, Shaul. (1994) "Islamic Reports Concerning Zoroastrianism." *Jerusalem Studies in Arabic and Islam* 17: 43–84.

West, Edward W., ed. and trans. (1965) *Pahlavi Texts* (translation of the Bundahisn). Sacred Books of the East, vol. 5. Delhi: Motilal Banarsidass.

List of Contributors

Akintunde E. Akinade
High Point University
Africa, Sub-Saharan

Jason Ardizzone
New York University
Free Spirit

William Sims Bainbridge
National Science Foundation
Ecstasy
Science Fiction Literature
Stress

Victor Balaban
Emory University
Fatima Cult
Marianism
Roman Catholicism

Michael Barkun
Syracuse University
Christian Identity
New World Order

Chip Berlet
Political Research Associates
Apocalypse
Conspiracism
Demagogues
Demonization
Militia Movements
Populism
Survivalism
Totalitarianism
Year 2000

Stephen Bowd
Manchester Metropolitan University
Papal Reform
Prophecy

John M. Bozeman
Nova Religion: Journal of Alternative and Emergent Religions
Technological Millennialism

Brenda E. Brasher
Mount Union College
Promise Keepers

Arndt Brendecke
Historisches Seminar, Abteilung Frühe Neuzeit
Century, Centennial, Centenarium
Fin de Siècle
Jubilee Traditions

Charles Cameron
The Arlington Institute
Y2K

Michael J. Christensen
Drew University
Chernobyl
Marking Millenial Moments (coauthor)
Russian Millenialism

Frederick Clarkson
Institute for Democracy
Christian Reconstructionists and Dominionists

William P. Collins
Library of Congress
Baha'i Faith

David Cook
University of Chicago
Akkadian and Babylonian Apocalypses
Chronology and Dating
Zoroastrianism

Ryan J. Cook
University of Chicago
Chen Tao
Heaven's Gate

Christy A. Cousineau
Indiana University
Age of Mary

Gary Dickson
University of Edinburgh
Joachism

Joel Elliott
University of North Carolina
Jehovah's Witnesses

Victoria L. Erickson
Drew University
Shakers (coauthor)

Beth Marie Forrest
Center for Millenial Studies
Witch-Hunts of Early Modern Europe

Lawrence Foster
Georgia Institute of Technology
Burned-over District

Timothy R. Furnish
Ohio State University
Islam

Eugene V. Gallagher
Connecticut College
Conversion
Cults

Martin Gardner
Science Writer, Hendersonville, NC
666
Rappites
Urantia

Blaine Gaustad
SUNY College at Fredonia
China

Yonder M. Gillihan
University of Chicago
Rapture

Matthew Goff
University of Chicago
Antichrist
Messianism

Ellen D. Haskell
University of Chicago
Sabbatian Movement

Johannes Heil
Technische Universitaet-Berlin
Judaism

James Hewitson
University of Toronto
Film
United States, Eighteenth Century

Dale T. Irvin
New York Theological Seminary
Camp Meetings
Holiness Movement
Shakers (coauthor)

Jeffrey Kaplan
Renvall Institute, Helsinki University
Violence

Catherine Keller
Drew University
Columbus/Colon

Philip Lamy
Castleton College
Aetherius Society
Armageddon Time Ark Base
Greater Community Way
Millennial Myth
New World Comforter
Outpost Kauai

Planetary Activation Organization
Summum
Ufology

Richard Landes
Center For Millennial Studies, Boston University
Millennialism in the Western World
Peace of God
Year 1000
Year 2000 Celebrations

Ronald Lawson
City University at New York
Seventh-Day Adventists

Michael C. Lazich
Buffalo State College
Asia

David Levinson
Berkshire Reference Works
Ghost Dance Movement
Rastafarianism

Lamont Lindstrom
University of Tulsa
Cargo Cults

Thomas L. Long
Thomas Nelson Community College
Defilement
Maps of Apocalyptic Time
Mysticism
Plague and Pestilence
Sexuality
Sodom
Utopia

Phillip Charles Lucas
Stetson University
Raelians

J. Gordon Melton
Institute for the Study of American Religion
New Age

Rebecca Moore
San Diego State University
Jubilee, Year of
Peoples Temple

David S. Nash
Oxford Brookes University
Secular Millennialism

Stephen O'Leary
University of Southern California
Media

Juan M. Ossio
Pontificia Universidad Católica del Perú
Israelites of the New Universal Covenant
Native South America

Susan J. Palmer
Dawson College
Apostles of Infinite Love
Family, The
Holy Tabernacle Ministry
Messianic Communities
Solar Temple
Women
Year of the Flagellants (1260)

William L. Pitts, Jr.
Baylor University
Davidians

Jerrold M. Post
George Washington University
Charisma

Ian Reader
Lancaster University
Aum Shinrikyo
Japan

David Redles
Center for Millennial Studies
Holocaust
Nazism

David L. Rowe
Middle Tennessee State University
Millerites
Protestantism

Carl E. Savage
Drew University
Marking Millennial Moments (coauthor)

Charles B. Strozier
City University of New York
Nuclear

Henry Sturcke
University of Zurich
Anabaptists
False Prophet
Worldwide Church of God

James D. Tabor
University of North Carolina—Charlotte
Ancient World
End Signs
Salvation

Bron Taylor
University of Wisconsin Oshkosh
Earth First!
Environmentalism

Diana Tumminia
California State University—Sacramento
Communism
Delaware Prophet
Great Peace of Deganaweda and Hiawatha
Handsome Lake
Indian Shakers
John Frum Movement
Ramtha School of Enlightenment
Unarius Academy of Science
White Buffalo Calf Woman

Grant Underwood
Brigham Young University—Hawaii
Mormonism

Catherine Wessinger
Loyola University
Assaulted Millennial Groups
Fragile Millennial Groups
Nativist Millennial Movements
Persecution
Progressive Millennialism
Revolutionary Millennial Movements

Robert K. Whalen
Chatham Township, NJ
Art
Dispensationalism
Doomsday
End of the World
Fundamentalism
Israel
Pentecostalism
Politics
Postmillennialism
Premillennialism
Zionism

Brad Whitsel
Pennsylvania State University
Church Universal and Triumphant

Daniel Wojcik
University of Oregon
Bayside (Our Lady of the Roses)
Fatalism

Andrew Corey Yerkes
Rice University
Literature

Index